The World of Retailing

The chapters in Section I provide background information about retail customers and competitors that you will need to understand the world of retailing and then develop and effectively implement a retail strategy.

Chapter 1 describes the functions that retailers perform and the variety of decisions they make to satisfy customers' needs in rapidly changing, highly competitive retail environments. The remaining chapters in this section give you further background information to understand the world of retailing.

Chapter 2 describes the different types of retailers.

Chapter 3 examines how retailers use multiple selling channels—stores, the Internet, catalogs—to reach their customers.

Chapter 4 discusses the factors consumers consider when choosing retail outlets and buying merchandise.

The chapters in Section II focus on the strategic decisions that retailers make.

The chapters in Sections III and IV explore tactical decisions involving merchandise and store management.

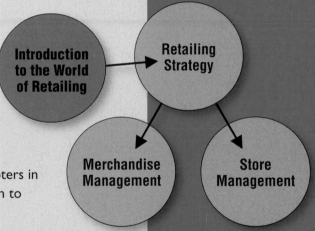

Introduction to the World of Retailing

EXECUTIVE BRIEFING
Maxine Clark, Chief Executive Bear,
Build-A-Bear Workshop

became President of Payless Shoe Stores, then a division of May Department Store with over 4,500 stores and $2 billion plus in annual sales at the time.

In early 1997, I decided to launch a retail concept I had been thinking about—Build-A-Bear Workshop®. While most retailers are merchandise driven, Build-A-Bear Workshop® offers highly interactive experiences like a theme park. It combines the universal appeal of plush animals with an interactive assembly line that allows children of all ages to create and accessorize their own huggable companions. We opened the first Build-A-Bear Workshop in St. Louis in the fall of 1997 and have now grown to over 200 stores and in 2003, $300 million in annual sales.

The keys to our success are great merchandise, great people, and great store execution. These three factors combine to create an environment where families share quality time and form irreplaceable memories. Our passion for serving our guests is emulated by our dedicated associates, known as "Master Bear Builders," who make every effort to ensure that each visit is memorable and enjoyable. Employees are empowered to make sure that

I had a passion for retailing even when I was a young girl. At an early age, I recognized the importance of having exciting merchandise and providing an engaging store experience for customers. But I never realized how significant these feelings would be in my life. I started my retail career, like many college graduates going into retailing, as an executive trainee at May Department Stores Company. Over the next 20 years I held a variety of store and merchandise positions of increasing responsibility. In 1992, I

CHAPTER 1

QUESTIONS

What is retailing?

What do retailers do?

Why is retailing important in our society?

What career and entrepreneurial opportunities does retailing offer?

What types of decisions do retail managers make?

every guest feels special every time they visit their stores. We have a company culture where great service and recognition are a daily occurrence. Ninety percent of guests rate the quality of experience in the highest two categories and 76 percent indicate that nothing could be done to improve their store experience.

We also believe strongly that we need to give back to the communities in which we have stores. For example, as part of our ongoing commitment to children's health and wellness, we introduced a series of Nikki's Bears to honor Nikki Giampolo, a young girl who lost her life to cancer. A portion of proceeds from the sale of Nikki's is donated to support programs that help children maintain normal lives while they struggle with difficult health issues including cancer, diabetes, and autism. To date, the program has raised nearly $700,000 for important children's health and wellness causes.

Most consumers shopping in their local stores don't realize that retailing is a high-tech, global industry. To illustrate the sophisticated technologies used by retailers, consider the following: If you are interested in buying an iPhone, Staples provides a Web site (www.staples.com) you can access to learn about the features of the different models. You can order the iPhone from the Web site and have it delivered to your home, or you can go to the store and buy it. If you decide to go to the store, Staples offers Web-enabled kiosks that you can use to review the information available on its Web site.

When you decide to buy an iPhone in the store, the point-of-sales (POS) terminal transmits data about the transaction to Staples' distribution center and then on to the manufacturer, Apple. When the in-store inventory level drops below a prespecified level, an electronic notice is automatically transmitted, authorizing the shipment of more units to the distribution center and then to the store. Data about your purchase are transmitted to a sophisticated inventory management system. A buyer at Staples analyzes the data to determine how many and which types of units should be stocked in your local store and what price the retailer should charge. Finally, the data about your purchase get stored in Staples' data warehouse and used to design special promotions for you.

Wanna buy a suit for interviewing? Since 1818, Brooks Brothers has been providing American men—and now women and boys—with traditional clothing.[1] If you visit a Brooks Brothers store today, you will find the same type of personal service that has made it famous, but you may also discover a few technological twists. Using the store's database, the sales associate realizes that you purchased a dark blue suit several months earlier, so she can coordinate several shirts and ties to go with it. In the future, salespeople will carry handheld devices that customers can use to view their virtual closet—everything they have ever purchased at Brooks Brothers. The sales associates then can help customers build a wardrobe, not just purchase a single item. New technologies also enable Brooks Brothers to offer reasonably priced custom suits in just seven days. Thus, like many retailers, Brooks Brothers uses technology to add value to its merchandise offering.

Historically, the retail landscape has been dominated by local retailers that bought and resold merchandise from local suppliers. Forty years ago, some of the largest retailers in the United States—Wal-Mart, The Gap, Home Depot, and Best Buy—either were small start-ups or did not even exist. Yet today, most retail sales are made by large national and international chains that buy merchandise from all over the world. Wal-Mart is the world's largest corporation. French-based Carrefour, the world's second-largest retailer, operates 12,000 hypermarkets in 30 countries (but not the United States). Some non–U.S.-based retailers that have gained a strong presence in the United States include Aldi (German grocer), Ahold (grocer from the Netherlands), IKEA (Swedish-based furniture and accessories retailer), and H&M (Swedish apparel).[2]

Retailing is such a common part of our everyday lives that we often just take it for granted. Retail managers make complex decisions in selecting their target markets and retail locations; determining what merchandise and services to offer; negotiating with suppliers; distributing merchandise to stores; training and motivating sales associates; and deciding how to price, promote, and present merchandise. Considerable skill and knowledge are required to make these decisions effectively. Working in this highly competitive, rapidly changing environment is both challenging and exciting, and it offers significant financial rewards.

This book describes the world of retailing and offers key principles for effectively managing retail businesses in highly competitive environments. Knowledge of retailing principles and practices will help you develop management skills for many business contexts. For example, managers at Procter & Gamble and Hewlett-Packard must have a thorough understanding of how retailers operate and make money so they can get their products on retail shelves and work with retailers to sell them to consumers. Financial and health care institutions use retail principles to develop their offerings, improve customer service, and provide convenient, easy access to their customers. Thus, any students interested in professional selling, marketing, or finance will find this book useful.

WHAT IS RETAILING?

Retailing is the set of business activities that adds value to the products and services sold to consumers for their personal or family use. Often people think of retailing only as the sale of products in stores, but retailing also involves the sale of services: overnight lodging in a motel, a doctor's exam, a haircut, a DVD rental, or a home-delivered pizza. Not all retailing is done in stores. Examples of nonstore retailing include Internet sales of hot sauces (www.firehotsauces. com), the direct sales of cosmetics by Avon, and catalog sales by L.L. Bean and Patagonia.

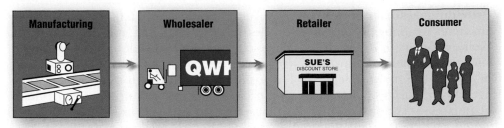

EXHIBIT 1–1
Example of a Supply Chain

A Retailer's Role in a Supply Chain

A **retailer** is a business that sells products and/or services to consumers for their personal or family use. Retailers are the final business in a supply chain that links manufacturers to consumers. A **supply chain** is a set of firms that make and deliver a given set of goods and services to the ultimate consumer. Exhibit 1–1 shows the retailer's position within a supply chain.

Manufacturers typically make products and sell them to retailers or wholesalers. When manufacturers like Nike and Apple sell directly to consumers, they are performing both production and retailing business activities. **Wholesalers,** in contrast, engage in buying, taking title to, often storing, and physically handling goods in large quantities, then reselling the goods (usually in smaller quantities) to retailers or industrial or business users. Wholesalers and retailers may perform many of the same functions described in the next section, but wholesalers uniquely satisfy retailers' needs, whereas retailers direct their efforts to satisfying the needs of ultimate consumers. Some retail chains, like Costco and Home Depot, function as both retailers and wholesalers: They perform retailing activities when they sell to consumers, but they engage in wholesaling activities when they sell to other businesses, like restaurants or building contractors.

In some supply chains, the manufacturing, wholesaling, and retailing activities are performed by independent firms, but most supply chains feature some vertical integration. **Vertical integration** means that a firm performs more than one set of activities in the supply chain, such as investments by retailers in wholesaling or manufacturing. **Backward integration** arises when a retailer performs some distribution and manufacturing activities, such as operating warehouses or designing private-label merchandise. **Forward integration** occurs when a manufacturer undertakes retailing activities, such as Ralph Lauren operating its own retail stores.

Most large retailers—such as Safeway, Wal-Mart, and Lowe's—engage in both wholesaling and retailing activities. They buy directly from manufacturers, have merchandise shipped to their warehouses for storage, and then distribute the merchandise to their stores. Other retailers, such as J. Crew and Victoria's Secret, are even more vertically integrated. They also design the merchandise they sell and then contract with manufacturers to produce it exclusively for them.

Retailers Create Value

Why are retailers needed? Wouldn't it be easier and cheaper to buy directly from companies that manufacture the products? The answer, generally, is no. Although in some situations, it is easier and cheaper to buy directly from manufacturers, such as at a local farmer's market or from Apple Inc., retailers provide important functions that increase the value of the products and services they sell to consumers and facilitate the distribution of those products and services for the manufacturers that produce them. These value-creating functions include

1. Providing an assortment of products and services.
2. Breaking bulk.
3. Holding inventory.
4. Providing services.

Providing Assortments   Supermarkets typically carry 20,000–30,000 different items made by more than 500 companies. Offering an assortment enables their customers to choose from a wide selection of brands, designs, sizes, colors, and prices at one location. Manufacturers specialize in producing specific types of products. For example, Frito-Lay makes snacks, Dannon makes dairy products, Skippy makes peanut butter, and Heinz makes ketchup. If each of these manufacturers had its own stores that only sold its own products, consumers would have to go to many different stores to buy the groceries needed to prepare a single meal.

All retailers offer assortments of products, but they specialize in the assortments they offer. Supermarkets provide assortments of food, health and beauty care, and household products, whereas Abercrombie & Fitch provides assortments of clothing and accessories. Most consumers are well aware of the product assortments retailers offer; even small children tend to know where to buy different types of products. But new types of retailers, offering unique assortments, appear each year. Steve and Barry's is a category specialist for licensed collegiate merchandise. Metropark is the lifestyle specialty store chain targeting trendsetting young adults that blends fashion, music, and art that is part club and part street boutique. Little Gym is a service retailer that helps children develop their motor skills by offering karate and gymnastic classes. Winestyles is a wine-store that arranges wine by taste category instead of region or type of wine and provides extensive information to reduce the complexity of buying wines.

Little Gym is a service retailer that helps children develop their motor skills by offering karate and gymnastic classes.

Breaking Bulk   To reduce transportation costs, manufacturers and wholesalers typically ship cases of frozen dinners or cartons of blouses to retailers. Retailers then offer the products in smaller quantities tailored to individual consumers' and households' consumption patterns in a process called **breaking bulk.** Breaking bulk is important to both manufacturers and consumers, because it provides cost efficiencies for manufacturers that can package and ship merchandise in larger, rather than smaller, quantities, and it gives consumers the chance to purchase merchandise in the smaller, more manageable quantities they prefer.

REFACT

The word *retail* is derived from the French word *retaillier,* meaning to cut a piece off or break bulk.

Holding Inventory   A major function of retailers is to keep inventory that has been broken into user-friendly sizes so that the products will be available when consumers want them. Thus, consumers can keep a smaller inventory of products at home because they know local retailers will have the products available when they need more. By maintaining an inventory, retailers provide a crucial benefit to consumers: They reduce the cost consumers would have to pay to store products. This function is particularly important to consumers with limited storage space and those who want to purchase perishable merchandise, like meat and produce, just before they consume it.

Providing Services   Retailers provide services that make it easier for customers to buy and use products. For example, they offer credit so consumers can have a product now and pay for it later. They display products so consumers can see and test them before buying. Some retailers employ salespeople in stores or maintain Web sites to answer questions and provide additional information about products.

Increasing the Value of Products and Services   By providing assortments, breaking bulk, holding inventory, and providing services, retailers increase the value that consumers receive from their products and services. To illustrate, consider a door in a shipping crate in an Iowa manufacturer's warehouse. The door cannot satisfy the needs of a do-it-yourselfer (DIYer) who wants to replace a closet door today. For the DIYer, a conveniently located home improvement center like Home Depot or Lowe's offers a door, available when the DIYer wants it. The home improvement center helps the customer select the door by displaying all available doors in an easy-to-see layout so the customer can examine them before selecting one to purchase. An employee helps the customer by explaining which door is best for closets and how the door should be hung. The store also provides an assortment of hardware, paint, and tools that the DIYer will need to complete the job. In this way, retailers increase the value of the products and services bought by their customers.

SOCIAL AND ECONOMIC SIGNIFICANCE OF RETAILING

Social Responsibility

Retailers are socially responsible businesses. **Corporate social responsibility** describes the voluntary actions taken by a company to address the ethical, social, and environmental impacts of its business operations and the concerns of its stakeholders.[3] Retailing View 1.1 illustrates how retailers provide value to their communities and society, as well as to their customers.

Retail Sales

Retailing affects every facet of life. Just think of how many daily contacts you have with retailers when you eat meals, furnish your apartment, have your car fixed, and buy clothing for a party or job interview. American retail sales are over $4 trillion, but even this sales level underestimates the impact of retailing, because it does not include the retail sales of automobiles and repairs.[4]

Although the majority of retail sales take place within large retail chains, most retailers are small businesses. Of the 1.9 million retail firms in the United States, 95 percent of them run only one store. Less than 1 percent of U.S. retail firms have more than 100 stores.[5]

Employment

Retailing also is one of the nation's largest industries in terms of employment. More than 24 million people were employed in retailing—approximately 18 percent of the nonagricultural U.S. workforce. Between 2004 and 2014, the retail industry expects to add 1.6 million jobs, making it one of the largest sectors for job growth in the United States.[6]

REFACT

Of all the sectors in the U.S. economy, retail, food service, and drinking establishments employ the most workers.[7]

Global Retailers

Retailing is becoming a global industry, as more and more retailers pursue growth by expanding their operations to other countries. The large retail firms are becoming increasingly international in the geographical scope of their operations. Amway, Avon, Ace Hardware, and Inditex (Zara) operate in more than 20 countries. The share of the global retail market accounted for by retailers operating in more than one country also is increasing, because these global retailers are growing at an even faster rate than are global retail sales. International operations account for a larger proportion of sales by these large firms, as is particularly apparent in European firms with their longer internationalization experience. Wal-Mart, Carrefour, Royal Ahold, Metro, and Schwarz each generate more than $20 billion annually in sales from their international operations.[8]

Exhibit 1–2 lists the 20 largest global retailers. With worldwide retail sales estimated at \$3.7 trillion, the 20 largest retailers represent a 35 percent share of the world market.[9] Wal-Mart remains the undisputed leader in the retail world, with sales more than three times as great as those of Carrefour, the second-largest retailer. Home Depot also has made significant sales gains over the last several years. Its third-place ranking in 2006 was up from 24th in 1996.

1.1   RETAILING VIEW   Socially Responsible Retailers

Many retailers are buying and designing biodegradable or environmentally sensitive merchandise, taking positive ecological actions, and giving to charities—all actions viewed by customers and shareholders as socially responsible stratgies. Bono, the lead singer of U2 and global activist, has introduced Edun, a fair-trade fashion brand that offers high-priced goods through stores such as Saks, Nordstrom, and FairIndigo.com. A fair-trade designation means that the items were produced in factories that pay workers far more than the prevailing minimum wage and offer other benefits, like onsite medical treatment. Not to be outdone, Starbucks pays its farmers 42 percent more than the going commodity price of Arabica coffee beans.

REFACT

Retail companies give away 1.7 percent of their profits each year before taxes, compared with approximately 0.9 percent by companies in other industries.[10]

Gap, Emporio Armani, Apple, and other high-end brands have launched their own Product Red lines in Europe, selling red t-shirts, cellphones, sunglasses, and other items and then donating a portion of the profits to the Global Fund to fight AIDS, tuberculosis, and malaria in Africa. But they are not the only retailers giving to charities. Saks Fifth Avenue donated a percentage of sales from a particular leather jacket to Help USA, a group that fights homelessness. Bloomingdale's gives to many charities annually, including the National Colorectal Cancer Research Alliance, the Juvenile Diabetes Research Foundation, and Autism Speaks. Wal-Mart helps the Salvation Army raise money and recently gave the charity a \$245 million donation. MAC Cosmetics' special line of lipsticks and greeting cards raised \$40 million for AIDS treatment

REFACT

One plastic bag can take up to 500 years to decay in a landfill.[11]

The United Kingdom's grocery giant, Tesco, launched a massive advertising campaign to raise awareness of a program that offers one loyalty card point for each bag that a customer reuses, saving the firm more than 10 million plastic bags a week. Taking a different approach to the problem of wasteful bags, Sweden's IKEA furniture stores charge U.K. shoppers 15 cents per plastic bag, which the company says are 100 percent biodegradable. Wal-Mart, Staples, Williams-Sonoma, Home Depot, and Safeway ensure that all of their wood and paper products come from sustainable forests (those that employ legal and renewable logging practices). Other firms are reducing unnecessary packaging and print marketing materials, and still others are incorporating more recycled paper in their catalogs. Retailers like Target are becoming more socially responsible in building and operating their stores by constructing energy-efficient buildings. These initiatives pay off not only in terms of social responsibility but also in cost savings. Through its Zero Waste initiative, Wal-Mart has

Edun is a fair-trade brand of apparel introduced by Bono the lead singer of U2 and global activist.

saved 478.1 million gallons of water, 20.7 million gallons of diesel fuel, and millions of pounds of solid waste. With its 100 percent renewable energy program, it hopes to reduce its energy consumption by 30 percent in all of its new stores by 2014.

Other firms take a more hands-on approach to helping the communities in which they reside. For example, Home Depot's 300,000 associates contribute more than 7 million hours of service through Team Depot, the retailer's volunteer corps. In addition, the corporation has donated more than \$25 million in four target areas: affordable housing, at-risk youth, the environment, and disaster preparedness and relief.

Sources: Johyn Vomhof Jr., "Target Starts Solar-Power Rollout," mlive. com, April 30, 2007; Steve Hochman, "Logistics: Green Supply Chains," Forbes.com, April 20, 2007; "Best Practices: It's Good to Be Green," www.smartreply.com, 2007; Michael Barbaro, "Candles, Jeans, Lipsticks: Products with Ulterior Motives," The New York Times, November 13, 2006; Stephanie Hanes, "Nice Clothes—But Are They Ethical?" Christian Science Monitor, October 15, 2006; Bob Tedeschi, "A Click on Clothes to Support Fair Trade," The New York Times, September 25, 2006.

EXHIBIT 1-2
20 Largest Global
Retailers

Rank	Retailer	Headquarters	2005 Retail Sales (US$mil)	Primary Format	Five-Year CAGR%*
1	Wal-Mart	U.S.	$312,427.00	Discount	11.60%
2	Carrefour	France	$92,778.00	Hypermarket	2.80
3	Home Depot	U.S.	$81,511.00	Category Specialist	12.30
4	Metro AG	Germany	$69,134.00	Multiple Food Formats	5.00
5	Tesco	U.K.	$68,866.00	Multiple Food Formats	12.80
6	Kroger	U.S.	$60,553.00	Supermarket	4.30
7	Target	U.S.	$52,620.00	Discount	7.40
8	Costco	U.S.	$51,862.00	Warehouse Club	10.40
9	Sears	U.S.	$49,124.00	Department Store	5.80
10	Schwarz	Germany	$45,891.00	Multiple Food Formats	13.00
11	Aldi	Germany	$45,096.00	Supermarket	4.50
12	Rewe	Germany	$44,039.00	Multiple Food Formats	3.00
13	Lowe's	U.S.	$43,243.00	Category Specialist	18.20
14	Walgreens	U.S.	$42,202.00	Drug Store	11.40
15	Groupe Auchan	France	$41,180.00	Multiple Food Formats	7.10
16	Albertsons	U.S.	$40,358.00	Supermarket	1.90
17	Edeka	Germany	$39,445.00	Multiple Food Formats	4.90
18	Safeway	U.S.	$38,416.00	Supermarket	3.70
19	CVS	U.S.	$37,006.00	Drug Store	13.00
20	AEON	Japan	$36,978.00	Specialty	10.60

Source: "2007 Global Powers of Retailing," *Stores*, January 2007, pp G17-18.

*CAGR = compounded annual growth rate.

Food retailing continues to dominate among the largest retailers. Eight of the ten largest retailers sell food, and more than 50 percent of the 250 largest retailers have supermarket, warehouse, hypermarket/supercenter, or convenience store formats, or some combination thereof. The dominance of food retailing would be even more pronounced if U.S. drug store chains and other stores that carry food were included as food retailers.

Of the top global retailers, 36 percent are headquartered in the United States, 36 percent in Europe, and 14 percent in Japan. Yet 43 percent of the largest retailers only operate in one country, and 14 percent operate in just two contiguous countries. European and American retailers have the largest international presence; the average European firm among the top 250 largest retailers operates in 9.9 countries. In contrast, the U.S. retailers in the top 250 average operations in 3.7 countries.[12]

STRUCTURE OF RETAILING AND SUPPLY CHAINS AROUND THE WORLD

The nature of retailing and distribution supply chains in various areas around the world differs. Some critical differences among the retailing and supply chain systems in the United States, European Union, China, and India are summarized in Exhibit 1–3. For example, the U.S. supply chain system has the greatest retail density and the greatest concentration of large retail firms. Many U.S. retail firms are large enough to operate their own warehouses, eliminating the need for wholesalers. And the fastest growing types of U.S. retailers sell through large stores with more than 20,000 square feet. The combination of large stores and large firms results in a very efficient supply chain.

EXHIBIT 1–3
Comparison of Retailing and Supply Chains across the World

	United States	European Union	India	China
Concentration (% of retail sales made by large retailers)	High	High	Low	Low
Retail density	High	Medium	Low	Low
Average store size	High	Medium	Low	Low
Role of wholesalers	Limited	Moderate	Extensive	Extensive
Infrastructure supporting efficient supply chains	Extensive	Extensive	Limited	Limited
Restriction on retail locations, store size, and ownership	Few	Considerable	Considerable	Few

Sources: Based on data from World Bank Indicators, http://web.worldbank.org/WBSITE/EXTERNAL/DATASTATISTICS/0,,menuPK:232599~pagePK:64133170~piPK:64133498~theSitePK: 239419,00.html (August 23, 2007); CIA World Fact Book, https://www.cia.gov/library/publications/the-world-factbook/ (August 23, 2007); University of Missouri Archive, http://www.umsl.edu/services/govdocs/wofact92/index.html (August 23, 2007); Retail analysis, www.igd.com/analysis/ (August 23, 2007).

The Chinese and Indian supply chain systems are characterized by small stores operated by relatively small firms and a large independent wholesale industry. To make the daily deliveries to these small retailers efficient, the merchandise often passes through several levels of distributors. In addition, the infrastructure to support retailing, especially the transportation and communication systems, are not as well developed as they are in Western countries. These efficiency differences then mean that a much larger percentage of the Indian and Chinese labor force is employed in supply chains and retailing than is the case in the United States.

The European supply chain system falls between the American and the Chinese and Indian systems on this continuum of efficiency and scale, but the northern, southern, and central parts of Europe should be distinguished. In northern European, retailing is similar to that in the United States, with high concentration levels—in some national markets, 80 percent or more of sales in a sector such as food or home improvements are accounted for by five or fewer firms. Southern European retailing is more fragmented across all sectors. For example, traditional farmers' market retailing remains important in some sectors, operating alongside large "big-box" formats.

Some factors that have created these differences in supply chain systems in the major markets include (1) social and political objectives, (2) geography, and (3) market size.

Social and Political Objectives   An important priority of the Indian and Chinese economic policy is to reduce unemployment by protecting small businesses such as neighborhood retailers. Several E.U. countries have passed laws protecting small retailers, as well as strict zoning laws to preserve green spaces, protect town centers, and inhibit the development of large-scale retailing in the suburbs.

Chinese supply chains are characterized by small stores operated by relatively small firms, making them less efficent than U.S. systems.

Geography   The population density in the United States is much lower than in India, China, or Europe. Thus, there is less low-cost real estate available for building large stores in these countries compared with in the United States.

Market Size   The U.S., Indian, and Chinese retail markets are larger than those in any single European country. In Europe, distribution centers and retail chains typically operate within a single country, which prevents them from achieving the scale economies that U.S. firms, which serve a broader customer base, enjoy. Even with the euro and other initiatives designed to make trade across European countries easier and more efficient, barriers to trade that are not found in the United States still exist.

OPPORTUNITIES IN RETAILING

Management Opportunities

To cope with a highly competitive and challenging environment, retailers hire and promote people with a wide range of skills and interests. Students often view retailing as part of marketing, because managing supply chains is part of a manufacturer's marketing function. But retailers operate businesses and, like manufacturers, undertake traditional business activities. Retailers raise capital from financial institutions; purchase goods and services; develop accounting and management information systems to control their operations; manage warehouses and distribution systems; design and develop new products; and undertake marketing activities such as advertising, promotions, sales force management, and market research. Thus, retailers employ people with expertise and interests in finance, accounting, human resource management, supply chain management, and computer systems, as well as marketing.

Retail managers are often given considerable responsibility early in their careers. Retail management is also financially rewarding. After completing a management trainee program in retailing, managers can double their starting salary in three to five years if they perform well. The typical buyer in a department store earns $50,000–$60,000 per year. Senior buyers and others in higher managerial positions and store managers make between $120,000 and $160,000.[13] (See Appendix 1A at the end of this chapter for a discussion of career opportunities in Retailing.)

Entrepreneurial Opportunities

Retailing also provides opportunities for people who wish to start their own business. Some of the world's richest people are retailing entrepreneurs. Many are well known because their names appear over the stores' door; others you may not recognize. Retailing View 1.2 examines the life of one of the world's greatest entrepreneurs, Sam Walton. Some other innovative retail entrepreneurs include Jeff Bezos, Anita Roddick, and Ingvar Kamprad.

Jeff Bezos (Amazon.com)   After his research uncovered that Internet usage was growing at a 2,300 percent annual rate in 1994, Jeffrey Bezos, the 30-year-old son of a Cuban refugee, quit his job on Wall Street and left behind a hefty bonus to start an Internet business.[14] While his wife MacKenzie was driving their car across country, Jeff pecked out his business plan on a laptop computer. By the time they reached Seattle, he had rounded up the investment capital to launch the first Internet book retailer. The company, Amazon.com, is named after the river that carries the greatest amount of water, symbolizing Bezos's objective of achieving the greatest volume of Internet sales. He was one of the few dot.com leaders to recognize that sweating the details was critical to success. Under his leadership, Amazon developed technologies to make shopping on the Internet faster, easier, and more personal than shopping in stores by offering personalized recommendations and home pages. Amazon.com has become more than a bookstore. It now provides its Web site and fulfillment services for retailers, in addition to hosting storefronts for thousands of smaller retailers.

REFACT

Jeff Bezos chose the domain name Amazon.com because at the time, Yahoo.com listed its search results in alphabetical order; therefore, Amazon would be at or near the top of the search results.[15]

Anita Roddick (The Body Shop)   Anita Roddick, who passed away in 2007, opened the first Body Shop in Brighton, England, to make some extra income for her family. She did not have any business background but was widely traveled and understood the body rituals of women. The small store that initially sold 15 product lines now sells more than 300 products in over 2,000 outlets throughout the world. From the start, Roddick recycled bottles to save money, but such actions also became the foundation for The Body Shop's core values. Today it endorses only environmentally friendly products and stands against animal testing. Roddick used her business as a means to communicate about human rights and environmental issues. Many of the products in the Body Shop contain materials bought from farming communities in

---

RETAILING VIEW   Sam Walton, Founder of Wal-Mart (1918–1992)

1.2

"Like Henry Ford with his Model T," said a professor of rural sociology at the University of Missouri, "Sam Walton and his Wal-Marts, for better or for worse, transformed small-town America." Others go even further and claim he transformed the entire nation and the global retail industry.

After graduating from the University of Missouri in 1940, Walton began working at a JCPenney store in Des Moines, Iowa. He served in the Army during World War II and then purchased a Ben Franklin variety store franchise in Newport, Arkansas. He boosted sales by finding suppliers who would sell to him lower than he could buy from Ben Franklin.

Walton lost his store, however, in 1950 when the landlord refused to renew his lease. He then moved to Bentonville, Arkansas, where he and a younger brother franchised another Ben Franklin store. Walton employed a new self-service system, one he had discovered at two Ben Franklin stores in Minnesota: no clerks or cash registers around the store, only checkout lanes in the front. By 1960, Walton had 15 stores in Arkansas and Missouri that laid the foundation for his own discount chain.

By the early 1960s, retailers had developed the discount concept using self-service, a limited assortment, low overhead costs, and massive parking lots. Walton joined them in 1962 when he opened his first Wal-Mart Discount City in Rogers, Arkansas. At least one observer called it a mess—with donkey rides and watermelons mixed together outside under the boiling sun and merchandise haphazardly arranged inside.

But Walton quickly brought order to his enterprise and pursued an innovative strategy: large discount stores in small towns. Walton felt cities were saturated with retailers and believed he could prosper in towns that the larger companies had ignored. By the 1980s, Walton started building stores in larger suburbs. Walton then started Sam's Clubs, warehouse-style stores that sold bulk merchandise at discount prices. Next came Wal-Mart Supercenters, ranging from 100,000 to 200,000 square feet, that featured a supermarket and a regular Wal-Mart under one roof. As a result of their success, Wal-Mart is now the largest food retailer in the United States.

Walton often visited his stores, dropping in unannounced to check the merchandise presentation or financial performance and talk to his "associates." He prided himself on a profit-sharing program and a friendly, open atmosphere, business practices he had learned when working for JCPenney. He often led his

Sam Walton believed in "Management by Walking Around."

workers in a cheer that some called corny, others uplifting. He once described it: "Give me a W! Give me an A! Give me an L! Give me a Squiggly! (Here, everybody sort of does the twist.) Give me an M! Give me an A! Give me an R! Give me a T! What's that spell? Wal-Mart! What's that spell? Wal-Mart! Who's number one? THE CUSTOMER!"

He offered his own formula for how a large company must operate: "Think one store at a time. That sounds easy enough, but it's something we've constantly had to stay on top of. Communicate, communicate, communicate: What good is figuring out a better way to sell beach towels if you aren't going to tell everybody in your company about it? Keep your ear to the ground: A computer is not—and will never be—a substitute for getting out in your stores and learning what's going on."

In 1991, due to the success of his concept and management practices, Walton became America's wealthiest person. He died of leukemia in 1992. Wal-Mart is now the world's largest corporation.

Sources: Michael Bergdahl, "10 Rules of Sam Walton," *Leadership Excellence*, September 2006, p. 4; Michael Bergdahl, *The 10 Rules of Sam Walton: Success Secrets for Remarkable Results* (Hoboken, NJ: John Wiley & Sons, 2006); "Sam Walton, http://en.wikipedia.org/wiki/Sam_Walton (November 26, 2007); http://littlerock.about.com/cs/homeliving/a/aasamwalton.htm; Wendy Zellner, "Sam Walton: King of the Discounters," *BusinessWeek*, August 9, 2004, p. 12; "The Waltons: Inside America's Richest Family," *Fortune*, November 15, 2004, pp. 86–101.

South America and thereby help those communities maintain their way of life. In 1989, Amazonian Indian tribes were protesting a hydroelectric project that would have flooded the rainforest and their native lands. Coming to their assistance, Roddick drew up a plan to prevent the project from moving forward. She then determined that Brazil nuts produced a moisturizing and conditioning oil and made a deal to buy the nuts from the Indians who gathered them. Today, The Body Shop continues its business relationship with this tribe.[16]

Ingvar Kamprad, IKEA's founder, started in business as a child by selling matches to neighbors from his bicycle.

 Ingvar Kamprad (IKEA)   Ingvar Kamprad, the founder of the Swedish-based home furnishing retailer chain IKEA, was always an entrepreneur; his first business was selling matches to neighbors from his bicycle.[17] By buying matches in bulk and selling them individually at a low price, he discovered he could make a good profit. He then expanded to selling fish, Christmas tree decorations, seeds, and ballpoint pens and pencils. By the time he was 17 years of age, he had earned a reward for succeeding in school: His father gave him the money to register a company. Like Sam Walton, the founder of Wal-Mart, Kamprad is known for his frugality. He drives an old Volvo, flies economy class, and encourages IKEA employees to write on both sides of a paper. This thriftiness has translated into a corporate philosophy of cost-cutting throughout IKEA so that it can offer quality furniture with innovative designs at low prices.

REFACT

The acronym IKEA is made up of the initials of the founder's name (**I**ngvar **K**amprad) plus those of **E**lmtaryd, his family farm, and the nearby village **A**gunnaryd.[18]

THE RETAIL MANAGEMENT DECISION PROCESS

This book is organized around the management decisions that retailers must make to provide value to their customers and develop an advantage over their competitors. Exhibit 1–4 identifies the chapters in this book associated with each type of decision.

REFACT

Fred Lazarus Jr., founder of the Lazarus department stores, which is now part of Macy's, promoted the idea of fixing Thanksgiving during the fourth weekend of November to expand the Christmas shopping season. Congress adopted his proposal in 1941.[19]

Understanding the World of Retailing—Section I

The first step in the retail management decision process, as Exhibit 1–4 shows, is understanding the world of retailing. Retail managers need to know the environment in which they operate before they can develop and implement effective strategies. The first section of this book therefore provides a general overview of the retailing industry and its customers.

The critical environmental factors in the world of retailing are (1) the macroenvironment and (2) the microenvironment. The impacts of the macroenvironment—including technological, social, and ethical/legal/political factors—on retailing are discussed throughout this book. For example, the influence of technology on the rise of multichannel retailing is reviewed in Chapter 3; the use of new information and supply chain technologies is examined in Chapters 10 and 11; and ethical, legal, and public policy issues are discussed throughout the book. The retailer's microenvironment focuses specifically on its competitors and customers.

EXHIBIT 1–4
Retail Management
Decision Process

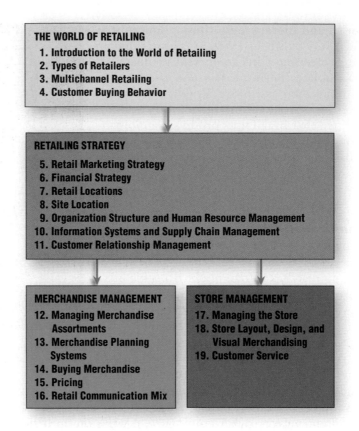

THE WORLD OF RETAILING
1. Introduction to the World of Retailing
2. Types of Retailers
3. Multichannel Retailing
4. Customer Buying Behavior

RETAILING STRATEGY
5. Retail Marketing Strategy
6. Financial Strategy
7. Retail Locations
8. Site Location
9. Organization Structure and Human Resource Management
10. Information Systems and Supply Chain Management
11. Customer Relationship Management

MERCHANDISE MANAGEMENT
12. Managing Merchandise Assortments
13. Merchandise Planning Systems
14. Buying Merchandise
15. Pricing
16. Retail Communication Mix

STORE MANAGEMENT
17. Managing the Store
18. Store Layout, Design, and Visual Merchandising
19. Customer Service

Competitors   At first glance, identifying competitors appears easy: A retailer's primary competitors are other retailers that use the same format. Thus, department stores compete against other department stores, and supermarkets compete with other supermarkets. This competition between the same type of retailers is called **intratype competition.**

Yet to appeal to a broader group of consumers, many retailers are increasing the variety of their merchandise. **Variety** is the number of different merchandise categories within a store or department. By offering greater variety in one store, retailers can provide one-stop shopping to satisfy more of the needs of their target market. For example, clothing and food are now available in grocery, department, discount, and drug stores. Walgreens has added jewelry, accessories, and apparel to its already extensive health and beauty categories to meet the lifestyle needs of its customers.[20] When retailers offer merchandise not typically associated with their type of store, such as clothing in a drug store, it results in **scrambled merchandising.** Scrambled merchandising increases **intertype competition,** or competition between retailers that sell similar merchandise using different formats, such as discount and department stores.

Increasing intertype competition has made it harder for retailers to identify and monitor their competition. In one sense, all retailers compete against one another for the dollars that consumers spend on goods and services. But the intensity of competition is greatest among retailers located near one another that sell offerings that are viewed as very similar.

Because the convenience of a location is important in store choice, a store's proximity to competitors is a critical factor in identifying competition. Consider two DVD rental stores, Blockbuster and Harry's Video, in two suburbs 10 miles apart. The stores are the only specialty DVD rental retailers within 50 miles, but a grocery store also rents a more limited selection of DVDs in the same strip center as Blockbuster. Due to the distance between Blockbuster and Harry's Video, they probably don't compete against each other intensely. Customers who live near Harry's Video will rent DVDs there, whereas customers close to

When a grocery store competes with a fast food restaurant, it is engaging in intertype competition.

Blockbuster will rent DVDs at Blockbuster or the grocery store. In this case, Harry's major competition may be movie theaters, cable television, and Netflix, a mail-order rental service, because it is too inconvenient for customers who live close to Harry's to rent DVDs elsewhere. In contrast, Blockbuster might compete most intensely with the grocery store.

Management's view of competition also may differ depending on the manager's position within the retail firm. For example, the manager of the Saks Fifth Avenue women's sportswear department in Bergen County, New Jersey, views the other women's sportswear specialty stores in the Riverside Square mall as her major competitors. But the Saks store manager views the Bloomingdale's store in a nearby mall as her strongest competitor. These differences in perspective arise because the department sales manager is primarily concerned with customers for a specific category of merchandise, whereas the store manager is concerned with customers seeking the entire selection of all merchandise and services offered by a department store.

The CEO of a retail chain, in contrast, views competition from a much broader geographic perspective. For example, Nordstrom might identify its strongest competitor as Macy's in the Northwest, Saks in northern California, and Bloomingdale's in northern Virginia. The CEO may also take a broader strategic perspective and recognize that other activities compete for consumers' disposable income. For example, Safeway's CEO adopts the consumer's perspective and recognizes that grocery stores are competing with pharmacies, convenience stores, and restaurants for customers' food dollars.

Retailing is intensely competitive, which means that understanding the different types of retailers and how they compete with one another is critical to developing and implementing a retail strategy. Chapter 2 discusses various types of retailers and their competitive strategies, and Chapter 3 concentrates on how retailers have adopted multichannel strategies to give themselves a competitive edge.

Customers   The second factor in the microenvironment is customers. Customer needs are changing at an ever-increasing rate. Retailers must respond to broad demographic and lifestyle trends in our society, such as the growth in the elderly and minority segments of the U.S. population or the importance of shopping convenience to the increasing number of two-income families. To develop and implement an effective strategy, retailers must understand why customers shop, how they select a store, and how they select among that store's merchandise—the information found in Chapter 4.

Developing a Retail Strategy—Section II

The next stages in the retail management decision-making process, formulating and implementing a retail strategy, are based on an understanding of the macro- and microenvironments developed in the first section. Section II focuses on decisions related to developing a retail strategy, whereas Sections III and IV pertain to decisions surrounding the implementation of the strategy.

The **retail strategy** indicates how the firm plans to focus its resources to accomplish its objectives. It identifies (1) the target market, or markets, toward which the retailer will direct its efforts; (2) the nature of the merchandise and services the retailer will offer to satisfy the needs of the target market; and (3) how the retailer will build a long-term advantage over its competitors.

The nature of a retail strategy can be illustrated by comparing the strategies of Wal-Mart and Circuit City. Initially, Wal-Mart identified its target market as small towns (fewer than 35,000 in population) in Arkansas, Texas, and Oklahoma. It offered name-brand merchandise at low prices in a broad array of categories, ranging from laundry detergent to girls' dresses. Today, even as Wal-Mart stores have expanded across the world and into many different categories of merchandise, the selection in each category remains limited. A store might have only three models of high-definition television sets, whereas an electronic category specialist might carry 30 models.

In contrast to Wal-Mart, Circuit City identified its target as consumers living in suburban areas of large cities. Rather than carrying a broad array of merchandise categories, Circuit City stores specialize in consumer electronics and carry most types and brands currently available in the market. Both Wal-Mart and Circuit City emphasize self-service: Customers select their merchandise, bring it to the checkout line, and then carry it to their cars. But Circuit City also offers knowledgeable, trained salespeople to assist customers in certain areas of the store, such as home entertainment centers, and provides delivery and installation of these systems.

Because Wal-Mart and Circuit City both emphasize low price, they have made strategic decisions to develop a cost advantage over their competitors. Both firms have sophisticated distribution and management information systems to manage inventory. Their strong relationships with their suppliers enable them to buy merchandise at low prices.

Strategic Decision Areas   The key strategic decision areas for a firm involve determining its target market, financial status, location, organizational and human resource structure, information systems, supply chain organization, and customer relationship management strategies.

Chapter 5 discusses how the selection of a retail market strategy requires analyzing the environment and the firm's strengths and weaknesses. When major environmental changes occur, the current strategy and the reasoning behind it must be reexamined. The retailer then decides what, if any, strategy changes are needed to take advantage of new opportunities or avoid new threats in the environment.

The retailer's market strategy must be consistent with the firm's financial objectives. Chapter 6 reviews how financial variables, such as sales, costs, expenses, profits, assets, and liabilities, can be used to evaluate the market strategy and its implementation.

Decisions regarding location strategy (reviewed in Chapters 7 and 8) are important for both consumer and competitive reasons. First, location is typically consumers' top consideration when selecting a store. Generally consumers buy gas at the closest service station and patronize the shopping mall that's most convenient to their home or office. Second, location offers an opportunity to gain a long-term advantage over competition. When a retailer has the best location, a competing retailer must settle for the second-best location.

A retailer's organization design and human resource management strategies are intimately related to its market strategy. For example, retailers that attempt to serve national or regional markets must make trade-offs between the efficiency of centralized buying and their need to tailor merchandise and services to local demands. Retailers that focus on customer segments seeking high-quality customer service must motivate and enable sales associates to provide the expected levels of service. The organization structure and human resources policies discussed in

Chapter 9 coordinate the implementation of the retailing strategy by buyers, store managers, and sales associates.

Retail information and supply chain management systems will offer a significant opportunity for retailers to gain strategic advantages in the coming decade. Chapter 10 reviews how some retailers are developing sophisticated computer and distribution systems to monitor flows of information and merchandise from vendors to retail distribution centers to retail stores. Point-of-sale (POS) terminals read price and product information coded into Universal Product Codes (UPCs) affixed to the merchandise. This information is then transmitted electronically to distribution centers or directly to vendors, computer to computer. These technologies are part of an overall inventory management system that enables retailers to (1) give customers a more complete selection of merchandise and (2) decrease their inventory investment.

Retailers, like most businesses, focus on loyalty from their best customers. Chapter 11 examines customer relationship management from a retailer-to-consumer perspective, including the process that retailers use to identify, design programs for, increase the share of wallet of, and build loyalty with their best customers.

JCPenney Moves from Main Street to the Mall

The interrelationships among these retail strategy decisions—market strategy, financial strategy, organization structure and human resource strategies, and location strategy—are illustrated by the strategic changes JCPenney has undertaken to cope with information and supply chain management changes in the retail landscape.[21]

In the late 1950s, Penney was one of the most profitable national retailers. Its target market was middle-income consumers living in small towns. In its Main Street locations, Penney sold staple soft goods—underwear, socks, basic clothing, sheets, tablecloths, and so forth—at low prices with friendly service. All sales were cash; the company didn't offer credit to its customers. Penney had considerable expertise in the design and purchase of private-label soft goods—brands developed by the retailer and sold exclusively at its stores.

Its organization structure was decentralized. Each store manager controlled the type of merchandise sold, the pricing of merchandise, and the management of store employees. Promotional efforts were limited and also controlled by store managers. Penney store managers were active participants in their community's social and political activities.

Although Penney was a highly successful retailer, there was a growing awareness among company executives that macroenvironmental trends would have a negative impact on the firm. First, as the nation's levels of education and disposable income rose, consumers grew more interested in fashionable rather than staple merchandise. Second, with the development of a national highway system, the growth of suburbs, and the rise of regional malls, small-town residents were attracted to conveniently located, large, regional shopping malls. Third, Sears (the nation's largest retailer at the time) was beginning to locate stores and auto centers in regional malls. These trends suggested a decline in small-town markets for staple soft goods.

In the early 1960s, Penney changed its strategy in response to these changes in its environment. All new Penney stores were located in regional malls across the United States. Penney opened several mall locations in each metropolitan area to create a significant presence in each market. (Of course, as JCPenney was moving from small towns to suburban malls, Wal-Mart began opening discount stores in small towns.) The firm began to offer credit to its customers and added new merchandise lines: appliances, auto supplies, paint, hardware, sporting goods, consumer electronics, and moderately priced fashionable clothing.

To effectively control its 1,150 department stores, Penney installed a national communication network. Store managers could monitor daily sales of each type of

REFACT

James Cash Penney opened the first JCPenney store, called Golden Rule, in Kemmerer, Wyoming, in 1902.[22]

JCPenney is upgrading its merchandise offering by adding Sephora "store-in-stores" (left) and improving the customer experience with centralized checkout counters.

merchandise in their store and every other store in the chain. Buyers at corporate headquarters in New York and then Dallas communicated daily with merchandise managers in each store over a satellite TV link, but store managers continued to make merchandise decisions for their stores.

In response to the increased time pressure on two-income and single-head-of household families, Penney launched its catalog operation and now is the largest catalog retailer in the United States. Penney has used its catalog distribution capability to aggressively move into selling merchandise over the Internet (www.jcpenney.com), a multichannel strategy that has been very successful.

The success of discount stores poses a growing threat for JCPenney. Department stores targeting middle-income families such as JCPenney and Sears are caught in the middle between higher-priced, fashion-oriented department store chains like Macy's that are lowering their prices through sales and lower-cost stores such as Kohl's, Target, and Wal-Mart that are offering more fashionable merchandise.

To compete effectively with the retailers targeting JCPenney's middle-income customers, the company has made some radical changes in how it operates, its organizational structure, where it locates its stores, its store atmospherics, and its merchandise/service offering:

- JCPenney is reducing its distribution costs by shipping merchandise through distribution centers rather than using direct delivery from vendors to stores.

- It has centralized merchandise management; rather than store managers making the merchandise decisions, buyers at corporate headquarters manage them. Centralization of merchandise decisions enables JCPenney to use its size to buy merchandise at a lower cost and respond more quickly to changing fashions.

- To increase customer convenience, JCPenney is building new stores away from malls in stand-alone locations and designing the stores with centralized checkout counters rather than checkout counters in each area of the store.

- It is improving its store atmospherics by widening aisles, adding "way-finding" signage, and upgrading fixtures in areas such as intimates and jewelry.

- It is upgrading its merchandise offering by adding France's cosmetics Sephora "store-in-stores," C7P by Chip and Pepper Foster jeans at $34.99 versus Chip and Pepper's regular line which sells for $150 to $200 at Neiman Marcus and Saks Fifth Avenue, a line of apparel by Polo Ralph Lauren called American Living, Nicole by Nicole Miller, Bisou Bisou, and special apparel lines by Liz Claiborne Inc. and Jones Apparel Group.

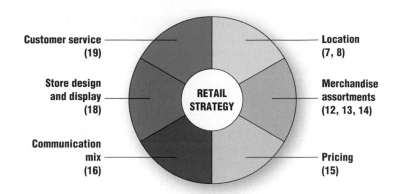

EXHIBIT 1–5
Elements in the Retail Mix

Implementing the Retail Strategy—Sections III and IV

To implement a retail strategy, management develops a retail mix that satisfies the needs of its target market better than that of its competitors. The **retail mix** includes the decision variables retailers use to satisfy customer needs and influence their purchase decisions. Elements in the retail mix (Exhibit 1–5) include the types of merchandise and services offered, merchandise pricing, advertising and promotional programs, store design, merchandise display, assistance to customers provided by salespeople, and convenience of the store's location. Section III reviews the implementation decisions made by buyers, and Section IV focuses on decisions made by store managers.

Managers in the buying organization must decide how much and what types of merchandise to buy (Chapters 12 and 13), the vendors to use and the purchase terms (Chapter 14), the retail prices to set (Chapter 15), and how to advertise and promote merchandise (Chapter 16).

Store managers must determine how to recruit, select, and motivate sales associates (Chapter 17), where and how merchandise will be displayed (Chapter 18), and the nature of services to provide customers (Chapter 19).

Whole Foods Market: An Organic and Natural Food Supermarket Chain

Whole Foods Market, one of the fastest-growing supermarket chains, illustrates the use of merchandise and store management activities to implement its retail strategy of providing a supermarket offering that targets health- and environmentally conscious consumers. Its stores are twice as productive as the typical supermarket.

It is easy to mistake John Mackey for an aging hippie rather than the founder and CEO of a retailer with $5.6 billion in annual sales.[23] At the University of Texas in Austin, Mackey developed a passion for philosophy and religion. When he found that textbooks weren't going to provide the answers he was looking for, he dropped out of college, lived in a vegetarian housing co-op, worked in an Austin natural food store, and eventually opened his own health food store and restaurant. Unlike other veggie joints, Mackey's store catered to a broad clientele by carrying items typically not found at health food stores, such as refined sugar and eggs. Then he teamed up with a local organic grocer to open the first Whole Foods, which was an instant success.

About 200 Whole Foods stores carry a much broader assortment than the typical natural and organic grocery store. It recently opened its first store outside the United States, in London.[24] The stores sell vegetarian no-nos, such as red meat, so that even health-conscious nonvegetarians can have a one-stop shopping experience. But it does not carry live lobsters or soft-shell crabs due to concerns about their humane treatment.[25] It has used its influence and buying power to demand that the meat it sells comes from animals that have been treated with a measure of dignity before being slaughtered.

The assortment includes seven lines of private-brand products that are free of artificial sweeteners, colorings, artificial flavorings, and preservatives.[26] Buyers work with artisan food producers and organic farmers to attain products sold under the superpremium Authentic Food Artisan brand. Its core private brands are called Whole Brands (department-specific products), Whole Foods (premium products), and Whole Kids Organic (organic products for children). The 365 Day Everyday Value and 365 Day Organic Everyday Value lines provides natural products at value prices. Finally, Allegro Coffee Company works with farmers to ensure its products meet fair-trade standards, meaning farmers get a fair share of profits generated by their labor.

The company communicates openly with its customers about issues related to the food it sells. Stores display placards detailing test results for PCB contamination in the chain's farm-raised and wild salmon, along with FDA limits. Curious about the life of a chicken in the display case? It comes with a 16-page booklet and an invitation to visit the live chickens at the company's Pennsylvania farm.

The flower power of the 1960s is reflected in Mackey's guiding management principles: love, trust, and employee empowerment. All employees are organized into self-managed teams that meet regularly to discuss issues and solve problems. Almost all team members have stock options in the firm. To ensure that employees are compensated equitably, the company has a cap on salaries so that no employee's total compensation, including executives', can be more than 14 times the average compensation of any employee.[28]

Whole Foods attempts to have a positive impact in the communities in which it operates and purchases products, as well as on the environment. Its Whole Planet Foundation funds collateral-free microloans to farmers and poor entrepreneurs in developing countries.[29] It has also made the largest-ever corporate purchase of sustainable wind energy credits—sufficient to supply 100 percent of its electricity needs.

"Americans love to eat. And Americans love to shop. But we don't like to shop for food. It's a chore, like doing laundry," laments John Mackey.[30] Whole Foods thinks shopping should be fun. So it is opening stores that synthesize

REFACT

Whole Foods CEO and founder John Mackey cut his salary to $1 in January 2007.[27]

Whole Foods has a retail mix that supports its strategy of targeting health conscious consumers.

RETAILING
MANAGEMENT

CHAPTER 19 CUSTOMER SERVICE 538

APPENDIX A STARTING YOUR OWN RETAIL BUSINESS 562

APPENDIX B STARTING A FRANCHISE BUSINESS 570

SECTION V CASES

CHAPTER 10   INFORMATION SYSTEMS AND SUPPLY CHAIN MANAGEMENT   276

CHAPTER 11   CUSTOMER RELATIONSHIP MANAGEMENT   304

SECTION III   MERCHANDISE MANAGEMENT

CHAPTER 12   MANAGING MERCHANDISE ASSORTMENTS   328

SECTION II RETAILING STRATEGY

TABLE OF CONTENTS

BRIEF CONTENTS

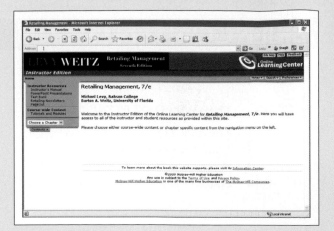

The online teaching center for instructors includes the instructor's manual, PageOut course management system, PowerPoint slides, Power-Web (an excellent research source), and archived retail newsletters.

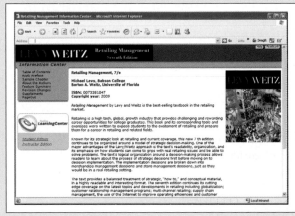

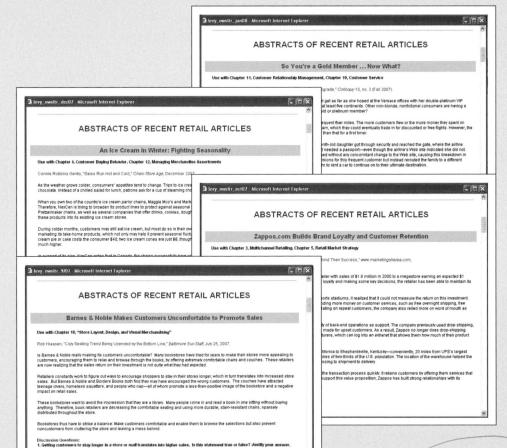

Each month, the authors prepare and distribute through email a Retailing Newsletter. The newsletters contain ten to twelve abstracts of articles appearing in the business or trade press about current issues facing retailers specifically and the industry in general.

Thirty-five video segments are available to illustrate issues addressed in the text. Topics addressed in the video include Rainforest Café's and Build-A-Bear's retail strategy, Domino Pizzas entry into Mexico, Starbuck's fair trade policy with its coffee growers, Staples' growth strategy in the copying business, Costco, Container Store's organizational culture, Netflix's distribution strategy, Wal-Mart's campaign to change its image, internet shopping behavior, supply chain management, pricing, management information systems, and suburban and lifestyle shopping centers. A number of the videos complement the cases.

SUPPORT FOR STUDENT LEARNING

The end-of-chapter Get Out and Do It exercises and the Online Learning Center involve students in the course and the material covered in the text.

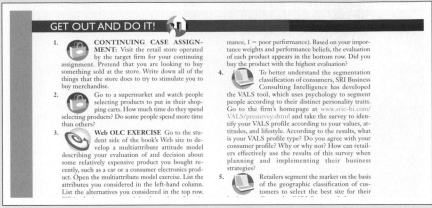

Get Out and Do It! Exercises Found at the end of each chapter, these exercises suggest projects that students can undertake by either visiting local retail stores, surfing the Internet, or using the student Web site. The exercises are designed to provide a hands-on learning experience for students. A continuing exercise is included in each chapter so that students can be involved in an experiential exercise involving the same retailer throughout the course.

The **Online Learning Center** provides students with exercises to evaluate international expansion opportunities, examine financial performance of retailers, analyze potential store locations, develop a merchandise budget plan, edit the assortment for a category, make pricing and markdown decisions, and determine break-even sales levels. Sample test questions and flash cards are provided for each chapter.

To **stimulate class discussion** about issues confronting retail managers, the text contains 38 cases. Cases include Tractor Supply, Retailing in India, Retail Pet Market, Macy's National Brand Strategy, Wal-Mart and social responsibility activities, Starbucks, Build-a-Bear Workshop, Financial Comparisons of Blue Nile and Tiffany's, Nordstrom's loyalty program, Retailing to Teens, and Sav-A-Lot.

To illustrate the opportunities and rewards from a career in retailing, each chapter begins with a **profile** of a retail manager—either a senior executive or recent college graduate—discussing their area of decision-making and their career path.

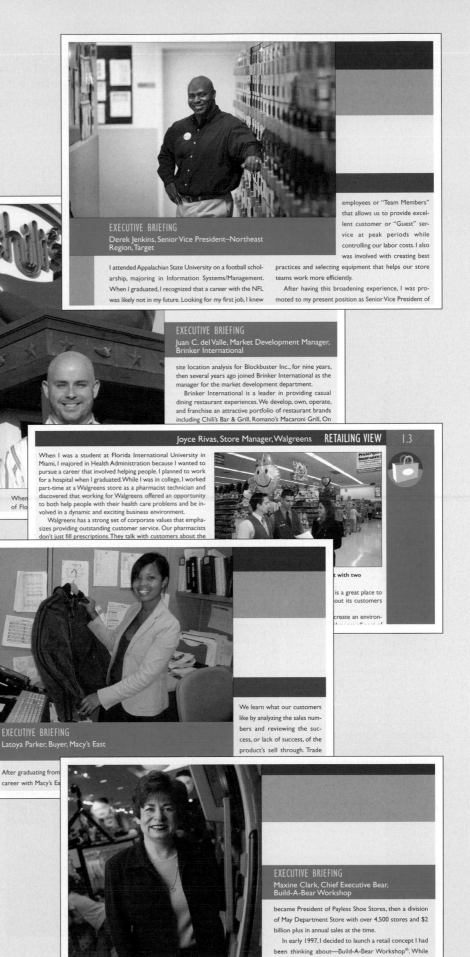

EXECUTIVE BRIEFING
Derek Jenkins, Senior Vice President–Northeast Region, Target

I attended Appalachian State University on a football scholarship, majoring in Information Systems/Management. When I graduated, I recognized that a career with the NFL was likely not in my future. Looking for my first job, I knew

employees or "Team Members" that allows us to provide excellent customer or "Guest" service at peak periods while controlling our labor costs. I also was involved with creating best practices and selecting equipment that helps our store teams work more efficiently.

After having this broadening experience, I was promoted to my present position as Senior Vice President of

EXECUTIVE BRIEFING
Juan C. del Valle, Market Development Manager, Brinker International

site location analysis for Blockbuster Inc., for nine years, then several years ago joined Brinker International as the manager for the market development department.

Brinker International is a leader in providing casual dining restaurant experiences. We develop, own, operate, and franchise an attractive portfolio of restaurant brands including Chili's Bar & Grill, Romano's Macaroni Grill, On

Joyce Rivas, Store Manager, Walgreens **RETAILING VIEW** 1.3

When I was a student at Florida International University in Miami, I majored in Health Administration because I wanted to pursue a career that involved helping people. I planned to work for a hospital when I graduated. While I was in college, I worked part-time at a Walgreens store as a pharmacist technician and discovered that working for Walgreens offered an opportunity to both help people with their health care problems and be involved in a dynamic and exciting business environment.

Walgreens has a strong set of corporate values that emphasizes providing outstanding customer service. Our pharmacists don't just fill prescriptions. They talk with customers about the

with two

is a great place to out its customers

create an environ-

When
of Flo

EXECUTIVE BRIEFING
Latoya Parker, Buyer, Macy's East

After graduating from
career with Macy's Ea

We learn what our customers like by analyzing the sales numbers and reviewing the success, or lack of success, of the product's sell through. Trade

EXECUTIVE BRIEFING
Maxine Clark, Chief Executive Bear, Build-A-Bear Workshop

became President of Payless Shoe Stores, then a division of May Department Store with over 4,500 stores and $2 billion plus in annual sales at the time.

In early 1997, I decided to launch a retail concept I had been thinking about—Build-A-Bear Workshop®. While

INTERESTING AND READABLE

This edition continues the emphasis placed on **creating interest and involving students** in the course and the industry. Refacts, Retailing Views, and retail manager profiles at the beginning of each chapter make the textbook a **"good read"** for students.

Refacts (retailing factoids) are interesting facts about retailing, related to the textual material, that are placed in the margins.

Retailing Views are vignettes in each chapter that relate concepts developed in the text to issues and problems confronting retailers.

CAREERS IN RETAILING

The challenges and rewards of retail careers are emphsized. In addition to discussing careers with national chains, entrepreneurial opportunites are also discussed. Some of issues relating to careers are:

Myths about retail careers.

training, placement, advancement, and welfare of employees. Because there are seasonal peaks in retailing (such as Christmas, when many extra people must be hired), human resource personnel must be flexible and highly efficient.

MYTHS ABOUT RETAILING

Sales Clerk Is the Entry-Level Job in Retailing

Most students and their parents think that people working in retailing have jobs as sales clerks and cashiers. They hold this view because, as customers in retail stores, they typically only interact with sales associates and store managers. But as we have discussed in this ch... are large, sophisticated corporations tha... ers with a wide variety of knowledge, sk...

Entry-level positions for college and university graduates are typically management trainees in the buying or store organization, not sales associates.

Management trainees in retailing are given more responsibility more quickly than in other industries. Buyers are responsible for choosing, promoting, pricing, distributing, and selling millions of dollars worth of merchandise each season. The department manager, generally the first position after a training program, is often responsible for merchandising one or more departments, as well as managing 10 or more full- and part-time sales associates.

College and University Degrees Are Not ...

Example of retail entrepreneurs.

Anita Roddick (The Body Shop) Anita Roddick, who passed away in 2007, opened the first Body Shop in Brighton, England, to make some extra income for her family. She did not have any business background but was widely traveled and understood the body rituals of women. The small store that initially sold 15 product lines now sells more than 300 products in over 2,000 outlets throughout the world. From the start, Roddick recycled bottles to save money, but such actions also became the foundation for The Body Shop's core values. Today it endorses only environmentally friendly products and stands against animal testing. Roddick used her business as a means to communicate about human rights and environmental issues. Many of the products in the Body Shop contain materials bought from farming communities in

New Appendices

APPENDIX A
Starting Your Own Retail Business

Starting a retail business can be an enticing and daunting prospect. On the one hand, you can be your own boss, enjoy complete creative control, and reap the full rewards of your hard work. On the other hand, retail business owners must assume large amounts of responsibility, bear the consequences of poor decisions, and ultimately shoulder the blame for the success or failure of the business. Owning your own business involves a great deal of effort, sacrifice, and patience. It is inherently risky, and consequently, fewer than 20 percent of new retail businesses survive to the five-year mark. Yet the rewards of successfully navigating the unpredictable landscape of business ownership can be enormous, both personally and financially. You might grow your business and become the next Sam Walton (Wal-Mart), Maxine Clark (Build-A-Bear Workshop), or John Mackey (Whole Food Markets).

APPENDIX B
Starting a Franchise Business

Like hot dogs, baseball, and apple pie, franchising in an American institution. A proven means to realize the entrepreneurial dream, franchising also is taking over much of the retail trade in the United States. This appendix explores franchising options in terms of their merits and drawbacks. With more than 2,300 franchises to choose from, finding the best one can be almost as hard as starting a business.

Franchises are popular largely because of their historical success. A 1999 study by the U.S. Chamber of Commerce found that 91 percent of new franchises remained in business after seven years, compared with only 20 percent of new, individual start-up businesses.[1] But not all franchises are secure investments. Arthur Treacher's Fish and Chips, Jerry Lewis Theaters, and Chicken Delight all have one thing in common: They failed. As a result, thousands of dreams were shattered, and millions of dollars were lost. Buying a franchise can be a dream come true, or it can be a nightmare. The key is buying smart, which re-

INNOVATIVE RETAILING APPROACHES

Retailers use advanced technologies and analytical tools to improve their operating efficiencies. Some of these technologies and tools, identified with a technology icon, examined in this edition are:

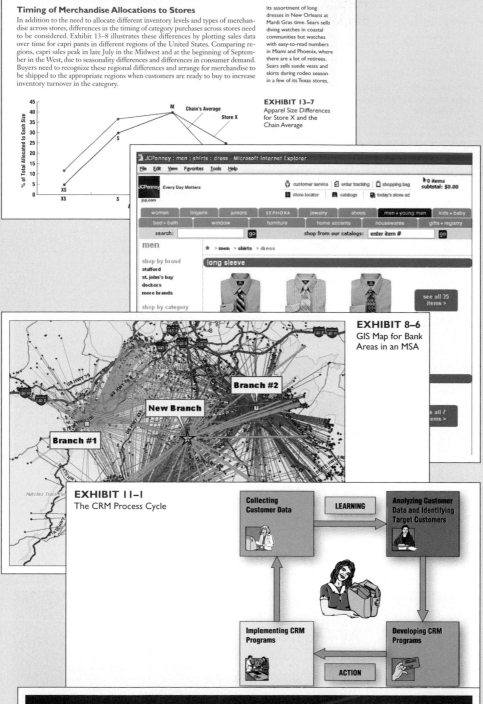

Timing of Merchandise Allocations to Stores

In addition to the need to allocate different inventory levels and types of merchandise across stores, differences in the timing of category purchases across stores need to be considered. Exhibit 13–8 illustrates these differences by plotting sales data over time for capri pants in different regions of the United States. Comparing regions, capri sales peak in late July in the Midwest and at the beginning of September in the West, due to seasonality differences and differences in consumer demand. Buyers need to recognize these regional differences and arrange for merchandise to be shipped to the appropriate regions when customers are ready to buy to increase inventory turnover in the category.

its assortment of long dresses in New Orleans at Mardi Gras time. Sears sells diving watches in coastal communities but watches with easy-to-read numbers in Miami and Phoenix, where there are a lot of retirees. Sears sells suede vests and skirts during rodeo season in a few of its Texas stores.

EXHIBIT 13–7
Apparel Size Differences for Store X and the Chain Average

EXHIBIT 8–6
GIS Map for Bank Areas in an MSA

EXHIBIT 11–1
The CRM Process Cycle

To build its employment brand, JCPenney uses the tagline "A Perfect Fit" on all correspondence and advertising directed toward potential employees.

Merchandise optimization. Methods of optimize merchandise decisions such as taking markdowns and allocating merchandise to stores.

RFID used by retailers to increase inventory turnover, reduce stockouts, and improve supply chain efficiency.

Geographic information systems for store location.

Customer relationship management for identifying the best customers and targeting promotion toward them.

Employment branding. As the sophistication in decision making by retailers increases, the demand for managers with analytical thinking skills is increasing. Retailers are undertaking employment branding programs to attract the best and brightest.

GLOBALIZATION OF THE RETAIL INDUSTRY

Retailing is a global industry. With a greater emphasis being placed on private-label merchandise, retailers are working with manufacturers located throughout the world to acquire merchandise. In addition, retailers are increasingly looking to international markets for growth opportunities. Some of the global retailing issues and illustrations, identified with an icon in the margin, examined in this edition are:

Global sourcing of merchandise.

Datang, China, Is Sock City RETAILING VIEW 14.3

Datang, China, is called Sock City because nine billion pairs of socks, more than one set for every person in the world, and 2.6 pairs for each American, are produced there each year. Its annual trade fair attracts 100,000 buyers from around the world. Southeast of Datang is Shenzhou, which is the world's necktie capital; to the west is Sweater City and Kids' Clothing City; and to the south is Underwear City.

This specialization creates the economies of scale that have made Chinese businesses the world's leading garment manufacturers. Buyers from New York to Tokyo can place orders for 500,000 pairs of socks all at once—or 300,000 neckties, 100,000 children's jackets, or 50,000 size 36B bras—in China's

needed to move products quickly to market. It has created networks of support businesses located near one another, such as the button capital that furnishes most of the buttons on the world's shirts, pants, and jackets. Private companies, with the support of the government, have built huge textile factory complexes, complete with dormitories and hospitals, that provide food, shelter, and health care, along with close supervision.

Huafang Group, one of China's largest textile companies, has over 100 factory buildings, 30,000 employees, and round-the-clock operations. More than 20,000 workers live free of charge in Huafang's dormitories.

As a result of government and private investment, China has become the leading manufacturer of private-label and national brand merchandise.

REFACT
Twelve percent of China's

Evaluation of non-domestic markets for potential entry.

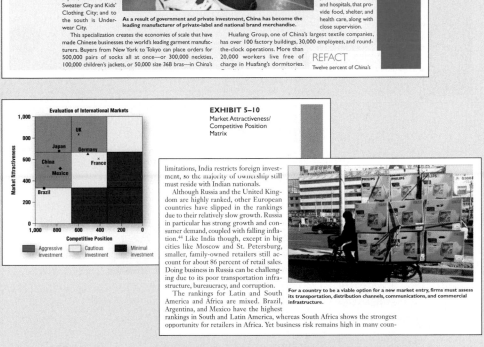

EXHIBIT 5–10
Market Attractiveness/Competitive Position Matrix

limitations, India restricts foreign investment, so the majority of ownership still must reside with Indian nationals.

Although Russia and the United Kingdom are highly ranked, other European countries have slipped in the rankings due to their relatively slow growth. Russia in particular has strong growth and consumer demand, coupled with falling inflation.[44] Like India though, except in big cities like Moscow and St. Petersburg, smaller, family-owned retailers still account for about 86 percent of retail sales. Doing business in Russia can be challenging due to its poor transportation infrastructure, bureaucracy, and corruption.

The rankings for Latin and South America and Africa are mixed. Brazil, Argentina, and Mexico have the highest rankings in South and Latin America, whereas South Africa shows the strongest opportunity for retailers in Africa. Yet business risk remains high in many coun-

For a country to be a viable option for a new market entry, firms must assess its transportation, distribution channels, communications, and commercial infrastructure.

Profiles of successful global retailers.

IKEA: Bringing Its Philosophy to a World Market RETAILING VIEW 5.3

Many consumers need to buy furniture and have sophisticated taste but either cannot or do not want to spend lots of money. These consumers don't necessarily want or need furniture that will last forever. Operating 254 stores in 35 countries, IKEA offers unique, well-designed, functional

Zara Delivers Fast Fashion RETAILING VIEW 10.1

Fast fashion is a retail business strategy that involves using supply chain management process to introduce fashionable merchandise rapidly and respond to customer demand for the merchandise quickly. This business strategy was pioneered by Zara, a global specialty apparel chain located in La Coruña, Spain, and adopted by other retailers such as H&M (headquartered in Sweden), TopShop (U.K.) and Forever 21 (U.S.).

The fast fashion process starts with receiving timely information from store managers. At Zara, its store managers are equipped with handheld devices linked directly to the company's corporate office in Spain. They report daily on what customers are buying and not buying and what they are asking for but not finding. For instance, when buyers find that customers are requesting a purple shirt that is similar to one they are selling in pink,

There is nothing more fashionable these days than an efficient supply chain. Just ask Zara.

SOCIAL RESPONSIBILITY AND ETHICAL RESPONSIBILITIES OF RETAILERS

Given the importance of retailers' societal role, both consumers and retailers are becoming more concerned about important legal, social, and ethical issues facing the world such as global warming, immigration, health care, and working condition in less-developed economies. Some of these issues, identified with an icon, discussed in this edition are:

1.1 RETAILING VIEW   Socially Responsible Retailers

Many retailers are buying and designing biodegradable or environmentally sensitive merchandise, taking positive ecological actions, and giving to charities—all actions viewed by customers and shareholders as socially responsible stratgies. Bono, the lead singer of U2 and global activist, has introduced Edun, a fair-trade fashion brand that offers high-priced goods through stores such as Saks, Nordstrom, and FairIndigo.com. A fair-trade designation means that the items were produced in factories that pay workers far more than the prevailing minimum wage and offer other benefits, like onsite medical treatment. Not to be outdone, Starbucks pays its farmers 42 percent more than the going commodity price of Arabica coffee beans.

REFACT
Retail companies give away 1.7 percent of their profits each year before taxes, compared with approximately 0.9 percent by companies in other industries.[10]

Gap, Emporio Armani, Apple, and other high-end brands have launched their own Product Red lines in Europe, selling red t-shirts, cellphones, sunglasses, and other items and then donating items and then donating of the profits to the Glob fight AIDS, tuberculosis, in Africa. But they are no retailers giving to charities. Saks Fifth Avenue donated age of sales from a particular leather jacket to He group that fights homelessness. Bloomingdale's gives charities annually, including the National Colorectal C search Alliance, the Juvenile Diabetes Research Found Autism Speaks. Wal-Mart helps the Salvation Army ra and recently gave the charity a $245 million donati Cosmetics' special line of lipsticks and greeting car

Illustrations of socially responsible activities undertaken by retailers.

Ethical and Legal Considerations

When making the strategic and tactical decisions discussed previously, managers need to consider the ethical and legal implications of their decisions, in addition to the effects that those decisions have on the profitability of their firms and the satisfaction of their customers. **Ethics** are the principles governing the behavior of individuals and companies to establish appropriate behavior and indicate what is right and wrong. Defining the term is easy, but determining what the principles are is difficult. What one person thinks is right, another may consider wrong.

What is ethical can vary from country to country and from industry to industry. For example, offering bribes to overcome bureaucratic roadblocks is an accepted practice in Middle Eastern countries but considered unethical, and even illegal, in the United States. An ethical principle also can change over time. For example, some years ago, doctors and lawyers who advertised their services were considered unethical. Today such advertising is accepted as common practice.

Framework of making ethical decisions.

Retailers Buy Socially Responsible Products   RETAILING VIEW   14.5

Corporate social responsibility describes the voluntary actions taken by a company to address the ethical, social, and environmental impacts of its business operations. Retailers act socially responsible in many ways, from giving to charity to donating time to philanthropic community activities. Recently, however, retailers are increasing their efforts to buy merchandise in a socially responsible way.

Whole Foods is increasing its efforts to provide locally grown produce to support the local ec save carbon emissions involved in transporting pro distant producers. It requires all its stores to buy fr four local farmers. It gives $10 million a year in l

U2 lead singer and activ called Edun that is sol

that a 5 percent reduction in packaging will prevent 667,000 metric tons of carbon dioxide from entering the atmosphere while also resulting in $3.4 billion in cost savings.

Other retailers are demanding smaller, eco-friendly packages from their suppliers. Smaller packages save in not only

Selling fair trade merchandise.

ISSUES IN RETAIL HUMAN RESOURCE MANAGEMENT

In this final section, we discuss three trends in HR management: (1) the increasing importance of a diverse workforce, (2) the growth in legal restrictions on HR practices, and (3) the use of technology to increase employee productivity.

Managing Diversity

Managing diversity is a human resource management activity designed to realize the benefits of a diverse workforce. Today, diversity means more than differences in race nationality, or gender, but managing a diverse workforce isn't a new issue for retailers. In the late 1800s and early 1900s, waves of immigrants entering America went to work in retail stores. The traditional approach for dealing with Minority employ male-oriented cul ed their ethnic or

Legal and ethical issues in human resource management.

customer. Imagine a customer purchases a computer at www.staples.com using a credit card and then uses the same credit card to purchase supplies at a Staples store. Then, the store's database can capture the customer's name and shipping address from the Web site transaction and update the customer's purchase record with the supplies obtained in the store.

the store three times as often as regular customers. Saks First shoppers spend five to ten times as much as non-Saks First card users.[19]

Privacy and CRM Programs

Although detailed information about individual customers helps retailers provide more benefits to their better customers, consumers also are concerned about retailers violating their privacy when they collect this information. If customers' data are not secure and susceptible to identity theft, customers would be reluctant to participate in loyalty programs. The data broker ChoicePoint was fined $15 million by the Federal Trade Co consumers' data were accessed. The FBI and ing to retailers that consumer privacy is a m

REFACT
The FTC says that data theft is now more profitable than illegal drug trafficking.[30]

REFACT
There are an estimated 25 million victims of identity theft each year.[21]

REFACT
Seventy-one percent of consumers believe that protecting personal information and privacy is more of a concern now than a few years ago.[23]

Privacy is becoming an increasing important issue as retailers collect data about their customers to support CRM Program.

Privacy Concerns   The degree to which consumers feel their privacy has been violated depends on:

- Their control over their personal information when engaging in marketplace transactions. Do they feel they can decide the amount and type of information collected by the retailer?
- Their knowledge about the collection and use of personal information. Do they know what information is being collected and how the retailer will be using it? Will the retailer be sharing the information with other parties?[22]

These concerns are particularly acute for customers using an electronic channel because many of them do not realize the extensive amount of information that can be collected without their knowledge. This information is easily collected when the user visits a Web site that installs a cookie on the visitor's computer. **Cookies** are text files that identify visitors when they return to a Web site and track their navigation at the Web site. Due to the data in the cookies, customers do not have to identify themselves or use passwords every time they visit a site. However, the cookies also collect information about other sites the person has visited and what pages they have downloaded.

ABOUT *RETAILING MANAGEMENT*, 7e

For six editions, Levy & Weitz's **Retailing Management** has been known for its strategic focus, decision-making emphasis, applications orientation, and readability. The authors and McGraw-Hill/Irwin are proud to introduce the seventh edition and invite you to see how this edition captures the exciting, dynamic nature of retailing.

MULTI-CHANNEL RETAILING

Retailers are **using the internet** and other technologies to provide more value to their customers, increase customer service, and improve operating efficiencies. Some of examples of these Internet applications examined in this edition are:

The role of the Internet to complement store offerings by multi-channel retailers.

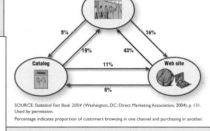

EXHIBIT 3–4
Percentage of Cross-Channel Shoppers

SOURCE: *Statistical Fact Book 2004* (Washington, DC: Direct Marketing Association, 2004), p. 131. Used by permission.
Percentage indicates proportion of customers browsing in one channel and purchasing in another.

REFACT
The luxury retailer Neiman Marcus claims that its multi-channel customers spend 3.6 times more than single-channel customers do.[10]

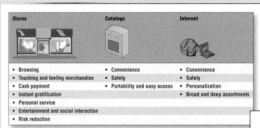

EXHIBIT 3–2
Benefits Provided by Different Channels

Use of virtual models and other technologies to overcome the limitation of an electronic channel.

SHOPPING IN THE FUTURE

The following hypothetical scenario illustrates the seamless interface across channels that customers in the future may experience.

Shopping Experience
It's Tuesday morning, and Judy Jamison is eating breakfast thinking about buying a new dress for the party she'll be attending this Friday night at the new club downtown. She logs onto her laptop, accesses her personal shopper program called FRED, and has the following interactive dialog:

Fred: Do you wish to browse, go to a specific store, or buy a specific item?
Judy: Specific item.

Shopping experience in the future, from collecting information on the Internet to automated checkout though RFID.

Communicating with customers through mobile devices.

M-Commerce As technology and customers together become more sophisticated, more retailers are augmenting their e-mail communications with m-commerce (mobile commerce), which involves communicating with and even selling to customers through wireless handheld devices, such as cellular telephones and personal digital assistants (PDAs).[20] Tech-savvy customers use their cellphones and PDAs to obtain sports scores, weather, music videos, and text messages in real time. It thus is a natural evolution for retailers to tap into this trend. Consider some of these innovative m-commerce applications:

• Grand Rapids, Michigan–based hypermarket Meijer offers consumers the opportunity to learn in advance when the retailer's gasoline prices are going to go up, before the hikes actually hit the pump.[21]

30 million

Instant chat for personal communication with customers visiting a retailer's Web site.

Amy Tomas
University of Vermont

Mary Weber
University of New Mexico

Kathleen Debevic Witz
University of Massachusetts

Janet Wagner
University of Maryland

Sandy White
Greenville Tech College

Merv Yeagle
University of Maryland

Gary Walk
Lima Technical College

Fred T. Whitman
Mary Washington College

Ron Zallocco
University of Toledo

We received cases from professors all over the world. Although we would like to have used more cases in the text and the Instructor's Manual, space was limited. We would like to thank all who contributed but are especially appreciative of the following authors whose cases were used in *Retailing Management* or in the Instructor's Manual:

Ronald Adams
University of North Florida

Laura Bliss
Stephens College

James Camerius
Northern Michigan University

Daphne Comfort
University of Gloucestershire

Hope Bober Corrigan
Loyola College, Maryland

Tina Brienne Curley
Loyola College, Maryland

David Ehrlich
Marymount University

Sunil Erevelles
University of North Carolina, Charlotte

Ann Fairhurst
Indiana University

Linda F. Felicetti
Clarion University

Joseph P. Grunewald
Clarion University

David Hillier
University of Glamorgan

K. Douglas Hoffman
University of North Carolina–Wilmington

Terence L. Holmes
Murray State University

Peter Jones
University of Gloucestershire

Kirthi Kalyanam
Santa Clara University

Dilip Karer
University of North Florida

Hean Tat Keh
National University, Singapore

Robert Kenny
Saint Michael's College

Nirmalya Kumar
London Business School

Marilyn Lavin
University of Wisconsin–Whitewater

Robert Letovsky
Saint Michael's College

Alicia Lueddemann
The Management Mind Group

Gordon H. G. McDougall
Wilfrid Laurier University

Debra Murphy
Saint Michael's College

Todd Nicolini
Loyola College, Maryland

Jan Owens
University of Wisconsin

Kristina Pacca
University of Florida

Michael Pearce
University of Western Ontario

James Pope
Loyola College, Maryland

Catherine Porter
University of Massachusetts

Richard Rausch
Hofstra University

Dan Rice
University of Florida

David Rosage
Loyola College, Maryland

Cecelia Schulz
University of Florida

Vidya Sundari
National University, Singapore

William R. Swinyard
Brigham Young University

Stephen Vitucci
Tarleton State University

Elizabeth J. Wilson
Suffolk University

Irvin Zaenglein
Northern Michigan University

Steven Keith Platt
Platt Retail Institute

Ann Rupert
Macy's Florida

John Thomas
Pinch-A-Penny

Susan Reda
Stores Magazine

Lori Schafer
SAS Retail

Suzanne Voorhees
The Grapevine Group

The seventh edition of *Retailing Management* has benefited from reviews by several leading scholars and many teachers of retailing and related disciplines. Together, these reviewers spent hundreds of hours reading and critiquing the manuscript. We gratefully acknowledge them and the following reviewers for their diligence and insight in helping us prepare previous editions:

Mark Abel
Kirkwood Community College

Stephen J. Anderson
Austin Peay State University

Jill Attaway
Illinois State University

Mary Barry
Auburn University

Lance A. Bettencourt
Indiana University

David Blanchette
Rhode Island College

Jeff Blodgett
University of Mississippi

George W. Boulware
Lipscomb University

Willard Broucek
Northern State University

Leroy M. Buckner
Florida Atlantic University

David J. Burns
Purdue University

Lon Camomile
Colorado State University

Donald W. Caudill
Bluefield State College

James Clark
Northeastern State University

Sylvia Clark
St. John's University

J. Joseph Cronin, Jr.
Florida State University

Angela D'Auria
Stanton Radford University

Irene J. Dickey
University of Dayton

Ann DuPont
University of Texas

Chloe I. Elmgren
Mankato State University

Richard L. Entrikin
George Mason University

David Erickson
Angelo University

Kenneth R. Evans
University of Missouri–Columbia

Richard Feinberg
Purdue University

Kevin Fertig
University of Illinois

Drew Ehrlich Fulton
Montgomery Community College

David M. Georgoff
Florida Atlantic University

Peter Gordon
Southeast Missouri State University

Larry Gresham
Texas A&M University

Tom Gross
University of Wisconsin

Sally Harmon
Purdue University

Susan Harmon
Middle Tennessee State University

Michael D. Hartline
Louisiana State University

Tony L. Henthorne
University of Southern Mississippi

Kae Hineline
McLennan Community College

David Horne
California State University–Long Beach

Joshua Holt
Brigham Young University

Michael Jones
Auburn University

Eugene J. Kangas
Winona State University

Herbert Katzenstein
St. John's University

Terrence Kroeten
North Dakota State University

Ann Lucht
Milwaukee Area Technical College

Elizabeth Mariotz
Philadelphia College of Textiles and Science

Tony Mayo
George Mason University

Harold McCoy
Virginia Commonwealth University

Michael McGinnis
University of South Alabama

Phyliss McGinnis
Boston University

Kim McKeage
University of Maine

Barbara Mihm
University of Wisconsin–Stevens Point

Robert Miller
Central Michigan University

Mary Anne Milward
University of Arizona

Cheryl O'Hara
Kings College

Dorothy M. Oppenheim
Bridgewater State University

Michael M. Pearson
Loyola University, New Orleans

Janis Petronis
Tarleton State University

Linda Pettijohn
Southern Missouri State University

John J. Porter
West Virginia University

Sue Riha
University of Texas–Austin

Nick Saratakes
Austin Community College

Laura Scroggins
California State University–Chico

Steve Solesbee
Aiken Technical College

Shirley M. Stretch
California State University–LA

William R. Swinyard
Brigham Young University

Web Site for Students and Instructors (www.mhhe.com/levy7e) Just as retailers are using the Internet to help their customers, we have developed a Web site to help students and instructors use the seventh edition of this textbook effectively. Some of the features on the Web site are:

- Multiple-choice questions on the student site.
- Experiential exercises for students.
- Chapter-by-chapter Instructor Manual coverage.
- Case and video notes.
- Retailing trade publications and professional associations.
- News articles about current events in retailing.
- PowerPoint slides summarizing key issues in each chapter.
- Hot links to retailing news sites and sites associated with the Internet exercises in the textbook.
- Additional cases about retailers.

ACKNOWLEDGMENTS

Throughout the development of this text, several outstanding individuals were integrally involved and made substantial contributions. First, we recognize the invaluable contributions of Hope Bober Corrigan (Loyola College in Maryland) for providing constructive comments and suggestions on the revised chapters, editing the cases and video package, and providing many useful teaching activities found in the Instructor's Manual. We also thank Britt Hackmann (Babson College) for her important assistance in doing research for the book, writing examples, and preparing the manuscript for publication. We express our sincere appreciation to Amy Tomas (University of Vermont) for preparing the Instructor's Manual and Hyunjoo Oh (University of Florida) for preparing the PowerPoint slides and Test Bank. Special thanks go to Tracy Meyer (University of North Carolina Wilmington) for preparing the "Starting a Franchise Business" Appendix, to Christian Tassin (University of Florida) for preparing the appendix on "Starting Your Own Retail Business," to Jim Lewis (Enhanced Retail and Solutions LLC) Zhen Zhu (Suffolk University) for assistance in updating chapters, and to Elisabeth Nevins Caswell for her excellent and insightful comments while copyediting the manuscript.

We'd like especially to acknowledge the contribution of Retail Forward, Inc. Their daily news briefing and research reports facilitated the research that has gone into this text.

We also appreciate the contributions of Margaret Jones, Cecilia Schulz and Betsy Trobaugh (David F. Miller Center for Retailing Education and Research, University of Florida), who provided invaluable assistance in preparing the manuscript.

The support, expertise, and occasional coercion from our Managing Developmental Editor, Nancy Barbour, are greatly appreciated. The book would also never have come together without the editorial and production staff at McGraw-Hill/Irwin: Doug Hughes, Harvey Yep, Lori Koetters, Carol Bielski, Cara Hawthorne, Jeremy Cheshareck, Keri Johnson, and Kerry Bowler.

Retailing Management has also benefited significantly from contributions by several leading executives and scholars in retailing and related fields. We would like to thank:

William Alcorn
JCPenney

Mark Blakeley
Oracle

Cynthia Cohen
Strategic Mindshare

John Gremer
Walgreens

Dhruv Grewal
Babson College

Linda Hyde
Retail Forward

Steve Knopik
Beall's Inc.

Doug Koch
Famous Footwear

Bradley Macullum
ESRI

Bruce Mager
Macy's East

Richard A. McAllister
Florida Retail Federation

Tracey Mullins
National Retail Federation

material in the chapter. These profiles range from Maxine Clark, Chief Executive Bear at Build-A-Bear Workshop, and Lori Anderson, the founder and manager of a dress shop in Tampa, to Lotoya Parker, a buyer at Macy's East, and Lee Donelly, Store Manager for Walgreens in California. They include people who have extensive experience in a specific aspect of retailing, like Bari Harlam, Vice President, Marketing Intelligence, CVS Caremark, Inc., and Juan del Valle, Market Development Manager, Brinker International.

The profiles illustrate how senior executives view the industry and suggest career opportunities for college students. They also provide students with firsthand information about what people in retailing do and the rewards and challenges of their jobs and careers.

OTHER UNIQUE ASPECTS OF LEVY AND WEITZ'S *RETAILING MANAGEMENT* TEXTBOOK

Chapter on Customer Relationship Management   Chapter 11 examines how retailers are using customer databases to build repeat business and realize a greater share of wallet from key customers. These customer relationship management activities exploit the 80–20 rule—20 percent of the customers account for 80 percent of the sales and profits. In this chapter, we discuss how retailers identify their best customers and target these customers with special promotions and customer services.

Chapter on Multichannel Retailing   Chapter 3 describes the opportunities and challenges retailers face interacting with customers through multiple channels—stores, catalogs, and the Internet. As markets for Internet-only retailers have diminished, traditional retailers are investing in using the Internet to complement their stores. This chapter discusses how multichannel retailers can and do provide more value to their customers.

SUPPLEMENTAL MATERIALS

To enhance the student learning experience, the seventh edition includes new cases and videos illustrating state-of-the-art retail practices, a Web-based computer exercise package for students, and a comprehensive online instructor's manual with additional cases and teaching suggestions.

Get Out and Do It! exercises are found at the end of each chapter. These exercises suggest projects that students can undertake by visiting local retail stores, surfing the Internet, or using the student Web site. A continuing assignment exercise is included so that students can engage in an exercise involving the same retailer throughout the course. The exercises are designed to provide a hands-on learning experience for students.

Monthly Newsletter with Short Cases based on recent retailing articles appearing in the business and trade press. Instructors can use these short cases to stimulate class discussions about current issues confronting retailers. The newsletter is e-mailed to instructors and archived on the text's Web page.

Twelve New Cases include discussions of corporate social responsibility at Wal-Mart, Tractor Supply, Sav-a-Lot, retailing using blogs, retailing diamonds, pet retailing, Macy's rebranding, retailing in India, Nordstrom's loyalty program, and Macy's store rebranding. All 38 cases in the textbook are either new or updated with current information. A number of the cases, such as Starbucks, Build-A-Bear, Rainforest Café, and Wal-Mart, have videos that complement the written case.

Ten New Videos among the thirty-five video segments available to illustrate issues addressed in the text. The topics addressed by the ten new videos include Domino's Pizza's entry into Mexico, Starbuck's fair trade policy with its coffee growers, Staples's growth strategy in the copying business, The Container Store's organizational culture, Netflix's distribution strategy, and Wal-Mart's campaign to change its image.

How-to Information   *Retailing Management* goes beyond this descriptive information to illustrate how and why retailers, large and small, make decisions. Step-by-step procedures with examples are provided for making the following decisions:

- Comparison shopping (Appendix 2A to Chapter 2).
- Managing a multichannel outreach to customers (Chapter 3).
- Scanning the environment and developing a retail strategy (Chapter 5).
- Analyzing the financial implications of retail strategy (Chapter 6).
- Evaluating location decisions (Chapter 8).
- Developing a merchandise assortment and budget plan (Chapters 12 and 13).
- Negotiating with vendors (Chapter 14).
- Pricing merchandise (Chapter 15).
- Recruiting, selecting, training, evaluating, and compensating sales associates (Chapter 17).
- Designing the layout for a store (Chapter 18).
- Providing superior customer service (Chapter 19).

Conceptual Information   *Retailing Management* also includes conceptual information that enables students to understand why decisions are made, as outlined in the text. As Mark Twain said, "There is nothing as practical as a good theory." Students need to know these basic concepts so they can make effective decisions in new situations. Examples of this conceptual information in the seventh edition are:

- Customers' decision-making process (Chapter 4).
- Market attractiveness/competitive position matrix for evaluating strategic alternatives (Appendix 5A to Chapter 5).
- The strategic profit model and approach for evaluating financial performance (Chapter 6).
- Price theory and marginal analysis (Chapters 15 and 16).
- Motivation of employees (Chapter 17).
- In-store shopping behaviors (Chapter 18).
- The Gaps model for service quality management (Chapter 19).

Student-Friendly Textbook   This seventh edition creates interest and involves students in the course and the industry by making the textbook a "good read" for students. We use Refacts (retailing factoids), Retailing Views, and retail manager profiles at the beginning of each chapter to engage students.

Refacts   We have updated and added more interesting facts about retailing, called Refacts, in the margins of each chapter. Did you know that a Montgomery Ward buyer created Rudolph the Red-Nosed Reindeer as a Christmas promotion in 1939? Or that the teabag was developed by a Macy's buyer, and pantyhose was developed by a JCPenney buyer?

Retailing Views   Each chapter contains either new or updated vignettes called Retailing Views to relate concepts to activities and decisions made by retailers. The vignettes look at major retailers, like Wal-Mart, Walgreens, JCPenney, Target, Kohl's, Neiman Marcus, and Macy's, that interview students on campus for management training positions. They also discuss innovative retailers like REI, Starbucks, The Container Store, Sephora, Curves, Chico's, and Bass Pro Shops. Finally, a number of Retailing Views focus on entrepreneurial retailers competing effectively against national chains.

Profiles of Retail Managers   To illustrate the challenges and opportunities in retailing, each chapter in the seventh edition begins with a brief profile, in their own words, of a manager or industry expert whose job or expertise is related to the

The text explores in depth the resources that retailers use to develop sustainable competitive advantage, such as

- Selecting store location (Chapters 7, 8).
- Developing and maintaining human resources (Chapter 9).
- Managing supply chain and information systems (Chapter 10).
- Managing customer relationship management and loyalty programs (Chapter 11).

Financial Analysis   The financial aspects of retailing are becoming increasingly important. The financial problems experienced by some of the largest retail firms, like Kmart, Sharper Image, and COMPUSA, highlight the need for a thorough understanding of the financial implications of strategic retail decisions. Financial analysis is emphasized in selected chapters, such as Chapter 6 on the overall strategy of the firm, Chapter 11 on the evaluation of customer lifetime value, and Chapter 13 on retail buying systems. Financial issues are also raised in the sections on negotiating leases, bargaining with suppliers, pricing merchandise, developing a communication budget, and compensating salespeople.

Implementing a Retail Strategy   Although developing a retail strategy is critical to long-term financial performance, the execution of strategies is as important as the development of the strategy. Traditionally, retailers have exalted the merchant prince—the buyer who knew what the hot trends were going to be. While we provide a thorough review of merchandise management issues, the emphasis in retailing is shifting from merchandise management to the block and tackling of getting merchandise to the stores and customers and providing excellent customer service and an exciting shopping experience. Due to this shift toward store management, most students embarking on retail careers go into distribution and store management rather than merchandise buying. Thus, this text devotes an entire chapter to information systems and supply chain management and an entire section to store management.

Up-to-Date Information   Retailing is a very dynamic industry, with new ideas and formats developing and traditional retailers constantly adapting to the changing environment or suffering financially. More than half of the Retailing Views are new, and the remaining ones have been updated.

Balanced Approach   The seventh edition continues to offer a balanced approach for teaching an introductory retailing course by including descriptive, how-to, and conceptual information in a highly readable format.

Descriptive Information   Students can learn about the vocabulary and practice of retailing from the descriptive information throughout the text. Examples of this material are:

- Leading U.S. and international retailers (Chapter 1).
- Management decisions made by retailers (Chapter 1).
- Types of store-based and nonstore retailers (Chapter 2 and 3).
- Approaches for entering international markets (Chapter 5).
- Locations (Chapter 7).
- Lease terms (Chapter 8).
- Organization structure of typical retailers (Chapter 9).
- Flow of information and merchandise (Chapter 10).
- Branding strategies (Chapter 14).
- Methods for communicating with customers (Chapter 16).
- Store layout options and merchandise display techniques (Chapter 18).
- Career opportunities (Appendix 1A to Chapter 1).

- EAS technology designed to reduce shoplifting (Chapter 17).
- Creating planograms to optimize sales and profits from merchandise categories (Chapter 18).
- Digital signage to reduce cost and increase message flexibility (Chapter 18).
- In-store kiosks, mobile devices, and the Internet to improve customer service (Chapter 19).
- Instant chat for servicing online customers (Chapter 19).

Globalization of the Retail Industry   Retailing is a global industry. With a greater emphasis being placed on private-label merchandise, retailers are working with manufacturers located throughout the world to acquire merchandise. In addition, retailers are increasingly looking to international markets for growth opportunities. For instance, Carrefour, France's hypermarket chain and the second-largest retailer in the world, is focusing its growth investments in 25 countries but not in France. Some of the global retailing issues, identified with icons in the margins, examined in this edition are:

- Retail efficiencies in different economies (Chapter 1).
- Illustrations of global expansion by retailers (Chapter 2).
- Cultural impacts on customer buying behavior (Chapter 4).
- Keys to successful entry into international markets (Chapter 5).
- Evaluation of international growth opportunities (Chapter 5).
- Differences in location opportunities in global markets (Chapter 7).
- Regulations affecting customer data collection in world markets (Chapter 10).
- Employee management issues in international markets (Chapters 9 and 17).
- Global sourcing of private-label merchandise (Chapter 14).
- Cultural differences in customer service needs (Chapter 19).

Entrepreneurship in Retailing   In this seventh edition, we have added two appendices that provide an overview of "How to Start Your Own Retail Business" and "How to Start a Franchise Business." Retailing continues to offer opportunities for people to start their own business. Some of the world's richest people are retailing entrepreneurs. Many are well known because their names appear over the stores' door, such as James Cash Penney and William H. Macy. But many other successful entrepreneurs are less well known, such as Donald Fisher (The Gap), Thomas Stemberg (Staples), Les Wexner (The Limited/Victoria Secret), Maxine Clark (Build-A-Bear Workshop).

BASIC PHILOSOPHY

The seventh edition of *Retailing Management* maintains the basic philosophy of the previous six editions. We continue to focus on key strategic issues with an emphasis on financial considerations and implementation through merchandise and store management. These strategic and tactical issues are examined for a broad spectrum of retailers, both large and small, domestic and international, selling merchandise and services.

Strategic Focus   The entire textbook is organized around a model of strategic decision making outlined in Exhibit 1–5 in Chapter 1. Each section and chapter relates back to this overarching strategic framework. In addition, the second section of the book focuses exclusively on critical strategic decisions, such as selecting target markets, developing a sustainable competitive advantage, building an organizational structure and information and distribution systems to support the strategic direction, building customer loyalty, and managing customer relationships.

Development of Exclusive Brands   To differentiate their offerings and build strategic advantages over competitors, most retailers are devoting more resources to the development of exclusive products—whether products that the retailer designs (private labels) or exclusive brands produced for the retailer by national brand manufacturers. For example, Ralph Lauren has developed American Style brand for JCPenney, and Estée Lauder has developed the American Beauty cosmetic line for Kohl's.

Retailers are placing more emphasis on developing their brand images, building strong images for their private-label merchandise, and extending their images to new retail formats. These exclusive brands, as the term implies, are only available from the retailer, and thus customers loyal to these brands can only find them in one store. Some examples of our extended treatment of exclusive brands in this edition are:

- Strategic importance of private labels (Chapter 5).
- Private-label approaches and types. (Chapter 14).
- Process for developing and sourcing private labels (Chapter 14).
- Building a strong brand image (Chapter 16).

Use of Technology in Retailing   Retailing is a high-tech industry with retailers increasingly using communications and information systems technologies and analytical models to increase operating efficiencies and improve customer service. Some of these new technology applications, identified with technology icons in the margins and discussed in the seventh edition, are:

- Use of Web sites to sell products and services to customers (Chapter 3).
- Providing a seamless multichannel (stores, Web sites, and catalogs) interface so that customers can interact with retailers anytime, anywhere (Chapter 3).
- Stores of the future that use technology to provide a more rewarding shopping experience (Chapter 3).
- Application of geographic information system (GIS) technology for store location decisions (Chapter 8).
- Internet applications for effective human resource management (Chapter 9).
- Integrated supply chain management systems (Chapter 10).
- RFID (radio frequency identification) technology to improve supply chain efficiency (Chapter 10).
- Analysis of customer databases to determine customer lifetime value, target promotions toward a retailer's best customers, and undertake market basket analyses (Chapter 11).
- Implementation of marketing programs to increase customer share of wallet (Chapter 11).
- CPFR (collaboration, planning, forecasting, and replenishment) systems for coordinating vendors and retailer activities (Chapter 12).
- Sophisticated inventory management systems (Chapter 13).
- Reverse auctions for buying merchandise (Chapter 14).
- Use of profit-optimization decision support systems for setting prices in different markets and taking markdowns (Chapter 15).
- Using m-commerce to communicate with potential customers with hand-held devices like cell phones and PDAs (Chapter 16).
- Adopting social marketing techniques to get customers involved in online product reviews (Chapter 16).
- Developing targeted promotions using customer databases (Chapter 16).
- Internet-based training for store employees (Chapter 17).
- Decision support systems for scheduling sales associates (Chapter 17).

PREFACE

Retailing is a high-tech, global, growth industry that plays a vital economic role in society. Our objective in preparing this seventh edition is to stimulate student interest in retailing courses and careers by capturing the exciting, challenging, and rewarding opportunities facing both retailers and firms that sell their products and services to retailers, such as IBM and Proctor & Gamble. The textbook focuses on the strategic issues facing the retail industry and provides a current, informative, "good read" for students.

NEW FEATURES

In preparing the seventh edition of *Retailing Management*, we have revised the textbook to address five important developments in retailing: (1) the evolving role of the Internet in retailing, (2) the greater emphasis on the social responsibility of retailers, (3) the increased emphasis retailers are placing on developing exclusive brands, (4) the use of technology and analytical methods for decision making, (5) globalization and (6) the entrepreneurial opportunities in retailing.

Evolving Role of the Internet   Ten years ago, many experts thought that the consumers would abandon the mall and shop for most products and services using the Internet. Traditional retailers would be replaced by a new breed of techno-savvy entrepreneurs. Now it is clear that the Internet is not transforming the retail industry but rather facilitating the activities undertaken by traditional retailers—retailers that use multiple channels (Internet, catalog, stores, and mobile) to interact with their customers.

In the seventh edition, we have increased our treatment of how these multichannel retailers provide information and sell products and services to customers. In this edition, we also go beyond Chapter 3, which is dedicated to multichannel retailing, to discuss Internet retailing applications throughout the textbook. For example,

- The impact of social networks on buying behavior (Chapter 4).
- Use of the Internet for training (Chapters 9 and 17).
- Communicating with customers through m-commerce, social shopping, e-mail, and Web sites (Chapter 16).
- Internet-based digital signage in stores (Chapter 18).
- Providing information and customer service through Web-enabled kiosks and POS terminals (Chapter 19).

Social Responsibility of Retailers   Retail institutions are pervasive in our society and thus have a major impact on the welfare of their customers, suppliers, and employees. Given the importance of their societal role, both consumers and retailers are becoming more concerned about social issues facing the world, such as global warming, immigration, health care, and working conditions in less developed economies. Some of these social responsibility issues, identified with legal/ethical icons in the margins and discussed in the seventh edition, are:

- Consumer interest in green products (Chapter 4).
- Issues in sourcing merchandise globally (Chapter 14).
- Considering sustainability issues in store operations (Chapter 17) and design (Chapter 18).
- Three new cases focusing on legal, ethical, and social responsibility issues facing retailers.

ABOUT THE AUTHORS

Michael Levy, Ph.D.
Babson College
mlevy@babson.edu

Michael Levy, Ph.D., is the Charles Clarke Reynolds Professor of Marketing and Director of the Retail Supply Chain Institute at Babson College. He received his Ph.D. in business administration from The Ohio State University and his undergraduate and MS degrees in business administration from the University of Colorado at Boulder. He taught at Southern Methodist University before joining the faculty as professor and chair of the marketing department at the University of Miami.

Professor Levy has developed a strong stream of research in retailing, business logistics, financial retailing strategy, pricing, and sales management. He has published over 50 articles in leading marketing and logistics journals, including the *Journal of Retailing, Journal of Marketing,* and *Journal of Marketing Research.* He currently serves on the editorial review boards of the *Journal of Retailing, Journal of the Academy of Marketing Science, International Journal of Logistics Management, International Journal of Logistics and Materials Management,* and *European Business Review,* as well as the Advisory Board for *International Retailing and Marketing Review.* He is co-author of *Marketing and M-Marketing* (McGraw-Hill, Irwin). Professor Levy also was co-editor of *Journal of Retailing* from 2001 to 2007.

Professor Levy has worked in retailing and related disciplines throughout his professional life. Prior to his academic career, he worked for several retailers and a housewares distributor in Colorado. He has performed research projects with many retailers and retail technology firms, including Accenture, Federated Department Stores, Khimetrics, Mervyn's, Neiman Marcus, ProfitLogic (Oracle), and Zale Corporation.

Barton A. Weitz, Ph.D.
University of Florida
bart.weitz@cba.ufl.edu

Barton A. Weitz, Ph.D., received an undergraduate degree in electrical engineering from MIT and an MBA and a Ph.D. in business administration from Stanford University. He has been a member of the faculty at the UCLA Graduate School of Business and the Wharton School at the University of Pennsylvania and is presently the JCPenney Eminent Scholar Chair in Retail Management in the Warrington College of Business Administration at the University of Florida.

Professor Weitz is the executive director of the David F. Miller Center for Retailing Education and Research at the University of Florida (www.cba.ufl.edu/crer). The activities of the center are supported by contributions from 35 retailers and firms supporting the retail industry, including JCPenney, Macy's, PetSmart, Office Depot, Walgreens, Target, Build-A-Bear, Bealls, City Furniture, NPD, and the International Council of Shopping Centers. Each year, the center places more than 250 undergraduates in paid summer internships and management trainee positions with retail firms and funds research on retailing issues and problems.

Professor Weitz has won awards for teaching excellence and made numerous presentations to industry and academic groups. He has published over 50 articles in leading academic journals on channel relationships, electronic retailing, store design, salesperson effectiveness, and sales force and human resource management. His research has been recognized with two Louis Stern Awards for his contributions to channel management research and a Paul Root Award for the *Journal of Marketing* article that makes the greatest contribution to marketing practice. He serves on the editorial review boards of the *Journal of Retailing, Journal of Marketing, International Journal of Research in Marketing, Marketing Science,* and *Journal of Marketing Research.* He is a former editor of the *Journal of Marketing Research.*

Professor Weitz has been the chair of the American Marketing Association and a member of the board of directors of the National Retail Federation, the National Retail Foundation, and the American Marketing Association. In 1989, he was honored as the AMA/Irwin Distinguished Educator in recognition of his contributions to the marketing discipline. He was selected by the National Retail Federation as Retail Educator of the Year in 2005 and been recognized for lifetime achievements by American Marketing Association Sales and Inter-Organizational Special Interests Groups.

To Marcia and Eva Levy and Shirley Weitz

Who enrich our lives with love, affection, and considerable patience

McGraw-Hill
Irwin

RETAILING MANAGEMENT

Published by McGraw-Hill/Irwin, a business unit of The McGraw-Hill Companies, Inc., 1221 Avenue of the Americas, New York, NY, 10020. Copyright © 2009, 2007, 2004, 2001, 1998, 1995, 1992 by The McGraw-Hill Companies, Inc. All rights reserved. No part of this publication may be reproduced or distributed in any form or by any means, or stored in a database or retrieval system, without the prior written consent of The McGraw-Hill Companies, Inc., including, but not limited to, in any network or other electronic storage or transmission, or broadcast for distance learning.

Some ancillaries, including electronic and print components, may not be available to customers outside the United States.

This book is printed on acid-free paper.

2 3 4 5 6 7 8 9 0 CTP/CTP 0 9 8

ISBN   978-0-07-338104-6
MHID   0-07-338104-7

Editor-in-chief: *Brent Gordon*
Publisher: *Paul Ducham*
Executive editor: *Doug Hughes*
Managing developmental editor: *Nancy Barbour*
Editorial assistant: *Devon Raemisch*
Associate marketing manager: *Dean Karampelas*
Senior project manager: *Harvey Yep*
Lead production supervisor: *Carol A. Bielski*
Lead designer: *Matthew Baldwin*
Senior photo research coordinator: *Jeremy Cheshareck*
Photo researcher: *Keri Johnson*
Senior media project manager: *Kerry Bowler*
Cover design: *Joanne Schopler*
Cover image: © *Raul Vasquez/Bloomberg News/Landov*
Interior design: *Kami Carter*
Typeface: *10.5/12 Janson*
Compositor: *Aptara, Inc.*
Printer: *CTPS*

Library of Congress Cataloging-in-Publication Data

Levy, Michael, 1950-
    Retailing management / Michael Levy, Barton A. Weitz. — 7th ed.
        p. cm.
    Includes bibliographical references and index.
    ISBN-13: 978-0-07-338104-6 (alk. paper)
    ISBN-10: 0-07-338104-7 (alk. paper)
    1. Retail trade—Management. I. Weitz, Barton A. II. Title.
HF5429.L4828 2009
658.8'7—dc22

                                                    2008006472

RETAILING MANAGEMENT

SEVENTH EDITION

Michael Levy, Ph.D.
Babson College

Barton A. Weitz, Ph.D.
University of Florida

Boston   Burr Ridge, IL   Dubuque, IA   New York   San Francisco   St. Louis
Bangkok   Bogotá   Caracas   Kuala Lumpur   Lisbon   London   Madrid   Mexico City
Milan   Montreal   New Delhi   Santiago   Seoul   Singapore   Sydney   Taipei   Toronto

The cover for this textbook illustrates that retailing has evolved into a global, high technology industry. The U.S. remains the world's most sophisticated retail market. However, retail sales in the BRIC countries (Brazil, Russia, India and China) are attractive markets with high potential growth. Traditional retailing in these countries has been dominated by small, independent retailers. Due to changing government policies and consumer demand, these markets are experiencing a transformation. Large national chains are developing, either through domestic investment or through the entry of foreign retailers. These national chains are increasing the efficiency of distribution systems, lowering prices, and making a greater variety of merchandise available to consumers in these countries. The Chinese mall displayed on the cover is an example of this transformation. Seven of the ten largest enclosed malls are now located in China.

In addition to addressing these global issues in the edition, the text also examines the technologies that are being developed by retailers and used domestically as well as in the emerging markets. Some examples of the technologies highlighted are the use of the Internet for providing information and selling products and services to customers; application of geographic information system (GIS) technology to determine store locations; integrated supply chain management systems, RFID, and CPFR (collaboration, planning, forecasting and replenishment) systems; analysis of customer databases to identify and tailor offerings to the best customers; and, the use of profit optimization decision support systems for setting prices in different markets, taking markdowns, and allocating merchandise.

This edition also highlights retailers' heightened concern for societal issues, the environment, and the people involved in making and transporting merchandise to markets. Retailers are buying merchandise with an eye toward its carbon footprint and other ecological factors. They have taken an active role in making sure that workers are treated humanely and can earn a living wage.

The Chinese characters on the signs are the same as the Chinese word for good fortune and happiness, written in different styles. Chinese people usually hang this character during the Chinese New Year season, hoping to bring good fortune to them in the coming year. Retailers also display this word in their stores (mostly during the Chinese New Year season), hoping that it can bring good fortune to their customers as well as to themselves.

health and pleasure. Take, for instance, its new store in Manhattan. It includes a humidy-controlled cheese cave, a pie shop, a Belgian-style french fry station, several salad bars for desserts and hot and cold foods, a gelato station, a sandwich shop, and a pizza oven. Upstairs, there is an Italian restaurant; a small clothing department featuring hemp T-shirts and other casual wear; a lifestyle department offering yoga mats, relaxation CDs, and related items; a health and beauty section; and a demonstration kitchen for cooking classes.[31] Whole Foods also is introducing spas in stores; some customers may even opt out of grocery shopping and head straight for their massage by handing a grocery list to the concierge, free of charge.

To round out its whole experience, Whole Foods has launched a weekly online cooking show and resource for home cooks seeking useful tips and exciting recipe ideas.[32] The video podcast available at www.wholefoodsmarket.com/secretingredient focuses on one ingredient per episode, so viewers can really get to know the featured item and how to prepare it.

Ethical and Legal Considerations

When making the strategic and tactical decisions discussed previously, managers need to consider the ethical and legal implications of their decisions, in addition to the effects that those decisions have on the profitability of their firms and the satisfaction of their customers. **Ethics** are the principles governing the behavior of individuals and companies to establish appropriate behavior and indicate what is right and wrong. Defining the term is easy, but determining what the principles are is difficult. What one person thinks is right, another may consider wrong.

What is ethical can vary from country to country and from industry to industry. For example, offering bribes to overcome bureaucratic roadblocks is an accepted practice in Middle Eastern countries but considered unethical, and even illegal, in the United States. An ethical principle also can change over time. For example, some years ago, doctors and lawyers who advertised their services were considered unethical. Today such advertising is accepted as common practice.

Some examples of difficult situations that retail manager face include the following:

- Should a retailer sell merchandise that it suspects was made using child labor?
- Should a retailer advertise that its prices are the lowest available in the market, even though some items are not?
- Should a retail buyer accept an expensive gift from a vendor?
- Should a retailer charge a supplier a fee to get a new item in its store?
- Should retail salespeople use a high-pressure sales approach when they know the product is not the best for the customer's needs?
- Should a retailer disclose product information that may affect whether or not it is purchased?
- Should a retailer promote a product as being "on sale" if it never sold at a higher, non-sale price?
- Should a retailer offer credit at a higher interest rate or sell products at higher prices in stores patronized mostly by low-income customers?

Laws dictate which activities society has deemed to be clearly wrong, those activities for which retailers and their employees will be punished through the federal or state legal systems. However, most business decisions are not regulated

EXHIBIT I–6

The Six Tests of Ethical
Action

The Publicity Test

- Would I want to see this action that I'm about to take described on the front page of the local paper or in a national magazine?
- How would I feel about having done this if everyone were to find out all about it, including the people I love and care about the most?

The Moral Mentor Test

- What would the person I admire the most do in this situation?

The Admired Observer Test

- Would I want the person I admire most to see me doing this?
- Would I be proud of this action in the presence of a person whose life and character I really admire?
- What would make the person I admire most proud of me in this situation?

The Transparency Test

- Could I give a clear explanation for the action I'm contemplating, including an honest and transparent account of all my motives, that would satisfy a fair and dispassionate moral judge?

The Person in the Mirror Test

- Will I be able to look at myself in the mirror and respect the person I see there?

The Golden Rule Test

- Would I like to be on the receiving end of this action and all its potential consequences?
- Am I treating others the way I'd want to be treated?

Source: Tom Morris, *The Art of Achievement: Success in Business and in Life,* Fine Communications, 2003.

by laws. Often retail managers have to rely on their firms' and industries' codes of ethics and/or their own codes of ethics to determine the right thing to do.

Many companies have codes of ethics to provide guidelines for their employees in making their ethical decisions. These ethical policies provide a clear sense of right and wrong so that companies and their customers can depend on their employees when questionable situations arise. However, in many situations, retail managers need to rely on their personal code of ethics—their personal sense of what is right or wrong.

Exhibit 1–6 lists some questions you can ask yourself to determine whether a behavior or activity is unethical. The questions emphasize that ethical behavior is determined by widely accepted views of what is right and wrong. Thus, you should engage only in activities about which you would be proud to tell your family, friends, employer, and customers.

If the answer to any of these questions is yes, the behavior or activity is probably unethical, and you should not do it.

Your firm can strongly affect the ethical choices you will have to make. When you view your firm's polices or requests as improper, you have three choices:

1. Ignore your personal values and do what your company asks you to do. Self-respect suffers when you have to compromise your principles to please an employer. If you take this path, you will probably feel guilty and be dissatisfied with your job in the long run.

2. Take a stand and tell your employer what you think. Try to influence the decisions and policies of your company and supervisors.

3. Refuse to compromise your principles. Taking this path may mean you will get fired or be forced to quit.

You should not take a job with a company whose products, policies, and conduct conflict with your standards. Before taking a job, investigate the company's procedures and selling approach to see if they conflict with your personal ethical standards. Throughout this text, we will highlight the legal and ethical issues associated with the retail decisions made by managers.

SUMMARY

Retailing is evolving into a global, high-tech industry that plays a major role in the global economy. About one in five U.S. workers is employed by retailers.[33] Increasingly, retailers are selling their products and services through more than one channel—such as stores, Internet, and catalogs. Firms selling services to consumers, such as dry cleaning and automobile repairs, are also retailers.

Retailing is defined as a set of business activities that add value to the products and services sold to consumers for their personal or family use. These value-added activities include providing assortments, breaking bulk, holding inventory, and providing services.

The retail management decision process involves developing a strategy for creating a competitive advantage in the marketplace and then developing a retail mix to implement that strategy. The strategic decisions, discussed in the first section of this textbook, involve selecting a target market, defining the nature of the retailer's offering, and building a competitive advantage through locations,

human resource management, information and supply chain management systems, and customer relationship management programs. The tactical decisions for implementing the strategy, discussed in the second half of this textbook, involve selecting a merchandise assortment, buying merchandise, setting prices, communicating with customers, managing the store, presenting merchandise in stores, and providing customer service. Large retail chains use sophisticated information systems to analyze business opportunities and make these decisions about how to operate their businesses in multiple countries.

Retailing offers opportunities for exciting, challenging careers, either by working for a retail firm or starting your own business. Aspects of retail careers are discussed in Appendix 1A, and Appendix 1B provides some sources of information about the retail industry. Suggestions about starting your own business and franchising appear in Appendix 1 and Appendix 2 at the end of the book.

KEY TERMS

backward integration, *7*
breaking bulk, *8*
corporate social responsibility, *9*
ethics, *23*
forward integration, *7*
intertype competition, *16*

intratype competition, *16*
retailer, *7*
retailing, *6*
retail mix, *21*
retail strategy, *18*
scrambled merchandising, *16*

supply chain, *7*
variety, *16*
vertical integration, *7*
wholesalers, *7*

GET OUT AND DO IT!

1. **CONTINUING CASE ASSIGNMENT** In most chapters of this textbook, there will be a GET OUT AND DO IT! assignment that will give you an opportunity to examine the strategy and tactics of one retailer. Your first assignment is to select a retailer and prepare a report on the retailer's history, including when it was founded and how it has evolved over time. To ensure that you can get information about the retailer for subsequent Continuing Case Assignments, the retailer you select should
   - Be a publicly held company so that you can access its financial statements and annual reports. Do not select a retailer that is owned by another company. For example, since Bath & Body Works is owned by Limited Brands, you can only get financial information about the holding company and not the individual companies it owns, such as Victoria's Secret, White Barn Candle, and so forth.
   - Focus on one type of retailing. For example, J. Crew just operates one type of specialty stores and thus would be a good choice. However, Wal-Mart operates discount stores, warehouse club

   stores, and supercenters and thus would not be a good choice.
   - Be easy to visit and collect information about. Some retailers and store managers may not allow you to interview them about the store, take pictures of the store, talk with sales associates, or analyze the merchandise assortment in the store. Try to pick a retailer with a local store manager who can help you complete the assignments.

   Some examples of retailers that meet the first two criteria are Whole Foods Market, Dress Barn, Burlington Coat Factory, Ross Stores, Ann Taylor, Cato, Chico's, Finish Line, Foot Locker, Brookstone, Claire's, CVS, Walgreens, Staples, Office Depot, Borders, American Eagle Outfitter, Pacific Sunwear, Abercrombie & Fitch, Tiffany & Co., AutoZone, Pep Boys, Hot Topic, Wet Seal, Best Buy, Family Dollar, Dollar General, Circuit City, Michaels, PetSmart, Dillard's, Pier 1 Imports, Home Depot, Lowe's, Bed Bath & Beyond, Men's Warehouse, Kroger, Kohl's, Radio Shack, Safeway, and Target.

2. Visit a local retail store and describe each of the elements in its retail mix.

3. Data on U.S. retail sales are available at the U.S. Bureau of the Census Internet site at http://www.census.gov/mrts/ www/mrts.html. Look at the unadjusted monthly sales by type of retailer. In which quarter are sales the highest? Which types of retailers have their greatest sales in the fourth quarter?

4. Go to the Macy's (http://www.macysjobs. com/college), Sears Holding (http://www. searsholdings.com/careers/), and National Retail Federation (http://www.nrf.com/retailcareers/) Web sites to find information about retail careers with these companies. Review the information about the different positions in these companies. In which positions would you be interested? Which positions are not of interest to you? Which company would interest you? Why?

DISCUSSION QUESTIONS AND PROBLEMS

1. What is your favorite retailer? Why do you like this retailer? What would a competitive retailer have to do to get your patronage?

2. From your perspective, what are the benefits and limitations of purchasing a pair of jeans directly from a manufacturer rather than from a retailer?

3. What retailers would be considered intratype competitors for a convenience store chain such as 7-Eleven? What firms would be intertype competitors?

4. Does Wal-Mart contribute to or detract from the communities in which it operates stores?

5. Choose a U.S.-based retailer that wants to open a new store outside the United States for the first time. Which country should it pursue? Why?

6. Why do retail managers need to consider ethical issues when making decisions?

7. Choose one of the top 20 retailers (Exhibit 1–2). Go to the company's Web site and find out how the company started and how it has changed over time.

8. From a personal perspective, how does retailing rate as a potential career compared with others you are considering?

9. How might managers at different levels of a retail organization define their competition?

10. Retailing View 1.1 describes how some retailers are acting socially responsibly. Take the perspective of a stockholder in the company. What effect will these activities have on the value of its stock? Why might they have a positive or negative effect?

SUGGESTED READINGS

Brunn, Stanley D. *Wal-Mart World: The World's Biggest Corporation in the Global Economy*. Oxford: Routledge, 2006.

Byers, Ann. *Jeff Bezos: The Founder of Amazon.com*. New York: Rosen Publishing Group, 2006.

Clark, Maxine, and Amy Joyner. *The Bear Necessities of Business: Building a Company with Heart*. Hoboken, NJ: John Wiley & Sons, 2006.

Draganska, Michaela and Daniel Klapper. "Retail Environment and Manufacturer Competitive Intensity." *Journal of Retailing* 83 (April 2007), pp. 183–93.

Etgar, Michael, and Dalia Rachman-Moore. "Determinant Factors of Failures of International Retailers in Foreign Markets." *The International Review of Retail, Distribution and Consumer Research* 17 (February 2007), pp. 79–81.

Foster, J. Lucia, John Haltiwanger, and C.J. Krizan. "Market Selection, Reallocation, and Restructuring in the U.S. Retail

Trade Sector in the 1990s." *The Review of Economics and Statistics* 88 (November 2006), pp. 748–63.

Koehn, Nancy F., and Katherine Miller. "John Mackey and Whole Foods Market." *Harvard Business Review*, May 14, 2007, accessed electronically.

Kraft, Manfred, and Murali K. Mantrala. *Retailing in the 21st Century*. Berlin, Germany: Springer, 2006.

Lewis, Elen. *Great Ikea!: A Brand for All the People*. London: Cyan Communications, 2005.

Plunkett, Jack (ed). *Plunkett's Retail Industry Almanac 2007*. Houston: Plunkett Research, Ltd., 2006.

Sharp Paine, Lynn. "Ethics: A Basic Framework." *Harvard Business Review*, May 14, 2007, accessed electronically.

"2007 Global Powers of Retailing," *Stores*, January 2007, pp. G1–45.

APPENDIX 1A   Careers in Retailing

Retailing offers exciting and challenging career opportunities. Few other industries grant as many responsibilities to young managers. When students asked Dave Fuente, former CEO of Office Depot, what they needed to become a CEO someday, he responded, "You need to have profit and loss responsibility and the experience of managing people early in your career." Entry-level retail

jobs for college graduates offer both of these opportunities. Most college graduates begin their retail careers as assistant buyers, merchandise planners, or department managers in stores, in which positions they have the responsibility for the profitability of a line of merchandise or an area of the store, and they also manage people who work for them.

Even if you work for a large company, retailing provides an opportunity for you to do your own thing and be rewarded. You can come with an idea, execute it almost immediately, and see how well it is doing by reviewing the sales data at the end of the day.

Retailing offers a variety of career paths, such as buying, store management, sales promotion and advertising, personnel, operations/distribution, loss prevention, and finance. In addition, retailing offers almost immediate accountability for talented people so they can reach key management positions fairly quickly. Starting salaries are competitive, and the compensation of top management ranks among the highest in any industry.

CAREER OPPORTUNITIES

In retail firms, career opportunities occur among the merchandising/buying, store management, and corporate staff functions. Corporate positions are found in such areas as accounting, finance, promotions and advertising, computer and distribution systems, and human resources.

The primary entry-level opportunities for a retailing career are in the areas of buying and store management. Buying positions are more numbers oriented, whereas store management positions are more people oriented. Entry-level positions on the corporate staff are limited. Retailers typically want all of their employees to understand their customers and their merchandise. Therefore, most executives and corporate staff managers begin their careers in store management or buying.

Store Management

Successful store managers must have the ability to lead and motivate employees. They also need to be sensitive to customers' needs by making sure that merchandise is available and neatly displayed.

Store management involves all the discipline necessary to run a successful business: sales planning and goal setting, overall store image and merchandise presentation, budgets and expense control, customer service and sales supervision, personnel administration and development, and community relations.

Store managers work directly in the local market, often at quite a distance from the home office, which means they have limited direct supervision. Their hours generally mirror their store's and can therefore include some weekends and evenings. In addition, they spend time during nonoperating hours tending to administrative responsibilities.

The typical entry-level store management position is a department manager with responsibility for merchandise presentation, customer service, and inventory control for an area of the store. The next level is an area or group manager with responsibility for executing merchandising plans and achieving sales goals for several areas, as well as supervising, training, and developing department managers. Beyond these positions, you might be promoted store manager, then a district manager responsible for a group of stores, and then regional manager responsible for a group of districts. Retailing View 1.3 describes Joyce Rivas's experience in store management.

Joyce Rivas, Store Manager, Walgreens   RETAILING VIEW   1.3

When I was a student at Florida International University in Miami, I majored in Health Administration because I wanted to pursue a career that involved helping people. I planned to work for a hospital when I graduated. While I was in college, I worked part-time at a Walgreens store as a pharmacist technician and discovered that working for Walgreens offered an opportunity to both help people with their health care problems and be involved in a dynamic and exciting business environment.

Walgreens has a strong set of corporate values that emphasizes providing outstanding customer service. Our pharmacists don't just fill prescriptions. They talk with customers about the medications that they are taking, answer questions, and try to address concerns customers might have.

I really like working in a store. I would be bored if I had to sit behind a desk all day. I need to walk around and talk with people. As a store manager, I interact with a wide variety of people including customers, store employees, and people in our district office. Every day at Walgreens is different. In a single day, I will handle some personnel issues, help customers find what they need, decide on how to display new merchandise, and review reports summarizing the financial performance of my store.

Being a store manager at Walgreens is like running your own business. The annual sales for my store, which employs 50 people, is over $15 million and I am responsible and rewarded for the store's performance. But the rewards I get are more than just monetary. I receive a great deal of satisfaction from

Joyce Rivas (right) discusses the sales report with two assistant managers.

working with and helping people. Walgreens is a great place to work because it is a company that cares about its customers and employees just like I do.

As the manager of this business, I try to create an environment in which my store employees feel that they are all part of a team working together to provide an attractive offering for our customers. I want all of my team members to learn more about how our store and company operates, develop their skills, and realize their potential. By working together and helping each other, we can all achieve our goals.

Merchandise Management

Merchandise management attracts people with strong analytical capabilities, an ability to predict what merchandise will appeal to their target markets, and a skill for negotiating with vendors as well as store management to get things done. Many retailers have broken the merchandising management activities into two different yet parallel career paths: buying and merchandise planning.

Retail merchandise buyers are similar to financial portfolio managers. They invest in a portfolio of merchandise, monitor the performance (sales) of the merchandise, and, on the basis of the sales, either decide to buy more merchandise that is selling well or get rid of (discount) merchandise that is selling poorly. Buyers are responsible for selecting the type and amount of merchandise to buy, negotiating the wholesale price and payment terms with suppliers, setting the initial retail price for the merchandise, monitoring merchandise sales, and making appropriate retail price adjustments. Thus buyers need to have good financial planning skills, knowledge of their customers' needs and wants and competitive activities, and the ability to develop good working relationships with vendors. To develop a better understanding of their customers, buyers typically stay in contact with their stores by visiting them, talking to sales associates and managers, and monitoring the sales data available through their merchandise management systems.

Planners have an even more analytical role than buyers. Their primary responsibility is to determine the assortment of merchandise sent to each store—how many styles, colors, sizes, and individual items to purchase for each store. Planners also are responsible for allocating merchandise to stores. Once the merchandise is in the stores, planners closely monitor sales and work with buyers on decisions such as how much additional merchandise to purchase if the merchandise is doing well or when to reduce the price on the merchandise if sales are below expectations.

The typical entry-level position of college graduates interested in merchandise management is either assistant buyer or assistant planner in a merchandise category such as men's athletic shoes or consumer electronics. In these positions, you will do the sales analysis needed to support the decisions eventually made by the planner or buyer for whom you work. From this entry-level position, you could be promoted to buyer and then divisional merchandise manager, responsible for a number of merchandise categories. Most retailers believe that merchandise management skills are not category specific. Thus, as you are promoted in the buying organization, you will probably work in various merchandise categories. Retailing View 1.4 provides a perspective on a JCPenney buyer's job.

Corporate Staff

The corporate staff positions in retail firms involve activities and require knowledge, skills, and abilities similar to comparable positions in nonretail firms. Thus many managers in these positions identify with their profession rather than the retail industry. For example, accountants in retail firms view themselves as accountant, not retailers.

Management Information Systems (MIS)   Employees in this area are involved with applications for capturing data and monitoring inventory, as well as the management of store systems such as POS terminals, self-checkout systems, and in-store kiosks.

Operations/Distribution   Operations employees are responsible for operating and maintaining the store's physical plant; providing various customer services; the receipt, ticketing, warehousing, and distribution of a store's inventory; and buying and maintaining store supplies and operating equipment. Students in operations and MIS typically major in production, operations, or computer information systems.

Marketing   Those activities include public relations, advertising, visual merchandising, and special events. This department attempts to build the retail firm's brand image and encourage customers to visit the retailer's stores and/or Web site. Managers in this area typically major in marketing or mass communications.

Loss Prevention   Loss prevention employees are responsible for protecting the retailer's assets. They develop systems and procedures to minimize employee theft and shoplifting. Managers in this area often major in sociology or criminology, though, as we discuss in Chapters 9 and 16, loss prevention is beginning to be viewed as a human resource management issue.

Finance/Control   Many retailers are large businesses involved in complicated corporate structures. Most retailers also operate with a tight net profit margin. With such a fine line between success and failure, retailers continue to require top financial experts—and they compensate them generously. The finance/control division is responsible for the financial health of the company. They prepare financial reports for all aspects of the business, including long-range forecasting and planning, economic trend analysis and budgeting, shortage control and internal audits, gross and net profit, accounts payable to vendors, and accounts receivable from charge customers. In addition, they manage the retailer's relationship with the financial community. Students interested in this area often major in finance or accounting.

Real Estate   Employees in the real estate division are responsible for selecting locations for stores, negotiating leases and land purchases, and managing the leasehold costs. Students entering this area typically major in real estate or finance.

Store Design   Employees working in this area are responsible for designing the store and presenting merchandise and fixtures in the store. Talented, creative students in business, architecture, art, and other related fields will have innumerable opportunities for growth in the area of retail store design.

Human Resource Management   Human resource management is responsible for the effective selection, training, placement, advancement, and welfare of employees. Because there are seasonal peaks in retailing (such as Christmas, when many extra people must be hired), human resource personnel must be flexible and highly efficient.

MYTHS ABOUT RETAILING

Sales Clerk Is the Entry-Level Job in Retailing

Most students and their parents think that people working in retailing have jobs as sales clerks and cashiers. They hold this view because, as customers in retail stores, they typically only interact with sales associates, not their managers. But as we have discussed in this chapter, retail firms are large, sophisticated corporations that employ managers with a wide variety of knowledge, skills, and abilities.

Entry-level positions for college and university graduates are typically management trainees in the buying or store organization, not sales associates.

Management trainees in retailing are given more responsibility more quickly than in other industries. Buyers are responsible for choosing, promoting, pricing, distributing, and selling millions of dollars worth of merchandise each season. The department manager, generally the first position after a training program, is often responsible for merchandising one or more departments, as well as managing 10 or more full- and part-time sales associates.

College and University Degrees Are Not Needed to Succeed in Retailing

While some employees are promoted on the basis of their retail experience, a college degree is needed for most retail management positions, ranging from store manager to

---

John Tighe, VP, Division Merchandise Manager, JCPenney   RETAILING VIEW   1.4

My interest in retailing was peaked when I took a retail seminar while I was an undergraduate at the University of Massachusetts. During the seminar, I spent a day shadowing a retail manager and was attracted to the variety of challenging issues he had to deal with everyday. After graduation, I went to work for a regional department store chain owned by the May Company. I started as a management trainee and eventual became a buyer. JCPenney presented me with an exciting opportunity that I accepted and moved to the corporate headquarters in Dallas. I am now the Divisional Merchandise Manager for junior sportswear. The twenty people including four buyers who work in my group are responsible for over $1 billion in annual sales.

I really love my job and can't image working in an industry other than retailing. Everyday there is something new and different to deal with. For example, I have recently worked with our supply chain management people to see how we can get some popular apparel in our stores faster; met with are marketing department to discuss the items we will feature in our new advertising campaign; talked with a well-known, national brand vendor about making a special line of merchandise to be sold exclusively at Penney; and developed a presentation to make to our store personnel over our closed circuit TV network about some new merchandise we are offering. And of course a lot of my time is spent working with our buyers to decide what merchandise we are going to offer and managing inventory levels. I feel as if I am an entrepreneur running a business with the resources of a large company supporting me.

Managing merchandise effectively is both an art and a science. Our information systems tell us what merchandise is sold each day, and even each hour, in every one of our 1100 stores. Our buyers and planners spend a lot of time developing merchandise budget plans and analyzing this data to see how they are doing, to plan and to understand what is selling, and where it is selling. We use sophisticated software to forecast sales and determine when and how deep to take markdowns. This part of the buyer's job is really like a financial analyst sitting in front of a computer and playing with the numbers.

And then there is the art. You also need to have a feel for what merchandise our customers will buy. Just like with any

John Tighe runs a $1 billion bussiness at JCPenney

business, you need to become an expert to be successful. So I spend a lot of time trying to understand the trends and what our customers want. I read the trade publications like *Womens Wear Daily* to see what the designers are showing and fashion leaders are wearing. I shop at our stores and those of competitors to see what is being offered and what customers are wearing and buying.

I am a very competitive person—I want to take business away from our competitors and have the best performing merchandise division in JCPenney. It gives me great satisfaction to turn on my computer and see that the merchandise we have bought is flying off the shelves. But it is also satisfying when we make a mistake and buy merchandise that does not sell to plan and then find the right price to move the inventory so we can replace it with something new and exciting.

CEO. More than 150 colleges and universities offer programs of study and degrees or majors in retailing.

Retail Jobs Are Low Paying

Starting salaries for management trainees with a college degree range from $35,000 to $65,000 a year, and the compensation of top management ranks with the highest in industry. For example, store managers with only a few years of experience can earn up to $100,000 or more, depending on their performance bonuses. A senior buyer for a department store earns from $50,000 to $90,000 or more. A department store manager can earn from $50,000 to $150,000; a discount store manager makes from $70,000 to $100,000 or more; and a specialty store manager earns from $35,000 to $60,000 or more.

Compensation varies according to the amount of responsibility. Specialty store managers are generally paid less than department store managers because their annual sales volume is lower. But advancements in this area can be faster. Aggressive specialty store managers often are promoted to district managers and run 8 to 15 units after a few years so that they quickly move into higher pay brackets.

Because information systems enable retailers to assess the sales and profit performance of each manager, and even each sales associate, the compensation of retail managers is closely linked to objective measures of their performance. As a result, in addition to salaries, retail managers are generally given strong monetary incentives based on the sales they create.

A compensation package consists of more than salary alone. In retailing, the benefits package is often substantial and may include a profit-sharing plan, savings plan, stock options, medical and dental insurance, life insurance, long-term disability protection and income protection plans, and paid vacations and holidays. Two additional benefits of retailing careers are that most retailers offer employees valuable discounts on the merchandise that they sell, and some buying positions include extensive foreign travel.

Retailing Is a Low Growth Industry with Little Opportunity for Advancement

While the growth rate of retail parallels the growth rate of the overall economy, many opportunities for rapid advancement exist simply because of the sheer size of the retail industry. With so many retail firms, there is always a large number of firms that are experiencing a high growth rate, opening many new stores, and needing store managers and support staff positions.

Working in Retailing Requires Long Hours and Frequent Relocation

Retailing has an often exaggerated reputation of demanding long and unusual hours. Superficially, this reputation is true. Store managers do work some evenings and weekends. But many progressive retailers have realized that if the unusual hours aren't offset by time off at other periods during the week, many managers become inefficient, angry, and resentful—in other words, burned out. It's also important to put the concept of long hours into perspective. Most professional careers require more than 40 hours per week for the person to succeed. In a new job with new tasks and responsibilities, the time commitment is even greater.

Depending on the type of retailer and the specific firm, retailing enables executives to change locations often or not at all. In general, a career path in store management has more opportunity for relocation than paths in buying/merchandising or corporate. Because buying and corporate offices are usually centrally located, these positions generally are not subject to frequent moves. In addition, employees in corporate positions and merchandise management tend to work during normal business hours.

Retailing Doesn't Provide Opportunities for Women and Minorities

Many people consider retailing to be among the most race- and gender-blind industries. Retailers typically think that their managers and executives will make better decisions if they mirror their customers. Because most purchases are made by women, and minorities are becoming an increasingly important factor in the market, most retailers have active programs designed to provide the experiences and support that will enable women and minorities to be promoted to top management positions.

APPENDIX 1B   Sources of Information about Retailing

RETAIL TRADE PUBLICATIONS AND WEB SITES

About.com. This Web site provides information about the retail industry. http://retailindustry.about.com/. For example, the listing of the largest retail firms appears at http://retailindustry.about.com/od/sales_retailers/Retail_Sales_by_Retailer.htm.

Advanstar Integrated marketing solutions for the fashion, life sciences and powersports industries. www.advanstar.com

Bizstats.com Instant access to useful financial ratios, business statistics and benchmarks. Effective and understandable analysis of businesses & industries. www.bizstats.com

Chain Store Age Monthly magazine for retail headquarters executives and shopping center developers. Deals with management, operations, construction, modernization, store equipment, maintenance, real estate, financing, materials handling, and advertising. More oriented to operations than stores. www.chainstoreage.com

Colloquy Trade publication and Web site targeting the loyalty marketing industry. It provides marketers with consulting, news, editorial, educational, and research services across all industries and around the globe on topics including loyalty marketing, reward programs, and customer retention. www.colloquy.com

Convenience Store News Monthly magazine for convenience store and oil retailing executives, managers, and franchisees. Covers industry trends, news, and merchandising techniques. www.csnews.com

DNR Daily newspaper about retail fashion, products, merchandising, and marketing for men's and boy's wear. Geared to retailers, wholesalers, and manufacturers. www.dnrnews.com

Dealerscope Monthly publication for retailers of consumer electronics, appliances, and computers. www.dealerscope.com

Direct Selling News Monthly magazine for executives in the direct selling industry. www.directsellingnews.com

Drug Store News Biweekly publication covering chain drug and combination store retailing. www.drugstorenews.com

ESRI Leading source of geodemographic data used for store location. A specific Web page on the ESRI site allows a person to enter a zip code and get a description of the geodemographic profile of that zip code. www.esri.com/data/community_data/ community-tapestry/index.html

E-Tailer's Digest. Moderated discussions of various issues confronting Internet retailing such as customer service, security issues, effective merchandising, shipping and tax issues, and warehousing and logistics. www.etailersdigest.com/

Furniture Today Weekly newspaper for retail executives in furniture and department stores and for executives in manufacturing firms. www.furnituretoday.com

Hobby Merchandiser Monthly trade publication for suppliers and retailers in the model hobby industry. www.hobbymerchandiser.com

Hoovers. A division of D&B that provides financial information about firms. The site for retail firms is premium.hoovers.com/subscribe/ind/factsheet. xhtml?HICID=1518. Video clips of analyst reports on retail firms are available on the site.

Internet Retailer Monthly magazine devoted to electronic retailing issues. www.internetretailer.com

InternetRetailing.Net InternetRetail.net (IR), based in the United Kingdom, provides news and analysis for today's net retailers. IR combines online information, a print magazine, and an annual conference. www.internetretailing.net

Mass Market Retailers Biweekly newspaper for executives in supermarket, chain drug, and chain discount headquarters. Reports news and interprets its effects on mass merchandisers. www.massmarketretailers.com

Modern Grocer Weekly newspaper covers regional and national news current events relating to food retailing. www.griffcomm.net

Modern Jeweler Monthly magazine for jewelry retailers. Looks at trends in jewelry, gems, and watches. www.modernjeweler.com

NACS Magazine Monthly publication for convenience stores. www.cstorecentral.com

NRF SmartBrief Daily e-mail newsletter highlighting links to the top retail headlines, often read by retail executives. www.nrf.com/RetailHeadlines

Planning Factory Limited Tools for merchandise planning. www.planfact.co.uk/abouttpf.htm A series of 12 articles developed by Retek about merchandise planning is available at www.planfact.co.uk/art_retk.htm.

Private Label Magazine Bimonthly magazine for buyers, merchandisers, and executives involved in purchasing private, controlled packer, and generic labeled products for chain supermarkets and drug, discount, convenience, and department stores. www.privatelabelmag.com

Progressive Grocer Monthly magazine reporting on the supermarket industry. In-depth features offer insights into trends in store development, technology, marketing, logistics, international retailing, human resources, and consumer purchasing patterns. www.progressivegrocer.com

RFID Journal Trade publication covering the uses and new developments of RFID technology. www.rfidjournal.com/article/verticals/13/

RIS (Retail Info Systems) News Monthly magazine addressing system solutions for corporate/financial, operations, MIS, and merchandising management in retail. www.risnews.com

Retailing Today. Published biweekly, providing news, trends, and research for decision makers in the 150 largest retailers. www.retailingtoday.com

Retail Merchandiser Published monthly for retail buyers, CEOs, financial investors, visual merchandisers, and consultants. www.retail-merchandiser.com

Retail Solutions Online Newsletter focusing on technology used to improve retail operations. www.retailsolutionsonline.com

RetailTraffic Monthly magazine for managers involved in real estate and location decisions. www.retailtrafficmag.com

RetailWire Online discussion forum that goes beyond conventional headline news reporting. Each business morning, RetailWire editors pick news topics worthy of commentary, according to its "Brain Trust" panel of industry experts and the general RetailWire membership. The results are virtual round tables of industry opinion and advice covering key dynamics and issues affecting the retailing industry. www.retailwire.com

Retail Worker. Labor news and discussion, by, for, and about retail workers. A project of the Industrial Workers of the World labor union. www.retailworker.com/

Retaildesign Monthly publication describing new trends and techniques in store design and merchandise presentation. www.retailreporting.com

RIS Trade publication focusing on the retail technology industry. Its media portfolio includes a monthly magazine, weekly e-newsletter, Web site, blogs, podcasts, online Web seminars, custom publishing, research studies, custom events, and four major summits and conferences. www.risnews.com

New York Times Specific content pertaining to entrepreneurship and small businesses. www.nytimes.com/business/smallbusiness/

Retail Bulletin Online information source aimed at meeting retailers' need for quick, accurate, and up-to-date news about the industry. The free online service delivers the latest company news, breaking stories, and summaries of media coverage of the retail sector. www.theretailbulletin.com

Retail Forward Reports on market change and assesses the impact of these changes on retailers' operations and performance. www.retailforward.com

Retail Systems Alert Group Covers the extended retail industry through conferences, print, and online channels. Its main focus is on the customer experience and how players in the extended retail industry can enhance it. www.retailsystems.com/

Retail Technology Milestones Tracks the changes, successes, and accomplishments achieved by the many solutions providers in the retail industry. It provides a platform to centralize and distribute all the news that retail solution providers offer. www.rtmilestones.com

Shopping Centers Today Monthly publication about the development of new shopping centers and the expansion of existing ones. http://www.icsc.org/srch/sct/sct0507/index.php

Stores Monthly magazine published by the National Retail Federation (NRF). Aimed at retail executives in department and specialty stores, it emphasizes broad trends in customer behavior, management practices, and technology. www.stores.org

StoreFrontBackTalk The information on the site covers issues involved in store operations, such as e-commerce, RFID, payment systems, security/fraud, CRM, contactless/wireless, IT strategy, and biometrics. www.storefrontbacktalk.com/

Supply Chain Brain.com Global logistics and supply chain strategies, offering case studies, executive interviews, and features with information on the latest technology, services, and processes needed to maximize supply chain efficiency. www.glscs.com

VM+SD (Visual Merchandising and Store Design) Monthly magazine for people involved in merchandise display, store interior design and planning, and manufacturing of equipment used by display and store designers. www.stmediagroup.com/index.php3?d=pubs&p=vm

Wal-Mart Information about Wal-Mart, including short videos. www.walmartstores.com/GlobalWMStoresWeb/navigate.do?catg=1

WWD (formerly *Women's Wear Daily*) Daily newspaper reports fashion and industry news on women's and children's ready-to-wear, sportswear, innerwear, accessories, and cosmetics. www.wwd.com

Workforce Management Trade publication Web site focusing on human resource management issues. www.workforce.com

Xtreme Retailing Sponsored by IBM, offers reports and video about new retail technologies. www.xr23.com/Page.cfm/1

RETAIL TRADE ASSOCIATIONS

Direct Marketing Association The leading global trade association of business and nonprofit organizations using and supporting direct marketing tools and techniques to generate sales. DMA advocates industry standards for responsible marketing, promotes relevance as the key to reaching consumers with desirable offers, and provides research, education, and networking opportunities to improve results throughout the entire direct marketing process. www.the-dma.org

Direct Selling Association The national trade association of the leading firms that manufacture and distribute goods and services sold directly to consumers. More than 200 companies are members of the association, including many well-known brand names. www.dsa.org

Electronic Retailing Association A trade association for companies that use the power of direct response to sell goods and services to the public on television, online, and radio. ERA serves as the cohesive voice for multichannel marketers while promoting government affairs initiatives and regulations designed to protect members' bottom line. www.retailing.org

Food Marketing Institute Membership includes 1,600 grocery retailers and wholesalers. Maintains liaisons with government and consumers and conducts research programs. Publishes *Facts About Supermarket Development* and *Supermarket Industry Financial Review*. Formed by the merger of the National Association of Food Chains and Supermarket Institute. www.fmi.org

In-Store Marketing Institute The institute serves brand marketers, retailers, agencies and manufacturers worldwide with information and educational events focused on improving retail marketing strategy. The Web site offers marketing profiles of leading retailers, 1,400 articles about promotions and display programs, 200 research studies, and 1,000 charts examining such issues as effectiveness measurement and consumer behavior, as well as summaries of 2,900 retail campaigns conducted since 1988, 15,000 images of displays, signs, and other forms of marketing material, and summaries of historical lawsuits and litigation affecting various aspects of retail marketing activity. www.instoremarketer.org

International Council of Shopping Centers Represents 35,000 owners, developers, retailers, and managers of shopping centers; architects, engineers, contractors, leasing brokers, promotion agencies, and others who provide services and products for shopping center owners, shopping center merchant associations, retailers, and public and academic organizations. Promotes professional standards of performance in the development, construction, financing, leasing, management, and operation of shopping centers throughout the world. Engages in research and data gathering on all aspects of shopping centers and compiles statistics. www.icsc.org

National Association of Chain Drug Stores Interprets actions by government agencies in such areas as drugs, public health, federal trade, labor, and excise taxes. www.nacds.org

National Association of Convenience Stores Membership includes 4,000 retail stores that sell gasoline, fast foods, soft drinks, dairy products, beer, cigarettes, publications, grocery items, snacks, and nonfood items and are usually open seven days per week. www.cstorecentral.com

National Mail Order Association Trade association provides business resources for small to medium-sized

companies involved in direct marketing. The site offers a free newsletter and statistics associated with direct mail retailing, such as response rates. www.nmoa.org/

National Retail Federation (NRF) The NRF conducts extensive conferences and educational programs for retailers, provides statistical information, and publishes *Stores Magazine*. www.nrf.com

Retail Industry Leaders Association Membership includes 750 mass retailing (discount) chains. Conducts research and educational programs on every phase of self-service general merchandise retailing. Publishes *Operating Results of Mass Retail Stores/Mass Retailers' Merchandising and Operating Results* annually. www.retail-leaders.org

Shop.org The only trade association to focus exclusively on Internet retailing. Its 300 members represent all segments of online retailing, including virtual retailers, conventional retailers, catalogers, manufacturers, and companies providing products and services for online retailers. Sponsors studies on electronic retailing. A division of the NRF. www.shop.org

Types of Retailers

EXECUTIVE BRIEFING
Keith Koenig, President, City Furniture

store for him. I still remember how excited I was when I called him and told him that we just had our first $1,000 sales day. When I finished the MBA program at the University of Florida, Kevin offered me a partnership in the business.

Waterbed styles in the 1970s were simple structures, consisting of basic wood frames. Kevin cut and stained the frames by night and sold them by day. And when Kevin wasn't building waterbeds, he was familiarizing the public with waterbeds. He spent every dime he could on advertising, and it paid off! Customers kept coming into our modest showroom, and we soon realized a bigger store was vital. Our first expansion was from 800 square feet to 1,400 square feet, and soon more showrooms followed.

At the end of the 1980s, waterbeds were going out of style, and we experienced our first decline in annual sales. Some waterbed stores converted to bedding and mattress outlets. But we decided to make a dramatic strategic change and become a full-line furniture store. In September of 1994, Waterbed City evolved into City Furniture. This evolution involved expanding our product line to include living and dining room furniture, wall units, home theatre, and ready-to-assemble furniture. We

In 1971, after graduating from college, my brother Kevin and his girlfriend wanted to escape the Florida heat and spend the summer at Cape Cod. To pay for their living expenses, they opened a waterbed store in Provincetown and cleared $5,000 before returning home to Fort Lauderdale in the fall. The Cape Cod experience was encouraging, so Kevin opened a waterbed store in the fall in Fort Lauderdale. His Waterbed City showroom was a mere 800 square feet and probably located in the worst place in the shopping center. Kevin went to the Cape the following summer, and I ran the

CHAPTER 2

QUESTIONS

What trends are shaping today's retailers?

What are the different types of retailers?

How do retailers differ in terms of how they meet the needs of their customers?

How do services retailers differ from merchandise retailers?

What are the types of ownership for retail firms?

implemented a new positioning that combines quality brand-name home furnishings with fantastic everyday low prices, and a strong commitment to great customer service.

We offer services that few modestly priced furniture stores offer, like same-day delivery and our Academy of Design program. Most customers are reluctant to hire an interior designer when they furnish their home. They are concerned about the price of the service and the merchandise suggested. We offer customers three levels of design service packages ranging from $295 to $695. Customers can go to our Web site, select one of the packages, and pick a design consultant who is located near their home. Then the consultant goes to the customer's home and suggests furniture, wall finishings, window treatments, and flooring. Using a laptop computer, the customer can visualize the décor, also know what the price will be, make changes to keep within a budget, and get suggestions for a subcontractor who might do the work. The customer is not obligated to buy from us. Our strategy at City Furniture is really working. Our sales have increased nearly eight fold from $45 million in 1994 to over $350 million in 2008 from our 21 locations, and we are the largest furniture chain in South Florida..

You want to have a good cup of coffee in the morning, not instant, but you don't want to bother with grinding coffee beans, boiling water, pouring it through ground coffee in a filter, and waiting. Think of all of the different retailers that could help you satisfy this need. You could get your cup of brewed coffee from the drive-through window at the local Starbucks, or you could decide to buy an automatic coffeemaker with a timer so your coffee will be ready when you wake up. You could purchase the coffeemaker at a discount store like Wal-Mart or Target, a department store like Macy's, a drugstore like Walgreens, or a category specialist like Circuit City. If you want to buy the coffeemaker without taking the time to visit a store, you could order it from the JCPenney catalog or go to www.shopping.yahoo.com, search for "coffee and espresso maker," and review the information on 12,000 models sold by more than 73 Internet retailers.

All these retailers are competing against one another to satisfy your need for a hassle-free, good cup of coffee. Many are selling the same brands, but they offer different services, prices, environments, and convenience. For example, if you want to buy a low-price, basic coffeemaker, you might go to a discount store. But if you are interested in a coffeemaker with more features and want to have someone explain the different features, you might visit a department store or a category specialist.

To develop and implement a retail strategy, retailers need to understand the nature of competition in the retail marketplace. This chapter describes the different types of retailers—both store and nonstore—and how they compete against one another by offering different benefits to consumers. These benefits are reflected in the nature of the retail mixes used by the retailers to satisfy customer needs: the types of merchandise and services offered, the degree to which their offerings emphasize services versus merchandise, and the prices charged (recall Exhibit 1–5).

RETAILER CHARACTERISTICS

The 1.9 million[1] U.S. retailers range from street vendors selling hot dogs to Internet retailers like Amazon.com to multichannel retailers such as Best Buy that have both an extensive physical store presence and an active Internet site. Each retailer survives and prospers when it satisfies a group of consumers' needs more effectively than its competitors can. The different types of retailers offer unique benefits, so consumers patronize different retail types when they have different needs. For example, you might value the convenience of buying a gift t-shirt from a catalog that will be shipped to a friend in another city. Alternatively, you might prefer to buy from a local store when making a purchase for yourself so you can try on the shirt. You might go to a discount store to buy an inexpensive t-shirt for a camping trip or a sporting goods specialty store to buy a t-shirt with the insignia of your favorite football team before you meet friends to watch your team's game.

As consumer needs and competition change, new retail formats are created and existing formats evolve. The initial category specialists in toys, consumer electronics, and home improvement supplies have been joined by a host of new specialists, including Zappos.com (shoes), Sephora (cosmetics), and PetSmart (pet supplies). Wal-Mart is closing its traditional discount stores to open supercenters—large stores that combine a discount store with a supermarket. eBay Motors, which allows consumers to buy cars and motorcycles from thousands of individuals as well as established dealers, competes with traditional automobile dealers that sell new and used cars using more conventional retailing methods. Kayak and Expedia both use the Internet to provide many of the services offered by traditional travel agents.

The most basic characteristics used to describe the different types of retailers is the retail mix, or the elements retailers use to satisfy their customers' needs (see Exhibit 1–5). Four elements of the retail mix are particularly useful for classifying retailers: the type of merchandise and/or services sold, the variety and assortment of merchandise sold, the level of customer service, and the price of the merchandise.

Type of Merchandise

REFACT

The NAICS replaces the Standard Industrial Classification (SIC) system that had been used by the U.S. Census Bureau since the 1930s.

The United States, Canada, and Mexico have developed a classification scheme, called the **North American Industry Classification System (NAICS),** to collect data on business activity in each country. Every business is assigned a hierarchical, six-digit code based on the type of products and services it produces and sells. The first two digits identify the firm's business sector, and the remaining four digits identify various subsectors.

The classifications for retail firms selling merchandise, based largely on the type of merchandise sold, are illustrated in Exhibit 2–1. Merchandise retailers constitute sectors 44 and 45, and the third digit breaks down these retailers further. For example, retailers selling clothing and clothing accessories are in classification 448, whereas general merchandise retailers are in classification 452. The fourth and fifth digits provide a finer classification. As shown in Exhibit 2–1, the fourth digit subdivides clothing and accessories retailers (448) into clothing stores (4481), shoe stores (4482), and jewelry, luggage, and leather goods stores (4483). The fifth digit provides a further breakdown into men's clothing stores (44811) and women's clothing stores (44812). The sixth digit, not illustrated in Exhibit 2–1, captures differences in the three North American countries using the classification scheme.

Most services retailers appear in sectors 71 (arts, entertainment, and recreation) and 72 (accommodation and food services). For example, food services and

EXHIBIT 2–1
NAICS Codes for
Retailers

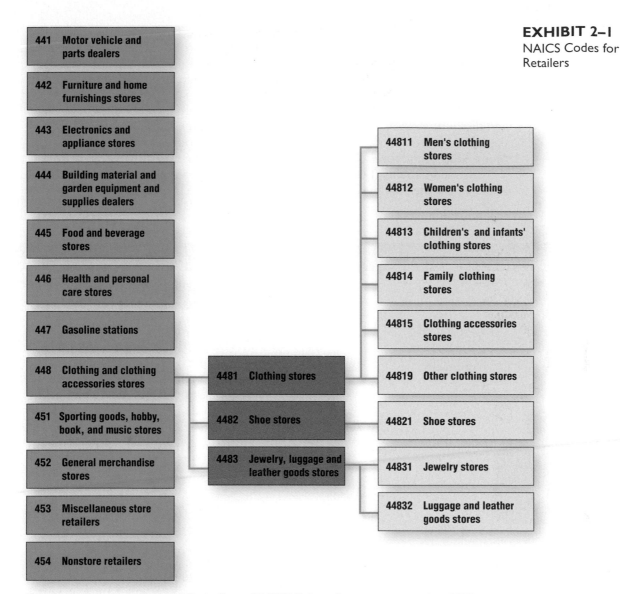

SOURCE: "North American Industry Classification System (NAICS)," U.S. Census Bureau, www.census.gov/naics/2007/ NAICOD07.HTM, (accessed February 14, 2008).

drinking places are in category (722), which gets subdivided into full-service restaurants (7221) and limited-service eating places like fast-food restaurants (7222).

Variety and Assortment

Even if retailers sell the same type of merchandise, they might not compete directly. For example, the primary classification for retailers selling clothing and clothing accessories is 448. But clothing can be purchased in sporting goods stores (45111), department stores (4521), warehouse clubs and supercenters (45291), and electronic shopping and mail-order houses (4541). These different types of retailers do not compete directly because they appeal to different customer needs and thus offer different assortments and varieties of merchandise and services. Retailing View 2.1 descibes an Internet retailer that is narrow on variety but deep on assortment.

Variety is the number of merchandise categories a retailer offers. **Assortment** is the number of different items in a merchandise category. Variety is often referred

REFACT

Twenty percent of all U.S. retail sales are for motor vehicles and parts dealers (441); department stores (4521) account for just 5 percent.[2]

to as the **breadth of merchandise** carried by a retailer; assortment is referred to as the **depth of merchandise.** Each different item of merchandise is called an **SKU (stockkeeping unit).** Some examples of SKUs include an original scent, 33-ounce box of Tide laundry detergent with bleach or a blue, long-sleeved, button-down-collar Ralph Lauren shirt, size medium.

Warehouse clubs, discount stores, and toy stores all sell toys, but warehouse clubs and discount stores sell many other categories of merchandise in addition to toys (i.e., they have greater variety). Stores specializing in toys stock more types of toys (more SKUs), and for each type of toy, such as dolls, the specialty toy retailer offers a greater assortment (i.e., greater depth in the form of more models, sizes, and brands) than the full-line discount stores or warehouse clubs.

2.1   RETAILING VIEW   Can't Afford to Buy? Then Bag Borrow or Steal

Can't afford this purse? Just rent it at Bag Borrow or Steal.

You no longer have to be wealthy to enjoy luxury goods. Businesses like Bag Borrow or Steal (www.Bagborroworsteal.com) are making luxury products like handbags and jewelry available to consumers for a fraction of the retail price. These goods are the current season's fashions, not last season's merchandise. So how do you do it?

Bag Borrow or Steal is an online luxury rental company. Consumers pay a monthly subscription fee, between $5 and $10, that enables them to choose from thousands of designer bags and jewelry, from Coach to Chanel. They also pay a monthly membership fee for each rented item. For example, a BCBG clutch is available for $6 per week or $20 per month for members and $20 per week and $35 per month for nonmembers.

There are various levels of designer merchandise on the Web site ranging in price from trendy to couture. The Couture category includes a Chloe Paddington bag that rents for $80 per week or $235 per month for members and $100 per week and $270 per month for nonmembers—a bag that otherwise retails for about $1600. If a customer "falls in love" with an item, she has the option to pay a reduced price for it, based on its condition and age. The Web site also offers an outlet store that sells items at 20–50 percent off, depending on their condition.

The target market for Bag Borrow or Steal is women between 25 and 49 years of age with an annual income averaging $113,000. Many of these consumers already have designer bags but cannot afford to buy the selection that would be available to them through Bag Borrow or Steal. A bag is an accessory item for which many consumers are willing to spend up to their limit, or above, because of the "noticeability" of it compared with other articles of clothing. "Fashionistas" especially value the ability to carry many designer bags throughout the year rather than just one or two. For $80 per week, the customer can rent 20 different Couture bags for the same price as purchasing just one bag.

Sources: Sarah Lacy, "The Tech Beat," *BusinessWeek*, March 7, 2006 (accessed December 24, 2007; Kate M. Jackson, "Renting a Handful of Luxury," *Boston Globe*, October 13, 2005 (accessed December 24, 2007 December 24, 2007; www.bagborroworsteal.com (accessed June 6, 2007).

Variety and Assortment of Kayaks in Different Retail Outlets   **EXHIBIT 2–2**

	White-Water & Surf	Recreational	Light Touring	Sea Kayak	Fishing
EMS (Eastern Mountain Sports)	Pyranha	Pyranha, Necky, Wilderness Systems, Ocean Kayak, Perception, Old Town, Mad River	Necky, Wilderness Systems, Old Town	Wilderness Systems, Necky	
	3 SKUs	18 SKUs	11 SKUs	6 SKUs	
	$549–$649	$330–$999	$850–$1325	$1299–1699	
Outdoorplay.com	WaveSport, Dagger, Necky, Riot, Perception, Aire, NRS	Wilderness Systems, Necky, Perception, Dagger, Old Town, Ocean Kayak, Mad River		Perception, Wilderness Systems, Old Town, Necky, Dagger	Old Town, Perceptions, Dagger, Wilderness Systems, Ocean Kayak, Mad River
	54 SKUs	52 SKUs		19 SKUs	23 SKUs
	$649–$1199	$549–$1199		$699–$1699	$599–$1074
Wal-Mart		Coleman, Stearns	Coleman		
		5 SKUs	1 SKU		
		$79.98–$299.98	$269.94		

Exhibit 2–2 shows the breadth and depth of kayaks carried by Eastern Mountain Sports, an outdoor gear and equipment store (specialty store); Outdoorplay.com, a kayak store (category specialist); and Wal-Mart (discount store). Although Eastern Mountain Sports carries the same number of categories as Outdoorplay.com, the former has a narrower assortment than the category specialist, which carries more SKUs within each of the kayak categories. Outdoorplay.com does not carry "Light Touring" kayaks but has a large assortment of "Fishing" kayaks. Wal-Mart offers the narrowest variety and smallest assortment. It has the fewest total SKUs (6) compared with EMS (38) and Outdoorplay.com (148).

Services Offered

Retailers also differ in the services they offer customers. For example, Eastern Mountain Sports offers assistance in selecting the appropriate kayak, as well as repairs. Outdoorplay.com and Wal-Mart do not provide any such services. Customers expect almost all retailers to provide certain services: displaying merchandise, accepting credit cards, providing parking, and being open at convenient hours. Some retailers charge customers for other services, such as home delivery and gift wrapping. Upscale retailers offer customers most of these services at no charge.

Prices and the Cost of Offering Breadth and Depth of Merchandise and Services

Stocking a deep and broad assortment, like the one Eastern Mountain Sports offers in kayaks, is appealing to customers but costly for retailers. When a retailer offers many SKUs, its inventory investment increases, because the retailer must have backup stock for each and every SKU.

Similarly, services attract customers to the retailer, but they also are costly. More salespeople are needed to provide information and assist customers, alter products to meet customers' needs, and demonstrate merchandise. Child care facilities, restrooms, dressing rooms, and check rooms take up valuable store space that could be used to stock and display merchandise. Offering delayed

Rate EMS's variety and assortment of kayaks compared to Outdoorplay.com and Wal-Mart

EXHIBIT 2–3
Sales and Growth Rate for
Retail Sectors

	Estimated 2010 Sales $ Millions	Estimated Percentage Compounded Sales Growth, 2005–2010
Food Retailers		
Conventional supermarkets	$521,126	2.4%
Supercenters	331,558	11.1
Warehouse clubs	125,114	6.6
Convenience stores	669,393	7.1
General Merchandise Retailers		
Department stores	79,813	−1.0
Apparel and accessory specialty stores	184,766	4.4
Jewelry stores	36,053	4.9
Shoe stores	27,011	1.9
Furniture stores	73,655	4.6
Home furnishing stores	35,242	4.8
Office supply stores	26,073	3.8
Sporting goods stores	40,417	5.4
Book stores	18,257	1.9
Building material, hardware, and garden supply stores	485,106	6.6
Consumer electronics and appliance stores	134,675	6.0
Drug stores	227,836	5.5
Full-line discount stores	134,220	1.0
Food and general merchandise extreme value stores	47,631	3.4
Nonstore Retailers		
Nonstore retailing	263,220	10.3
E-commerce	285,000	26.5

Sources: *Softgoods Economic Forecast: Outlook to 2010* (Columbus, OH: Retail Forward, May 2006); *Homegoods Economic Forecast: Outlook to 2010* (Columbus, OH: Retail Forward, May 2006); *Food Drug Mass Economic Forecast: Outlook to 2010* (Columbus, OH: Retail Forward, May 2006).

billing, credit, or installment payments requires a financial investment that could be used to buy more merchandise.

To make a profit, retailers that offer broader variety, deeper assortments, and/or additional services need to charge higher prices. For example, department stores have higher prices because of their higher costs, which result from stocking a lot of fashionable and seasonal merchandise, discounting merchandise when they make errors in forecasting consumer tastes, providing some personal sales service, and having expensive mall locations. In contrast, discount stores appeal to customers who are looking for lower prices and are less interested in services but want to see a broad range of merchandise brands and models. Thus, a critical retail decision involves the trade-off between the costs and benefits of maintaining additional inventory or providing additional services. Chapters 6 and 12 address the considerations required in making this trade-off.

To compare their offering with competitive offerings, retailers often shop their competitors' stores. Appendix 2A provides a template used by retailers for their comparison shopping. In the next section, we discuss the different types of food retailers, then general merchandise and nonstore retailers. Exhibit 2–3 contains information about the size and growth rates for each of these retail sectors.

FOOD RETAILERS

The food retailing landscape is changing dramatically. Twenty years ago, consumers purchased food primarily at conventional supermarkets. Now conventional supermarkets account for only 56 percent of food sales (not including restaurants).

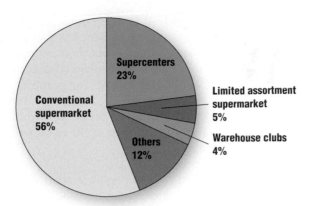

SOURCE: *Industry Outlook: Food Channel* (Columbus, OH: Retail Forward, April 2007), p. 7. Used by permission of TNS Retail Forward.

EXHIBIT 2–4
Where Grocery Shoppers Do Most of Their Food Shopping

The fastest growing segment of the food retail market is the remaining 44 percent of food sales made by supercenters, warehouse clubs, convenience stores, and new concepts such as limited assortment supermarket or extreme value food retailers (see Exhibit 2–4).[3] While Wal-Mart and other general merchandise retailers are offering more food items, traditional supermarkets are carrying more nonfood items, and many offer pharmacies, health care clinics, photo processing centers, banks, and cafés.

The world's largest food retailer, Wal-Mart, has more than $134 billion in sales of supermarket-type merchandise, followed by Kroger (U.S. corporate headquarters), Carrefour (France), Ahold (Netherlands), and Albertson's (U.S.).[4] The largest supermarket chains in the United States are Kroger, Safeway, Supervalu, Ahold USA, and Publix.[5]

Most of Wal-Mart's food sales are generated from its supercenter format, whereas Carrefour garners most of its sales using the hypermarket format that it developed. The remaining larger food retailers primarily sell through conventional supermarkets. Exhibit 2–5 shows the retail mixes for different types of food retailers.

Supermarkets

A **conventional supermarket** is a self-service food store offering groceries, meat, and produce with limited sales of nonfood items, such as health and beauty aids and general merchandise.[6] Perishables like meat and produce account for 50 percent of supermarket sales and typically have higher margins than packaged goods.[7]

Whereas conventional supermarkets carry about 30,000 SKUs, **limited assortment supermarkets,** or **extreme value food retailers,** only stock about 1250 SKUs.[8] The two largest limited assortment supermarket chains in the United States are Save-A-Lot and ALDI. Retailing View 2.2 describes ALDI, a firm that makes Wal-Mart seem luxurious.

REFACT

The first self-service grocery store was opened in 1930 by King Kullen in Jamaica, New York.[9]

EXHIBIT 2–5
Characteristics of Food Retailers

	Conventional Supermarket	Limited Assortment Supermarket	Supercenter	Warehouse Club	Convenience Store
Percentage food	70–80	80–90	30–40	60	90
Size (000 sq ft)	20–30	7–10	150–220	100–150	2–3
SKUs (000)	20–40	1–1.5	100–150	20	2–3
Variety	average	narrow	broad	broad	narrow
Assortment	average	shallow	deep	shallow	shallow
Ambience	pleasant	minimal	average	minimal	average
Service	modest	limited	limited	limited	limited
Prices	average	lowest	low	low	high
Gross margin (%)	20–22	10–12	15–18	12–15	25–30

Rather than carrying twenty brands of laundry detergent, limited assortment stores offer one or two brands and sizes, one of which is a store brand. Stores are designed to maximize efficiency and reduce costs. For example, merchandise is shipped in cartons on pallets that can serve as displays so that no shelf stocking is needed. Some costly services that consumers take for granted, such as free bags and paying with credit cards, are not provided. Stores are typically located in second- or third-tier shopping centers with low rents. By trimming costs, limited assortment supermarkets can offer merchandise at 40 to 60 percent lower prices than conventional supermarkets.[10]

REFACT

By 2010, less than half of the $1 trillion annual grocery and consumable sales will be by traditional grocers.[11]

Trends in Supermarket Retailing   Although conventional supermarkets still sell a majority of food merchandise, they are under substantial competitive pressure. Everyone wants a piece of the food retail pie. Supercenters are rapidly attracting conventional supermarket customers with their broader assortments of food and general merchandise at attractive prices. Full-line discount chains, like Target and Wal-Mart, and extreme value retailers like Dollar General and Family

---

2.2   RETAILING VIEW   ALDI: Germany's Wal-Mart

At first glance, an ALDI store in Germany reminds you of the sparse retail stores in Eastern Europe in 1975. Jars of asparagus and cans of beans are displayed in cardboard boxes piled on top of pallets. There are only two brands of toilet paper and one brand of pickles. The line at the cash registers is 10 customers deep. But the prices are really low—three frozen pizzas for $3.24, a $2.36 bottle of decent Cabernet, and a trench coat for $21.

ALDI stores are found not only in working-class neighborhoods but also in wealthy communities. An astonishing 89 percent of German households shopped at least once at ALDI during the year. ALDI, short for "Albrecht Discount," after its founder Karl Albrecht, has a cult following, including a Web site for fans of the retailer. Some attribute Wal-Mart's exit from Germany to the strong competition posed by ALDI.

ALDI now operates 4,100 stores in Germany and 6,600 worldwide, including 800 stores in 26 U.S. states. Like Wal-Mart, ALDI focuses relentlessly on reducing costs, has considerable buying power with vendors, is very profitable, and seems to enjoy unstoppable growth.

ALDI has a simple but highly effective strategy: A typical ALDI store stocks about 700 to 1,000 products, compared with as many as 150,000 at a Wal-Mart Supercenter. A Wal-Mart Supercenter has 10 to 15 brands, types, and sizes of peanut butter, but Aldi offers just one size and type.

ALDI provides quality merchandise at low prices by reducing its assortment to control store operating expenses.

Almost everything sold is an ALDI exclusive label, such as Millville Raisin Bran at $1.49 a box and Sweet Valley root beer for $1.89 a 12 pack. However, the quality of the store brands is comparable to that of nationally advertised brands like Nestlé and Kraft. Because it sells so few products, ALDI can exert strong control over quality and price and simplify shipping and handling.

ALDI reduces its labor costs by keeping limited store staff. Its stores typically have four or five workers, compared with about fifteen at a normal supermarket. Meat and bakery items are shipped to stores to eliminate the need for costly "specialist" clerks, such as butchers or bakers. Time and effort spent arranging products on shelves is minimized. Food gets stacked in its original packing boxes with the tops removed, piled high either on top of pallets against the walls or on simple shelving units. Prices are plainly listed on paper signs attached to molding hung from the ceiling, and shoppers bag their own groceries. Due to this mode of operations, ALDI's labor cost are only 6 percent of sales compared with 12–16 percent for the typical supermarket.

Sources: Nirmalya Kumar, "Strategies to Fight Low-Cost Rivals," *Harvard Business Review*, 84, no. 12 (December 2006) (accessed December 24, 2007); "Food Retail in Germany: Industry Profile, Reference Code 0165-2058," May 2006, www.datamonitor.com (accessed December 24, 2007); Mark Hamstra, "Wal-Mart Plans to Exit Germany," *Supermarket News*, August 7, 2006, p. 6; Rodger Brown, "Germany's ALDI Discount Grocery Chain Expands in U.S.," *SCT*, November 2006, pp. 16–18.

Dollar stores are increasing the amount of space they devote to consumables. Convenience stores are also selling more fresh merchandise.

Low-cost competitors, supercenters, and warehouse clubs are particularly troublesome for supermarkets because of their superior operating efficiencies. These stores have tremendous buying power in the market because they can buy such large quantities. They can concentrate on buying special deals, because they do not carry the deep assortment found in supermarkets. They also have invested heavily in state-of-the-art supply chain, assortment planning, and pricing systems, which reduce their inventories while increasing their sales and margins. These activities are discussed in more detail in Chapters 10 and 12.

To compete successfully against intrusions by other food retailing formats, conventional supermarkets are differentiating their offerings by (1) emphasizing fresh perishables, (2) targeting health-conscious and ethnic consumers, (3) providing a better in-store experience, and (4) offering more private-label brands. For example, fresh merchandise categories, the areas around the outside walls known as the **"power perimeter,"** have long been the mainstays of conventional supermarkets. These areas include the dairy, bakery, meat, florist, produce, deli, and coffee bar departments—high traffic, profitable departments that pull shoppers through the store. The dairy and produce sections in particular are high need items that, if of high quality and priced competitively, can increase store loyalty among customers. Conventional supermarkets are building on this strength by devoting more space to fresh merchandise with cooking exhibitions and "action" stations, such as store-made sushi and freshly grilled meat.

At Wegmans, customers can eat a meal overlooking the European-style Market Cafe.

Another example of the emphasis on "fresh" is the meal solutions offered to time-pressured consumers. At Wegmans (an upstate New York–based supermarket chain), customers can eat lunch overlooking the European-style Market Cafe or buy prepared meals to take home. Chefs in monogrammed white jackets and tall pleated paper hats staff the separate pizza, deli, and fresh-baked bread stations. Along one wall, Caesar salads are made to order. At another station, customers have a choice of Alfredo, marinara, or vodka sauce on their hot pasta. At a station called the Outer Loop, the store offers open-face sandwiches of crab cakes and grilled salmon criss-crossed with bacon. Turkey chili is served in a hollowed-out round loaf of crusty bread. Folks who keep kosher have their own area for, say, meat-stuffed cabbage and potato pancakes or a Waldorf salad.[12]

Conventional supermarkets also are offering more natural, organic, and fair-trade foods for the growing segment of consumers who are health and environmentally conscious.[13] **Fair trade** means purchasing from factories that pay workers a living wage, well more than the prevailing minimum wage, and offer other benefits, like onsite medical treatment. Although Whole Foods continues to be the leader in the natural/organic food categories, other supermarket chains like Safeway and Sainsbury's are devoting significant space to natural and organic foods.[14]

Furthermore, conventional supermarkets are adjusting their merchandise mix to attract more ethnic shoppers. Hispanics, who now constitute 14 percent of the U.S. population, have significantly different shopping and eating patterns

REFACT

Natural/organic product sales represented almost 8 percent of total food-at-home sales in 2005, up from 6.5 percent in 2000.[15]

than the general population. They are more likely to prepare meals from scratch, spend more on groceries, prefer stores with bilingual staff and signage, and place importance on fresh food.[16] Many smaller chains continue to serve this market, but larger regional and national grocery stores are competing for the group. Kroger has opened Fry's Mercado in Phoenix, which features, in addition to typical grocery departments with names in Spanish, a restaurant, a Hispanic tortilleria and made-from-scratch bakery, and space leased to independent merchants selling items such as clothing, bridal wear, jewelry, and accessories.[17]

Conventional supermarket chains such as HEB and Publix are leveraging their quality reputation to offer more private-label merchandise. Private-label brands (discussed in Chapter 14) benefit both customers and retailers. The benefits to customers include having more choices, finding the same ingredients and quality as in national brands, relying on the reputation of the store, enjoying availability in many categories, and saving 5–15 percent without coupons. The benefits of private-label brands to retailers include increased store loyalty, the ability to differentiate themselves from the competition, high customer awareness and acceptance of store brands, minimal promotional costs, and higher gross margins compared with national brands.

The online grocery market also represents a growing category.[18] During the dot-com boom, many online grocers failed, but today, supermarket chains and Amazon.com are rebuilding this market. Different retailers have different online strategies. Amazon sells bulk nonperishable items, such as what one might find at a warehouse club like Costco. Expert in selling online and shipping, Amazon can exploit its huge customer base by considering food and consumer products just another category that it can add to its offerings. As the only retailer offering bulk orders, Amazon's model may be more popular among businesses than consumers. For nutrition fact buffs, Peapod.com allows users to sort items by calories, fat, or other nutritional information. FreshDirect.com gives cooking and food preparation advice, such as noting that "grape tomatoes are better in kabobs than in sandwiches."

Creating an enjoyable shopping experience through wider variety, better store ambiance, and customer service is another approach that supermarket chains use to differentiate themselves from low-cost, low-price competitors. Supermarkets are increasingly incorporating "food as theater" concepts, such as open-air market designs, cooking and nutrition classes, demonstrations, baby-sitting services, and food tasting. The newest Super Stop & Shop markets in New York, for example, offer DVDs, video games, and books.[20] Customers can also buy toilet seats and towels, Play-Doh and Barbies. A dining area equipped with wireless Internet service represents another example of an extended shopping experience.

Supercenters

Supercenters, the fastest growing retail category, are large stores (150,000–220,000 square feet) that combine a supermarket with a full-line discount store. Wal-Mart operates 2,300 supercenters in the United States—four times more than its leading competitors Meijer, Kmart, Fred Meyer (a division of Kroger), and Target combined. By offering broad assortments of grocery and general merchandise products under one roof, supercenters provide a one-stop shopping experience. Customers will typically drive farther to shop at these stores than to visit conventional supermarkets (which offer a narrower variety of general merchandise).

General merchandise (nonfood) items are often purchased on impulse when customers' primary reason for coming to the supercenter is to buy groceries. General merchandise has higher margins, enabling the supercenters to price food items more aggressively. However, supercenters are very large, so some customers find them inconvenient because it can take a long time to find the items they want.

REFACT

Private-label brands account for approximately 25 percent of total U.S. sales by food retailers, compared with 45 percent in Europe.[19]

REFACT

Supercenters have the highest revenue growth of all retail formats, at 13 percent annually. About four new supercenters open each week in the United States.[21]

Hypermarkets are also large (100,000–300,000 square feet) combination food (60–70 percent) and general merchandise (30–40 percent) stores. The world's second largest retailer, Carrefour, operates hypermarkets. Hypermarkets typically stock fewer SKUs than supercenters—between 40,000 and 60,000 items, ranging from groceries, hardware, and sports equipment to furniture and appliances to computers and electronics.

Hypermarkets were created in France after World War II. By building large stores on the outskirts of metropolitan areas, French retailers could attract customers and not violate strict land-use laws. They have spread throughout Europe and become popular in some South American countries such as Argentina and Brazil.

Hypermarkets are not common in the United States, though hypermarkets and supercenters are similar. Both hypermarkets and supercenters are large, carry grocery and general merchandise categories, offer self-service, and are located in warehouse-type structures with large parking facilities. However, hypermarkets carry a larger proportion of food items than supercenters with a greater emphasis on perishables—produce, meat, fish, and bakery items. Supercenters, in contrast, have a larger percentage of nonfood items and focus more on dry groceries, such as breakfast cereal and canned goods, instead of fresh items.

Although supercenters and hypermarkets are the fastest growing segments in food retailing, they face challenges in finding locations for new **big box** (large, limited service) stores. In Europe and Japan, land for building large stores is limited and expensive. New supercenters and hypermarkets in these areas often have to be multistory, which increases operating costs and reduces shopper convenience. Furthermore, some countries place restrictions on the size of new retail outlets. In the United States, there has been a backlash against large retail stores, particularly Wal-Mart outlets. These opposing sentiments are based on local views that big box stores drive local retailers out of business, offer low wages, provide nonunion jobs, have unfair labor practices, threaten U.S. workers due to their purchase of imported merchandise, and cause excessive automobile and delivery truck traffic.

Warehouse Clubs

Warehouse clubs are retailers that offer a limited and irregular assortment of food and general merchandise with little service at low prices for ultimate consumers and small businesses. The largest warehouse club chains are Costco, Sam's Club (a division of Wal-Mart), and BJ's Wholesale Club, a distant third. Costco differentiates itself by offering unique upscale merchandise not available elsewhere at low prices. For example, you can buy a 5-carat diamond ring for $127,999.99 or a Marc Jacobs handbag for $649.99—much lower than can be found elsewhere. Sam's Club focuses more on small businesses, providing services such as group health insurance as well as products.

Warehouse clubs are large (at least 100,000–150,000 square feet) and typically located in low-rent districts. They have simple interiors and concrete floors. Aisles are wide so forklifts can pick up pallets of merchandise and arrange them on the selling floor. Little service is offered. Customers pick merchandise off shipping pallets,

People go to warehouse clubs like Costco to search for treasures like computers at prices lower than competitors.

take it to checkout lines in the front of the store, and usually pay with cash. Warehouse clubs can offer low prices because they use low-cost locations, inexpensive store designs, and little customer service; they further keep inventory holding costs low by carrying a limited assortment of fast selling items. In addition, they buy merchandise opportunistically. For example, if Hewlett-Packard is introducing new models of its printers, warehouse clubs will buy the inventory of the older models at a significant discount and then offer them for sale until the inventory is depleted.

Most warehouse clubs have two types of members: wholesale members who own small businesses and individual members who purchase for their own use. For example, many small restaurants are wholesale customers who buy their supplies, food ingredients, and desserts from a warehouse club rather than from food distributors. To cater to their business customers, warehouse clubs sell food items in very large containers and packages—sizes that also appeal to larger families. Typically, members must pay an annual fee of around $50.[22]

Convenience Stores

Convenience stores provide a limited variety and assortment of merchandise at a convenient location in 2,000–3,000 square foot stores with speedy checkout. They are the modern version of the neighborhood mom-and-pop grocery/general store. Convenience stores enable consumers to make purchases quickly, without having to search through a large store and wait in a long checkout line. Over half the items bought are consumed within 30 minutes of purchase.

Due to their small size and high sales, convenience stores typically receive deliveries every day. Convenience stores only offer limited assortments and variety, and they charge higher prices than supermarkets. Milk, eggs, and bread once represented the majority of their sales, but now the majority of sales come from gasoline and cigarettes.

Convenience stores also face increased competition from other formats. Sales tend to increase during periods of rising gasoline prices, but their dependency on gasoline sales is a problem because gasoline sales have low margins. In addition, supercenter and supermarket chains are attempting to increase customer store visits by offering gasoline and tying gasoline sales to their frequent shopper programs. Drugstores and full-line discount stores also are setting up easily accessed areas of their stores with convenience store merchandise.

In response to these competitive pressures, convenience stores are taking steps to decrease their dependency on gasoline sales, tailoring assortments to local markets, and making their stores even more convenient to shop. To get gasoline customers to spend more on other merchandise and services, convenience stores are offering more fresh food and healthy fast food that appeals to today's on-the-go consumers, especially women and young adults. Some convenience stores are adding fast casual restaurants, like BP's Wild Bean Cafe. 7-Eleven is selling more fruits, vegetables, salads, and reduced-calorie fare. The U.K. supermarket giant, Tesco's Fresh & Easy stores sell fresh produce, meats, and ready-to-eat meals targeted at customers who do not want to visit a regular grocery store or spend too much time cooking.[24] Finally, convenience stores are adding new services, such as financial service kiosks that give customers the opportunity to cash checks, pay bills, and buy prepaid telephone minutes, theater tickets, and gift cards.

To increase convenience, convenience stores are opening smaller stores close to where consumers shop and work. For example, 7-Eleven has stores in airports, office buildings, and schools. Easy access, storefront parking, and quick in-and-out access are key benefits offered by convenience stores. They also are exploring the use of technology to increase shopping convenience. For example, Sheetz, a Pennsylvania-based convenience store chain, has self-service food-ordering kiosks at its gasoline pumps. Customers can order a custom-made sandwich while filling their tank and pick it up in the store when they are finished.[25]

GENERAL MERCHANDISE RETAILERS

The major types of general merchandise retailers are department stores, full-line discount stores, specialty stores, category specialists, home improvement centers, off-price retailers, and extreme value retailers. Exhibit 2–6 summarizes the characteristics of general merchandise retailers that sell through stores.

Department Stores

Department stores are retailers that carry a broad variety and deep assortment, offer customer services, and organize their stores into distinct departments for displaying merchandise. The largest department store chains in the United States are Macy's, Sears, JCPenney, Kohl's, Nordstrom, Dillards, and Saks.[27]

Traditionally, department stores attracted customers by offering a pleasing ambience, attentive service, and a wide variety of merchandise under one roof. They sold both soft goods (apparel and bedding) and hard goods (appliances, furniture, and consumer electronics). But now most department stores focus almost exclusively on soft goods. The major departments are women's, men's, and children's apparel and accessories; home furnishings; cosmetics; and kitchenware and small appliances. Each department within the store has a specific selling space allocated to it, as well as salespeople to assist customers. The department store often resembles a collection of specialty shops.

Department store chains can be categorized into three tiers. The first tier includes upscale, high fashion chains with exclusive designer merchandise and excellent customer service, such as Neiman Marcus, Bloomingdale's (part of Macy's Inc.), Nordstrom, and Saks Fifth Avenue (part of Saks Inc.). Macy's and Dillards are in the second tier of upscale traditional department stores, in which retailers sell more modestly priced merchandise with less customer service. The value-oriented third tier—Sears, JCPenney, and Kohl's—caters to more price-conscious consumers. The retail chains in the first tier have established a clearly differentiated position and are producing strong financial results, whereas the value-oriented tier is facing significant competitive challenges from discount stores, particularly Target. Retailing View 2.3 describes the innovative strategy of Kohl's, a successful value-oriented department store chain.

Department stores still account for some of retailing's traditions—special events and parades (Macy's Thanksgiving parade in New York City), Santa Claus lands, and holiday decorations—and offer exclusive designer brands that are not available from other retailers. But many consumers are questioning the benefits

REFACT

T. Stewart was the first U.S. department store, opening in 1847 in New York.[28]

REFACT

While overall retail sales rose some 24.2 percent during the past six years, to $2.2 trillion, department store sales declined nearly 14 percent.[29]

Characteristics of General Merchandise Retailers   **EXHIBIT 2–6**

Type	Variety	Assortment	Service	Prices	Size (000 sq. ft.)	SKUs (000)	Location
Department stores	Broad	Deep to average	Average to high	Average to high	100–200	100	Regional malls
Discount stores	Broad	Average to shallow	Low	Low	60–80	30	Stand alone, power strip centers
Specialty stores	Narrow	Deep	High	High	4–12	5	Regional malls
Category specialists	Narrow	Very deep	Low to high	Low	50–120	20–40	Stand alone, power strip centers
Home improvement centers	Narrow	Very deep	Low to high	Low	80–120	20–40	Stand alone, power strip centers
Drugstores	Narrow	Very deep	Average	Average to high	3–15	10–20	Stand alone, strip centers
Off-price stores	Average	Deep but varying	Low	Low	20–30	50	Outlet malls
Extreme value retailers	Average	Average and varying	Low	Low	7–15	3–4	Urban, strip

and costs of shopping at department stores. Department stores are not as convenient as discount stores, such as Target, because they are located in large regional malls rather than local neighborhoods, though JCPenney and Sears are following Kohl's by opening stores in non-mall locations. Customer service has diminished in the second- and third-tier stores because of the retailers' desire to increase profits by reducing labor costs. In addition, department stores have not been as successful as discount stores and food retailers in reducing costs by working with their vendors to establish just-in-time inventory systems, so prices remain relatively high.

To deal with their eroding market share, department stores are (1) attempting to increase the amount of exclusive merchandise they sell, (2) undertaking marketing campaigns to develop strong images for their stores and brands, and (3) expanding their online presence.

2.3   RETAILING VIEW   Kohl's—A Rapidly Growing Department Store Chain

Kohl's, a combination department and discount store, is one of the fastest growing retail firms in the United States. From 76 stores in 1992, Kohl's has grown to more than 600 stores in 45 states. Its formula for success involves offering shopping convenience for time-pressured soccer moms interested in buying national brand apparel and soft home merchandise at reasonable prices. Some of the national brands it sells include Chaps by Ralph Lauren, Dockers and Arrow menswear, Healthtex and Oshkosh children's clothing, KitchenAid appliances, and Nike and Sketchers footwear. To capture younger professionals, it has signed some trendy, fashion-forward names such as designer Vera Wang, Elle magazine, skateboard icon Tony Hawk, and the Food Network to design private-label lines. Kohl's also is now the exclusive dealer of Candie's Shoes, which are being promoted by the celebrity artist Fergie. In addition, it has exclusive subbrand arrangements with some national brands sold at second-tier department stores, such as Estée Lauder cosmetics and Laura Ashley home textile and bedroom accessories.

But the key to Kohl's success is convenience. Its stores, located in suburban neighborhood centers, are easy to shop. The stores are smaller (80,000 square feet) than traditional, mall-based department stores and are on one floor. The aisles and fixture spacings are wider than those of the typical department store, so that customers pushing a shopping cart or baby

Kohl's department stores place the checkout counters in a convenient centralized location near the store entrances.

stroller can easily navigate the store. Rather than having POS terminals in each department, like most other department stores, the stores features centralized cash wraps (checkout stations) near the store entrances so that customers can select merchandise from different areas of the store and pay for it all at once when they are ready to leave.

Because Kohl's does not carry designer brands that require "store-within-a-store" displays, it groups different brands by the type of item rather than brand. Kohl's avoids a cluttered look by positioning display racks in amphitheater style, making all the merchandise visible. Colors are displayed from light to dark, a pattern that is most appealing to the eye. And unlike most stores, which try to straighten up merchandise all day, Kohl's keeps presentations sharp with a daily 2:00 PM "recovery period," when everyone in the store—from secretaries to store managers—is called upon to straighten up displays. Night crews do something similar. The total effect is to allow salesclerks to concentrate solely on customers.

Sources: Kelly Nolan, "Kohl's Draws New Battle Lines Out West," *Retailing Today*, May 21, 2007, pp. 4–7; Cheryl Lu-Lien Tan, "Hot Kohl's" *The Wall Street Journal Online*, April 16, 2007 (accessed December 24, 2007); www.kohls.com (accessed June 15, 2007); Eric Wilson and Michael Barbaro, "Can You Be Too Fashionable?" *The New York Times*, June 17, 2007, p. 3.1

To differentiate their merchandise offering and strengthen their image, department stores are aggressively seeking exclusive arrangements with nationally recognized designers. For example, Macy's has introduced exclusive women's apparel lines from designers Elie Tahari and Oscar de la Renta. Estée Lauder developed an exclusive private-label line of cosmetics for Kohl's, and Ralph Lauren designed a line of casual apparel exclusively for JCPenney. In addition, department stores are placing more emphasis on developing their own private-label brands. Macy's has been very successful in developing a strong image for its brands, such as I.N.C. (women's clothing) and Tools of the Trade (housewares). Saks Fifth Avenue is introducing Signature, geared to the slightly younger customer with respect to style and fit, and Classics and Sport with more generous cuts.[30]

In recent years, department stores' discount sales events have increased dramatically to the point that consumers have been trained to wait for items to be placed on sale rather than buy them at full price. Department stores are shifting their marketing activities from promotional sales to brand-building activities involving television advertising and specialty publications, such as seasonal glossy magazine-type publications by Saks Fifth Avenue, Neiman Marcus, and Barney's New York.

Finally, most department stores are becoming full participants in the multichannel retailing revolution by beefing up their Internet presence.[32] JCPenney, for instance, does more than $1 billion in online sales, and part of its success is due to its strong catalog business. It knows how to sell to nonstore customers, and many of its traditional catalog customers have migrated to the Internet.[33]

Full-Line Discount Stores

Full-line discount stores are retailers that offer a broad variety of merchandise, limited service, and low prices. Discount stores offer both private labels and national brands, but except for Target, these brands are typically less fashion oriented than the brands in department and specialty stores. The largest full-line discount store chains are Wal-Mart, Kmart (part of Sears Holding), and Target.

Wal-Mart alone accounts for almost 66 percent of full-line discount store retail sales, so the most significant trend in this sector is Wal-Mart's conversion of discount stores to supercenters. Currently, Wal-Mart has 1,051 discount stores, 2,307 supercenters, and 118 Neighborhood markets in the United States, along with 2,701 international stores.[34] Wal-Mart is expected to reach 3,300 supercenters by 2010, while conventional stores should decrease to around half their current level.[35] This change in emphasis is the result of the increased competition faced by full-line discount stores and the operating efficiencies of supercenters. Full-line discount stores confront intense competition from discount specialty stores that focus on a single category of merchandise, such as Dick's Sporting Goods, Office Depot, Circuit City, Bed Bath & Beyond, Sports Authority, and Lowe's.

As Wal-Mart closes its full-line discount stores, Target is becoming one of the most successful retailers in terms of sales growth and profitability. Target succeeds because its stores offer fashionable merchandise at low prices in a pleasant shopping environment. It has developed an image of "cheap chic" by teaming with designers such as Behnaz Sarafpour, Proenza Schouler, and Patrick Robinson to produce inexpensive, exclusive merchandise.

Specialty Stores

Specialty stores concentrate on a limited number of complementary merchandise categories and provide a high level of service in relatively small stores. Exhibit 2–7 lists some of the largest U.S. specialty store chains.

Specialty stores tailor their retail strategy toward very specific market segments by offering deep but narrow assortments and sales associate expertise. For example, Victoria's Secret is the leading specialty retailer of lingerie and beauty products in the United States. Using a multipronged location strategy that includes

REFACT
JCPenney now sells about 46 percent of its merchandise under private labels. Kohl's and Dillards sell about 25 percent, and Macy's comes in at about 16 percent.[31]

REFACT
Hudson's Bay Company, the oldest retailer in North America, conquered the Canadian wilderness by trading furs more than 300 years ago. Today, it is one of the largest retailers in Canada, operating chains of discount, department, and home stores.[36]

EXHIBIT 2–7
Specialty Store Retailers

Accessories	Electronics/Software/Gifts	Jewelry
Claire's	RadioShack	Zales
	Sharper Image	Tiffany & Co.
Apparel		
The Gap	**Entertainment**	**Optical**
J. Crew	GameStop	LensCrafters
The Limited	Blockbuster	**Shoes**
Victoria's Secret	**Food Supplements**	Foot Locker
Lane Bryant	GNC	**Sporting Goods**
Abercrombie & Fitch	**Furniture**	Hibbett Sports
Talbots	Ethan Allen	Play It Again
Michaels	Thomasville	
Auto Parts	**Housewares**	
AutoZone	Williams-Sonoma	
Advance Auto Parts	Crate & Barrel	
	Pottery Barn	

Sephora is an innovative specialty store selling perfume and cosmetics.

malls, lifestyle centers, and central business districts, Victoria's Secret offers fashion-oriented lingerie collections, fragrances, and cosmetics. Its message is conveyed using supermodels and world-famous runway shows.[37] Hot Topic focuses on selling licensed, music-inspired apparel to teenagers in mall-based stores. Its sales associates know what is new on the radio and in record stores, concert tours, and pop culture.[38]

Sephora, France's leading perfume and cosmetic chain—a division of luxury-goods conglomerate LVMH (Louis Vuitton–Moet Hennessy)—is another example of an innovative specialty store concept. In the United States, prestige cosmetics are typically sold in department stores. Each brand has a separate counter with a commissioned salesperson stationed behind the counter to help customers. Sephora is a cosmetic and perfume specialty store offering a deep assortment in a self-service, 6,000–9,000-square foot format. Its stores offer over 15,000 SKUs and more than 200 brands, including its own, private-label brand. Merchandise is grouped by product category with the brands displayed alphabetically so customers can locate them easily. Customers are free to shop and experiment on their own. Sampling is encouraged. The knowledgeable salespeople, always available to assist customers, are paid a salary by Sephora, unlike department store cosmetic salespeople who are compensated in part by incentives provided by the vendors. The low-key, open-sell environment results in customers spending more time shopping.

Competitors from other countries also are making some of the most successful specialty stores in the United States rethink how they satisfy their customer's needs. The Spanish Zara chain and Sweden's H&M have introduced cheap and chic "fast fashion" to the United States.[39] Fast-fashion companies introduce new products two to three times per week, compared with 10 to 12 times per year at traditional specialty stores, to ensure that they offer the most trendy and up-to-date fashions. Because of the constantly fresh atmosphere, customers develop "buy it now" shopping behavior; next week, the store will have different merchandise. As a result, fast-fashion retailers actually sell 85 percent of their merchandise at full price compared with only 60 percent at traditional stores.

Drugstores

Drugstores are specialty stores that concentrate on health and personal grooming merchandise. Pharmaceuticals often represent more than 50 percent of drugstore sales and an even greater percentage of their profits. The largest drugstore chains in the United States are Walgreens, CVS, and Rite Aid—three chains that account for about 66 percent of U.S. drugstore sales, up from only 43 percent in 2000.[40]

Drugstores, particularly the national chains, are experiencing sustained sales growth because the aging population requires more prescription drugs. Although the profit margins for prescription pharmaceuticals are higher than for other drugstore merchandise, these margins are shrinking due to government health care policies, HMOs, and public outcry over lower prices in other countries, especially Canada.

Drugstores are also being squeezed by considerable competition from pharmacies in discount stores and supermarkets, as well as prescription mail-order retailers. In response, the major drugstore chains are building larger stand-alone stores to offer a wider assortment of merchandise, more frequently purchased food items, the convenience of drive-through windows for picking up prescriptions, and in-store medical clinics. Walgreens is even adding women's apparel, most of which is priced below $15.[41] To build customer loyalty, the chains are changing the role of their pharmacists from simply dispensing pills (referred to as "count, pour, lick, and stick") to providing health care assistance, such as explaining how to use a nebulizer.

Drugstore retailers also are using systems to allow pharmacists time to provide personalized service. For example, at Walgreens, customers can order prescription refills via the phone or Internet and receive automatic notifications when the prescription is ready. On the basis of the time these customers plan to pick up their prescriptions, a computer system automatically schedules the workload in the pharmacy. It also offers a multilingual counseling system called Dial-a-Pharmacist that searches for on-duty pharmacists who can speak to a patient in one of 14 languages.[43]

Category Specialists

Category specialists are big box discount stores that offer a narrow but deep assortment of merchandise. Exhibit 2–8 lists some of the largest category specialists in the United States.

Most category specialists predominantly use a self-service approach, but they offer assistance to customers in some areas of the stores. For example, Staples stores have a warehouse atmosphere, with cartons of copy paper stacked on pallets, plus equipment in boxes on shelves. But in some departments, such as computers and other high-tech products, it provides salespeople who man the display area to answer questions and make suggestions. Bass Pro Shops' Outdoor World is a category specialist offering merchandise for outdoor recreational activities. The stores offer everything a person needs for hunting and fishing—from 27-cent plastic bait to boats and recreational vehicles costing $45,000. Sales associates are knowledgeable outdoors people. Each is hired for a particular department that matches that person's expertise. All private-branded products are field tested by Bass Pro Shops' professional teams: Redhead Pro Hunting Team and Tracker Pro Fishing Team.

REFACT

Due to increased competition, the drugstore industry's share of retail pharmacy sales was 59.2 percent in 2005, down from 64.1 percent in 2000.[42]

EXHIBIT 2–8
Category Specialists

Apparel/Accessories
Disney Store
Famous Footwear
Men's Warehouse
Toys "R" Us

Books
Barnes & Noble
Borders

Consumer Electronics
Best Buy
Circuit City

Crafts
Michaels

Entertainment
Chuck E. Cheese
Dave & Busters

Food
Fresh Market
Trader Joe's
Whole Foods

Furniture
Crate & Barrel
IKEA
Pier 1
Sofa Express

Home
Bed Bath & Beyond
Linens 'n Things
The Great Indoors
World Market

Home Improvement
Home Depot
Lowe's
Menards

Musical Instruments
Guitar Center

Office Supply
Office Depot
Staples
Office Max

Off-Price
DSW
TJX

Pet Supplies
PetSmart
PETCO

Sporting Goods
Bass Pro Shop
Cabela's
Dick's Sporting Goods
L.L. Bean
Golfsmith

By offering a complete assortment in a category at low prices, category specialists can "kill" a category of merchandise for other retailers and thus are frequently called **category killers.** Using their category dominance, they exploit their buying power to negotiate low prices and are assured of supply when items are scarce. Department stores and full-line discount stores located near category specialists often have to reduce their offerings in the category because consumers are drawn to the deep assortment and low prices at the category killer.

Category specialists, like the **Bass Pro Shops,** offer a deep assortment of merchandise at low prices.

One of the largest and most successful types of category specialists is the home improvement center. A **home improvement center** is a category specialist offering equipment and material used by do-it-yourselfers and contractors to make home improvements. The largest U.S. home improvement chains are Home Depot and Lowe's. Like warehouse clubs and office supply category specialists, home improvement centers operate as retailers when they sell merchandise to consumers and as wholesalers when they sell to contractors and other businesses. Although merchandise in home improvement centers is displayed in a warehouse atmosphere, salespeople are available to assist customers in selecting merchandise and to tell them how to use it.

Although category specialists compete with other types of retailers, competition between them is intense, such as the intense competition between Lowe's and Home Depot; Staples and Office Depot; and Bed Bath & Beyond and Linens 'n Things. These retailers have difficulty differentiating themselves on most of the elements of their retail mixes. They all provide similar assortments, because they have similar access to national brands, and they all provide the same level of service. Primarily then, they compete on price. In an attempt to gain an edge, the category killers continue to concentrate on reducing costs by increasing their operating efficiencies and acquiring smaller chains to gain scale economies. As a result of this consolidation, just a few firms dominate each category.

Some category specialists are attempting to differentiate themselves with service. For example, Home Depot and Lowe's hire licensed contractors as sales associates to help customers with electrical and plumbing repairs. They also provide classes to train home owners in tiling, painting, and other tasks to give shoppers the confidence to tackle their do-it-yourself projects on their own.

Extreme Value Retailers

Extreme value retailers are small, full-line discount stores that offer a limited merchandise assortment at very low prices. The largest extreme value retailers are Family Dollar Stores and Dollar General.[44]

Like limited assortment food retailers, extreme value retailers reduce costs and maintain low prices by offering a limited assortment and operating in low-rent locations. They offer a broad but shallow assortment of household goods, health and beauty aids, and groceries. Many value retailers, particularly Family Dollar and Dollar General, target low-income consumers, whose shopping behavior differs from typical discount store or warehouse club customers. For instance, though these consumers demand well-known national brands, they often cannot afford to buy large-size packages.

Despite some of these chains' names, few just sell merchandise for a dollar. In fact, the two largest—Family Dollar and Dollar General—do not employ a strict dollar limit and sell merchandise for up to $20. The names imply a *good value* but do not limit customers to the arbitrary dollar price point. Because this segment of the retail industry is growing rapidly, vendors often create special, smaller packages just for them.

Dollar Tree and 99 Cents Only are true dollar stores, meaning that all of the merchandise is $1 or less. True dollar stores offer a wide array of gift bags, party supplies, housewares, seasonal decor, candy and food, toys, health and beauty care items, gifts, stationery, and books. In the past, these true dollar stores were considered low-status retailers that catered to lower-income consumers. Today, however, higher-income consumers are increasingly patronizing dollar stores for the thrill of the hunt. Some shoppers see extreme value retailers as an opportunity to find some hidden treasure among the bric-a-brac.[46]

Off-Price Retailers

Off-price retailers, also known as **close-out retailers,** offer an inconsistent assortment of brand name merchandise at low prices. America's largest off-price

REFACT

Second to supercenters, extreme value retailers are the fastest growing segment in retail. The industry adds about five new such stores a day.[45]

Why are designer handbags so inexpensive at off-price retailers line T.J. Maxx?

REFACT

Selling close-outs out of her Brooklyn home in 1920, Frieda Loehmann started the first off-price retail business.[48]

retail chains are TJX Companies (which operates T.J. Maxx and Marshalls, Winners, HomeGoods, TKMaxx, AJWright, and HomeSense), Ross Stores, Burlington Coat Factory, Loehmann's, Big Lots Inc., and Tuesday Morning. Off-price retailers sell brand name and even designer-label merchandise at 20–60 percent lower than department store prices through their unique buying and merchandising practices.[47] Most merchandise is bought opportunistically from manufacturers or other retailers with excess inventory at the end of the season. End-of-season merchandise that will not be used in following seasons is called **close-outs.** The merchandise might be in odd sizes or unpopular colors and styles, or it may be **irregulars** (merchandise that has minor mistakes in construction). Typically, merchandise is purchased at one-fifth to one-fourth of the original wholesale price. Off-price retailers can buy at low prices because they do not ask suppliers for advertising allowances, return privileges, markdown adjustments, or delayed payments. (Terms and conditions associated with buying merchandise are detailed in Chapter 14.)

Due to this pattern of opportunistic buying, customers cannot be confident that the same type of merchandise will be in stock each time they visit the store. Different bargains will be available on each visit. To improve their offerings' consistency, some off-price retailers complement their opportunistically bought merchandise with merchandise purchased at regular wholesale prices.

A special type of off-price retailer are outlet stores. **Outlet stores** are off-price retailers owned by manufacturers or department or specialty store chains. Those owned by manufacturers are also referred to as **factory outlets.** Outlet stores are typically found in outlet malls, discussed in Chapter 7. Manufacturers view outlet stores as an opportunity to improve their revenues from irregulars, production overruns, and merchandise returned by retailers. Outlet stores also allow manufacturers some control over where their branded merchandise may be sold at discount prices. Retailers with strong brand names such as Saks (Saks OFF 5th) and Brooks Brothers operate outlet stores too. By selling excess merchandise in outlet stores rather than at markdown prices in their primary stores, these department and specialty store chains can maintain an image of offering desirable merchandise at full price.

NONSTORE RETAILERS

In the preceding sections, we examined retailers whose *primary* channel is their stores. In this section, we will discuss types of retailers that operate primarily through nonstore channels. The major nonstore channels are the Internet, catalogs and direct mail, direct selling, television home shopping, and vending machines.

Electronic Retailers

Electronic retailing (also called **e-tailing, online retailing,** and **Internet retailing**) is a retail format in which the retailers communicate with customers and offer products and services for sale over the Internet. Perspectives on electronic retailing have changed dramatically over the past 10 years. In 1998, most retail experts were predicting that a new breed of high-tech, Web-savvy entrepreneurs would dominate the retail industry. Everyone would be doing their shopping over the Internet; stores would close due to lack of traffic, and paper catalogs would become obsolete. The prospects for electronic retailing were so bright that billions of dollars were invested, and then lost, in Internet retail entrepreneurial ventures like Webvan, eToys, and Garden.com—companies that no longer appear in the retail landscape.

Even though online retail sales continue to grow much faster than retail sales through stores and catalogs, we now realize the Internet is not a revolutionary new retail format that will replace stores and catalogs. Although the Internet continues to provide opportunities for entrepreneurs in the retail industry, it is now primarily used by traditional retailers as a tool to complement their store and catalog offerings, grow their revenues, and provide more value for their customers. In Chapter 3, we discuss how traditional store-based retailers are using the Internet to evolve into multichannel retailers.

Some of the most well-known Internet-based companies associated with retailing, Amazon.com and eBay, are not pure retailers. Amazon does sell merchandise to consumers, but a significant portion of its revenues is generated by providing Web site development and fulfillment services to other retailers, ranging from individual consumers selling used books to large, store-based retailers such as Borders. eBay is not directly involved in the transactions between buyers and sellers who participate in the auctions on its Web site. Thus, eBay is more like a mall or shopping center operator providing a platform for buyers and sellers to interact with one another.

Catalog and Direct-Mail Retailers

Catalog retailing is a nonstore retail format in which the retail offering is communicated to a customer through a catalog, whereas **direct-mail retailers** communicate with their customers using letters and brochures. Historically, catalog and direct-mail retailing were most successful with rural consumers who lacked ready access to retail stores. With the growth of two-income and single-head-of-household families, however, consumers have found catalogs to be a convenient and time-saving shopping alternative. Exhibit 2–9 lists some of the nation's largest catalog retailers.

REFACT

Internet sales are approaching $200 billion but still only represent about 5 percent of non-auto retail sales.[49]

REFACT

Mail-order catalogs began in 1856 when Orvis began selling fishing gear. In 1872, Aaron Montgomery Ward started selling farming equipment. Richard Warren Sears started his mail-order business selling watches in 1886.[50]

EXHIBIT 2–9
Largest Catalog Retailers

	2005 Sales ($millions)	Merchandise Sold
JCPenney Co.	$2,838	General merchandise
Sears (includes Lands' End)	2,400	General merchandise
Williams-Sonoma	1,290	Home décor
Limited Brands (includes Victoria's Secret)	9,699	Apparel, beauty
L.L. Bean	1,114	Outdoor merchandise

Source: *Statistical Fact Book 2007* (New York: Direct Marketing Association, 2006), p. 68. Used by permission of Direct Marketing Association.

Notes: These sales may include some noncatalog sales.

About half of U.S. consumers shop through catalogs, and more than 19 billion catalogs are distributed in the United States each year. The merchandise categories with the greatest catalog sales are apparel, gifts, books/music/videos, home décor, and toys/games. The Internet has become a natural extension to most catalogers' selling strategy.[51]

Types of Catalog and Direct-Mail Retailers   Two types of firms selling products through catalogs are (1) general merchandise and specialty catalog retailers and (2) direct-mail retailers. **General merchandise catalog retailers** offer a broad variety of merchandise in catalogs that are periodically mailed to their customers. For example, Neiman Marcus distributes a 100-page Christmas book every year with more than 500 gifts ranging in price from $12 to $20 million. The highly anticipated catalog offers exclusive products and is crucial for the strength of the brand. It also distributes many specialty catalogs throughout the year.[52] **Specialty catalog retailers** focus on specific categories of merchandise, such as Victoria's Secret (intimate apparel and accessories), Sharper Image (gifts and electronic gadgets), and Lands' End (apparel).

Direct-mail retailers typically mail brochures and pamphlets to sell a specific product or service to customers at one point in time. For example, a Victoria's Secret customer is likely to receive numerous mailings within a very short time period, all with slightly different appearance and content. As opposed to most direct-mail retailers that are primarily interested in making a single sale from a specific mailing, retailers like Victoria's Secret typically maintain relationships with customers over time.

Catalog retailing is very challenging. First, it is difficult for smaller catalog and direct-mail retailers to compete with large, well-established firms with sophisticated customer relationship management (CRM) and fulfillment systems. Second, the mailing and printing costs are high and increasing. Third, it is difficult to get consumers' attention, because they are mailed so many catalogs and direct-mail promotions. Fourth, the length of time required to design, develop, and distribute catalogs makes it difficult for catalog and direct-mail retailers to respond quickly to new trends and fashions.

Eddie Bauer's customers maintain relationships with its customers by mailing numerous catalogs within a very short time period.

Direct Selling

Direct selling is a retail format in which salespeople, frequently independent businesspeople, contact customers directly in a convenient location, either at the customer's home or at work; demonstrate merchandise benefits and/or explain a service; take an order; and deliver the merchandise or perform the service. Direct selling is a highly interactive form of retailing in which considerable information is conveyed to customers through face-to-face discussions with salespeople. However, providing this high level of information, including extensive demonstrations, is costly.

Annual U.S. sales through direct selling are over $30 billion; worldwide, they are more than $100 billion.[53] The largest categories of merchandise sold through direct selling are personal care (e.g., cosmetics, fragrances), home/family care (e.g., cooking and kitchenware), wellness (e.g., weight loss products, vitamins), other services, and leisure/educational items (e.g., books, videos, toys). Similar to catalog retailers and television shopping networks, direct sellers are using the Internet to complement their face-to-face selling. Approximately 73 percent of all direct sales are made face to face, mostly in homes.[54]

Almost all of the 14 million salespeople who work in direct sales are independent agents.[55] They are not employed by the direct sales firm but rather act as independent distributors, buying merchandise from the firms and then reselling it to consumers. In addition, 87 percent of the direct salespeople work part time (fewer than 30 hours per week). In most cases, direct salespeople may sell their merchandise to anyone, but some companies, such as Avon, assign territories to salespeople who regularly contact households in their territory.

Two special types of direct selling are the party plan and multilevel selling. About 27 percent of all direct sales are made using a **party plan system,** in which salespeople encourage customers to act as hosts and invite friends or coworkers to a "party" at which the merchandise is demonstrated.[56] Sales made at the party are influenced by the social relationship of the people attending with the host or hostess, who receives a gift or commission for arranging the meeting. A party plan system can be, but does not have to be, used in a multilevel network.

Multilevel networks are a popular way to achieve wide distribution. In a **multilevel network,** people serve as master distributors, recruiting other people to become distributors in their network. The master distributors either buy merchandise from the firm and resell it to their distributors or receive a commission on all merchandise purchased by the distributors in their network. In addition to selling merchandise themselves, the master distributors are involved in recruiting and training other distributors.

Some multilevel direct-selling firms are illegal pyramid schemes. A **pyramid scheme** develops when the firm and its program are designed to sell merchandise and services to other distributors rather than to end users. The founders and initial distributors in pyramid schemes profit from the inventory bought by later participants, but little merchandise is sold to consumers who use it. Citing hundreds of fraudulent multilevel direct-selling complaints, the Federal Trade Commission (FTC) has proposed rules that would require companies to tell potential recruits how many sales representatives have failed to earn more than their start-up costs and how many customers have filed lawsuits over deceptive practices.[57]

Television Home Shopping

Television home shopping, also known as **T-commerce** or **teleshopping,** is a retail format in which customers watch a television program that demonstrates merchandise and then place orders for that merchandise, usually by telephone. Recent technology advances even allow viewers to purchase products using their TV's remote control.[58] The three forms of electronic home shopping retailing are (1) cable channels dedicated to television shopping, (2) infomercials, and (3) direct-response advertising. **Infomercials** are programs, typically 30 minutes long, that mix entertainment with product demonstrations and then solicit orders placed by telephone. **Direct-response advertising** includes advertisements on television and radio that describe products and provide an opportunity for consumers to order them.

The two largest home shopping networks are QVC and HSN, followed by ShopNBC, Jewelry Television, and Shop At Home. Although all Americans with cable television have access to a television shopping channel, relatively few watch on a regular basis. Furthermore, most of the purchases are made by a relatively small proportion of viewers. Like catalogs, TV home shopping networks are embracing the Internet; the major home shopping networks all have online operations.

The major advantage of TV home shopping, compared with catalog retailing, is that customers can see the merchandise demonstrated on their television screens. However, customers cannot examine a particular type of merchandise or a specific item when they want, as they could with catalogs, but instead must wait for the specific time the merchandise shows up on the screen. To address this limitation, home shopping networks schedule categories of merchandise for specific times so customers looking for specific merchandise can plan their viewing time. Television home shopping retailers appeal primarily to lower-income consumers, though the Ultimate Shopping Network (USN) sells luxury products priced from $100 to $100,000.[60] Still, most TV home shopping sales are inexpensive jewelry, apparel, cosmetics, kitchenware, and exercise equipment.

Vending Machine Retailing

Vending machine retailing is a nonstore format in which merchandise or services are stored in a machine and dispensed to customers when they deposit cash or use a credit card. Vending machines are typically placed at convenient, high-traffic locations, such as in the workplace or on university campuses, and primarily contain snacks or drinks.

Vending machine sales growth has been declining during the past few years. The vast majority of vending machine sales are cold beverages, candy, and snacks, but sales in these categories are being adversely affected by growing concerns among consumers about healthy eating habits.

Popular new vending machine applications are emerging in the entertainment industry. Redbox rents DVDs and now has 3,000 kiosks in the United States, mostly in supermarkets.[62] Vending machines that sell do-it-yourself CDs, much like purchasing songs from Apple Inc.'s iTunes, are found in record stores, Starbucks, book stores, and big box electronics stores.[63] The cost of these CDs is typically 99 cents per song, plus $3 for a jewel case, customized labels, and the CD, so 10 songs would cost $12.90. Customers can also plug in their MP3 player or a music-playing mobile telephone into these vending machines and pay only 99 cents per song.

One new retail concept, Get & Go Express, combines a convenience store with vending machines.[64] No one works at these stores, nothing gets stolen, and they are open 24 hours a day, 7 days a week. The "store" consists of 16 vending machines that accept credit or debit cards and cash. They supply up to 500 different varieties of snacks, packaged beverages, fresh sandwiches, and DVD rentals but none of the traditional convenience store merchandise, like tobacco, gasoline, lottery tickets, or alcoholic beverages.

REFACT

QVC has shipped 890 million packages since its launch in 1986. It can be viewed by over 90 million homes.[59]

REFACT

The Greek mathematician Hero invented the first vending machine in 215 BC to vend holy water in Egyptian temples. The first commercial coin-operated vending machines were introduced in London, England, in the early 1880s to dispense post cards.[61]

Get & Go Express is a convenience store with vending machines.

SERVICES RETAILING

The retail firms discussed in the previous sections sell products to consumers. However, **services retailers,** or firms that primarily sell services rather than merchandise, are a large and growing part of the retail industry. Consider a typical Saturday: After a bagel and cup of coffee at a nearby Einstein Bros. Bagels, you go to the laundromat to wash and dry your clothes, drop a suit off at a dry cleaner, leave film to be developed at a Walgreens drugstore, and make your way to Jiffy Lube to have your car's oil changed. In a hurry, you drive through a Taco Bell so you can eat lunch quickly and not be late for your haircut at 1:00 PM. By midafternoon, you're ready for a workout at your health club. After stopping at home for a change of clothes, you're off to dinner, a movie, and dancing with a friend. Finally, you end your day with a café latte at Starbucks, having interacted with 10 different services retailers during the day.

Several trends suggest considerable future growth in services retailing. For example, the aging population will increase demand for health care services. Younger people are also spending more time and money on health and fitness. Busy parents in two-income families are willing to pay to have their homes cleaned, lawns maintained, clothes washed and pressed, and meals prepared so they can spend more time with their families.

Exhibit 2–10 shows the wide variety of services retailers, along with some national companies that provide these services. These companies are retailers because they sell goods and services to consumers. However, some are not just retailers. For example, airlines, banks, hotels, and insurance and express mail companies sell their services to businesses as well as consumers. Also, many services retailers,

Service providers, like this automobile oil change service, are retailers too.

EXHIBIT 2–10
Services Retailers

Type of Service	Service Retail Firms
Airlines	American, Southwest, British Airways, JetBlue
Alternative	I-Soldit
Automobile maintenance and repair	Jiffy Lube, Midas, AAMCO
Automobile rental	Hertz, Avis, Budget, Enterprise
Banks	Citibank, Wachovia, Bank of America
Child care centers	Kindercare, Gymboree
Credit cards	American Express, VISA, MasterCard
Education	Babson College, University of Florida, Princeton Review
Entertainment	Disney, Six Flags, Chuck E. Cheese, Dave & Busters
Express package delivery	Federal Express, UPS, DHL
Fast food	Wendy's, McDonald's, Starbucks
Financial services	Merrill Lynch, Dean Witter
Fitness	Jazzercise, Bally's, Gold's Gym
Health care	Humana, HCA, Kaiser
Home maintenance	Chemlawn, Mini Maid, Roto-Rooter
Hotels and motels	Hyatt, Sheraton, Marriott, Days Inn
Income tax preparation	H&R Block
Insurance	Allstate, State Farm
Internet access/electronic information	Google
Movie theaters	AMC, Odeon/Cineplex
Real estate	Century 21, Coldwell Banker
Restaurants	TGI Friday's, Cheesecake Factory
Truck rentals	U-Haul, Ryder
Weight loss	Weight Watchers, Jenny Craig, Curves
Video rental	Blockbuster
Vision centers	Lenscrafters, Pearle

EXHIBIT 2–11   Continuum of Merchandise and Service Retailers

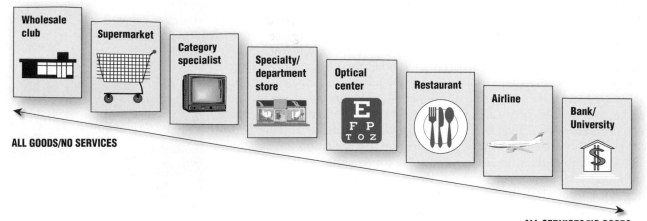

such as lawyers, doctors, and dry cleaners, do not appear in the exhibit because they focus on local markets and do not have a national presence.

Organizations such as banks, hospitals, health spas, legal clinics, entertainment firms, and universities that offer services to consumers traditionally have not considered themselves retailers. Yet due to increased competition, these organizations are adopting retailing principles to attract customers and satisfy their needs. For example, Zoots is a dry cleaning chain in the Boston area.[65] Founded by a former Staples executive, Zoots has adopted many retailing best practices: It has convenient locations, and it offers pickup and delivery service. Zoots stores also provide extended hours, are open on weekends, and offer a drop-off option for those who cannot get to the store during operating hours. The stores are bright and clean. Customers can check their order status, schedule a pickup, and provide special instructions using the online MY ZOOTS service. Clerks are taught to welcome customers and acknowledge their presence, especially if there is a line.

All retailers provide goods and services for their customers. However, the emphasis placed on the merchandise versus the service differs across retail formats, as Exhibit 2–11 shows. On the left side of the exhibit are supermarkets and warehouse clubs. These retail formats consist of self-service stores that offer very few services, except perhaps displaying merchandise, cashing checks, and assisting customers. Moving along the continuum from left to right, department and specialty stores provide higher levels of service. In addition to assistance from sales associates, they offer services such as gift wrapping, bridal registries, and alterations.[66] Optical centers and restaurants lie somewhere in the middle of the merchandise/service continuum. In addition to selling frames, eyeglasses, and contact lenses, optical centers provide important services like eye examinations and eyeglass fittings. Similarly, restaurants offer food plus a place to eat, music in the background, a pleasant ambience, and table service. As we move to the right end of the continuum, we encounter retailers whose offerings are primarily services. However, even these retailers have some products associated with the services offered, such as a meal on the airplane or a checkbook at a bank.

Differences between Services and Merchandise Retailers

Four important differences in the nature of the offerings provided by services and merchandise retailers are (1) intangibility, (2) simultaneous production and consumption, (3) perishability, and (4) inconsistency of the offering to customers.

Intangibility   Services are generally intangible—customers cannot see, touch, or feel them. They are performances or actions rather than objects. For example, health care services cannot be seen or touched by a patient. Intangibility introduces several challenges for services retailers. Because customers cannot touch and feel services, it is difficult for them to evaluate services before they buy them, or even after they buy and consume them. Due to the intangibility of their offerings, services retailers often use tangible symbols to inform customers about the quality of their services. For example, lawyers frequently have elegant, carpeted offices with expensive antique furniture. Services retailers also have difficulty evaluating the quality of services they are providing.[67] For example, it can be hard for a law firm to evaluate how well its lawyers are performing their jobs. To determine the quality of their offering, services retailers often solicit customer evaluations and complaints.

Simultaneous Production and Consumption   Products are typically made in a factory, stored and sold by a retailer, and then used by consumers in their homes. Service providers, however, create and deliver the service as the customer is consuming it. For example, when you eat at a restaurant, the meal is prepared and consumed almost at the same time. The simultaneity of production and consumption also creates some special problems for services retailers. First, the customers are present when the service is produced, may even have an opportunity to see it produced, and in some cases may be part of the production process, as in making their own Teddy Bear at Build-A-Bear Workshops. Second, other customers consuming the service at the same time can affect the quality of the service provided. For example, an obnoxious passenger next to you on an airplane can make the flight very unpleasant. Third, the services retailer often does not get a second chance to satisfy the needs of its customers. Whereas customers can return damaged merchandise to a store, customers who are dissatisfied with services have limited recourse. Thus, it is critical for services retailers to get it right the first time.

Because services are produced and consumed at the same time, it is difficult to reduce costs through mass production. For this reason, most services retailers are small, local firms. Large national retailers are able to reduce costs by "industrializing" the services they offer. They make substantial investments in equipment and training to provide a uniform service. For example, McDonald's has a detailed procedure for cooking French fries and hamburgers to make sure they come out the same, whether cooked in Paris, France, or Paris, Illinois.

Perishability   Because the creation and consumption of services are inseparable, services are perishable. They cannot be saved, stored, or resold. Once an airplane takes off with an empty seat, the sale is lost forever. In contrast, merchandise can be held in inventory until a customer is ready to buy it. Due to the perishability of services, services retailing must match supply and demand. Most services retailers have a capacity constraint, and their capacity cannot be changed easily. There are a fixed number of tables in a restaurant, seats in a classroom, beds in a hospital, and electricity that can be generated by a power plant. To increase capacity, services retailers need to make major investments, such as buying more airplanes or building an addition to increase the size of the hospital or restaurant. In addition, demand for service varies considerably over time. Consumers are most likely to fly on airplanes during holidays and the summer, eat in restaurants at lunch and dinner time, and use electricity in the evening rather than earlier in the day.

Thus, services retailers often suffer times when their services are underutilized and other times when they have to turn customers away because they cannot accommodate them. Services retailers use a variety of programs to match demand and supply. For example, airlines and hotels set lower prices on weekends, when they have excessive capacity because businesspeople are not traveling. To achieve more capacity flexibility, health clinics stay open longer during flu season, and tax preparation services are open on weekends during March and April. Restaurants increase staffing on weekends, may not open until dinner

This Chinese restaurant adjusts its capacity by having more waiters during lunch and dinner time, but fewer waiters at other times during the day.

time, and use a reservation system to guarantee service delivery at a specific time. Finally, services retailers attempt to make customers' waiting time more enjoyable. For example, videos and park employees entertain customers while they wait in line at Disney theme parks.

Inconsistency   Products can be produced by machines with very tight quality control so customers are reasonably assured that all boxes of Cheerios will be identical. But because services are performances produced by people (employees and customers), no two services will be identical. For example, tax accountants can have different knowledge and skills for preparing tax returns. The waiter at the Olive Garden can be in a bad mood and make your dining experience a disaster. Thus, an important challenge for services retailers is to provide consistently high-quality services. Many factors that determine service quality are beyond the control of the retailers; however, services retailers expend considerable time and effort selecting, training, managing, and motivating their service providers.

TYPES OF OWNERSHIP

Previous sections of this chapter discussed how retailers may be classified in terms of their retail mix and the merchandise and services they sell. Another way to classify retailers is by their ownership. The major classifications of retail ownership are (1) independent, single-store establishments, (2) corporate chains, and (3) franchises.

Independent, Single-Store Establishments

Retailing is one of the few sectors in our economy in which entrepreneurial activity is extensive. Many of these retail start-ups are owner managed, which means management has direct contact with customers and can respond quickly to their needs. Small retailers are also very flexible and can react quickly to market changes and customer needs. They are not bound by the bureaucracies inherent in large retail organizations.

Whereas single-store retailers can tailor their offerings to their customers' needs, corporate chains can more effectively negotiate lower prices for merchandise and advertising because of their larger size. In addition, corporate chains have a broader management base, with people who specialize in specific retail activities. Single-store retailers typically must rely on their owner–managers' capabilities to make the broad range of necessary retail decisions.

To compete against corporate chains, some independent retailers join a **wholesale-sponsored voluntary cooperative group,** which is an organization operated by a wholesaler offering a merchandising program to small, independent retailers on a voluntary basis. The Independent Grocers Alliance (IGA), Tru Serv (supplier to True Value Hardware), and Ace Hardware are wholesale-sponsored voluntary cooperative groups. In addition to buying, warehousing, and distribution, these groups offer members services such as advice on store design and layout, site selection, bookkeeping and inventory management systems, and employee training programs.

Corporate Retail Chains

A **retail chain** is a company that operates multiple retail units under common ownership and usually has centralized decision making for defining and implementing its strategy. Retail chains can range in size from a drugstore with two locations to retailers with thousands of stores, such as Safeway, Wal-Mart, Target, and JCPenney. Some retail chains are divisions of larger corporations or holding companies. For example, The Gap owns Old Navy, Baby Gap, GapKids, and Banana Republic. Royal Ahold owns 14 retail chains, including Stop and Shop, Giant, Peapod, and Tops in the United States and ICA, Hypernova, and Albert Heigh in Europe.

Franchising

Franchising is a contractual agreement between a franchisor and a franchisee that allows the franchisee to operate a retail outlet using a name and format developed and supported by the franchisor. More than 40 percent of all U.S. retail sales are made by franchisees.[68] Exhibit 2–12 lists some retailers governed by franchise agreements.

Food Retailers	
7-Eleven	InterContinental hotels
Arby's	Jackson Hewitt Tax Service
Ben & Jerry's	Jani-King
Cold Stone Creamery	Jazzercise
Denny's	Jiffy Lube
Domino's Pizza	LA Weight Loss
Dunkin' Donuts	Lawn Doctor
Johnny Rockets	Liberty Tax Service
McDonald's	Mail Boxes
Olive Garden	Midas
Panera Bread	Payless Car Rental
Subway	RE/MAX
YUM! Brands (KFC and Taco Bell)	Rent-a-Wreck
	UPS Stores
Services Retailers	**Merchandise Retailers**
1-800-GOT-JUNK?	Ace Hardware
AAMCO	Culligan
Cash Now	GNC
Century 21 Real Estate	Matco Tools
Coldwell Banker	Merle Norman
Curves	Pearle Vision
Hampton Inn	Sign-A-Rama
I-Sold It	

EXHIBIT 2–12
Retailers Using Franchise Business Model

In a franchise contract, the franchisee pays a lump sum plus a royalty on all sales for the right to operate a store in a specific location. The franchisee also agrees to operate the outlet in accordance with procedures prescribed by the franchisor. The franchisor provides assistance in locating and building the store, developing the products or services sold, training managers, and advertising. To maintain each franchisee's reputation, the franchisor also makes sure that all outlets provide the same quality of services and products.

The franchise ownership format attempts to combine the advantages of owner-managed businesses with the efficiencies of centralized decision making in chain store operations. Franchisees are motivated to make their stores successful because they receive the profits (after the royalty is paid). The franchisor is motivated to develop new products and systems and to promote the franchise because it receives a royalty on all sales. Advertising, product development, and system development are efficiently performed by the franchisor, with costs shared by all franchisees. Retailing View 2.4 describes iSold It, the largest seller on eBay and the top-ranked among *Entrepreneur* magazine's top 50 new franchises for 2007. Appendix A at the end of the book provides a more detailed description of franchising.

2.4   RETAILING VIEW   Want to Sell on eBay? Leave It to iSold It

eBay, the largest online marketplace, is visited by over 9 million people annually. Responding to this demand, a new category, eBay drop-off stores, was born. iSold It was founded in Pasadena, California, in December 2003 by Elise Wetsel, a mother who was trying to raise money for her children's school. She wanted to sell items on eBay that the family no longer needed. In doing so, she found that it was much harder to sell on eBay than it was to buy items on the auction site. It was then that she realized the opportunity of selling other people's items.

This business idea turned into a retail store and then became a rapidly growing franchise throughout the country. iSold It is a brick-and-mortar interface to the Internet. iSold It stores are found in convenient strip mall locations, normally in a Wal-Mart or supermarket shopping center. Customers drop off the items that they want sold, and the staff at iSold It take care of the entire selling process, including researching the item, professionally photographing it, listing it for sale on eBay, storing it while it is for sale, answering all questions pertaining to the item from potential buyers, shipping the item, and finally sending the seller a check for the item.

The retailer takes a fee as a percentage of the selling price, as well as being reimbursed for the auction fees. The sales commission is 30 percent on sales up to $500 and 20 percent on sales of more than $500. The average product that iSold It sells on eBay goes for about $100, netting the seller approximately $63 after the commissions and selling fees. The average household has about $2,200 worth of merchandise that it no longer uses. Thus, the eBay drop-off stores make it much easier for consumers to cash out on items that they no longer need or want.

One of iSold It's founding principles is to raise money for charitable purposes. It continues to accept items for sale on eBay and donates the net sales to a charity.

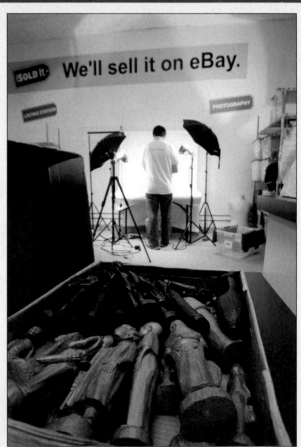

iSold It makes everyone a winner. The franchisees and the franchisor make money, and their customers get rid of unwanted items on eBay.

Sources: Reed Richardson, "Business Ideas to Make Every Minute Count," *Priority*, September 2006; Sara Wilson, "#17 iSold It LLC," *Entrepreneur* 34, No. 6 (June 2006), p. 84; www.isold-it.com (accessed June 3, 2007); Alison Ledger, "Treasure Hunt," *Business Franchise*, October 2006; "The Urge to Purge and Leasing Luxury Goods," *The Oprah Magazine*, September 2006, p. 326; "The eBay Evolution," *Business Franchise*, July/August 2006; Jaime Ciavarra, "eBay Shop is King of Yardsale Circuit," *Gazette.Net*, September 20, 2006; "Rising Stars," *Entrepreneur*, April 2007.

SUMMARY

This chapter has explained the different types of retailers and how they compete with different retail mixes to sell merchandise and services to customers. To collect statistics about retailing, the federal government classifies retailers by the type of merchandise and services they sell. But this classification method may not be useful to determine a retailer's major competitors. A more useful approach for understanding the retail marketplace is to classify retailers on the basis of the retail mix, merchandise variety and assortment, services, location, pricing, and promotion decisions they make to attract customers.

During the past 30 years, U.S. retail markets have been characterized by the emergence of many new retail institutions. Traditional institutions (supermarkets, convenience, department, discount, and specialty stores) have been joined by category specialists, superstores, hypermarkets, convenience stores, warehouse clubs, off-price retailers, catalogers, and nonstore retailers. In addition, there has been substantial growth in services retailing.

The inherent differences between services and merchandise result in services retailers emphasizing store management, whereas merchandise retailers emphasize inventory control issues. Traditional retail institutions have changed in response to these new retailers. For example, department stores have increased their emphasis on fashion-oriented apparel and improved the services they offer. Supermarkets are focusing more attention on meal solutions and perishables.

Retailers can also be classified by ownership. Some retailers are independently owned, single-store establishments. These stores can rapidly react to the marketplace, but often do not have the buying power or breadth of management skills to compete effectively with its larger competitors. A second type of retailer is a corporate retail chain. Chains can be relatively small with as few as two locations, or include thousands of locations, as is the case for the largest retailer in the world, Wal-Mart. The final ownership alternative is a franchise. Franchisees own their stores, but pay fees to a franchisor to use its name and format.

KEY TERMS

assortment, *37*

big box, *45*

breadth of merchandise, *38*

catalog retailing, *53*

category killers, *52*

category specialist, *51*

close-out retailers, *53*

close-outs, *54*

convenience store, *46*

conventional supermarket, *41*

department store, *47*

depth of merchandise, *38*

direct-mail retailer, *55*

direct-response advertising, *58*

direct selling, *57*

drugstore, *51*

electronic retailing, *55*

e-tailing, *55*

extreme value food retailers, *41*

extreme value retailers, *53*

factory outlet, *54*

fair trade, *43*

franchising, *63*

full-line discount store, *49*

general merchandise catalog retailer, *56*

home improvement center, *53*

hypermarket, *45*

infomercial, *58*

Internet retailing, *55*

Irregulars, *54*

limited assortment supermarket, *41*

multilevel network, *57*

NAICS (North American Industry Classification System), *36*

off-price retailer, *53*

online retailing, *55*

outlet store, *54*

party plan system, *57*

power perimeter, *43*

pyramid scheme, *57*

retail chain, *63*

services retailer, *59*

SKU (stockkeeping unit), *38*

specialty catalog retailer, *56*

specialty store, *49*

supercenter, *44*

t-commerce, *57*

teleshopping, *57*

television home shopping, *57*

variety, *37*

vending machine retailing, *58*

warehouse club, *45*

wholesale-sponsored voluntary cooperative group, *63*

GET OUT AND DO IT!

1. **CONTINUING CASE ASSIGNMENT:** The Comparison Shopping Exercise in Appendix 2A gives you the opportunity to see a retail store through the eyes of a retailer instead of a consumer. The objective of this assignment is to have you take the retailer's perspective and think about the different strategies that the retailer you selected and another retailer might have, as well as how these strategies result in different retail mixes. The assignment is to conduct a comparison of the retail offering for a specific merchandise category, such as PDAs, men's suits, country/western CDs, women's athletic shoes, or house paint, for two different retailers. The other retailer selected might be a direct competitor using the same format or a retailer selling similar merchandise with a different format.

Your comparison should include the following:
- The strategy pursued by the two retailers—each retailer's target market and general approach to satisfying the needs of that target market.
- The retail mixes (store location, merchandise, pricing, advertising and promotion, location of merchandise category in store, store design, customer service) used by each of the retailers.
- With respect to the merchandise category, a detailed comparison of the variety and depth of assortment. In comparing the merchandise offering, use the table and questions in Appendix 2A.

To prepare this comparison, you need to visit the stores, observe the retail mixes in the stores, and play the role of a customer to observe the service.

2. Go to an athletic footwear specialty store such as Foot Locker, a department store, and a discount store. Analyze their variety and assortment of athletic footwear by creating a table similar to that in Exhibit 2–2.

3. Keep a diary of where you shop, what you buy, and how much you spend for two weeks. Get your parents to do the same thing. Tabulate your results by type of retailer. Are your shopping habits significantly different or are they similar to those of your parents? Do you and your parents' shopping habits coincide with the trends discussed in this chapter? Why or why not?

4. Data on U.S. retail sales are available from the U.S. Bureau of the Census Internet site at www.census.gov/mrts/www/mrts.html. Look at the unadjusted monthly sales by NAICS. Which categories of retailers have the largest percentage of sales in the fourth quarter (the holiday season)?

5. Four large associations of retailers are the National Retail Federation (www.nrf.com), the Food Marketing Institute (www.fmi.org), the National Association of Chain Drug Stores (www.nacds.org), and the National Association of Convenience Stores (www.nacsonline.com). Visit these sites and report on the latest retail developments and issues confronting the industry.

6. Go to *Entrepreneur Magazine*'s Franchise Zone Web page at http://www.entrepreneur.com/franchise500 and view the top 500 franchises for the past year. How many of the retailers in the top ten have you patronized as a customer? Did you know that they were operated as a franchise? Look at the lists from previous years to see changes in the rankings. Click on the link "About the Franchise 500" and describe which factors were used to develop the list. Finally, what is the nature of the businesses that seem to lend themselves to franchising?

DISCUSSION QUESTIONS AND PROBLEMS

1. Distinguish between variety and assortment. Why are these important elements of the retail market structure?

2. Choose a small, independent retailer and explain how it can compete against a large national chain.

3. What do off-price retailers need to do to compete against other formats in the future?

4. Compare and contrast the retail mixes of convenience stores, traditional supermarkets, supercenters, and warehouse stores. Can all of these food retail institutions survive over the long run? How? Why?

5. Why are retailers in the limited assortment supermarket and extreme value discount store sectors growing so rapidly?

6. The same brand and model of a personal computer is sold by specialty computer stores, discount stores, category specialists, and warehouse stores. Why would a customer choose one store over the others?

7. Choose a product category that both you and your parents purchase (e.g., business clothing, casual clothing, music, electronic equipment, shampoo). In which type of store do you typically purchase this merchandise? What about your parents? Explain why there is, or is not, a difference in your store choices.

8. At many optical stores, you can get your eyes checked *and* purchase glasses or contact lenses. How is the shopping experience different for the service as compared to the product? Design a strategy designed to get customers to purchase both the service and the product. In so doing, delineate specific actions that should be taken to acquire and retain optical customers.

9. Which of the store-based retail formats discussed in this chapter is most vulnerable to competition from Internet retailers? Why? Which is least vulnerable? Why?

10. Many experts believe that customer service is one of retailing's most important issues. How can retailers that emphasize price (e.g., discount stores, category specialists, off-price retailers) improve customer service without increasing costs and, thus, prices?

SUGGESTED READINGS

Granger, Michele, and Tina Sterling. *Fashion Entrepreneurship.* New York: Fairchild, 2003.

Kim, Sang-Hoon, and S. Chan Choi. "The Role of Warehouse Club Membership Fees in Retail Competition." *Journal of Retailing* 83, no. 2, 2007, pp. 171–181.

Kumar, Nirmalya. "Strategies to Fight Low-Cost Rivals." *Harvard Business Review*, December 1, 2006, pp. 1–12. Mitchell, Stacy. *Big-Box Swindle: The True Cost of Mega-Retailers and the Fight for America's Independent Businesses.* Boston: Beacon Press, 2006.

Rivkin, Jan W., and Troy Smith. "Organic Growth at Wal-Mart." *Harvard Business Review*, January 23, 2007, pp. 1–4.

Spector, Robert. *Category Killers: The Retail Revolution and its Impact on Consumer Culture.* Boston: Harvard Business School, 2005.

"State of the Industry–Top 100 U.S. Retailers." *Chain Store Age,* August 2007, pp. A1–A9.

"Top 100 Retailers." *Stores*, August 2007, pp. 15+.

Weitz, Barton A., and Mary Brett Whitfield. "Trends in U.S. Retailing." in *Retailing in the 21st Century–Current and Future Trends,* eds. Manfred Kraft and Murali Mantrala. Berlin: Springer, 2006, pp. 59–75.

Whitaker, Jan. *Service and Style: How the American Department Store Fashioned the Middle Class.* New York: St. Martin's Press, 2006.

Windsperger, Josef, and Rajiv P. Dant. "Contractibility and Ownership Redirection in Franchising: A Property Rights View." *Journal of Retailing* 82, no. 3, 2006, pp. 259–272.

APPENDIX 2A   Comparison Shopping

All retailers learn about their competitors through comparison shopping. Comparison shopping might be as informal as walking through a competitor's store and looking around, but a structured analysis is more helpful in developing a retail offering that will attract consumers from a competitor's store.

The first step in the process is to define the scope of the comparison. For example, the comparison might be between two retail chains, two specific stores, two departments, or two categories of merchandise. The appropriate scope depends on the responsibilities of the person undertaking the comparison. For example, CEOs of retail chains would be interested in comparing their chain with a competitor's. Such comparisons might focus on the chains' financial resources, inventory levels, number of stores and employees, store locations, merchandise sold, employee compensation programs, and return policies. Thus, CEOs would examine factors for which the corporate office is responsible. In contrast, store managers would be interested in comparing their store with a competing store. For example, department store managers would want to know more about other department stores anchoring the mall in which they're located. Buyers and department managers would focus on specific areas of merchandise for which they're responsible.

Exhibit 2–13 lists questions to consider when comparison shopping. Exhibit 2–14 suggests a format for comparing merchandise, in this case lugsole shoes in JCPenney and a men's shoe store.

EXHIBIT 2–13

Some Issues to Address in Comparison Shopping

Merchandise Presentation

1. How is the selling floor laid out? What selling areas are devoted to specific types of merchandise? How many square feet are devoted to each area?

2. Where are the different selling areas located? Are they in heavy traffic areas? By restrooms? On the main aisle? On a secondary aisle? How does this location affect sales volume for merchandise in the area?

3. What kind of fixtures are used in each selling area (faceouts, rounders, cubes, bunkers, tables, gondolas)?

4. Are aisles, walls, and columns used to display merchandise?

5. What is the lighting for sales areas (focus, overhead, bright, toned down)? How is the merchandise organized in the selling areas (by type, price point, vendor, style, color)?

7. Evaluate the housekeeping of the selling areas. Are they cluttered or messy? Are they well maintained and organized?

8. What's the overall atmosphere or image of the selling areas? What effect does the lighting, fixturing, spacing, and visual merchandising have on customers?

9. What type of customer (age, income, fashion orientation) would be attracted to the store and each selling area within it?

Sales Support/Customer Services

1. How many salespeople are in each department? Is the department adequately staffed?

2. How are salespeople dressed? Do they have an appropriate appearance?

3. Do salespeople approach customers promptly? How soon after entering a selling area is a customer greeted? How do customers respond to the level of service?

4. Evaluate salespeople's product knowledge.

5. Do salespeople suggest add-on merchandise?

6. Where, if applicable, are fitting rooms in relation to the selling floor? In what condition are they? Are they supervised? Are there enough fitting rooms to meet demand?

7. How many registers are on the selling floor? Are they well staffed and well stocked with supplies?

8. What services (credit card acceptance, gift wrapping, delivery, special ordering, bridal registry, alterations, other) does the store offer?

9. What level of customer service is provided in the selling area?

Merchandise (Each Category)

1. Who are the key vendors?

2. How deep are the assortments for each vendor?

3. What are the private labels and how important are they?

4. What are the low, average, and top prices for merchandise in the category?

Summary and Conclusions

1. Who is the store's target customer?

2. What are the competitor's strengths and weaknesses?

3. How can we capture more business from the competitor?

Format for Merchandise Comparison   **EXHIBIT 2–14**

Retailer	Factors	Lug sole casual shoes			Comments
JCPenney	Style	3 eyelet oxford			
	Brands	St. Johns Bay (private)			
	Price	$35			
	% mix	5%			
	SKUs	36 pair			
Father/Son Shoes	Style	3 eyelet oxford	Tie suede	Chakka suede	
	Brands	British Knights Private	Private	Private	
	Price	$38.99–39.99	$29.99	$37.95	
	% mix	10%	5%	5%	
	SKUs	24 pairs	36 pairs	12 pairs	
Harwyns	Style	2 eyelet oxford	Tie suede		
	Brands	British Knights	Private		
	Price	$39.99	$29.95		
	% mix	5%	5%		
	SKUs	36 pairs	36 pairs		

Style For clothing, style might be the fabric or cut. For example, sweater styles might be split into wool, cotton, or polyblend and V-neck, crewneck, or cardigan.

Brands The identifying label. Indicate whether or not the brand is a national brand or store brand.

Price The price marked on the merchandise. If the item has been marked down, indicate the original price and the marked-down price.

Percent mix The percentage of the total assortment devoted to this style of merchandise.

SKUs The number of different items in this subcategory.

Multichannel Retailing

Office Depot's multichannel offering increases the value we can provide our customers. Customers can search for detailed information about products on our Web site; place orders at the Web site or through our call centers; and have their order delivered to them or pick up the merchandise at a local store. In addition, our Web site has a Business Resource Center that provides our small business customers with the tools, information, and business solutions that help them improve their business operations.

One of the challenges that multichannel retailers like Office Depot have is coordinating the merchandise

EXECUTIVE BRIEFING
Kristin Micalizo, Vice President
Direct Sales, Office Depot

offered and prices in the different channels. At Office Depot, the merchandise decisions are made by a centralized group. This merchandise management group has buyers with responsibility for product categories and experts in catalog and Internet retailing who tailor the assortment and prices for our different channels.

I am responsible for the sales and marketing of the merchandise and services Office Depot offers to consumers and small and medium businesses through our nonstore channels. My group manages our Web site, www.officedepot.com; our catalogs; and our Internet-based promotions including e-mails, paid search, online banners, and viral marketing.

One of our more recent innovations is adding green pages to our catalogs and Web site. These pages promote products that are environmental friendly. By offering a broad assortment of green office products, covering a wide range of everyday office requirements, we can help our customers contribute toward a greener way of doing business and help them comply with legislation and certification (e.g., ISO14001). In addition, these pages provide information on recycling services and expert advice and guides on how to select the best green products for our customers' businesses.

CHAPTER 3

QUESTIONS

What are the unique customer benefits offered by the three retail channels: stores, catalogs, and the Internet?

Why are retailers moving toward using all three channels?

How do multichannel retailers provide more value to their customers?

What are the key success factors in multichannel retailing?

How might technology affect the future shopping experience?

My college degree is in economics, and my initial jobs were in finance. When I joined Office Depot, I worked on the budgeting, forecasting, and financial analysis of capital projects for Office Depot's supply chain management system, including its distributions systems. And then I got a great opportunity. I was offered the position of running our eight distribution centers. While I was familiar with the activities undertaken in the distribution centers, all of a sudden I went from managing a couple of assistants to managing 2,000 people.

To be a senior general manager, you need to walk in the shoes of managers responsible for different facets of the business. While I had considerable experience in finance and operations, I wanted to broaden my experience in marketing and sales so I could continue to advance my career. Office Depot was great in accommodating my desire to be more well-rounded and offered me my present position. One of the benefits of working for a retailer is that you have the opportunities to be involved in all aspects of the business.

Widespread access to and use of the Internet has significantly changed the retailing industry. Even though sales over the Internet continue to grow at double-digit rates, more than five times faster than store or catalog sales, Internet sales are expected to represent less than 10 percent of non-auto retail sales by 2010.[1] However, the Internet has and will continue to have a substantial influence on consumer store choice and purchase decisions. For example, more than 50 percent of U.S. consumers review information on Web sites about such products as consumer electronics, home décor and appliances, and tools/hardware/garden supplies before buying offline.[2] The Internet thus has become a frequently used place to shop as well as buy.

In this chapter, we take a strategic perspective in our discussion of three different channels—stores, catalogs, and the Internet—through which retailers can communicate with and sell merchandise and services to their customers. Then we look at how retailers can increase revenues and improve their customers' shopping experience by using all of these channels to interact with their customers. At the end of the chapter, we illustrate how integrating these channels and using new technologies will create a compelling shopping experience in the future.

In other chapters, we examine how retailers use the Internet in specific applications, including managing employees, buying merchandise, managing customer relationships, advertising and promoting merchandise, and providing customer service.

RETAIL CHANNELS FOR INTERACTING WITH CUSTOMERS

Many store-based retail chains sell merchandise from their Web sites and communicate with their customers through the Internet. Many small retailers also offer products online as a key way to increase sales and attract a wider customer base. For example, locals can visit one of Little Pie's three Manhattan locations and enjoy an assortment of flavors, from Old-Fashioned Apple Pie to the company's most famous taste, Sour Cream Apple Walnut. With annual sales of less than $5 million, Little Pie still receives orders for over 100 pies a week from its Web site. Mary Jo Slatter, an independent casting company director who lives in California and describes herself as a "Little Pie groupie," says, "I order early in the morning, and I get it the next day. It tasted like you got it right out of the oven."[3]

At the same time, Internet retailers are opening actual stores. Epicenter Collection (www.epicenter.net) has stores that showcase online and catalog companies, as well as branded manufacturers that generally don't have their own stores.[4] Shoppers are issued a handheld shopping device called a Spree-go that enables them to select and buy products without waiting at the checkout line or finding a sales associate, and then can cross-shop all the brands and companies within the Epicenter store.

Multichannel retailers are retailers that sell merchandise or services through more than one channel. By using a combination of channels, retailers can leverage the unique benefits provided by each to attract and satisfy more customers. In addition, a multichannel offering is particularly attractive to a retailer's best customers. As seen in Exhibit 3–1, JCPenney's best customers use the catalog, store, and Internet channels to purchase merchandise.

Exhibit 3–2 lists the unique benefits of stores, catalogs, and the Internet to illustrate how the channels can be used to complement one another.

Store Channel

Stores offer several benefits to customers that they cannot get when they shop through catalogs or on the Internet.

Browsing   Shoppers often have only a general sense of what they want (e.g., a sweater, something for dinner, a gift) but don't know the specific item they want. They go to a store to see what is available before they decide what to buy. Although some consumers surf the Web and look through catalogs for ideas, most consumers still prefer browsing in stores.

REFACT

More than 600,000 small retailers in the United States have Web sites.[5]

EXHIBIT 3–1
Average Annual Dollars Spent by JCPenney's Customers

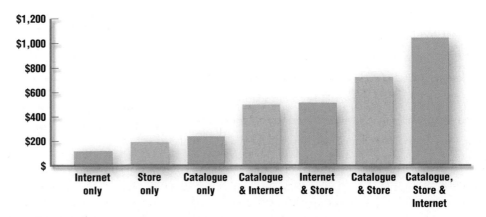

SOURCE: Roger A. Kerin et al., "Instructor's Resource Package," in *Marketing, 5th ed.* (Boston: McGraw-Hill Irwin, 2006). Used by permission.

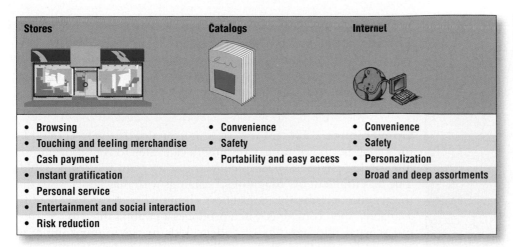

EXHIBIT 3–2
Benefits Provided by
Different Channels

Stores	Catalogs	Internet
• Browsing	• Convenience	• Convenience
• Touching and feeling merchandise	• Safety	• Safety
• Cash payment	• Portability and easy access	• Personalization
• Instant gratification		• Broad and deep assortments
• Personal service		
• Entertainment and social interaction		
• Risk reduction		

Touching and Feeling Products   Perhaps the greatest benefit offered by stores is the opportunity for customers to use all five of their senses—touching, smelling, tasting, seeing, and hearing—when examining products. Although new technologies can provide 3D representations on a computer screen, these visual improvements do not provide the same level of information you get when actually trying on a swimsuit or smelling the fragrance of a candle.

Personal Service   Although shoppers might be critical of the personal service they get in stores, sales associates still have the capability to provide meaningful, personalized information. They can tell you if a suit looks good on you, suggest a tie to go with a dress shirt, or answer questions you might have about what is appropriate to wear at a business-casual event. In your own buying experience for a complicated purchase such as a snowboard and boots, wouldn't a good salesperson's advice be more useful than advertising, friends, an online chat or blog on the Internet, or *Consumer Reports* in making your purchase?[6]

Cash and Credit Payment   Stores are the only channel that accepts cash payments. Some customers prefer to pay with cash because it is easy, resolves the transaction immediately, and does not result in potential interest payments. Some customers also prefer to use their credit card or debit card in person rather than electronically sending the payment information via the Internet.

Entertainment and Social Experience   In-store shopping can be a stimulating experience for some people, providing a break in their daily routine and enabling them to interact with friends. All nonstore retail formats are limited in the degree to which they can satisfy these entertainment and social needs. Even the most attractive and inventive Web pages and video clips will not be as exciting as the displays and activities in a Bass Pro Shop or REI store.

Immediate Gratification   Stores have the advantage of allowing customers to get the merchandise immediately after they buy it. For example, if you have a fever, you are not going to wait a day or two for the delivery of a prescription from Drugstore.com.

Risk Reduction   When customers purchase merchandise in stores, the physical presence of the store reduces their perceived risk of buying and increases their confidence that any problems with the merchandise will be corrected. The store is easily accessible in case the merchandise is defective or unsuitable, and customers can simply receive credit for it. Customers don't have to worry about a returned item getting lost in the mail or being processed incorrectly.

Under what circumstances are catalogs more convenient than shopping in stores or over the Internet?

Catalog Channel

The catalog channel provides some benefits to customers that are not available from the store or Internet channels. Catalogs, like all nonstore formats, offer the convenience of looking at merchandise and placing an order from almost anywhere 24/7. However, catalogs also have some advantages over other nonstore formats.

Convenience   The information in a catalog is easily accessible for a long period of time. Consumers can refer to the information in a catalog anytime by simply picking it up from the coffee table. The development of **"magalogs,"** catalogs with magazine-type editorial content, enhances consumers' desire to keep catalogs readily available. Abercrombie & Fitch produces a popular magalog featuring sensual photographs of college kids in rustic environments alongside the clothing that contributes to this lifestyle.

Information   Catalogs are no longer just a description of available products. They offer more information on how the products can enhance consumer's lifestyle and be used effectively. For example, Williams-Sonoma's catalog features beautiful photographs of the gourmet dishes that can be prepared using the kitchen items and foods sold in the catalog. It is also replete with recipes illustrating how to make these fine dishes.

Safety   Security in malls and shopping areas is becoming an important concern for many shoppers, particularly the elderly. Nonstore retail formats have an advantage over store-based retailers in that they enable customers to review merchandise and place orders from a safe environment—their homes.

Internet Channel

Shopping over the Internet provides the convenience offered by catalogs and other nonstore formats. However, the Internet, compared with store and catalog channels, also has the potential to offer a greater selection of products and more personalized information about products and services in a relatively short amount of time. It also offers retailers the unique opportunity to collect information about how consumers shop—information that they can use to improve the shopping experience across all channels.

Broader Selection   One benefit of the Internet channel, compared with the other two channels, is the vast number of alternatives available to consumers. By shopping on the Internet, consumers can easily "visit" and select merchandise from a broader array of retailers. People living in Columbus, Ohio, can shop electronically at Harrod's in London in less time than it takes them to visit their local supermarket. Retail Web sites typically offer deeper assortments of merchandise (more colors, brands, and sizes) than are available in stores. This offering enables them to satisfy consumer demand for less popular styles, colors, or sizes and still keep their overall inventory costs low.[8]

More Information to Evaluate Merchandise   An important service offered by retailers is the provision of information to help customers make better buying decisions. The retail channels differ in terms of how much information they provide and whether customers can format the information to compare different brands easily. For instance, some catalogs provide only a few facts about each item, such as price, weight, and brand/model, along with a photograph. Other catalogs offer much more detail about each item carried. For many clothing items, Lands' End not only provides color pictures but also gives extensive information about the construction process, stitching, and materials.

REFACT

E-commerce was born on August 11, 1994, when a CD by Sting was sold by NetMarket over the Internet.[7]

The depth of information available at a retailer's Web site can provide solutions to customer problems. For example, Williams-Sonoma's Web site can help customers plan a margarita party or a picnic. It describes everything that you might need for the occasion. By taking the focus off of each product and aggregately thinking about the purpose for which the products will be used, such deep information prompts customers to view more products than they otherwise would have considered online. Home Depot walks customers on its Web site through the steps of installation and repair projects, thereby giving do-it-yourselfers confidence prior to tackling home improvement tasks. The directions include the level of difficulty and a list of the tools and materials needed to complete the project successfully.

Stores differ in the depth of information they make available to consumers. Specialty and department stores typically have trained, knowledgeable sales associates, whereas most discount stores do not. However, the personal knowledge of sales associates is often limited. The space available in self-service stores and catalogs to provide information is constrained to the size of a printed page, a sign, or a package on a shelf.

Using an Internet channel, retailers can provide as much information as each customer wants and more information than he or she could get through store or catalog channels. Customers shopping electronically can drill down through Web pages until they have enough information to make a purchase decision. Unlike in catalogs, the information on an electronic channel database can be frequently updated and will always be available—24/7, 365 days per year. Furthermore, retaining knowledgeable sales associates is difficult and, in many cases, not cost effective. The cost of adding information to an Internet channel is likely to be far less than the cost of continually training thousands of sales associates.

In addition, when using the Internet channel, customers can format the information so that they can effectively use it when evaluating products. Exhibit 3–3 illustrates how Circuit City provides information in a side-by-side comparison

REFACT

Thirty to forty percent of shoppers use retailers' or manufacturers' Web sites to research purchases before going to stores.[9]

EXHIBIT 3–3
Side-By-Side Comparison Available through the Internet Channel

	Apple® 4GB iPod® mini (M9800LL/A)	Apple® 1GB iPod® shuffle (M9725LL/A)	Apple® 4GB iPod® mini (M9806LL/A)
Price	$199.99 `add to cart`	$149.99 `add to cart`	$199.99 `add to cart`
Availability	**Availability** ✓ Shipping ✓ Pick up in most stores	**Availability** ✓ Shipping ✓ Pick up in most stores	**Availability** ✓ Shipping ✓ Pick up in most stores
Customer rating	▭ 4.6	▭ 4.6	▭ 4.4
Memory			
Built-in memory ⑦	4GB	1GB	4GB
Maximum memory	4GB	1GB	4GB
Expandable memory	No	No	No
Memory media/type	Hard Drive	Internal Flash Memory	Hard Drive
Storage capacity	1,000 songs in 128-Kbps AAC format	240 songs in 128-Kbps AAC format	1,000 songs in 128-Kbps AAC format
Note:	MB = megabytes, GB = gigabytes; actual formatted capacity may vary.	MB = megabytes, GB = gigabytes; actual formatted capacity may vary.	MB = megabytes, GB = gigabytes; actual formatted capacity may vary.
File formats supported			
WMA ⑦	No	No	No
WAV ⑦	Yes	Yes	Yes
OGG ⑦	No	No	No
Radio			
Digital tuner ⑦	No	No	No
# of AM/FM tuner presets ⑦	N/A	N/A	N/A
Music/data transfer			

format. In contrast, customers in stores usually have to inspect each brand, one item at a time, and then remember the different attributes to make a comparison. At Glimpse.com, customers can view side-by-side images of similar merchandise available from about 100 Web sites in a single screen, eliminating the need to open several to view each retailer's selection separately.[10]

Virtual communities, networks of people who seek information, products, and services and communicate with one another about specific issues, also help customers solve problems by providing information not readily available through other channels. People who participate in these networks, known as **social shoppers,** seek not just information for future use but also an enhanced emotional connection to other participants in the shopping experience.[11] Some of these social shoppers may spend two or three times the amount of time traditional shoppers spend shopping, and then not make a purchase. It is the experience of shopping they enjoy more than the product or service.

Pricegrabber.com and Epinions.com are long-established sites for buyers to compare products and write reviews for more technical products.[12] Other sites, like ThisNext.com, Kaboodle.com, Wists.com, and StyleHive.com, are spearheading a new type of community dedicated to social shopping, which combines shopping and social networking.[13] For instance, if a person is interested in Kona coffee, she would go to www.ThisNext.com and register to create her own pages to collect information on items she finds. In addition to describing the items and posting Web addresses, she would post images and rate the products. Other people interested in Kona coffee then could find this and similar information easily.[14]

Many retailers have added the ability for customers to post apparel reviews to their Web sites. These reviews are not only helpful to their customers but also provide valuable feedback to buyers about what customers like and don't like. Retailers are ideally suited to offer these problem-solving sites for customers because they have the skills to put together merchandise assortments, services, and information to attract members. Retailing View 3.1 describes how Web sites can help couples plan their weddings.

Personalization   The most significant potential benefit of the Internet channel is its ability to personalize the information for each customer economically. Catalogers cannot economically tailor their merchandise and information to the needs and preferences of all individual consumers. To be cost effective, they have to send the same catalog to a large segment of customers.

Sales associates in high service-oriented retailers like department and specialty stores can provide this benefit however. They know what their preferred customers want. They can select a few outfits and arrange to show these outfits before the store opens or even take the outfits to the customer's office or home. However, store-based retailers can only provide this benefit when their sales associates are working, and even then, providing it is costly. The Internet offers an opportunity to provide "personal" service at a low cost.

PART OF DIFFERENCE

Personalized Customer Service   Traditional Internet channel approaches for responding to customer questions—such as FAQ (frequently asked questions) pages and offering an 800 number or e-mail address to ask questions—often do not provide the timely information customers are seeking. To improve customer service from an electronic channel, many retailers are offering live, online chats. An **online chat** provides customers with the opportunity to click a button at anytime and have an instant messaging e-mail or voice conversation with a customer service representative. This technology also enables electronic retailers to send a proactive chat invitation automatically to customers on the site. The timing of these invitations can be based on the time the visitor has spent on the site, the specific page the customer is viewing, or a product on which the customer has clicked. At Bluefly.com, for example, if a visitor searches for more than three items in five minutes, thereby demonstrating more than a passing interest, Bluefly will display a pop-up window with a friendly face offering help.[17]

Offering online chats is economically attractive for retailers. The average cost per electronic customer service session is less than an e-mail and about one-third the cost of a telephone customer session. Retailers vary in how they make the trade-off between stimulating sales and increasing customer satisfaction versus the cost of providing online instant chat services.

Personalized Offering   The interactive nature of the Internet provides an opportunity for retailers to personalize their offerings for each of their customers. For example, at many Web sites, you can create a personal homepage, like MyYahoo,

---

The Wedding Channel Helps Couples Get Ready for the Big Day   RETAILING VIEW   3.1

The WeddingChannel.com offers merchandise, services, and information for couples planning their wedding.

The typical engagement/wedding planning process lasts 14 months, costs almost $20,000, and involves many emotionally charged decisions, such as how many people and whom to invite, what print style to use on the invitations, where to hold the reception, what music to play during the ceremony, and what gifts to list in the registry. Traditionally, the bride's family managed the wedding planning process. But with more couples getting married when they are older, both working, and living farther from their parents, wedding planning is more challenging.

Internet wedding sites, such as WeddingChannel.com (www. weddingchannel.com), offer couples and their families planning guides, tips, and an opportunity to chat with other couples getting married. Gift registries can be created at different retailers and broadcast to guests through e-mail. The couple can collect information from home rather than by making appointments with different suppliers. Potential places for the reception can be ruled out by looking at photos on the Web, and instead of going to hear different bands play, audio clips also can be downloaded from the Web. Hotel reservations for out-of-town guests can be made over the Internet, and maps can be created to show those guests how to get to the hotel and reception. Finally, couples can have their own personal site on which they post their wedding pictures.

Sources: Carlye Adler, "Till Death Do Us Part," *Fortune Small Business*, July/August 2007, pp. 30–32 (accessed August 13, 2007); www.weddingchannel.com; www.theknot.com.

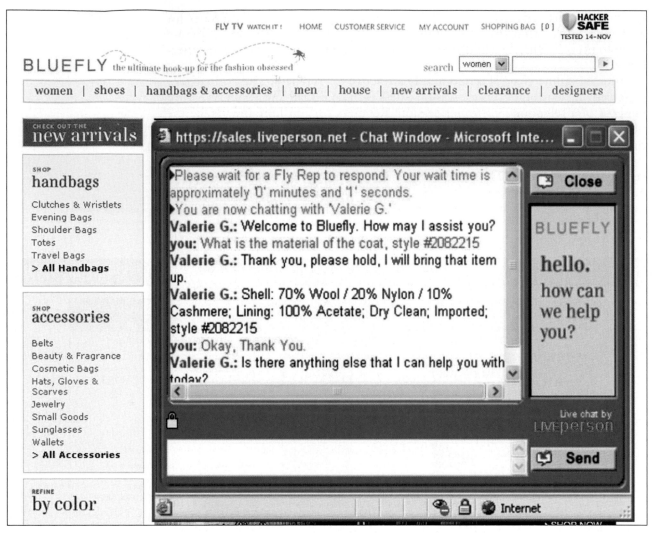

At Bluefly.com, if a visitor lingers on certain items, a window will pop-up offering help.

that is tailored to your individual needs. Using a **cookie** (a small computer program that provides identifying information installed on your hard drive), Amazon serves you a personalized homepage with information about books and other products of interest based on your past purchases. Amazon.com will also send interested customers customized e-mail messages that notify them that their favorite author or recording artist has published a new book or released a new CD. Another personalized offering that online retailers are able to present to customers is recommendations of complementary merchandise. Just as a well-trained salesperson would make recommendations to customers prior to checkout, an interactive Web page can make suggestions to the shopper about items that he or she might like to see, such as what other customers who bought the same item also purchased.

Some Internet retailers, like Overstock.com, are able to personalize promotions and homepages on the basis of several attributes tied to the shopper's current or previous Web sessions, such as the time of day, time zone as determined by a computer's Internet address, and assumed gender.[18] Overstock.com claims it can determine a shopper's gender after about five to ten clicks. Using this information, a retailer can target promotions for collectables to those who have previously searched for similar merchandise or deals on down parkas to those living in colder climates. It can also test the effectiveness of different promotions in real time. For instance, if a 5 percent discount works better than $5 off, it will stick with the more successful promotion.

Selling Merchandise with "Touch-and-Feel" Attributes   When you buy products, some critical information might include "look-and-see" attributes, like color, style, and grams of carbohydrates, or "touch-and-feel" attributes, like how the shirt fits, the ice cream flavor tastes, or the perfume smells. Fit can only be predicted well if the apparel has consistent sizing and the consumer has learned over time which size to buy from a particular brand. Due to the problems of providing touch-and-feel information, apparel retailers experience return rates of more than 20 percent on purchases made through an electronic channel but only 10 percent for purchases made in stores.

Role of Brands   Brands provide a consistent experience for customers that helps overcome the difficulty of not being able to touch and feel merchandise prior to purchase online. Because consumers trust familiar brands, products with important touch-and-feel attributes, such as clothing, perfume, flowers, and food, with well-known name brands sell successfully through nonstore channels including the Internet, catalogs, and TV home shopping.

Consider branded merchandise like Nautica perfume or Levi's 501 jeans. Even though you can't smell a sample of the perfume before buying it, you know that it will smell like your last bottle when you buy it electronically because the manufacturer of Nautica makes sure each bottle smells the same. Similarly, if you wear size 30-inch waist/32-inch inseam Levi's 501 jeans, you know the pair you order electronically will still fit.

The retailer's brand can also provide information about the consistency and quality of merchandise. For example, consumers might be reluctant to buy produce using an electronic channel because they cannot see the fruits and vegetables before purchasing. However, the same consumers would likely feel comfortable buying fruit from Harry & David catalogs or its Internet site, because Harry & David has established a strong reputation for selling only the highest quality fruit. Retailing View 3.2 describes how Blue Nile sells high-priced diamonds over the Internet and thus is making traditional jewelry stores very nervous.

Using Technology   Retailers with electronic channels are using technology to convert touch-and-feel information into look-and-see information that can be communicated through the Internet. Web sites are going beyond offering the basic image to giving customers the opportunity to view merchandise from different angles and perspectives using 3D imaging and/or zoom technology. JCPenney.com has a new interactive shopping tool, for instance, that lets shoppers mix and match 142,000 combinations of window treatments in visual room settings to preview how a particular choice might look at home.[20] The use of these image-enhancing technologies has increased **conversion rates** (the percentage of consumers who buy the product after viewing it) and reduced returns.

To overcome the limitations associated with trying on clothing, apparel retailers have started to use virtual models on their Web sites. These virtual models enable consumers to see how selected merchandise looks on an image with similar proportions to their own and then rotate the model so the "fit" can be evaluated from all angles. The virtual models are either selected from a set of "prebuilt" models or, as H&M (www.hm.com) does, constructed on the basis of the shopper's response to questions about his or her height, weight, facial, leg, and other body dimensions. At MyShape.com and Zafu.com, consumers respond to a series of questions about their bodies' shape.[21] On the basis of the answers, the site recommends the best-fitting clothing. Landsend.com was among the first to offer custom clothing, such as jeans and khakis featuring selected details like type of wash, rise, and leg shape. At Timberland.com, customers can design custom boots in a variety of colors, monograms, sole colors, and stitching.

Not too long ago, most people believed that consumers would only buy staple items, such as books or CDs, over the Internet. Clearly they were wrong. Today, many products that experts believed were too personal, too unique, too expensive, or too difficult to visualize or assess in terms of their fit or touch-and-feel quality are being successfully sold on the Internet. Blue Nile (www.bluenile.com), the second largest seller of diamond rings, behind only Tiffany's, is one of the companies making those experts eat their words. Blue Nile is an Internet-only jewelry company that mainly sells diamond engagement rings. They are the leading seller of diamonds in the bridal and engagement category.

Buying a diamond in general and an engagement ring in particular is not something that people do everyday. Diamonds are particularly difficult to buy because their value is difficult for ordinary people to

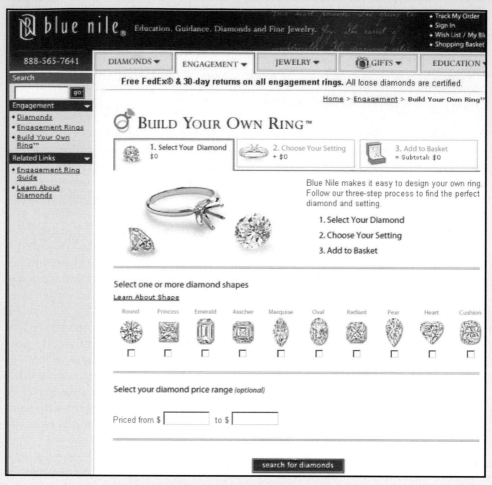

Blue Nile takes the "black box" and risk out of buying a diamond.

assess. Furthermore, some traditional jewelers can put off customers with their pretentious settings and touch of snobbishness. Blue Nile therefore took on the traditional jeweler by providing easy-to-understand educational information about diamonds, eliminating the sometimes alienating store environment, and reducing the risk of purchasing the hard-to-value, generally expensive product by providing a comprehensive warranty and return policy.

Founder Mark Vadon discovered the hassle of buying a diamond ring when he took a trip to Tiffany & Co. Because he was casually dressed in a t-shirt and shorts, the salespeople ignored him at first and eventually were not very helpful. As one salesperson said to him, "Buy the one that speaks to you," Vadon, who like many men did not know the first thing about diamonds, found the statement absurd.

Vadon decided to do some research online and ended up purchasing a comparable diamond to the one Tiffany & Co was offering for about half of the price. This experience in turn made him realize the potential for a good online diamond jewelry store. He decided to buy the very Internet company from which he had purchased his diamond.

Blue Nile makes buying a diamond easy. The Web site educates customers about the cut, clarity, shape, weight, color, and certification of diamonds so that they are better positioned to choose an appropriate stone. A customer can "Build Your Own Ring" by first choosing the shape of diamond and then the clarity, size, and color, as well as the setting. The Web site clearly shows, in a grid format, the price differences as each dimension of the diamond improves. For example, a 3-carat, "fair" quality diamond may be less expensive than a 2-carat, "very good" quality diamond. The GIA (Gemological Institute of America) report that certifies the quality of diamonds also appears on the Web site for viewing before a customer purchases the diamond.

The average diamond sells for $5,500 on Blue Nile, which is twice as much as the industry average of $2,700. Everyday, a ring sells for $20,000 to $40,000, and quite a few sell for more than $50,000. Blue Nile also offers free shipping and delivers in a timely manner.

Sources: www.bluenile.com (accessed June 18, 2007); Gary Rivlin, "When Buying a Diamond Starts With a Mouse," *The New York Times*, January 7, 2007.

Many retailers, like H&M, use virtual models on their Web site to let customers "try on" apparel before they buy it.

Gifts   In some situations, touch-and-feel information might be important, but the information in a store is not much better than the information provided electronically. For example, suppose you're buying a bottle of perfume for your mother. Even if you go to the store and smell the samples of all the new scents, you might not get much information to help you determine which one your mother would like. In this situation, stores offer little benefit over an electronic channel in terms of useful information provided about the merchandise. But buying gifts electronically offers the benefit of saving you the time and effort of packing and sending the gift to your mother. For this reason, gifts represent a substantial portion of sales made through the Internet channel.

Services   Some service retailers have been very successful over the Internet, because the look-and-see attributes of their offering can be presented very effectively online. For example, REI Adventures (www.rei.com/adventures/) is a subsidiary of REI, the multichannel outdoor sporting goods retailer. You can shop for trips by location, activity, or specialty, such as family, private departures, women, and youth. The site provides biographies of the tour guides in each region and vivid descriptions that make you want to pack your bags and go. Diningin.com (www.diningin.com), available in Boston, Chicago, Dallas, and Philadelphia, delivers food from a variety of restaurants directly to your door. You provide the address and the preferred delivery time; it provides you with a list of restaurants available in your area. You select the restaurant and the items, provide credit card information, and then wait for your meal.

Using the Internet to Improve Multichannel Shopping Experience[23]   An electronic channel can provide valuable insights into how and why customers shop and are dissatisfied or satisfied with their experiences. For example, information on how customers shop a merchandise category would be useful for designing a store or a Web site.

The store and Web site layouts need to reflect whether customers shop by brands, size, color, or price point. Customer willingness to substitute one brand for another, for example, is valuable information for assortment planning. To

REFACT

Consumers are still largely reluctant to buy clothing online, at least compared with products like computers. They made only 8 percent of all apparel purchases on the Web, compared with 41 percent of computers, 21 percent of books, and 15 percent of baby gifts. However, apparel sales are one of the fastest growing categories for Interent purchases.[22]

collect this information from store or catalog shoppers would be quite difficult; someone would have to follow them around the store or observe them going through catalog pages. However, collecting data as customers navigate through a Web site is quite easy.

Perceived Risks in Electronic Shopping   Although most consumers have had the opportunity to try out electronic shopping, they also have some concerns about buying products through an electronic channel. The two critical perceived

3.3   RETAILING VIEW   Recreational Equipment Inc. (REI)—A Leader in Multichannel Retailing

In 1938, mountain climbers Lloyd and Mary Anderson joined with 21 fellow northwestern climbers to found Recreational Equipment Inc. (REI) so that high-quality, European ice axes and climbing equipment could be purchased locally. REI develops its own outdoor gear and apparel in addition to selling national brands. Products are evaluated in one of the industry's most complete quality assurance labs and tested extensively in the most important laboratory of them all: the outdoors. REI's product quality assurance team is made up of avid outdoor people who test products in all types of conditions.

The company, based in Kent, Washington, is a 90-store category specialist in the outdoor gear and clothing market. Its stores provide an exciting place for outdoor enthusiasts to shop. For example, the Seattle flagship store has a 65-foot, freestanding climbing rock; mountain bike trails; camp stove demonstration tables; and "rain rooms" so customers can test all their equipment before buying it. REI also sells merchandise domestically and internationally through catalogs and its Web site (www.rei.com). The company operates REI Adventures, a full-service travel agency for outdoor adventures, as well as an outlet store through its Web site.

REI was a pioneer in electronic retailing when, in 1996, it started selling merchandise over the Internet. The Internet offered a way for REI to "deliver any product, any time, any place, and answer any question":

- *Any product:* a larger selection on the Internet.
- *Any time:* 24 hours/seven days a week.
- *Any place:* Internet/stores/catalog, domestic and international.
- *Any question:* rich product information on the Web.

By using all three channels synergistically, REI increases its sales to customers. For example, 35 percent of the products

Customers at REI get to enjoy the excitement of rock climbing and trying the equipment when visiting the store. This experience cannot be duplicated with the retailer's other retail channels.

and more than 40 percent of the sale products bought over the Internet are picked up in stores. When customers come to pick up their orders, they end up spending $70–85 buying additional merchandise.

REI brings the Internet into its stores by linking its point-of-sale (POS) terminals to the Internet. Through the connection, cashiers gain Internet access and additional product-search functionality. Because the in-store kiosks are linked to the Internet, even its smallest stores are able to offer the company's full assortment.

REI also uses its Web site to build loyalty by creating a community of outdoor enthusiasts who, through dozens of message boards, exchange stories about their adventures, seek guidance on products, and post snapshots of their travels. The site also includes primers written by expert users, covering topics such as how to choose gear and what to do "If You Become Lost."

Sources: www.rei.com (accessed June 15, 2007); "R.E.I.," http://en.wikipedia.org/wiki/R.E.I. (accessed June 15, 2007); Jordan K. Speer, "REI Continues Its Transformation with PLM," *Apparel Magazine* 47, no. 8 (2006).

risks are (1) the security of credit card transactions on the Internet and (2) potential privacy violations. Although many consumers remain concerned about credit card security, extensive security problems have been rare. Almost all retailers use sophisticated technologies to encrypt communications.[24] In 2006 however, the security encryption systems for TJX companies (owners of Marshall's and TJ Maxx) were hacked, exposing 45.7 million credit and debit cards to theft. As a result, customers are leery, and banks are suing the retailer for neglecting to encrypt this secure information properly.[25]

Consumers also are concerned about the ability of retailers to collect information about their purchase history, personal information, and search behavior on the Internet. Consumers may be worried about how this information will be used in the future. Will it be sold to other retailers, or will the consumer receive unwanted promotional materials online or in the mail? Issues related to privacy, and the steps that retailers are taking to allay these concerns, are discussed in more detail in Chapter 11.

REFACT

Since 2005, more than 150 million credit card records have been compromised. If each of the 150 million compromised records represented one discrete person, the number would constitute nearly half the U.S. population.[26]

EVOLUTION TOWARD MULTICHANNEL RETAILING

Traditional store-based and catalog retailers are placing more emphasis on their electronic channels and evolving into multichannel retailers for four reasons. First, the electronic channel gives them an opportunity to overcome the limitations of their primary existing format. Second, by using an electronic channel, retailers can reach out to new markets. Third, providing a multichannel offering builds "**share of wallet**," or the percentage of total purchases made by a customer from that retailer. Fourth, an electronic channel enables retailers to gain valuable insights into their customers' shopping behavior.   Loyalty card

Retailing View 3.3 illustrates how REI, a chain that sells outdoor equipment and apparel, uses all three channels to interact with its customers.

REFACT

Forty-one percent of North American households shop online at least once a month. By 2010, this level is expected to reach 61 percent.[27]

Overcoming the Limitations of an Existing Format

One of the greatest constraints facing store-based retailers is the size of their stores. The amount of merchandise that can be displayed and offered for sale in stores is limited. By blending stores with Internet-enabled kiosks, retailers can dramatically expand the assortment offered to their customers. For example, Wal-Mart and Home Depot have a limited number of major appliance floor models in their stores, but customers can used a Web-enabled kiosk to look at an expanded selection of appliances, get more detailed information, and place orders.

Another limitation that store-based retailers face is inconsistent execution. The availability and knowledge of sales associates can vary considerably across stores or even within a store at different times during the day. This inconsistency is most problematic for retailers selling new, complex merchandise. For example, consumer electronic retailers such as Best Buy find it difficult to communicate the features and benefits of the newest products to all of their sales associates. To address this problem, Best Buy installed kiosks designed to be used by sales associates and customers to obtain product information.

A catalog retailer also can use its electronic channel to overcome the limitations of its catalog. Once a catalog is printed, it cannot be updated with price changes and new merchandise. Therefore, Lands' End uses its Internet site to provide customers with real-time information about stock availability and price reductions on clearance merchandise.

REFACT

Fifty-one percent of consumers research online and then go offline to buy. Decisions regarding consumer electronics, home décor, and appliances are most likely to be purchased in this manner.[28]

Expanding Market Presence
Adding an electronic channel is particularly attractive to firms with strong brand names but limited locations and distribution.

For example, retailers such as Harrod's, Henri Bendel, IKEA, and Neiman Marcus are widely known for offering unique, high-quality merchandise, but they require customers to travel to England or major U.S. cities to buy many of the items they carry. Interestingly, most of these store-based retailers currently are multichannel retailers through their successful catalog offerings. Retailing View 3.4 illustrates how small retailers can also expand their markets using the Internet.

3.4 RETAILING VIEW   Zingerman's: Yesterday Ann Arbor, Today the World

Zingerman's (www.zingermans.com) began simply as a delicatessen in Ann Arbor, Michigan, and has grown its business through its Internet and catalog channels to $30 million a year. Its businesses now include:

Zingerman's Bakehouse (www.zingermansbakehouse.com),

Zingerman's Roadhouse (www.zingermansroadhouse.com),

Zingerman's Creamery (www.zingermanscreamery.com),

Zingerman's Coffee Company (www.zingermanscoffee.com),

Zingerman's Training (www.zingtrain.com),

Zingerman's Catering (www.zingermanscatering.com), and

Zingerman's Delicatessen (www.zingermansdeli.com).

It is considering plans to add a microbrewery, a small hotel, a fish- and meat-smoking business, and a publishing house.

The local deli, which focuses on high-quality products, with friendly employees to service customers, has been a foundation for the multiple businesses that the company has developed into one brand. The deli offers New York–style sandwiches that cost $10.99 for a Reuben, $9.50 for a B.L.T., or $7.99 for a bacon, cheddar, and ketchup hot dog. The company imports unique foods, like meats from a specialty California producer, Niman Ranch; cheeses from Europe; honeys from France; vinegars and olive oils from Italy—and hosts an entire wall of olive oils. It also makes its own breads at Zingerman's Bakehouse.

The Web sites are as exciting as its stores. Along with its posted nutrition facts for each product, the site posts a pop-up window with a message from the owner: "We confess, Yes, it's true: at Zingerman's Bakehouse, we like to know the fat in our baked goods. Our pastries are made with a bunch of really good butter, plenty of heavy cream, hand-ladled cream cheese from Zingerman's Creamery, thick farm-fresh sour cream, lots of freshly-cracked whole eggs, and all sorts of other known-fat ingredients."

The Web sites also are clearly laid out and easy to navigate, which enables them to emulate the friendly service that the company has in its store with an immature font, bright colors, and almost child-like atmosphere.

Although it has grown to be more well known and appreciated throughout the country than in southeast Michigan, Zingerman's remains committed to its roots on Detroit Street. It has 545 employees, but its focus stays on maintaining localized atmosphere even as it grows internationally.

Sources: www.zingermans.com (accessed June 18, 2007); Micheline Maynard, "A Corner Deli with International Appeal," *The New York Times*, May 3, 2007.

Before the Internet, Zingerman's was unknown outside of Ann Arbor, Michigan. Today it sells over $30 million per year through its Internet, catalog, and store channels.

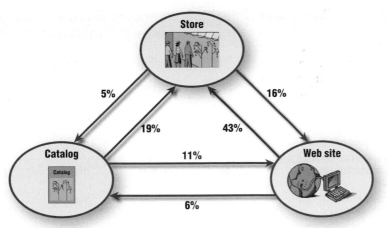

SOURCE: *Statistical Fact Book 2004* (Washington, DC: Direct Marketing Association, 2004), p. 131. Used by permission.

Percentage indicates proportion of customers browsing in one channel and purchasing in another.

EXHIBIT 3–4
Percentage of Cross-
Channel Shoppers

REFACT

The luxury retailer Neiman Marcus claims that its multi-channel customers spend 3.6 times more than single-channel customers do.[30]

USE 3 diff typo increase sales

Increasing Share of Wallet[29]   Although offering an electronic channel may lead to some cannibalization, using it synergistically with other channels can result in consumers making more total purchases from a retailer. Exhibit 3–4 illustrates the multichannel shopping behavior of customers. Forty-three percent of customers visiting a retailer's Web site and 19 percent of those looking at a retailer's catalog make purchases in the retailer's store. Thus, the electronic and catalog channels drive more purchases to the stores, and the stores drive more purchases to the Web site.

Traditional single-channel retailers can use one channel to promote the services offered by other channels. For example, the URL of a store's Web site can be advertised on in-store signs, shopping bags, credit card billing statements, POS receipts, and the print or broadcast advertising used to promote the stores. The physical stores and catalogs are also advertisements for all of the retailer's channels. The retailer's electronic channel can be used to stimulate store visits by announcing special store events and promotions. Store-based retailers can leverage their stores to lower the cost of fulfilling orders and processing returned merchandise if they use the stores as "warehouses" for gathering merchandise for delivery to customers. Customers also can be offered the opportunity to pick up and return merchandise at the retailer's stores rather than pay shipping charges. Many retailers will waive shipping charges when orders are placed online or through the catalog if the customer physically comes in the store.

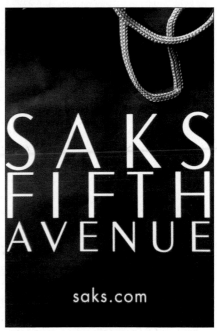

Saks Fifth Avenue, a multichannel retailer, uses its shopping bags to promote its Internet channel.

CAPABILITIES NEEDED FOR MULTICHANNEL RETAILING

As we noted in Chapter 2, in the late 1990s, there was a large group of new Internet-only retailers that ultimately failed. As a result, many traditional retailers and catalog firms moved into electronic retailing very cautiously. Today, electronic retailing activity is not controlled by Internet-only retailers but rather by retailers that have their roots in either traditional stores or catalogs. These traditional retailers have found that substantial opportunities exist for growing their businesses by integrating the electronic channel into their operations and becoming multichannel retailers. These retailers also recognize than an electronic channel can complement and even enhance their traditional channel, and thus, they are no longer concerned that one channel will cannibalize another.[31]

EXHIBIT 3–5
Capabilities Needed for
Multichannel Retailing

Capabilities	Store-Based Retailers	Catalog Retailers	Niche Retailers	Merchandise Manufacturers
Develop assortments and manage inventory	High	High	Low	Low
Manage people in remote locations	High	Low	Low	Low
Efficiently distribute merchandise to stores	High	Low	Low	High
Present merchandise effectively in a printed format and distribute catalogs	Medium	High	Low	Low
Present merchandise effectively on a Web site	Medium	High	High	Low
Process orders from individual customers electronically	Medium	High	High	Low
Efficiently distribute merchandise to homes and accept returns	Medium	High	Low	Low
Integrate information systems to provide a seamless customer experience across channels	Low	Medium	High	Low

To effectively operate and realize the benefits of multichannel retailing, firms need to have the skills to (1) develop assortments and manage inventory—the basic merchandise management activities; (2) manage store operations including managing employees in distant locations; and (3) distribute merchandise efficiently from distribution centers to stores; (4) undertake nonstore retail activities, including presenting merchandise in both catalogs and Web sites; (5) process orders from individual customers electronically; (6) efficiently distribute individual orders to homes and accept returns; and (7) integrate information systems to provide a seamless customer experience across channels. Some retailer types and merchandise manufacturers are better at these skills than others. Exhibit 3–5 provides an assessment of the degree to which the different types of retailers and merchandise manufacturers possess these skills.[32]

Who Has These Critical Resources?

As indicated in Exhibit 3–5, catalog retailers are best positioned to add an electronic channel offering. They have very efficient systems for taking orders from individual customers, packaging the merchandise ordered for shipping, delivering the shipments, and handling returned merchandise. They also have extensive information about their customers and the database management skills needed to personalize their service effectively. For example, many catalog retailers presently have systems that their telephone operators use to search their customer databases and make suggestions for complementary merchandise. Finally, the visual merchandising skills necessary for preparing catalogs are similar to those needed to set up an effective Web site.

Store-based and catalog retailers both are ideally suited to offer assortments and efficiently manage merchandise inventories. Typically, they have more experience and greater skills in putting together merchandise assortments, a skill that most manufacturers and specialty retailers lack. In addition, store-based and catalog retailers typically have more credibility than manufacturers to suggest merchandise to customers because they offer an assortment of brands from multiple suppliers. These traditional retailers also have relationships with vendors, purchasing power, and information/distribution systems in place to manage the supply chain from vendors to distribution centers. However, most store-based retailers and manufacturers lack the appropriate systems for shipping individual orders to households. Their distribution center systems are designed to fill large orders from retail firms or stores and deliver truckloads of goods to retailers' distribution centers or stores. However, store-based retailers with broad market coverage can use their stores as convenient places for Internet shoppers to pick up their merchandise and return unsatisfactory purchases.

Whereas specialty retail entrepreneurs at one time were highly valued by investors, Exhibit 3–5 suggests that most of them do not possess sufficient resources to evolve into multichannel retailers. These niche retailers were immersed in Internet technology and had considerable skills in designing Web sites and developing systems to manage transactions. They also had the opportunity to exploit this unique interactive feature of the Internet, but they lacked the brand recognition and retailing skills necessary to create consumer trust, build merchandise assortments, manage inventory, and fulfill small orders to households.

To illustrate the skills that a traditional store and catalog retailer has over an electronic only retailer, let's examine the women's specialty apparel chain Talbots. Operating under the brands Talbots and J. Jill, Talbots, Inc. is a leading international specialty retailer, cataloger, and e-tailer of women's, apparel, shoes, and accessories.[34] The combined company operates more than 1,300 stores and circulates approximately 118 million catalogs.

Because Talbots was both a catalog and store-based retailer, it had a natural and relatively easy transition to the Internet. Talbots rates high on each of the issues needed for multichannel retailing in Exhibit 3–5. In particular, its distribution center is set up to handle stores, catalogs, and Internet orders under one roof. After merchandise is received from vendors, it is handled differently depending on whether it is destined to go out in bulk to stores or one at a time to customers. Talbots is particularly adept at integrating the store's image on the Internet. For instance, its signature red doors are transposed to an Internet setting. Each packaged order through the Internet or catalog is wrapped in tissue with the same care one would find in its stores. On the Web site, customers can consult an online style guide offering seasonal fashion tips and articles about how to buy a swimsuit in the right size, the art of layering, and petite sizing. Talbots's commitment to "friendly" service is reinforced by the availability of 24-hour online, personal service.

Will Manufacturers Bypass Retailers and Sell Directly to Consumers?

Disintermediation occurs when a manufacturer sells directly to consumers, bypassing retailers. Retailers are concerned about disintermediation because manufacturers can get direct access to their consumers by establishing a retail site on the Internet. Naturalizer brand shoes and accessories are sold through its Web site (www.naturalizer.com), its own

Talbots retains its inviting red door appearance on its Internet site.

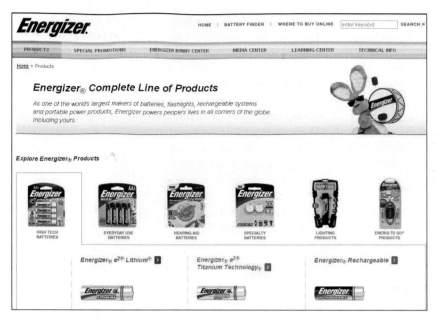

Energizer uses its Web site to provide information about its products but only sells the products through retailers.

stores, and at the same time directly to retailers such as Zappos.com (www.zappos.com) or Macy's.[36] However, Exhibit 3–5 illustrates why most manufacturers are reluctant to engage in retailing.

Manufacturers lack many of the critical skills necessary to sell merchandise electronically, and retailers are typically more efficient in dealing with customers directly than are manufacturers. They have considerably more experience than manufacturers in distributing merchandise directly to customers, providing complementary assortments, and collecting and using information about customers. Retailers also have an advantage because they can provide a broader array of products and services, such as various brands or special offerings, to solve customer problems. For example, if consumers want to buy the components for a home entertainment center from a variety of manufacturers, they must go to several different Internet sites and still cannot be sure that the components will work together or arrive at the same time.

Manufacturers that sell directly to consumers risk losing the support of the retailers they bypass. Therefore, many manufacturers, such as Energizer, the world's largest producer of batteries and flashlights, use its Web site (www.energizer.com) only as a marketing tool to show customers which products that are available and then directing them to nearby stores at which they can purchase the products.[37]

Which Channel Is the Most Profitable?

Many people thought that the electronic channel would enable retailers to sell products at a lower price because they would not have to incur the costs of building and operating stores and compensating sales associates working in those stores. However, the electronic channel involves significant costs to design, maintain, and refresh a Web site; attract customers to the site; maintain distribution systems and warehouses dedicated to selling to individual customers; and deal with a high level of returns. These costs associated with operating an electronic channel may even be greater than the costs of operating physical stores. For example, Amazon.com employs more than 12,000 employees.[38]

ISSUES IN MULTICHANNEL RETAILING

Customers want to be recognized by a retailer, whether they interact with a sales associate or kiosk in a store, log on to the retailer's Web site, or contact the retailer's call center by telephone. At J. Crew, for instance, store associates are trained to greet customers, but it is usually not by name. When contacting a call center, the associate quickly ascertains the customer's name and retrieves the purchasing record. The retailer can address its customers by first name as soon as they log onto its Web page.

However, to provide a consistent image to customers across multiple channels, retailers integrate their customer databases and the systems used to support each

EXHIBIT 3–6
Multichannel Services and
Features

Features/Services	Description
Return policy	Online purchases can be returned in the store
Promotions	Web sites and stores feature offline and online sales, promotions, and events
Information	Customers and sales associates can access the Web site in the store (sometimes through kiosks) to get product and availability information
Selection	Web sites and stores access larger merchandise selection online
Store pick-up	Online orders can be picked up at the local store
Inventory	Web site indicates where inventory is available in the store
Shipping	Free shipping, especially for in-store pick up

channel. In addition to the information technology issues, other critical issues facing retailers that want to provide an integrated, customer-centric offering include brand image, merchandise assortment, and pricing.

Integrated Shopping Experience

When retailers initially went online, they simply displayed products for sale on their Web sites. Now, to get ahead of the competition, multichannel retailers provide features and services that enhance the customer's experience across channels. Some of these features and services are listed in Exhibit 3–6.

Many retailers are still struggling to integrate the shopping experience across all their channels. Legacy systems (first installed long ago) and disconnected customer and inventory databases hamper retailers' ability to maintain consistency across channels. For some large stores with a large array of inventory, it's impossible to mirror online exactly what is offered in stores. This problem is more acute with fashion retailers, because they must maintain adequate inventories to stay in stock on their Internet items. What's more, the expensive technology upgrades are difficult to justify. Online sales still account for such a small fraction of all sales. Many retailers are finding it easier to offer integration one step at a time rather than trying to link everything from the start, which could be financially and technologically daunting for them and alienate consumers if things don't go well.

Brand Image

Multichannel retailers need to project the same image to their customers across all channels. For example, Patagonia reinforces its image of selling high-quality, environmentally friendly sports equipment in its stores, catalogs, and Web site.[39] Patagonia's product descriptions emphasize function, not fashion. It explains its environmental orientation and specific programs in great detail. For instance, it donates time, services, and at least 1 percent of its sales to hundreds of grassroots environmental groups all over the world

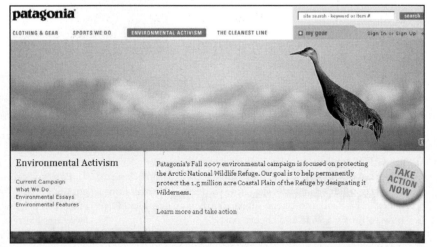

Is Patagonia's online and store image the same?

that work to help reverse the erosion in environmental quality. It explains that it strives to minimize its negative impact on the environment by carefully lighting its stores and using recycled polyester in many of its clothes, as well as only organic, rather than pesticide-intensive, cotton. Its Web log, www.thecleanestline.com, is dedicated to essays and other features on environmental activism, innovative design, and sports. Retailing View 3.5 describes Pottery Barn's different strategy for integrating its brand image across channels.

Merchandise Assortment

Typically, customers expect that most merchandise they see in a retailer's store will also be available on its Web site and vice versa. Significant product overlap across channels reinforces the brand image in the customer's mind. However, the amount of product overlap across channels varies dramatically across retailers. The key is to develop assortments that match customer expectations. Some retailers, like Costco, have little overlap between stores and the Internet site. It might sell some large, bulky items in both places to help customers get them home, or it might stock a sofa at the warehouse and complementary pieces online. But many of the online items are more high-end than the store items. For instance, a good midrange digital camera would appear on store shelves, but the professional model with interchangeable lenses would be at Costco.com.[40] Most multichannel retailers use their Internet channels to expand the assortment they can offer to customers. For example, a typical Staples office supply store sells about 9,000 items, whereas Staples.com has about 50,000 items.

Online can showcase more.

3.5   **RETAILING VIEW**   Living the Pottery Barn Lifestyle

Pottery Barn successfully integrates multiple retailing channels. The home furnishings store, owned by Williams-Sonoma, created a strong brand so that its customers would identify with its "comfortable style" and work it into their lifestyle.

Pottery Barn has 180 stores, along with 90 Pottery Barn Kids stores. It also has a strong catalog and online business. Given that it has many competitors in the home furnishings industry, particularly Crate & Barrel and Restoration Hardware, it must maintain that strong brand across all of its channels to add value for its customers.

Each of its retail channels are integrated so that customers can utilize the stores, the catalogs, and the Web site for more tips, products, and ideas on how to obtain the "Pottery Barn lifestyle." Customers can take the catalogs with them as they run errands or as they relax at home. The catalog has beautiful photographs with products located just as they would look in a home. It also gives interior design advice, like "how to design for small living spaces." The Web site offers similar lifestyle advice, including "how to throw a wine and cheese party."

Its in-store experience continues to connect the customer with the Pottery Barn lifestyle, combining a natural calm environment with comfortable scents and sounds. It is a similar experience to walking through a show house that is perfectly decorated and ready to move in. Pottery Barn e-mails its customers about special store events, such as complementary holiday decorating classes.

The "Pottery Barn lifestyle" is consistently portrayed in its stores, catalogs and Internet site.

Pottery Barn was featured on CBS's *Early Show* in segments entitled "Home Trends for 2007" and "Rugs 101." The company uses each channel to help its customer come a little closer to living this lifestyle. It thus has gone past the point of selling furniture and decorations and become an interior designer and party planner as well.

Sources: www.potterybarn.com (accessed June 18, 2007); "Williams-Sonoma," http://en.wikipedia.org/wiki/Williams-Sonoma (accessed June 19, 2007); Lois Boyle, "Cracking the Multichannel Code: The Brand Experience," *Multichannel Merchant* 3, no. 3 (2007), (accessed December 24, 2007.)

Pricing

Pricing represents another difficult decision for a multichannel retailer. Customers expect pricing consistency across channels (excluding shipping charges and sales tax). However, in some cases, retailers need to adjust their pricing strategy because of the competition they face in different channels. For example, Barnes & Noble.com offers lower prices through its electronic channel than its stores to compete effectively against Amazon.com.

Retailers with stores in multiple markets often set different prices for the same merchandise to deal with differences in local competition. Typical customers do not realize these price differences because they are only exposed to the prices in their local markets. However, multichannel retailers may have difficulties sustaining these regional price differences when customers can easily check prices on the Internet. Some retailers, such as Staples, are able to offer their Internet customers different prices in different markets by asking their online customers for their zip code and screens with unique prices for that zip code.

In conclusion, there is a growing expectation among customers that they should be able to interact with retailers anytime, anywhere, any place and that the retailer should recognize them and their transaction history, regardless of the channel used to contact the retailer. Multichannel retailers face a difficult challenge in providing the seamless interface that their customers expect. While the Internet channel continues to grow at a healthy pace, that growth has slowed in recent years. In the next section, we take a look into the future of Internet shopping.

SHOPPING IN THE FUTURE

The following hypothetical scenario illustrates the seamless interface across channels that customers in the future may experience.

Shopping Experience

It's Tuesday morning, and Judy Jamison is eating breakfast thinking about buying a new dress for the party she'll be attending this Friday night at the new club downtown. She logs onto her laptop, accesses her personal shopper program called FRED, and has the following interactive dialog:

Fred: Do you wish to browse, go to a specific store, or buy a specific item?

Judy: Specific item.

Fred: Item? [Menu appears and Judy selects.]

Judy: Dress.

Fred: Type of dress? [Menu appears.]

Judy: Cocktail dress.

Fred: Price range? [Menu appears.]

Judy: $75–$100.
[Now FRED goes out and literally shops the world electronically, visiting the servers for companies selling cocktail dresses in Europe, Asia, Africa, Australia, and North and South America.]

Fred: 1,231 items have been identified. How many do you want to review?
[Menu appears.]

Judy: Just 5
[FRED selects the five best alternatives on the basis of information it has about Judy's style preferences. The five cocktail dresses appear on the screen with the price, brand name, and retailer listed beneath each one. Judy clicks on each dress to get more information about it. With another click, she sees a full-motion video of a woman who looks similar to Judy modeling the dress. She selects the dress she finds most appealing.]

However, Judy decides not to buy the dress because she wants to wear it tonight. She likes the Robert Rodriguez styles FRED found, so she goes to Brand-Habit.com, types in the designer and her zip code, and finds the closest store that carries his designs.[41] The site directs her to the store's Web site to look at more dresses; she decides to visit the store after work.

Shortly after Judy walks into the store, a chip in her credit card signals her presence and status as a frequent shopper to a PDA (personal digital assistant) held by the store sales associate responsible for preferred clients. Information about items in which Judy might be interested, including the items she viewed on the Web site through FRED, is downloaded from the store server to Judy's and the sales associate's PDAs.

A sales associate approaches Judy and says, "Hello, Ms. Jamison. My name is Joan Bradford. How can I help you?" Judy tells the associate she needs to buy a dress for a party. She has seen some dresses on the store's Web site and would like to look at them in the store. The sales associate takes Judy to a virtual dressing room.

In the dressing room, Judy sits in a comfortable chair and views the dresses displayed on her image, which has been drawn from a body scan stored in Judy's customer file. Information about Judy's recent visit to the retailer's Web site and past purchases is used to select the dresses displayed.

Using her PDA, Judy shares this personalized viewing with her friend, who is still at work in California. They discuss which dress looks best on Judy. Then using her PDA again, Judy drills down to find more information about the dress—the fabric, cleaning instructions, and so forth. Finally, she selects a dress and purchases it with one click.

Using information displayed on her PDA, the sales associate Joan suggests a handbag and scarf that would complement the dress. These accessories are added to the image of Judy in the dress. Judy decides to buy the scarf but not the handbag. Finally, Judy is told about the minor alterations needed to make the dress a perfect fit. She can check the retailer's Web site to find out when the alterations are completed and then indicate whether she wants the dress delivered to her home or if she will pick it up at the store.

As Judy passes through the cosmetics department on her way to her car, she sees an appealing new lipstick shade. She purchases the lipstick and a three-ounce bottle of her favorite perfume and walks out of the store. The store systems sense her departure, and the merchandise she has selected is automatically charged to her account by sensing an RFID (radio frequency identification) chip on the merchandise and her credit card.

Supporting the Shopping Experience

This scenario illustrates the advantages of having a customer database shared by all channels and integrated across all systems. The sales associate and the store systems are able to offer superior customer service based on this database, which contains information about Judy's body scan image, her interaction with the retailer's Web site, and her past purchases and preferences. The technology also supports the retailer's business model, which promises to offer customers the products and services that will provide the best shopping experience.

Judy's interest in buying a new dress was stimulated by an upcoming event, but before she went into the store, she interacted with a search engine to find where the particular brand and product she was looking for could be found. She then interacted with the retailer's Web site to review the available merchandise before she went to the store, check the status of her alterations, and decide about having the merchandise delivered to her home. The scenario also includes some new technologies that will exist in the store of the future, such as RFID, self-checkout, and personalized virtual reality displays.

SUMMARY

Traditional store-based and catalog retailers are adding electronic channels and evolving into integrated, customer-centric, multichannel retailers. This evolution toward multichannel retailing has been driven by the increasing desire of customers to communicate with retailers anytime, anywhere, anyplace.

Each of the channels (stores, catalogs, and Web sites) offers unique benefits to customers. The store channel enables customers to touch and feel merchandise and use the products immediately after they are purchased. Catalogs enable customers to browse through a retailer's offering anytime and anyplace. A unique benefit offered by the electronic channel is the opportunity for consumers to search across a broad range of alternatives, develop a smaller set of alternatives based on their needs, get specific information about the alternatives they want, and make an order with a few clicks.

By offering multiple channels, retailers overcome the limitations of each channel. Thus, Web sites can be used to extend the geographical presence and assortment offered by the store channel, communicate promotions, educate consumers, and provide an intimate link between the retailer and the customer. Stores can be used to provide a multiple sensory experience and an economical method of getting merchandise to both stores and Internet customers.

The type of merchandise sold most effectively through the Internet channel depends on shipping costs, shipping time, the degree to which electronic retailers can provide prepurchase information that helps customers determine whether they will be satisfied with the merchandise, and their customer service return policies to lessen the online risk. The successful use of an electronic channel overcomes its limitations by offering testimonials from other buyers or providing brand, size, and usage information. For consumers who have previously purchased a branded product, brand name alone may be enough information to predict their satisfaction with the purchase decision.

Some critical resources needed for successful multichannel retailing include operating each of the channels efficiently and then having the systems needed to provide a seamless customer experience across channels. Traditional store-based and catalog retailers possess most of these assets and thus are better positioned to evolve into multichannel retailers than are the entrepreneurial electronic retailers that first started using the Internet to reach customers. Widespread disintermediation by manufacturers is unlikely because most manufacturers do not have the capability to distribute merchandise efficiently to individual consumers or provide sufficient assortments.

Providing a seamless interface across channels is challenging for multichannel retailers. Meeting the shopper's expectations will require the development and use of common customer databases and integrated systems. In addition, multichannel retailers will have to make decisions about how to use the different channels to support the retailer's brand image, as well as how to present consistent merchandise assortments and pricing across channels.

KEY TERMS

conversion rate, *79*

cookie, *78*

disintermediation, *87*

magalogs, *74*

multichannel retailer, *72*

online chat, *76*

share of wallet, *83*

social shoppers, *76*

virtual communities, *76*

GET OUT AND DO IT!

1. **CONTINUING CASE ASSIGNMENT:** Assume that you are shopping on the Internet for an item in the same merchandise category you analyzed for the Comparison Shopping exercise in Chapter 2. Go to the retailer's Web site and compare the merchandise assortment offered, the prices, and the shopping experience in the store and on the store's Web site. How easy was it to locate what you were looking for? What were the assortment and pricing like? What was the checkout like? What features of the sites do you like and dislike, such as the look and feel of the site, navigation, special features, and so forth?

2. Go to the Web sites of J. Crew (www. jcrew.com), JCPenney (www.jcp.com), and Lands' End (www.landsend.com) and shop for a pair of khaki pants. Evaluate your shopping experience at each site. Compare and contrast the sites and your experiences on the basis of characteristics you think are important to consumers.

3. Assume that you are getting married and planning your wedding. Compare and contrast the usefulness of www.theknot. com and www.weddingchannel.com for planning your wedding. What features of the sites do you like and dislike? Indicate the specific services offered by these sites that you would use.

4. Go to the Center for Democracy and Technology's homepage at http://www. cdt.org/ and click on Consumer Privacy, then Privacy Guide (http://www.cdt.org/privacy/guide/basic/topten.html). Why is privacy a concern

for Internet shoppers? What are the top ten recommended ways for consumers to protect their privacy online? How many of these recommendations have you employed when using the Internet?

5. Go to the list of the top 50 Internet retailers at http://images10.newegg.com/uploadfilesfornewegg/pressroom/PDFs/IRAnnouncesTop50for2006.pdf. How are these online retailers improving the multichannel shopping experience? Look at the list of Top 50 Retailing Sites. Which of these Internet retailers have you visited in the past? Which would you add to the list? Why should they be included in the list of top retail Web sites?

6. Look up the Estimated Quarterly U.S. Retail Sales: Total and E-commerce, tabulated by the Retail Indicators Branch of the U.S. Census Bureau at http://www.census.gov/mrts/www/ecomm.html. First, using Excel, create a bar graph of the E-Commerce Retail Sales in Millions of Dollars for the past five years. How would you describe the growth trend? Project the E-Commerce Retail Sales for the second quarter of 2008. How did you make this forecast? Second, again using Excel, create a bar graph of the E-Commerce Retail Sales as a Percentage of Total Retail Sales for the past five years. How would you describe the growth trend? Project the E-Commerce Retail Sales as a Percentage of Total Retail Sales for the second quarter of 2008. How did you make this forecast?

7. What information do search engines collect about visitors to their Web sites? Watch the video on You Tube called "Google Privacy: Plain and Simple," available at http://www.youtube.com/watch?v=kLgJYBRzUXY to help you answer this question.

DISCUSSION QUESTIONS AND PROBLEMS

1. Why are store-based retailers aggressively pursuing sales through electronic channels?

2. What capabilities are needed to be an effective multichannel retailer?

3. From a customer's perspective, what are the benefits and limitations of stores? Catalogs? Retail Web sites?

4. Would you buy clothes based upon the way they looked on a customized virtual model? Why or why not?

5. Why are the electronic and catalog channels so popular for gift giving?

6. Should a multichannel retailer offer the same assortment of merchandise for sale on its Web site at the same price as it sells in its stores? Why or why not?

7. Which of the following categories of merchandise do you think could be sold effectively through an electronic channel: jewelry, TV sets, computer software, high-fashion apparel, pharmaceuticals, and health care products such as toothpaste, shampoo, and cold remedies? Why?

8. Assume you are interested in investing in a virtual community targeting people who enjoy active outdoor recreation, such as hiking, rock climbing, and kayaking. What merchandise and information would you offer on the site? What type of a entity do you think would be most effective in running the site: a well-known outdoors person, a magazine targeting outdoor activity, or a retailer selling outdoor merchandise such as Patagonia or REI? Why?

9. Outline a strategy for an electronic-only retail business that is involved in selling merchandise or services in your town. Outline your strategy in terms of your target market and the offering available on your Internet site. Who are your competitors in terms of providing the merchandise or service? What advantages and disadvantages do you have over your competitors?

10. When you shop online for merchandise, how much time do you spend browsing versus buying? When you shop in a store for merchandise, how much time do you spend browsing versus buying? Explain your responses.

SUGGESTED READINGS

Cho, Jinsook. "The Mechanism of Trust and Distrust Formation and their Rational Outcomes." *Journal of Retailing* 82, no. 1 (2006), pp. 25–35.

Dwyer, Paul. "Measuring the Value of Electronic Word of Mouth and Its Impact in Consumer Communities." *Journal of Interactive Marketing* 21, no. 2 (2007), pp. 63–79.

Gopal, Ram D., Bhavik Pathak, and Rvind K. Tripathi. "From Fatwallet to eBay: An Investigation of Online Deal-Forums and Sales Promotions." *Journal of Retailing* 82, no. 2 (2006), pp. 155–64.

Kleijnen, Mirella, Ko De Ruyter, and Martin Wetzels. "An Assessment of Value Creation in Mobile Service Delivery and the Moderating Role of Time Consciousness." *Journal of Retailing* 83, no. 1 (2007), pp. 33–46.

Lewis, Michael. "The Effect of Shipping Fees on Customer Acquisition, Customer Retention, and Purchase Quantities." *Journal of Retailing* 82, no.1 (2006), pp. 13–23.

Lueg, Jason E., Nicole Ponder, Sharon E. Beatty, and Michael L. Capella. "Teenagers' Use of Alternative Shopping

Channels: A Consumer Socialization Perspective." *Journal of Retailing* 82, no. 2 (2006), pp. 137–53.

Mendelsohn, Tamara, Brian Tesch, and Carrie A. Johnson. *Trends 2007: Multichannel Retail.* Cambridge: Forrester, 2007.

Neslin, Scott A., Dhruv Grewal, Robert Leghorn, Venkatesh Shankar, Marije L. Teerling, Jacquelyn S. Thomas, and Peter C. Verhoef. "Challenges and Opportunities in Multichannel Customer Management." *Journal of Service Research* 9, no. 2 (2006), pp. 95–112.

Payn, Yue, and George M. Zinkhan. "Exploring the Impact of Online Privacy Disclosures on Consumer Trust." *Journal of Retailing* 82, no. 4 (2006), pp. 331–38.

Sonneck, Peter, and Cirk Soren Ott. "Future Trends in Multi-channel Retailing." In *Retailing in the 21st Century–Current and Future Trends*, eds. Manfred Kraft and Murali Mantrala. Berlin: Springer, 2006, pp. 176–92.

Weitz, Barton A. "Electronic Retailing." In *Retailing in the 21st Century–Current and Future Trends*, eds. Manfred Kraft and Murali Mantrala. Berlin: Springer, 2006, pp. 309–23.

Customer Buying Behavior

Cynthia Cohen started her career in retailing working in an inner-city supermarket. Prior to founding Strategic Mindshare, she was a Partner in Management Consulting at Deloitte & Touche. She is a member of the Board of Directors for Bebe and Hot Topic. Her consulting firm is known for its insightful research into customer behavior, specifically, inner-city and urban consumers, Hispanic consumers, Speeders, and the various life stages of Boomer women. She discusses some of her research on Generation Y consumers:

EXECUTIVE BRIEFING
Cynthia Cohen, Founder and Chief Executive Officer, Strategic Mindshare

"There are a lot of definitions of the cohort called Generation Y but I think the most useful definition is people born between 1978 to 1989. Our research finds that consumers in this cohort have similar shopping behaviors but they shop differently than their Baby Boomers parents. Generation Yers are the first cohort that is truly techno-savvy. They grew up with the Internet and mobile phones. For this group of consumers, the Yellow Pages isn't relevant. They find out who is selling products they want through the Internet and collect information and make price comparisons from Web sites before they visit stores and buy products. Thus Gen Y consumers are very knowledgeable about products and the retailers selling them.

"While Gen Y consumers are attracted to branded merchandise, they are more adventuresome than their parents. They know what they want and are comfortable mixing and matching products—wearing a top from Target with a scarf from H&M and a Coach handbag. This generation is a driving force behind the growth of masstige—products with prestige appeal but mass market prices. While Gen Yers like their brands, they are quick to switch retailers if the retailer fails to deliver on its brand

CHAPTER 4

QUESTIONS

How do customers make decisions about what retailer to go to and what merchandise to buy?

What social and personal factors affect customer purchase decisions?

How can retailers get customers to visit their stores more frequently and buy more merchandise during each visit?

Why and how do retailers group customers into market segments?

As discussed in Chapter 1, an effective retail strategy satisfies customer needs better than do competitors' strategies. Thus, understanding customer needs and buying behavior is critical for effective retail decision making. Successful retailers have made the customer a priority in every business activity performed. Customers are never an afterthought but always at the forefront of all business decisions.

This chapter focuses on the needs and buying behavior of customers and groups of customers, or market segments. It describes the stages customers go through to purchase merchandise and the factors that influence the buying process. We then use information about the buying process to discuss how consumers can be grouped into market segments.[1] The appendix to this chapter examines special aspects of consumer behavior that concern retailers selling fashion merchandise.

promise—if the quality of its products or the customer service declines.

"But within the Gen Y cohort are two distinct segments—the pre-nesters and nesters. In making the transition from college to the workforce, Gen Yers experience a significant increase in their income; however, pre-nesters and nesters spend this new income in different ways. The pre-nesters haven't married, started a family, or settled down. They spend their disposable income on entertainment, buy big screen TVs, and shop for furniture at IKEA. The nesters, in contrast, are starting a family and buying home furnishing for their first home. However, unlike their parents, nesters view their homes as investments, rather than a place they expect to spend the next twenty years of their life. They want to get into the housing market to build equity for their next home.

"To be successful, retailers need to understand the needs of customers in their target market, what sources of information they use in selecting products and retailers, and how and why they make purchase decisions. But even more important, retailers need to continuously monitor their customers and competitors and be responsive to changes in customer buying behaviors."

THE BUYING PROCESS

The following scenario illustrates the steps consumers go through when purchasing merchandise. Eva Carlyn, a student at the University of Washington, is beginning to interview for jobs. For the first interviews on campus, Eva had planned to wear the blue suit her parents bought her three years ago. But looking at her suit, she realizes that it's not very stylish and that the jacket is beginning to show signs of wear. Wanting to make a good first impression during her interviews, she decides to buy a new suit.

Eva surfs the Internet for tips on dressing for interviews (www.collegegrad.com/jobsearch/Competitive-Interview-Prep/Dressing-for-Interview-Success/ and jobsearch.about.com/od/interviewattire/a/interviewdress.htm) and looks through some catalogs to see the styles and prices being offered. She then decides to go to a retail store so she can try on the suit and have it for her first interview next week. She likes to shop at Abercrombie & Fitch and American Eagle Outfitters, but neither sells business suits. Before going to her favorite mall in Seattle, she goes to BrandHabit.com (www.brandhabit.com), a site that allows her to examine and compare all of the suits currently available at the mall. Armed with a list of possibilities, she goes directly to the stores in the mall that she already reviewed on BrandHabit.com.

She likes to shop with her friend Britt, but Britt is in Paris for the semester. Because she values and wants Britt's opinion, she shares her shopping list with her on Kaboodle.com (www.kaboodle.com).

Eva first wanders into Macy's and is approached by a salesperson in the career women's department. After asking Eva what type of suit she wants and her size, the salesperson shows her three suits. Eva takes photos of the suits with her cell phone and sends them via text message to Britt in Paris. Britt likes all three, so Eva tries them on.

When Eva comes out of the dressing room, she is unsure which suit to select, but after text messaging Britt some more photos, she, Britt, and the salesperson decide the second suit is the most attractive and appropriate for interviewing. Eva is happy with the color, fit, fabric, and length of the suit, but she is concerned that it will require dry cleaning and that she is spending more than she had planned. Eva decides to buy the suit after another customer in the store tells her she looks very professional.

Eva doesn't have a Macy's charge card, so she asks if she can pay with a personal check. The salesperson says yes but notes that the store also takes Visa and MasterCard. Eva decides to pay with her Visa card. As the salesperson walks with Eva to the cash register, they pass a display of scarves. The salesperson stops, picks up a scarf, and shows Eva how well the scarf complements the suit. Eva decides to buy the scarf also.

Consider Eva's shopping trip as we describe the customer buying process. The **buying process,** the steps consumers go through when buying a product or service, begins when customers recognize an unsatisfied need. They seek information about how to satisfy the need, such as what products might be useful and how they can be bought. Customers evaluate the alternative retailers and channels available for purchasing the merchandise, such as stores, catalogs, and the Internet, and then choose a store or Internet site to visit or a catalog to review. This encounter with a retailer provides more information and may alert customers to additional needs. After evaluating the retailer's merchandise offering by weighing both objective and subjective criteria, customers may make a purchase or go to another retailer to collect more information. Eventually, customers make a purchase, use the product, and then decide whether the product satisfies their needs during the postpurchase evaluation stage of the customer buying process.

Exhibit 4–1 outlines the buying process—the stages in selecting a retailer and buying merchandise. Retailers attempt to influence consumers as they go through the buying process to encourage them to buy their merchandise and services. Each stage in the buying process is addressed in the following sections.

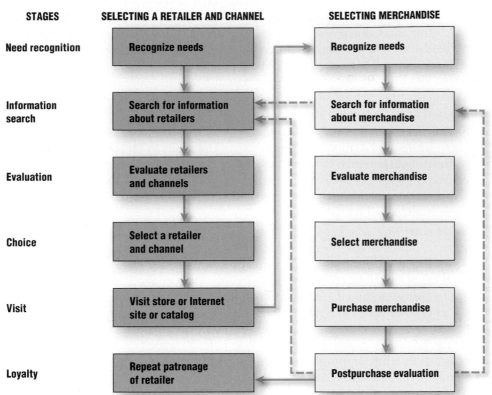

EXHIBIT 4–1
Stages in the Buying
Process

As we discuss the stages in the buying process, you should recognize that customers might not go through the stages in the same order shown in Exhibit 4‡1. For example, imagine that Eva wanted to find a suit that she saw Gabrielle Solis (Eva Longoria) wear on the television show *Desperate Housewives*. In this case, she would search SeenOn.com (www.seenon.com) to find out she could buy it at Banana Republic. Thus, she decides what product she wants and subsequently selects the specific retailer. Alternatively, she might decide she wants to buy a skirt on the Internet, go to a shopping Web site such as Shopping.com (www.shopping.com), and then buy the garment from the retailer that offered the lowest price.

Need Recognition

The buying process is triggered when consumers recognize they have an unsatisfied need. An unsatisfied need arises when a customer's desired level of satisfaction differs from his or her present level of satisfaction. For example, Eva Carlyn recognized that she had a need when she was faced with the prospect of interviewing for jobs in her blue suit. She needed a suit that would make a good impression and realized her worn, outdated blue suit would not satisfy this need. Need recognition can be triggered by realizing you need a haircut, by feeling the need for an uplifting experience after a final exam, or by a message from a Facebook group member about an addition to his or her profile.

Types of Needs   The needs that motivate customers to go shopping and purchase merchandise can be classified as utilitarian or hedonic. When consumers go shopping to accomplish a specific task, such as Eva buying a suit for job interviews, they are seeking to satisfy **utilitarian needs.** When consumers go shopping for pleasure, they are seeking to satisfy their **hedonic needs**[a]their needs for an entertaining, emotional, and recreational experience. Thus, from the consumer's perspective, utilitarian needs are associated with work, whereas hedonic needs are associated with fun.[2]

Successful retailers attempt to satisfy both the utilitarian and hedonic needs of their customers. Consumers motivated by utilitarian needs typically shop in a more deliberate and efficient manner; thus, retailers need to make the shopping experience easy and effortless for them by providing the desired merchandise in a way that can be easily located and purchased. Some hedonic needs that retailers can satisfy include stimulation, social experience, learning new trends, status and power, self-reward, and adventure.[3]

1. *Stimulation.* Retailers and mall managers use background music, visual displays, scents, and demonstrations in stores and malls to create a carnival-like, stimulating experience for their customers. These environments encourage consumers to take a break from their everyday lives and visit stores.[4] Retailers also attempt to stimulate customers with exciting graphics and photography in their catalogs and on their Web sites.[5]

2. *Social experience.* Marketplaces traditionally have been centers of social activity, places where people could meet friends and develop new relationships. Regional shopping malls in many communities have replaced open markets as social meeting places, especially for teenagers. Mall developers are focusing on mixed-use developments to satisfy consumers' need for social experiences. Lifestyle centers are allocating significant space to restaurants, movie theaters, outdoor entertainment, and even condominium living. Barnes & Noble bookstores host cafés in which customers can discuss novels while sipping lattes. Online retailers provide similar social experiences by enabling customers to e-mail products to their friends, create personal blogs with their shopping lists to be shared with other people, or participate in a particular interest-driven forum. For example, visitors to Amazon.com (www.amazon.com) can write reviews and opinions about books they have read and make them available to all potential customers on the Web site.

3. *Learning new trends.* By visiting retailers, people learn about new trends and ideas. These visits satisfy customers' needs to be informed about their environment. For example, teens might go to The Body Shop to learn about new products, as well as ways they can live an environmentally friendly lifestyle. Customers also learn about trends through normal social encounters and surfing the Web.

4. *Status and power.* For some people, a store or a service provider is one of the few places where they get attention and respect. Canyon Ranch offers upscale health resorts in Tucson, Arizona, and Lenox, Massachusetts, as well as spa clubs in Las Vegas, Nevada, and Kissimmee, Florida. All Canyon Ranch resorts and spas make the customer the center of attention, offering spa services, medical and nutritional consultations and workshops, spiritual pursuits, and healthy gourmet cuisine.

5. *Self-reward.* Customers frequently purchase merchandise to reward themselves when they have accomplished something or want to dispel depression. Per-

REFACT

Some people view shopping as a leisure-time activity, just like any other sport. Frequent leisure-time shoppers spend an average of $113.33 per shopping trip, making this segment of consumers one of most profitable and informed. They buy primarily apparel, health and beauty aids, entertainment and leisure items, and electronics.[6]

What type of utilitarian or hedonic need is getting a makeover?

fume, cosmetics, apparel, and jewelry are common self-gifts. Retailers satisfy these needs by, for example, "treating" customers to personalized makeovers while they are in the store.

6. *Adventure*. Often consumers go shopping because they enjoy finding bargains, looking for sales, and finding discounts or low prices. They treat shopping as a game to be "won." Off-price retailers like Marshalls, warehouse clubs like Costco, discount stores like Target, and fast-fashion retailers like Zara cater to this need by constantly changing their assortment so customers never know what kind of treasure they will find.

Conflicting Needs   Most customers have multiple needs. Moreover, these needs often conflict. For example, Eva Carlyn would like to wear a DKNY suit, which would enhance her self-image, earn her the admiration of her college friends, and be appropriate for her upcoming job interviews. But this hedonic need conflicts with her budget and her utilitarian need to get a job. Employers might feel that she's not responsible if she wears a suit that is too expensive for an interview for an entry-level position. Typically, customers make trade-offs between their conflicting needs. Later in this chapter, we will discuss a model of how customers make such trade-offs.

Because needs often cannot be satisfied in one store or by one product, consumers may appear to be inconsistent in their shopping behavior. For example, a skier may purchase expensive Spyder goggles but wear an inexpensive snow suit from Target. A grocery shopper might buy an inexpensive store brand of paper towels and a premium national brand of orange juice like Tropicana. The pattern of buying both premium and low-priced merchandise or patronizing both expensive, status-oriented retailers and price-oriented retailers is called **cross-shopping.**

Although all cross-shoppers seek value, their perception of value varies across product classes. Thus, a cross-shopper might feel it is worth the money to dine at an expensive restaurant but believe there is little quality difference between kitchen utensils at Target and designer brands at a specialty store. Similarly, consumers may cut back on their vacations at costly resorts but still want to treat themselves to expensive, high-quality jams, mustards, and olive oils from the supermarket. Retailers might not be able to discern how the buying patterns of cross-shoppers make sense, but they certainly make sense to their customers.

To stimulate need recognition, the Saks Fifth Avenue store in Manhattan uses its 310 feet of window displays to showcase new merchandise. Each day at lunchtime, about 3,000 people walk by the 31 window displays. Saks produces 1,200 different window displays each year, with the Fifth Avenue windows changing each week.

Stimulating Need Recognition   As we have noted, customers must recognize unsatisfied needs before they are motivated to visit a store or go online to buy merchandise. Sometimes these needs are stimulated by an event in a person's life. For example, Eva's department store visit to buy a suit was stimulated by her impending interview, her examination of her current wardrobe, and her visit to BrandHabit.com. Retailers use a variety of approaches to stimulate problem recognition and motivate customers to visit their stores and buy merchandise. Advertising, Internet promotions, direct mail, publicity, and special events communicate the availability of merchandise or special prices. SeenOn.com (www.seenon.com) stimulates need recognition by showing products that celebrities or television actors have worn. Within the store, visual merchandising and salespeople can stimulate need recognition. For example, the salesperson showed Eva a scarf to stimulate her need for an accessory to complement her new suit.

Information Search

Once customers identify a need, they may seek information about retailers or products to help them satisfy that need. Eva's search started on the Internet, then narrowed to the three suits shown to her by the salesperson at Macy's. She was satisfied with this level of information search because she and her friend Britt had confidence in Macy's merchandise and pricing, and she was pleased with the selection of suits presented to her. More extended buying processes may involve collecting a lot of information, visiting several retailers, or deliberating a long time before making a purchase.[7]

Amount of Information Searched   In general, the amount of **information search** depends on the value customers feel they can gain from searching versus the cost of searching. Consumers will often spend more time searching for information when they have little prior experience with the merchandise category. The value of the search stems from how it improves the customer's purchase decision. Will the search help the customer find a lower-priced product or one that will give superior performance? The costs of search include both time and money. Traveling from store to store can cost money for gas and parking, but the major cost incurred is the customer's time.

Technology can dramatically reduce the cost of information search. For example, NearbyNow.com (www.nearbynow.com) sends promotions to customers' cell phones via a text message and enables them to search their local malls for products and brands via text messages. This way, customers can save time in the search process by going directly to the retailer that sells the desired product.[8] Vast information about merchandise sold across the world is just a mouse click away. Retailing

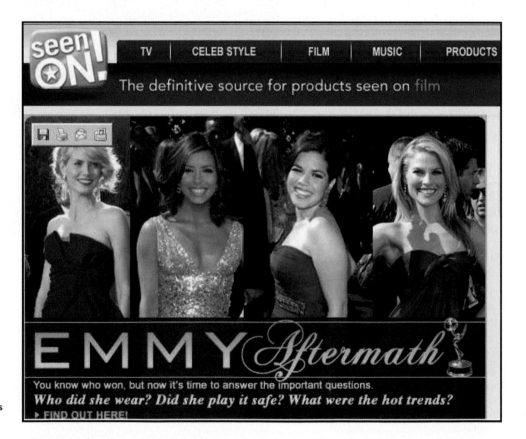

Consumers use Internet sites like SeenOn to search for information about products worn by celebrities and where to buy them.

View 4.1 describes how readily available information on the Web is affecting the automobile buying process.

Factors influencing the amount of information search include (1) the nature and use of the product being purchased, (2) characteristics of the individual customer, and (3) aspects of the market and buying situation in which the purchase is made. Some people search more than others. For example, as we discussed in Chapter 3, social shoppers spend more time shopping than other customers, and do so for the sheer enjoyment of the process and interacting with other potential customers and retailer customer service and sales representatives.[9] Also, customers who are self-confident or have prior experience purchasing and using the product or service tend to search less.

Marketplace and situational factors affecting information search include (1) the number of competing brands and retail outlets and (2) the time pressure under which the purchase must be made. When competition is greater and there are more alternatives to consider, the amount of information search increases. However, the amount decreases as time pressure increases.

Sources of Information   Customers have two sources of information: internal and external. **Internal sources** are information in a customer's memory, such as names, images, and past experiences with different stores. The major source of internal information is the customer's past shopping experience. Eva relied on her memory of an ad when choosing to visit Macy's. Even if they remember only a small fraction of the information to which they are exposed, customers have an extensive internal information bank to draw upon when deciding where to shop and what to buy.

External sources refer to information provided by ads and other people. When customers feel that their internal information is inadequate, they turn to external information sources. Remember how Eva Carlyn asked her friend, Britt, to help her make the purchase decision? External sources of information play a major role in the acceptance of fashions, as discussed in the appendix to this chapter.

The Internet has had a profound impact on consumers' ability to gather external information. If consumers want to search for something specific, they can try specialized search engines such as Like.com (www.like.com).[10] The site relies on artificial intelligence technology to search images on the Web and then serves up goods for sale that visually match items on a shopper's wish list. Visitors to the site can

---

How the Internet Changed the Car Buying Process   **RETAILING VIEW**   **4.1**

Ten years ago, if consumers wanted to buy a car, they would visit several dealers, look at different models, test drive the cars sold by each dealer, and then negotiate price and financing with the dealer. Many consumers viewed this traditional process of buying a car as about as pleasurable as a visit to the dentist. But now the Internet is changing this experience, as well as the nature of automobile retailing.

The Internet is giving consumers more control over the car buying process. Consumers can go to Web sites such as Autobytel.com www.autobytel.com, Cars.com www.cars.com, or Edmunds.com www.edmunds.com; access a wealth of information, including the dealer's costs for cars and options; compare vehicles in a side-by-side chart that lists their price, features, horsepower, mileage, legroom, and options; read multiple reviews for most models; and even take a 360-degree photo tour of car interiors that gives them an idea of what the view looks like from the driver's seat. Through the sites' relationships with car dealers, consumers can request prices from retailers in their area. A handy calculator tells them how much the monthly payment would be if they were to buy a car on credit. The sites also

have calculators to help car buyers figure out how much they can afford to spend on a car, whether they should buy a new or used car, and whether they should lease or buy. This information enables consumers to walk into a dealership knowing as much or more than the dealer's salespeople.

CarFax (www.carfax.com) goes further; it allows customers to gain access to any vehicle's history report by typing in its VIN (vehicle identification number). This history describes any accidents, its past ownership, odometer fraud, and any other events that might show up for a vehicle. Services such as CarFax make it much easier for customers to purchase used cars with confidence.

Sources: www.cars.com (accessed July 9, 2007); www.autobytel.com (accessed July 9, 2007); www.edmunds.com (accessed July 9, 2007); www.carfax.com (accessed July 9, 2007); "Buy Better on the Web," *Consumer Reports* 72, no. 4 (2007), pp. 21–28; Andreas Herrmann, Lan Xia, Kent B. Monroe, and Frank Huber, "The Influence of Price Fairness on Customer Satisfaction: An Empirical Test in the Context of Automobile Purchases," *Journal of Product and Brand Management* 16, no. 1 (2007), pp. 48–49.

search for products in one of two ways. First, they may type in, say, "silver earrings" and receive pages filled with images that match the description, along with prices and links to the product pages of the Web sites on which the items are sold. Second, users may browse through selected items in the wardrobes of about a dozen celebrities, including Scarlett Johansson and Jessica Simpson, and choose, perhaps, the dress that Johansson wore on the cover of *Esquire* magazine. The site then searches for similar dresses, returning more than 5,000 ranging in price from $40 to $8,000.

Two other sites, NearbyNow.com (www.nearbynow.com) and GPShopper.com (www.gpshopper.com), have introduced mobile Internet applications that allow shoppers to use their cellphones and PDAs to search inventory and prices while at a particular mall, saving them wasted time and sometimes turning up last-minute bargains and promotions.[11]

Increasingly, retailers are encouraging their customers to post information on their Web sites too, such as product reviews, ratings, and, in some cases, photos and videos.[12] Consumers can also get product reviews from other consumers on retailer sites like Amazon and Golfsmith (www.golfsmith.com). The result is that customer reviews are emerging as a prime source for online shoppers as they collect information during the buying process.

REFACT

Macys.com adds approximately 350 product reviews a day from customers.[13]

REFACT

Internet retailers' conversion rate, or the percentage of browsers who actually purchase, is only about 3 percent.[14]

Reducing Information Search   The retailer's objective at the information search stage of the buying process is to limit the customer's search to its store or Web site. Each element of the retailing mix can be used to achieve this objective. Category specialists such as Best Buy and Lowe's provide a very deep assortment of merchandise, everything a customer might want in the category, so that the customer can collect all of the information and make the necessary comparisons in their stores or on their Web sites.

Services provided by retailers can also limit search to the retailer's location. The availability of credit and delivery may be important for consumers who want to purchase large durable goods, such as furniture and appliances. Salespeople can provide enough information to customers that they don't feel the need to collect additional information by visiting other stores. For example, most men have no idea how to buy lingerie for their girlfriends or wives and are embarrassed to ask female sales associates. So London's Marks & Spencer department store used several "Stocking Fellas" as a one-time holiday promotion to help them shop for these items.[15] Thanks to the Stocking Fellas, lingerie sales are up, and merchandise returns are down.

Everyday low pricing is another way retailers increase the chance that customers will buy in their store and not search for a better price elsewhere. An **everyday low pricing strategy** maintains the continuity of retail prices at a level somewhere between the regular nonsale price and the deep discount sale price of the retailer's competitors. Wal-Mart and Circuit City have everyday low pricing policies, which makes customers confident that they won't find that merchandise at a lower price at another retailer. Many stores with everyday low pricing offer money-back guarantees if a competitor offers the same merchandise at a lower price. Chapter 15 talks about the benefits and limitations of this and other pricing strategies.

This "Stocking Fella" at U.K.'s Marks & Spencer helped men buy lingerie for their girlfriends or wives at a one-time holiday promotion.

Although retailers hope to confine their customers' information search to their stores and Web sites, they also want to encourage customers to spend as much time shopping in their channels as possible. The more time customers spend shopping, the more they will buy. Stores use food and personal service to create a comfortable environment that encourages customers to keep shopping.[16] For instance, Talbots offers the personal attention of a sales associate, by appointment, along with a light snack. American Eagle Outfitter's Martin + Osa Division, which targets a slightly older audience, serves bottled water and apples. Macy's is expanding its dressing room waiting areas and adding restaurants to some stores. The off-price retailer Stein Mart hires socially networked women to serve iced tea and cookies and provide advice in the higher-end boutique clothing department. Gymboree provides a television playing videos at the back of its stores to keep its youngest customers occupied while their parents shop.

Evaluation of Alternatives: The Multiattribute Model

The multiattribute attitude model provides a useful way to summarize how customers use the information they have and collect about alternative products, evaluate the alternatives, and select the one that best satisfies their needs. We discuss it in detail because it offers a framework for developing a retailing strategy.[18]

The **multiattribute attitude model** is based on the notion that customers see a retailer, a product, or a service as a collection of attributes or characteristics. The model is designed to predict a customer's evaluation of a product, service, or retailer based on (1) its performance on relevant attributes and (2) the importance of those attributes to the customer.

Beliefs about Performance   To illustrate this model, consider the store choice decision confronting a young, single, professional, Milwaukee woman who needs groceries. She considers three alternatives: a supercenter in the next suburb, her local supermarket, or an Internet grocery retailer such as Peapod (www.peapod.com), as compared in Exhibit 4–2.

The customer mentally processes the "objective" information about each grocery retailer in Exhibit 4–2A and forms an impression of the benefits each one provides. Exhibit 4–2B shows her beliefs about these benefits. Notice that some

REFACT

Customers who spend 40 minutes in a store are more than twice as likely to buy as someone who spends 10 minutes, and they typically buy twice as many items.[17]

EXHIBIT 4–2
Characteristics of Food Retailers

A. INFORMATION ABOUT STORES SELLING GROCERIES			
Store Characteristics	**Supercenter**	**Supermarket**	**Internet Grocer**
Grocery prices	20% below average	average	10% above average
Delivery cost ($)	0	0	10
Total travel time (minutes)	30	15	0
Typical checkout time (minutes)	10	5	2
Number of products, brands, and sizes	40,000	30,000	40,000
Fresh produce	Yes	Yes	Yes
Fresh fish	Yes	Yes	No
Ease of finding products	Difficult	Easy	Easy
Ease of collecting nutritional information about products	Difficult	Difficult	Easy

B. BELIEFS ABOUT STORES' PERFORMANCE BENEFITS*			
Performance Benefits	**Supercenter**	**Supermarket**	**Internet Grocer**
Economy	10	8	6
Convenience	3	5	10
Assortment	9	7	5
Availability of product Information	4	4	8

*10 = excellent, 1 = poor.

benefits combine several objective characteristics. For example, the convenience benefit combines travel time, checkout time, and ease of finding products. Grocery prices and delivery cost affect her beliefs about the economy of shopping at the various retail outlets.

The degree to which each retailer provides each benefit is represented on a 10-point scale: 10 means the retailer performs well in providing the benefit; 1 means it performs poorly. Here, no retailer has superior performance on all benefits. The supercenter performs well on economy and assortment but is low on convenience. The Internet grocer offers the best convenience but is weak on economy and assortment.

Importance Weights   The young woman in the preceding example forms an overall evaluation of each alternative on the basis of the importance she places on each benefit the stores provide. The importance she places on a benefit can also be represented using a 10-point rating scale, with 10 indicating the benefit is very important and 1 indicating it's very unimportant. Using this rating scale, the importance of the retailer benefits for the young woman and for a parent with four children are shown in Exhibit 4–3, along with the performance beliefs previously discussed. Notice that the single woman values convenience and the availability of product information much more than economy and assortment. But the parent places a lot of importance on economy, assortment is moderately important, and convenience and product information aren't very important.

The importance of a retailer's benefits differs for each customer and also may differ for each shopping trip. For example, the parent with four children may stress economy for major shopping trips but place more importance on convenience for a fill-in trip.

In Exhibit 4–3, the single woman and parent have the same beliefs about each retailer's performance, but they differ in the importance they place on the benefits the retailers offer. In general, customers can differ in their beliefs about the retailers' performance as well as in their importance weights.

Evaluating Stores   Research has shown that a customer's overall evaluation of an alternative (in this situation, two stores and the Internet channel) relates closely to the sum of the performance beliefs multiplied by the importance weights.[19] Thus, we calculate the young, single woman's overall evaluation or score for the supercenter as follows:

$$
\begin{aligned}
4 \times 10 &= 40 \\
10 \times 3 &= 30 \\
5 \times 9 &= 45 \\
9 \times 4 &= \underline{36} \\
& 151
\end{aligned}
$$

EXHIBIT 4–3
Evaluation of Retailers

	IMPORTANCE WEIGHTS*		PERFORMANCE BELIEFS		
Characteristic	Young Single Woman	Parent with Four Children	Supercenter	Supermarket	Internet Grocer
Economy	4	10	10	8	6
Convenience	10	4	3	5	10
Assortment	5	8	9	7	5
Availability of product information	9	2	4	4	8
OVERALL EVALUATION					
Young single woman			151	153	221
Parent with four children			192	164	156

*10 = very important, 1 = very unimportant.

Exhibit 4–3 shows the overall evaluations of the three retailers using the importance weights of the single woman and the parent. For the single woman, the Internet grocer has the highest score, 221, and thus the most favorable evaluation. Therefore, on the one hand, she would probably select this retailer for most of her grocery shopping. On the other hand, the supercenter has the highest score, 192, for the parent, who'd probably buy the family's weekly groceries there.

Based on the multiattribute analysis, where would you expect the young single woman (left) and the parent with children (right) to shop? The supercenter, the supermarket, or the Internet grocer?

When customers are about to select a retailer, they don't actually go through the process of listing store characteristics, evaluating retailers' performances on these characteristics, determining each characteristic's importance, calculating each store's overall score, and then patronizing the retailer with the highest score! The multiattribute attitude model does not reflect customers' actual decision process, but it does predict their evaluation of alternatives and their choice.[20] In addition, the model provides useful information for designing a retail offering. For example, if the supermarket could increase its performance rating on assortment from 7 to 10 (perhaps by adding a bakery and a wide selection of prepared meals), customers like the parent might shop at the supermarket more often than at the supercenter. Later in this chapter, we'll discuss how retailers can use the multiattribute attitude model to improve their store's evaluation.

The application of the multiattribute attitude model in Exhibit 4–3 deals with a customer who is evaluating and selecting a retail store. The same model can also be used to describe how a customer evaluates and selects which channel to use (store, Internet, or catalog) or what merchandise to buy from a retailer. For example, Exhibit 4–4 shows Eva Carlyn's beliefs and importance weights about the three suits shown to her by the salesperson. Eva evaluated only three suits at one store and bought suit "B" because it met most of her original needs, even though she didn't bother to fully evaluate "A" and "C" by assessing their fit. Its overall

		BELIEFS ABOUT PERFORMANCE		
Benefits Provided by Suits	Importance Weights	Suit A	Suit B	Suit C
Economy	6	6	5	8
Quality	6	10	7	5
Conservative look	8	6	6	10
Complement to wardrobe	8	7	6	9
Fashion	4	7	10	5
Fit	10	?	?	8
Overall evaluation				330

EXHIBIT 4–4
Information Eva Carlyn Used in Buying a Suit

evaluation passed some minimum threshold (which, in terms of this multiattribute attitude model, might be a score of 330).

Customers often make choices as Eva did. They don't thoroughly evaluate all alternatives, as is suggested by the multiattribute attitude model. Instead, they simply buy merchandise that's good enough or very good on one particular attribute. In general, customers don't spend the time necessary to find the very best product. Once they've found a product that satisfies their need, they stop searching.[21]

Implications for Retailers   How can a retailer use the multiattribute attitude model to encourage customers to shop at it more frequently? First, the model indicates what information customers use to decide which retailer to patronize and which channel to use. Second, it suggests tactics that retailers can undertake to influence customer store choices and merchandise selection.

Thus, to develop a program for attracting customers, the retailer must do market research to collect the following information:

1. Alternative retailers that customers consider.
2. Characteristics or benefits that customers consider when evaluating and choosing a retailer.
3. Customers' ratings of each retailer's performance on the characteristics.
4. The importance weights that customers attach to the characteristics.

Armed with this information, the retailer can use several approaches to influence customers to patronize its store or Internet site.

Getting into the Consideration Set   The retailer needs to make sure that it is included in the customer's **consideration set,** or the set of alternatives the customer evaluates when making a selection. To be included in the consideration set, retailers develop programs to increase the likelihood that customers will remember them when they're about to go shopping. Retailers influence this top-of-the-mind awareness through Internet, advertising, and location strategies. They get exposure on search engines like Google or Yahoo by placing ads that are shown on pages related to the search items. Advertising expenditures that stress the retailer's name can increase top-of-the-mind awareness. When a retailer such as Starbucks locates several stores in the same area, customers are exposed more frequently to the store name as they drive through the area.[22]

After ensuring that it is in consumers' consideration set, a retailer can use four methods to increase the chances that customers will select its store for a visit:

1. Increase beliefs about the store's performance.
2. Decrease the performance beliefs for competing stores in the consideration set.
3. Increase customers' importance weights.
4. Add a new benefit.

Changing Performance Beliefs   The first approach involves altering customers' beliefs about the retailer's performance by increasing the retailer's performance rating on a characteristic. For example, the supermarket in Exhibit 4–3 would want to increase its overall rating by improving its rating on all four benefits. The supermarket could improve its rating on economy by lowering prices and its assortment rating by stocking more gourmet and ethnic foods. Retailing View 4.2 illustrates how Lowe's altered the performance beliefs of women for its stores.

Because it can get costly for a retailer to improve its performance on all benefits, retailers must focus on improving their performance on those benefits that are important to customers in their target markets. For example, Best Buy knows that its customers don't want to be without their computers for lengthy amounts of time when they are in need of repair.[23] So it has a 165,000 square-foot "Geek Squad City" warehouse designed to cut the time it takes to repair and return a PC to one to three days. Inside the facility's sprawling repair room, PC parts and precision tools are spread over the rows and rows of desks where hundreds of computer techs—Geek Squad's "agents"—fix more than 2,000 laptops a day. Best Buy recognizes the sizable investment this warehouse requires, but it also believes it is worth it to achieve high ratings on a service attribute that is very important to its customers.

A change in a performance belief about an important benefit results in a large change in customers' overall evaluations. In Exhibit 4–3, the supermarket should attempt to improve its convenience ratings if it wants to attract more young, single women who presently shop on the Internet. If its convenience rating rose from 5 to 8, its overall evaluation among young, single women would increase from 153 to 183 and thus be much higher than their evaluation of supercenters. Note that an increase in the rating from 8 to 10 for a less important benefit, such as economy, would have less effect on the store's overall evaluation. The supermarket might try to improve its rating on convenience by increasing the number of checkout stations, using customer scanning to reduce checkout time, or providing more in-store information so customers could locate merchandise more easily.

Research further suggests that consumers in Germany, France, and the United Kingdom place different weights on three important attributes—price/value, service/quality, and relationships—when selecting a retailer to patronize. German

---

Do It Herself at Lowe's   **RETAILING VIEW**   4.2

You might think that home improvement centers are a retail recreation destination mostly for men. Men visit the stores on the weekends to check out the new tools and buy material for do-it-yourself (DIY) projects. But more than 50 percent of the sales at home improvement centers actually are made to women. Women not only make the decisions about what materials to use for home improvement projects but also end up doing much of the work themselves.

Lowe's was early to recognize the importance of female customers. It redesigned its stores to be brighter, lose the warehouse look, and feature departments more appealing to women. Aisles were widened to help eliminate "butt brush," the uncomfortable contact that can occur as customers navigate narrow, crowded aisles—and something that women particularly dislike.

What has Lowe's done to make its stores and services more appealing to women?

REFACT

The importance of women to retailers has grown in part because more households are headed by women—27 percent at last count, a fourfold increase since 1950.[24]

To make the store feel less intimidating, Lowe's made the shelves shorter and used aisle markers like those in grocery stores, with maps to help customers find products. However, Lowe's needed to balance the performance beliefs and importance weights that women have about their store with those of men. Its male customers might shun stores if they find them too feminine. Yet Lowe's also

found that women held the same negative view of overly feminine home improvement stores, so it decided to teach women about tools rather than carrying tools specifically designed for women. One section of its Web site, www.lowes.com/howto, provides online clinics and videos to help all customers successfully implement their own DIY projects at home.

Sources: John Birger, "Second Mover Advantage," *Fortune*, April 20, 2006, pp. 10–11; Patricia Anstett, "Hammer Time: Women Who Want To Tackle Repairs Around The House Can Get Help From Home Improvement Stores," *Knight Ridder Tribune Business News*, November 4, 2006 (accessed December 24, 2007).

consumers tend to place more weight on price/value, whereas customer service and product quality are more important for French consumers, and affinity benefits such as loyalty cards and preferred customer programs are more important for English consumers. Thus, in general, retailers that emphasize price and good value will be more successful in Germany than in France or the United Kingdom.[25]

Another approach tries to decrease customers' performance ratings of a competing store. This approach may be illegal and usually isn't very effective, because bad-mouthing competitors generally backfires and customers typically don't believe a firm's negative comments about its competitors anyway.

Changing Importance Weights   Altering customers' importance weights is another approach to influencing store choice. A retailer wants to increase the importance customers place on benefits for which its performance is superior and decrease the importance of benefits for which it has inferior performance.

For example, if the supermarket in Exhibit 4–3 tried to attract families who shop at supercenters, it could increase the importance of convenience for them. Typically, changing importance weights is harder than changing performance beliefs, because importance weights reflect customers' personal values.[26]

Adding a New Benefit   Finally, retailers might try to add a new benefit to the set of benefits customers consider when selecting a store. For example, Fair Indigo (www.fairindigo.com), along with other retailers, is adding a new benefit that is important to many consumers: the degree to which the retailer is socially responsible. Fair Indigo emphasizes that the apparel sold through its multiple channels is made by workers who are paid a fair wage, not just a minimum wage. A fair wage means that workers are able to live relatively comfortably within the context of their local area, with enough money for housing, food, health care, education for their children, and some disposable income. To get a high evaluation on this new benefit, Fair Indigo handpicked the most ethical factories around the globe to make its apparel.[27] The approach of adding a new benefit is often effective, because it's easier to change customer evaluations of new than of old benefits.

Purchasing the Merchandise or Service

Customers don't always purchase a brand or item of merchandise with the highest overall evaluation. The product or service offering the greatest benefits (having the highest evaluation) may not be available in the store, or the customer may feel that its risks outweigh the potential benefits. One measure of retailers' success at converting positive evaluations to purchases is the number of real or virtual abandoned carts in the retailer's store and Web site.

Retailers use various tactics to increase the chances that customers will convert their positive merchandise or service evaluations into purchases. Retailers can reduce the number of abandoned carts by making it easier to purchase merchandise. They reduce the actual wait time to buy merchandise by having more checkout lanes open and placing them conveniently inside the store. To reduce perceived wait times, they install digital displays to entertain customers waiting in line. On a Web site, the ease of navigation is critical for decreasing the number of abandoned virtual carts.

Customers' perceived risk in making a purchase decision can be reduced by providing sufficient information that reinforces the customer's positive evaluation. For example, her friend Britt, the salesperson, and another potential customer provided Eva with positive feedback to support her purchase decision. For those customers who do not have other friends to consult, especially those browsing the Internet, retailers offer online reviews.[28] Finally, risks are reduced when retailers offer liberal return policies, money-back guarantees, and refunds if customers find the same merchandise available at lower prices from another retailer.

Postpurchase Evaluation

The buying process doesn't end when a customer purchases a product. After making a purchase, the customer uses the product and then evaluates the experience to determine whether it was satisfactory or unsatisfactory. **Satisfaction** is a postconsumption evaluation of how well a store or product meets or exceeds customer expectations. This **postpurchase evaluation** then becomes part of the customer's internal information and affects future store and product decisions. Unsatisfactory experiences can motivate customers to complain to the retailer, patronize other stores, and select different brands in the future.[30] Consistently high levels of satisfaction build store and brand loyalty, important sources of competitive advantage for retailers.

Chapters 17 and 19 discuss some means to increase customer satisfaction, such as offering quality merchandise, providing accurate information about merchandise, and contacting customers after a sale.

REFACT

Negative word of mouth is expensive. Only 6 percent of shoppers who experienced a problem with a retailer contacted the company, but 31 percent told someone what happened, and many of those went on to tell others. Overall, if 100 people have a bad experience, a retailer stands to lose between 32 and 36 current or potential customers.[31]

TYPES OF BUYING DECISIONS

In some situations, customers like Eva Carlyn spend considerable time and effort selecting a retailer and evaluating the merchandise—going through all the steps in the buying process described in the preceding section. In other situations, buying decisions are made automatically with little thought. Three types of customer decision-making processes are extended problem solving, limited problem solving, and habitual decision making.

Extended Problem Solving

Extended problem solving is a purchase decision process in which customers devote considerable time and effort to analyzing their alternatives. Customers typically engage in extended problem solving when the purchase decision involves a lot of risk and uncertainty. Financial risks arise when customers purchase an expensive product or service. Physical risks are important when customers feel that a product or service may affect their health or safety. Social risks arise when customers believe a product will affect how others view them. Lasik eye surgery, for instance, involves all three types of risks: It can be expensive, potentially damage the eyes, and change a person's appearance.

Consumers engage in extended problem solving when they are making a buying decision to satisfy an important need or when they have little knowledge about the product or service. Due to the high risk in these situations, customers go beyond their personal knowledge to consult with friends, family members, or experts. They may visit several retailers before making a purchase decision.

Retailers stimulate sales from customers engaged in extended problem solving by providing the necessary information in a readily available and easily understood manner and by offering money-back guarantees. For example, retailers that sell merchandise involving extended problem solving provide information on their Web site describing the merchandise and its specifications, have informational displays in the store (such as a sofa cut in half to show its construction), and use salespeople to demonstrate features and answer questions.

Limited Problem Solving

Limited problem solving is a purchase decision process involving a moderate amount of effort and time. Customers engage in this type of buying process when they have had some prior experience with the product or service and their risk is moderate. In these situations, customers tend to rely more on personal knowledge than on external information. They usually choose a retailer they have shopped at before and select merchandise they have bought in the past. The majority of customer purchase decisions involve limited problem solving.

Retailers attempt to reinforce this buying pattern when customers are buying merchandise from them. If customers are shopping elsewhere, however, retailers need to break this buying pattern by introducing new information or offering different merchandise or services.

Eva Carlyn's buying process illustrates both limited and extended problem solving. Her store choice decision was based on her prior knowledge of the merchandise in various stores she had shopped in and her search on Brandhabit.com. Considering this information, she felt the store choice decision was not very risky; thus, she engaged in limited problem solving when deciding to visit Macy's. But her buying process for the suit was extended. This decision was important to her; thus, she spent time acquiring information from a friend, the salesperson, and another shopper to evaluate and select a suit.

One common type of limited problem solving is **impulse buying,** which is a buying decision made by customers on the spot after seeing the merchandise.[32] Eva's decision to buy the scarf was an impulse purchase.

Why do retailers put candy at their cash registers?

Retailers encourage impulse buying behavior by using prominent point-of-purchase or point-of-sale (POP or POS) displays to attract customers' attention. Retailers have long recognized that the most valuable real estate in the store is at the POP (point of purchase). An increasing number of nonfood retailers such as Dick's Sporting Goods and Staples are looking to increase impulse buys from customers by offering candy, gum, and mints at their cash registers.[33] Electronic shoppers are also stimulated to purchase impulsively when Internet retailers put special merchandise on their homepages and suggest complementary merchandise just before checkout.

Habitual Decision Making

Habitual decision making is a purchase decision process involving little or no conscious effort. Today's customers have many demands on their time. One way they cope with these time pressures is by simplifying their decision-making process. When a need arises, customers may automatically respond with, "I'll buy the same thing I bought last time from the same store." Typically, this habitual decision-making process occurs when decisions aren't very important to customers and involve familiar merchandise they have bought in the past. When customers are loyal to a brand or a store, they are involved in habitual decision making.

Brand loyalty means that customers like and consistently buy a specific brand in a product category. They are reluctant to switch to other brands if their favorite brand isn't available. Thus, retailers can satisfy these customers' needs only if they offer the specific brands desired.

Brand loyalty creates both opportunities and problems for retailers. Customers are attracted to stores that carry popular brands, but because retailers must carry these high-loyalty brands, they may not be able to negotiate favorable terms with the suppliers of the popular national brands. If, however, the high-loyalty brands are private-label brands (i.e., brands owned by the retailer), both brand and store loyalty is heightened. Chapter 14 covers buying and stocking branded and private-label merchandise.

Store loyalty means that customers like and habitually visit the same store to purchase a type of merchandise. All retailers would like to increase their customers'

REFACT

The product categories with the highest brand loyalty are beverages, cosmetics, health and beauty aids, and snacks.[34]

store loyalty and might do so by selecting a convenient location (see Chapters 7 and 8), offering complete assortments of national and private-label brands (Chapter 14), reducing the number of stockouts (Chapter 13), rewarding customers for frequent purchases (Chapters 11 and 16), or providing good customer service (Chapter 19).

SOCIAL FACTORS INFLUENCING THE BUYING PROCESS

Exhibit 4–5 illustrates how customer buying decisions are influenced by the customer's social environment: family, reference groups, and culture.

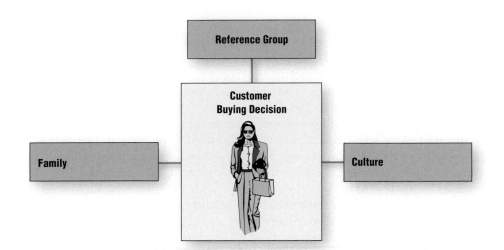

EXHIBIT 4–5
Social Factors Affecting
Buying Decisions

Family

Many purchase decisions involve products that the entire family will consume or use. Thus, retailers must understand how families make purchase decisions and how various family members influence these decisions. The previous discussion of the buying process focused on how one person makes a decision. When families make purchase decisions, they often consider the needs of all family members. When choosing a vacation site, for example, all family members may participate in the decision making. In other situations, one member of the family may assume the decision-making role. For example, the husband might buy the groceries, which the wife then uses to prepare their child's lunch, which the child consumes in school. In this situation, the store choice decision might be made by the husband, but the brand choice decision might be made by the mother, though it likely is greatly influenced by the child.

REFACT

Kids in the United States spend more than $200 billion each year on personal items. They also directly influence the purchase of another $300 billion worth of items, such as food and clothing.[35]

Children play an important role in family buying decisions. Resort hotels now realize they must satisfy children's needs as well as those of adults. For example, Hyatt hotels greet families by offering books and games tailored to the children's ages. Parents checking in with infants receive a first-day supply of baby food or formula and diapers at no charge. Baby-sitting and escort services to attractions for children also are offered.

Retailers can attract consumers who shop with other family members by satisfying the needs of all those family members. For example, IKEA, the worlds leading home furnishings retailer, have play facilities with ball-rooms in all their stores, in which children can play while their parents shop. Nordstrom provides sitting areas in its store where men may watch a football game while their wives shop.

IKEA has a "ball-pit" in which children can play while their parents shop.

By accommodating the needs of men and children who might not be interested in shopping, the retailer keeps the family in the stores longer and thereby encourages them to buy more merchandise. Retailing View 4.3 profiles some retailers that target tweens who shop with their parents.

Reference Groups

A **reference group** includes one or more people whom a person uses as a basis of comparison for beliefs, feelings, and behaviors. A consumer might have a number of different reference groups, though the most important is the family, as we discussed in the previous section. These reference groups affect buying decisions by (1) offering information, (2) providing rewards for specific purchasing behaviors, and (3) enhancing a consumer's self-image.

Reference groups provide information to consumers directly through conversation or indirectly through observation. For example, Eva received valuable information from her friend about the suits she was considering. On other occasions, Eva might look to women like soccer player Mia Hamm and tennis player Maria Sharapova to guide her selection of athletic apparel, or Jessica Simpson and Rachel Bilson for casual fashion advice. The role of reference groups in creating fashion is discussed in the appendix to this chapter.

By identifying and affiliating with reference groups, consumers create, enhance, and maintain their self-image. Customers who want to be seen as members of an elite social class may shop at prestige retailers, whereas others who want to create an image of an outdoors enthusiast might buy merchandise from the L.L. Bean Web site.

Retailers are particularly interested in identifying and reaching out to those in a reference group who act as store advocates and actively influence others in the group. **Store advocates** are customers who like a store so much that they actively share their positive experiences with friends and family. Consumers see so much advertising that they have become suspicious of the claims being made. So they are relying more on their own social networks for information about stores to patronize and merchandise to buy. Trader Joe's, a specialty supermarket chain, has built its business largely through the word of mouth of store advocates. Research has found that advocacy for a particular supermarket is not built on low prices. It is stimulated by a store design that enables advocates to find items easily, by courteous and helpful employees, and by having a wide selection of fresh vegetables and fruits.[36]

Alpha moms are good examples of store advocates. Educated, tech-savvy, Type A moms have a common goal: mommy excellence.[38] An Alpha mom is a multitasker, kidcentric, and hands-on. She may or may not work outside the home, but at home, she views motherhood as a job that can be mastered with diligent research. As the label implies, she is a leader of the pack who influences how other moms spend. She's also wired—online 87 minutes a day, she spends a hefty 7 percent more than the typical Internet user. The impact of her purchases or what she touts can spread on the Internet, far beyond her personal e-mail list or blog.

Culture

Culture is the meaning, beliefs, morals, and values shared by most members of a society. For example, an important value in most Western cultures is individualism—people should only look out for themselves and their immediate family. Thus, consumers in individualistic cultures rely on their own inner standards and beliefs when making decisions. However, Eastern cultures value collectivism, emphasizing that consideration of others, particularly family, should guide behavior. Thus, social relationships are more important and material goods are less important to consumers in collectivist cultures.

REFACT

Victoria's Secret has the highest percentage of advocates among its customers. Twenty-three percent of its customers are store advocates, compared with 13 percent for average retailers.[37]

Research has found that collectivists are more price sensitive than individualistic consumers about private goods—products and services consumed privately such as personal hygiene products—but less price sensitive about goods consumed in public, such as apparel.[39] In addition, consumers in collectivist cultures are more prone to shop in groups than are individualistic consumers. Chinese shoppers have even started shopping in teams to bargain for bigger discounts. The practice, called *tuangou*, or team purchase, begins on Internet chat rooms, where like-minded consumers develop plans to buy appliances, furnishings, food, and even cars in bulk. Then they go together to stores and demand discounts. In an increasingly competitive marketplace, retailers in China are bending to the demands of these groups.[40]

REFACT

In 1994, the Swedish furniture retailer IKEA aired the first mainstream television ad targeted toward the gay subculture by featuring a gay relationship.[41]

Retailing to Tweens **RETAILING VIEW** 4.3

Tween shoppers, between the ages of 5 and 13 years, are the fastest growing age segment in the United States. The 10 million tweens spend $11 billion annually using their own money and influence the $175 billion their parents spend on them. The tween girl may want to emulate her older sister, but sex and romance are not part of her life yet. She is still a little girl at heart. She likes fun, frilly, glittery, sensory environments that tap into the kid in her. She wants to be treated as young, but not babyish.

Tweens Brands Inc., operating over 700 Limited Too and Justice stores, is a market leader in the tween segment. It realizes that the tween girl might want to look like her 16-year-old sister but that apparel assortments need to be fine-tuned to her younger body type and be more modest and sensible. Its stores create a mood of power and excitement for the tween girl. They include colorful storefront windows, light displays, photographic sticker booths, ear-piercing stations, and gumball machines. Special fixtures are placed at eye level for younger girls, even though the girls will be visiting the store with mom, because the tweens choose and the parents pay. The stores have interactive elements, such as music listening stations, to encourage tweens to spend more time in the stores.

Club Libby Lu, with more than 90 mall-based stores, offers an even more interactive format for the tween girl. At the center of the activities are birthday parties, where the girls can dress up, get makeovers, and, of course, buy things. Girls can dress up in costumes at Club Libby Lu as well as make their own charm bracelets. One of the favorite makeovers is the "Rock Princess". The girl-centered environment of Club Libby Lu includes a palette of pinks and purples, accented by glitter and sparkle. Each store is sectioned into key shopping zones:

- *The Style Studio.* During a "Libby Du™," girls dress up as pretend characters, such as a rock star or princess.

- *Sparkle Spa.* Includes all bath products, cosmetics, fragrances and the "Create-your-own" stations, where girls mix spa products like "Soapy Sundae" Body Scrub and "Kool Karma" Body Spray.

Everything Club LibbyLu does is designed to appeal to Tweens.

- *Ear Piercing.* A simply "Ear-isistable" experience at Club Libby Lu includes a song, sticker, certificate, and free Libby Charmette™.

- *Pooch Parlor.* Girls can make their own furry pup or kitty to take home in a fancy carrier with a collar and a pooch t-shirt.

- *Shopping/Products.* Designed around what is important to tween girls—their rooms, sleepovers, and cool apparel.

Sears also hosts a dynamic Web site, www.sear.com/e-me, targeting tweens. After creating a personalized E-Me, or avatar, tween visitors can dress it with Sears apparel and shoes and save the selections in their virtual closets. Visitors can print the contents of the closet and give to their parents, who then get a 10 percent discount if they buy the items at a Sears store. The site also has an E-Me Fashion Show, where kids can submit their E-Me outfits to be rated by other site users, and a variety of interactive elements allowing E-Me characters to dance, flip burgers, and more.

Sources: Tween Brands, 10k, SEC Filing, April 3, 2007; www.clublibbylu. com (accessed December 24, 2007); Jane O'Donnell, "Marketers Keep Pace with 'Tweens'", *USA Today*, April 11, 2007 (accessed August 22, 2007); www.sears.com/e-me (accessed September 5, 2007).

Subcultures are distinctive groups of people within a culture. Members of a subculture share some customs and norms with the overall society but also have some unique perspectives. Subcultures can be based on geography (southerners), age (Gen Y), ethnicity (Asian Americans), lifestyle (preppies), or a college. For instance, the culture at your college may evoke an "intellectual," "athletic," or "party" reputation among potential students. This subcultural environment influences, to some extent, the way students spend their leisure time and select the stores, brands, and merchandise they purchase.

Many retailers and shopping center managers have adjusted their strategies to appeal to different cultures and subcultures.

Many retailers and shopping center managers have recognized the importance of appealing to different cultures and subcultures. For instance, the U.S. Hispanic population is growing faster than any other market segment, and their purchasing power is rising faster than that of the general population. Many retailers, particularly supermarkets in areas with large Hispanic populations, have dedicated significant space to products that are indigenous to particular Spanish-speaking countries. The product mix will, however, differ depending on the region of the country. Merchandise should reflect that, for instance, Miami has a large Cuban and Latin American population, whereas Los Angeles and Texas have more people from Mexico. Bilingual employees are a critical success factor for stores catering to the Hispanic population. Recent research found that Hispanic families tend to shop together, particularly on Sunday.[42] To appeal to this group, shopping centers are adding Mexican restaurants to their food courts and Hispanic-targeted entertainment.

MARKET SEGMENTATION

The preceding discussion focused on (1) how individual customers evaluate and select stores and merchandise and (2) the factors affecting their decision making. To be cost effective, retailers identify groups of these customers (market segments) and target their offerings to meet the needs of typical customers in that segment rather than the needs of a specific customer. At one time, Wal-Mart used a "one size fits all" strategy.[43] The merchandise selection was very similar across the United States, without much regard to geographical or demographic variations. This approach worked well when most of its stores were located in rural areas in the Southeast. But as it opened stores in more diverse locations, it realized it had to develop different retail mixes for different market segments. It now targets and provides different offerings in stores that serve African Americans, Hispanics, affluent customers, empty-nesters, suburbanites, and rural residents.

A **retail market segment** is a group of customers whose needs are satisfied by the same retail mix because they have similar needs. For example, families traveling on a vacation have different needs than executives on business trips. Thus, Marriott offers hotel chains with different retail mixes for each of these segments. The Internet enables retailers to target individual customers efficiently and market products to them on a one-to-one basis. This one-to-one marketing concept is discussed in Chapter 11, as it pertains to customer relationship management.

Criteria for Evaluating Market Segments

Customers can be grouped into segments in many different ways. Exhibit 4–6 shows some different methods for segmenting retail markets. There's no simple way to determine which method is best, though four criteria useful for evaluating whether a retail segment is a viable target market are as follows: actionable, identifiable, substantial, and reachable.

Actionable   The fundamental criteria for evaluating a retail market segment are that (1) customers in the segment must have similar needs, seek similar benefits, and be satisfied by a similar retail offering and (2) those customers' needs must differ from the needs of customers in other segments. **Actionable** means that the definition of the segment clearly indicates what the retailer should do to satisfy its needs. According to this criterion, it makes sense for Lane Bryant to segment the apparel market on the basis of the demographic characteristic of physical size. Customers who wear large sizes have different needs than those who wear small sizes, so they are attracted to a store offering a unique merchandise mix. In the context of the multiattribute attitude model discussed previously, women who wear large sizes place more importance on fit and fashion because it's relatively hard for them to satisfy these needs.

In contrast, it wouldn't make sense for a supermarket to segment its market on the basis of customer size. Large and small men and women probably have the same needs, seek the same benefits, and go through the same buying process for groceries. This segmentation approach wouldn't be actionable for a supermarket retailer because the retailer couldn't develop unique mixes for large and small customers. Thus, supermarkets usually segment markets using demographics such as income or ethnic origin to develop their retail mix.

Identifiable   **Identifiable** means that the retailer is able to determine which customers are in the market segment. When customers are identifiable, the retailer can determine the (1) the segment's size and (2) the consumers to whom the retailer needs to target its promotion. Continuing with the preceding example, grocery retailers use customer demographics to identify where they should put their stores and the merchandise that they carry. For instance, more prepared foods, gourmet foods, fancy produce, and meat would go into stores in neighborhoods with higher average incomes. It is equally important to ensure that the segments are distinct from one another, because too much overlap between segments means that distinct marketing strategies aren't needed. If, for example, a regional grocery store chain had stores located in neighborhoods containing people with similar demographics, then there would be no need to vary its merchandise selection.

Substantial   If a market is too small or its buying power insignificant (i.e., not **substantial**), it cannot generate sufficient profits to support the retailing mix activities. For example, the market for pet pharmaceuticals is probably not large enough in one local area to support a unique segmentation strategy, but a national market could be serviced through the Internet channel.

Reachable   **Reachable** means that the retailer can target promotions and other elements of the retail mix to consumers in the segment. For example, AutoZone targets men who repair their own automobiles themselves. Potential customers in this segment are reachable because they read car magazines, listen to *Car Talk* on NPR, and have distinct television viewing habits.

Approaches for Segmenting Markets

Exhibit 4–6 illustrates the wide variety of approaches for segmenting retail markets. No one approach is best for all retailers. Instead, they must explore various factors that affect customer buying behavior and determine which factors are most important for them.

Geographic Segmentation   **Geographic segmentation** groups customers according to where they live. A retail market can be segmented by countries (Japan,

EXHIBIT 4–6
Methods for Segmenting
Retail Markets

Segmentation Descriptor	Example of Categories
GEOGRAPHIC	
Region	Pacific, Mountain, Central, South, Mid-Atlantic, Northeast
Population density	Rural, suburban, urban
Climate	Cold, warm
DEMOGRAPHIC	
Age	Under 6, 6–12, 13–19, 20–29, 30–49, 50–65, over 65
Gender	Male, female
Family life cycle	Single, married with no children, married with youngest child under 6, married with youngest child over 6, married with children no longer living at home, widowed
Family income	Under $19,999, $20,000–29,999, $30,000–49,999, $50,000–$74,999, over $75,000
Occupation	Professional, clerical, sales, craftsperson, retired, student, homemaker
Education	Some high school, high school graduate, some college, college graduate, graduate degree
Religion	Catholic, Protestant, Jewish, Muslim
Race	Caucasian, African American, Hispanic, Asian
Nationality	American, Japanese, British, French, German, Italian, Chinese
PSYCHOSOCIAL	
Social class	Lower, middle, upper
Lifestyle	Striver, driver, devoted, intimate, altruist, fun seeker, creative
Personality	Aggressive, shy, emotional
FEELINGS AND BEHAVIORS	
Attitudes	Positive, neutral, negative
Benefit sought	Convenience, economy, prestige
Stage in decision process	Unaware, aware, informed, interested, intend to buy, bought previously
Perceived risk	High, medium, low
Innovativeness	Innovator, early adopter, early majority, late majority, laggard
Loyalty	None, some, completely
Usage rate	None, light, medium, heavy
Usage situation	Home, work, vacation, leisure
User status	Nonuser, ex-user, potential user, current user

Mexico) or by areas within a country, such as states, cities, and neighborhoods. Because customers typically shop at stores convenient to where they live and work, individual retail outlets usually focus on the customer segment reasonably close to the outlet.

Even though national retailers such as Safeway and Sears have no geographic focus, they do tailor their merchandise selections to different regions of the country. Snow sleds don't sell well in Florida, and surfboards don't sell well in Colorado. Even within a metropolitan area, stores in a chain must adjust to the unique needs of customers in different neighborhoods. As we noted previously, supermarkets typically feature more products used in a Hispanic family's diet in areas with larger Hispanic populations.

Segments based on geography can be identifiable, substantial, and reachable. It's easy to determine who lives in a geographic segment, such as the Paris metropolitan area, and then determine how many potential customers are in that area. It is also relatively simply to target communications and locate retail outlets for customers in Paris and then determine if they are being responsive to those communications. However, when customers in different geographic segments have similar needs, it is inefficient to develop unique retail offerings by geographic markets. For example, a fast-food customer in Detroit probably seeks the same benefits as a fast-food customer in Los Angeles. Thus, it wouldn't be useful to segment the U.S. fast-food market geographically.

Demographic Segmentation   **Demographic segmentation** groups consumers on the basis of easily measured, objective characteristics such as age, gender, income, and education. Demographic variables are the most common means to define segments, because consumers in these segments can be easily identified, the market size can be determined, and the degree to which they can be reached by and are responsive to media can be easily assessed.

A challenge facing many retailers is how to continue to appeal to one of their most lucrative market segments, Generation Y, who now are in their 20s and completing college or starting their first jobs. Who is going to dress them as they move into a different phase of their lives? Abercrombie & Fitch has Ruehl No. 925, Aeropostale has JIMMY'Z, and American Eagle Outfitters has Martin + Osa, all aimed at 20–35-year-olds.[44]

However, demographics may not be useful for defining segments for some retailers. For example, demographics are poor predictors of users of activewear, such as jogging suits and running shoes. At one time, retailers assumed that activewear would be purchased exclusively by young people, but the health and fitness trend has led people of all ages to buy this merchandise. Relatively inactive consumers also find activewear to be comfortable.

Geodemographic Segmentation   **Geodemographic segmentation** uses both geographic and demographic characteristics to classify consumers. This segmentation scheme is based on the principle that "birds of a feather flock together."[45] Consumers in the same neighborhoods tend to buy the same types of cars, appliances, and apparel and shop at the same types of retailers.

One widely used tool for geographic segmentation is PRIZM (Potential Rating Index by Zip Market), developed by Claritas (www.claritas.com). Claritas identified 66 geodemographic segments, called neighborhoods or clusters, using detailed demographic and consumption information and data about the media habits of the people who live in each zip code.

In addition to providing demographic information about each cluster, Claritas provides indexes comparing the buying behavior and media habits of consumers in each cluster to the national average, which is set to 100. Thus, an index of 155 for a cluster indicates that the cluster is 55 percent higher than the national average for those variables. The information in the table below describes three PRIZM clusters:

Cluster name	Town & Gown	Gray Collars	Latino American
Cluster number	31	42	44
Description	College-town singles	Aging couples in near suburbs	Hispanic middle class
Lifestyle/products	Foreign videos (551)*	Lottery tickets (169)	Boxing (443)
	Online services (216)	Six-month CDs (140)	Dance music (194)
	Dogs (54)	Museums (68)	Campers (45)
	Sewing (35)	Tennis (42)	Barbecuing (57)
Food and drink	Tequila (183)	Fresh cold cuts (136)	Avocado (230)
	Coca-Cola (145)	Fast food (134)	Pita bread (115)
	Pasta salad (141)	Frozen dinners (130)	Chewing gum (105)
	Fast food (105)	Non-alcoholic beer (129)	Coca-Cola (108)
Media used	*Cosmopolitan* (183)	*Ebony* (159)	*Cosmopolitan* (228)
	Sports Illustrated (182)	*McCall's* (141)	*Touched by an Angel* (193)
	Friends (222)	*Good Morning America* (139)	*Court TV* (156)
	Face the Nation (164)	TV Wrestling (137)	*Seventeen* (117)

*Index based on 100 = average.

EXHIBIT 4–7
Location of Gray-Collar
Neighborhoods

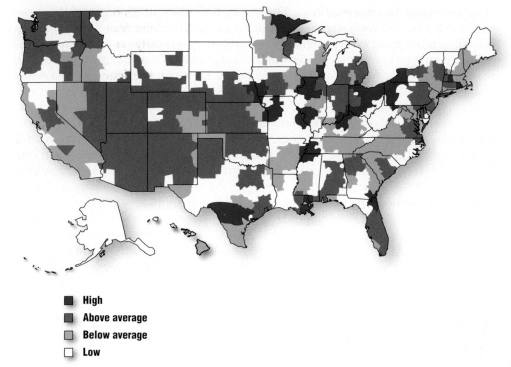

■ **High**
■ **Above average**
■ **Below average**
□ **Low**

SOURCE: Michael J. Weiss, *The Clustered World* (Boston: Little, Brown, 2000), p. 262. Reprinted with permission of Hachette Book Groups, USA.

These neighborhoods, with their similar demographics and buying behaviors, can be any place in the United States. For example, Exhibit 4–7 outlines the location of gray-collar areas in the United States.

Geodemographic segmentation is particularly appealing to store-based retailers, because customers typically patronize stores close to their neighborhood. Thus, retailers can use geodemographic segmentation to select locations for their stores and tailor the assortment in the stores to the preferences of the local community. In Chapter 8, we illustrate how geodemographic segmentation is used to make store location decisions.

Lifestyle Segmentation   Of the various methods of segmenting, lifestyle is the one that incorporates consumer needs.[46] **Lifestyle,** or **psychographics,** refers to how people live, how they spend their time and money, what activities they pursue, and their attitudes and opinions about the world in which they live. For example, a person may have a strong need for adventure. This need then motivates the person to buy products that make them feel like they fit in such a lifestyle segment. For instance, Harley-Davidson motorcycle owners share a slice of the American Dream—the freedom to conquer the open road. Retailing View 4.4 describes male lifestyle segments.

Lifestyle segments can be identified through consumer surveys that ask respondents to indicate whether they agree or disagree with statements such as, "My idea of fun in a national park would be to stay in an expensive lodge and dress up for dinner," "I often crave excitement," or "I could not stand to skin a dead animal." Retailers today are placing more emphasis on lifestyles than on demographics to define a target segment.

One of the most widely used tools for **lifestyle segmentation** is **VALS™,** developed by SRI Consulting Business Intelligence (www.sric-bi.com/VALS).[47] On the basis of responses to the VALS survey, consumers are classified into the eight segments shown in Exhibit 4–8. On the horizontal dimension, the segments are described by their resources, including their income, education, health, and energy level, as well as their degree of innovativeness. The segments on top have more resources and are more innovative; those on the bottom have fewer resources and are less innovative. The segments are also grouped vertically on the basis of their primary motivation.

Firms are finding that lifestyles are often more useful for predicting consumer behavior than are demographics. For instance, some college students and some day laborers may have similar demographics based on their income, but they spend that income quite differently because of their very different values and lifestyles. There are limitations to using lifestyle segmentation, however. Lifestyles are not as objective as demographics, and it is harder to identify potential customers. With demographics, a firm like Nike can easily identify its customers as men or women and direct its marketing strategies to each group differently. For these reasons, lifestyle segmentation is often used in conjunction with other segmentation methods.[48]

More than Metro   RETAILING VIEW   4.4

Most retailers target women, because women are typically the purchasing managers for their households. In fact, its common for retail executives to refer to their customers always as "she." But men are now doing more shopping and becoming an appealing market segment. Men are considered the primary shoppers for about 20 percent of U.S. households and buy more than 70 percent of their apparel, whereas 10 years ago, women bought the vast majority of men's apparel.

This recognition of the male market began several years ago with an interest in a segment of males referred to as "metrosexuals." Metrosexuals are urban men who are in touch with their feminine side. They have a strong aesthetic sense, spend a great deal of time and money on their appearance and lifestyle, and enjoy shopping. Descriptions of them characterize them shopping Barney's New York, getting $100 haircuts and chemical tans, watching *Queer Eye for the Straight Guy* on cable, and reading *Cargo*, a shopping magazine (of all things) for men. This metrosexual image became so popular in the urban subculture that some "regular guys" were concerned that if they weren't metro, they would be considered beer-guzzling, sports-watching troglodytes.

In which market segment does the man buying the digital camera on the right most likely belong?

Retailers actually note several lifestyle segments within the male market. Metros only account for about 20 percent of the male market. Several additional male segments include mature teens, modern men, and dads. Mature teens are responsible and pragmatic, because their baby boomer parents treated them as equals. They are techno-savvy, do their research using the Internet, and serve as the in-house shopping experts for their families.

Modern men are sophisticated shoppers in their 20s and 30s who enjoy shopping more than their fathers, but they still like watching pro football games with the guys. They are comfortable with women but don't find shopping with them much fun. They buy moisturizers and hair gels but refuse to get manicures.

And then there are the dads. At one time, when men got married and had children, they delegated the shopping to their stay-at-home wives. Now, with so many two-income families, dads are almost as likely as moms to be found walking down the diaper aisle.

Sources: Diana Middleton, "Capturing the Hunter," Knight Ridder Tribune Business News, June 25, 2007 (accessed December 24, 2007); Blanca Torres, "More and More, Men Like Shopping," *Contra Costa Times*, October 12, 2006; Nanette Byrnes, "Secrets Of The Male Shopper," *BusinessWeek*, September 4, 2006.

EXHIBIT 4–8
VALS™ American Lifestyle
Segments

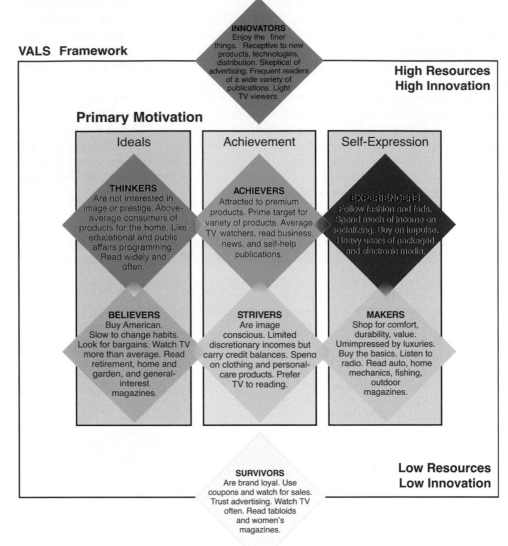

VALS Framework

INNOVATORS
Enjoy the finer things. Receptive to new products, technologies, distribution. Skeptical of advertising. Frequent readers of a wide variety of publications. Light TV viewers.

High Resources
High Innovation

Primary Motivation

Ideals   Achievement   Self-Expression

THINKERS
Are not interested in image or prestige. Above-average consumers of products for the home. Like educational and public affairs programming. Read widely and often.

ACHIEVERS
Attracted to premium products. Prime target for variety of products. Average TV watchers, read business, news, and self-help publications.

EXPERIENCERS
Follow fashion and fads. Spend much of income on socializing. Buy on impulse. Heavy users of packaged and electronic media.

BELIEVERS
Buy American. Slow to change habits. Look for bargains. Watch TV more than average. Read retirement, home and garden, and general-interest magazines.

STRIVERS
Are image conscious. Limited discretionary incomes but carry credit balances. Spend on clothing and personal-care products. Prefer TV to reading.

MAKERS
Shop for comfort, durability, value. Unimpressed by luxuries. Buy the basics. Listen to radio. Read auto, home mechanics, fishing, outdoor magazines.

SURVIVORS
Are brand loyal. Use coupons and watch for sales. Trust advertising. Watch TV often. Read tabloids and women's magazines.

Low Resources
Low Innovation

Buying Situation Segmentation   The buying behavior of customers with the same demographics or lifestyle can differ depending on their buying situation. Thus, retailers may use **buying situations,** such as fill-in versus weekly shopping, to segment a market. For example, in Exhibit 4–3, the parent with four children evaluated the supercenter more positively than the Internet grocer or supermarket for weekly grocery purchases. But if the parent ran out of milk during the week, he or she would probably go to the convenience store rather than the wholesale club for this fill-in shopping. In terms of Exhibit 4–3's multiattribute attitude model, convenience would be more important than assortment in the fill-in shopping situation. Similarly, an executive might stay at a convention hotel on a business trip and a resort during a family vacation.

Buying situation segmentation rates high among the criteria for evaluating market segments. The segments are actionable, because it is relatively easy to determine what a retailer should do to satisfy the needs of a particular segment. They are identifiable and accessible, because the retailer or service provider can determine who the customers are on the basis of who has purchased the product or service and under what circumstances. Once they have identified the customer segment, they can assess its size.

Benefit Segmentation   Another approach for defining a target segment is to group customers seeking similar benefits; this method is called **benefit segmentation.** In the multiattribute attitude model, customers in the same benefit segment would have a similar set of importance weights for the attributes of a store or product. For example, customers who place high importance on fashion and style and low importance on price might form a fashion segment, whereas customers who place more importance on price would form a price segment.

Benefit segments are very actionable. The benefits sought by customers in the target segment clearly indicate how retailers should design their offerings to appeal to those customers. But customers in benefit segments aren't easily identified or accessed; it's hard to look at a person and determine what benefits he or she is seeking. Typically, the audience for the media used by retailers is described by demographics rather than by the benefits they seek.

Composite Segmentation Approaches

As we've seen, no one approach meets all the criteria for useful customer segmentation. For example, segmenting by demographics and geography is ideal for identifying and accessing customers, but these characteristics often are unrelated to customers' needs. Thus these approaches may not indicate the actions necessary to attract customers in these segments. In contrast, knowing what benefits customers are seeking is useful for designing an effective retail offering; the problem is identifying which customers are seeking these benefits. For these reasons, **composite segmentation** uses multiple variables to identify customers in the target segment according to their benefits sought, lifestyles, and demographics.

Best Buy has introduced its "Customer Centricity" program to target five composite segments.[49] Each of these segments, referred by a first name, has a manager responsible for developing a retail strategy for the market segment. "Barrys" are the best customers. They are affluent professional men, 30–60 years of age, who make a minimum of $150,000 a year and drive luxury cars. Barry is the kind of guy who walks in to Best Buy, sees a $30,000 home theater system, and says, "I'll take it." In contrast, "Jills" are the busy suburban moms, "Buzzes" are focused, active younger men, and "Rays" are family men who like their technology practical. The fifth segment consists of small businesses buying their consumer electronics at Best Buy.

A group of stores has been redesigned to focus on a specific segment or two with significant representation in the local area. For example, Jill stores have personal shoppers and areas for children to play while mom shops. The soundtrack playing in the background is often children's music. Stores catering to Barrys have special areas to display high-end entertainment systems and experts in mobile technology; stores for Jills dedicate more inventory to things like learning software and feature softer colors and a children's technology department. The Buzz-oriented stores, by contrast, feature the very latest technologies and video games. They have comfortable places in which customers can sample technologies, complete with sofas and flat-screen televisions for testing video games and consoles. Ray stores focus more on low price.

SUMMARY

To satisfy customer needs, retailers must thoroughly understand how customers make store choice and purchase decisions and the factors they consider when deciding. This chapter describes the six stages in the buying process (need recognition, information search, evaluation of alternatives, choice of alternatives, purchase, and postpurchase

evaluations) and how retailers can influence their customers at each stage.

The importance of the stages depends on the nature of the customer's decision. When decisions are important and risky, the buying process is longer because customers spend more time and effort on information search and evaluating alternatives. When buying decisions are less important to customers, they spend little time in the buying process, and their buying behavior may become habitual.

The buying process of consumers is influenced by their personal beliefs, attitudes, and values and by their social environmental. The primary social influences are provided by the consumers' families, reference groups, and culture.

To develop cost-effective retail programs, retailers group customers into segments. Some approaches for segmenting markets are based on geography, demographics, geodemographics, lifestyles, usage situations, and benefits sought. Because each approach has its advantages and disadvantages, retailers typically define their target segment by several characteristics.

KEY TERMS

actionable, *117*

benefit segmentation, *123*

brand loyalty, *112*

buying process, *98*

buying situations, *122*

compatibility, *128*

complexity, *128*

composite segmentation, *123*

consideration set, *108*

cross-shopping, *101*

culture, *114*

demographic segmentation, *119*

everyday low pricing strategy, *104*

extended problem solving, *111*

external sources, *103*

fashion, *126*

geodemographic segmentation, *119*

geographic segmentation, *118*

habitual decision making, *112*

hedonic needs, *100*

identifiable, *117*

impulse buying, *112*

information search, *102*

internal sources, *103*

knockoffs, *128*

lifestyle, *120*

lifestyle segmentation, *120*

limited problem solving, *111*

mass-market theory, *128*

multiattribute attitude model, *105*

observability, *129*

postpurchase evaluation, *111*

psychographics, *120*

reachable, *118*

reference group, *114*

retail market segment, *116*

satisfaction, *111*

store advocates, *114*

store loyalty, *112*

subcultures, *116*

subculture theory, *128*

substantial, *118*

trialability, *128*

trickledown theory, *128*

utilitarian needs, *100*

VALS™, *120*

GET OUT AND DO IT!

1. **CONTINUING CASE ASSIGN-MENT:** Visit the retail store operated by the target firm for your continuing assignment. Pretend that you are looking to buy something sold at the store. Write down all of the things that the store does to try to stimulate you to buy merchandise.

2. Go to a supermarket and watch people selecting products to put in their shopping carts. How much time do they spend selecting products? Do some people spend more time than others?

3. **Web OLC EXERCISE** Go to the student side of the book's Web site to develop a multiattribute attitude model describing your evaluation of and decision about some relatively expensive product you bought recently, such as a car or a consumer electronics product. Open the multiattribute model exercise. List the attributes you considered in the left-hand column. List the alternatives you considered in the top row. Fill in the importance weights for each attribute in the second column (10 = very important, 1 = very unimportant), then fill in your evaluation of each product on each attribute (10 = excellent perfor-

mance, 1 = poor performance). Based on your importance weights and performance beliefs, the evaluation of each product appears in the bottom row. Did you buy the product with the highest evaluation?

4. To better understand the segmentation classification of consumers, SRI Business Consulting Intelligence has developed the VALS tool, which uses psychology to segment people according to their distinct personality traits. Go to the firm's homepage at www.sric-bi.com/VALS/presurvey.shtml and take the survey to identify your VALS profile according to your values, attitudes, and lifestyle. According to the results, what is your VALS profile type? Do you agree with your consumer profile? Why or why not? How can retailers effectively use the results of this survey when planning and implementing their business strategies?

5. Retailers segment the market on the basis of the geographic classification of customers to select the best site for their businesses. Go to the ESRI Business Information Solutions homepage at http://www.esri.com/data/community_data/community-tapestry/index.html and type in the zip code for your hometown or your

campus and read the results. How would a retailer, such as a local restaurant, use the information in this report when making a decision about whether to open a location in this zip code?

6. Go to the following Internet sites offering information about the latest fashions: www.style.com (*Vogue, W*),

www.fashioninformation.com (U.K.), and www.telegraph.co.uk/fashion/index.jhtml (U.K.), and http://www.infomat.com/trend/index.html. Write a report describing the latest apparel fashions that are being shown by designers. Which of these fashions do you think will be popular? Why?

DISCUSSION QUESTIONS AND PROBLEMS

1. Does the customer buying process end when a customer buys some merchandise? Explain your answer.

2. What would make a consumer switch from making a habitual or routine decision to eat at one type of quick service restaurant to making a limited or extended choice decision and trying a new restaurant?

3. Considering the steps in the consumer buying process (Exhibit 4–1), describe how you (and your family) used this process to select your college/university. How many schools did you consider? How much time did you invest in this purchase decision? When you were deciding on which college to attend, what objective and subjective criteria did you use in the alternative evaluation portion of the consumer buying process?

4. Why do retailers use geodemographic segmentation to locate stores?

5. Any retailer's goal is to get customers in its store so that they can find the merchandise that they are looking for and make a purchase at this location. How

could a sporting goods retailer ensure that the customer buys athletic equipment at its outlet?

6. A family-owned used book store across the street from a major university campus wants to identify the various segments in its market. What approaches might the store owner use to segment its market? List two potential target market segments based on this segmentation approach. Then contrast the retail mix that would be most appropriate for the two potential target segments.

7. How would you expect the buying decision process to differ when shopping on the Internet compared with shopping in a store?

8. Using the multiattribute attitude model, identify the probable choice of a local car dealer for a young, single woman and for a retired couple with limited income (see the table below). What can the national retail chain do to increase the chances of the retired couple patronizing its dealership? You can use the multiattribute model template on the student side of the book's Web site to analyze this information.

Performance Attributres	IMPORTANCE WEIGHTS		PERFORMANCE BELIEFS		
	Young, Single Woman	Retired Couple	Local Gas Station	National Service Chain	Local Car Dealer
Price	2	10	9	10	3
Time to complete repair	8	5	5	9	7
Reliability	2	9	2	7	10
Convenience	8	3	3	6	5

9. When the Nintendo Wii launched, customers camped out overnight and waited outside in the bitter cold for stores to open to have the chance to buy this $250 videogame machine. Other customers went online to eBay and paid up to $750 for the same unit. Describe the segmentation characteristics (based on Exhibit 4–6) of the Nintendo Wii customer that would spend the extra time and money to purchase this game console.

10. According to *Confectioner* magazine, seasonal sales of candy have increased for four major holidays. Describe the stages in the buying process for candy using

Exhibit 4–1. How does need recognition differ for each of the four key candy holidays: Christmas, Easter, Valentine's Day, and Halloween? Where would customers purchase candy for each of these holidays? How would the buying process differ when buying candy for personal consumption versus buying candy as a gift? Consider Godiva and Hershey and explain the importantace of brand name recognition to a candy purchase. What can candy manufacturers and retailers do to continue the positive trend in sales growth?

SUGGESTED READINGS

Grohmann, Bianca, Eric R. Spangenberg, and David E. Sprott. "The Influence of Tactile Input on the Evaluation of Retail Product Offerings." *Journal of Retailing* 83, no. 2 (2007), pp. 237–45.

Hawkins, Delbert, David L. Mothersbaugh, and Roger J. Best. *Consumer Behavior*, 10th ed. New York: McGraw-Hill/Irwin, 2007.

Hines, Tony and Margaret Bruce. *Fashion Marketing, Second Edition: Contemporary Issues*. Burlington, MA: Butterworth-Heinemann, 2007.

Mcgoldrick, Peter J., and Natalie Collins. "Multichannel Retailing: Profiling the Multichannel Shopper." *International Review of Retail, Distribution & Consumer Research* 17, no. 2 (2007), pp. 139–58.

Pan, You, and George M. Zinkhan. "Determinants of Retail Patronage: A Meta-Analytical Perspective." *Journal of Retailing* 82, no. 3 (2006), pp. 229–43.

Peter, J. Paul, and Jerry Olson. *Consumer Behavior and Marketing Strategy*, 7th ed. New York: McGraw-Hill/Irwin, 2005.

Reda, Susan. "What Are Shoppers Saying About You?" *Stores*, February 2007.

Uncles, Mark D. "Understanding Retail Customers." In *Retailing in the 21st Century–Current and Future Trends*, eds. Manfred Kraft and Murali Mantrala Berlin: Springer, 2006, pp. 159–73.

Underhill, Paco. *Why We Buy: The Science of Shopping*. New York: Simon & Schuster, 1999.

Wagner, Tillmann. "Shopping Motivation Revised: A Means–End Chain Analytical Perspective." *International Journal of Retail & Distribution Management* 35, no. 7 (2007), pp. 569–82.

APPENDIX 4A   Customer Buying Behavior and Fashion

Many retailers, particularly department and specialty stores, sell fashionable merchandise. To sell this type of merchandise profitably, retailers need to (1) understand how fashions develop and diffuse throughout the marketplace and (2) use operating systems that enable them to match supply and demand for this seasonal merchandise. This appendix reviews the consumer behavior aspects of fashion; the operating systems for matching supply and demand for fashion merchandise are discussed in Chapters 12 and 13.

Fashion is a type of product or a way of behaving that is temporarily adopted by a large number of consumers because the product, service, or behavior is considered socially appropriate for the time and place.[50] For example, in some social groups, it is or has been fashionable to have brightly colored hair, play golf, wear a coat made from animal fur, have a beard, or go to an expensive health spa for a vacation. In many retail environments, however, the term *fashion* is associated with apparel and accessories.

CUSTOMER NEEDS SATISFIED BY FASHION

Fashion gives people an opportunity to satisfy many emotional and practical needs. Through fashions, people develop their own identity. They also can use fashions to manage their appearance, express their self-image and feelings, enhance their egos, and make an impression on others. Through the years, fashions have become associated with specific lifestyles or the roles people play. You wear different clothing styles when you are attending class, going out on a date, or interviewing for a job.

Fashion also can be used to communicate with others. For example, a salesperson might wear a classic business suit when making a sales call at Best Buy but more informal and fashion-forward attire when calling on Abercrombie & Fitch. These different dress styles indicate the salesperson's understanding of the differences in the corporate cultures of these firms.

People use fashions to both develop their own identity and gain acceptance from others. These two benefits of fashion can be opposing forces. If you choose to wear something radically different, you will achieve recognition for your individuality but might not be accepted by your peers. To satisfy these conflicting needs, manufacturers and retailers offer a variety and combination of designs that are fashionable and still enable consumers to express their individuality.

Consumers also adopt fashions to overcome boredom. People get tired of wearing the same clothing and seeing the same furniture in their living room. They seek changes in their lifestyles by buying new clothes or redecorating their houses to meet their changing tastes, preferences, and income.

HOW DO FASHIONS DEVELOP AND SPREAD?

Fashions are not universal. A fashion might be accepted in one geographic region, country, or age group and not in another. Consider how your idea of "fashionable" differs from your parents'. Many of you might have a hard time imagining them dressed in distressed, hip-hugging jeans and a tight t-shirt. Well, they might have just as much trouble picturing you in a double-breasted business suit. One interesting sports fashion trend has been the uniforms for college and NBA basketball players. Thirty years ago, they sported long hair and wore tight, short shorts and Converse shoes. Now they have short hair and wear baggy shorts and Nike shoes (see www.nba.com/photostore/).

The stages in the fashion life cycle are shown in Exhibit 4–9. The cycle begins with the creation of a new design or style. Then some consumers recognized as fashion

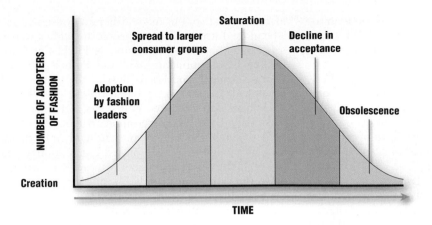

EXHIBIT 4–9
Stages in the Fashion
Life Cycle

leaders or innovators adopt the fashion and start a trend in their social group. The fashion spreads from the leaders to others and is accepted widely as a fashion. Eventually, the fashion is accepted by most people in the social group and can become overused. Saturation and overuse set the stage for the decline in popularity and the creation of new fashions. The time span of a fashion life cycle varies depending on the type of product and the market. Apparel fashions for "tweens," or young teenagers, is measured in months or even weeks, whereas the fashion cycle for home furnishings may last several years.

Creation

New fashions arise from a number of sources. Fashion designers are one source of creative inspirations, but fashions are also developed by creative consumers, celebrities, and even retailers. When high-profile actors, performers, and athletes wear the latest styles in television shows and movies, on stage, or on the red carpet, consumers interested in fashion often adopt and follow these trends.

Adoption by Fashion Leaders

The fashion life cycle really starts when the fashion is adopted by leading consumers. These initial adopters of a new fashion are called *fashion leaders*, *innovators*, or *trendsetters*, and they are the first people to display the new

Retailers scrutinize the designer-inspired fashion trends and produce merchandise suitable for their target markets.

fashion in their social group. If the fashion is too innovative or very different from currently accepted fashion, it might not be accepted by the social group, thus prematurely ending its life cycle.

Three theories have been proposed to explain how fashion spreads within a society. The **trickledown theory** suggests that fashion leaders are consumers with the highest social status—wealthy, well-educated consumers. After they adopt a fashion, the fashion trickles down to consumers in lower social classes. When the fashion is accepted in the lowest social class, it is no longer acceptable to the fashion leaders in the highest social class.

Manufacturers and retailers stimulate this trickledown process by copying the latest styles displayed at designer fashion shows and sold in exclusive specialty stores. These copies, referred to as **knockoffs,** are sold at lower prices through retailers targeting a broader market. For example, designers at JCPenney view fashion shows on their computers in Plano, Texas, and interpret the designs for their market.[51] If the designers in Paris and Milan are showing turtlenecks, the JCPenney designers determine what aspects of that fashion will appeal to their broader market and have them manufactured in Asia. It is likely that the knockoff turtlenecks will be on the shelves at JCPenney well before the higher-priced originals get to the high-end specialty and department stores.

Other retailers have gotten one step closer to the designers: They hire them! After spending four years as design director for women's wear at Giorgio Armani in the early 1990s, and at Paco Rabanne, Patrick Robinson today is designing clothes for less than $50 for Target.[52] Robinson notes his surprise that he didn't have to compromise as much on design and materials as he expected.

REFACT

The profile of a U.S. apparel fashion innovator is a woman, 16 to 24 years of age, who spends more than $1,000 a year on clothes.[53]

The second theory, the **mass-market theory,** suggests that fashions spread across different peer groups. Each group has its own fashion leaders who play key roles in their own social networks. Fashion information trickles across groups rather than down from the upper classes to the lower classes. For instance, motorcycle jackets and other gear have become fashion for many who have never been on a motorcycle, thanks to designers' interpretations of traditional garments and fashion leaders' desire to try something different.

The third theory, the **subculture theory,** is based on the development of recent fashions. Subcultures of mostly young and less affluent consumers, such as urban youth, started fashions for such things as colorful fabrics, t-shirts, sneakers, jeans, black leather jackets, and surplus military clothing. Many times, fashions are started unintentionally by people in lower-income consumer groups and trickle up to mainstream consumer classes. For example, workers wear blue jeans that have holes in them and are distressed from manual labor, their t-shirts are faded from working in the sun, and people who paint houses are covered in splashes of paint. These looks have been adapted by manufacturers and sold to many different consumer groups. The more distress, the more people are willing to pay.

Retailers such as Abercrombie & Fitch, The Gap, and J. Crew at the moderate end and Polo/Ralph Lauren, Giorgio Armani, and Hugo Boss at the upper end have developed "casual luxury" based on the distressed look. They have also distressed golf shirts and khaki pants to make them look old. Abercrombie, Banana Republic, and J. Crew add to "the look" by presenting their clothes wrinkled, as though they were picked out of a dirty laundry basket. In the extreme, designer Michael Kors sent models down the runway in wrinkled business suits. To enhance the crinkliness, he inserted metal into the fabric, giving more dimensionality to the wrinkles.

These theories of fashion development indicate that fashion leaders can come from many different places and social groups. In our diverse society, many types of consumers have the opportunity to be the leaders in setting fashion trends.

Spread to Large Consumer Groups

During this stage, the fashion is accepted by a wider group of consumers referred to as *early adopters*. The fashion becomes increasingly visible, receives greater publicity and media attention, and is readily available in retail stores. The relative advantage, compatibility, complexity, trialability, and observability of a fashion affect the time it takes for that fashion to spread through a social group. New fashions that provide more benefits have a higher relative advantage compared with existing fashions, and these new fashions spread faster. Fashions are often adopted by consumers because they make people feel special. Thus, more exclusive fashions like expensive clothing are adopted more quickly in an affluent target market. On a more utilitarian level, clothing that is easy to maintain, such as wrinkle-free pants, will diffuse quickly in the general population.

Compatibility is the degree to which the fashion is consistent with existing norms, values, and behaviors. When new fashions aren't consistent with existing norms, the number of adopters and the speed of adoption are lower. Skinny jeans are only compatible with a relatively small percentage of the public that wears jeans. Although it may be moderately successful for a few seasons, it will never achieve widespread acceptance.[54]

Complexity refers to how easy it is to understand and use the new fashion. Consumers have to learn how to incorporate a new fashion into their lifestyle. For example, a platform, 6-inch, stiletto-heeled pump is difficult to walk in unless you are only taking a quick strut down the runway.

Trialability refers to the costs and commitment required to adopt the fashion initially. For example, designers that have trunk shows to preview and presell the new season's fashions often bring only a sample of each piece. The consumer has to make a guess as to their size and hope that it will have a good fit and style. Consumers need to spend a lot of money buying a new type of expensive apparel to be in fashion, so the rate of adoption is faster if consumers can see how it looks on them without having to buy it.

Observability is the degree to which the new fashion is visible and easily communicated to others in the social group. Clothing fashions are very observable compared with fashions for the home, such as sheets and towels. It is therefore likely that a fashion in clothing will spread more quickly than a new color scheme or style for the bedroom.

Fashion retailers engage in many activities to increase the adoption and spread of a new fashion throughout their target market. Compatibility is increased and complexity is decreased by showing consumers how to coordinate a new article of fashion clothing with other items the consumer already owns. Trialability is increased by providing dressing rooms so customers can try on clothing and see how it looks on them. Providing opportunities for customers to return merchandise also increases trialability. Retailers increase observability by displaying fashion merchandise in their stores and advertising it in the media.

Saturation
In this stage, the fashion achieves its highest level of social acceptance. Almost all consumers in the target market are aware of the fashion and have decided to either accept or reject it. At this point, the fashion has become old and boring to many people.

Decline in Acceptance and Obsolescence
When fashions reach saturation, they have become less appealing to consumers. Because most people have already adopted the fashion, it no longer provides an opportunity for people to express their individuality. Fashion creators and leaders thus are beginning to experiment with new fashions. The introduction of a new fashion speeds the decline of the preceding fashion.

Retailing Strategy

Section I described retail management decisions; the different types of retailers, including how retailers use multiple selling channels—stores, the Internet, and catalogs—to reach their customers; and factors that affect consumers' choices of retailers, channels, and merchandise. This broad overview of retailing provided the background information needed to develop and implement an effective retail strategy.

Section II discusses strategic decisions made by retailers.

Chapter 5 describes the development of a retail market strategy.

Chapter 6 examines the financial strategy associated with the market strategy.

Chapters 7 and 8 discuss the location strategy for retail outlets.

Chapter 9 looks at the firm's organization and human resource strategy.

Chapter 10 examines systems used to control the flow of information and merchandise.

Chapter 11 details approaches that retailers take to manage relationships with their customers.

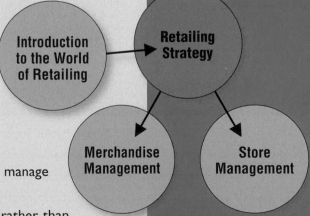

As outlined in Chapter 1, these decisions are strategic rather than tactical because they involve committing significant resources to developing long-term advantages over the competition in a target market segment.

Sections III and IV review the tactical decisions regarding merchandise and store management that serve to implement the retail strategy. These implementation or tactical decisions affect a retailer's efficiency, but their impact is shorter term than that of the strategic decisions reviewed in Section II.

Retail Market Strategy

EXECUTIVE BRIEFING
Jim Cossin, Director of Strategy Support,
Publix Super Markets, Inc.

Manufacturing, Distribution, Fresh Products, Engineering, and Strategic Planning. I also was Director of Fulfillment for PublixDirect, our online shopping and home delivery test.

As Director of Strategy Support, my primary responsibility is to support and facilitate the development and implementation of strategy at Publix. Each year, our various business areas are required to update their annual business plan. My department is responsible for assisting these business units through a rigorous process of strategy development and helping them to define the initiatives that will best achieve their desired goals. We also assist with implementation by providing project management support for these initiatives, and by measuring and reporting progress.

Another area of responsibility is to facilitate the development of our corporate business plan. I constantly monitor and evaluate the supermarket industry and gather information that helps to identify potential opportunities and threats facing Publix. I provide this information to our President, CEO, and CFO, and work with them to determine our best course of action.

With annual sales approaching $23 billion, Publix Super Markets, Inc., is one of the 10 largest supermarket chains in the United States. We operate over 900 stores, primarily in Florida, but also have stores in Georgia, Alabama, South Carolina, and Tennessee.

My background began in operations, with my first job out of college being a production supervisor at Frito Lay. I also spent time in the software consulting industry prior to joining Publix in 1994. Since coming to Publix, I've spent time in a wide variety of business areas including

CHAPTER 5

QUESTIONS

What is a retail strategy?

How can a retailer build a sustainable competitive advantage?

What steps do retailers go through to develop a strategy?

What different strategic growth opportunities can retailers pursue?

What retailers are best positioned to become global retailers?

In addition to supporting strategic planning and implementation, I am also responsible for the Process Improvement team (a group of 22 Industrial Engineers and Assistants), as well as our Continuous Quality Improvement programs.

At Publix, our strategy centers on customer service. We have a long tradition of providing premier service to our customers. We continually look for ways to improve this service, as well as ways to improve our operations so we can continue to provide the products and services our customers want at a good value.

Being part of the Strategy Support group at Publix has allowed me to be involved in many new and promising opportunities we are investigating. Publix is currently rolling out our "Pix" convenience stores and gas kiosks, and building several of our natural and organic formats called the "Greenwise Market." We also continue to enhance the customer experience through Supply Chain automation and associate training programs. These are just a few of the exciting opportunities that we experience everyday. It's an aspect of retail that I never knew existed prior to my coming to Publix.

The growing intensity of retail competition— due to the emergence of new competitors, formats, and technologies, as well as shifts in customer needs—is forcing retailers to devote more attention to long-term strategic planning. As the retail management decision-making process (discussed in Chapter 1) indicates, retailing strategy (Section II) is the bridge between understanding the world of retailing—that is, the analysis of the retail environment (Section I)—and the more tactical merchandise management and store operations activities (Sections III and IV) undertaken to implement the retail strategy. The retail strategy provides the direction retailers need to deal effectively with their environment, customers, and competitors.[1]

The first part of this chapter defines the term *retail strategy* and discusses three important elements of retail strategy: the target market segment, retail format, and sustainable competitive advantage. Next, we outline approaches for building a sustainable competitive advantage. The chapter concludes with a discussion of the strategic retail planning process.

WHAT IS A RETAIL STRATEGY?

REFACT

The word *strategy* comes from the Greek word meaning the "art of the general."[2]

The term *strategy* is frequently used in retailing. For example, retailers talk about their merchandise strategy, promotion strategy, location strategy, or private brand strategy. The term is used so commonly that it appears that all retailing decisions are strategic decisions, but retail strategy isn't just another expression for retail management.

Definition of Retail Market Strategy

A **retail strategy** is a statement identifying (1) the retailer's target market, (2) the format the retailer plans to use to satisfy the target market's needs, and (3) the bases upon which the retailer plans to build a sustainable competitive advantage.[3] The **target market** is the market segment(s) toward which the retailer plans to focus its resources and retail mix. A **retail format** describes the nature of the retailer's operations—that is, its retail mix (type of merchandise and services offered, pricing policy, advertising and promotion program, approach to store design and visual merchandising, typical locations, and customer services)—that is designed to satisfy the needs of its target market. A **sustainable competitive advantage** is an advantage over the competition that is not easily copied and thus can be maintained over a long period of time. The following are a few examples of retail strategies.

- **Steve & Barry's.** Steven Shore and Barry Prevor opened their first store near Philadelphia's University of Pennsylvania in 1985. Initially, the chain sold university-logoed sportswear at low prices. Its 200 stores now have expanded to offering humorous t-shirts and basic clothing for men, women, and children. Nearly all of its merchandise is priced at less than $15, but the quality is surprisingly high. The Starbury brand of shoes (licensed from NBA player Stephon Marbury) appear on NBA courts, worn by professional basketball players. The key to its success is gaining aggressive incentives from mall owners, applying creative approaches to working with vendors, and relying on virtually no advertising.[4]

- **Chico's.** The chain's 600 specialty stores sell fashionable apparel designed for women between 35 and 55 years of age. The company sells only its own private-label brands and is verticly integrated, handling everything from sourcing to designing to supervising merchandise, manufacturing, and delivery. Chico's does not use a cookie-cutter approach to its stores, so its merchandise assortment is adjusted to fit local tastes. The retailer stocks three collections. The Traveler's collection is its core assortment, whereas the other two collections are available in limited quantities and adapted from the latest trends. Chico's 5 million loyalty club members get a 5 percent discount, notice of store sales, free shipping, catalog discounts, and other perks, and they constitute 78 percent of Chico's sales. These shoppers spend more too— $110 per visit, compared with $70 for nonmembers. Chico's delivers high-quality customer service and devotes considerable time and effort to training its sales associates to work hard to establish personal relationships with each of its customers.[5]

- **Curves.** With more than 10,000 franchises in all 50 states and more than 30 countries, Curves has become the world's top fitness center in terms of number of clubs. One in every four fitness clubs in the United States is a Curves. Whereas other clubs go after the prized 18- to 34-year-old demographic segment, Curves's customers are aging baby boomers, typically living in small towns. This retailer's fitness centers don't have treadmills, saunas, locker rooms, mirrors, aerobics classes, or free weights. Members work out on eight to twelve hydraulic resistance machines, stopping between stations to walk or jog in place. The clubs' standard routine finishes in 30 minutes and is designed to burn 500 calories. Club members usually pay $29 a month, far less than they would in conventional fitness clubs. Rather than attracting customers from other clubs, Curves generates customers who haven't considered joining a fitness club before.[6]

- **Magazine Luiza.** Brazil's third-largest nonfood retailer targets low-income consumers by selling consumer electronics and appliances on installment payment plans and offering affordable credit in a country with some of the world's highest interest rates. The company requires customers to return to the store each month to make payments in person, enticing many customers to make new

Steve & Barry's offers sportswear at surprisingly low prices and surprisingly high quality.

purchases upon seeing the appealing merchandise on sale. In a country where almost half the population does not have a checking account, the retailer also provides services—including personal loans and insurance policies—that would otherwise be out of reach to most customers. Even though 80 percent of its sales are paid for in installments, its default rate is 50 percent lower than that of other Brazilian retailers.[7]

Each of these retail strategies involves (1) selecting target market segment(s), (2) selecting a retail format (the elements in the retail mix), and (3) developing a sustainable competitive advantage that enables the retailer to reduce the level of competition it faces. Now let's examine these central concepts of a retail strategy.

TARGET MARKET AND RETAIL FORMAT

The **retailing concept** is a management orientation that focuses a retailer on determining the needs of its target market and satisfying those needs more effectively and efficiently than its competitors do. The selection of a target market concentrates the retailer on a group of consumers whose needs it will attempt to satisfy, and the selection of a retail format outlines the retail mix to be used to satisfy the needs of those customers. Successful retailers satisfy the needs of customers in their target segment better than their competition does.

A **retail market** is a group of consumers with similar needs (a market segment) that a group of retailers can service using a similar retail format to satisfy them.[8] Exhibit 5–1 illustrates a set of retail markets for women's clothing and lists various retail formats in the left-hand column. Each format offers a different retail mix to its customers. Market segments are listed in the exhibit's top row. As mentioned in Chapter 4, these segments could be defined in terms of the customers' geographic location, demographics, lifestyle, buying situation, or benefits sought. In this exhibit, we divide the market into three fashion-related segments: conservative, or consumers who place little importance on fashion; traditional, who want classic styles; and fashion-forward, or those who want the latest fashions.

EXHIBIT 5–1   Retail Markets for Women's Apparel

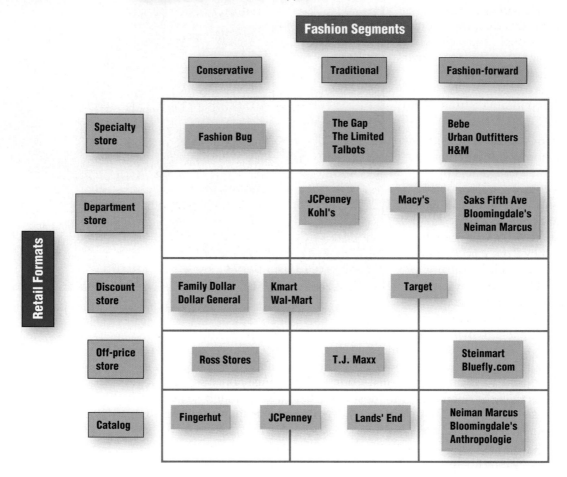

Each square of the matrix shown in Exhibit 5–1 describes a potential retail market in which retailers can compete. For example, Wal-Mart and Kmart stores in the same geographic area compete with each other using a discount store format to target conservative customers, whereas Bloomingdale's and Neiman Marcus compete against each other using a department store format that appeals to the fashion-forward segment. Each fashion segment—conservative, traditional, and fashion-forward—is likely to shop multiple formats. For instance, a fashion-forward customer might shop Urban Outfitters for casual wear and Neiman Marcus for business attire.

The women's clothing market in Exhibit 5–1 is just one of several representations that we could have used. Retail formats might be expanded to include outlet stores and category specialists. Rather than being segmented by fashion orientation, the market could be segmented using the other approaches described in Chapter 4. Although Exhibit 5–1 isn't the only way to describe the women's retail clothing market, it does illustrate how retail markets may be defined in terms of retail format and customer market segments and portrays a retail market in each square.

Exhibit 5–1's matrix also describes the battlefields on which women's apparel retailers compete. The position in each battlefield (cell in the matrix) indicates the first two elements of a retailer's strategy: the fashion segment (the x-axis) and the retail format (the y-axis).

Consider the situation confronting Target as it refines its retail strategy for the women's clothing market. Should Target compete in all 15 retail markets shown in Exhibit 5–1, or should it focus on a limited set of markets? If Target decides to focus on a limited set of markets, which should it pursue? Target's answers to these questions define its retail strategy and indicate how it should focus its resources.

BUILDING A SUSTAINABLE COMPETITIVE ADVANTAGE

The final element in a retail strategy is the retailer's approach to building a sustainable competitive advantage. Any business activity that a retailer engages in can be the basis for a competitive advantage, but some advantages are sustainable over a long period of time, whereas others can be duplicated by competitors almost immediately.[9] For example, it would be hard for Seattle's Best Coffee to establish a long-term advantage over Starbucks by simply offering the same coffee specialties at lower prices. If Seattle's Best's lower prices were successful in attracting customers, Starbucks would know what Seattle's Best had done and quickly match the price reduction. Similarly, it's hard for retailers to develop a long-term advantage by offering broader or deeper merchandise assortments. If broader and deeper assortments attract a lot of customers, competitors will simply go out and buy the same merchandise for their stores.

Establishing a competitive advantage means that the retailer, in effect, builds a wall around its position in a retail market. When the wall is high, it will be hard for competitors outside the wall (i.e., retailers operating in other markets or entrepreneurs) to enter the market and compete for the retailer's target customers.

Over time, all advantages erode due to competitive forces, but by building high, thick walls, retailers can sustain their advantage, minimize competitive pressures, and boost profits for a longer time. Thus, establishing a sustainable competitive advantage is the key to positive long-term financial performance.

Seven important opportunities for retailers to develop sustainable competitive advantages are as follows: (1) customer loyalty, (2) location, (3) human resource management, (4) distribution and information systems, (5) unique merchandise, (6) vendor relations, and (7) customer service. Exhibit 5–2 indicates which aspects of these sources of competitive advantage are more and less sustainable. Let's look at each of these approaches.

EXHIBIT 5–2
Methods of Developing Sustainable Competitive Advantage

Sources of Advantage	SUSTAINABILITY OF ADVANTAGE	
	Less Sustainable	**More Sustainable**
Customer loyalty (Chapters 11 and 16)	Habitual repeat purchasing; repeat purchases because of limited competition in the local area	Building a brand image with an emotional connection with customers; using databases to develop and utilize a deeper understanding of customers
Location (Chapters 7 and 8)		Convenient locations
Human resource management (Chapter 9)	More employees	Committed, knowledgeable employees
Distribution and information systems (Chapter 10)	Bigger warehouses; automated warehouses	Shared systems with vendors
Unique merchandise (Chapters 12 to 14)	More merchandise; greater assortment; lower price; higher advertising budgets; more sales promotions	Exclusive merchandise
Vendor relations (Chapter 14)	Repeat purchases from vendor due to limited alternatives	Coordination of procurement efforts; ability to get scarce merchandise
Customer service (Chapter 19)	Hours of operation	Knowledgeable and helpful salespeople

Customer Loyalty

Customer loyalty means that customers are committed to buying merchandise and services from a particular retailer. Other bases for sustainable competitive advantage discussed in this section help attract and maintain loyal customers; for instance, having dedicated employees, unique merchandise, and superior customer service all help solidify a loyal customer base. But having loyal customers is, in and of itself, an important method of sustaining an advantage over competitors.

Loyalty is more than simply liking one retailer over another.[10] Loyalty means that customers will be reluctant to patronize competitive retailers. For example, loyal customers will continue to have their car serviced at Jiffy Lube, even if a competitor opens a store nearby and provides slightly lower prices. Some ways that retailers build loyalty are by (1) developing a strong brand image for the retailer or its private label brands, (2) developing clear and precise positioning strategies, and (3) creating an attachment with customers through loyalty programs.[11]

Retail Branding   Retailers use brands to build loyalty in much the same way that manufacturers do. In retailing, however, a retailer may put its name on the merchandise, such as Hot Topic, or use a name that is sold exclusively at that retailer, such as Kenmore appliances at Sears. These store brands are also known as private-label brands and are discussed in Chapter 14.

A retail brand, whether it is the name of the retailer or a private label, can create an emotional tie with customers that builds their trust and loyalty. People know, for instance, that when they buy the L.L. Bean brand, they can be assured that the products are "guaranteed to give 100% satisfaction in every way. Return anything purchased from us at any time if it proves otherwise. We do not want you to have anything from L.L. Bean that is not completely satisfactory. [We] do not consider a sale complete until goods are worn out and [the] customer [is] still satisfied."[12] Retail brands also facilitate loyalty because they stand for a predictable level of quality that customers feel comfortable with and often seek. Retail branding is discussed in Chapter 16. A strong retail brand also becomes part of a retailer's positioning strategy, the topic discussed next.

Positioning   A retailer builds customer loyalty by developing a clear, distinctive image of its retail offering and consistently reinforcing that image through its merchandise and services. **Positioning** involves the design and implementation of a retail mix to create an image of the retailer in the customer's mind relative to its competitors.[13]

Furthermore, positioning emphasizes that the image in the customer's mind (not the retail manager's mind) is critical. Thus, the retailer needs to research what its image is and make sure that it is consistent with what customers in its target market want. A perceptual map is frequently used to represent the customer's held image and preferences for retailers.

Exhibit 5–3 offers a hypothetical perceptual map of retailers selling women's clothing in the Washington, DC, area. The two dimensions in this map, fashion/style and service, represent the two primary characteristics that consumers in this example use in forming their impressions of retail stores. Perceptual maps are developed so that the distance between two retailers' positions on the map indicates how similar the stores appear to consumers. For example, Neiman Marcus and Saks Fifth Avenue are very close to each other on the map because consumers in this illustration see them as offering similar services and fashion. In contrast, Nordstrom and Marshalls are far apart, indicating consumers think they're quite different. Note that stores close to each other compete vigorously because consumers feel they provide similar benefits.

According to this example, Macy's has an image of offering fashionable women's clothing with good service. T. J. Maxx offers a similar level of fashionable clothing with less service. Sears is viewed as a retailer offering women's clothing that is not fashionable with relatively limited service.

Hypothetical Perceptual Map of Women's Apparel Market in Washington, DC   **EXHIBIT 5–3**

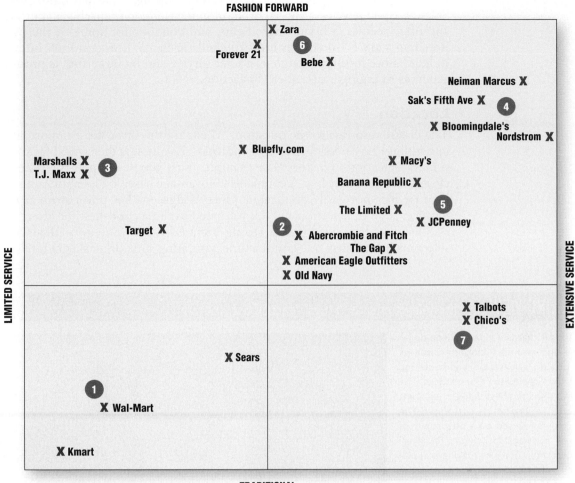

The ideal points (marked by red dots on the map) indicate the characteristics of an ideal retailer for consumers in different market segments. For example, consumers in segment 3 prefer a retailer that offers high-fashion merchandise with low service, whereas consumers in segment 1 want more traditional apparel and aren't concerned about service. The ideal points are located so that the distance between a retailer's position (marked with a blue "x") and the ideal point indicates how consumers in the segment evaluate that retailer.

Retailers that are closer to an ideal point are evaluated more favorably by the consumers in the segment than are retailers located farther away. Thus, consumers in segment 6 prefer Forever 21 and Bebe to Neiman Marcus because these retailers are more fashion forward, and their target customers do not require such high service levels.

Loyalty Programs   Loyalty programs are part of an overall customer relationship management (CRM) program, examined in Chapter 11. These programs are prevalent in retailing, from department stores to the local pizza shop.

Customer loyalty programs work hand-in-hand with CRM. Members of loyalty programs are identified when they buy because they use some type of loyalty card. Their purchase information then is stored in a huge database known as a **data warehouse.** From this data warehouse, analysts determine what types of merchandise and services certain groups of customers are buying. Using this information, retailers can tailor their offerings to better meet the needs of their loyal customers.

For instance, by analyzing its database, Safeway might identify those customers who buy expensive wines and gourmet food. Having identified these customers, Safeway could develop a special promotion focusing on preparing a gourmet meal and offer recipes, a list of ingredients, and coupons for some of the products. Retailing View 5.1 describes how Mitchells/Richards uses customer information to build store loyalty through customer service and by targeting its promotional activities to improve customer satisfaction.

Location

The classic response to the question, "What are the three most important things in retailing?" is "location, location, location." Location is the critical factor in consumers' selection of a store. For example, most people shop at the supermarket closest to where they live. A competitive advantage based on location is sustainable because it is not easily duplicated. Once Walgreens has put a store at the best location at an intersection, CVS is relegated to the second-best location.

Starbucks has developed a strong competitive advantage with its location selection. It conquers one city at a time, saturating a major market before entering

---

5.1   **RETAILING VIEW**   Mitchells/Richards "Hugs" each Customer

Mitchells/Richards is a multimillion-dollar men's and women's clothing business with one store in Westport and a second store in Greenwich, Connecticut. The family-owned business delivers excellent personal service to its customers. The company is focused on a philosophy of building relationships, always "hugging" the customer, not just making transactions. The Mitchells family view their staff as a critical component of their customer-centered business model. On average, the tenure of sales associates at the Connecticut stores is 15 years or more, and these long-term employees treat all customers as celebrities or CEOs.

To empower employees to serve clients properly, Mitchells/Richards uses a sophisticated customer relationship management (CRM) program. Mitchells/Richards designed its computer system around its business model. The system includes a profile for not only each individual customer but also

Stores like Mitchells/Richards build a sustainable competitive advantage by building a loyal customer base with excellent customer service.

each household member, which may include the primary customer, a spouse or significant other, children, and even pets. The financial returns from this CRM system are significant. Achieving $1 million in sales was once unheard of but is now expected during the first year a sales associate joins the company. Some customers' annual purchases range up to $100,000, and some even spend $250,000.

The retailer's customer service goes far beyond just offering complimentary tailoring. The employees, including the sales associates, the tailors, the fitters, and the delivery people, know everything about their customers. They study their customers' profiles, which include merchandise they have bought recently, merchandise they have *not* bought recently, upcoming events

such as family birthdays, changes in spending habits, golf handicaps, and so forth.

Mitchells/Richards does not do traditional advertising but rather communicates with its existing and new customers via personalized gestures. For instance, customers in the area that have bought million-dollar homes receive a box of wooden hangers and a $100 gift certificate. With these efforts, the retailer reminds customers of its loyalty and service to the customer.

Sources: Edmondson, Amy C. and John A. Davis, "The Mitchell Family and Mitchells/Richards," Boston: Harvard Business Press, 2007; http://www. mitchellsonline.com (accessed July 30, 2007); Keiko Morris, "Venerable Men's Store 'Hugs' Women," *Knight Ridder Tribune Business News,* September 11, 2006, p. 1.

a new market. For example, there were more than 100 Starbucks outlets in the Seattle area before the company expanded to a new region. Starbucks will frequently open several stores close to one another. It has two stores on two corners of the intersection of Robson and Thurlow in Vancouver. Starbucks has such a high density of stores that it makes it very difficult for a competitor to enter a market and find good locations. Approaches for evaluating and selecting locations are discussed in Chapters 7 and 8.

Human Resource Management

Retailing is a labor-intensive business, in which employees play a major role providing services for customers and building customer loyalty. Knowledgeable and skilled employees committed to the retailer's objectives are critical assets that support the success of companies such as Southwest Airlines, Whole Foods, and The Container Store.[14]

Starbucks creates a competitive advantage by picking good locations, by saturating an area.

JCPenney chairman and CEO Mike Ullman believes in the power of the employee for building a sustainable competitive advantage.[15] As he notes, "The associates are the first customers we sell. If it doesn't ring true to them, it's impossible to communicate and inspire the customer." To build involvement and commitment among its employees, Penney has dropped many of the traditional pretenses that define an old-style hierarchical organization. For instance, at the Plano, Texas, corporate headquarters, all employees are on a first-name basis, workweeks are flexible, and leadership workshops help build the executive team for the future.

Recruiting and retaining great employees does not come easy. Chapter 9 examines how retailers can gain a sustainable competitive advantage by developing programs to motivate and coordinate employee efforts, providing appropriate incentives, fostering a strong and positive organizational culture and environment, and managing diversity.

Distribution and Information Systems

All retailers strive to reduce operating costs—the costs associated with running the business—and make sure the right merchandise is available when and where customers want it. The use of sophisticated distribution and information systems offers an opportunity for retailers to achieve these efficiencies.[16] For instance, merchandise sales information flows seamlessly from Wal-Mart to its vendors, like Procter & Gamble, to facilitate quick and efficient merchandise replenishment that avoids costly stockouts and reduces inventory levels. Wal-Mart has the largest data warehouse in the world, enabling the company to fine-tune its merchandise assortments on a store-by-store, category-by-category basis. Wal-Mart's distribution and information systems have enabled this retailer to become the lowest cost provider of merchandise in every market in which it competes. This component of competitive advantage is discussed in Chapter 10.

Unique Merchandise

It is difficult for retailers to develop a competitive advantage through merchandise because most competitors can purchase and sell the same popular national brands. But many retailers realize a sustainable competitive advantage by developing **private-label brands** (also called **store brands**), which are products developed and marketed by a retailer and available only from that retailer.[17]

Sears has a strong private label program. If you want to buy Craftsman tools or Kenmore appliances, you have to purchase them from Sears or Kmart.

For example, three of Sears powerful private-label brands are Kenmore, Die Hard, and Craftsman. Each of these brands has strong loyalty among a significant group of consumers and thus generates considerable store traffic. The quality image of these brands also makes a significant contribution to the image of Sears and the value of Sears Holding Company.[18] Issues pertaining to the development of private label brand merchandise are discussed in Chapter 14.

Vendor Relations

By developing strong relations with vendors, retailers may gain exclusive rights to (1) sell merchandise in a specific region, (2) obtain special terms of purchase that are not available to competitors that lack such relationships, or (3) receive popular merchandise in short supply. Relationships with vendors, like relationships with customers, are developed over a long time and may not be easily offset by a competitor.[19] For example, IKEA, the Swedish-based furniture retailer, works very closely with its suppliers to design low cost furniture and keep inventory to a minimum so it can offer its furniture at low prices.[20] Chapter 14 examines how retailers work with their vendors to build mutually beneficial, long-term relationships.

Customer Service

Retailers also can build a sustainable competitive advantage by offering excellent customer service.[21] Offering good service consistently is difficult because customer service is provided by retail employees, and humans are less consistent than machines. Have you ever received less than perfect service from a salesperson or customer service representative? It is possible that the employee wasn't trained properly, that she didn't like her job, or that he was either inept or just plain rude. It is also possible that you were the 497th customer the salesperson interacted with that day, and she was at the end of her shift. Retailers that offer good customer service instill its importance in their employees over a long period of time through coaching and training. In this way, customer service becomes part of the retailer's organizational culture, a topic examined in Chapter 9.

It takes considerable time and effort to build a tradition and reputation for customer service, but good service is a valuable strategic asset. Once a retailer has earned a service reputation, it can sustain this advantage for a long time because it's hard for a competitor to develop a comparable reputation. Chapter 19 discusses how retailers develop a service advantage.

Multiple Sources of Advantage

To build a sustainable competitive advantage, retailers typically don't rely on a single approach, such as low cost or excellent service.[22] Instead, they need multiple approaches to build as high a wall around their position as possible. For example, McDonald's success is based on providing customers with a good value that meets their expectations, having good customer service, possessing a strong brand name, and having great locations. By pursuing all of these strategies concurrently, McDonald's has developed a strong competitive position in the quick service restaurant market.

McDonald's has always positioned itself as providing a good value—customers get a lot for not much money. Its customers don't have extraordinary expectations;

they don't expect a meal prepared to their specific tastes. But customers do expect and get hot, fresh food that is reasonably priced.

McDonald's customers also don't expect friendly table service with linen table cloths and sterling silverware. Their service expectations, which are typically met, are simple. By developing a system for producing its food and using extensive training for its store employees, McDonald's reduces customers' waiting time.

Furthermore, McDonald's has a strong brand name with very high levels of awareness around the world. When most people think of fast food, they think of McDonald's. The brand also has a number of favorable brand associations, such as Ronald McDonald, fast, clean, and french fries.

Finally, McDonald's has a large number of great locations, which is very important for convenience products such as fast food. Given its market power, it has been successful in finding and opening stores in prime retail locations. In every great city in which it operates around the world, McDonald's has outstanding locations.

By developing these unique capabilities in a number of areas, McDonald's has built a high wall around its position as a service retailer, using a fast-food format directed toward families with young children. Each of the retail strategies outlined at the beginning of the chapter involves multiple sources of advantage. For example, Chico's has developed a strong competitive position through its unique merchandise, strong brand name, high-quality service provided by committed employees, and effective loyalty program. Retailing View 5.2 describes The

---

The Container Store—Selling Products that Make Life Simpler   **RETAILING VIEW**   **5.2**

Customers go to The Container Store to solve a problem. For example, when approached by a salesperson, a customer may say, "My wife loves romance novels. She's got them scattered all over the house. I need something to keep them in." And the salesperson helps the customer solve the problem, or challenge, as the company likes to call them.

The Container Store sells products to help people organize their lives. Multipurpose shelving and garment bags are available to organize closets. Portable file cabinets and magazine holders create order in home offices. Backpacks, modular shelving, and CD holders can make dorm rooms less cluttered. Recipe holders, bottles, jars, and recycling bins bring harmony to kitchens.

The Container Store also owns Elfa International, one of its main suppliers of shelving and storage units. Although Elfa is sold throughout the world, The Container Store decided in 2007 to be the exclusive dealer of it in North America. Elfa products are compatable, interlocking items that can be built to the desired size and shape needed.

Its more than 40 stores range in size from 22,000 to 30,000 square feet and showcase more than 10,000 innovative products. The stores are divided into lifestyle sections marked with brightly colored banners, such as Closet, Kitchen, Office, and Laundry. Wherever you look in the store, there's always someone in a blue apron ready to help solve everything from the tiniest of storage problems to the most intimidating organizational challenges. The annual sales per square foot for this retailer average approximately $400. Although storage items and many other similar products are available at other retailers such as Linens 'N Things and Bed Bath & Beyond, few competitors offer The Container Store's customer service. The Container Store spends considerable time educating sales associates about the merchandise, who are then empowered to use their own intuition and creativity to solve customer problems. It actively recruits customers who are intrigued with helping people organize

The Container Store spends considerable time training sales associates about its unique merchandise that simplifies its customers' lives.

their lives and thus may hire people who were not even looking for employment. The Container Store has appeared on *Fortune*'s list of 100 Best Companies to Work For in each of the last eight years.

Over the years, the company has developed strong vendor relations. Most of its vendors' primary focus has been to manufacture products for industrial use. Yet over time, the company has worked closely with its vendors to develop products that are appropriate for the home.

Sources: Katherine Field, "Containing Culture," *Chain Store Age*, April 2007, pp. 22–24; Sara Schaefer Munoz, "Why The Container-Store Guy Wants to Be Your Therapist," *The Wall Street Journal*, March 29, 2007, p. D.1; www.containerstore.com (accessed July 16, 2007).

Container Store, a retail chain that built a sustainable competitive advantage through unique merchandise, excellent customer service, and strong customer and vendor relations.

GROWTH STRATEGIES

Four types of growth opportunities that retailers may pursue—market penetration, market expansion, retail format development, and diversification—are shown in Exhibit 5–4.[23] The vertical axis indicates the synergies between the retailer's present markets and the growth opportunity—whether the opportunity involves markets the retailer is presently pursuing or new markets. The horizontal axis indicates the synergies between the retailer's present retail mix and the retail mix of the growth opportunity—whether the opportunity exploits the retailer's skills in operating its present format or requires a new set of skills to operate.

Market Penetration

A **market penetration growth opportunity** involves realizing growth by directing efforts toward existing customers using the retailer's present retailing format. These opportunities involve either attracting consumers from the current target market who don't patronize the retailer currently or devising approaches that get current customers to visit the retailer more often or buy more merchandise on each visit. For example, many retailers allow products bought through their Web sites to be picked up at their stores. This initiative has been successful not only in bringing customers into the stores more often but also in encouraging them to purchase more items while in the store.[24]

Market penetration approaches include opening more stores in the target market and keeping existing stores open for longer hours. Other approaches involve displaying merchandise to increase impulse purchases and training salespeople to cross-sell. **Cross-selling** means that sales associates in one department attempt to sell complementary merchandise from other departments to their customers. For example, a sales associate who has just sold a DVD player to a customer will take the customer to the accessories department to sell special cables to improve the performance of the player.

EXHIBIT 5–4
Growth Opportunities

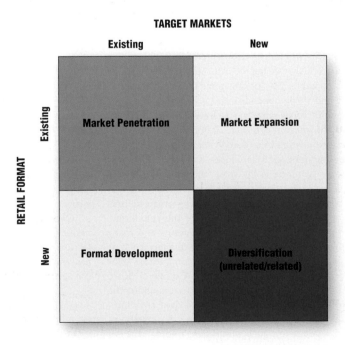

Market Expansion

A **market expansion growth opportunity** involves using the existing retail format in new market segments. For example, Dunkin' Donuts gradually has been opening new stores outside its northeastern U.S. stronghold. The plan calls for Dunkin' eventually to increase the number of its U.S. outlets from the current level of more than 5,300 (out of a total of 7,000-plus stores) to 15,000 while also moving into more foreign countries, including China.[26] Abercrombie & Fitch's (A&F) primary target market is college students, not high-schoolers. Because college-aged people don't particularly like to hang out with teens, A&F opened a new, lower-priced chain called Hollister Co. Although the merchandise and ambience are slightly different than A&F, the retail format is essentially the same.[27]

Retail Format Development

A **retail format development growth opportunity** is an opportunity in which a retailer develops a new retail format—a format with a different retail mix—for the same target market. Multichannel retailing is an example of retail format development, because a bricks-and-mortar retailer is offering an Internet channel as a new format, in addition to its exisiting channel.

The U.K.-based retailer Tesco has employed a retail format development growth strategy by operating several different food store formats that all cater to essentially the same target markets. The smallest is Tesco Express, up to 3,000 square feet. These stores are located close to where customers live and work. Tesco Metro stores are 7,000–15,000 square feet, bring convenience to city center locations, and specialize in offering a wide range of ready-to-eat-meals. Tesco Superstores (up to 50,000 square feet), are the oldest format. In recent years, the company has added nonfood products, such as DVDs and books, to improve customer satisfaction. Finally, Tesco Extra stores (more than 60,000 square feet) are designed to be a one-stop destination, with the widest range of food and nonfood products, from housewares and clothing to garden furniture.[28]

Diversification

A **diversification growth opportunity** is one in which a retailer operates a new retail format directed toward a market segment that's not currently served by the retailer. Diversification opportunities are either related or unrelated.

Related versus Unrelated Diversification   In a **related diversification growth opportunity**, the retailer's present target market or retail format shares something in common with the new opportunity. This commonality might entail purchasing from the same vendors, operating in similar locations, using the same distribution or management information system, or advertising in the same newspapers to similar target markets. In contrast, an **unrelated diversification** lacks any commonality between the present business and the new business.

Through acquisition, Home Depot built a wholesale building supply business, called HD Supply, that generated over $3 billion annual sales. Management felt that this growth opportunity would be synergistic with the firm's retail business, because its stores were selling similar merchandise to contractors. Thus, Home Depot viewed this growth opportunity as a related diversification, because customers (i.e., contractors) would be similar, and the new market of large contractors could be serviced using the same warehouse-like format. In addition, Home Depot would realize cost savings by placing larger orders with vendors because it would be selling to both retail and wholesale businesses.

In hindsight though, the HD Supply actually was an unrelated diversification. HD Supply sold primarily pipes, lumber, and concrete—products with limited sales in retail stores. Selling these supplies for large construction jobs often involved competitive bidding that reduced margins. So Home Depot sold this unrelated diversification to concentrate on its retail/small contractor business.[29]

Vertical Integration   **Vertical integration** describes diversification by retailers into wholesaling or manufacturing.[30] For example, some retailers go beyond designing their private-label merchandise to owning factories that manufacture the merchandise. When retailers integrate by manufacturing products, they are making risky investments because the requisite skills to make products are different from those associated with retailing them. In addition, retailers and manufacturers have different customers; the immediate customers for a manufacturer's merchandise are retailers, whereas a retailer's customers are consumers. Thus, a manufacturer's marketing activities are very different from those of a retailer. Note that designing private-label merchandise is a related diversification because it builds on the retailer's knowledge of its customers, but actually making the merchandise is considered an unrelated diversification.

Strategic Opportunities and Competitive Advantage

Typically, retailers have the greatest competitive advantage when they engage in opportunities that are similar to their present retail strategy. Thus, retailers would be most successful engaging in market penetration opportunities that don't involve entering new, unfamiliar markets or operating new, unfamiliar retail formats.

When retailers pursue market expansion opportunities, they build on their strengths in operating a retail format and apply this competitive advantage in a new market. Those retailers that successfully expand globally are able to translate what they do best—their core competencies—to a new culture and market.

A retail format development opportunity builds on the retailer's reputation and success with its present customers. Even if a retailer doesn't have experience and skills in operating the new format, it hopes to attract its loyal customers to it. For example, as discussed in Chapter 3, some retailers have successfully developed multichannel strategies by seamlessly integrating stores, the Internet, and catalogs to provide extra convenience and multiple opportunities for their current customers to shop. Retailers have the least opportunity to exploit a competitive advantage when they pursue diversification opportunities.

REFACT

Brooks Brothers, a men's specialty store chain, sold the rights to the Polo brand name to Ralph Lauren.[31]

GLOBAL GROWTH OPPORTUNITIES

International expansion is a market expansion growth opportunity that many retailers find attractive. Of the 50 largest global retailers, 38 operate in more than one country.[32] But international expansion can be risky, because retailers must deal with different government regulations, cultural traditions, supply chain considerations, and languages. We first discuss the types of retailers that successfully compete globally, followed by a look at some of the pitfalls of global expansion. Then we examine the key success factors for global expansion and, finally, evaluate the strategies for entering a nondomestic market.

Who Is Successful and Who Isn't?

Retailers with an offering that has universal appeal, based on strong brand images, distinctive merchandise or low cost, are the most successful at exploiting global markets. For example, some of the most successful global retailers are specialty store retailers with strong brand images and/or unique merchandise, such as Starbucks, McDonald's, Zara, and H&M; those that offer deep assortments and low prices, which appeal to consumers in different cultures; or discount and food retailers with low prices, such as Wal-Mart, Carrefour, Royal Ahold, and Metro AG. Retailing View 5.3 discusses some of the successes and problems IKEA has encountered on its way to being a global retailer.

Category specialists and supercenter retailers may be particularly well suited to succeed globally because of their operating efficiencies. First, these retailers are leaders in their use of technology to manage inventories, control global logistical systems, and tailor merchandise assortments to local needs. Second, retailers like Wal-Mart and Carrefour enjoy scale economies for buying merchandise globally. Third, despite idiosyncrasies in the global environment, category specialists and

---

IKEA: Bringing Its Philosophy to a World Market RETAILING VIEW 5.3

Many consumers need to buy furniture and have sophisticated taste but either cannot or do not want to spend lots of money. These consumers don't necessarily want or need furniture that will last forever. Operating 254 stores in 35 countries, IKEA offers unique, well-designed, functional furniture at low prices displayed in realistic room settings.

At IKEA, customers are encouraged to get actively involved in the shopping experience by sitting on the sofas and opening and closing drawers. Price and product information is clearly marked on large, easy-to-read tags, making it easier for customers to serve themselves. The guid-

IKEA has adjusted its unique furniture retail offering to satisfy the needs of U.S. consumers.

ing philosophy is: "You do your part. We do our part. Together, we save money."

The stores are designed to put the customer on a logical buying path. One starts in the living rooms, then moves to bedrooms, closets/bureaus, then kitchens and bathrooms. After the furniture has been chosen for the rooms, the accessories are bought: lighting, dinnerware, art, rugs, and so on. To complete the shopping experience, customers pick up their own furniture and carry the pieces to the register. Self-service items include small tables, chairs, and other manageable pieces. The larger pieces that are too large are brought out from another warehouse. The unassembled furniture is packed flat, suitable for tying to the top of cars. For those customers that do not want to be as involved, IKEA offers delivery service and a recommendation for third-party assembly providers. Couple all this activity with the long checkout lines, and an IKEA shopping trip can run between four to six hours. Yet IKEA customers see tremendous value in the offering and low prices, so they are happy to make the self-service trade-off.

As a bonus to its customers, IKEA maintains the Swedish-style food offered in its cafeterias. In the onsite restaurant, customers can take a shopping break and have breakfast, lunch,

dinner, dessert, or a snack. The food is low priced, and customers can even buy some delicacies, such as Swedish sausages, to take home.

When entering the United States in 1987, IKEA had to make some functional changes to its products. For example, Scandinavian beds were the wrong size for American bed linens, Scandinavian-styled bookshelves were too small to hold a television for Americans who wanted shelving for an entertainment system, its glasses were deemed too small for the super-sized thirsts of Americans, and the dining room tables weren't big enough to fit a turkey in the center on Thanksgiving. But IKEA quickly adapted its products to meet U.S. market needs.

REFACT

Approximately 1.1 million customers visit IKEA each day, and 150 million Swedish meatballs are served per year, or 41,000 each day.[33]

Sources: www.ikea.com (accessed July 19, 2007); Marianne Barner, "Be a Socially Responsible Corporation," *Harvard Business Review*, July/August 2007, pp. 59–60; Jérôme Barthélemy, "The Experimental Roots of Revolutionary Vision," *MIT Sloan Management Review*, Fall 2006, p. 81; R Michelle Breyer, "Marketing Tactics Involve Nuance Within Each Culture," *DSN Retailing Today*, March 27, 2006, pp. 5–6.

supercenter retailers have developed unique systems and standardized formats that facilitate control over multiple stores. Fourth, at one time, U.S.-based retailers believed that consumers outside the United States, who were used to high levels of personalized service, would not embrace the self-service concept employed by category killers and supercenter retailers. However, the experience of chains such as Carrefour (France) and ALDI (Germany) has shown that consumers around the globe are willing to forgo service for lower prices.[34]

Some U.S. retailers have a competitive advantage in global markets because American culture is emulated in many countries, particularly among young people. Due to rising prosperity and the rapidly increasing access to cable TV that features American programming, fashion trends in the United States are spreading to young people in emerging countries. The global MTV generation prefers Coke to tea, athletic shoes to sandals, Chicken McNuggets to rice, and credit cards to cash. China's major cities have sprouted American stores and restaurants, including KFC, Pizza Hut, and McDonald's. Shanghai and Beijing have 57 and 95 Starbucks stores, respectively, even though coffee had never been the drink of choice until Starbucks came to town. But these Chinese urban dwellers go there to impress a friend or because it's a symbol of a new kind of lifestyle. Although Western products and stores have gained a reputation for high quality and good service in China, in some ways, it is the American culture that many Chinese consumers want.

Keys to Success

Four characteristics of retailers that have successfully exploited international growth opportunities are (1) a globally sustainable competitive advantage, (2) adaptability, (3) global culture, and (4) financial resources.[35] A hypothetical evaluation of international growth opportunities appears in the appendix to this chapter.

 Globally Sustainable Competitive Advantage   Entry into nondomestic markets is most successful when the expansion opportunity is consistent with the retailer's core bases of competitive advantage. Some core competitive advantages for global retailers are shown in the following table:

Core Advantage	Global Retailer Example
Low-cost, efficient operations	Wal-Mart, Carrefour, ALDI
Strong private-label brands	Starbucks, KFC
Fashion reputation	H&M, Zara
Category dominance	Office Depot, IKEA, Toys 'R Us

Thus, Wal-Mart, Carrefour, and ALDI are successful in international markets in which price plays an important role in consumer decision making and a distribution infrastructure is available to enable these firms to exploit their logistical capabilities. In contrast, H&M and Zara are more successful in international markets that value lower-priced, fashionable merchandise.

Adaptability   Although successful global retailers build on their core competencies, they also recognize cultural differences and adapt their core strategy to the needs of local markets.[36] Color preferences, the preferred cut of apparel, and sizes differ across cultures. For example, in China, white is the color of mourning, and brides wear red dresses. Food probably has the greatest diversity of tastes around the world. Carrefour is an expert at understanding and integrating itself in local regions, such as its early realization that the merchandising of fish differs for each local market. In San Francisco, fish is dead and filleted; in France, the fish is dead but whole on ice with the head still intact; and in China, fish is sold live. However, consumers in the middle and western parts of China have more confidence in frozen fish, because they are so far from the ocean.[37]

Selling seasons also vary across countries. In the United States, many stores experience a sales increase in August, when families stock up on back-to-school supplies and apparel; however, this month is one of the slowest sales periods in Europe, because most people are on vacation. Back-to-school season in Japan occurs in April.

Store designs and layouts often need to be adjusted in different parts of the world. In the United States, for instance, discount stores are usually quite large and on one level. In other parts of the world, such as Europe and parts of Asia, where space is at a premium, stores must be designed to fit a smaller space and are often housed in multiple levels. In some cultures, social norms dictate that men's and women's clothing cannot be displayed next to each other.

Government regulations and cultural values can also affect store operations. Some differences, such as holidays, hours of operation, and regulations governing part-time employees and terminations, are easy to identify. Other factors require a deeper understanding. For example, Latin American culture is very family oriented, so traditional U.S. work schedules would need to be adjusted so that Latin American employees could have more time with their families. Boots, a U.K. drugstore chain, has the checkout clerks in its Japanese stores standing up because it discovered that Japanese shoppers found it offensive to pay money to a seated clerk, but retailers have to provide seating for checkout clerks in Germany. Retailers in Germany also must recycle packaging materials sold in their stores. Also in Germany, seasonal sales can be held only during specific weeks and apply only to specific product categories, and the amount of the discounts are limited.

Starbucks has been pleasantly surprised at how quickly consumers around the world have accepted the products it sells in the United States. In terms of assortment, there isn't great variation from country to country. Outside the United States, food is a bigger part of business—much more important in China, Japan, and the United Kingdom than it is in the United States. Frappuccino-type products, however, are popular everywhere, though Starbucks has developed some unique drinks for different markets. For example, the green tea Frappuccino, sold only in Taiwan and Japan, is the best selling Frappuccino in those countries, and a strawberries-and-cream Frappuccino was developed expressly for the United Kingdom.[38]

Global Culture   To be global, retailers must think globally. It is not sufficient to transplant a home-country culture and infrastructure into another country. In this regard, Carrefour is truly global. In the early years of its international expansion, it started in each country slowly, which reduced the company's ethnocentrism. Further enriching its global perspective, Carrefour has always encouraged the rapid development of local management and retains few expatriates in its overseas operations. Carrefour's management ranks are truly international. One is just as likely to run across a Portuguese regional manager in Hong Kong as a French or Chinese one. Finally, Carrefour discourages the classic overseas "tour of duty" mentality often found in U.S. firms. International assignments are important in themselves, not just as stepping stones to ultimate career advancement back in France. The globalization of Carrefour's culture is perhaps most evident in the speed with which ideas flow throughout the organization. A global management structure of regional "committees," which meet regularly, advances the awareness and implementation of global best practices. The proof of Carrefour's global commitment lies in the numbers: It has had more than 30 years of international experience in 30 countries, both developed and developing.[39]

Coffee was not the drink of choice until Starbucks came to China. But now Shanghai and Beijing each have more than two dozen Starbucks.

Financial Resources   Expansion into international markets requires a long-term commitment and considerable upfront planning. Retailers find it very difficult to generate short-term profits when they make the transition to global retailing. Although firms like Wal-Mart, Carrefour, Office Depot, and Costco often initially have difficulty achieving success in new global markets, these large firms generally are in a strong financial position and therefore have the ability to keep investing in projects long enough to become successful.

Evaluating Global Growth Opportunities

In their efforts to grow, many retailers have sought opportunities to open stores in other countries. However, some countries represent better opportunities than others. Exhibit 5–5 shows the top 20 countries ranked by overall opportunity.[40] These rankings are based on a weighted score according to their growth (55 percent), risk (25 percent), and market size (20 percent).

China, India, Japan, Australia, and Malaysia—all Asia-Pacific countries—are in the top 10. Following the lifting of international restrictions on foreign investments international food retailers (Auchan, Carrefour, Ito-Yokado, Metro, Tesco, and Wal-Mart) have already entered China.[42] Although much of this retail development has been in the largest cities of Shanghai and Beijing, international retailers are now moving into interior cities. Doing business in China is still a challenge, however. Operating costs are increasing, managerial talent is becoming more difficult to find and retain, and an underdeveloped and inefficient supply chain predominates.

India is an attractive market for retailers because it has a population of over 1 billion, solid economic growth, rising affluent urban middle-class, and it has rescinded some restrictions on foreign investment.[43] The challenge facing global retailers in India is that the majority of the population, especially in rural areas, still prefers small, family-owned shops. In addition, despite some loosening of the

REFACT

China sells more washing machines and television sets than the United States, while Indians buy more refrigerators and televisions than Germans.[41]

REFACT

India's compounded annual population growth rate is expected to be 1.12 percent between now and 2020—more than double the forecast for China for the same period. If these rates continue, India will have more people than China by 2035.

EXHIBIT 5–5
Global Retail Opportunity Rankings

2006 Ranking	Country	Index*
1	China	76
2	United States	63
3	India	61
4	Russia	59
5	United Kingdom	57
6	Malaysia	48
7	Japan	46
8	Australia	46
9	Canada	44
10	Spain	41
11	Philippines	40
12	Turkey	40
13	South Africa	40
14	Germany	40
15	France	39
16	Taiwan	39
17	Vietnam	38
18	Thailand	37
19	Netherlands	36
20	Sweden	35

*Weighted index.

SOURCE: Ayuna Kidder, "Global Retail Outlook," Columbus, OH: Retail Forward, Inc., March 2007.

limitations, India restricts foreign investment, so the majority of ownership still must reside with Indian nationals.

Although Russia and the United Kingdom are highly ranked, other European countries have slipped in the rankings due to their relatively slow growth. Russia in particular has strong growth and consumer demand, coupled with falling inflation.[44] Like India though, except in big cities like Moscow and St. Petersburg, smaller, family-owned retailers still account for about 86 percent of retail sales. Doing business in Russia can be challenging due to its poor transportation infrastructure, bureaucracy, and corruption.

The rankings for Latin and South America and Africa are mixed. Brazil, Argentina, and Mexico have the highest

For a country to be a viable option for a new market entry, firms must assess its transportation, distribution channels, communications, and commercial infrastructure.

rankings in South and Latin America, whereas South Africa shows the strongest opportunity for retailers in Africa. Yet business risk remains high in many countries in these parts of the world.

The three opportunity ranking dimensions—growth, risk, and market size—are used to portray the top 30 countries graphically in Exhibit 5–6. The horizontal axis represents growth, the vertical axis represents risk, and the size of the circle represents market size. The United States, United Kingdom, Taiwan, and Malaysia fall into the "Best Opportunity" quadrant (upper right). Australia and Canada are on the fringe of this quadrant. China, India, and Russia dominate the lower-right

Growth, Risk, and Market Size of the Top 30 Countries   **EXHIBIT 5–6**

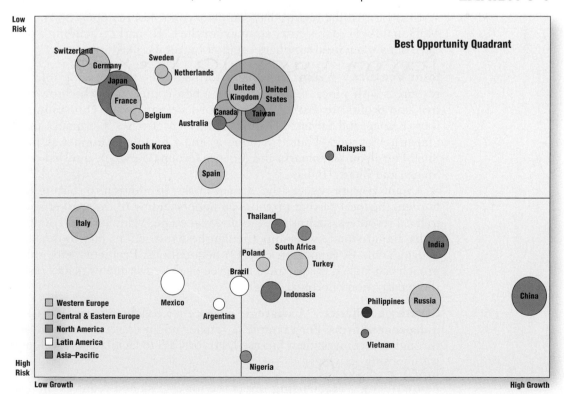

SOURCE: Ayuna Kidder, "Global Retail Outlook," Columbus, OH: Retail Forward, March 2007. Used by permission of TNS Retail Forward.

quadrant because they have high growth but relatively high risk. Although most of the Western European countries remain stable, their growth is stagnant, putting them in the upper-left quadrant. The appendix to this chapter describes a process for evaluating growth opportunities.

Moving into global markets requires all the same success factors as starting any business—a good strategy that is sustainable, a strong financial position, and a little luck. But global expansions require a lot more. First, firms must act like they are local and understand their customers' needs.[45] For example, France-based Carrefour and U.K.-based Tesco makes sure that more than 90 percent of the merchandise they sell is produced in the country in which it is sold.[46] Second, retailers must understand and act appropriately in response to the subtle nuances between markets and countries. For instance, Spanish and French retailers work under government-controlled operating hours and must mind policies prohibiting mid-season sales. Average rental space in the United Kingdom is more than twice as much as that in Spain. Spain also has a $4.70 minimum wage, compared with almost $11.00 in France. Third, retailers must ensure their timing is right. In 1995, for example, the Japanese retailer Yachan opened one of the world's biggest department stores in Shanghai and planned to open 1,000 more stores in China. But at that time, the affluent market was too small to support the store, and in 1997, Yachan filed for bankruptcy. Fourth and finally, a global retailer must be selective. Tesco has opened convenience stores in California but is avoiding supermarkets, because the food retailer believes this market is saturated.

Entry Strategies

Four approaches that retailers can take when entering nondomestic markets are direct investment, joint venture, strategic alliance, and franchising.[47]

Direct Investment   **Direct investment** occurs when a retail firm invests in and owns a division or subsidiary that operates in a foreign country. This entry strategy requires the highest level of investment and exposes the retailer to significant risks, but it also has the highest potential returns. One advantage of direct investment is that the retailer has complete control of the operations. For example, McDonald's chose this entry strategy for the U.K. market, building a plant to produce buns when local suppliers could not meet its specifications.

Joint Venture   A **joint venture** is formed when the entering retailer pools its resources with a local retailer to form a new company in which ownership, control, and profits are shared. Examples of successful joint ventures include Carrefour (France) and Sabanci Holding (Turkey); Metro AG (Germany) and Marubeni (Japan); Monsoon (United Kingdom) and Charming Shoppes (United States); Shell Petroleum (Denmark) and Alliance Group (Ukraine); and Wal-Mart (United States) and Bharti (India).

A joint venture reduces the entrant's risks. In addition to sharing the financial burden, the local partner provides an understanding of the market and has access to local resources, such as vendors and real estate. Many foreign countries, such as India, require joint ownership, though these restrictions may loosen as a result of World Trade Organization (WTO) negotiations. Problems with this entry approach can arise if the partners disagree or the government places restrictions on the repatriation of profits.

Strategic Alliance   A **strategic alliance** is a collaborative relationship between independent firms. For example, a retailer might enter an international market through direct investment but use DHL or UPS to facilitate its local logistical and warehousing activities.

Franchising   **Franchising** offers the lowest risk and requires the least investment. However, the entrant has limited control over the retail operations in the foreign country, its potential profit is reduced, and the risk of assisting in the creation of a local domestic competitor increases. The U.K.-based Marks & Spencer, for example, has franchised stores in 30 countries.[48] The Franchising appendix at the end of the text provides a thorough discussion of this ownership approach.

THE STRATEGIC RETAIL PLANNING PROCESS

The **strategic retail planning process** entails the set of steps a retailer goes through to develop a strategic retail plan[49] (see Exhibit 5–7). It describes how retailers select target market segments, determine the appropriate retail format, and build sustainable competitive advantages. As indicated in Exhibit 5–7, it is not always necessary to go through the entire process each time an evaluation is performed (step 7). For instance, a retailer could evaluate its performance, find that its present strategy is working well, and then go to step 5 to update its objective.

The planning process can be used to formulate strategic plans at different levels within a retail corporation. For example, the corporate strategic plan of Tesco indicates how to allocate resources across the corporation's various divisions, such as Tesco, Tesco Extra, Tesco Express, Tesco Metro, Tesco Homeplus, and One Stop. Each division, in turn, develops its own strategic plan.

As we discuss the steps in the retail planning process, we will apply each step to the planning process Kelly Bradford is undertaking. Kelly owns Gifts To Go, a small, two-store chain in the Chicago area. One of her 1,000 square foot stores is located in the downtown area; the other is in an upscale suburban mall. The target market for Gifts To Go is upper-income men and women looking for gifts in the $50–500 price range. The stores have an eclectic selection of merchandise, including handmade jewelry and crafts, fine china and glassware, perfume, watches, writing

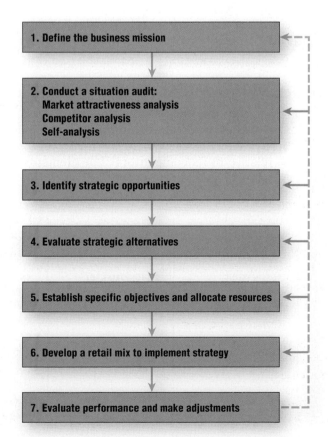

EXHIBIT 5–7
Stages in the Strategic
Retail Planning Process

instruments, and a variety of one-of-a-kind items. Gifts To Go also has developed a number of loyal customers who are contacted by sales associates when family anniversaries and birthdays come up. In many cases, customers have a close relationship with a sales associate and enough confidence in the associate's judgment that they tell the associate to pick out an appropriate gift. The turnover of Gifts To Go sales associates is low for the industry, because Kelly treats associates as part of the family. The company pays for medical insurance for all associates, and they share in the profits of the firm.

Step 1: Define the Business Mission

The first step in the strategic retail planning process is to define the business mission. The **mission statement** is a broad description of a retailer's objectives and the scope of activities it plans to undertake.[50] Whereas the objective of a publicly held firm is to maximize its stockholders' wealth by increasing the value of its stock and paying dividends,[51] owners of small, privately held firms frequently have other objectives, such as achieving a specific level of income and avoiding risks rather than maximizing income.

The mission statement defines the general nature of the target segments and retail formats on which the firm will focus. For example, the mission statement of an office supply category specialist, "Serve the customer, build value for shareholders, and create opportunities for associates," is too broad. It fails to provide a sense of strategic direction.

In developing the mission statement, managers need to answer five questions: (1) What business are we in? (2) What should our business be in the future? (3) Who are our customers? (4) What are our capabilities? (5) What do we want to accomplish? Gifts To Go's mission statement is "The mission of Gifts To Go is to be the leading retailer of higher-priced gifts in Chicago and provide a stable income of $100,000 per year for the owner."

Because the mission statement defines the retailer's objectives and the scope of activities it plans to undertake, Gifts To Go's mission statement clarifies that its management won't consider retail opportunities outside the Chicago area, for selling low-priced gifts, or that would jeopardize its ability to generate $100,000 in annual income.[52]

Step 2: Conduct a Situation Audit

After developing a mission statement and setting objectives, the next step in the strategic planning process is to conduct a **situation audit**, an analysis of the opportunities and threats in the retail environment and the strengths and weaknesses of the retail business relative to its competitors. The elements in the situation analysis are shown in Exhibit 5–8.[53]

EXHIBIT 5–8
Elements in a Situation Audit

MARKET FACTORS	COMPETITIVE FACTORS	ENVIRONMENTAL FACTORS	ANALYSIS OF STRENGTHS AND WEAKNESSES
Size	Barriers to entry	Technology	Management capabilities
Growth	Bargaining power of vendors	Economic	Financial resources
Seasonality	Competitive rivalry	Regulatory	Locations
Business cycles		Social	Operations
			Merchandise
			Store management
			Customer loyalty

Market Factors   Some critical factors related to consumers and their buying patterns are the target market size and growth, sales cyclicity, and seasonality. Market size, typically measured in retail sales dollars, is important because it indicates a retailer's opportunity to generate revenues to cover its investment. Large markets are attractive to large retail firms, but they are also attractive to small entrepreneurs because they offer more opportunities to focus on a market segment. Some retailers, however, prefer to concentrate on smaller markets because they face less competition. Cato, for instance, sells value-priced women's fashion in more than 1,000 stores located in 31 U.S. states, primarily in small towns.[54]

Growing markets are typically more attractive than mature or declining markets. For example, retail markets for limited assortment, extreme value retailers are growing faster than are those for department stores. Typically, the return on investment is higher in growing markets because competition is less intense than in mature markets. Because new customers are just beginning to patronize stores in growing markets, they may not have developed strong store loyalties and thus might be easier to attract to new outlets.

Firms are often interested in minimizing the business cycle's impact on their sales. Thus, those retail markets for merchandise affected by economic conditions (such as cars and major appliances) are less attractive than retail markets unaffected by economic conditions (such as food).

In general, markets with highly seasonal sales are unattractive because a lot of resources are needed to accommodate the peak season, but then resources are underutilized the rest of the year. To minimize problems due to seasonality, ski resorts promote summer vacations to generate sales during all four seasons.

To conduct an analysis of the market factors for Gifts To Go, Kelly Bradford went on the Internet to get information about the size, growth, and cyclical and seasonal nature of the gift market in general and, more specifically, in Chicago. On the basis of her analysis, she concluded that the market factors were attractive; the market for more expensive gifts was large, growing, and not vulnerable to business cycles. The only negative aspect was the high seasonality of gifts, with peaks at Valentine's Day, June (due to weddings), Christmas, and other holidays.

Competitive Factors   The nature of the competition in retail markets is affected by barriers to entry, the bargaining power of vendors, and competitive rivalry.[55] Retail markets are more attractive when competitive entry is costly. **Barriers to entry** institute conditions in a retail market that make it difficult for other firms to enter the market, such as scale economies, customer loyalty, and the availability of good locations.

Scale economies are cost advantages due to a retailer's size. Markets dominated by large competitors with scale economies are typically unattractive. For example, a small entrepreneur might avoid becoming an office supply category specialist because the market is an oligopoly dominated by three large firms: Staples, Office Depot, and OfficeMax. These firms have a considerable cost advantage over the entrepreneur because they can buy merchandise cheaper and operate more efficiently by investing in the latest technology and spreading their overhead across more stores. However, Retailing View 5.4 discusses how some small retailers develop sustainable advantages over national chains with significant scale economies.

Retail markets dominated by a well-established retailer that has developed a loyal group of customers also are unattractive. For example, Home Depot's high customer loyalty in Atlanta, where it has its corporate offices, makes it hard for a competing home improvement center to enter the Atlanta market.

Finally, the availability of locations may impede competitive entry. Staples, for instance, attributes part of its success over its rivals in the northeastern United States to its first-mover advantage. The Northeast has a preponderance of mature but stable retail markets, so finding new locations is more difficult there than it is in most of the rest of the United States. Because Staples started in the Northeast, it was able to open stores in the best locations.

Entry barriers are a double-edged sword. A retail market with high entry barriers is very attractive for retailers presently competing in that market, because those barriers limit competition. However, markets with high entry barriers are unattractive for retailers not already in the market. For example, the lack of good retail locations in Hong Kong makes this market attractive for retailers already in the region but less attractive for retailers desiring to enter the market.

Another competitive factor is the **bargaining power of vendors.** Markets are less attractive when only a few vendors control the merchandise sold in it. In these situations, vendors have the opportunity to dictate prices and other terms (like delivery dates), reducing the retailer's profits. For example, the market for retailing fashionable cosmetics is less attractive because only two suppliers, Estée Lauder (Estée Lauder, Clinique, Prescriptives, Aveda, Jo Malone, Bumble and Bumble, Tommy Hilfiger, MAC, and Origins) and L'Oréal (Maybelline, Giorgio Armani, RedKen, Lancôme, Garnier, and Ralph Lauren), provide very desirable premium brands. Because department stores need these brands to support a fashionable image, the suppliers have the power to sell their products to retailers at high prices.

The final competitive factor is the level of competitive rivalry in the retail market. **Competitive rivalry** is the frequency and intensity of reactions to actions undertaken by competitors. When rivalry is high, price wars erupt, employee raids occur, advertising and promotion expenses increase, and profit potential falls. Conditions that

5.4   RETAILING VIEW   Competing Against the Giants

When small businesses compete for the same customers as big box retailers, the story goes, they lose. But a small paper goods, office furnishing, and gift shop called Quill & Press, located near a Staples megastore in Acton, Massachusetts, in the Boston area, has managed to achieve great results.

The small store offers niche products that cannot be found in Staples. Its product assortment ranges from a 35¢ ballpoint pen to a $3,500 fountain pen by Graf von Faber-Castel. To its upscale customer base, the retailer offers special products available only in the store, including top-of-the-line stationary, invitations, leather goods, art supplies, and writing utensils.

This small retailer manages to keep 35,000–40,000 items in inventory, but its assortment differs significantly from that of Staples, which appeals to the mass market. Whereas Staples offers convenience for customers shopping for basic office and school supplies, the small retailer stocks more emotionally valuable products, like a $2,500 ergonomic leather desk chair.

Customers value the special service that they receive from the small retailer; it knows its clientele better, so it not only stocks products they desire but also helps them navigate the product selection. As another perk, customers feel as though they are supporting local businesses rather than a national chain. The local retailer makes contributions to local schools and ballet activities—investments a national chain is not likely to support.

Quill & Press in Acton, MA competes with Staples with unusual merchandise and outstanding service.

Both the big box retailer and the small local retailer thus appear to have found room in the market. Depending on what the customer is searching for, he or she prefers one retailer over the other. However, the service and unique, high-end products that the small retailer provides appear to be offerings that prompt true customer loyalty.

Source: Davis Bushnell, "Thriving Retailer's Personal Stamp," *Boston Globe,* April 12, 2007. Reprinted by permission of The Boston Globe.

may lead to intense rivalry include (1) a large number of competitors that are all about the same size, (2) slow growth, (3) high fixed costs, and (4) a lack of perceived differences between competing retailers. Dunkin' Donuts and Starbucks have an intense rivalry in some markets. Starbucks has extended its food/lunch menu, while Dunkin' is encroaching on Starbucks' gourmet coffee turf. Pricing for similar items is close, though Starbucks is still more expensive. To provide easier accessibility, Starbucks is offering Dunkin'-style drive-through windows in some locations.

When Kelly Bradford started to analyze the competitive factors for Gifts To Go, she realized that identifying her competitors wasn't easy. Although there were no gift stores carrying similar merchandise at the same price points in the Chicago area, there were various other retailers from which a customer could buy gifts. She identified her primary competitors as department stores, craft galleries, catalogs, and Internet retailers. Kelly felt there were some scale economies in developing customer databases to support gift retailing. The lack of large suppliers meant that vendors' bargaining power wasn't a problem, and competitive rivalry was minimal because the gift business was not a critical part of the department store's overall business. In addition, merchandise carried by the various retailers offered considerable differentiation opportunities.

Environmental Factors Environmental factors that can affect market attractiveness span technological, economic, regulatory, and social changes. When a retail market is going through significant changes in technology, existing competitors are vulnerable to new entrants that are skilled at using the new technology. Many traditional store-based retailers were slow to develop their multichannel Internet strategies fully. For instance, in the 1990s, few retailers offered the ability for customers to purchase over the Internet and return merchandise to a store. Today, however, the larger multichannel retailers set the standards for services provided through technology.

Some retailers may be more affected by economic conditions than others. During tough economic times, retailers that offer a perceived high value offering, such as discount, off-price, warehouse clubs, and extreme value retailers, are in a much better position than retailers specializing in luxury goods, such as jewelry stores, designer apparel specialty stores, and gourmet and organic grocers.

Government regulations can reduce the attractiveness of a retail market. For example, until recently, government regulations have made it difficult for foreign-owned retailers to open stores in India.[56] Also, many local governments within the United States have tried to stop Wal-Mart from entering their markets in an attempt to protect locally owned retailers.

Finally, trends in demographics, lifestyles, attitudes, and personal values affect retail markets' attractiveness. Apple specializes in developing aesthetically designed products in areas of popular technology. Its stores also mimic the high-tech design of its products and are known to have "Apple Style." The products are appealing to aficionados of technology, as well as to nontechnological consumers. Apple Stores are simple to navigate and friendly, and the architecture is similar to a fashion or luxury store. The stores feature circular signage inspired by the thumbwheel on the iPod and hosts the "Genius Bar" that staffs technical support. Apple has partnered with AT&T to make it the exclusive distributor of the iPhone.[57]

Retailers need to answer three questions about each environmental factor:

1. What new developments or changes might occur, such as new technologies and regulations or different social factors and economic conditions?

2. What is the likelihood that these environmental changes will occur? What key factors affect whether these changes will occur?

3. How will these changes affect each retail market, the firm, and its competitors?

Kelly Bradford's primary concern when she did an environmental analysis was the potential growth of Internet gift retailers such as RedEnvelope. Gifts seem

EXHIBIT 5–9
Elements in a Strengths
and Weaknesses Analysis

In performing a self-analysis, the retailer considers the potential areas for developing a competitive advantage listed below and answers the following questions:

At what is our company good?
In which of these areas is our company better than our competitors?
In which of these areas does our company's unique capabilities provide a sustainable competitive advantage or a basis for developing one?

 MANAGEMENT CAPABILITY
Capabilities and experience of top
  management
Depth of management—capabilities of
  middle management
Management's commitment to firm

 MERCHANDISING CAPABILITIES
Knowledge and skills of buyers
Relationships with vendors
Capabilities in developing private brands
Advertising and promotion capabilities

 FINANCIAL RESOURCES
Cash flow from existing business
Ability to raise debt or equity financing

 STORE MANAGEMENT CAPABILITIES
Management capabilities
Quality of sales associates
Commitment of sales associates to firm

 OPERATIONS
Overhead cost structure
Quality of operating systems
Distribution capabilities
Management information systems
Loss prevention systems
Inventory control systems

 LOCATIONS

 CUSTOMERS
Loyalty of customers

ideal for an electronic channel, because customers can order the item over the Internet and have it shipped directly to the gift recipient. Kelly also recognized that the electronic channel could effectively collect information about customers and then target promotions and suggestions to them when future gift-giving occasions arose.

Strengths and Weaknesses Analysis   The most critical aspect of the situation audit is for a retailer to determine its unique capabilities in terms of its strengths and weaknesses relative to the competition. A **strengths and weaknesses analysis** indicates how well the business can seize opportunities and avoid harm from threats in the environment. Exhibit 5–9 outlines some issues to consider in performing a strength and weakness analysis.

Here is Kelly Bradford's analysis of Gifts To Go's strengths and weaknesses:

Management capability	Limited—Two excellent store managers and a relatively inexperienced person helped Kelly buy merchandise. An accounting firm kept the financial records for the business but had no skills in developing and utilizing customer databases.
Financial resources	Good—Gifts To Go had no debt and a good relationship with a bank. Kelly had saved $255,000 that she had in liquid securities.
Operations	Poor—While Kelly felt Gifts To Go had relatively low overhead, the company did not have a computer-based inventory control system or management and customer information systems. Her competitors (local department stores, catalog, and Internet retailers) certainly had superior systems.
Merchandising capabilities	Good—Kelly had a flair for selecting unique gifts, and she had excellent relationships with vendors providing one-of-a-kind merchandise.
Store management capabilities	Excellent—The store managers and sales associates were excellent. They were very attentive to customers and loyal to the firm. Employee and customer theft were kept to a minimum.
Locations	Excellent—Both of Gifts To Go's locations were excellent. The downtown location was convenient for office workers. The suburban mall location was at a heavily trafficked juncture.
Customers	Good—While Gifts To Go did not achieve the sales volume in gifts done in department stores, the company had a loyal base of customers.

Step 3: Identify Strategic Opportunities

After completing the situation audit, the next step is to identify opportunities for increasing retail sales. Kelly Bradford presently competes in gift retailing using a specialty store format. The strategic alternatives she is considering are defined in terms of the growth opportunities in Exhibit 5–4. Note that some of these growth strategies involve a redefinition of her mission.

Step 4: Evaluate Strategic Opportunities

The fourth step in the strategic planning progress is to evaluate opportunities that have been identified in the situation audit. The evaluation determines the retailer's potential to establish a sustainable competitive advantage and reap long-term profits from the opportunities being evaluated. Thus, a retailer must focus on opportunities that utilize its strengths and its competitive advantage.

Both the market attractiveness and the strengths and weaknesses of the retailer need to be considered in evaluating strategic opportunities. The greatest investments should be made in market opportunities for which the retailer has a strong competitive position. A formal method for performing such an analysis is described in the appendix to this chapter. Here's Kelly's informal analysis:

Growth Opportunity	Market Attractiveness	Competitive Position
Increase size of present stores and amount of merchandise in stores	Low	High
Open additional gift stores in Chicago area	Medium	Medium
Open gift stores outside the Chicago area (new geographic segment)	Medium	Low
Sell lower-priced gifts in present stores or open new stores selling low-priced gifts (new benefit segment)	Medium	Low
Sell apparel and other nongift merchandise to same customers in same or new stores	High	Medium
Sell similar gift merchandise to same market segment using the Internet	High	Low
Open apparel stores targeted at teenagers	High	Low
Open a category specialist selling low-priced gifts	High	Low

Step 5: Establish Specific Objectives and Allocate Resources

After evaluating the strategic investment opportunities, the next step in the strategic planning process is to establish a specific objective for each opportunity. The retailer's overall objective is included in the mission statement; the specific objectives are goals against which progress toward the overall objective can be measured. Thus, these specific objectives have three components: (1) the performance sought, including a numerical index against which progress may be measured; (2) a time frame within which the goal is to be achieved; and (3) the level of investment needed to achieve the objective. Typically, the performance levels are financial criteria such as return on investment, sales, or profits. Kelly's objective is to increase profits by 20 percent in each of the next five years. She expects she will need to invest an additional $25,000 in her apparel and other nongift merchandise inventory.

Step 6: Develop a Retail Mix to Implement Strategy

The sixth step in the planning process is to develop a retail mix for each opportunity in which an investment will be made and control and evaluate performance. Decisions related to the elements in the retail mix are discussed in Sections III and IV.

Step 7: Evaluate Performance and Make Adjustments

The final step in the planning process is to evaluate the results of the strategy and implementation program. If the retailer is meeting or exceeding its objectives, changes aren't needed. But if the retailer fails to meet its objectives, reanalysis is required. Typically, this reanalysis starts with reviewing the implementation programs, but it may indicate that the strategy (or even the mission statement) needs to be reconsidered. This conclusion would result in starting a new planning process, including a new situation audit. Retailing View 5.5 illustrates how changes in the competitive environment forced Blockbuster to reevaluate its entire retail format.

Strategic Planning in the Real World

The planning process in Exhibit 5–7 suggests that strategic decisions are made in a sequential manner. After the business mission is defined, the situation audit is performed, strategic opportunities are identified, alternatives are evaluated, objectives are set, resources are allocated, the implementation plan is developed, and, finally, performance is evaluated and adjustments are made. But actual planning processes have interactions among the steps. For example, the situation audit may uncover a logical alternative for the firm to consider, even though this alternative isn't included in the mission statement. Thus, the mission statement may need to be reformulated. The development of the implementation plan might reveal that the resources allocated to a particular opportunity are insufficient to achieve the objective. In that case, the objective would need to be changed, the resources would need to be increased, or the retailer might consider not investing in the opportunity at all.

5.5   RETAILING VIEW   Can Blockbuster Stay a Blockbuster?

Netflix (www.netflix.com), the largest online DVD rental business, began in 1998, causing many consumers to stop patronizing Blockbuster (www.blockbuster.com) Many consumers preferred to have movies delivered to their home rather than go to a Blockbuster store. Not only was the service easy to use, but Netflix did not charge late fees, which was customary in the video rental industry at the time.

In 2004, Blockbuster launched Blockbuster Online to compete with Netflix. In November 2006, it launched the Total Access plan, which allows customers to return online rentals to stores, giving customers the convenience of using either channel and allowing them to borrow another movie immediately rather than waiting for return mail. In response to Blockbuster's Total Access plan, Netflix launched a feature that allowed customers to view their movie and television show selections immediately on their computers.

Blockbuster remains committed to growing its online business. It has elected to lower its prices (and profitability) to increase its subscriber base. Blockbuster is now the largest chain of DVD and game rental stores in the world and has signed up more than 3 million Internet subscribers, compared with 6.8 million Netflix subscribers. Both companies face the threat of movies-on-demand from cable and satellite providers.

Sources: www.netflix.com (accessed July 18, 2007); www.blockbuster.com (accessed July 18, 2007); "Blockbuster, Inc.," http://en.wikipedia.org/wiki/Blockbuster_Inc. (accessed July 18, 2007); Angela Pruitt, "Blockbuster's Online Plan Undercuts Netflix Rates," *The Wall Street Journal*, June 13, 2007; Doug Desjardins, "Blockbuster's Recent Moves Shifts Focus to Digital Business," *Retailing Today*, March 19, 2007; Russ Britt, "Blockbuster, Netflix Settle Patent Dispute," *The Wall Street Journal*, June 28, 2007.

Who is winning the DVD rental battle, Blockbuster (left) or Netflix (right)?

SUMMARY

A retailer's long-term performance is largely determined by its strategy. A strategy coordinates employees' activities and communicates the direction the retailer plans to take. Thus, retail market strategy describes both the strategic direction and the process by which the strategy is to be developed.

The retail strategy statement includes an identification of a target market and the retail format (its offering) to be directed toward that target market. The statement also needs to indicate the retailer's methods to build a sustainable competitive advantage. Seven important opportunities for retailers to develop sustainable competitive advantages are (1) customer loyalty, (2) location, (3) human resource management, (4) distribution and information systems, (5) unique merchandise, (6) vendor relations, (7) and customer service.

The strategic planning process consists of a sequence of steps, including (1) defining the business mission, (2) conducting a situation audit, (3) identifying strategic opportunities, (4) evaluating the alternatives, (5) establishing specific objectives and allocating resources, (6) developing a retail mix to implement strategy, and (7) evaluating performance and making adjustments.

Strategic planning is an ongoing process. Every day, retailers audit their situations, examine consumer trends, study new technologies, and monitor competitive activities. But the retail strategy statement does not change every year or every six months; the strategy statement is reviewed and altered only when major changes in the retailer's environment or capabilities occur.

When a retailer undertakes a major reexamination of its strategy, the process for developing a new strategy statement may take a year or two. Potential strategic directions are generated by people at all levels of the organization, then evaluated by senior executives and operating personnel to ensure that the eventual strategic direction is profitable in the long run and can be implemented.

KEY TERMS

bargaining power of vendors, *156*
barriers to entry, *155*
competitive rivalry, *156*
cross-selling, *144*
customer loyalty, *138*
data warehouse, *139*
direct investment, *152*
diversification growth opportunity, *145*
franchising, *152*
joint venture, *152*
market attractiveness/competitive position matrix, *163*

market expansion growth opportunity, *145*
market penetration growth opportunity, *144*
mission statement, *154*
positioning, *138*
private-label brands, *141*
related diversification growth opportunity, *145*
retail format, *134*
retail format development growth opportunity, *145*
retailing concept, *135*
retail market, *135*

retail strategy, *134*
scale economies, *155*
situation audit, *154*
strategic alliance, *152*
strategic retail planning process, *153*
strengths and weaknesses analysis, *158*
sustainable competitive advantage, *134*
target market, *134*
unrelated diversification, *145*
vertical integration, *146*

GET OUT AND DO IT!

1. **CONTINUING CASE ASSIGNMENT:** Prepare an analysis of the company you selected for the continuing assignment. Identify its direct competitors, its target market and positioning, its strategy with respect to its competitors, its retail format (the elements in its retail mix—merchandise variety and assortment, pricing, locations), and its bases for developing a competitive advantage relative to its competitors. Outline the retailer's strengths, weaknesses, opportunities, and threats relative to its competitors. Pick a specific country in which the firm does not operate and make a recommendation of whether the retailer should enter the country, and if so, how it should do so.

2. Visit the Web sites for IKEA (www.ikea.com) and Starbucks (www.starbucks.com). Is the look/feel of these Internet sites consistent with the in-store experience of these stores?

3. Go to the Web sites for Wal-Mart (www.walmartstores.com), Carrefour (www.carrefour.fr), Royal Ahold (www.ahold.com), and Metro AG (www.metro.de). Which chain has the most global strategy? Justify your answer.

4. Visit two stores that sell similar merchandise categories and cater to the same target segment(s). How are their retail formats (the elements in their retail mixes) similar? Dissimilar?

On what bases do they have a sustainable competitive advantage? Explain which you believe has a stronger position.

5. Go to the student side of the book's Web site and click on Market Position Matrix. Exercise 1: This spreadsheet reproduces the analysis of international growth opportunities discussed in the appendix to Chapter 5. What numbers in the matrices would have to change to make China and France more attractive opportunities? To make Brazil and Mexico less attractive opportunities? Change the numbers in the matrices and see what effect it has on the overall position of the opportunity in the grid. Exercise 2: The market attractiveness/competitive position matrix can also be used by a department store to evaluate its merchandise categories and determine how much it should invest in each category. Fill in the importance weights (10 = very important, 1 = not very important) and the evaluations of the merchandise categories (10 = excellent, 1 = poor), and then see what is recommended by the plot on the opportunity matrix. Exercise 3: Think of another investment decision that a retailer might make and analyze it using the strategic analysis matrix. List the alternatives and the characteristics of the alternatives, and then put in the importance weights for the characteristics (10 = very important, 1 = not very important) and the evaluation of each alternative on each characteristic (10 = excellent, 1 = poor).

DISCUSSION QUESTIONS AND PROBLEMS

1. For each of the four retailers discussed at the beginning of the chapter (Steve & Barry's, Chico's, Curves, and Magazine Luiza), describe its strategy and the basis of its competitive advantage.

2. Choose a retailer and describe how it has developed a competitive strategic advantage.

3. Give an example of a market penetration, a retail format development, a market expansion, and a diversification growth strategy that Best Buy might use.

4. Choose your favorite retailer. Draw and explain a positioning map, like that shown in Exhibit 5–3, that includes your retailer, retailers that sell the same types of merchandise, and the target customer segments (ideal points).

5. Do a situation analysis for McDonald's. What is its mission? What are its strengths and weaknesses? What environmental threats might it face over the next 10 years? How could it prepare for these threats?

6. What are Neiman Marcus's and Save-A-Lot's bases for sustainable competitive advantage? Are they really sustainable, or are they easily copied?

7. Assume you are interested in opening a restaurant in your town. Go through the steps in the strategic planning process shown in Exhibit 5–6. Focus on conducting a situation audit of the local restaurant market, identifying and evaluating alternatives, and selecting a target market and a retail mix for the restaurant.

8. Abercrombie & Fitch (A&F) owns several chains, including abercrombie that targets ages 7 to 14 years, Hollister Co. that targets ages 14–18 years, Abercrombie & Fitch that targets the 18–22 year old crowd, and Ruehl No. 925 that appeals to the 22–35 year old group. What type of growth opportunity was A&F pursuing when it opened each of these retail concepts? Which is most synergistic with the original A&F chain?

9. Identify a store or service provider that you believe has an effective loyalty program. Explain why it is effective.

10. Choose a retailer that you believe could be, but is not yet, successful in other countries. Explain why you think it could be successful.

11. Amazon.com started as an Internet retailer selling books. Then it expanded to groceries, DVDs, apparel, software, travel services, and basically everything under the sun. Evaluate these growth opportunities in terms of the probability that they will be profitable businesses for Amazon.com. What competitive advantages does Amazon.com bring to each of these businesses?

SUGGESTED READINGS

Aaker, David. *Strategic Market Management.* 8th ed. New York: Wiley, 2007.

Ander, Willard, and Neil Stern. *Winning at Retail: Developing a Sustained Model for Retail Success.* Hoboken, NJ: Wiley, 2004.

Dawson, John A., and Jung-Hee Lee. *International Retailing Plans and Strategies in Asia.* New York: International Business Press, 2005.

De Mooij, Marieke K. *Global Marketing and Advertising: Understanding Cultural Paradoxes,* 2nd ed. Thousand Oaks, CA: Sage Publications, 2005.

Etgar, Michael, and Dalia Rachman-Moore. "Determinant Factors of Failures in Foreign Markets." *International Review of Retail, Distribution and Consumer Research* 17, no. 1 (2007), pp. 79–100.

Fox, Edward J., and Raj Sethuraman. "Retail Competition." In *Retailing in the 21st Century–Current and Future Trends*, eds. Manfred Kraft and Murali Mantrala. Berlin: Springer, 2006, pp. 193–208.

"Global Retail Outlook." Columbus, OH: Retail Forward, March 2007.

Kumar, Nirmalya. "The Global Retail Challenge." *Business Strategy Review* 16 (Spring 2005), pp. 5–14.

Lehmann, Donald and Russell Winer. *Analysis for Marketing Planning.* 7th ed. Burr Ridge, IL: McGraw-Hill/Irwin, 2007.

Megicks, Phil. "Levels of Strategy and Performance in UK Small Retail Businesses." *Management Decision* 45, no. 3 (2007), pp. 484–502.

Souitaris, Vangelis, and George Balabanis. "Tailoring Online Retail Strategies to Increase Customer Satisfaction and Loyalty." *Long Range Planning* 40, no. 2 (2007), pp. 244–61.

APPENDIX 5A   Using the Market Attractiveness/Competitive Position Matrix

The following example illustrates an application of the **market attractiveness/competitive position matrix**.[58] The matrix (Exhibit 5–10) provides a method for analyzing opportunities that explicitly considers both the retailer's capabilities and the retail market's attractiveness. Its underlying premise is that a market's attractiveness and the retailer's competitive position indicates the long-term profit potential for the opportunity. That is, the matrix indicates that the greatest investments should be made in attractive markets where the retailer has a strong competitive position.

There are six steps in using the matrix to evaluate opportunities for strategic investments:

1. Define the strategic opportunities to be evaluated. For example, a store manager could use the matrix to evaluate departments in a store; a vice president of stores for a specialty store chain could use it to evaluate stores or potential store sites; a merchandise vice president could use it to evaluate merchandise categories sold by the retailer; or a retail holding company's CEO could use it to evaluate international growth opportunities.

2. Identify key factors determining market attractiveness and the retailer's competitive position. Factors that might be selected are discussed in the market attractiveness, competitor analysis, and self-analysis sections of the situation audit.

3. Assign weights to each factor used to determine market attractiveness and competitive position to indicate that factor's importance. Typically, weights are selected so they add up to 100.

4. Rate each strategic investment opportunity on (a) the attractiveness of its market and (b) the retailer's competitive position in that market. Typically, opportunities are rated on a 1 to 10 scale, with 10 indicating a very attractive market or very strong competitive position and 1 indicating a very unattractive market or very weak competitive position.

5. Calculate each opportunity's score for market attractiveness and competitive position. Scores are calculated by (a) multiplying the weights by each factor's rating and (b) adding across the factors.

6. Plot each opportunity on the matrix in Exhibit 5–10.

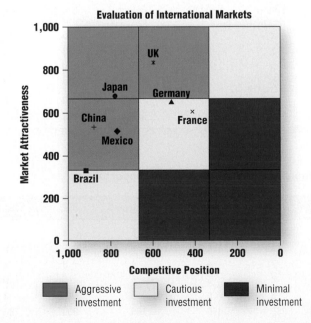

Evaluation of International Markets

EXHIBIT 5–10

Market Attractiveness/ Competitive Position Matrix

EXHIBIT 5–11   Data about International Markets

	U.S.	Mexico	Brazil	Germany	France	U.K.	Japan	China
Population, 2006 (Millions)	299.1	108.3	186.8	82.4	61.2	60.5	127.8	1311
Projected population change 2006–2050 (%)	40	28	39	−9	5	14	−21	10
Retail sales market size 2006 (Billions)	3428	288	188	800	665	750	1206	629
Per capita retail sales, 2006 ($)	11,461	2,659	1,006	9,709	10,866	12,397	9,437	480
Retail sales compounded annual growth rate 2006–2011 (%)	4.3	2.8	4	1.4	2	4.1	1.9	9
Population density (per sq. mile)	80	143	57	598	287	640	876	355
% living in urban areas	79	75	81	88	74	89	48	41
Business environment ranking	4	33	37	15	13	5	27	38

SOURCE: "2007 Global Powers of Retailing," *Stores*, January 2007; "2006 World Population Data Sheet," Population Reference Bureau, 2006; "Global Retail Outlook," Columbus, OH: Retail Forward, March 2007.

In this example, a fashion-oriented U.S. women's apparel retailer is evaluating seven countries for international expansion: Mexico, Brazil, Germany, France, the United Kingdom, Japan, and China. Some information about the markets appears in Exhibit 5–11.

To evaluate each country's market attractiveness, the retailer's management identified five market factors, assigned a weight to each factor, rated the markets on each factor, and calculated a market attractiveness score for each alternative (Exhibit 5–12). Here, management assigned the highest weight to the attitude that consumers in the country have toward the United States (30) and gave the lowest weight to market growth (10). Ratings for market size and market growth are based on country data;

the firm also had to consider size of its target market—middle-class women between the ages of 25 and 50 years. For this reason, Brazil and Mexico had low ratings on market size. These countries are also low on economic stability; however, the retailer did not find that factor particularly important because the buying power of its target segment is relatively insensitive to the country's economy. The business climate factor includes an assessment of the degree to which the government supports business and foreign investment. The European countries and Japan are high on this dimension.

Exhibit 5–13 shows the factors, weights, and ratings used to evaluate the retailer's position in each country versus the competition. In evaluating the competitive

EXHIBIT 5–12   Market Attractiveness Ratings for International Growth Opportunities

	Weight	Mexico	Brazil	Germany	France	U.K.	Japan	China
Market size	20	2	2	7	6	5	10	4
Market growth	10	10	7	3	3	3	2	6
Economic stability	15	2	2	10	9	9	5	2
Business climate	25	4	2	7	7	10	6	2
Attitude toward U.S.	30	7	5	8	3	10	10	2
Total	**100**	**480**	**340**	**735**	**550**	**815**	**745**	**280**

EXHIBIT 5–13   Competitive Position for International Growth Opportunities

	Weight	Mexico	Brazil	Germany	France	U.K.	Japan	China
Cost	10	9	10	5	5	5	7	10
Brand image	30	8	10	4	3	7	9	6
Vendor relations	20	7	7	4	4	3	8	8
Locations	20	6	8	6	5	7	6	10
Marketing	20	8	8	6	3	6	8	10
Total	**100**	**750**	**860**	**490**	**380**	**630**	**780**	**840**

position, management felt that its brand name was the most critical aspect because image is particularly important in selling fashionable merchandise. Because cost was viewed as the least important factor in determining the competitive position of a high-fashion retailer, it received a weight of only 10.

In terms of the retailer's competitive position within each country, the firm believed its brand name was very well known in Japan and Brazil but not in France or Germany. Brazil, Mexico, and China offer the best opportunities to operate efficiently due to the low labor costs in these countries. Evaluations of each of the countries are plotted on the market attractiveness/competitive position matrix in Exhibit 5–10. According to the recommended investment level and objectives associated with each cell in the exhibit, the retailer should invest substantially in Japan, the United Kingdom, Mexico, and China and be cautious about investments in Brazil, Germany, and France.

Financial Strategy

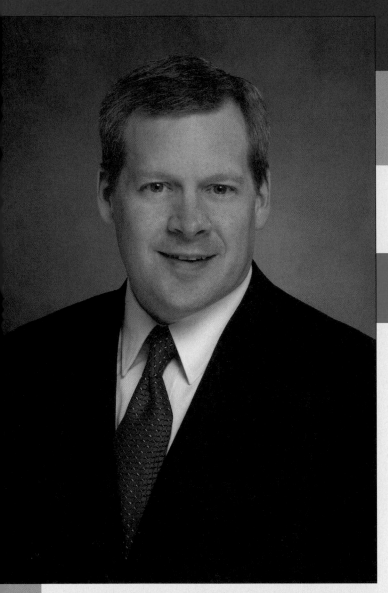

EXECUTIVE BRIEFING
Steve Stagner, President and Chief Operating Officer, Mattress Firm

After I graduated from college, I worked in a variety of sales and marketing positions for leading mattress manufacturers, Sealy and Simmons. But I had always had an interest in starting my own business. So some colleagues and I spent two years developing a comprehensive plan for franchising Mattress Firm stores in Atlanta and ultimately the surrounding Southeast—a strong bedding market/region that Mattress Firm did not participate in.

A lot of our success in launching our company was due to the thoroughness of our business plan. A key element in our plan was the financial analysis, the pro forma income and cash flow statements, and the balance sheets. These analyses showed we could develop a profitable business, but the plan outlined in detail how we were going to generate the profits. The plan described the locations we were considering, the design of the stores, the store expenses, type of people we were going to hire, and how we were going to train and develop our employees.

In March 1996, we launched the business with $1,300 and over the next eight years grew it into a $62 million business (our financials were almost identical to our plan for the first year). The plan was instrumental in raising capital, hiring people, and getting good locations. Most shopping centers are looking for hot retailers like Starbucks and didn't find a mattress retailer particularly attractive. But they were much more receptive when they saw our store build out (hardwood floors, unique wall treatments, etc.) and learned of our plan to staff the stores with college graduates, not used car salespeople.

Mattress retailing is a very fragmented business, dominated by small local retailers. Our large-term vision has always been to become the first national mattress retailer.

CHAPTER 6

QUESTIONS

How is a retail strategy reflected in retailers' financial objectives?

Why do retailers need to evaluate their performance?

What is the strategic profit model, and how is it used?

What measures do retailers use to assess their performance?

By 2005, we had saturated the Atlanta market and surrounding areas. Gary Fazio, CEO of Mattress Firm's corporate entity, and I agreed to merge our franchise operation with Mattress Firm corporate in 2005. Through additional acquisitions, we now have over 420 stores (only 50 are franchised).

Metrics are really critical in running a retail business. Some of the metrics we look at are the number of shoppers coming to the stores, conversion rate (shoppers converted to buyers), average sale (ticket), and margins by store, vendor, and even salesperson. We also have mystery shoppers evaluate their shopping experience in our stores. These factors drive profitability.

But our inventory turnover is also critical to our performance. Mattresses are bulky and have low labor content. Thus, there is little advantage to manufacturing them abroad. Buying from domestic suppliers reduces our inventory pipeline. We don't have inventory on ships coming from China. So we can turn our inventory more than 10 times a year—sometimes before we have paid for it.

Financial objectives and goals are an integral part of a retailer's market strategy. In Chapter 5, we examined how retailers develop their strategy and build a sustainable competitive advantage to generate a continuing stream of profits. In this chapter, we look at how financial analysis can be used to assess the retailer's market strategy—to monitor the retailer's performance, assess the reasons its performance is above or below expectations, and provide insights into appropriate actions that can be taken if performance falls short of those expectations.

For example, Kelly Bradford, the owner of Gifts To Go, whom we described in Chapter 5, needs to know how well she is doing because she wants to stay in business, be successful, increase the profitability of her company, and realize her goal of generating an annual income over $100,000. To assess her performance, she can count the number of customers who buy something at her stores and total the receipts at the end of the day. But these simple measures don't indicate how well her business is doing. For instance, she might find that sales are good, and her accountant tells her the business is profitable, but she doesn't have the cash to buy new merchandise. When this happens, Kelly needs to analyze her business to determine the cause of the problem and what can be done to overcome it.

In this chapter, we first review the importance of establishing objectives and measuring performance against specific goals. After considering the various objectives retailers might have, we introduce the strategic profit model, used to analyze the factors affecting the financial performance of a firm. To illustrate the use of this model, we examine and compare the factors affecting the performance of Macy's Inc. (Macy's and Bloomingdale's) and Costco, the largest warehouse club chain. Then we demonstrate how the model can be used to evaluate one of the growth opportunities Kelly Bradford is considering. In the last part of this chapter, we examine productivity measures that assess the performance of retail activities, merchandise management, and store operations.

OBJECTIVES AND GOALS

As we discussed in Chapter 5, the first step in the strategic planning process involves articulating the retailer's objectives and the scope of activities it plans to undertake. These objectives guide the development of the retailer's strategy,[1] and specific performance goals determine whether the retailer's objectives are being achieved. When the goals are not being achieved, the retailer knows that it must take corrective actions. Three types of objectives that a retailer might have are (1) financial, (2) societal, and (3) personal.[2]

Financial Objectives

When assessing financial performance, most people focus on profits: What were the retailer's profits or profit margin (profit as a percentage of sales) last year, and what will they be this year and into the future? But the appropriate financial performance measure is not profits but rather return on investment (ROI). Kelly Bradford set a financial objective of making a profit of at least $100,000 a year, but she really needs to consider how much she needs to invest to make the $100,000, the profit she desires from her investment.

Think of the decisions you might make when planning how to invest some money you might have. In making this investment, you want to determine the highest percentage return you can—the highest interest rate or greatest percentage increase in stock price—not the absolute amount of the return. You can always get a greater absolute return by investing more money. For example, Kelly Bradford would be delighted if she made $100,000 and only needed to invest $500,000 (a 20 percent ROI) in the business but disappointed if she had to invest $4,000,000 to make $100,000 profit (a 2.5 percent ROI). A commonly used measure of the return on investment is **return on assets (ROA),** or the profit return on all the assets possessed by the firm.

Societal Objectives

Societal objectives are related to broader issues that provide benefits to society—that is, making the world a better place to live. For example, retailers might be concerned about providing employment opportunities for people in a particular area or more specifically for minorities or the handicapped. Other societal objectives might include offering people unique merchandise, such as environmentally sensitive products; providing an innovative service to improve personal health, such as weight reduction programs; or sponsoring community events.

Ben & Jerry's remains committed to being a green company. The company partnered with Dave Matthews Band and Save Our Environment to launch a new product flavor. All of the proceeds from the purchase of this flavor support Dave Matthews Band's Bama Works Fund, which supports charitable organizations. Ben & Jerry's also sponsored a "Campus Consciousness Tour" with the rock band Guster to educate students about global warming. The company launched an environmental awareness campaign, called "Lick Global Warming," with a Web site (www.lickglobalwarming.org) designed to educate people about global warming and encourage them to write their congressperson about these issues. Ben & Jerry's measures its carbon-dioxide emissions, including corporate employee air travel, and for every mile logged, it buys clean renewable energy from Native Energy, an energy provider with methane-capture, wind, and solar energy projects.[3]

REFACT

When Congress opened the Artic National Wildlife Refuge for oil drilling in 2005, Ben & Jerry's created the world's largest baked Alaska for Earth Day, then placed the 1,140-pound, 4-foot dessert in front of the U.S. Capitol to represent the environmental damage the drilling in the wildlife preserve would cause.[4]

Jerry Greenfield (left) and Ben Cohen (right), are committed to making Ben & Jerry's Homemade Ice Cream a green company.

Performance with respect to societal objectives is more difficult to measure than that affiliated with financial objectives. But explicit societal goals can be set, such as reductions in energy usage and excess packaging, increased use of renewable resources, and support for nonprofit organizations such as United Way and Habitat for Humanity.

Personal Objectives

Many retailers, particularly owners of small, independent businesses, have important personal objectives, including self-gratification, status, and respect. For example, the owner/operator of a book store may find it rewarding to interact with others who like reading and authors who visit the store for book-signing promotions. By operating a popular store, a retailer might become recognized as a well-respected business leader in the community.

Whereas societal and personal objectives are important to some retailers, financial objectives should be the primary focus of managers of publicly held retailers—those whose stocks are listed on and bought through a stock market. Investors in publicly held companies, namely, the people who buy stock in a company, are primarily interested in getting a return on their investment, and the managers of these companies must have the same objectives as the investors. Therefore, the remaining sections of this chapter focus on financial objectives and the factors affecting a retailer's ability to achieve financial goals.

STRATEGIC PROFIT MODEL

The **strategic profit model,** illustrated in Exhibit 6–1, is a method for summarizing the factors that affect a firm's financial performance, as measured by ROA. The model decomposes ROA into two components: (1) net profit margin and (2) asset turnover. The **net profit margin** is simply how much profit (after taxes, interest income, and extraordinary gains and losses) a firm makes, divided by its net sales. Thus, it reflects the profits generated from each dollar of sales. If a retailer's net profit margin is 5 percent, it generates income of $.05 for every dollar of merchandise or services it sells.

EXHIBIT 6–1
Components of the
Strategic Profit Model

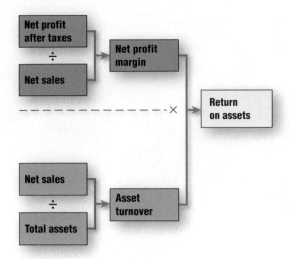

Asset turnover is the retailer's net sales divided by its assets. This financial measure assesses the productivity of a firm's investment in its assets and indicates how many sales dollars are generated by each dollar of assets. Thus, if a retailer's asset turnover is 3.0, it generates $3 in sales for each dollar invested in the firm's assets.

The retailer's ROA is determined by multiplying the two components together:

$$\text{Net profit margin} \quad \times \quad \text{Asset turnover} \quad = \quad \text{Return on assets (ROA)}$$

$$\frac{\text{Net profit}}{\text{Net sales}} \quad \times \quad \frac{\text{Net sales}}{\text{Total assets}} \quad = \quad \frac{\text{Net profit}}{\text{Total assets}}$$

These two components of the strategic profit model illustrate that ROA is determined by two sets of activities—profit margin management and asset turnover management—and that a high ROA can be achieved by various combinations of net profit margins and asset turnover levels.

To illustrate the different approaches for achieving a high ROA, consider the financial performance of two very different hypothetical retailers in Exhibit 6–2. La Chatelaine Bakery has a net profit margin of only 1 percent and asset turnover of 10, resulting in an ROA of 10 percent. Its profit margin is low due to the highly competitive nature of its business. Consumers can buy baked goods from a wide variety of retailers, as well as from the other bakeries in the area. However, its asset turnover is relatively high, because the firm has a very low level of inventory assets. It has very little inventory because it sells everything the same day it is baked.

On the other hand, Lehring Jewelry Store has a net profit margin of 10 percent—ten times higher than that of the bakery. Even though it has a much higher net profit margin, the jewelry store has the same ROA because it has a very low asset turnover of 1. Lehring's asset turnover is low compared with the bakery's because Lehring has a high level of inventory and stocks a lot of items that take many months to sell. In addition, the jewelry store offers liberal credit to customers, increasing its assets in accounts receivable.

Thus, La Chatelaine Bakery is achieving its 10 percent ROA by having a relatively high asset turnover—the asset management path. Lehring Jewelry Store, in contrast, achieves its same ROA with a relatively high net profit margin—the profit margin management path.

EXHIBIT 6–2
Different Approaches for
Achieving an Acceptable
ROA (Bakery and Jewelry
Store)

	Net Profit Margin	×	Asset Turnover	=	Return on Assets
La Chatelaine Bakery	1%		10 times		10%
Lehring Jewelry	10%		1 time		10%

Project:
use template on web link.

CSS for navigation style in separate file.

Save as: nav-govan
address

3.00 | nav
8.15
9.30

In the next section, we take a close look at these two components of ROA. Specifically, we examine the relationship between these ratios and a firm's retail strategy and describe how these financial measures can be used to assess performance with traditional accounting information. To illustrate the financial implications of different retail strategies, we compare the financial performance of Macy's Inc. and Costco.

Macy's Inc, as described in Retailing View 6.1, operates two national department store chains, Macy's and Bloomingdale's. Similar to other department store chains, Macy's Inc. offers a wide variety of fashionable apparel and home furnishings, a relatively high level of customer service provided by sales associates, and an attractive shopping environment. Costco's warehouse stores, in contrast, offers a limited assortment of food and general merchandise in a self-service, warehouse environment. Retailing View 6.2 provides some background information about Costco.

Profit Margin Management Path

Information used to examine the profit margin management path comes from the retailer's income statement, which summarizes a firm's financial performance over

---

Macy's, Inc.   **RETAILING VIEW**   6.1

Federated Department Stores was founded in 1929 as a holding company composed of several family-owned, regional department store chains including Jordan Marsh (in Boston), Lazarus (Columbus, Ohio), and Abraham & Straus (New York). Over the next 60 years, Federated acquired additional regional department stores chains—Bon Marche (Seattle), Rike's (Dayton, Ohio), Goldsmith's (Memphis), Burdines (Miami), and Rich's (Atlanta). Its most significant acquisitions were Macy's in 1994 and the May Company in 2005.

The regional department store chains owned by Federated were operated autonomiously. Each chain had its own buying departments and distribution systems. During the past 15 years, Federated has centralized various functions, including the development of private-label merchandising, management information systems, and supply chain management. In 2005, Federated rebranded all its regional department store chains to Macy's. In February 2007, Federated Department Stores changed its corporate name to the Macy's Group, Inc., and converted its stock ticker symbol to "M."

Macy's has now reached the point that it can implement its long-term strategy of operating two national retail chains (Bloomingdale's and Macy's), each positioned at different points on the price/quality continuum. Macy's and Bloomingdale's are two of retailing's strongest brand names. Macy's Group operates more than 850 stores with greater than $27 billion in annual sales. By listening to its customers' needs and remodeling stores to offer the amenities that shoppers desire, Macy's is enhancing its brand. Its Internet channel, www.macys.com, generates more than $1 billion in annual sales.

Macy's primary target market is a female shopper between 25 and 54 years of age, who typically works outside the house, has children and an average family income of more than $75,000, and spends $5,000 on merchandise sold at Macy's for herself, her family, and as gifts. Macy's has been particularly effective in developing private-label and exclusive merchandise, such as I.N.C., Charter Club, The Cellar, Alfani, Greendog, and Tools of the Trade, as well as the exclusive T Tahari line from designer Elie Tahari and O Oscar from Oscar De La Renta. These private labels presently account for 33 percent of sales, and the sales rate

The Macy's store located at Herald Square in New York City is the United States' largest department store.

is growing three times faster than its national brands merchandise.

The Bloomingdale's chain of 36 stores targets fashion-forward women who are interested in the latest styles of designer apparel and accessories. In addition to offering exclusive designer merchandise, Bloomingdale's provides a high level of personalized customer service. Sales associates regularly contact their top customers to announce new merchandise, invite them to store events, and follow up to ensure high levels of customer satisfaction.

REFACT

Macy's was named one of the top 10 companies for executive women by the National Association of Female Executives and one of the top 100 companies providing the best opportunities for Latinos by *Hispanic Magazine.*[5]

Sources: Macy's 2007 Fact Book, www.macysinc.com/ir/vote/2007_fact_book.pdf (accessed July 1, 2007); www.macys.com (accessed July 1, 2007); Kelly Nolan, "Given Its Past, Federated Has Experience to Succeed in Future," *Retailing Today*, May 7, 2007, pp. 3–4; Kelly Nolan, "Macy's to Woo May Patrons with Marketing Revamp," *Retailing Today*, June 4, 2007, pp. 5–6.

a period of time. For example, the income statement in a retailer's annual report provides a summary of the retailer's performance during the previous fiscal year, which may not coincide with a calendar year. For instance, to capture all the sales and returns from the Christmas season, many retailers define their fiscal year as beginning on February 1 and ending January 31.

Exhibit 6–3 shows income statements adapted[6] from the annual reports of Macy's Inc. and Costco. The profit margin management path portion of the strategic profit model that summarizes these data appears in Exhibit 6–4. In the following sections, we consider each element in the profit margin management path.

Net Sales   The term **net sales** refers to the total revenue received by a retailer after refunds have been paid to customers for returned merchandise and payments have been collected from vendors for promotions. Costco accrued more than $1 billion in membership fees, at $50 per person, which are included in the net sales.

Customer returns represent the value of merchandise that customers return and for which they receive a refund of cash or a credit. **Promotional allowances**

6.2   RETAILING VIEW   Costco Wholesale Corporation

As the largest warehouse club, Costco enjoys higher sales, sales per store, and sales per square foot than its two biggest competitors, Sam's Club and BJ's Wholesale Club. The $61 billion company runs more than 500 stores, most of which are located in the United States. The large, 155,000 square foot warehouses consist of commodity items, such as dairy products and toilet paper, as well as special unique items that are always a surprise. The "treasure hunt" environment gives the customer a sense of urgency to buy the item immediately. Some limited availability products include 4-carat diamond ring, Louis Vuitton handbag, or Versace china set. Costco is committed to delivering both value and quality to its customers.

Costco's target market is not only low-income customers who need to shop for the lowest prices. This retailer also attracts a loyal, upscale clientele that enjoys finding bargains and unique merchandise. The retailer marks products up no more than 14 percent, giving its customers true value, whether the product is a quart of ketchup or an LCD television.

Costco carries only 4,000 SKUs though with a greater variety of products than a conventional supermarket. However, the retailer still sold $900 million worth of seafood in 2006, $150 million in rotisserie chickens, and 7 percent of the organic milk sold to U.S. consumers. In the food sector, Costco keeps only 110 frozen and 72 refrigerated SKUs, which allows its buyers to maintain strong control on the movement and quality of the goods.

Private-label merchandise accounts for 15 percent of its overall sales and 40 percent of Costco's commodity sales. To grow its private label, Kirkland Signature, which offers a diverse selection of Kirkland wines and champagnes, bakery items, and so forth, Costco's buyers develop quality relationships with vendors and can thus capitalize on the trend to develop products for the popular store. Many of its items are cobranded with manufacturers, such as Hormel bacon, Stonyfield Farm organic smoothies, Dannon Activia, and Borghese upscale cosmetics. The cobranded products signal to customers that they will receive a quality product from a trusted name at a value price.

Costco also is committed to healthy products and environmental responsibility. It ensures that the raw materials used in the products that it sells, like cocoa, coffee, or seafood, were

Costco, the fourth-largest U.S. retailer, has strong financial performance and provides good value to its customers by controlling costs and offering a limited assortment.

all grown and produced in a fair and healthy way. This retailer is also trying to cut down on the amount of packaging it uses. The company evaluates its suppliers closely; to check up on one seafood supplier, the company sent representatives to meet the ships when they docked to determine how the products were being iced, how they were unloaded, and how the seafood company maintained the temperature from the boat to the plant. Protocols such as this one enable the company to maintain its consistent quality.

REFACT

Costco's 68,000 hourly U.S. workers sell more per square foot than those at Sam's Club. Sam Club's 102,000 U.S. employees generated $35 billion in sales last year, whereas Costco earned $34 billion with one-third fewer employees.[7]

Sources: Warren Thayer, "Costco Wholesale: Our Retailer of the Year," *RFF Retailer*, April 2007; Katia Watson, "Costco: What's the Buzz?" Columbus, OH: Retail Forward, December 2006; www.costco.com (accessed June 3, 2007).

	Macy's Inc.	Costco
Net sales	$26,970	$60,151
Less Cost of goods sold	16,197	52,745
Gross Margin	10,773	7,406
Less operating expenses	8,937	5781
Less net interest expense/income	390	(126)
Total Expenses	9327	5655
Net Profit Before Tax	1,446	1,751
Less taxes	451	648
Net Profit After Taxes	995	1103
Ratios		
Gross margin percentage	39.9%	12.3%
Operating expenses as percentage of sales	33.1	9.6
Net operating income percentage	6.8	2.7
Net profit percentage after taxes	3.7	1.8

EXHIBIT 6–3
Fiscal Annual Income Statement for Macy's Inc. and Costco ($ millions)

SOURCE: Macy's 10K Report, filed April 4, 2007, for fiscal year ending January 31, 2007, p. F6; Costco 10K Report, filed November 17, 2006, for fiscal year ending September 3, 2006, p. 42.

are payments made by vendors to retailers in exchange for the retailer's promotions of the vendor's merchandise. For example, consumer packaged good manufacturers frequently pay supermarket chains to stock a new product (called slotting fees) or advertise a product.

Net sales = Gross amount of sales + Promotional allowances − Customer returns

Sales are an important measure of performance because they indicate the activity level of the merchandising function. Costco's net revenues, which include both merchandise sales and club membership fees, are more than double those of Macy's.

Profit Management Path for Macy's Inc. and Costco   **EXHIBIT 6–4**

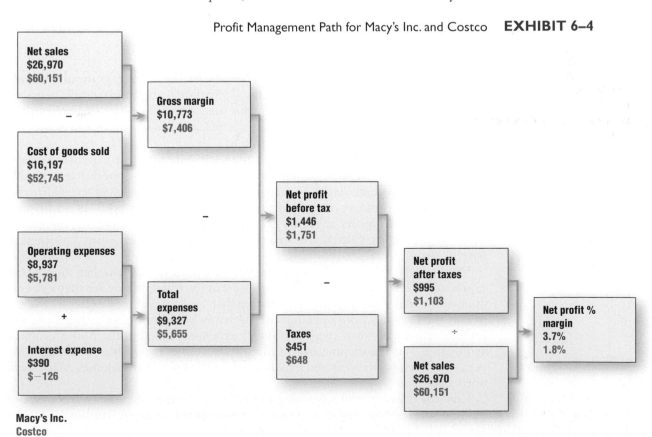

Macy's Inc.
Costco

Gross Margin   The **gross margin,** also called **gross profit,** is the net sales minus the cost of the goods sold. It is an important measure in retailing because it indicates how much profit the retailer is making on merchandise sales, without considering the expenses associated with operating the store and corporate overhead expenses.

Gross margin = Net sales − Cost of goods sold

Gross margin, similar to other performance measures, also can be expressed as a percentage of net sales so retailers can compare (1) the performances of various types of merchandise and (2) their own performance with other retailers with higher or lower levels of sales.

$$\frac{\text{Gross margin}}{\text{Net sales}} = \text{Gross margin \%}$$

Macy's: $\dfrac{10,773}{\$26,970} = 39.9\%$

Costco: $\dfrac{7,406}{\$60,151} = 12.3\%$

Even though Costco has more than double the sales of Macy's, Macy's has a much higher gross margin percentage. This difference in gross margin percentage can be traced back to the retail strategies of the companies. Warehouse clubs generally have lower gross margin percentages than department stores because they buy merchandise opportunistically, sell primarily staples with predictable sales and lower clearance discounts, and, thus, offer low prices because they target price-conscious, bargain-hunting customers. Department stores, in contrast, sell more fashionable merchandise, and charge higher prices because their customers are less price conscious. It is important for department stores to achieve a relatively high gross margin because their operating expenses to provide customer service and pay rent in prime locations are higher than those of warehouse clubs.

Operating Expenses   **Operating expenses** are the **selling, general, and administrative expenses (SG&A),** plus the depreciation and amortization of assets. The SG&A includes costs, other than the cost of merchandise, incurred in the normal course of doing business, such as salaries for sales associates and managers, advertising, utilities, office supplies, and rent.

Both Macy's and Costco's income statements contain some expenses beyond the normal SG&A expenses, which we include in the total operating expenses in Exhibit 6–4. When Macy's acquired the May company, it incurred additional expenses for inventory reevaluation and integration, as well as additional income from selling its accounts receivables (the money owed by customers who buy on credit). Costco also incurred some additional expenses for opening new stores.

When analyzing a retailer's performance, one must decide whether these other expenses are related to the normal operations of the retail firm or are they extraordinary expenses that will only arise during that specific year. For example, the expenses for Costco's store openings are probably going to occur each year as the retailer opens new stores, whereas Macy's expenses related to the May Company acquisition and the income from selling its accounts receivables probably only occur for that specific year and may not reflect the operating expenses Macy's will normally incur.

Like the gross margin, operating expenses can be expressed as a percentage of net sales to facilitate comparisons across items, stores, and merchandise categories with different sales levels. Macy's has significantly higher operating expenses, as a percentage of its net sales, than Costco does.

$$\frac{\text{Operating expenses}}{\text{Net sales}} = \text{Operating expenses \%}$$

Macy's: $\dfrac{8{,}937}{\$26{,}970}$ $= 33.1\%$

Costco: $\dfrac{5{,}781}{\$60{,}151}$ $= 9.6\%$

The operating expenses percentage for Costco is about one-quarter as large as that for Macy's because Costco has lower selling expenses and spends less maintaining the appearance of its stores. Finally, warehouse club stores operate with a smaller administrative staff than do department stores. For instance, Costco's buying expenses are much lower because fewer buyers are needed to conduct the simpler buying process for commodity-type merchandise, like packaged foods and fresh meat and produce, compared with fashion apparel. Also, its buyers do not have to travel to fashion markets around the world, as department store buyers do.

Interest and Taxes   Two other major expense categories are **interest,** which includes the cost of borrowing money to finance everything from inventory to the purchase of new store locations, and taxes. Offsetting the interest expense is the **interest income** a retailer can generate through proprietary credit cards, bank deposits, bonds, treasury bills, fixed income investments, and other investments. Exhibit 6–4 reports the net interest expense/income, which is interest expense minus interest income.

Most retailers incur expenses for interest and taxes. However, these costs of doing business may not reflect the retailer's performance in its primary business activity, which is selling its merchandise and services. That is, the interest expense is a financial, not an operating, decision, based on the evaluation of the relative cost of borrowing money or raising funds by selling more stock in the company. Taxes can be affected by the retailer's losses in the previous year and/or changes in government regulations and laws.

Net Operating Income   Due to the lack of control over taxes, interest, and extraordinary expenses, a commonly used profit measure is the net profit percentage before interest expenses/income, taxes, and extraordinary expenses. Like the gross margin and operating expenses, net operating income is often expressed as a percentage of net sales to facilitate comparisons across items, merchandise categories, and departments with different sales levels.

$$\frac{\text{Gross margin} - \text{Operating expenses}}{\text{Net sales}} = \text{Net operating income \%}$$

Macy's: $\dfrac{10{,}773 - 8{,}937}{\$26{,}970}$ $= 6.81\%$

Costco: $\dfrac{7{,}406 - 5{,}781}{\$60{,}151}$ $= 2.70\%$

Net Profit   **Net profit** (after taxes) is the gross margin minus operating expenses, net interest, and taxes:

Net profit = Gross margin − Operating expenses − Net interest − Taxes

It is a measure of overall performance with respect to the profit margin management path and can also be expressed before taxes. Net profit margin, like gross margin, is often expressed as a percentage of net sales:

$$\frac{\text{Net profit after taxes}}{\text{Net sales}} = \text{Net profit \% after taxes}$$

Macy's: $\dfrac{995}{\$26{,}970} = 3.70\%$

Costco: $\dfrac{1103}{\$60{,}151} = 1.83\%$

In this examination of their profit management paths, it appears that even though Costco has more than double the sales that Macy's has, both companies generate about the same amount of profit dollars. Therefore, due to Macy's lower sales revenues, it has a much higher net profit margin percent. Note that Macy's net profit margin would be even greater if the extraordinary costs involved in the May Company acquisiton were removed from the calculation of net profit margin. Thus, this component of the strategic profit model suggests that Macy's is outperforming Costco, but the following examination of the asset management path tells a different story.

Asset Management Path

The information used to analyze a retailer's asset management path primarily comes from the firm's balance sheet. Whereas the income statement summarizes financial performance over a period of time (usually a year or quarter), the balance sheet summarizes a retailer's financial position at a given point in time, typically the end of its fiscal year. The information about Macy's and Costco's assets from their balance sheets is shown in Exhibit 6–5, and the asset management path components in the strategic profit model are shown in Exhibit 6–6.

Assets are economic resources (e.g., inventory, buildings, computers, store fixtures) owned or controlled by a firm. There are two types of assets, current and fixed.

Current Assets   By accounting definition, **current assets** are assets that can normally be converted to cash within one year. In retailing, current assets are primarily cash, accounts receivable, and merchandise inventory. **Accounts receivable** are primarily the monies owed to the retailer because it has sold merchandise on credit to customers.

Current assets = Cash + Accounts receivable + Merchandise inventory + Other current assets

EXHIBIT 6–5

Asset Information from Macy's and Costco's Balance Sheets ($ millions)

	Macy's	Costco
Cash and short-term investments	$ 1,211	$ 2,833
Accounts receivable	517	565
Merchandise inventory	5,317	4,569
Other current assets	126	265
Total current assets	7,422	8,232
Total fixed assets	22,128	9,263
Total assets	$29,550	$17,495
Ratios		
Inventory turnover (cost of goods sold ÷ inventory at cost)	3.04	11.54
Asset turnover	0.91	3.44
ROA (net profit margin × asset turnover)	3.37%	6.19%

SOURCES: Macys 10K Report, filed April 4, 2007, for fiscal year ending January 31, 2007, p. F7; Costco 10K Report, filed November 17, 2006, for fiscal year ending September 3, 2006, p. 43.

EXHIBIT 6–6
Asset Management Path
for Macy's Inc. and Costco

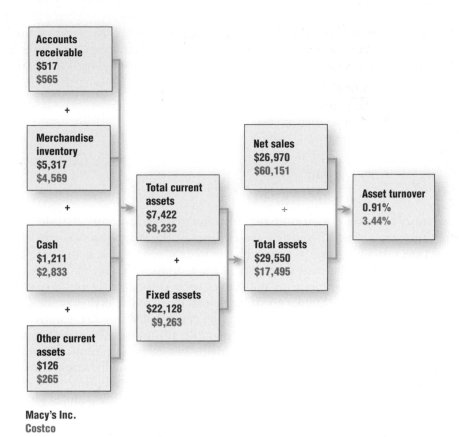

Accounts receivable
$517
$565

+

Merchandise inventory
$5,317
$4,569

+

Cash
$1,211
$2,833

+

Other current assets
$126
$265

Total current assets
$7,422
$8,232

+

Fixed assets
$22,128
$9,263

Net sales
$26,970
$60,151

÷

Total assets
$29,550
$17,495

Asset turnover
0.91%
3.44%

Macy's Inc.
Costco

Current assets are substantial for some retailers. From a marketing perspective, the accounts receivable generated from a **proprietary store credit card system** provide an important service to customers. This system, also known as an **in-house credit system** is one in which credit cards have the store's name on them, and the accounts receivable are administered by the retailer, not a credit card company like Visa or Master Card or a financial institution.[8] The retailer's ability to provide credit, particularly if it can offer a low interest rate as an incentive, can make the difference between making or losing a sale, because paying cash for a sizable purchases may be difficult for many people. But offering this service is costly, because it increases accounts receivable and thus the total amount of assets needed by the retailer. When merchandise is sold on credit, the proceeds of the sale are tied up in accounts receivable until the retailer collects the debt. The money invested in accounts receivable costs the retailer interest expenses and keeps it from investing the money generated by the sale elsewhere. To ease the financial burden of carrying accounts receivable, retailers often use third-party credit cards, such as Visa or MasterCard, and collect from delinquent accounts quickly.

Merchandise inventory is a retailer's lifeblood. The principle benefit retailers offer customers is having the right merchandise inventory available at the right time and place. **Inventory turnover,** indicates how effectively retailers utilize their investment in inventory. It is the cost of goods sold from the income statement divided by the average inventory level (at cost) from the balance sheet.

Since credit card sales can be expensive for retailers, why do they take them?

REFACT

Note that the inventory level reported on the balance sheet is the level on the last day of the fiscal year, not the average level. To measure the average inventory level more accurately, we would have to measure the level on each day of the year and divide by 365 or by each month. (See Chapter 12).

$$\frac{\text{Cost of goods sold}}{\text{Average inventory at cost}} = \text{Inventory turnover}$$

$$\text{Macy's:} \quad \frac{\$16,197}{\$5,317} = 3.04$$

$$\text{Costco:} \quad \frac{\$52,746}{\$4,569} = 11.54$$

Inventory turnover is a measure of the productivity of inventory that shows how many times, on average, inventory cycles through the store during a specific period of time (usually a year). Costco's higher inventory turnover is to be expected, due to the nature of its retail strategy and the merchandise it sells. That is, most items in Costco are commodities and staples such as food, batteries, housewares, and basic apparel items. Unlike apparel fashions that are the mainstay for department stores like Macy's, these staples can be replenished quickly. Costco stores also have only 4,000 SKUs in total; for example, it may only offer one brand of ketchup in two different sizes, which represents two inventory items. Department stores, however, usually stock more than 100,000 SKUs—including as many as 500 SKUs of men's dress shirts (different colors, sizes, styles, and brands). Larger assortments, like those in department stores, require relatively higher inventory investments, which slows inventory turnover.

To provide a more attractive store environment, department store retailers (top) have higher fixed assets than wholesale club retailers (bottom).

Fixed Assets   **Fixed assets** are those that require more than a year to convert to cash. In retailing, the principal fixed assets are buildings (if store property is owned rather than leased), fixtures (e.g., display racks), equipment (e.g., computers, delivery trucks), and other long-term investments such as stock in other firms.

Typically, large retailers such as Wal-Mart and Home Depot own their store locations.[9] Other retailers rent their retail space and use the money they would have used to buy the land to remodel stores or buy merchandise. Yet ownership appeals to many retailers, because it enables them to secure their costs and avoid the possibility of increasing rents. When a retailer owns though, the area around the location may change and become unattractive, which would force the retailer to sell the location at a loss.

When a retailer remodels a store, it removes and replaces, for example, old fixtures, carpeting, and lights. Thus, like inventory, these assets cycle through the store. The difference is that the process is a lot slower. The life of a fixture in a Macy's store may be five years (instead of two months, as it might be for a Sony digital camera), yet the concept of turnover is the same. When a retailer decides to invest in a fixed asset, it needs to determine how many sales dollars can be generated from that asset.

Suppose that Macy's is considering the purchase of a new fixture for displaying dinnerware. It has a choice of buying an expensive antique display cabinet for $20,000 or having a simple plywood display constructed for $5,000. Using the expensive antique, it forecasts incremental sales of $50,000 in the first year, whereas the plywood display is expected to generate only $25,000. Ignoring all other assets for a moment,

$$\frac{\text{Net sales}}{\text{Fixed assets}} = \text{Asset turnover}$$

Antique cabinet: $\dfrac{\$50,000}{\$20,000} = 2.5$

Plywood cabinet: $\dfrac{\$25,000}{\$5,000} = 5.0$

The antique cabinet will certainly help create an atmosphere conducive to selling expensive dinnerware. Exclusively from a sales perspective, the antique cabinet would thus appear appropriate. But it costs much more than the plywood shelves. Clearly, by considering only asset turnover, the plywood shelves are the way to go. In the end, a combination of marketing and financial factors should be considered when making the appropriate asset purchase decision.[10]

Asset Turnover   Asset turnover is an overall performance measure derived from the asset management component in the strategic profit model.

$$\frac{\text{Net sales}}{\text{Total assets}} = \text{Asset turnover}$$

Macy's: $\dfrac{\$26,970}{\$29,550} = .91$

Costco: $\dfrac{\$60,151}{\$17,494} = 3.44$

Costco's asset turnover thus is more than three times as much as Macy's. Again, this difference reflects the different retail strategies pursued by the companies. Costco targets consumers who are more interested in low prices than in an extensive assortment of merchandise. Thus, Costco stocks fewer SKUs, has limited inventory, and experiences higher inventory turnover. In addition, it uses fewer fixed assets (e.g., fixtures, lighting, mannequins) in its stores compared with Macy's stores.

Macy's targets a market segment interested in buying fashionable apparel. Consumers in its target segment are less price conscious; want to choose from a broad assortment of colors, sizes, and brands; and like to shop in a more attractive environment, and certainly not a warehouse. Thus, Macy's needs to invest in more current assets (merchandise inventory) and fixed assets (store design elements), which results in its lower asset turnover.

Return on Assets

In terms of the profit margin management path, Macy's performs better than Costco, but Costco has a higher asset turnover and thus performs better on the asset management path. But overall performance, as measured by ROA, is determined

EXHIBIT 6–7
Strategic Profit Model
Ratios for Selected
Retailers

	Net Profit Margin (%)	Asset Turnover	Return on Assets (%)
Category specialists			
Best Buy	3.80%	2.65	10.07
Home Depot	6.30	1.74	10.96
Lowe's	6.60	1.69	11.15
PetSmart	4.40	2.06	9.06
Barnes & Noble	2.90	1.65	4.79
Borders	−3.70	1.57	−5.81
Specialty stores			
The Gap	4.90	1.87	9.16
Chico's	10.10	1.56	15.76
Abercrombie & Fitch	12.70	1.48	18.80
The Limited Brands	6.30	1.50	9.45
Urban Outfitters	9.50	1.36	12.92
Drugstores			
CVS	3.10	2.13	6.60
Walgreens	3.70	2.77	10.25
Discount			
Family Dollar	3.10	2.54	7.87
Dollar General	1.50	3.02	4.53
Wal-Mart	3.20	2.31	7.39
Target	4.70	1.59	7.47
Supermarkets			
Safeway	2.20	2.47	5.43
Albertson's	1.10	2.26	2.49

SOURCE: 2007 Hoovers Online.

by considering the effects of both paths by multiplying the net profit margin by asset turnover:

	Net profit margin	×	Asset turnover	=	Return on assets
Macy's:	3.70%	×	.91	=	3.37%
Costco:	1.8%	×	3.44	=	6.19%

Although the ROA calculated here shows the return on assets for a specific time period, this number may not be a good indicator of future performance. If we were to use the net operating income percentage in making the calculation, rather than the net profit margin, the ROAs would be as follows:

	Net operating income	×	Asset turnover	=	Return on assets
Macy's:	6.81%	×	.91	=	6.20%
Costco:	2.70%	×	3.44	=	6.29%

This difference arises because Macy's incurred some extraordinary expenses during the year, associated with its acquisiton of the May Company.

In the end, the two firm's ROAs tell two stories about the companies that are based on two different financial paths. Macy's has the higher net profit margin; Costco has the higher asset turnover. Return on assets is a very important performance measure, because it shows how much money the retailer is making on its investment in assets and how good that return is relative to other investments. For instance, if a retailer can achieve a 4 percent ROA by opening a new store and 6 percent by investing in a risk-free Treasury bill, the retailer should make the higher-yield, lower-risk investment.

The strategic profit model illustrates two important issues. First, retailers and investors need to consider both net profit margin and asset turnover when evaluating their financial performance. Firms can achieve high performance (high ROA) by effectively managing both net profit margins and asset turnover. Second, retailers need to consider the implications of their strategic decisions on both components of the strategic profit model. For example, simply increasing prices will increase the gross margin and net profit margins (profit margin management path). However, increasing prices will result in fewer sales, and assuming the level of assets stays the same, asset turnover will decrease. Thus profit margin increases, assets turnover decreases, and the effect on ROA depends on how much the profit margin increases compared with the decrease in asset turnover.

Exhibit 6–7 shows the strategic profit model ratios for a variety of retailers. The exhibit illustrates that supermarket and discount chains typically have higher asset turnovers and lower net profit margin percentages. The apparel specialty stores have lower asset turnovers and higher net profit margin percentages; however, the drug store chains are just the opposite. Note also the range in ROA ratios among specialty stores, with Chico's, Urban Outfitters, and Abercrombie & Fitch at the top and Safeway and Albertson's supermarkets at the bottom.

Although ROA and its components are important indicators of a retailers performance, Retailing View 6.3 discusses some other considerations that private equity firms consider when making investments in retailers.

Illustration: Kelly Bradford's Evaluation of the Gifts-To-Go.com Growth Opportunity

To illustrate the use of the strategic profit model for evaluating a growth opportunity, let's look at the opportunity that Kelly Bradford, from Chapter 5, is considering. Recall that Kelly Bradford owns Gifts To Go, a two-store chain in the Chicago area. She's considering several growth options, one of which is to open a new Internet channel called www.Gifts-To-Go.com. She determined that the market size for this channel is high but very competitive. Now she needs to conduct a financial

REFACT
Gas stations, on average, have a gross margin of only 15.5 percent but an inventory turnover of 39.3 percent.[11]

Barbarians at the Gate   RETAILING VIEW   6.3

Private equity firms make significant investments in buying retail firms. For example, Blackstone Group and Bain Capital teamed up to buy the craft-store chain Michaels for $6 billion, and KKR and several other firms bought Toys "R" Us for $6.6 billion; Texas Pacific, with its partners, bought Neiman Marcus for $5.1 billion, and Leonard Green & Partner bought The Container Store.

Private equity firms, formerly known as corporate raiders or "Barbarians at the Gate," are firms that invest their money and the money of others, such as union pension funds and university endowments. Rather than buying stock in companies, private equity investors buy the entire company from its stockholders, improve the efficiency of the firm (often by hiring new senior managers), and then sell the acquired company several years later. Because shares for the acquired company after the acquisition are not traded on the stock exchange, the company can take a long-term perspective toward improving the firm's operations, because it does not have to issue the quarterly reports required by the Securities and Exchange Commission (SEC). The managers of the acquired firms thus can reengineer a business to move away from Wall Street's ceaseless scrutiny of monthly comparable store sales and quarterly growth in earnings.

Private equity firms find retailers attractive investments because many of them have strong cash flows and undervalued assets and respond quickly to efficiency improvements and changes in strategic direction. Whereas the typical small investor focuses

on profits and return on assets, private equity firms are interested in cash flow—the money that the retailer generates from its operations. A company with a higher cash flow reduces the risk of bankruptcy and provides money to invest in improving efficiencies, such installing information systems or remodeling stores.

Retailers frequently have undervalued assets, such as well-known private-label brands, leases for space in attractive locations, or the land on which their stores are located. A private equity company can sell these assets after it acquires a retailer or use these assets as collateral to get loans. For example, a private equity firm might sell the rights to use a well-known private-label brand to a company that would license the brands to other firms. Thus, the whole of the retailer is often less than the sum of its parts.

"The issue is never whether private equity firms can grow a company, but whether they can make it more efficient and improve the cash flows," said George Smith, a professor of economics with the Leonard Stern School of Business. "Sometimes that means downsizing. Sometimes it means a change of strategy. Sometimes it means growing. It all depends on the particular circumstances."

Sources: Dan Freed, "Stocking Up: Why Buyout Firms Love Retail," *Investment Dealers' Digest*, July 23, 2007, pp. 16–20; Susan Reda, "Following the Cash Flow," *Stores*, November 2006 (accessed January 4, 2008); Steve Rosenbush, "Private Equity Takes a Shine to Retail," *BusinessWeek*, July 5, 2006 (accessed January 4, 2008).

EXHIBIT 6–8

Income Statement Information for Gifts To Go Stores and Proposed Gifts To-Go.com Internet Channel

Income Statement	Gifts To Go Stores	Gifts-To-Go.com (Projected)	Businesses Combined
Net sales	$700,000	$440,000	$1,140,000
Less: Cost of goods sold	350,000	220,000	570,000
Gross margin	350,000	220,000	570,000
Less: Operating expenses	250,000	150,000	400,000
Less: Interest expenses	8,000	0	8,000
Total expenses	258,000	150,000	408,000
Net profit before tax	92,000	70,000	162,000
Less: Taxes	32,200	24,500	56,700
Net profit after taxes	59,800	45,500	105,300
Gross margin %	50.00%	50.00%	50.00%
Operating expenses %	35.7	34.1	35.1
Net profit % after taxes	8.54	10.34	9.2
Net operating income %	14.3	15.9	14.9

analysis for the proposed online channel, compare the projections with Gifts To Go stores, and determine the financial performance of the combined businesses. We'll first look at the profit margin management path, followed by the asset turnover management path. Exhibit 6–8 shows income statement information for Kelly's Gifts To Go stores, her estimates for Gifts-To-Go.com, and the combined businesses.

Profit Margin Management Path   Kelly thinks she can develop Gifts-To-Go.com into a business that will generate annual sales of $440,000. She anticipates some cannibalization of her store sales by the Internet channel; some customers who will buy merchandise at Gifts-To-Go.com will no longer go into her stores to make their purchases. She also thinks the Internet channel will stimulate some store sales; customers who see gift items on her Web site will visit the stores and make their purchases there. Thus, she decides to perform the analysis with the assumption that her store sales will remain the same after the introduction of the Internet channel.

Gross Margin Percentage   Kelly plans to charge the same prices and sell basically the same merchandise, with an extended assortment, on Gifts-To-Go.com as she sells in her stores. Thus, she expects the gross margin percentage for store sales will be the same as the gross margin percentage for Gifts-To-Go.com sales.

$$\frac{\text{Gross margin}}{\text{Net sales}} = \text{Gross margin \%}$$

$$\text{Stores:} \quad \frac{350,000}{\$700,000} = 50\%$$

$$\text{Gifts-To-Go.com:} \quad \frac{220,000}{\$440,000} = 50\%$$

Operating Expenses   Initially, Kelly thought that her operating expenses as a percentage of sales would be lower for Gifts-To-Go.com because she would not need to pay rent or highly trained salespeople. But she discovered that her operating expenses as a percentage of sales will be only slightly lower for Gifts-To-Go.com, because she needs to hire a firm to maintain the Web site, process orders, and get orders ready for shipment. Also, Gifts To Go stores have an established clientele and highly trafficked locations with good visibility. Although some of her current customers will learn about the Web site from her in-store promotions, Kelly will have to invest in advertising and promotions to create awareness for her new channel and inform people who are unfamiliar with her stores.

$$\frac{\text{Operating expenses}}{\text{Net sales}} = \text{Operating expenses \%}$$

Stores: $\dfrac{250,000}{\$700,000} = 35.7\%$

Gifts-To-Go.com: $\dfrac{150,000}{\$440,000} = 34.1\%$

Net Profit Margins   Because the gross margin and operating expenses as a percentage of sales for the two operations are projected to be the same, Gifts-To-Go.com is expected to generate a slightly higher net profit margin percentage:

$$\frac{\text{Net profit}}{\text{Net sales}} = \text{Net profit \%}$$

Stores: $\dfrac{59,800}{\$700,000} = 8.5\%$

Gifts-To-Go.com: $\dfrac{45,500}{\$440,000} = 10.3\%$

Asset Turnover Management Path   Now let's compare the two operations using the asset turnover management path with the balance sheet information from Exhibit 6–9.

Accounts Receivable   Like Gifts To Go, Gifts-To-Go.com will have accounts receivable because many customers use credit cards to buy gifts. Because the percentage of credit card sales is higher over the Internet channel than in stores, Kelly expects that the accounts receivable for the Internet channel will be higher than for the store channel.

Inventory Turnover   Kelly estimates that Gifts-To-Go.com will have a higher inventory turnover than Gifts To Go stores, because it will consolidate the inventory at one centralized distribution center that services a large sales volume, as opposed to Gifts to Go, which has inventory sitting in several stores with relatively lower sales volumes.

REFACT

The average inventory turnover for grocery stores is 12.7 compared with 3.5 for hardware stores.[12]

$$\frac{\text{Cost of goods}}{\text{Average inventory}} = \text{Inventory turnover}$$

Stores: $\dfrac{350,000}{\$175,000} = 2.0$

Gifts-To-Go.com: $\dfrac{220,000}{\$70,000} = 3.1$

Balance Sheet Information	Gifts To Go Stores	Gifts-To-Go.com (Projected)	Businesses Combined
Accounts receivable	$140,000	$120,000	$260,000
Merchandise inventory	175,000	70,000	245,000
Cash	35,000	11,000	46,000
Total current assets	350,000	201,000	551,000
Fixed assets	30,000	10,000	40,000
Total assets	380,000	211,000	591,000
Ratios			
Inventory turnover	2.0	3.1	2.3
Asset turnover	1.84	2.09	1.93
ROA	15.70%	21.60%	17.80%

EXHIBIT 6–9
Balance Sheet Information for Gifts To Go Stores and Proposed Internet Channel

Fixed Assets   Gifts To Go's store space is rented. Thus, Kelly's fixed assets consist of the fixtures, lighting, and other leasehold improvements for her stores, as well as equipment such as point-of-sale terminals. Kelly also has invested in assets that make her stores aesthetically pleasing. Gifts-To-Go.com is outsourcing the fulfillment of orders placed on its Web site, so it has no warehouse assets. Thus, its fixed assets are its Web site and order processing computer system.

Asset Turnover   As she expects, Gifts-To-Go.com's projected asset turnover is higher than that of Gifts To Go's stores, because Kelly estimates that Gifts-To-Go.com will have a higher inventory turnover, and its other assets are lower.

$$\frac{\text{Net sales}}{\text{Total assets}} = \text{Asset turnover}$$

Stores: $\dfrac{700,000}{\$380,000} = 1.84$

Gifts-To-Go.com: $\dfrac{440,000}{\$211,000} = 2.09$

Return on Assets   Because Kelly's estimates for the net profit margin and asset turnover for Gifts-To-Go.com are higher than those for her stores, Gifts-To-Go.com achieves a higher ROA. Thus, this strategic profit model analysis indicates that Gifts-To-Go.com is a financially viable growth opportunity for Kelly.

	Net profit margin	×	Asset turnover	=	Return on assets
Stores:	8.54%	×	1.84	=	15.7%
Gifts-To-Go.com:	10.3%	×	2.09	=	21.5%

Using the Strategic Profit Model to Analyze Other Decisions   The strategic profit model is useful to retailers because it combines two decision-making areas: profit margin management and asset turnover management. Managers can use the model to examine interrelationships between the components. For example, Kelly might consider an investment in a computerized inventory control system that would help her make better decisions about which merchandise to order, when to reorder merchandise, and when to lower prices on merchandise that is not being bought.

If she buys the system, her sales will increase because she will have a greater percentage of merchandise that is selling well and fewer stockouts. However, even though her cost of goods sold will increase, it will not do so proportionally, because she will have fewer price discounts to sell slow-moving merchandise.

Looking at the asset turnover management path, the purchase of the computer system will increase her fixed assets by the amount of the system, but her inventory turnover will increase and the level of inventory assets will decrease, because she is able to buy more efficiently. Thus, her asset turnover will probably increase, because sales will increase at a greater percentage than will total assets. Total assets may actually decrease if the additional cost of the inventory system is less than the reduction in inventory.

SETTING AND MEASURING PERFORMANCE OBJECTIVES

Setting performance objectives is a necessary component of any firm's strategic planning process. A retailer would not know how it has performed if it doesn't have specific objectives in mind to compare its actual performance against. Performance objectives should include (1) a numerical index of the performance desired against which progress may be measured, (2) a time frame within which the objective is to be achieved, and (3) the resources needed to achieve the objective. For example, "earning reasonable profits" isn't a good objective. It doesn't provide specific goals that can be used to evaluate performance. What's reasonable? When do you want to realize the profits? A better objective would be "earning $100,000 in profit during calendar year 2010 on a $500,000 investment in inventory and building."

Top-Down versus Bottom-Up Process

Setting objectives in large retail organizations entails a combination of the top-down and bottom-up approaches to planning.

Top-down planning means that goals get set at the top of the organization and are passed down to the lower operating levels. In a retailing organization, top-down planning involves corporate officers developing an overall retail strategy and assessing broad economic, competitive, and consumer trends. With this information, they develop performance objectives for the corporation. These overall objectives are then broken down into specific objectives for each buyer and merchandise category and for each region, store, and even each department within stores and the sales associates working in those departments.

The overall strategy determines the merchandise variety, assortment, and product availability, plus the store size, location, and level of customer service. Then the merchandise vice presidents decide which types of merchandise are expected to grow, stay the same, or shrink. Next, performance goals are established for each buyer and merchandise manager. This process is reviewed in Chapters 12 and 13.

Similarly, regional store vice presidents translate the company's performance objectives into objectives for each district manager, who then develop objectives with their store managers. The process then trickles down to department managers in the stores and individual sales associates. The process of setting objectives for sales associates in stores is discussed in Chapter 17.

This top-down planning is complemented by a bottom-up planning approach. **Bottom-up planning** involves lower levels in the company developing performance objectives that are aggregated up to develop overall company objectives. Buyers and store managers estimate what they can achieve, and their estimates are transmitted up the organization to the corporate executives.

Frequently there are disagreements between the goals that have trickled down from the top and those set by lower-level employees of the organization. For example, a store manager may not be able to achieve the 10 percent sales growth set for his or her region because a major employer in the area has announced plans to lay off 2,000 employees. These differences between bottom-up and top-down plans are resolved through a negotiation process involving corporate executives and operating managers. If the operating managers aren't involved in the objective-setting process, they won't accept the objectives and thus will be less motivated to achieve them.

Accountable for Performance

At each level of the retail organization, the business unit and its manager should be held accountable only for the revenues, expenses, and contribution to ROA that they can control. Thus, expenses that affect several levels of the organization (e.g., labor and capital expenses associated with operating a corporate headquarters) shouldn't be arbitrarily assigned to lower levels. In the case of a store, for example, it may be appropriate to set performance objectives based on sales, sales associate productivity, store inventory shrinkage due to employee theft and shoplifting, and energy costs. If the buyer lowers prices to get rid of merchandise and therefore profits suffer, it is not fair to assess a store manager's performance on the basis of the resulting decline in store profit.

Performance objectives and measures can be used to pinpoint problem areas. The reasons that performance may be above or below planned levels must be examined. Perhaps the managers involved in setting the objectives aren't very good at making estimates. If so, they may need to be trained in forecasting. Also, buyers may misrepresent their business unit's ability to contribute to the firm's financial goals to get a larger inventory budget than is warranted and consequently earn a higher bonus. In either case, investment funds would be misallocated.

Actual performance may be different than the plan predicts due to circumstances beyond the manager's control. For example, there may have been a recession. Assuming the recession wasn't predicted, or was more severe or lasted longer than anticipated, there are several relevant questions: How quickly were plans adjusted? How rapidly and appropriately were pricing and promotional policies modified? In short, did the manager react to salvage an adverse situation, or did those reactions worsen the situation?

Performance Objectives and Measures

Many factors contribute to a retailer's overall performance, which makes it hard to find a single measure to evaluate performance. For instance, sales is a global measure of a retail store's activity level. However, a store manager could easily increase sales by lowering prices, but the profit realized on that merchandise (gross margin) would suffer as a result. Clearly, an attempt to maximize one measure may lower another. Managers must therefore understand how their actions affect multiple performance measures. It's usually unwise to use only one measure, because it rarely tells the whole story.

The measures used to evaluate retail operations vary depending on (1) the level of the organization at which the decision is made and (2) the resources the manager controls. For example, the principal resources controlled by store managers are space and money for operating expenses (such as wages for sales associates and utility payments to light and heat the store). Thus, store managers focus on performance measures like sales per square foot and employee cost as a percent of sales.

REFACT

The average annual sales per employee is $89,169 for women's apparel specialty store retailers, $181,833 for home improvement centers, and $361,795 for catalog and e-retailers.[13]

Types of Measures

Exhibit 6–10 breaks down a variety of retailers' performance measures into three types: input measures, output measures, and productivity measures. **Input measures** are the resources or money allocated by a retailer to achieve outputs, or results. For example, the amount and selection of merchandise inventory, the number of stores, the size of the stores, the employees, advertising, markdowns, store hours, and promotions are managerial decisions involving resource allocations.

EXHIBIT 6–10   Performance Objectives and Measures Used by Retailers

Level of Organization	Output	Input	Productivity (output/input)
Corporate (measures for entire corporation)	Net sales Net profits Growth in sales, profits, comparable store sales	Square feet of store space Number of employees Inventory Advertising expenditures	Return on assets Asset turnover Sales per employee Sales per square foot
Merchandise management (measures for a merchandise category)	Net sales Gross margin Growth in sales	Inventory level Markdowns Advertising expenses Cost of merchandise	Gross margin return on investment (GMROI) Inventory turnover Advertising as a percentage of sales* Markdown as a percentage of sales*
Store operations (measures for a store or department within a store)	Net sales Gross margin Growth in sales	Square feet of selling areas Expenses for utilities Number of sales associates	Net sales per square foot Net sales per sales associate or per selling hour Utility expenses as a percentage of sales* Inventory shrinkage*

*These productivity measures are commonly expressed as an input/output ratio.

Output measures assess the results of a retailer's investment decisions. For example, sales revenue, gross margin, and net profit margin are all output measures and ways to evaluate a retailer's input or resource allocations decisions. A **productivity measure** (the ratio of an output to an input) determines how effectively retailers use their resources—what return they get on their investments.

In general, because productivity measures are ratios of outputs to inputs, they are very useful for comparing the performance of different business units. Suppose Kelly Bradford's two stores are different sizes: One has 5,000 square feet, and the other has 10,000 square feet. It's hard to compare the stores' performances using just output or input measures, because the larger store will probably generate more sales and have higher expenses. But if the larger store has lower space productivity because it generates $210 net sales per square foot and the smaller store generates $350 per square foot, Kelly knows that the smaller store is operating more efficiently, even though it's generating lower sales.

Corporate Performance   At a corporate level, retail executives have three critical resources (inputs)—merchandise inventory, store space, and employees—that they can manage to generate sales and profits (outputs). Thus, effective productivity measures of the utilization of these assets include asset and inventory turnover, sales per square foot of selling space, and sales per employee.

As we have discussed, ROA is an overall productivity measure combining the profit margin percentage and asset turnover management. **Comparable store sales growth** (also called **same-store sales growth**) is a commonly used measure of a retailer's performance. There are two sources of annual sales growth, sales from new stores opened during the year and sales growth from stores that were open during the previous year. Comparable store sales growth is the sales growth in stores that have been open for at least a year – the second source of sales growth. Thus growth in comparable store sales assesses how well the retailer is doing with its core business strategy and execution. Comparable store sales growth is a preferable measure to overall sales growth because the inclusion of new store sales clouds the long-term performance assessment. For example, overall sales might be increasing because the retailer is opening new stores, but, over time the sales in the retailer's stores, new and existing, is decreasing. Thus, when the new store openings slow down, the retailer will experience negative sales growth. By excluding the sales from new stores, retailers and investors can better assess how the overall strategy and implementation are working. Comparable store sales growth assesses how well the retailer's fundamental business approach is not being well received by its customers.

Merchandise Management Measures   The critical resource (input) controlled by merchandise managers is merchandise inventory. Merchandise managers also have the authority to set initial prices and lower prices when merchandise is not selling (i.e., take a markdown). Finally, they negotiate with vendors over the price paid for merchandise.

Inventory turnover is a productivity measure of the management of inventory; higher turnover means greater inventory management productivity. Gross margin percentage indicates the performance of merchandise managers in negotiating with vendors and buying merchandise that can generate a profit. Discounts (markdowns) as a percentage of sales are also a measure of the quality of the merchandise buying decisions. If merchandise managers have a high percentage of markdowns, they may not be buying the right merchandise or the right quantities, because they weren't able to sell some of it at its original retail price. Note that gross margin and discount percentages are productivity measures, but they are typically expressed as an input divided by an output as opposed to the typical productivity measures that are outputs divided by inputs.

Store Operations Measures   The critical assets controlled by store managers are the use of the store space and the management of the store's employees. Thus, measures of store operations productivity include sales per square foot of selling space and sales per employee (or sales per employee per working hour, to take into account that some employees work part-time). Store management is also responsible for controlling theft by employees and customers (referred to as inventory shrinkage), store maintenance, and energy costs (lighting, heating, and air conditioning). Thus, some other productivity measures used to assess the performance of store managers are inventory shrinkage and energy costs as a percentage of sales. Retailing View 6.4 describes how self-checkout increases labor productivity.

Assessing Performance: The Role of Benchmarks

As we have discussed, the financial measures used to assess performance reflect the retailer's market strategy. For example, because Costco has a different business strategy than Macy's. It has a lower profit margin. It earns an acceptable ROA because it increases its inventory and asset turnovers by stocking a more limited merchandise assortment of less fashionable, staple items. In contrast, Macy's specializes in apparel and accessories, which requires a broad and deep merchandise assortment. Thus, it has lower inventory and asset turnover but achieves an acceptable ROA through its higher profit margins. In other words, the performance of a retailer cannot be assessed accurately simply by looking at isolated measures, because they are affected by the retailer's strategy. To get a better assessment of a retailer's performance, we need to compare it to a benchmark. Two commonly used benchmarks are (1) the performance of the retailer over time and (2) the performance of the retailer compared with that of its competitors.

6.4   RETAILING VIEW   Self-Checkout Increases Labor Productivity

Self-checkout retailers have been around for a long time in gas stations, ATM machines, and FastLanes. As retailers aim for higher efficiency, self-checkout also is increasingly replacing human labor at grocery stores, home improvement centers, discount stores, and fast-food restaurants. Estimates suggest that the value of self-service transactions will rise from $161 billion in 2005 to $450 billion by 2008.

Self-checkout terminals allow customers to scan and bag their own purchases and pay for them without a cashier. Stores generally have four terminals overseen by one employee. Some customers find self-checkout faster and more convenient than traditional checkout stations, especially when they have fewer items.

Retailers that embrace self-service argue that the option of self-service is a service in itself that can make customers feel accommodated. In addition, freeing up cashiers allows store employees to stock shelves and help customers. Some customers enjoy not having to interact with a young cashier in need of an attitude adjustment or avoiding the awkwardness associated with looking into the eyes of a cashier when they buy personal items.

On the other side, some retailers, such as Safeway and Macy's, claim that personal service is a hallmark of their business, so self-checkout would detract from their image. Some customers are hesitant to try out the technology with unique items they may have trouble scanning, such as a head of radicchio. An item that does not scan immediately can cause repetitive automated voices and incessant beeping, which may even force a customer to choose the wrong product option to forgo being embarrassed at the front of a queue of people.

The next generation of self-checkout technology should dramatically increase the convenience and reduce the potential

Home Depot implemented self-checkout lanes in its stores to improve customer service, increase labor productivity, and lower labor costs.

for theft. Using radio frequency identification (RFID) technology, computer chips embedded in each product will transmit a signal identifying the product and price. Customers can load up a shopping cart and simply walk through a "reader" that totals up the purchases and even automatically deducts the balance from a bank account by reading the signal from the chip on a key chain or bank card.

Sources: Paul Burel, "Checking Out Self Checkout," *Chain Store Age*, July 2007, p. 58; Suzanne Barlyn and Jim Carlton, "Do-It-Yourself Supermarket Checkout," *The Wall Street Journal*, April 5, 2007, p. D3; Paul Lukas, "Whither The Checkout Girl?" *Fast Company*, November 2006, pp. 50–51.

Macy's and Costco's Three-Year Financial Performance   **EXHIBIT 6–11**

	MACY'S			COSTCO		
	2006	**2005**	**2004**	**2006**	**2005**	**2004**
Gross margin %	39.90%	40.60%	40.50%	12.30%	12.40%	12.50%
Operating expenses %	33.10%	30.00%	31.66%	9.60%	9.76%	9.60%
Net profit %	3.70%	6.30%	4.40%	1.80%	2.00%	1.80%
Asset turnover	0.91	0.68	1.05	3.44	3.21	3.19
ROA	3.37%	4.28%	4.62%	6.19%	6.42%	5.84%
Inventory turnover	3.04	2.35	2.88	11.54	11.54	11.55
Sales per employee	$143,457	$96,509	$140,857	$473,632	$448,748	$425,751
Sales per square foot	$172	$141	$189	$937	$897	$1,062
Growth in same-store sales	4.40%	1.30%	2.40%	7%	6%	9%

SOURCES: Calculations based on data in Macy's 10K Report, filed April 4, 2007, for fiscal year ending February 3, 2007; Macy's 10K Report, filed April 13, 2006, for fiscal year ending January 28, 2006; Macy's 10K Report, filed March 29, 2005, for fiscal year ending January 28, 2005; Costco 10K Report, filed November 17, 2006, for fiscal year ending September 3, 2006; Costco 10K Report, filed November 10, 2005, for fiscal year ending August 28, 2006; Costco 10K Report, filed November 11, 2004, for fiscal year ending August 29, 2004.

Performance over Time   One useful approach for assessing a retailer's performance compares its recent performance with its performance in the preceding months, quarters, or years. Exhibit 6–11 shows the performance measures for Macy's Inc. and Costco over a three-year period.

Costco experiences greater inventory turnover and sales per square foot, due to the type of merchandise sold (food and staples versus fashion apparel), as well as lower sales per employees due to its self-service offering compared with the customer service provided by the sales associates at Macy's. In terms of the strategic profit model components, Costco's ROA shows a general upward trend, whereas Macy's seems to be decling over time. This difference in ROA trends probably occurs because Costco's asset turnover has been increasing over time, while Macy's has been decreasing, perhaps as a result of the May Company acquisition. Macy's, however, seems to be rebounding as it continues to assimilate the May Company holdings.

Performance Compared to Competitors   A second approach for assessing a retailer's performance involves comparing it with that of its competitors. Exhibit 6–12 compares the performance of Macy's Inc. with other national department store chains.

Financial Performance of Macy's Inc. and Other National Department Store Chains   **EXHIBIT 6–12**

	Macy's	JCPenney	Sears	Dillard's	Nordstrom	Kohl's
Net sales (millions $)	26,970	19,903	53,012	7,810	8,561	15,544
Gross margin %	39.90%	39.30%	28.70%	35.60%	37.50%	36.40%
Net profit %	3.70%	5.80%	2.80%	3.10%	7.90%	7.10%
Asset turnover	0.91	1.57	1.76	1.44	1.77	1.72
Return on assets	3.37%	9.11%	4.93%	4.48%	13.98%	12.21%
Inventory turnover	3.04	3.55	3.82	2.84	5.37	3.82
Sales per square foot	$172	$193	$181	$135	$424	$256
Sales per employee	$143,457	$131,808	$168,292	$148,604	$161,828	$136,352
Growth in sales 2006/2005	16.98%	5.64%	7.33%	1.11%	9.79%	13.78%
Comparable store sales % change	4.40%	3.70%	−3.70%	0%	7.50%	5.90%

SOURCES: Calculations based on data in Macy's 10K Report, filed April 4, 2007, for fiscal year ending March 23, 2007; JCPenney 10K Report, filed April 4, 2007, for fiscal year ending February 3, 2007; Sears Holding 10K Report, filed April 4, 2007, for fiscal year ending February 3, 2007; Dillard's 10K Report, filed March 23, 2007, for fiscal year ending February 3, 2007; Nordstrom 10K Report, filed March 23, 2007, for fiscal year ending February 3, 2007; Kohl's10K Report, filed March 23, 2007, for fiscal year ending February 3, 2007.

Macy's has the lowest ROA because its has the lowest asset turnover and lowest net profit margin, even though it has highest gross margin percentage. The May Company acquisition might be affecting these numbers. For example, Macy's might have more SG&A expenses because of the temporary duplication in staff—two distribution systems, two sets of buyers, and so forth. Due to the May acquisition, its also has the highest growth in sales, but the comparable store sales growth is about average, less than Nordstrom or Kohl's. Macy's also is about average in terms of labor and space productivity.

SUMMARY

This chapter explains some basic elements of the retailing financial strategy and examines how retailing strategy affects the financial performance of a firm. The strategic profit model is a vehicle for understanding the complex interrelations between financial ratios and retailing strategy. Different types of retailers have different financial operating characteristics. Specifically, department store chains like Macy's generally have higher profit margins and lower turnover ratios than warehouse clubs like Costco. Yet when margin and turnover are combined into return on assets, it is possible to achieve similar financial performance.

Financial performance measures are used to evaluate different aspects of a retailing organization. Although the return on assets ratio in the strategic profit model is appropriate for evaluating the performance of the retail executives responsible for managing the firm, other measures are more appropriate for more specific activities. For instance, inventory turnover and gross margin are appropriate for buyers, whereas store managers should be concerned with sales or gross margin per square foot or per employee.

KEY TERMS

accounts receivable, *176*
assets, *176*
asset turnover, *170, 179*
bottom-up planning, *185*
comparable store sales growth, *187*
current assets, *176*
customer returns, *172*
fixed assets, *178*
gross margin, *174*
gross profit, *174*

in-house credit system, *177*
input measures, *186*
interest, *175*
interest income, *175*
inventory turnover, *177*
net profit, *175*
net profit margin, *169*
net sales, *172*
operating expenses, *174*
output measures, *187*

productivity measure, *187*
promotional allowances, *172*
proprietary store credit card
    system, *177*
return on assets, *168*
same-store sales growth, *187*
selling, general, and administrative
    expenses (SG&A), *174*
strategic profit model, *169*
top-down planning, *185*

GET OUT AND DO IT!

1.   **CONTINUING CASE ASSIGN-
    MENT** Evaluate the financial performance of the retailer you have selected for the continuing case assignment and another store that sells similar merchandise categories but to a very different target market. If yours is a high margin/low turnover store, compare it with a low margin/high turnover store. You can get this information from your chosen store's latest annual report, available in the "investor relations" area of its Web site, Hoovers Online, or the Edgar files at www.sec.gov. Explain why you would expect the gross margin percentage, operating expenses-to-sales ratio, net profit margin, inventory turnover, asset turnover, sales per square foot, and sales per employee to differ between the two stores. Assess which chain achieves better overall financial performance.

2.   Go to the latest annual reports and use the financial information to update the numbers in the net profit margin management model and the asset turnover management models for Macy's Inc. and Costco. Have there been any significant changes in their financial performance? Why are the key financial ratios for these two retailers so different?

3. Go to your favorite store and interview the manager. Determine how the retailer sets its performance objectives. Evaluate its procedures relative to the procedures presented in the text.

Go to the Strategic Profit Model (SPM) on the student side of the book's Web site. The SPM tutorial was designed to provide a refresher course on the basic financial ratios leading to return on assets and walks you through the process step-by-step. A "calculation page" is also included that will calculate all the ratios. You can type in the numbers from a firm's balance sheet and income statement to see the financial results produced with the current financial figures. You can also access an Excel spreadsheet for SPM calculations. The calculation page or the Excel spreadsheet can be used for Case 13 Tiffany's and Blue Nile: Comparing Financial Performance, page 589.

DISCUSSION QUESTIONS AND PROBLEMS

1. Why does a retailer need to use multiple performance measures to evaluate its performance?

2. Describe how a multiple-store retailer might set its annual performance objectives.

3. Buyers' performance is often measured by their gross margin percentage. Why is this measure more appropriate than net profit percentage?

4. How does the strategic profit model assist retailers in planning and evaluating their marketing and financial strategies?

5. Neiman Marcus (a chain of high-service department stores) and Wal-Mart target different customer segments. Which retailer would you expect to have a higher gross margin? Higher expense-to-sales ratio? Higher inventory turnover? Higher asset turnover? Net profit margin percentage? Why?

6. What elements in the strategic model are affected if a retailer decides to build and open 10 new stores?

7. What differences would you expect to see when comparing Gifts To Go's specialty store strategic profit model with that of two dry cleaning service businesses?

8. Using the following information about Lowe's 2007 income statement and balance sheet from Hoovers, determine its asset turnover, net profit margin percentage, and ROA. (Figures are in $ millions.)

Net sales	$46,927
Total assets	$27,285
Net profit	$ 3,259

9. Using the following information taken from the 2007 balance sheet and 2007 income statement for Urban Outfitters, develop a strategic profit model. (Figures are in $ millions.) You can access an Excel spreadsheet for SPM calculations on the student side of the book's Web site.

Net sales	$1,224.7
Cost of goods sold	$ 772.8
Operating expenses	$ 287.9
Inventory	$ 154.4
Accounts receivable	$ 25.5
Other current assets	$ 27.3
Fixed assets	$ 445.7

10. Examine Circuit City's and Best Buy's financial performance on the basis of the competitive information on www.hoovers.com. Which results are similar, and which are different for these two electronics retailers? Why?

Key Numbers	Circuit City	Best Buy
Annual sales ($ millions)	12,429.8	35,934.0
Employees	43,011	140,000
Gross profit margin	23.20%	24.10%
Pretax profit margin	(0.60%)	5.60%
Net profit margin	(0.60%)	3.60%
Return on assets	(1.7%)	10.9%
Inventory turnover	5.1	7.0
Asset turnover	3.1	3.0

SUGGESTED READINGS

Brealey, Richard; Stewart C. Myers; and Franklin Allen. *Principles of Corporate Finance*, 9th ed. New York: McGraw-Hill, 2008.

Brewer, Peter; Ray Garrison; and Eric Noreen. *Introduction to Managerial Accounting*, 3rd ed. New York; McGraw-Hill, 2006.

Castellano, Joseph; Saul Young; and Harper Roehm. "The Seven Fatal Flaws of Performance Measurement." *The CPA Journal* 74 (June 2004), pp. 32–36.

Chiquan, Guo; and Pornsit Jiraporn. "Customer Satisfaction, Net Income and Total Assets: An Exploratory Study." *Journal of Targeting, Measurement and Analysis* 13, no. 4 (2005), pp. 346–53.

Devan, Janamitra; Anna Kristina Millan; and Pranav Shirke. "Balancing Short- and Long-Term Performance." *McKinsey Quarterly* 1 (2005), pp. 31–35.

Lehmann, Donald R.; and David J. Reibstein. *Marketing Metrics and Financial Performance*. Cambridge, MA: Marketing Science Institute, 2006.

Keiningham, Timothy L.; Bruce Cooil; Tor Wallin Andreassen; and Lerzan Aksoy. "A Longitudinal Examination of Net Promoter and Firm Revenue Growth." *Journal of Marketing* 71, no. 3 (2007), pp. 39–51.

O'Sullivan, Don; and Andrew V. Abela. "Marketing Performance Measurement Ability and Firm Performance," *Journal of Marketing* 71, no. 2 (2007), pp. 79–93.

Retail Locations

EXECUTIVE BRIEFING

Michael Kercheval, President and CEO,
International Council of Shopping Centers

Based on my experiences, I observed keenly how retail developments are a catalyst for economic development. They create a virtuous cycle: retail developments → more goods, more choice, lower prices, and greater income → more retail development. The shopping centers provided goods to people with higher quality at lower prices and greater convenience. By saving people money on necessities, they can have a higher standard of living and greater disposable income. In addition, the retail developments provide jobs that increased the incomes. Then the increased incomes spurred more retail developments.

We recently had an event in Dubai, and the Ruler of Dubai, His Highness Sheikh Mohammed bin Rashid Al Maktoum, asked me to meet him in his palace. He said that he wants to open 700 shopping centers in the Middle East because these shopping centers would lead to economic development and world peace. He feels that if young people in the Middle East have jobs and more opportunities to get ahead, they will forsake terrorism and war.

Seven years ago, I became President of the International Council for Shopping Centers (ICSC) because it offered me a chance to serve an industry that is very involved in economic development around the world, as

While I was going to college, I became very concerned about the poor quality of life—disease, poor health care, lack of opportunity, etc.—in much of the world and volunteered to work on several economic development projects in Latin America sponsored by the Peace Corps and the Pan American Health Organization. From these experiences, I decided to go to medical school, become a doctor, and then return to Latin America. But pre-med chemistry did not agree with me. I discover economics and majored in developmental economics.

After graduate school, I went to work for Equitable Life Insurance and eventually became involved in managing real estate investment activities in Latin America.

CHAPTER 7

QUESTIONS

What types of locations are available to retailers?

What are the relative advantages of each location type?

Why are some locations particularly well suited to specific retail strategies?

Which types of locations are growing in popularity with retailers?

well as in urban and rural communities in the United States. ICSC is the global trade association of the shopping center industry. Its more than 70,000 members in the United States, Canada, and more than 80 other countries include shopping center owners, developers, managers, marketing specialists, investors, lenders, retailers, and other professionals, as well as academics and public officials. The principal aim of ICSC is to advance the development of the retail real estate industry and to establish shopping centers as major institutions in their communities. Our organization is involved in providing educational programs and undertaking research to help our members better serve their markets.

The retail development industry is at interesting crossroads now. Demand for retail space across the globe is far greater than supply, and there is considerable capital available to invest in new retail developments. The primary restraint to growth is from government policymakers who are tempering new development out of concern for small retail businesses, the environment, and what they see as suburban sprawl. ICSC and its members are working on ways to meet the retail needs of consumers, stimulate economic growth, and address the concerns of policymakers.

The oft-referenced response to the question, "What are the three most important things in retailing?" is "Location, location, location." Why is store location such an important decision for a retailer? First, location is typically one of the most influential considerations in a customer's store choice decision. For instance, when choosing where you're going to have your car washed, you usually pick the location closest to your home or work. Most consumers similarly shop at the supermarket closest to them.

Second, location decisions have strategic importance because they can be used to develop a sustainable competitive advantage. If a retailer has the best location, that is, the location that is most attractive to its customers, competitors can't easily copy this advantage. They are relegated to occupying the second-best location.

Third, location decisions are risky. Typically, when retailers select a location, they must either make a substantial investment to buy and develop the real estate or commit to a long-term lease with developers. Retailers often commit to leases for 5 to 15 years.

As you will see, there are a wide variety of locations available for retailers, ranging from renovated historical buildings such as the oldest shopping center in the country, The Country Club Plaza in Kansas City, to enclosed malls to outdoor lifestyle centers. However, location decisions are more restricted in Western Europe and Asia than in the United States. These areas of the world have higher population densities and more people living and shopping in urban environments. Thus,

REFACT

Currently, the United States contains 20 square feet of retail space in shopping centers for every person, up from 11 square feet in 1980. The second-highest country in terms of retail space per citizen is Sweden, with 3.1 square feet per person.[1]

less space is available for retailing, and the space that is available is costly. In addition, many Western European countries restrict retailing to specific areas and then restrict the sizes of the stores that can be built.

In the first part of this chapter, we discuss the types and relative advantages of locations available to retailers. We then examine how the location decision fits into the retailer's strategy. For example, the best locations for a 7-Eleven convenience store are not the best locations for a category specialist such as a Bed Bath and Beyond. In the next chapter, we discuss the issues involved in selecting areas of the country in which to locate stores and how to evaluate specific locations and negotiate leases.

TYPES OF LOCATIONS

Many types of locations are available for retail stores, each with its own strengths and weaknesses. Retailers have three basic types of locations to choose from: freestanding, city or town business district, or shopping center. Retailers can also locate in a nontraditional location like an airport or within another store. Retailing View 7.1 describes some of Subway's nontraditional locations and its accommodations to secure those locations.

7.1   RETAILING VIEW   Subway Goes to Church

Subway Restaurants, with 20,000 outlets, is finding it increasingly difficult to maintain its growth by opening new locations. Its traditional locations in strip malls and alongside highways are being taken by other brands of fast-food restaurants, so in response, it is exploring some unusual locations. In the past several years, Subway has opened restaurants inside a church in upstate New York, a laundromat in California, a Goodwill Industries store in South Carolina, a car dealership in Germany, and 110 hospitals throughout the United States.

With its menu of sandwiches, Subway has an easier time opening in unusual venues because it has a simpler kitchen than traditional fast-food restaurants, which require frying and grilling equipment. Hospitals and religious facilities have a favorable attitude toward Subway because it promotes its sandwiches as a fresher, healthier alternative to traditional fast food.

To maintain growth, Subway has opened outlets in non-traditional locations like this one in a Goodwill Industries store.

Subway often has to make accommodation when opening stores in nontraditional locations though. For example, when a franchisee opened a Subway in the Jewish Community Center of Cleveland, he had to make the menu kosher. He replaced the cheese with a soy-based product and removed ham and bacon from sandwiches. In observance of the Jewish Sabbath, the restaurant is closed on Friday afternoon and all day Saturday.

When a Subway opened in the True Bethel Baptist Church of Buffalo, New York, in a low-income area of town, the franchisee worked closely with church leaders. To support the congregation and create jobs, church leaders had approached several fast-food franchisors about opening a franchise in a corner of the church. Subway was the only chain that was flexible enough toward the space available and the operating hours to accommodate the church. The chain agreed to waive its requirement of a Subway sign on the outside of the building and created a parking pattern to keep restaurant traffic from displacing churchgoers during services.

Sources: Howard Riell, "When Only a QSR Will Do," *Food Service Director*, February 15, 2007, pp. 46–47; Janet Adamy, "For Subway, Every Nook And Cranny on the Planet Is Possible Site for a Franchise," *The Wall Street Journal*, September 1, 2006, p. A1.

	Size (000 sq. ft.)	Trading Area (Miles)	Annual Occupancy Cost ($ per sq. ft.)	Shopping Convenience	Pedestrian Traffic	Vehicular Traffic	Restrictions on Operations	Typical Tenants
UNPLANNED AREAS								
Free standing	Varies	3–7	15–30	High	Low	High	Limited	Convenience, drug stores, category specialists
Urban locations/ Central business district	Varies	Varies	8–20	Low	High	Low	Limited to medium	Specialty stores
SHOPPING CENTERS								
Neighborhood and Community shopping centers	30–350	3–7	8–20	High	Low	High	Medium	Supermarkets, discount stores
Power centers	250–600	5–10	10–20	Medium	Medium	Medium	Limited	Category specialists
Enclosed malls	400–1,000	5–25	10–70	Low	High	Low	High	Department and specialty apparel stores
Lifestyle centers	500+	5–15	15–35	Medium	Medium	Medium	Medium to high	Specialty apparel and home stores, restaurants
Fashion/specialty centers	80–250	5–15	10–70	Medium	High	Low	High	High-end fashion-oriented specialty stores
Outlet centers	400+	25–75	8–15	Low	High	High	Limited	Off-price retailers and factory outlets
Theme/festival centers	80–250	N/A	20–70	Low	High	Low	Highest	Specialty stores and restaurants

Source: Personal communications with industry executives; "North American Retail Highlights 2006," http://www.colliers.com/Content/Repositories/Base/Corporate/English/Market_Report_Corporate/PDFs/RetailNAHighlights2006.pdf.

Choosing a particular location type requires evaluating a series of trade-offs. These trade-offs generally involve the size of the trade area, the occupancy cost of the location, the pedestrian and vehicle customer traffic location, the restrictions placed on store operations by the property managers, and the convenience of the location for customers. The **trade area** is the geographic area that encompasses most of the customers who would patronize a specific retail site.

The following sections describe the characteristics of each type of location, as summarized in Exhibit 7–1. The first two types of locations are unplanned areas occupied by retail stores, and planned and managed shopping center developments.

UNPLANNED RETAIL LOCATIONS

Some retailers put their stores in unplanned locations for which there is no centralized management to determine where the specific stores are and how they will be operated. Two types of unplanned retail locations are freestanding sites and city or town locations.

Freestanding Sites

Freestanding sites are retail locations for an individual, isolated store unconnected to other retailers; however, they might be near other freestanding retailers, a shopping center, or, in the case of a kiosk, inside an office building or shopping center. The advantages of freestanding locations are their convenience for customers (easy access and parking); high vehicular traffic and visibility to attract those customers driving by; modest occupancy costs; and fewer restrictions on signs, hours, or merchandise, typically imposed in shopping centers. **Outparcels** are stores that are

Some Sears stores are located in freestanding structures away from the mall to provide easy parking and convenience for customers.

not connected to other stores in a shopping center but are located on the premises, typically in a parking area. These free-standing locations that are popular for fast-food restaurants, such as McDonalds or Dunkin' Donuts, or banks. Outparcels enable retailers to have a drive-through window, dedicated parking, and clear visibility from the street.

However, freestanding locations have a limited trade area when there are no other nearby retailers to attract customers interested in shopping at multiple outlets on one trip. In addition, freestanding locations have higher occupancy costs than strip centers because they do not have other retailers to share the cost of outside lighting, parking lot maintenance, or trash collection. Finally, freestanding locations generally appear in areas with little pedestrian traffic, limiting the number of customers who might drop in because they are walking by.

Although most U.S. retailers locate in shopping centers, freestanding locations, due to the convenience they offer customers, are becoming more popular. For example, based on Kohl's success with its freestanding locations, JCPenney and Sears are opening off-the-mall stores in freestanding locations.[2] The three major drugstore chains also have shifted their emphasis to freestanding locations because they want accessible drive-through windows for pharmacies, more floor space, or better access for receiving merchandise.

Merchandise Kiosks   **Merchandise kiosks** are small selling spaces, typically located in the walkways of enclosed malls, airports, train stations, or office building lobbies. Some are staffed and resemble a miniature store or cart that could be easily moved. Others are twenty-first century versions of a vending machine. For instance, Redbox, a division of McDonald's Corporation, operates more than 3,000 DVD rental kiosks in the United States, many of them in supermarkets.[3] It charges about $1 per day to rent a DVD and requires a credit or debit card. A Redbox kiosk carries approximately 80 titles, mostly new releases. Although Redbox and its kiosk competitors still represent only about 1 percent of the DVD rental market, its sales are growing rapidly.

For mall operators, kiosks are an opportunity to generate rental income in otherwise vacant space and offer a broad assortment of merchandise for visitors. They also can generate excitement, leading to additional sales for the entire mall. Dell Computers' mall kiosks offer the same products, prices, and services that are offered through the company's Web site, Dell Direct. Many cell phone companies such as Sprint or T-Mobile also take advantage of mall kiosks. Moreover, mall kiosks can be changed quickly to match seasonal demand.

When planning the location of kiosks in a mall, operators are sensitive to their regular mall tenants' needs. They are careful to avoid kiosks that block any storefronts, create an incompatible image, or actually compete directly with permanent tenants by selling similar merchandise.

Office building managers view kiosks as a way to provide services for people working in the building. Thus, kiosks in office lobbies often sell newspapers, flowers, or snacks.

City or Town Locations

Most retailers followed U.S. families as they have moved from the downtown areas to the surrounding suburbs. However, some retailers are finding urban locations attractive, particularly in cities that are redeveloping their downtowns and surrounding urban areas. Big box retailers like Target, Wal-Mart, Home Depot, and Costco, which usually locate in the suburbs, are now opening new outlets in cities, sometimes with smaller stores and on multiple floors.[4]

In general, urban locations have lower occupancy costs, and locations in central business districts often have high pedestrian traffic. However, vehicular traffic is limited due to congestion in urban areas, and parking problems reduce consumer convenience. Unlike freestanding locations, store signage can be restricted in these locations.

Many urban areas are going through a process of **gentrification**—the renewal and rebuilding of offices, housing, and retailers in deteriorating areas—coupled with an influx of more affluent people that displaces the former poorer residents. Young professionals and retired empty-nesters are moving into these areas to enjoy the convenience of shopping, restaurants, and entertainment near where they live.

Redevelopment opportunities for retailers also are emerging in so-called brownfields—former industrial locations with a history of chemical pollutants. In the 1980s, most developers avoided abandoned industrial sites, but investors and their lenders are taking a second look at such sites because of changes in environmental law in the mid-1990s and increased protection from legal complications. Liability insurance is increasingly available to developers who clean up industrial sites, and local governments have offered more guarantees to shield developers against future lawsuits.[5] The three types of urban locations are central business districts, Main Streets, and inner city locations.

Central Business District   The **central business district (CBD)** is the traditional downtown business area in a city or town. Due to its daily activity, it draws many people and employees into the area during business hours. The CBD is also the hub for public transportation, and there is a high level of pedestrian traffic. Finally, many CBDs have a large number of residents living in the area.

Although CBD locations in the United States declined in popularity among retailers and their customers for years, many are experiencing a revival as they become gentrified, drawing in new retailers and residents that crave an urban experience and want to be able to walk to do errands and shopping.

Because shoplifting can be common, and parking is often limited, CBDs generally require the retailers to hire security. Parking problems and driving times can discourage suburban shoppers from patronizing stores in a CBD. Shopping flow in the evening and on weekends is also slow in many CBDs. Finally, unlike shopping centers, CBDs tend to suffer from a lack of planning. One block may contain upscale boutiques, and the next may be populated with low-income housing, which means consumers may not have access to enough interesting retailers that they can visit in one shopping trip.

Main Street   **Main Street** refers to the traditional shopping area in smaller towns or a secondary business district in a suburb or within a larger city. Streets in these areas often have been converted into pedestrian walkways. They represent an effort by cities to draw people from the suburbs and revitalize areas as a destination for shopping and recreation.

Main Streets share most of the characteristics of a primary CBD, but their occupancy costs are generally lower because they do not draw as many people as the primary CBD, fewer people work in the area, and the fewer stores generally mean a smaller overall selection. In addition, Main Streets typically don't offer the range of entertainment and recreational activities available in the more successful primary CBDs. Finally, the planning organization for the town or redevelopment often imposes some restrictions on store operations.

In the European Union, Main Street locations (called High Street in the United Kingdom) are threatened by large big box retailers located outside the city limits. Local governments in these countries are trying to restrain superstores' growth by limiting their size and subsidizing the redevelopment of Main Street areas to help

In the United Kingdom, small retailers High Street locations remain popular but face competition from larger retailers such as supermarkets and hypermarkets.

local retailers compete. Europe has greater population density and less space, and strict planning and greenbelt laws provide a sharp division between town and country. Suburbs are few, thus minimizing urban sprawl. But preserving the environment comes at a cost for Europe. The limits on out-of-town, big box retailing reduce competition and retailing efficiency, causing higher prices.[7]

REFACT

Baby boomers and echo boomers are moving to downtown areas for easy access to everything; 75 percent of U.S. urban retail locations are growing as a result.[8]

Inner City   The **inner city** in the United States refers to high density urban areas that have higher unemployment and lower median incomes than the surrounding metropolitan area. Some retailers have avoided opening stores in the inner city because they believe it is riskier and achieves lower returns than other areas. As a result, inner-city consumers often have to travel to the suburbs to shop, even for food items. Conservatively, inner-city consumers constitute $85 billion in annual retail spending power—equal to the entire country of Mexico.[9] Although income levels are lower in inner cities than in other neighborhoods, most inner-city retailers achieve a higher sales volume and often higher margins, resulting in higher profits.

Retailing can play an important role in inner-city redevelopment activities by providing needed services and jobs for inner-city residents, as well as property taxes to support the redevelopment. Due to the potential of this untapped market and incentives from local governments, developers are increasing their focus on opportunities in the inner city. Often local governments will use the right of eminent domain to buy buildings and land, then sell it to developers at an attractive price. However, inner-city redevelopments can be controversial. For instance, people are concerned about the residents displaced by the development, increased traffic, and parking difficulties.[10]

In a monumental redevelopment project of an inner-city location, the Harlem area of Manhattan is attracting high-profile and high-fashion national chains that historically have not been represented there.[11] One 300,000 square foot space is earmarked for national chains, local retailers, restaurants, a movie theater, nonprofit cultural groups, and 1,000 units of affordable housing. Throughout Harlem, there are new FedEx Kinkos, Staples, Starbucks, Marshall's, The Children's Place stores, Old Navy and H&M outlets, a Chuck E. Cheese restaurant, and a Chase bank. Not only do these retailers bring needed goods and services to the area, they also bring jobs. Retailing View 7.2 describes how Magic Johnson has brought retailing to the inner city. Although we have discussed these urban developments in terms of unplanned locations, they also may be managed shopping centers, as discussed in the following section.

SHOPPING CENTERS

A **shopping center** is a group of retail and other commercial establishments that are planned, developed, owned, and managed as a single property. By combining many stores at one location, the developer attracts more consumers to the shopping center than if the stores were at separate locations. It's not uncommon, for instance, for a store's sales to increase when a competing store enters the shopping center. However, the developer and shopping center management carefully select a set of retailers that are complementary to provide consumers with a comprehensive shopping experience, including a well thought out assortment of retailers.

The shopping center management maintains the common facilities (referred to as common area maintenance [CAM]), such as the parking area. The management is also responsible for activities such as providing security, parking lot lighting, outdoor signage for the center, and advertising and special events to attract consumers. Lease agreements typically require retailers in the center to pay a portion of the CAM costs and promotional expenses for the center according to

---

Magic Johnson Brings Retailing to the Inner City   **RETAILING VIEW**   **7.2**

In 13 unparalleled years in the National Basketball Association, Earvin "Magic" Johnson rewrote the record books and dazzled fans with his no-look passes and clutch jump shots. He led the Los Angeles Lakers to five championships. After he announced to the world in 1991 that he had contracted HIV, many thought he would retire from public life. Instead, for Johnson, basketball was just the beginning. He makes over 100 public appearances every year, which exceeds those in his basketball career.

Post-basketball, he took his game to a different arena, one in which the obstacles are higher and the challenges greater. His new career began with a relatively modest partnership with Loews Cineplex Entertainment, formerly Sony Retail Entertainment. After doing some research, Magic and his partners realized that minorities make up approximately 32 to 35 percent of the nationwide movie audience, but there were few theaters in minority neighborhoods. Minorities living in the inner city were driving 30 to 40 minutes to get to a theater. So it seemed natural to build movie theaters in urban neighborhoods across the country.

With the theaters in place, the next step was finding other businesses that would complement these theatres. What they found was most casual sit-down restaurants targeted similar demographics. However, eateries weren't willing to commit to urban locations. Magic and his partners had customers coming in saying they loved the theaters, but they had to go all the way across town if they wanted to get something to eat. So next Magic collaborated with Starbucks and TGI Fridays.

Magic Johnson Enterprises is dedicated to urban business development. It partners with Burger King, 24 Hour Fitness, Starbucks, and many more businesses to facilitate their operations in inner-city locations. His Burger King locations outperform others in the same market by 10 percent.

No longer a presence on the basketball court, Magic Johnson has become a leader in urban retail developments.

Magic Johnson Foundation is a nonprofit organization that educates and creates innovative programs for the advancement of minority groups. Magic Johnson actively promotes HIV/AIDS awareness education to prevent the spread of the disease.

Currently, he is also developing shopping centers and malls in African American neighborhoods around the country. A $1.1 billion, 2.5 million square feet, mixed-use development of offices, hotels, residences, and retail is to be completed in 2009 and named the "Midtown Mile" in Atlanta, Georgia

Sources: www.magicjohnsonenterprises.com (accessed July 24, 2007); www.magicjohnson.org (accessed July 24, 2007); Jill Lerner, "999 Peachtree Aims for Slot in 'Midtown Mile'," *Atlanta Business Chronicle,* February 9, 2007; Claire Heininger, "Magic Johnson Tells Newark to Get Smart on HIV/AIDS," www.nj.com, July 17, 2007 (accessed January 4, 2008).

the size of their space and/or sales volume. The shopping center management can also place restrictions on the operating hours, signage, and even the type of merchandise sold in the stores.

Most shopping centers have at least one or two major retailers, referred to as **anchors.** These retailers are courted by the center developer because they attract a significant number of consumers and consequently make the center more appealing for other retailers. To get these anchor retailers to locate in a center, developers frequently make special deals, such as reduced lease costs, for the anchor tenants.

In strip shopping centers, supermarkets and discount stores are typically anchors, whereas department stores traditionally anchor enclosed shopping malls. However, a lifestyle center may not have anchors, whereas power centers consist primarily of multiple "anchor" stores. The different types of shopping centers are discussed next.

Neighborhood and Community Shopping Centers

Neighborhood and **community centers** (also called **strip shopping centers**) are attached rows of stores managed as units, with onsite parking usually located in the front of the stores. Because the common areas are not enclosed, these centers are often referred to as "open air centers." The most common layouts are linear, L-shaped, and inverted U-shaped. Historically, the term "strip center" has applied to the linear configuration.

Smaller centers (neighborhood centers) are typically anchored by a supermarket and designed for convenient shopping. The larger centers (community centers) are typically anchored by a discount department store such as Wal-Mart or Target and may have additional anchors, such as off-price retailers or category specialists. These anchors are supported by smaller specialty stores offering hardware, flowers, and a variety of personal services, such as barber shops and dry cleaners.

The primary advantages of these centers are that they offer customers convenient locations and easy parking, and they have relatively low occupancy costs. The primary disadvantage is that smaller centers have a limited trade area due to their size, and they lack entertainment and restaurants. In addition, there is no protection from the weather. As a result, neighborhood and community centers do not attract as many customers as larger, enclosed malls.

Neighborhood shopping centers are attached rows of stores managed as units, with onsite parking usually located in front of the stores.

Current neighborhood and community centers have fewer local, independent stores than in the past. National chains such as The Children's Place, Borders, Kohl's, Radio Shack, and Marshall's compete effectively against their rival mall-based stores by offering the convenience of a neighborhood or community center. In these locations, they can offer lower prices, partly because of the lower occupancy cost, and their customers can drive right up to the door.

These centers also have started to take on nontraditional, service-oriented tenants. For example, 80 percent of Orthodontics Centers of America's patients are children. Thus, it looks to locate in neighborhood and community centers or professional buildings near retailers with a complementary consumer base, such as Toy "R" Us and Home Depot.

Power Centers

Power centers are shopping centers that consist primarily of collections of big box retail stores, such as discount stores (Target), off-price stores (Marshall's), warehouse clubs (Costco), and category specialists (Lowe's, Staples, Michaels, Barnes & Noble, Circuit City, Sports Authority, Toys "R" Us). In contrast to traditional strip centers power centers have few small specialty tenants. Many power centers are located near an enclosed shopping mall.

Power centers were virtually unknown before the 1990s, but they have steadily grown in number as the sales of category specialists have grown. Many are now larger than some regional malls and have trade areas as large as regional malls. Power centers offer low occupancy costs and modest levels of consumer convenience and vehicular and pedestrian traffic.

Shopping Malls

Shopping malls are enclosed, climate controlled, lighted shopping centers with retail stores on one or both sides of an enclosed walkway. Parking is usually provided around the perimeter of the mall. Shopping malls are classified as either **regional malls** (less than 1 million square feet) or **super regional malls** (more than 1 million square feet). Super regional centers are similar to regional centers, but because of their larger size, they have more anchors, specialty stores, and recreational opportunities and draw from a larger geographic area. They often are considered tourist attractions.[15] Retailing View 7.3 describes some of Asia's mega malls.

Shopping malls have several advantages over alternative locations. First, because of the many different types of stores, the merchandise assortments available within those stores, and the opportunity to combine shopping with entertainment, shopping malls attract many shoppers and have a large trade area. They generate significant pedestrian traffic inside the mall and provide an inexpensive form of entertainment. Older citizens get their exercise by walking the malls, and teenagers hang out and meet their friends, though some malls are restricting their admittance in the evenings. Second, customers don't have to worry about the weather, and thus, malls are appealing places to shop during cold winters and hot summers. Third, malls offer retailers a strong level of homogeneous operations with the other stores. For instance, most major malls enforce uniform hours of operation.

However, malls also have some disadvantages. First, mall occupancy costs are higher than those of strip centers, freestanding sites, and most central business districts. Second, some retailers may not like mall management's control of their operations. For example, most malls have strict rules governing window displays and signage. Third, competition within shopping centers can be intense. Several specialty and department stores might sell very similar merchandise and be located in close proximity.

In addition, shopping malls face several challenges. First, many people do not have the time for a leisurely stroll through a mall. Freestanding locations, strip centers, and power centers are more convenient because customers can park in front of a store, go in and buy what they want, and go about their other errands.

Second, most retailers in shopping malls sell fashionable apparel, a merchandise category that has seen limited growth due to more casual lifestyles. Third, some malls were built more than 40 years ago and have not been subject to any significant remodeling, so they appear rundown and unappealing to shoppers. Furthermore, these older malls are now located in areas with unfavorable demographics, because the population has shifted from the near suburbs to outer suburbs and exerbs. Fourth, the consolidation in retailing, particularly in the department store segment, has decreased the number of potential anchor tenants, leaving some malls with diminished drawing power.

For these reasons, mall traffic and sales have been declining, and limited resources are being spent on new mall development. At least 300 older malls in the United States, each with one or two anchor stores, have shut down since the mid-1990s. Only five new malls opened per year between 2000 and 2005. To address this decline, mall managers and developers are trying to enhance the mall shopping experience and redevelop failing malls.

REFACT

In the past 15 years, the sales generated by mall-based retailers has dropped from 39 percent of total nonfood retail sales to 18.5 percent.[17]

7.3   RETAILING VIEW   Mega Malls in Asia

Seven of the ten largest malls in the world are located in Asia, and of these, six were built since 2004. Fourteen years ago, The Mall of America in Bloomington, Minnesota was the largest mega-mall in the world, but with economic expansions in Asia, only two American malls, The King of Prussia mall in Pennsylvania and the South Coast Plaza mall in Costa Mesa, California still make the top 10 list.

Mall development is rapidly growing to keep up with the lifestyle and income changes in this part of the world. Mega-malls are mixed-use centers with retail, dining, entertainment, and residential living. They house many familiar, global, luxury brands, including Gucci, Hermes, Versace, and Cartier. Although the malls, located in places like Dubai, Singapore, Hong Kong, and Kuala Lumpur, are impressive because of their large size and the entertainment choices they offer (cinemas, bowling alleys, windmills, children's theme parks, skating rinks, and an abundance of restaurants), they also have taken on some of the less desirable features of U.S. malls. For instance, the malls are favoring chains over local proprietors, thus diluting local culture. This effect doesn't seem to bother the tourists though, who make up about one-third of the malls' business.

The South China Mall in Dongguan City, just north of Hong Kong, is one of the world's biggest shopping center at 9.6 million square feet. The indoor and outdoor center spreads over about 100 acres, with some stores facing sidewalks along the

The South China Mall in Dongguan, China is the largest mall in the world with over 9.6 million square feet and 1,500 stores.

streets. It has seven "zones" modeled on international cities, nations, and regions: Amsterdam, Paris, Rome, Venice, Egypt, the Caribbean, and California. Considerable attention is paid to the details so that each area feels like the real thing. For example, the security guards in the Parisian section are dressed as gendarmes. Shoppers can circumnavigate the perimeter by gondolas and water taxis on a Venetian-inspired canal that stretches more than a mile.

Enhancing the Mall Experience   Mall managers are devising ways to make the mall shopping experience more enjoyable, because the more time customers spend in a mall, the more money they spend. Some malls have common areas that look like a typical living room, with wide-armed club chairs, overstuffed sofas, and coffee tables strewn with newspapers, all bordering a plush rug.[18] The Westfield Group is opening 500 square foot family lounges in its 68 U.S. shopping malls, featuring chairs, sofas, tables, and rugs, as well as televisions playing children's programming, bottle warmers, changing stations, games, and toys.

Malls have also realized that great food is another method for attracting customers. At the 200-store International Plaza mall next to Tampa International Airport in Florida, for instance, shoppers can eat at an indoor court that has nine fast-food establishments, but they also have their pick of 15 full-service restaurants, including about a dozen that sit within a large outdoor area adjacent to the mall.[20] The area, called Bay Street, includes destination restaurants like Blue Martini, a bar that also serves food, and a Capital Grille steakhouse, where white tablecloths preside. Other malls contain dental clinics, dry cleaners, wedding chapels, or high-tech playgrounds.

Another strategy shopping mall developers are employing to deal with the changing demographics in their mall's trade area is to tailor their offerings to their local markets. For instance, older shopping centers are being repositioned to appeal to large Hispanic markets.[21] The centers typically have both national and

REFACT
J. Crew, Little Gym International, lucy, ULTA, UNIQLO, and WineStyles currently are the hottest retailers, that is, the retailers that developers would like to have in their malls.[19]

Large Mega Malls

Shopping Mall	Year Opened	GLA* (square feet)	Total Area (square feet)	Stores	Comments
South China Mall in Dongguan, China	2005	7.1-million	9.6-million	1,500	One of the world's largest shopping mall, arrayed in six separate themed areas.
Jin Yuan (Golden Resources Shopping Mall) in Beijing, China	2004	6.0-million	7.3-million	1,000+	Also known as the "Great Mall of China," this mega mall has six floors and is located near the Fourth Ring Road, west of Beijing.
West Edmonton Mall in Edmonton, Alberta, Canada	1981	3.8-million	5.3-million	800	Largest shopping mall in North America; includes indoor wave pool, amusement areas, hotel, restaurants, and 20,000 parking spaces.
Cevahir Istanbul in Istanbul, Turkey	2005	3.8-million	4.5-million	280	The largest shopping mall in Europe; has six floors, cinemas, a roller coaster, and a theater.
Berjaya Times Square in Kuala Lumpur, Malaysia		3.4-million	7.5-million (700,000)	1,000+	Includes 45 restaurants, a theme park, and a 3D Digi-IMAX theater.
Beijing Mall in Beijing, China	2005	3.4-million	4.7-million	600	Four levels of shopping with interior residences; located near Fifth Ring Road, southeast of Beijing.
Zhengjia Plaza (Grandview Mall) in Guangzhou, China	2005	3.0-million	4.5-million		Enclosed in a complex that includes a 48-story hotel and 30-story office building.
King of Prussia Mall in Philadelphia, Pennsylvania, USA	1962	2.8-million		327	Created by connecting together three adjacent malls, managed by a single company.
South Coast Plaza in Costa Mesa, California, USA	1967	2.7-million		280	The highest revenue volume mall in the United States. It also is home to the Orange Lounge, a branch of the Orange County Museum of Art.
Central World Plaza in Bangkok, Thailand	2006	2.6-million		500+	21-screen cinemas, bowling lanes, and restaurants; also a convention center (not included in the GLA).

*GLA stands for gross leasable area. It is the total usable, rental space in a building.

Sources: Stan Sesser, "The New Spot for Giant Malls: Asia," *The Wall Street Journal*, September, 16, 2006; Tom Van Riper, "World's Largest Malls," *Forbes*, January 9, 2007; www.easternct.edu/depts/amerst/MallsWorld.htm (accessed July 25, 2007)

Hispanic-focused retailers and plenty of outdoor space and seating to accommodate families that go shopping together. Because these centers are often situated in dense urban areas where parks are scarce, the malls substitute for the town square.

The Plaza Fiesta Mall in Atlanta celebrates Cinco de Mayo with 14 bands playing mariachi, reggaeton, and banda. There are carnival rides and special Mexican foods. Although the mall is anchored by Burlington Coat Factory and Marshall's, it also has many Hispanic retailers and a sprawling market where almost 300 vendors in booths sell everything from *quinceanera* dresses (worn during celebrations of girls' 15th birthdays) to Western wear to religious statues.

Mall Renovation and Redevelopment   Another approach for rejuvenating malls is the renovation and redevelopment of existing malls. For example, the 1.3 million square foot South Park Mall in Charlotte, North Carolina, could be a candidate for the reality show *Extreme Makeover*. The owners of the 30-year-old mall decided to remake South Park from a typical regional mall into a destination retail center that would attract the discriminating shoppers who patronize upscale stores in Atlanta. The makeover cost $100 million and involved adding an additional anchor and specialty stores and creating an adjoining park with an amphitheater for the Charlotte Symphony Orchestra's summer pops series.

Lifestyle Centers

Lifestyle centers, the fastest growing type of retail development, are shopping centers with an open-air configuration of specialty stores, entertainment, and restaurants with design ambience and amenities such as fountains and street furniture.[23] In the next few years, there are plans to build 100 to 150 lifestyle centers but only one or two enclosed malls.[24] Although exposure to the weather may be a disadvantage, lifestyle centers are also being built in Northern climates.

Lifestyle centers resemble the main streets in small towns, where people stroll from store to store, have lunch, and sit for awhile on a park bench talking to friends. Thus, they cater to the "lifestyles" of consumers in their trade areas. Lifestyle centers are particularly attractive to specialty retailers, typically located in malls, such as Talbots, Victoria Secret, Chico's, The Gap, Banana Republic, Williams-Sonoma, and American Eagle Outfitters. Some lifestyle centers are anchored by smaller versions of department stores such as Sears, Macy's, and Dillard's or by discounters such as Wal-Mart or even grocery stores such as Wegmans Food Market.[25]

Due to the ease of parking, lifestyle centers are very convenient for shoppers. But they typically have less retail space than enclosed malls and thus smaller trade areas, and they attract fewer customers than enclosed malls. However, men, who typically eschew shopping malls, like the relaxed, open environments of lifestyle centers.[26] Many lifestyle centers are located near higher income areas so the

The Plaza Fiesta Mall in Atlanta emphasizes a Hispanic theme.

higher purchases per visit compensate for the fewer number of shoppers. Pedestrian traffic is greater than at strip malls. Finally, occupancy costs and operating restrictions

Lifestyle centers are shopping centers with an open-air configuration of specialty stores, entertainment, and restaurants with design ambiance and amenities such as fountains and street furniture.

REFACT

The average income of lifestyle center customers is approximately double that of mall shoppers. They visit 2.5 times more often, and they spend 50 percent more per visit.[28]

are less than those of enclosed malls, because there is no need to climate control the common areas, though the common area maintenance costs are greater than those of strip centers.

Chapel View lifestyle center in Cranston, Rhode Island, transformed a historic old school and church into a village-style retail, residential, and office complex. The complex that formerly housed a state-owned correctional and educational facility was converted into a lifestyle center. The developer worked with local agencies to preserve its historical features while transforming the facility into retail and residential space. The buildings combine ground-floor retail with residential and/or office space above.[27]

Fashion/Specialty Centers

Fashion/specialty centers are shopping centers composed mainly of upscale apparel shops, boutiques, and gift shops carrying selected fashions or unique merchandise of high quality and price. These centers need not be anchored, though sometimes upscale department stores, gourmet restaurants, drinking establishments, and theaters can function as anchors. The physical design of these centers is very elegant, emphasizing a rich decor and high-quality landscaping.

Fashion/specialty centers usually are found in trade areas with high income levels, in tourist areas, or in some central business districts. These centers' trade areas are larger than the typical enclosed mall because of the distinctive nature of the tenants and their products. Occupancy costs are also higher than those of the typical enclosed mall because the common areas are more elegant.

An example of a fashion/specialty center is Phipps Plaza. Located in the exclusive Buckhead area of Atlanta, Phipps Plaza was named a "Southern Best" in *Southern Living* magazine's Readers' Choice Awards. This fashion/specialty mall is anchored by Nordstrom, Parisian, and Saks Fifth Avenue. As Atlanta's premier upscale shopping center, Phipps Plaza is home to more than 100 specialty stores including Tiffany, Gucci, Max Mara, Giorgio Armani, and Tommy Bahama's.

Outlet Centers

Outlet centers are shopping centers that contain mostly manufacturers' outlets, such as Ralph Lauren/Polo and Nautica, and retailers' outlets, such as Pottery Barn and Ann Taylor. The merchandise offered is predominately apparel, accessories, and home furnishings with strong brand names.[29] Outlet centers have progressed from no-frills warehouses to well-designed buildings with landscaping, gardens, and food courts that make them hard to distinguish from more traditional shopping centers and lifestyle centers. The newest outlet centers have a strong entertainment component, including movie theaters and theme restaurants to keep customers on the premises longer.[30] For example, Prime Outlets San Marcos (Texas) has a "Venice" section with a canal and singing gondoliers. Outlet center tenants have also upgraded their offerings by adding credit, dressing rooms, high-quality fixtures and lighting, and other amenities.

Fifteen years ago, the number of outlet centers in the United States peaked at 329 and has since dwindled to 220. Although fewer in number, outlet centers today are larger in size than they were a decade ago—up from 148,000 square feet to 362,000 square feet, with some outlet centers having over 1 million square feet. In the United States, only two or three new outlet centers open each year. Many outlet retailers are locating redeveloped enclosed malls. However, outlet centers are becoming very popular outside the United States.[31]

More than 400 new outlet centers are being developed in Europe and Asia.[32] For example, Japan is particularly attractive, given its large population, interest in American brands, and growing consumer enthusiasm for value retailing concepts. At the foot of Mount Fuji, the Gotemba Premium Outlet is flooded with people, young and old, seeking brand name items. This outlet center, Japan's largest, covers an area seven times that of the Tokyo Dome and houses 165 shops. Many of the visitors to the Gotemba outlet come from Hong Kong on packaged tours that include visits to (Tokyo) Disneyland and Hakone, a famous sightseeing spot, west of Tokyo, where the outlet is located. On weekends, more than 10,000 vehicles and 100 buses arrive at the outlet center, and the number of visitors on each Saturday and Sunday is estimated at about 30,000.[33]

Tourism is an important factor in generating traffic for many outlet centers. Thus, many are located with convenient interstate access and close to popular tourist attractions. For instance, the 1.2 million square foot Factory Outlet Mega Mall in Niagara Falls, New York, offers an interesting diversion for the 15 million tourists per year visiting Niagara Falls. Some center developers actually organize bus tours to bring people hundreds of miles to their malls. As a result, the primary trade area for some outlet centers is 50 miles or more.

Ghirardelli Square in San Francisco is a Theme Center because of its historical architectural interest.

Theme/Festival Centers

Theme/festival centers are shopping centers that typically employ a unifying theme reflected in the individual shops, the architectural design and, to an extent, in their merchandise. The biggest appeal of these centers is for tourists. Theme/festival centers can be anchored by restaurants and entertainment facilities.

A theme/festival center might be located in a place of historical interest, such as Quincy Market and Faneuil Hall in Boston or Ghirardelli Square in San Francisco. Alternatively, they may attempt to replicate a historical place (such as the Old Mill Center in Mountain View, California) or create a unique shopping environment (like MCA's CityWalk in Los Angeles).

Larger, Multiformat Developments—Omnicenters

New shopping center developments are combining enclosed malls, lifestyle centers, and power centers.[34] Although centers of this type do not have an official name, they may be referred to as **omnicenters**.

Omnicenters represent a response to several trends in retailing, including the desire of tenants to lower common area maintenance charges by spreading the costs among more tenants and function inside larger developments that generate more pedestrian traffic and longer shopping trips. In addition, they reflect the growing tendency of consumers to cross-shop, such as when a Wal-Mart customer also patronizes the Cheesecake Factory and Nordstrom's, as well as the desire for time-scarce consumers to go to one place that offers everything. For example, the 1.3 million square foot St. John's Town Center in Jacksonville, Florida, is divided into three components: a lifestyle center with a Dillard's department store anchor, a community center anchored by Dick's Sporting Goods and a Barnes & Noble bookstore, and a Main Street with Cheesecake Factory and P.F. Chang's restaurants as anchors.[35]

Mixed Use Developments

Instead of just blending different shopping center types in one location called an omnicenter, **mixed use developments (MXDs)** combine several different uses into one complex, including shopping centers, office towers, hotels, residential complexes, civic centers, and convention centers. These developments offer an all-inclusive environment so that consumers can work, live, and play in a proximal area. They appeal to people who have had enough of long commutes to work and the social fragmentation of their neighborhoods and are looking for a lifestyle that gives them more time for the things they enjoy and an opportunity to live in a genuine community. In addition, MXDs are popular with retailers because they bring additional shoppers to their stores. They are also popular with governments, urban planners, and environmentalists, because they provide a pleasant, pedestrian environment and are an efficient use of space. Developers also like MXDs because they use space productively. For instance, land costs the same whether a developer builds a shopping mall by itself or an office tower on top of the mall or parking structure.

The Boca Mall, a 430,000 square foot regional shopping mall in Boca Raton, Florida, opened in 1974. Decades later, the mall was plagued by two trends: population

Minzer Park in Boca Raton, Florida is an MXD that combines retail, residential and entertainment offerings in one location with unique boutiques, eateries, music, movies, and art galleries conveniently located close to ocean-front apartments and condos.

growth occurring west of the city and competing malls, such as the 1.3 million square foot Town Center Mall, that were attracting most of its patrons. The original anchors and many of the specialty stores departed. The Boca Mall was demolished and replaced with a mixed use development called Mizner Park. Mizner Park has commercial office space located above the ground-floor retail space on one side of the street, and residential units sit above the retail space on the opposite side of the street.[36]

OTHER LOCATION OPPORTUNITIES

Airports, temporary stores, resorts and stores within a store are other location alternatives for many retailers. Retailing View 7.4 examines Second Life virtual locations.

7.4 RETAILING VIEW   A 3D Virtual Shopping Experience

In the Second Life virtual, 3D community, people can create personalities, called avatars, buy and sell land, build houses and furnish them, buy apparel, and go to bars and restaurants by themselves or with friends. The Second Life world has its own currency, the Linden dollar, which residents can swap for U.S. greenbacks at a dynamic exchange rate; $1 U.S. is roughly equivalent to 270 Linden dollars.

More than 8 million people are involved in this virtual reality. A number of retailers have located their stores in this virtual world and link these virtual stores to their own Internet site. For example,

- American Apparel is believed to be the first "real-world" retailer to have a Second Life store. It features a minimalist design with racks of bright, solid-colored clothing. It sells 20 basic items, for real, and reportedly has sold 12,000 pairs of virtual jeans for $2 each.
- Best Buy has opened a Geek Squad Island, where technical support workers, wearing white, short-sleeve, button-down shirts and badges, offer free computer advice. It plans to start selling products and hosting events on its Geek Squad Island soon.
- Circuit City is experimenting with an interactive home theater set-up where customers can recreate their own home environments and determine the optimal size television to purchase.

Retailers are experimenting with locations in virtual reality or Second Life.

- Sears's virtual store allows customers to experiment with changing the color of cabinets and countertops in a virtual kitchen and learn how to organize a garage with customized storage accessories.

Although these initiatives may seem modest today, they are expected to be simply the precursors of virtual locations in the future.

Sources: Susan Reda, "Retailers Explore Opportunities on the Latest Virtual Frontier," *Stores*, May 2007 (accessed January 4, 2008); Vanessa Facenda, "Retail's Newest Frontier," *Retail Merchandiser*, February 2007, p. 4; www.secondlife.com (accessed February 19, 2008).

REFACT

Second Life residents spend more than $1.5 million a day (U.S. dollars, not their virtual equivalent) buying everything from clothing to real estate. That figure is growing at 20 percent per month.

Airports

A high-pedestrian area that has become popular with national retail chains is airports. After all, what better way to spend waiting time than to have a Starbucks coffee or buy a gift at Brookstone? Sales per square foot at airport stores are often much higher than at regular mall stores. However, rents are higher too. Also, costs can be higher—hours are longer, and because the location is often inconvenient for workers, the businesses have to pay higher wages. The best airport locations tend to be ones where there are many connecting flights (Atlanta and Frankfurt) and international flights (Washington Dulles and London Heathrow), because customers have downtime to browse through stores. The best-selling products are gifts, necessities, and easy-to-pack items.

Temporary Locations

Retailers and manufacturers sometimes open temporary or pop-up stores to focus on a new product or a limited group of products. These temporary stores introduce and remind customers of a brand or store, but they are not designed primarily to sell the product.[37] One of the first pop-up stores was a temporary Target store that briefly opened on a boat off Chelsea Piers in Manhattan, because of the lack of retail space available in Manhattan. Target used this transient store to create buzz, and one year later, it launched the Isaac Mizrahi clothing collection from a pop-up store in Rockefeller Center.[38]

Other retailers, often one-person operations, open temporary stores to take advantage of the holiday season in December or to get visibility and additional sales at festivals or concerts, such as the Newport Jazz Festival, or weekend crafts fairs. For instance, in New York's Columbus Circle, 100 vendors sell a variety of gifts from Yogawear to handmade glass jewelry.[39] Cities around the United States generally welcome these temporary retailers because they bring in people, and therefore excitement and money, to the area. Local retailers, who pay high rents, aren't necessarily so enthusiastic, because some of the temporary retailers attract their customers.

Temporary retailers, like this street vendor, create excitement and therefore bring people and money to an area.

Resorts

Retailers view resorts as prime location opportunities. There is a captive audience of well-to-do customers with time on their hands. As noted previously, outlet malls are popular in tourist areas. In fact, some outlet malls, such as Sawgrass Mills in Sunrise, Florida, or Silver Sands Factory Stores of Destin, Florida, actually draw tourists to the area. Resort retailing also attracts small, unique, local retailers and premium national brands like Scoop in Miami's The Shore Club or Roberto Cavalli and Dolce & Gabbana in Las Vegas's Ceasar's Palace Forum shops. Resorts like Aspen in Colorado can support dozens of art galleries and fashion retailers with high-end designers. After all, it isn't unusual for visitors at such places to have a net worth of several million dollars.

Store within a Store

Another nontraditional location for retailers is within other, larger stores. Retailers, particularly department stores, have traditionally leased space to other retailers, such as sellers of fine jewelry or furs. Grocery stores have been experimenting with the store-within-a-store concept for years with service providers like dry cleaners, coffee bars, banks, film processors, clinics, and video outlets.[40]

LOCATION AND RETAIL STRATEGY

The selection of a location type must reinforce the retailer's strategy. Thus, the location type decision needs to be consistent with the shopping behavior and size of the target market and the retailer's positioning in its target market. Each of these factors is discussed next. Retailing View 7.5 summarizes the description offered by Steve Knopik, president of Bealls, a value-oriented, off-price retailer, regarding how the company's location decisions fit its retail strategy.

Shopping Behavior of Consumers in Retailer's Target Market

A critical factor affecting the location that consumers select to visit is the shopping situation in which they are involved. Three types of shopping situations are convenience shopping, comparison shopping, and specialty shopping.

Convenience Shopping   When consumers are engaged in **convenience shopping situations**, they are primarily concerned with minimizing their effort to get the product or service they want. They are indifferent about which brands to buy or the retailer's image and are somewhat insensitive to price. Thus, they don't spend much time evaluating different brands or retailers; they simply want to make the purchase as quickly and easily as possible. Examples of convenience shopping situations are getting a cup of coffee during a work break, buying gas for a car, or buying milk for breakfast in the morning.

Retailers targeting customers involved in convenience shopping, such as convenience stores and gas stations, usually locate their stores close to where their customers are and make it easy for them to access the location and park, find what they want, and go about their other business. Thus, convenience stores are generally located in neighborhood strip centers, freestanding spots, and city and town locations. Drugstores and fast-food restaurants also cater to convenience shoppers and thus select locations with easy access, parking, and the added convenience of a drive-through window. Convenience also plays an important role for supermarkets and full-line discount stores. Often, shoppers at these stores are not particularly brand or store loyal and do not find shopping in these stores enjoyable. Thus, these stores typically are also located in neighborhood strip centers and freestanding locations.

Comparison Shopping   Consumers involved in **comparison shopping situations** have a general idea about the type of product or service they want, but they do not have a strong preference for a brand, model, or specific retailer to patronize. Similar to many convenience shopping situations, consumers are not particularly brand or store loyal. However, the purchase decisions are more important to them, so they seek information and are willing to expend considerable effort planning and making their purchase decisions. Consumers typically engage in this type of shopping behavior when buying furniture, appliances, apparel, consumer electronics, hand tools, and cameras.

Furniture retailers, for instance, often locate next to one another to create a "furniture row." In New York City, a number of retailers selling houseplants and flowers are all located in Chelsea between 27th and 30th streets on 6th Avenue, and diamond dealers are located on West 47th Street between 5th and 6th avenues. These competing retailers locate near one another because doing so facilitates comparison shopping and thus attracts customers to the locations. To compare different types of houseplants and prices, New Yorkers just need to walk from store to store on 6th Avenue, and they know they will see most types of houseplants. Similarly, the advantage of attracting a large number of shoppers to West 47th Street outweighs the disadvantage of sharing these customers with other jewelers.

Bealls's Locations Support Its Strategy   **RETAILING VIEW**   **7.5**

In addition to its Florida-based department stores, Bealls operates more than 500 Bealls Outlet and Burke's Outlet stores in Sunbelt states from South and North Carolina to California. Its strategy is to sell, to price-sensitive customers, value-priced apparel in 15,000 to 25,000 square foot stores. To service these customers, Bealls needs to keep its prices and costs down. Its no-advertising strategy makes it very important to locate stores in heavily trafficked intersections or strip shopping centers to attract customers

Bealls uses a geodemographic service to identify and evaluate potential markets. It knows the geodemographic profiles of its customers and tries to locate its stores where a lot of those customers live. Once it identifies a community that meets its criteria, the next step is to find a specific location in the area. Its best locations are in strip shopping centers with an anchor like Wal-Mart, Target, or a grocery store that attracts a lot of shoppers.

Sometimes it finds an appealing site that is 30,000 to 40,000 square feet, bigger than it would prefer. To take advantage of these opportunities, it sometimes will partner with a complementary retailer, like Big Lots, an off-price retailer focusing on hard goods, and approach the property owner together.

Left: Steve Knopik, president of Bealls, Inc., visits one of the Bealls locations. Right: Bealls Outlet attracts customers by locating stores in heavily trafficked strip shopping centers with trade areas that match the profile of its target market.

Enclosed malls offer the same benefits to consumers interested in comparison shopping for fashionable apparel. For example, Eva Carlyn, the student described in Chapter 4 who was looking for a business suit for job interviews, could easily compare the suits offered at JCPenney and Ann Taylor with the suits she saw at Macy's by simply walking to these other stores located in the same mall. Thus, department stores and specialty apparel retailers locate in enclosed malls for the same reason that houseplant retailers locate together on 6th Avenue in New York City. By colocating in the same mall, they attract more potential customers interested in comparison shopping for fashionable apparel. Even though the enclosed mall might be inconvenient compared with a freestanding location, comparison shopping is easier after the customers have arrived.

Category specialists offer the same benefit of comparison shopping as a collection of colocated specialty stores like those described previously. Rather than going to a set of small specialty stores when comparison shopping for consumer electronics, consumers know they can see almost all of the brands and models they would want to buy in either Best Buy or Circuit City. Thus, category specialists are **destination stores**, places where consumers will go even if it is inconvenient, just like enclosed malls are destination locations for fashionable apparel comparison shopping. Category specialists locate in power centers, primarily to reduce their costs and create awareness of their location and secondarily to benefit from multiple retailers that attract more consumers and the resulting potential for cross-shopping. Basically, power centers are a collection of destination stores.

Specialty Shopping   When consumers go **specialty shopping**, they know what they want and will not accept a substitute. They are brand and/or retailer loyal and will pay a premium or expend extra effort, if necessary, to get exactly what they want. Examples of these shopping occasions include buying an expensive designer brand perfume, adopting a dog from the animal shelter, or buying a new, high-quality stovetop and oven. The retailer they patronize when specialty shopping also becomes a destination store. Thus, consumers are willing to travel to an inconvenient location to patronize a unique gourmet restaurant or a health food store that specializes in organic vegetables. Having a convenient location is not as important for retailers selling unique merchandise or services.

Size of Target Market

A second, but closely related, factor that affects the choice of location type is the size of the retailer's target market near the location. A good location has many people in the target market who are drawn to it. So a convenience store located in a CBD can be sustained by the many consumers who live and work in fairly close proximity to the store. It is not as important to have high customer density near a store that sells specialty merchandise, because people are willing to search out this type of merchandise. A Porsche dealer, for instance, need not be near other car dealers or in close proximity to its target market, because those seeking this luxury car will drive to wherever the dealer may be.

Uniqueness of Retail Offering

Finally, the convenience of their locations is less important for retailers with unique, differentiated offerings than for retailers with an offering similar to other retailers. For example, Bass Pro Shops provide a unique merchandise assortment and store atmosphere. Customers will travel to wherever the store is located, and its location will become a destination.

LEGAL CONSIDERATIONS

Legal considerations need to be examined when evaluating different location types. Laws regarding how land may be used have become so important that they are an important consideration in a site search. Legal issues that affect the location decision include environmental issues, zoning, building codes, signs, and licensing requirements.

Environmental Issues

The Environmental Protection Agency, as well as state and local agencies, has become increasingly involved with issues that could affect retail stores. Two environmental issues have received particular attention in recent years. The first is above-ground risks, such as asbestos-containing materials or lead pipes used in construction. These materials can be removed relatively easily.

The second issue is hazardous materials that have been stored in the ground. This consideration can be particularly important for a dry cleaner because of the chemicals it uses or for an auto repair shop because of its need to dispose of used motor oil and battery fluid. The costs of cleaning up hazardous materials can range from several thousand to many millions of dollars per site.

Real estate transactions almost always require an environmental impact statement on the property. But relying on past public filings of buried tanks and other potential hazards can be unreliable and does not provide protection in court. Retailers have two remedies to protect themselves from these environmental hazards. The best option at their disposal is to stipulate in the lease that the lessor is responsible for the removal and disposal of any such material if it is found. Alternatively, the retailer can buy insurance that specifically protects it from these risks.

Although laws related to the environment restrict the nature of retail developments, many new developments go beyond these legal requirements to address sustainability and energy efficiency issues. New retail developments are using energy-efficient building materials, lighting, and refrigeration systems; renewable power sources such as solar panels and wind turbines; water conservation systems; day-to-day waste recycling; and recycled materials in buildings.[41]

Zoning and Building Codes

Zoning determines how a particular site can be used. For instance, some parts of a city are zoned for residential use only; others are zoned for light industrial and retail uses. Building codes are similar legal restrictions that specify the type of building, signs, size and type of parking lot, and so forth that can be used at a particular location. Some building codes require a certain sized parking lot or a particular architectural design. In Santa Fe, New Mexico, for instance, building codes require buildings to keep a traditional mud stucco (adobe) style.

The building code in Santa Fe, New Mexico, requires buildings to keep a traditional mud stucco (adobe) style.

Signs   Restrictions on the use of signs can affect a particular site's desirability. Sign sizes and styles may be restricted by building codes, zoning ordinances, or even the shopping center management. At the Bal Harbour Shops in North Miami

Beach, for example, all signs (even sale signs) must be approved by the shopping center management prior to implementation by each individual retailer.

Licensing Requirements   Licensing requirements may vary in different parts of a region. For instance, some Dallas neighborhoods are dry, meaning no alcoholic beverages can be sold; in other areas, only wine and beer can be sold. Such restrictions can affect retailers other than restaurants and bars. For instance, a theme/festival shopping center that restricts the use of alcoholic beverages may find its clientele limited at night.

Legal issues such as those mentioned here can discourage a retailer from pursuing a particular site. These restrictions aren't always permanent, however. Although difficult, time consuming, and possibly expensive, lobbying efforts and court battles can change these legal restrictions.

SUMMARY

Decisions about where to locate a store are critical to any retailer's success. Location decisions are particularly important because of their high-cost, long-term commitment and impact on customer patronage. Choosing a particular location type involves evaluating a series of trade-offs. These trade-offs generally include the occupancy cost of the location, the pedestrian and vehicle customer traffic associated with the location, the restrictions placed on store operations by the property managers, and the convenience of the location for customers. In addition, legal issues need to be considered when selecting a site.

Retailers have a plethora of types of sites from which to choose. Each type of location has advantages and disadvantages. Many central business districts, inner-city, and Main Street locations have become more viable options than in the past due to gentrification of the areas, tax incentives, and the lack of competition. There also are a wide variety of shopping center types for retailers. They can locate in a strip or power center, or they can go into an enclosed mall or a lifestyle, fashion/specialty, theme/festival, or outlet center. Other nontraditional sites are mixed use developments, virtual locations, airports, resorts, stores within a store, and temporary locations.

KEY TERMS

anchor, *200*

central business district (CBD), *197*

community center, *200*

comparison shopping situation, *211*

convenience shopping situation, *210*

destination store, *212*

fashion/specialty center, *205*

freestanding site, *195*

gentrification, *197*

inner city, *198*

merchandise kiosk, *196*

lifestyle center, *204*

Main Street, *197*

mixed use development (MXD), *207*

neighborhood center, *200*

omnicenter, *206*

outlet center, *205*

outparcel, *195*

power center, *201*

regional mall, *201*

shopping center, *199*

shopping mall, *201*

specialty shopping, *212*

strip shopping center, *200*

super regional mall, *201*

theme/festival center, *206*

trade area, *195*

GET OUT AND DO IT!

1.   **CONTINUING CASE ASSIGN- MENT** Interview the manager of the shopping center that contains the retailer you selected for the continuing assignment. Write a report summarizing which retailers the shopping center manager thinks are his or her best tenants and why they are valued. How does the manager rate the retailer you have selected? What criteria does he or she use?

2.   Go to www.faneuilhallmarketplace.com and www.galleryatcocowalk.com. What kinds of centers are these? List their similarities and differences.

3.   Go to your favorite shopping center and analyze the tenant mix. Do the tenants appear to complement one another? What changes would you make in the tenant mix to increase the overall health of the center?

4. Visit a lifestyle center near your college or hometown. What tenants are found in this location? Describe the population characteristics around this center. How far would people drive to shop at this lifestyle center? What other types of retail locations does this lifestyle center compete with?

5. Go to the homepage for Regency Commercial Associates, LLC, at www.regency-prop.com and read about this property development company that oversees nearly two million square feet of shopping center and office space in five states. Describe this firm's strategy to build relationships with retail tenants.

6. Go to the homepage of your favorite fashion mall and describe it in terms of the following characteristics: number of anchor stores, number and categories of specialty stores, number of sit-down and quick service restaurants, and types of entertainment offered. What are the strengths and weaknesses of this assortment of retailers?

7. Visit a power center near your home or college that contains a Target, Staples, Sports Authority, Home Depot, or other category specialists. What other retailers are in the same location? How is this mix of stores beneficial to both shoppers and retailers?

DISCUSSION QUESTIONS AND PROBLEMS

1. Why is store location such an important decision for retailers?
2. Pick your favorite store. Describe the advantages and disadvantages of its current location, given its target market.
3. Home Depot, a rapidly growing chain of large home improvement centers, typically locates in either a power center or a freestanding site. What are the strengths of each location for a store like Home Depot?
4. As a consultant to 7-Eleven convenience stores, American Eagle Outfitters, and Porsche of America, what would you say is the single most important factor in choosing a site for these three very different types of stores?
5. Retailers are developing shopping centers and freestanding locations in central business districts that have suffered decay. Some people have questioned the ethical and social ramifications of this process, which is known as gentrification. What are the benefits and problems associated with gentrification?
6. Staples and Office Depot both have strong multichannel strategies. How does the Internet affect their strategies for locating stores?
7. In many malls, fast-food retailers are located together in an area known as a food court. What are this arrangement's advantages and disadvantages to the fast-food retailers? What is the new trend for food retailers in the shopping environment?
8. Why would a Payless ShoeSource store locate in a neighborhood shopping center instead of a regional shopping mall?
9. How does the mall that you shop at frequently combine the shopping and entertainment experience?
10. Consider a big city that has invested in an urban renaissance. What components of the gentrification project attract both local residents and visiting tourists to spend time shopping, eating, and sightseeing in this location?
11. Different brands of car dealerships are usually located near one another on the same street. What are the pros and cons of this strategy?

SUGGESTED READINGS

Anselmsson, Johan. " Sources of Customer Satisfaction with Shopping Malls: A Comparative Study of Different Customer Segments." *International Review of Retail, Distribution and Consumer Research* 16, no. 1 (2006), pp. 115–38.

Chebat, Jean-Charles; M. Joseph Sirgy; and Valerie St-James. "Upscale Image Transfer from Malls to Stores: A Self-Image Congruence Explanation." *Journal of Business Research* 59, no. 12 (2006), pp. 1288–96.

Cohen, Nancy. *America's Marketplace: The History of Shopping Centers.* Lyme, CT: Greenwich Publishing Group, 2002.

Hazel, Debra. "Life as a Lifestyle Center." *Chain Store Age*, March 2007.

ICSC. *Brief Notes Shopping Center Management.* New York: ICSC, 2006.

ICSC. *Winning Shopping Center Designs*, 30th ed. New York: ICSC, 2007.

Kramer, Anita. *Dollars & Cents of Shopping Centers/The SCORE 2006.* Washington DC: Urban Land Institute, 2006.

Maronick, Thomas. "Specialty Retail Center's Impact on Downtown Shopping, Dining, and Entertainment." *International Journal of Retail and Distribution Management* 35, no. 7 (2007), pp. 556–68.

Morgan, Michael. "Making Space for Experiences." *Journal of Retail and Leisure Property* 5, no. 4 (2006), pp. 305–13.

Retail Site Location

When I was an undergraduate student at the University of Florida, I mostly studied physical geography, learning about natural systems involving glaciers, geomorphology, and geology. While intellectually challenging, I wanted something a little different and sought knowledge from the economic geography discipline. While in graduate school, I took a course in Business Geography and was fascinated with the use of geographic information systems (GIS) to provide insights into a wide range of real-world problems—problems ranging from understanding the growth patterns of urban areas to selecting sites for retail stores. After completing my undergraduate and Master's degree in geography at UF, I began my career working in

EXECUTIVE BRIEFING
Juan C. del Valle, Market Development Manager, Brinker International

site location analysis for Blockbuster Inc., for nine years, then several years ago joined Brinker International as the manager for the market development department.

Brinker International is a leader in providing casual dining restaurant experiences. We develop, own, operate, and franchise an attractive portfolio of restaurant brands including Chili's Bar & Grill, Romano's Macaroni Grill, On The Border Mexican Grill & Cantina, and Maggiano's Little Italy. Founded in 1975, we have grown to over 1,600 restaurants worldwide with 100,000 employees and system-wide sales of over $4 billion annually.

Finding profitable locations and managing our portfolio are critical to the success of our restaurants. The company devotes significant efforts to the investigation of new locations and reexamining existing locations. Our research group undertakes a wide range of location analysis studies. At a broad strategic level, we use geodemographic data to identify areas of the country that are attractive for opening new restaurants and determine the number of restaurants that a geographic area might support. For example, we might do an analysis of the Anywhere, USA, metro market and determine that the market can support 20 Chili's restaurants. Then we would determine the appropriate location for these 20 restaurants so that they would serve the entire market by maximizing system profitability while minimizing sales cannibalization between locations.

We also undertake detailed analyses of the potential for restaurants at specific sites identified by our real estate

CHAPTER 8

QUESTIONS

What factors do retailers consider when determining where to locate their stores?

What is a trade area for a store, and how do retailers determine the trade area?

What factors do retailers consider when deciding on a particular site?

How do retailers forecast sales for new store locations?

Where can retailers get information to evaluate potential store locations?

What issues are involved in negotiating leases?

Chapter 5 emphasized the strategic importance of location decisions. Although location decisions can create strategic advantage, like all strategic decisions, they are also risky because they involve a significant commitment of resources. Opening a store at a site often involves committing to a lease of five years or more or purchasing land and building a store. If the store's performance is below expectations, the retailer may not be able to recover its investment easily by having another party move in and assume the lease or buy the building.

Chapter 7 reviewed the different types of locations available to retailers and why certain types of retailers gravitate toward particular locations. This chapter takes a closer look at how retailers choose specific sites to locate their stores.

Selecting retail locations involves the analysis of a lot of data and the use of sophisticated statistical models. Because most retailers make these decisions infrequently, it may not be economical for them to employ full-time real estate analysts with state-of-the-art skills. Thus, small retailers often use firms that provide the geographic and demographic data and consulting services needed to evaluate specific sites. However, there continues to be an element of art in making these location decisions.

This chapter reviews the steps retailers go through in selecting their store locations and negotiating leases. The first part of the chapter examines the factors retailers consider in selecting a general area for locating stores and determining the number of stores to operate in an area. Next, this chapter reviews different approaches used to evaluate specific sites and estimate the expected sales if and when a store is located at that site. Finally, the chapter looks at the various terms that are negotiated when a retailer commits to leasing space for its store.

department. When completing these studies, we consider a wide range of factors including: trade area demographics, such as target population density and household income levels; physical site characteristics, such as visibility, accessibility and automobile traffic volume; relative proximity to activity centers, such as shopping centers, hotel/entertainment complexes and office buildings; supply and demand trends, such as proposed infrastructure improvements and new developments; and existing and potential competition. In addition to considering traditional locations we also evaluate nontraditional locations (such as airports, toll plazas, and food courts) that can adequately support our restaurant brands.

Our brands offer different types of food and have different atmospheres. Consequently, there are some important differences we consider when analyzing sites. For example, Maggiano's restaurants are larger than our other restaurant brands and cater to a different strata of consumer because of its value platform. Maggiano's also has banquet rooms that cater to business meetings and weddings, thus consequently having a larger geographic trade area than other chains. This translates into unique target demographics and site requirements, as well as a different level of revenue requirements.

Leveraging GIS technology, spatial analysis tools, and location theory sheds a unique light on business location challenges. Visualization of business and market patterns allows the business manager to uncover valuable insight otherwise not available with traditional data analysis tools. Any budding retail manager would be wise to tap the invaluable geography toolbox.

EVALUATING SPECIFIC AREAS FOR LOCATIONS

REFACT

There are 363 MSAs and 576 micropolitan statistical areas in the United States.[1]

Areas that retailers consider for locating stores might be countries, areas within a country such as a province in France or a state in the United States, particular cities, or areas within cities. In the United States, retailers often focus their analysis on a **metropolitan statistical area (MSA)** because consumers tend to shop within an MSA, and media coverage and demographic data for analyzing location opportunities often are organized by MSA.

An MSA is a core urban area containing a population of more than 50,000 inhabitants, together with adjacent communities that have a high degree of economic and social integration with the core community. For example, many people in an MSA commute to work in the urban core but live in the surrounding areas. An MSA can consist of one or several counties and usually is named after the major urban area in the MSA. For example, the Cincinnati–Middleton MSA consists of fifteen counties (three in Indiana, seven in Kentucky, and five in Ohio) with a population of 2,104,218; the Missoula, Montana, MSA consists of one county with a population of 101,417. A **micropolitan statistical area** is a smaller unit of analysis with only about 10,000 inhabitants in its area.[2]

The best areas for locating stores are those that generate the highest long-term profits for a retailer. Some factors affecting the long-term profit generated by stores that should be considered when evaluating an area include (1) the economic conditions, (2) competition, (3) the strategic fit of the area's population with the retailer's target market, and (4) the costs of operating stores (see Exhibit 8–1). Note that these factors are similar to those that retailers consider when evaluating an investment in a new business growth opportunity or entry into a foreign market, as discussed in Chapter 5.

Economic Conditions

Because locations involve a commitment of resources over a long time horizon, it is important to examine an area's level and growth of population and employment. A large, fully employed population means high purchasing power and high levels of retail sales. Exhibit 8–2 shows the population growth for MSAs in the United States.

But population and employment growth alone aren't enough to ensure a strong retail environment in the future. Retail location analysts must determine how long such growth will continue and how it will affect demand for merchandise sold in

EXHIBIT 8–1

Factors Affecting the Demand for a Retail or Trade Area

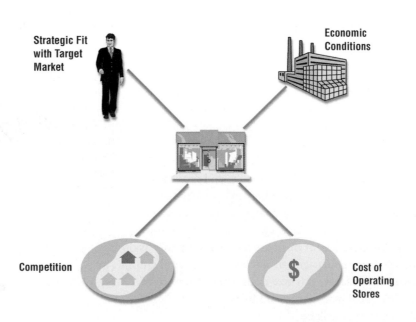

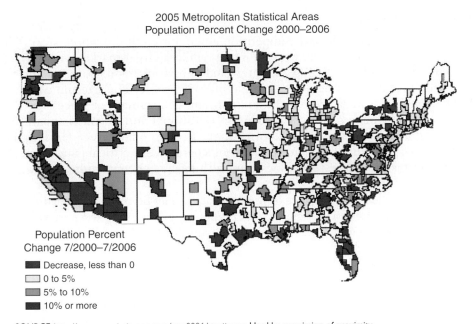

2005 Metropolitan Statistical Areas
Population Percent Change 2000–2006

Population Percent
Change 7/2000–7/2006

- ■ Decrease, less than 0
- □ 0 to 5%
- ▨ 5% to 10%
- ■ 10% or more

SOURCE: http://www.proximityone.com/msa0006.htm#maps. Used by permission of proximity.

EXHIBIT 8–2
Population Growth of
Metropolitan Statistical
Areas

its stores. For instance, the economies of some Rust Belt cities like Flint, Michigan, experience greater peaks and valleys due to their dependence on specific industries such as automobiles. If economic activity is not diversified in various industries, the area may be unattractive because of extreme cyclical trends. However, many areas that have been traditionally dependent on agriculture, a declining industry, have attempted to bring in new industries, such as manufacturing and high-tech, to help diversify their economies.

Also, it is useful to determine which areas are growing quickly and why. For instance, the east side of Seattle, Washington, has become a desirable retail location because of its proximity to Microsoft's corporate headquarters. But the performance of these retail locations is inextricably linked to the financial performance of Microsoft.

In most cases, areas where the population is large and growing are preferable to those with declining populations. However, some retailers, such as Subway, often go into new strip shopping centers with few nearby households with the anticipation that the surrounding suburban area will eventually be built up enough to support the stores.

Competition

The level of competition in an area clearly affects the demand for a retailer's merchandise. Wal-Mart's early success was based on a location strategy of opening stores in small towns with little competition. It offered consumers in small towns quality merchandise at low prices. Previously, rural consumers either shopped in small stores with limited assortments or drove to larger towns.

Although they once were viewed as undesirable areas, inner-city neighborhoods today host many full-service restaurant chains. Full-service operators like IHOP, T.G.I. Friday's, Chili's, and Denny's are moving into urban areas from Oakland, California, to New York. They are discovering that these previously underserved markets are attractive because of the lack of competition, the relatively high level of disposable income of the residents, and the large, untapped labor force. Retailing View 8.1 describes how Whole Foods caters to an urban market segment.

REFACT

The first Wal-Mart Discount City opened in Rogers, Arkansas, in 1962.[3]

Strategic Fit

Population level, growth, and competition alone don't tell the whole story. The area needs to have consumers who are in the retailer's target market—who are attracted to the retailer's offering and interested in patronizing its stores. Thus, the area must have the right demographic and lifestyle profile. The size and composition of households in an area can be an important determinant of success. For instance, Ann Taylor (a chain specializing in traditional and business apparel for women) generally locates in areas with high-income, dual-career families and tourist areas. Household size, however, is not a particularly critical issue. Toys "R" Us, in contrast, is interested in locations with heavy concentrations of families with young children.

Finally, lifestyle characteristics of the population may be relevant, depending on the target market(s) that a particular retailer is pursuing. For example, areas with consumers interested in outdoor activities are attractive for R.E.I. and Bass Pro Shops.

Operating Costs

The cost of operating stores can vary across areas. For example, store rental and advertising costs in the Missoula, Montana MSA are significantly lower than those in the Cincinnati–Middletown MSA. But of course, the potential sales and profits from stores located in the Cincinnati–Middletown MSA are substantially greater due to its larger and denser population.

Operating costs are also affected by the proximity of the area being considered to other areas in which the retailer operates stores. For example, if a store is located near other stores and the retailer's distribution centers, the cost of shipping merchandise to the store is lower, as is the cost and travel time spent by the district manager supervising the stores' operations.

The local and state legal and regulatory environment can have a significant effect on operating costs. Some retailers are reluctant to locate stores in California

---

8.1   RETAILING VIEW   Whole Foods Market Is Just Downstairs

Whole Foods opened its fourth Manhattan, New York, location in 2007 in the Lower East Side. Its three existing locations in Chelsea, Union Square, and Columbus Circle are all located on major transit hubs, but this one provides a different advantage: Its customers live on top of it!

This two-story, 71,000 square foot store is the largest in the northeastern United States and is located at the bottom of a 361-unit luxury apartment building, in an up and coming commercial and residential neighborhood.

Most Whole Foods supermarkets are located in stand-alone sites. But this mixed-use location offers a win–win–win situation for Whole Foods, the apartments' developer, and tenants. The luxury apartments rent for $56 per square foot—which translates into $3,400 for a 700 square foot one-bedroom, and $4500–$6,500 for a 1,190 square foot two-bedroom. Tenants that can afford these prices demand a lot.

Although this luxury apartment building has all the usual amenities, for many perspective tenants, the onsite Whole Foods is the deal maker. Whole Foods has joined the gym and the concierge as a must-have amenity in several luxury condominium towers being built in cities across the country. With the intense competition and millions of apartments available in New York City, this apartment building has a competitive advantage over many others.

Upscale supermarkets in condominium developments are popular with urban residents and attractive locations for Whole Foods Markets.

Source: Michael Stoler, "Luxury Seems to be Set for the Lower East Side," *The New York Sun,* May 17, 2007; Mark Hamstra, "Slow Start for Newest Whole Foods," *Supermarket News,* April 9, 2007; www.avalonchrystieplace.com (accessed July 31, 2007); www.wholefoods.com (accessed July 31, 2007).

because they feel that the state and local governments, its political process of vote-initiated referendums, and a legal environment that fosters class-action lawsuits result in higher operating costs. For example, the California legislature has considered or passed laws requiring employers to pay for health care benefits, lower requirements for workers' compensation claims, require the payment of overtime wages to employees classified as managers (but who do some of the same activities as hourly employees), and make it easier for employees to sue employers for wage and work condition violations.

In addition, some state courts have supported class-action suits affecting retail operations, such as making retail stores more accessible to the handicapped. Various cities have passed "living wage" laws that raise the minimum wage above the nationally set level. Although these political and legal activities provide benefits to employees and consumers, they also increase the operating costs for retailers and eventually increase the prices consumers pay for merchandise.

NUMBER OF STORES IN AN AREA

Having selected an area in which to locate its stores, a retailer's next decision is how many stores to operate in the area. At first glance, you might think that a retailer should choose the one best location in each MSA, but clearly, larger MSAs can support more stores than smaller MSAs. But there is a limit to how many stores can be operated in even the largest MSAs. When making the decision about how many stores to open in an area, retailers must consider the trade-offs between lower operating costs and potential sales cannibalization from having multiple stores in an area.

Economies of Scale from Multiple Stores

Most retail chains open multiple stores in an area because promotion and distribution economies of scale can be achieved. A retailer's total promotional costs are the same for newspaper advertising that promotes 20 stores in an area or only one store. Multiple stores in an area are needed to justify the cost of building a new distribution center. Thus, chains like Wal-Mart expand into areas only where they have a distribution center in place to support the stores. When Kohl's entered the Florida market, it opened 14 stores in Jacksonville and Orlando on the same day.

Opening multiple stores in an area can increase sales per store as well as reduce costs. For instance, Davenport, Iowa–based Von Maur is a family-owned, 22-store regional department store chain. Although it cannot compete with larger, national chains on costs due to its smaller scale economies, one of its advantages stems from its regional orientation. It maintains a loyal customer base that identifies with the local communities. Moreover, its merchandising, pricing, and promotional strategies specifically target the needs of a regional rather than a national market. Finally, the management team can have a greater span of control over a regional market; managers can easily visit the stores and assess competitive situations.

Cannibalization

Although retailers gain scale economies from opening multiple locations in an area, they also suffer diminishing returns associated with locating too many additional stores in an area. For example, suppose the first four stores opened in an MSA by a specialty store retailer generate sales of $2 million each. Because they are located far apart from one another, customers only consider patronizing the store nearest to them, and there is no cannibalization. When the retailer opens a fifth store close to one of the existing stores, it anticipates a net sales increase for the area of $2 million; the new store should generate the same sales level as the four existing stores. The next sales gain might be $1.5 million because the sales in the nearest existing store drop to $1.7 million, and sales from the new store are only $1.8 million because its location is only the fifth best in the area.

Because a primary retailing objective is to maximize profits for the entire chain, retailers should continue to open stores only as long as profits continue to increase or, in economic terms, as long as the marginal revenues achieved by opening a new store are greater than the marginal costs. Wal-Mart opens over 250 supercenters a year in the United States. When Wal-Mart analyzes a potential new location, it takes into account the impact that the new store will have on existing store sales—the cannibalized sales. However, Wal-Mart has found that it can profitably put su-percenters closer together than it originally thought. It deliberately plans to cannibalize sales in existing stores when those stores reach annual sales volumes of $100 million or more. Basically, Wal-Mart prefers operating two supercenters, each with annual sales of $80 million, to one location with annual sales over $100 million. The cannibalization that results from opening new stores near existing stores reduces its sales growth potential for stores that are currently open by a percentage point or two. In the long run, however, this intentional cannibal-ization builds a competitive advantage because the shopping experience for customers is enhanced—two stores, less congestion. In addition, having multiple stores in an area makes it less attractive for a competitor to enter the area.[4]

Why might the location objectives of franchisees and a franchisor differ?

For franchise retail operations, the objectives of the franchisor and franchisee differ, and thus, dis-putes can arise over the number of locations in an area. The franchisor is interested in maximizing the sales of all stores because it earns a royalty based on total store sales. The franchisee is interested in just the sales and profits from its store(s). Thus, the franchisor is not as concerned about cannibaliza-tion as the franchisee is. To reduce the level of conflict, most franchise agree-ments grant franchisees an exclusive territory to protect them from another franchisee cannibalizing their sales.

EVALUATING A SITE FOR LOCATING A RETAIL STORE

Having decided to locate stores in an area, the retailer's next step is to evaluate and select a specific site. In making this decision, retailers consider three factors: (1) the characteristics of the site, (2) the characteristics of the trading area for a store at the site, and (3) the estimated potential sales that can be generated by a store at the site. The first two sets of factors are typically considered in an initial screening of potential sites. The methods used to forecast store sales, the third factor, can involve a more complex analytical approach. Each of these factors is discussed in the following sections.

Site Characteristics

Some characteristics of a site that affect store sales and thus are considered in se-lecting a site are (1) the traffic flow past the site and accessibility to the site, (2) the characteristics of the location, and (3) the costs associated with locating at the site (see Exhibit 8–3). The section at the end of the chapter on negotiating a lease re-views the cost factors associated with sites.

EXHIBIT 8–3
Site Characteristics

Traffic Flow and Accessibility	Restrictions
vehicular traffic	zoning
ease of vehicular access	signage
access to major highways	restrictions on tenant mix
street congestion	safety code restrictions
pedestrian traffic	
availability of mass transit	
Location Characteristics	**Costs**
parking spaces	rental fee
access to store entrance and exit	common area maintenance cost
visibility of store from street	local taxes
access for deliveries	advertising and promotion fees
size and shape of store	length of lease
condition of building	
adjacent retailers	

Traffic Flow and Accessibility

One of the most important factors affecting store sales is the number of vehicles and pedestrians that pass by the site, or the **traffic flow.** When the traffic is greater, more consumers are likely to stop in and shop at the store. Thus, retailers often use traffic count measures to assess a site's attractiveness. Traffic counts are particularly important for retailers offering merchandise and services bought on impulse or on frequent trips. For example, good traffic flow and accessibility are more important for car washes or grocery stores than for destination retailers like The Container Store.

Wireless Toyz is a specialty retailer that provides a one-stop shopping destination for all brands of cell phone service, equipment, and accessories. When it evaluates new sites, it looks for locations in high-traffic outdoor lifestyle centers, next to an anchor store, or at a corner with a stoplight. This retailer plans to have 1,000 stores by 2011, a threefold increase over its current number of locations.[5]

More traffic flow is not always better; rather, traffic flow is a question of balance. The site should have a substantial number of cars per day but not so many cars that traffic congestion impedes access to the store.

To assess the level of vehicular traffic, the retailer can either perform site visits or commission a specialized firm to do the study. The number of vehicles going by the site may not tell the whole story, however. For instance, the data may need to be adjusted for the time of day. Areas congested during rush hours may have a good traffic flow during the rest of the day when most shopping takes place.

The **accessibility** of the site, which can be as important as traffic flow, is the ease with which customers can get into and out of the site. Accessibility is greater for sites located near major highways, on uncongested highways, and with traffic lights and lanes that enable turns into the site. Retailing View 8.2 describes the importance of accessibility to a retailer's business.

Natural barriers, such as rivers or mountains, and **artificial barriers,** such as railroad tracks, divided or limited access highways, or parks, may also affect accessibility. These barriers' impact on a particular site primarily depends on whether the merchandise or services will appeal to customers so strongly that they cross the barrier. For example, a supermarket on one side of a divided highway with no convenient cross-over point will only appeal to consumers going in one direction.

In the United States, most consumers drive to shopping centers, and thus, vehicular traffic is an important consideration when evaluating a site. However, pedestrian traffic flow and access by public transportation is more important for site analysis in a country where consumers do not drive to shop or for evaluating urban sites and sites within an enclosed mall.

Location Characteristics

Some factors associated with specific locations that retailers consider when evaluating a site are (1) parking, (2) store visibility, and (3) adjacent retailers.

Parking   The amount and quality of parking facilities are critical for evaluating a shopping center and specific site within the center. On the one hand, if there aren't enough spaces or the spaces are too far from the store, customers will be discouraged from patronizing the site and the store. On the other hand, if there are too many open spaces, the shopping center may be perceived as having unpopular stores. A standard rule of thumb is 5.5:1,000 (five and one-half spaces per thousand square feet of retail store space) for a shopping center and 10 to 15 spaces per 1,000 square feet for a supermarket.

Retailers need to observe the shopping center at various times of the day, week, and season. They also must consider the availability of employee parking, the proportion of shoppers using cars, parking by nonshoppers, and the typical length of a shopping trip.

An issue closely related to the amount of available parking facilities but extended into the shopping center itself is the relative congestion of the area. **Congestion** is an excess level of traffic that results in customer delays. There is an optimal level of congestion for customers. Too much congestion can make shopping slow, irritate customers, and generally discourage sales. However, a relatively high level of activity in a shopping center creates excitement and can stimulate sales.

Visibility   Visibility refers to customers' ability to see the store from the street. Good visibility is less important for stores with a well-established and loyal customer base, but most retailers still want a direct, unimpeded view of their store. In

---

One retailer's demise can be another retailer's opportunity. Jones Hardware & Building Supply in Wake Forest, North Carolina, survived the Great Depression and the relocation of the town's largest employer, so it believed it could survive Home Depot coming to town. However, the traffic pattern near the store was changed to accommodate new Home Depot and Target stores. The hardware store's once-accessible, prized corner lot location was crippled by a new intersection that prevented a left turn into the store's parking lot. Customers turning left into the store were forced to make a U-turn and access Jones Hardware through an adjoining Winn-Dixie parking lot. Whether it was this inconvenience or the arrival of Lowe's Home Improvement across from Home Depot, the fate of the smaller retailer was sealed, and within two years, Jones Hardware closed.

That same corner lot soon became the site of the market's first Walgreens, because the location satisfies Walgreens' fundamental real estate strategy: to be easily accessible for residents as they return home from work. Walgreens positions its stores so that evening commuter traffic can make an easy right turn into the store's parking lot. The former Jones Hardware store fronts a key artery for afternoon commuter traffic, and the CVS store in the shopping center across from the Walgreens has to rely on customer loyalty to motivate those same

Walgreens selects locations that enable it to offer drive-through prescription pickup—a value-added customer service.

commuters to make the less convenient left-hand turn into its parking area.

Source: Jim Frederick, "The Hedgehog vs. the Elephant: Winning the Walgreen Way," *Drug Store News,* March 19, 2007; Connie Gentry, "Science Validates Art." Reprinted by permission from *Chain Store Age,* April 2005, pp. 83–84. Copyright Lebhar-Friedman, Inc., 425 Park Avenue, New York, NY 10022.

an area with a highly transient population, such as a tourist center or large city, good visibility from the road is particularly important.

Adjacent Tenants   Locations with complementary, as well as competing, adjacent retailers have the potential to build traffic. Complementary retailers target the same market segment but have a different, noncompeting merchandise offering. For example, Save-A-Lot, a limited assortment supermarket targeting price-sensitive consumers, prefers to be co-located with other retailers targeting price-sensitive consumers, such as Big Lots, Family Dollar, or even Wal-Mart.

Have you ever noticed that competing fast food restaurants, automobile dealerships, antique dealers, or even shoe and apparel stores in a mall are located next to one another? Consumers looking for these types of merchandise are involved in convenience or comparison shopping situations, as we described in Chapter 7. They want to be able to make their choice easily in the case of convenience shopping, or they want to have a good assortment so they can "shop around."

This grouped location approach is based on the principle of **cumulative attraction,** which states that a cluster of similar and complementary retailing activities will generally have greater drawing power than isolated stores that engage in the same retailing activities.

Store visibility is an important consideration when evaluating a site. The Banana Republic store (left) is clearly visible; whereas the stores going up the stairs (right) are not.

REFACT

Seventy percent of Lowe's Home Improvement stores are within 10 miles of a Home Depot store.[6]

Restrictions and Costs

As we will learn later in this chapter, retailers may place restrictions on the type of tenants that are allowed in a shopping center in their lease agreement. Some of these restrictions can make the shopping center more attractive for a retailer. For example, a specialty men's apparel retailer may prefer a lease agreement that precludes other men's specialty apparel retailers from locating in the same center. A florist in a strip center may specify that if the grocery anchor tenant vacates the center, it can be released from its lease. Retailers would look unfavorably on a shopping center with a sign size restriction that prevented easy visibility of the store's name from the street. At the end of the chapter, we discuss some other restrictions and cost issues involved in negotiating a lease.

Locations within a Shopping Center

Locating within a shopping center affects both sales and occupancy costs, in that the better locations have higher occupancy costs. In a strip shopping center, the more expensive locations are closest to the supermarket, so a flower shop or sandwich shop that may attract impulse buyers should be close to the supermarket. But a shoe repair store, which does not cater to customers shopping on impulse, could be in a lower traffic location farther away from the supermarket because customers in need of this service will seek out the store. In other words, it is a destination store.

The same issues apply to evaluating locations within a multilevel, enclosed shopping mall. Stores that cater to consumers engaging in comparison shopping, such as shoppers buying fashionable apparel, benefit from being located in more expensive locations near the department store anchors, which are destinations for comparison apparel shoppers. As apparel shoppers enter and leave the department store, they walk by and may be attracted to neighboring specialty store retailers. In contrast, a retailer such as Foot Locker, another destination store, need not be in the most expensive location, because many of its customers know they're in the market for this type of product before they even go shopping.

Another consideration is how to locate stores that appeal to similar target markets. In essence, customers want to shop where they'll find a good assortment of merchandise. The principle of cumulative attraction applies to both stores that sell complementary merchandise and those that compete directly with one another. Consider Exhibit 8–4, a map of the Columbia Mall, the centerpiece of the planned community of Columbia, Maryland. The mall's trade area includes about three-quarters of a million people, located in wealthy Howard County, which is positioned halfway between Baltimore, Maryland, and Washington, DC. This mall underwent a major expansion, completed in 2003, that added 80,000 square feet of new merchandise space and entertainment venues. The new tenants include three restaurants located along the perimeter of the center: P.F. Chang's, Uno Chicago Grill, and Champs; a 14-screen, state-of-the-art, stadium-seating cinema; and L.L. Bean, Domain, Restoration Hardware, Banana Republic, Bebe, Build-A-Bear Workshop, Abercrombie & Fitch, Starbucks, J. Crew, and GUESS? stores.

During the expansion, many tenants were repositioned within the mall into category zones to better match their target audience. A good example of this repositioning is the location of retailers selling children's apparel and related merchandise. Gymboree and Abercrombie Kids are located side-by-side in Section B on the lower level. A short escalator ride to the upper level takes busy parents

EXHIBIT 8–4   Grouping Retailers in an Enclosed Mall

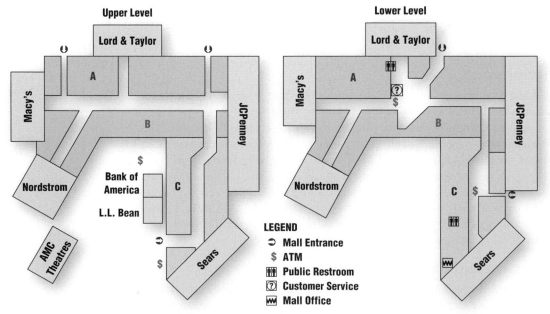

During the expansion of the Columbia Mall in Columbia, Maryland, many tenants were repositioned to better match their target audience. For instance, GapKids, BabyGap, and Limited Too are all near each other.

and their children to the Build-A-Bear Workshop, The Disney Store, and Club Libby Lu, all located in Section B. Directly across the walkway in Section A, shoppers can visit GapKids, BabyGap, and Limited Too for more children's clothing and accessories.

TRADE AREA CHARACTERISTICS

After identifying several sites that have acceptable traffic flow, accessibility, and other location characteristics, the next step is to collect information about the trade area that can be used to forecast sales for a store located at the sites. The retailer first needs to define the trade area for each site. Once the trade area is defined, the retailer can use several different information sources to develop a detailed understanding of the nature of consumers in the site's trade area.

Trade Area Definition

A **trade area** is a contiguous geographic area that accounts for the majority of a store's sales and customers. Trade areas can be divided into three zones, as shown in Exhibit 8–5. The exhibit of the trade area for a shopping center located at the red square shows the five-minute drive time zone (light brown), the ten-minute zone (blue), and the fifteen-minute zone (green).

The trade area zones shown in Exhibit 8–5 are not concentric circles based on distance from the store but rather are irregular polygons based on the location of roads, highways, and natural barriers, like rivers and valleys, that affect the driving time to the store. The location of competitive stores can also affect the actual trade area configuration.

The **primary trading area** is the geographic area from which the shopping center or store site derives 50–70 percent of its customers. The **secondary trading area** is the geographic area of secondary importance in terms of customer sales, generating about 20–30 percent of the site's customers. The **tertiary trading area** or **fringe** (the outermost area) includes the remaining customers who shop at the site but come from widely dispersed areas. These customers might travel an

EXHIBIT 8–5
Where are the primary, secondary, and tertiary trade areas for the store denoted by the red square?

unusually long distance because they do not have comparable retail facilities closer to home, or they may drive near the store or center on their way to or from work.

The best way to define the three zones is based on driving time rather than distance. Thus, the primary trading might be defined as customers within five minutes' driving time of the site; the secondary trading area as customers with a fifteen-minute drive, and the tertiary zone as customers more than fifteen minutes away from the site by car. In bigger cities where driving times are lengthy, such as Los Angeles, the primary trading area may be 15 minutes, the secondary trading area 40 minutes, and the tertiary trading area more than 1 hour. However, it is much easier to collect information about the number of people and their characteristics in the different zones by geographical distance than driving time. Thus, retailers often define the zones by distance—such as three, five, and ten miles from the site—rather than driving time.

Factors Affecting the Size of the Trade Area

The actual boundaries of a trade area are determined by the store's accessibility, natural and physical barriers, and level of competition, which we discussed previously in this chapter. The boundaries are also affected by the type of shopping area and type of store.

Trade area size is influenced by the type of store or shopping area. A Starbucks in a central business district, for example, may have a primary trade area of only two or three blocks; a category specialist like Best Buy may draw customers from 10 miles away; and The Container Store, which is the only store of its kind in a city, might draw customers from 30 miles away. The size of the trading area is determined by the nature of the merchandise sold, the assortment offered, and the location of alternative sources for the merchandise. People go to convenience stores because they can buy products like milk and bread quickly and easily; thus, their trade areas are relatively small. Category specialists, in contrast, offer a large choice of brands and products for which customers are engaged in comparison shopping. Thus, customers generally drive some distance to shop at these stores.

Recall from Chapter 7 that a destination store is a place where consumers will go even if it is inconvenient. In general, destination stores have a large trade area—people are willing to drive farther to shop there. Examples of destination stores are anchor stores in shopping malls such as department stores, certain specialty stores such as IKEA, category killers such as Staples and Office Depot, and some service providers such as IMAX theaters.

A **parasite store** is one that does not create its own traffic and whose trade area is determined by the dominant retailer in the shopping center or retail area. A co-located dry cleaner would be a parasite store to a Wal-Mart store because people tend to stop at the dry cleaner on the way to or from Wal-Mart and other stores. Its business is thus derived from Wal-Mart and other businesses in the area. Some retail experts have noted that Wal-Mart can be a destructive force to competition in a trade area because it is so dominant. Yet some parasite stores and stores that have learned to provide product or service offerings that complement, rather than compete with, Wal-Mart actually benefit from its presence.

For example, Party City, the world's largest party supply retailer, has 249 company-owned stores and 258 franchised stores in 41 states. They offer a wide selection of merchandise for celebratory occasions, such as birthdays and anniversaries, as well as for seasonal events, such as Halloween and Thanksgiving. Party City looks for regional centers with nationally recognized co-tenants such as Wal-Mart, Target, or Kohl's because of the traffic these stores bring to the center. It chooses locations that have a high density of solid middle-income shoppers, a growing population, and a high percentage of children. Party City carries a broader assortment and deeper variety of party supplies than Wal-Mart or Target.[7] Other examples of parasite stores are food court restaurants and kiosks in a mall.

Measuring the Trade Area for a Retail Site

Retailers can determine the trade area for their existing stores by customer spotting. **Customer spotting** is the process of locating the residences of customers for a store on a map and displaying their positions relative to the store location. The addresses for locating the customers' residences usually are obtained by asking the customers, recording the information from a check or Internet channel purchases, or collecting the information from customer data warehouses developed through loyalty programs. An older method observes automobile license plates in the parking lot and traces them to the owner by purchasing the information from state governments or private research companies. However, this method is not believed to be very accurate and is illegal in some states, though it may be the easiest way to understand competitors' trade areas. The data collected from customer spotting can be processed in two ways: manually plotting the location of each customer on a map or using a geographic information system like those described later in this chapter. Retailing View 8.3 describes how multichannel retailers use their nonsales data to spot customers and potential store locations.

It is more challenging to estimate the trade area for a new store location than for existing locations. However, retailers typically use information about the trade areas for existing stores to estimate the trade areas for new stores. For example, a

This Factory Card & Party Outlet store picks up customers from Best Buy. It is therefore a parasite store.

sporting goods retail chain with 7,000 square foot stores located in neighborhood shopping centers might find that the primary trading area for its stores is a drive of less than 10 minutes, the secondary trade area is a drive of 10–20 minutes, and the tertiary trade zone is more than a 20-minute drive. Assuming the site under consideration is located in an area that has similar demographic and lifestyle characteristics, the retailer assumes the trade areas for the new site will be defined by the same 10- and 20-minute drive times.

Sources of Information about the Trade Area

To further analyze the attractiveness of a potential store site, a retailer needs information about both the consumers and the competitors in the site's trade area. Two widely used sources of information about the nature of consumers in the trade area are (1) data published by the U.S. Census Bureau based on the *Decennial Census of the United States* and (2) data from GIS (geographic information systems) provided by several commercial firms.

REFACT

The United States was the first country to institute a periodic census.[8]

REFACT

California, Florida, and New York account for one-quarter of the U.S. population.[9]

Demographic Data from U.S. Census Bureau   A **census** is a count of the population of a country as of a specified date. The first U.S. decennial census was undertaken in 1790 as part of a Constitutional mandate to periodically reapportion state representation in the House of Representatives on the basis of states' population.

Every ten years, census takers attempt to gather demographic information (sex, age, ethnicity, education, marital status, etc.) from every household in the United States. Many questions on the decennial census are mandated by federal law, and questions change over time to reflect changes in data needs and national interests. For example, current census questionnaires no longer ask about household use of electric lights and television ownership, but they do ask about foster children and stepchildren, the presence of solar heat in the home, and, most recently, grandparents as primary caregivers of children. The decennial census is more than just a head count; it provides a snapshot of the country's demographic, social, and economic characteristics.

The U.S. Census Bureau prepares periodic reports summarizing the data from two sources: the census demographics for each person and additional data collected

---

8.3   RETAILING VIEW   Customer Spotting for Multichannel Retailers

Multichannel retailers that sell merchandise using catalogs and the Internet have an advantage over store-based retailers in locating and evaluating potential store sites because they can apply their customer data to help them determine which locations are more likely to be profitable. For example, Talbots, a specialty apparel multichannel retailer, relies primarily on catalog and Internet sales data when determining whether and where to open a store. It has developed and validated a formula for taking its nonstore sales data to tell where its customers are and what they're buying. Hypothetically, if Talbots did $150,000 in catalog sales in a particular area last year, it knows it can put a store there and do $1–$1.5 million in retail sales.

Using these nonstore sales data, Talbots opens successful stores in locales that other retailers overlook. At one time, Talbots thought its classic

Talbots uses the addresses of its catalog customers to determine promising locations for its future stores.

styles only appealed to women in the Northeast and Midwest, but strong catalog sales in the Sun Belt states encouraged the company to open stores in warmer climates. Nonstore sales data also identified some locations it would not normally consider. For instance, though Fishkill, New York— some 75 miles north of New York City—has a population of fewer than 20,000 people, it is the site of a profitable Talbots store. Some of the company's best-performing stores are in these overlooked areas. Talbots is often a destination location, and it knows it has established customer bases in these towns and surrounding areas.

Source: Bruce Soderholm, Senior Vice President, Operations, Talbots, personal communication, April 2006; Paul Miller, "Location, Location, Location," *Catalog Age*, May 2004, pp. 55–56. Reprinted with the permission of Primedia Business Magazines & Media. Copyright 2004. All rights reserved.

from a sample of the population. The smallest geographic entity for which census data is available is the **census block,** an area bounded on all sides by visible (roads, rivers, etc.) and/or invisible (county, state boundaries) features. There are seven million census blocks in the United States, each containing the residences of about 40 people. The smallest unit for the sample data is the **block group,** a collection of adjacent blocks that contain between 300 and 3,000 people. Data are also available at higher levels of aggregation, including zip code, census tract (collections of adjacent block groups), county, state, and region.[10]

Although the data from the U.S. Census Bureau can be used to develop a better understanding of the nature of consumers in a region or trade area, it has several limitations. First, because it is based on data collected every ten years, it is not very current, though its projections are reasonably accurate. Second, only demographic data about an area are available. As we discussed in Chapter 4, demographics are not always the best predictor of buying behavior. Third, the data are not particularly user friendly. It is difficult to utilize census data to examine the trade areas for various locations for specific products or services. Thus, most retailers rely on GIS data offered by a number of companies to examine trade areas for potential stores.

Geographic Information System (GIS) Suppliers GIS is a system of hardware and software used to store, retrieve, map, and analyze geographic data, along with the operating personnel and the data that go into the system. The key feature of GIS data is that they are linked to a coordinate system (latitude/longitude) that references a particular place on Earth. The data in the systems include spatial features such as rivers and roads, as well as descriptive information associated with the spatial features, such as the street address and characteristics of the household at the address.

Firms such as ESRI (www.esri.com), Claritas (www.claritas.com), and MapInfo (www.mapinfo.com) that construct and offer services involving GIS combine updated demographic census data with data from other sources that describe consumer spending patterns and lifestyles in a geographic area. In addition, they provide a user-friendly interface so the data can be accessed and analyzed easily. Frequently, the outputs from the system are maps that enable retailers to visualize the implications of the data quickly. For example, the map in Exhibit 8–6 shows

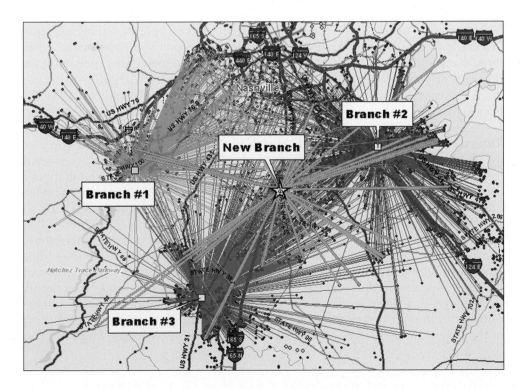

EXHIBIT 8–6
GIS Map for Bank Trade Areas in an MSA

the trading areas for three branch banks that a retailer has in an MSA and a fourth branch it is considering, as well as the residences of its customers who bank at each branch. This map suggests that people bank near their work, and thus, the new location might cannibalize from the other branches.

A retailer interested in developing a deeper understanding of the trade areas for several sites can provide ESRI with the latitude and longitude or street addresses for the sites under consideration. The system then provides the data shown in the table below for 2009 and projected for 2014 pertaining to people living within a three-, five-, and ten-mile radius of the sites.

gender	occupation
income	travel time to work
disposible income	transportation mode to work
net worth	household composition
education	household expenditures by NAICS categories
age	geodemographic market segment
race/ethnicity	market potential index
employment status	spending potential index

Not too long ago, Wendy's used demographic data like household income to make site selection decisions.[11] Now it uses a model based on GIS data that help it decide on which markets to focus, such as whether to concentrate on Miami or Salt Lake City. On a micro level, the GIS tools help Wendy's select a site within the market. Working with a Web-based tool the GIS team accesses data about Wendy's' existing stores to create projected sales forecasts for new sites.

The analysis takes less than a minute and provides maps with great detail, such as traffic counts, shopping center locations, competitors, and surrounding neighborhoods. Also, the information is updated whenever the market changes, which is a big improvement over old paper wall maps with color-coded sticky dots all over them.

An example of a report on the retail goods and services purchased by residents in a trade area is shown in Exhibit 8–7. In addition to the demographic data, this sample report contains some special data—the lifestyle segments represented in the trade area and the spending power index for various retail categories—that are discussed next. But first consider how the hamburger chain Wendy's utilizes GIS information.

Tapestry Segments   ESRI and other GIS suppliers have developed schemes for classifying geographical areas in the United States by combining census and survey data about people's lifestyles and purchasing behavior with the mapping capabilities of GIS. The analysis is based on the premise that "birds of a feather flock together." Specifically, people that live in the same neighborhoods tend to have similar lifestyle and consumer behavior patterns.

The ESRI Community Tapestry segmentation scheme classifies neighborhoods into 65 categories. Exhibit 8–7 is a hypothetical report for a 1.5 mile radius around 100 S. Wacker Drive in Chicago. Each segment provides a description of the typical person in that segment. The largest segment in the trade area report in Exhibit 8–7 is metro renters.[12] Metro renters are young (approximately 30 percent are in their 20s), well-educated singles beginning their professional careers in the largest cities, such as New York, Chicago, and Los Angeles. Their median

GIS Data for Retail Expenditures in Trade Area **EXHIBIT 8–7**

Retail Goods and Services Expenditures

Sample

ESRI

Proposed Location	Latitude:	41.880499
100 S Wacker Dr	Longitude:	-87.637123
Chicago, IL 60606 **Site Type: Radius**	Radius:	1.5 miles

Top Tapestry Segments:		**Demographic Summary**	**2007**	**2012**
Metro Renters	48.8%	Population	99,551	109,128
Laptops and Lattes	30.8%	Households	55,684	60,991
City Strivers	5.7%	Families	17,466	18,495
Trendsetters	5.1%	Median Age	35.9	37.7
City Commons	1.8%	Median Household Income	$76,509	$93,848

	Spending Potential Index	**Average Amount Spent**	**Total**
Apparel and Services	162	$4,444.21	$247,471,207
Men's	164	$814.22	$45,339,170
Women's	155	$1,487.88	$82,851,060
Children's	159	$696.51	$38,784,351
Footwear	149	$758.66	$42,245,409
Watches & Jewelry	178	$351.17	$19,554,657
Apparel Products and Services	227	$335.76	$18,696,560
Computer			
Computers and Hardware for Home Use	176	$384.83	$21,429,014
Software and Accessories for Home Use	174	$51.98	$2,894,710
Entertainment & Recreation	156	$5,346.95	$297,739,447
Fees and Admissions	165	$1,005.79	$56,006,451
Membership Fees for Clubs	156	$247.73	$13,794,616
Fees for Participant Sports, excl. Trips	152	$172.55	$9,608,284
Admission to Movie/Theatre/Opera/Ballet	189	$283.75	$15,800,064
Admission to Sporting Events, excl. Trips	164	$94.05	$5,237,000
Fees for Recreational Lessons	159	$207.72	$11,566,487
TV/Video/Sound Equipment	169	$1,965.82	$109,464,907
Community Antenna or Cable Television	164	$1,093.62	$60,897,100

SOURCE: Retail Goods and Services Expenditures Sample reprinted courtesy of ESRI.

household income of $50,400 has been increasing faster than that of most market segments. A majority are renters, often in older high-rise units. They live alone or share with roommates. Metro renters spend money on themselves, buying designer jeans, ski apparel, and workout clothing. They also enjoy time with friends and entertain at home. For leisure, they attend rock concerts, go to the movies, and go dancing, as well as play racquetball and tennis, practice yoga, work out regularly, ski, and jog. Surfing the Internet is an important part of their lives; they go online to search for jobs, listen to the radio, and order airline and concert tickets.

Metro renters are young well-educated singles beginning their professional careers in the largest cities such as New York, Chicago, and Los Angeles.

Several similar and competing GIS are currently commercially available, including PRIZM (Potential Rating Index for Zip Markets), which was developed by Claritas and is described in Chapter 4.

Spending Potential Index   The **spending potential index (SPI)** also shown in Exhibit 8–7, compares the average expenditure for a particular product or service to the amount spent on that product or service nationally. The average expenditure across the United States is indexed to 100, so the 162 SPI for men's apparel in Exhibit 8–7 means that men in the trade area spend 62 percent more than the average for the rest of the United States. This particular trading area is higher than the national average for all merchandise and service categories.

Exhibit 8–8 shows the location of customers who have the desired geodemographic profile on a trade area map for a shopping center. Note that most of the retailer's desirable customers are not even in the tertiary trade area; thus, this shopping center would not be a desirable location. (The shopping center is designated by the red star. The primary trade area is green; the secondary trade area is lavender; and the tertiary trade area is turquoise.

Competition in the Trade Area

In addition to information about the residents in a trade area, retailers need to know about the amount and type of competition in the trade area. Although GIS vendors provide data on the location of competitive retailers, there are other sources for this information. For example, most retailer Web sites list not only all current store locations but future sites as well. A more traditional method of accessing competitive information is to look through the Yellow Pages of the telephone book. Other sources of competitive information include directories published by trade associations, chambers of commerce, *Chain Store Guide* (published by CSG Information Services, www.csgis.com), and municipal and county governments.

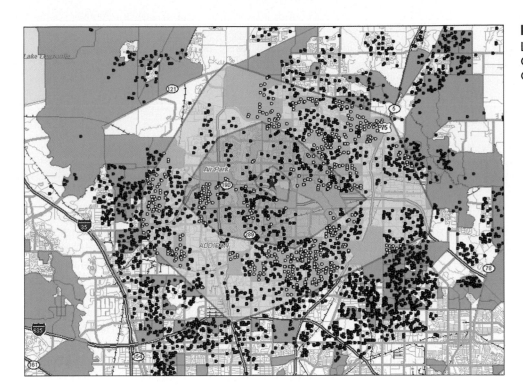

EXHIBIT 8–8
Location of Target
Customers in Shopping
Center Trade Area

ESTIMATING POTENTIAL SALES FOR A STORE SITE

Three approaches for using the information about the trade area to estimate the potential sales for a store at the location are (1) the Huff gravity model, (2) regression analysis, and (3) the analog method.

Huff Gravity Model

The **Huff gravity model**[13] for estimating the sales of a retail store is based on the concept of gravity: Consumers are attracted to a store location, just like Newton's falling apple was attracted to the Earth. In this model, the force of the attraction is based on two factors: the size of the store (larger stores have more pulling power) and the time it takes to travel to the store (stores that take more time to get to have less pulling power). The mathematical formula to predict the probability of a customer going to a specific store location is as follows:

$$P_{ij} = \frac{S_j / T_{ij}^{\lambda}}{\sum S_j / T_{ij}^{\lambda}}$$

where

P_{ij} = probability that customer i shops at location j,

S_j = size of the store at location j, and

T_{ij} = travel time for customer i to get to location j.

The formula indicates that the larger the size (S_j) of the store compared with competing stores' sizes, the greater the probability that a customer will shop at the location. A larger size is generally more attractive in consumers' eyes because it means more merchandise assortment and variety. Travel time or distance (T_{ij}) has the opposite effect on the probability that a consumer will shop at a location. The greater the travel time or distance from the consumer, compared with that of competing

EXHIBIT 8–9
Application of Huff
Gravity Model for
Estimating Store Sales

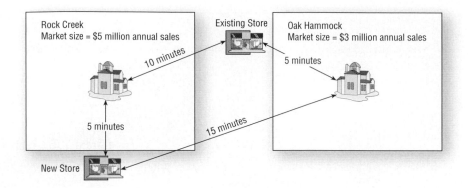

locations, the lower the probability that the consumer will shop at the location. Generally, customers would rather shop at a close store than a distant one.

The exponent λ reflects the relative effect of travel time versus store size. When λ is equal to 1, store size and travel time have an equal but opposite effect on the probability of a consumer shopping at a store location. When λ is greater than 1, travel time has a greater effect, and when λ is less than 1, store size has a greater effect. The value of λ is affected by the nature of the shopping trips consumers generally take when visiting the specific type of store. For instance, travel time or distance is generally more important for convenience goods than for specialty goods because people are less willing to travel a great distance for a quart of milk than they are for a new pair of shoes. Thus, a larger value for λ is assigned if the store being studied specializes in convenience goods rather than specialty goods. The value of λ is usually estimated statistically using data that describe shopping patterns at existing stores.

To illustrate the use of the Huff model, consider the situations shown in Exhibit 8–9. A small town has two communities, Rock Creek and Oak Hammock. The town currently has one 5,000 square foot drugstore with annual sales of $8 million, $3 million of which come from Oak Hammock residents and $5 million from Rock Creek residents. A competitive chain is considering opening a 10,000 square foot store. As the exhibit illustrates, the driving time for the average Rock Creek resident to the existing store is ten minutes but would only be five minutes to the new store. In contrast, the driving time for the typical Oak Hammock resident to the existing drug store is five minutes and would be fifteen minutes to the new store. Based on its past experience, the drug store chain has found that λ equals 2 for its store locations. Using the Huff formula, the probability of a Rock Creek resident shopping at the new location, P_{RC}, is

$$P_{RC} = \frac{10,000/5^2}{10,000/5^2 + 5,000/10^2} = .889.$$

The probability of Oak Hammock residents shopping at the new location, P_{OH}, is

$$P_{OH} = \frac{10,000/15^2}{10,000/15^2 + 5,000/5^2} = .182.$$

The expected sales (probability of patronage times market size) for the new location thus would be

.889 × $5 million + .182 × $3 million = $4,991,000.

This simple application assumes that the market size for drug stores in the community will remain the same at $8 million with the addition of the new store. We also could have considered that two drug stores would increase the total size of the market. In addition, rather than do the calculations for the average customer located in the middle of each community, we could have calculated the probabilities that each customer in the two communities would go to the new location.

Even though the Huff gravity model only considers two factors affecting store sales—travel time and store size—its predictions are quite accurate because these two factors typically have the greatest effect on store choice.[14] The regression approach discussed in the next section provides a way to incorporate additional factors into the sales forecast for a store under consideration.

Regression Analysis

The **regression analysis** approach is based on the assumption that factors that affect the sales of existing stores in a chain will have the same impact on stores located at new sites being considered. When using this approach, the retailer employs a technique called multiple regression to estimate a statistical model that predicts sales at existing store locations. The technique can consider the effects of the wide range of factors discussed in this chapter, including site characteristics, such as visibility and access, and characteristics of the trade area, such as demographics and lifestyle segments represented.

Consider the following example: A chain of sporting goods stores has analyzed the factors affecting sales in its existing stores and found that the following model is the best predictor of store sales (the weights for the factors, such as 275 for the number of households, are estimated using multiple regression):

Stores sales = 275 × number of households in trade area (15-minute drive time)
    + 1,800,000 × percentage of households in trade area with children under 15 years of age
    + 2,000,000 × percentage of households in trade area in Tapestry segment "aspiring young"
    + 8 × shopping center square feet
    + 250,000 if visible from street
    + 300,000 if Wal-Mart in center.

The sporting goods chain is considering the following two locations:

Variable	Location A	Location B
Households within 15 minute drive time	11,000	15,000
% of households with children under 15 years old	70%	20%
% of households in aspiring young geodemographic segment	60%	10%
Sq ft of shopping center	200,000	250,000
Visible from street	yes	no
Wal-Mart in shopping center	yes	no

Using the statistical model, the forecasted sales for location A are:

Stores sales at location A = $7,635,000 = 275 × 11,000
    + 1,800,000 × 0.7
    + 2,000,000 × 0.6
    + 8 × 200,000
    + 250,000
    + 300,000,

and forecasted sales for location B are:

Store sales at location B = $6,685,000 = 275 × 15,000
    + 1,800,000 × 0.2
    + 2,000,000 × 0.1
    + 8 × 250,000.

Note that location A has greater forecasted sales, even though it has a smaller trading area population and shopping center size, because the profile of its target market fits the profile of the trade area better.

Analog Approach

To develop a regression model, a retailer needs data about the trade area and site characteristics from a large number of stores. Because small chains cannot use the regression approach, they use the similar but more subjective analog approach. When using the **analog approach,** the retailer simply describes the site and trade area characteristics for its most successful stores and attempts to find a site with similar characteristics. The use of this approach is described in the following illustration.

ILLUSTRATION OF SITE SELECTION: EDWARD BEINER OPTICAL

Edward Beiner Optical is a six-store Florida retailer specializing in upper-end, high-fashion eyewear. Its store in South Miami is in a Main Street location. Although a Main Street location does not draw from a trade area as large as a central business district or a shopping center, it serves the people working and living in the area.

The retailers in this Main Street location recognize that their location lacks the entertainment and recreation found in shopping centers, so they sponsor art and music festivals to bring people to the area. On Halloween, each store provides candy to its future customers and their parents.

Edward Beiner Optical recognizes other issues that make its South Miami Main Street location less than perfect. There's no protection against the heavy rains that characterize the area's subtropical climate. Security also could be an issue, though most stores are closed at night (when most of their customers have time to shop). Although most of the stores in the area cater to upscale customers living in surrounding neighborhoods, the tenant mix is not always balanced. For instance, Edward Beiner shares its block with a secondhand clothing store and an inexpensive diner. Finally, parking is often a problem.

In general though, Edward Beiner finds its Main Street location attractive. The rent is much less than it would be in a shopping mall. There is usually good pedestrian traffic. Because the properties in the Main Street location are owned by several individuals, the landlords have less control over the tenants than they would in a

Edward Beiner Optical specializes in high-fashion eyewear and targets affluent consumers.

Competitive Analysis of Potential Locations   **EXHIBIT 8–10**

Trade Area (1)	Eyeglasses/ Year/ Person (2)	Trade Area Population (3)	Total Eyeglasses Potential (4)	Estimated Eyeglasses Sold (5)	Trade Area Potential Units (6)	Trade Area Potential Percentage (7)	Relative Level of Competition (8)
South Miami	0.2	85,979	17,196	7,550	9,646	56.09%	Low
Site A	0.2	91,683	18,337	15,800	2,537	13.83	Medium
Site B	0.2	101,972	20,394	12,580	7,814	38.32	Low
Site C	0.2	60,200	12,040	11,300	740	6.15	High
Site D	0.2	81,390	16,278	13,300	2,978	18.29	Medium

planned shopping center. Finally, though there are other optical stores in the area, the competition is not intense due to the exclusive lines Edward Beiner carries.

Edward Beiner Optical wants to open a new location. Because the South Miami site is its best store, it would like to find a location whose trade area has similar characteristics. It has identified several potential locations that it is evaluating.

Using the analog approach, Edward Beiner undertakes the following steps:

1. Do a competitive analysis.
2. Define present trade area.
3. Analyze trade area characteristics.
4. Match characteristics of present trade area with potential sites.

Competitive Analysis

The competitive analysis of the four potential sites being considered by Edward Beiner is shown in Exhibit 8–10. To perform the analysis, Edward Beiner first estimated the number of eyeglasses sold per year per person (column 2), obtained from industry sources. Then the area population was taken from information provided by ESRI (column 3). Column 4 is an estimate of the trade area potential reached by multiplying column 2 times column 3.

The estimates of the number of eyeglasses sold in the trade areas, column 5, are based on visits to competitive stores. Column 6 represents the unit sales potential for eyeglasses in the trade areas, or column 4 minus column 5. Then the trade area potential penetration is calculated by dividing column 6 by column 4. For instance, because the total eyeglasses potential for the South Miami store trade area is 17,196 pairs and an additional 9,646 pairs could be sold in that trade area, 56.09 percent of the eyeglasses market in this area remains untapped. The bigger the number, the lower the competition. Column 8, the relative level of competition, is subjectively estimated on the basis of column 7.

Unlike other optical stores in the trade area, Edward Beiner Optical carries a very exclusive merchandise selection. In general, however, the higher the trade area potential, the lower the relative competition will be.

On the basis of the information in Exhibit 8–10, Edward Beiner Optical should locate its new store at site B. The trade area potential is high, and competition is relatively low. Of course, relative competition is only one issue to consider. Later in this section, we'll consider competition along with other issues to determine which is the best new location for Edward Beiner Optical.

Define Present Trade Area

On the basis of customer spotting data gathered from its data warehouse of current customers, the trade area map in Exhibit 8–11 was generated using ESRI's GIS. The zones are based on drive times: 5 minutes for the primary trade area (red), 10 minutes for the secondary trade area (purple), and 20 minutes for the tertiary trade area (green). Note that the trade area boundaries are oblong because the major highways, especially U.S. 1, run north and south. Not only do the

EXHIBIT 8–11   Trade Area for Edward Beiner Optical

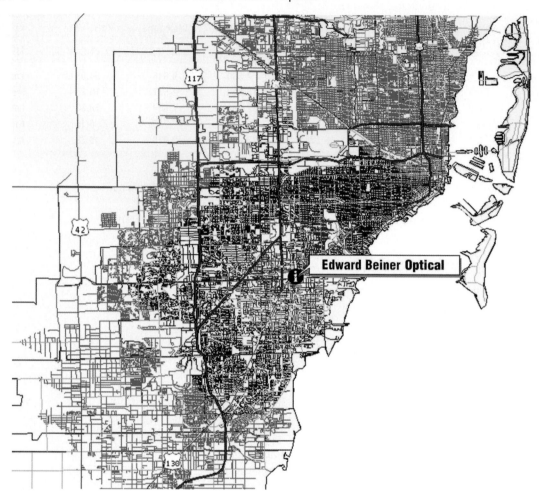

north–south highways bring traffic to the area, but heavy traffic often makes them difficult to cross. Biscayne Bay also limits the trade area on the east.

Because Edward Beiner Optical has a Main Street location, its trade area is smaller than it would be if it were located in a regional shopping mall. However, Edward Beiner Optical is one of several optical shops in this business district. Having similar shopping goods stores in the same vicinity expands its trade area boundaries; more people are drawn to the area to shop because of its expanded selection. In addition, Edward Beiner Optical's trade area is limited on the south by a large regional shopping center that has several stores carrying similar merchandise.

Trade Area Characteristics

Having defined its trade area, Edward Beiner Optical reviewed a number of reports describing the characteristics of its trade area according to the ESRI GIS. Some of interesting findings from these reports were

- The average household income is $92,653. In addition, 27.6 percent of the households have incomes between $75,000 and $149,000, and 13.7 percent have incomes over $150,000. The three-mile ring surrounding Edward Beiner Optical is very affluent.

- The area surrounding Edward Beiner Optical has a population that is 53.1 percent Hispanic.

- The major geodemographic segments in the trade area are High-Rise Renters, Thriving Immigrants, Top One Percenters, and Wealthy Seaboard Suburbs.

Four Potential Locations for a New Edward Beiner Optical Store **EXHIBIT 8-12**

Store Location	Average Household Income	White-Collar Occupations	Percentage Residents Age 45 and Over	Predominant Geodemographic Segments	Level of Competition
Edward Beiner Optical	$100,000	High	37%	Top One Percent	Low
Site A	60,000	High	25	Young Immigrant Families	Medium
Site B	70,000	Low	80	Gray Power	Low
Site C	100,000	High	30	Young Literate	High
Site D	120,000	High	50	Upper-Income Empty-Nesters	Medium

Match Characteristics of Present Trade Area with Potential Sites

Edward Beiner Optical believes that the profile of its current trade area is high income, predominantly white-collar occupations, a relatively large percentage of older residents, upscale geodemographic segments, and relatively low competition for expensive, high-fashion eyewear. Exhibit 8–12 compares Edward Beiner's current location with four potential locations on these five factors.

Although the potential customers of site A typically have white-collar occupations, they also have relatively low incomes and are comparatively young. Young Immigrant Families also tend to have young families, so expensive eyewear may not be a priority purchase. Finally, there's a medium level of competition in the area.

The Gray Power residents surrounding site B have moderate incomes and are mostly retired. Even though competition would be low and most residents need glasses, these customers are more interested in value than in fashion.

Site C has strong potential because the Young Literate residents in the area are young and have a strong interest in fashion. Although working, they are busy furnishing their first homes and apartments and paying off college loans. They probably would appreciate Edward Beiner's fashionable assortment, but they won't appreciate the high prices. Also, other high-end optical stores are entrenched in the area.

Site D is the best location for Edward Beiner. The residents are older professionals or early retirees with high incomes. Upper-Income Empty-Nesters are sophisticated consumers of adult luxuries like high-fashion eyewear. Importantly, this geodemographic segment is similar to Top One Percenters and Wealthy Seaboard Suburbs—two large segments in Edward Beiner's current location.

Finding analogous situations isn't always as easy as in this example. The weaker the analogy, the more difficult the location decision will be. When a retailer has a relatively small number of outlets (say, 20 or fewer), the analog approach is often best. Even retailers with just one outlet like Edward Beiner Optical can use the analog approach. As the number of stores increases, it becomes more difficult for the analyst to organize the data in a meaningful way. More analytical approaches, such as regression analysis, then are necessary.

NEGOTIATING A LEASE

Once a particular site is chosen, retailers still face a multitude of decisions, including the types and terms of the lease.

Types of Leases

Most retailers lease store sites. Although there are advantages to owning a store site (such as stable mortgage payments and freedom from lease covenants), most retailers don't wish to tie up their capital by owning real estate. Also, most of the best locations—such as in shopping malls—are only available by leasing. There are two basic types of leases: percentage and fixed-rate.

Percentage Leases   Although there are many combinations within each type of lease, the most common form is a **percentage lease,** in which the rent is based on a percentage of sales. In addition to the percentage of sales, retailers typically pay a maintenance fee based on a percentage of their square footage of leased space. Most malls use some form of percentage lease. Because retail leases typically run for five to ten years, they appear equitable to both parties if rents go up (or down) with sales and inflation.

A **percentage lease with a specified maximum** is a lease that pays the lessor, or landlord, a percentage of sales up to a maximum amount. This type of lease rewards good retailer performance by allowing the retailer to hold rent constant above a certain level of sales. A similar variation, the **percentage lease with a specified minimum,** specifies that the retailer must pay a minimum rent, no matter how low sales are.

Another type of percentage lease is a **sliding scale lease** in which the percentage of sales paid as rent decreases as the sales go up. For instance, a retailer may pay 4 percent on the first $200,000 in sales and then 3 percent on sales greater than $200,000. Similar to the percentage lease with a specified maximum, the sliding scale rewards high-performing retailers.

Fixed-Rate Leases   The second basic type of lease is a **fixed-rate lease,** most commonly used by community and neighborhood centers. A retailer pays a fixed amount per month over the life of the lease. With a fixed-rate lease, the retailer and landlord know exactly how much will be paid in rent, but as noted previously, this type of lease does not appear as popular as the various forms of percentage leases.

A variation of the fixed-rate lease is the **graduated lease,** in which rent increases by a fixed amount over a specified period of time. For instance, rent may be $1,000 per month for the first three years and $1,250 for the next five years.

A **maintenance-increase–recoupment lease** can be used with either a percentage or fixed-rate lease. This type of lease allows the landlord to increase the rent if insurance, property taxes, or utility bills increase beyond a certain point.

Terms of the Lease

Although leases are formal contracts, they can be changed to reflect the relative power and specific needs of the retailer. Because the basic format of most leases is developed by the lessor (the property owner), the lease's terms may be slanted in favor of the lessor. It is therefore up to the lessee (the party signing the lease, in this case, the retailer) to be certain that the lease reflects the lessee's needs. Let's look at some clauses retailers may wish to include in a lease.

Prohibited Use Clause   A **prohibited use clause** limits the landlord from leasing to certain kinds of tenants. Many retailers don't want the landlord to lease space to establishments that take up a lot of parking spaces but do not bring in shoppers, such as a bowling alley, skating rink, meeting hall, dentist, or real estate office. Retailers may also wish to restrict the use of space from those establishments that could harm the shopping center's wholesome image. Prohibited use clauses often specify that bars, pool halls, game parlors, off-track betting establishments, massage parlors, and pornography retailers are unacceptable.

Exclusive Use Clause   An **exclusive use clause** prohibits the landlord from leasing to retailers that sell competing products. For example, a discount store's lease may specify that the landlord cannot lease to other discount stores, variety stores, extreme value stores, or discount clothing outlet stores.

Some retailers also are particular about how the storefront appears. For instance, a women's specialty store may specify that the storefront must have floor-to-ceiling glass to maximize window displays to improve customers' ability to see into the store. Other retailers believe it is important that nothing blocks the view of the store from the street, so they specify that the landlord cannot place any outparcels in the parking lot. An **outparcel** is a building (like a bank or McDonald's) or kiosk (like an automatic teller machine) that sits in the parking lot of a shopping center but is not physically attached to the center.

It is crucial to some retailers that they be in shopping centers with specific types of tenants. For instance, a chain of moderately priced women's apparel shops benefits from the traffic flow of Kmart and Wal-Mart stores. It therefore specifies in its leases that if the major retailer leaves the shopping center, it has the option of canceling its lease or paying a reduced rent.

Escape Clause   An interesting feature that any retailer would want to have in a lease, if it could get away with it, is an escape clause. An **escape clause** allows the retailer to terminate its lease if sales don't reach a certain level after a specified number of years or if a specific co-tenant in the center terminates its lease.

SUMMARY

Location decisions have great strategic importance because they have significant effects on store choice and are difficult advantages for competitors to duplicate. Picking good sites for locating stores is part science and part art.

Some factors retailers consider when evaluating an area to locate stores are (1) the economic conditions, (2) competition, (3) the strategic fit of the area's population with the retailer's target market, and (4) the costs of operating stores. Having selected an area to locate stores, the next decision is how many stores to operate in that area.

When making the decision about how many stores to open in an area, retailers have to consider the trade-offs between lower operating costs and potential cannibalization from multiple stores in an area. Most retail chains open multiple stores in an area because promotion and distribution economies of scale can be achieved. Although scale economies can be gained from opening multiple locations in an area, there also are diminishing returns associated with locating too many additional stores in an area due to cannibalization.

The next step for a retailer is to evaluate and select a specific site. In making this decision, retailers consider three factors: (1) the characteristic of the site, (2) the characteristics of the trading area for a store at the site, and (3) the estimated potential sales that can be generated by a store at the site.

Trade areas are typically divided into primary, secondary, and tertiary zones. The boundaries of a trade area are determined by how accessible it is to customers, the natural and physical barriers that exist in the area, the type of shopping area in which the store is located, the type of store, and the level of competition.

Once retailers have the data that describe their trade areas, they use several analytical techniques to estimate demand. The Huff gravity model predicts the probability that a customer will choose a particular store in a trade area, based on the premise that customers are more likely to shop at a given store or shopping center if it is conveniently located and offers a large selection. Regression analysis is a statistically based model that estimates the effects of a variety of factors on existing store sales and uses that information to predict sales for a new site. The analog approach—one of the easiest to use—can be particularly useful for smaller retailers. Using the same logic as regression analysis, the retailer can make predictions about sales by a new store based on sales in stores in similar areas.

Finally, retailers need to negotiate the terms of a lease. These lease terms affect the cost of the location and may restrict retailing activities.

KEY TERMS

accessibility, *223*
analog approach, *238*
artificial barrier, *223*
block group, *231*
census, *230*
census block, *231*
congestion, *224*
cumulative attraction, *225*
customer spotting, *229*

escape clause, *243*
exclusive use
   clause, *242*
fixed-rate lease, *242*
fringe, *227*
geographic information
   system (GIS), *231*
graduated lease, *242*
Huff gravity model, *235*

maintenance–increase–recoupment
   lease, *242*
metropolitan statistical
   area (MSA), *218*
micropolitan statistical area, *218*
natural barrier, *223*
outparcel, *243*
parasite store, *229*
percentage lease, *242*

GET OUT AND DO IT!

1. **CONTINUING CASE ASSIGN-MENT** Evaluate the location of a store operated by the retailer you have selected for the continuing case assignment. What is the size and shape of the retailer's trade area? Describe the positive and negative aspects of its location. Compare the store's location with the locations of its competitors.

2. See if the expression "birds of a feather flock together" really is true and if similar groups are clustered together by going to www.claritas.com/MyBestSegments/Default.jsp?ID=20. Type in the zip code for your home or school address. Does the information you get accurately describe you and your family? Compare the Claritas description to the one provided by ESRI at www.gis.com under "Zip Code Fast Facts." Note the similarities and differences in these two reports for the same zip code.

3. Go to www.gis.com, the homepage for ESRI Geographical Information Systems, and click on "Demo: What is GIS?" After watching the three-minute video, explain how retailers can make better decisions with GIS.

4. The U.S. Census Bureau tracks key population characteristics, such as age, gender, disability, employment, income, language, poverty, race, and so forth. Go to the U.S. Census Bureau homepage at http://factfinder.census.gov/home/saff/main.html?_lang=en and, using the Population Finder, look up key demographic data for your state. Which segmentation characteristics are changing for this location? Why? Which factors would be most importat for retailers considering this location to evaluate?

5. Go to a shopping mall. Get or draw a map of the stores. Analyze whether the stores are clustered in some logical manner. For instance, are all the high-end stores together? Is there a good mix of retailers catering to comparison shoppers near one another?

6. Visit a jewelry store in an enclosed mall and one in a neighborhood strip shopping center. List the pros and cons for each location. Which location is the most desirable? Why is this the case?

7. Go to the student side of the book's Web site and click on "Location." You will see an Excel spreadsheet that contains the sales for 45 retail locations of a sporting goods retail chain, plus the characteristics of each location: number of households in trading area, percentage of households with children under 15 years old, percentage of households in appropriate Tapestry segments that the retailer is targeting, distance from a Wal-Mart store, and distance from a Sports Authority store. Estimate a multiple regression model that predicts sales as a function of the site characteristics, and use the estimate weights to evaluate the two sites at the bottom of the spreadsheet.

DISCUSSION QUESTIONS AND PROBLEMS

1. Which factors do retailers consider when evaluating an area of the country to locate stores? How do retailers determine the trade area for a store?

2. When measuring trade areas, why is the analog approach not a good choice for a retailer with several hundred outlets?

3. True Value Hardware plans to open a new store. Two sites are available, both in middle-income neighborhood centers. One neighborhood is 20 years old and has been well maintained. The other was recently built in a newly planned community. Which site is preferable for True Value? Why?

4. Trade areas are often described as concentric circles emanating from the store or shopping center. Why is this practice used? Suggest an alternative method. Which would you use if you owned a store in need of a trade area analysis?

5. Under what circumstances might a retailer use the analog approach for estimating demand for a new store? What about regression analysis?

6. Some specialty stores prefer to locate next to or close to an anchor store. But Little Caesars, a takeout pizza retailer typically found in strip centers, prefers to be at the end of the center, away from the supermarket anchor. Why?

7. Retailers have a choice of locating on a mall's main floor or second or third level. Typically, the main floor offers the best, but most expensive, locations. Why would specialty stores such as Radio Shack and Foot Locker choose the second or third floor?

8. What retail locations are best for department stores, consumer electronics category killers, specialty apparel stores, and warehouse stores? Discuss your rationale.

9. If you were considering the ownership of a Taco Bell franchise, what would you want to know about the location in terms of traffic, population, income, employment, and competition? What else would you need to research about a potential location?

10. A drugstore is considering opening a new location at shopping center A, with hopes of capturing sales from a new neighborhood under construction. Two nearby shopping centers, B and C, will provide competition. Using the following information and the Huff gravity model, determine the probability that residents of the new neighborhood will shop at shopping center A:

Shopping center	Size (000's sq. ft.)	Distance from new neighborhood (miles)
A	3,500	4
B	1,500	5
C	300	3

Assume that $\lambda = 2$.

SUGGESTED READINGS

Birkin, Mark; Graham Clarke; and Martin Clarke. *Retail Geography and Intelligent Network Planning*. Chichester, UK: Wiley, 2002.

Chen, Rachel J. C. "Significance and Variety of Geographic Information System (GIS) Applications in Retail, Hospitality, Tourism, and Consumer Services." *Journal of Retailing and Consumer Services* 14, no. 4 (2007), pp. 247–48.

DeMers, Michael N. *Fundamentals of Geographic Information Systems*. New York: Wiley Publishing, 2002.

González-Benito, Óscar; César Bustos-Reyes; and Pablo Muñoz-Gallego. "Isolating the Geodemographic Characterisation of Retail Format Choice from the Effects of Spatial Convenience." *Marketing Letters* 18, no. 1/2 (2007), pp. 45–59.

Hernandez, Tony. "Enhancing Retail Location Decision Support: The Development and Application of Geovisualization." *Journal of Retailing and Consumer Services* 14, no. 4 (2007), pp. 249–58.

Maantay, Juliana; John Ziegler; and John Pickles. *GIS for the Urban Environment*. ESRI Publishing, 2006.

Miller, Fred; Glynn W. Mangold; and Terry Holmes. "Integrating Geographic Information Systems (GIS) Applications into Business Courses Using Online Business Geographics Modules." *Journal of Education for Business* 82, no. 2 (2006), pp. 74–79.

Peterson, Keith (ed.). *The Power of Place: Advanced Customer and Location Analytics for Market Planning*. San Diego: Integras, 2004.

Wood, Steve; and Sue Browne. "Convenience Store Location Planning and Forecasting—a Practical Research." *International Journal of Retail and Distribution Management* 35, no. 4 (2007), pp. 233–55.

Human Resource Management

EXECUTIVE BRIEFING

Derek Jenkins, Senior Vice President–Northeast Region, Target

I attended Appalachian State University on a football scholarship, majoring in Information Systems/Management. When I graduated, I recognized that a career with the NFL was likely not in my future. Looking for my first job, I knew that I wanted to work with people and find a way to use the team skills that I had developed while playing football. I never imagined that I would end up in retail.

I was offered a good opportunity with a regional department store chain and eventually went to work for Target as a store manager. I was promoted to district manager in charge of 12 stores, then group director responsible for 70 stores, and eventually promoted to Vice President of Store Operations.

As Vice President of Store Operations, I championed the development and implementation of several systems that we use at Target, including a new way of scheduling employees or "Team Members" that allows us to provide excellent customer or "Guest" service at peak periods while controlling our labor costs. I also was involved with creating best practices and selecting equipment that helps our store teams work more efficiently.

After having this broadening experience, I was promoted to my present position as Senior Vice President of our 350-plus stores in the northeast region of the country. In this role, I am directly involved with each store, from openings to remodeling to helping build world-class teams and relationships with the leaders in our communities.

Working for Target brings up many of the things that I liked about playing football. I am a driven individual who likes competition, and I want the stores in my region to perform well. One of the nice things about working in this industry is that you get a scorecard. If your department, store, district, or region performs well, you and your coworkers feel a rewarding sense of accomplishment. In

CHAPTER 9

QUESTIONS

In what way does the management of human resources play a vital role in a retailer's performance?

How do retailers build a sustainable competitive advantage by developing and managing their human resources?

What activities do retail employees undertake, and how are they typically organized?

How does a retailer coordinate employees' activities and motivate them to work toward the retailer's goals?

What are the human resource management programs for building a committed workforce?

How and why do retailers manage diversity among their employees?

retail, there is not a lot of subjectivity in evaluating performance—and you know when you have scored a touchdown.

The other aspect of football that I see in retail is being part of a team and working closely with others to accomplish goals. Team is a priority at Target. We call our store and department managers "Team Leaders," and they are expected to create a strong sense of morale in their stores and to develop their employees or "Team Members" so that everyone has the opportunity to achieve his or her career goals.

Target's team orientation goes beyond our stores and is reflected by our commitment to being a good community partner. Our store team leaders are encouraged to build local relationships and to help improve the social, economic, and environmental well-being of their communities. This year alone, Target team members, retirees, and families will donate more than 300,000 hours to volunteer initiatives, and from a corporate philanthropy perspective, Target is an industry leader and gave 5 percent of its income, totaling $3 million a week in 2007, to making a positive impact in education, social services and the arts.

Retailers achieve their financial objectives by effectively managing their five critical assets: locations, merchandise inventory, stores, employees, and customers. This chapter focuses on the organization and management of employees—the retailer's human resources. As Howard Schultz, CEO of Starbucks, emphasizes, "the relationship that we have with our people and the culture of our company is our most sustainable competitive advantage."[1]

Sherry Hollock, Vice President of Organization Development at Macy's, emphasizes the importance of human resources in retailing: "One of the biggest challenges facing Macy's, and most other retail chains, is hiring and retaining managers to lead our company in the coming years. The changing demographics are working against our hiring and retention objectives. Over the next ten years, a lot of our senior managers, members of the Baby Boomer generation, will be retiring. So we are going to be competing with other retailers and firms in other industries for a smaller pool of available managers in the generations behind the Boomers. In addition, retailing is becoming a much more sophisticated business. Our managers need to be comfortable with new technologies, information and supply chain management systems, and international business as well as managing a diverse workforce and buying merchandise."[2]

Human resource management is particularly important in retailing because employees play a major role in performing its critical business functions. In manufacturing firms, capital equipment (machinery, computer systems, robotics) often is used to perform the jobs employees once did. But retailing and other service businesses remain labor intensive. Retailers still rely on people to perform the basic retailing activities, such as buying, displaying merchandise, and providing service to customers.

Two chapters in this text are devoted to human resource management because it is such an important issue for the performance of retail firms. This chapter focuses on the broad strategic issues involving organization structure; the general approaches used for motivating and coordinating employee activities; and the management practices for building an effective, committed workforce and reducing turnover.

The activities undertaken to implement the retailer's human resource strategy, including recruiting, selecting, training, supervising, evaluating, and compensating sales associates, are typically undertaken by store management. Such operational issues will be discussed in more detail in Chapter 17 in the Store Management section of this textbook.

GAINING COMPETITIVE ADVANTAGE THROUGH HUMAN RESOURCE MANAGEMENT

REFACT

A study of Sears' employees found that a 5 percent increase in employee satisfaction resulted in a 1.3 percent increase in customer satisfaction, which led to a 0.5 percent growth in sales.[3]

Human resource management can be the basis of a sustainable competitive advantage for three reasons. First, labor costs account for a significant percentage of a retailer's total expenses. Thus, the effective management of employees can produce a cost advantage. Second, the experience that most customers have with a retailer is determined by the activities of employees who select merchandise, provide information and assistance, and stock displays and shelves. Thus, employees can play a major role in differentiating a retailer's offering from its competitor's. Third, these potential advantages are difficult for competitors to duplicate. For example, every department store executive knows that Nordstrom employees provide outstanding customer service; however, they are not able to develop the same customer-oriented culture in their firms. Retailing View 9.1 describes how Men's Wearhouse built a competitive advantage through effective human resource management.

Objectives of Human Resource Management

The strategic objective of human resource management is to align the capabilities and behaviors of employees with the short- and long-term goals of the retail firm. One human resource management performance measure is **employee productivity**—the retailer's sales or profit divided by the number of employees. Employee productivity can be improved by increasing the sales generated by existing employees, reducing the number of employees without affecting sales, or both.

Whereas employee productivity is directly related to the retailer's short-term profits, employee attitudes, such as job satisfaction and commitment, have important effects on customer satisfaction and loyalty and the subsequent long-term performance of the retailer. In addition to survey measures of these attitudes, a behavioral measure of these attitudes is employee turnover. **Employee turnover** equals

$$\frac{\text{Number of employees leaving their job during the year}}{\text{Number of positions}}.$$

So if a store owner had five sales associate positions but three employees left and were replaced during the year, the turnover would be $3 \div 5 = 60$ percent. Note that turnover can be greater than 100 percent if a substantial number of people are replaced more than once during the year. In our example, if the replacements for the three employees that left also left during the year, the turnover would be $6 \div 5 = 120$ percent.

A failure to consider both long- and short-term objectives can result in the mismanagement of human resources and a downward performance spiral, as shown in

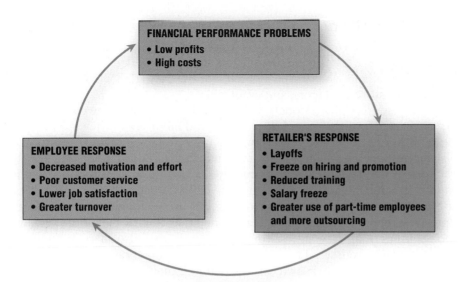

EXHIBIT 9–1
Downward Performance
Spiral

Exhibit 9–1. Sometimes, when retailers' sales and profits decline due to increased competition, they respond by decreasing labor costs. They reduce the number of sales associates in stores, hire more part-timers, and spend less on training. Although these actions may increase short-term productivity and profits, they have an adverse effect on long-term performance because employee morale and customer service decline.[4]

The Men's Wearhouse: Using Human Resources to Build a Competitive Advantage   RETAILING VIEW   9.1

While the sale of men's tailored clothing has declined during the past 30 years, Men's Wearhouse, founded by George Zimmer when he was only 24 years of age, has continued to gain market share, becoming one of the largest specialty retailers of men's apparel in North America. Men's Wearhouse sales have grown to over $1.8 billion through more than 1,200 retail store locations in the United States and Canada.

The core of the company's strategy is to offer superior customer service delivered by knowledgeable, caring salespeople, called wardrobe consultants. The term *wardrobe consultant* was chosen intentionally to emphasize that sales associates are professionals, like physicians or attorneys.

George Zimmer believes in a win–win–win philosophy, in which the customer, the wardrobe consultant, and the company all do well. Because the company believes that its job is to develop the untapped human potential in its employees, it devotes considerable attention to training. Some of Men's Wearhouse's core philosophies include the following:

Fulfillment at Work   Job satisfaction—everyone wants to have it. So how does Men's Wearhouse help its employees find it? It all starts with trust and respect.

Don't Be Afraid of Mistakes   You can tell a lot about a company by observing the way they handle mistakes. Men's Wearhouse focuses on the learning opportunities that mistakes provide. It likes to say that it celebrates its successes and its failures.

Balancing Work and Family Life   Men's Wearhouse encourages employees to balance the worlds inside and outside of the workplace.

Having Fun at Work with Friends   A workplace filled with fun among friends is GOOD for business.

Celebrate Individual and Team Success   Men's Wearhouse recognizes that individual and team excellence

Extensive training and teamwork enable Men's Wearhouse sales personnel to provide excellent customer service and build a competitive advantage for the firm.

are interrelated—they support each other. That's why it celebrates both individual and team achievements.

Promote from Within   Skills and experience at a job are only part of the picture. When picking its leaders, it looks for people who care about others, take the time to listen, and show enthusiasm when working toward team and individual goals. That's why it promotes people it already knows.

Source: Sharon Edelson, "The Training Advantage," *WWD*, April 2, 2007, p. 14; "Give People a Second Chance" *Business 2.0*, May 2007, p. 67; Men's Wearhouse 2007 Annual Report, http://www.menswearhouse.com (accessed September 14, 2007).

The Human Resource Triad

Many retailers believe that human resources are too important to be left to the human resources (HR) department. The full potential of a retailer's human resources is realized when three elements of the HR triad work together—HR professionals, store managers, and employees.

Human resources professionals, who typically work out of the corporate office, have specialized knowledge of HR practices and labor laws. They are responsible for establishing HR policies that reinforce the retailer's strategy and provide the tools and training used by line managers and employees to implement those policies. Store or line managers, who primarily work in the stores, are responsible for bringing the policies to life through their daily management of the employees who work for them. The issues confronting HR professionals are discussed in this chapter; Chapter 17, in the Store Management section of this book, reviews the responsibilities of line managers. Finally, the employees also share in the management of human resources. They can play an active role by providing feedback on the policies, managing their own careers, defining their job functions, and evaluating the performance of their managers and coworkers. These three elements of the HR triad are illustrated in Exhibit 9–2.

Special HR Conditions Facing Retailers

Human resource management in retailing is very challenging due to (1) the need to use part-time employees, (2) the emphasis on expense control, and (3) the changing demographics of the workforce. Retailers operating in international markets face additional challenges.

Part-Time Employees   Most retailers are open long hours and weekends to respond to the needs of family shoppers and working people. In addition, peak shopping periods occur during lunch hours, at night, and during sales. To deal with these peak periods and long hours, retailers have to complement their one or two shifts of full-time (40 hours per week) store employees with part-time workers. Part-time workers can be more difficult to manage than full-time employees because they often are less committed to the company and their jobs and more likely to quit than full-time employees.

Expense Control   Retailers must control their expenses if they are to be profitable. Thus, they are cautious about paying high wages to hourly employees who perform low-skill jobs. To control costs, retailers often hire people with little or no experience to work as sales associates, bank tellers, and waiters. High turnover, absenteeism, and poor performance often result from this use of inexperienced, low-wage employees.

The lack of experience and motivation among many retail employees is particularly troublesome because these employees are often in direct contact with customers. Poor appearance, manners, and attitudes can have a negative effect on

EXHIBIT 9–2
Human Resource Triad

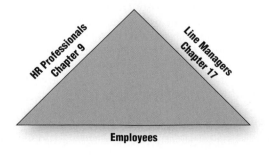

sales and customer loyalty. Research has shown that in some types of retail operations, a modest investment in hiring more staff will result in a significant increase in sales.[6]

Employee Demographics   The changing demographic pattern will result in a chronic shortage of qualified sales associates. Annual percentage growth in the U.S. labor market in 1980 was 14 percent. In 2010, it is forecasted to be only 4 percent and then drop to 2 percent in 2020. Thus, retailers need to explore various approaches for operating effectively in a tight labor market—increase retention; recruit, train, and manage minority, handicapped, and mature workers; and use incentives and technology to increase productivity.

To satisfy their HR needs, retailers will need to increase the diversity of their workforces and employ more minorities, handicapped people, and elderly. The work values of young employees are quite different than those of their Baby Boomer supervisors, which causes many older managers to feel that younger employees have poor work ethics. Younger employees respond by saying, "Get a life," as they strive to balance their personal and professional lives. Managers find it necessary to constantly praise younger workers to keep them motivated, even if it is less than deserved, because these workers have been brought up with constant praise from their parents, teachers, and coaches. Managing this growing diversity and the changing values in the retail workforce creates both opportunities and problems for human resource managers.[9]

More and more retailers are encouraging older workers to work for them, because older workers prove to be more reliable employees. The attraction of older workers stems from their lower turnover rates and often better work performance. Home Depot even offers winter work in Florida and summer work in Maine for retirees who move to follow the nice weather. By building relationships with groups like the American Association of Retired Persons (AARP), Home Depot hopes to help people like military retirees find jobs in the future. Training and recruitment costs are much lower for older people, evening out any increased costs in missed days for medical problems.[10]

International Human Resource Issues   Finally, the management of employees working for international retailers is especially challenging. Differences in work values, economic systems, and labor laws mean that HR practices that are effective in one country might not be effective in another. For example, U.S. retailers rely heavily on individual performance appraisals and rewards tied to individual performance—a practice consistent with the individualistic U.S. culture. However, in countries with a collectivist culture, such as China and Japan, employees downplay individual desires and focus on the needs of the group. Thus, group-based evaluations and incentives are more effective in those countries.[11]

The legal/political system in countries often dictates the human resource management practices that retailers can use. For example, the United States has led the world in eliminating workplace discrimination. However, in Singapore, it is perfectly legal to place an employment ad specifying that candidates must be male, between the ages of 25 and 40 years, and ethnic Chinese. In the Netherlands, a retailer can make a substantial reduction in its workforce only if it demonstrates to the government that the cutback is absolutely necessary. In addition, a Dutch retailer must develop a plan for the cutback, which must then be approved by unions and other involved parties.[12]

Finally, the staffing of management positions in foreign countries raises a wide set of issues. Should management be local, or should expatriates be used? How should the local managers or expatriates be selected, trained, and compensated? For example, at the France-based hypermarket chain Carrefour, a Brazilian might be managing a store in China. The company prides itself in grooming managers for global experiences.

team work.

legal system

management

The following sections of this chapter examine three important strategic issues facing retail HR professionals:

1. The design of the organization structure for assigning responsibility and authority for tasks to people and business units,

2. The approaches used to coordinate the activities of the firm's departments and employees and motivate employees to work toward achieving company goals, and

3. The programs used to build employee commitment and retain valuable human resources.

DESIGNING THE ORGANIZATION STRUCTURE FOR A RETAIL FIRM

The **organization structure** identifies the activities to be performed by specific employees and determines the lines of authority and responsibility in the firm. The first step in developing an organization structure is to determine the tasks that must be performed. Exhibit 9–3 shows tasks typically performed in a retail firm.

These tasks are divided into four major categories in retail firms: strategic management, administrative management (operations), merchandise management, and store management. The organization of this textbook is based on these tasks and the managers who perform them.

EXHIBIT 9–3   Tasks Performed by a Typical Retail Firm

STRATEGIC MANAGEMENT
- Develop a retail strategy
- Identify the target market
- Determine the retail format
- Design organizational structure
- Select locations

MERCHANDISE MANAGEMENT
- Buy merchandise
  - Locate vendors
  - Evaluate vendors
  - Negotiate with vendors
  - Place orders
- Control merchandise inventory
  - Develop merchandise budget plans
  - Allocate merchandise to stores
  - Review open-to-buy and stock position
- Price merchandise
  - Set initial prices
  - Adjust prices

STORE MANAGEMENT
- Recruit, hire, and train store personnel
- Plan work schedules
- Evaluate performance of store personnel
- Maintain store facilities
- Locate and display merchandise
- Sell merchandise to customers
- Repair and alter merchandise
- Provide services such as gift wrapping and delivery
- Handle customer complaints
- Take physical inventory
- Prevent inventory shrinkage

ADMINISTRATIVE MANAGEMENT (OPERATIONS)
- Promote the firm, its merchandise, and its services
  - Plan communication programs
  - Plan special promotions
  - Design special displays
  - Manage public relations
- Manage human resources
  - Develop policies for managing store personnel
  - Recruit, hire, and train managers
  - Keep employee records
- Distribute merchandise
  - Locate warehouses
  - Receive merchandise
  - Store merchandise
  - Ship merchandise to stores
  - Return merchandise to vendors
- Establish financial control
  - Provide timely information on financial performance
  - Forecast sales, cash flow, and profits
  - Raise capital from investors

Section II of this text focuses on strategic and administrative tasks. Strategic market and finance decisions (discussed in Chapters 5 and 6) are undertaken primarily by senior management: the CEO, chief operating officer, vice presidents, and the board of directors that represents shareholders in publicly held firms. Administrative tasks (discussed in Chapters 7–11) are performed by corporate staff employees who have specialized skills in human resource management, finance, accounting, real estate, distribution, and management information systems. People in these administrative functions develop plans, procedures, and information to assist operating managers in implementing the retailer's strategy.

In retail firms, the primary operating or line managers are involved in merchandise management (Section III) and store management (Section IV). These operating managers implement the strategic plans with the assistance of administrative personnel. They make the day-to-day decisions that directly affect the retailer's performance.

To illustrate the connection between the tasks performed in Exhibit 9-3 and the organization structure presented in the following sections, the tasks are color coded. Red is used to represent the strategic tasks, orange for the administrative tasks, brown for the merchandising tasks, and yellow for the store management tasks.

Matching Organization Structure to Retail Strategy

The design of the organization structure needs to match the firm's retail strategy.[13] For example, category specialists and warehouse clubs such as Best Buy and Costco target price-sensitive customers and thus are very concerned about building a competitive advantage based on low cost. They minimize the number of employees by assigning decisions to a few people at corporate headquarters. These centralized organization structures are very effective when there are limited regional or local differences in customer needs.

In contrast, high-fashion clothing customers often aren't very price sensitive, and their tastes vary across the country. Retailers targeting these segments tend to have more managers and make decisions at the local store level. When more decisions are made at the local store level, human resource costs are higher, but sales also increase because the merchandise and services are tailored to meet the needs of local markets. Retailing View 9.2 illustrates how elements of the human resource strategy are used to reinforce PetSmart's strategy.

Organization of a Single-Store Retailer

Initially, the owner–manager of a single store may be the entire organization. When he or she goes to lunch or heads home, the store closes. As sales grow, the owner–manager hires employees. Coordinating and controlling employee activities is easier in a small store than in a large chain of stores; the owner–manager simply assigns tasks to each employee and watches to see that these tasks are performed properly. Because the number of employees is limited, single-store retailers have little **specialization**. Each employee must perform a wide range of activities, and the owner–manager is responsible for all management tasks.

As sales continue to increase, specialization in management may occur when the owner–manager hires additional management employees. Exhibit 9–4 illustrates the common division of management responsibilities into merchandise and store management. The owner–manager continues to perform strategic management tasks. The store manager may be responsible for administrative tasks associated with receiving and shipping merchandising and managing the employees. The merchandise

REFACT

More than 95 percent of all U.S. retailers own and operate a single store, but single-store retailers account for less than 50 percent of all retail store sales.[14]

REFACT

Mellerio dits Meller, the French jeweler founded in 1591, is one of the oldest family-owned retail chains still operating.[15]

EXHIBIT 9–4   Organization Structure for a Small Retailer

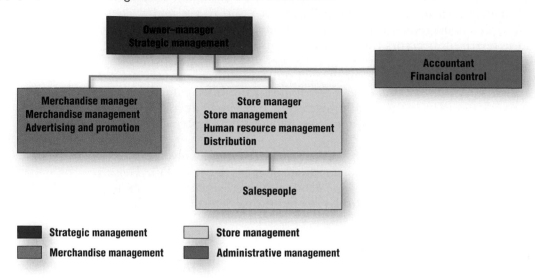

Owner–manager
Strategic management

Accountant
Financial control

Merchandise manager
Merchandise management
Advertising and promotion

Store manager
Store management
Human resource management
Distribution

Salespeople

■ **Strategic management**   □ **Store management**

■ **Merchandise management**   ■ **Administrative management**

9.2   RETAILING VIEW   PetSmart's HR Practices Support Its Retail Strategy

When PetSmart launched its concept for a pet supply category killer in 1988, it followed the lead of other category killers and emphasized its low prices, broad product assortment, limited customer service, and warehouse atmosphere. But it discovered that pet owners wanted more. They viewed their pets as part of the family, not just animals that needed to be fed. They wanted to be good "pet parents" and deal with a company that was as concerned about their pets' health and well-being as they were. Thus, PetSmart undertook a strategy to reposition its brand from category killer to a caring and trusted source of products and service for pets.

To implement this new positioning, PetSmart started to provide some new services in its stores, such as pet grooming, veterinary services, and training classes. Rather than hire veterinarians, the retailer arranged to have the clinics operated by Banfield, The Pet Hospital, a trusted source of "human"-quality medical care for pets. PetSmart also decided to provide facilities and space for shelters to make homeless pets available rather than sell dogs and cats. Finally, the company changed its marketing communications to be less price oriented and more service driven, with all messages highlighting that pets are as welcome in the store as the rest of their family is. Promotional tie-ins with major animal shelters and pet rescue services became major focal points nationally and at the local store level.

PetSmart also recognized that its employees would play a crucial role in the development of a new brand image. Its frontline employees have to understand and accept the brand's values and the promise the brand is making to its customers. To develop these values in its employees, PetSmart changed the criteria it used to select sales associates. The company no longer looks for people who can just stock the shelves; it now hires people who have a deep love for dogs or cats or tropical fish. The groomers in its styling salons love making a pet look

PetSmart hires caring pet groomers and trainers to offer complementary services to pet owners in one convenient location.

beautiful. To develop its employees, PetSmart provides extensive training so that the store employees can become even more knowledgeable about the pets with which they work.

Sources: PetSmart 2007 Annual Report, http://www.petsmart.com (accessed August 15, 2007); http://www.petsmartjobs.com/ (accessed August 15, 2007); Betsy Spethmann "Pet Friendly," *Promo,* February 1, 2007; Patricia Odell, "Play Money," *Promo,* February 1, 2007.

manager or buyer may handle the advertising and promotion tasks, as well as merchandise selection and inventory management tasks. Often the owner–manager contracts with an accounting firm to perform financial control tasks for a fee.

Organization of a National Retail Chain

In contrast to the management of a single store, retail chain management is complex. Managers must supervise units that are geographically distant from one another. In this section, we use Macy's Inc. to illustrate the organization structure for a national retail chain. Macy's Inc. is a corporation consisting of six regionally based divisions of Macy's, Bloomingdale's, the Macy's catalog and Internet channels, and corporate support functions for its regionally based divisions.

Traditionally, retailers were family-owned and -managed. Organization of these firms was governed by family circumstances. Executive positions were designed to accommodate family members involved in the business. Then, in 1927, Paul Mazur proposed a functional organization plan that has since been adopted by most retailers.[16] The organization structures of retail chains, including Macy's Florida, continue to reflect principles of the Mazur plan, such as separating buying and store management tasks into different divisions.

Exhibit 9–5 shows the organization structure of Macy's Florida, one of the six store-based operating divisions of Macy's Inc.'s organization structures. Vice presidents

Organization of Macy's Florida   **EXHIBIT 9–5**

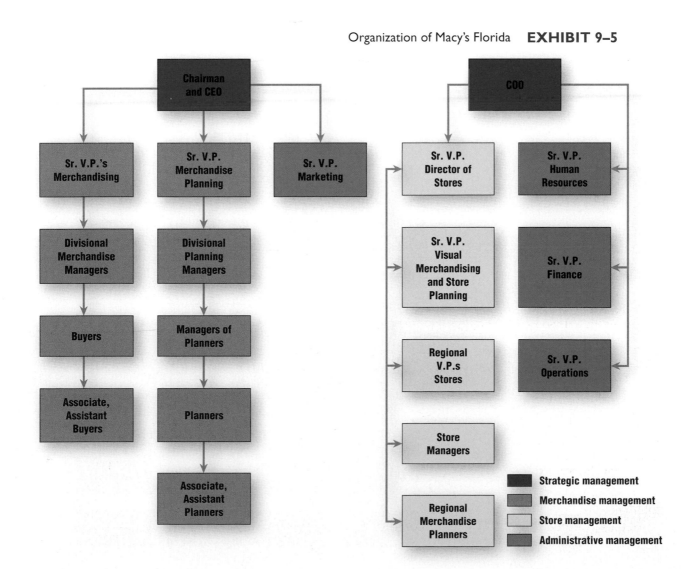

responsible for administrative tasks (orange), specific merchandise categories (brown), and stores (yellow) report to the chairperson and president.

In most retail firms, the two senior executives, typically called the CEO and COO, work closely together to manage the firm. They are frequently referred to as the principals or partners. One member of the partnership is primarily responsible for the merchandising activities of the firm—the merchandise and marketing divisions. The other partner is primarily responsible for the operating divisions—stores, human resources, operations, information systems, and finance divisions. In Macy's Florida, the CEO is responsible for merchandising, whereas the COO is responsible for operations. However, these responsibilities might be switched in other retail firms.

Most managers and employees in the stores division work in stores located throughout the geographic region—in this case, the state of Florida. Merchandise, planning, marketing, finance, visual merchandising, and human resource managers and employees work at corporate headquarters in Miami.

Merchandise Division   The merchandise division is responsible for procuring the merchandise sold in the stores and ensuring that the quality, fashionability, assortment, and pricing of merchandise is consistent with the firm's strategy. Chapters 12 through 15 discuss major activities performed in the merchandise division.

Exhibit 9–6 shows a detailed organization structure of Macy's Florida merchandise division. This exhibit provides a more detailed view of the brown boxes on the left side of Exhibit 9–5. Each senior vice president/general merchandise manager (GMM) is responsible for specific categories of merchandise. The GMMs report directly to the chairperson and CEO, that is, the partner in charge of the merchandising activities.

Buyers   **Buyers** are responsible for procuring merchandise, setting prices and markdowns, and managing inventories for specific merchandise categories. They

EXHIBIT 9–6
Merchandise Division Organization: Macy's Florida

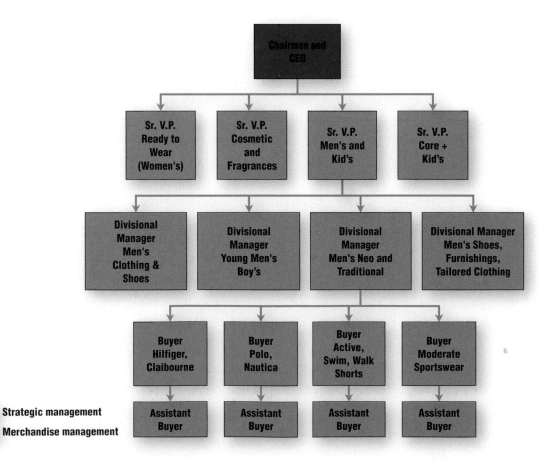

attend trade and fashion shows and negotiate with vendors over prices, quantities, assortments, delivery dates, and payment terms. In addition, they might specify private-label merchandise or request modifications to tailor the merchandise to the retailer's target market and/or differentiate it from competitive offerings.

Although buyers have considerable autonomy to "run their own business," they must adhere to an inventory budget that will vary from season to season. The budget is the result of a negotiation between the buyers and their superiors, the divisional merchandise managers. The issues involved in managing the inventory budget are discussed in Chapters 12 and 13, and merchandise buying activities are reviewed in Chapter 14.

In recent years, the buyer's role in supermarket chains has evolved into a category manager. Traditional supermarket buyers were very vendor focused. For example, they would just be responsible for buying merchandise from a vendor such as Campbell or Kraft. They developed close relationships with vendors and were more concerned with maintaining these vendor relationships than selling products to customers. This focus was partially caused by an evaluation system that rewarded supermarket buyers more for securing price discounts than for sales, gross margins, or inventory turns.

Category managers are responsible for a set of products that customers likely view as substitutes. For example, a category manager might be in charge of all pastas: fresh, frozen, packaged, or canned. Category managers are evaluated on the profitability of their category and thus are motivated to eliminate "me-too" products and keep essential niche products. Note that buyers in most other types of retail firms have always been responsible for merchandise categories. This term, category manager, is used primarily by supermarket and big box retailers.

Planners   Traditionally, buyers or category managers were also responsible for determining the assortment stocked in each store, allocating merchandise to the stores, monitoring sales, and placing reorders. Giving this responsibility to buyers took away from their primary responsibility of selecting and procuring merchandise. As a result, the assortment and allocation decisions did not get the attention they deserved. To address these problems, most retail chains created merchandise planners, supervised by a Senior VP of planning and distribution who is at the same level as the merchandise managers in the buying organization. (See Exhibit 9–5.) Each **merchandising planner** is responsible for allocating merchandise and tailoring the assortment of several categories for specific stores in a geographic area. For example, the planner at Michaels, the nation's largest specialty retailer of arts and crafts materials, would alter the basic assortment of artificial plants for the different climates in south Texas and the Pacific Northwest.

Stores Division   The stores division shown in yellow of Exhibit 9–5 is responsible for the group of activities undertaken in stores. Each vice president is in charge of a set of stores. A store manager, also called a general manager, is responsible for activities performed in each store.

Exhibit 9–7 shows the organization chart of a Macy's Florida store. General managers in large stores have two assistant store managers who report to them. The assistant store manager for sales manages the sales associates. The assistant manager for administration manages the receiving, restocking, and presentation of the merchandise in the store; human resources, including selecting, training, and evaluating employees; operations such as store maintenance; and store security.

Sales managers and the salespeople work with customers in specific areas of the store. For example, a sales manager might be responsible for the entire area in which kitchen appliances, gifts, china, silver, and tableware are sold.

Corporate Organization of Macy's Inc.   Exhibit 9–8 shows the organization chart of Macy's Inc.'s corporate headquarters in Cincinnati, Ohio. The decisions

EXHIBIT 9–7
Organization of a Macy's
Florida Store

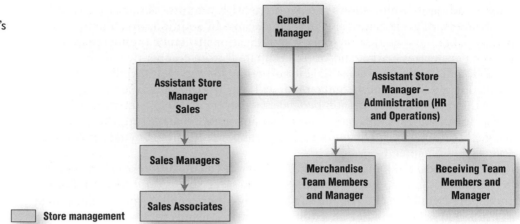

made at the corporate office involve activities that set strategic directions and increase productivity by coordinating the regional divisions' activities. For example, managing one corporate management information system and one private-brand merchandise program is much more efficient and effective than having separate systems and programs for each regional chain. Activities performed at the Macy's Inc. corporate office, rather than at the regional division level, include:

- Provide support services and counsel to operating divisions, including tax, audit, accounting, cash management and finance, planning, insurance, statistical analysis and forecasting, law, vendor development programs, diversity training, communications, and real estate recommendations.

- Conceptualize, design, source, and market private-label and exclusive merchandise sold at Macy's and, in some cases, Bloomingdale's. Some of Macy's private brands include I·N·C, Charter Club/Club Room, Alfani, Style & Co., Tasso Elba, Tools of the Trade, Hotel Collection, The Cellar, Greendog, and First Impressions.

- Create overall strategy, product development, merchandising, and marketing of home-related merchandise in Macy's stores, including design, planning, and marketing for textiles, tabletop, housewares, and furniture.

- Support logistics, distribution, and operations functions for all Macy's and Bloomingdale's retail divisions. The primary responsibility is to ensure the efficient and timely flow of fresh goods to the selling floor of the company's stores. To this end, the division operates small-ticket and large-ticket

EXHIBIT 9–8   Corporate Organization of Macy's Inc.

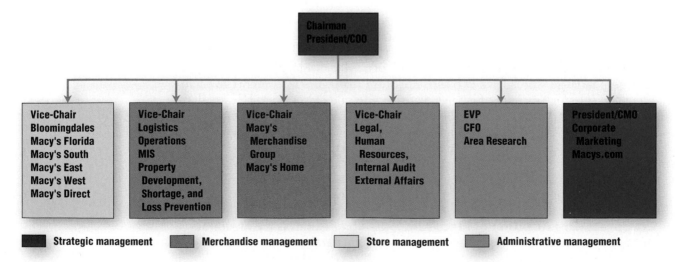

distribution centers, coordinates transportation and shuttle deliveries, and handles vendor returns and merchandise liquidation.

- Service all Bloomingdale's and Macy's proprietary and VISA credit card accounts.

- Perform most other non-store services for customers and employees, including telephone orders for the retail divisions and Bloomingdale's By Mail; furniture/bedding customer service; e-commerce support (e-mails, telephone calls) for www.macys.com, www.bloomingdales.com, and Wedding Channel bridal businesses; human resources services; and payroll and benefits.

- Develop distinctive sales promotion programs for the Macy's brand that are national in scope but remain locally responsive. Manage national public relations and annual events, credit marketing, and cause-related marketing initiatives for the Macy's brand.

- Provide integrated electronic commerce and data warehouse systems for use at all levels within Macy's Inc. Develop and implement merchandise planning systems; provide customer service devices (e.g., price and gift card value checking) and other new technologies; institute new technology on the sales floor to help process transactions more quickly, accurately, and efficiently; and analyze data to maximize and focus marketing.[17]

Organization Structures of Other Types of Retailers

Most retail chains have organization structures very similar to the Macy's Florida structure in Exhibit 9–5, with people in charge of the merchandising, store management, and administrative tasks reporting to the CEO and president. Only corporations that operate several different chains, such as Macy's, Kroger, and The Gap, have an overarching corporate structure similar to that in Exhibit 9–8, in which each division operates as a semi-independent unit with its own merchandise and store management staff, as illustrated in Exhibit 9–5.

The primary difference between the organization structure of a department store and other retail formats is the number of people and management levels in the merchandising and store management areas. Many national retailers such as The Gap, Kohl's, JCPenney, and Circuit City centralize merchandise management activities at corporate headquarters. As a result, they have fewer buyers and management levels in the merchandise group. However, these national retailers also have many more stores than a regional department store division like Macy's Florida, so they have more managers and management levels in the stores division.

RETAIL ORGANIZATION DESIGN ISSUES

Two important issues in the design of a retail organization are (1) the degree to which decision making is centralized or decentralized and (2) the approaches used to coordinate merchandise and store management. The first issue translates into whether the decisions about activities such as merchandise management, information and distribution systems, and human resource management are made by regional, district, or store managers or by managers in the corporate headquarters. The second issue arises because retailers divide merchandise and store management activities into different organizations within the firm. Thus, they need to develop ways to coordinate these interdependent activities.

Centralization versus Decentralization

Centralization is when authority for retailing decisions is delegated to corporate managers rather than to geographically dispersed managers; **decentralization** is when authority for retail decisions is assigned to lower levels in the organization.

[Handwritten margin notes:
Centralize:
+ reduce cost
+ reduce personnel
+ lower prices
+ better decision maker
+ efficiency
– adaptability
– responsibility
– management at low level]

JCPenney is an example of a retail corporation that has migrated from geographically decentralized decision making to centralized decision making. Now most retailing management decisions are made by corporate managers.

Retailers reduce costs when decision making is centralized in corporate management. First, overhead falls because fewer managers are required to make the merchandise, human resource, marketing, and financial decisions. For example, Macy's operates six regional divisions and thus has seven women's blouse buyers (six in the Macy's regional offices, and a corporate buyer who coordinates the regional chains and buys private-label blouses). In contrast, JCPenney has two buyers for women's blouses at the corporate headquarters. Centralized retail organizations can similarly reduce personnel in administrative functions, such as marketing, real estate, information systems, and human resources.

Second, by coordinating buying across geographically dispersed stores, the company can achieve lower prices from suppliers. The retailer can negotiate better purchasing terms by placing one large order rather than a number of smaller orders.

Third, centralization provides an opportunity to have the best people make decisions for the entire corporation. For example, in a centralized organization, people with the greatest expertise in areas such as management information systems (MIS), buying, store design, or visual merchandise can offer all stores the benefit of their skills.

Fourth, centralization increases efficiency. Standard operating policies apply to store and personnel management; these policies limit the decisions made by store managers. For example, corporate merchandisers perform considerable research to determine the best method for presenting merchandise. They provide detailed guides for displaying merchandise to each store manager so that all stores look the same throughout the country. Because they offer the same core merchandise in all stores, centralized retailers can achieve economies of scale by advertising through national media rather than more costly local media.

Although centralization has advantages in reducing costs, its disadvantage is that it makes it more difficult for a retailer to adapt to local market conditions. For example, Gainesville is located in central Florida, and thus, the manager in charge of the fishing category at the Sports Authority corporate office might think that the Gainesville store customers primarily engage in freshwater lake fishing. But the local store manager knows that most of his customers drive 90 miles to go saltwater fishing in either the Gulf of Mexico or the Atlantic Ocean.

In addition to problems with tailoring its merchandise to local needs, a centralized retailer may have difficulty responding to local competition and labor markets. Because pricing is established centrally, individual stores may not be able to respond quickly to competition in their market. Finally, centralized personnel policies may make it hard for local managers to pay competitive wages in their area or hire appropriate types of salespeople.

However, centralized retailers are relying more on their information systems to react to local market conditions. For example, centralized buyers can vary pricing, markdowns, and merchandise allocations on a store-by-store or region-by region basis.

Coordinating Merchandise and Store Management

Small, independent retailers have little difficulty coordinating their stores' buying and selling activities. Owner–managers typically buy the merchandise and work with their salespeople to sell it. In close contact with customers, the owner–managers know what their customers want.

In contrast, large retail firms organize the buying and selling functions into separate divisions. Buyers specialize in buying merchandise and have limited contact with the store employees responsible for selling it. While this specialization increases buyers' skills and expertise, it makes it harder for them to understand customers' needs. Three approaches large retailers use to coordinate buying and selling are (1) improving buyers' appreciation for the store environment, (2) making store visits, and (3) assigning employees to coordinating roles.

Improving Appreciation for the Store Environment   To improve coordination, retailers try to increase buyers' contact with customers and improve informal communication between buyers and the store personnel who sell the merchandise they buy. Management trainees, who eventually become buyers, are required by most retailers to work in the stores before they enter the buying office. During this 6–10-month training period, prospective buyers gain appreciation for the activities performed in the stores, the problems salespeople and department managers encounter, and the needs of customers.

Making Store Visits   Another approach to increasing customer contact and communication is to have buyers visit the stores and work with the departments for which they buy. At Wal-Mart, all managers (not just the buyers) are required to visit stores frequently and practice the company philosophy of CBWA (coaching by wandering around). Managers leave corporate headquarters in Bentonville, Arkansas, on Sunday night and return to share their experiences at the traditional Saturday morning meetings. This face-to-face communication provides managers with a richer view of store and customer needs than they could get from impersonal sales reports from the company's management information system. Spending time in the stores improves buyers' understanding of customer needs, but this approach is costly because it reduces the time the buyer has to review sales patterns, plan promotions, manage inventory, and locate new sources of merchandise.

Sam Walton, founder of Wal-Mart, symbolized Wal-Mart's philosophy of management by practicing CBWA (coaching by wandering around).

Assigning Employees to Coordinating Roles   Some retailers, like TJX, maintain people in both the merchandise division (planners and allocators who work with buyers) and stores who are responsible for coordinating buying and selling activities. Many national retail chains have regional and even district personnel to coordinate buying and selling activities. For example, Target's regional merchandise managers in Chicago work with stores in the north-central U.S. region to translate plans developed by corporate buyers into programs that meet the regional needs of consumers.

In addition to developing an organization structure, HR management undertakes a number of activities to attract effective employees, improve employee performance, build commitment among employees, and reduce turnover. In the following two sections of this chapter, we examine these human resource management activities.

WINNING THE TALENT WAR

As we indicated at the beginning of the chapter, the pool of potential employees is decreasing due to changing demographics. There is, however, a need for managers that can effectively deal with the increased complexities of retail jobs, such as the use of new technologies, increased global competition, and a diverse wortkforce. Thus, retailers are engaged in a "war" with their competitors for talent, that is, for effective employees and managers.[18] Corporate HR departments are generals in the war for talent. They are responsible for developing programs that will attract, develop, motivate, and keep talent.

Attracting Talent: Employment Marketing

The HR departments for retailers such as Starbucks and Marriott develop marketing programs to attract the "best and brightest" potential employees. These programs, called **employment marketing** or **employment branding,** involve undertaking marketing research to understand what potential employees are seeking, as well as what they think about the retailer; developing a value proposition and an employment brand image; communicating that brand image to potential employees; and then fulfilling the brand promise by ensuring the employee experience matches that which was advertised. Retailers often use advertisng agencies that specialize in employment marketing to develop creative approaches to attract employees.[19]

For example, Starbucks's research revealed that prospective and existing employees like their jobs. The rewards they receive from working at Starbucks go beyond pay and promotion opportunities. So Starbucks developed an employment marketing program based on the theme "Love What You Do." Southwest uses a similar tagline for its employment marketing program: "Feel Free to Actually Enjoy What You Are Doing."

Starbucks uses the "Love What You Do" theme in its printed material, available to prospective employees in stores, and in videos designed to describe the Starbucks employee experience. In this collateral material, real employees describe why they love what they do.

Starbucks encourages all of its partners (employees) to get involved in recruiting potential employees. Employees in its stores are trained to respond to customer inquiries about job opportunities and questions about working in stores. The company also provides store managers with WOW business cards that they can hand out to anyone who has provided them with great customer service, such as a server in another restaurant or a teller in a bank. The WOW says, "WOW, that is great service you provided." The WOW card thanks the service provider, provides the name and contact information of the store manager, and provides a space for the store manager to write a personal note inviting the service provider to stop by his or her Starbucks store, have a free latté, and discuss job opportunities at Starbucks.[20]

The profile of Derek Jenkins at the beginning of this chapter illustrates the theme on which Target's employment marketing is based. When marketing to potential employees, Target stresses its team environment and spirit. This positioning is reinforced by referring to its employees as team members and its managers as team leaders.

Developing Talent: Selection and Training

Two activities that retailers undertake to develop knowledge, skills, and abilities in their human resources are selection and training. Retailers that build a competitive

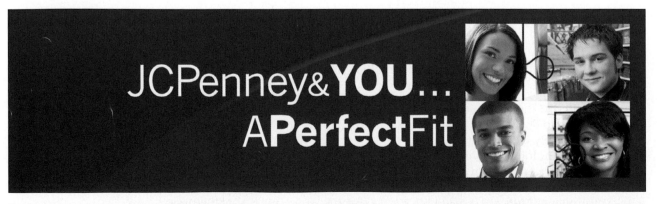

To build its employment brand, JCPenney uses the tagline "A Perfect Fit" on all correspondence and advertising directed toward potential employees.

advantage through their human resources are very selective in hiring people and make significant investments in training.

Selective Hiring   The first step in building an effective workforce is to recruit the right people. Singapore Airlines, one of Asia's most admired companies, is consistently ranked among the top airlines in terms of service quality. Because its flight attendants are the critical point of contact with its customers, senior management is personally involved in their selection. Only 10 percent of the applicants make it through the initial screening, and only 2 percent are eventually hired.

The job requirements and firm strategy dictate the type of people hired. Simply seeking the best and the brightest often may not be the most effective approach. For example, at Recreational Equipment Inc. (REI), a category specialist in outdoor gear, the motto is "You live what you sell." Outdoor enthusiasts are hired as sales associates so they can help customers and serve as a resource for the buying staff. Borders Books and Music similarly wants avid readers in its workforce.[21]

Training   Training is particularly important in retailing because more than 60 percent of retail employees have direct contact with customers, which means they are responsible for helping customers satisfy their needs and resolve their problems.

REFACT
Averaging only seven hours per employee per year, the retail industry spends less time on training than all other industries.[22]

A key to success at Rochester, N.Y.–based supermarket chain Wegmans is how it treats its employees and its emphasis on training.[23] It instills a sense of ownership with its employees, which translates into them taking responsibility for how the company operates and how it performs. Colleen Wegman, president of the privately held company, says, "We listen to our people. We get ideas from all over the company. We try out the ideas. If they don't work, we change course." Wegmans cultivates its young workers through its schlarship program. Since 1984, the Wegmans Scholarship Program has given $63 million to more than 20,000 full- and part-time employees. It also invests in its employees by providing training. In-depth product knowledge makes the job more fulfilling. The employees learn about new cooking techniques, which they share with customers.

An interesting challenge facing retailers is how to train younger employees. They have recognized that Generation Y, the first generation to grow up with the Internet and Internet-based games, learns differently than previous generations. So, for example, the children's apparel retailer The Children's Place developed a series of training modules about loss prevention and store safety modeled after the television series *CSI: Crime Scene Investigation*, called "Place Scene Investigation" or PSI.[24] These modules are much more interactive than the typical click-next modules typically found in retailing. Retailing View 9.3 illustrates another approach that illustrates Peet's Coffee and Tea's commitment to training.

Motivating Talent: Aligning Goals

The task of aligning employees' and the firm's goals is often difficult, because employees' goals usually differ from those of the firm. For example, a sales associate might find it more personally rewarding to arrange a display creatively than to help a customer. Retailers generally use three methods to motivate their employees' activities: (1) written policies and supervision, (2) incentives, and (3) organization culture.[25]

Policies and Supervision   Perhaps the most fundamental method of coordination is to prepare written policies that indicate what employees should do, and then have supervisors enforce these policies. For example, retailers may set policies about when and what merchandise can be returned by customers. If employees use the written policies to make these decisions, their actions will be consistent with the retailer's strategy. But strict reliance on written policies also can reduce employee motivation, because employees have little opportunity to use their own initiative to improve performance in their areas of responsibility. As a result, they eventually might find their jobs uninteresting.

Relying on rules as a method of coordination leads to a lot of red tape. Situations will arise that aren't covered by a rule, in which case employees may need to talk to a supervisor. Alternatively, many retailers empower their employees to make decisions on their own. Empowerment is discussed subsequently in this chapter and in Chapter 19.

Incentives   The second method of motivating and coordinating employees uses incentives to encourage them to perform activities consistent with the retailer's objectives. For example, buyers will be motivated to focus on the firm's profits if they receive a bonus based on the profitability of the merchandise they buy.

REFACT

The late Mary Kay Ash, founder of Mary Kay Cosmetics, was fond of saying, "There are two things that people want more than sex and money—recognition and praise."[26]

9.3   RETAILING VIEW   Peet's Knows Its Tea

Why would someone pay $2 or more for a cup of tea when it costs only pennies to buy a Lipton tea bag and put it in a cup of hot water? Because companies like Peet's Coffee & Tea have learned to create value by training employees to provide great customer service. Peet's, known as the "grandfather of specialty coffee," was started by Alfred Peet in 1966 a few blocks away from University of California, Berkeley. Although its primary business is coffee, Peet's managers know that if everything they sell—including tea—isn't as good as it can be, business will suffer.

Peet's first priority is educating its staff. In addition to knowing how to brew tea, employees need to know about the beverage they're serving. How are green, black, and oolong teas grown and processed? How do they differ? How do they taste? What about their caffeine content?

Once the staff knows all there is to know about tea, they can educate their customers, who generally fall into two categories: those few who know a lot about tea and everyone else. Knowledgeable tea enthusiasts may ask very specific questions, whereas most neophyte tea buyers probably don't understand why tea is so expensive. Most customers also grew up with tea bags, so they need to be educated about how to brew the loose tea that Peet's sells.

At Peet's, the staff also has a "cheat sheet" for every tea container with information they can pass on to customers. The sheet illustrates how much tea should be used, how long it should brew for optimal taste, and how hot the water should be. If the staff doesn't know the answer to a customer's question, they find out by asking their manager or the home office.

Selling and consuming tea can be a very personal experience, so Peet's staff are encouraged to interact with customers. For instance, they might ask drinkers to describe their favorite tea and how it tastes, then use those details to suggest new, alternative teas. But the best way to sell tea is to drink it. Getting the staff to test and taste different teas gives them the confidence and knowledge to be good tea emissaries. Peet's has figured out that the key to its success is not just

At Peet's Coffee and Tea, the staff is provided in-depth product knowledge to serve their customers better than the competition.

good coffee and tea but excellent service delivered by knowledgeable employees.

Sources: http://www.peets.com (accessed August 15, 2007); Gray W. Blake, "Coffee Drinks Give 'I'm Buzzed' a Double Meaning," *San Francisco Chronicle*, February 23, 2006; Gene G. Marcial, "Peet's Tempting Aroma," *BusinessWeek*, June 13, 2004.

Types of Incentive Compensation   Two types of incentives are commissions and bonuses. A commission is compensation based on a fixed formula, such as 2 percent of sales. Many retail salespeople's compensation is based on a fixed percentage of the merchandise they sell.

A bonus is additional compensation awarded periodically on the basis of an evaluation of the employee's performance. For example, store managers often receive bonuses at the end of the year based on their store's performance relative to its budgeted sales and profits. Chapter 17 details the advantages and disadvantages of compensation plans compared with other nonfinancial incentives like recognition and promotions.

In addition to incentives based on individual performance, retail managers often receive income based on their firm's performance. These profit-sharing arrangements can be offered as a cash bonus based on the firm's profits or a grant of stock options that link additional income to the performance of the firm's stock.

Some retailers use stock incentives to motivate and reward all employees, including sales associates. Employees are encouraged to buy shares in their companies at discounted prices through payroll deduction plans. These stock incentives align employees' interests with those of the company and can be very rewarding when the company does well. However, if growth in the company's stock price declines, employee morale declines too, corporate culture is threatened, and demands for higher wages and more benefits develop.

Drawbacks of Incentives   Incentives are very effective at motivating employees to perform the activities on which the incentives are based. But incentives also may cause employees to ignore other activities. For example, salespeople whose compensation is based entirely on their sales may be reluctant to spend time restocking fixtures and shelves. Excessive use of incentives to motivate employees also can reduce employee commitment. Company loyalty falls because employees feel that the firm hasn't made a commitment to them (because it is unwilling to guarantee their compensation). Thus, if a competitor offers to pay a higher commission rate, they'll feel free to leave.[27]

Organization Culture   The final method for motivating and coordinating employees is to develop a strong organization culture. An **organization culture** is the set of values, traditions, and customs of a firm that guides employee behavior. These guidelines aren't written down as a set of policies and procedures; they are traditions passed along by experienced employees to new employees.

Many retail firms have strong organization cultures that give employees a sense of what they ought to do on their jobs and how they should behave to be consistent with the firm's strategy. For example, Nordstrom's strong organization culture emphasizes customer service, whereas Wal-Mart's focuses on reducing costs so the firm can provide low prices to its customers.

An organization culture often has a much stronger effect on employees' actions than do rewards offered through compensation plans, directions provided by supervisors, or written company policies. Nordstrom emphasizes the strength of its organization culture in the policy manual given to new employees.[28] The

[handwritten margin notes: "- ignore other activity - reduce commitment"]

Nordstrom has one rule in its policy manual, "Use your best judgment to do anything you can to provide service to our customers."

manual has one rule: Use your best judgment to do anything you can to provide service to our customers. Lack of written rules doesn't mean that Nordstrom employees have no guidelines or restrictions on their behavior; rather, its organization culture guides employees' behavior. New salespeople learn from other employees that they should always wear clothes sold at Nordstrom, that they should park their cars at the outskirts of the parking lot so customers can park in more convenient locations, that they should approach customers who enter their department, that they should accept any merchandise returned by a customer even if the merchandise wasn't purchased at a Nordstrom store, and that they should offer to carry packages to the customer's car.

Developing and Maintaining a Culture   Organization cultures are developed and maintained through stories and symbols.[30] Values in an organization culture are often explained to new employees and reinforced by present employees through stories. For example, each day at every Ritz-Carlton around the world, employees from every department meet to review guest experiences, resolve issues, and discuss ways to improve service.[31] During the meeting, a "wow story" is read. The same story is told in every Ritz-Carlton, and it singles out a staff person that offers exemplary service. For instance, a family staying at the Ritz-Carlton in Bali had carried specialized eggs and milk for their son who suffered from food allergies. Upon arrival, they saw that the eggs had broken and the milk had soured. When the staff failed to find the special items locally, the executive chef contacted his mother-in-law in Singapore and asked that she buy the products and fly to Bali to deliver them, which she agreed to do.

Whole Foods strengthens its organization culture by working in teams and using its employees during the hiring process.[32] Each store is organized into approximately 10 teams, each responsible for a different category or aspect of store operations, such as customer service or checkout lines. Store operations are highly decentralized, so many purchasing and operational decisions are made by the teams. When hiring, team leaders screen candidates, but a two-thirds majority of the team must approve each hire.

Using symbols is another technique for managing organization culture and conveying its underlying values. Symbols are an effective means of communicating with employees because the values they represent can be remembered easily. Wal-Mart makes extensive use of symbols and symbolic behavior to reinforce its emphasis on controlling costs and keeping in contact with its customers. Photocopy machines at corporate headquarters have cups on them for employees to use to pay for any personal copying. At the traditional Saturday morning executive meeting, employees present information on the cost-control measures they've recently undertaken. Managers who have been traveling in the field report on what they've seen, unique programs undertaken in the stores, and promising merchandise. Headquarters are Spartan. Founder Sam Walton, one of the world's wealthiest people before he died, lived in a modest house and drove a pickup truck to work.

Keeping Talent: Building Employee Commitment

Having attracted and developed effective employees, an important challenge in retailing is to keep them, that is, to reduce turnover. High turnover reduces sales and increases costs. Sales are lost because inexperienced employees lack the skills and knowledge about company policies and merchandise to interact effectively with customers. Costs increase due to the need to recruit and train new employees. Retailing View 9.4 illustrates how Wal-Mart builds a committed workforce by investing in it.

Consider what happens when Bob Roberts, meat department manager in a supermarket chain, leaves the company. His employer promotes a meat manager from a smaller store to take Bob's position, promotes an assistant department manager to the position in the smaller store, promotes a meat department trainee to the assistant manager's position, and hires a new trainee. Now the supermarket chain needs to train two meat department managers and one assistant manager and hire and train one trainee. The estimated cost for replacing Bob Roberts is almost $10,000.

To reduce turnover, retailers need to build an atmosphere of mutual commitment in their firms. When a retailer demonstrates its commitment, employees respond by developing loyalty to the company. Employees improve their skills and work hard for the company when they feel the company is committed to them over the long run, through thick and thin. Some approaches that retailers take to build mutual commitment are (1) empowering employees and (2) creating a partnering relationship with employees.[33] Research indicates that engaging in these HR management practices increases the firm's financial performance.

Empowering Employees   **Empowerment** is a process in which managers share power and decision-making authority with employees. When employees have the authority to make decisions, they are more confident in their abilities, have a greater opportunity to provide service to customers, and are more committed to the firm's success.[34]

Wal-Mart Cares About Its Employees   **RETAILING VIEW**   9.4

Is the corporation's commitment to environmentalism, personal fitness, and a healthy lifestyle why people work at Wal-Mart? IBM, Microsoft, and other white-collar companies already sponsor fitness and lifestyle improvement programs for their employees. But now the world's largest retailer, which employs 1.3 million people who make an average of less than $20,000 per year, is launching a voluntary personal sustainability project.

Approximately 50 percent of its employees are participating in the program. Wal-Mart is holding workshops to teach employees the benefits of carpooling to work with three colleagues, discontinuing cigarette smoking, and turning off the television. Employees are learning the importance of environmental sustainability, reducing carbon emissions, and consuming healthy and environmentally friendly food.

As a result of the seminars, employees have already taken the initiative to tailor environmental practices that fit with their new lifestyles. Employees have pledged to start recycling at home and improve their physical health with healthier food and more exercise. One employee created a "zero waste" break room, where the employees had to use mugs instead of Styrofoam cups and recycling bins were set up for aluminum cans and plastic bottles. Employees are also lobbying for healthier Subway restaurants in the Wal-Mart stores instead of McDonald's.

Wal-Mart's personal sustainability program is part of its environmental initiative, which includes minimizing its use of packaging and pressuring its vendors to follow its lead.

What was first thought to be a public relations stunt for Wal-Mart is turning out to be a positive project that could improve the quality of life and the productivity of its employees, reduce health care costs for the company, improve its image among its customers, and help it become a corporate leader in environmentalism.

Sources: Michael Barbaro, "At Wal-Mart, Lessons in Self-Help," *The New York Times*, April 5, 2007; http://www.walmart.com (accessed August 6, 2007).

The first step in empowering employees is reviewing employee activities that require a manager's approval. For example, Parisian, an upscale department store chain owned by Belk, changed its check authorization policy, thereby empowering sales associates to accept personal checks of up to $1,000 without a manager's approval. Under the old policy, a customer often had to wait more than 10 minutes for the sales associate to locate a manager. Then the busy manager simply signed the check without reviewing the customer's identification. When the sales associates were empowered to make approvals, service improved, and the number of bad checks decreased, because the sales associates felt personally responsible to check identification carefully.

Empowerment of retail employees transfers authority and responsibility for making decisions to lower levels in the organization. These employees are closer to the customers and in a good position to know what it takes to satisfy customers. For empowerment to work, managers must have an attitude of respect and trust, not control and distrust.

Creating Partnering Relationships   Three HR management activities that build commitment by developing partnering relationships with employees are (1) reducing status differences, (2) promoting from within, and (3) enabling employees to balance their careers and families.

Reducing Status Differences

Many retailers attempt to reduce status differences among employees. With limited status differences, employees feel that they play important roles in the firm's ability to achieve its goals and that their contributions are valued.

Status differences can be reduced symbolically through the use of language and substantively by lowering wage differences and increasing communications among managers at different levels in the company. For example, hourly workers at JCPenney are referred to as associates and managers are called partners, a practice that Sam Walton adopted when he started Wal-Mart.

Whole Foods has a policy of limiting executive compensation to less than fourteen times the compensation of the average full-time salaried employee. When Herb Kelleher was CEO of Southwest Airlines, he negotiated a five-year wage freeze for his employees in exchange for stock options. He also agreed to freeze his base salary at $380,000. Sam Walton typically appeared on lists of the most underpaid CEOs.

Promotion from Within

This staffing policy involves hiring new employees only for positions at the lowest level in the job hierarchy and then promoting experienced employees to openings at higher levels in the hierarchy. While many retailers use promotion-from-within policies, other retailers frequently hire people from competitors when management positions become available.

Promotion-from-within policies establish a sense of fairness. When employees do an outstanding job and then outsiders are brought in over them, the employees feel that the company doesn't respect them. Promotion-from-within policies also commit the retailer to developing its own employees.[35]

Balancing Careers and Families

The increasing number of two-income and single-parent families makes it difficult for employees to effectively do their jobs and manage their households simultaneously. Retailers can build employee commitment by offering services like job sharing, childcare, and employee assistance programs to help their employees manage these problems.

Flextime is a job scheduling system that enables employees to choose the times they work. With **job sharing,** two employees voluntarily are responsible for a job that was previously held by one person. Both programs let employees accommodate their work schedules to other demands in their life, such as being home when their children return from school.[36]

Best Buy has gone one step further with its ROWE, or "results-only work program environment." In a classic flextime structure, workers arrange their schedules with their supervisors in advance. In the ROWE program, the supervisor has no say in scheduling. Employees work as long as it takes to get their assigned tasks completed. They are evaluated only on the tasks successfully completed—even if they did not complete any of them in the office.[37]

Many retailers offer childcare assistance as well. Sears' corporate headquarters near Chicago has a 20,000 square foot daycare center. At Eddie Bauer in Seattle, the corporate headquarters cafeteria stays open late and prepares takeout meals for time-pressed employees. Some companies will even arrange for a person to be at an employee's home waiting for the cable guy to come or pick up and drop off dry cleaning.

ISSUES IN RETAIL HUMAN RESOURCE MANAGEMENT

In this final section, we discuss three trends in HR management: (1) the increasing importance of a diverse workforce, (2) the growth in legal restrictions on HR practices, and (3) the use of technology to increase employee productivity.

Managing Diversity

Managing diversity is a human resource management activity designed to realize the benefits of a diverse workforce. Today, diversity means more than differences in race, nationality, or gender, but managing a diverse workforce isn't a new issue for retailers. In the late 1800s and early 1900s, waves of immigrants entering America went to work in retail stores. The traditional approach for dealing with these diverse groups was to blend them into the "melting pot." Minority employees were encouraged to adopt the values of the majority, white, male-oriented culture. To keep their jobs and get promoted, employees abandoned their ethnic or racial distinctiveness.

But times have changed. Minority groups now embrace their differences and want employers to accept them for who they are. The appropriate metaphor now is a salad bowl, not a melting pot. Each ingredient in the salad is distinctive, preserving its own identity, but the mixture of ingredients improves the combined taste of the individual elements.[38]

Some legal restrictions promote diversity in the workplace by preventing retailers from practicing discrimination based on non–performance-related employee characteristics. But retailers now recognize that promoting employee diversity also can improve financial performance. By encouraging diversity in their workforce, retailers can better understand and respond to the needs of their customers and deal with the shrinking labor market.

To compete in this changing marketplace, retailers need management staffs that match the characteristics of their target markets. For example, the majority of merchandise sold in department stores and home improvement centers is bought by women. To better understand customer needs, department stores and home improvement retailers feel that they must have women in senior management positions—people who really understand their female customers' needs.

In addition to gaining greater insight into customer needs, retailers must deal with the reality that their employees will become more diverse in the future. Many retailers have found that emerging groups are more productive than traditional employees. After renovating its national reservation center to accommodate workers with disabilities, Days Inn found that turnover among disabled workers was only 1 percent annually, compared with 30 percent for its entire staff. Lowe's, a home improvement center chain, changed floor employees' responsibilities so they wouldn't have to lift heavy merchandise. By assigning these tasks to the night crew, the firm was able to shift its floor personnel from male teenagers to older employees who provided better customer service and had personal experience with do-it-yourself projects. Effectively managing a diverse workforce isn't just morally correct; it's necessary for business success.[39]

The fundamental principle behind managing diversity is the recognition that employees have different needs and require different approaches to accommodating those needs. Managing diversity goes beyond meeting equal employment opportunity laws. It means accepting and valuing differences. Some programs that retailers use to manage diversity involve offering diversity training, providing support groups and mentoring, and managing career development and promotions.

Diversity Training   Diversity training typically consists of two components: developing cultural awareness and building competencies. The cultural awareness component teaches people about how their own culture differs from the culture of other employees and how the stereotypes they hold influence the way they treat people, often in subtle ways that they might not realize. Then role playing is used to help employees develop their competencies, such as better interpersonal skills that enable them to show respect and treat people as equals.

Support Groups and Mentoring   **Mentoring programs** assign higher-level managers to help lower-level managers learn the firm's values and meet other senior executives. Many retailers help form minority networks that exchange information and provide emotional and career support for members who traditionally haven't been included in the majority's networks. In addition, mentors are often assigned to minority managers. At Giant Foods, a Maryland-based supermarket chain, the mentoring program has reduced turnover of minorities by making them more aware of the resources available to them and giving them practical advice for solving problems that might arise on their jobs.

REFACT

In 1866, Macy's employed the first female executive in retailing when Margaret Getchell was promoted to the position of store superintendent.[40]

Career Development and Promotions   Although laws provide entry-level opportunities for women and minority groups, these employees often encounter a glass ceiling as they move through the corporation. A **glass ceiling** is an invisible barrier that makes it difficult for minorities and women to be promoted beyond a certain level. To help employees break through this glass ceiling, JCPenney monitors high-potential minority and female employees and makes sure they have opportunities for store and merchandise management positions that are critical for their eventual promotion to senior management.

Similarly, women in the supermarket business have traditionally been assigned to peripheral departments like the bakery and deli, while men were assigned to the critical departments in the store like meat and grocery. Even in the supermarket chain corporate office, women traditionally have been in staff-support areas like HR management, finance, and accounting, whereas men have been more involved in store operations and buying. To make sure that more women have an opportunity to break through the glass ceiling in the supermarket industry, more firms are placing them in positions critical to the firm's success.

Legal and Regulatory Issues in Human Resource Management

The proliferation of laws and regulations affecting employment practices in the 1960s was a major reason for the emergence of human resource management as an important organization function. Managing in this complex regulatory environment required expertise in labor laws, as well as skills in helping other managers comply with those laws. The major legal and regulatory issues involving the management of retail employees are (1) equal employment opportunity, (2) compensation, (3) labor relations, (4) employee safety and health, (5) sexual harassment, and (6) employee privacy.

United Food and Commercial Workers Union members strike to maintain wages and benefits earned from southern California supermarkets that are facing stiff competition from nonunion retailers.

Equal Employment Opportunity   The basic goal of equal employment opportunity regulations is to protect employees from unfair discrimination in the workplace. **Illegal discrimination** refers to the actions of a company or its managers that result in members of a protected class being treated unfairly and differently than others. A protected class is a group of individuals who share a common characteristic as defined by the law. Companies cannot treat employees differently simply on the basis of their race, religion, sex, national origin, age, or disability status. There are a very limited set of circumstances in which employees can be treated differently. For example, it is illegal for a restaurant to hire young, attractive servers because that is what its customers prefer. Such discrimination must be absolutely necessary, not simply preferred.

In addition, it is illegal to engage in a practice that disproportionately excludes a protected group, even though it might seem nondiscriminatory. For example, suppose that a retailer uses scores on a test to make hiring decisions. If a protected group systematically performs worse on the test, the retailer is illegally discriminating, even if there was no intention to discriminate.

Compensation   Laws relating to compensation define the 40-hour work week, the pay rate for working overtime, the minimum wage, and protection for employee pensions. In addition, they require that firms provide the same pay for men and women who are doing equal work.

A recent issue related to compensation involves the criteria used to classify employees as managers who are paid a salary and not eligible for overtime pay. A number of lawsuits have been filed by assistant managers claiming that they do the same job as hourly employees but are classified as managers so that their retail employer can avoid paying them overtime wages. For example, one lawsuit claimed a retailer's district managers frequently encourage store managers to send hourly workers home before their shift is over to avoid overtime pay and then cause assistant managers to continue working to compensate for the absence of hourly workers.

These lawsuits point out the difficulty in distinguishing the tasks of assistant managers and hourly workers. Federal law requires that managers be paid overtime if more than 40 percent of their time is not spent supervising or if their jobs do not include decision making. However, many retailers feel managers perform other activities, such as interviewing job candidates, making schedules, and handling other supervisory duties. Because so many lawsuits regarding overtime pay are filed each year, the Labor Department has developed overtime rules and regulations, such as defining specific jobs as managerial and paying overtime to managers who earn less than $23,660 a year but denying overtime to employees who earn more than $100,000 annually.[41]

Labor Relations   Labor relations laws describe the process by which unions can be formed and the ways in which companies must deal with the unions. They indicate how negotiations with unions must take place and what the parties can and cannot do.

Wal-Mart has vigorously challenged attempts by unions to represent their employees. Supermarket chains, in contrast, are typically unionized, and therefore believe they have a labor cost disadvantage that makes it difficult for them to compete effectively with Wal-Mart. Safeway was involved in a four and a half month strike in Southern California, which affected 289 stores, representing about 16 percent of its total store base. Approximately 77 percent of its employees are covered by 400 or so collective bargaining agreements. The agreements generally have three-year terms and are negotiated with 10 different international unions. Thus, every three years, Safeway renegotiates with several labor unions for greater concessions for the growing costs of health care and other benefits.[42]

Employee Safety and Health   The basic premise of health and safety laws is that the employer is obligated to provide each employee with an environment that is free of hazards that are likely to cause death or serious injury. Compliance officers from the Department of Labor enforce the Occupational Safety and Health Act (OSHA) by conducting inspections to ensure that employers are providing such an environment for their workers.[43]

Sexual Harassment   Sexual harassment includes unwelcome sexual advances, requests for sexual favors, and other inappropriate verbal and physical conduct. Harassment is not confined to requests for sexual favors in exchange for job considerations such as a raise or promotion. Simply creating a hostile work environment can be considered sexual harassment. For example, actions considered sexual harassment include lewd comments, joking, and graffiti, as well as showing obscene photographs, staring at a coworker in a sexual manner, alleging that an employee got rewards by engaging in sexual acts, and commenting on an employee's moral reputation.

Customers can engage in sexual harassment as much as supervisors and coworkers. For example, if a male customer is harrassing a female server in a restaurant, and the restaurant manager knows about it and does nothing to stop the harrassment, the employer can be held responsible for that sexual harrassment.[44]

Employee Privacy   Employees' privacy protection is very limited. For example, employers can monitor e-mail and telephone communications, search an employee's work space and handbag, and require drug testing. However, employers cannot discriminate among employees when undertaking these activities unless they have a strong suspicion that specific employees are acting inappropriately.

Developing Policies   The HR department is responsible for developing programs and policies to make sure that managers and employees are aware of these legal restrictions and know how to deal with potential violations. The legal and regulatory requirements are basically designed to treat people fairly. Employees want to be treated fairly, and companies want to be perceived as treating their employees fairly. The perception of fairness encourages people to join a company and leads to the trust and commitment of employees to a firm. When employees believe they are not being treated fairly, they can complain internally, stay and accept the situation, stay but engage in negative behavior, quit, or complain to an external authority or even sue the employer.

Perceptions of fairness are based on two perceptions: (1) distributive justice and (2) procedural justice. **Distributive justice** arises when the outcomes received are viewed as fair with respect to the outcomes received by others. However, the perception of distributive justice can differ across cultures. For example, in the individualistic culture of the United States, merit-based pay is perceived as fair, whereas in collectivist cultures such as China and Japan, equal pay is viewed as fair. **Procedural justice** is based on the fairness of the process used to determine the outcome. American workers consider formal processes as fair, whereas group decisions are considered fairer in collectivist cultures.[45] Some illustrations of policies that pertain to procedural justice are presented in Chapter 17.

Use of Technology

Retail chains are using intranets to automate and streamline their HR operations. For example, JCPenney's 150,000 employees use kiosks in the 1,200 Penney stores to make changes in their personnel records, request time off, register for training classes, review the company's policies and procedures manual, and request services such as direct deposit of their paychecks. These self-service kiosks are also used by job applicants to review open positions, submit applications, and take prescreening tests. The use of these kiosks, connected through an intranet to a centralized database, dramatically reduces the time human resources administrators spend on paperwork.[46]

SUMMARY

Human resource management plays a vital role in supporting a retailing strategy. The organization structure defines supervisory relationships and employees' responsibilities. The four primary groups of tasks performed by retailers are strategic decisions by the corporate officers, administrative tasks by the corporate staff, merchandise management by the buying organization, and store management.

In developing an organization structure, retailers must make trade-offs between the cost savings gained through centralized decision making and the benefits of tailoring the merchandise offering to local markets—benefits that arise when decisions are made in a decentralized manner.

Retailers are engaged in a war of talent. To win the war, retailers develop programs to attract, develop, motivate, and keep talent. A key factor in reducing turnover is developing an atmosphere of mutual commitment.

Managing diversity also is important in retailing because customers are becoming more diverse, and new entrants into the retail workforce will come largely from the ranks of women and minorities. Programs for managing diversity include diversity training, support groups and mentors, and promotion management.

The human resource department is also responsible for making sure that its firm complies with the laws and regulations that prevent discriminatory practices against employees and making sure that employees have a safe and harassment-free work environment.

KEY TERMS

buyer, *256*

category manager, *257*

centralization, *259*

decentralization, *259*

distributive justice, *273*

employee productivity, *248*

employee turnover, *248*

employment branding, *262*

employment marketing, *262*

empowerment, *267*

flextime, *268*

glass ceiling, *270*

illegal discrimination, *271*

job sharing, *268*

managing diversity, *269*

mentoring program, *270*

merchandising planner, *257*

organization culture, *265*

organization structure, *252*

procedural justice, *273*

specialization, *253*

GET OUT AND DO IT!

1. **CONTINUING CASE ASSIGNMENT** Meet with the store manager of the retailer you have chosen for this continuing assignment. Ask the store manager which company HR policies he or she feels are very effective and which are not effective. Why? Also ask the manager about the store's policies concerning the legal and regulatory issues discussed in the chapter. Does the retailer have written policies that enable the manager to deal effectively with any situations that arise? Have situations arisen that were not covered by the policies? How was the situation addressed? To what degree does the manager feel he or she is empowered to make decisions that affect the performance of the store? Would the manager like more or less decision-making authority? Why?

2. Go to the Society of Human Resource Management's home page, www.shrm.org. An organization of human resource professionals, SHRM publishes *HR Magazine*, with articles available online at www.workforce.com. Find and summarize the conclusions of articles addressing the HR challenges that retailers are facing, such as the management of a diverse workforce, international expansion, and the use of technology to increase productivity.

3. The Fair Measures Law Consulting Group provides training and legal services for employers. Go to its Web site, www.fairmeasures.com, and choose one of the legal areas to investigate (anti-harassment, wrongful termination, and so forth). Another source of information about legal issues regarding employees is www.law.cornell.edu/topics/employment.html. Read the most recent court opinions and articles about employment issues, and summarize the implications for human resource management in retailing.

4. Go to Club Med's recruitment home page at www.clubmedjobs.com/index.php. Take a few minutes to become familiar with the information offered about the interview process, job descriptions, and the competencies that this global leisure company is looking for when hiring. What are some of the unique challenges that this employer faces when hiring internationally?

5. Go to the National Retail Federation's Retail Careers & Advancement home page at www.nrf.com/RetailCareers/ and click on "Is retail for me?" Read about the different career paths in Marketing/Advertising, Store Operations, Loss Prevention, Store Management, Finance, Human Resources, IT and E-Commerce, Sales and Sales-Related, Distribution Logistics Supply Chain Management, Merchandise Buying/Planning, and Entrepreneurship. Which area(s) appeals to you the most? Why is this the case?

6. Talk with a salesperson in a store. Ask him or her how committed he or she is to working for the retailer. Why does the salesperson feel that way? What could the retailer do to build a great sense of commitment?

7. A. Go to the student side of the book's Web site and review the student resumes. Which resumes do you think are effective? Ineffective? Why?

   B. Update your resume and prepare for an interview for a Manager Training program with a large lumber and building supply retailer. This full-time position promises rapid advancement upon completion of the training period. A college degree and experience in retail, sales, and marketing are preferred. The base pay is between $28,000 and $34,000 per year. This retailer promotes from within, and a new Manager Trainee can become a Store Manager within two to three years, with an earning potential of $100,000 or more. The benefits package is generous, including medical/hospitalization/dental/disability/life insurance, a 401k plan, profit sharing, awards and incentives, paid vacations, and holidays. Your resume should include your contact information, education and training, skills, experience and accomplishments, and honors and awards.

   C. Role play a practice interview for this position. Pair up with another student and read each others' resumes; then spend 20 to 30 minutes on each side of the interview. One student should be the Human Resource Manager screening applicants, and the other person should be the candidate for the Manager Training program. Here are some questions to use in the role-play scenario:
   - Why are you applying for this position?
   - What are your strengths and weaknesses for this position?
   - Why should this organization consider you for this position?
   - Why are you interested in working for this company?
   - What are your career goals for the next five to ten years?
   - Describe your skills when working in a team setting.
   - What questions do you have about the company?

DISCUSSION QUESTIONS AND PROBLEMS

1. Why is human resource management more important in retailing than in manufacturing firms?

2. Describe the similarities and differences between the organization of small and large retail companies. Why do these similarities and differences exist?

3. Some retailers have specific employees (merchandise assistants) assigned to restock the shelves and maintain the appearance of the store. Other retailers have sales associates perform these tasks. What are the advantages and disadvantages of each approach?

4. How can national retailers like Best Buy and Victoria's Secret, which both use a centralized buying system, make sure that their buyers are aware of the local differences in consumer needs?

5. What are the positive and negative aspects of employee turnover? How can a retailer reduce the turnover of its sales associates?

6. To motivate employees, several major department stores are experimenting with incentive compensation plans, though frequently, compensation plans with a lot of incentives don't promote good customer service. How can retailers motivate employees to sell merchandise aggressively and at the same time not jeopardize customer service?

7. Assume that you're starting a new restaurant that caters to college students and plan to use college students as servers. What human resource management problems would you expect to have? How could you build a strong organization culture in your restaurant to provide outstanding customer service?

8. Three approaches for motivating and coordinating employee activities are policies and supervision, incentives, and organization culture. What are the advantages and disadvantages of each?

9. Why should retailers be concerned about the needs of their employees? What can retailers do to satisfy these needs?

10. You've been promoted to manage a general merchandise discount store. Your assistant managers are an African-American male, a Hispanic male, a white female, and a female who has worked for the company for 35 years. What are the strengths of your management group, and what problems do you foresee arising?

11. What HR trends are helping meet employees' needs, increase job satisfaction, and lower turnover?

SUGGESTED READINGS

"The 100 Best Companies to Work For," *Fortune,* January 8, 2007, pp. 148–68.

Booth, Simon, and Kristian Hamer. "Labour Turnover in the Retail Industry." *International Journal of Retail and Distribution Management* 35, no. 4 (2007), pp. 289–307.

Burke, Ronald, and Cary Cooper (eds.). *Reinventing Human Resource Management: Challenges and New Directions.* London: Routledge, 2005.

Feuti, Norman. *Pretending You Care: The Retail Employee Handbook.* New York: Hyperion, 2007.

Hart, Cathy; Grazyna B. Stachow; Andrew M. Farrell; and Gary Reed. "Employer Perceptions of Skills Gaps in Retail: Issues and Implications for UK Retailers." *International Journal of Retail and Distribution Management* 35, no. 4 (2007), pp. 271–88.

Henly, Julia R.; H. Luke Shaefer; and Elaine Waxman. "Nonstandard Work Schedules: Employer-and Employee-Driven Flexibility in Retail Jobs." *Social Service Review* 80, no. 4 (2006), pp. 609–34.

Ivancevich, John. *Human Resource Management.* 10th ed. Boston: McGraw-Hill/Irwin, 2006.

McBride, Dwight. *Why I Hate Abercrombie & Fitch: Essays on Race and Sexuality (Sexual Cultures Series).* New York: NYU Press, 2005.

McKay, Patrick F.; Derek R. Avery; Scott Tonidandel; Mark A. Morris; Morela Hernandez; and Michelle R. Hebl. "Racial Differences in Employee Retention: Are Diversity Climate Perceptions the Key?" *Personnel Psychology* 60, no. 1 (2007), pp. 35–62.

Noe, Raymond; John Hollenbeck; Barry Gerhart; and Patrick Wright. *Human Resource Management.* 6th ed. Burr Ridge, IL: McGraw-Hill/Irwin, 2007.

Rothwell, William J.; Carolyn K. Hohne; and Stephen B. King. *Human Performance Improvement, 2d ed.: Building Practitioner Competence.* Boston: Butterworth-Heinemann, 2007.

Information Systems and Supply Chain Management

EXECUTIVE BRIEFING

Jim LaBounty, Senior Vice-President and
Director of Supply Chain Management, JCPenney

Jim LaBounty (center) with Marie Lacertosa (left), Vice President and Director of Supply Chain Operations, and Marice McNeal (right), Operations/Inventory Manager for the JCPenney Alliance Distribution Center in Fort Worth, Texas.

At JCPenney, I provide the strategic and operational leadership for managing the pipeline that moves merchandise from our vendors around the world to our stores and Internet/catalog customers. Over 8,000 Penney's associates and $1 billion in annual expenses are involved in these supply chain activities that make sure we have the right product at the right place at the right time.

Before joining JCPenney, I served over 28 years in the U.S. Army. Prior to my retirement from the military, I was the Commander (CEO/COO) of the Defense Distribution Region West. I learned how to move people and material quickly and efficiently during my military career, but the most important thing I learned in the military was leadership—how to provide a vision of what needs to be done, organize and motivate people to do it effectively, and respond quickly to changes in the environment.

Shortly before I arrived at JCPenney in 2001, the company made a strategic decision to change its supply chain management approach from having vendors ship merchandise directly to stores (direct store delivery) to using distribution centers for storing inventory and consolidating merchandise for store shipments. The old approach got the merchandise to the stores slightly faster but resulted in excess inventory in the supply chain and greater labor costs. Store employees had to receive deliveries from a lot of different vendors and then get it ready to be displayed on the sales floor. We can do these "floor-ready" activities much more efficiently in our distribution centers and have just one delivery to the store each day.

Even though most of what my colleagues and I do is behind the scenes, it's very important for us to visit the stores to understand how we can better service them.

CHAPTER 10

QUESTIONS

How do merchandise and information flow from the vendor to the retailer to consumers?

What information technology (IT) developments are facilitating vendor–retailer communications?

How do retailers and vendors collaborate to make sure the right merchandise is available when customers are ready to buy it?

What are the benefits to vendors and retailers of collaborating on supply chain management?

What is RFID, and how will it affect retailing?

For example, during some visits I made when I first joined Penney's, store associates told me they spent a lot of time taking plastic wrappers off apparel. The vendors wrap each garment in plastic so they will remain clean during shipment. A test we conducted revealed that we could take the plastic wrap off in the distribution center for all garment except suits and white apparel and the garments would remain clean. By removing the wrappers in the distribution centers, we saved a lot of labor hours for store associates, hours they now spend on providing customer service, and we also generated some revenue by gathering and recycling the plastic.

Retailing is an exciting business. New problems and challenges come up every day. One day we are helping a buyer get hot merchandise from China into our stores faster and the next day we have to deal with a longshoremen's strike at a major port. There's never a dull moment.

Joe Jackson wakes up in the morning, takes a shower, dresses, and goes to his kitchen to make a cup of coffee and toast a bagel. He slices the bagel and puts it in his toaster oven, but to his dismay, the toaster oven is not working. As he reads the newspaper and eats his untoasted bagel with his coffee, he notices that Target is having a sale on Michael Graves toaster ovens. The toaster ovens look great. So, on his way home from work, he stops at a Target store to buy one. He finds the advertised Michael Graves model on the shelf and buys it.

Joe expects to find a Michael Graves and other toaster oven models available at Target, but he probably doesn't realize that Target uses sophisticated information and supply chain management systems to make sure that the Michael Graves toaster ovens and other brands are available in stores whenever he and other customers want them. When Joe bought the toaster oven, the information about his transaction was automatically forwarded through Target's information systems to its regional distribution center, the home appliance planner at Target's corporate headquarters in Minneapolis, and the manufacturer in China. A computer information system monitors all toaster oven sales and inventory levels in every Target store and decides when to have toaster ovens shipped from the manufacturer in China to the regional distribution centers and then from the centers to the stores. Shipments to the distribution centers and stores are monitored using a satellite tracking system that locates the ships and trucks transporting the toaster ovens.

Of course, Target could ensure the availability of toaster ovens and other merchandise by simply keeping a large number of units in the stores at all times. But stocking a large number of each stockkeeping unit (SKU) would require much more space to store the items and a significant investment in additional inventory. So the challenge for Target is to limit its inventory investment but still make sure products are always available when customers want them.

This chapter begins by outlining how retailers can gain a strategic advantage through supply chain management and information systems. Then the chapter describes supply chain information and product flows and the activities undertaken in distribution centers. Next it examines how vendors and retailers work together to efficiently manage the movement of merchandise from the vendor through the retailer's distribution centers to its stores. The chapter concludes with a discussion of a new technology, radio frequency identification (RFID), being used to improve supply chain efficiency.

CREATING STRATEGIC ADVANTAGE THROUGH SUPPLY MANAGEMENT AND INFORMATION SYSTEMS

As discussed in Chapter 1, retailers connect customers with vendors who provide the merchandise. It is the retailers' responsibility to gauge customers' wants and needs and work with the other members of the supply chain—distributors, vendors, and transportation companies—to make sure the merchandise that customers want is available when they want it. A simplified supply chain is illustrated in Exhibit 10–1. Vendors ship merchandise either to a **distribution center** operated by a retailer (as is the case for vendors V1 and V3) or directly to stores (as is the case for vendor V2). The relative advantages of shipping directly to stores versus to distribution centers are discussed later in this chapter.

Supply chain management refers to a set of approaches and techniques firms employ to efficiently and effectively integrate their suppliers, manufacturers, warehouses, stores, and transportation intermediaries to efficiently have the right quantities, at the right locations, and at the right time.[1] Retailers are increasingly

EXHIBIT 10–1   Illustration of a Supply Chain

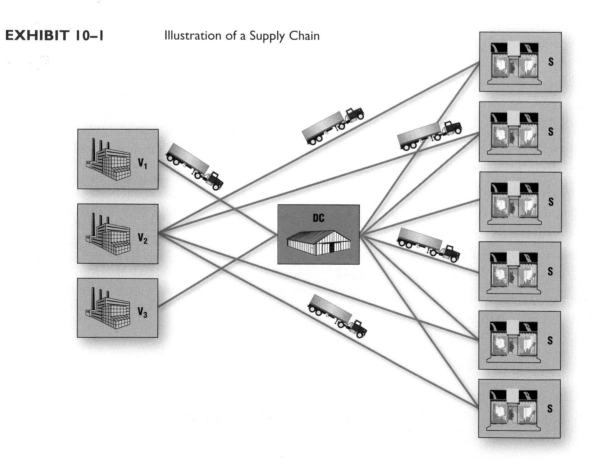

taking a leadership role in managing their respective supply chains. When retailers were predominantly small, family-owned businesses, larger manufacturers and distributors dictated when, where, and how merchandise was delivered. But with the emergence of larger, national retail chains, retailers now play an active role in coordinating supply chain management activities. The size of these national retailers typically makes them more powerful than their vendors and thus better able to control their supply chains. In addition, retailers are more knowledgeable about their customers. They are in the unique position to collect purchase information customer by customer, transaction by transaction. As we will discuss later in the chapter, this information is being shared with suppliers to plan production, promotions, deliveries, assortments, and inventory levels. But first we'll explore why efficient supply chain management is so important to retailers—because it provides improved product availability, higher return on investment, and a strategic advantage.

Improved Product Availability

Efficient supply chain management provides two benefits to customers: (1) reduced stockouts and (2) tailored assortments. These benefits translate into greater sales, lower costs, higher inventory turnover, and lower markdowns for retailers.

Reduced Stockouts   A **stockout** occurs when an SKU that a customer wants is not available. What would happen if Joe went to the Target store, and the store had stocked out of Michael Graves toaster ovens because the distribution center did not ship enough to the store? The store would give Joe a rain check so he could come back and still pay the sale price when the store received a new shipment, but Joe would have made a wasted trip to the store. As a result of the stockout, Joe might decide to buy another model, or he might go to a nearby Wal-Mart to buy a toaster oven. While at Wal-Mart, he could purchase other items in addition to the toaster oven. He also might be reluctant to shop at Target in the future and tell all of his friends about the negative experience he had. This bad experience could have been avoided if Target had done a better job of managing its supply chain.

In general, stockouts have significant short- and long-term effects on sales and profits. Data show that the first time a customer experiences a stockout, he or she will purchase a substitute item 70 percent of the time.[2] With a second out-of-stock occurrence, that rate drops to 50 percent, with customers going to a competitor the other 50 percent of time. By the third instance, there is a 70 percent chance that the retailer has lost the sale entirely, and, most likely, the customer's loyalty as well. The customer may never come back.

Tailored Assortments   Another benefit provided by information systems that support supply chain management is making sure that the right merchandise is available at the right store. National retail chains have long adjusted assortments in their stores on the basis of climate—stocking more wool sweaters in northern stores and cotton sweaters in southern stores during the winter. Now retailers use sophisticated statistical methods to analyze sales transaction data and adjust store assortments for a wide range of merchandise on the basis of the customer demand characteristics of the store's local market. For example, when Oracle's assortment planning software was used at a $650 million national specialty store chain, it increased profits by $60 million by just getting the right products in the right stores at the right time.[4]

Higher Return on Investment

From the retailer's perspective, an efficient supply chain and information system can improve its return on investment because it increases sales, net profit margins,

REFACT

Retailers are out of stock an average of 8 percent across all items but 13 percent on promoted items.[3]

and assets (inventory turnover).[5] Net sales increase because customers are offered more attractive assortments that are in stock. Consider Joe Jackson's toaster oven purchase. Target, with its excellent information systems, could accurately estimate how many Michael Graves toaster ovens each store would sell during the special promotion. Using its supply chain management system, it made sure sufficient stock was available at Joe's store so all of the customers that wanted to buy one, could.

Net profit margin is improved by increasing the gross margin and lowering expenses. An information system that facilitates coordination between the buying staff and vendors allows retailers to take advantage of special buying opportunities and obtain the merchandise at a lower cost, thus improving their gross margin. Retailers also can lower their operating expenses by coordinating deliveries, thus reducing transportation expenses. With more efficient distribution centers, merchandise can be received, prepared for sale, and shipped to stores with minimum handling, further reducing expenses.

By efficiently managing their supply chain, retailers can carry less backup inventory to stay in stock. Thus, inventory levels are lower, and with a lower inventory investment, the total assets are also lower, so the asset and inventory turnovers are both higher. Retailing View 10.1 describes how supply chain management is changing the way fashion comes to market.

Strategic Advantage

Of course, all retailers strive to increase sales and reduce costs by using high-performance information systems and efficient supply chain management. But not all retailers can develop a competitive advantage from their information and supply chain systems. However, if they do develop an advantage, the advantage is sustainable; that is, it is difficult for competitors to duplicate. For example, a critical factor in Wal-Mart's success is its information and supply chain management systems. Even though competitors recognize this advantage, they have difficulty achieving the same level of performance as Wal-Mart's systems for two reasons. First, Wal-Mart has made a substantial investment in developing its systems and has the scale economies to justify this investment. It is so well-regarded for its advanced supply chain systems that it has entered into a joint venture with Bharti Enterprises in India to wholesale food and other products to small retailers. With Wal-Mart's supply chain management systems in place, farmers and small manufacturers will be directly linked to retailers, thus streamlining the supply chain.[6] Second, its systems are not simply a software package any firm can buy from a supplier. Through experience and learning, changes are always being made to improve the performance of these systems. In addition, the effective use of these systems requires the coordinated effort of employees and functional areas throughout the company.

To illustrate the complexity of the tasks performed by these systems and the need for coordinated efforts, consider the various activities required to keep stores in stock:

- Forecast accurately.
- Stock stores with adequate/correct shelf space and appropriate frequency.
- Utilize storage areas.
- Place accurate, timely orders with vendors and distribution centers.
- Replenish merchandise from distribution centers with the right quantities when the stores need it.
- Ensure buyers and marketing managers coordinate merchandise delivery with special sales and promotional materials.

Fast fashion is a retail business strategy that involves using supply chain management process to introduce fashionable merchandise rapidly and respond to customer demand for the merchandise quickly. This business strategy was pioneered by Zara, a global specialty apparel chain located in La Coruña, Spain, and adopted by other retailers such as H&M (headquartered in Sweden), TopShop (U.K.) and Forever 21 (U.S.).

The fast fashion process starts with receiving timely information from store managers. At Zara, its store managers are equipped with handheld devices linked directly to the company's corporate office in Spain. They report daily on what customers are buying and not buying and what they are asking for but not finding. For instance, when buyers find that customers are requesting a purple shirt that is similar to one they are selling in pink, they pass this information onto the designers in Spain, who initiate a process that results in making and shipping purple shirts to its stores in a very short period of time.

There is nothing more fashionable these days than an efficient supply chain. Just ask Zara.

Zara successfully reduces lead time by communicating electronically with the factory, using automated equipment, assemblers who are in close proximity to the factory, and premium transportation. Although Zara buys undyed fabric from Asia, the bulk of its apparel manufacturing occurs in Spain and Portugal. On the basis of its new design concepts and customer response in stores, fabric gets cut and dyed by robots in the company's 23 highly automated factories in Spain. The final assembly is entrusted to a network of 300 or so small suppliers located near the factories in Galicia, Spain, and northern Portugal. To ensure the apparel is delivered in a timely manner, merchandise is shipped by truck to stores in Europe and by air express to stores in the rest of the world.

Zara makes deliveries to each of its stores every few days. New products like the purple shirts would be in stores in several weeks—compared with the several months it would take for most department stores and other specialty apparel stores to accomplish the same feat. For instance, if a Zara store is running low on a medium kelly green sweater, its fast fashion system will ensure a shorter lead time than that of more traditional retailers. As a result, it's less likely that the Zara store will be out of stock before the next sweater shipment arrives. Limiting the stock in stores also creates a sense of scarcity among its customers. If they don't buy now, the item might not be available next time they visit the store. Finally, by producing and shipping small quantities, Zara can quickly recover from a fashion faux pas.

Due to the efficiency of its supply chain, Zara does not have to discount merchandise that is not selling as much as other specialty store apparel retailers. At Zara, the number of items that end up marked down is about half the industry average. Zara is able to achieve these results and still have 10,000 new designs and 40,000 new SKUs each year.

H&M uses a slightly different strategy. About one-quarter of its assortment is made up of fast fashion items that are designed in-house and produced by independent, local factories. As at Zara, these items move quickly through the stores and are replaced frequently with fresh designs. But H&M also keeps a significant inventory of basic, items sourced from low cost Asian factories.

The fast fashion approach is particularly effective for specialty apparel retailers targeting customers who are very fashion conscious and always want to have a new look, not the same things their friends are wearing. Consumers attracted to fast fashion buy new apparel more frequently, discarding items that are only a few months old. Thus, the sales of fast fashion merchandise in second-hand stores is growing dramatically.

REFACT

Consumers in central London visit the average apparel store four times annually, but Zara's customers visit its shops an average of 17 times a year.[7]

Sources: Anita Hamilton, "Fast Fashion, the Remix," *Time*, June 11, 2007, p. 85; Elizabeth Esfahani, "High Class, Low Price," *Business 2.0*, November 2006, p. 74; Margaret Bruce, "Buyer Behaviour for Fast Fashion," *Journal of Fashion Marketing and Management* 10 (2006), pp. 329–40; Jeanine Poggi, "Retail Market Feels Fast Fashion Effect," *WWD*, October 23, 2006, p. 13; Brian Dunn, "Inside The Zara Business Model," *DNR*, March 20, 2006, p. 11; Michael A. Lewis and Jose A.D. Machuca, "Rapid-Fire Fulfillment," *Harvard Business Review* 82, no. 11 (November 2004).

EXHIBIT 10–2
Information and
Merchandise Flows

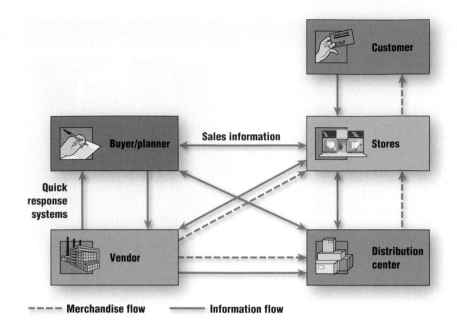

The complexities of the merchandise and information flows in a typical multi-store chain are illustrated in Exhibit 10–2. Although information and merchandise flows are intertwined, in the following sections, we describe first how information about customer demand is captured at the store, which triggers a series of responses from buyers and planners, distribution centers, and vendors that is designed to ensure that merchandise is available at the store when the customer wants it. Then, we discuss the physical movement of merchandise from vendors through distribution centers to the stores.

INFORMATION FLOWS

When Joe Jackson bought his toaster oven at Target, he initiated the information flows illustrated in Exhibit 10–3 (the numbers in parentheses refer to the path in the exhibit):

EXHIBIT 10–3
Information Flows

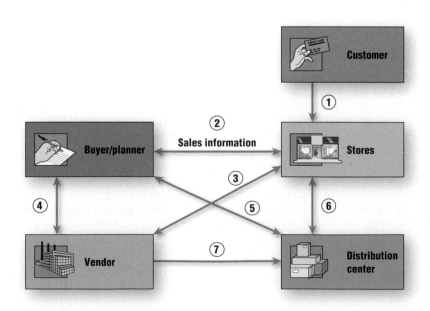

The Target cashier scans the **Universal Product Code (UPC)** tag on the toaster oven box (1), and a sales receipt is generated for Joe. The UPC tag is a black-and-white bar code containing a 13-digit code that indicates the manufacturer of the item, a description of the item, information about special packaging, and special promotions.[8] The codes for all products are issued by GS1 US (www.gs1us.org), formerly the Uniform Code Council. In the future, RFID tags, discussed at the end of this chapter, may replace UPC tags. Retailing View 10.2 describes how a retailer uses UPC tags to keep track of your dry cleaning.

scan.

The information about the transaction is captured at the point-of-sale (POS) terminal and sent to Target's information system, where it can be accessed by the planner for the toaster oven product category (2). The planner uses this information to monitor and analyze sales and to decide to reorder more toaster ovens or reduce its prices if sales are below expectations.

send info to planner.

The sales transaction data also are sent to the distribution center (6). When the store inventory drops to a specified level, more toaster ovens are shipped to the store, and the shipment information is sent to the Target computer system (5) so the planner knows the inventory level that remains in the distribution center.

data sent to distribution center.

When the inventory drops to a specified level in the distribution center (4), the planner negotiates terms and shipping dates and places an order with the manufacturer of the toaster ovens. The planner then informs the distribution centers about the new order and when the store can expect delivery (5).

When the manufacturer ships the toaster ovens to the Target distribution centers, it sends an advanced shipping notice to the distribution centers (7). An **advanced shipping notice (ASN)** is a document that tells the distribution center what specifically is being shipped and when it will be delivered. The distribution

---

Zoots Doesn't Lose Your Shirt   RETAILING VIEW   10.2

Newton, Massachusetts-based Zoots has made dry cleaning and laundry a quick, easy, and reliable process. But Zoots didn't always run so smoothly. When it started in 1998, it was spending 6 percent of its revenues on damages or lost items. Since then however, it has built a $15 million, state-of-the-art technology system, supported by a $1 million annual budget dedicated to achieving high customer convenience. It now suffers less than 1 percent loss claims.

Zoots attaches a permanent UPC-type identification tag in an inconspicuous place on each garment. This tag contains customer information and dry cleaning or laundering specifications. For example, a customer may specify "no starch" or "light press." Not only does this process speed up the check-in process, but if garments are lost, they can be easily tracked down.

Zoots offers lockers so customers can pick up their clothing 24/7, or they can have it delivered. Going to Zoots is as simple as going to an ATM machine.

Sources: Jenn Abelson, "Bar-Code Tags, ATM-Style Machines Drive High-Tech Laundry Business," *Boston Globe,* July 3, 2006; www.zoots.com (accessed August 18, 2007).

Going to Zoots to pick up laundry and dry cleaning is as easy as going to an ATM machine.

center then makes appointments for trucks to make the delivery at a specific time, date, and loading dock.

When the shipment is received at the distribution center, the planner is notified (5) and then authorizes payment to the vendor.

In some situations, discussed later in this chapter, the sales transaction data are sent directly from the store to the vendor (3), and the vendor decides when to ship more merchandise to the distribution centers and stores. In other situations, especially when merchandise is reordered frequently, the ordering process is done automatically, bypassing the planners.

Data Warehouse

Purchase data collected at the point of sale goes into a huge database known as a data warehouse. The information stored in the data warehouse is accessible on various dimensions and levels, as depicted in the data cube in Exhibit 10–4.

As shown on the horizontal axis, data can be accessed according to the level of merchandise aggregation—category (dresses), vendor (Jones New York), SKU (black, size 5) or all merchandise. Along the vertical axis, data can be accessed by level of the company—store, division, or the total company. Finally, along the third dimension, data can be accessed by point in time—day, season, or year.

The CEO might be interested in how the corporation is generally doing and could look at the data aggregated by quarter for a merchandise division, a region of the country, or the total corporation. A buyer may be more interested in a particular vendor in a certain store on a particular day. Analysts from various levels of the retail operation extract information from the data warehouse to make a plethora of decisions about developing and replenishing merchandise assortments.

Data warehouses also contain detailed information about customers, which is used to target promotions and group products together in stores. These applications are discussed in Chapter 11.

EXHIBIT 10–4   Retail Data Warehouse

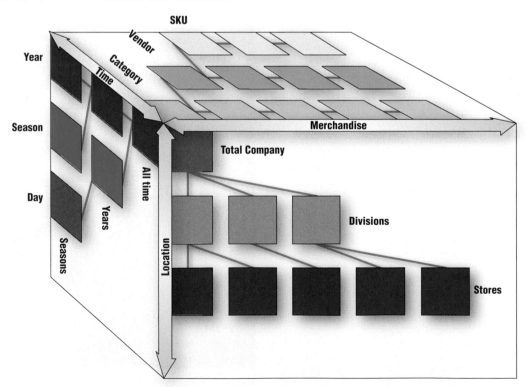

SOURCE: SAS Retail.

Electronic Data Interchange

In the past, these information flows were accomplished by sending handwritten or typed documents through the mail or by fax. Now most communications between vendors and retailers occur via electronic data interchange. **Electronic data interchange (EDI)** is the computer-to-computer exchange of business documents in a structured format, which means that the data transmissions use a standard format to communicate the data. For example, specific symbols are used to delineate the purchase order number, the vendor's name, the address the merchandise is being shipped to, and so forth.

Standards   In the retail industry, two data transmission standards are used: (1) the Uniform Communication Standard (UCS), used initially by the grocery sector, though it has now been adopted in many supply chains, including those for alcoholic beverages, convenience stores, the foodservice industry, discount stores, and wholesale pharmaceuticals,[11] and (2) the Voluntary Interindustry Commerce Solutions (VICS),[12] used by the general merchandise retailing sector. Using these standards, retailers and vendors can exchange information about purchase order changes, order status, transportation routings, advance shipping notices, on-hand inventory status, and vendor promotions, as well as information that enables vendors to put price tags on merchandise. The development and use of these standards is critical to the use of EDI, because they enable all retailers to use the same format when transmitting data to their vendors.

[handwritten margin note: UCS ← grocery. VICS ← general merchandise]

Transmission Systems   In larger retail firms, communications among employees within a company, such as the communications among store managers, planners, and distribution center employees, are done through an intranet. An **intranet** is a local area network (LAN) that employs Internet technology in an organization to facilitate communication and access to information internally.

[handwritten margin note: intranet (LAN) extranet]

To communicate with people outside the organization, such as vendors and transportation companies, large retailers like Wal-Mart initially developed their own propriety transmission systems. But now EDI transmissions between retailers and vendors occur over the Internet through extranets. An **extranet** is a collaborative network that uses Internet technology to link businesses with their suppliers, customers, or other businesses. Extranets are typically private and secure and can be accessed only by authorized parties.

An extranet is generally an extension of a company's intranet, modified to allow access to specified external users. The shift from a propriety transmission network to Internet-based networks enables small retailers and vendors to take advantage of EDI economically. For example, Target Corporation has shifted its propriety EDI network to an extranet system called Partners Online, and Wal-Mart's extranet is called Retail Link. These companies make certain time-sensitive procedures, confidential information, and general supplier information, such as shipping requirements and prerequisites for packing cartons, available to vendors via the extranet.

Security   Because the Internet is a publicly accessible network, its use to communicate internally and externally with vendors and customers raises security issues. Some potential implications of security failures are the loss of business data essential to conducting business, disputes with vendors and customers, loss of public confidence and its effect on brand image, bad publicity, and the loss of revenue from customers using an electronic channel.[13]

Internet security can be expensive and necessary for even the smallest retailer or service provider. For example, Groople, a small online travel company, has invested $55,000 to upgrade its information technology security so it can continue to do business with large customers like Travelocity and large hotel corporations. It believes this upgrade is a small price to pay for keeping its business out of reach of hackers, cyberthieves, and even disgruntled employees.[14]

Security has become a bigger challenge in recent years as a result of EDI using extranets and the operation of Internet retail channels. Now vendors and customers all need some form of access to the retailer's information system.

To help control this changing information environment, retailers have incorporated security policies. A **security policy** is the set of rules that apply to activities involving computer and communications resources that belong to an organization. However, in addition to instituting these policies, retailers train employees and add the necessary software and hardware to enforce the rules. The objectives of the security policy are:

- *Authentication.* The system assures or verifies that the person or computer at the other end of the interaction really is who or what it claims to be.

- *Authorization.* The system assures that the person or computer at the other end of the interaction has permission to carry out the request.

- *Integrity.* The system assures that the arriving information is the same as that sent, which means that the data have been protected from unauthorized changes or tampering through a data encryption process.

Benefits of EDI   The use of EDI provides three main benefits to retailers and their vendors. First, EDI reduces the **cycle time,** or the time between the decision to place an order and the receipt of merchandise. Information flows quicker using EDI, which means that inventory turnover is higher. Second, EDI improves the overall quality of communications through better recordkeeping; fewer errors in inputting an order, order receipt, and ASNs; and less human error in the interpretation of data. Third, the data transmitted by EDI are in a computer-readable format that can be easily analyzed and used for a variety of tasks ranging from evaluating vendor delivery performance to automating reorder processes.

Due to these benefits, many retailers are asking their vendors to interface with them using EDI. However, small- to medium-sized vendors and retailers face significant barriers, specifically, cost and the lack of information technology (IT) expertise, to become EDI enabled.

Pull and Push Supply Chains

Information flows such as that described previously illustrate a **pull supply chain**—a supply chain in which orders for merchandise are generated at the store level on the basis of sales data captured by POS terminals. Basically, in this type of supply chain, the demand for an item pulls it through the supply chain. An alternative and less sophisticated approach is a **push supply chain,** in which merchandise is allocated to stores on the basis of forecasted demand. Once a forecast is developed, specified quantities of merchandise are shipped (pushed) to distribution centers and stores at predetermined time intervals.

In a pull supply chain, there is less likelihood of being overstocked or out of stock because the store orders merchandise as needed on the basis of consumer demand. A pull approach increases inventory turnover and is more responsive to changes in customer demand. A pull approach becomes even more efficient than a push approach when demand is uncertain and difficult to forecast.[15]

Although generally more desirable, a pull approach is not the most effective in all situations. First, a pull approach requires a more costly and sophisticated information system to support it. Second, for some merchandise, retailers do not have the flexibility to adjust inventory levels on the basis of demand. For example, commitments must be made months in advance for fashion and private-label apparel. Because these commitments cannot be easily changed, the merchandise has to be preallocated to the stores at the time the orders are formulated. Third, push supply chains are efficient for merchandise that has steady, predictable demand, such as milk and eggs, basic men's underwear, and bath towels. Because both pull and push supply chains have their advantages, most retailers use a combination of these approaches.

THE PHYSICAL FLOW OF MERCHANDISE—LOGISTICS

Exhibit 10–5 illustrates the physical flow of merchandise within the supply chain:

1. Merchandise flows from vendor to distribution center.

2. Merchandise goes from distribution center to stores.

3. Alternatively, merchandise can go from vendor directly to stores.

Logistics is the aspect of supply chain management that refers to the planning, implementation, and control of the efficient flow and storage of goods, services, and related information from the point of origin to the point of consumption to meet customers' requirements.[16] In addition to managing the inbound and outbound transportation, logistics involves the activities undertaken in the retailer's distribution center. For example, sometimes merchandise is temporarily stored at the distribution center; other times it is immediately prepared for shipment to individual stores. This preparation may include breaking received shipping cartons into smaller quantities that can be more readily utilized by the individual stores as well as affixing price tags or stickers, UPC codes, and the store's label.

Distribution Centers versus Direct Store Delivery

As indicated in Exhibit 10–5, retailers can have merchandise shipped directly to their stores—direct store delivery (path 3)—or to their distribution centers (paths 1 and 2). The appropriate decision depends on the characteristics of the merchandise and the nature of demand. To determine which distribution system—distribution centers or direct store delivery—is better, retailers consider the total cost associated with each alternative and the customer service criterion of having the right merchandise at the store when the customer wants to buy it.

There are several advantages to using a distribution center:

• More accurate sales forecasts are possible when retailers combine forecasts for many stores serviced by one distribution center rather than doing a forecast for each store. Consider a set of 50 Target stores, serviced by a single distribution center, that each carry Michael Graves toasters. Each store normally stocks 5 units for a total of 250 units in the system. By carrying the item at each store,

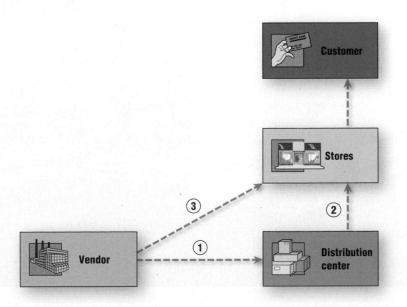

EXHIBIT 10–5
Merchandise Flow

a ccwrate forecast
carry less invu
less storage cost
avoid over stock/out of stock

the retailer must develop 50 individual forecasts, each with the possibility of errors that could result in either too much or too little merchandise. Alternatively, by delivering most of the inventory to a distribution center and feeding the stores additional toasters as they need them, the effects of forecast errors for the individual stores are minimized, and less backup inventory is needed to prevent stockouts.

- Distribution centers enable the retailer to carry less merchandise in the individual stores, which results in lower inventory investments systemwide. If the stores get frequent deliveries from the distribution center, they need to carry relatively less extra merchandise as backup stock.

- It's easier to avoid running out of stock or having too much stock in any particular store because merchandise is ordered from the distribution center as needed.

- Retail sto0re space is typically much more expensive than space at a distribution center, and distribution centers are better equipped than stores to prepare merchandise for sale. As a result, many retailers find it cost effective to store merchandise and get it ready for sale at a distribution center rather than in individual stores.

But distribution centers aren't appropriate for all retailers or types of merchandise. If a retailer has only a few outlets, the expense of a distribution center is probably unwarranted. Also, if many outlets are concentrated in metropolitan areas, merchandise can be consolidated and delivered by the vendor directly to all the stores in one area economically. Direct store delivery gets merchandise to the stores faster and thus is used for perishable goods (meat and produce), items that help create the retailer's image of being the first to sell the latest product (e.g., video games), or fads. For example, by developing a supply chain that bypasses the distribution center, ProFlowers reduced the delivery time from flower cutting to store delivery from 12 to 3 days.[17] Finally, some vendors provide direct store delivery for retailers to ensure that their products are on the store's shelves, properly displayed, and fresh. For example, employees delivering Frito-Lay snacks directly to supermarkets replace products that have been on the shelf too long and are stale, replenish products that have been sold, and arrange products so they are neatly displayed.

REFACT

About half of a video game's sales are made within three days of its release, and 70 percent are rung up within the first week.

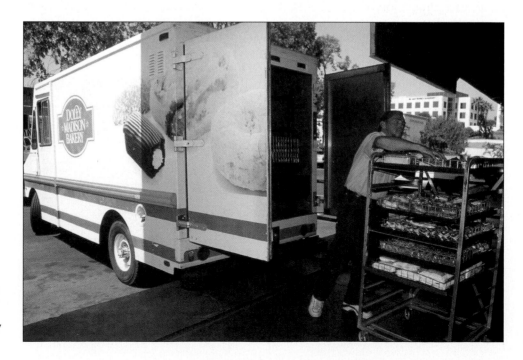

Why would a grocery store prefer direct store delivery of Dolly Madison Bakery products instead of delivery to a distribution center?

Thus, the types of retail stores and merchandise that are most efficiently supplied through distribution centers are:

- nonperishable merchandise.

- merchandise that has highly uncertain demand, such as fashionable apparel, because more accurate sales forecasts are possible when demand from many stores is aggregated at distribution centers.

- merchandise that needs to be replenished frequently, like grocery items, because a direct store delivery system requires stores to spend too much time receiving and processing deliveries from many vendors.

- retailers that carry a relatively large number of items that are shipped to stores in less than full-case quantities, such as drug stores.

- retailers with a large number of outlets that are not geographically concentrated within a metropolitan area but are within 150 to 200 miles of a distribution center.

- retailers that do not require in-store servicing, such as snacks, soda, or non–store-made baked goods.

THE DISTRIBUTION CENTER

The distribution center performs the following activities: coordinating inbound transportation; receiving, checking, storing, and crossdocking; getting merchandise "floor-ready"; and coordinating outbound transportation.[18] To illustrate these activities being undertaken in a distribution center, consider a shipment of Sony plasma televisions arriving at a Sears distribution center.

Management of Inbound Transportation   Traditionally, buyers focused their efforts, when working with vendors, on developing merchandise assortments, negotiating prices, and arranging joint promotions. Now, buyers and planners are much more involved in coordinating the physical flow of merchandise to the stores. The plasma TV buyer has arranged for a truckload of televisions to be delivered to its Houston, Texas, distribution center on Monday between 1:00 and 3:00 p.m. The buyer also specifies how the merchandise should be placed on pallets for easy unloading.

The truck must arrive within the specified time because the distribution center has all of its 100 receiving docks allocated throughout the day, and much of the merchandise on this particular truck is going to be shipped to stores that evening. Unfortunately, the truck was delayed in a snow storm. The **dispatcher**—the person who coordinates deliveries to the distribution center—reassigns the truck delivering the TVs to a Wednesday morning delivery slot and charges the firm several hundred dollars for missing its delivery time. Although many manufacturers pay transportation expenses, some believe they can lower their net merchandise cost and better control merchandise flow if they pay their own transportation and negotiate directly with trucking companies and consolidate shipments from many vendors.

Receiving and Checking   **Receiving** is the process of recording the receipt of merchandise as it arrives at a distribution center. **Checking** is the process of going through the goods upon receipt to make sure they arrived undamaged and that the merchandise ordered was the merchandise received.

In the past, checking merchandise was a very labor-intensive and time-consuming process. Today, however, many distribution systems using EDI are designed to minimize, if not eliminate, these processes. The advance shipping notice (ASN) tells the distribution center what should be in each carton. A UPC label on the

In a crossdocking distribution center, merchandise moves from vendors' trucks to the retailer's delivery trucks in a matter of hours.

REFACT

Crossdocking can cut 35 to 45 cents off a vendor's total cost of 60 to 70 cents per case to deliver products to a supermarket chain.[19]

shipping carton that identifies the carton's contents is scanned and recorded as it is being received and checked. A few stores, most notably Wal-Mart, require that vendors replace the UPC label with an RFID tag, which are discussed at the end of the chapter.

Storing and Crossdocking   After the merchandise is received and checked, it is either stored or crossdocked. When merchandise is stored, the cartons are transported by a conveyor system and forklift trucks to racks that go from the distribution center's floor to its ceiling. Then, when the merchandise is needed in the stores, a forklift driver goes to the rack, picks up the carton, and places it on a conveyor system that routes the carton to the loading dock of a truck going to the store.

Merchandise cartons that are **crossdocked** are prepackaged by the vendor for a specific store. The UPC labels on the carton indicate the store to which it is to be sent. The merchandise is routed from an incoming truck dock to a dock used for loading trucks going to stores—thus, the name crossdocked. The cartons are routed on the conveyor system automatically by sensors that read the UPC label on the cartons. Crossdocked merchandise is only in the distribution center for a few hours before it is shipped to the stores.

Merchandise size and the sales rate typically determine whether cartons are crossdocked or stored. For instance, because Sony's plasma TVs are so large and sell so quickly, it is in Sears' best interest not to store them in a distribution center. Thus, they are unloaded and reloaded onto store delivery trucks within hours.

Getting Merchandise Floor Ready   For some merchandise, additional tasks are undertaken in the distribution center to make the merchandise floor ready. **Floor-ready merchandise** is merchandise that is ready to be placed on the selling floor. Getting merchandise floor ready entails ticketing, marking, and, in the case of some apparel, placing garments on hangers.

Ticketing and marking refers to affixing price and identification labels to the merchandise. It is more efficient for a retailer to perform these activities at a distribution center than in its stores. In a distribution center, an area can be set aside and a process implemented to efficiently add labels and put apparel on hangers. Conversely, getting merchandise floor ready in stores can block aisles and divert salespeople's attention from their customers. An even better approach

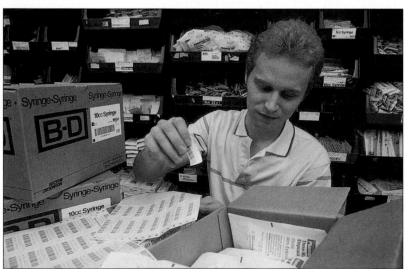

An important activity undertaken in distribution centers is ticketing and marking merchandise so it is floor ready.

from the retailer's perspective is to get vendors to ship floor-ready merchandise, thus totally eliminating the expensive, time-consuming ticketing and marking process.

Preparing to Ship Merchandise to a Store   At the beginning of the day, the computer system in the distribution center generates a list of items to be shipped to each store on that day. For each item, a pick ticket and shipping label is generated. The **pick ticket** is a document or display on a screen in a forklift truck indicating how much of each item to get from specific storage areas. The forklift driver goes to the storage area, picks up the number of cartons indicated on the pick ticket, places UPC shipping labels on the cartons that indicate the stores to which the items are to be shipped, and puts the cartons on the conveyor system, where they are automatically routed to the loading dock for the truck going to the stores.

Pick tickets and labels are also generated for the break pack area. In the break pack area, the number of items for a store are selected by employees from open cartons and put into a new carton. Then shipping labels indicating the store destinations are attached to the new cartons, and the cartons are placed on the conveyor system and routed to the appropriate loading dock.

So the conveyor system feeds cartons from three sources to the loading dock for a truck going to a specific store: (1) crossdocked cartons directly from the vendor's delivery trucks, (2) cartons stored in the distribution center, and (3) cartons from the break pack area. These cartons are then loaded onto the trucks by employees.

Management of Outbound Transportation   The management of outbound transportation from distribution center to stores has become increasingly complex. Most distribution centers run 50–100 outbound truck routes in one day. To handle this complex transportation problem, the centers use sophisticated routing and scheduling computer systems that consider the locations of the stores, road conditions, and transportation operating constraints to develop the most efficient routes possible. As a result, stores are provided with an accurate estimated time of arrival, and vehicle utilization is maximized.

Dollar General offers lower-income families a limited assortment of basic necessities and consumable merchandise at low prices in convenient, hassle-free locations. Controlling cost and distributing merchandise efficiently to its 8,000 stores is key to maintaining its low prices and still making a profit. Each week, more than 2,000 cartons would be delivered to a typical store, and 12 person hours would be required to unload a delivery truck—time the employees could have spent helping customers. Labor scheduling was a real problem, because store managers had to schedule additional staff on truck days, and then in some cases, the drivers could not make deliveries at the preplanned time. In addition, many of its stores are located in urban areas that can make it difficult to park delivery trucks at a convenient location for an extended time period.

To address these challenges, Dollar General invested $100 million in a delivery system called EZ store. The EZ store system involves packing merchandise for shipment to stores in easy-to-move containers called roll-tainers. Instead of having store staff unload the truck when it arrives, the truck drivers alone can unload the 25 roll-tainers for the typical store in about 90 minutes. Store staff no longer need to wait for the truck to arrive, and then walk three to eight miles, lifting 6,000 pounds of merchandise on truck days. Instead, they can unload the roll-tainers and stock shelves with merchandise in the roll-tainers during slow times in the day. The roll-tainers are also designed to protect the merchandise. When drivers make their next delivery, they offload the filled roll-tainers and pick up the empty ones. The system has led to significant reductions in employee injuries and turnover, reduced labor hours, and greater customer satisfaction.[20]

Retailing View 10.3 describes similar activities in Wal-Mart's distribution centers.

Reverse Logistics

Reverse logistics is the process of moving returned goods back through the supply chain from the customer, to the stores, distribution centers, and vendors. It includes processing returned merchandise due to damage, excess merchandise, or recalls.[22] Reverse logistics can be an important issue. Product returns cost U.S. manufacturers and retailers $100 billion every year in lost sales, transportation, handling, processing, and disposal.[23]

Reverse logistics systems are challenging. The returned items may be damaged or lack the original shipping carton and thus require special handling. Transportation costs can be high because items are shipped back in small quantities.

Guaranteed
You Have Our Word™

Our products are guaranteed to give 100% satisfaction in every way. Return anything purchased from us at any time if it proves otherwise. We do not want you to have anything from L.L.Bean that is not completely satisfactory.

From kayaks to slippers, fly rods to sweaters, everything we sell at L.L.Bean is backed by the same rock-solid guarantee of satisfaction. It's been that way since our founder sold his very first pair of Bean Boots in 1912. Today we're proud to continue the tradition – by offering quality products and standing behind them.

Of course, we want you to be the final judge of quality. If you're not satisfied with your purchase, we'll replace it or give you your money back. It's that simple.

NOTICE
I DO NOT CONSIDER A SALE COMPLETE UNTIL GOODS ARE WORN OUT AND CUSTOMER STILL SATISFIED.
L.L.BEAN, 1916

L.L. Bean placed this notice on the wall of our Freeport store.

L.L. Bean takes returns seriously. After all, its guarantee is unconditional.

Of the 48 million units L.L. Bean ships in a year, approximately 6 million will be returned, with a larger proportion coming back after the holiday season.[24] About 85 percent of returns are refunds, and 15 percent are exchanges. L.L. Bean considers how it handles returns as the way to protect its guarantee. For whatever reason, the products have disappointed the customer once. It has to get it right the second time. Although the returned merchandise moves through the system on a conveyor belt, one person handles each return from the time it is picked up off the conveyor to be scanned, processed, and prepped to the time it is sorted and placed back on the conveyor for reintroduction into the inventory system. This process has streamlined the return process and reduced errors.

Logistics for Fulfilling Catalog and Internet Orders

Fulfilling Internet and catalog orders from customers is very different than distributing merchandise to stores. The typical retail distribution center is designed to ship a large number of cartons in truckloads to a relatively small number of stores. These distribution centers typically have automated material-handling equipment and warehouse-management software. In contrast, when fulfilling orders from individual consumers, retailers ship small packages with one or two items to a large number of different places. Thus, a completely different distribution center design is required for supplying Internet and catalog channels compared with that for a store channel.

Catalog retailers use distribution centers designed to pick and pack orders for individual consumers. Traditional store-based retailers, as they evolve into multichannel retailers,

Retailers like Staples use hi-tech robots (the orange boxes on the ground) created by Kiva Systems in their distribution centers.

have had to either redesign their distribution centers or outsource the fulfillment. Some multichannel retailers, like Staples, use different distribution centers to service stores and Internet and catalog customers. Sharper Image, which started as a catalog merchant and now operates 190 stores in the United States, uses its two distribution centers to service all three retail formats.

Outsourcing Logistics   *3rd party logistic.*

To streamline their operations and make more productive use of their assets and personnel, retailers consider **outsourcing** logistical functions if those functions can be performed better or less expensively by third-party logistics companies. **Third-party logistics companies** are firms that facilitate the movement of merchandise from manufacturer to retailer but are independently owned. Specifically, they provide transportation, warehousing, consolidation of orders, and/or documentation.

Transportation   Retailers are careful in choosing their shippers. They demand reliable, customized services because, to a large extent, the retailer's cycle time and its variations are determined by the transportation company. Also, many retailers are finding that it is worth the added cost of airfreight to get merchandise into stores quicker.

One cost advantage of independent transportation companies is they are better able to fill trucks on the return trip (backhaul) than is the retailer. By arranging a   *lower cost* productive round-trip, they can offer their services at a lower cost than most retailers can achieve themselves.

Some retailers mix modes of transportation to reduce overall costs and time delays. For example, many Japanese shippers send Europe-bound cargo by ship to the U.S. West Coast. From there, the cargo is flown to its final destination in Europe. By combining the two modes of transport, sea and air, the entire trip takes about two weeks, as opposed to four or five weeks with an all-water route, and the cost is about half that of an all-air route.

Warehousing   To meet the increasingly stringent demands retailers are placing on their vendors to meet specific delivery times for floor-ready merchandise, many vendors must store merchandise close to their retail customers. Rather than owning these warehouses themselves, vendors typically use **public warehouses** that are owned and operated by a third party. By using public warehouses, vendors can provide their retailers with the level of service demanded without having to invest in warehousing facilities.

Freight Forwarders   **Freight forwarders** are companies that purchase transport services. They then consolidate small shipments from a number of shippers into large shipments that move at a lower freight rate. These companies offer shippers lower rates than the shippers could obtain directly from transportation companies because small shipments generally cost more per pound to transport than do large shipments.

One of the most daunting tasks for a retailer involved in importing merchandise to the United States is government bureaucracy. International freight forwarders not only purchase transportation services but also prepare and expedite all documentation, such as government-required export declarations and consular and shipping documents.

Integrated Third-Party Logistics Services   Traditional definitions distinguishing among transportation, warehousing, and freight forwarding have become blurred in recent years. Some of the best transportation firms, for example, now provide public warehousing and freight forwarding. The same diversification strategy is being used by other types of third-party logistics providers.

Retailers are finding this one-stop shopping quite useful. For instance, LUSH Fresh Handmade Cosmetics in Canada produces handmade bath and beauty products

10.3   RETAILING VIEW   Wal-Mart's Muscle: Its Distribution Centers

Wal-Mart has always been a leader in supply chain management, but because of the company's large size, customers still experience stockouts. It has 240 distribution centers (DCs), supplied by 8,000 drivers who travel more than 900 million miles per year to 6,000 stores worldwide.

Half of the merchandise that a DC processes is crossdocked and ships out fewer than 24 hours after it arrives. The other half, called "pull stock," is stored at the DC. Eighty-five percent of the pull stock is processed through the facility's approximately 20 miles worth of conveyors. Automated, conveyor-mounted shoes push cartons off the lane and down one of the facility's 100 chutes to a waiting truck at a rate of 200 cartons per minute.

The remaining 15 percent of pull stock consists of "non-conveyables": merchandise that is too bulky to be carried on the conveyors, such as Christmas trees or home gyms. These items are transported to the waiting trucks by forklift. A voice-based guidance system directs the forklift drivers to the right trucking bay.

Wal-Mart continues to concentrate on its supply chain efficiency. Currently, Wal-Mart's goal is to grow its inventory half as fast as its sales growth. All too often, however, a leaner inventory translates into stockouts for customers.

Wal-Mart has also been a leader in the adoption of RFID technology to communicate better with its manufacturers and retail stores. In 2005, it required that its top 100 suppliers put RFID tags on all cases and pallets, and now it has more than 600 suppliers using RFID. Its hope is that a more extensive RFID rollout will result in a more efficient supply chain with even fewer stockouts.

Sources: Marc L. Songini, "Wal-Mart Shifts RFID Plans," *Computerworld* 41, no. 9 (February 26, 2007); Mike Troy, "Wal-Mart's Inventory Equation," September 11, 2006; "Financial Outlook: Restoring the Productivity Loop," *Retailing Today*, June 26, 2006.

State-of-the-art technology helps move merchandise efficiently through Wal-Mart's 80 distribution centers, keeping its 6,000 stores well stocked.

LUSH Fresh Handmade Cosmetics partners with FedEx to facilitate shipment of merchandise from Canada to the United States.

for sale through catalogs and on the Internet (www.lush.com).[26] The U.S. market accounts for the majority of LUSH's online business. But the supply chain from LUSH's warehouse to its customers was complicated by U.S. Customs and customers' inability to track orders. LUSH teamed up with FedEx to help streamline and speed up its order processing and fulfillment. Now FedEx consolidates multiple orders in Canada, then moves bulk shipments to the border, reducing LUSH's transportation costs. FedEx then clears the bulk shipment through customs and breaks it down into individual shipments at a FedEx facility in the United States.

COLLABORATION BETWEEN RETAILERS AND VENDORS IN SUPPLY CHAIN MANAGEMENT

As we discussed previously, retailers' and vendors' objectives for supply chain management are to make sure that merchandise is available in the stores when customers want it, minimize stockouts, respond to changing customers, introduce new products, and accomplish all these tasks with the minimum investments in inventory and costs. Retailing View 10.1 at the beginning of this chapter illustrated how fast fashion specialty retailers, such as Zara and H&M, excel at coordinating their stores, designers, and production capability to achieve these objectives.

Supply chain efficiency dramatically improves when vendors and retailers share information and work together. By collaborating, vendors can plan their purchases of raw materials and production process to match the retailer's merchandise needs. Thus, vendors can make sure that the merchandise is available "just in time," when the retailer needs it, without having to stock excessive inventory in the vendor's warehouse or the retailer's distribution centers or stores.

When retailers and vendors do not coordinate their supply chain management activities, excess inventory builds up in the system, even if the retail sales rate for the merchandise is relatively constant. This buildup of inventory in an uncoordinated channel is called the **bullwhip effect.** The effect was first discovered by Procter & Gamble, which saw that its orders from retailers for Pampers disposable diapers were shaped like a bullwhip, with wide swings in quantity ordered, even though retail sales were relatively constant (see Exhibit 10–6). Its retailers were ordering, on average, more inventory than they really needed.[27]

EXHIBIT 10–6
Bullwhip Effect in Uncoordinated Supply Chain

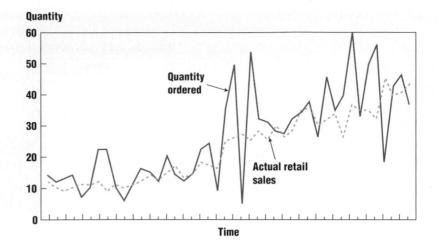

Research has found that the bullwhip effect in an *uncoordinated supply chain* is caused by the following factors:

- *Delays in transmitting orders and receiving merchandise.* Even when retailers can forecast sales accurately, there are delays in getting orders to the vendor and receiving those orders from the vendor. In an uncoordinated supply chain, retailers might not know how fast they can get the merchandise, and thus, they overorder to prevent stockouts.

- *Overreacting to shortages.* When retailers find it difficult to get the merchandise they want, they begin to play the shortage game. They order more than they need to prevent stockouts, hoping they will receive a larger partial shipment. So, on average, the vendor ships more than the retailer really needs.

- *Ordering in batches.* Rather than generating a number of small orders, retailers wait and place larger orders to reduce order processing and transportation costs and take advantage of quantity discounts.

These factors cause the bullwhip effect even when sales are fairly constant. However, for many retailers, sales are not constant; they go up dramatically when retailers put merchandise on sale and during special gift-giving times of the year. These irregularities in sales heighten the bullwhip effect and the buildup of inventory in the supply chain.

Vendors and retailers have found that by working together, they can reduce the level of inventory in the supply chain and the number of stockouts in the stores. Four approaches for coordinating supply chain activities, in order of the level of collaboration, are (1) using EDI; (2) exchanging information; (3) using vendor-managed inventory; and (4) employing collaborative planning, forecasting, and replenishment (CPFR).[28] Retailing View 10.4 describes the historical forces motivating retailers and vendors to collaborate on supply chain management.

Using EDI

The use of EDI to transmit purchase order information reduces the time it takes for retailers to place orders and for vendors to acknowledge the receipt of orders and communicate delivery information about those orders. In addition, EDI facilitates the implementation of other collaborative approaches discussed in the following sections. However, the use of EDI without other collaborative approaches only addresses one factor discussed previously—the delay in transmitting and receiving orders—that causes the buildup of inventory in the supply chain.

Sharing Information

One of the major factors causing excessive inventory in the supply chain is the inability of vendors to know what the actual level of retail store sales are. For instance, suppose a grocery store vendor offered discounts to its retailers several times a year, hoping that the savings would be passed on to customers.[29] Instead, however, the retailers purchased extra inventory and kept the extra discounts to increase their margins. The bullwhip effect caused wild fluctuations in retail orders and inventory, causing an inventory buildup and retail and production difficulties for the vendor. Once the retailer started sharing sales information with the vendor, the vendor began to give discounts on retail sales, not on purchases, and the inventory problem vanished.

solve.

Sharing sales data with vendors is an important first step in improving supply chain efficiency. With these sales data, vendors can improve their sales forecasts, improve production efficiency, and reduce the need for excessive backup inventory. But additional levels of collaboration are needed to use this information effectively. The sales data reflect historical data, not what the retailer's plans are for the future. For example, the retailer might decide to delete a vendor's SKU from its assortment—a decision that clearly affects future sales.

Vendor-Managed Inventory

Vendor-managed inventory (VMI) is an approach for improving supply chain efficiency in which the vendor is responsible for maintaining the retailer's inventory levels in each of its stores.[30] As illustrated in Exhibit 10–7, the vendor determines a reorder point—a level of inventory at which more merchandise is required. The retailer shares sales data with the vendor via EDI. When inventory drops to

---

Quick Response and Efficient Consumer Response (ECR)   **RETAILING VIEW**   **10.4**

Retailer–vendor collaboration in supply chain management grew out of activities undertaken by apparel manufacturers and retailers, called quick response (QR), and by consumer packaged goods (CPG) manufacturers and supermarket retailers, called efficient consumer response (ECR). In the mid-1980s, Milliken, a U.S. textile manufacturer facing severe price competition from imports, developed a strategy to compete on its speed to market rather than price. At the time, it took 66 weeks for the apparel industry to go from yarn at the manufacturer to clothing on a retail store fixture. But because no one in the supply chain knew what would be selling in a month, much less a year, the cost of that lengthy supply cycle was devastating. The apparel industry as a whole lost billions of dollars each year through price reductions on items customers didn't want and because they did not have enough of what they did want.

To address this supply chain inefficiency, Milliken joined with The Warren Featherbone Company, a children's apparel maker, and Mercantile Stores, a large retail chain, to compete through what they called quick response. Quick response was modeled after the just-in-time (JIT) initiatives undertaken by manufacturers and adapted to retailing. Mercantile developed a sales forecast for a season. Milliken manufactured the fabric to meet the forecast but kept most of the fabric as "grey goods" that could be dyed different colors when orders for the specific colors came in. Featherbone cut and sewed a small initial assortment of garments and shipped them to Mercantile. Mercantile monitored the initial sales of colors and sizes, then transmitted this information to Featherbone and Milliken so the remaining fabric could be dyed, cut, and sewed in the colors and sizes that consumers were buying.

Wal-Mart and other discount store chains were the motivating force for collaboration between CPG manufacturers and supermarket retailers. Through the Food Marketing Institute, supermarkets, facing price competition from discount stores, commissioned Kurt Salmon Associates (KSA) to find out how they could compete more effectively. KSA found that the supermarkets had a significant cost disadvantage due to their inefficient supply chains. When CPG manufacturers held special trade promotions (discounted the wholesale price), supermarket chains would buy a six-month supply of the products, leaving them with $30 billion of excess inventory in their distribution centers. In 1993, the KSA report recommended a multipronged approach called ECR that involved collaboration between manufacturers and retailers to achieve efficient replenishment and promotions.[32]

Since these initiatives were launched, the grocery industry has made greater strides in improving its supply chain efficiencies than the apparel industry, because the manufacturing process for apparel is more complex and the number of SKUs is significantly greater.

REFACT

Potential sales growth of 5 percent, or €42 billion, is available to retailers that better meet shoppers' and consumers' needs through new products, improved information, and service offerings in-store.[31]

REFACT

Top-tier ECR adopters enjoy 6 percent better service levels, 5 percent higher on-shelf availability, and 10 days lower finished goods inventories than do low or non-adopters of ECR practices.[33]

Sources: "Backgrounder: Efficient Consumer Response," http://www.fmi.org/media/bg/ecr1.htm (accessed August 19, 2007); Joerg Hofstetter, "Assessing the Contribution of ECR," *ECR Journal* 6, no. 1 (Spring 2006), pp. 20–29.

EXHIBIT 10–7
Vendor-Managed
Inventory

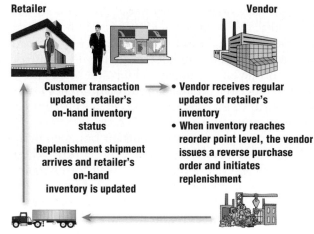

Retailer   Vendor

• **Customer transaction**   • **Vendor receives regular**
  updates retailer's   **updates of retailer's**
  on-hand inventory   **inventory**
  status   • **When inventory reaches**
                                               reorder point level, the vendor
Replenishment shipment   **issues a reverse purchase**
arrives and retailer's   **order and initiates**
on-hand   **replenishment**
inventory is updated

SOURCE: Adapted from Terrance L. Pohlen and Thomas J. Goldsby, "VMI and SMI Programs," *International Journal of Physical Distribution & Logistics Management* 33, no. 7 (2003), p. 567.

the order point, the vendor generates the order (i.e., a reverse purchase order) and delivers the merchandise. Although VMI can be used to replenish inventory at retail stores, the approach is usually applied to replenish inventories at the retailer's distribution center.[34]

In ideal conditions, the vendor replenishes inventories in quantities that meet the retailer's immediate demand, reducing stockouts with minimal inventory. In addition to better matching retail demand to supply, VMI can reduce the vendor's and the retailer's costs. Vendor salespeople no longer need to spend time generating orders on items that are already in the stores, and their role shifts to selling new items and maintaining relationships. Retail buyers and planners no longer need to monitor inventory levels and place orders.

For example, TAL Apparel Ltd., a Hong Kong shirt maker, produces garments for labels such as J.Crew, Calvin Klein, Banana Republic, and JCPenney, and it supplies one in seven dress shirts sold in the United States. It now manages JCPenney's men's dress shirt inventory. TAL collects POS data for JCPenney's shirt sales directly from stores in North America and then runs the numbers through a computer model it designed. Next, TAL decides how many shirts to make and in what styles, colors, and sizes. It sends the shirts directly to each JCPenney's store, bypassing the retailer's distribution centers and merchandise managers. Because TAL manages the entire process, from design to ordering yarn, it can bring a new style from the testing stage to full retail rollout in four months, much faster than JCPenney's could on its own. The system, in effect, lets consumers, not merchandise managers, pick the styles.[35]

The use of VMI is not a new approach. Frito-Lay and other snack food, candy, and beverage vendors have managed the stocks of their products on supermarket shelves for a long time. However, technological advances have increased the sophistication of VMI. The sharing of POS transaction data, for instance, allows vendors to sell merchandise on **consignment;** the vendor owns the merchandise until it is sold by the retailer, at which time the retailer pays for the merchandise. Consignment selling provides an incentive for the vendor to pick SKUs and inventory levels that will minimize inventory and generate sales. Because the vendor is bearing the financial cost of owning the inventory, retailers are more willing to allow the vendor to be responsible for determining the inventory plan and appropriate assortment for each store.

Although it is a more advanced level of collaboration than simply using EDI and sharing information, VMI has its limitations. Whereas the vendor coordinates the supply chain for its specific products, it does not know what other actions the retailer is taking that might affect the sales of its products in the future. For example, Pepsi might not know that a supermarket will be having a big promotion in three weeks for a new beverage introduced by Coca-Cola. Without this knowledge, Pepsi would ship too much merchandise to the supermarket.

REFACT

Improvements in vendor-managed inventory can result in the elimination of between 20 and 30 percent of the previously required supply chain inventory.[36]

Hong Kong shirt maker TAL apparel Ltd produces shirts and manages the inventory for JCPenney.

Collaborative Planning, Forecasting, and Replenishment

Collaborative planning, forecasting, and replenishment (CPFR) is the sharing of forecast and related business information and collaborative planning between retailers and vendors to improve supply chain efficiency and product replenishment.[37] Although retailers share sales and inventory data when using a VMI approach, the vendor remains responsible for managing the inventory. In contrast, CPFR is a more advanced form of retailer–vendor collaboration that involves sharing proprietary information such as business strategies, promotion plans, new product developments and introductions, production schedules, and lead time information.

CPFR was more formally developed by Voluntary Interindustry Commerce Standards, or VICS (www.vics.org) and adopted by ECR Europe (www.ecrnet.org). The software used to exchange CPFR information is Internet based and thus more easily and inexpensively accessible to all parties. Retail exchanges such as WorldWide Retail Exchange (www.worldwideretailexchange.org) and Global NetXchange (www.gnx.com) now offer CPFR software to their members. Retailing View 10.5 illustrates how West Marine uses CPFR to improve its supply chain efficiency.

REFACT

A precursor to the Internet-based systems used for CPFR occurred in 1987 when Wal-Mart and Procter & Gamble forged a partnership to control their inventory. The partnership program improved product availability, decreased inventory, and reduced costs, which Wal-Mart passed on as savings to its customers in the form of lower prices.

RADIO FREQUENCY IDENTIFICATION (RFID)

Radio frequency identification (RFID) is a technology that allows an object or person to be identified at a distance using radio signals. The electronic chips are inserted into oceangoing containers, on shipping cartons, or even behind merchandise labels; they then transmit data about the object in which they are embedded.

REFACT

Supply chain collaboration can add as much as three percentage points to profit margins for all types of supply chain players.[38]

RFID technology has advantages over bar codes. First, the chips can hold more data and update data stored on the device. For instance, it can keep track of where an item is in the supply chain and even where it is stored in a distribution center. Second the data on the device can be acquired without a visual line of sight and in harsh environments in which bar code labels won't work.

The promise of RFID is the dream of every supply chain manager, because it enables the accurate, real-time tracking of every single product, from manufacturers to checkout in stores. It eliminates the manual point-and-read operations needed to get data from UPC bar coding. Thus, RFID can significantly decrease warehouse, distribution, and inventory costs; increase margins; and provide better in-stock positions.

Several of the most prominent retailers are already taking advantage of this new technology. Wal-Mart has demanded its top 600 suppliers put RFID tags on all pallets,

---

10.5   RETAILING VIEW   West Marine Uses CPFR to Build a Competitive Advantage

West Marine's founder and chairman, Randy Repass, channeled his passion for boating into a business that revolutionized the way people shop for boating supplies. Forty years ago, when Randy started selling nylon rope out of his garage, boat supply stores were dark, disorganized places staffed by a couple of salty but indifferent clerks who preferred swapping sea stories with one another to helping customers find what they came in to buy. Randy's vision was to provide a one-stop shopping experience with great customer service for boaters. Today, West Marine has more than 370 stores across the United States and Canada and sells supplies through catalog and Internet channels. The company offers more than 50,000 products, ranging from the rope that started it all to the latest in marine electronics.

The boating market is highly seasonal; more than 50 percent of sales occur between April and October. Whereas the holiday season and Christmas are the peak seasons for most retailers, West Marine's peak sales occur during the week before the 4th of July. In addition, boat supply retailers are very promotional, which introduces more variation and uncertainty into sales forecasts. West Marine found that these wide variations in demand resulted in lost sales due to inefficiencies in its supply chain.

To address this issue, West Marine and its key suppliers implemented collaboration, planning, forecasting, and replenishment (CPFR) programs following the Voluntary Interindustry Commerce Standards Association (VICS) model. The first step West Marine took was to meet with key suppliers to develop a better forecasting system. Now, every night, West Marine collects SKU-level sales and inventory information for each of its stores, and every day, it generates a 52-week forecast for demand by store at the SKU level. The forecasts factor in all marketing and promotional events. The forecast is shared with the suppliers so they can order parts and schedule production.

How does West Marine use CPFR to improve its supply chain?

West Marine has made CPFR an integral part of its merchandising and planning operations. Each West Marine category manager (CM) partners with a merchandise planner (MP). The CM is responsible for the vendor strategies and marketing relationships; the MP is responsible for directing the supply chain relationship. West Marine MPs and CMs conduct quarterly supply chain planning meetings with each CPFR supplier. These meetings involve teams from both companies and include the key marketing, forecasting, production planning, distribution, and transportation players. In addition, the planners from both sides engage in a monthly collaborative meeting that reviews results, manages current initiatives, and identifies and resolves any supply issues based on the order forecast. Team members beyond the primary planners frequently attend and contribute to these monthly meetings as well.

Sources: www.westmarine.com (accessed October 11, 2007); Larry Smith, "West Marine: A CPFR Success Story," *Supply Chain Management Review*, March 1, 2006, pp. 29–36.

cases, cartons, and high-margin items, and another 700 are expected to be added to the mandate.[39] Metro (Germany's largest retailer), Target, Best Buy, and Albertson's are also experimenting with RFID programs.[40] To meet these demands, vendors have been forced to make significant investments to acquire the necessary technology and equipment.

Benefits of RFID

Some of the benefits of RFID include

Reduced warehouse and distribution labor costs, Warehouse and distribution costs typically represent 2 to 4 percent of operating expenses for retailers. Replacing point-and-read, labor-intensive operations with sensors that track pallets, cases, cartons, and individual products anywhere in the facility can significantly reduce labor costs by as much as 30 percent.

Reduced point-of-sale labor costs. Using RFID at the product level can help retailers reduce the labor costs needed for checking shelf inventory. In addition, RFID-enabled products will improve self-scan checkouts and increase the use of self-scans, thus shortening checkout times and reducing employee fraud.

Inventory savings. RFID reduces inventory errors, ensuring that the inventory recorded is actually available. By tracking pieces more exactly, companies have more accurate information about what was sold and what inventory is actually needed.

Magicmirror™ uses RFID to provide product information to customers. Magicmirror™ is also used to deter shoplifting since the mirror keeps track of the items the customer has brought into the dressing room.

Eliminate counterfeit merchandise. Using RFID on individual items can help eliminate counterfeit merchandise.[41] For example, California will require all drug makers to utilize this technology by January 1, 2009. Oregon and New York, as well as France, Japan, and Spain, are all making moves toward similar legislation.

Facilitates the selling process. Magicmirror™ is a new technological innovation that links an RFID reader to a digital display to provide product information to consumers.[42] When a customer brings a tagged item near the mirror, the system displays a description of the garment, as well as other available colors and sizes. If the shopper wants a different item, he or she taps the mirror, and a sales associate is alerted to the request through a mobile device. The technology also suggests accompanying accessories to help salespeople up- and cross-sell.

Reduced theft. With RFID, products can be tracked through the supply chain to pinpoint where a product is at all times, which helps reduce theft in transportation, at the distribution centers, or in the stores. RFID has already been successfully deployed in stores, particularly on costly items prone to theft, such as Gillette Mach 3 razor blades. The Magicmirror™ can also be used to deter shoplifting. When a shopper enters the dressing room, the mirror keeps track of all the items and sizes the customer has brought in with him or her.[43]

Reduced out-of-stock conditions. Because RFID facilitates accurate product tracking, forecasts are more accurate, which decreases stockouts. Using RFID, store managers can be automatically notified when specific SKUs are not on the shelves and need to be stocked.[44]

Impediments to the Adoption of RFID

A major obstacle to the widespread adoption of RFID has been the high costs, which make the present return on investment low. The cost of RFID tags is 15 cents per tag,

REFACT

A recent study found that the use of RFID trimmed out-of-stocks by up to 16 percent.[45]

cost ??
data ??
labor coll ??
privacy

down from 40 cents in 2002. However, with demand increasing and tag production costs declining, the tags are expected to reach 5 cents per tag, and they are reusable.[46]

Another reason RFID has not been adopted by more retailers is that it generates more data than can be efficiently processed, and therefore, retailers find it difficult to justify the implementation costs. Most retailers are not capable of transmitting, storing, and processing the data that would be available about the location of pallets, cases, cartons, totes, and individual products in the supply chain.

Suppliers are pushing back as well. Some claim that instead of saving labor, RFID tagging actually takes more: Bar codes are printed on cases at the factory, but because most manufacturers have yet to adopt RFID, those tags have to be put on by hand at the warehouse.

Finally, consumers, particularly in the United States, are wary that once the tags are on individual items, they could be used to track individual buyers—an obvious invasion of privacy.[47] The problem is less acute in the European Union, where retailers have educated consumers on RFID use and changed procedures to accommodate consumers' fears by developing tag-removal policies. Germany's Metro and England's Marks & Spencer are both using item-level RFID on a limited basis.

SUMMARY

Supply chain management and information systems have become important tools for achieving a sustainable competitive advantage. Developing more efficient methods of distributing merchandise creates an opportunity to reduce expenses and improve customer service levels.

The systems used to control the flow of information to buyers and then on to vendors have become quite sophisticated. Retailers have developed data warehouses that provide them with intimate knowledge of who their customers are and what they like to buy. These data warehouses are being used to strengthen the relationships with their customers and improve the productivity of their marketing and inventory management efforts.

Some retailers are using distribution centers for crossdocking instead of storing merchandise. Others have their vendors supply them with floor-ready merchandise and adhere to strict delivery schedules. Still other retailers are having vendors deliver merchandise directly to their stores and use pull supply chains that base inventory policies on consumer demand. Retailers are outsourcing many of these logistics functions to third-party logistics companies.

Retailers and vendors are collaborating to improve supply chain efficiency. Electronic data interchange enables retailers to communicate electronically with their vendors. The Internet has accelerated the adoption of EDI, especially among smaller, less sophisticated vendors. Other more involving and effective collaborative approaches include information sharing, VMI, and CPFR. These approaches represent the nexus of information systems and logistics management. They reduce lead time, increase product availability, lower inventory investments, and reduce overall logistics expenses.

Finally, RFID has the potential of further streamlining the supply chain. These small devices are affixed to pallets, cartons, and individual items and can be used to track merchandise through the supply chain and store information, such as when an item was shipped to a distribution center. Although still relatively expensive to be placed on all items, RFID technology can reduce labor, theft, and inventory costs.

KEY TERMS

GET OUT AND DO IT!

1. **CONTINUING ASSIGNMENT** Interview the store manager working for the retailer you have selected for the continuing assignment. Write a report that describes and evaluates the retailer's information and supply chain systems. Use this chapter as a basis for developing a set of questions to ask the manager. Some of the questions might include: Where is the store's distribution center? Does the retailer use direct store delivery from vendors? How frequently are deliveries made to the store? Does the merchandise come in ready for sale? What is the store's percentage of stockouts? Does the retailer use a push or pull system? Does the store get involved in determining what merchandise is in the store and in what quantities? Does the retailer use VMI, EDI, CPFR, or RFID?

2. Go to Barcoding Incorporated's Web page at http://www.barcoding.com/success_stories/ and read some of the posted success stories in the retail industry. How has this company solved problems for retailers with automatic data collection systems?

3. Go to the Metro Group, Future Store Initiative, homepage and watch the video called "RFID Innovation Center" at http://www.future-store.org/servlet/PB/menu/1007054/index.html. After watching the six-minute video clip, describe how electronic product codes and radio frequency identification can make the shopping experience better for consumers and improve efficiency in the supply chain.

DISCUSSION QUESTIONS AND PROBLEMS

1. Retail system acronyms include VMI, EDI, CPFR, and RFID. How are these terms related to one another?

2. Explain how an efficient supply chain system can increase a retailer's level of product availability and decrease its inventory investment.

3. This chapter presents some trends in logistics and information systems that benefit retailers. How do vendors benefit from these trends?

4. What type of merchandise is most likely to be cross-docked at retailers' distribution centers? Why is this the case?

5. Why haven't more fashion retailers adopted an integrated supply chain system similar to Zara's?

6. Explain the differences between pull and push supply chains.

7. Why is global logistics much more complicated than domestic logistics?

8. Consumers have five key reactions to stockouts: buy the item at another store, substitute a different brand, substitute the same brand, delay purchase, or do not purchase the item. Consider your own purchasing behavior and describe how various categories of merchandise would result in different reactions to a stockout.

9. Abandoned purchases as a result of stockouts can mean millions of dollars a year in lost sales. How are retailers and manufacturers using technology to reduce stockouts and improve sales?

10. In the past, manufacturers dominated the relationship between vendors and retailers. Today, retailers have more leverage, and both parties are investing in and seeing the benefits of a more trusting relationship with two-way communication. How has the emergence of mega-formats, mergers and acquisitions, and technology enabled this shift to greater cooperation between retailers and manufacturers?

SUGGESTED READINGS

Bernon, Michael, and John Cullen. "An Integrated Approach to Managing Reverse Logistics." *International Journal of Logistics: Research & Applications* 10, no. 1 (2007), pp. 41–56.

Chang, Tien-Hsiang; Hsin-Pin Fu; Wan-I Lee; Yichen Lin; and Hsu-Chih Hsueh. "A Study of an Augmented CPFR Model for the 3C Retail Industry." *Supply Chain Management* 12, no. 3 (2007), pp. 200–209.

Chopra, Sunil, and Peter Meindl. *Supply Chain Management*, 3rd ed. Englewood Cliffs, NJ: Prentice Hall, 2006.

Hugos, Michael, and Chris Thomas. *Supply Chain Management in the Retail Industry.* New York: Wiley, 2005.

Niederman, Fred; Richard G. Mathieu; Roger Morley; and Kwon Ik-Whan. "Examining RFID Applications in Supply Chain Management." *Communications of the ACM* 50, no. 7 (2007), pp. 93–101.

Parker, Philip M. *The 2007–2012 World Outlook for Retail Logistics.* San Diego: ICON Group International, Inc., 2006.

Seung-Kuk, Paik, and Prabir K. Bachi. "Understanding the Causes of the Bullwhip Effect in a Supply Chain." *International Journal of Retail & Distribution Management* 35, no. 4 (2007), pp. 308–24.

Vaidyanathan, Jayaraman. "Creating Competitive Advantages Through New Value Creation: A Reverse Logistics Perspective." *Academy of Management Perspectives* 21, no. 2 (2007), pp. 56–73.

Wong, Chien Yaw and Duncan McFarlane. "Radio Frequency Identification Data Capture and Its Impact on Shelf Replenishment." *International Journal of Logistics: Research & Applications* 10, no. 1 (2007), pp. 71–93.

Customer Relationship Management

Our group is responsible for analyzing the purchasing data we have on our customers and developing programs and promotions that increase CVS pharmacy's share of wallet. These customer relationship management activities drive off the data we collect from the 50 million cardholders enrolled in our ExtraCare® program. Customers in the program earn ExtraBucks®—2 percent on most in-store and online purchases and $1 for every two prescriptions purchased—that can be used when shopping in our stores or online. ExtraCare® customers also receive

EXECUTIVE BRIEFING
Bari Harlam, Vice President, Marketing Intelligence, CVS Caremark, Inc.

e-mails and direct mailings with helpful health and beauty insights, new product information, and valuable coupons, in addition to free merchandise when we have special vendor promotions.

By analyzing the buying behavior of our ExtraCare® customers, we discover some interesting opportunities for cross-promotions. For example, about two-thirds of our customers buying toothpaste did not buy toothbrushes from us. To encourage these customers to buy toothbrushes as well as toothpaste, we target these customers for a special toothbrush promotion.

We also use targeted special promotions to increase the average size of a customer's market basket. For example, we offer a $4 coupon to customers with an average market basket of $15 who buy $25. Customers who normally purchase $25 of merchandise get a $10 coupon if they make a $50 purchase.

Each quarter we distribute over five million messages to our customers. These messages contain information and offers tailored to the customers' buying behavior. Like most drugstore chains, over 20 percent of our sales involve some form of promotion. These promotions

CHAPTER 11

QUESTIONS

What is customer relationship management?

Why do retailers want to treat customers differently?

How do retailers determine who their best customers are?

How can retailers build customer loyalty?

What can retailers do to increase their share of wallet?

What can retailers do to alleviate the privacy concerns of their customers?

increase sales but can lower our gross margin. We experiment with different messaging and offerings and then analyze customer buying behavior to determine which promotions are more profitable.

We are very concerned about our customers' privacy. Our program is an opt-in one, and therefore, we only send mailings to customers who give us permission to do so. At times, we use outside processing companies as our agents to help print and send mailings. But these agents never receive any personal customer information beyond name and address. We value our customers' privacy and never give or sell any specific information about them to any manufacturer or direct marketers.

Ms. Harlam earned a Ph.D. in marketing from the Wharton School at the University of Pennsylvania. Prior to joining CVS, she was a marketing professor at the University of Rhode Island and Columbia University's Graduate School of Business.

The business press and companies are talking a lot about the importance of managing customer relationships. Companies are spending billions of dollars on computer systems to help them collect and analyze data about their customers. With all of this buzz, you'd think that the customer is a popular new kid in the neighborhood. However, the customer is more like an old friend who's been taken for granted—until now.

Consider the following example. Shari Ast is on her third business trip this month. She takes a cab from Boston Logan airport to the Ritz-Carlton, her favorite hotel. As the doorman opens the car door for her, he greets her with, "Welcome back to the Ritz-Carlton, Ms. Ast." When she goes to the registration desk, the receptionist gives her a room key. Then she goes to her room and finds just what she prefers—a room with a view of the Boston Commons, a single queen-size bed, an extra pillow and blanket, a fax machine connected to her telephone, and a basket with her favorite fruits and snacks.

Shari Ast's experience is an example of the Ritz-Carlton's customer relationship management program. **Customer relationship management (CRM)** is a business philosophy and set of strategies, programs, and systems that focuses on identifying and building loyalty with a retailer's most valued customers. Based on the philosophy that retailers can increase their profitability by building relationships with their better customers, the goal of CRM is to develop a base of loyal customers who patronize the retailer frequently. In the following sections of this chapter, we discuss in more depth the objective of CRM programs and the elements of the CRM process.

When guests check into 5-star hotels like the Ritz-Carlton, they are greated by name. Their preferences are known based on past vists. Everything possible is done to meet their needs and wants.

THE CRM PROCESS

Traditionally, retailers have focused their attention on encouraging customers to visit their stores, look through their catalogs, and visit their Web sites. To accomplish this objective, they have used mass media advertising and sales promotions, treating all of their customers the same.

Now retailers are beginning to concentrate on providing more value to their best customers using targeted promotions and services to increase their **share of wallet** from a customer—the percentage of the customers' purchases made from the retailer. This change in perspective is supported by research indicating that all customers are not equally profitable and that more and less profitable customers need to be treated differently.[1]

What Is Loyalty?

emotional connection

Customer loyalty, the objective of CRM, is more than having customers make repeat visits to a retailer and being satisfied with their experiences. **Customer loyalty** to a retailer means that customers are committed to purchasing merchandise and services from the retailer and will resist the activities of competitors attempting to attract their patronage. They have a bond with the retailer, and the bond is based on more than a positive feeling about the retailer.[2] Retailing View 11.1 describes how Neiman Marcus builds loyalty with its best customers.

Loyal customers have an emotional connection with the retailer. They feel like the retailer is a friend. Their reasons for continuing to patronize a retailer go beyond the convenience of the retailer's store or the low prices and specific brands offered by the retailer. They feel such goodwill toward the retailer that they will encourage their friends and family to buy from it.

Programs that encourage repeat buying by simply offering price discounts can be easily copied by competitors. In addition, these types of price-promotion programs encourage customers to always look for the best deal rather than develop a relationship with one retailer. However, when a retailer develops an emotional connection with a customer, it is difficult for a competitor to attract that customer.[3]

Emotional connections develop when customers receive personal attention. For example, many small, independent restaurants build loyalty by functioning as neighborhood cafés, where waiters and waitresses recognize customers by name and know their preferences. Larger stores like Nordstrom have found that paying personal attention to customers by inviting them to grand opening celebrations, pampering them during private shopping parties, and offering them concierge services,free alterations, and shipping is more important than giving them discounts.[4]

CRM activity

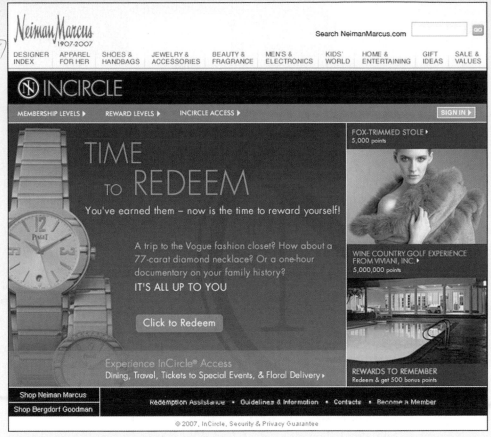

Neiman Marcus's InCircle program provides special benefits to build its share of wallet with its best customers.

One of the best examples of a CRM activity designed to build customer loyalty is Neiman Marcus's InCircle program. The program is designed to focus on its best customers.

Customers spending more than $5,000 annually on their Neiman Marcus credit card are enrolled in the program and get special gifts, awards, and services. Customers whose higher spending levels place them in the "Platinum" or "Chairman's" categories generate additional rewards and services for themselves. There are currently 100,000 InCircle members, whose median household income is $285,000 and who spend an average of over $12,000 per year.

Customers earn one point for each dollar charged on a Neiman Marcus credit card. The points can be redeemed for prizes ranging from a limited-edition Emilio Pucci silk scarf to an eight-night excursion through India or a complete Sony home movie theater. Each year, for 5,000,000 points, a limited edition luxury vehicle is a reward choice. This year, it is the 2008 Lexus LS600h L. Reward options are refined and expanded annually, but the options are always designed to enhance Neiman's exclusive image and reputation for uniqueness.

InCircle members receive frequent communications from Neiman Marcus throughout the year, including the quarterly InCircle newsletter and the semiannual InCircle *Entrée* magazine, a quality publication produced by the creators of *Southern Living* and *Southern Accents*.

Customer relationships are also nurtured at the store level. Neiman's sales associates can tap into information about customers' past purchases and shopping behaviors and are encouraged to contact these customers personally. Sales associates have the freedom to be creative in helping InCircle customers shop in multiple departments and use the various services Neiman Marcus offers, from gift wrapping to travel services. Store managers invite InCircle members to free luncheons on their birthdays.

Recognizing the value of these preferred customers, Neiman invites InCircle members to sit on a board that provides feedback and suggestions as to how Neiman can improve its customers' shopping experience and enhance and broaden its role in the community. These board meetings help Neiman Marcus maintain a genuine, ongoing dialogue with its best customers and make these customers feel that the company respects them and values their opinions.

REFACT

In 1984, Neiman Marcus launched the first frequent shopper program sponsored by a retailer.[5]

Sources: Vanessa O'Connell, "Posh Retailers Pile on Perks for Top Customers," *The Wall Street Journal*, April 26, 2007; www.incircle.com (accessed August 29, 2007); www.neimanmarcus.com (accessed August 29, 2007).

EXHIBIT 11–1
The CRM Process Cycle

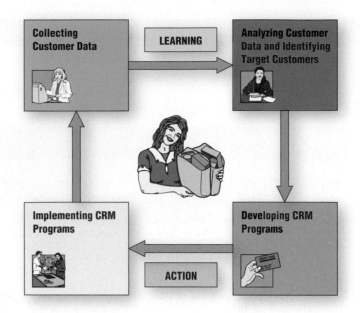

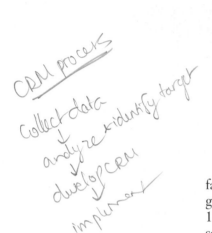

Unusual positive experiences also build emotional connections. For example, a family was shopping for shoes at Nordstrom for their teenage daughter, who was going through a growth spurt. One of her feet was a size 10, and the other was a 10½. The salesperson broke up two pairs of shoes to make the sale and ensure a satisfied customer. The gesture paid off—that day, the family purchased five pairs of shoes and have remained loyal customers ever since.[6] Providing such memorable experiences is an important avenue for building customer loyalty.[7]

Overview of the CRM Process

REFACT

The modern age of loyalty marketing began in 1981 with the launch of the American Airlines Advantage program. Airlines now have over 255 million members, the most of any industry.[8]

Exhibit 11–1 illustrates that CRM is an iterative process that turns customer data into customer loyalty through four activities: (1) collecting customer data, (2) analyzing the customer data and identifying target customers, (3) developing CRM programs, and (4) implementing CRM programs. The process begins with the collection and analysis of data about a retailer's customers and the identification of target customers. The analysis translates the customer information into activities that offer value to the targeted customers. Then these activities are executed through communication programs undertaken by the marketing department and customer service programs implemented by customer contact employees, typically sales associates. Each of the four activities in the CRM process is discussed in the following sections.

COLLECTING CUSTOMER DATA

The first step in the CRM process is to construct a **customer database.** This database is part of the data warehouse described in Chapter 10. It contains all of the data the firm has collected about its customers and is the foundation for subsequent CRM activities.

Customer Database

Ideally, the database should contain the following information:

- *Transactions.* A complete history of the purchases made by the customer, including the purchase date, the SKUs purchased, the price paid, the amount of profit, and whether the merchandise was purchased in response to a special promotion or marketing activity.
- *Customer contacts.* A record of the interactions that the customer has had with the retailer, including visits to the retailer's Web site, inquiries made through in-store kiosks, and telephone calls made to the retailer's call center, plus information about

contacts initiated by the retailer, such as catalogs and direct mail sent to the customer.

• *Customer preferences.* What the customer likes, such as favorite colors, brands, fabrics, and flavors, as well as apparel sizes. At a Brooks Brothers store in New York, a sales associate looked up a customer's recent purchases at its POS terminal. She saw that the customer purchased a navy pinstripe suit several months ago. Using this information, she knew exactly which dress shirts would go with the suit and took the opportunity to show him some coordinating ties, too. By the time she rang up the sale, it included three dress shirts, two ties, underwear, and socks.[9]

• *Descriptive information.* Demographic and psychographic data describing the customer that can be used in developing market segments.

• *Responses to marketing activities.* Analyses of transaction and contact data provide information about the customer's responsiveness to marketing activities.

Different members of the same household also might also have interactions with a retailer. Thus, to get a complete view of the customer, retailers need to be able to combine individual customer data from each member of a household. For example, at Mitchells or Richards, stores in a family-owned apparel chain in Westport and Greenwich, Connecticut, husbands and wives buy things for each other. The chain's database keeps track of both household-level purchases and individual purchases so sales associates can help one spouse buy a gift for the other. The database also keeps track of spending changes and habits. Anniversaries, birthdays, and even divorces and second marriages are tracked along with style, brand, size, and color preferences; hobbies; and sometimes pets' names and golf handicaps.[10] Retailing View 11.2 describes how Harrah's uses its customer database for its loyalty program.

With today's technology, independent companies are able to network with their larger suppliers to increase sales. For example, George Matick Chevrolet in Redford, Michigan, doubled its sales when it installed a CRM program that helped it keep track of potential sales leads. The leads originate both from its own and General Motors' Web site.[11]

Customers' sales information is recorded at POS terminals, stored in data warehouses, and used in CRM systems.

Identifying Information

Constructing a database for catalog and Internet shoppers and customers who use the retailer's credit card when buying merchandise in stores is relatively easy. Customers buying merchandise through nonstore channels must provide their contact information, name, and address so that the purchases can be sent to them. When retailers issue their own credit cards, they can collect the contact information for billing when customers apply for the card. In these cases, the identification of the customer is linked to the transaction. However, identifying most customers who are making in-store transactions is more difficult because they often pay for the merchandise with a check, cash, or a third-party credit card such as Visa or MasterCard.

Three approaches that store-based retailers use to overcome this problem are (1) asking customers for their identifying information, (2) offering frequent shopper programs, and (3) connecting Internet purchasing data with store purchases.

Asking for Identifying Information   Some retailers have their sales associates ask customers for identifying information, such as their phone number or name and address, when they ring up a sale.[12] This information is then used to create a transaction database for the customer. However, some customers may be reluctant to provide the information and feel that the sales associates are violating their privacy.

REFACT

Eighty-nine percent of consumers believe that retailers are not doing everything they should to protect personal information.[13]

Offering Frequent Shopper Programs   **Frequent shopper programs,** also called **loyalty programs,** are programs that identify and provide rewards to customers who patronize a retailer. Some retailers issue customers a frequent shopper card, whereas others use a **private-label credit card**—a credit card that has the store's name on it. In both cases, customer information is automatically captured when the card is scanned at the point of sale terminal. When customers enroll in one of these programs, they provide some descriptive information about themselves or their household. The customers then are offered an incentive to use the card when they make purchases from the retailer. Research has shown that customers generally prefer to get something extra—a reward—for their purchases, rather than lower prices.[15] As we see in Retailing Views 11.1 and 11.2, Neiman Marcus and Harrah's both give points for every dollar spent or gambled. The points can be redeemed for special gifts, special privileges, complementary food, drinks, hotel rooms, and even vacations.

11.2   RETAILING VIEW   Harrah's CRM

Harrah's is an innovator in using customer relationship management in the gaming industry. In the 1990s, casinos were competing against each other by building more and more elaborate facilities. Harrah's, with more limited resources than some of the large casinos, took a different approach for developing a competitive advantage. It decided to focus on CRM to build customer loyalty and increase share of wallet. Gary Loveman, a Harvard Business School professor, was hired as a consultant to analyze Harrah's customer data and develop its CRM program. He is now the CEO of the company.

Developing customer loyalty in the gaming industry is a challenge. Slot machines and gaming tables are a commodity offered by all casinos. Loveman starting building Harrah's CRM program by collecting customer data from which he could calculate the life time value of each customer. Harrah's decided to focus on avid experience players, who were not really the "high rollers." Avid experience players gamble $100–$500 per trip, visit several times per year, and provide $5,000 in annual revenue.

From this research, Harrah's Total Rewards loyalty card program was born to create closer customer relationships. The program contains four tiers: Gold, Platinum, Diamond, and the highest, Seven Stars, according to the customer's lifetime value. Less than 1 percent of its 40 million customers reach the Seven Stars level, but this group is significant to the company's revenue. Each of the four segments comprises approximately 90 different groups based on geodemographics, psychographics, and play patterns.

Harrah's sophisticated database boasts customer detail like, "Tom likes NASCAR, Clint Holmes, thick steaks." Its CRM program allows it to measure four key metrics: (1) share of its customers' gaming dollars, (2) percentage of revenues from customers visiting more than one site, (3) percentage of Total Rewards members upgraded to a higher tier, and (4) customer satisfaction scores for all properties. Just as it focuses on servicing customers and helping them move up to the next level, it also terminates relationships

Harrah's best customers earn points toward benefits and upgrades on the basis of how much they spend through the Total Rewards loyalty card program. The program helps Harrah's determine the lifetime value of each customer.

wih customers that are not significant enough. Dropping nonlucrative customers saves the company $20 million annually and helps it focus on its true customers. The company's share of its customers' wallet increased to more than 43 percent from 36 percent in 1998.

A key CRM component is Harrah's ability to empower its 80,000 employees to take control over customer satisfaction. Employee performance is taken seriously to ensure they do not just provide a minimum service level but really work to make a difference. Gary Loveman, the CEO says, "From housekeepers to slot attendants, from valets to stewards, from receptionists to chefs, all employees are told daily as they arrive at work: If your service can persuade one customers to make one more visit with us, you've had a good shift. If you can persuade three, you've had a great shift." For those casinos that improve customer service by 3 percent in one year,[16] the company pays bonuses to all nonmanagement employees. In the first four years of the program's existence, the company paid out $43 million in bonuses.

With 38 casinos in 15 states, customers have many chances to accumulate points. When a gamer—casino lingo for a customer— gambles, he or she swipes a card through the slot machine or a pit boss estimates his or her bets at a table. As the points accumulate, card holders earn new status titles: 4,000 points earns a gamer Platinum status and a few privileges, such as shorter wait times in line. With 10,000 points, a gamer earns the Diamond card, which entitles him or her to benefits such as free valet parking, room upgrades, and free weekend reservations. Gamers are rewarded on the basis of their value to the hotel chain and encouraged to earn the next loyalty card status level.

Sources: Sudhir H. Kale and Peter Klugsberger, "Reaping Rewards," *Marketing Management,* July/August 2007; Richard Slawsky, "Harrah's Finds Better Service Through Technology," http://www.selfservice.org/article_3094_2.php, August 20, 2007 (accessed August 23, 2007); www.harrahs.com (accessed August 23, 2007).

Frequent shopper programs offer two benefits from the retailer's perspective: (1) customers provide demographic and other information when they sign up for the program and then are motivated to identify themselves at each transaction and (2) customers are motivated by the rewards offered to increase the number of visits and the amount purchased on each visit to the retailer.

Other retailers and service providers are experimenting with technology to increase customer loyalty and spending. As described in the Executive Briefing at the beginning of the chapter, CVS has implemented its *ExtraCare* loyalty program, in which customers can accrue rewards and are eligible for discounts according to scans of their card.[17] The drugstore chain has partnered with the bank holding company HSBC to launch its innovative loyalty program. Using HSBC's OptiPay technology, the ExtraCare Plus card acts as a debit card and a loyalty card all in one. The card is linked to customers' checking accounts so CVS can better personalize and measure its marketing promotions. This link also eliminates the customer's need for two cards, shortens queue times at the register, and allows a closer relationship with the customer.

Frequent shopper cards are becoming so common that consumers cannot carry all their many cards.

Rather than asking for identifying information or requiring a frequent shopper card, some retailers, especially those in the services sector, use a cardless, cashless payment and loyalty system. Using fingerprint scanners, a customer can pay efficiently, and the company can store the customer information quickly and accurately.

Dayton, Ohio–based Dorothy Lane Market is using this technology in its stores. Customers entering the store can either use a finger scan or swipe a card to receive a printout of their personalized product discounts. At check-out, customers can pay using the finger scan and automatically debit the amount from a checking account. This system eliminates all cards completely and fully integrates loyalty programs and customer data, and makes rewards easily available with the simple act of a fingerprint scan.[18]

Connecting Internet Purchasing Data with the Stores   When customers use third-party credit cards such as Visa or MasterCard to make a purchase in a store, the retailer cannot identify the purchase by the customer. However, if the customer used the same credit card while shopping the retailer's Web site and provided shipping information, the retailer could connect the credit card purchases with the customer. Imagine a customer purchases a computer at www.staples.com using a credit card and then uses the same credit card to purchase supplies at a Staples store. Then, the store's database can capture the customer's name and shipping address from the Web site transaction and update the customer's purchase record with the supplies obtained in the store.

REFACT

Saks Fifth Avenue has found that shoppers carrying its Saks First credit card visit the store three times as often as regular customers. Saks First shoppers spend five to ten times as much as non-Saks First card users.[19]

Privacy and CRM Programs

Although detailed information about individual customers helps retailers provide more benefits to their better customers, consumers also are concerned about retailers violating their privacy when they collect this information. If customers' data are not secure and susceptible to identity theft, customers would be reluctant to participate in loyalty programs. The data broker ChoicePoint was fined $15 million by the Federal Trade Commission (FTC) because 163,000 consumers' data were accessed. The FBI and the Secret Service also are signaling to retailers that consumer privacy is a much more serious issue than it ever has been before.

Privacy Concerns   The degree to which consumers feel their privacy has been violated depends on:

- Their control over their personal information when engaging in marketplace transactions. Do they feel they can decide the amount and type of information collected by the retailer?

- Their knowledge about the collection and use of personal information. Do they know what information is being collected and how the retailer will be using it? Will the retailer be sharing the information with other parties?[22]

These concerns are particularly acute for customers using an electronic channel because many of them do not realize the extensive amount of information that can be collected without their knowledge. This information is easily collected when the user visits a Web site that installs a cookie on the visitor's computer. **Cookies** are text files that identify visitors when they return to a Web site and track their navigation at the Web site. Due to the data in the cookies, customers do not have to identify themselves or use passwords every time they visit a site. However, the cookies also collect information about other sites the person has visited and what pages they have downloaded.

Protecting Customer Privacy   What is personal information? The definition is debatable. Some people define personal information as all information that is not publicly available; others include both public (e.g., driver's license, mortgage data) and private (hobbies, income) information. Retailers need to take the necessary precautions to protect personal information by incorporating privacy safety software such as firewalls to keep out hackers and encrypting data every time it is transferred to prevent it being intercepted.[24]

In the United States, Americans rely on retailers to protect consumer privacy. Existing legislation for consumer privacy is restricted to the protection of information associated with credit reporting, video rentals, banking, and health care. However, the European Union (EU), Australia, New Zealand, and Canada have different and more stringent consumer privacy laws. Some of the provisions of the EU directive on consumer privacy include the following:

- Businesses can collect consumer information only if they have clearly defined the purpose, such as completing the transaction.

- The purpose must be disclosed to the consumer from whom the information is being collected.

- The information can only be used for that specific purpose.

- The business can only keep the information for the stated purpose. If the business wants to use the information for another purpose, it must initiate a new collection process.

- Businesses operating in Europe can only export information from the 27 EU countries to importing countries with similar privacy policies. Thus, U.S. retailers, hotel chains, airlines, and banks cannot transfer information from Europe to the United States because the United States does not have similar privacy policies.

Basically, the EU perspective is that consumers own their personal information, so retailers must get consumers to agree explicitly to share this personal information. This agreement is referred to as an **opt in.** In contrast, personal information in the United States is generally viewed as being in the public domain, and retailers can use it in any way they desire. American consumers must explicitly tell retailers not to use their personal information—they must **opt out.**[25]

The EU has delayed enforcement of its directive. The United States is currently negotiating a safe harbor program that would enable U.S. companies abiding by the EU directives to export information. However, due to increasing concerns about consumer privacy, Congress is considering new legislation on consumer privacy. The Federal Trade Commission has developed the following set of principles for fair information practices:

- *Notice and awareness.* Covers the disclosure of information practices, including a comprehensive statement of information use, such as information storage, manipulation, and dissemination.

- *Choice/consent.* Includes both opt-out and opt-in options and allows consumers the opportunity to trade information for benefits.

- *Access/participation.* Allows for the confirmation of information accuracy by consumers.

- *Integrity/security.* Controls for the theft of and tampering with personal information.

- *Enforcement/redress.* Provides a mechanism to ensure compliance by participating companies.[26]

In summary, there is growing consensus that personal information must be fairly collected; that the collection must be purposeful; and that the data should be relevant, maintained as accurate, essential to the business, subject to the rights of the owning individual, kept reasonably secure, and transferred only with the permission of the consumer. To address these concerns, many retailers that collect customer information have privacy policies. The Electronic Privacy Information Center (www.epic.org) recommends that privacy policies clearly state what information is collected from each visitor and how it will be used, give consumers a choice as to whether they give information, and allow them to view and correct any personal information held by an online retail site. Retailers need to ensure their customers that information about them is held securely and not passed on to other companies without the customer's permission.

ANALYZING CUSTOMER DATA AND IDENTIFYING TARGET CUSTOMERS

The next step in the CRM process is to analyze the customer database and convert the data into information that will help retailers develop programs for building customer loyalty. **Data mining,** one approach commonly used to develop this information, identifies patterns in data, typically those that the analyst is unaware of prior to searching through the data. For example, DeBijenkorf, a department store in Amsterdam, Netherlands, was able to increase customers' purchases using data mining. It predicted which customers would not go on vacation in the current year on the basis of whether they went on vacation the year before. Then it targeted the non-vacation goers with double loyalty points and, based on their purchasing history, a special offer in one product category. A striking 45 percent of shoppers responded to the promotion.[27]

Market basket analysis is a specific type of data analysis that focuses on the composition of the basket, or bundle, of products purchased by a household during a single shopping occasion. This analysis is often useful for suggesting where to place merchandise in a store. For example, on the basis of market basket analyses, Wal-Mart changed the traditional location of several items:

- Because bananas are the most common item in Americans' grocery carts, Wal-Mart Supercenters sell bananas in the cereal aisle, as well as in the produce section.

DeBijenkorf department store in Amsterdam uses data mining to targeted non-vacation goers.

- Tissues are in the paper goods aisle and also mixed in with cold medicine.

- Measuring spoons appear in the housewares section and also hang next to baking supplies such as flour and shortening.

- Flashlights are placed in the hardware aisle and with a seasonal display of Halloween costumes.

- Snack cakes are found in the bread aisle and also next to the coffee.

- Bug spray is merchandised with the hunting gear and houshold cleaning supplies.

Retailing View 11.3 examines how U.K.-based Tesco uses the information from its market basket analysis.

Identifying the Best Customers

Traditionally, customer data analysis has focused on identifying market segments—groups of customers who have similar needs, purchase similar merchandise, and respond in a similar manner to marketing activities. But one of the goals of CRM is to identify and cater to the best, most profitable customers. For instance, Home Depot realized that 70 to 80 percent of its kitchen renovation department was coming from 20 to 30 percent of the department's customers.[28] It speculated that these heavy spenders might spend even more if it organized the department around meeting their needs. It knew that heavy spenders want lots of choices and information. So it added more assortment, better-trained associates, a computer-aided design system, and suites of innovative kitchen layouts arranged so that customers could readily sense what their kitchen would look like after a renovation. The results—higher sales and profit per square foot than traditional departments designed to satisfy all customers.

Using information in the customer database, retailers can develop a score or number indicating how valuable customers are to the firm. This score can then be used to determine which customers to target. A commonly used measure to score each customer is called lifetime customer value. **Lifetime customer value (LTV)** is the expected contribution from the customer to the retailer's profits over his or her entire relationship with the retailer.

To estimate LTV, retailers use past behaviors to forecast future purchases, the gross margin from these purchases, and the costs associated with servicing the customers. Some of the costs associated with a customer include the costs of advertising, promotions used to acquire the customer, and processing merchandise that the customer has returned. Thus, a customer who purchases $200 of groceries from a supermarket every other month would have a lower LTV for that supermarket than a customer who buys $30 on each visit and shops at the store three times a week. Similarly, a customer who buys apparel only when it is on sale in a department store would have a lower LTV than a customer who typically pays full price and buys the same amount of merchandise.

These assessments of LTV are based on the assumption that the customer's future purchase behaviors will be the same as they have been in the past. Sophisticated statistical methods are typically used to estimate the future contributions from past purchases.[29] For example, these methods might consider how recent purchases have occurred. The expected LTV of a customer who purchased $600 on one visit six months ago is probably less than the LTV of a customer who has been purchasing $100 of merchandise every month for the last six months, because the $600 sale might have be a one-time purchase by a person visiting from out of town.

Customer Pyramid   Most retailers realize that their customers differ in terms of their profitability or LTV. In particular, they know that a relatively small number of customers account for the majority of their profits. This realization is often called the **80–20 rule**—80 percent of the sales or profits come from 20 percent of the customers. Thus, retailers could group their customers into two categories on the basis of their LTV scores. One group would be the 20 percent of the customers with the highest LTV scores, and the other group would be the rest. However, this two-segment scheme, "best" and "rest," does not consider important differences among the 80 percent of customers in the

---

Tesco Analyzes Market Baskets   **RETAILING VIEW   11.3**

Tesco uses information collected from its loyalty Clubcards to better serve its customers, tailor assortments, determine prices, develop new product lines, build new stores, and leverage itself against the competition. Up to 80 percent of Tesco shoppers are Clubcard members.

Tesco encourages customers to sign up for the Clubcard to be eligible for promotions on products they purchase and gives them discounts if they provide their name, address, and other personal information.

Tesco receives data on 15 million transactions every week. Each product is rated on 50 different characteristics, including price and size, so that the food retailer can compare the shopping baskets of customers who bought similar products. The system then segments the customer into six categories, such as the "Finer Foods" segment, which includes affluent, time-strapped shoppers who buy upscale products, or "Traditional" shoppers who are homemakers with time to cook a meal.

Tesco analyzes customers' market baskets to alter its merchandise selection in stores, develop new products, and target specific customer groups.

Each quarter, Tesco sends a coupon package to Clubcard members. Three coupons are for products the customer normally buys, and three coupons are for products that the retailer believes the customer may like to try, based on their previous purchases. Approximately 15 to 20 percent of Tesco's coupons are redeemed, compared with the industry average redemption rate of 1 to 2 percent.

Tesco introduced "World Foods," which features Asian herbs and other ethnic food, in Indian and Pakistani neighborhoods. The retailer found that 36 percent of all its shoppers were buying from the line. When it looked at the locations from which the customers traveled, it found that more than 25 percent of customers buying the World Foods line were coming from non-Asian neighborhoods and were not Asian. This discovery spurred an initiative to expand its distribution to more stores.

Using its market basket analyis, Tesco also was able to hold onto its price-sensitive customers in the face of rising price competition from Wal-Mart's Asda chain. Tesco lowered its prices on 300 products that price-sensitive customers considered staples. This change in pricing strategy resulted in a 17 percent increase in Tesco's sales.

Tesco develops its new product lines on the basis of its analysis of Clubcard customers. One of its new lines, Tesco Finest, includes duck pâté and other gourmet food items. It decided to roll out this new line in response to a market basket analysis showing that its higher spending customers were not buying wine, cheese, fruit, and other higher priced/higher margin items from Tesco.

Market basket analysis has helped Tesco experience enormous growth, international expansion, and loyal and satisfied customers.

Sources: Cecile Rohwedder, "No. 1 Retailer in Britain uses 'Clubcard' to Thwart Wal-Mart," *The Wall Street Journal*, June 6, 2006, pp. A1–A16; www.tesco.com (accessed August 30, 2007).

EXHIBIT 11–2
The Customer Pyramid

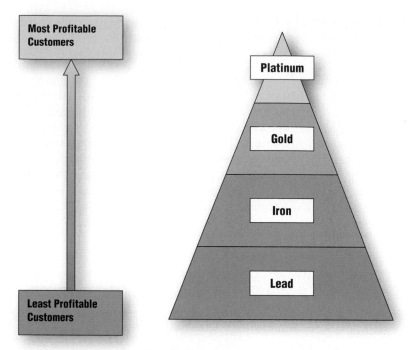

SOURCE: Valarie Zeithaml, Roland Rust, and Katherine Lemon, "The Customer Pyramid: Creating and Serving Profitable Customers," *California Management Review* 43 (Summer 2001), p. 125. Reprinted by permission.

"rest" segment.[30] A commonly used segmentation scheme divides customers into four segments, as illustrated in Exhibit 11–2. This scheme allows retailers to develop more appropriate strategies for each of the segments. Each of the four segments is described next.

- *Platinum segment.* This segment is composed of the customers who possess the top 25 percent LTVs. Typically, these are the most loyal customers who are not overly concerned about merchandise price and place more value on customer service.
- *Gold segment.* The next 25 percent of customers in terms of their LTV make up the gold segment. These customers have a lower LTV than platinum customers because they are more price sensitive. Even though they buy a significant amount of merchandise from the retailer, they are not as profitable as platinum customers and probably patronize some of the retailer's competitors.
- *Iron segment.* Customers in this third tier probably do not deserve much special attention from the retailer due to their modest LTV.
- *Lead segment.* Customers in the lowest segment can cost the company money. They often demand a lot of attention but do not buy much from the retailer, or they buy a lot of sale merchandise and abuse return privileges. For example, some retailers, like Target and Best Buy, have tightened their return policies to help disuade the "lead" segment.

Target and Best Buy have tightened their return policies to help dissuade the least profitable customers who abuse return privileges.

Many segmentation schemes are based on past or future sales, but the profitability of sales actually is a more appropriate measure for classifying customers. For example, airlines assign rewards in their frequent flier programs on the basis of miles flown. These programs provide the same rewards to customers who take low-cost flights as those who fly first class and pay non-discounted prices. Recently, however, some airlines, such as Lufthansa, have adopted an LTV measure based on the profitability of the miles flown instead of the number of miles.[31]

RFM Analysis   An **RFM** (recency, frequency, monetary) **analysis,** often used by catalog retailers and direct marketers, is a scheme for determing the LTV of customers according to how recently they have made a purchase, how frequently they make purchases, and how much they have bought. Exhibit 11–3 is an example of an RFM analysis done by a catalog apparel retailer that mails a catalog each month to its customers.

The catalog retailer divides its customers into 32 groups or segments on the basis of how many orders each customer has placed during the last year, how much merchandise the customer has purchased, and the last time the customer placed an order. Each segment is represented by one cell in Exhibit 11–3. For example, the customers in the upper-left cell have made one or two purchases in the last year, made a purchase within the last two months, and purchased less than $50 of merchandise.

Catalog retailers often use this type of analysis to determine which customer groups should receive catalogs. For each of the RFM groups, they will determine the percentage of customers in the group who made a purchase from the last catalog sent to them. For example, 5 percent of the customers in the upper-left corner of Exhibit 11–3 placed an order from the last catalog sent to them. With information about the response rate and the average gross margin from orders placed by customers in each cell, the catalog retailer can calculate the expected profit from sending catalogs to different customers. For example, if the average gross margin from orders placed by customers in the upper-left cell is $20 and the cost of sending a catalog to customers in the cell is $0.75, the catalog would make $0.25 per customer from each catalog mailed to those customers.

$20 contribution × .05 response
= $1.00 expected contribution − $.75 cost
= $.25 per customer.

Thus, RFM analysis is basically a method of estimating the LTV of a customer using the recency, frequency, and monetary value of his or her past

EXHIBIT 11–3
RFM Analysis for a Catalog Retailer

Frequency	Monetary	RECENCY			
		0–2 months	3–4 months	5–6 months	Over 6 months
1–2	<$50	5.0%*	3.5%	1.0%	0.1%
1–2	Over $50	5.0	3.6	1.1	0.1
3–4	< $150	8.0	5.0	1.5	0.6
3–4	Over $150	8.8	5.0	1.7	0.8
5–6	<$300	10.0	6.0	2.5	1.0
5–6	Over $300	12.0	8.0	2.7	1.2
Over 6	<$450	15.0	10.0	3.5	1.8
Over 6	Over $450	16.0	11.0	4.0	2.0

*Percentage of customers in the cell who made a purchase from the last catalog mailed to them.

EXHIBIT 11–4
RFM Target Strategies

Frequency	Monetary	RECENCY			
		0–2 months	3–4 months	5–6 months	Over 6 months
1–2	<$50	First-time customers		Low-value customers	
1–2	Over $50				
3–4	<$150	Early repeat customers		Defectors	
3–4	Over $150				
5–6	<$300	High-value customers		Core defectors	
5–6	Over $300				
Over 6	<$450				
Over 6	Over $450				

SOURCE: Reprinted by permission of Harvard Business School Press. Adapted from Robert Blattberg, Gary Getz, and Jacquelyn Thomas, *Customer Equity: Building and Managing Relationships as Valuable Assets* (Boston: Harvard Business School Press, 2001), p. 18. Copyright © 2001 by the Harvard Business School Publishing Corporation; all rights reserved.

purchases. Exhibit 11–4 illustrates how RFM can be used to develop customer target strategies.

Customers who have made infrequent, small purchases recently are often first-time customers. The objective of CRM programs directed toward this segment of customers is to convert them into early repeat customers and eventually high-value customers. The CRM programs directed toward customers in the high-value segment (high RFM value) attempt to maintain loyalty, increase retention, and gain a greater share of wallet by selling more merchandise to them. However, customers who have not purchased recently either have a low lifetime value (low-value customers) and therefore are not worth pursuing or are committed to another retailer and may be difficult to recapture (defectors or core defectors). The CRM programs designed to realize objectives related to these different segments are discussed in the following section.

DEVELOPING CRM PROGRAMS

Having segmented customers according to their future profit potential, the next step in the CRM process (see Exhibit 11–1) is to develop programs for the different customer segments. In the following sections, we discuss programs retailers use to (1) retain their best customers, (2) convert good customers into high-LTV customers, and (3) get rid of unprofitable customers.

Customer Retention

Four approaches that retailers use to retain their best customers are (1) frequent shopper programs, (2) special customer services, (3) personalization, and (4) community.

Frequent Shopper Programs   As mentioned previously, frequent shopper programs are used to both build a customer database by identifying customers with their transactions and encourage repeat purchase behavior and retailer loyalty.[32] Retailers provide incentives to encourage customers to enroll in the program and use the card. These incentives are either discounts on purchases made from the retailer or points for every dollar of merchandise purchased. The points are then redeemable for special rewards. Some recommendations concerning the nature of the rewards offered are as follows:

• *Tiered.* Rewards should be tiered according to the customer's purchases to motivate them to increase the level of their purchases. These tiers can be based on individual or cumulative transactions. Some programs combine both discounts and points for rewards. For example, a $5 discount on purchases between $100 and $149.99, $10 dollars off purchases from $150 to $249.99, and $15 off purchases of $250 or more. Beyond $250, customers accumulate points that can be redeemed for rewards, such as free merchandise. Customers generally accept the idea that people who spend more should receive greater rewards.

• *Offer choices.* Not all customers value the same rewards. Thus, the most effective frequent shopper programs offer customers choices. For example, Coles Myer, a leading Australian retailer, originally offered customers air miles but shifted to a menu of rewards when it discovered that many customers did not value air miles. Sainsbury, a U.K. supermarket chain, allows customers to use their Nectar points for vouchers at a variety of retail partners, such as Blockbuster and BP Gas.

Some retailers link their frequent shopper programs to charitable causes. For example, Target donates 1 percent of all purchases charged to Target's REDcard to a program that benefits local schools. Although these altruistic rewards can be an effective part of a frequent shopper program, such incentives probably should not be the focal point of the program. Research indicates that the most effective incentives benefit the recipient directly, not indirectly, as is the case with charitable contributions.

• *Reward all transactions.* To ensure they collect all customer transaction data and encourage repeat purchases, programs need to reward all purchases, not just purchases of selected merchandise.

• *Transparency and simplicity.* Customers need to be able to understand quickly and easily when they will receive rewards, what the rewards are, how much they have earned, and how they can redeem the points they have accumulated. The ground rules need to be clearly stated. There should be no surprises or confusion. Some companies mail a separate catalog to customers that describes its reward levels and available prizes. Knowing exactly what the rewards are push customers to move to the next spending level to receive the desired prizes.

Problems with Frequent Shopping Programs   Four factors limit the effectiveness of frequent shopping programs.

1. They can be expensive. For example, a 1 percent price discount can cost large retailers over $100 million a year. In addition, for a large retailer, the initial launch and maintenance investments (store training, marketing, fulfillment support, and information technology and systems costs) can be as high as $30 million. Annual maintenance costs can reach $5–$10 million when marketing, program support, offer fulfillment, customer service, and IT infrastructure costs are included. Then there are the marketing support costs needed to maintain awareness of the program.

2. It is difficult to make corrections in programs when problems arise. Programs become part of the customer's shopping experience, so customers must be informed about even the smallest changes in programs. They react negatively to any perceived "take away" once a program is in place, even if they are not actively involved in it. Negative reactions can reduce customer trust in and loyalty toward the retailer.

3. It is not clear that these programs increase customer spending behavior and loyalty toward the retailer.[34] For example, the Wisconsin-based Sun Prairie grocery store polled shoppers throughout its 39 stores regarding its frequent shopper program. Over 80 percent of those surveyed would rather not have to use a card to receive the discounts on their purchases.[35]

4. Perhaps most important, it is difficult to gain a competitive advantage based on a frequent shopper program. Because the programs are visible, they can be easily duplicated by competitors. Between 50 and 70 percent of all grocery retailers offer a loyalty card to their customers, and 80 percent of households have at least one of these grocery stores' cards in their wallets. Yet the perceived value of the

REFACT

U.S. companies spend more than $1.2 billion a year on customer loyalty programs.[33]

cards is low. Supermarkets' loyalty cards allow customers access to price discounts, which encourages the low-price shopper but not necessarily the loyal customer who would shop at the store regardless of whether it offered discounts or points for prizes. In general, consumers see little difference between the programs when they all provide a discount of $.50 on detergent.[36]

To avoid this problem, retailers are offering more personalized benefits to their best customers based on their unique knowledge of the customer; these benefits thus are more "invisible" to competitors.

Special Customer Services   Some retailers provide unusually high-quality customer service to build and maintain the loyalty of their best customers. Nordstrom holds complementary private parties for invitees to view new clothing lines. Saks Fifth Avenue offers free fur storage, complementary tailoring, and dinner at the captain's table on a luxury cruise line. Neiman Marcus will provide lunch or champagne to customers that hold a Nieman Marcus credit card, without even asking them to make any purchases.

Personalization   An important limitation of CRM strategies developed for market segments, such as a platinum segment in the customer pyramid (Exhibit 11–2) or early repeat customers in the RFM analysis (Exhibit 11–3), is that each segment is composed of a large number of customers who are not identical. Thus, any strategy will be most appealing for only the typical customer and not as appealing to the majority of customers in the segment. For example, customers in the platinum segment with the highest LTVs might include a 25-year-old single woman who has quite different needs than a 49-year-old working mother with two children.

With the availability of customer-level data and analysis tools, retailers can now economically offer unique benefits and target messages to individual customers. They have the ability to develop programs for small groups of customers and even specific individuals. For example, at Harry Rosen, a Canadian men's apparel specialty retailer, customers are occasionally contacted by the salesperson with whom they have developed a personal relationship. If Harry Rosen receives a new shipment of Armani suits, the sales clerk will contact customers who have purchased Armani in the past. If a customer has been relatively inactive, the retailer might send him a $100 certificate on something he has not bought in a while.[37]

Developing retail programs for small groups or individual customers is referred to as **1-to-1 retailing.** Many small, local retailers have always practiced 1-to-1 retailing. They know each of their customers, greet them by name when they walk in the store, and then recommend merchandise they know the customers will like. These local store owners do not need customer databases and data mining tools; they have the information in their heads. But most large retail chains and their employees do not have this intimate knowledge of their customers. Thus, the CRM process enables larger retailers to efficiently develop relationships similar to those that many small local retailers have with customers.

The Internet channel provides an opportunity for retailers to automate the practice of 1-to-1 retailing. Some use site registration to customize what the shopper sees according to his or her known demographic data and expressed interests.[38] Others have shoppers rate specific products they like the most so they receive "similar item" recommendations.

Nearly every online retailer allows shoppers to search selectively for the items in which they are most interested. Some retailers attempt to match specialized promotions to the customer's search. If someone is searching for cell phones, for instance, the online retailer can offer a "10 percent off" sale on cell phones. The retailer can also customize its homepage so that the next time the customer logs on, he or she will see special promotions on items similar to those previously searched. Amazon.com, for instance, greets customers by name on its homepage, and the products displayed are based on the company's analysis of past purchasing behavior.

The personalized rewards or benefits that customers receive are based on unique information possessed by the retailer and its sales associates. This information, in the retailer's customer database, cannot be accessed or used by competitors. Thus, it provides an opportunity to develop a sustainable competitive advantage.

The effective use of this information creates the positive feedback cycle in the CRM process (see Exhibit 11–1). Increasing repeat purchases from a retailer increases the amount of data collected from the customer, which enables the retailer to provide more personalized benefits, which in turn increases the customer's purchases from the retailer.

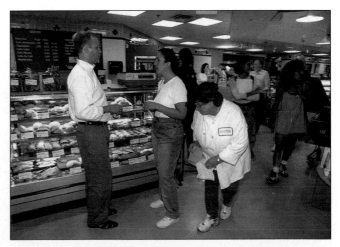

Amazon.com provides personalized recommendations based on the past purchases of its customers.

Community A fourth approach for building customer retention and loyalty is to develop a sense of community among customers. The Internet channel offers an opportunity for customers to exchange information using bulletin boards and develop more personal relationships with one another and the retailer. By participating in such a community, customers become more reluctant to leave the "family" of other people patronizing the retailer.

In Seattle, Whole Foods holds a "singles" night every month, during which it offers wine tastings and snacks, as well as an opportunity for people to mingle and interact. The "singles" night extends the brand experience for its customers to more than just a place to buy food.

The Nike store in Portland, Oregon, hosts running groups that meet two times per week, after which the runners meet at the Niketown store for refreshments. Members who have logged more than 100 miles earn special recognition, and the Nike Plus Web site communicates with runners' Apple iPods to track their running metrics. More than half of the 200,000 runners involved in Nike's program use this system, visiting the Web site more than four times per week. In comparison, even Starbucks's core customers frequent its stores only about 15 times per month.[39]

Converting Good Customers into Best Customers

In the context of the customer pyramid (Exhibit 11–2), increasing the sales made to good customers is referred to as *customer alchemy*—converting iron and gold customers into platinum customers.[40] A way to achieve customer alchemy is through **add-on selling**, which involves offering and selling more products and services to existing customers and increasing the retailer's share of wallet with these customers.

Oprah Winfrey is a master of add-on selling. She has capitalized on her popularity by building on her daytime television show (*The Oprah Winfrey Show*) to sell and promote books, movies, and television specials (Harpo Productions), a cable channel (Oxygen Media), a Web site (www.oprah.com), and a widely read

Singles night at Whole Foods offers wine tastings and snacks, as well as an opportunity for people to mingle and interact.

This Shopping Buddy on Stop & Shop's carts stimulates all-on sales.

magazine (*O*) to her target audience—women interested in self-improvement and empowerment. For viewers of the television show, each of these products provides additional value. For example, when a respected celebrity appears on her television show, an article with more detailed information about the celebrity will be published in *O*. Winfrey builds community by using her television show and magazine to encourage her customers to exchange experiences with her and others through her Web site. For example, a customer reading an article about one of "Oprah's Favorite Things" can go online and share her interests and experiences with others interested in purchasing similar items.[41]

Tesco, the U.K. supermarket chain, added a second tier to its frequent shopper program to increase its share of wallet. The first tier has a traditional design to gather customer data. The second tier, targeted at its better customers, is more innovative. Customers earn a "key" when they spend $38 or more in a single transaction. Fifty keys make the customer a "keyholder," 100 keys a "premium keyholder." When customers achieve these higher levels, they get discounts on popular entertainment events, theater tickets, sporting events, and hotel vacations. The key program seeks to convert iron and gold customers into platinum customers.

A retailer's customer database also reveals opportunities for add-on selling. For example, Stop & Shop Co. equipped some of its grocery stores in the New England area with a "shopping buddy," a wireless computer device attached to shopping carts. It utilizes the retailer's loyalty card and the shopping history it collects to alert customers of sale items that they previously purchased and might want to buy again while they are on sale. If the customer's history shows she frequently purchases hamburgers but not ketchup, the shopping buddy might provide her with a special coupon for each. It also shows the running total of the purchases in the cart and gives the customer the ability to order deli products without waiting in line.[42]

Dealing with Unprofitable Customers

In many cases, the bottom tier of customers actually has a negative LTV. Retailers lose money on every sale they make to these customers. For example, catalog retailers have customers who repeatedly buy three or four items and return all but one of them. The cost of processing two or three returned items is much greater than the profits coming from the one item that the customer kept. Customers in the bottom tier may also be there because they stopped buying from the store and then started again. For example, customers may vanish because a competitor is offering a more attractive offer or they are dissatisfied, and then return months or years later as a new customer. The costs of their (re)acquisition make them unprofitable. The process of no longer selling to these unprofitable customers can be referred to as "getting the lead out," in terms of the customer pyramid.[43] Retailing View 11.4 describes how Limited Express and Best Buy are dealing with undesirable customers.

Other approaches for getting the lead out are (1) offering less costly approaches to satisfy the needs of lead customers and (2) charging customers for the services they are abusing. Fidelity Investments has about 550,000 Web site visits a day and more than 700,000 daily calls, about three-quarters of which go to automated systems that cost the company less than a $1 each. The remaining calls are handled by call center agents, who cost $13 per call. Fidelity contacted 25,000 lower-tier customers who placed a lot of calls to agents and told them they must use the Web site or automated calls for simple account and price information. Each name was flagged and routed to a special representative who would direct callers back to automated services and tell them how to use it. "If all our customers chose to go through live reps, it would be cost prohibitive," said a Fidelity spokeswoman.

IMPLEMENTING CRM PROGRAMS

As discussed throughout this chapter, increasing sales and profits through CRM programs is a challenge. Effective CRM strategies require more than appointing a CRM manager, installing a computer system to manage and analyze a customer database, and making speeches about the importance of customers. The effective implementation of CRM programs requires the close coordination of activities by different functions in a retailer's organization. The IT department needs to collect, analyze, and make the relevant information readily accessible to the employees implementing the programs—the frontline service providers and sales associates and the marketers responsible for communicating with customers through impersonal channels (mass advertising, direct mail, e-mail). Store operations and human resource management needs to hire, train, and motivate the employees who will be using the information to deliver personalized services.

Most retailers are product-centric, not customer-centric; as shown in Chapter 9, buyers in a retail firm are organized by type of product. Typically, there is no area of a retail firm organized by customer type and responsible for delivering products and services to different types of customers. Perhaps in the future, retailers will have market managers to perform this coordinating function.

Getting the Lead Out   RETAILING VIEW   11.4

One source of unprofitable customers is the practice of fraudulent returns, which costs retailers more than $15 billion each year. Some examples of these costly returns include people who buy a large-screen television for their Super Bowl party and then return it after the game or an expensive dress for a special occasion, returned after they wear it once. Professional returners even use the Internet to make money on fraudulent returns. Some people steal merchandise from a store, return it for credit slips, and then turn the credit slips into cash by selling them at a discount on eBay or other online auction sites.

Retailers like The Limited and Best Buy are fighting back against such high-tech fraud with high-tech defenses. Limited Express's return policy says consumers have up to 60 days to return items. However, the company's return policy also notes that it uses an industrywide service operated by Return Exchange to authorize returns and that "under certain circumstances we reserve the right to deny returns." Return Exchange, based in Irvine, California, analyzes Express's customer database and identifies customers who have an unusually high propensity for returning merchandise. When these customers return merchandise, the POS terminal generates a slip of paper that says "RETURN DECLINED," and the sales associate tells the customer to call the toll-free number at the bottom for more information.

Best Buy is undertaking a strategy to focus on gold and platinum customers and get rid of lead customers. To lure high spenders, it is providing more effective customer service. To discourage undesirable customers, it is reducing promotions that tend to draw them into the store and removing them from direct marketing lists. The trickiest challenge may be to deter bad customers without turning off good ones.

Best Buy's campaign against undesirable customers pits it against dozens of Web sites like FatWallet.com, SlickDeals.net, and TechBargains.com that trade electronic coupons and tips from former clerks and insiders, hoping to gain extra advantages against the stores. At SlickDeals.net, whose subscribers boast about techniques for gaining hefty discounts, a visitor recently bragged about his practice of shopping at Best Buy only when he thinks he can buy at below the retailer's cost.

Best Buy cannot bar undesirable customers from its stores, but it is taking steps to put a stop to their most damaging practices. It's enforcing a restocking fee of 15 percent of the purchase price on returned merchandise. To discourage customers who return items with the intention of repurchasing them at a "returned merchandise" discount, it is experimenting with reselling returned merchandise over the Internet, so the goods don't reappear in the store where they were originally purchased. Best Buy also cut ties to FatWallet.com, an online "affiliate" that had collected referral fees for delivering customers to Best Buy's Web site.

Rejecting customers is a delicate business. Filene's Basement was criticized on television and in newspapers for asking two Massachusetts customers not to shop at its stores because of their frequent returns and complaints. Best Buy's CEO apologized in writing to students at a Washington, DC, school after employees at one store barred a group of black students while admitting a group of white students.

Sources: Jennifer Davis, "Retailers Use Technology to Thwart Would-Be Thieves," *San Diego Tribune*, June 13, 2007; http://www.fashion era.com/Trends_2006/2006_spring_fashion_trends_returns_consumer_fraud.htm (accessed September 20, 2007); http://www.oracle.com/applications/retail/mom/retail-returns-management.html (accessed September 20, 2007).

SUMMARY

To develop a strategic advantage, retailers must effectively manage their critical resources—their finances (Chapter 6), human resources (Chapter 9), real estate and locations (Chapters 7 and 8), inventory and information (Chapter 10), and customers (Chapter 11). This chapter focuses on activities that retailers are undertaking now and will undertake in the future to increase the sales and profits they get from their better customers.

Customer relationship management is a business philosophy and set of strategies, programs, and systems that focuses on identifying and building loyalty with a retailer's most valued customers. Loyal customers are committed to patronizing a retailer and are not prone to switch to a competitor. In addition to building loyalty, CRM programs are designed to increase the share of wallet from the retailer's best customers.

Customer relationship management is an iterative process that turns customer data into customer loyalty through four activities: (1) collecting customer data, (2) analyzing the customer data and identifying target customers, (3) developing CRM programs, and (4) implementing CRM programs. The first step of the process is to collect and store data about customers. One of the challenges in collecting customer data is identifying the customer in connection with each transaction. Retailers use a variety of approaches to overcome this challenge.

The second step is to analyze the data to identify the most profitable customers. Two approaches used to rank customers according to their profitability are calculating the customer's lifetime value and categorizing customers on the basis of characteristics of their buying behavior—their recency, frequency, and monetary value.

Using this information about customers, retailers can develop programs to build loyalty in their best customers, increase their share of wallet with better customers (e.g., converting gold customers into platinum customers), and deal with unprofitable customers (getting the lead out). Four approaches that retailers use to build loyalty and retain their best customers are (1) launching frequent shopper programs, (2) offering special customer services, (3) personalizing the services they provide, and (4) building a sense of community. Unprofitable customers are dealt with by developing lower-cost approaches for servicing them. Effectively implementing CRM programs is difficult because it requires coordinating a number of different areas in a retailer's organization.

KEY TERMS

add-on selling, *321*
cookies, *312*
customer database, *308*
customer loyalty, *306*
customer relationship
   management (CRM), *305*

data mining, *313*
80–20 rule, *315*
frequent shopper program, *310*
lifetime customer value (LTV), *314*
loyalty program, *310*
market basket analysis, *313*

1-to-1 retailing, *320*
opt in, *313*
opt out, *313*
private-label credit card, *310*
RFM analysis, *317*
share of wallet, *306*

GET OUT AND DO IT!

1. **CONTINUING ASSIGNMENT** Interview the store manager working for the retailer you have selected for the continuing assignment. Ask the manager if the store offers a frequent shopper program and how effective it is in terms of increasing the store's sales and profits. Find out why the manager has these views and what could be done to increase the effectiveness of the program. Then talk to some customers in the store. Ask them why they are members or not. Find out how membership in the program affects their shopping behavior and loyalty toward the retailer.

2. Go to some of the retail sites that you frequent and compare their privacy policies. Which policies make you less concerned about violations of your privacy? Why? Which policies, or lack of policies, raise your concern? Why?

3. Go to the Web site for the Electronic Privacy Information Center (www.epic.org) and review the issues raised by the organization. What does this watchdog organization feel are the most important issues? How will these issues affect retailers and their customers?

4. Go to Macy's credit card homepage at http://www1.macys.com/service/credit/overview.ognc. Read about the different levels of membership for this customer rewards program. Describe how Macy's is using the customer pyramid (Exhibit 11–2) in its CRM program to target and classify customers.

5. Go to the homepage for 1-800-Flowers at www.1800flowers.com. How does this company's CRM program help it grow its business and increase customer loyalty?

DISCUSSION QUESTIONS AND PROBLEMS

1. What is CRM?

2. Why do retailers want to determine the lifetime value of their customers?

3. Why do customers have privacy concerns about the frequent shopper programs that supermarkets offer, and what can supermarkets do to minimize these concerns?

4. What are some examples of opportunities for add-on selling that might be pursued by (a) travel agents, (b) jewelry stores, and (c) dry cleaners?

5. Which of the following types of retailers do you think would benefit most from instituting CRM: (a) supermarkets, (b) banks, (c) automobile dealers, or (d) consumer electronic retailers? Why?

6. Develop a CRM program for a local store that sells apparel and gifts with your college's or university's logo. What type of information would you collect about your customers, and how would you use this information to increase the sales and profits of the store?

7. What are the different approaches retailers can use to identify customers by their transactions? What are the advantages and disadvantages of each approach?

8. A CRM program focuses on building relationships with a retailer's better customers. Some customers who do not receive the same benefits as the retailer's best customers may be upset because they are treated differently. What can retailers do to minimize this negative reaction?

9. Think of one of your favorite places to shop. How does this retailer create customer loyalty and satisfaction, encourage repeat visits, establish an emotional bond between the customer and the retailer, know the customer's preferences, and provide personal attention and memorable experiences to its "best customers"?

10. How would a retailer use transactions, customer contacts, customer preferences, descriptive information, and responses to marketing activities in its customer database?

SUGGESTED READINGS

Bell, Chip R., and John R. Patterson. *Customer Loyalty Guaranteed: Create, Lead, and Sustain Remarkable Customer Service.* Cincinatti, OH: Adams Media Corporation, 2007.

Bell, Simon; Seigyoung Auh; and Karen Smalley. "Customer Relationship Dynamics: Service Quality and Customer Loyalty in the Context of Varying Levels of Customer Expertise and Switching Costs," *Journal of the Academy of Marketing Science* 33 (Spring 2005), pp. 169–84.

Bligh, Philip, and Douglas Turk. *CRM Unplugged: Releasing CRM's Strategic Value.* Hoboken, NJ: Wiley, 2004.

Greenberg, Paul. *CRM at the Speed of Light: Capturing and Keeping Customers in Internet Real Time,* 3d ed. New York: Osborne/McGraw-Hill, 2004.

Gupta, Sunil and Donald R. Lehmann. *Managing Customers as Investments.* Philadelphia, PA: Wharton School Publishing, 2005.

Kumar, V.; Denish Shah; and Rajkumar Venkatesan. "Managing Retailer Profitability—One Customer at a Time!" *Journal of Retailing* 82, no. 4 (2006).

Meyer-Waarden, Lars. "The Effects of Loyalty Programs on Customer Lifetime Duration and Share of Wallet." *Journal of Retailing* 83, no. 2 (2007).

Shugan, Steven. "Brand Loyalty Programs: Are They Shams?" *Marketing Science* 24 (Spring 2005), pp. 185–94.

Tokman, Mert; Lenita M. Davis; and Katherine N. Lemon. "The WOW Factor: Creating Value through Win-Back Offers to Reclaim Lost Customers." *Journal of Retailing* 83, no. 1, (2007).

Venkatesh, Shankar, and Russel S. Winer. "When Customer Relationship Management Meets Data Mining." *Journal of Interactive Marketing* 20, no. 3/4 (2006), pp. 2–4.

Merchandise Management

Section II reviewed the strategic decisions made by retailers—the development of their retail market strategy, their financial strategy associated with the market strategy, their store location opportunities and choices, their organization and human resource strategy, the systems they use to control the flow of information and merchandise, and the approaches they take to manage relationships with their customers. These decisions are strategic rather than tactical because they involve committing significant resources to developing long-term advantages over the competition in a target retail market segment.

This section, Section III, examines the tactical merchandise management decisions undertaken to implement the retail strategy.

Chapter 12 provides an overview of how retailers manage their merchandise inventory—how they organize the merchandise planning process, evaluate their performance, forecast sales, establish an assortment plan, and determine the appropriate inventory levels.

Chapter 13 examines the buying systems used to manage basic and fashion merchandise inventories.

Chapter 14 explores how retailers buy merchandise from vendors—their branding options, negotiating processes, and vendor relationship-building activities.

Chapter 15 addresses the question of how retailers set and adjust prices for the merchandise and services they offer.

Chapter 16 looks at the approaches that retailers take to build their brand image and communicate with their customers.

The following section, Section IV, focuses on store management implementation decisions.

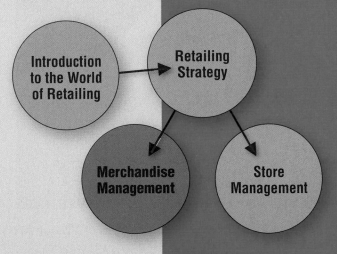

Managing Merchandise Assortments

After graduating from the University of Wisconsin-Madison, I took a position as a Business Analyst in Target's merchandise division at their corporate headquarters in Minneapolis, Minnesota. My primary responsibility on the Denim/Woven team was to analyze sales data and propose inventory plans for each of the different merchandise categories, in the varying sized stores. After determining the correct inventory levels, I would analyze styles, colors, sizes, and selling history across the different store volume classifications. I then used the merchandise planning systems to monitor sales and suggest a course of action to

EXECUTIVE BRIEFING
Jeanna Hesse, Buyer,
Sears Holding Company

ensure the right amount of inventory was being sent to the right stores—at the right time.

For personal reasons, I moved to Chicago, Illinois. I really liked the fast pace of retailing; in addition, there are new challenges and opportunities every day. I wanted to continue my career in retailing and was fortunate to obtain a position in the merchandise division for Sears Holding Corp. (SHC). One of the attractive aspects of retailing is that there are retail headquarters in practically every major U.S. city.

I have received several promotions in the buying organization during my five years at SHC, and I am now a buyer responsible for two brands: Apostrophe and First Issue by Liz Claiborne. Apostrophe is a private-label brand, designed primarily by the SHC design team and domestic market partners. First Issue is a national-brand vendor but sold exclusively at Sears. These brands generate over $175 million in annual sales volume.

I really like working for Sears Holding because of the team spirit in our organization. We all work together to provide fashionable, reasonably priced merchandise for our customers. My team consists of Associate Buyers who report to me, and an Inventory Manager, Senior Inventory Analyst, Inventory Analyst, and Design and Sourcing teams.

CHAPTER 12

QUESTIONS

How is the merchandise management process organized?

Why do the merchandise management processes differ for staple and fashion merchandise?

How do retailers evaluate the quality of their merchandise management decisions?

How do retailers forecast sales for merchandise classifications?

How do retailers plan their assortments and determine the appropriate inventory levels?

What trade-offs must buyers make in developing merchandise assortments?

The Inventory Manager and Analysts allocate the merchandise to the stores and monitor inventory levels.

To be successful, our team needs to quickly react to the ever-changing customer preferences. I continually monitor the fastest Juniors' apparel fashions shown in stores and trade publications and offered by high fashion retailers in order to predict my customers' needs. For example, I recently saw that some high-end specialty chains were selling a "club top" in updated styling and great prints. I felt this top would appeal to our customers in urban markets—Miami, New York, Chicago, and Los Angeles. I worked with a domestic market vendor to design and produce the top for the Apostrophe line and ensure the cost would be consistent with our margin goals. Our inventory team will plan and eventually distribute this top to our urban market stores.

Each promotion I have received at SHC has involved more responsibility and provided the opportunity to further develop my merchandising and management skills. I enjoy my job and continue to develop my career at Sears. I am given all the responsibility I can handle and the support I need to be successful. It's rewarding to work in an atmosphere where I am committed to improving the lives of our customers by providing quality services, products, and solutions that earn their trust and build lifetime relationships.

Merchandise management activities are undertaken primarily by buyers and their superiors, divisional merchandise managers (DMMs) and general merchandise managers (GMMs). Many people view these jobs as very exciting and glamorous. They think that buyers spend most of their time trying to identify the latest fashions and trends, attending designer shows replete with celebrities in Paris and Milan, and going to rock concerts and other glamorous events to see what the trendsetters are wearing. But in reality, the lives of retail buyers are more like Wall Street investment analysts than globe-trotting trend gurus.

Investment analysts manage a portfolio of stocks. They buy stock in companies they think will increase in value and sell stocks in companies they believe do not have a promising future. They continuously monitor the performance of the stocks they own to see which are increasing in value and which are decreasing. Sometimes they make mistakes and invest in companies that do not perform well. So they sell their stock in these companies and lose money, but they use the money from the sold stocks to buy more attractive stocks. Other times, the stocks they buy increase dramatically in price, and they wish they had bought more shares.

Rather than managing a portfolio of stocks, retail buyers manage a portfolio of merchandise inventory. They buy merchandise they think will be popular with their customers. Like investment analysts, they use their retailer's information system to monitor the performance of their merchandise portfolio—to see what is selling and what is not. Retail buyers also make mistakes. When the merchandise they bought is not selling well, they get rid of it by putting it on sale so they can use the money to buy better selling merchandise. However, they also might take a chance and buy a lot of a new product and be rewarded

Traders on the stock exchange floor manage a portfolio of stocks, and retail buyers manage a portfolio of merchandise inventory. Both continually assess the risks associated with their purchase decisions.

when it sells well, whereas competitors, who were more conservative, don't have enough of the product.

Chris Manning, a former swimwear buyer at Macy's South, draws an analogy between surfing and buying merchandise: "My job is like surfing. Sometimes you catch a big wave (trend) and it's exhilarating and sometimes you think you've caught a good wave and brown turns out not to be the color this season. But the real fun is getting the most out of the wave you can. Let me give you an example of how I worked a big wave. Vendors started to show tankinis—women's bathing suits with bikini bottoms and tank tops. My customers were women in their 40s that had a couple of kids. I thought they would really go for this new style because it had the advantages of a two-piece bathing suit, but wasn't much more revealing than a one-piece suit. I bought a wide color assortment—bright reds, yellows, pink, and black—and put them in our fashion-forward stores in January for a test. The initial sales were good, but our customers thought they were a little too skimpy. Then I started to work the wave. I went back to the vendor and got them to recut the top so that the suit was less revealing, and I placed a big order for the colors that were selling best. Sales were so good that the other Macy's divisions picked up on it, but we rode the wave the longest and had the best swimwear sales of all of the divisions."[1]

Merchandise management refers to the process by which a retailer attempts to offer the right quantity of the right merchandise in the right place at the right time and meet the company's financial goals. Buyers need to be in touch with and anticipate what customers will want to buy, but this ability to sense market trends is just one skill needed to manage merchandise inventory effectively. Perhaps an even more important skill is the ability to analyze sales data continually and make appropriate adjustments in prices and inventory levels.

The first section of this chapter outlines the process retailers use to manage their merchandise assortments. Then, several steps in the process—forecasting sales, formulating an assortment plan, and determining the appropriate inventory level—are examined in more detail. Other steps in the merchandise management process reviewed in subsequent chapters are merchandise management planning (Chapter 13), buying merchandise (Chapter 14), and pricing (Chapter 15).

MERCHANDISE MANAGEMENT PROCESS OVERVIEW

This section provides an overview of the merchandise management process, including the organization of a retailer's merchandise management activities and the objectives and measures used to evaluate merchandise management performance. The section concludes with an outline of the steps in the merchandise management process and a discussion of the differences in the process for managing fashion and seasonal merchandise versus basic merchandise.

The Buying Organization

Every retailer has its own system for grouping categories of merchandise, but the basic structure of the buying organization is similar for most retailers. Exhibit 12–1 illustrates this basic structure by depicting the organization of the merchandise division for a department store chain such as Macy's, Belk, or Dillard's. Exhibit 12–1 shows the organization of buyers and planners in the merchandise division. The buyers negotiate with vendors to buy the merchandise and the planner (also called assorters) focus on distribution to specific stores and replenishment.

Merchandise Group   The highest classification level is the **merchandise group.** The organization chart shown in Exhibit 12–1 has four merchandise

Illustration of Merchandise Classifications and Organization   **EXHIBIT 12-1**

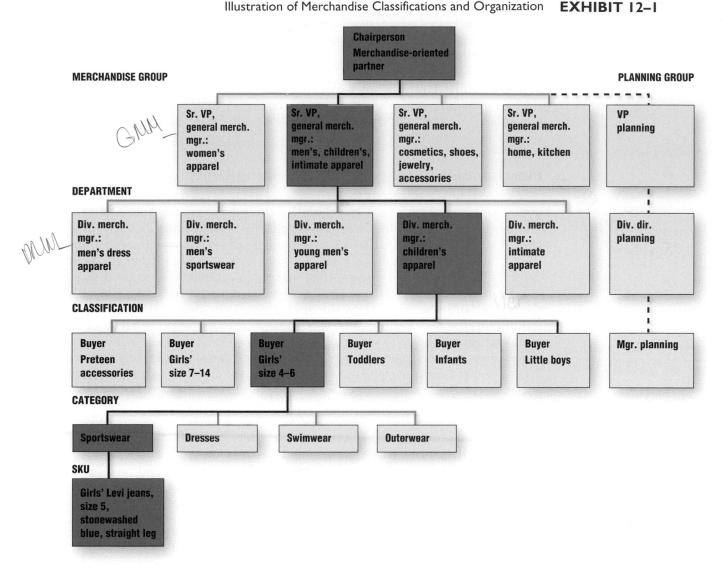

groups: women's apparel; men's, children's, and intimate apparel; cosmetics, shoes, jewelry, and accessories; and home and kitchen. Each of the four merchandise groups is managed by a general merchandise manager (GMM), who is often a senior vice president in the firm. Each of these GMMs is responsible for several departments. For example, the GMM for men's, children's, and intimate apparel makes decisions about how the merchandise inventory is managed in the five departments he or she manages: men's dress apparel, men's sportswear, young men's apparel, children's apparel, and intimate apparel.

Department The second level in the merchandise classification scheme is the **department.** Departments are managed by divisional merchandise managers (DMMs). For example, the DMM highlighted in Exhibit 12–1 is in charge of children's apparel and manages the buyers responsible for six merchandise classifications: preteen accessories, girls' sizes 7 to 14, girls' sizes 4 to 6, toddlers, infants, and little boys.

Classification The classification is the third level for categorizing merchandise and organizing merchandise management activities. A **classification** is a group of items targeting the same customer type, such as girls' sizes 4 to 6.

Categories   Categories are the next lower level in the classification scheme. Each buyer manages several merchandise categories. For example, the girls' sizes 4 to 6 buyer manages the sportswear, dresses, swimwear, and outerwear categories for girls who wear sizes 4 to 6.

Stock-Keeping Unit   A **stock-keeping unit (SKU)** is the smallest unit available for inventory control. In soft goods merchandise, a SKU usually means a particular size, color, and style. For example, a pair of size 5, stonewashed, blue, straight-legged Levi jeans is an SKU.

Merchandise Category—The Planning Unit

include substitutable items

The merchandise category is the basic unit of analysis for making merchandising management decisions. A **merchandise category** is an assortment of items that customers see as substitutes for one another. For example, a department store might offer a wide variety of girls' dresses sizes 4 to 6 in different colors, styles, and brand names. But a mother buying a dress for her daughter might consider the entire set of dresses when making her purchase decision. Lowering the price on one dress may increase the sales of that dress but also decrease the sales of other dresses. Thus, the buyers' decisions about pricing and promoting specific SKUs in the category will affect the sales of other SKUs in the same category.

Retailers and their vendors may have different definitions of a category. A vendor might assign shampoos and conditioners, for example, to different categories, on the basis of their significant differences in product attributes. However, a grocery store might put them and other combination shampoo–conditioner products into a single category on the basis of consumers' common buying behavior. Paper towels could be assigned to a "paper products" category or combined with detergent, paper tissues, and napkins in a "cleaning products" category.

Some retailers may define categories in terms of brands. For example, Tommy Hilfiger might be one category and Polo/Ralph Lauren another category because the retailer feels that the brands are not substitutes for each other. A "Tommy" customer buys Tommy and not Ralph. Also, it is easier for the buyer to purchase merchandise and plan distribution and promotions if the entire line of branded merchandise is coordinated.

failto interdependency

Category Management   Whereas department stores, in general, manage merchandise at the category level, supermarkets and other general merchandise retailers traditionally have organized their merchandise around brands or vendors. For instance, in a supermarket chain, three different buyers—one each for Kellogg's, General Mills, and General Foods—might buy breakfast cereal.[2]

Managing merchandise within a category by brand can lead to inefficiencies because it fails to consider the interdependencies between SKUs in the category. For example, a breakfast cereal category manager might make the decision to stock specific SKUs for corn flakes from Kellogg's, General Mills, General Foods, a private-label vendor, and a popular locally produced brand. An analysis might indicate that there is relatively little demand for the giant-sized box of corn flakes, so the category manager would decide to stock only one giant-sized corn flakes SKU. But if the decision were being made by each of the three buyers, the supermarket chain might stock three giant-sized corn flakes SKUs, one from each vendor. The analysis might also indicate that though the locally produced brand is not a top seller, it has a strong following among customers who have a high lifetime value. If the retailer drops the local brand, it may lose some very good customers. Finally, the supermarket chain might make a greater profit by setting three different prices (high, medium, and low) for the corn flakes offered by the three vendors rather than pricing them all at the same level.

Thus, the **category management** approach to managing breakfast cereals should have one buyer or category manager who oversees all merchandising activities for the entire category.[3] Managing by category can help ensure that the store's assortment includes the "best" combination of sizes and vendors— the one that will get the most profit from the allocated space.

Category Captain   Some retailers turn to a preferred vendor to help them manage a particular category. The vendor, known as the **category captain,** works with the retailer to develop a better understanding of customer behavior, create assortments that satisfy consumer needs, and improve the profitability of the merchandise category. Vendors are often in a better position to manage a category than retailers because they have superior information through their focus on a specific category and acquired insights from managing the category for different retailers.

For example, Frito-Lay acts as the snack food category captain for many retail chains. To help Frito-Lay manage the category, supermarket chains give it access to their market and store information, including their costs and the sales of competitors. In return, Frito-Lay works with the supermarkets' category managers to make decisions about assortments, product placement on shelves, promotions, and pricing for all brands in the category. Before category management, these decisions were often based on whichever vendor was able to make the best sales pitch to the buyer. Shelf space allocation, for instance, could change frequently, depending on which vendor's salesperson offered a better promotional price.

Appointing vendors as category captains has its advantages for retailers. It makes merchandise management tasks easier and can increase profits. But retailers are becoming increasingly reluctant to turn over these important decisions to their vendors. They have found that working with their vendors and carefully evaluating their suggestions is a much more prudent approach.[5]

A potential problem with establishing a vendor as a category captain is that vendors could take advantage of their position. It is somewhat like "letting the fox into the henhouse." Suppose, for example, that Frito-Lay chose to maximize its own sales at the expense of its competition. It could suggest an assortment plan that included most of its SKUs and exclude SKUs that contributed to the retailer's profit, such as high margin, private-label SKUs.

There are also antitrust considerations. The vendor category captain could collude with the retailer to fix prices. It could also block other brands, particularly smaller ones, from access to shelf space. Category captains need to temper their zeal for control over retailers as well. Some actions that vendor category captains take to avoid antitrust problems are:

- Divulge all information obtained from the retailer to the other brands in the category.

- Appoint another large brand as a "category adviser" to oversee the captain's decisions.

- To circumvent potential collusion in price setting, refuse to serve as captain for two retailers in the same market.

Should the dairy aisle be managed by category or by brand for optimum efficiency?

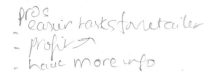

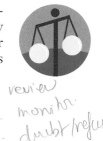

Evaluating Merchandise Management Performance—GMROI

As we discussed in Chapter 6, a good performance measure for evaluating a retail firm is ROI. Return on investment is composed of two components, asset turnover and net profit margin. But ROI is not a good measure for evaluating the performance of merchandise managers because they do not have control over all of the retailer's assets or all the expenses that the retailer incurs. Merchandise managers only have control over the merchandise they buy (the retailer's merchandise inventory assets), the price at which the merchandise is sold, and the cost of the merchandise. Thus, buyers generally have control over the gross margin but not operating expenses, such as store operations, human resources, real estate, and logistics and information systems.

A financial ratio that assesses a buyer's ROI performance on the basis of the factors that the buyer can control is gross margin return on inventory investment (GMROI, typically pronounced *jim-roy*).[6] It measures how many gross margin dollars are earned on every dollar of inventory investment made by the buyer.

Thus, GMROI is a similar concept to ROI, except that its components are under the control of the buyer rather than other managers in the firm. Instead of combining net profit margin and asset turnover, GMROI combines gross margin percentage and the sales-to-stock ratio, which is related to inventory turnover.

$$GMROI = \text{Gross margin percentage} \times \text{Sales-to-stock ratio}$$

$$= \frac{\text{Gross margin}}{\text{Net sales}} \times \frac{\text{Net sales}}{\text{Average inventory at cost}}$$

$$= \frac{\text{Gross margin}}{\text{Average inventory at cost}}$$

The difference between the stock-to-sales ratio and inventory turnover is the numerator of the equation. When calculating the sales-to-stock ratio, the numerator is net sales; when calculating inventory turnover, the numerator is the cost of goods sold. To convert the sales-to-stock ratio to inventory turnover, simply multiply the sales-to-stock ratio by $(1 - \text{gross margin percentage})$. Thus, if the sales-to-stock ratio is 9.0 and the gross margin percentage is .40, the inventory turnover for the category is 5.4:

$$\text{Inventory turnover} = (1 - \text{Gross margin percentage}) \times \text{Sales-to-stock ratio}$$
$$5.4 = (1 - .4) \times 9.0$$

Buyers have control over both components of GMROI. The gross margin component is affected by the prices they set and the prices they negotiate with vendors when buying merchandise. The sales-to-stock ratio is affected by the popularity of the merchandise they buy. If they buy merchandise that customers want, it sells quickly, and the sales-to-stock ratio is high.

Like ROI, GMROI assesses not just the profitability of merchandise decisions but also how effectively the merchandise assets (inventory) are used. Thus, merchandise categories with different margin/turnover profiles can be compared and evaluated. For instance, within a supermarket, some categories (e.g., wine) are high margin/low turnover, whereas other categories (e.g., milk) are low margin/high turnover. If the wine category's performance were compared with that of milk using inventory turnover alone, the contribution of wine to the supermarket's performance would be undervalued. In contrast, if only gross margin were used, wine's contribution would be overvalued.

Consider the situation in Exhibit 12–2, in which a supermarket wants to evaluate the performance of two categories: fresh bakery bread and gourmet

EXHIBIT 12–2
Illustration of GMROI

			Fresh Bakery Bread	Gourmet Canned Food		
		sales	$1,000,000	200,000		
		gross margin	200,000	100,000		
		average inventory	100,000	50,000		
	GMROI	= $\dfrac{\text{Gross Margin}}{\text{Net Sales}}$	× $\dfrac{\text{Net Sales}}{\text{Average Inventory}}$	= $\dfrac{\text{Gross Margin}}{\text{Average Inventory}}$		
Fresh Bakery Bread	GMROI	= $\dfrac{200{,}000}{1{,}000{,}000}$	× $\dfrac{1{,}000{,}000}{100{,}000}$	= $\dfrac{200{,}000}{100{,}000}$		
		= 20%	× 10	= 200%		
Gourmet Canned Food	GMROI	= $\dfrac{100{,}000}{200{,}000}$	× $\dfrac{200{,}000}{50{,}000}$	= $\dfrac{50{,}000}{100{,}000}$		
		= 50%	× 4	= 200%		

canned food. If evaluated on gross margin percent alone, gourmet canned food has the best performance with 50% gross margin percent, versus only a 20% gross margin percent for the fresh bakery bread. However, the fresh bakery bread stock-to-sales ratio is 10, much higher than the gourmet canned food category with only 4. When the GMROI is calculated for both categories, they have the same financial performance, with a GMROI of 200%.

Exhibit 12–3 shows the GMROI percentages for selected departments in discount stores. Jewelry, apparel, and housewares have the highest gross margin percentages. Their sales-to-stock ratios range from 8.75 (food) to 3.24 (jewelry). We might expect food to have the highest sales-to-stock ratio because it is perishable; it is either sold quickly or spoils. However, as a luxury item, jewelry has a relatively low sales-to-stock ratio. Furniture also has a low sales-to-stock ratio because a relatively large assortment of costly items is needed to support the sales level.

In this case, GMROI ranges from 235 (apparel) to 90 (furniture). Thus, it's not surprising that Wal-Mart and Target currently are emphasizing apparel and have deemphasized furniture. They continue to carry consumer electronics and health and beauty products—both with low GMROIs—because these categories have traditionally brought customers into the store. These retailers hope that while customers buying products from these categories are in the store, they will also purchase higher GMROI items.

Could a fresh bakery and a gourmet canned food department in a grocery store have the same GMROI?

EXHIBIT 12–3
GMROI for Selected Departments in Discount Stores

Department	Gross Margin %	Sales-to-Stock Ratio	GMROI
Apparel	37	6.35	235
Housewares	35	4.63	162
Food	20	8.75	175
Jewelry	38	3.24	123
Furniture	31	4.09	90
Health and beauty supplies	22	5.14	113
Consumer electronics	21	5.05	106

Measuring Sales-to-Stock Ratio Retailers normally express sales-to-stock ratios (and inventory turnover) on an annual basis rather than for part of a year. If the sales-to-stock ratio for a three-month season equals 2.3, the annual sales-to-stock ratio will be four times that number (9.2). Thus, to convert a sales-to-stock ratio based on part of a year to an annual figure, multiply it by the number of such time periods in the year.

The most accurate measure of average inventory is to measure the inventory level at the end of each day and divide the sum by 365. Most retailers can use their information systems to get accurate average inventory estimates by averaging the inventory in stores and distribution centers at the end of each day. Another method is to take the end-of-month (EOM) inventories for several months and divide by the number of months. For example,

Month	End-of-Month Inventory at Retail Prices
January	$22,000
February	33,000
March	38,000
Total inventory	93,000
Average inventory	31,000

This approach is adequate only if the EOM figure does not differ in any appreciable or systematic way from any other day. For instance, January's EOM inventory is significantly lower than that of February or March because it assesses the inventory position at the end of the winter clearance sale and before the spring buildup.

Managing Inventory Turnover

As we discussed at the beginning of this chapter, buyers are responsible for investing in and managing merchandise inventory. Inventory turnover (and the related sales-to-stock ratio) helps assess the buyer's performance in managing this asset. Retailers want to achieve a high inventory turnover, but just focusing on increasing inventory turnover can actually decrease gross margin and GMROI. Thus, buyers need to consider the trade-offs associated with managing their inventory turnover.

Benefits of High Turnover Increasing inventory turnover can increase sales volume, improve salesperson morale, reduce the risk of obsolescence and markdowns, and provide more resources to take advantage of new buying opportunities. Higher inventory turnover increases sales because new merchandise is continually available to customers, and new merchandise sells better and faster than old merchandise. New merchandise attracts customers to visit the store more frequently because they know they will be seeing different merchandise each time they visit the store. When inventory turnover is low, the merchandise begins to look shop-worn—slightly damaged from being displayed and handled by customers for a long time. Increasing the amount of new merchandise also improves sales associates' morale. Salespeople are excited about and more motivated to sell the new merchandise, and thus, sales increase, increasing inventory turnover even further.

The value of fashion and other perishable merchandise starts declining as soon as it is placed on display. When inventory is selling quickly, merchandise isn't in the store long enough to become obsolete. As a result, sale price discounts are reduced, and gross margins increase.

Finally, when inventory turnover increases, the increased rate of sales generates more money that can be used to buy new merchandise. Having money available to buy merchandise late in a fashion season can open up profit opportunities. For instance, buyers can take advantage of special prices offered by vendors that have too much inventory left over. Buyers can acquire this overstocked merchandise at low costs, sell it to customers at the normal price, and increase their gross margins. Or the buyer can sell the overstocked merchandise at a lower than normal price and increase its sales. In either case, the higher inventory turnover rate enables buyers to make opportunistic buys and increase GMROI.

Potential Problems with Approaches for Improving Inventory Turnover

Retailers need to strike a balance in their rate of inventory turnover. Some approaches for improving inventory turnover can lower GMROI by lowering sales volume, increasing the cost of goods sold, and increasing operating expenses.

One approach to increase turnover is to reduce the number of merchandise categories, the number of SKUs within a category, or the number of items within an SKU. However, if customers can't find the size or color they seek—or even worse, if they can't find the brand or product line at all—due to the reduced assortment, patronage and sales can decrease. Customers who are disappointed on a regular basis will shop elsewhere and possibly urge their friends to do the same.

Another approach for increasing inventory turnover is to buy merchandise more often and in smaller quantities, which reduces average inventory without reducing sales. But by buying smaller quantities, the gross margin decreases because buyers can't take advantage of quantity discounts and transportation economies of scale. Buying merchandise frequently in small quantities can also increase operating expenses, in that buyers spend more time placing orders and monitoring deliveries.

Merchandise Management Process

Exhibit 12–4 outlines the activities and decisions that are involved in the merchandise management process. First, buyers forecast category sales, develop an assortment plan for merchandise in the category, and determine the amount of inventory needed to support the forecasted sales and assortment plan. Each of these activities is discussed in the remaining sections of this chapter.

Second, buyers develop a plan outlining the sales expected for each month, the inventory needed to support the sales, and the money that can be spent on replenishing sold merchandise and buying new merchandise. Along with the plan, the buyer or planners decide what type and how much merchandise should be allocated to each store. The development of these merchandise plans is discussed in Chapter 13.

Third, having developed a plan, the buyer negotiates with vendors and buys the merchandise. These merchandise buying activities are reviewed in Chapter 14.

Excessively high inventory turnover results in stockouts.

EXHIBIT 12–4
Merchandise Planning
Process

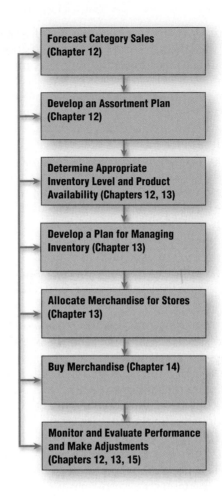

Forecast Category Sales
(Chapter 12)

Develop an Assortment Plan
(Chapter 12)

Determine Appropriate
Inventory Level and Product
Availability (Chapters 12, 13)

Develop a Plan for Managing
Inventory (Chapter 13)

Allocate Merchandise for Stores
(Chapter 13)

Buy Merchandise (Chapter 14)

Monitor and Evaluate Performance
and Make Adjustments
(Chapters 12, 13, 15)

Buyers continually monitor the sales of merchandise in the category and make adjustments. For example, if category sales are less than the forecast in the plan and the projected GMROI for the category falls below the buyer's goal, the buyer may decide to dispose of some merchandise by putting it on sale and using the money generated to buy merchandise with greater sales potential or to reduce the number of SKUs in the assortment to increase inventory turnover.

Although Exhibit 12–4 suggests that these decisions follow each other sequentially, in practice, some decisions may be made at the same time or in a different order. For example, a buyer might first decide on the amount of inventory to invest in the category, and this decision might determine the number of SKUs that can be offered in the category.

Types of Merchandise Management Planning Processes

Retailers use two distinct types of merchandise management planning systems for managing (1) staple and (2) fashion merchandise categories. **Staple merchandise categories,** also called **basic merchandise categories,** consist of items that are in continuous demand over an extended time period. The number of new product introductions in these categories is limited. Some examples of staple merchandise categories include most categories sold in supermarkets, housewares, white paint, copy paper, hosiery, inexpensive watches, basic casual apparel such as t-shirts, and men's underwear.

Because sales of staple merchandise are relatively steady from day to day, it is relatively easy to forecast demand, and the consequences of making mistakes in forecasting are not great. For example, if a buyer overestimates the demand for canned soup and buys too much, the retailer will have excess inventory for a short period of time, but eventually the canned soup will be sold without having to resort to discounts or special marketing efforts. Because the demand for basic merchandise is predictable, merchandise planning systems for staple categories focus on continuous replenishment. These systems involve continuously monitoring merchandise sales and generating replacement orders, often automatically, when inventory levels drop below predetermined levels.

Fashion merchandise consists of items that are only in demand for a relatively short period of time. New products are continually introduced into these categories, making the existing products obsolete. In some cases, the basic product does not change, but the colors and styles change to reflect what is "hot" that season. Some examples of fashion merchandise categories are athletic shoes, mobile phones, laptop computers, and women's apparel. Retailing View 12.1 describes how Mango creates and manages fashion merchandise.

Fast Fashion at Mango   **RETAILING VIEW**   12.1

"We know how to improvise," says David Egea, Mango's merchandising director and a top executive. "To react and have what people want, we have to break some rules." Mango/MNG Holding SL, with over 850 stores in 81 countries, including the United States, typifies the new retail trend of "fast fashion," pioneered by Spain's Zara and Sweden's H&M. These chains fill their racks with a steady stream of new, gotta-have-it merchandise. Their retail strategy combines stylistic and technological resources built on flexibility and speed, from design sketch to the store shelf.

Mango is famous for an eclectic mix of body-hugging styles. A black pinstriped jacket sells for $60 and a tight black minidress for $40. It maintains tight controls over the design and manufacturing of its private-label merchandise. Last minute changes, like substituting a fabric or dropping a hemline, are a built-in part of the creative process. So long as the company has fabric in stock, it can move a design from sketchpad to store in four weeks.

Mango's merchandise planning cycle begins every three months when designers meet to discuss important new trends for each of its main collections, which contain five or six mini-collections. So shops receive a near-constant stream of new merchandise, ranging from clingy short dresses to work wear and sparkly evening gowns. New items are sent to its stores once a week, roughly six times as often as the typical American clothing chain.

To get ideas for each collection, designers attend the traditional fashion shows and trade fairs. But they also stay close to the customer. They take photos of stylish young women and note what people are wearing on the streets and in nightclubs. "To see what everyone's going to do for next season is very easy," says Egea. "But that doesn't mean this is the thing that is going to catch on." Hoping to stay au courant, design teams meet each week to adjust to ever-changing trends. Mango commissioned Penelope Cruz and her sister Monica to design a 25-piece collection to compete with the other fast fashion companies that have used celebrities as designers. Top Shop released its Kate Moss collection, and H&M came out with a Madonna collection.

When collection designs are set, Mango's product management and distribution team assigns them personality traits, denoting SKUs as trendy, dressy, or suitable for hot weather. Depending on

Mango stocks high-fashion, trendy merchandise to attract its target shoppers.

an item's personality, it heads to one of Mango's 731 stores, which also has its own set of traits, such as the climate, where the shop is located, and whether large or small sizes sell best. A proprietary computer program then matches compatible shops and styles.

Orders are sent to a distribution center where clothes are scanned and dropped into one of 466 store-specific slots. Then they're boxed and shipped to shops, where managers can adjust store layouts daily on the basis of input from regional supervisors and headquarters.

Mango stores only display a limited merchandise assortment. On each rack, only one size per item is hung. This policy encourages a sense of urgency by playing on customers' worst fear: Maybe your size is going to run out.

Sources: www.mangoshop.com (accessed September 18, 2007); Beth Wilson, "Mango's Fast-Fashion Approach To Expansion," *WWD*. December 7, 2006, p. 23; Sally Raikes, "Cruz Control," *Scotland on Sunday*, September 16, 2007 (accessed September 18, 2007).

Sales of seasonal merchandise, such as Christmas tree ornaments, fluctuate dramatically depending on the time of year.

Forecasting the sales for fashion merchandise categories is much more challenging than for staple goods. Buyers for fashion merchandise categories have much less flexibility in correcting forecasting errors. For example, if the mobile phone buyer for Best Buy buys too many units of a particular model, the excess inventory cannot be easily sold when a new replacement model is introduced. Due to the short life cycle of fashion merchandise, buyers often do not have a chance to reorder additional merchandise after an initial order is placed. So if buyers initially order too little fashion merchandise, the retailer may not be able to satisfy the demand for the merchandise and will develop a reputation for not having the most popular merchandise in stock. Thus, an important objective of merchandise planning systems for fashion merchandise categories is to be as close to out of stock as possible when the SKUs become out of fashion or the season ends.

Seasonal merchandise categories consist of items whose sales fluctuate dramatically depending on the time of year. Some examples of seasonal merchandise are Halloween candy, Christmas ornaments, swimwear, and snow shovels. Both staple and fashion merchandise can be seasonal categories. For example, swimwear is a fashion merchandise category, whereas snow shovels are a staple merchandise category. However, from a merchandise planning perspective, retailers buy seasonal merchandise in much the same way that they buy fashion merchandise. Retailers could store unsold snow shovels at the end of the winter season and sell them the next winter, but it is typically better from a financial perspective to sell the shovels at a steep discount near the end of the season rather than incur the cost of carrying this excess inventory until the beginning of the next season. Thus, buyers for seasonal merchandise develop plans for getting rid of all of their seasonal merchandise at the end of the season.

These two different merchandise planning systems are discussed in more detail in Chapter 13. The remaining sections in this chapter examine three elements in the merchandise management process: (1) forecasting sales, (2) developing an assortment plan, and (3) determining the appropriate inventory level.

FORECASTING SALES

As indicated in Exhibit 12–4, the first step in merchandise management planning is to develop a forecast for category sales. To develop a category forecast, one needs to understand the nature of category life cycles and the factors that might affect the shape of the life cycle in the future. The methods and information used for forecasting basic and fashion merchandise categories are also discussed in this section.

Category Life Cycles

Merchandise categories typically follow a predictable sales pattern: Sales start off low, increase, plateau, and then ultimately decline. This sales pattern, referred to as the **category life cycle** (Exhibit 12–5), is divided into four stages: introduction, growth, maturity, and decline. Knowing where a category is in its life cycle is important in developing a sales forecast and merchandising strategy.

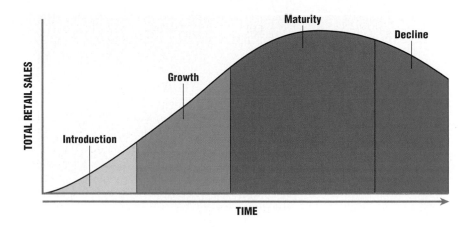

EXHIBIT 12–5
The Category Product
Life Cycle

For example, when high-definition TV (HDTV) systems were first introduced in the 1980s, the target market was producers in the film industry.[7] Compared with regular analog televisions, HDTVs were very expensive, not readily available in stores, and, most important, only a few TV shows were broadcast in HD. Today, HDTV is still in its growth stage. Although many households do not yet own HDTVs, HDTV programming is available in most market areas in the United States.[8] As this product category reaches maturity, most programs will be broadcast in HD, and only HDTVs will be available for sale.

The shape of the life cycle is not only determined by how quickly consumers adopt the product or service and environmental factors such as the economy and government regulations. It is also affected by the activities undertaken by retailers and vendors. For instance, a vendor might set a low introductory price for a new product to increase its adoption rate or a high price to generate more profits even though sales might not grow as fast. When first introduced, HDTVs were very expensive. Although the prices have declined, they continue to be significantly more expensive than analog televisions.

Care must be taken, however, when using the category life cycle as a predictive tool. If a product is classified as being in the decline stage of its product life cycle, it's likely that retailers will stock less variety and limit promotions. Naturally, sales will go down. Thus, the declining classification may actually become a self-fulfilling prophesy. Many products have been successfully maintained at the maturity stage because their buyers have maintained innovative strategies to market the mature product. For instance, Kellogg's Corn Flakes has been the best-selling ready-to-eat cereal over many decades because it has innovative advertising and competitive pricing.

Variations in Category Life Cycles   The characteristics of common variations of the category life cycle—fad, fashion, and staple—are shown in Exhibit 12–6. The distinguishing attributes between these classifications are the number of seasons sales are sustained, whether specific styles also sell for many seasons, and whether sales vary dramatically from one season to the next.

A **fad** is a merchandise category that generates a lot of sales for a relatively short time, often less than a season. Examples are pogs, skinny jeans, Crocs, "Livestrong"

Are Crocs a fashion or a fad?

EXHIBIT 12–6
Variations in Category Life Cycles

	FAD	FASHION	STAPLE
Sales over many seasons	No	Yes	Yes
Sales of a specific style over many seasons	No	No	Yes
Sales vary dramatically from one season to the next	No	Yes	No
Illustration (Sales against Time)	Sales / Time	Sales / Time	Sales / Time

bracelets,[9] some licensed characters like Star Wars action figures, and some electronic games. The art of retailing a fad comes in recognizing the fad in its earliest stages, taking a significant inventory position, and having it available in stores nationwide before the competition does. However, retailing fads are risky because even if the company properly identifies a fad, it must still know when the peak occurs so it isn't stuck with a warehouse full of merchandise.

Unlike a fad, fashion categories typically last several seasons; however, like fads, sales of specific SKUs (styles and colors) can vary dramatically from one season to the next. For instance, black apparel might be popular one year, and the same style in purple is popular the next year. Some questions that help buyers distinguish between fads and more enduring fashions are:

- *Is it compatible with a change in consumer lifestyles?* Innovations that are consistent with lifestyles are more enduring. For example, denim jeans are an enduring fashion because they are comfortable to wear, are easily laundered, and can be worn on multiple occasions. Leather pants, in contrast, are uncomfortable and expensive to clean and thus more fadish.
- *Does the innovation provide real benefits?* The switch to poultry and fish from beef is not a fad because it provides real benefits to a health-conscious society.
- *Is the innovation compatible with other changes in the marketplace?* For example, PDAs are more enduring because they are compatible with a mobile, time-pressured society.
- *Who is adopting the trend?* If the product is being adopted by a large and growing segment, such as working mothers, Baby Boomers, Generation Y, or the elderly, it is more likely to endure. Alternatively, if it is being adopted by teenagers, who are known to be fickle in their tastes, it is likely to fade quickly.

Staple merchandise categories experience relatively steady sales over an extended period of time. However, even staple merchandise categories go into decline eventually. For example, changing technology resulted in the decline of CD sales with the growth in demand for downloadable music. Retailing View 12.2 questions whether jeans are a fad, a fashion, or a staple.

Forecasting Staple Merchandise

The sales of staple merchandise are relatively constant from year to year. Thus, forecasts are typically based on extrapolating historical sales. Because there are substantial sales data available, statistical techniques can be used to forecast future sales for each SKU. Exhibit 12–7 illustrates the analysis of past unit sales data for a 12-inch, cast iron, Lodge frying pan at a national home store chain to forecast sales for 2009.

Exhibit 12–7a contains the sales data by quarter for the past eight years. The annual sales data are plotted in Exhibit 12–7b, and the quarterly sales data are plotted in Exhibit 12–7c. The annual sales pattern reveals a slight annual growth in sales. Average annual growth rate has been 3.6 percent; however, sales actually decreased in 2007 and then jumped 7.6 percent in 2008.

The graph of quarterly sales shows a seasonal pattern, with sales greatest during the fourth quarter and lowest during the third quarter. The average percentage of annual sales for each quarter is 21 percent for the first quarter, 26 percent for the second quarter, 18 percent in the third quarter, and 35 percent in the fourth quarter. Even though people use frying pans throughout the year, there is a tendency to give them as holiday gifts, and people tend to cook more on the stove when the weather gets cold.

On the basis of these past unit sales data, the buyer could simply project the sales data and estimate the annual unit sales for the frying pans for 2009 as

2009 annual sales = 1.036 (3.6 percent growth) × 118,963 (2008 annual sales)
= 123,245.

Are Jeans a Fad, a Fashion, or a Staple? **RETAILING VIEW** **12.2**

The answer to the question, whether jeans are a fad, a fashion, or a staple, all depends on what style and market segment you are considering. For example, skinny jeans hit the market in 2005–2007. After a decade of boot-cut pants, the skinny look was a major silhouette change. Designers and retailers attempted to change women's looks to upside-down triangle silhouettes, characterized by larger tops and narrower bottoms. At the same time, clothes steadily are becoming less flashy, with details like darts, stitching, and pleats instead of sequins, embroidery, and holes.

It doesn't take a fashion guru to realize that skinny jeans wouldn't look good on all women. But those retailers that could accurately predict the fashion lifecycle of these jeans profited handsomely.

A jeans fad like skinny jeans is more likely to succeed for retailers that cater to younger women, such as Urban Outfitters, Abercrombie & Fitch, and Bebe. Retailers that target older women, such as Chico's, Talbots, and Ann Taylor, approached this silhouette more cautiously.

Although not as trendy as skinny jeans, boot-cut jeans have been a fashionable cut for several years. What's the difference between the relatively long-term success of the boot-cut fashion and the short-lived skinny jean? First and foremost, the boot-cut is a complementary silhouette for most bodies. As a result, it appeals to many large market segments.

Some jeans are considered staples from a merchandise management perspective. Levi's 501 jean, for instance, was introduced in 1873 and remains popular all over the world. Wrangler, Lee, L.L. Bean, Lands' End, and private labels from JCPenney and other retailers are purchased by people of all ages and walks of life for work and play.

Can you predict the fashion cycle for high-waisted jeans?

How long did the skinny jeans fad last?

Sources: Helen Tither, "Flares: Bigger, Better, Beautiful," *Manchester Evening News*, September, 10, 2007 (accessed January 15, 2008); Chelsea Emery, "Fashion Shift May Help Teen Retailers, Hurt Others," www.washingtonpost.com, June 11, 2006 (accessed January 15, 2008).

EXHIBIT 12–7   Sales of 12-Inch Lodge Frying Pans at a National Home Store Chain

EXHIBIT 12–7a   Unit Sales by Quarter

Year	Quarter	Sales by Quarter	Annual Sales	Annual Sales Growth Rate	% Annual Sales by Quarter
2001	1	21,074			23%
	2	24,123			26
	3	16,066			17
	4	32,145	93,408		34
2002	1	20,728			23
	2	23,656			26
	3	15,867			18
	4	30,135	90,387	−3.2%	33
2003	1	21,076			22
	2	25,259			26
	3	18,585			19
	4	33,064	97,984	8.4	34
2004	1	20,617			21
	2	26,084			26
	3	18,308			18
	4	34,921	99,931	2.0	35
2005	1	21,464			20
	2	27,568			26
	3	18,996			18
	4	38,163	106,192	6.3	36
2006	1	24,401			21
	2	28,057			25
	3	21,092			18
	4	40,843	114,394	7.7	36
2007	1	23,859			22
	2	27,441			25
	3	19,537			18
	4	39,726	110,562	−3.3	36
2008	1	24,588			21
	2	30,788			26
	3	19,869			17
	4	43,718	118,963	7.6	37

EXHIBIT 12–7b
Plot of Sales by Year

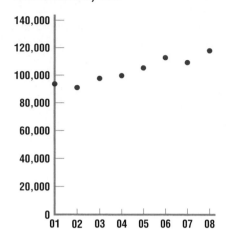

EXHIBIT 12–7c
Plot of Sales by Quarter

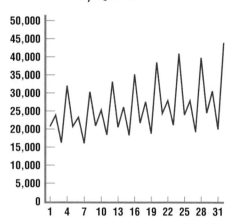

The estimated quarterly sales would be

First-quarter sales $= 123,245 \times .21 = 25,881.$
Second-quarter sales $= 123,245 \times .26 = 32,044.$
Third-quarter sales $= 123,245 \times .18 = 22,184.$
Fourth-quarter sales $= 123,245 \times .35 = 43,136.$

However, these projections are based on the assumption that the factors affecting 12-inch, cast iron, Lodge frying pan sales in 2009 will be the same and have the same effect as they have had for the past eight years. Even though sales for staple merchandise categories such as cookwear are relatively predictable, controllable and uncontrollable factors can have a significant impact on them.

Controllable factors include openings and closings of stores, the price set for the merchandise in the category, special promotions for the category, the pricing and promotion of complementary categories, and the placement of the merchandise categories in the stores. Some factors beyond the retailer's control are the weather, general economic conditions, special promotions or new product introductions by vendors, the availability of products and pricing and promotional activities by competitors. Retailing View 12.3 illustrates how retailers use long-range weather forecasts to improve their merchandise planning.

In this case, the buyer might adjust the annual unit sales projection downward for the 12-inch frying pan because the manufacturer, and thus the retailer, has increased its prices. Also, third-quarter sales might be adjusted upward because the chain, for the first time, is holding a series of in-store cooking demonstrations in which the guest chef will use this particular pan.

Forecasting Fashion Merchandise Categories

Forecasting sales for fashion merchandise categories is challenging because some or all of the items in the category are new and different than units offered in previous years. Some sources of information that retailers use to develop forecasts for fashion merchandise categories are (1) previous sales data, (2) personal awareness, (3) fashion and trend services, (4) vendors, and (5) traditional market research.

Previous Sales Data   Although items in fashion merchandise categories might be new each season, the basic merchandise in many categories is the same, and thus, accurate forecasts might be generated by simply projecting past sales data. For example, women's fashion dresses might change from season to season with new colors, styles, and fabrics. Whereas the SKUs are different each season, the total number of fashion dresses sold each year might be relatively constant and very predictable.

Personal Awareness   Buyers for fashion merchandise categories need to be aware of trends that can affect their category sales. To find out what customers are going to want in the future, they immerse themselves in customers' worlds: go into Internet chat rooms and blogs, look in their closets, attend soccer games and rock concerts. They visit hot spots around town like restaurants and nightclubs and attend

---

Forecasting the Weather   **RETAILING VIEW**   12.3

Retailers know that when hurricane season comes, they need to be ready with batteries, flashlights, plywood, water, and prepared meals. But what about the more subtle influences of weather, like a warmer than normal holiday season? Many retailers forecast sales, including seasonality, on the basis of past seasons' sales. Unfortunately, they can be wrong 75 to 80 percent of the time.

Long-range weather forecasting services like those provided by Planalytics and Weather Trends International help retailers manage severe weather events like hurricanes, as well as more subtle year-to-year changes. Retail executives, buyers, and planners, can use the information provided by these firms to make decisions about the timing of supply chain flow, promotions, and price discounts that can have huge gross margin implications. For example, weather can influence what types of gifts shoppers will buy during the holiday season. So, if it is expected to be warmer this year than last during the pre-holiday season, from November 17 until before Christmas, retailers can expect to sell more electronics rather than winter apparel. Then, if the temperatures are expected to drop during the second half of the holiday season, which goes from December 17 until January 18, apparel sales will pick up, and retailers can refrain from taking deep discounts until later. This type of information can have a significant impact on gross margins, but it doesn't come cheap. Retailers pay between $35,000 and $1 million a year for the information.

When analyzing the effects of weather, one needs to recognize that it is relative. What's cold to a Texan is very different from what cold feels like to someone who lives in Buffalo. Another good example is Los Angeles. If it's cloudy and rainy in L.A. in November, consumers react as if winter is upon them and start buying fleece and Duraflame logs, even though the temperature is still in the 60s.

REFACT

On average, weather can affect monthy sales by 5 to 10 percent. But during extreme conditions, it can affect monthly sales by as much as 50 to 60 percent.[10]

Tropical storms, hurricanes, thunderstorms, and other severe weather can cause serious damage to homes and property. Retailers should stock merchandise that homeowners and contractors need to make repairs and help get the community back to normal after the damage caused by catastrophic weather events.

Sources: Pia Sarkar, "Retailers Use Weather to Forecast Their Sales," *San Francisco Chronicle*, December 4, 2006 (accessed January 15, 2008); "Home Depot Prepares for Upcoming Storms," *Chain Store Age*, August 1, 2006 (accessed January 15, 2008); Susan Reda, "Whither Forecasting?" *Stores*, December 2004, pp. 23–27.

football games and concerts. Some suggestions to help buyers keep abreast of what Gen Y customers will want to buy are shop, converse, act, and notice (SCAN):

- *Shop* the retail stores, Web sites, and catalogs of competitors as a customer would. When visiting your own stores, don't identify yourself. When store employees know you are coming, they are on their best behavior. Surprise them: Watch how your staff interacts with shoppers. Pretend to be a customer. The key is to open your eyes to things that are new and different.

- *Converse* with consumers, sales clerks, and neighbors. Ask them: What are your favorite bands? Why are you buying a $16 Gap t-shirt to wear with a $200 suit? What TV and radio shows are you tuning in to? What do you do in your spare time? Talk to vendors and other people who are close to consumers, such as beauticians and real estate agents.

- *Act* like your customer. For one weekend, become your customer and see your merchandise or stores through the eyes of the consumer. Buy yourself a pair of high-waisted jeans, Saucony shoes, and a "green" cotton t-shirt. Spend the day in a mall, pick up a copy of *Us Weekly* and *Vogue*, listen to Rihanna and Justin Timberlake, go to a trendy nightclub, watch MTV, and then log on to MTV.com (www.mtv.com) to find out about the after-shows. Check out Web sites such as Alloy.com (www.alloy.com) and Perezhilton.com's (www.perezhilton.com) cool-hunting polls to see how Gen Y really feels about reality shows, celebrities, and inflatable furniture.

- *Notice*, notice, notice. Become a cultural sleuth by noticing the things that make you uncomfortable or seem strange and different. What movies are hits at the box office? Who is going to see them? What books and albums are on the top 10 lists? What magazines are consumers purchasing? Become an information junkie and read voraciously. Are there themes that keep popping up? All of these clues are cultural trend posts that can become an on-ramp into the mainstream.

Fashion and Trend Services   There are many services such as Trendzine (www.FashionInformation.com), Doneger Creative Services (www.Doneger.com), and Fashion Snoops (www.fashionsnoops.com) that buyers, particularly buyers of apparel categories, can subscribe to that forecast the latest fashions, colors, and styles. For example, Doneger Creative Services offers a range of services related to trend and color forecasting and analysis for apparel, accessories, and lifestyle markets in the women's, men's, and youth merchandise categories through its print publications, online content, and live presentations. Its color forecast service provides color direction for each season using dyed-to-specification color standards plus suggested color combinations and applications for specific categories. Its online clipboard reports present actionable information and style news from the runways to the streets.

Kim Hastreiter, the cofounder and editor of *Paper* magazine, is a cool hunter.[11] To most people, *Paper* is just a glossy magazine filled with clothes they can't imagine ever wearing. But exploring the underground has been *Paper*'s mission for 25 years—discovering and documenting provocateurs, places, and ideas in their earliest, rawest, and often most disconcerting form. *Paper* doesn't pride itself on being trendy. It is pretrendy.

"Trends don't start with trendy people," Hastreiter says. So you won't find Hastreiter dining at the latest restaurant where reservations can only be made using a secret number. Instead, Hastreiter will be at the restaurant off the alley behind a seedy street. "We prefer to write about things when they're still in garages, when they're more rough," Hastreiter says. "Years ago we put a local waitress with tattoos all over her body on the cover of the magazine. We lost ads because of it. But we had never seen that before." Now, of course, tattoos and body piercings are common, and their wearers are models for such mainstream brands as The Gap and Pepsi.

Japan's youth have become the world's trendsetters.[12] Some retailers, notably Abercrombie & Fitch and Sweden's H&M, have set up shop in Tokyo and are using the stores to test new fashion concepts. Others, such as Gola, an English brand of athletic shoes and apparel, have teamed up with Euro-Pacific (Japan) Ltd., a Tokyo-based retailer of fashion footwear to test new concepts. For instance, after testing shin-high boxing boots to young women in Japan, Gola successfully introduced them in Europe. Japan has its own "cool hunter" entrepreneurs that take foreign visitors around to boutiques. They typically spend $20,000 or more buying up merchandise that they send back to their companies' design teams or directly to factories in China to adapt and make for the U.S. market.

Since Japan's youth have become the world's trendsetters, retailers test new fashion concepts there.

Vendors   Vendors have proprietary information about their marketing plans, such as new product launches and special promotions, that can have a significant impact on retail sales for their products and the entire merchandise category. In addition, vendors tend to be knowledgeable about market trends for merchandise categories because they typically specialize in fewer merchandise categories than retailers. Thus, information from vendors about their plans and market research about merchandise categories is very useful to buyers as they develop category sales forecasts. Retailing View 12.4 describes how JCPenney manages the risks associated with developing private label fashion.

Market Research   Information on how customers will react to new merchandise can be obtained by asking customers about the merchandise or measuring their reactions to it through sales tests. For example, a cashier at a restaurant may ask how a customer liked a new item on the menu. But retailers need to have a systematic way to collect this information and relay it to the appropriate buyers. As we discussed in Chapter 11, some retailers incorporate information about customer requests in their CRM systems. This information is then accessed by buyers for making forecasts and purchasing decisions.

Customer information also can be collected through traditional forms of marketing research like depth interviews and focus groups. The **depth interview** is an unstructured personal interview in which the interviewer uses extensive probing to get individual respondents to talk in detail about a subject. For example, one grocery store chain goes through the personal checks received each day and selects all customers with large purchases of groceries and several with small purchases. Representatives from the chain call these customers and interview them to find out what products they would like to buy in the store.

A more informal method of interviewing customers is to require buyers to spend some time on the selling floor waiting on customers. In most national retail chains, buyers are physically isolated from their customers. For example, buying offices for Target and The Gap are in Minnesota and northern California, respectively, yet their stores are throughout the United States. It has become increasingly hard for buyers in large chains to be attuned to local customer demand. Frequent store visits help resolve the situation. Some retailers require their buyers to spend a specified period of time, like one day a week, in a store.

A **focus group** is a small group of respondents interviewed by a moderator using a loosely structured format. Participants are encouraged to express their views and comment on the views of others in the group. To keep abreast of the teen market, for instance, some stores have teen boards comprised of opinion leaders who meet to discuss merchandising and other store issues. Abercrombie & Fitch brings in groups of teenagers and has them rate their preferences for different items.

Finally, many retailers have a program for conducting merchandise experiments. For example, Claire's, an international specialty accessory retail chain targeting teens, continually runs tests to determine whether new merchandise concepts will produce adequate sales. It introduces the new merchandise into a representative group of stores and sees what sales are generated for the items. Multichannel retailers often run similar tests by offering new items on their Web sites before making a decision to stock them in their stores.

Sales Forecasting for Service Retailers

Due to the perishable nature of services, service retailers face a more extreme problem than fashion retailers. Their offering perishes at the end of the day, not at the end of the season. If there are empty seats when a plane takes off or the rock

---

12.4   RETAILING VIEW   Transforming Runway Fashions into JCPenney Fashions

Buyers no longer have to travel to fashion shows in New York, Paris, or Milan to scrutinize the latest designer clothing. Style Web sites like www.style.com, *New York Magazine's* www.nymag.com, WGSN, and Style Sight show images of runway models that retailers can use to spot new trends. Of course, buyers still go to trade shows, subscribe to fashion and trend services, and travel to trend-setting locations around the world like Toyko, Sweden, Milan, and Montreal.

Buyers at JCPenney, Dillard's., Kohl's., Wal-Mart, Target, and other large apparel retailers look for the trends, trying to spot a common theme across several designers, then modify it to appeal to their more mainstream, middle-income customers. For instance, the bodies of supermodels aren't the same as those of the average woman, so the stores might lengthen hemlines, modify necklines, or remove embroidery.

REFACT

JCPenney employs about 100 in-house designers and creates approximately 35,000 items of clothing a year—roughly half of them for women.[13]

Ten years ago, JCPenney and other large apparel retailers waited as long as two years after runway fashions arrived at more upscale department and specialty stores before their customers would see similar items in their stores. But the Internet and increased competition has forced these stores to speed up their fashion cycle.

When a firm like JCPenney decides to make a commitment to a particular style sold under one of its private labels, it better be right. About 45 percent of its revenue comes from sales of apparel it creates in house. Unlike nationally branded merchandisers that may take back unsold merchandise or grant allowances for markdowns, all the risk of its private-label merchandise rests on its shoulders.

When JCPenney makes its commitment to buy into a new trend, such as turtlenecks for fall, it buys a limited number of styles but fabric in very large quantities. The introductory styles gets prominent floor space and plenty of online communications. If buyers miscalculate demand for specific styles and colors, Penney can still make style and color adjustments for the second round of shipments for later in the season.

Mid-tier fashion retailers modify runway fashions to fit the needs of their target markets.

Sources: Vanessa O'Connell, "How Fashion Makes Its Way From the Runway to the Rack," *The Wall Street Journal,* February 8, 2007, p. D1; Christina Binkley, "After the Show: The Real Business of Fashion," *The Wall Street Journal,* March 1, 2007, p. D6.

concert is over, the revenue that might have been generated from these seats is lost forever. However, if more people are interested in dining at a restaurant than there are tables available, a revenue opportunity also is lost. So service retailers have devised approaches for managing demand for their offering so that it meets but does not exceed capacity.

Some service retailers attempt to match supply and demand by taking reservations or making appointments. Physicians often overbook their appointments so many patients have to wait. They do this so they will always fill their capacity and not have unproductive, non–revenue-generating time. Restaurants take reservations so that customers will not have to wait for a table. In addition, the reservations indicate the staffing levels needed for that meal. Another approach is selling advance tickets for a service.[14]

DEVELOPING AN ASSORTMENT PLAN

After forecasting sales for the category, the next step in the merchandise management planning process is to develop an assortment plan. An **assortment plan** is a list of the SKUs that a retailer will offer in a merchandise category. The assortment plan thus reflects the variety and assortment that the retailer plans to offer in a merchandise category.

Category Variety and Assortment

In Chapter 2, the **variety** or breadth of a retailer's merchandise was defined as the number of different merchandising categories offered, and the retailer's **assortment** or depth of merchandise was defined as the number of SKUs within a category. For example, Target, a full-line discount store chain, offers a wide variety of merchandise categories ranging from consumer electronics to women's dresses but only a limited number of the most popular SKUs in each category. Thus, Target's merchandise offering is high on variety (broad) and low on assortment (shallow). A category specialist such as Circuit City, in contrast, focuses on consumer electronics and thus sells fewer merchandise categories (less variety or breadth) but has a greater assortment of merchandise in each category (depth).

Services retailers also make assortment decisions. For example, some health clubs offer a large variety of activities and equipment from exercise machines to swimming, wellness programs, and New Age lectures. Others, like Gold's Gym, don't offer much variety but have deep assortments of body-building equipment and programs. Some hospitals, such as big municipal hospitals found in most urban areas, offer a large variety of medical services, whereas others specialize in services such as trauma or prenatal care.

In the context of merchandise planning, the concepts of variety and assortment are applied to a merchandise category rather than a retail firm. At the category level, variety reflects the number of different types of merchandise, and assortment is the number of SKUs per type. For example, the assortment plan for girls' jeans in Exhibit 12–8 includes 10 types or varieties (traditional or boot cut, regular denim or stonewashed, and three price points reflecting different brands). For each type, there are 81 SKUs (3 colors × 9 sizes × 3 lengths). Thus, this retailer plans to offer 810 SKUs in girls' jeans.

Determining Variety and Assortment

In attempting to determine the variety and assortment for a category like jeans, the buyer considers the following factors: the firm's retail strategy, GMROI of the merchandise mix, physical characteristics of the store, trade-off between too much versus too little assortment, and degree to which categories of merchandise complement one another.

EXHIBIT 12–8   Assortment Plan for Girls' Jeans

Styles	Traditional	Traditional	Traditional	Traditional	Traditional	Traditional
Price levels	$20	$20	$35	$35	$45	$45
Fabric composition	Regular denim	Stonewashed	Regular denim	Stonewashed	Regular denim	Stonewashed
Colors	Light blue	Light blue	Light blue	Light blue	Light blue	Light blue
	Indigo	Indigo	Indigo	Indigo	Indigo	Indigo
	Black	Black	Black	Black	Black	Black

Styles	Boot-Cut	Boot-Cut	Boot-Cut	Boot-Cut
Price levels	$25	$25	$45	$45
Fabric composition	Regular denim	Stonewashed	Regular denim	Stonewashed
Colors	Light blue	Light blue	Light blue	Light blue
	Indigo	Indigo	Indigo	Indigo
	Black	Black	Black	Black

Retail Strategy   The number of SKUs to offer in a merchandise category is a strategic decision. Costco focuses on customers who are looking for a good value for both commodity-type merchandise and special higher-end treasures. Thus, it offers few SKUs per category. In contrast, Circuit City focuses on consumers interested in comparing alternatives for specific consumer electronic categories and thus offers more SKUs per category.

The breath and depth of the assortment in a merchandise category can affect the retailer's brand image. In general, retailers need to offer enough SKUs to satisfy the customers' needs and maintain their brand image with respect to the merchandise category but not too many so that their image is compromised. Selecting the right assortment is referred to as **editing the assortment.**

Tiffany & Co., for example, has gone through a significant editing process for its assortment. In an effort to increase sales, it introduced silver charm bracelets priced at about $100. Although these bracelets were very popular with teens and generated significant sales, Tiffany was worried that the "low-priced" items would alienate its older, wealthier, and more conservative customers and damage Tiffany's reputation for luxury. So Tiffany decided to kill its "silver" goose. It increased prices on its fast-growing, highly profitable line of cheaper silver jewelry and simultaneously introduced pricier jewelry collections to its assortment plan.[15]

It is important to have a properly balanced assortment. Customers want to feel like they are getting a lot of choices. But having too much choice can confuse customers and make them question whether they ultimately made the right choice. Too much choice can also dilute the retailer's image of being able to provide exactly what its target market wants. Furthermore, the more SKUs a retailer carries, the higher its inventory investment.

Recent research has shown that customers actually buy more if there are modest reductions of redundant items in assortments, such as reducing the number of different ketchup bottle sizes or low-share brands carried by a supermarket.[16] Some retailers, such as Circuit City and Staples, have increased sales by reducing the number of choices in each of their product categories.[17] Another option is to present customers with a strong selection but feature certain items. This method, borrowed from the restaurant industry, is popular with Internet retailers.[18] Retailing View 12.5 looks at the tough decisions that Victoria's Secret has to deal with in evaluating its assortment of bras.

GMROI of Merchandise Assortment   Buyers are constrained by the amount of money they have to invest in a merchandise category and the store space available to display the merchandise. They must deal with the trade-off of increasing sales by offering more breadth and depth but potentially reducing inventory turn-over and GMROI by stocking more SKUs.

Increasing breadth and depth also can increase the need to put merchandise on sale and thus negatively affect the gross margin. For example, the more SKUs offered, the greater the chance of **breaking sizes**—that is, stocking out of a specific size SKU. If a stockout occurs for a popular SKU in a fashion merchandise category and the buyer cannot reorder during the season, the buyer will typically discount the entire merchandise type. The buyer's objective is to remove the merchandise type from the assortment altogether so that customers will not be disappointed when they don't find the size and color they want.

Physical Characteristics of the Store   Retailers must consider how much space to devote to the category. If many SKUs are in the assortment, more space will be required to display and store the merchandise properly. For example, a wall may hold 20 plasma TVs. It wouldn't be aesthetically pleasing to display only five units on the wall or to mix the TVs with another merchandise category. Thus, the buyer might include 20 SKUs in the assortment plan.

For some merchandise categories, a lot of space is needed to display individual items, limiting the number of SKUs that can be offered in stores. For example, furniture takes up a lot of space, and thus, furniture retailers typically display one model of a chair or sofa and then have photographs and cloth swatches or a virtual room on a computer to show how the furniture would look with different upholstery.

Multichannel retailers address the space limitations in stores by offering a greater assortment through their Internet and catalog channels than they do in stores. For example, Staples offers more types of notebook computers and printers

Evaluating Victoria's Secret's Bra Assortment   RETAILING VIEW   12.5

In a busy Victoria's Secret store in New York's SoHo district, Amanda White, 27, picks up a matching set of a leopard-print bra and under-wear, a black negligee, a turquoise lace bra, and three simple cotton bras in pale blue, white, and yellow. After about a half-hour in the fitting room, she walks out of the store carrying three items: the simple cotton bras. "My boyfriend won't love these, but I need something I can wear everyday," she says.

Victoria's Secret has more bad news for White's boyfriend. The chain, which built its image as a sexy lingerie retailer with expensive ad campaigns featuring famous models, wants to include more basic, less expensive styles of lingerie. American women seem to prefer them. The move carries risks but has a clear business logic: A large majority of the bras sold at Victoria's Secret fall into the so-called "glamour" category with lace or push-up features. But according to analysts, between 70 to 80 percent of the total bra market in the United States still consists of what some women call "workhorse" bras—simple styles that are comfortable and durable.

Victoria's Secret wants a larger "share of drawer" in its customers' dressers and hopes to grab a good chunk of the everyday market currently dominated by other lingerie players and away from retailers such as The Gap and J. Crew, which have their own lingerie lines.

Victoria's Secret is continually adjusting its lingerie assortment to attract more customers and increase sales to each of those customers.

Adjusting an assortment from sexy to practical is a tricky business. So far, however, the strategy is working: The company launched its "Body by Victoria" collection in 1999, a simple line of bras in nylon and spandex that promised its wearers, "all you see is curves." It quickly became a best seller.

The move to plainer styles is risky because the company could smudge its image as a purveyor of fancy lingerie. Its brand says "sexy," but being too sexy has given the company problems in the past, such as when Victoria's Secret made a misstep in its sleepwear. It offered a lot of see-through negligees and too few flannel pajamas. Sales fell.

Also, if it is going to continue to grow, the company must expand its market. Although its image is still "26 and sexy," not every Victoria's Secret client fits that image anymore. To broaden its appeal, instead of featuring models in black lace, thigh-high stockings on the cover, one recent catalog touted, "NEW! SEXY SUPPORT." Underneath, in smaller print, was written, "Sizes 34B–40DD."

Sources: Emily Bryson York, "Bra Just Won't Fit? Playtex Offers Some Support," *Advertising Age*, September 17, 2007; Margaret Pressler, "Under Where? Retail's Unmentionable Is What She Won't Put On," *Washington Post*, February 8, 2004, p. F.06.

on its Internet site than it stocks in its stores. If customers do not find the computer or printer they want in the store, sales associates direct them to the company's Internet site and can even order the merchandise for them from a POS terminal.

Complementary Merchandise   When retailers plan to alter their assortment, they must consider whether the merchandise under consideration complements other merchandise in the department. For instance, DVD players may stimulate the sales of DVDs, accessories, and cables. Whereas the DVD players might have a low GMROI that does not justify a significant assortment, the complementary accessories might have very high GMROIs. Thus, retailers may decide to carry more DVD player SKUs to build up accessory sales.

SETTING INVENTORY AND PRODUCT AVAILABILITY LEVELS

Assortment plans typically include the desired inventory levels of each SKU stocked in the store, as illustrated in Exhibit 12–9. This summary of the typical store inventory support for a merchandise category is referred to as the **model stock plan.** For example, the model stock plan in Exhibit 12–9 includes nine units of size 1, short, which represent 2 percent of the 429 total units for girls' traditional $20 denim jeans in light blue. Note that there is more stock for more popular sizes.

The retailer might have different model stock plans for each store size in a chain. For example, retailers typically classify their stores as A, B, and C stores on the basis of their sales volume. The basic assortment in a category is stocked in C stores. For the larger stores, more space is available, and thus, the number of SKUs increases. The larger A and B stores may have more brands, colors, styles, and sizes of apparel or more models for hard goods such as appliances and consumer electronics.

Product Availability

The backup stock in the model stock plan determines product availability. **Product availability** is defined as the percentage of demand for a particular SKU that is satisfied. For instance, if 100 people go into a Macy's department store to purchase a pair of traditional, light blue, denim jeans, and only 90 people can make the purchase before the stock in the store is depleted, product availability for that SKU is 90 percent. Product availability is also referred to as the **level of support** or **service level.**

The higher the desired product availability, the greater the amount of backup stock, or **buffer stock,** needed to ensure that the retailer won't be out of stock on a particular SKU when customers want it. Choosing an appropriate amount of backup stock is critical to successful assortment planning because if the backup stock is too low, the retailer will lose sales, and possibly customers too. If the level is too

EXHIBIT 12–9
Model Stock Plans

LENGTH		SIZE								
		1	2	4	5	6	8	10	12	14
Short	%	2	4	7	6	8	5	7	4	2
	units	9	17	30	26	34	21	30	17	9
Medium	%	2	4	7	6	8	5	7	4	2
	units	9	17	30	26	34	21	30	17	9
Long	%	0	2	2	2	3	2	2	1	0
	units	0	9	9	9	12	9	9	4	0
Total 100%										
429 units										

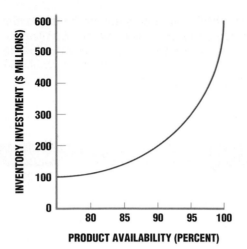

EXHIBIT 12–10
Inventory Investment and Product Availability

high, scarce financial resources will be wasted on needless inventory that could be more profitably invested to increase variety or assortment in the category.

Exhibit 12–10 shows the trade-off between inventory investment and product availability. Although the actual inventory investment varies in different situations, the general relationship shows that prohibitively high levels of inventory are needed to provide very high levels of availability.

Several factors need to be considered to determine the appropriate level of buffer stock and thus the product availability for each SKU. Retailers often classify merchandise categories or individual SKUs as A, B, or C items, reflecting the product availability the retailer wants to offer. For A items, the retailer rarely wants to risk a stockout, whereas lower product availability is acceptable for C items. For example, white paint is an A item for Sherwin Williams, and copy paper is an A item for Office Depot. Stocking out of these very popular SKUs would diminish the image of these retailers.

Some other factors considered in determining backup stock levels and product availability are the fluctuations in demand, the lead time for delivery from the vendor, fluctuations in vendor lead time, and the frequency of store deliveries. These factors are discussed in more detail in Chapter 13, along with the merchandising planning systems for staple and fashion merchandise categories, the allocation of merchandise to stores, and the performance evaluation for merchandise categories.

The trade-off among variety, assortment, and product availability is a crucial issue in determining a retailer's merchandising strategy. Buyers have a limited budget for the inventory investments they can make in a category. Thus, they are forced to sacrifice breadth of merchandise if they opt to increase depth or reduce both depth and breadth to increase product availability.

SUMMARY

This chapter provides an overview of the merchandise management planning process and examines sales forecasting and assortment planning in more detail. Merchandise is broken down into categories for planning purposes. Buyers and planners, manage these categories, often with the help of their major vendors.

Performance measures used to assess merchandise management are GMROI, sales-to-stock ratios and inventory turnover, and gross margin percent. Retailers use GMROI to plan and evaluate merchandise performance.

The GMROI planned for a particular merchandise category is derived from the firm's overall financial goals, broken down to the category level. Gross margin percentage and inventory turnover work together to form this useful merchandise management tool.

High inventory turnover is important for a retailer's financial success. But if the retailer attempts to push inventory turnover to its limit, stockouts and increased costs may result.

When developing a sales forecast, retailers need to know what stage of the life cycle a particular category is in and whether the product is a fad, fashion, or staple item so they can plan their merchandising activities accordingly. Creating a sales forecast involves such sources of information as (1) previous sales data, (2) personal knowledge, (3) fashion and trend services, (4) vendors, and (5) traditional market research.

The next step in the merchandise planning process is developing an assortment plan and model stock list. The assortment plan reflects the retailer's merchandise strategy with respect to the depth and breadth of merchandise carried in the category.

KEY TERMS

assortment, *349*

assortment plan, *349*

basic merchandise categories, *338*

breaking sizes, *351*

buffer stock, *352*

category captain, *333*

category life cycle, *340*

category management, *333*

classification, *331*

department, *331*

depth interview, *347*

editing the assortment, *350*

fad, *341*

fashion merchandise, *339*

focus group, *347*

level of support, *352*

merchandise category, *332*

merchandise group, *330*

merchandise management, *330*

model stock plan, *352*

product availability, *352*

seasonal merchandise, *340*

service level, *352*

staple merchandise categories, *338*

stock-keeping unit (SKU), *332*

variety, *349*

GET OUT AND DO IT!

1. **CONTINUING EXERCISE** Go to a retailer's store and audit the variety and assortment for a specific merchandise category. Record the breadth and depth of the assortment and the level of support (average number of items for the SKUs in each category). Compare the variety, assortment, and support for the same category in a competing retail store.

2. Go to www.badfads.com. Choose some fads. Ask the four questions related to Variations in Category Life Cycles, listed on page 342 in this chapter. According to your answers, how did these fads develop into a fashion or else crash and die?

3. Go to the Beanie Babies homepage at www.ty.com/BeanieBabies_home and then go to the Webkinz homepage at www.webkinz.com. How is Ganz trying to keep its Webkinz merchandise offerings from being a fad, as Ty experienced in the late 1990s with Beanie Babies? How can a toy company develop an enduring brand?

4. Go to www.macys.com and www.jcp.com. Which seems to have the largest variety? Choose a merchandise category and determine which retailer offers the largest assortment.

5. Go to Oracle Retail Merchandise Planning at www.oracle.com/applications/retail/MP/index.html and read about its merchandise planning software. How does the software use sales and inventory data to help retailers make more informed merchandise planning decisions?

6. Go to the home page for the following three retail trade publications: *WWD* at www.wwd.com, *Chain Store Age* at www.chainstoreage.com, and *Retailing Today* at www.retailingtoday.com. How can the articles found in these sources assist retailers with merchandise planning decisions?

7. Go to the student online learning center (OLC) and develop an assortment plan for Star Hardware's wrench category. Use the data on unit sales, sales-to-stock ratios, and gross margin percentages in the Excel spreadsheet found under the heading "Merchandise Assortment Plan." The tradeoffs you need to consider include (1) increasing the GMROI for the category, (2) maintaining the level of sales in the category, (3) providing a full line of wrenches at different price points, and (4) potentially reducing the number of vendors.

DISCUSSION QUESTIONS AND PROBLEMS

1. What are the differences among a fashion, a fad, and a staple? How should a merchandise planner manage these types of merchandise differently?

2. How and why would you expect variety and assortment to differ between a traditional bricks-and-mortar store and its Internet counterpart?

3. Simply speaking, increasing inventory turnover is an important goal for a retail manager. What are the consequences of turnover that's too slow? Too fast?

4. Assume you are the grocery buyer for canned fruits and vegetables at a five-store supermarket chain. Del Monte has told you and your boss that it would be responsible for making all inventory decisions for those merchandise categories. Del Monte will now determine how much to order and when shipments should be made. It promises a 10 percent increase in gross margin dollars in the coming year. Would you take Del Monte up on its offer? Justify your answer.

5. A buyer at Old Navy has received a number of customer complaints that the category he manages has been out of stock on some sizes of men's t-shirts. The buyer subsequently decides to increase this category's product availability from 80 percent to 90 percent. What will be the impact on backup stock and inventory turnover? Would your answer be the same if the product category were men's fleece sweatshirts?

6. Variety, assortment, and product availability are the cornerstones of the merchandise planning process. Provide examples of retailers that have done an outstanding job of positioning their stores on the basis of one or more of these issues.

7. The fine jewelry department in a department store has the same GMROI as the small appliances department, even though characteristics of the merchandise are quite different. Explain this situation.

8. Calculate the GMROI and inventory turnover given annual sales of $20,000, average inventory (at cost) of $4,000, and a gross margin of 45 percent.

9. Give examples of products that you have purchased that are fad, fashion, and staple items according to the category life cycle. How does each item fit the definitions given in Exhibit 12–6?

10. As the athletic shoe buyer for Sports Authority, how would you go about forecasting sales for a new Nike running shoe?

SUGGESTED READING

Brannon, Evelyn. *Fashion Forecasting: Research, Analysis and Presentation*. 2nd ed. New York: Fairchild, 2005.

Caro, Felipe, and Jérémie Gallien. "Dynamic Assortment with Demand Learning for Seasonal Consumer Goods." *Management Science* 53, no. 2 (2007), pp. 276–92.

Clodfelter, Richard. *Retail Buying: From Basics to Fashion*, 2nd ed. New York: Fairchild, 2002.

Diamond, Jay, and Gerald Pintel. *Retail Buying*, 8th ed. Upper Saddle River, NJ: Prentice Hall, 2007.

Donnellan, John. *Merchandise Buying and Management*. 2nd ed. New York: Fairchild, 2002.

Dupre, Kyle, and Thomas Gruen. "The Use of Category Management Practices to Obtain a Sustainable Competitive Advantage in the Fast-Moving Consumer-Goods Industry." *Journal of Business & Industrial Marketing* 19 (2004), pp. 444–60.

Hariga, Moncer A.; Abdulrahman Al-Ahmari; and Abdel-Rahman A. Mohamed. "A Joint Optimisation Model for Inventory Replenishment, Product Assortment, Shelf Space and Display Area Allocation Decisions." *European Journal of Operational Research* 181, no. 1 (2007), pp. 239–51.

Hart, Cathy and Mohammed Rafiq. "The Dimensions of Assortment: A Proposed Hierarchy of Assortment Decision Making." *International Review of Retail, Distribution & Consumer Research* 16, no. 3 (2006), pp. 333–51.

Jones, Jen. *Fashion Trends: How Popular Style Is Shaped (The World of Fashion)*. Pasadena: Snap, 2007.

Kalyanam, Kirthi; Sharad Borle; and Peter Boatwright. "Deconstructing Each Item's Category Contribution." *Marketing Science* 26, no. 3 (2007), pp. 327–41.

Thomas, Chris. *Management of Retail Buying*. New York: Wiley, 2005.

Varley, Rosemary. *Retail Product Management: Buying and Merchandising*. 2nd ed. New York: Routledge, 2005.

Merchandise Planning Systems

EXECUTIVE BRIEFING
Latoya Parker, Buyer, Macy's East

After graduating from Florida A&M University, I began my career with Macy's East in New York City as an Assistant Buyer for Men's Collections (Claiborne, DKNY, Kenneth Cole). Within 1½ years, I was promoted to Associate Buyer in Men's Collections and given specific responsibility for Timberland and Lacoste. After 2½ years, I was promoted to Buyer for Men's Nautica, Tommy, and Timberland Collections. Currently, I now manage and buy, with an Associate Buyer and an Assistant Buyer, about $80 million in sales for around 15 young men's brands including Levi's, Ecko, Quiksilver, and Macy's private-label brand, American Rag.

Sometimes people outside the business are surprised when I tell them I buy young men's merchandise. They say, "What do you know about what young men like to wear?" I have to explain to them that we buy what our customers like and expect to see when they come into a Macy's.

We learn what our customers like by analyzing the sales numbers and reviewing the success, or lack of success, of the product's sell through. Trade publications are also helpful in determining future trends. At Macy's, we put our customers first. Buying is more than having a sense of fashion and what's hot at the moment. You also have to know how to analyze the numbers.

Every season my planner and I build merchandise sales plans for each of my brands. These plans are reviewed by my DMM and GMM. They make sure that the plans developed by the buyers and planners are consistent with our division's goals. If we identify a good opportunity, I can get additional funding outside of the plan to pursue it. For example, last year one of my vendors had excess inventory in plaid shorts. They approached me about buying some of the excess inventory at a significant discount. I had been analyzing the performance of shorts and noticed that plaids were really selling well in our stores, but I didn't have the open-to-buy to take advantage of this

CHAPTER 13

QUESTIONS

How does a staple merchandise buying system operate?

What are a merchandise budget plan and open-to-buy systems, and how are they developed?

How do multistore retailers allocate merchandise to stores?

How do retailers evaluate their merchandising performance?

great offer. I presented a plan to my DMM and GMM, and they gave me more open-to-buy. It was really exciting to come to work, turn on the computer, and track how well those plaid shorts were selling.

One great thing about retailing is that you get immediate feedback on the quality of decisions that you make. I really look forward to reviewing my daily financial results, which is basically a report card that tracks the sales generated within my departments. It's a great feeling to see strategies we implemented be successful. And even when sales are below expectations, I am excited about the challenge of turning things around. For example, when we acquired the May Company stores, we started stocking them with the same merchandise assortment that had done well in our Macy's stores. We noticed that in some cases we had to make assortment changes because the customer was not responding to the merchandise mix. We adjusted our mix for these stores and started to see positive results.

I am really happy that I decided to go into retailing. My job is exciting and challenging. It keeps me busy every day. And it's rewarding, both personally and financially.

Chapter 12 provided an overview of the process for managing inventory for a merchandise category and the measures—GMROI, gross margin, and inventory turnover—used to evaluate the performance of buyers in managing their inventory investments. Issues related to forecasting sales and developing assortment plans indicated in very general terms what and how much inventory should be carried in a particular merchandise category. But the actual management of a retail inventory on a daily basis is quite complex. For example, Sears' buyers have to place orders and keep track of inventory levels for 500,000 SKUs.

Retailers employ computer-based information and planning support systems to assist buyers in this challenging management task. These systems help buyers and planners determine when and how much to buy and what adjustments might be needed in the pricing and allocation of merchandise to specific stores.

As discussed in Chapter 12, retailers use two different merchandise planning systems—one for staple merchandise categories and another for fashion and seasonal merchandise categories. Because staple merchandise items are continuously sold over a number of years, there is a sales history for each SKU. Thus statistical techniques can be used to forecast sales. In addition, the risks associated with inaccurate forecasts are minimal because excess inventory can be sold during subsequent time periods. Thus, staple merchandise planning systems manage inventory at the level of the SKU.

In contrast, fashion merchandise categories typically consist of many SKUs that are new products without a sales history available for accurate forecasts. In addition, the potential losses from forecasting errors are significant because if the merchandise does not sell during the season, it can no longer be sold because it will be out of fashion. Therefore, fashion merchandise planning systems manage inventory at the category level. After determining the appropriate inventory levels in dollars, buyers for fashion merchandise categories develop assortment plans to determine the quantity of specific SKUs to purchase. Open-to-buy systems keep track of merchandise flow (orders, sales, and merchandise receipts) so buyers don't spend too much or too little.

Some retailers have developed their own merchandise planning systems, whereas others use systems developed by software companies, such as SAS; Retek, a division of Oracle; and JDA. In some retail firms, these merchandise planning systems are part of the firm's enterprise resource planning (ERP) system, which integrates merchandise planning with systems for managing supply chains and other business activities. In small retail firms, the software for merchandise planning might be installed on the owner's personal computer. Retailing View 13.1 describes how some retailers are utilizing these merchandise management systems.

This chapter begins with a look at buying systems for staple merchandise. Buying systems for fashion merchandise are examined next, followed by an examination of open-to-buy systems. SAS systems illustrate the functions of the reports generated by these systems. The chapter then discusses how multistore retailers allocate merchandise among stores and how merchandise management performance is evaluated. At the end of this chapter, Appendix 13A describes the retail inventory method (RIM).

13.1   RETAILING VIEW   Retailers Utilize State-of-the-Art Merchandise Management Systems

SAS has developed an integrated system to maximize retailers' profitability using several modules. These and similar systems are discussed in this and subsequent chapters. SAS's system provides a merchandise planning and forecasting module that forecasts sales and provides buyers with suggestions about how much of a particular category to buy. It also helps planners determine assortments, plan space in stores and allocate merchandise to stores. Its revenue optimization module helps buyers determine optimal initial prices on the basis of costs, regional demand patterns, and competitive price information. This module also helps buyers determine optimal prices for promotions and markdowns.

The Children's Place has been a SAS customer since 2005. It uses the software to optimize regular and clearance pricing strategies, promotion decisions, and preseason planning. The system also allows its buyers to make adjustments throughout the selling season and review actual performance with respect to planned performance.

Loehmann's, the national, upscale, off-price specialty store, has experienced greater gross margins and overall profitability as a result of using Oracle's Retail merchandising application, which competes with SAS's systems. This type of application allows the retailer to recognize underperforming merchandise categories and make changes faster to increase inventory

Off-price retailer, Loehmann's, has increased its gross margins and profits as a result of using Oracle's Retail merchandising application.

turnover. As a result, customers can have the best selection of merchandise available.

Sources: www.sas.com/industry/retail/merchandise/ (accessed October 24, 2007); "Loehmann's Uses Oracle (R) Retail Application to Deliver Best Selection of In-Season Merchandise at Discount Prices," *CNN Money*, September 10, 2007; "The Children's Place Retail Stores Inc. Chooses SAS for Advanced Merchandise Planning at Disney Store North America," *SAS*, March 7, 2007.

STAPLE MERCHANDISE MANAGEMENT SYSTEMS

Exhibit 13–1 illustrates the merchandise flow in a staple merchandise management system. At the beginning of week 1, the retailer had 150 units of the SKU in inventory, and the buyer placed an order for 96 additional units. During the next two weeks, customers purchased a lot of the SKU, and the inventory level decreased to 20 units. At the end of week 2, the 96-unit order from the vendor arrived, and the inventory level jumped up to 116 units. The buyer placed another order with the vendor that will arrive in two weeks, before customer sales decrease the inventory level to 0 and the retailer stocks out.

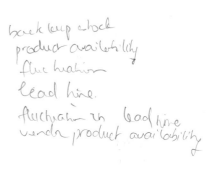

Inventory for which the level goes up and down due to the sales and replenishment process is called **cycle stock** or **base stock.** The retailer hopes to reduce the base stock inventory to keep its inventory investment low. One approach for reducing the base stock is to reorder and receive merchandise from the vendor more often instead of once every other week. But more frequent ordering and shipments increase administrative and transportation costs.

Because sales of the SKU and receipts of orders from the vendor cannot be predicted with perfect accuracy, the retailer has to carry **backup stock,** also known as **safety stock** or **buffer stock,** as a cushion so it doesn't stock out before the next order arrives. Backup stock is shown in yellow in Exhibit 13–1.

Several factors determine the level of required backup stock. First, it depends on the product availability the retailer wishes to provide. As discussed in Chapter 12 (recall Exhibit 12–10), the greater the backup stock, the lower the chances of a stockout, and the greater the availability of the SKU. Thus, if Lowe's rarely wants to stock out of white paint, it needs to have a higher level of backup stock. However, if it is willing to accept a 75 percent product availability for melon-colored paint, a lower level of buffer stock is needed for that SKU.

Second, the greater the fluctuation in demand, the more backup stock is needed. Suppose a Lowe's store sells an average of 30 gallons of purple paint in two weeks. Yet, in some weeks, sales are 50 gallons, and some weeks they are only 10 gallons. When sales are less than average, the store ends up carrying a little more merchandise than it needs. But when sales are much more than average, there must be more backup stock to ensure that the store does not stock out. Note in Exhibit 13–1 that during week 4, sales were greater than average, so the retailer had to dip into its backup stock to avoid a stockout.

Third, the amount of backup stock needed is affected by the lead time from the vendor. **Lead time** is the amount of time between the recognition that an order needs to be placed and the point at which the merchandise arrives in the store and is ready for sale. If it took two months to receive a shipment of purple paint, the possibility of running out of stock is greater than if the lead time were only two weeks. The shorter lead times inherent in collaborative supply chain management

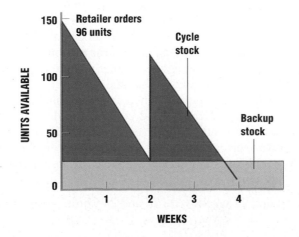

EXHIBIT 13–1
Inventory Levels for
Staple Merchandise

When planning the amount of inventory to order for a staple merchandise category, such as paint, Lowe's buyers must consider current inventory, customer demand, lead time for replenishment, and backup stock need to avoid stockouts in the department.

systems like CPFR (described in Chapter 10) result in a lower level of backup stock required to maintain the same level of product availability.

Fourth, fluctuations in lead time also affect the amount of backup stock. If Lowe's knows that the lead time for purple paint is always two weeks, plus or minus one day, it can more accurately plan its inventory levels. But if the lead time is one day on one shipment and then ten days on the next shipment, the stores must carry additional backup stock to cover this uncertainty in lead time. Many retailers using collaborative supply chain management systems require their vendors to deliver merchandise within a very narrow window—sometimes two or three hours—to reduce the fluctuations in lead time and thus the amount of required backup stock.

Fifth, the vendor's product availability also affects the retailer's backup stock requirements. For example, Lowe's can more easily plan its inventory requirements if the vendor normally ships every item that is ordered. If, however, the vendor only ships 75 percent of the ordered items, Lowe's must maintain more backup stock to be certain that the paint availability for its customers isn't adversely affected. The percentage of complete orders received from a vendor is called the **fill rate.**

Staple merchandise planning systems provide the information needed to determine how much to order and when to place orders for SKUs. These systems assist buyers by performing three functions:

- Monitoring and measuring current sales for items at the SKU level.
- Forecasting future SKU demand with allowances for seasonal variations and changes in trends.
- Developing ordering decision rules for optimum restocking.

The inventory management report, discussed in the next section, provides the information to perform these functions.

The Inventory Management Report

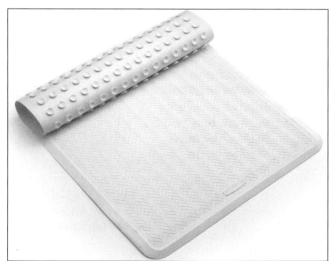

Staple merchandise management systems are used for items like Rubbermaid bath mats.

The inventory management report provides information about the current sales rate or velocity, sales forecasts, inventory availability, the amount on order, decision variables such as product availability, the backup stock needed to provide the product availability desired, performance measures such as planned and actual inventory turnover, and the appropriate ordering decisions for each SKU.

Exhibit 13–2 is an inventory management report for Rubbermaid bath mats.

This report shows a retailer's inventory management report for Rubbermaid SKUs. Rubbermaid is a large manufacturer of household plastic products. The suggested order point and quantity are the critical decisions that the buyer for a staple merchandise category needs to make. They indicate when and how much to order.

The first five columns of Exhibit 13–2 contain the descriptions of each item, how many items are on hand and on order, and sales for the past 4 and 12 weeks. The first-row SKU is a Rubbermaid bath mat in avocado green. There are 30 units on hand and 60 on order. Thus, the quantity available of this SKU is 90.

Quantity on hand + quantity on order = quantity available.

Sales for the past 4 and 12 weeks were 72 and 215 units, respectively.

	Quantity On Hand	Quantity On Order	Sales Last 4 Wks	Sales Last 12 Wks	Forecast Next 4 Wks	Forecast Next 8 Wks	Product Availability	Backup Stock	Turnover Planned	Turnover Actual	Order Point	Order Quantity
RM- Bath												
RM Bath Mat - Avocado	30	60	72	215	152	229	99	18	12	11	132	42
RM Bath Mat - Blue	36	36	56	130	115	173	95	12	9	10	98	26
RM Bath Mat - Gold	41	72	117	325	243	355	99	35	12	13	217	104
RM Bath Mat - Pink	10	12	15	41	13	25	90	3	7	7	13	0

Sales forecasts for the next 4 and 8 weeks are determined by the system using a statistical model that considers the trends in past sales and the seasonal pattern for the SKU. However, in this case, the buyer made an adjustment in the forecast for the next 4 weeks to reflect an upcoming special promotion on avocado, blue, and gold bath mats.

The product availability is a decision variable input by the buyer. For the avocado bath mat SKU, the buyer wants 99 out of every 100 customers to find it in stock. But the buyer is less concerned about stocking out of pink bath mats and thus sets its product availability at 90 percent. The system then calculates the necessary backup stock for the avocado bath mat, 18 units, based on a predetermined formula—18 units. This number is determined by the system on the basis of the specified product availability, the variability in demand, the vendor delivery lead time, and the variability in the lead time, as discussed in Chapter 12.

The planned inventory turnover for the SKU, 12 times, is a decision variable also set by the buyer on the basis of the retailer's overall financial goals; it drives the inventory management system. For this SKU, the system determined that the actual turnover, based on the cost of goods sold and average inventory, is 11.

Order Point   The **order point** is the amount of inventory below which the quantity available shouldn't go or the item will be out of stock before the next order arrives. This number tells the buyer that when the inventory level drops to this point, additional merchandise should be ordered. The order point is defined as:

Order point = Sales/Day × (Lead time + Review time) + Backup stock.

Lead time is the time between the recognition that an order needs to be placed and the receipt of the merchandise in stores, ready for sale. However, buyers might not review each SKU every day. **Review time** is the maximum time between reviews of the SKU. In a situation in which the lead time is two weeks, the buyer reviews the SKU once a week, 18 units of backup stock are needed to maintain the product availability desired, and the sales rate forecasted for the next four weeks is (152 ÷ 28) = 5.43 units per day. The order point is:

Order point = [(5.43 units) × (14 + 7 days)] + (18 units) = 132 units.

For this SKU, the buyer needs to place an order if the quantity in inventory falls to 132 or fewer units to produce the desired product availability.

Order Quantity   When inventory reaches the order point, the buyer needs to order enough units so the cycle stock isn't depleted and sales dip into backup stock before the next order arrives. This order quantity is the difference between the quantity available and the order point. Using the avocado bath mats in Exhibit 13–2 as an example, because the quantity available is 90, the buyer orders 42 units, because the order point is 132 (i.e., 132 − 90 = 42).

Order quantity = Order point − Quantity available.

Now that we've seen how inventory management systems work for staple merchandise, let's look at a system designed for fashion merchandise.

FASHION MERCHANDISE MANAGEMENT SYSTEMS

REFACT

More than 40 percent of retailers do not have a well-defined process for adjusting the four parameters of their inventory control system: product availability, order points, safety stock levels, and lead times.[1]

The system for managing fashion merchandise categories is typically called a merchandise budget plan. The **merchandise budget plan** specifies the planned inventory investment in dollars in a fashion merchandise category over time. It is a financial plan that specifies how much money will be spent each month to support sales and achieve the desired inventory turnover and GMROI objectives. However, it isn't a complete buying plan because it doesn't indicate the specific assortment of SKUs to buy or the quantities.

Exhibit 13–3 shows a six-month merchandise budget plan for men's casual slacks at a national specialty store chain. For a category like this, the buyer probably completes the plan in the fall for the following spring and summer. The buyer needs to plan how much merchandise should be delivered in each month to achieve the financial goals for the period.

Actual sales might differ from the sales forecasted in the merchandise budget plan. Even with this uncertainty though, the plan is used to coordinate the supply and demand for merchandise and ensure that the financial goals are realized.

The remaining part of this section describes the steps in developing the merchandise budget plan and determining the bottom line, line 8, the "Monthly Additions to Stock," in Exhibit 13–3. The "Monthly Additions to Stock" tells the buyer how much merchandise in retail dollars he or she needs to have, on average, at the beginning of each month for the retailer's financial goals to be met.

Monthly Sales Percentage Distribution to Season (Line 1)

Line 1 of the plan projects what percentage of the total sales is expected to be sold in each month. In Exhibit 13–3, 21 percent of the six-month sales are expected to occur in April.

		SPRING			SUMMER		
	Six-Month Data	April	May	June	July	August	September
Sales % Distribution to 1 Month	100.00%	21.00%	12.00%	12.00%	19.00%	21.00%	15.00%

Historical sales data provide the starting point for determining the percentage distribution of sales by month. The percentage of total category sales that occurs

EXHIBIT 13–3   Six-Month Merchandise Budget Plan for Men's Casual Slacks

	Spring	April	May	June	July	August	September
1. Sales % Distribution to Season	100.00%	21.00%	12.00%	12.00%	19.00%	21.00%	15.00%
2. Monthly Sales	$130,000	$27,300	$15,600	$15,600	$24,700	$27,300	$19,500
3. Reduc % Distribution to Season	100.00%	40.00%	14.00%	16.00%	12.00%	10.00%	8.00%
4. Monthly Reductions	$16,500	$6,600	$2,310	$2,640	$1,980	$1,650	$1,320
5. BOM Stock to Sales Ratio	4.00	3.60	4.40	4.40	4.00	3.60	4.00
6. BOM Inventory	$98,280	$98,280	$68,640	$68,640	$98,800	$98,280	$78,000
7. EOM Inventory	$65,600	$68,640	$68,640	$98,800	$98,280	$78,000	$65,600
8. Monthly Additions to Stock	$113,820	$4,260	$17,910	$48,400	$26,160	$8,670	$8,420

Retail sales are very seasonal. The Christmas season often accounts for more than 40 percent of a retailer's annual sales.

in a particular month doesn't vary much from year to year. However, the buyer might adjust the historical percentages to reflect changes in buying patterns and special promotions. For instance, the buyer might feel that the autumn selling season for men's casual slacks continues to be pushed further back into summer and thus increase the percentages for July and decrease the percentages for August and September. The buyer might also decide to hold a special Easter sale promotion, increasing the April percentage and decreasing the other percentages.

Monthly Sales (Line 2)

Monthly sales are the forecasted total sales for the six-month period in the first column ($130,000) multiplied by each monthly sales percentage (line 1). In Exhibit 13–3, monthly sales for April = $130,000 × 21 percent = $27,300.

		SPRING			SUMMER		
	Six-Month Data	April	May	June	July	August	September
Sales % Distribution to							
1 Month	100.00%	21.00%	12.00%	12.00%	19.00%	21.00%	15.00%
2 Monthly sales	$130,000	$27,300	$15,600	$15,600	$24,700	$27,300	$19,500

Monthly Reductions Percentage Distribution to Season (Line 3)

To have enough merchandise every month to support the monthly sales forecast, the buyer needs to consider other factors that reduce the inventory level in addition to sales made to customers. Although sales are the primary reduction, the

		SPRING			SUMMER		
	Six-Month Data	April	May	June	July	August	September
3 Reduction % Distribution to Season	100.00%	40.00%	14.00%	16.00%	12.00%	10.00%	8.00%

Clothing at this children's apparel store is marked down at the end of the spring season to make room for summer merchandise.

value of the inventory is also reduced by markdowns (sales discounts), shrinkage, and discounts to employees. The merchandise budget planning process builds these additional reductions into the planned purchases. If these reductions were not considered, the category would always be understocked. Note that in Exhibit 13–3, 40 percent of the season's total reductions occur in April as a result of price discounts (markdowns) during end-of-season sales.

Markdowns also can be forecasted from historical records. However, changes in markdown strategies—or changes in the environment, such as competition or general economic activity—must be taken into consideration when forecasting markdowns.

Discounts to employees are like markdowns, except that they are given to employees rather than to customers. The level of the employee discount is tied fairly closely to the sales level and number of employees. Thus, employee discounts also can be forecasted from historical records.

Shrinkage refers to inventory losses caused by shoplifting, employee theft, merchandise being misplaced or damaged, and poor bookkeeping. Retailers measure shrinkage by taking the difference between (1) the inventory's recorded value based on merchandise bought and received and (2) the physical inventory actually in stores and distribution centers. Shrinkage varies by department and season, but typically it varies directly with sales as well. So if sales of men's casual pants increase by 10 percent, then the buyer can expect a 10 percent increase in shrinkage.

Shrinkage = recorded inventory − actual inventory in store

Monthly Reductions (Line 4)

Monthly reductions are calculated by multiplying the total reductions by each percentage in line 3. The total reductions for this example are based on historical data. In Exhibit 13–3, April reductions = $16,500 × 40 percent = $6,600.

		SPRING			SUMMER		
	Six-Month Data	April	May	June	July	August	September
3 Reduction % Distribution to Season	100.00%	40.00%	14.00%	16.00%	12.00%	10.00%	8.00%
4 Monthly reductions	$16,500	$6,600	$2,310	$2,640	$1,980	$1,650	$1,320

BOM (Beginning-of-Month) Stock-to-Sales Ratio (Line 5)

The **stock-to-sales ratio,** listed in line 5, specifies the amount of inventory that should be on hand at the beginning of the month to support the sales forecast and maintain the inventory turnover objective for the category. Thus, a stock-to-sales ratio of 2 means that the retailer plans to have twice as much inventory on hand at the beginning of the month as there are forecasted sales for the month. Both the BOM stock and forecasted sales for the month are expressed in retail sales dollars.

		SPRING			SUMMER		
	Six-Month Data	April	May	June	July	August	September
5 BOM stock-to-sales ratio	4.0	3.6	4.4	4.4	4.0	3.6	4.0

Rather than specifying the stock-to-sales ratio, many retailers specify a related measure, weeks of inventory. A stock-to-sales ratio of 4 means there are 16 weeks of inventory, or approximately 112 days, on hand at the beginning of the month. A stock-to-sales ratio of 1/2 indicates a two-week supply of merchandise, or enough for approximately 14 days. The stock-to-sales ratio is determined so the merchandise category achieves its targeted performance—its planned GMROI and inventory turnover. The steps in determining the stock-to-sales ratio for the category are shown next.

Step 1: Calculate Sales-to-Stock Ratio   The GMROI is equal to the gross margin percentage times the sales-to-stock ratio. The sales-to-stock ratio is conceptually similar to inventory turnover except the denominator in the stock-to-sales ratio is expressed in retail sales dollars, whereas the denominator in inventory turnover is the cost of goods sold (sales at cost). The buyer's target GMROI for the category is 123 percent, and the buyer feels the category will produce a gross margin of 45 percent. Thus,

GMROI = Gross margin percent × Sales-to-stock ratio

Sales-to-stock ratio = GMROI/Gross margin percent = 123/45 = 2.73

Because this illustration of a merchandise budget plan is for a six-month period rather than a year, the sales-to-stock ratio is based on six months rather than annual sales. So for this six-month period, sales must be 2.73 times the inventory cost to meet the targeted GMROI.

Step 2: Convert the Sales-to-Stock Ratio to Inventory Turnover   Inventory turnover is

Inventory turnover = Sales-to-stock ratio × (1.00 − Gross margin %/100)

$$= \quad 2.73 \quad × (1.00 − 45/100)$$

$$1.50 = \quad 2.73 \quad × .55$$

This adjustment is necessary because the sales-to-stock ratio defines sales at retail and inventory at cost, whereas inventory turnover defines both sales and inventory at cost. Like the sales-to-stock ratio, this inventory turnover is based on a six-month period.

Step 3: Calculate Average Stock-to-Sales Ratio   The average stock-to-sales ratio is

Average stock-to-sales ratio = 6 months/Inventory turnover

$$4 = 6/1.5$$

If preparing a 12-month plan, the buyer divides 12 by the annual inventory turnover. Because the merchandise budget plan in Exhibit 13–3 is based on retail dollars, it's easiest to think of the numerator as BOM retail inventory and the denominator as sales for that month. Thus, to achieve a six-month inventory turnover of 1.5, on average, the buyer must plan to have a BOM inventory that equals four times the amount of sales for a given month, which is equivalent to four months, or 16 weeks of supply.

One needs to be careful when thinking about the average *stock-to-sales ratio*, which can be easily confused with the *sales-to-stock ratio*. These ratios are not the inverse of each other. Sales are the same in both ratios, but stock in the sales-to-stock ratio is the average inventory at cost over all days in the period, whereas stock in the stock-to-sales ratio is the average BOM inventory at retail. Also, the BOM stock-to-sales ratio is an average for all months. Adjustments are made to this average in line 5 to account for seasonal variation in sales.

Step 4: Calculate Monthly Stock-to-Sales Ratios   The monthly stock-to-sales ratios in line 5 must average the stock-to-sales ratio calculated previously to achieve the planned inventory turnover. Generally, monthly stock-to-sales ratios vary in the opposite direction of sales. That is, in months when sales are larger, stock-to-sales ratios are smaller, and vice versa.

To make this adjustment, the buyer needs to consider the seasonal pattern for men's casual slacks in determining the monthly stock-to-sales ratios. In the ideal situation, men's casual slacks would arrive in the store the same day and in the same quantity that customers demand them. Unfortunately, the real-life retailing world isn't this simple. Note in Exhibit 13–3 (line 8) that men's casual slacks for the spring season start arriving slowly in April ($4,260 for the month), yet demand lags behind these arrivals until the weather starts getting warmer. Monthly sales then jump from 12 percent of annual sales in May and June to 19 percent in July (line 1). But the stock-to-sales ratio (line 5) decreased from 4.4 in May and June to 4.0 in July. Thus, in months when sales increase (e.g., July), the BOM inventory also increases (line 6) but at a slower rate, which causes the stock-to-sales ratios to decrease. Likewise, in months when sales decrease dramatically, like in May (line 2), inventory also decreases (line 6), again at a slower rate, causing the stock-to-sales ratios to increase (line 5).

When creating a merchandise budget plan for a category such as men's casual slacks with a sales history, the buyer also examines previous years' stock-to-sales ratios. To judge how adequate these past ratios were, the buyer determines if inventory levels were exceedingly high or low in any months. Then the buyer makes minor corrections to adjust for a previous imbalance in inventory levels, as well as for changes in the current environment. For instance, assume the buyer is planning a promotion for Memorial Day. This promotion has never been done before, so the stock-to-sales ratio for the month of May should be adjusted downward to allow for the expected increase in sales. Note that monthly stock-to-sales ratios don't change by the same percentage that the percentage distribution of sales by month is changing. In months when sales increase, stock-to-sales ratios decrease but at a slower rate. Because there is no exact method of making these adjustments, the buyer must make some subjective judgments.

BOM Stock (Line 6)

The amount of inventory planned for the beginning-of-the-month (BOM) inventory for April equals

BOM inventory = Monthly sales (line 2) × BOM stock-to-sales ratio (line 5)
$98,280   = $27,300   × 3.6

| | Six-Month Data | SPRING | | | SUMMER | | |
		April	May	June	July	August	September
6 BOM inventory	$98,280	$98,280	$68,640	$68,640	$98,800	$98,280	$78,000

EOM (End-of-Month) Stock (Line 7)

The BOM stock for the current month is the same as the EOM (end-of-month) stock in the previous month. That is, BOM stock in line 6 is simply EOM inventory in line 7 from the previous month. Thus, in Exhibit 13–3, the EOM stock for April is the same as the BOM stock for May, $68,640. Forecasting the ending inventory for the last month in the plan is the next step in the merchandise budget

| | Six-Month Data | SPRING | | | SUMMER | | |
		April	May	June	July	August	September
7 EOM inventory	$65,600	$68,640	$68,640	$98,800	$98,280	$78,000	$65,600

plan. Note that EOM inventory for June is high, which indicates planning for a substantial sales increase in July.

Monthly Additions to Stock (Line 8)

The monthly additions to stock needed is the amount to be ordered for delivery in each month to meet the inventory turnover and sales objectives.

Additions to stock = Sales (line 2) + Reductions (line 4)
                     + EOM inventory (line 7) − BOM inventory (line 6)

Additions to stock (April) = $27,300 + 6,600 + 68,640 − 98,280 = $4,260

At the beginning of the month, the inventory level equals BOM stock. During the month, merchandise is sold, and various inventory reductions affecting the retail sales level occur, such as markdowns and theft. So the BOM stock minus monthly sales minus reductions equals the EOM stock if nothing is purchased. But something must be purchased to get back up to the forecast EOM stock. The difference between EOM stock if nothing is purchased (BOM stock − sales − reductions) and the forecast EOM stock is the additions to stock.

		SPRING			SUMMER		
	Six-Month Data	April	May	June	July	August	September
8 Monthly additions to stock	$113,820	$4,260	$17,920	$48,400	$26,160	$8,670	$8,420

Evaluating the Merchandise Budget Plan

Inventory turnover, GMROI, and the sales forecast are used for both planning and control. The previous sections have described how they all fit together in planning the merchandise budget. Buyers negotiate GMROI, inventory turnover, and sales forecast goals with their superiors, the GMMs and DMMs. Then merchandise budgets are developed to meet these goals. Well before the season, buyers purchase the amount of merchandise found in the last line of the merchandise budget plan to be delivered in those specific months—the monthly additions to stock.

After the selling season, the buyer must determine how the category actually performed compared with the plan. If the actual GMROI, turnover, and forecast are greater than those in the plan, performance is better than expected. However, performance evaluations should not be based just on any one of these measures. Several additional questions should be answered to evaluate the buyer's performance: Why did the performance exceed or fall short of the plan? Was the deviation from the plan due to something under the buyer's control? (For instance, was too much merchandise purchased?) Did the buyer react quickly to changes in demand by either purchasing more or having a sale? Was the deviation instead due to some external factor, such as a change in competitive level or economic activity? Every attempt should be made to discover answers to these questions. Later in this chapter, several additional tools used to evaluate merchandise performance will be examined.

OPEN-TO-BUY SYSTEM

The open-to-buy system is used after the merchandise is purchased and is based on the merchandise budget plan or staple merchandise management system. The merchandise management systems discussed previously provide buyers with a plan for purchasing merchandise. The **open-to-buy** system keeps track of merchandise flows while they are occurring. It keeps a record of how much is actually spent purchasing merchandise each month and how much is left to spend.

In the same way that you must keep track of the checks you write, buyers need to keep track of the merchandise they purchase and when it is to be delivered. Without the open-to-buy system keeping track of merchandise flows, buyers might

Open-to-buy is like the buyer's checkbook. It keeps track of how much money has been spent and how much money is left to spend.

buy too much or too little. Merchandise could be delivered when it isn't needed and be unavailable when it is needed. Thus, sales and inventory turnover would suffer. For consistency, we will continue with our example of an open-to-buy system using the merchandise budget plan previously discussed. The open-to-buy system is also applicable to staple goods merchandise management systems.

To make the merchandise budget plan successful (i.e., meet the sales, inventory turnover, and GMROI goals for a category), the buyer attempts to buy merchandise in quantities with delivery dates such that the actual EOM stock for a month will be the same as the forecasted EOM stock. For example, at the end of September, which is the end of the spring/ summer season, the buyer would like to be completely sold out of spring/summer men's casual slacks so there will be room for the fall styles. Thus, the buyer would want the projected EOM stock and the actual EOM stock for this fashion and/or seasonal merchandise to both equal zero.

Calculating Open-to-Buy for the Current Period

Buyers develop plans indicating how much inventory for the merchandise category will be available at the end of the month. However, these plans might be inaccurate. Shipments might not arrive on time, sales might be greater than expected, and/or reductions (price discounts due to sales) might be less than expected.

The open-to-buy is the difference between the planned EOM inventory and the projected EOM. Thus, open-to-buy for a month is:

Open-to-buy = Planned EOM inventory − Projected EOM inventory

If open-to-buy is positive, then the buyer still has money in the budget to purchase merchandise for that month. If the open-to-buy is negative, then the buyer has overbought, meaning he or she has spent more than was in the budget.

The planned EOM inventory is taken from the merchandise budget plan, and the projected EOM inventory is calculated as follows:

Projected EOM inventory = Actual BOM inventory
  + Monthly additions actual
    (received new merchandise)
  + On order (merchandise to be delivered)
  − Sales plan (merchandise sold)
  − Monthly reductions plan

Exhibit 13–4 presents the six-month open-to-buy for the same category of men's casual slacks discussed in the fashion merchandise planning section of this chapter. Consider May as the current month. The BOM stock (inventory) actual level is $59,500, but there is no EOM actual inventory yet because the month hasn't finished. When calculating the open-to-buy for the current month, the projected EOM stock plan comes into play. Think of the projected EOM stock plan as a new and improved estimate of the planned EOM stock from the merchandise budget plan. This new and improved version takes information into account that wasn't available when the merchandise budget plan was made. The formula for projected EOM inventory for the category is

Six-Month Open-to-Buy System Report   **EXHIBIT 13–4**

open to buy Ex. 13–4.bmp							
In-Season Planning - Worksheet: Mens department (Business View: 'OTB : Global')							_ □ ×
Worksheet						In-Season Management	
Plan Edit View Tools Help							
Skip To Month ▼							

Loc - 10	Spring						
Merch - Aged Soft ...	**April**	**May**	**June**	**July**	**August**	**September**	
EOM Stock Plan	$68,640	$68,640	$98,800	$98,280	$78,000	$65,600	
EOM Actuals	$69,950						
BOM Stock Plan	$98,280	$68,640	$68,640	$98,800	$98,280	$78,000	
BOM Stock Actual	$95,000	$59,500					
Monthly Additions Plan	$4,260	$17,910	$48,400	$26,160	$8,670	$8,420	
Monthly Additions Actuals	$3,500	$7,000					
OnOrder	$45,000	$18,000	$48,400				
Sales Plan	$27,300	$15,600	$15,600	$24,700	$27,300	$19,500	
Sales Actuals	$26,900						
Monthly Reductions Plan	$6,600	$2,310	$2,640	$1,980	$1,650	$1,320	
Monthly Reductions Actuals	$1,650						
Projected EOM Stock Plan	$59,500	$66,590	$96,750	$70,070	$41,120	$20,300	
Projected BOM Stock Plan	$24,570	$59,500	$66,500	$96,750	$70,070	$41,120	
OTB	$0.00	$2,050	$2,050	$28,210	$36,880	$45,300	

Projected EOM inventory = Actual BOM inventory	$59,500
+ Monthly additions actual	7,000
+ On order	18,000
− Sales plan	15,600
− Monthly reductions plan	2,310
=	$66,590

The open-to-buy for the current month is:

$$\text{Open-to-buy plan} = \text{EOM inventory planned} - \text{Projected EOM inventory}$$
$$\$2,050 = \$68,640 - \$66,590$$

Therefore, the buyer has $2,050 left to spend in May to reach the planned EOM stock of $68,640. This is a relatively small amount, so we can conclude that the buyer's plan is right on target. But if the open-to-buy for May were $20,000, the buyer could then go back into the market and look for some great buys. If one of the vendors had too much stock of men's casual slacks, the buyer might be able to use the $20,000 to pick up some bargains that could be passed on to customers.

If, however, the open-to-buy was a negative $20,000, the buyer would have over-spent the budget. Similar to overspending your checkbook, the buyer would have to cut back on spending in future months so the total purchases would be within the merchandise budget. Alternatively, if the buyer believed that the overspending was justified because of changes in the marketplace, a negotiation could take place between the buyer and the divisional merchandise manager to get more open-to-buy.

ALLOCATING MERCHANDISE TO STORES

After developing a plan for managing merchandise inventory in a category, the next step in the merchandise management process is to allocate the merchandise purchased and received to the retailer's stores (see Exhibit 12–4). Research indicates that these allocation decisions have a much bigger impact on profitability than does the decision about the quantity of merchandise to purchase.[3] In other words, buying too little or too much merchandise has less impact on a category's profitability than making mistakes in allocating the right amount and type of merchandise to stores. Thus, many retailers have created positions called either "allocators" or "planners" to specialize in making store allocation decisions. Allocating merchandise to stores involves three decisions: (1) how much merchandise to allocate to each store, (2) what type of merchandise to allocate, and (3) when to allocate the merchandise to different stores.

EXHIBIT 13–5

Inventory Allocation Based on Sales Volume and Stock-to-Sales Ratios

1 Type of Store	2 Forecasted Sales per Store	3 Proportional Allocation	4 Stock-to-Sales Ratio	5 Allocation Based on Store Size (Column 2 × Column 4)
A	$15,000	$30,000	1.8	$27,000
B	10,000	20,000	2	20,000
C	7,500	15,000	2.4	18,000

Amount of Merchandise Allocated to Each Store

An approach for allocating merchandise to stores is illustrated in Exhibit 13–5. Initially the planner makes the allocation in proportion to the forecasted sales for each store (column 3). Thus, if the average stock-to-sales ratio for the chain is 2, and the sales for store A are $15,000 (column 2, row 1), store A would be allocated $30,000 (column 3, row 1). The planner fine tunes the allocation by recognizing that smaller stores require a proportionally higher inventory allocation than larger stores because if the depth of the assortment or the level of product availability is too small, customers will perceive it as being inferior. Hence, smaller stores require a higher than average stock-to-sales ratio. The opposite is true for stores with greater than average sales. Thus, in Exhibit 13–5, column 4, the larger store A has a smaller stock-to-sales ratio (27,000/15,000 = 1.8), so its allocation in column 5 is less than proportional to its size. The smaller store C has a greater than average stock-to-sales ratio (18,000/7,500 = 2.4), so its allocation is more than proportional to its size. The determination of the best stock-to-sales ratios for each type of store depends on the size constraints of the store, the physical characteristics of the merchandise, and the depth of assortment and level of product availability that the firm wishes to portray for the store.

Type of Merchandise Allocated to Stores

In addition to classifying stores on the basis of their size and sales volume, retailers classify stores according to the characteristics of the stores' trading area. As discussed in Chapter 8, the profiles of trading areas are used in making store location decisions. Store trade area geodemographics are also used to develop merchandise assortments for specific stores. Consider the allocation decision of a national supermarket for its ready-to-eat cereal assortment. Some stores are located in areas dominated by segments called "Rustbelt Retirees," and other areas are dominated by the "Laptops and Lattes" segment, as described in Exhibit 13–6.

EXHIBIT 13–6

Example of Different Geodemographic Segments

Laptops and Lattes: The most eligible and unencumbered marketplace	Rustbelt Retirees
Laptops and Lattes are affluent, single, and still renting. They are educated, professional, and partial to city life, favoring major metropolitan areas such as New York, Boston, Chicago, Los Angeles, and San Francisco. Median household income is more than $87,000; median age is 38 years. Technologically savvy, the Laptops and Lattes segment is the top market for notebook PCs and PDAs. They use the Internet on a daily basis to trade stocks and make purchases and travel plans. They are health conscious and physically fit; they take vitamins, use organic products, and exercise in the gym. They embrace liberal philosophies and work for environmental causes.	Rustbelt Retirees can be found in older, industrial cities in the Northeast and Midwest, especially in Pennsylvania and other states surrounding the Great Lakes. Households are mainly occupied by married couples with no children and singles who live alone. The median age is 43.8 years. Although many residents are still working, labor force participation is below average. More than 40 percent of the households receive Social Security benefits. Most residents live in owned, single-family homes, with a median value of $118,500. Unlike many retirees, these residents are not inclined to move. They are proud of their homes and gardens and participate in community activities. Some are members of veterans' clubs. Leisure activities include playing bingo, gambling in Atlantic City, going to the horse races, working crossword puzzles, and playing golf.

SOURCE: www.esri.com/library/whitepapers/pdfs/community-tapestry.pdf.

In which store would higher priced, low sugar, organic, whole wheat breakfast cereals do best—one dominated by the geodemographic segment "laptops and lattes" (left) or "rustbelt retirees" (right)?

The ready-to-eat breakfast cereal buyer would certainly want to offer different assortments for stores in these two areas. Stores with a high proportion of Rustbelt Retirees in their trading areas would have better results with an assortment of lower priced, well-known brands and more private-label cereals. Stores in areas dominated by the Laptops and Lattes geodemographic segment would do better with an assortment with higher priced brands that were low in sugar, organic, and whole wheat. Private-label cereals would be deemphasized.

Even the sales of different apparel sizes can vary dramatically from store to store in the same chain. Exhibit 13–7 illustrates this point. Notice that Store X sells significantly more large sizes and fewer small sizes than is average for the chain. If the buyer allocated the same size distribution of merchandise to all stores in the chain, Store X would stock out of large sizes, have an oversupply of small sizes, and be out of some sizes sooner than other stores in the chain. Retailing View 13.2 provides a glimpse of how Saks Fifth Avenue allocates merchandise to stores on the basis of customer characteristics.

Timing of Merchandise Allocations to Stores

In addition to the need to allocate different inventory levels and types of merchandise across stores, differences in the timing of category purchases across stores need to be considered. Exhibit 13–8 illustrates these differences by plotting sales data over time for capri pants in different regions of the United States. Comparing regions, capri sales peak in late July in the Midwest and at the beginning of September in the West, due to seasonality differences and differences in consumer demand. Buyers need to recognize these regional differences and arrange for merchandise to be shipped to the appropriate regions when customers are ready to buy to increase inventory turnover in the category.

REFACT

Saks Fifth Avenue increases its assortment of long dresses in New Orleans at Mardi Gras time. Sears sells diving watches in coastal communities but watches with easy-to-read numbers in Miami and Phoenix, where there are a lot of retirees. Sears sells suede vests and skirts during rodeo season in a few of its Texas stores.

EXHIBIT 13–7
Apparel Size Differences for Store X and the Chain Average

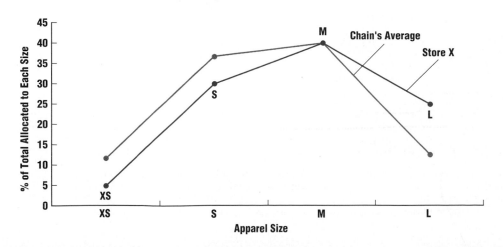

13.2   RETAILING VIEW   Customer-Centric Merchandise Allocation at Saks Fifth Avenue

Having the right merchandise in the right stores is the key to merchandising success for fashion retailers like Saks Fifth Avenue. For instance, Saks Fifth Avenue considers its core shopper at its New York flagship store in Manhattan to be a woman, in her late forties, with a largely "classic" style, especially when it comes to work clothes. She has a taste for slightly more modern looks when she goes out with friends on weekends. But it also recognizes the merchandise selection for stores located elsewhere need to be less New York-centric. Even stores closely situated to New York City attract different types of shoppers. In Greenwich, Connecticut, Saks Fifth Avenue caters to a slightly older shopper than does the Saks Fifth Avenue in Stamford, Connecticut, about five miles away. Stamford shoppers tend to be women who work in town, whereas Greenwich attracts a higher proportion of women who are at home full-time. Shoppers on Saks.com, now the chain's second-biggest revenue generator after its New York flagship store, average approximately seven years younger than the typical Saks Fifth Avenue customer and spend more per transaction.

To better match its assortments with its stores, Saks Fifth Avenue has developed a nine-box grid. Along the top of the matrix are style categories: "Park Avenue" classic; "uptown," or modern; and "Soho," meaning trendy or contemporary. On the side axis are pricing levels, from "good" (brands such as Dana Buchman, Ellen Tracy, and Lafayette 148) to "better" (Piazza Sempione, Armani Collezioni, and some Ralph Lauren) to "best" (Chanel, Gucci, Louis Vuitton, Oscar de la Renta, and Bill Blass). By cross-referencing the preferred styles and spending levels at each location, the grid charts the best mix of brands and vendors to stock at each store by product category.

Saks Fifth Avenue must take care, however, to balance its assortment planning by store with its goal to project a consistent personality through national marketing. In its Semi-annual "Want It" ad campaign, highlighting Key items for each season Saks Fifth Avenue promoted velour sweaters for men in fall 2006. Since many men, especially older ones and those who live in the South, don't especially go for this fabric, Saks Fifth Avenue included more classic items with broader appeal, such as navy blazers. At the same time, it is increasing its efforts to tailor its marketing to local markets.

Sources: Vanessa O'Connell, "Park Avenue Classic or Soho Trendy?" *The Wall Street Journal*, April 20, 2007, p. B1; www.saks.com (accessed September 25, 2007).

Saks Fifth Avenue's customer-centric merchandise allocation system divides its merchandise into "good", "better" (like the Ralph Lauren Black Label outfit on the left), and "best" (like the Oscar de la Renta dress on the right).

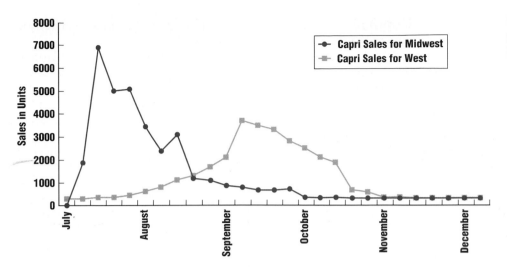

EXHIBIT 13–8
Sales of Capri Pants
by Region

ANALYZING MERCHANDISE MANAGEMENT PERFORMANCE

The next step in the merchandise planning process is to analyze the performance of the process and make adjustments, such as ordering more or less merchandise, lowering prices to increase sales, allocating different assortments to specific stores, or changing the assortment and model stock plans. Three types of analyses related to the monitoring and adjustment step are (1) sell-through analysis, (2) ABC analysis of assortments, and (3) multiattribute analysis of vendors. The first analysis provides an ongoing evaluation of the merchandise management plan compared with actual sales. The remaining two analyses offer approaches for evaluating and altering the assortment plan using the specific SKUs in the plan and the vendors that provide the merchandise to support the plan.

Sell-Through Analysis Evaluating Merchandise Plan

A **sell-through analysis** compares actual and planned sales to determine whether more merchandise is needed to satisfy demand or if price reductions (markdowns) are required. Exhibit 13–9 shows a sell-through analysis for blouses for the first two weeks of the season.

These blouses are high-fashion items that experience significant uncertainty in sales. Thus, after two weeks in the stores, the buyer reviews sales and determines if adjustments are needed. The need to make adjustments depends on a variety of factors, including experience with the merchandise in the past, plans for featuring the merchandise in advertising, and the availability of markdown money from

Stock Number		Description	WEEK 1			WEEK 2		
			Plan	Actual-to-Plan Actual	Percentage	Plan	Actual-to-Plan Actual	Percentage
1011	Small	White silk V-neck	20	15	−25%	20	10	−50%
1011	Medium	White silk V-neck	30	25	−16.6	30	20	−33
1011	Large	White silk V-neck	20	16	−20	20	16	−20
1012	Small	Blue silk V-neck	25	26	4	25	27	8
1012	Medium	Blue silk V-neck	35	45	29	35	40	14
1012	Large	Blue silk V-neck	25	25	0	25	30	20

EXHIBIT 13–9
Example of a Sell-Through Analysis

vendors (**Markdown money** are funds that a vendor gives a retailer to cover lost gross margin dollars that results from markdowns).

In this case, the white blouses are selling significantly less well than planned. Therefore, the buyer makes an early price reduction to ensure that the merchandise isn't left unsold at the end of the season. The decision regarding the blue blouses isn't as clear. The small blue blouses are selling slightly ahead of the plan, and the medium blue blouses are also selling well, but the large blue blouses start selling ahead of plan only in the second week. In this case, the buyer decides to wait another week or two before taking any action. If actual sales stay significantly ahead of planned sales, a reorder might be appropriate.

Evaluating the Assortment Plan and Vendors

ABC Analysis   An **ABC analysis** identifies the performance of individual SKUs in the assortment plan. It is used to determine which SKUs should be in the plan and how much backup stock and resulting product availability is provided for each SKU in the plan. In an ABC analysis, the SKUs in a merchandise category are rank ordered by several performance measures, such as sales, gross margin, inventory turnover, and GMROI. Typically, this rank order reveals the general 80–20 principle; namely, approximately 80 percent of a retailer's sales or profits come from 20 percent of the products. This principle suggests that retailers should concentrate on the products that provide the biggest returns.

After rank ordering the SKUs, the next step is to classify the items; on the basis of the classification, determine whether to maintain the item in the assortment plan; and, if so, what level of product availability to offer. For example, a men's dress shirt buyer might identify the A, B, C, and D SKUs by rank ordering them by sales volume. The A items account for only 5 percent of the SKUs in the category but represent 70 percent of sales. The buyer decides that these SKUs should never be out of stock and thus plans to maintain more backup stock for A items, such as keeping more sizes of long- and short-sleeved white, blue, and pink dress shirts than of the B and C items.

The B items represent 10 percent of the SKUs and 20 percent of sales. These items include some of the other better-selling colors and patterned shirts and contribute to the retailer's image of having fashionable merchandise. Occasionally, the retailer will run out of some SKUs in the B category because it does not carry the same amount of backup stock as for A items.

The C items account for 65 percent of SKUs but contribute to only 10 percent of sales. The planner may plan to carry some C items only in very small or very large sizes of the most basic shirts, with special orders used to satisfy customer demand.

Finally, the buyer discovers that the remaining 20 percent of the SKUs, D items, have virtually no sales until they are marked down. Not only are these items excess merchandise and an unproductive investment, but they also distract from the rest of the inventory and clutter the store shelves. The buyer decides to eliminate most of these items from the assortment plan.

Multiattribute Method for Evaluating Vendors   The **multiattribute analysis** method for evaluating vendors uses a weighted average score for each vendor. The score is based on the importance of various issues and the vendor's performance on those issues. This method is similar to the multiattribute approach that can be used to understand how customers evaluate stores and merchandise, as we discussed in Chapter 4. Retailing View 13.3 describes Home Depot's system for vendor evaluation.

Which of these shirts is an A item? B item?

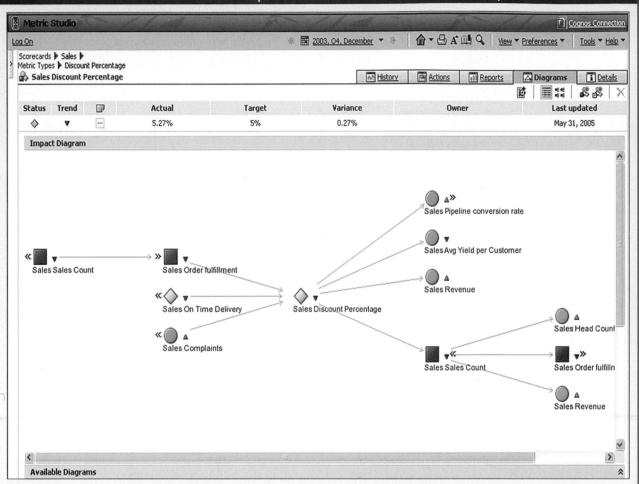

Home Depot's vendor analysis scorecard gives everyone a quick view of how the vendor is doing. Green is good, but red isn't.

Until recently, Home Depot had no easy way to keep tabs on its 10,000–12,000 vendors and monitor their compliance with its rules for product quality, order fulfillment, and delivery. For the most part, communications took place by fax and phone.

To improve this situation, Home Depot developed a vendor evaluation program that focuses on three criteria for excellence. The first, the behavioral criterion, helps it protect the reputation of its brand while instilling social and environmental responsibility into its vendor relationships. The second, the manufacturing criterion, is designed to improve product quality, cost, and innovation. Finally, the supply chain criterion is intended to reduce overall costs through process integration and standardization.

Home Depot has always had high expectations in terms of product quality, innovation, availability, on-time delivery, safety in production and shipping, compliance with laws and codes of conduct, and sensitivity to brand reputation. But it had no clear system to measure these issues and ensure compliance. For example, it used 8,000 different paper versions of buying agreement with vendors, and no good way of tracking who actually received which one.

The new system is designed to measure service and ensure compliance specifically through the Vendor Center Web site. It features continuously updated information about how to do business with Home Depot, including the corporate performance policy, updates, news, information on events and training, and scorecards. Included in the laundry list of expectations is Home Depot's Social and Environmental Responsibility (SER) program, which addresses a wide range of issues related to vendors' proper treatment of their workers and the environment, including age requirements, wages, working conditions, emergency planning, health and safety, and prohibitions against forced labor, fraud, and discrimination. The program combines regular audits of vendor factories with extensive education to help vendors understand the retailer's expectations.

Home Depot posts online vendor scorecards, providing graphical representations of their performance levels. Each participating vendor is rated on criteria such as compliance with shipping-platform standards and import on-time delivery. The vendors and Home Depot can observe trends over 13-month periods. Green, yellow and red "lights" for each category let vendors know how they have been rated at a glance.

Although Home Depot's compliance program focuses on education instead of punishment, vendors pay a price if they fail to meet the company's strict requirements. Fines for noncompliance with its shipping standards amount to $10,000 for the first violation and $25,000 each time thereafter.

Source: "Retail Supply Chains: 'Back end' or Business Value?," www.cognos.com, November 29, 2006; Robert J. Bowman, "Home Depot Turns Its Attention to Vendor Performance Management," www.supplychainbrain.com, June 2006.

EXHIBIT 13–10
Multiattribute Model for
Evaluating Vendors

Issues (1)	Importance Evaluation of Issues (I) (2)	PERFORMANCE EVALUATIONS OF INDIVIDUAL BRANDS ACROSS ISSUES			
		Brand A (P_a) (3)	Brand B (P_b) (4)	Brand C (P_c) (5)	Brand D (P_d) (6)
Vendor reputation	9	5	9	4	8
Service	8	6	6	4	6
Meets delivery dates	6	5	7	4	4
Merchandise quality	5	5	4	6	5
Markup opportunity	5	5	4	4	5
Country of origin	6	5	3	3	8
Product fashionability	7	6	6	3	8
Selling history	3	5	5	5	5
Promotional assistance	4	5	3	4	7
Overall evaluation a $\sum_{i=1}^{n} I_j \times P_{ij}$		280	298	212	341

$\sum_{i=1}^{n}$ = Sum of the expression.

I_j = Importance weight assigned to the ith dimension.

P_{ij} = Performance evaluation for jth brand alternative on the ith issue.

1 = Not important.

10 = Very important.

To illustrate the multiattribute method for evaluating vendors, either current or proposed, consider the example in Exhibit 13–10 for a vendor of men's casual slacks.

A buyer can evaluate vendors using the following five steps:

1. Develop a list of issues to consider in the evaluation (column 1).

2. Determine the importance weights for each issue in column 1, in conjunction with the GMM (column 2) on a 1–10 scale, where 1 equals not important and 10 equals very important. For instance, the buyer and the merchandise manager believe that vendor reputation should receive a 9 because it's very important to the retailer's image. Merchandise quality receives a 5 because it's moderately important. Finally, a vendor's selling history is less important, so it could be rated 3.

3. Make judgments about each individual brand's performance on each issue (remaining columns). Note that some brands have high ratings on some issues but not on others.

4. Develop an overall score by multiplying the importance of each issue by the performance of each brand or its vendor. For instance, vendor reputation importance (9) multiplied by the performance rating (5) for brand A is 45. Promotional assistance importance (4) multiplied by the performance rating (7) for vendor D is 28. This type of analysis illustrates an important point: It doesn't pay to perform well on issues that retailers don't believe are very important. Although vendor D performed well on promotional assistance, the buyer didn't rate this issue highly in importance, so the resulting score was still low.

5. To determine a vendor's overall rating, add the products for each brand for all issues. In Exhibit 13–10, brand D has the highest overall rating (341), so D is the preferred vendor.

SUMMARY

This chapter reviews the merchandise planning and buying systems for staple and fashion merchandise. Buying systems for staple merchandise are very different from those for fashion merchandise. Because information is available about past sales for each SKU, it is relatively straightforward to forecast future merchandise needs.

The sales forecast and inventory turnover described in Chapter 12 work together to drive the merchandise budget plan for fashion merchandise. The sales forecast is broken down by month, based on historical seasonality patterns. It is necessary to purchase more in months when sales are forecast to be higher than average. Planned inventory turnover is converted to stock-to-sales ratios and used in the merchandise budget plan to determine the inventory level necessary to support sales. Monthly stock-to-sales ratios are then adjusted to reflect seasonal sales patterns. The end product of the merchandise budget planning process is the dollar amount of merchandise a buyer should purchase each month for a category if the sales forecast and inventory turnover goals are to be met.

The open-to-buy system begins where the merchandise budget plan and staple goods inventory management systems leave off. It tracks how much merchandise is purchased

for delivery in each month. Using an open-to-buy system, buyers know exactly how much money they've spent compared with how much they plan to spend.

Once the merchandise is purchased, merchandise buyers in multistore chains must allocate the merchandise to stores. Buyers must look at the differences in not only sales potential among stores but also the characteristics of the customer base.

In the end, the performance of buyers, vendors, and individual SKUs must be determined. Three different approaches can evaluate merchandise performance. The sell-through analysis is more useful for examining the performance of individual SKUs in the merchandise plan. The buyer compares actual with planned sales to determine whether more merchandise needs to be ordered or if the merchandise should be put on sale. In an ABC analysis, merchandise is rank ordered from highest to lowest. The merchandising team uses this information to set inventory management policies. For example, the most productive SKUs should carry sufficient backup stock to never be out of stock. Finally, the multiattribute method is most useful for evaluating vendors' performance. This chapter concludes with Appendix 13A, in which we examine the retail inventory method.

KEY TERMS

ABC analysis, *374*
backup stock, *359*
base stock, *359*
buffer stock, *359*
cycle stock, *359*
fill rate, *360*

lead time, *359*
markdown money, *373*
merchandise budget plan, *362*
multiattribute analysis, *374*
open-to-buy, *367*
order point, *361*

review time, *361*
safety stock, *359*
sell-through analysis, *373*
shrinkage, *364*
stock-to-sales ratio, *364*

GET OUT AND DO IT!

1. Go to www.oracle.com/retek. How are Retek products being used by retailers today?

2. Go to www.sas.com/industry/retail/merchandise, the SAS Merchandise Intelligence group Web site.
How are their products different from Retek's? Which would you hire, Retek or SAS?

3. The merchandise budget plan determines how much merchandise should be purchased in each month of a fashion buying season (in dollars), given the sales and reduction forecast, inventory turnover goals, and seasonal monthly fluctuations in sales. Go to the student side of the Online Learning Center and click on the Merchandise Budget Plan. The merchandise budget plan generally covers one fashion season for one merchandise category. This application presents both a one-month and a six-month example. In addition,

practice calculations are presented for the one-month example. Have your calculator ready! In the calculation section, you have access to an Excel-based six-month merchandise budget plan that can be used to complete Case number 21 (McFadden's Department Store) in the text.

4. The vendor evaluation model utilizes the multiattribute method to evaluate vendors described in the chapter. Go to the student side of the Online Learning Center and click on Vendor Evaluation Model. There are two spreadsheets. Open the first spreadsheet, vendor evaluation 1.xls. This spreadsheet is the same as Exhibit 13–10. If you were selling Brand A to the retailer, which numbers would change? Change the numbers in the matrix and see the effect of that change on the overall evaluation. Go to the second spreadsheet, labeled evaluation 2.xls. This spreadsheet can be used to evaluate brands or merchandise you might stock in your

store. Assume you own a bicycle shop. List the brands you might consider stocking and the issues you would consider in selecting the brands to stock. Fill in the importance of the issues (10 = very important, 1 = not very important) and the evaluation of each brand on each characteristic (10 = excellent, 1 = poor). Determine which is the best brand for your store.

5. According to Target's homepage, available at www.targetcorp.com, the company has a "Merchandise Focus with an emphasis on basic merchandise—staple, everyday items that consumers use and need most. Combined with an aggressive fashion strategy, this foundation in basics enables Target to compete as a life-style trend merchandiser in all merchandise categories, from apparel to personal care, home decor to automotive." Based on this statement, how does this discounter manage a buying system to ensure that both staple and fashion merchandise are properly stocked to meet customer demand?

DISCUSSION QUESTIONS AND PROBLEMS

1. Inventory shrinkage can be a problem for many retailers. How does the merchandise budget planning process account for inventory shrinkage?

2. Using the following information, calculate additions to stock:
   a. Sales $26,000
   b. EOM stock $100,000
   c. BOM stock $88,000

3. Using the following information, calculate the average BOM stock-to-sales ratio for a six-month merchandise budget plan:
   a. GMROI 130%
   b. Gross margin 46%

4. Today is July 19. Buyers at two different stores are attempting to assess current open-to-buy given the following information:

	Store A	Store B
Actual BOM stock	$50,000	$75,000
Monthly additions actual	$25,000	$30,000
Merchandise on order to be delivered	$10,000	$12,000
Planned monthly sales	$30,000	$40,000
Planned reductions	$5,000	$6,000
Planned EOM stock	$65,000	$75,000

What is the open-to-buy on July 19? What does this number mean to you for each store?

5. Typically, August school supply sales are relatively low. In September, sales increase tremendously. How does the September stock-to-sales ratio differ from the August ratio?

6. Using the 80–20 principle, how can a retailer make certain it has enough inventory of fast selling merchandise and a minimal amount of slow selling merchandise?

7. What is the order point and how many units should be reordered if a food retailer has an item with a 7-day lead time, 10-day review time, and daily demand of 8 units? Say 70 units are on hand, and the retailer must maintain a backup stock of 20 units to maintain a 98 percent service level.

8. A buyer at a sporting goods store in Denver receives a shipment of 400 ski parkas on October 1 and expects to sell out by January 31. On November 1, the buyer still has 350 parkas left. What issues should the buyer consider in evaluating the selling season's progress?

9. If you have a stock-to-sales ratio of 2, how many months of supply do you have? How many weeks of supply?

10. A buyer is trying to decide from which vendor to buy a certain item. Using the information in this table, determine from which vendor the buyer should buy.

	VENDOR PERFORMANCE		
	Importance Weight	Vendor A	Vendor B
Reputation for collaboration	8	9	8
Service	7	8	7
Meets delivery dates	9	7	8
Merchandise quality	7	8	4
Gross margin	6	4	8
Brand name recognition	5	7	5
Promotional assistance	3	8	8

SUGGESTED READINGS

Amato-McCoy, Deena. "'Tis the Season For Item Movement." *Chain Store Age*, December 2006, p. 80.

Belcher, Leslie. "Inventory Management: Measure, Plan and Optimize." *Stores Magazine*, May 2005, p. 146.

Bragg, Steven. *Inventory Accounting: A Comprehensive Guide.* Hoboken, NJ: Wiley, 2005.

Cachon, Gérard; Christian Terwiesch; and Yi Xu. "Retail Assortment Planning in the Presence of Consumer Search." *Manufacturing & Service Operations Management*, 7 (Fall 2005), pp. 330–47.

"Cross-Channel Operations, Demand Planning and Item Management Top Enterprise Retail System Spending." *Stores Magazine*, July 2006, special section, p. IT9.

Dong, Yan; Venkatesh Shankar; and Martin Dresner. "Efficient Replenishment in the Distribution Channel." *Journal of Retailing*, 83(August 2007), pp. 253–67.

Donnellan, John. *Merchandise Buying and Management.* New York: Fairchild Books & Visuals, 2007.

Mollo, George. "An Inside Look at Open-to-Buy." *Catalog Age*, April 2004, pp. 50–52.

Murphy, Samantha. "The Future of Automated Forecasts and Ordering." *Chain Store Age*, May 2007, p. 134.

Tepper, Bette K. *Mathematics for Retail Buying.* 6th ed. New York: Fairchild Books, 2005.

Varley, Rosemary. *Retail Product Management: Buying and Merchandising.* 2nd ed. New York: Routledge, 2005.

APPENDIX 13A   Retail Inventory Method

Similar to firms in most industries, retailers can value their inventory at cost—and some retailers do just that. Yet many retailers find it advantageous to value their inventory at retail and use the retail inventory method (RIM), which has two objectives:

1. To maintain a perpetual or book inventory in terms of retail dollar amounts.

2. To maintain records that make it possible to determine the cost value of the inventory at any time without taking a physical inventory.

THE PROBLEM

Retailers generally think of their inventory at retail price levels rather than at cost. They take their initial markups, markdowns, and so forth as percentages of retail. (These terms are thoroughly defined in Chapter 15.) When retailers compare their prices with competitors', they compare retail prices. The problem is that when retailers design their financial plans, evaluate performance, and prepare financial statements, they also need to know the cost value of their inventory.

One way to keep abreast of their inventory cost is to take physical inventories. Anyone who has worked in retailing knows that this process is time consuming, costly, and not much fun. So retailers usually only take physical inventories once or twice a year. By the time management receives the results of these physical inventories, it's often too late to make any changes.

Many retailers use POS terminals that easily keep track of every item sold, its original cost, and its final selling price. The rest of the retail world faces the problem of not knowing the cost value of its inventory at any one time. Therefore, RIM can be used by retailers with either computerized or manual systems.

ADVANTAGES OF RIM

The RIM has five advantages over a system of evaluating inventory at cost.

• The retailer doesn't have to "cost" each time. For retailers with many SKUs, keeping track of each item at cost is expensive and time consuming, and it increases the cost of errors. It's easier to determine the value of inventory with the retail prices marked on the merchandise than with unmarked or coded cost prices.

• It follows the accepted accounting practice of valuing assets at cost or market, whichever is lower. The system lowers the value of inventory when markdowns are taken but doesn't allow the inventory's value to increase with additional markups.

• As a by-product of RIM, the amounts and percentages of initial markups, additional markups, markdowns, and shrinkage can be identified. This information can then be compared with historical records or industry norms.

• It is useful for determining shrinkage. The difference between the book inventory and the physical inventory can be attributed to shrinkage.

• The book inventory determined by RIM can be used in an insurance claim in case of a loss (e.g., due to fire).

DISADVANTAGES OF RIM

However, RIM is a system that uses an average markup. When markup percentages change substantially during a period or when the inventory on hand at a particular time isn't representative of the total goods handled in terms of markups, the resulting cost figure may be distorted. As with inventory turnover, merchandise budget planning, and open-to-buy, RIM should be applied on a category basis to avoid this problem.

The record-keeping process involved in RIM is burdensome. Buyers must take care so that changes made to the cost and retail inventories are properly recorded.

STEPS IN RIM

Exhibit 13–11 is an example of RIM in action. The following discussion, which outlines the steps in RIM, is based on this exhibit.

EXHIBIT 13–11
RIM Example

Total Goods Handled	Cost		Retail	
Beginning Inventory		$60,000		$84,000
Purchases	$50,000		$70,000	
– Return to vendor	(11,000)		(15,400)	
Net purchases		39,000		54,600
Additional markups			4,000	
– Markup cancellations			(2,000)	
Net markups				2,000
Additional transportation		1,000		
Transfers in	1,428		2,000	
– Transfers out	(714)		(1,000)	
Net transfers		714		1,000
Total goods handled		$100,714		$141,600

Reductions	Retail	
Gross sales	$82,000	
– Customer returns and allowances	(4,000)	
Net sales		$78,000
Markdowns	6,000	
– Markdown cancellations	(3,000)	
Net markdowns		3,000
Employee discounts		3,000
Discounts to customers		500
Estimated shrinkage		1,500
Total reductions		$86,000

Calculate Total Goods Handled at Cost and Retail

To determine the total goods handled at cost and retail, retailers take the following steps:

1. *Record beginning inventory at cost ($60,000) and at retail ($84,000).* The initial markup is reflected in the retail inventory.

2. *Calculate net purchases ($39,000 at cost and $54,600 at retail)* by recording gross purchases ($50,000 at cost and $70,000 at retail) and adjusting for merchandise returned to vendor ($11,000 at cost and $15,400 at retail).

3. *Calculate net additional markups ($2,000)* by adjusting gross additional markups ($4,000) by any additional markup cancellations ($2,000). (An additional markup is a markup that occurs in addition to the normal markup for an item. A markup cancellation occurs if an item has an additional markup, and then the price is reduced. The price reduction is a markup cancellation until it reaches the initial markup price. Any reduction below the initial markup price is a markdown.) Note: These figures are recorded only at retail because markups affect only the retail value of inventory.

4. *Record transportation expenses ($1,000).* Transportation is recorded at cost because it affects only the cost of the inventory.

5. *Calculate net transfers ($714 at cost and $1,000 at retail)* by recording the amount of transfers in and out. A transfer can be from one department to another or from store to store. Transfers are generally made to help adjust

inventory to fit demand. For instance, a sweater may be selling well at one store but not at another. A transfer is, in effect, just like a purchase (transfer in) or a return (transfer out). Thus, it's recorded at both cost and retail.

6. *Calculate the sum as the total goods handled ($100,714 at cost and $141,600 at retail).*

Calculate Retail Reductions

Reductions are the transactions that reduce the value of inventory at retail (except additional markup cancellations, which were included as part of the total goods handled). Reductions are calculated as follows:

1. *Record net sales.* The largest reduction in inventory is sales. Gross sales ($82,000) are reduced to net sales ($78,000) by deducting customer returns and allowances ($4,000).

2. *Calculate markdowns.* Net markdowns ($3,000) are derived by subtracting any markdown cancellations ($3,000) from gross markdowns ($6,000). (A markdown cancellation is the amount by which the price of an item increases after a markdown is applied, such as when a weekend sale occurs and the price goes back up after the weekend.)

3. *Record discounts to employees ($3,000) and customers ($500).*

4. *Record estimated shrinkage ($1,500).* Estimated shrinkage is used to determine the ending book inventory if the buyer is preparing an interim financial statement. The

estimate is based on historical records and presented as a percentage of sales. Estimated shrinkage wouldn't be included, however, if a physical inventory was taken at the time the statement was being prepared. In this case, the difference between the physical inventory and the book inventory would be the amount of shrinkage due to loss, shoplifting, and so forth.

5. *Calculate the sum as the total reductions* ($86,000).

Calculate the Cumulative Markup and Cost Multiplier

The cumulative markup is the average percentage markup for the period. It's calculated the same way the markup for an item is calculated:

$$\text{Cumulative markup} = \frac{\text{Total retail} - \text{Total cost}}{\text{Total retail}}$$

$$28.87\% = \frac{\$141,600 - \$100,714}{\$141,600}$$

The cumulative markup can be used as a comparison against the planned initial markup. If the cumulative markup is higher than planned, the category is doing better than planned.

The cost multiplier is similar to the cost of goods sold percentage, also called the cost complement.

$$\text{Cost multiplier} = (100\% - \text{Cumulative markup \%})$$

$$71.13\% = 100\% - 28.7\%$$

$$\frac{\text{Total cost}}{\text{Total retail}} = \frac{\$100,714}{\$141,600} = 71.13\%$$

The cost multiplier is used in the next step to determine the ending book inventory at retail.

Determine Ending Book Inventory at Cost and Retail

$$\text{Ending book} = \text{Total goods handled at retail inventory at retail} - \text{Total reductions}$$

$$\$55,600 = \$141,600 - \$86,000$$

The ending book inventory at cost is determined in the same way that retail has been changed to cost in other situations—by multiplying the retail times (100% − gross margin).

$$\text{Ending book inventory at cost} = \text{Ending book inventory at retail} \times \text{Cost multiplier}$$

$$\$39,548 = \$55,600 \times 71.13\%$$

Buying Merchandise

EXECUTIVE BRIEFING

Michael Jeppesen, Divisional Senior Vice-President for Global Sourcing and Product Development, Payless ShoeSource

I joined Payless ShoeSource to implement our new strategy to democratize fashion and design in footwear and accessories, and to become the retailer of choice for fashion-oriented products featuring well-recognized brands. In the past, Payless sold shoes to budget-minded customers at its 4,500 convenient locations. When Matt Rubel became CEO in 2005, he directed a strategic shift to ensure continued growth and to differentiate Payless against other discount mass retailers. Under his direction, we have increased the value to our customers by developing stylish products featuring the latest trends

and well-recognized brands, still offering merchandise at affordable prices.

I am responsible for designing, developing, commercializing, and manufacturing all of our merchandise. The 275 people who work in the product development and sourcing division are located in our corporate headquarters in Topeka, Kansas; in our design center in New York City; and in our nine offices in Asia where our products are manufactured.

For our House of Brands effort, Payless offers well-recognized brands in Payless stores through acquisitions and through licensing agreements. We license some brands like Champion, Tailwind, Dunkman, and Dexter, and own American Eagle, Airwalk, as well as develop "co-brands" with fashion designers. For example, Laura Poretzky, our first "Guest Designer" for Payless, is a highly regarded, young SoHo-based fashion designer known for her hip, modern apparel sold at Bergdorf Goodman and other high-end retailers. Known as an up-and-coming clothing designer, she had not yet designed shoes. We approached her about working with Payless to develop a line of shoes under her label Abaete, which would be sold exclusively at Payless. Our footwear designers and commercialization team

What branding options are available to retailers?

How do retailers buy national brands?

What issues do retailers consider when buying and sourcing private-label merchandise internationally?

How do retailers prepare for and conduct negotiations with their vendors?

Why are retailers building strategic relationships with their vendors?

What legal and ethical issues are involved in buying merchandise?

CHAPTER 14

worked with her to develop shoes that are well aligned with their apparel designs for their upcoming seasonal collection. We provide handmade samples of shoes that are worn by models and unveiled with their collections on the runway at the premier fashion event: New York Fashion Week.

But our mission and strategy isn't just about fashion; it's about authentic performance shoes as well. Shaquille O'Neil wanted to endorse a line of athletic shoes that young people could buy at a reasonable price—$25, not the $150 charged for most shoes endorsed by star athletes. Several years ago Shaq approached us about designing and offering a line of basketball shoes. Shaq is very involved in the design process, working directly with our designers, and he wears his Dunkman shoes from Payless when on the court.

After earning my first degree in business administration at the Copenhagen Business School in Denmark and an MBA at Cranfield University in the United Kingdom, I worked for eight years managing production operations for ECCO Shoes in Portugal and in Indonesia and managed product development for Adidas, Saucony, and Coach the following 10 years. To be effective in designing and developing footwear, you need to know about the production issues as well as the fashion trends.

The preceding two chapters outlined the merchandise management process and the steps in the process that buyers go through to determine what and how much merchandise to buy. After creating an assortment plan for the category, forecasting sales, and developing a plan outlining the flow of merchandise (how much merchandise needs to be ordered and when it needs to be delivered), the next step in the merchandise management process is to buy the merchandise.

The first strategic decision that needs to be made is the type of merchandise to buy for the category—well-known national brands or private-label brands that are available exclusively from the retailer. When buying merchandise, buyers meet with vendors at retail markets or in their offices and negotiate many issues such as prices, delivery dates, payment terms, and advertising and markdown support.

The development and buying process for private-label merchandise is often more complex. Some retailers have their own design and sourcing departments that work with buyers to specify the merchandise designs and then negotiate with manufacturers to produce the merchandise. Because merchandise is often manufactured outside the United States, these retailers need to deal with the complexities of international business transactions. In other cases, buyers might negotiate with national brand vendors or manufacturers to buy merchandise designed by the supplier exclusively for the retailer.

Although buyers meet and negotiate with national brand vendors and private-label manufacturers each season concerning new merchandise, there is a trend toward developing long-term strategic relationships with key suppliers. These partnerships enable the collaboration needed to develop the efficient supply chains discussed in Chapter 10, as well as joint merchandise and marketing programs.

This chapter begins with a description of the different merchandise branding alternatives. Then the issues involved in buying national brands and private-label merchandise are reviewed. The chapter concludes with a discussion of the development of strategic partnering relationships between retailers and their suppliers.

BRAND ALTERNATIVES

Retailers and their buyers face a strategic decision about the mix of national brands and private-label brands sold exclusively by the retailer. The advantages and disadvantages of these branding alternatives are discussed in this section.

REFACT

The world's 10 most valuable company brands are Coca-Cola, Microsoft, IBM, GE, Nokia, Toyota, Intel, McDonald's, Disney, and Mercedes.[1]

National Brands

National brands, also known as **manufacturer's brands** are products designed, produced, and marketed by a vendor and sold to many different retailers. The vendor is responsible for developing the merchandise, producing it with consistent quality, and undertaking a marketing program to establish an appealing brand image. In some cases, vendors use an umbrella or family brand associated with their company and a subbrand associated with the product, such as Kellogg's (family brand) Frosted Flakes (subbrand) or Ford (family brand) F150 truck (subbrand). In other cases, vendors use individual brand names for different product categories and don't associate the brands with their companies. For example, most consumers probably don't know that Procter & Gamble makes Iams pet food, Crest toothpaste, Ivory soap, Max Factor cosmetics, Folgers coffee, Hugo by Hugo Boss cologne, and Pringles potato chips.

By offering these national brands, retailers attract customers to their stores and Web sites and therefore do not have to incur the cost of developing and promoting the brand's image and associated merchandise.

Some retailers organize their buying activities around national brand vendors that cut across merchandise categories. For instance, buyers in department stores may be responsible for all cosmetic brands offered by Estée Lauder (Estée Lauder, Origins, Clinique, and Prescriptives) rather than for a product category such as skin care, eye makeup, and so forth. Managing merchandise by vendor, rather than by category, gives retailers more clout when dealing with vendors. However, as indicated in Chapter 12, there are inefficiencies associated with managing merchandise at the brand or vendor rather than the category level.

Private-Label Brands

Private-label brands, also called **store brands, house brands,** or **own brands,** are products developed by retailers. In many cases, retailers develop the design and specifications for their private-label products and then contract with manufacturers to produce those products. In other cases, national brand vendors work with a retailer to develop a special version of its standard merchandise offering to be sold exclusively by the retailer. In these cases, the national brand vendor or manufacturer is responsible for the design and specification as well as the production of the merchandise. Retailing View 14.1 describes Asda's private label strategy.

REFACT

Private-label product sales are growing faster than their national brand counterparts. Between 1997 and 2004, private-label dollar sales in the United States grew at a rate that was more than twice as fast as that for branded items.[2]

U.K.'s Asda Loves Private Labels **RETAILING VIEW** 14.1

The British supermarket retailer Asda, owned by Wal-Mart, has a private-label portfolio that accounts for 45 percent of its grocery and 50 percent of its nonfood sales. Asda has extended its own label into such categories as healthy eating, organics, and food for kids and now is placing more emphasis on developing premium-priced private labels.

Asda offers six private-label brands in the food, health and beauty, and household categories. In addition, it has its successful George private-label clothing brand and a selection of Asda-branded financial services, including home, motor, and life insurance. Some of its brands include:

Asada, a U.K. chain owned by Wal-Mart, developed George, a private-label apparel and footwear brand. Although very successful in the U.K, it has not been as successful in Wal-Mart stores in the U.S.

- Smart Price—Economy-value, no-frills food and general merchandise essentials.
- Best-in-market everyday food and general merchandise items at low prices.
- Good for you!—Foods with lower fat content than standard Asda brand alternatives.
- Organic—Best-value organic "everyday" products.
- Onn—Mid-level eclectic brand with stylized designs.
- Extra Special—Asda's premium private-label food brand.
- More for Kids—Healthier, fun products for kids across the food and health and beauty categories.

The Extra Special premium private-label brand has grown from 40 SKUs in 2000 to more than 750 across categories that include confectionery, soft drinks, snacks, trifles, specialty breads, prepared meat and fish meals, and a wide range of cheeses and sliced meats. The criteria for an Extra Special branded product include better taste and the finest ingredients compared with standard alternatives or national premium equivalents, but affordable at a 10–15 percent lower price than competitors' premium private-label equivalents.

Asda's private-label clothing and footwear brand, George, is the fourth largest apparel brand in the United Kingdom. Created by George Davies, the former owner of a successful chain of British apparel stores, George merchandise comprises sleek but inexpensive clothing, accessories, and undergarments for women and men. Wal-Mart is importing George merchandise and selling it in its U.S. stores as part of its effort to upgrade its apparel offering. But George merchandise has not been as successful in the United States.

REFACT

Private labels are big business in Europe: Aldi and Lidl's private brands account for 80–90 percent of their merchandise; Tesco 50 percent; Wal-Mart 40 percent; and Carrefour 25 percent.[3]

Sources: www.asda.co.uk (accessed October 16, 2007); "Odin Drives ASDA 'Extra Special' Range onto Shelves," *The Retail Bulletin,* August 30, 2007; Bill Condie, "Asda Plans to Spruce Up Tired George Label as Growth Slows Down," *Knight Ridder Tribune Business News,* September 14, 2007.

REFACT

Private-label sales of food and nonalcoholic beverages in the United States are increasing at approximately 4.3 percent, to $44 billion per year, excluding sales by Wal-Mart. In contrast, sales of branded food and nonalcoholic beverages are rising at only 2.2 percent.[5]

REFACT

Macy's was among the first department stores to pioneer the concept of private-label brands for fashion goods. In the 1890s, its "Macy's" and "Red Star" brands were the rage in New York.[6]

In the past, sales of private label brands were limited. National brands had the resources to develop loyalty toward their brands through aggressive marketing. It was difficult for smaller local and regional retailers to gain the economies of scale in design, production, and promotion needed to develop well-known brands.

In recent years, as the size of retail firms has increased through consolidation, more retailers have the scale economies to develop private-label merchandise and use this merchandise to establish a distinctive identity. In addition, manufacturers and national brand suppliers are more willing to accommodate the needs of retailers and develop exclusive private labels for them. Private-label products now account for an average of 16 percent of the purchases in North America and roughly 22 percent in Europe.[4]

Similar to national brands, retailers can use their names to create a private label for merchandise in many different categories or develop category-specific private brands. For example, The Gap and Victoria's Secret use a family brand approach, in which all of their private-label merchandise is associated with their name. In contrast, Macy's has a portfolio of private-label brands associated with different merchandise types, such as Charter Club, First Impressions, Greendog, INC, The Cellar, Martha Stewart Collection, and Tools of the Trade.

There are four categories of private brands: premium, generic, copycat, and exclusive co-brands. **Premium brands** offer the consumer a private label that is comparable to, or even superior to, a manufacturer's brand quality, sometimes with modest price savings. Examples of premium private labels include Wal-Mart's Sam's Choice (U.S.), Loblaw's President's Choice (Canada), Tesco Finest (U.K.), Marks & Spencer's St. Michael (U.K.), Woolworth Select (Australia), Pick and Pay's Choice (South Africa), and Albert Heijn's AH Select (Netherlands).[7]

President's Choice is Canadian retailer Loblaw's premium private label. It competes on quality, not price. Kellogg has two scoops of raisins in its cereal, but President's Choice cereal has four and is still cheaper. The Decadent chocolate chip cookie under the President's Choice label has 39 percent chocolate chips by weight, compared with 19 percent in Chips Ahoy! In addition, it uses real butter instead of hydrogenated coconut oil and quality chocolate instead of artificial chips. The resulting product is Canada's market leader in chocolate chip cookies, despite being sold only in 20 percent of the market held by Loblaw.[8]

The Martha Stewart Collection is just one of many private-label brands available at Macy's.

Generic brands target a price-sensitive segment by offering a no-frills product at a discount price. These products are used for commodities like milk or eggs in grocery stores and underwear in discount stores.

Copycat brands imitate the manufacturer's brand in appearance and packaging, generally are perceived as lower quality, and are offered at lower prices. Copycat brands abound in drugstores. As discussed in Chapter 12, many retailers monitor the introduction of new national brands and then modify them to meet the needs of their target customers. For instance, CVS or Walgreen's brands are placed next to the manufacturer's brands and often look like them.

Exclusive Co-Brands   An **exclusive co-brand** is a brand that is developed by a national brand vendor, often in conjunction with a retailer, and is sold exclusively by the retailer. The simplest form of an exclusive co-brand is when a national brand manufacturer assigns different model numbers and has different exterior features for the same basic product sold by different retailers. For example, a Canon digital camera sold at Best Buy might have a different model number than a Canon digital camera with similar features available at Circuit City. These exclusive models make it difficult for consumers to compare prices for virtually the same camera sold by different retailers. Since, the retailers are less likely to compete on price when selling these exclusive co-brands, their margins for the products reach higher, and they are motivated to devote more resources toward selling the exclusive co-brands than they would for similar national brands.[9]

A more sophisticated form of exclusive co-branding is when a manufacturer develops an exclusive product or product category for a retailer. For example, cosmetics powerhouse Estée Lauder sells three brands of cosmetics and skin care products—American Beauty, Flirt, and Good Skin—exclusively at Kohl's. The products are priced between mass-market brands such as Cover Girl or Maybelline, sold mainly in drugstores, discount stores, and supermarkets, and Lauder's higher-end brands, sold primarily in more fashion-forward department stores such as Macy's and Dillard's. Levi's has also developed the Signature brand jeans for sale at Wal-Mart. Examples of these and several other exclusive co-brands you might recognize are found in Exhibit 14–1.

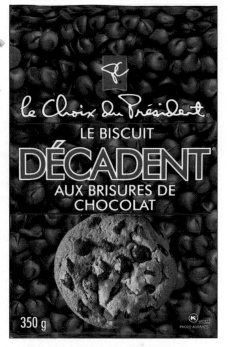

President's Choice Decadent chocolate chip cookie is a premium private label that is Canada's market leader because of its high quality ingredients.

Estee Lauder sells three exclusive co-brands at Kohl's—American Beauty, Flirt, and Good Skin.

EXHIBIT 14–1
Exclusive Brands

Retailer	Manufacturer/ Designer	Product Category	Product Name
Kohl's	Estée Lauder	Cosmetics	American Beauty, Flirt, and Good Skin
Wal-Mart	Mary Kate and Ashley Olsen	Apparel and accessories	Mary Kate and Ashley
Wal-Mart, Best Buy,[10]	Hewlett-Packard	Computers	
Circuit City Stores[11]	Toshiba	Computers	
Macy's[12]	Martha Stewart	Soft home (sheets, towels)	Martha Stewart
JCPenney[13]	Ralph Lauren	Home goods, apparel, and accessories	American Living
KB Toys, Toys "R" Us[14]	Mattel	Toys	

National Brands or Private Labels?   Exhibit 14–2 outlines the advantages and disadvantages of national versus private-label brands. Buying from vendors of national brands can help retailers build their image and traffic flow and reduce their selling/promotional expenses. Many customers have developed loyalty to specific national brands. They patronize retailers selling the national brand merchandise and ask for it by name. This loyalty toward the brand develops because customers know what to expect from the products, like them, and trust them. If a retailer does not offer these national brands, customers might decide to patronize a retailer that does.

National brand vendors devote considerable resources to creating images of their brands that build customer loyalty. As a result, retailers need to spend relatively less money selling and promoting national brands. For instance, Sony attempts to communicate a constant and focused message about the quality and performance of its products to its customers by coordinating advertising with in-store promotions and displays. Thus, Best Buy and Circuit City do not need to engage in image advertising for Sony products.

But because vendors of national brands assume the expenses of designing, manufacturing, distributing, and promoting the brand, retailers typically realize lower gross margins for them compared with those for their private-label brands. Also, because national brands are sold by other retailers, competition can be intense. Customers compare prices for these brands across stores, which means retailers often have to offer significant discounts on some national brands to attract customers to their stores, further reducing their gross margins. Large retailers, however, can push some of the financial risk of buying the merchandise back onto the national brand vendor. If, for instance, a product doesn't sell, the retailer can negotiate to either send the merchandise back to the vendor or require the vendor to make up the difference in lost gross margin if the merchandise has to be marked down.

EXHIBIT 14–2
Relative Advantages of National Versus Private Brands

	TYPE OF VENDOR	
Impact on Store	National Brands	Private-Label Brands
Store loyalty	?	+
Store image	+	+
Traffic flow	+	+
Selling and promotional expenses	+	−
Restrictions	−	+
Differential advantages	−	+
Margins	?	?

+ advantage to the retailer, − disadvantage to the retailer, ? depends on circumstances.

Stocking national brands can increase or decrease store loyalty. If the national brand is available through a limited number of retail outlets (e.g., Kiehl's skin care products, Diesel jeans), customers loyal to the brand will also become loyal to the limited number of stores selling the brand. If, however, manufacturer brands are readily available from many retailers in a market, store loyalty may decrease because the retailer can't differentiate itself from its competition.

Another problem with manufacturer's brands is that they can limit a retailer's flexibility. Vendors of strong brands can dictate how their products are displayed, advertised, and priced. Jockey underwear, for instance, tells retailers exactly when and how its products should be advertised.

The exclusivity of strong private labels boosts store loyalty. Well-known and highly desirable private labels and exclusive brands can enhance the retailer's image and draw customers to the store. For instance, Kohl's exclusive co-brands, as discussed in Retailing View 14.2, are not available from its competitors.

But there are drawbacks to private labels. Although gross margins may be higher for private-label brands than for national brands, other expenses aren't as readily apparent. Retailers must make significant investments to design merchandise, manage global manufacturers, create customer awareness, and develop a favorable image for their private-label and exclusive brands. If the private-label or exclusive merchandise doesn't sell, retailers may not be able to negotiate to either return the merchandise or receive compensation from the lost margin from the manufacturer.

Only at Kohl's   **RETAILING VIEW**   14.2

Kohl's is a department store chain offering fashionable merchandise in convenient, off the mall locations. Previously known as a discount apparel store, Kohl's is changing its image by offering trendy exclusive co-brands, such as Daisy Fuentes, featuring the former MTV host; Candies, which uses several celebrity spokespeople; Ralph Lauren's Home Chaps, and an *ELLE Magazine* apparel line. Its exclusive brands currently make up 8 percent of its business.

Kohl's has been very successful with its exclusive co-branded private-label products. Its Ralph Lauren Home Chaps line was introduced in 2007 for men. Not only is the company doing more brand extensions with its other private labels, like the Daisy Fuentes intimate apparel line, it is also building entire marketing campaigns behind a single private-label product. Kohl's has introduced Simply Vera by Vera Wang, a famous designer, best known for her luxury bridal gowns. She expanded her line to include high-end runway apparel that features $1700 jackets and $2800 gowns.

Thus, Wang's introduction into Kohl's delineates a new and bold step for both. Kohl's is attracting a slightly more hip, upscale customer. Wang is able to sell dresses and accessories at a fraction of the runway line prices. Wang is following in the footsteps of her former employer, Ralph Lauren. Lauren has brilliantly translated the fashion market from the upper echelons to the middle masses. Like Lauren, Wang's high-end line is made with the finest materials and workmanship, whereas the Kohl's line, though still fashionably designed, is made with less expensive materials and less labor-intensive details. Yet Simply Vera for Kohl's excites consumers! Customers recognize the Vera Wang brand name and are attracted to Kohl's as a result.

Simply Vera by Vera Wang is one of Kohl's exclusive co-brands. The Simply Vera brand sells at a fraction of Vera Wang's runway line.

Sources: Vanessa O'Connell, "Is Discount a Good Fit for Vera Wang?" *The Wall Street Journal,* September 5, 2007; Kelly Nolan, "Striking a Balance between Mass & Fashion," *Retailing Today,* August 13, 2007; Kelly Nolan, "Kohl's Plans to Keep Shoppers Shopping—Across the Store," *Retailing Today,* June 18, 2007; www.kohls.com/VeraWang (accessed November 28, 2007); "Vera Wang to Design Line Just for Kohl's," *USA Today,* August 24, 2006.

BUYING NATIONAL BRAND MERCHANDISE

After developing a merchandise budget plan and determining how much merchandise needs to be bought, the next step is to buy the merchandise. Buyers of fashion apparel and accessory categories typically make major merchandise buying decisions five or six times a year for their core merchandise. These purchases are made many months before delivery to allow vendors to produce and deliver the merchandise. Because fashion changes so rapidly, retailers will withhold some of their open to buy to infuse their core assortment with trendier items that they procure much closer to the selling season. Buyers of staple merchandise categories make decisions about buying new merchandise items less frequently. The next sections review how retail buyers of national brands meet with vendors and review the merchandise they have to offer at wholesale markets.

Meeting National Brand Vendors

A **wholesale market** for retail buyers is a concentration of vendors within a specific geographic location, perhaps even under one roof or over the Internet. These markets may be permanent wholesale market centers or annual trade shows or trade fairs. Retailers also interact with vendors at their corporate headquarters. A listing of more than 350,000 trade shows, designer show rooms, retailers, and global manufacturers for the fashion industry can be viewed at Infomat (www.infomat.com).

Wholesale Market Centers   For many types of merchandise, particularly fashion apparel and accessories, buyers regularly visit with vendors in established market centers. Wholesale market centers have permanent vendor showrooms that retailers can visit throughout the year. At specific times during the year, these wholesale centers host **market weeks** during which buyers make appointments to visit the various vendor showrooms. Vendors that do not have permanent showrooms at the market center lease temporary space to participate in market weeks.

Probably the world's most well-known wholesale market center for many merchandise categories is in New York City. The Fashion Center, also known as the Garment District, is located from Fifth to Ninth avenues and from 34th to 41st streets. An estimated 22,000 apparel buyers visit every year for five market weeks and 65 annual trade shows. The Garment District hosts more than 5,000 showrooms and 4,500 factories.[15] There are also major wholesale market centers in London, Milan, Paris, and Tokyo.

The United States also has various regional wholesale market centers. The Dallas Market Center, is a 7-million-square-foot complex of four buildings.[16] More than 26,000 manufacturers and importers display their international products in its 2,200 permanent showrooms and 460,000 square feet of temporary spaces. The Dallas Market Center conducts 50 market weeks annually, attended by more than 200,000 buyers for products ranging from floor coverings to toys, apparel, jewelry, and gifts.

These regional merchandise marts are used by smaller retailers to view and purchase merchandise. For example, the owner of a gift shop in Birmingham, Alabama, might go to the Atlanta Merchandise Mart several times a year to buy merchandise for his store. Some regional centers have developed into national markets for specific merchandise categories. For example, the Miami Merchandise Mart is now an international market for swimwear.

Trade Shows   Trade shows provide another opportunity for buyers to see the latest products and styles and interact with vendors. For example, consumer

REFACT

An estimated $7.5 billion of wholesale transactions are conducted within the Dallas Market Center complex annually.[17]

electronics buyers attend the annual International Consumer Electronics Show (CES) in Las Vegas, the world's largest trade show for consumer technology (www.cesweb.org). The trade show, like most, is closed to the public, but vendors, developers, and suppliers of consumer technology hardware, content, technology delivery systems, and related products and services are among the more than 140,000 attendees from over 110 countries. Nearly 2,700 vendor exhibits take up 1.8 million net square feet of exhibit space, showcasing their latest products and services. Vendors often use CES to introduce new products, such as the first camcorder (1981), high definition television (HDTV) (1998), and Internet protocol television (IP TV) (2005). In addition to providing an opportunity for retail buyers to see the latest products, CES has a conference program featuring prominent speakers from the technology sector, such as Bill Gates.[18]

Buyers for sporting equipment and apparel attend The Super Show® (www.thesupershow.com), sponsored by the Sporting Goods Manufacturers Association. One of the features of this trade show is that world-renowned athletes participate to promote their licensed merchandise.

Everyone who is anyone in the book industry attends the Frankfurt Book Fair (www.frankfurter-buchmesse.de)—authors and publishers, book retailers and librarians, art dealers and illustrators, agents and journalists, information brokers and readers. Not only is the Frankfurt Book Fair the meeting place for the business, it is also the world's largest marketplace for trading in publishing rights and licenses.

Trade shows are typically staged at convention centers not associated with wholesale market centers. McCormick Place in Chicago (the nation's largest convention complex, with more than 2.7 million square feet) hosts over 65 meetings and trade shows per year, including the National Hardware Show and National Housewares Manufacturers Association International Exposition.[19] At these trade shows, the vendors display their merchandise in designated areas and have sales representatives, company executives, and sometime even celebrities available to talk with buyers as they walk through the exhibit area.

Vendors from outside the United States and private brand manufacturers have started to attend trade shows to learn about the market and pick up trend information. Some private-label manufacturers attend and display at trade shows, but most participants are national brand vendors.

The International Consumer Electronics Show (CES) in Las Vegas, is the world's largest trade show for consumer technology.

National Brand Buying Process

When attending market weeks or trade shows, buyers and their supervisors typically make a series of appointments with key vendors. During these meetings, the buyers discuss the performance of the vendor's merchandise during the previous season, review the vendor's offering for the coming season, and possibly place orders for the coming season. These meetings take place in conference rooms in the vendors' showrooms at wholesale market centers. During trade shows, these meetings typically are less formal. The meetings during market weeks offer an opportunity for an in-depth discussion, whereas trade shows provide the opportunity for buyers to see a broader array of merchandise in one location and gauge reactions to the merchandise by observing the level of activity in the vendor's display area.

Often buyers do not negotiate with vendors and place orders, referred to as "writing paper," during the market week or trade show. They typically want to see what merchandise and prices are available from all the potential vendors before deciding what items to buy. So after attending a market week or trade show, buyers return to their offices, review requested samples of merchandise sent to them by vendors, meet with their supervisors to review the available merchandise, make decisions about which items are most attractive, and then negotiate with the vendors before placing an order. The issues involved in negotiating the purchase of national brand merchandise are discussed later in this chapter.

DEVELOPING AND SOURCING PRIVATE-LABEL MERCHANDISE

Retailers use a variety of different processes to develop and buy private-label merchandise.

Developing Private-Label Merchandise

Larger retailers that offer a significant amount of private-label merchandise, such as JCPenney, Macy's, The Gap, and American Eagle Outfitters, have large divisions with people devoted to the development of that private-label merchandise. Employees in these divisions specialize in identifying trends, designing and specifying products, selecting manufacturers to make the products, maintaining a worldwide staff to monitor the conditions under which the products are made, and managing facilities to test the quality of the manufactured products. For example, Limited Brands acquired MAST Industries in 1978. MAST is now one of the world's biggest contract manufacturers, importers, and distributors of apparel, with manufacturing operations and joint ventures in more than a dozen countries including China, Israel, Mexico, and Sri Lanka. In addition to being the major private-label supplier of Limited Brands (Victoria's Secret and Bath & Body Works), it provides private-label merchandise for Abercrombie & Fitch, Lane Bryant, New York & Company, and Chico's. However, most retailers do not own and operate manufacturing facilities.

Smaller retail chains can offer private-label merchandise without making a significant investment in the supporting infrastructure. Smaller retailers often ask national brand or private label suppliers to make minor changes to products they offer and then provide the merchandise with the store's brand name or a special label copyrighted by the national brand. Alternatively, private-label manufacturers will sell to them from a predetermined stock selection. Hollander, for instance, makes 150,000 private-label pillows a day for companies like Laura Ashley and Simmons Beautyrest.[20]

Retailing View 14.3 describes how Chinese manufacturers achieve low costs by developing economies of scale without exploiting workers.

Retailers with private-label departments or divisions use different processes to develop merchandise. For some retailers, designers in the private label division use their insight about market trends to develop a product line. They then present the designs to buyers. The buyers then make decisions about which items to buy from the merchandise developed by the division. In some firms, the buyers are instructed to buy specific items or a specific amount of private-label merchandise from the firm's division. In other retail firms, the private-label division operates somewhat independently, like a national brand vendor, and the buyers are free to buy the private-label merchandise offered by the divisions or buy national brands. In retailing firms that only sell private-label merchandise, the buyers and designers typically work together closely to develop the merchandise.

Datang, China, Is Sock City RETAILING VIEW 14.3

Datang, China, is called Sock City because nine billion pairs of socks, more than one set for every person in the world, and 2.6 pairs for each American, are produced there each year. Its annual trade fair attracts 100,000 buyers from around the world. Southeast of Datang is Shenzhou, which is the world's necktie capital; to the west is Sweater City and Kids' Clothing City; and to the south is Underwear City.

As a result of government and private investment, China has become the leading manufacturer of private-label and national brand merchandise.

This specialization creates the economies of scale that have made Chinese businesses the world's leading garment manufacturers. Buyers from New York to Tokyo can place orders for 500,000 pairs of socks all at once—or 300,000 neckties, 100,000 children's jackets, or 50,000 size 36B bras—in China's giant new specialty textile cities.

Textile production is a prime example of how the Chinese government guides development indirectly through local planning instead of state ownership. In the late 1970s, Datang was a rice-farming village with 1,000 people, who gathered in small groups and stitched socks together at home, then sold them in baskets along the highway. But the government designated Datang's sock makers as producers and ordered them to stop retailing socks. Now, they produce over one-third of the world's output. Due to the policy, there are many rags-to-riches tales in Datang, such as that of Dong Ying Hong, who in the 1970s gave up a $9-a-month job as an elementary school teacher to make socks at home. Now, she is the owner of Zhejiang Socks and a sock millionaire.

The Chinese government has also designated large areas for development, formed giant industrial parks, given tax benefits, and developed the infrastructure and transportation networks

needed to move products quickly to market. It has created networks of support businesses located near one another, such as the button capital that furnishes most of the buttons on the world's shirts, pants, and jackets. Private companies, with the support of the government, have built huge textile factory complexes, complete with dormitories and hospitals, that provide food, shelter, and health care, along with close supervision.

Huafang Group, one of China's largest textile companies, has over 100 factory buildings, 30,000 employees, and round-the-clock operations. More than 20,000 workers live free of charge in Huafang's dormitories. Conditions aren't great, but they are often better than the conditions in the inland provinces from which the workers come. Many women go there after high school, stay for a few years, and then return home to be married. As they return home, another 10,000 are bused in from the countryside.

Sources: Geoffrey Colvin, "Saving America's Socks—but Killing Free Trade," *Fortune*, August 22, 2005, p. 38; Evan Clark, "China's Foothold on Socks," *Women's Wear Daily*, December 5, 2005.

REFACT
Twelve percent of China's exports to the United States are sent to Wal-Mart. Wal-Mart's purchases account for 1 percent of China's gross domestic product.[21]

REFACT
Workers in China cost about 92 cents an hour compared with $1.20 in Thailand, $1.70 in Mexico, and about $21.80 in the United States. Only India among the major export countries, at about 70 cents an hour, is cheaper.[22]

Sourcing Merchandise

Once the decision has been made about which and how much private-label merchandise will be acquired, the designers develop a complete specification and work with the sourcing department to find a manufacturer for the merchandise. For example, JCPenney has sourcing and quality assurance offices in 18 countries. These offices take the specification developed by the designer, negotiate a contract to produce the item with manufacturers, and monitor the production process.[23]

Reverse Auctions   Rather than negotiating with a specific manufacturers to produce the merchandise, some retailers use reverse auctions to get quality private-label merchandise at low prices. The most common use of reverse auctions is to buy the products and services used in retail operations rather than merchandise for resale. Some operating materials that are frequently bought through reverse auctions are store carpeting, fixtures, and supplies. However, reverse auctions also are being used by retailers to procure private-label merchandise, such as commodities and seasonal merchandise like lawn furniture.[24] For example, Bashas', a privately owned supermarket chain based in Chandler, Arizona, uses reverse auctions to purchase about 70 percent of its meat. Twice weekly, seven competing suppliers bid for the business.[25]

In traditional auctions like those conducted on eBay, there is one seller and many buyers. Auctions conducted by retailer buyers of private-label merchandise are called **reverse auctions** because there is one buyer, the retailer, and many potential sellers, the manufacturing firms. In reverse auctions, retail buyers provide a specification for what they want to a group of potential vendors. The competing vendors then bid on the price at which they are willing to sell until the auction is over. However, the retailer is not required to place an order with the lowest bidder. The retailer can choose to place an order at the offered price from whichever vendor the retailer feels will provide the merchandise in a timely manner and with the specified quality.[26]

Reverse auctions are not popular with vendors. Few vendors want to be anonymous contestants in bidding wars where price alone, not service or quality, seems to be the sole basis for winning the business. Strategic relationships are also difficult to nurture when the primary interactions with vendors are through electronic auctions.[27]

Global Sourcing

An important issue facing large retailers that design and contract for the production of private-label merchandise is the best way to select a manufacturer. Barriers to international trade are diminishing, which means that retailers can consider sources of production from across the globe. In this section, factors affecting global sourcing costs and human rights and child-labor violations are examined.

Costs Associated with Global Sourcing Decisions   Retailers use production facilities located in developing economies for much of their private-label merchandise because of the very low labor costs in these countries. To counterbalance the lower acquisition costs, however, there are other expenses that can increase the costs of sourcing private-label merchandise from other countries. These costs include relative value of foreign currencies, tariffs, longer lead times, and increased transportation costs.

Retailers can hedge against short-term foreign currency fluctuations by buying contracts that lock the retailer into a set price regardless of how the currency fluctuates. But in the longer term, the relative value of foreign currencies can have a strong influence on the cost of imported merchandise. For example, if the Indian rupee has a sustained and significant increase relative to the U.S. dollar, the cost of private-label merchandise produced in India and imported for sale into the United States will increase. **Tariffs,** also known as **duties** are taxes placed by a government on imports that increase the cost of merchandise imported from international sources. Import tariffs have been used to shield domestic manufacturers from foreign competition. Inventory turnover also is likely to be lower when purchasing from foreign suppliers. Because lead times are longer and more uncertain, retailers using foreign sources must maintain larger inventories to ensure that the merchandise is available when the customer wants it. Larger inventories mean larger inventory carrying costs. Finally, transportation costs are higher when merchandise is produced in foreign countries.

The decline of the value of the U.S. dollar against the Euro and other important world currencies has made imports to the United States more expensive and exports from the United States less expensive.

Managerial Issues Associated with Global Sourcing Decisions   Whereas the cost factors associated with global sourcing are easy to quantify, some more subjective issues include quality control, time to market, and social/political risks. When sourcing globally, it's harder to maintain consistent quality standards than when sourcing domestically. Quality control problems can cause delays in shipment and adversely affect a retailer's image.

The collaborative supply chain management approaches described in Chapter 10 are more difficult to implement when sourcing globally. Collaborative systems are based on short and consistent lead times. Vendors provide frequent deliveries of smaller quantities. For a collaborative system to work properly, there must be a strong alliance between the vendor and the retailer that is based on trust and sharing of information. These activities are more difficult to perform globally than domestically.

A final issue related to global sourcing is the problem of policing potential violations of human rights and child-labor laws. Many retailers have had to publicly defend themselves against allegations of human rights, child-labor, or other abuses involving the factories and countries in which their goods are made.[28] Due to the efforts of U.S. retailers, and nonprofit organizations, fewer imported goods are produced in sweatshop conditions today. Some retailers are quite proactive in enforcing the labor practices of their suppliers. Limited Brands, for instance, was one of the first U.S. apparel manufacturers to develop and implement policies requiring observance by vendors and their subcontractors and suppliers of core labor standards as a condition of doing business. Among other things, this requirement insures that each supplier pays minimum wages and benefits; limits overtime to local industry standards; does not use prisoners, forced labor, or child labor; and provides a healthy and safe environment.[29] Many other companies that produce or sell goods made in low-wage countries conduct similar self-policing. Self-policing allows companies to avoid painful public revelations. For example, The Gap Inc. provides a 40-page "social-responsibility report" that details the problems it found in the 3,000 factories it has contracted with to produce clothing for its outlets.[30]

SUPPORT SERVICES FOR BUYING MERCHANDISE

Two services available to buyers that can help them acquire merchandise more effectively are resident buying offices and Internet exchanges.

Resident Buying Offices

Many retailers purchasing private-label merchandise use **resident buying offices,** which are organizations located in major market centers that provide services to help retailers buy merchandise. As retailers have become larger and more sophisticated, these third-party independent resident buying offices have become less important. Now many retailers have their own buying offices in other countries.

To illustrate how buying offices operate, consider how David Smith of Pockets Men's Store in Dallas utilizes his resident buying offices when he goes to market in Milan. Smith meets with market representative Alain Bordat of the Doneger

Group. Bordat, an English-speaking Italian, knows Smith's store and his upscale customers, so in advance of Smith's visit, he sets up appointments with Italian vendors he believes will fit Pockets' image.

When Smith is in Italy, Bordat accompanies him to the appointments and acts as a translator, negotiator, and accountant. Bordat informs Smith of the cost of importing the merchandise into the United States, taking into account duty, freight, insurance, processing costs, and so forth.

Once the orders are placed, Bordat writes the contracts and follows up on delivery and quality control. The Doneger Group also acts as a home base for buyers like Smith, providing office space and services, travel advisers, and emergency aid. Bordat and his association continue to keep Smith abreast of what's happening on the Italian fashion scene through reports and constant communication. Without the help of a resident buying office, it would be difficult, if not impossible, for Smith to access the Italian wholesale market.

Retail Exchanges

Retail exchanges are providers of Internet-based solutions and services for retailers. One of their functions is similar to a trade show, except that they are virtual and, as such, available 24/7. In addition to providing a virtual meeting place for buyers and vendors, they offer software and services to help retailers, manufacturers, and their trading partners reduce costs and improve efficiency by streamlining and automating sourcing and supply chain processes. They provide an opportunity for vendors and retailers to interact electronically rather than meet face-to-face in a physical market.

Agentrics is an international business-to-business exchange that serves the retail e-marketplace. It connects more than 250 retailers with 80,000 suppliers that provide members with supply-chain and e-commerce services. The company was formed in the late 2005 merger of the WorldWide Retail Exchange (WWRE) with GlobalNetXchange (GNX), another supplier of e-commerce software and services.

Global Sources provides an online business-to-business marketplace for import/export traders. Its Web site allows some 420,000 buyers to search through products from 130,000 suppliers located in 200 countries, with a strong focus on the Chinese market. Global Sources also sponsors exhibitions and provides such e-commerce services as private online catalogs and supply chain management. The company concentrates primarily on such industries as fashion accessories, hardware, electronics, and gifts.

NEGOTIATING WITH VENDORS

William Alcorn, JCPenney's Chief Purchasing Officer, (far left) watches the bids on a reverse auction with his associates.

When buying national brands or sourcing private-label merchandise, buyers and firm employees responsible for sourcing typically enter into negotiations with suppliers To describe how buyers negotiate with vendors, consider a hypothetical situation in which Carolyn Swigler, women's jeans buyer at Bloomingdale's, is preparing to meet with Dario Carvel, the salesperson from Juicy Couture, in his office in New York City. Swigler, after reviewing the merchandise during the womenswear market week in New York, is ready to buy Juicy Couture's spring line, but she has some merchandising problems that have yet to be resolved from last season.

Retailing View 14.4 illustrates how a small vendor can effectively resolve its differences with a very large retailer.

Knowledge Is Power

The more Carolyn Swigler knows about her situation and Juicy Couture's, as well as the trends in the marketplace, the more effective she will be during the negotiations. First, Swigler assesses the relationship she has with the vendor. Although Swigler and Carvel have only met a few times in the past, their companies have had a long, profitable relationship. A sense of trust and mutual respect has been established, which Swigler feels will lead to a productive meeting.

Although Juicy Couture jeans have been profitable for Bloomingdale's in the past, three styles sold poorly last season. Swigler plans to ask Carvel to let her return some merchandise. Swigler knows from past experience that Juicy Couture normally doesn't allow merchandise to be returned but does provide **markdown money**—funds vendors give retailers to cover lost gross margin dollars due to the markdowns needed to sell unpopular merchandise.

Vendors and their representatives are excellent sources of market information. They generally know what is and isn't selling. Providing good, timely information about the market is an indispensable and inexpensive marketing research tool. So Swigler plans to spend at least part of the meeting talking to Carvel about market trends.

Just as Carvel can provide market information to Swigler, she can provide information to him. For example, on one of her buying trips to England, she found a great new wash made by a

When negotiating with a vendor, the more knowledge that is available about the vendor, the market, and the products, the more successful the negotiation will be.

David versus Goliath: Negotiating with the Big Boys   RETAILING VIEW   14.4

If Wal-Mart says jump, usually its suppliers simply ask how high, but not always. Global Vision Inc. is one of 61,000 U.S. suppliers to Wal-Mart. It buys excess inventory of name-brand clothing and accessories, such as Ray Ban sunglasses, Polo Ralph Lauren shirts, and Calvin Klein jeans, and sells them to discount retailers based in Latin America, Europe, and Asia.

Global Vision's disagreement with Wal-Mart began when a buyer for the company's Sam's Club 9 outlets in Puerto Rico called the company's owner, Romano Pontes with a request. She wanted about 4,000 Ocean Pacific cargo pants in a special cut. Pontes delivered the order, but within a few months, the buyer said they weren't selling well. Pontes says that he told Wal-Mart he would try to resell the clothes to stores in another nearby country, but before he could do so, Wal-Mart shipped the merchandise back to his La Jolla, California, warehouse and deducted the purchase price from what it owed his company. Wal-Mart disputes this claim, saying Global agreed to take the pants back and that the reason for the return was that the merchandise was defective.

Pontes recalls some advice that Wal-Mart's founder Sam Walton gave him: "If you believe in a point, scream it as loud as you can to whomever will listen to you." Taking Walton's advice, Pontes tried to work with his Wal-Mart buyers. When that didn't work, he told a senior executive in the finance department that he could produce documentation that the merchandise wasn't defective and challenged Wal-Mart to prove that it was. Pontes also indicated that he wasn't going to

deliver Sam's Club's next order for its Puerto Rico stores. He then contacted his warehouse employees and told them to stop shipment of pending Wal-Mart orders to stores in about three or four countries.

A conference call was set up between Pontes and a general merchandise manager. But two hours before the scheduled call, Pontes canceled and sent an e-mail instead, claiming he had stopped shipments on Wal-Mart orders to locations around the world. He added that other buyers in Puerto Rico were interested in buying Wal-Mart's 1,296-piece order of t-shirts and board shorts by Quicksilver, a trendy teen brand. Less than two hours later, Wal-Mart e-mailed back, saying it would pay for the original Ocean Pacific order and wanted it shipped back to Puerto Rico.

Global's hard-line approach to this problem worked. Pontes recognized that his firm's long-term relationship with Wal-Mart was important to both parties. Wal-Mart wanted Global's merchandise in the future and was willing to sacrifice a little profit in the short term to make much more profit in the future. Pontes presented a sound rationale for taking the action he did, based on a thorough knowledge of what had happened and a sense of history regarding how things work at Wal-Mart. Pontes stood up for what he thought was right. This time, he won.

Source: Ann Zimmerman, "Working Things Out With a Giant Customer," *The Wall Street Journal*, October 17, 2006 (accessed **January 25, 2008**); www.globalvision.us (accessed October 15, 2007).

small English firm. She bought a pair and gave it to Carvel, who passed it along to Juicy Couture's designers. They used the jeans to develop a new wash that was a big success.

Swigler also knows that Carvel will want her to buy some of the newest and most avant-garde designs in Juicy Couture's spring product line. Carvel knows that many U.S. buyers go to market in New York and that most stop at Bloomingdale's to see what's new, what's selling, and how it's displayed. Thus, Carvel wants to make sure that Juicy Couture is well represented at Bloomingdale's.

Negotiation Issues

In addition to taking care of last season's leftover merchandise, Swigler is prepared to discuss six issues during the upcoming meeting: (1) prices and gross margin, (2) special margin-enhancing opportunities, (3) terms of purchase, (4) exclusivity, (5) advertising allowances, and (6) transportation.

Price and Gross Margin   Of course, Swigler wants to buy the merchandise at a low price so she will have a high gross margin. In contrast, Carvel wants to sell the jeans at a higher price because he is concerned about Juicy Couture's profits. Two factors that affect the price and gross margin are margin guarantees and slotting allowances.

Margin Guarantees   Swigler, like most buyers, has a gross margin goal for each merchandise category that is quantified in her merchandise budget plans (Chapter 13). The wholesale price Swigler negotiates for the Juicy Couture merchandise might enable her to achieve her gross margin goal. However, if the merchandise does not sell as expected, Swigler might have to put the items on sale, and she will not make her margin goal. Faced with this uncertainty, Swigler, and other buyers, may seek a commitment from Juicy Couture to "guarantee" that she will realize her gross margin goal on the merchandise. If she has to markdown the merchandise, she wants Juicy Couture to provide her with markdown money.

Carvel, like many vendors, might be willing to provide this gross margin guarantee. However, Carvel is concerned that Swigler might not aggressively promote Juicy Couture's merchandise if she knows that her gross margin is guaranteed. Thus, Carvel will only offer the guarantee in exchange for a commitment from Swigler that she will feature Juicy Couture merchandise in the store and advertise the product line.

Slotting Allowances   In addition to negotiating the wholesale price, supermarket buyers often negotiate slotting fees. **Slotting allowances** or **slotting fees** are charges imposed by a retailer to stock a new item. When a vendor agrees to pay that fee, the retailer will stock the product for period of time, assess its sales and margin, and, if successful, continue to offer the product after the trial period. For example, when Kraft wants to introduce a new product, supermarket chains might charge between $1 and $2 million for a national rollout to stock the product. The fee varies depending on the nature of the product and the relative power of the retailer. Products with low brand loyalty pay the highest slotting allowances. Likewise, large supermarket chains can demand higher slotting allowances than small, independent retailers.

Vendors may view slotting allowances as extortion, and small vendors believe these fees preclude their access to retail stores. However, retailers, and most economists, argue that slotting allowances are a useful method for retailers to determine which new products merit inclusion in their assortment. The vendor has more information than the retailer about the quality of its new product. Thus, the slotting fee is a method for getting the vendor to reveal this private information. If the new product is good, the vendor will be willing to pay the fee, because it knows the product will sell and generate adequate margins during the trial period. However, a vendor promoting a poor product will be reluctant to pay the fee.[31]

Additional Markup Opportunities   At times in the past, Juicy Couture has offered Swigler discounted prices to take excess merchandise. This excessive merchandise arises from order cancellations, returned merchandise from other retailers, or simply an overly optimistic sales forecast. Although Swigler can realize higher-than-normal gross margins on this merchandise or put the merchandise on sale and pass the savings on to customers, Bloomingdale's has to preserve its image as a fashion leader, and thus, Swigler is not very interested in any excess inventory that Juicy Couture has to offer.

Terms of Purchase   Swigler would like to negotiate for a long time period in which to pay for merchandise. A long payment period improves Bloomindale's cash flow, lowers its liabilities (accounts payable), and can reduce its interest expense if it's borrowing money from financial institutions to pay for its inventory. But Juicy Couture also has its own financial objectives it wants to accomplish and thus would like to be paid soon after it delivers the merchandise.

Exclusivity   Retailers often negotiate with vendors for an exclusive arrangement so that no other retailer can sell the same item or brand. Through these exclusive arrangements, retailers can differentiate themselves from competitors and realize higher margins due to reduced price competition. In some cases, vendors also benefit by making sure that the image of retailers selling their merchandise is consistent with their brand image. For example, Prada might want to give exclusive rights for its apparel to only one store in a major market, such as Neiman Marcus. In addition, an exclusive arrangement offers a monopoly to the retailer and, thus, a strong incentive to promote the item.

In fashion merchandise categories, being the first retailer in a market to carry certain products helps that retailer hold a fashion-leader image and achieve a differential advantage. Swigler wants her shipment of the new spring line to arrive as early in the season as possible and would like to have some jeans styles and washes that won't be sold to competing retailers. In contrast, Juicy Couture wants to have its products sold by many different retailers to maximize its sales.

Advertising Allowances   Retailers often share the cost of advertising through a cooperative arrangement with vendors known as **co-op (cooperative) advertising**—a program undertaken by a vendor in which the vendor agrees to pay for all or part of a pricing promotion. As a fashion leader, Bloomingdale's advertises heavily. Swigler would like Juicy Couture to support an advertising program with a generous advertising allowance.

Transportation   Transportation costs can be substantial, though this point isn't a big issue for the Juicy Couture jeans because their merchandise has a high unit price and low weight. Nonetheless, the question of who pays for shipping merchandise from the vendor to the retailer will be a significant negotiating point.

Now that some of the issues involved in the negotiation between Juicy Couture and Bloomingdale's are on the table, the next section presents some tips for effective negotiations.

Tips for Effective Negotiating[32]

Have at Least as Many Negotiators as the Vendor   Retailers have a psychological advantage at the negotiating table if the vendor is outnumbered. At the very least, retailers want the negotiating teams to be the same size. Swigler plans to invite her DMM (divisional merchandise manager) into the discussion if Carvel comes with his sales manager.

Choose a Good Place to Negotiate   Swigler may have an advantage in the upcoming meeting because it will be in her office. She'll have ready access to information, plus secretarial and supervisory assistance. From a psychological perspective, people generally feel more comfortable and confident in familiar surroundings. However, Swigler also might get more out of the negotiation if Carvel feels comfortable. In the end, selecting the location for a negotiation is an important decision.

Be Aware of Real Deadlines   Swigler recognizes that Carvel must go back to his office with an order in hand, because he has a quota to meet by the end of the month. She also knows that she must get markdown money or permission to return the unsold jeans by the end of the week or she won't have sufficient open-to-buy to cover the orders she wishes to place. Recognizing these deadlines will help Swigler come to closure quickly in the upcoming negotiation.

Separate the People from the Problem   Suppose Swigler starts the meeting with, "Dario, you know we've been friends for a long time. I have a personal favor to ask. Would you mind taking back $10,000 in shirts?" This personal plea puts Carvel in an uncomfortable situation. Swigler's personal relationship with Carvel isn't the issue here and shouldn't become part of the negotiation. An equally detrimental scenario would be for Swigler to say, "Dario, your line is terrible. I can hardly give the stuff away. I want you to take back $10,000 in jeans. After all, you're dealing with Bloomingdale's. If you don't take this junk back, you can forget about ever doing business with us again." Threats usually don't work in negotiations. They put the other party on the defensive. Threats may actually cause negotiations to break down, in which case no one wins.

Insist on Objective Information   The best way to separate the people from the business issues is to rely on objective information. Swigler must know exactly how many jeans need to be returned to Juicy Couture or how much markdown money is necessary to maintain her gross margin. If Carvel argues from an emotional perspective, Swigler will stick to the numbers. For instance, suppose that after Swigler presents her position, Carvel says that he'll get into trouble if he takes back the merchandise or provides markdown money. With the knowledge that Juicy Couture has provided relief in similar situations in the past, Swigler should ask what Juicy Couture's policy is regarding customer overstock problems. She should also show Carvel a summary of Bloomingdale's buying activity with Juicy Couture over the past few seasons. Using this approach, Swigler forces Carvel to acknowledge that providing assistance in this overstock situation— especially if it has been done in the past—is a small price to pay for a long-term profitable relationship.

Invent Options for Mutual Gain   Inventing multiple options is part of the planning process, but knowing when and how much to give, or give up, requires quick thinking at the bargaining table. Consider Swigler's overstock problem. Her objective is to get the merchandise out of her inventory without significantly hurting her gross margin. Carvel's objective is to maintain a healthy yet profitable relationship with Bloomingdale's. Thus, Swigler must invent options that could satisfy both parties, such as offering to buy some of Juicy Couture's most avant-garde jeans in return for markdown money for her excess inventory.

Let Them Do the Talking   There's a natural tendency for one person to continue to talk if the other person involved in the conversation doesn't respond. If used properly, this phenomenon can work to the negotiator's advantage. Suppose Swigler asks Carvel for special financial support for Bloomingdale's Christmas catalog. Carvel begins with a qualified no and cites all the reasons he can't cooperate. But Swigler doesn't say a word. Although Carvel appears nervous, he continues to talk. Eventually, he comes around to a yes. In negotiations, those who break the silence first, lose.

Know How Far to Go   There's a fine line between negotiating too hard and walking away from the table without an agreement. If Swigler negotiates too aggressively for the markdown money, better terms of purchase, and a strong advertising allowance, the management of Juicy Couture may decide that other retailers are more worthy of early deliveries and the best styles. Carvel may not be afraid to say no if Swigler pushes him beyond a legal, ethical, profitable relationship.

Don't Burn Bridges   Even if Swigler gets few additional concessions from Carvel, she shouldn't be abusive or resort to threats. Bloomingdale's may not wish to stop doing business with Juicy Couture on the basis of this one encounter. From a personal perspective, the world of retailing is relatively small. Swigler and Carvel may meet at the negotiating table again, possibly both working for different companies. Neither can afford to be known in the trade as unfair, rude, or worse.

Don't Assume   Many issues are raised and resolved in any negotiating session. To be certain there are no misunderstandings, participants should orally review the outcomes at the end of the session. Swigler and Carvel should both summarize the session in writing as soon as possible after the meeting.

STRATEGIC RELATIONSHIPS

Chapter 5 emphasized that maintaining strong vendor relationships is an important method to develop a sustainable competitive advantage. Chapters 10 and 12 discussed some of the ways partnering relations can improve information exchange, planning, and the management of supply chains. For example, collaborative planning, forecasting, and replenishment (CPFR) systems cannot operate effectively without the vendor and retailer making a commitment to work together and invest in the relationship. In this section, we examine how retailers can develop strategic relationships and the characteristics of successful long-term relationships.

Defining Strategic Relationships

Traditionally, relationships between retailers and vendors have focused on haggling over how to split up a profit pie.[33] The relationships were basically win–lose encounters because when one party got a larger portion of the pie, the other party got a smaller portion. Both parties were interested exclusively in their own profits and unconcerned about the other party's welfare. These relationships continue to be common, especially when the products being bought are commodities and have limited impact on the retailers' performance. Thus, there is no benefit to the retailer to enter into a strategic relationship.

A **strategic relationship,** also called a **partnering relationship,** emerges when a retailer and vendor are committed to maintaining the relationship over the long term and investing in opportunities that are mutually beneficial to both parties. In these relationships, it's important for the partners to take risks to expand the profit pie to give the relationship a strategic advantage over other companies. In addition, the parties have a long-term perspective. They are willing to make short-term sacrifices because they know that they will get their fair share in the long run.

Strategic relationships are win–win relationships. Both parties benefit because the size of the profit pie increases. —Both the retailer and vendor increase their sales and profits because the parties in strategic relationships work together to develop and exploit joint opportunities. They depend on and trust each other heavily. They share goals and agree on how to accomplish those goals and they thus reduce the risks of investing in the relationship and sharing confidential information.

A strategic relationship is like a marriage. When businesses enter strategic relationships, they're wedded to their partners for better or worse. For example, Michaels Stores Inc., the largest retail arts and crafts store chain in the United States, was having lots of supply chain problems with some of its vendors.[34] Vendors shipped items in inconvenient quantities from a storage perspective, shipping cartons came into their distribution center improperly marked, vendors combined orders without informing Michaels, and merchandise was coming in damaged. Instead of replacing the offending retailers, Michaels formed a Supply Chain Vendor Relations team to inform, educate, and interact with its vendors and prevent problems that kept merchandise from flowing efficiently throughout the supply chain.

Maintaining Strategic Relationships

The four foundations of successful strategic relationships are mutual trust, open communication, common goals, and credible commitments.

Mutual Trust   The glue in a strategic relationship is trust. **Trust** is a belief that a partner is honest (reliable and stands by its word) and benevolent (concerned about the other party's welfare).[36] When vendors and buyers trust each other, they're more willing to share relevant ideas, clarify goals and problems, and communicate efficiently. Information shared between the parties becomes increasingly comprehensive, accurate, and timely. There's less need for the vendor and buyer to constantly monitor and check up on each other's actions, because each believes the other will not take advantage, even given the opportunity.[37]

Strategic relationships and trust are often developed initially between the leaders of organizations. For example, when Wal-Mart started to work with Procter & Gamble to coordinate its buying activities, Sam Walton got together with P&G's vice president of sales on a canoeing trip. They discussed the mutual benefits of cooperating and the potential risks associated with altering their normal business practices. In the end, they concluded that the potential long-term gains were worth the additional risks and short-term setbacks that would probably occur as they developed the new systems.

Open Communication   To share information, develop sales forecasts together, and coordinate deliveries, Wal-Mart and P&G have open and honest communication. This requirement may sound easy in principle, but most businesses don't like to share information with their business partners. They believe it is none of the other's business. But open, honest communication is a key to developing successful relationships. Buyers and vendors in a relationship need to understand what is driving each other's business, their roles in the relationship, each firm's strategies, and any problems that arise over the course of the relationship.

Common Goals   Vendors and buyers must have common goals for a successful relationship to develop. Shared goals give both members of the relationship an incentive to pool their strengths and abilities and exploit potential opportunities between them. They also create an assurance that the other partner will not do anything to hinder goal achievement within the relationship.

For example, Wal-Mart and P&G recognized that it was in their common interest to remain business partners—they needed each other—and to do so, both

REFACT

Bentonville, Arkansas, the corporate headquarters for Wal-Mart, has a population of 32,000. More than 450 companies that are suppliers to Wal-Mart have opened offices in Bentonville, otherwise known as Vendorville, including Microsoft, Oracle, Rubbermaid, Disney, Dreamworks, and Procter & Gamble.[35]

had to be allowed to make profitable transactions. Wal-Mart can't demand prices so low that P&G won't make money, and P&G must be flexible enough to accommodate the needs of its biggest customer. With a common goal, both firms have an incentive to cooperate, because they know that by doing so, each can boost sales. Common goals also help sustain the relationship when expected benefit flows aren't realized. If one P&G shipment fails to reach a Wal-Mart store on time due to an uncontrollable event like misrouting by a trucking firm, Wal-Mart won't suddenly call off the whole arrangement. Instead, Wal-Mart is likely to view the incident as a simple mistake and remain in the relationship, because it knows that it and P&G are committed to the same goals in the long run.

Credible Commitments   Successful relationships develop because both parties make credible commitments. Credible commitments are tangible investments in the relationship. They go beyond just making the hollow statement, "I want to be your partner." Credible commitments involve spending money to improve the supplier's products or services provided to the customer. For example, one of the strengths of the Wal-Mart–P&G partnership is the obvious and significant investments both parties have made in CPFR systems and material handling equipment.

Building Partnering Relationships

Although not all retailer–vendor relationships should or do become strategic partnerships, the development of strategic partnerships tends to go through a series of phases characterized by increasing levels of commitment: (1) awareness, (2) exploration, (3) expansion, and (4) commitment.

Awareness   In the awareness stage, no transactions have taken place. This phase might begin with the buyer seeing some interesting merchandise at a retail market or an ad in a trade magazine. The reputation and image of the vendor can play an important role in determining if the buyer moves to the next stage.

Exploration   During the exploration phase, the buyer and vendor begin to explore the potential benefits and costs of a partnership. At this point, the buyer may make a small purchase and try to test the demand for the merchandise in several stores. In addition, the buyer will get information about how easy it is to work with the vendor.

Expansion   Eventually, the buyer has collected enough information about the vendor to consider developing a longer-term relationship. The buyer and the vendor determine if there is the potential for a win–win relationship. They begin to work on joint promotional programs, and the amount of merchandise sold increases.

Commitment   If both parties continue to find the relationship mutually beneficial, it moves to the commitment stage and becomes a strategic relationship. The buyer and vendor then make significant investments in the relationship and develop a long-term perspective toward it.

It is difficult for retailer–vendor relationships to be as committed as some supplier–manufacturer relationships. Manufacturers can enter into monogamous (sole source) relationships with other manufacturers. However, an important function of retailers is to provide an assortment of merchandise for their customers. Thus, they must always deal with multiple, sometimes competing suppliers.

Regardless of which partner-building phase a retailer is in with a supplier, it is constantly involved in the give-and-take process of negotiations. The next section looks at some of the legal and ethical issues that arise when buying merchandise.

LEGAL AND ETHICAL ISSUES FOR BUYING MERCHANDISE

Given the many negotiations and interactions between retail buyers and vendors, ethical and legal issues are bound to arise. This section reviews some practices that arise in buyer–vendor negotiations that may have legal and/or ethical implications. Retailing View 14.5 examines some recent socially responsible retail buying initiatives.

Terms and Conditions of Purchase   The Robinson-Patman Act, passed by the U.S. Congress in 1936, potentially restricts the prices and terms that vendors can offer to retailers. The Act forbids vendors from offering different terms and conditions to different retailers for the same merchandise and quantity. Sometimes called the "Anti-Chain-Store Act," it was passed to protect independent retailers from chain-store competition. Thus, if a vendor negotiates a good deal on the issues discussed in the previous section (price, advertising allowance, markdown money, transportation), the Robinson-Patman Act requires the vendor to offer the same terms and conditions to other retailers.

However, vendors can offer different terms to retailers for the same merchandise and quantities if the costs of manufacturing, selling, or delivery are different. The cost of manufacturing is usually the same, but selling and delivery could be more expensive for some retailers. For example, vendors may incur larger transportation expenses due to smaller shipments to independent retailers.

Different prices can also be offered if the retailers are providing different functions. For example, a large retailer can get a lower price if its distribution centers store the merchandise or its stores provide different services valued by customers. In addition, lower prices can be offered to meet competition and dispose of perishable merchandise.[38]

Resale Price Maintenance   Resale price maintenance (RPM) is a requirement imposed by a vendor that a retailer cannot sell an item for less than a specific price—the **manufacturer's suggested retail price (MSRP).** Such RPM has been in effect, off and on, since the passage of the Sherman Antitrust Act almost 100 years ago. Recently, however, the U.S. Supreme Court ruled that RPMs are not automatically an antitrust violation.

Vendors place this restriction on retail prices so that the retailers will have an adequate margin to provide the services needed to sell the vendors' products. For example, suppose Bose feels that its retailers need to have a specially designed soundproof room to demonstrate the quality of its speakers to customers. An audio specialty retailer selling Bose speakers would incur the additional cost of building and maintaining this special room in its stores. But the retailer might not make additional sales. Consumers experiencing the quality of Bose speakers in the specialty store may buy the speakers at a discount store for a lower price. The discount store can sell the speakers at a lower cost because it did not have to incur the costs of building and maintaining the special room.

In this situation, the discount store is **free riding** on the specialty store's services. It is taking more than its fair share of the benefits but not incurring its fair share of the costs. Thus, RPM is an approach for reducing free riding. If all retailers are required to charge the same price for Bose speakers, they will have an incentive to compete on service rather than price, which will enable Bose to demonstrate the superior quality of its speakers to consumers. Although RPM has been viewed as a restraint of competition and thus illegal in the past, it is now legal, as long as it promotes interbrand competition—competition between Bose and other speaker vendors. Vendors can require retailers to sell its products at the MSRP and refuse to sell its products to a discounter if they price products below the MSRP.

Some retailers, however, do not appreciate RPM. Their position is that they own the merchandise, and they should be able to sell it for whatever they like.

Corporate social responsibility describes the voluntary actions taken by a company to address the ethical, social, and environmental impacts of its business operations. Retailers act socially responsible in many ways, from giving to charity to donating time to philanthropic community activities. Recently, however, retailers are increasing their efforts to buy merchandise in a socially responsible way.

Whole Foods is increasing its efforts to provide locally grown produce to support the local economy and save carbon emissions involved in transporting produce from distant producers. It requires all its stores to buy from at least four local farmers. It gives $10 million a year in low-interest loans to help small, local farmers and producers of grass-fed and humanely raised meat, poultry, and dairy animals. It also has hired an "animal compassionate field buyer" to work with producers to ensure they meet standards of humane care for the animals that supply meat, eggs, and dairy to its stores.

Some retailers are getting involved in **fair trade,** a socially responsible movement that ensures that producers receive fair prices for their products. The coffee retailers Starbucks and Peet's offer some, but not all, blends that use fair trade coffee. Wal-Mart is investing heavily in fair trade coffee, partially in response to a new corporate philosophy that goes beyond "everyday low prices" to "doing well by doing good." Fair Indigo is an online store that features fair trade apparel. Bono, the U2 lead singer and activist, is selling his high-priced fair trade apparel line, Edun, to stores like Saks and Nordstrom

Barneys, the upscale specialty apparel retail chain, has introduced organic and eco-friendly products in all of the product categories it offers. But Barneys also is determined not to make green a "crunchy, granola" affair and plans to include green products as permanent, and growing, parts of its offering. All of the apparel in its Loomstate for Barneys Green product line are made from organic cotton, and two new private-label cosmetic lines are organic and natural. It offers non-leather shoes from Stella McCartney and is developing its own line of non-leather handbags.

Home Depot is encouraging its suppliers to apply to include their products in its Eco Options marketing campaign. Some products are obviously attractive to green customers, such as organic gardening products and high-efficiency light bulbs. But a number of less obvious products are also good for the environment. Electric chain saws are green, because they are not gas-powered, and bug zappers reduce the use of poisonous sprays. Home Depot also has introduced some new environmentally sensitive products into its assortment, including solar-powered landscape lighting, biodegradable peat pots, and paints that discharge fewer pollutants. Home Depot encourages its vendors to use recyclable plastic or cardboard packaging. It estimates

U2 lead singer and activist, Bono, has developed a fair trade line of apparel called Edun that is sold in upscale stores like Saks and Nordstrom.

that a 5 percent reduction in packaging will prevent 667,000 metric tons of carbon dioxide from entering the atmosphere while also resulting in $3.4 billion in cost savings.

Other retailers are demanding smaller, eco-friendly packages from their suppliers. Smaller packages save in not only materials but also energy. Because more packages can be transported on a truck, the transportation cost per unit goes down. Wal-Mart plans to reduce packaging by 5 percent by 2013, a move that could save $3.4 billion.

Another packaging option is to favor paper bags, which are more environmentally friendly than plastic. The U.K. grocery chain Tesco is saving more than 10 million plastic bags a week by offering one loyalty point for every bag returned. A rival U.K. grocer, Sainsbury, has introduced a bag made of one-third recycled plastic. Kroger, Bigg's, Remke Markets, Wild Oats, and Trader Joe's all promote shopping bag recycling programs. Trader Joe's, for example, offers a gift certificate drawing every month for those who reuse their bags. Whole Foods has eliminated plastic bags altogether in favor of paper or BYOB (bring your own bag). Some retailers, like Limited Brands' Victoria's Secret, are considering programs to use more recycled paper in their catalogs.

McDonald's Europe has helped persuade agribusiness giants to stop buying soybeans from newly deforested tracts in protected regions of the Amazon. Wal-Mart is urging its suppliers to combat global warming by using less energy and incorporating alternative sources. Tiffany & Co. has been calling on gold miners to end waste dumping in pristine lakes and adhere to international labor standards.

These initiatives and many others suggest a complicated business model. Are socially responsible activities good for business? Some are more expensive than traditional products and initiatives. In the end, should retailers force more socially responsible products on their customers, or should they wait for customers to ask for them?

Sources: Michelle: Moran, "Green Is the New Black?" *Gourmet Retailer,* August 2007 (accessed October 11, 2007); Clifford Krauss, "At Home Depot, How Green Is That Chainsaw?" *The New York Times,* June 25, 2007 (accessed June 26, 2007); Sharon Edelson, "Barneys' Goal: Bringing Green to Luxury," *WWD,* February 26, 2007 (accessed October 11, 2007); www.globalexchange.org/campaigns/fairtrade/coffee/starbucks.html (accessed October 9, 2007); www.bsi.org (accessed October 9, 2007); Carol Ness, "Whole Foods, Taking Flak, Thinks Local," *San Francisco Chronicle,* July 26, 2006 (accessed January 25, 2008; "Retailers Push Packagers to Think 'Green'," *Reuters,* September 4, 2007; G. Jeffrey MacDonald, "Stopping the Outcry Before It Starts," *Christian Science Monitor,* August 28, 2006 (accessed January 25, 2008); Bob Tedeschi, "A Click on Clothes to Support Fair Trade," *The New York Times,* September 25, 2006 (accessed January 25, 2008); Ylan Q. Mui, "For Wal-Mart, Fair Trade May Be More Than a Hill of Beans," *Washington Post,* June 12, 2006, p. A01.

Suppose Best Buy purchased more Toshiba computers than it really needed for the back-to-school season. It would want the flexibility to reduce the price below the MSRP to either get rid of the excess or generate traffic into the store.

Commercial Bribery   **Commercial bribery** occurs when a vendor or its agent offers or a buyer asks for "something of value" to influence purchase decisions. Say a salesperson for a ski manufacturer takes a sporting goods retail buyer to lunch at a fancy private club and then proposes a ski weekend in Vail. These gifts could be construed as bribes or kickbacks, which are illegal unless the buyer's manager is informed of them. To avoid these problems, many retailers forbid employees to accept any gifts from vendors. Because some Home Depot buyers allegedly accepted large cash kickbacks from suppliers, the retailer has tightened its ethics code to ban buyers from accepting any gifts or entertainment from vendors—a zero tolerance policy.[40] Other retailers have a policy that it is fine to accept limited entertainment or token gifts, such as flowers or wine for the holidays. In either case, they want their buyers to decide on purchases solely on the basis of what is best for the retailer.[41]

Chargebacks   A **chargeback** is a practice used by retailers in which they deduct money from the amount they owe a vendor. Retailers often chargeback vendors when the vendor did not meet the agreed upon terms, such as improperly applied labels to shipping containers or merchandise, missing items in the shipments, or late shipments. Chargebacks are especially difficult for vendors because once the money is deducted from an invoice and the invoice is marked "paid," it is difficult to dispute the claim and get the amount back. Vendors sometime feel that the chargebacks retailers take are not justifiable and thus unethical.[42]

Buybacks   Similar to slotting allowances, **buybacks,** also known as **stocklifts** or **lift-outs,** are activities engaged in by vendors and retailers to get products into retail stores. Specifically, in a buyback situation, a retailer either allows a vendor to create space for its merchandise by "buying back" a competitor's inventory and removing it from a retailer's system, or the retailer forces a vendor to buy back slow-moving merchandise. A vendor with significant market power can violate federal antitrust laws if it stocklifts from a competitor so often as to shut it out of a market, but such cases are difficult to prove.

Counterfeit Merchandise   Selling counterfeit merchandise can negatively affect a retailer's image and its relationship with the vendor of the legitimate brand. **Counterfeit merchandise** includes goods made and sold without the permission of the owner of a trademark or copyright. Trademarks and copyrights are **intellectual property,** that is, intangible and created by intellectual (mental) effort as opposed to physical effort. A **trademark** is any mark, word, picture, device, or nonfunctional design associated with certain merchandise (e.g., the crown on a Rolex watch, the GE on General Electric products). A **copyright** protects the original work of authors, painters, sculptors, musicians, and others who produce works of artistic or intellectual merit. This book is copyrighted, so these sentences cannot be used by anyone without the consent of the copyright owners.

It is illegal for this "street retailer" to sell counterfeit watches, because it violates the watch manufacturers' rights to control the use of their trademarks.

The nature of counterfeiting has changed during the past decade. Counterfeit name-brand merchandise, such as women's handbags, have improved in quality, making them more expensive and difficult to distinguish from the real merchandise. Also, there is a thriving business in counterfeit information products such as software, CDs, and CD-ROMs. This type of merchandise is attractive to counterfeiters because it has a high unit value, is relatively easy to duplicate and transport, and prompts high consumer demand. The ease of illegally downloading and distributing music means that neither the record label nor the artist receives any money for their investment, work, or talent, and thus, both may be less motivated to develop and produce music.

Gray Markets and Diverted Merchandise   **Gray-market goods,** also known as **parallel imports,** refer to the flow of merchandise through distribution channels other than those authorized or intended by the manufacturer or producer. For example, to increase its profits, McGraw-Hill, the publisher of this textbook, charges a higher wholesale price for this textbook in the United States than in other countries. An importer can buy textbooks at a low price in other countries, import them into the United States, and sell them at a price lower than U.S. bookstores.

Diverted merchandise is similar to gray-market merchandise except there need not be distribution across international boundaries. Suppose, for instance, the fragrance manufacturer Givenchy grants an exclusive scent to Saks Fifth Avenue. The Saks buyer has excess inventory and sells the excess inventory at a low price to a discount retailer, such as an off-price retailer or a extreme value retailer. In this case, the merchandise has been diverted from its legitimate channel of distribution, and Saks would be referred to as the diverter. While Saks may benefit from this transaction, the vendor is concerned about gray markets and diversions. Making the product available at discount stores at low prices may reduce the vendor's brand image and the service normally provided with the brand.

Vendors engage in a number of activities to avoid gray-market/diverting problems. They require all of their retail and wholesale customers to sign a contract stipulating that they will not engage in gray marketing. If a retailer is found in violation of the agreement, the vendor will refuse to deal with it in the future. Another strategy is to produce different versions of products for different markets. For instance, McGraw-Hill sells a different version of this textbook in India than it sells in the United States. Retailing View 14.6 examines why it is hard to tell whether merchandise is gray market or counterfeit.

Exclusive Dealing Agreements   **Exclusive dealing agreements** occur when a vendor restricts a retailer to carrying only its products and nothing from competing vendors. For example, Ford may require its dealers to sell only Ford cars and no cars made by General Motors. The effect of these arrangements on competition is determined by the market power of the vendor. For example, it may be illegal for the market leader like Coca-Cola to only sell its products to a small supermarket chain, if the chain agrees not to sell a less popular Cola product like R.C. Cola.

Tying Contract   A **tying contract** exists when a vendor requires a retailer to take a product it doesn't necessarily desire (the tied product) to ensure that it can buy a product it does desire (the tying product). Tying contracts are illegal if they substantially lessen competition or tend to create a monopoly, but the complaining party has the burden of proof. Thus, it is typically legal for a vendor to require a buyer to buy all items in its product line. For example, if a gift store sued a postcard manufactuer for requiring that it purchase as many "local view" postcards (the tied product) as it did licensed Disney character postcards (the tying product), the court would probably dismiss the case because the retailer would be unable to prove a substantial lessening of competition.

Refusal to Deal   The practice of refusing to deal (buy or sell to) can be viewed from both vendors' and retailers' perspectives. Generally, both vendors and retailers have the right to deal or refuse to deal with anyone they choose. But there are exceptions to this general rule when there's evidence of anticompetitive conduct by one or more firms that wield market power. A vendor may refuse to sell to a particular retailer, but it can't do so for the sole purpose of benefiting a competing retailer. For example, Mattel decided not to offer certain popular Barbie packages to wholesale clubs. This action in itself would have been legal. However, it was

---

14.6   **RETAILING VIEW**   Where Did T.J. Maxx Get Its Coach Handbags?

The national brands that off-price retailers like T.J. Maxx, Marshalls, Ross, and Loehmann's sell at lower prices than their department and specialty store competition come from a variety of sources. Sometimes the merchandise comes directly from manufacturers like Coach, the luxury leather goods maker, because the item was last year's model, it didn't sell well at retail and was returned by its luxury retail customer, or Coach overestimated demand and therefore had excess inventory leftover. Coach in particular sells less than 1% of its bags to off-price stores. Although luxury manufacturers prefer not to have their merchandise sold in off-price stores, having these off-price stores provide an excellent opportunity to rid the luxury manufacturers of excess inventory.

Another source of Coach bags for off-price retailers may be luxury retailers. These retailers may have bought too many bags or specific styles that did not sell and need to dispose of them at them at the end of a season. One alternative is for the retailers to mark down the price and put the handbags on sale. But sales on luxury products like Coach bags might damage the retailer's image. Also, Coach may not want their bags sold at a discount at luxury stores. So, the retailer might sell the excess inventory to off-price retailers like T.J. Maxx. This diverting of merchandise to an unauthorized retailer is creating a gray market for the Coach bags. If Coach discovers that one of its luxury retailers is diverting its newer merchandise to off-price retailers, it might refuse to sell to the retailer in the future.

Luxury brands' vendors hope that their products don't end up in off-price outlets, but they definitely fight to make sure that counterfeit products are not sold anywhere. While it is relatively harmless for gray market luxury branded products to end up in an off-price store, it is quite harmful to the luxury brands if a counterfeit bag is sold in a Wal-Mart store.

Off-price stores like T.J. Maxx regularly sell gray market, but not counterfeit merchandise.

Since the sale of counterfeit goods is illegal. Luxury brand vendors are taking steps to insure that national retailers will not partake in their sale. Coach recently sued Target for selling counterfeit Coach bags in its stores. Similarly, the luxury conglomerate, LVMH, sued Wal-Mart Stores for selling fake Fendi bags in its stores. In both of these cases, the vendors are very concerned that the image of their products will be damaged by having counterfeit merchandise sold in a discount store. Although it has not been confirmed as to whether these products were authentic or not, the publicity surrounding these lawsuits raise the question in consumers' minds as to whether luxury brands sold in discount stores such as Wal-Mart and Target are real.

REFACT

TJX, owner of TJ Maxx and Marshalls, employs 400 buyers who purchase from more than 10,000 vendors in over 60 countries.[43]

determined that Mattel agreed to do so as part of a conspiracy among 10 toy manufacturers orchestrated by Toys "R" Us to prevent wholesale clubs from underselling the same toy packages that Toys "R" Us sold. The refusal to deal then became an illegal group boycott.[44]

In summary, any time buyers and vendors interact, there's a potential for ethical and legal problems. Buyers face issues such as how much to charge a vendor for shelf space in their stores or whether they should accept a gift or favor from a vendor with no strings attached. An eye toward fairness and the desire to maintain a strong relationship should dictate behavior in these areas. Retailers must also be concerned with the origin of their merchandise. Specifically, is it counterfeit or gray-market merchandise?

SUMMARY

This chapter examines issues surrounding purchasing merchandise and vendor relations. Retailers can purchase either national brands or private-label brands. Each type has its own relative advantages. Choosing appropriate brands and a branding strategy is an integral component of a firm's merchandise and assortment planning process.

Buyers of manufacturer's brands attend trade shows and wholesale market centers to meet with vendors, view new merchandise, and place orders. Virtually every merchandise category has at least one annual trade show at which retailers and vendors meet.

The process for buying private-label merchandise can be more complicated than that for buying national brands, because the retailer takes on some of the responsibilities that a national brand manufacturer normally would have, such as designing and specifying products and selecting manufactuers to make the products. A large percentage of private-label merchandise is manufactured outside of the United States. The cost, managerial, and ethical issues surrounding global sourcing decisions must be considered.

Buying merchandise sometimes is facilitated by resident buying offices. Market representatives of these resident buying offices facilitate merchandising purchases in foreign markets.

Buyers of both national brands and private labels engage in negotiating a series of issues with their vendors, including markdown money, slotting fees, advertising allowances, terms of purchase, exclusivity, and transportation costs. Successful vendor relationships depend on planning for and being adept at negotiations.

Retailers that can successfully team up with their vendors can achieve a sustainable competitive advantage. There needs to be more than just a promise to buy and sell on a regular basis. Strategic relationships require trust, shared goals, strong communications, and a financial commitment.

Buyers need to be aware of ethical and legal issues to guide them in their negotiations and purchase decisions. There are also problems associated with counterfeit and gray-market merchandise and issues that vendors face when selling to retailers, such as exclusive territories and tying contracts. Care should be taken by vendors when placing restrictions on which retailers they will sell to, what merchandise, how much, and at what price.

KEY TERMS

buybacks, *406*

chargeback, *406*

commercial bribery, *406*

cooperative advertising, *399*

copycat brands, *387*

copyright, *406*

corporate social responsibility, *405*

counterfeit merchandise, *406*

diverted merchandise, *407*

duties, *394*

exclusive co-brands, *387*

exclusive dealing agreements, *407*

fair trade, *405*

free riding, *404*

generic brands, *387*

gray-market goods, *407*

house brands, *385*

intellectual property, *406*

lift-outs, *406*

manufacturer's brands, *384*

manufacturer suggested retail price (MSRP), *404*

markdown money, *397*

market weeks, *390*

national brands, *384*

own brands, *385*

parallel imports, *407*

partnering relationship, *401*

premium branding, *386*

private-label brands, *385*

resale price maintenance (RPM), *404*

resident buying offices, *395*

retail exchanges, *396*

reverse auctions, *394*

slotting allowances, *398*

slotting fees, *398*

stocklifts, *406*

store brands, *385*

strategic relationship, *401*

tariffs, *394*

trade shows, *390*

trademark, *406*

trust, *402*

tying contract, *407*

wholesale market, *390*

GET OUT AND DO IT!

1. **CONTINUING ASSIGNMENT** Go visit the retailer you have selected for the continuing assignment and perform an audit of its manufacturer's and private brands. Interview a manager to determine whether the percentage of private brands has increased or decreased during the past five years. Ask the manager to comment on the store's philosophy toward manufacturer's versus private brands. On the basis of what you see and hear, assess its branding strategy.

2. Go to the Immigration and Customs Enforcement (ICE) homepage, an investigative branch of the Department of Homeland Security (DHS), at www.ice.gov, and find out what this federal agency is responsible for in terms of preventing counterfeit merchandise from entering the United States.

3. Go to the home page for the Private Label Manufacturers Association (PLMA) and read the "Market Profile," which can be found at www.plma.com/storeBrands/sbt05.html. What are store brand products? Who purchases store brands? Who makes store brands? What store brands are you purchasing on a regular basis?

4. Read the feature article, "Changing the Face of Private Labels," written by Dale Buss about private-label cosmetics at Kohl's, available at www. brandchannel.com/features_ effect.asp?pf_id5209. What are the major benefits from the retailer's perspective of offering an Estée Lauder–developed private-label brand of cosmetics in Kohl's department stores? Discuss why Estée Lauder is interested in developing a private-label brand of cosmetics, based on the forces fueling retailer power and the interdependence between retail business partners.

5. Go to your favorite food store and look up the prices for the items in the following table. Be sure to select the same-sized packages for this price comparison of manufacturer's brands and store brands. How much can consumers save by purchasing private label brands of these products? How would you compare the percentage of savings on different categories of merchandise? How did the various grocery stores selected by the class compare in terms of price savings on their private label brands versus the national brands?

	Raspberry Cereal Bars	Coffee	Macaroni & Cheese Mix	Tissues	Cola
National brand					
Private label brand					

DISCUSSION QUESTIONS AND PROBLEMS

1. Assume you have been hired to consult with The Gap on sourcing decisions for sportswear. What issues would you consider when deciding whether you should buy from Mexico or China, or find a source within the United States?

2. What is the difference between counterfeit and gray-market merchandise? Is the selling of either legal? Do you believe that the selling of counterfeit merchandise should be allowed? What about gray-market merchandise? Provide a rationale for your positions.

3. What are the advantages and disadvantages of manufacturer's brands versus private-label brands? Does your favorite clothing store have a strong private-label brand strategy? Should it?

4. How can a private-label brand help a retailer build store loyalty?

5. Explain why a grocery store, such as Kroger, offers more than one private-label brand within a particular product category.

6. Why have retailers found exclusive private labels to be an appealing branding option? Choose a department store, a discount store, and a grocery store. What exclusive private-label brands do they offer? How are they positioned in relation to their national brand counterparts?

7. For which product categories do you prefer private labels or national brands? Explain your preference.

8. What are retailers doing to be more socially responsible in buying merchandise? Why are they becoming more socially responsible? Do you buy products that you believe were produced in a socially responsible manner, even if they cost more?

9. You have decided that you don't want to take the final in this class. Explain how you would plan and operationalize a negotiation with the instructor.

SUGGESTED READINGS

Amrouche, Nawel and Georges Zaccour. "Shelf-Space Allocation of National and Private Brands." *European Journal of Operational Research* 180, no. 2 (2007), pp. 648–63.

Anderson, Erin and Sandy D. Jap. "The Dark-Side of Close Relationships." *Sloan Management Review* 46, no. 3 (2005), pp. 75–82.

Deleersnyder, Barbara; Marnik G. Dekimpe; Jan-Benedict E.M. Steenkamp; and Oliver Koll. "Win–Win Strategies at Discount Stores." *Journal of Retailing & Consumer Services* 14 (September 2007), pp. 309–18.

Diamond, Jay. *Retail Buying*, 8th ed. Upper Saddle River, NJ: Pearson, 2007.

Hsiu-Li, Chen. "Gray Marketing and its Impacts on Brand Equity." *Journal of Product & Brand Management* 16, no. 4/5 (2007), pp. 247–56.

Jap, Sandy D. "The Impact of Online Reverse Auction Design on Buyer-Supplier Relationships." *Journal of Marketing* 71, no. 1 (2007), pp. 146–59.

Shell, Richard G. *Bargaining for Advantage: Negotiation Strategies for Reasonable People*, 2d ed. New York: Penguin, 2006.

Timmor, Yaron. "Manufacturing for Overseas Private Labels: A Win–Win Strategy for Retailers and Producers." *International Review of Retail, Distribution & Consumer Research* 17, no. 2 (2007), pp. 121–138.

Varley, Rosemary. *Retail Product Management: Buying and Merchandising*, 2nd ed. New York: Routledge, 2005.

Retail Pricing

EXECUTIVE BRIEFING
Mike Pepe, Private Label Brand Manager,
Price Chopper Supermarkets

During high school and college, I worked as a cashier and on the night shift restocking shelves for Grand Union, a Northeast U.S. regional supermarket chain headquartered in New Jersey. I continued to work for Grand Union after graduation and then entered the management-training program at Price Chopper Supermarkets.

Price Chopper Supermarkets were founded in Schenectady, New York, in 1932 by Ben and Bill Golub. The Golubs were innovators in the supermarket industry. Working with other regional supermarkets, they created the Food Marketing Institute and were the first supermarket to offer S&H Green Stamps and be open 24-hours. The Golubs opened stores across upstate New York and eventually five other states. In 1973, the Golubs made a strategic change converting, their Central Markets with their Green Stamps to the Price Chopper Discount

Supermarket concept offering high-quality products at low prices. We now operate 116 stores in six states and are continually expanding.

After completing the training and some assignments as a department manager in stores, I was promoted to managing our weekly sales promotion program. Price Chopper is a traditional HI-LO supermarket. Each week we selected about 500 items and offered them at deeply discounted prices that represent a tremendous value to our consumers. The specials for the week are promoted on our Web site and in inserts in local newspapers. We tailor the weekly specials to appeal to the demographics of the local markets. So each week I select specials and set prices for 20 different markets.

I assumed my present position several years ago and am now responsible for building our private-label business. Private-label products play an important role in building loyalty to Price Chopper and increasing our margins and profitability. Our first foray into private labels was offering private-label products at lower prices but

CHAPTER 15

QUESTIONS

What factors do retailers consider when pricing merchandise?

What are the legal restrictions on retail pricing?

How do retailers set retail prices?

How do retailers make adjustments to prices over time and for different market segments?

Why do some retailers have frequent sales while others attempt to maintain an everyday low price strategy?

What pricing tactics do retailers use to influence consumer purchases?

having the same quality as the leading national brands such as Breyers ice cream and Maxwell House coffee. Typically we price these private labels, called Price Chopper, at 10 to 15 percent lower than the national brands; however, for commodity-type products like flour, the price differential is less. We also place the Price Chopper private labels to the right of the national brands on shelves in stores so as customers scan the shelf from left to right, they will see the national brand and then a similar private-label brand at a lower price. Now I am developing a premium line of 200 private-label SKUs, called Central Market Classics. Central Market Classics items have superior quality to the national brand but are priced the same as the national brands. Even through the quality-to-price ratio for our private brands is higher than national brands, our private labels have significantly higher margins.

Trying to understand how price and quality affect our customers' buying decisions is challenging, but it is very exciting when developing products that move quickly out of the store. Retailing is my passion, and I enjoy working for a company that deals directly with the ultimate customer.

The decisions examined in this textbook are directed toward facilitating exchanges between retailers and their customers. As discussed in Chapter 1, retailers offer a number of benefits to their customers, including making merchandise available to customers when they want it, at a convenient location, and in the quantities they want. In addition, retailers provide services such as the opportunity for customers to see and try out merchandise before buying it. In exchange for these benefits, customers pay money for the merchandise and services provided by retailers.

The importance of pricing decisions is growing because today's customers have more alternatives to choose from and are better informed about the alternatives available in the marketplace. Thus, they are in a better position to seek a good value when they buy merchandise and services. **Value** is the ratio of what customers receive (the perceived benefit of the products and services offered by the retailer) to what they have to pay for it:

$$\text{Value} = \frac{\text{Perceived Benefits}}{\text{Price}}$$

Thus, retailers can increase value and stimulate more sales (exchanges) by either increasing the perceived benefits offered or reducing the price. To some customers, a good value means simply paying the lowest price because other benefits offered by retailers are not important to them. Others are willing to pay extra for additional benefits as long as they believe they're getting their money's worth in terms of product quality or service.

If retailers set prices higher than the benefits they provide, sales and profits will decrease. In contrast, if retailers set prices too low, their sales might increase, but profits might decrease due to the lower profit margin. In addition to offering an attractive value to customers, retailers need to consider the value proposition offered by their competitors and legal restrictions related to pricing. Thus, setting the right price can be challenging.

The first section of this chapter reviews the factors retailers consider in setting retail prices. Then the actual process that retailers use to determine prices is described. The next section examines methods that retailers use to charge different prices over time based on changes in demand, different market segments, and even individual customers. After discussing the different pricing strategies used by retailers, the chapter concludes with some special issues in pricing, such as loss leaders, category and odd pricing, and the potential increase in price competition due to the Internet.

CONSIDERATIONS IN SETTING RETAIL PRICES

As illustrated in Exhibit 15–1, the four factors retailers consider in setting retail prices are (1) the price sensitivity of consumers, (2) the cost of the merchandise and services, (3) competition, and (4) legal restrictions.

Customer Price Sensitivity and Cost

Generally, as the price of a product increases, the sales for the product will decrease because fewer and fewer customers feel the product is a good value. The price sensitivity of customers determines how many units will be sold at different price levels. If customers in the target market are very price sensitive, sales will decrease significantly when prices increase. If customers are not very price sensitive, sales will not decrease significantly if the prices are increased.

One approach that can be used to measure the price sensitivity of customers is a price experiment. Consider the following situation: A movie theater chain wants to determine how many movie tickets it can sell at different price levels. It selects six theaters in the chain with very similar trading areas and sets prices at different levels in each of the theaters for a week. Assume that the variable cost per ticket, the royalty paid to the movie distributor, is $5.00 per ticket sold, and the fixed cost of operating the theater for a week, the cost for rent, labor and energy, is $8,000.

The results of this experiment are shown in Exhibit 15–2. Notice in Exhibit 15–2a that as prices increase, the fixed costs remain the same, sales and variable costs both decrease, but sales decrease at a faster rate than variable costs (Exhibit 15–2b). So the highest profit level occurs at a $7.00 ticket price (Exhibit 15–2c). If the movie theater only considers customers' price sensitivity and cost in setting prices, it would set prices for theaters with these demand characteristics at $7.00 to maximize profits.

EXHIBIT 15–1
Considerations in Setting
Retail Prices

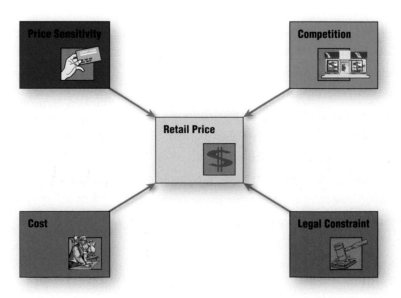

Results of Price Experiment   **EXHIBIT** 15–2

Data from Price Experiment   **EXHIBIT** 15–2a

Theater	Price	Quantity Sold	Column (1) × Column (2) Revenue	Column (2) × $5 Variable Cost per Ticket Variable Cost	Fixed Cost	Column (3) − Column (4) − Column (5) Contribution to Profit
1	$6.00	9,502	$57,012	$47,510	$8,000	$1,502
2	6.50	6,429	41,789	32,145	8,000	1,644
3	7.00	5,350	37,450	26,750	8,000	2,700
4	7.50	4,051	30,383	20,255	8,000	2,128
5	8.00	2,873	22,984	14,365	8,000	619
6	8.50	2,121	18,029	10,605	8,000	−577

EXHIBIT 15–2b
Quantity Sold at Different Prices

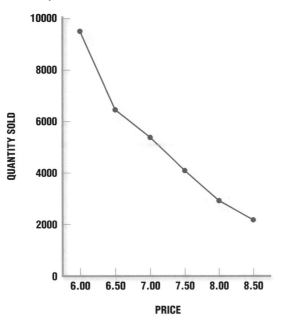

EXHIBIT 15–2c
Profit at Different Prices

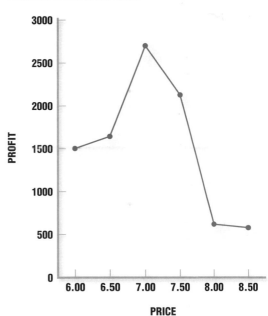

Price Elasticity   A commonly used measure of price sensitivity is **price elasticity,** or the percentage change in quantity sold divided by the percentage change in price:

$$\text{Elasticity} = \frac{\text{Percentage change in quantity sold}}{\text{Percentage change in price}}$$

Assume that a retailer originally priced a private-label DVD player at $90 and then raised the price to $100. Prior to raising the price, the retailer was selling 1,500 units a week. When the price increased, sales dropped to 1,100 units per week. The calculation of the price elasticity is as follows:

$$\begin{aligned}
\text{Elasticity} &= \frac{\text{Percentage change in quantity sold}}{\text{Percentage change in price}} \\[6pt]
&= \frac{(\text{New quantity sold} - \text{Old quantity sold}) \div (\text{Old quantity sold})}{(\text{New price} - \text{Old price}) \div (\text{Old price})} \\[6pt]
&= \frac{(1100 - 1500)/1500}{(10 - 9)/9} = \frac{-0.2667}{.1111} = -2.4005
\end{aligned}$$

Because the quantity sold usually decreases when prices increase, price elasticity is a negative number.

The target market for a product is generally viewed to be price insensitive (referred to as inelastic) when its price elasticity is greater than −1—that is, when a 1 percent decrease in price results in less than a 1 percent increase in quantity sold. The target market for a product is price sensitive (referred to as elastic) when the price elasticity is less than −1—that is, when a 1 percent decrease in price produces more than a 1 percent increase in quantity sold. The price elasticity for a product can be estimated by conducting an experiment as described previously or by using statistical techniques to analyze how sales have changed in the past when prices changed.

Various factors affect the price sensitivity for a product. First, the more substitutes a product or service has, the more likely it is to be price elastic (sensitive). For example, there are many alternatives for McDonald's sandwich meals, and thus, fast food prices are typically price elastic, but branded luxury goods almost no substitutes and is price inelastic (insensitive). Second, products and services that are necessities are price inelastic. Thus, medical care is price inelastic, whereas airline tickets for a vacation are price elastic. Third, products that are expensive relative to a consumer's income are price elastic. Thus, cars are price elastic, and books and movie tickets tend to be price inelastic. The estimated elasticities for some commonly purchased items are shown below.[1]

Product Class	PRICE ELASTICITY	
	Short Run	Long Run
Clothing	−0.90	−2.90
Wine	−0.88	−1.17
Jewelry and watches	−0.44	−0.67
Gasoline	−0.20	−0.60

Based on these estimates, a 1 percent decrease in the price of clothing would result in only a 0.90 percent increase in the quantity sold in the short run but a 2.90 percent increase in the long run. So if you must have that new sweater today, you are much less responsive to a low price than if you can wait for the sweater to be on sale three months from now. In contrast, Americans aren't going to change their gasoline purchases much in the short or long run, regardless of slight price decreases or increases. However, these elasticity estimates are based on relatively small changes in prices and might be different for large price changes.

For products with price elasticities less than −1, the price that maximizes profits can be determined by the following formula:

$$\text{Profit-maximizing price} = \frac{\text{Price elasticity} \times \text{Cost}}{\text{Price elasticity} + 1}$$

So, if the private-label DVD player described in the preceding example cost $50, the profit-maximizing price would be:

$$\text{Profit-maximizing price} = \frac{\text{Price elasticity} \times \text{Cost}}{\text{Price elasticity} + 1}$$
$$= \frac{-2.4005 \times \$50}{-2.4005 + 1} = \$85.70$$

Competition

The previous discussion about setting price on the basis of customer price sensitivity (elasticity) and cost ignores the effects of competitors' prices. For example, assume the movie theater chain that conducted the experiment had a $7.50 ticket price and, following the results of its experiment, dropped its price to $7.00 to increase sales and profits. If the increased sales occurred, competitors would see a decline in their sales and react by dropping their prices to $7.00, and the experimenting theater might not realize the sales and profit increases it anticipated.

Retailers can price above, below, or at parity with the competition. The chosen pricing policy must be consistent with the retailer's overall strategy and its relative market position. Consider, for instance, Wal-Mart and Tiffany and Co. Wal-Mart's overall strategy is to be the low-cost retailer for the merchandise it sells. It tries to price the products it sells below its competition. Tiffany, in contrast, offers significant benefits to its customers beyond just the merchandise. Its brand name and customer service assure customers that they will be satisfied with the jewelry they purchase. Due to the unique nature of Tiffany's offering, it is able to set prices higher than competitors.

Collecting and Using Competitive Price Data
Most retailers routinely collect price data about their competitors to see if they need to adjust their prices to remain competitive. Competitive price data are typically collected using store personnel, but pricing data also are available from business service providers like ACNielsen and IRI.

A hypothetical example of such price comparison data appears in Exhibit 15–3. In this example, CVS, the national drugstore chain, sets its prices generally above Winn-Dixie and Wal-Mart; however, pricing for shampoo, toothpaste, and shaving gel is very competitive. Similarly, Winn-Dixie, a grocery chain, is moderately priced with low prices on select items, like baby food. Wal-Mart is generally priced below its competitors.

Reducing Price Competition
Retailers attempt to reduce price competition by utilizing some of the branding strategies described in Chapter 14 to offer unique merchandise. For instance, they can develop lines of private-label or exclusive merchandise or negotiate with manufacturer's brands for exclusive distribution rights. Because the competition doesn't offer this merchandise, customers cannot make price comparisons easily.

Historically, the price elasticity of gasoline has been greater than –1, so increases in price have not led to a proportional decrease in sales.

REFACT

When Wal-Mart cut its price of 42-inch flat-panel TVs to less than $1,000, it triggered a disastrous financial meltdown among some consumer electronics retailers whose sales were adversely affected by the move.[2]

SKU	CVS	Winn-Dixie	Wal-Mart
Centrum Vitamins (130 tablets)	$9.49	$9.99	$8.26
Tylenol Liquid	6.49	4.69	5.47
Emfamil Liquid Baby Food	3.29	2.99	3.13
VO5 Shampoo	0.99	1.19	0.97
Pedialyte (1 liter)	5.79	5.29	
Colgate Toothpaste (6 oz.)	2.99	2.99	2.84
Duracell AA Batteries (4 pack)	4.79	3.49	3.24
9 Lives Canned Cat Food	1.49	1.29	0.98
Advil (50 caps)	5.99	5.59	
Edge Shaving Gel (7 oz.)	2.39	2.39	2.14
Competitive Price Index*	100%	91%	85%

EXHIBIT 15–3
Competitive Price Data

*Only common items are indexed.

Legal and Ethical Pricing Issues

In addition to customer price sensitivity, cost, and competition, retailers need to consider legal and ethical issues when setting prices. For example, pricing has been particularly difficult for Carrefour hypermarkets in France, where regulation prohibits how much it can lower its prices on branded merchandise. Carrefour has been hurt by competitors, such as two German chains, ALDI and Lidl, both of which sell private-label merchandise that is not subject to the French rules and thus can be priced more cheaply than Carrefour's products. Both of these retailers aggressively entered the French market, winning over many Carrefour shoppers.[3]

Some of these legal and ethical pricing issues include price discrimination, resale price maintenance, horizontal price fixing, predatory pricing, bait-and-switch tactics, and scanned versus posted prices.

Price Discrimination   **Price discrimination** by retailers occurs when a retailer charges different prices for identical products and/or services sold to different customers. Price discrimination between retailers and their customers is generally legal.

Different customers typically receive different prices when buying products and services with coupons or meeting specified conditions, such as eating at a restaurant before 6:00 PM. It is common for customers to negotiate for different prices when buying merchandise such as cars, jewelry, or collectibles. Women are often charged more for haircuts and dry cleaning, even though the costs of providing these services to women and men are about the same.[4] Some states have laws against retail price discrimination based on gender, race, or ethnicity, as Retailing View 15.1 describes.

15.1   RETAILING VIEW   Oh Yes, It's Ladies' Night … No More

Despite the enduring popularity of Kool and the Gang's 1979 hit, it may not be ladies' night anymore in several states. In 2004, New Jersey became the latest state to fall in the battle to outlaw ladies' nights in bars. Traditionally, bars have chosen one night per week and designated it "ladies' night," the night when women are admitted either for free or at a reduced rate and, once inside, served drinks at reduced prices. A New Jersey man named David Gillespie went to the Coastline Bar on one ladies' night and was charged a $5 admission and full price for drinks; when he requested the discounted ladies' night prices, he was refused.

Gillespie sued under New Jersey's Law Against Discrimination and won. Because the bar offered public accomodation, it could not charge higher prices to men. The bar offered in its defense that the difference in prices had a legitimate business purpose and no intent of hostility toward men. It argued that the ladies night discounts attracted more women and subsequently men, thus increasing sales and profits.

Other similar arguments have been made successfully in court, but not in this case. Regardless of motive, the practice was deemed to discriminate purely on the basis of gender. The court's decision opens the doors for reviews of other types of discount pricing programs, such as children's or senior prices in restaurants.

The decision has been met with mixed reviews. The former governor of New Jersey, James McGreevey, issued a written statement denouncing it as "bureaucratic nonsense" and an overreaction that reflects a "complete lack of common sense and good judgement." One television commentator cried, "Is there nothing sacred?" For now, however, the law stands, and it is ladies' night no more in New Jersey.

Should bars be allowed to have "ladies' night" when women are admitted either for free or at a reduced rate and, once inside, served drinks at reduced prices? Is this illegal price discrimination?

Source: Berny Morson, "Ladies' Night Foe Aims Complaint at Rockies," *Rocky Mountain News,* October 16, 2007; Brittany Bacon, "'Ladies' Night' Lawsuit on the Rocks?" *ABC News,* July 25, 2007; DeWayne Wickham, "'Ladies' Night' Ban in N.J. Sends the Wrong Message," *USA Today,* June 7, 2004.

How and why retailers engage in price discrimination is discussed later in the chapter. In many cases, customers are not aware that they are being charged different prices. For example, online retailers are able to target price promotions to customers based on their gender, location, shopping time of day, speed of Internet connection, or even Google browsing habits.[5] So a woman with a high-speed Internet connection in the South may get a free shipping offer, while her male counterpart in the West may be offered live customer service instead. If, however, customers become aware of this practice, they may feel they are being treated unfairly and be reluctant to patronize the retailer in the future.[6]

Predatory Pricing   **Predatory pricing** arises when a dominant retailer sets prices below its costs to drive competitive retailers out of business. Eventually, the predator hopes to raise prices when the competition is eliminated and earn back enough profits to compensate for its losses.

Some states have old statutes that declare it illegal to sell merchandise at unreasonably low prices, usually below their cost. However, a retailer generally may sell merchandise at any price so long as the motive isn't to eliminate competition. For instance, independent retailers in small towns accuse Wal-Mart of selling goods below cost to drive them out of business, but Wal-Mart maintains that it hasn't violated the law because it didn't intend to hurt competitors. It admits, however, it has sold some products below cost, as do other retailers, to attract customers into the store in the hope that they will then buy other products during their visit.

Resale Price Maintenance   As discussed in Chapter 14, vendors often encourage retailers to sell their merchandise at a specific price, known as the manufacturer's suggested retail price (MSRP). Vendors set MSRP prices to reduce retail price competition among retailers, eliminate free riding, and stimulate retailers to provide complementary services. Vendors enforce MSRPs by withholding benefits such as cooperative advertising or even refusing to deliver merchandise to noncomplying retailers. The Supreme Court recently ruled that the ability of a vendor to require retailers to sell merchandise at MSRP should be decided on a case-by-case basis, depending on the individual circumstances.[8]

Horizontal Price Fixing   **Horizontal price fixing** involves agreements between retailers that are in direct competition with each other to set the same prices. This practice clearly reduces competition and is illegal. As a general rule of thumb, retailers should refrain from discussing prices or terms and conditions of sale with competitors. If buyers or store managers want to know competitors' prices, they can look at a competitor's advertisements, its Web sites, or its stores.

Bait-and-Switch Tactics   A **bait-and-switch** is an unlawful, deceptive practice that lures customers into a store by advertising a product at a lower-than-normal price (the bait) and then, once they are in the store, induces them to purchase a higher-priced model (the switch). Bait-and-switch usually involves the store either having inadequate inventory for the advertised product or pushing salespeople to disparage the quality of the advertised model and emphasize the superior performance of a higher-priced model. To avoid disappointing customers and risking problems with the Federal Trade Commission (FTC), the retailer needs to have sufficient inventory of advertised items and offer customers rain checks if stockouts occur.

Scanned versus Posted Prices   Although many customers and regulators are concerned about price scanning accuracy, studies usually find a high level of accuracy. In general, retailers lose money from scanning errors because the scanned price is below the posted price.[9] Periodic price audits are an essential component of good pricing practices. Price audits of a random sample of items should be done periodically to identify the extent and cause of scanning errors and develop procedures to minimize errors.

SETTING RETAIL PRICES

As described in the previous section, theoretically, retailers maximize their profits by setting prices on the basis of the price sensitivity of customers and the cost of merchandise. One limitation of just using price sensitivity and cost for setting prices is that it fails to consider the prices being charged by competitors. Another problem is that implementing this approach requires knowledge of the price sensitivity (price elasticity) of each item. Many retailers have to set prices for more than 50,000 SKUs and make thousands of pricing decisions each month. From a practical perspective, they cannot conduct experiments or do statistical analyses to determine the price sensitivity for each item.

Setting Prices Based on Costs

Most retailers either use the MSRP (manufacturer's suggested retail price) or set prices by marking up the item's cost to yield a profitable gross margin. Then these cost-based prices are adjusted on the basis of insights about customer price sensitivity and competitive pricing. The following section describes how retailers set prices solely on the basis of merchandise cost.

Retail Price and Markup   When setting prices based on merchandise cost, retailers start with the following equation:

Retail price = Cost of merchandise + Markup

The **markup** is the difference between the retail price and the cost of an item. Thus, if a sporting-goods retailer buys a tennis racket for $75 and sets the retail price at $125, the markup is $50. The appropriate markup is determined to cover all of the retailer's operating expenses (labor costs, rent, utilities, advertising, etc.) needed to sell the merchandise and produce a profit for the retailer. As discussed later in the chapter, retailers may price some merchandise below their costs and sell it at a loss because these low-priced items generate store traffic.

The **markup percentage** is the markup as a percentage of the retail price:

$$\text{Markup percentage} = \frac{\text{Retail price } - \text{ Cost of merchandise}}{\text{Retail price}}$$

Thus, the markup percentage for the tennis racket is:

$$\text{Markup percentage} = \frac{\$125 - \$75}{\$125} = 40\%$$

The retail price based on the cost and markup percentage is:

Retail price = Cost of merchandise + Markup

Retail price = Cost of merchandise + Retail price × Markup percentage

$$\text{Retail price} = \frac{\text{Cost of merchandise}}{1 - \text{Markup percentage (as a fraction)}}$$

Thus, if a buyer for an office supply category specialist purchases calculators at $14 and needs a 30 percent markup to meet the financial goals for the category, the retail price needs to be:

$$\text{Retail price} = \frac{\text{Cost}}{1 - \text{Markup percentage}} = \frac{\$14.00}{1 - 0.30} = \$20$$

Traditionally, apparel retailers used a 50 percent markup, referred to as **keystoning,** that set the retail price by simply doubling the cost.

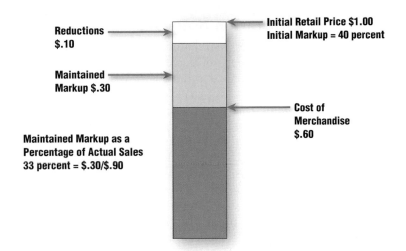

EXHIBIT 15–4
Difference between Initial Markup and Maintained Markup

Initial Markup and Maintained Markup The previous discussion is based on the assumption that the retailer sells all items at an initially set price. However, retailers rarely sell all items at the initial price. They frequently reduce the price of items for special promotions or to get rid of excess inventory at the end of a season. In addition, discounts are given to employees, and some merchandise is lost to theft and accounting errors (inventory shrinkage). These factors that reduce the actual selling price from the initial sales price are called **reductions.** Thus, there is a difference between the initial and the maintained markup. The **initial markup** is the retail selling price initially set for the merchandise, minus the cost of the merchandise. The **maintained markup** is the actual sales realized for the merchandise, minus its costs. Thus, the maintained markup is equivalent to the gross margin for the product.

The difference between the initial and maintained markup is illustrated in Exhibit 15–4. The item illustrated costs $0.60, and the initial price for the item is $1.00, so the initial markup is $0.40, and the initial markup percentage is 40 percent. However, the average actual sale price for the item is $.90. The reductions are $0.10, so the maintained markup is $0.30, and the maintained markup percentage is 33 percent (0.30/0.90).

The relationship between the initial and the maintained markup percentage is:

$$\text{Initial markup percentage} = \frac{\begin{array}{c}\text{Maintained markup percentage} \\ \text{(as a percentage of planned} \\ \text{actual sales)}\end{array} + \begin{array}{c}\text{Percent reductions} \\ \text{(as a percentage of planned} \\ \text{actual sales)}\end{array}}{100\% + \begin{array}{c}\text{Percent reductions} \\ \text{(as a percentage of planned} \\ \text{actual sales)}\end{array}}$$

Thus, if the buyer setting the price for the item shown in Exhibit 15–4 planned on reductions of 10 percent of actual sales and wanted a maintained markup of 33 percent, the initial markup should be:

$$\text{Initial markup percentage} = \frac{33\% + (\$0.10/\$0.90 = 11.111\%)}{100\% + 11.111\%} = 40\%$$

and the initial retail price should be:

$$\text{Initial retail price} = \frac{\text{Cost}}{1 - \text{Initial markup percentage}} = \frac{\$0.60}{1 - 0.40} = \$1.00$$

Merchandising Optimization Software

Setting prices by simply marking up merchandise cost neglects a number of other factors that retailers need to consider, such as price sensitivities, competition, and the sales of complementary products. A relatively new approach to setting retail prices takes a more comprehensive approach using **merchandising optimization software.** These software programs use a set of algorithms that analyze past and current merchandise sales and prices, estimate the relationship between prices and sales generated, and then determine the optimal (most profitable) initial price for the merchandise and the appropriate size and timing of markdowns. To set initial prices, the software uses historical sales data from its own and competitors' stores. It determines the price/sales relationship of complementary items—those that have a similar sales pattern, such as Pepsi and Lays Potato Chips. So, not only can the software tell buyers the best price for Pepsi, but it also suggests a price for the chips. Buyers can also determine how much Pepsi they will sell at a given price if they lower the price of Coke or their private-label brand. The software can incorporate other factors, such as whether a store has a cheap or premium price image; the proximity of the nearest rival, seasonal factors (e.g., soft drinks sell better in the summer than in the winter), or whether an item is featured in coupons.[11]

Merchandising optimization software can be expensive, costing upwards of a million dollars, and is therefore currently used by less than 200 retailers worldwide.[12] But its use can have an impressive impact on bottom-line profitability. For instance, New York City's Duane Reade pharmacy chain used merchandising optimization software to boost its sales of diapers.[13] The chain had tried discounts and coupons, but the category was losing ground to the competition. The software told it that the markup should be a function of the child's age. Therefore, it made newborn sizes more expensive and big-kid pull-ups cheaper. After a year, the increased diaper sales helped boost baby care revenues by 27 percent, and the category's gross margin rose 2 percent. A traditional analysis could not provide the insight that parents of newborns are far less price-sensitive than parents of toddlers.

Profit Impact of Setting a Retail Price: The Use of Break-Even Analysis

Retailers often want to know the number of units they need sell to begin making a profit. For example, a retailer might want to know:

- Break-even sales to generate a target profit.
- Break-even volume and dollars to justify introducing a new product, product line, or department.
- Break-even sales change needed to cover a price change.

A useful analytical tool for making these assessments is a **break-even analysis,** which determines, on the basis of a consideration of fixed and variable costs, how much merchandise needs to be sold to achieve a break-even (zero) profit.

The **break-even point quantity** is the quantity at which total revenue equals total cost, and then profit occurs for additional sales.

The formula for calculating the sales quantity needed to break even is:

$$\text{Break-even quantity} = \frac{\text{Total fixed costs}}{\text{Actual unit sales price} - \text{Unit variable cost}}$$

The following examples illustrate the use of this formula in determining the break-even volume of a new private-label product and the break-even change in volume needed to cover a price change.

Calculating Break-Even for a New Product   Hypothetically, PetSmart is considering an introduction of a new private-label, dry dog food targeting owners of older dogs. The cost of developing this dog food is $700,000, including salaries for the design team and testing the product. Because these costs do not change with the quantity of product produced and sold, they're known as **fixed costs.** PetSmart plans to sell the dog food for $12 a bag—the unit price. The **variable cost** is the retailer's expenses that vary directly with the quantity of product produced and sold. Variable costs often include direct labor and materials used in producing the product. PetSmart will be purchasing the product from a private-label manufacturer. Thus, the only variable cost is the dog food's cost, $5, from the private-label manufacturer.

$$\text{Break-even quantity} = \frac{\text{Fixed cost}}{\text{Actual unit sales price} - \text{Unit variable cost}}$$

$$= \frac{\$700,000}{\$12 - \$5} = 100,000 \text{ bags}$$

Thus, PetSmart needs to sell 100,000 bags of dog food to break even, or make zero profit, and for every additional bag sold, it will make $7 profit.

Now assume that PetSmart wants to make $100,000 profit from the new product line. The break-even quantity now becomes:

$$\text{Break-even quantity} = \frac{\text{Fixed cost}}{\text{Actual unit sales price} - \text{Unit variable cost}}$$

$$= \frac{\$700,000 + \$100,000}{\$12 - \$5} = 114,286 \text{ bags}$$

Calculating Break-Even Sales   A closely related issue to the calculation of a break-even point is determining how much unit sales would have to increase to make a profit from a price cut or how much sales would have to decline to make a price increase unprofitable. Continuing with the PetSmart example, assume the break-even quantity is 114,286 units, based on the $700,000 fixed cost, the $100,000 profit, a selling price of $12, and a cost of $5. Now PetSmart is considering lowering the price of a bag of dog food to $10. How many units must it sell to break, even if it lowers its selling price by 16.67 percent to $10? Using the formula,

$$\text{Break-even quantity} = \frac{\text{Fixed cost}}{\text{Actual unit sales price} - \text{Unit variable cost}}$$

$$= \frac{\$700,000 + \$100,000}{\$10 - \$5} = 160,000 \text{ bags}$$

So if PetSmart decreases its price by 16.67 percent from $12 to $10, unit sales must increase by 40 percent: (160,000 − 114,286) ÷ 114,286.

PRICE ADJUSTMENTS

The preceding section reviewed how retailers initially set prices on the basis of the merchandise cost and desired maintained margin. However, retailers adjust prices over time (markdowns) and for different customer segments (variable pricing). Retailing View 15.2 describes how some retailers are trying to raise their gross margin percentage by avoiding markdowns.

REFACT

Marked-down goods, which accounted for just 8 percent of department store sales three decades ago, have climbed to around 20 percent of sales.[14]

Markdowns

Markdowns are price reductions or discounts from the initial retail price. This section examines why retailers take markdowns, how they optimize markdown decisions, how they reduce the amount of markdowns by working with vendors, how they liquidate markdown merchandise, and the mechanics of taking markdowns.

Reasons for Taking Markdowns

Retailers' reasons for taking markdowns can be classified as either clearance (to dispose of merchandise) or promotional (to generate sales).

Clearance Markdowns   When merchandise is selling at a slower rate than planned, will become obsolete at the end of its season, or is priced higher than competitors' goods, buyers generally mark it down for clearance purposes. As

---

15.2   RETAILING VIEW   Get Them While They're Hot

For years, retailers have lured customers into stores with sales and markdowns. Shoppers know when items will go on sale and often wait for bargains. Although this policy helps retailers sell more merchandise, it also decreases their gross margins. Frequent sales also may signal to customers that there might be something wrong with the merchandise or that it isn't good quality. Frequent sales can also damage retailer's overall image. So retailers have devised tactics to reverse this cycle and encourage more customers to pay full price.

Wal-Mart uses an Everday Low Price Strategy, which implies merchandise is already at low prices and won't be further discounted.

Macy's, long known for its everyday sales, is promoting "Every Day Value," or EDV, on many of its racks. Costco doesn't need to advertise its low prices. Loyal customers return time after time to look for low-priced treasures.

A handful of retailers, like Coach and Apple, have taken a dramatically different approach. They focus on quality and image and therefore simply don't have sales! Customers accept this full-price message. It is an enviable position, to which most retailers can only aspire.

One method of reducing markdowns is to better control the quantities bought. By adopting a just-in-time inventory policy, in which small amounts of merchandise arrive just in time to be sold, customers perceive a scarcity and purchase at full price. (See Chapter 14 for more on this strategy.) Even if there are adequate quantities of merchandise available in the stock room or in a distribution center, displaying just a few items on the sales floor sends a signal to the customer to "buy them now, while they last!" If retailers simply change their displays frequently, customers will perceive that the merchandise is new and available in limited quantities.

Some retailers, such as Wal-Mart advertise everyday low prices, which implies that their products are already at low prices and therefore will not be further discounted. Even

These tactics for preventing bargain hunting increase gross margins as well as inventory turnovers. When more products are sold at full price, gross margins naturally increase. As retailers trim their inventories to give a feeling of "buy now or be sorry," sales also will increase, and inventory will decrease, thus resulting in greater inventory turnover.

Sources: Allison Kaplan, "Rough Weather Behind Them, Retailers Are Starting to Trim Their Sales," *St. Paul Pioneer Press*, January 26, 2007 (accessed January 25, 2008).; Jayne O'Donnell, "Retailers Try to Train Shoppers to Buy Now," *USA TODAY*, September 25, 2006 (accessed January 25, 2008); Linda Whitaker, *Managing Markdowns: Why Prevention Is Better than the Optimization Cure* (Carlsbad, CA: Quantum Retail Technology, 2007), (accessed January 25, 2008); Kris Hudson, "Turning Shopping Trips into Treasure Hunts," *The Wall Street Journal*, August 27, 2007, p. B1.

discussed in Chapter 12, slow-selling merchandise decreases inventory turnover; prevents buyers from acquiring new, better selling merchandise; and can diminish the retailer's image for selling the most current styles and trends.

Markdowns are part of the cost of doing business, and thus, buyers plan for them. They tend to order more fashion merchandise than they forecast actually selling because they are more concerned about underordering and stocking out of a popular item before the end of the season than about overordering and having to discount excess merchandise at the end of the season. Stocking out of popular merchandise can have a detrimental effect on a fashion retailer's image, whereas discounting merchandise at the end of the season just reduces maintained markup.

Thus, a buyer's objective isn't to minimize markdowns. If markdowns are too low, the buyer is probably pricing the merchandise too low, not purchasing enough merchandise, or not taking enough risks with the merchandise being purchased. So buyers set the initial markup price high enough that, even after markdowns and other reductions have been taken, the planned maintained markup is still achieved.

Promotional Markdowns   Buyers also employ markdowns to promote merchandise and increase sales. Markdowns can increase customer traffic flow. Retailers plan promotions in which they take markdowns for holidays, for special events, and as part of their overall promotional program. In fact, small portable appliances (such as toasters) are called *traffic appliances* because they're often sold at promotional or reduced prices to generate in-store traffic. Retailers hope that customers will purchase other products at regular prices while they're in the store. Another opportunity created by markdowns is to increase the sale of complementary products. For example, a supermarket's markdown on hot dog buns may be offset by increased demand for hot dogs, mustard, and relish—all sold at regular prices.

Optimizing Markdown Decisions   Retailers have traditionally created a set of arbitrary rules for taking markdowns. One retailer, for instance, identifies markdown candidates when its weekly sell-through percentages fall below a certain level. Another retailer cuts prices on the basis of how long the merchandise has been in the store—marking products down by 20 percent after 8 weeks, then by 30 percent after 12 weeks, and finally by 50 percent after 16 weeks. Such a rules-based approach, however, is limited because it does not consider the demand for the merchandise at different price points and thus produces less-than-optimal profits.

The optimization software described previously in this chapter, used to set initial retail prices, can also indicate when to take markdowns and how much they should be.[15] It works by continually updating its pricing forecasts on the basis of actual sales throughout the season and factoring in differences in price sensitivities. For example, the software recognizes that in early November, a winter item's sales are better than expected, so it delays taking a markdown that had been planned. Each week, as new sales data become available, it readjusts the forecasts to include the latest information. It computes literally thousands of scenarios for each item—a process that is too complicated and time consuming for buyers to do on their own. It then evaluates the outcomes on the basis of expected profits and other factors and selects the action that produces the best results.

Bloomingdale's implemented markdown optimization in 40 percent of its apparel business across all stores, accounting for about 10 percent of its total sales. The software changed the mindset of its buyers. Buyers now take markdowns quicker, don't feel locked into particular patterns, and don't think that every

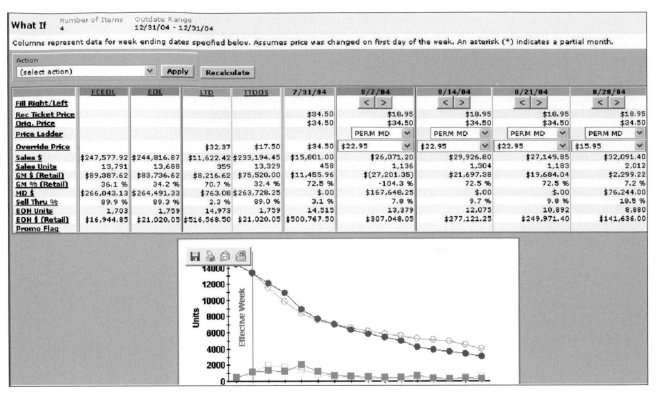

What If	Number of Items 4	Outdate Range 12/31/04 - 12/31/04							

Columns represent data for week ending dates specified below. Assumes price was changed on first day of the week. An asterisk (*) indicates a partial month.

	FCEOL	EOL	LTD	TTOOS	7/31/04	8/7/04	8/14/04	8/21/04	8/28/04
Fill Right/Left						< >	< >	< >	< >
Rec Ticket Price					$34.50	$18.95	$18.95	$18.95	$18.95
Orig. Price					$34.50	$34.50	$34.50	$34.50	$34.50
Price Ladder						PERM MD	PERM MD	PERM MD	PERM MD
Override Price			$32.37	$17.50	$34.50	$22.95	$22.95	$22.95	$15.95
Sales $	$247,577.92	$244,816.87	$11,622.42	$233,194.45	$15,801.00	$26,071.20	$29,926.80	$27,149.85	$32,091.40
Sales Units	13,791	13,688	359	13,329	458	1,136	1,304	1,183	2,012
GM $ (Retail)	$89,387.62	$83,736.62	$8,216.62	$75,520.00	$11,455.96	$(27,201.35)	$21,697.38	$19,684.04	$2,299.22
GM % (Retail)	36.1 %	34.2 %	70.7 %	32.4 %	72.5 %	-104.3 %	72.5 %	72.5 %	7.2 %
MD $	$266,043.13	$264,491.33	$763.08	$263,728.25	$.00	$167,648.25	$.00	$.00	$76,244.00
Sell Thru %	89.9 %	89.3 %	2.3 %	89.0 %	3.1 %	7.8 %	9.7 %	9.8 %	18.5 %
EOH Units	1,703	1,759	14,973	1,759	14,515	13,379	12,075	10,892	8,880
EOH $ (Retail)	$16,944.85	$21,020.05	$516,568.50	$21,020.05	$500,767.50	$307,048.05	$277,121.25	$249,971.40	$141,636.00
Promo Flag									

The output from the **Oracle Retail** markdown model indicates that the model's recommended markdown of $18.95 will result in more than $5,000 greater profit than the buyer's planned markdown of $22.95.

markdown has to be the same. By taking the first markdown when there is still customer demand, Bloomingdale's sells more units at a first markdown price and has fewer units selling at the second markdown price. In one instance, a buyer had planned to wait until after Christmas to take markdowns, but the software indicated that the buyer should start taking markdowns right after Thanksgiving. There was a great deal of risk, but it worked. Bloomingdale's sold through the product before Christmas at a higher price than it had planned to run post-Christmas.[16]

The output from the Oracle Retail markdown model above indicates that the model's recommended markdown of $18.95 will result in more than $5,000 greater profit than the buyer's planned markdown of $22.95.

Reducing the Amount of Markdowns by Working with Vendors   Retailers work closely with their vendor partners to coordinate deliveries and help share the financial burden of taking markdowns. Supply chain management systems (discussed in Chapter 10) reduce the lead time for receiving merchandise so that retailers can monitor changes in trends and customer demand more closely, thus reducing markdowns.

Vendors have a partnering relationship with their retailers and thus a vested interest in their success. Vendors that are knowledgeable about the market and competition can help with stock selections. Of course, a retailer must also trust its own taste and intuition; otherwise, its store will have the same merchandise as all other stores. As discussed in Chapter 14, buyers can often obtain markdown money—funds a vendor gives the retailer to cover lost gross margin dollars that result from markdowns and other merchandising issues.

Liquidating Markdown Merchandise   Even with the best planning, some merchandise may remain unsold at the end of a season. Retailers use one of five strategies to liquidate this unsold merchandise:

1. Sell the merchandise to another retailer.
2. Consolidate the unsold merchandise.
3. Place the remaining merchandise on an Internet auction site like eBay or have a special clearance location on its own Web site.
4. Donate the merchandise to charity.
5. Carry the merchandise over to the next season.

Selling the unsold merchandise to another retailer has been very popular among retailers. For instance, off-price retailers such as TJX Corporation (owners of T.J. Maxx and Marshalls) and Bluefly.com (www.bluefly.com) purchase end-of-season merchandise from other retailers and sell it at deep discounts. However, this approach for liquidating unsold merchandise only enables retailers to recoup a small percentage of the merchandise's cost—often a mere 10 percent.

Markdown merchandise can be consolidated in a number of ways. First, the consolidation can be made into one or a few of the retailer's regular locations. Second, markdown merchandise can be consolidated into another retail chain or an outlet store under the same ownership. Saks Fifth Avenue (OFF Fifth) and Neiman Marcus (Last Call Clearance Center) use this approach. Third, unsold merchandise can be shipped to a distribution center or rented space such as a convention center (Barney's New York and J. Crew) for final sale. However, consolidation sales can be complex and expensive due to the extra transportation and record-keeping involved.

The Internet is increasingly useful for liquidating unsold merchandise. For example, an electronics store might utilize eBay to sell goods it has received from trade-ins. Many retailers have separate areas of their Web sites for clearance merchandise.

Donating clearance merchandise to charities is a common practice. Charitable giving is always a good corporate practice. It is a way of giving back to the community and has strong public relations benefits. Also, the cost value of the merchandise can be deducted from income.

The final liquidation approach—to carry merchandise over to the next season—is used with relatively high-priced nonfashion merchandise, such as traditional men's clothing and furniture. Generally, however, it is not profitable to carry over merchandise because of excessive inventory carrying costs.

Variable Pricing and Price Discrimination

Retailers use a variety of techniques to maximize profits by charging different prices to different customers.

Individualized Variable Pricing   Ideally, retailers could maximize their profits if they charged each customer as much as the customer was willing to pay. For instance, if a wealthy, price-insensitive customer wants to buy a new car battery, AutoZone would like to price the battery at $200 but then price the same battery at $125 to make a sale to a more price-sensitive, lower-income customer. Charging each individual customer a different price based on their willingness to pay is called **first-degree price discrimination.**

Pricing merchandise through auction bidding is an example of first-degree price discrimination. A retailer offering a 1960 Porsche Speedster on eBay maximizes its profits because the customer with the highest willingness to pay bids and pays the highest price. Another example of retailers practicing first-degree price discrimination is when they allow customers to haggle over price, as described in Retailing View 15.3

REFACT

R.H. Macy, founder of Macy's, did away with bargaining over price by initiating fixed prices when he opened his first dry goods store in 1858. He was the first to advertise these fixed prices in a newspaper.[17]

Customers can get discount codes for their favorite retailers at Reesycakes.com.

Out shopping a few weeks ago, Regina Ranonis was trying to decide between trendy low-heeled boots or a more conservative style. Then the sales associate spoke up: If she would spring for both pairs, he would knock $270 off the total price.

Does this sound like the local flea market? It wasn't. An array of retailers is hoping to reel in sales by allowing haggling, or some form of it. The practice isn't entirely new—and it remains officially denied by most companies—but good consumers say they're getting deals everywhere, from Sunglass Hut to the trendy Kenneth Cole boutique. Big-name stores like Saks and Macy's say savvy shoppers who can cite competitors' prices may also find some wiggle room.

The Internet has given a real boost to haggling for bargains. Fashion sites such as Reesycakes.com list discount codes that can be used online at checkout. Because many retailers honor a lower price on the same item found at a competitor's store or Internet site, savvy customers use search engines to find the best deal.

Chinese consumers even have taken haggling to a new level—group haggling! The practice, called *tuangou*, or team purchase, begins in Internet chat rooms, where consumers devise plans to buy items like appliances, food, or even cars in bulk. Next, they show up together at the stores and demand discounts.

Many of the biggest U.S. retailers, from The Gap to Pottery Barn, say they're sticking to firm no-haggling policies. Many retailers use cash registers that won't accept unauthorized discount prices without managerial approval. Some even have video cameras not only to watch shoppers but also to make sure the staff isn't cutting sweetheart deals for their friends.

Some of the best negotiating territory is at franchises, where owners have the flexibility to operate more like mom-and-pop shops. But even at major department stores and small chains, a growing number of managers are now authorized to lower a price to meet the competition or throw in free alterations or delivery. Many stores take pains to insist that haggling is off limits, even as customers and sales associates say it goes on all the time. The policy is, "Try not to come down in price too much, but don't let the business walk out."

Sources: David Welch, "Haggling Starts to Go the Way of the Tail Fin," *BusinessWeek,* October 29, 2007; "The Fine Art of Haggling," *Consumer Reports Money Advisor* 4, no. 7 (July 2007), p. 14; Cheryl Lu-Lien Tan, "Haggling 2.0," *The Wall Street Journal,* June 23, 2007, p. P1; James T. Areddy, "Chinese Consumers Overwhelm Retailers with Team Tactics," *The Wall Street Journal,* February 28, 2006, p. A1; Rick Popely, "For Some, Haggling Is Part of the Fun," *Knight Ridder Tribune Business News,* April 24, 2005, p. 1.

If this Porsche were on eBay, would the seller be using first-, second-, or third-degree price discrimination?

REFACT

One of the world's oldest pairs of Levi's Jeans, made in the 1880s and originally sold for around $1, was reacquired by Levi Strauss & Co. for $46,532 during an online eBay auction.[18]

Although first-degree price discrimination is legal and widely used in some retail sectors, such as automobile and antique dealers, it is impractical in most retail stores. First, it is difficult to assess each customer's willingness to pay, and second, retailers cannot change the posted prices in stores as customers with different willingness to pay enter the store. In addition, customers might feel they are being treated unfairly if they realize that they are being charged a higher price than other customers.

However, first-degree price discrimination is possible when selling merchandise on the Internet. Retailers can assess each customer's willingness to pay by analyzing past purchase behavior and then serve up Web pages with unique pricing based on the customer's willingness to pay.[19]

Self-Selected Variable Pricing An alternative approach for variable pricing is to offer the same multiple price schedule to all customers but require that customers do something to get the lower price—something that discourages customers with a high willingness to pay to take advantage of the lower price. This approach is referred to as **second-degree price discrimination.** For example, restaurants often have early-bird specials, lower prices for meals served before 6:00 PM. Anyone can take advantage of this discount; however, price-sensitive consumers are more likely to be attracted by the offer. Clearance markdowns, coupons and rebates, bundling, and multiunit pricing are other examples of this approach.

Clearance Markdowns for Fashion Merchandise Clearance markdowns result in higher prices being charged at the beginning of the season than at the end of the season. Thus, fashion-conscious customers who have a high willingness to pay because they want to be the first to wear the latest fashions self-select to pay higher prices. More price-sensitive customers wait to buy the merchandise at the end of the season when prices are lower.

Coupons **Coupons** offer a discount on the price of specific items when they're purchased. Coupons are issued by manufacturers and retailers in newspapers, on products, on the shelf, at the cash register, over the Internet, and through the mail. Retailers use coupons because they are thought to induce customers to try products for the first time, convert those first-time users to regular users, encourage large purchases, increase usage, and protect market share against competition.

Coupons are also considered a form of second-degree price discrimination because, in general, price-sensitive customers will expend the extra effort to collect and redeem coupons, whereas price-insensitive customers will not. However, the impact of coupons on profitability is questionable.

Coupon promotions, like all temporary promotions, may be stealing sales from a future period without any net increase in sales. For instance, if a supermarket runs a coupon promotion on sugar, households may buy a large quantity of sugar and stockpile it for future use. Thus, unless the coupon is used mostly by new buyers, the net impact on sales is negligible, and there will be a negative impact on profits due to the amount of the redeemed coupons and cost of the coupon redemption procedures. Coupons may annoy, alienate, and confuse consumers and therefore do little to increase store loyalty. Customers see an ad for a supermarket with a headline reading "Double Coupons" but don't realize there might be conditions, such as a minimum purchase required, or that it may only apply to manufacturers' paper coupons.

Recognizing these problems, some retailers like Macy's are reducing coupon usage.[20] Grocery stores like Ukrop's are using coupons more strategically by tying them to their customer relationship management (CRM) systems.[21] Shoppers scan their loyalty cards at a kiosk located near the store entrance and receive up to eight coupons and messages selected just for them, based on their shopping history. This program allows Ukrop's and its vendors to give unadvertised personalized offers to the chain's most valuable customers.

Rebates   **Rebates** provide another form of discounts for consumers off the final selling price; however, in this case, the manufacturer, instead of the retailer, issues the refund as a portion of the purchase price returned to the buyer in the form of cash. Rebates can be even more frustrating than coupons for consumers, but the idea is similar. Whereas a coupon provides instant savings when presented, a rebate promises savings, usually mailed to the consumer at some later date, only if the consumer carefully follows the rules. The "hassle factor" for rebates thus is higher than for coupons—the consumer must first buy the item during a specified time period, mail in the required documentation (which usually includes the

Shoppers at Ukrop's use their loyalty card at a kiosk and receive unadvertised personalized coupons.

original sales receipt), and finally wait four to six weeks (or more!) for a check to arrive.

Manufacturers generally like rebates because as much as 90 percent of consumers never bother to redeem them. Manufacturers also embrace this form of price reduction because they let them offer price cuts to consumers directly. With a traditional wholesale price cut from its vendors, retailers can keep the price on the shelf the same and pocket the difference. Rebates can also be rolled out and shut off quickly. That allows manufacturers to fine-tune inventories or respond quickly to competitors without actually cutting prices. Finally, because buyers are required to fill out forms with names, addresses, and other data, rebates become a great way for vendors to build a customer data warehouse. From the retailer's perspective, rebates are more advantageous than coupons since they increase demand in the same way coupons may, but the retailer has no handling costs.

Price Bundling   **Price bundling** is the practice of offering two or more different products or services for sale at one price. For instance, McDonald's offers a bundle of a sandwich, French fries, and a soft drink in a Value Meal® at a discount compared with buying the items individually. Price bundling increases both unit and dollar sales by increasing the amount of merchandise bought during a store visit. The practice is also an example of second-degree price discrimination because it offers more price-sensitive customers a lower-priced alternative.

Multiple-Unit Pricing **Multiple-unit pricing** or **quantity discounts** refer to the practice of offering two or more similar products or services for sale at one lower total price. For example, a convenience store may sell 3 liters of soda for $2.39 when the price per unit is 99 cents—a savings of 58 cents. Like price bundling, this variable pricing approach is used to increase sales volume. Depending on the type of product, however, customers may stockpile for use at a later time, thus having no impact on sales over time.

Multiunit pricing is an example of second-degree price discrimination because customers who buy and consume more of a product are presumably more price sensitive and thus attracted by the lower prices if they buy more units.

Multiple-unit pricing refers to the practice of offering two or more similar products for sale at one lower price.

Variable Pricing by Market Segment Retailers often charge different prices to different demographic market segments, a practice referred to as **third-degree price discrimination.** For example, movie theaters have lower ticket prices for seniors and college students, presumably because these segments are more price sensitive than other customers.

Another example of third-degree price discrimination is zone pricing. **Zone pricing** refers to the practice of charging different prices in different stores, markets, regions, or zones. Retailers generally use zone pricing to address different competitive situations in their various markets. For example, some multichannel retailers implement zone pricing by asking customers to enter their zip code before they are quoted a price. Food retailers often have up to four or five pricing zones in a single city. They'll have one zone if they're next to a Wal-Mart, and another zone if they're next to a less price-competitive regional chain. Drugstores and supermarkets have been known to charge higher prices in poor urban areas and neighborhoods populated by elderly retirees, because customers in those areas have relatively few shopping choices and therefore tend to be relatively insensitive to price. Third-degree price discrimination, when used in this manner to discriminate on the basis of income and age, is considered an unethical practice by many.

The preceding sections focus on how retailers set prices and then adjust them over time and for different market segments. The following sections examine the two prevalent pricing strategies used by retailers, pricing issues that confront services retailers, and special pricing techniques that retailers use.

PRICING STRATEGIES

Retailers use two basic retail pricing strategies: high/low pricing and everyday low pricing (EDLP). Each of these strategies and its advantages and disadvantages is discussed in this section.

High/Low Pricing

Retailers using a **high/low pricing** strategy frequently—often weekly—discount the initial prices for merchandise through frequent sales promotions. This strategy is in response to competitive moves and the positive response from value-conscious customers. Some retailers have found, however, that adopting a high/low pricing strategy can be dangerous. As customers learn to expect frequent sales, many simply wait until the merchandise they want goes on sale, which has an adverse effect on profits. Furthermore, as competing stores try to outdo one another's sales, price wars erupt. So many retailers have tried to wean customers from the "sale" habit by offering everyday low prices.

(+) excitement
(+) profits thru price discrimination

Which store is using a high/low pricing strategy, and which is using everyday low pricing?

Everyday Low Pricing

(f) assure low price
reduce ad + operating cost
reduce stock out + inv.
management

Many retailers, particularly supermarkets, home improvement centers, and discount stores, have adopted an **everyday low pricing (EDLP)** strategy. This strategy emphasizes the continuity of retail prices at a level somewhere between the regular nonsale price and the deep-discount sale price of high/low retailers. Although EDLP retailers embrace their consistent pricing strategy, they occasionally have sales, just not as frequently as their high/low competitors.

The term *everyday low pricing* is somewhat misleading, because low doesn't mean lowest. Although retailers using EDLP strive for low prices, they aren't always the lowest priced in the market. At any given time, a sale price at a high/low retailer may be the lowest price available in a market.

To reinforce their EDLP strategy, many retailers have adopted a **low price guarantee policy** that guarantees customers they will have the lowest price in a market for products they sell. The guarantee usually promises to match or better any lower price found in the market and might include a provision to refund the difference between the seller's offer price and the lower price.

Advantages of the Pricing Strategies

The high/low pricing strategy has the following advantages:

• *Increases profits through price discrimination* High/low pricing allows retailers to charge higher prices to customers who are not price sensitive and are willing to pay the "high" price and lower prices to price-sensitive customers who will wait for the "low" sale price.

• *Sales create excitement* A "get them while they last" atmosphere often occurs during a sale. Sales draw a lot of customers, and a lot of customers create excitement. Some retailers augment low prices and advertising with special in-store activities, like product demonstrations, giveaways, and celebrity appearances.

• *Sells merchandise* Sales allow retailers to get rid of slow-selling merchandise.

The EDLP approach has its own advantages, as follows:

• *Assures customers of low prices* Many customers are skeptical about initial retail prices. They have become conditioned to buying only on sale—the main characteristic of a high/low pricing strategy. The EDLP strategy lets customers know that they will get the same low prices every time they patronize the EDLP retailer. Customers do not have to read the ads and wait for items they want to go on sale.

• *Reduces advertising and operating expenses* The stable prices caused by EDLP limit the need for the weekly sale advertising used in the high/low strategy. In addition, EDLP retailers do not have to incur the labor costs of changing price tags and signs and putting up sales signs.

• *Reduces stockouts and improves inventory management* The EDLP approach reduces the large variations in demand caused by frequent sales with large markdowns. As a result, retailers can manage their inventories with more certainty. Fewer stockouts mean more satisfied customers, higher sales, and fewer rain checks. (**Rain checks** are written promises given to customers when merchandise is out of stock to sell customers that merchandise at the sale price when the merchandise arrives.) In addition, a more predictable customer demand pattern enables the retailer to improve inventory turnover by reducing the average inventory needed for special promotions and backup stock.

PRICING SERVICES

Additional challenges arise when pricing services due to (1) the need to match supply and demand and (2) the difficulties customer have in determining service quality.[22]

Matching Supply and Demand

Services are intangible and thus cannot be inventoried. When retailers are selling products, if the products don't sell one day, they can be stored and sold the next day. However, when a plane departs with empty seats or a play is performed without a full house, the potential revenue from this unused capacity is lost forever. In addition, most services have limited capacity. For example, restaurants are limited in the number of customers that can be seated. Due to capacity constraints, services retailers might encounter situations in which they cannot realize as many sales as they could make.

To maximize sales and profits, many services retailers engage in yield management.[23] **Yield management** is the practice of adjusting prices up or down in response to demand to control the sales generated. Airlines are masters at yield management. Using sophisticated computer programs, they monitor the reservations and ticket sales for each flight and adjust prices according to capacity utilization. Prices are lowered on flights when sales are below forecasts and there is significant excess capacity. As ticket sales approach capacity, prices are increased.

Other services retailers use less sophisticated approaches to match supply and demand. For example, more people want to go to a restaurant for dinner or see a movie at 7:00 PM than at 5:00 PM. Restaurants and movie theaters thus might not be able to satisfy the demand for their services at 7:00 PM but have excess capacity at 5:00 PM. Thus, restaurants and movie theaters often price their services lower for customers who use them at 5:00 PM compared with 7:00 PM in an effort to shift demand from 7:00 PM to 5:00 PM.

Theaters use a variety of strategies to try to ensure that the seats are sold and sold at prices equivalent to what customers are willing to pay. Targeted direct mail coupons are often used when the play opens, and two-for-one tickets are introduced about halfway through the run. In some cities, like New York and Boston, theaters partner with half-price ticket brokers, which sell unsold tickets for 50 percent off the ticket price, but only for performances that same day.

Priceline.com offers a unique pricing scheme for booking airline flights, hotel rooms, and rental cars that helps service

REFACT

Yield management can increase revenues by 7 percent and increase net profit by as much as 100 percent.[24]

Because air travel, like most services, cannot be inventoried, when this plane took off with empty seats, the opportunity to sell the seats was lost forever.

providers match supply and demand and captures some profit through price discrimination. Customers can visit its Web site and specify the price they are prepared to pay and the acceptable range of times, days, and/or quality for a particular leisure travel service. For example, a customer can indicate she wants to fly from Miami to Chicago, anytime between 6:00 AM and 10:00 PM on September 14 or stay in any four-star hotel in Maui from January 15 to January 20. Thus, the service for which the customer is paying is opaque; the customer does not know the specific nature of the service that will be offered. Then, Priceline.com (www.priceline.com) accesses databases of participating suppliers to determine whether it can fulfill the customer's offer and whether it wants to accept the price designated by the consumer. Consumers agree to hold their offers open for a specified period of time (generally, not longer than a minute) to determine whether they can or want to accept the offer. Once fulfilled, offers generally cannot be canceled, making such purchases nonrefundable.

The service that Priceline.com offers benefits both buyers and sellers. Price-sensitive buyers save money, and sellers generate incremental revenue by selling their services at below retail prices but without disrupting their existing retail pricing structures.[25] Retailing View 15.4 provides another example of how the Internet has enabled third parties to capture profits that could have accrued to retailers had they used price discrimination tactics.

15.4   RETAILING VIEW   Hey, Wanna Buy a Ticket?

Typically, promoters of entertainment and sports events offer tickets for a specific seat and date at a fixed price. Individual brokers buy the tickets at the list price, then make a profit by reselling them at a premium to price-insensitive consumers. Software even allows brokers to buy tickets from Ticketmaster, the leading broker of sports, concerts, and theater events, in bulk and then resell them at three or four times the face value price.

Prior to the Internet, these broker or individuals, often called scalpers, would stand in front of the venue for the event and raise their hand with tickets for sale. However, StubHub, owned by eBay, and other online businesses have created a legitimate $2 billion-plus secondary market for seats at plays, concerts, and sports events. Brokers or individuals with tickets to events can list them on an Internet site that people around the world can access. In addition to providing a market by bringing buyers and sellers together, StubHub guarantees customers similar or better seats if anything goes wrong.

To prevent scalpers from making money in the secondary market, some sports teams are threatening to revoke season ticketholders' rights to put their seats up for sale without authorization. However, major league baseball teams are capturing the profits from this form of price discrimination by reselling their own tickets online and collecting a transaction fee.

Event promoters and sports teams engage in price discrimination by varying the prices for different seats at the event. Price-sensitive customers pay a lower price for seats a greater distance from the stage or field of play, while price-insensitive customers pay to sit closer. Now sports teams are engaging in even more sophisticated forms of price discrimination, including increasing the prices of tickets for special games, such as those against important rivals or on special holidays.

Seats for some Hannah Montana (Miley Cyrus) concerts go for $237 on StubHub, when the face value for the ticket was $63.

Sources: Ethan Smith, "Hannah Montana Battles the Bots," *The Wall Street Journal*, October 5, 2007, p. B1; Amy Feldman, "Hot Tickets," *Fast Company*, September 2007, pp. 44–46.

Determining Service Quality

Due to the intangibility of services, it is often difficult for customers to assess service quality, especially when other information is not available.[26] Thus, if consumers are unfamiliar with a service or service provider, they may use price to make quality judgments. For example, most consumers have limited information about lawyers and the quality of legal advice they offer. They may therefore base their assessment of the quality of legal services offered on the fees they charge. They may also use other non-diagnostic cues to assess quality such as the size and décor of the lawyer's office.

Another factor that increases the dependence on price as a quality indicator is the risk associated with a service purchase. In high-risk situations, many of which involve credence services such as medical treatment or legal consulting, the customer will look to price as a surrogate for quality.

Because customers depend on price as a cue of quality and because price creates expectations of quality, service prices must be determined carefully. In addition to being chosen to manage capacity, prices must be set to convey the appropriate quality signal. Pricing too low can lead to inaccurate inferences about the quality of the service. Pricing too high can set expectations that may be difficult to match in service delivery.

PRICING TECHNIQUES FOR INCREASING SALES

This section reviews three techniques used by retailers to increase sales. Each of these techniques—leader pricing, price lining, and odd pricing—takes advantage of the way customers process information.

Leader Pricing

Leader pricing involves a retailer pricing certain items lower than normal to increase customers' traffic flow or boost sales of complementary products. Some retailers call these products **loss leaders.** In a strict sense, loss leaders are sold below cost. But a product doesn't have to be sold below cost for the retailer to use a leader-pricing strategy.

Music CDs and video DVDs appear to be popular loss leaders for some retailers. Amazon, for instance, is selling some downloaded tracks for 89 cents, which is within a penny or so of its cost.[27] Fry's Electronics sells DVDs for $11.99, about $10 below the going rate at other retail outlets.[28]

The best items for leader pricing are frequently purchased products like white bread, milk, and eggs or well-known brand names like Coca-Cola and Kellogg's Corn Flakes. Customers take note of ads for these products because they're purchased weekly. The retailer hopes consumers will also purchase their entire weekly grocery list while buying the loss leaders.

One problem with leader pricing is that it might attract shoppers, referred to as **cherry pickers,** who go from one store to another, buying only items that are on special. These shoppers are clearly unprofitable for retailers.[29]

Price Lining

Retailers frequently offer a limited number of predetermined price points within a merchandise category. For instance, a tire store may offer tires at $69.99, $89.99, and $129.99 that reflect good, better, and best quality. This practice is referred to as **price lining.** Both customers and retailers can benefit from such a strategy for several reasons:

• Confusion that often arises from multiple price choices is essentially eliminated. The customer can choose the tire with the low, medium, or high price.
• From the retailer's perspective, the merchandising task is simplified. That is, all products within a certain price line are merchandised together. Furthermore,

when going to market, the firm's buyers can select their purchases with the predetermined price lines in mind.

- Price lining can also give buyers greater flexibility. If a strict formula is used to establish the initial retail price (initial markup), there could be numerous price points. But with a price-lining strategy, some merchandise may be bought a little below or above the expected cost for a price line. Of course, price lining can also limit retail buyers' flexibility. They may be forced to pass up potentially profitable merchandise because it doesn't fit into a price line.

Although many manufacturers and retailers are simplifying their product offerings to save distribution and inventory costs and make the choice simpler for consumers, price lining can be used to get customers to "trade up" to a more expensive model. Research indicates a tendency for people to choose the product in the middle of a price line. So, for example, if a camera store starts carrying a "super deluxe" model, customers will be more likely to purchase the model that was previously the most expensive. Retailers must decide whether it's more profitable to sell more expensive merchandise or save money by paring down their stock selection.[30]

Odd Pricing

Odd pricing refers to the practice of using a price that ends in an odd number, typically a 9. Odd pricing has a long history in retailing. In the nineteenth and early twentieth centuries, odd pricing was used to reduce losses due to employee theft. Because merchandise had an odd price, salespeople typically had to go to the cash register to give the customer change and record the sale, making it more difficult for salespeople to keep the customer's money. Odd pricing was also used to keep track of how many times an item had been marked down. After an initial price of $20, the first markdown would be $17.99, the second markdown $15.98, and so on.

The results of empirical studies in this area are mixed;[32] however, many retailers believe that odd pricing can increase profits. For example, the computerized pricing system at CVS Stores begins by applying the necessary markup to an item's cost. After that is completed, the program takes the pennies digit of the resulting price and raises it to the nearest 5 or 9. Wal-Mart takes a different approach to this fine tuning. The exact prices are determined by marking costs up by a fixed percent, thus producing a variety of price endings.[33]

The theory behind odd pricing is the assumption that shoppers don't notice the last digit or digits of a price, so that a price of $2.99 is perceived as $2. An alternative theory is that 9 endings signal low prices. Thus, for products that are believed to be sensitive to price, many retailers will round the price down to the nearest nine to create a positive price image. If, for example, the price would normally be $3.09, many retailers will lower the price to $2.99.

Research results suggest the following guidelines for making price-ending decisions:

- When the price sensitivity of the market is high, it is likely to be advantageous to raise or lower prices so that they end in high numbers such as 9.
- When the price sensitivity of the market is not especially high, the risks to the retailer's image of using 9 endings are likely to outweigh the benefits. In such cases, the use of even dollar prices and round number endings would be more appropriate.
- Many upscale retailers appeal to price-sensitive segments of the market through periodic discounting, which suggests the value of a combination strategy: Only break from a standard policy of round number endings to use 9 endings when communicating discounts and special offers.[34]

Many retailers set prices to end in 9s because they believe customers will perceive the prices as lower than they actually are.

THE INTERNET AND PRICE COMPETITION

Retailers are concerned that the growth of electronic retailing will intensify price competition. Traditionally, price competition between store-based retailers offering the same merchandise was reduced by geography because consumers typically shop at the stores and malls closest to where they live and work. However, using shopping bots and search engines, consumers can search for merchandise across the globe at a low cost. The number of stores that a consumer can visit to compare prices is no longer limited by physical distance.

Although consumers shopping electronically can collect price information with little effort, they also can get a lot of other information about the quality and performance of products at a low cost. For instance, an electronic channel offering custom-made Oriental rugs can clearly show real differences in the patterns and materials used for construction. Electronic grocery services offered by Safeway (www.shop.safeway.com) and Albertson's (www.albertsons.com) allow customers to sort cereals by nutritional content, thus making it easier to use that attribute in their decision making. The additional information about product quality might lead customers to pay more for high-quality products, thus decreasing the importance of price.

Retailers using an electronic channel can reduce the emphasis on price by providing better services and information. Because of these services, customers might be willing to pay higher prices for the merchandise. For example, Amazon.com provides customers with the table of contents and synopsis of a book, as well as reviews and comments by the author, or authors, and people who have read the book. When the customer finds an interesting book, Amazon's system is programmed to suggest other books by the same author or of the same genre. Finally, customers can tell Amazon about their favorite authors and subjects and then receive e-mails about new books that might be of interest. The classic response to the question, What are the three most important things in retailing? used to be "location, location, location." In the world of electronic retailing, the answer will be "information, information, information."

SUMMARY

Setting prices is a critical decision in implementing a retail strategy, because price is a critical component in customers' perceived value. In setting prices, retailers consider the price sensitivity of customers in their target market, the cost of the merchandise and services offered, competitive prices, and legal restrictions. Theoretically, retailers maximize their profits by setting prices on the basis of the price sensitivity of customers and the cost of merchandise. However, this approach does not consider the prices being charged by competitors. Another problem with attempting to set prices on the basis of customer price sensitivity is the implementation challenges associated with the large number of pricing decisions a retailer must make. Although some large retailers are using pricing optimization software to set prices, most retailers just mark up the item's cost to yield a profitable maintained margin. Then these cost-based initial prices might be adjusted according to the retail buyer's insights about customer price sensitivity and competitive pricing.

Initial prices are adjusted over time using markdowns and for different market segments using variable pricing strategies. Retailers take markdowns to either dispose of merchandise or generate sales. Markdowns are part of the cost of doing business, and thus, buyers plan for them.

Retailers use a variety of techniques to maximize profits by charging different prices to different customers. These techniques include setting different prices for individual customers, providing an offering that enables customers to self-select the price they are willing to pay, and setting different prices according to customer demographics.

Retailers use two basic retail pricing strategies: everyday low pricing (EDLP) and high/low pricing. Each of these strategies has its advantages and disadvantages. The high/low strategy increases profits through price discrimination, creates excitement, and provides an opportunity to sell slow-moving merchandise. The EDLP approach assures customers of low prices, reduces advertising and operating expenses, reduces stockouts, and improves supply chain management.

Additional challenges arise when pricing services, due to the need to match supply and demand and the difficulties customers have in determining service quality. Retailers use yield management techniques to match supply and demand for services.

Finally, retailers use a variety of pricing techniques to stimulate sales, including price lining, leader pricing, and odd pricing.

KEY TERMS

bait-and-switch, *419*
break-even analysis, *422*
break-even point quantity, *423*
cherry picker, *435*
coupons, *429*
everyday low pricing (EDLP), *432*
first-degree price discrimination, *427*
fixed cost, *423*
high/low pricing, *431*
horizontal price fixing, *419*
initial markup, *421*
keystoning, *420*
leader pricing, *435*

loss leader, *414*
low-price guarantee policy, *432*
maintained markup, *421*
markdowns, *424*
markup, *420*
markup percentage, *420*
merchandising optimization
    software, *422*
multiple-unit pricing, *431*
odd pricing, *436*
predatory pricing, *419*
price bundling, *430*
price discrimination, *418*

price elasticity, *415*
price lining, *435*
quantity discount, *431*
rain check, *433*
rebates, *430*
reductions, *421*
second-degree price
    discrimination, *429*
third-degree price discrimination, *431*
value, *413*
variable cost, *423*
yield management, *433*
zone pricing, *431*

GET OUT AND DO IT!

1. **CONTINUING ASSIGNMENT** Go shopping at the retailer you have selected for the continuing assignment. Does the retailer use a high/low pricing or EDLP strategy? Ask the store manager how markdown decisions are made and how the store decides how much a markdown should be. What rule-based approaches does it use to make markdowns? Does the retailer use techniques for stimulating sales such as price lining, leader pricing, and odd pricing? Are the prices on its Web site the same as in the store? Evaluate your findings. Do you believe the retailer is using the best pricing strategies and tactics for its type of store? What, if anything, could it do to improve?

2. Go to the Web page for Overstock.com and look at its top selling merchandise. Select a few key items and compare the price of each to other online retail sites, such as Target.com, Amazon.com, and Macys.com. How do the prices

compare for this Internet outlet to a discount store, online retailer, and department store?

3. Price bundling is very common in the travel and vacation industry. Go to the Web site for Sandals (www.sandals.com) and see what you can get at an all-for-one, all-inclusive price.

4. Go to three different types of stores and try to bargain your way down from the tagged price. Explain your experience. Was there any difference in your success rate as a result of the type of store or merchandise? Did you have better luck if you spoke to a manager?

5. Go to your favorite food store and your local Wal-Mart to find the prices for the market basket of goods at the bottom of the page. What was the total cost of the market basket at each store? How did the prices compare? Did Wal-Mart live up to its slogan of "Always lower prices"?

Competitive Pricing: Grocery Store vs. Wal-Mart

Item	Size	Brand	Grocery	Wal-Mart	Price Difference	Percent Savings
Grocery						
Ground coffee	11.5 oz can	Folgers				
Raisin Bran	25.5 oz box	Kellogg's				
Pet Supplies						
Puppy Chow	4.4 lb bag	Purina				
Cleaning						
Liquid laundry detergent	100 oz bottle	All				
Dryer sheets	80 count	Bounce				
Liquid dish detergent	25 oz bottle	Palmolive				
Health and Beauty						
Shampoo	12 oz bottle	Dove				
Toothpaste	4.2 oz tube	Colgate Total				
Total Cost of the Market Basket of Goods						

6. Go to the student side of the online learning center. Click on pricing and then on markdown model. Oracle Retail has provided you the opportunity to play buyer and test your analytical abilities for taking markdowns. You will be given the opportunity to make markdown decisions for several products over several weeks. You can either play this simulation game on your own or against your classmates.

DISCUSSION QUESTIONS AND PROBLEMS

1. How does merchandising optimization software help buyers make better initial pricing and markdown decisions?

2. When Apple introduced the iPhone, the initial price was $599. Just two months later, the manufacturer dropped the price by one-third. Loyal buyers were upset, and Chief Executive Steve Jobs, offered a partial rebate as an apology. Why did Apple reduce the price? Explain in terms of the product life cycle and competition in the mobile electronics industry. Was it a good idea to offer a partial rebate? Why or why not?

3. Do you know any retailers that have violated any of the legal issues discussed in this chapter? Explain your answer.

4. Re-read Retailing View 15.1, "Oh Yes, It's Ladies' Night . . . No More." Putting aside your own potential gender biases for a moment, do you agree with the governor or the court concerning offering reduced prices on admission and/or drinks to only women in clubs, bars, and restaurants? Is this a real case of discrimination that should be protected under the law or an effective pricing strategy? Explain your reasoning.

Note: For questions 5–9, you may use the student side of the online learning center. Click on pricing.

5. A department store's maintained markup is 38 percent, reductions are $560, and net sales are $28,000. What's the initial markup percentage?

6. Maintained markup is 39 percent, net sales are $52,000, and reductions are $2,500. What are the gross margin in dollars and the initial markup as a percentage? Explain why initial markup is greater than maintained markup.

7. The cost of a product is $150, markup is 50 percent, and markdown is 30 percent. What's the final selling price?

8. Manny Perez bought a tie for $9 and priced it to sell for $15. What was his markup on the tie?

9. Answer the following questions: (a) The Limited is planning a new line of leather jean jackets for fall. It plans to retail the jackets for $100. It is having the jackets produced in the Dominican Republic. Although The Limited does not own the factory, its product development and design costs are $400,000. The total cost of the jacket, including transportation to the stores, is $45. For this line to be successful, The Limited needs to make $900,000 profit. What is its break-even point in units and dollars? (b) The buyer has just found out that The Gap, one of The Limited's major competitors, is bringing out a similar jacket that will retail for $90. If The Limited wishes to match The Gap's price, how many units will it have to sell?

SUGGESTED READINGS

DelVecchio, Devon; H. Shanker Krishnan; and Daniel C. Smith. "Cents or Percent: The Effects of Promotion Framing on Price Expectations and Choice." *Journal of Marketing* 71, no. 3 (2007), pp. 158–70.

Foubert, Bram and Els Gijsbrechts. "Shopper Response to Bundle Promotions for Packaged Goods." *Journal of Marketing Research* 44, no. 4 (2007), pp. 647–62.

Gupta, Diwakar; Arthur V. Hill; and Tatiana Bouzdine-Chameeva. "A Pricing Model for Clearing End-of-Season Retail Inventory." *European Journal of Operational Research* 170, no. 2 (2006), pp. 518–40.

Hardesty, David M.; William O. Bearden; and Jay P. Carlson. "Persuasion Knowledge and Consumer Reactions to Pricing Tactics." *Journal of Retailing* 83, no. 2 (2007), pp. 199–210.

Kamakura, Wagner A. and Wooseong Kang. "Chain-Wide and Store-Level Analysis of Cross-Category Management." *Journal of Retailing* 83, no. 2 (2007), pp. 159–70.

Kukar-Kinney, Monika; Rockney G. Walters; and Scott B. MacKenzie. "Consumer Responses to Characteristics of

Price-Matching Guarantees: The Moderating Role of Price Consciousness." *Journal of Retailing* 83, no. 2 (2007), pp. 211–22.

Levy, Michael; Dhruv Grewal; Praveen Kopalle; and James Hess. "Emerging Trends in Retail Pricing Practice: Implications for Research." *Journal of Retailing* 80, no. 3 (2004), pp. xiii–xxi.

Marn, Michael V.; Eric V. Roegner; and Craig C. Zawada. *The Price Advantage.* New York: Wiley, 2004.

Monroe, Kent. *Pricing: Making Profitable Decisions.* 3rd ed. New York: McGraw-Hill, 2002.

Nagle, Thomas T. and John Hogan. *The Strategy and Tactics of Pricing: A Guide to Growing More Profitably.* 4th ed. Upper Saddle River, NJ: Prentice Hall, 2005.

Thomas, Manoj and Geeta Menon. "When Internal Reference Prices and Price Expectations Diverge: The Role of Confidence." *Journal of Marketing Research* 44, no. 3 (2007), pp. 401–409.

Retail Communication Mix

EXECUTIVE BRIEFING

Spencer Knisely, Director of In-Store Communications, Best Buy

I started working at Best Buy as a store employee when I was attending the University of Wisconsin in Madison in 1994, holding various roles in the field, and ultimately in our corporate support group. Today I oversee an integrated team of visual communication designers, producers, writers, engineers, and vendors responsible for all customer-facing communication in our stores.

Our store environment, as the core of our brand, plays a critical role in communicating our brand message and information about the products we sell to our customers. We strive to provide a fun, interactive shopping atmosphere that presents our merchandise in an approachable way, highlighting the connections between technology and the customer's lifestyle. The goal of our in-store communications is to help customers find the products they want, teach them about the products' benefits, inform them about prices and sales, and provide an entertaining environment that makes them want to come to our stores and stay longer.

In 1997, Best Buy launched the first all-day, country-wide, HDTV in-store network. The network broadcasted and demonstrated the picture quality of HDTV and included entertainment with some messages about Best Buy and vendors' products. The network at that time enabled Best Buy to fill a gap in the consumers' understanding of the marvelous benefits of HD pictures. Best Buy's investment in our network put a real HDTV demonstration in front of the customer and generated the necessary adoption and interest to convince manufacturers and broadcasters to accelerate their commitment. The work has been recognized by the National Academy of Television Arts and Science, which considered the Best Buy retail network, and its creators, for receiving an Emmy award in appreciation for this contribution to a fledgling technology in the industry.

Fast forward to today, we find ourselves in a world with addressable-IP technology available for the delivery of content and communication. Now the possibility of directing different messages to each of the televisions and

CHAPTER 16

QUESTIONS

How can retailers build brand equity for their stores and their private-label merchandise?

How are retailers using new approaches to communicate with their customers?

What are the strengths and weaknesses of the different methods for communicating with customers?

Why do retailers need to have an integrated marketing communication program?

What steps are involved in developing a communication program?

How do retailers establish a communication budget?

How can retailers use the different elements in a communication mix to alter customers' decision-making processes?

digital displays in each store is real. This opens a whole new world of capability, allowing us to provide messaging that is most appealing for the customers in a store's trading area, at the time they need it, making it most relevant to them. In addition, we can change the messaging for different day parts. For example, if we find that the soccer mom segment shops in the morning and the sophisticated gamers shop in the evening, we can show basic information about big-screen TVs with family oriented programming in the morning and information on the latest games in the evening.

Connecting it all together, at Best Buy, we rely on our 5 Families™ group, comprised of the directors responsible for different aspects of our communication programs, to insure that we deliver a consistent message to our customers across all our channels. As a member, I meet regularly with the directors of broadcast advertising, Internet communications, print communications, internal communications to our employees, and public relations. My group also works closely with our merchandising team so that we support the rollout of new merchandising initiatives and campaigns. The goal of our 5 Families™ work is always to be a connected, brand-right, single voice to our customer, from the store outward into every touchpoint.

The preceding chapters in this section on merchandise management described how retailers develop an assortment and merchandise budget plan and then buy and price merchandise. The next step in the retail management decision-making process is to develop and implement a communication program to build appealing brand images, attract customers to stores and Internet sites, and encourage those customers to buy merchandise. The communication program informs customers about the retailer as well as the merchandise and services it offers and plays a role in developing repeat visits and customer loyalty.

Communication programs can have both long- and short-term effects on a retailer's business. From a long-term perspective, communications programs can be used to create and maintain a strong, differentiated image of the retailer and its private-label brands. This image develops customer loyalty and creates a strategic advantage. Thus, brand image–building communication programs complement the objectives of a retailer's CRM program, as discussed in Chapter 11.

In addition, retailers frequently use communication programs to realize the short-term objective of increasing sales during a specified time period. For example, retailers often have sales, during which some or all merchandise is priced at a discount for a short time. Supermarkets usually place weekly ads with coupons that can be used to save money on purchases made during the week.

The first part of this chapter examines the role of communication programs in building brand images. The second part of the chapter focuses on developing and implementing communication programs. The appendix includes more detailed material related to the implementation of advertising programs, including developing the ad message and selecting media for distributing the message.

The ad on the left focuses on a short-term objective—building sales during Mothers Day—while the Old Navy ad on the right is directed toward building Old Navy's brand image—a long term objective.

USING COMMUNICATION PROGRAMS TO DEVELOP BRAND IMAGES AND BUILD CUSTOMER LOYALTY

A **brand** is a distinguishing name or symbol, such as a logo, that identifies the products or services offered by a seller and differentiates those products and services from the offerings of competitors.[1] In a retailing context, the name of the retailer is a brand that indicates to consumers the type of merchandise and services offered by that retailer. As we discussed in Chapter 14, some retailers develop private-label brands that are exclusively sold through their channels. In some cases, this private-label merchandise bears the retailer's name, such as Walgreens aspirin and Victoria's Secret lingerie. In other cases, special brand names are used, such as Macy's INC apparel and Sears' Die Hard batteries.

Value of Brand Image

Brands provide value to both customers and retailers. Brands convey information to consumers about the nature of the shopping experience—the retailer's mix—they will encounter when patronizing a retailer. They also affect customers' confidence in their decisions to buy merchandise from a retailer. Finally, brands can enhance customers' satisfaction with the merchandise and services they buy. Consumers feel different when wearing jewelry bought from Tiffany rather than from Zales or by staying at a Ritz-Carlton hotel rather than a Fairfield Inn.

The value that a brand image offers retailers is referred to as **brand equity.** Strong brand names can affect the customer's decision-making process, motivate repeat visits and purchases, and build loyalty. In addition, strong brand names enable retailers to charge higher prices and lower their marketing costs.

Customer loyalty to brands arises from heightened awareness of the brand and emotional ties to it. For example, Chapter 4 discussed the need for retailers to be in a customer's consideration set. Some retail brands such as Wal-Mart and Sears are so well known by consumers that they typically appear in those consumers' consideration set. In addition, customers identify and have strong emotional relationships with some brands. For example, going to Target has become a cool experience, because people think it is trendy to save money and buy fashionable merchandise in the same store. Customers affectionately use the faux French pronunciation of "Tar-zhay" when referring to Target. High brand awareness and strong emotional connections reduce the incentive of customers to switch to competing retailers.

[handwritten margin notes:]
- affect customer's decision making process
- motivate repeat purchase & visit
- build loyalty
- competitive advantage

A strong brand image also enables retailers to increase their margins. When retailers have high customer loyalty, they can engage in premium pricing and reduce their reliance on price promotions to attract customers. Brands with weaker images are forced to offer low prices and frequent sales to maintain their market share.

Finally, retailers with strong brand names can leverage their brands to introduce new retail concepts with only a limited amount of marketing effort. For example, The Gap has efficiently extended its brand to GapKids, gapbody, GapMaternity, and babyGap, and Toys "R" Us has extended its brand name to Kids "R" Us, Babies "R" Us, Toys "R" Us Toy Box, and Toys "R" Us Express.

As we discussed in Chapter 5, a strong brand name creates a strategic advantage that is very difficult for competitors to duplicate. Just think how hard it would be for Kmart to change its image to that of Wal-Mart or Target, the more successful discount store chains. Retailing View 16.1 examines how JCPenney has worked to reposition its brand.

Building Brand Equity

The activities that a retailer needs to undertake to build the brand equity for its firm or its private-label merchandise are (1) create a high level of brand awareness, (2) develop favorable associations with the brand name, and (3) consistently reinforce the image of the brand.

JCPenney Shifts Its Brand Image **RETAILING VIEW** **16.1**

It is difficult for a store that is more than 100 years old to reposition its brand, but this effort is exactly what JCPenney has undertaken, and just in the nick of time. JCPenney was losing money in 2003 but has moved well into the black as a result of its head-to-toe makeover.

JCPenney broadened its merchandise, with both its own labels and through partnerships with Chris Madden, who developed an exclusive home collection with the retailer, and Ralph Lauren who developed an exclusive, casual apparel line called American Living. JCPenney also sells nicole by Nicole Miller and Bisou Bisou and is adding Sephora cosmetics shops inside its stores.

The changes that have permeated the entire organization started at the top. JCPenney chairperson and chief executive officer Mike Ullman has been remaking the corporate culture so that JCPenney's workforce could communicate their own good feelings to customers. With the new overall brand positioning, "Every Day Matters," sales associates are encouraged to be "prepared to offer encouragement, be their [customers'] friend, and inspire them and to show them we know every day matters," says Ullman.

At the heart of the makeover is a new integrated promotion campaign. Playing off "Every Day Matters," it introduced a series of fast-moving domestic vignettes that celebrate family moments. The original song in the ad, "So Say I," has been downloaded more than 75,000 times on iTunes. The boldest part of the campaign features several online shows, or Webisodes, hosted by the clothing designers and twin brothers Chip and Pepper Foster, who are developing another new line for JCPenney. The series was taped at a public school in New Jersey using real students rather than actors. Called "Flipped," the Webisodes challenge

This scene comes from JCPenney's "Doodle Heart," a 30-second television ad that follows a young girl who finally finds the courage to reveal her true feelings to her secret crush.

students to leave the comfort of their cliques and join a new group. JCPenney hosts the series at www.jcp.com and teases teenagers with an extended commercial to be shown in movie theaters. The goal is for the videos to become a YouTube hit, which teenagers will e-mail to their friends—all of which should drive more and more teenagers to the Web site.

Although "Every Day Matters" isn't designed to sell specific merchandise per se, it features people dressed in JCPenney clothes in everyday situations. Thus, it is selling a way of life and a way of thinking.

Sources: Maria Halkias, "Penney Hoping Love Is in Store," *The Dallas Morning News*, February 13, 2007 (accessed January 25, 2008); Michael Barbaro, "Old Notions Put Aside, Penney Takes Aim at the Heartstrings," The New York Times, July 11, 2007 (accessed January 25, 2008); www.jcp.com (accessed March 7, 2008).

Brand Awareness **Brand awareness** refers to a potential customer's ability to recognize or recall that the brand name is a particular type of retailer or product/service. Thus, brand awareness is the strength of the link between the brand name and the type of merchandise or service in the minds of customers.

There is a range of awareness, from aided recall to top-of-mind awareness. **Aided recall** is when consumers indicate they know the brand when the name is presented to them. **Top-of-mind awareness,** the highest level of awareness, occurs when consumers mention a specific brand name first when they are asked about the type of retailer, a merchandise category, or a type of service. For example, Best Buy has a high top-of-mind awareness if most consumers respond "Best Buy" when asked about retailers that sell consumer electronics. High top-of-mind awareness means that a retailer probably will be in the consideration set when customers decide to shop for a type of product or service.

Retailers build top-of-mind awareness by having memorable names; repeatedly exposing their name to customers through advertising, locations, and sponsorships; and using memorable symbols. Some brand names are easy to remember, such as the name Home Depot. Because "Home" is in its brand name, it probably is more memorable and closely associated with home improvements than the name Lowe's.

Starbucks does very little advertising but has high awareness because of the large number of stores it has. Customers walk and drive by the stores on their way to and from work. The sheer number of stores provides substantial exposure to its brand.

Symbols involve visual images that typically are more easily recalled than words or phrases and thus are useful for building brand awareness. For example, the image of an apple and the golden arches enhances the ability of customers to recall the names Apple Stores and McDonald's.

Sponsorships of well-publicized events also can provide considerable exposure to a retailer's name and increase awareness. For example, watching the Macy's Thanksgiving Parade in New York City (www.macys.com/campaign/parade/parade.jsp) has become a holiday tradition for many families. The Macy's brand name is exposed to tens of millions of television viewers for three hours. In addition, newspaper articles are devoted to previewing the parade and describing it afterward.

Associations Building awareness is only one step in developing brand equity, but the value of the brand is largely based on the associations that customers make with the brand name. **Brand associations** are anything linked to or connected with the brand name in a consumer's memory. For example, some of the associations that consumers might have with Apple are its innovative products, such as the iPhone, iPod, and Macintosh computers, as well as its easy-to-use computer interface and innovative stores. These strong associations influence consumer buying behavior.

Some common associations that retailers develop with their brand name are as follows:

1. *Merchandise category* The most common association is to link the retailer to a category of merchandise. For example, Office Depot would like to have consumers associate its name with office supplies. Then when a need for office supplies arises, consumers immediately think of Office Depot.

2. *Price/quality* Some retailers, such as Saks Fifth Avenue, want to be associated with offering unique,

REFACT

The first Macy's Thanksgiving Day Parade, held in 1924, was organized by a handful of volunteer, immigrant employees.[3]

Macy's annual Thanksgiving day parade and the accompanying publicity builds top-of-mind awareness for the retailer.

high-fashion merchandise. Other retailers, such as Wal-Mart, want associations with low prices and good value.

3. *Specific attribute or benefit* A retailer can link its stores to attributes, such as 7-Eleven's association with providing convenience or Nordstrom's connection with offering a high level of customer service.

4. *Lifestyle or activity* Some retailers associate their name with a specific lifestyle or activity. For example, Patagonia, a retailer offering outdoor sports equipment, is linked to an active, environmentally friendly lifestyle. Pottery Barn is associated with comfortable living in the home.

When people think of Patagonia, they think about an active environmentally friendly lifestyle.

The **brand image** consists of a set of associations that are usually organized around some meaningful themes. Thus, the associations that a consumer might have about McDonald's might be organized into groups such as kids, service, and type of food. Retailing View 16.2 illustrates how L.L. Bean nurtures its brand image of selling high-quality, functional products and providing helpful service for outdoor living.

Consistent Reinforcement The retailer's brand image gets developed and maintained through the elements of the retailer's offering, such as its merchandise assortment, customer service, and pricing, as well as its communications through its store design, Web site and advertising. To develop a strong set of associations and a clearly defined brand image, retailers need to be consistent in portraying the same message to customers over time and across all of the elements of their retail mix.

Retailers need to develop an **integrated marketing communication program**—a program that integrates all of the communication elements to deliver a comprehensive, consistent message. Without this coordination, the communication methods might work at cross-purposes. For example, the retailer's televised advertising campaign might attempt to build an image of exceptional customer service, but the firm's sales promotions might all emphasize low prices. If communication methods aren't used consistently, customers may become confused about the retailer's image and therefore not patronize the store.

For example, Finish Line, the athletic shoe retailer, has developed an integrated marketing communications program that includes television advertising, in-store promotions, and a company-sponsored social networking site.[4] Aimed at its core, young adult target market, the communications ask, "What do your shoes say?" To answer the question, the communications show a skateboarder with the words "Be Bold," a person running upstairs with the words "Be Quick," and someone walking down the street with the words "Be Fresh." The tagline notes, "Your Voice, Your Choice." Instead of organizing shoes by sport, the company divides them into, for example, "Be Fresh" for new products, "Be Strong" for basketball shoes, and "Be Clean" for casual shoes.

Providing a consistent image can be challenging for multichannel retailers. American Eagle Outfitter wants its home page, at www.ae.com, to have the same look and feel as the front windows of its stores. However, each channel has its own needs for image displays. Images used in its stores stress lifestyle connotations, but its online images need to provide more product images. Stores can rely on lifestyle images without highlighting product details because in-store shoppers can see and feel the actual products on display. In addition, images for in-store displays and ads often are difficult to fit within a 17-inch computer screen to promote products effectively online. To address these issues, American Eagle Outfitters considers the needs of all its channels early in the planning of its communication program.[5]

16.2   RETAILING VIEW   L.L. Bean Celebrates the Outdoors

Leon Leonard Bean, an outdoorsman living in Freeport, Maine, founded L.L. Bean in 1912. The first product he sold through the mail was boots (The Maine Hunting Shoe) with waterproof rubber bottoms and lightweight leather tops. The boots provided significant benefits over heavyweight, all-leather boots in wet weather. However, the first pairs he sold had a stitching problem. Bean decided to refund each customer's money, which led to L.L. Bean's legendary "Guarantee of 100% Satisfaction." Some of the associations that L.L. Bean reinforces through its advertising and Web site, as well as other elements in its retail mix, are

L.L. Bean uses its Web site to reinforce its image of offering expertise in practical, economical outdoor merchandise.

- *Friendly*—L.L. Bean is comfortable and familiar, easy to approach.
- *Honest*—L.L. Bean is straightforward and honest. It would never mislead its customers. It provides factual information about its products.
- *Expertise*—L.L. Bean's employees are experts about their products and the outdoors. They'll do anything they can to help customers choose which product is best for them or even help them find the best place to camp.

- *Practical and economical*—Building on its Yankee New England roots, L.L. Bean offers products that are functional, with no-nonsense features, at fair prices. As Bean once said, "I attribute our success to the fact that, to the best of my judgment, every article we offer for sale is practical for the purpose for which we recommend it."

Some of Bean's associates might be unfavorable to its image. For example, the association with its New England heritage may lead some consumers to associate L.L. Bean, with old-fashioned and out-of-date merchandise and an antiquated way of doing business. The brand might also be viewed as very male oriented and not appealing to women or families.

Sources: Leon Gorman and Aaron Pressman, "Want Some Pajamas with that Kayak?" *BusinessWeek,* November 20, 2006, p. 76; *L.L. Bean: The Making of an American Icon* (Boston: Harvard Business School Press, October 3, 2006); Edward Murphy, "Portland, Maine–Based L.L. Bean Ranks High in Customer Loyalty," *Knight Ridder Tribune Business News,* April 8, 2005, p. 1; www.llbean.com (accessed November 14, 2007).

Extending the Brand Name

Retailers can leverage their brand names to support the growth strategies discussed in Chapter 5. For example, IKEA used its strong brand image to enter the U.S. home furnishing retail market successfully; Talbots introduced Talbots Mens; and Pottery Barn launched its Pottery Barn Kids catalog to target families with children. In other cases, retailers have pursued growth opportunities using a new and unrelated brand name. For example, Abercrombie & Fitch uses the brand name Hollister stores that target high school students, and Sears named its home store concept The Great Indoors.

There are both pluses and minuses to extending a brand name to a new concept. An important benefit of extending the brand name is that minimal communication expenses are needed to create awareness and a brand image for the new concept. Customers will quickly transfer their awareness and associations about the original concept to the new concept. However, in some cases, the retailer might not want to have the original brand's associations connected with the new concept. For example, The Limited Brands decided to invest in building a new and different brand image for Victoria's Secret rather than branding the new concept with a name like Limited Secret.

These issues also arise as a retailer expands internationally. Associations with the retailer's brands that are valued in one country may not be valued in another. For example, French consumers prefer to shop at supermarkets that offer good service and high-quality grocery products, whereas German shoppers prefer supermarkets that offer low prices and good value. Thus, a French supermarket retailer with a brand image of quality and service might not be able to leverage its image if it decides to enter the German market.

Retailers communicate with customers using a mix of methods, such as advertising, sales promotion, publicity, Web sites, and e-mail. This chapter focuses on these and other communication vehicles; Chapter 18 will examine how retailers communicate with customers through their store layout, design, and visual merchandising; and Chapter 19 touches on how they communicate through personal selling, as it relates to customer service.

In large retail firms, the communication mix elements examined in this chapter are managed by the firm's marketing or advertising department and the buying organization. The other elements, such as store atmosphere and salespeople, are managed by store personnel and are thus discussed in Section IV. The following sections of this chapter examine the methods that retailers use to communicate with their customers and how they plan and implement communication programs to build brand equity as well as short-term sales.

METHODS OF COMMUNICATING WITH CUSTOMERS

Exhibit 16–1 classifies the communication methods used by retailers. This classification is based on whether the methods are impersonal or personal and paid or unpaid.

Paid Impersonal Communications

Advertising, sales promotions, store atmosphere, and Web sites are examples of paid impersonal communications.

Advertising   Advertising is a form of paid communication to customers using impersonal mass media such as newspapers, TV, radio, direct mail, and the Internet. Following automobile manufacturers, retailers are the seond largest group of national advertisers, spending over $19 billion annually. Walt Disney, McDonald's,

REFACT

McDonald's spends more than $1.7 billion annually on advertising and is the sixteenth largest advertiser in the United States. Sears Holding ranked 17, and Macy's is number 20.[6]

EXHIBIT 16–1
Communication Methods

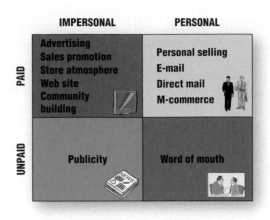

	IMPERSONAL	PERSONAL
PAID	Advertising Sales promotion Store atmosphere Web site Community building	Personal selling E-mail Direct mail M-commerce
UNPAID	Publicity	Word of mouth

REFACT

France recently lifted a ban on television advertising by supermarkets, department stores, hypermarkets, and other retailers. On the first day after the ban was lifted, only minutes after midnight, merchants monopolized all 11 spots on TF1, the most-watched television channel in France.[8]

REFACT

The Christmas story about Rudolph the Red-Nosed Reindeer was developed by a Montgomery Ward copy-writer in 1939 for a store promotion.[12]

Sears Holding, Macy's, JCPenney, Target, and Home Depot are among the 30 largest advertisers, each spending more than $1 billion a year.[7]

Sales Promotions   **Sales promotions** offer extra value and incentives to customers to visit a store or purchase merchandise during a specific period of time. The most common promotion is a sale. Other sales promotions involve special events, in-store demonstrations, contests, and coupons.

Special Events   A **special event** is a sales promotion program comprising a number of sales promotion techniques built around a seasonal, cultural, sporting, musical, or other event.[9] For example, when *The Simpsons Movie* debuted, the convenience store chain 7-Eleven offered real products from the fictional brands featured on the television show in its temporarily renamed Kwik-E-Mart stores. Customers lined up for "Squishees"—the fictional frozen equivalent to 7-Eleven's Slurpees. Others snapped up Krusty Burgers, KrustyO's cereal, and Buzz Cola. Employees even wore bright-green uniforms like that modeled by the show's convenience store proprietor, Apu.[10]

In-Store Demonstrations   Some retailers use in-store demonstrations and offer free samples of merchandise to build excitement in the store and stimulate purchases. In department stores, fashion shows and cooking demonstrations draw customers to the store and encourage impulse purchases. To attract young customers to its downtown Minneapolis store, Macy's brought in the town's most famous rock star, Prince, to perform.[11]

Contests are promotional games of skill or chance. They differ from traditional sales in that (1) only a few customers receive rewards and (2) winners are often determined by luck. For example, fast-food restaurants frequently have contests associated with major films (e.g., *Spiderman*) or sports events (e.g., the World Series).

H&M, a fast-fashion specialty apparel retailer, has developed an interesting contest for Sims 2 players.[13] Using an in-game tool, "Body Shop," and official kits available on the Sims Web site, players design clothes that fit a particular theme, such as "party time" or "skate park." H&M then chooses the best designs and features them in virtual runway shows, where viewers vote for their favorites. The winning design is produced and distributed in select stores worldwide. The public then votes with real

Boxes of KrustyO's cereal at a New York 7-Eleven store, temporarily converted into a Kwik-E-Mart, to promote *The Simpsons Movie*.

money—the designs either succeed in the real world or not. Programs like these generate tremendous excitement and provide valuable information to the retailer.

Coupons   **Coupons** offer a discount on the price of specific items at the time of purchase at the store. Coupons are the most common promotional tool used by supermarkets. Retailers distribute them in their newspaper ads, from in-store kiosks, and through direct mail programs. For example, Publix, a Florida-based supermarket chain, targets promotions at affluent customers using a direct-mail piece that includes recipes for a gourmet meal with coupons to purchase the products needed to prepare it. Manufacturers also distribute coupons for their products that can be used at retailers that stock their products. To attract customers, some supermarkets accept coupons distributed by competing retailers.

A new product, the Mediacart, delivers point-of-decision promotions from a shopping cart.[15] Although it doesn't provide paper coupons in a traditional way, it does inform customers about special deals as they pass them in the aisle. Each video screen is embedded with a radio frequency identification (RFID) chip that interacts with chips installed on store shelves. In addition to promoting special offers, it can record shopping habits, shopper dwelling times, and how shoppers travel through the store—all critical information that the retailer can use to provide a better shopping experience for customers and thus increase sales.

Pop-up Stores   An extreme type of sales promotion is a pop-up store. Pop-up stores are temporary storefronts that exist for only a limited time and generally focus on a new product or limited group of products offered by a retailer, manufacturer, or service provider. They give consumers a chance to interact with the brand and build brand awareness, but they are not designed primarily to sell the product. Retailing View 16.3 describes Meow Mix's pop-up store.

Although most sales promotions are effective at generating short-term interest among customers, they aren't very useful for building long-term loyalty. Customers who participate in the promotion might learn more about a store and return to it, but typically customers attracted by sales promotions are interested in the promoted merchandise, not the retailer. Unfortunately, when a specific promotion is effective for a retailer, competing retailers learn about it quickly and offer the same promotion, which prevents the innovating retailer from gaining any long-term advantage.

Mediacart delivers point-of-decision promotions from a shopping cart.

Store Atmosphere   The retail store itself provides paid, impersonal communications to its customers. **Store atmosphere** reflects the combination of the store's physical characteristics, such as its architecture, layout, signs and displays, colors, lighting, temperature, sounds, and smells, which together create an image in the customer's mind. The atmosphere communicates information about the store's service, its pricing, and the fashionability of its merchandise.[17] Chapter 18 discusses elements of store atmosphere further.

Web Site   Retailers are increasing their emphasis on communicating with customers through their Web sites. Retailers use their Web sites to build their brand image; inform customers of store locations, special events, and the availability of merchandise in local stores; and sell merchandise and services. For example, in addition to selling merchandise, Office Depot's Web site has a Business Resource Center that provides advice and product knowledge, as well as a source of networks to other businesses. There are forms that businesses use to comply with Occupational Safety and Health Act (OSHA) requirements, check job applicant records, estimate cash flow, and develop a sexual harassment policy; workshops for running a business; and local and national business news. By providing this information on its Web site, Office Depot reinforces its image as the essential source of products, services, and information for small businesses.

Community Building   As described in previous chapters, many retailers operate Web sites devoted to community building. These sites offer an opportunity for customers with similar interests to learn about products and services that support their hobbies and share information with others. Visitors to these Web sites can also post questions seeking information and/or comments about issues, products, and services. For example, at the The Knot (www.theknot.com), a community building site targeting couples planning their weddings, a bride-to-be might ask how to deal with a mother-in-law who is too involved in the wedding plans. Others who have experienced this problem then post their advice. REI, an outdoor apparel and equipment retailer, offers adventure travel planning resources for hiking trips, bike tours, paddling, adventure cruises, whitewater rafting, climbing, wildlife viewing, and snowshoeing. Customers can select from more than 90 trips worldwide, including weekend getaways, and experience travel REI-style, with small groups and experienced local guides. By offering these trips, REI creates a community of customers who engage in activities using the merchandise that REI sells. The community thus reinforces REI's brand image.

16.3   RETAILING VIEW   The Cat's Meow

Meow Mix Co. had planned to keep its Fifth Avenue storefront in New York City open for only a week, but the traffic and media attention were so great that it quickly decided to add a second week. The pop-up store, named "the Meow Mix Café," welcomed cats and their owners in for a bit of pampering. The idea was to use the café to introduce consumers to a new "wet" food line, as well as a new cat toy product line.

Meow Mix, the top dry cat food brand, hoped to transition cat owners to wet food through a campaign that generated both publicity and brand trials. The café idea accomplished both beautifully. Cat owners brought their cats to what the Meow Mix team termed an "ESPN Zone for cats," with lots of interactive games, fun, and food. The café's rousing success garnered it 100 million press mentions and enabled the company to distribute 14,000 sample pouches of cat food. A side benefit of the campaign was the calls from potential franchisees wanting information about how to open their own Meow Mix cafés. In total, the firm estimated that its $150,000 investment would yield about $50 million in incremental sales the following year—not a bad return. The café idea was so popular that Meow Mix is planning another pop-up store event, as well as a mobile café that will tour the country on a route determined by visitors to its Web site.

Meow Mix isn't the only firm to use a pop-up store. Kraft Foods was the first to try the concept by setting up a temporary pizzeria on Michigan Avenue in Chicago in an effort to

The Meow Mix Café is a pop-up store—it temporarily pops-up, and then disappears.

generate buzz about a new frozen pizza. Lexus and Motorola have also used pop-ups for short time periods to introduce new models. JCPenney introduced its Chris Madden home collection, sneaker maker Fila a new sportswear line, and Nike a special edition basketball shoe named after NBA All-Star LeBron James, all using pop-up stores.

Sources: www.meowmix.com/newsevents/meowcafe.asp (accessed June 20, 2007); Sandra Jones, "Pop-up Stores Aim to Creat a Buzz in Fleeting Existence," *Chicago Tribune*, February 27, 2007 (accessed January 28, 2007).

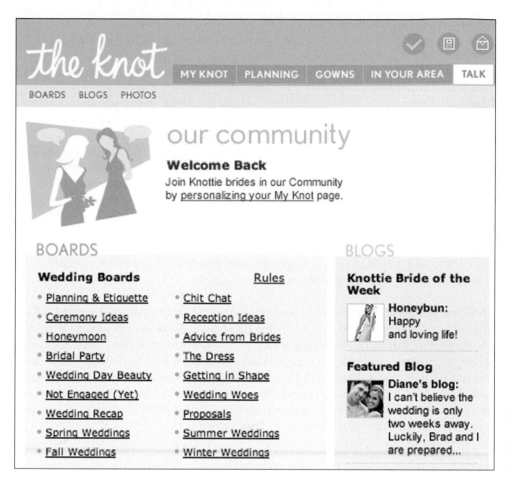

The Knot is a Web site designed to provide information, services, and products for couples planning a wedding. Web site visitors form a community of people with like interests.

Paid Personal Communications

Paid forms of personal communications are growing as new technologies emerge. This section details personal selling, e-mail, and direct mail, along with a newer form of paid personal communications, namely, m-commerce. All of these personal communication vehicles can be tailored to individual customers, whether through a face-to-face interchange, as is the case with personal selling, or by using the customer relationship management (CRM) systems described in Chapter 11. In some cases, however, all customers get the same message.

Personal Selling   Retail salespeople are the primary vehicles for providing paid personal communications to customers. **Personal selling** is a communication process in which salespeople help customers satisfy their needs through face-to-face exchanges of information.

E-mail   **E-mail** is another paid personal communication vehicle that involves sending messages over the Internet. E-mail, like other forms of electronic communications (e.g., Web sites, m-commerce), can be personalized to the specific consumer and thus is similar to communication delivered by salespeople. However, when the same message is delivered electroncially to all recipients, electronic communications more closely resemble advertising. Retailers use e-mail to inform customers of new merchandise and special promotions, confirm the receipt of an order, and indicate when an order has been shipped.

Direct Mail   **Direct mail** refers to any brochure, catalog, advertisement, or other printed marketing material delivered directly to the consumer through the mail or a private delivery company.[19] Retailers have communicated with their

REFACT

Sixty-eight percent of national retailers run e-mail marketing programs, but only one-quarter of the retailers that send e-mails personalize their messages.[18]

customers through the mail for as long as the mail has existed. The direct mail piece can go to all customers, a subset of the customers according to their previous purchases, or even on a personalized basis to individual customers.

Retailers frequently use data collected at POS terminals to target their direct mail promotions (see Chapter 11). For example, Neiman Marcus keeps a database of all purchases made by its credit card customers. With information about each customer's purchases, Neiman Marcus can target direct mail about a new perfume to customers with a history of purchasing such merchandise.

Retailers also can purchase a wide variety of lists that help them target consumers with specific demographic profiles, interests, and lifestyles. For example, a home furnishings store could buy a list of subscribers to *Architectural Digest* in its trading area and then mail a catalog or specific information about home furnishings to those upscale consumers. Finally, many retailers encourage their salespeople to maintain a preferred customer list and use it to mail personalized invitations and notes.

Although relatively expensive on a per customer basis, because of printing, mail costs, and a relatively low response rate, direct mail is still extensively used by many retailers because people respond favorably to personal messages.

M-Commerce   As technology and customers together become more sophisticated, more retailers are augmenting their e-mail communications with **m-commerce (mobile commerce),** which involves communicating with and even selling to customers through wireless handheld devices, such as cellular telephones and personal digital assistants (PDAs).[20] Tech-savvy customers use their cellphones and PDAs to obtain sports scores, weather, music videos, and text messages in real time. It thus is a natural evolution for retailers to tap into this trend. Consider some of these innovative m-commerce applications:

- Grand Rapids, Michigan–based hypermarket Meijer offers consumers the opportunity to learn in advance when the retailer's gasoline prices are going to go up, before the hikes actually hit the pump.[21]
- GPShopper is an Internet-style search engine that lets shoppers search a chain's entire inventory to see if an item is in stock at a nearby store.[22] This service is available for stores such as Best Buy, Toys "R" Us, and Sports Authority.
- Retailers can send coupons directly to shoppers' cellphones.[23] Redemptions rates have been as high as 40 percent, compared with less than 2 percent for many print and online campaigns. Shoppers text a code found on store signs to get the coupon, then display on their phone at checkout.
- Customers can buy products instantly using text messages, a process that eliminates the need to go to a store or even visit a Web site.[24] If a customer sees an ad for a coat in a magazine, he or she can order it by sending the text code that appear next to item through a cellphone or PDA. Not limited to merchandise, some concert halls are using this technology to sell tickets, and some charities are taking donations by text message.

The Gap and other retailers have partnered with (Product)RED, a brand designed to engage businesses in the fight against AIDS in Africa.

Unpaid Impersonal Communications

The primary method for generating unpaid impersonal communication is publicity. **Publicity** is communication through significant, unpaid presentations about the retailer, usually a news story, in impersonal media. Examples of publicity are newspaper and TV coverage of Linens-n-Things pink gift card, which donates $1 per card to the National Breast Cancer Foundation.[26] The Gap, Emporio Armani, and Apple are several of the companies that have partnered with

(Product)^RED, a brand designed to engage businesses in the fight against AIDS in Africa. Up to 50 percent of the profits from all (Product)^RED–branded items go to the Global Fund to counter AIDS in Africa. Other retailers receive positive publicity for selling products that benefit humanitarian causes, including Bath and Body Works, a division of Limited Brands Inc., which sells a line of candles and fragrances that benefit the Elton John AIDS Foundation, and Macy's, which is selling baskets made by Rwandan widows to help support that African nation's developing economy.

For years, Wal-Mart did little to promote itself as a positive social force, believing its low prices would speak for themselves. But it increasingly has been subjected to public criticism from labor unions and environmentalists, so Wal-Mart hired its first public relations firm. The public relations firm set up a war room to respond quickly to attacks or adverse news. Internet blogs and grass-roots initiatives were developed to stimulate popular support for Wal-Mart. The firm also looked for proactive opportunities to demonstrate Wal-Mart's social consciousness. For example, after Hurricane Katrina, Wal-Mart rushed to reopen its stores and speed supplies to storm-damaged areas. Evacuees and local officials proclaimed in the news that Wal-Mart had outhustled the federal government. Wal-Mart quickly made a $15 million donation to the hurricane-relief fund organized by former presidents Clinton and Bush. These two ex-presidents then praised Wal-Mart's generosity.[27] Retailing View 16.4 describes how Neiman Marcus annually creates newsworthy events by offering unusual gifts in its Christmas catalog and thus further builds its image of offering unique merchandise.

Most communications are directed toward potential customers. Publicity, however, often serves to communicate with employees and investors. Favorable news stories generated by publicity can build employee morale and help improve employee performance. Much of the communication to employees is done through internal e-mails, newsletters, magazines, bulletin board notices, handbooks, and inserts into pay envelopes. However, news about the retailer published in newspapers or broadcast over TV and radio can have a greater impact on employees than internally distributed information. Just like customers, employees place more credibility on information provided by news media than on that generated by the retailer. Similarly, stockholders, the financial community, vendors, and government agencies are influenced by publicity generated by retailers.

Unpaid Personal Communications

Finally, retailers communicate with their customers through **word of mouth (WOM),** or communication between people about a retailer.[29] A relatively new pathway for WOM communication is through social shopping. **Social shopping** is a communication channel in which consumers use the Internet to engage in the shopping process by exchanging preferences, thoughts, and opinions among friends, family, and others.[30] Customers or users review, communicate about, and aggregate information about products, prices, and deals.

Many retailers encourage customers to post reviews of products they have bought or used and even have visitors to their Web sites rate the quality of the reviews. Research has shown that these online product reviews increase customer loyalty and provide a competitive advantage for sites that offer them.[31] One survey reveals that of the shoppers who bought from sites with reviews, 40 percent said the review was the main reason they made the purchase. That group of product review users was also 21 percent more satisfied with its purchases than other buyers and 18 percent more likely than other buyers to buy from that site the next time it needed similar products.

The Internet site Shopstyle.com (www.shopstyle.com) features clothing and accessories from hundreds of other Internet stores. Shoppers can browse different looks that feature items across several retailers, put together outfits on their own, and then share and discuss them with friends. Some retailers are actively influencing

REFACT

People who have an unsatisfactory experience with retail service typically tell nine other people, on average, about their experience.[28]

the social shopping process. In these cases, it becomes a form of paid personal communication. For example, Shopstyle.com featured a contest with a prize donated by Shopbop.com (www.shopbop.com), an online retailer.[32] Customers exposed to the contest on Shopstyle may have been lured to Shopbop's site to buy. Nordstrom and Bluefly.com (www.bluefly.com) also host pages on Shopstyle.com that feature outfits they sell. The Gap maintains interactive pages on Stylehive.com (www.stylehive.com), a MySpace-like site on which shoppers exchange tips and post pictures of their favorite sites.

It is sometimes unclear whether the outfits posted or the advice given on a Web site is paid for by the retailer, which creates an ethically troubling issue for many consumers.[33] For instance, a Stylehive user named "Nataliezee" posts her favorite picks for outfits. Although her biography notes that she's an associate editor of *Craft Magazine*, it doesn't mention that the magazine has a deal with Stylehive to feature its wares prominently and use the advice of "Nataliezee."

Many retailers, feature customer reviews on their own Web sites.[34] In some cases, these reviews pose a potential risk if the review is negative. A dissatisfied customer's online comments could criticize the retailer or the products it offers. Even a negative online review can have a silver lining for retailers though. Negative reviews can help customers affirm that they've considered all of the issues before making a decision, as long as the reviews aren't overwhelmingly negative. Some negative reviews also add a sense of legitimacy to the information offered.

REFACT

Today, more than half the people in the United States trust their peers for information about a company or product more than they trust experts, such as doctors and academics. In 2003, only one-fifth of people surveyed picked their peers as their most trusted source.[35]

16.4   RETAILING VIEW   The Ultimate Gifts

The Neiman Marcus Christmas book is perhaps the nation's best-known retail catalog. Its reputation is largely due to its annual tradition of ultra-extravagant his-and-hers gifts. The Christmas book was first distributed in 1915 as a Christmas card inviting Neiman Marcus customers to visit the store during the holiday season. In the late 1950s, customers were asking Neiman Marcus about unique gifts and merchandise not available in the store or from other catalogs.

In 1959, the gift of a black angus steer, delivered on the hoof or in steaks, generated a lot of publicity and elevated the catalog to national prominence. The most expensive gift was a an unfinished Boeing business jet for more than $35 million. Most of these gifts do not sell. A highly publicized chocolate Monopoly set was purchased by Christie Hefner, president of Playboy Enterprises, for her father, Hugh Hefner, founder of *Playboy* magazine.

The 2007 Christmas book featured a $1.59 million private holiday concert for 500 people featuring piano virtuoso Lola Astanova. The evening, hosted by Regis Philbin, would be filmed as a party favor for guests. The Steinway Concert Grand piano on which the artist plays, and featuring her autograph, gets left for the host. The Neiman Marcus Christmas Book is mailed to 1.8 million customers and is also available on its Web site.

The Neiman Marcus 2007 Christmas book featured an under-the-sea dream machine with leather seats, a panorama window, air conditioning, and a two-day training course for $1.4 million.

Sources: Nathalie Atkinson "Who Wants Another Lexus?" *National Post,* November 8, 2007; Maria Halkias, "Marcus Unwraps Its Christmas Catalog," *The Dallas Morning News,* October 3, 2007; www.neimanmarcus.com (accessed November 14, 2007); www.incircle.com (accessed November 14, 2007).

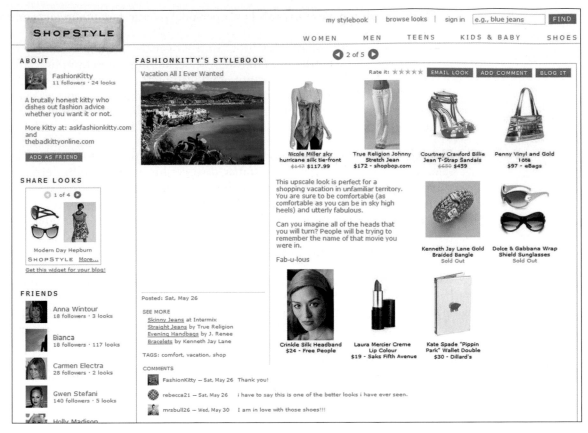

At www.shopstyle.com **shoppers can browse different items across several retailers, put together outfits, and then share and discuss them with friends.**

Strengths and Weaknesses of Communication Methods

Exhibit 16–2 compares these communication methods in terms of control, flexibility, credibility, and cost.

Control   Retailers have more control when using paid versus unpaid methods. When using advertising, sales promotions, store atmosphere, Web site, direct mail, and m-commerce, retailers determine the message's content. With advertising, sales promotion, e-mail, direct mail, and m-commerce, they also control the time of its delivery. Because salespeople have their own style and might deliver different

	Control	Flexibility	Credibility	Cost
Paid Impersonal				
Advertising	High	Lowest	Lowest	Modest
Sales promotion	High	Lowest	N/A	Modest
Store atmosphere	High	Lowest	N/A	Modest
Web site	High	Modest	Low	Modest
Community building	Modest	High	N/A	Moderate
Paid Personal				
Personal selling	Modest	Highest	Low	Highest
E-mail	Highest	High	Low	Low
Direct mail	Highest	High	Low	Highest
M-commerce	High	High	Low	Moderate
Unpaid Impersonal				
Publicity	Low	Low	High	Low
Unpaid Personal				
Word of mouth	Low	Low	High	Low

EXHIBIT 16–2
Comparison of Communication Methods

messages, retailers have less control over personal selling than other paid communication methods.

In contrast, retailers have very little control over the content or timing of publicity and word-of-mouth communications. Because unpaid communications are designed and delivered by people not employed by the retailer, they can communicate unfavorable as well as favorable information. For example, news coverage of a food poisoning incident at a restaurant or racial discrimination at a hotel can result in significant declines in sales.

Flexibility   Personal selling is the most flexible communication method, because salespeople can talk with each customer, discover his or her specific needs, and develop unique presentations. E-mails, direct mail, and m-commerce are also more flexible because they can be personalized to specific customer interests, and Web sites can be tailored to individual visitors on the basis of their past buying behavior. Other communication methods are less flexible. For example, mass media ads deliver the same message to all customers.

Credibility   Because publicity and word of mouth are typically communicated by independent sources, their information is usually more credible than the information in paid communication sources. For example, customers tend to doubt claims made by salespeople and in ads because they know retailers are trying to promote their merchandise. Recognizing that younger consumers have greater doubts about the credibility of advertising, retailers increasingly are using newer electronic methods of communications, such as encouraging WOM through social shopping and posting reviews.

REFACT

Eighty-six percent of teens and young adults, ages 14 to 30 years, ranked word of mouth as the most credible source among nine information sources, and 46 percent said friends were their leading source of information about fashion merchandise.[36]

Cost   Publicity and word of mouth are classified as unpaid communication methods, but retailers do incur costs to stimulate them. For example, the retailer and manufacturer Perry Ellis International (PEI) has an agreement with the Miami Dolphins and Dolphins Stadium to promote the company's brands at Dolphins games.[37] Its Cubavera logo appears on one backlit, permanent sign for all stadium events, including Dolphins games, Florida Marlins games, the FedEx Orange Bowl, and Monster Truck Jam events, which host a combined 2.5 million attendees each year. The agreement also gives PEI the rights to place the Dolphins Stadium logo on PEI merchandise and stadium employee uniforms. PEI also has the right to promote the company as an exclusive apparel supplier of Dolphins Stadium and an official

Perry Ellis International's Cubavera logo is seen by 2.5 million people each year at Miami Dolphins' Stadium.

sponsor of the Miami Dolphins and Dolphins Stadium. Paid impersonal communications often are economical. For example, a full-page advertisement in the *Los Angeles Times* costs about two cents per person to deliver the message in the ad.

In contrast, personal selling, because of its flexibility, is more effective than advertising, but it is more costly. A 10-minute presentation by a retail salesperson paid $12 per hour costs the retailer $2—100 times more than exposing a customer to a newspaper, radio, or TV ad. While maintaining a Web site on a server is relatively inexpensive, it is costly to design, continuously update, and promote the site to attract visitors; however, e-mails can be sent to customers at low cost.

Due to these differences, communication methods differ in their effectiveness in terms of performing communication tasks, as well as at different stages of the customer's decision-making process (see Chapter 4). Typically, advertising through mass media advertising and m-commerce are most effective for building awareness. Web sites, e-mail, direct mail, m-commerce, sales promotions, and newspaper advertising are effective for conveying information about a retailer's offerings and prices. Personal selling, community building, and WOM through social shopping are most effective at persuading customers to purchase merchandise. Television advertising, salespeople, community building, publicity, Web sites, and store atmosphere do the best job building the retailer's brand image and encouraging repeat purchases and store loyalty.

PLANNING THE RETAIL COMMUNICATION PROGRAM

Exhibit 16–3 illustrates the four steps involved in developing and implementing a retail communication program: establish objectives, determining a budget, allocating the budget, and implementing and evaluating the mix. The following sections detail each of these steps.

Establish Objectives

Retailers establish objectives for their communication programs to provide (1) direction for people implementing the program and (2) a basis for evaluating its effectiveness. As discussed at the beginning of this chapter, some communication programs can have a long-term objective, such as creating or altering a retailer's brand image. Other communication programs focus on improving short-term performance, such as increasing store traffic on a specific weekend.

Communication Objectives   Although retailers' overall objective is to generate long- and short-term sales and profits, they often use communication objectives rather than sales objectives to plan and evaluate their communication programs. **Communication objectives** are specific goals related to the retail communication mix's effect on the customer's decision-making process.

Exhibit 16–4 shows some hypothetical information about customers in the target market for a Safeway supermarket. This information illustrates the goals

Steps in Developing a Retail Communication Program   **EXHIBIT 16–3**

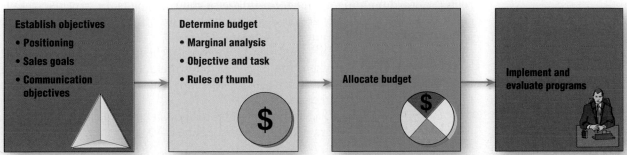

EXHIBIT 16–4
Communication Objectives
and Stages in Consumers'
Decision-Making Process

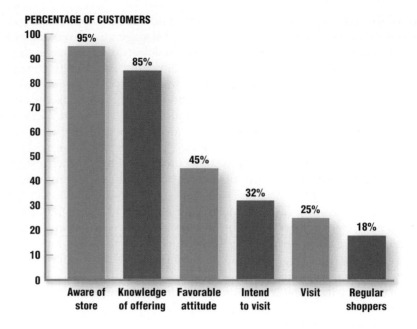

related to the stages in the consumer decision-making process outlined in Chapter 4. Note that 95 percent of the customers are aware of the store (the first stage in the decision-making process), and 85 percent know the type of merchandise it sells. But only 45 percent of the customers in the target market have a favorable attitude toward the store. Thirty-two percent intend to visit the store during the next few weeks; 25 percent actually visit the store during the next two weeks; and 18 percent regularly shop at the store.

In this hypothetical example, most people know about the store and its offering. The major problem confronting the Safeway supermarket is the big drop between knowledge and favorable attitudes. Thus, the store should develop a communication program with the objective of increasing the percentage of customers with a favorable attitude toward it.

To effectively implement and evaluate a communication program, its objectives must be clearly stated in quantitative terms. The target audience for the communication mix needs to be defined, along with the degree of change expected and the time period during which the change will be realized.

For example, a communication objective for a Safeway program might be to increase from 45 percent to 55 percent within three months the percentage of customers within a five-mile radius of the store who have a favorable attitude toward the store. This objective is clear and measurable. It indicates the task that the program should address. The people who implement the program thus know what they're supposed to accomplish.

The communication objectives and approaches used by vendors and retailers differ, and these differences can lead to conflicts. Some of these points of conflict are as follows:

- *Long-term versus short-term goals* Most communications by vendors are directed toward building a long-term image of their products. In contrast, retailer communications typically are used to announce promotions and special sales that generate short-term revenues.
- *Product versus location* When vendors advertise their branded products, they aren't concerned about where the customer buys them, as long as they buy their brand. In contrast, retailers aren't concerned about what brands customers buy as long as they buy them in their store.
- *Geographic coverage* Because people tend to shop at stores near their homes or workplaces, most retailers use local newspapers, TV, and radio to target their

communications. National retailers, however, increasingly are utilizing national media such as magazines and television, particularly for brand-building programs. Because most manufacturer's brands are sold nationally, these vendors tend to use national TV and magazines.

• *Breadth of merchandise* Typically, because vendors have a small number of products to promote, they can devote a lot of attention to developing consistent communication programs for each brand they make. Retailers have to develop communications programs that promote a much wider range of products.

Even though vendors and retailers have different goals, they frequently work together to develop mutually beneficial outcomes, as illustrated by Wal-Mart and Coppertone's sunscreen promotion program. The program was based on the idea that the spokescharacter Little Miss Coppertone had lost her dog in a Wal-Mart store. For three months prior to the event, the program was promoted to sales associates through Wal-Mart's internal communication channels, including its satellite TV broadcasts, headquarters meetings, and sell sheets distributed to sales associates. On the day of the event, a scavenger hunt, Wal-Mart greeters wore "Spot the Dog" buttons and distributed game pieces to children and their parents. The game pieces described the scavenger hunt and encouraged customers to find clues located in different areas of the store—sun care, lawn and garden, and pet food. The pieces also promoted Coppertone's innovative rub-free sprays and offered a $2 Wal-Mart coupon for the products. **Shelf talkers**—signs on shelves providing information about the merchandise and its price—in each area provided answers to the clues. When all three answers were filled in, the customer turned in the game pieces for a free beach ball at the "Scavenger Hunt Center" in the store.

The co-marketing promotion benefited both Wal-Mart and Coppertone. It built sun care customers' loyalty to Wal-Mart and Coppertone, kept customers in the Wal-Mart store longer while encouraging them to visit different areas of the store, and increased sunscreen sales for Wal-Mart and Coppertone. Almost 2,500 stores participated in the one-day event. Over 1.2 million prizes were delivered. Wal-Mart's sales of Coppertone sunscreen increased by 6 percent, and sales in other categories also increased.[38]

Determine the Communication Budget

The second step in developing a retail communication program is determining a budget (see Exhibit 16–3). The economically correct method for setting the communication budget is marginal analysis. Even though retailers usually don't have enough information to perform a complete marginal analysis, the method shows managers how they should approach budget-setting programs. The marginal analysis method for setting a communication budget is the approach that retailers should use when making all of their resource allocation decisions, including the number of locations in a geographic area (Chapter 8), the allocation of merchandise to stores (Chapter 14), the staffing of stores (Chapter 17), and the floor and shelf space devoted to merchandise categories (Chapter 18).

Marginal Analysis Method   **Marginal analysis** is based on the economic principle that firms should increase communication expenditures as long as each additional dollar spent generates more than a dollar of additional contribution. To illustrate marginal analysis, consider Diane West, the owner and manager of a specialty store selling women's business clothing. Exhibit 16–5 shows her analysis to determine how much she should spend next year on her communication program.

For 21 different communication expense levels (column 1), she estimates her store sales (column 2), gross margin (column 3), and other expenses (columns 4 and 5). Then she calculates the contribution, excluding expenses on communications (column 6), and the profit when the communication expenses are considered (column 7). To estimate the sales generated by different levels of communications,

EXHIBIT 16–5   Marginal Analysis for Setting Diane West's Communication Budget

Level	Communication expenses (1)	Sales (2)	Gross margin realized (3)	Rental expense (4)	Personnel expense (5)	Contribution before communication expenses (6) = (3) − (4) − (5)	Profit after communication expenses (7) = (6) − (1)	
1	$0	$240,000	$96,000	$44,000	$52,200	$ (200)	$ (200)	
2	5,000	280,000	112,000	48,000	53,400	10,600	5,600	
3	10,000	330,000	132,000	53,000	54,900	24,100	14,100	
4	15,000	380,000	152,000	58,000	56,400	37,600	22,600	
5	20,000	420,000	168,000	62,000	57,600	48,400	28,400	
6	25,000	460,000	184,000	66,000	58,800	59,200	34,200	
7	30,000	500,000	200,000	70,000	60,000	70,000	40,000	Last year
8	35,000	540,000	216,000	74,000	61,200	80,800	45,800	
9	40,000	570,000	228,000	77,000	62,100	88,900	48,900	
10	45,000	600,000	240,000	80,000	63,000	97,000	52,000	
11	50,000	625,000	250,000	82,500	63,750	103,750	53,750	
12	55,000	650,000	260,000	85,000	64,500	110,500	55,500	Chosen budget
13	60,000	670,000	268,000	87,000	65,100	115,900	55,900	
14	65,000	690,000	276,000	89,000	65,700	121,300	56,300	Best profit
15	70,000	705,000	282,000	90,500	66,150	125,350	55,350	
16	75,000	715,000	286,000	91,500	66,450	128,050	53,050	
17	80,000	725,000	290,000	92,500	66,750	130,750	50,750	
18	85,000	735,000	294,000	93,500	67,050	133,450	48,450	
19	90,000	745,000	298,000	94,500	67,350	136,150	46,150	
20	95,000	750,000	300,000	95,000	67,500	137,500	42,500	
21	100,000	750,000	300,000	95,000	67,500	137,500	37,500	

West can simply rely on her judgment and experience, or she might analyze past data to determine the relationship between communication expenses and sales. Historical data also provide information about the gross margin and other expenses as a percentage of sales.

Notice that at low levels of communication expenses, an additional $5,000 in communication expenses generates more than a $5,000 incremental contribution. For example, increasing the communication expense from $15,000 to $20,000 increases the contribution by $10,800 (or $48,400 – $37,600). When the communication expense reaches $65,000, further increases of $5,000 generate less than $5,000 in additional contributions. For example, increasing the budget from $65,000 to $70,000 generates only an additional $4,050 in contribution ($125,350 – $121,300).

In this example, West determines that the maximum profit would be generated with a communication expense budget of $65,000. But she notices that expense levels between $55,000 and $70,000 all result in about the same level of profit. Thus, West makes a conservative decision and establishes a $55,000 budget for her communication expenses.

In most cases, it's very hard to perform a marginal analysis because managers don't know the relationship between communication expenses and sales. Note that the numbers in Exhibit 16–5 are simply West's estimates; they may not be accurate.

Sometimes retailers perform experiments to get a better idea of the relationship between communication expenses and sales. Say, for example, a catalog retailer selects several geographic areas in the United States with the same sales potential. The retailer then distributes 100,000 catalogs in the first area, 200,000 in the second area, and 300,000 in the third. Using the sales and costs for each distribution level, it could conduct an analysis like the one in Exhibit 16–5 to determine the

Objective: Increase the percentage of target market (working women) who know of our store's location and that purchase business attire from 25 percent to 50 percent over the next 12 months.		
Task: 480, 30–second radio spots during peak commuting hours	$12,000	
Task: Sign with store name near entrance to mall	4,500	
Task: Display ad in the Yellow Pages	500	
Objective: Increase the percentage of target market who indicate that our store is their preferred store for buying their business wardrobe from 5 percent to 15 percent in 12 months.		
Task: Develop TV campaign to improve image and run 50, 30–second commercials	$24,000	
Task: Hold four "Dress for Success" seminars followed by a wine-and-cheese party	8,000	
Objective. Sell merchandise remaining at end of season.		
Task: Special event	$6,000	
Total budget	**$55,000**	

EXHIBIT 16–6

Illustration of Objective-and-Task Method for Setting a Communication Budget

most profitable distribution level. (Chapter 15 described the use of experiments to determine the relationship between price and sales.)

Some other methods that retailers use to set communication budgets are the objective-and-task and rules of thumb methods, which includes the affordable, percentage-of-sales, and competitive parity methods. These methods are less sophisticated than marginal analysis but easier to use.

Objective-and-Task Method   The **objective-and-task method** determines the budget required to undertake specific tasks to accomplish communication objectives. To use this method, the retailer first establishes a set of communication objectives, then determines the necessary tasks and their costs. The total of all costs incurred to undertake the tasks is the communication budget.

Exhibit 16–6 illustrates how Diane West could use the objective-and-task method to complement her marginal analysis. West establishes three objectives: to increase awareness of her store, to create a greater preference for her store among customers in her target market, and to promote the sale of merchandise remaining at the end of each season. The estimated communication budget she requires to achieve these objectives is $55,000.

In addition to defining her objectives and tasks, West rechecks the financial implications of the communication mix by projecting the income statement for next year using the communication budget (see Exhibit 16–7). This income statement includes an increase of $25,000 in communication expenses compared with last year. But West believes this increase in the communication budget will boost annual sales from $500,000 to $650,000. According to West's projections, the increase in communication expenses will raise store profits. The results of both the marginal analysis and the objective-and-task methods suggest a communication budget between $55,000 and $65,000.

Rule-of-Thumb Methods   The previous two methods set the communication budget by estimating communication activities' effects on the firm's future sales or communication objectives. The **rule-of-thumb methods** discussed in this section use the opposite logic. They use past sales and communication activities to determine the present communication budget.[39]

	Last Year	Next Year
Sales	$500,000	$650,000
Gross margin (realized)	200,000	260,000
Rental, maintenance, etc.	−70,000	−85,000
Personnel	−60,000	−64,500
Communications	−30,000	−55,000
Profit	$ 40,000	$55,500

EXHIBIT 16–7

Financial Implications of Increasing Communication Budget

Affordable Budgeting Method   When using the **affordable budgeting method**, retailers first forecast their sales and expenses, excluding communication expenses, during the budgeting period. The difference between the forecast sales and expenses plus the desired profit is then budgeted for the communication mix. In other words, the affordable method sets the communication budget by determining what money is available after operating costs and profits are subtracted.

The major problem with the affordable method is that it assumes that communication expenses don't stimulate sales and profit. Communication expenses are just a cost of business, like the cost of merchandise. When retailers use the affordable method, they typically cut "unnecessary" communication expenses if sales fall below the forecast rather than increasing communication expenses to increase sales.

REFACT

Supermarkets spend about 1 percent of their annual sales revenue on advertising, whereas department store retailers spend almost 4 percent of sales, and women's apparel specialty retailers spend 5 percent.[40]

"fightin budget"

x

Percentage-of-Sales Method   The **percentage-of-sales method** sets the communication budget as a fixed percentage of forecast sales. Retailers use this method to determine the communication budget by forecasting sales during the budget period and then applying a predetermined percentage to set the budget. The percentage may be the retailer's historical percentage or the average percentage used by similar retailers.

The problem with the percentage-of-sales method is that it assumes that the same percentage used in the past, or used by competitors, is appropriate for the future. Consider a retailer that hasn't opened new stores in the past but plans to open many new stores in the current year. It must create customer awareness for these new stores, so the communication budget should be much larger in the current year than in the past.

Using the same percentage as competitors also may be inappropriate. For example, a retailer might have better locations than its competitors. Due to these locations, customers may already have a high awareness of the retailer's stores. Thus, the retailer may not need to spend as much on communications as competitors with poorer locations.

One advantage of both the percentage-of-sales method and the affordable method for determining a communication budget is that the retailer won't spend beyond its means. Because the level of spending is determined by sales, the budget will only go up when sales go up and as the retailer generates more sales to pay for the additional communication expenses. When times are good, these methods work well because they allow the retailer to communicate more aggressively with customers. But when sales fall, communication expenses are cut, which may accelerate the sales decline.

Competitive Parity Method   Under the **competitive parity method,** the communication budget is set so that the retailer's share of its communication expenses equals its share of the market. For example, consider a sporting goods store in a small town. To use the competitive parity method, the owner manager would first estimate the total amount spent on communications by all sporting goods retailers in town. Then the owner-manager would estimate his or her store's market share for sporting goods and multiply that market share percentage by the sporting goods stores' total advertising expenses to set the budget. Assume that the owner-manager's estimate of advertising for sporting goods by all stores is $5,000 and the estimate of his or her store's market share is 45 percent. On the basis of these estimates, the owner-manager would set the store's communication budget at $2,250 to maintain competitive parity.

Similar to the other rule-of-thumb methods, the competitive parity method doesn't allow retailers to exploit the unique opportunities or problems they confront in a market. If all competitors used this method to set communication budgets, their market shares would stay about the same over time (assuming that the retailers develop equally effective campaigns and other retail mix activities).

Allocate the Promotional Budget

After determining the size of the communication budget, the third step in the communication planning process is to allocate the budget (see Exhibit 16–3). In this step, the retailer decides how much of its budget to allocate to specific communication elements, merchandise categories, geographic regions, or long- and short-term objectives. For example, Dillard's must decide how much of its communication budget to spend in each area it has stores: Southeast, Mid-Atlantic, Southwest, Midwest, and West Coast. Michaels decides how much to allocate to merchandise associated with different crafts. The sporting goods store owner-manager must decide how much of the store's $2,250 communication budget to spend on promoting the store's image versus generating sales during the year and how much to spend on advertising and special promotions.

Research indicates that allocation decisions are more important than the decision about the amount to spend on communications.[41] In other words, retailers often can realize the same objectives by reducing the size of the communication budget but allocating it more effectively.

An easy way to make such allocation decisions is to spend about the same in each geographic region or for each merchandise category. But this allocation rule probably won't maximize profits because it ignores the possibility that communication programs might be more effective for some merchandise categories or for some regions than for others. Another approach is to use rules of thumb, such as basing allocations on the sales level or contributions for the merchandise category.

Allocation decisions, like budget-setting decisions, should use the principles of marginal analysis. The retailer should allocate the budget to areas that will yield the greatest return. This approach for allocating a budget is sometimes referred to as the **high-assay principle.** Consider a miner who can spend his time digging on two claims. The value of the gold on one claim is assayed at $20,000 per ton, whereas the assay value on the other claim is $10,000 per ton. Should the miner spend two-thirds of his time at the first mine and one-third of his time at the other mine? Of course not! The miner should spend all of his time mining the first claim until the assay value of the ore mined drops to $10,000 a ton, at which time he can divide his time equally between the claims.

Similarly, a retailer may find that its customers have a high awareness and very favorable attitude toward its women's clothing but not know much about its men's clothing. In this situation, a dollar spent on advertising men's clothing might generate more sales than a dollar spent on women's clothing, even though the sales of women's clothing is greater than the sales of men's clothing.

Plan, Implement, and Evaluate Communication Programs—Two Illustrations

The final stage in developing a retail communication program is its implementation and evaluation (see Exhibit 16–3). This chapter's appendix discusses some specific issues in implementing advertising programs, including developing the message, selecting the media used for delivering the message, and determining the timing and frequency for presenting the message. This final section of the chapter illustrates the planning and evaluation process for two communication programs: an advertising campaign by a small specialty retailer, and a sales promotion opportunity confronting a supermarket chain.

Advertising Campaign   Hypothetically, imagine South Gate West is one of several specialty import home furnishing stores competing for upscale shoppers in Charleston, South Carolina. The store has the appearance of both a fine antique store and a traditional home furnishing shop, but most of its merchandise is new Asian imports.[42]

Harry Owens, the owner, realized his communication budget was considerably less than the budget of the local Pier 1 store. (Pier 1 is a large national chain that sells imported home furnishings.) He decided to concentrate his limited budget on a specific segment and use very creative copy and distinctive artwork in his advertising. His target market was knowledgeable, sophisticated consumers of housewares and home decorative items. His experience indicated the importance of personal selling for more seasoned shoppers because they (1) make large purchases and (2) seek considerable information before making a decision. Thus, Owens spent part of his communication budget on training his sales associates.

The advertising program Owens developed emphasized his store's distinctive image. He used the newspaper as his major vehicle. Competitive ads contained line drawings of furniture with prices. His ads emphasized imagery associated with Asian furniture by featuring off-the-beaten-path scenes of Asian countries with unusual art objects. This theme was also reflected in the store's atmosphere.

To evaluate his communication program, Owens needed to compare the results of his program with the objectives he had developed during the first part of the planning process. To measure his campaign's effectiveness, he conducted an inexpensive tracking study. Telephone interviews were performed periodically with a representative sample of furniture customers in his store's trading area. Communication objectives were assessed using the following questions:

Communication Objectives	Questions
Awareness	What stores sell East Asian furniture?
Knowledge	Which stores would you rate outstanding on the following characteristics?
Attitude	On your next shopping trip for East Asian furniture, which store would you visit first?
Visit	Which of the following stores have you been to?

Here are the survey results for one year:

Communication Objective	Before Campaign	6 Months After	One Year After
Awareness (% mentioning store)	38%	46%	52%
Knowledge (% giving outstanding rating for sales assistance)	9	17	24
Attitude (% first choice)	13	15	19
Visit (% visited store)	8	15	19

The results show a steady increase in awareness, knowledge of the store, and choice of the store as a primary source of East Asian furniture. This research provides evidence that the advertising was conveying the intended message to the target audience.

Sales Promotion Opportunity Many sales promotion opportunities undertaken by retailers are initiated by vendors. For example, Colgate-Palmolive might offer the following special promotion to Kroger: During a one-week period, Kroger can order Fab laundry detergent in the 48-ounce size at 15 cents below the standard wholesale price. However, if Kroger elects to buy Fab at the discounted price, the grocery chain must feature the 48-ounce container of Fab in its Thursday newspaper advertisement at $1.59 (20 cents off the typical retail price). In addition, Kroger must have an end-aisle display of Fab.

Before Kroger decides whether to accept such a trade promotion and then promote Fab to its customers, it needs to assess the promotion's impact on its own profitability. Such a promotion may be effective for the vendor but not for the retailer.

To evaluate a trade promotion, the retailer considers

* The realized margin from the promotion.
* The cost of the additional inventory carried due to buying more than the normal amount.
* The potential increase in sales from the promoted merchandise.
* The potential loss suffered when customers switch to the promoted merchandise from more profitable private-label brands.
* The additional sales made to customers attracted to the store by the promotion.[43]

When Fab's price is reduced to $1.59, Kroger will sell more Fab than it normally does. But Kroger's margin on Fab will be less because the required retail discount of 20 cents isn't offset by the wholesale discount of 15 cents. In addition, Kroger might suffer losses because the promotion encourages customers to buy Fab, which has a lower margin than Kroger's private-label detergent that those customers might have bought. Customers may even stockpile Fab, buying several boxes, which will reduce sales of Kroger's private-label detergent for some time after the special promotion ends. In contrast, the promotion may attract customers who don't normally shop at Kroger but who will visit to buy Fab at the discounted price. These customers might buy additional merchandise, providing a sales gain to the store that it wouldn't have realized if it hadn't promoted Fab.

The end-aisle display of Fab is part of a special Colgate-Palmolive promotion in which the supermarket bought Fab at a discount in exchange for the prominent display.

SUMMARY

A communication program can be designed to achieve a variety of objectives for the retailer, such as building a brand image of the retailer in the customer's mind, increasing sales and store traffic, providing information about the retailer's location and offering, and announcing special activities.

Retailers communicate with customers through advertising, sales promotions, store atmosphere, Web sites, salespeople, e-mail, direct mail, m-commerce, community building, publicity, and word of mouth. These elements in the communication mix must be coordinated so customers have a clear, distinct image of the retailer and are not confused by conflicting information.

Many retailers use rules of thumb to determine the size of the promotion budget. Marginal analysis, the most appropriate method for determining how much must be spent to accomplish the retailer's objectives, should be used to determine whether the level of spending maximizes the profits that could be generated by the communication mix.

The largest portion of a retailer's communication budget is typically spent on advertising and sales promotions. A wide array of media can be used for advertising. Each medium has its pros and cons. For example, newspaper advertising is effective for announcing sales, whereas TV ads are useful for developing an image. Sales promotions and m-commerce are typically used to achieve short-term objectives, such as increasing store traffic over a weekend. Personal selling, community building, and word of mouth through social shopping activities help achieve more long-term goals and customer loyalty. Publicity and word of mouth are typically low-cost communications, but they are very difficult for retailers to control.

KEY TERMS

advertising, *447*

affordable budgeting method, *462*

aided recall, *444*

brand, *442*

brand associations, *444*

brand awareness, *444*

brand equity, *442*

brand image, *445*

communication objectives, *457*

GET OUT AND DO IT!

1. **CONTINUING ASSIGNMENT** Evaluate the communication activities undertaken by the retailer you have selected for the continuing assignment. List all of the specific elements and information in the retailer's store and on its Web site that communicate the store's image and the merchandise it is offering to customers. What image does the retailer communicate through its store atmosphere, sales associates, Web site, and advertising? Does it engage in community building activities, m-commerce, or social shopping? What are the associations it attempts to develop with its brand? Are the elements in its communication program consistent in terms of communicating the same image? Why or why not?

2. Got to the homepage for ipsh!, a full service, global mobile marketing agency, at www.ipsh.com. How does this company support clients with mobile marketing campaignes?

3. Retailers and manufacturers now deliver coupons through the Internet rather than by mail or in inserts. Go to www.coolsavings.com for coupons offered over the Internet. How does this coupon distribution system compare with more traditional distribution systems?

4. Trader Joe's has an interesting retail concept: It's an off-price retailer that sells gourmet food and wine. Go to www.traderjoes.com and see how the firm uses its Internet site to promote its retail offering. How effective do you think the site is in promoting the store and building its image?

5. Go to the homepage for Rate My Professor at www.ratemyprofessors.com. Have you ever consulted this community Web site to evaluate a professor at your college or university prior to registering for a course? Why or why not? How credible is the information in these posts?

6. Go to the homepage for Floorgraphics at www.floorgraphics.com. Read about this in-store medium for communicating with shoppers. How does in-store advertising support the other elements of the communication mix? Have you seen floor ads in your own shopping experiences? Describe the store, aisle, and product/brand. Rate the effectiveness of this in-store communication tool.

7. Go to the homepage for Target's *Take Charge of Education* program at http://sites.target.com/site/en/corporate/page.jsp?contentId=PRD03-001825. How does this education fund-raising effort generate publicity for this retailer?

DISCUSSION QUESTIONS AND PROBLEMS

1. How do brands benefit consumers? Retailers?

2. How can advertising, personal selling, and sales promotion complement one another in an integrated marketing communications program? How can a retailer's customer relationship management program support these activities?

3. As a means of communicating with customers, how does mass media advertising differ from publicity?

4. For which of the following growth opportunities do you think the retailer should use its brand name when pursuing the opportunity? Why? (*a*) McDonald's starts a new chain of restaurants to sell seafood in a sit-down environment competing with Red Lobster. (*b*) Sears starts a chain of stand-alone stores that sell just home appliances. (*c*) Target begins to acquire regional grocery stores.

5. What factors should be considered in dividing up the advertising budget among a store's different merchandise areas? Which of the following should receive the highest advertising budget: staple, fad, fashion, or seasonal merchandise? Why?

6. Outline some elements in a communication program that can be used to achieve the following objectives: (a) Increase store loyalty by 20 percent. (b) Build awareness of the store by 10 percent. (c) Develop an image as a low-price retailer. How would you determine whether the communication program met each of these objectives?

7. Retailers use television advertising to build brand image. Television advertisers have identified many types of markets on the basis of the day, time, and type of show during which their ads may appear. During which days, times, and types of shows should retailers advertise the following categories of merchandise: fresh produce and meat, power tools, beer, cars, and health club memberships? Why?

8. A retailer plans to open a new store near a university. It will specialize in collegiate merchandise such as t-shirts, fraternity/sorority accessories, and sweatshirts. Develop an integrated communication program for the retailer. What specific media should the new store use to capture the university market?

9. Cooperative (co-op) advertising is a good way for a retailer to extend an advertising budget (see Appendix 16A). Why isn't it always in a retailer's best interests to rely extensively on co-op advertising?

10. What retailer's catalogs do you currently read and order from? What about other members of your family? How are catalogs an effective communication tool?

11. Why do some online retailers include editorial and customer reviews along with product information on their Web sites?

SUGGESTED READINGS

Aaker, David A. *Brand Portfolio Strategy: Creating Relevance, Differentiation, Energy, Leverage, and Clarity.* New York: The Free Press, 2004.

Belch, George, and Michael Belch. *Advertising and Promotion: An Integrated Marketing Communications Perspective.* 7th ed. New York: McGraw-Hill, 2007.

DelVecchio, Devon; David H. Henard; and Traci H. Freling. "The Effect of Sales Promotion on Post-Promotion Brand Preference: A Meta-Analysis." *Journal of Retailing* 82, no. 3 (2006), pp. 203–13.

Grewal, Dhruv; Michael Levy; and Donald Lehmann. "Retail Branding and Customer Loyalty: An Overview." *Journal of Retailing* 80 (Winter 2004), pp. 249–53.

Hastings, Gerard. *Social Marketing: Why Should the Devil Have All the Best Tunes?* Oxford, Butterworth-Heinemann, 2007.

Hughes, Mark. *Buzzmarketing.* New York: Penguin/Portfolio, 2005.

Keh, Hean Tat, and Yih hwai Lee. "Do Reward Programs Build Loyalty for Services? The Moderating Effect of Satisfaction on Type and Timing of Rewards." Journal of Retailing 82, no. 2 (2006), pp. 127–36.

Orth, Ulrich R.; Harold F. Koenig; and Zuzana Firbasova. "Cross-National Differences in Consumer Response to the Framing of Advertising Messages." *European Journal of Marketing* 41, no. 3/4 (2007), pp. 327–48.

Prins, Remco and Peter C. Verhoef. "Marketing Communication Drivers of Adoption Timing of a New E-Service Among Existing Customers." *Journal of Marketing* 71, no. 2 (2007), pp. 169–83.

Scott, David Meerman. *The New Rules of Marketing and PR: How to Use News Releases, Blogs, Podcasting, Viral Marketing and Online Media to Reach Buyers Directly.* New York: Wiley, 2007.

Smith, Steve. *How to Sell More Stuff: Promotional Marketing that Really Works.* Chicago: Dearborn Trade Publishers, 2005.

APPENDIX 16A   Implementing Retail Advertising Programs

Implementing an advertising program involves developing the message, choosing the specific media to convey the message, and determining the frequency and timing of the message. Each of these decisions is examined in this section.

DEVELOPING THE ADVERTISING MESSAGE

Most retail advertising messages have a short life and are designed for immediate impact. This immediacy calls for a copywriting style that grabs the reader's attention. Exhibit 16–8 outlines specific suggestions for developing local newspaper ads.[44]

Assistance in Advertising

Retailers get assistance in developing advertising campaigns from vendors through their cooperative (co-op) programs, advertising agencies, and media companies.

Co-op Programs   **Co-op (cooperative) advertising** is a promotional program undertaken by a vendor and a retailer working together. The vendor pays for part of the retailer's advertising but dictates some conditions. For example, Sony may have a co-op program that pays for half of a consumer electronics retailer's ads for Sony digital televisions.

Co-op advertising enables a retailer to increase its advertising budget. In the previous example, Best Buy would only pay for half of its expenses for ads including Sony digital TVs. In addition to lowering costs, co-op advertising enables a small retailer to associate its name with well-known national brands and use attractive artwork created by the national brand.

Co-op advertising has some drawbacks though. First, vendors want the ads to feature their products, whereas retailers are more interested in featuring their store's name, location, and assortment of merchandise and services offered. This conflict in goals can reduce the effectiveness of co-op advertising from the retailer's perspective. Second,

EXHIBIT 16–8   Suggestions for Developing Local Ads

Have a dominant headline	The first question a consumer asks is, What's in it for me? Thus, retailers need to feature the principal benefit being offered in the headline along with a reason why the consumer should act immediately. The benefit can be expanded on in a subhead.
Use a dominant element	Ads should include a large picture or headline. Typically, photographs of real people attract more attention than drawings. Action photographs are effective in getting readers' attention.
Stick to a simple layout	The ad's layout should lead the reader's eye through the message from the headline to the illustration and then to the explanatory copy, price, and retailer's name and location. Complex elements, decorative borders, and many different typefaces distract the reader's attention from the retailer's message.
Provide a specific, complete presentation	Ad readers are looking for information that will help them decide whether to visit the store. The ad must contain all of the information pertinent to this decision, including the type of merchandise, brands, prices, sizes, and colors. Consumers are unlikely to make a special trip to the store on the basis of vague information. Broadcast ads, particularly radio ads, tend to be very creative but often leave the consumer thinking, Gee, that was a clever ad, but what was it advertising?
Use easily recognizable, distinct visuals	Consumers see countless ads each day. Thus, to get the consumers' attention, retailers must make their ads distinct from those of the competition. Ads with distinctive art, layout, design elements, or typeface generate higher readership.
Give the store's name and address	The store's name and location are the two most important aspects of a retail ad. If consumers don't know where to go to buy the advertised merchandise, the retailer won't make a sale. The retailer's name and location must be prominently displayed in print ads and repeated several times in broadcast ads.

ads developed by the vendor often are used by several competing retailers and may list the names and locations of all retailers offering their brands. Thus, co-op ads tend to blur distinctions between retailers. Third, restrictions the vendor places on the ads may further reduce their effectiveness for the retailer. For example, the vendor may restrict advertising to a period of time when the vendor's sales are depressed, but the retailer might not normally be advertising during this time frame.

Agencies   Most large retailers have a department that creates advertising for sales and special events. Large retailers often use advertising agencies to develop ads for image building campaigns but develop promotional newspaper advertisements with their in-house staff. Many small retailers use local agencies to plan and create all of their advertising. These local agencies are often more skilled in planning and executing advertising than the retailer's employees are. Agencies also work on other aspects of the communication programs, such as contests, direct mail, and special promotions.

Media Companies   In addition to selling newspaper space and broadcast time, the advertising media offer services to local retailers, ranging from planning an advertising program to actually designing the ads. Media companies also do market research on their audiences and can provide information about shopping patterns in the local area.

CHOOSING THE MOST EFFECTIVE ADVERTISING MEDIA

After developing the message, the next step is to decide which medium to use to communicate the message. The media used for retail advertising are newspapers, magazines, radio, TV, outdoor billboards, the Internet, shopping guides, and the Yellow Pages. Exhibit 16–9 summarizes their characteristics.

REFACT

Thirty-six percent of retail advertising is spent in newspapers, 28 percent on network television, 5 percent on cable televsion, 11 percent on radio, 11 percent in magazines, 2 percent on outdoor, and 7 percent online.[45]

Simmons paid for part of the co-op advertisement, enabling Back To Bed Sleep Centers to stretch its advertising budget and associate itself with a well-respected national brand.

Newspapers

Retailing and newspaper advertising grew up together over the past century. But the growth in retail newspaper advertising has slowed recently as retailers have begun using other media. Still, 24 percent of newspapers' advertising dollars are generated by retailers.[46] In addition to displaying ads with their editorial content, newspapers distribute freestanding inserts. A **freestanding insert (FSI),** also called a **preprint,** is an advertisement printed at the retailer's expense and distributed as an insert in the newspaper.

EXHIBIT 16–9
Media Capabilities

Media	Targeting	Timeliness	Information Presentation Capacity	Life	Cost
Newspapers	Good	Good	Modest	Short	Modest
Magazines	Modest	Poor	Modest	Modest	High
Direct mail	Excellent	Modest	High	Short	Modest
Television	Modest	Modest	Low	Short	Modest
Radio	Modest	Good	Low	Short	Low
Internet					
Banner	Excellent	Excellent	Low	Modest	High
Web site	Excellent	Excellent	High	Long	Modest
E-mail	Excellent	Excellent	Modest	Short	Low
Outdoor billboards	Modest	Poor	Very low	Long	Modest
Shopping guides	Modest	Modest	Low	Modest	Low
Yellow Pages	Modest	Poor	Low	Long	Low

Because newspapers are distributed in well-defined local market areas, they're effective at targeting retail advertising. Often the local market covered by a newspaper is similar to the market served by the retailer. Newspapers offer opportunities for small retailers to target their advertising by developing editions for different areas of a city. For example, the *Boston Globe* has five special editions for the North, Northwest, West, South, and the City.

Newspapers also offer a quick response. There's only a short time between the deadline for receiving the advertisement and the time that the advertisement will appear. Thus, newspapers are useful for delivering messages on short notice.

Newspapers, like all print media, effectively convey a lot of detailed information. Readers can go through an advertisement at their own pace and refer back to part of the advertisement when they want. In addition, consumers can save the advertisement and take it to the store with them, which makes newspaper ads effective at conveying information about the prices of sale items. But newspaper ads aren't effective for showing merchandise, particularly when it's important to illustrate colors, because of the poor reproduction quality.

There are so many FSIs in local newspapers that it is difficult for a retailer to get consumers to notice its FSI.

Although newspapers are improving their printing facilities to provide better reproductions and color in ads, retailers continue to rely on preprints (FSIs) to get good reproduction quality. However, there are so many FSIs in some newspapers that readers can become overwhelmed. As a result, some retailers have reduced the number of FSIs they use because of the clutter and because younger readers, who may be their primary target markets, don't regularly read newspapers.

The life of a newspaper advertisement is short because the newspaper is usually discarded after it's read. In contrast, magazine advertising has a longer life because consumers tend to save magazines and read them several times during a week or month.

Finally, the cost of developing newspaper ads is very low. Newspaper ads can be developed by less experienced people and don't require expensive color photography or typesetting. However, the cost of delivering the message may be high if the newspaper's circulation is broader than the retailer's target market, which would require the retailer to pay for exposures that won't generate sales.

Magazines

Retail magazine advertising is mostly done by national retailers such as Target and The Gap. But magazine advertising is increasing with the growth of local magazines, regional editions of national magazines, and specialized magazines. Retailers tend to use this medium for image advertising because the reproduction quality is high. Due to the lead time—the time between submitting the advertisement and publication—a major disadvantage of magazine advertising is that the timing is difficult to coordinate with special events and sales.

Television

Television commercials can be placed on a national network or local station. A local television commercial is called a **spot**. Retailers typically use TV for image advertising, to take advantage of the high production quality and the opportunity to communicate through both visual images and sound. Television ads can also demonstrate product usage. For example, TV is an excellent medium for car, furniture, and consumer electronics dealers.

Sports Authority uses billboards to create awareness and remind customers to consider Sports Authority when they need sports equipment.

In addition to its high production costs, broadcast time for national TV advertising is expensive. Spots have relatively small audiences, but they may be economical for local retailers. To offset the high production costs, many vendors provide modular commercials, in which the retailer can insert its name or a "tag" after information about the vendor's merchandise.

Radio

Many retailers use radio advertising because messages can be targeted to a specific segment of the market.[47] Some radio stations' audiences are highly loyal to their announcers. When these announcers promote a retailer, listeners are impressed. The cost of developing and broadcasting radio commercials is quite low.

One disadvantage of radio advertising, however, is that listeners generally treat the radio broadcast as background, which limits the attention they give the message. As with all broadcast media, consumers must get the information from a radio commercial when it's broadcast. They can't refer back to the advertisement for information they didn't hear or remember.

Internet

Three uses of the Internet by retailers to communicate with customers are (1) banner ads and affiliate programs to generate awareness, (2) Web sites to provide information about merchandise and special events, and (3) e-mails to target messages. Banner ads and affiliate programs are very effective for targeting communication, but they are not cost effective for building awareness. Using information from a visitor's navigation and purchase behavior and IP address, banner ads can be targeted to specific individuals. For example, www.sportsline.com visitors who look at the box scores for Kansas City Royals baseball games are shown ads for Royals logo apparel and hats. DoubleClick, an Internet advertising agency, downloads different banner ads from its server to host Web sites on the basis of the information it has about the specific visitor. However, Internet advertising is not cost effective for building awareness because the large number of Web sites reduces the number of customers who might visit a site and see a particular ad.

Although the Internet is not effective for building awareness, it is an excellent vehicle for conveying information to customers. In addition to selling merchandise on a Web site, retailers can provide a wide array of information, ranging from store locations to the availability and pricing of merchandise in specific stores. The interactivity of the Internet gives customers the opportunity to quickly sift through a vast amount of information. For example, visitors to the Circuit City Web site can find detailed information about specific digital camera models and generate a table to compare a select group of cameras on features important to them. Finally, retailers can use the Internet to send e-mails to customers informing them of special events and new merchandise.

Outdoor Billboards

Billboards and other forms of outdoor advertising are effective vehicles for creating awareness and providing a very limited amount of information to a narrow audience. Thus, outdoor advertising has limited usefulness in providing information about sales. Outdoor advertising is typically used to remind customers about the retailer or inform people in cars of nearby retail outlets.

Shopping Guides

Shopping guides are free papers delivered to all residents in a specific area. This medium is particularly useful for retailers that want to saturate a trading area. Shopping guides are cost effective and assure the local retailer of 100 percent coverage. In contrast, subscription newspapers typically offer only 30 to 50 percent coverage. An extension of the shopping guide concept is the coupon book or magazine. These media contain coupons offered by retailers for discounts. Shopping guides and coupon books make no pretense about providing news to consumers; they're simply delivery vehicles for ads and coupons.

Yellow Pages

The Yellow Pages are useful for retailers because they have a long life. The Yellow Pages are used as a reference by consumers who are definitely interested in making a purchase and seeking information.

Considerations in Selecting Media

To convey their message with the most impact to the most consumers in the target market at the lowest cost, retailers need to evaluate media in terms of the coverage, reach, cost, and impact that they will deliver for advertising messages.

Coverage   **Coverage** refers to the number of potential customers in the retailer's target market that could be exposed to an advertisement in a given medium. For example, assume that the size of the target market is 100,000 customers. The local newspaper is distributed to 60 percent of the customers in the target market, 90 percent of the potential customers have a TV set that picks up the local station's signal, and 5 percent of the potential customers

Effectiveness of Media for Communication Objectives **EXHIBIT 16–10**

Communication Task	Newspapers	Magazine	Direct Mail	TV	Radio	Web sites	E-Mail	Outdoor
Getting attention	Low	Medium	Medium	Medium	Low	Low	High	Medium
Identifying name	Medium	High	Low	Low	Low	Low	Medium	High
Announcing events	High	Low	High	High	Medium	Low	High	Low
Demonstrating merchandise	Low	Medium	High	High	Low	High	Low	Low
Providing information	Low	High	High	Low	Low	High	Medium	Lowest
Changing attitudes	High	Medium	High	High	Medium	High	Low	Low
Building brand image	Low	Medium	High	High	Low	High	Low	Low

drive past a billboard. Thus, the coverage for newspaper advertising would be 60,000; for TV advertising, 90,000; and for the specific billboard, 5,000.

Reach   In contrast to coverage, **reach** is the actual number of customers in the target market exposed to an advertising medium. If on any given day, 60 percent of the potential customers who receive the newspaper actually read it, then the newspaper's reach would be 36,000 (or 60 percent of 60,000). Retailers often run an advertisement several times, in which case they calculate the **cumulative reach** for the sequence of ads. For example, if 60 percent of the potential customers receiving a newspaper read it each day, 93.6 percent (or 1 minus the probability of not reading the paper three times in a row [0.40 × 0.40 × 0.40]) of the potential customers will read the newspaper at least one day over the three-day period in which the advertisement appears in the paper. Thus, the cumulative reach for running a newspaper advertisement for three days is 56,160 (or 93.6 percent × 60,000), which almost equals the newspaper's coverage. When evaluating Internet advertising opportunities, the measure used to assess reach is the number of unique visitors who access the Web page on which the advertisement is located.

Cost   The **cost per thousand (CPM)** measure is often used to compare media. Typically, CPM is calculated by dividing an ad's cost by its reach. Another approach for determining CPM is to divide the cost of several ads in a campaign by their cumulative reach. If, in the previous example, one newspaper ad costs $500 and three ads cost $1,300, the CPM using simple reach is $13.89, or $500/(36,000/1,000). Using cumulative reach, the CPM is $23.15, or $1,300/ (56,160/1,000). Note that the CPM might be higher using cumulative reach instead of simple reach, but the overall reach is also higher, and many potential customers will see the ad two or three times. Thus, CPM is a good method for comparing similarly sized ads in similar media, such as full-page ads in the *Los Angeles Times* and the *Orange County Register*. But CPM can be misleading when comparing the cost effectiveness of ads in different types of media, such as newspaper and TV. A televised ad may have a lower CPM than a newspaper ad, but the newspaper ad may be much more effective at achieving the ad's communication objectives, such as giving information about a sale.

Impact   **Impact** is an ad's effect on the audience. Due to their unique characteristics, different media are particularly effective at accomplishing different communication tasks. Exhibit 16–10 shows the effectiveness of various media for different communication tasks. Television is particularly effective at getting an audience's attention, demonstrating merchandise, changing attitudes, and announcing events. Magazines are appropriate for emphasizing the quality and prestige of a store and its offering and providing detailed information to support quality claims. Newspapers are useful for providing price information and announcing events. Web sites are particularly effective for demonstrating merchandise and providing information. Outdoor advertising is most effective at promoting a retailer's name and location.

DETERMINING ADVERTISING FREQUENCY AND TIMING

The frequency and timing of ads determine how often and when customers will see the retailer's message.

Frequency

Frequency is how many times the potential customer is exposed to an ad. Frequency for Internet advertising, is typically assessed by measuring the number of times a Web page with the ad is downloaded during a visit to the site.

The appropriate frequency depends on the ad's objective. Typically, several exposures to an ad are required to influence a customer's buying behavior. Thus, campaigns directed toward changing purchase behavior rather than creating awareness emphasize frequency over reach. Ads announcing a sale are often seen and remembered after one exposure. Thus, sale ad campaigns emphasize reach over frequency.

Timing

Typically, an ad should appear on, or slightly precede, the days consumers are most likely to purchase merchandise. For example, if most consumers buy groceries Thursday through Sunday, then supermarkets should advertise on Thursday and Friday. Similarly, consumers often go shopping after they receive their paychecks at the middle and the end of the month. Thus, advertising should be concentrated at these times.

ONE PRICE. ONE SPOT.
ONE DOLLAR.

EXPRESS

3

Store Management

Section IV focuses on the implementation issues associated with store management, including managing store employees and controlling costs (Chapter 17), presenting merchandise (Chapter 18), and providing customer service (Chapter 19).

Traditionally, the issues pertaining to merchandise management were considered the most important retail implementation decisions, and buying was considered the best career path for achieving senior retail management positions. Now, developing a strategic advantage through merchandise management is becoming more and more difficult. Competing stores often have similar assortments of national-brand merchandise.

Because customers can find the same assortments in a number of conveniently located retail outlets and through the Internet, store management issues have become a critical basis for developing strategic advantage. Retailers are increasing their emphasis on differentiating their offering from competitive offerings on the basis of the experience that customers have in the stores, including the service they get from store employees and the quality of the shopping environment.

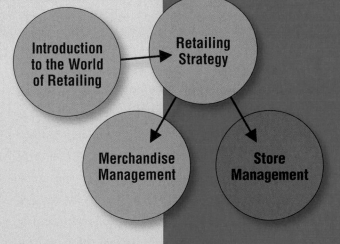

Managing the Store

EXECUTIVE BRIEFING
Lee Donelly (left), Store Manager, Walgreens

While I was in high school and college, I worked part-time at a Walgreens store and grew to appreciate the company's values. Walgreens really cares about its customers and employees. We want our customers to make fully informed, good decisions when they fill their prescriptions and buy other merchandise in the store. Walgreens has an open-door policy for everyone working for the company. There is always someone you can talk with about a problem. If employees feel their assistant manager is not addressing an issue, they can always go to their store manager or even the district manager or Regional Vice-President.

So when I graduated from Minnesota State University Moorhead, I was very excited about going into the management training program as a store assistant manager. When Walgreens expanded in the Southern California market, I jumped at the opportunity to transfer to California and open a new store. Over the last five years,

I have opened and managed six new stores and am now managing our store in Tustin.

The annual sales at my store are over $10 million. It employs 30 people, and I am responsible and rewarded for its performance. But the rewards I get are more than just monetary. I like to work with and help people, our customers and employees. I feel that many of our regular customers are my friends. I enjoy talking with them when they come into the store. I miss them when I have moved on to manage a new store. I also have close relationships with the people who work in my store. Many of them have transferred and followed me when I changed stores.

I really like working in a store because it gives me an opportunity to work with people. I would miss these human connections if I had to sit behind a desk all day. As a store manager, I interact with a lot of people—customers, store employees, people in our district office—and I do a lot of different things. In a typical day I could work on introducing a new product, handle some personnel issues, demonstrate a product to a customer, and review reports

CHAPTER 17

QUESTIONS

What are the responsibilities of store managers?

How do store managers recruit, select, motivate, train, and evaluate their employees?

How do store managers compensate their salespeople?

What legal and ethical issues must store managers consider in managing their employees?

What can store managers do to increase productivity and reduce costs?

How can store managers reduce inventory losses due to employee theft and shoplifting?

summarizing my store's performance. Every day is different, and I am constantly learning new things. I can't remember who said this, but it really sums up my feelings: "If you are happy at what you are doing, you never have to work again."

Store managers are on the firing line in retailing. Due to their daily contact with customers, they have the best knowledge of customer needs and competitive activity. From this unique vantage point, store managers play an important role in formulating and executing retail strategies. Buyers can develop exciting merchandise assortments and procure them at low cost, but the retailer only realizes the benefits of the buyers' efforts when the merchandise is sold. Good merchandise doesn't sell itself. Store managers must make sure that the merchandise is presented effectively and offer services that stimulate and facilitate customer buying decisions.

Even in national chains, store managers are treated as relatively independent managers of a business within the corporation. Some store managers are responsible for $150 million in annual sales and manage more than 1,000 employees. For example, James Nordstrom, former CEO of Nordstrom, told his store managers, "This is your business. Do your own thing. Don't listen to us in Seattle, listen to your customers. We give you permission to take care of your customers."

The first portion of this chapter focuses on the management of store employees and complements the strategic human resource management issues discussed in Chapter 9. Whereas Chapter 9 examined the organization of the tasks performed by retailers and the general approaches for motivating retail employees and building their commitment to the firm, this chapter discusses how store managers implement the retailer's human resource strategy.

STORE MANAGEMENT RESPONSIBILITIES

- increase productivity of employees & estate

The responsibilities of store managers are shown in Exhibit 17–1. These functions are divided into four major categories: managing employees, controlling costs, managing merchandise presentation, and providing customer service. Issues pertaining to the management of store employees and controlling costs also are discussed in this chapter. Subsequent chapters examine the store manager's responsibilities in presenting and managing merchandise and providing customer service.

Store managers are responsible for increasing the productivity of two of the retailer's most important assets: the firm's investments in its employees and its real estate. Most of this chapter is devoted to increasing labor productivity, namely, the sales generated by each store employee, by effectively managing them through recruiting and selecting good employees, training them to be more effective, and motivating them to perform at high levels.

In addition to increasing labor productivity, store managers affect their stores' profits by controlling costs. The major costs are compensation and benefits for employees. Store managers are responsible for controlling these costs by efficiently scheduling labor. But store managers are also responsbile for costs associated with operating and maintaining their buildings. Retailers are engaging in innovative cost-cutting initiatives that are also friendly to the environment. Another important retail cost controlling activity is reducing inventory shrinkage resulting from shoplifting and employee theft. These cost-control issues are discussed at the end of the chapter.

Exhibit 17–2 outlines the steps in the employee management process that affect store employees' productivity: (1) recruiting and selecting effective people, (2) improving their skills through socialization and training, (3) motivating them to perform at higher levels, (4) evaluating them, and finally (5) compensating and rewarding them.[1] Store managers also need to develop employees who can assume more responsibility and be promoted to higher-level management positions. By developing subordinates, managers help both their firms and themselves. The firm benefits from having more effective managers, and the manager benefits because the firm has a qualified replacement when the manager is promoted.

EXHIBIT 17–1

Responsibilities of Store Managers

MANAGING STORE EMPLOYEES (Chapter 17)
Recruiting and selecting
Socializing and training
Motivating
Evaluating and providing constructive feedback
Rewarding and compensating

CONTROLLING COSTS (Chapter 17)
Increasing labor productivity
Reducing maintenance and energy costs
Reducing inventory losses

MANAGING MERCHANDISE
Displaying merchandise and maintaining visual standards (Chapter 18)
Working with buyers
    Suggesting new merchandise
    Buying merchandise
    Planning and managing special events
    Marking down merchandise

PROVIDING CUSTOMER SERVICE (Chapter 19)

Steps in the Process of Managing Store Employees   **EXHIBIT 17–2**

1. Recruit and select employees
2. Socialize and train new employees
3. Motivate and manage employees to achieve store performance goals
4. Evaluate employee performance and provide feedback
5. Compensate and reward employees

RECRUITING AND SELECTING STORE EMPLOYEES

The first step in the employee management process is recruiting and selecting employees. To recruit employees effectively, store managers need to undertake a job analysis, prepare a job description, find potential applicants with the desired capabilities, and screen the best candidates to interview. (Appendix 1A to Chapter 1 describes the recruiting and selection process from the perspective of people interested in pursuing retail careers and applying for management trainee positions.)

Job Analysis

The **job analysis** identifies essential activities to be performed by the employees. It is used to determine the qualifications of potential employees. For example, retail salespeople's responsibilities vary from company to company and department to department within a store. Retail employees in stores such as grocery, discount, and drugstores typically help customers find merchandise, bring out and display merchandise, and ring up sales. In contrast, those who work in jewelry stores, high-end apparel departments, or furniture stores get involved in the selling process by trying to discover what customers really want and then finding solutions. The skill level required for those involved in actually selling merchandise is much greater than for those who rarely interact with customers.

Managers can obtain the information needed for a job analysis by observing employees presently doing the job and determining the characteristics of exceptional performers. Exhibit 17–3 lists some questions that managers should consider in a job analysis for sales associates. Information collected in the job analysis then is used to prepare a job description.

- How many salespeople will be working in the department at the same time?
- Do the salespeople have to work together in dealing with customers?
- How many customers will the salesperson have to work with at one time?
- Will the salesperson be selling on an open floor or working behind the counter?
- How much and what type of product knowledge does the salesperson need?
- Does the salesperson need to sell the merchandise or just ring up the orders and provide information?
- Is the salesperson required to make appointments with customers and develop a loyal customer base?
- Does the salesperson have the authority to negotiate price or terms of the sale?
- Does the salesperson need to demonstrate the merchandise?
- Will the salesperson be expected to make add-on sales?
- Is the salesperson's appearance important? How should an effective salesperson look?
- Will the salesperson be required to perform merchandising activities such as stocking shelves and setting up displays?
- Whom will the salesperson report to?
- What compensation plan will the salesperson be working under?

EXHIBIT 17–3

Questions for Undertaking a Job Analysis

Job Description

A **job description** includes (1) activities the employee needs to perform and (2) the performance expectations expressed in quantitative terms. The job description is a guideline for recruiting, selecting, training, and, eventually, evaluating employees.

Locating Prospective Employees

Staffing stores is becoming a critical problem because changing demographics are reducing the size of the labor pool. Some approaches being used by retailers to recruit applicants, in additon to placing ads in local newspapers and posting job openings on Web sites such as monster.com, are listed below:

Recruiting Minorities, Immigrants, and Older Workers   Retailers that aggressively pursue the growing number of Hispanic immigrant workers print application forms in English and Spanish. They also develop training programs for people who aren't familiar with U.S. business practices. For example, many foreign-born workers do not understand benefits like life insurance and are reluctant to report job-related injuries for fear of being fired.

Seniors are another attractive sourse for new recrits. Borders, Home Depot, and Walgreens are working with the American Association of Retired Persons (AARP) to form the Workforce Initiative, which matches seniors with job openings at those companies. Retailing often is attractive to seniors because its wide range of store hours fits seniors' need for flexible work schedules. In addition, some retailers pay health care benefits to part-time workers, an important consideration for seniors. Exclusively targeting seniors or minorities would violate antidiscrimination laws, but retailers can advertise in publications that are typically read by seniors. The AARP Web site lists companies interested in hiring seniors, with links to the employment areas of those companies' Web sites.[2]

Partnering with Government Agencies   National drugstore chain CVS is partnering with the government and churches to help it recruit the unemployed and former welfare recipients.[3] CVS doesn't just work with these groups in recruiting drives. It also has developed partnerships around the country to improve recruiting, training, and retention. The company established seven Regional Learning Centers, co-located with local government employment offices. For example, when the Washington, DC, Department of Employment Services interviews someone who matches CVS's qualifications, it sends that person to the company for further talks. If the person is selected, he or she may be sent back to the one-stop center—this time for training in a mock CVS store. A smaller version of the simulated store also is located in a building owned by Mount Lebanon Baptist Church, a 1,500-member congregation that has worked with CVS since 2001. After the store has completed a hire, the government still stays involved by helping connect new CVS employees with services such as transportation and childcare that enable them to transition to work. The partnership among CVS, the government, and faith-based organizations benefits all the parties: CVS staffs its stores; the public sector moves people off the unemployment rolls; and churches fulfill their role of ministering to their congregations' economic needs.

Using Employees as Talent Scouts   Retailers often ask their own employees if they know someone the retailer could hire, if they have recently encountered a particularly good salesperson when shopping at another store, or if they know of a customer whom they believe would make a good employee. The women's specialty store chain Chico's, for instance, often hires its best customers because they already know and love the store, and they can relate to other customers like them.

Many retailers provide incentives for such referrals by employees. For example, at The Container Store, recruiting is part of everybody's job. Employees get $500 for every full-time hire and $200 for every part-timer. All employees, from stockers to managers, carry recruiting cards to pull out when chatting with customers. The program is so successful that the company often goes six to eight months without placing a single classified ad.[4]

Using the Storefront Creatively   Retailers are going beyond posting a simple "Help Wanted" sign. A more effective sign might read "Thank you! Business is great. Because things are so good, we're hiring additional staff. Please stop in to discuss career opportunities."

Screening Applicants to Interview

The screening process matches applicants' qualifications with the job description. Many retailers use automated prescreening programs as a low-cost method to identify qualified candidates. Applicants either interact with a Web-enabled store kiosk or call a toll-free telephone number. The applicants then answer some basic questions using the keyboard or telephone buttons in response to a computer program.

The questions are tailored to the retailer's specific needs and environment. For example, Finish Line, the athletic retailer, asks a series of questions of applicants in a prescreening process. The company has set up online applications for the initial interview through kiosks in the stores and on the Web. By automating a portion of the application process, the retailer can select from a larger pool of applicants and allow managers to focus more on managing the store, not just interviewing new applicants. More than 75 percent of applicants apply online, and 30 percent are eliminated in the automated portion of the interview. After implementing this automated application tool, Finish Line's average sales/hour for associates have increased from $112 to $135, and employee retention has increased by 9 percent.[5]

Application Forms   Job application forms contain information about the applicant's employment history, previous compensation, reasons for leaving his or her previous employment, education and training, personal health, and references. This information enables the manager to determine whether the applicant has the minimum qualifications and also provides information useful when interviewing the applicant.

References and Online Checks   A good way to verify the information given on an application form is to contact the applicant's references or do an online check. Contacting references is helpful for collecting additional information from people who have worked with the applicant. In addition, store managers should check with former supervisors not listed as references and not rely solely on references from colleagues or friends. Because people are more likely to be frank in conversation, managers should always talk to the references, not rely on written references. Due to potential legal problems, however, many companies have a policy of not commenting on prior employees.

Store managers generally expect to hear favorable comments from an applicant's references or previous supervisors, even if they may not have thought highly of the applicant. One approach for reducing this positive bias is to ask the reference to rank the applicant relative to others in the same position. For example, the manager might ask, "How would you rate Pat's customer service skill in relation to other retail sales associates you have worked with?" Another approach is to ask specific questions, rather than yes/no questions or vague "tell me about John," type questions.

The Internet has become an excellent source of information on prospective employees. A quick look at someone's Facebook entry can often reveal more about the person than a face-to-face interview. A Google search can also be useful for finding out information that may not appear on the job application or emerge through contacts with references.[7] For instance, a search could reveal that an applicant was once involved in illegal or otherwise undesirable activities. Cyberspace records of previous activities can haunt a person forever.

Testing   Intelligence, ability, personality, and interest tests can provide insights about potential employees. For example, intelligence tests yield data about the applicant's innate abilities and can be used to match applicants with job openings and develop training programs. However, tests must be scientifically and legally valid. They can only be used when the scores have been shown to be related to job performance. It is illegal to use tests that assess factors that are not job related or that discriminate against specific groups.

Due to potential losses from theft, many retailers require applicants to take drug tests. Some retailers also use tests to assess applicants' honesty and ethics. Paper-and-pencil honesty tests include questions to find out if an applicant has ever thought about stealing and if he or she believes other people steal ("What percentage of people take more than $1 from their employer?").

Realistic Job Preview   Turnover declines when applicants understand both the attractive and unattractive aspects of the job.[10] Many retailers want their new hires to have previous retail experience. They have found that experience, even if the previous job was significantly different than the new opportunity, gives the applicant an appreciation for what a life in retailing is all about. Thus, retailing internships for potential management trainees are mutually beneficial—the employee gains experience and gets a realistic view of what a more permanent job might entail, and the retailer gets access to good talent that it may be able to hire in the future.

PetSmart, a pet supply category specialist, shows each applicant a 10-minute video that begins with the advantages of being a company employee and continues with scenes of employees dealing with irate customers and cleaning up animal droppings. This type of job preview typically screens out 15 percent of the applicants who would most likely quit within three months if they were hired.

Selecting Applicants

After screening applicants, the selection process typically involves a personal interview. Because the interview is usually the critical factor in the hiring decision, the store manager needs to be well prepared and have complete control over the interview.

Preparation for the Interview   The objective of the interview is to gather relevant information, not simply to ask a lot of questions. The most widely used interview technique, called the *behavioral interview*, asks candidates how they have handled actual situations they have encountered in the past, especially those situations requiring the skills outlined in the job description. For example, applicants applying for a job requiring them to handle customer complaints would be asked to describe a situation in which they were confronted by someone who was angry with something they had done. Candidates might be asked to describe the situation, what they did, and the outcomes of their actions. These situations also can be used to interview references for the applicants.[11]

An effective approach to interviewing involves some planning by the managers but also allows some flexibility in question selections. Managers should develop objectives for what they want to learn about the candidate. Each topic area covered in the interview starts with a broad question, such as "Tell me about your last job," which is designed to elicit a lengthy response. The broad opening question is followed by a sequence of more specific questions, such as "What did you learn from that job?" or "How many subordinates did you have?" Finally, managers need to avoid asking questions that are discriminatory.

Interviewing Questions **EXHIBIT 17–4**

EDUCATION

What were your most and least favorite subjects in college? Why?

What types of extracurricular activities did you participate in? Why did you select those activities?

If you had the opportunity to attend school all over again, what, if anything, would you do differently? Why?

How did you spend the summers during college?

Did you have any part-time jobs? Which of your part-time jobs did you find most interesting? What did you find most difficult about working and attending college at the same time? What advice would you give to someone who wanted to work and attend college at the same time?

What accomplishments are you most proud of?

PREVIOUS EXPERIENCE

What's your description of the ideal manager? Subordinate? Coworker?

What did you like most/least about your last job?

What kind of people do you find it difficult/easy to work with? Why?

What has been your greatest accomplishment during your career to date?

Describe a situation at your last job involving pressure. How did you handle it?

What were some duties on your last job that you found difficult?

Of all the jobs you've had, which did you find the most/least rewarding?

What is the most frustrating situation you've encountered in your career?

Why do you want to leave your present job?

What would you do if . . . ?

How would you handle . . . ?

What would you like to avoid in future jobs?

What do you consider your greatest strength/weakness?

What are your responsibilities in your present job?

Tell me about the people you hired on your last job. How did they work out? What about the people you fired?

What risks did you take in your last job, and what were the results of those risks?

Where do you see yourself in three years?

What kind of references will your previous employer give?

What do you do when you have trouble solving a problem?

QUESTIONS THAT SHOULD NOT BE ASKED PER EQUAL EMPLOYMENT OPPORTUNITY GUIDELINES

Do you have plans for having children/a family?

What are your marriage plans?

What does your husband/wife do?

What happens if your husband/wife gets transferred or needs to relocate?

Who will take care of your children while you're at work?

(Asked of men) How would you feel about working for a woman?

How old are you?

What is your date of birth?

How would you feel working for a person younger than you?

Where were you born?

Where were your parents born?

Do you have any handicaps?

As a handicapped person, what help are you going to need to do your work?

How severe is your handicap?

What's your religion?

What church do you attend?

Do you hold religious beliefs that would prevent you from working on certain days of the week?

Do you feel that your race/color will be a problem in your performing the job?

Are you of _____ heritage/race?

Managing the Interview Exhibit 17–4 shows some questions the manager might ask. Here are some suggestions for questioning the applicant during the interview:

- Encourage long responses by asking questions like "What do you know about our company?" rather than "How familiar are you with our company?"
- Avoid asking questions that have multiple parts.
- Avoid asking leading questions like "Are you prepared to provide good customer service?"
- Be an active listener. Evaluate the information being presented and sort out the important comments from the unimportant ones. Some techniques for active listening include repeating or rephrasing information, summarizing the conversation, and tolerating silences.

Legal Considerations in Selecting and Hiring Store Employees

Heightened social awareness and government regulations emphasize the need to avoid discriminating against hiring the handicapped, women, minorities, and older workers. Title VII of the Civil Rights Act prohibits discrimination on the basis of race, national origin, sex, or religion in company personnel practices. Discrimination is specifically prohibited in the following human resource decisions: recruitment, hiring, discharge, layoff, discipline, promotion, compensation, and access to training. In 1972, the act was expanded by the **Equal Employment Opportunity Commission (EEOC)** to allow employees to sue employers that violate the law. Several major retailers have been successfully sued because they discriminated in hiring and promoting minorities and women.

Discrimination arises when a member of a protected class (women, minorities, etc.) is treated differently from nonmembers of that class (**disparate treatment**) or when an apparently neutral rule has an unjustified discriminatory effect (**disparate impact**). An example of disparate treatment is if a qualified woman does not receive a promotion given to a less qualified man. Disparate impact occurs when a retailer requires high school graduation for all its employees, thereby excluding a larger proportion of disadvantaged minorities, when at least some of the jobs (e.g., custodian) could be performed just as well by people who did not graduate from high school. In such cases, the retailer is required to prove the imposed qualification is actually needed to be able to perform the job. The **Age Discrimination and Employment Act** also makes it illegal to discriminate in hiring and terminating people over the age of 40 years.

Finally, the **Americans with Disabilities Act (ADA)** opens up job opportunities for the disabled by requiring employers to provide accommodating work environments. A **disability** is defined as any physical or mental impairment that substantially limits one or more of an individual's major life activities or any condition that is regarded as being such an impairment. Although merely being HIV positive does not limit any life activities, it may be perceived as doing so and is therefore protected as a disability. Similarly, extreme obesity may be either actually limiting or perceived as such and be protected as long as the obese person can perform the duties of the job.

ORIENTATION AND TRAINING PROGRAMS FOR NEW STORE EMPLOYEES

After hiring employees, the next step in developing effective employees (as Exhibit 17–2 shows) is introducing them to the firm and its policies. Retailers want the people they hire to become involved, committed contributors to the firm's successful performance. Moreover, newly hired employees want to learn about their job responsibilities and the company they've decided to join.

Orientation Programs

REFACT

It costs retailers more than $4,000 to replace a store employee.[12]

Orientation programs are critical in overcoming entry shock and socializing new employees.[13] Even the most knowledgeable and mature new employees encounter some surprises. College students who accept management trainee positions often are quite surprised by the differences between their student and their employee roles. Retailing View 17.1 describes some of these differences.

Orientation programs can last from a few hours to several weeks. The orientation and training program for new salespeople might be limited to several hours during which the new salesperson learns the retailer's policies and procedures and how to use the POS terminal. Other retailers, like The Container Store, have a much more intensive training program. Selected by *Fortune* magazine as one of the best places to work, new Container Store employees go through a program called Foundation Week.[14] First, they receive a handbook and assignment before employment even begins. The first day of Foundation Week begins with the company philosophy and a visit from the store manager. Employees immediately see this introduction as different from the traditional first day, which typically entails completing forms and learning where to park. Days two through five continue with hands-on, on-the-floor training, including interaction with and instruction from various positions in the store. The culmination of Foundation Week is a ceremony during which the new employees finally receive their aprons, signifying their membership in this elite organization. The orientation process also continues past Foundation Week. Customer service is the company's core competency, so every first-year, full-time salesperson receives about 241 hours of training, compared with 8 hours in the retail industry on average. Training continues throughout an employee's career.

Disney overhauled its orientation program to emphasize emotion rather than company policies and procedures. The new program begins with current employees, referred to as cast members, discussing their earliest memories of Disney, their visions of great service, and their understanding of teamwork. Then trainers relate "magic moments" they have witnessed to emphasize that insignificant actions can have a big impact on a guest. For example, a four-year-old trips and falls, spilling his box of popcorn. The boy cries, the mother is concerned, and a costumed cast member, barely breaking stride, picks up the empty box, takes it to the popcorn stand for a refill, presents it to the child, and goes on his way.

The orientation program is just one element in the overall training program. It needs to be accompanied by a systematic follow-up to ensure that any problems and concerns arising after the initial period also are considered.

Training Store Employees

Effective training for new store employees includes both structured and on-the-job learning experiences.

Structured Program   During a **structured training program,** new employees learn the basic skills and knowledge they'll need to do their job. For example, salespeople learn what the company policies are, how to use the point-of-sale terminal, and how to perform basic selling skills. Stockroom employees learn procedures for receiving merchandise. This initial training might be done using virtual or real classrooms or with manuals and correspondence distributed to the new employees.

In this structured training program, newly hired Men's Wearhouse salespeople learn about merchandise they will be selling.

Transition from Student to Management Trainee   RETAILING VIEW   17.1

Many students have some difficulty adjusting to the demands of their first full-time job, because student life and professional life are very different. Students typically "report" to three or four supervisors (professors), but the student selects new "supervisors" every four months. In contrast, management trainees have limited involvement, if any, in selecting the one supervisor they'll report to, often for several years.

Student life has fixed time cycles—one- to two-hour classes with a well-defined beginning and end. Retail managers, however, are involved in a variety of activities with varied time horizons, ranging from a five-minute interaction with a customer to season-long development and implementation of a merchandise budget.

The decisions students encounter differ dramatically from the decisions retail managers encounter. For example, business

students might make several major decisions a day when they discuss cases in class. These decisions are made and implemented in one class period, and then a new set of decisions is made and implemented in the next class. In a retail environment, strategic decisions evolve over a long time period. Most decisions, such as those regarding merchandise buying and pricing, are made with incomplete information. Buyers in real life often lack the extensive information provided in many business cases studied in class. Finally, there are long periods of time when retail managers undertake mundane tasks associated with implementing decisions and no major issues are being considered. Students typically don't have these mundane tasks to perform.

Source: Professor Daniel Feldman, University of Georgia.

Some larger firms are finding that structured programs using e-training over the Internet have some benefits over on-the-job training. For example, there is greater consistency, because the training takes place with one computer-based program rather than several supervisors. Costs are lower; once the system is set up, there is no need for human instructors or travel, and employees can undertake the training whenever they want. It is efficient to organize and launch major marketing and service programs nationwide and respond rapidly to market opportunities. In addition, virtual training has contributed to strengthening vendor relationships. For example, many vendors provide briefings on new products to Circuit City so that store associates can learn about new product features and benefits.

The JCPenney e-training system uses one-way video with two-way audio and data exchange capability, which allows instructors to chat online with students during training programs.[15] Along with the presentations from the instructors, the training includes pre- and postclass testing to measure comprehension levels. Instructors also can break students into groups, in which they are given case studies and asked to make recommendations.

Nike's training system for its store employees and those of retailers selling its merchandise is called Sports Knowledge Underground.[16] The layout for Sports Knowledge Underground resembles a subway map, with different stations representing different training themes. As an example, Apparel Union Station branches off into the apparel technologies line, the running products line, and the Nike Pro products line. The Cleated Footwear Station offers paths to football, whereas the Central Station offers such broad lines as customer skills. Each node has a three to seven minute video that gives the associate the basic knowledge he or she needs about various products. As new products are introduced each season, the training is updated. Nike customizes the program for each retailer if requested. When stores implement Sports Knowledge Underground, they see a 4–5 percent increase in sales.

However, structured training programs also need to be supplemented with on-the-job training. New employees can learn about company policies and skills needed to perform their jobs, such as how to ring up orders on POS terminals, but they must be able to apply the information they have learned from structured training programs on the job.

On-the-Job Training   In **on-the-job training,** employees are assigned a job, given responsibilities, and coached by their supervisors. The best way to learn is to practice what is being taught. New employees learn by engaging in activities, making mistakes, and then learning how not to make those mistakes again. Research has shown that on-the-job training produces some of the biggest increases in knowledge.[17]

The outdoor equipment retailer Recreational Equipment Inc. (REI), for instance, spends hours helping new salespeople spot the difference between transactional customers, who want a specific product, and consultative customers, who want to chat about choices.[18] This knowledge helps salespeople engage in a productive selling interaction and provides a pleasant experience for customers. It would be difficult to teach this type of skill using a structured program.

Blended Approach   Because of the relative advantages of structured and on-the-job training, many firms use a blended approach. Best Buy associates attend

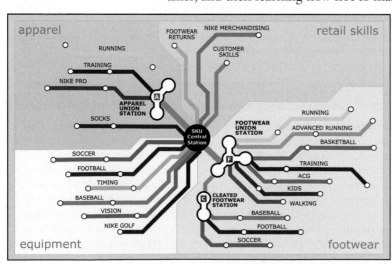

This diagram outlines the product knowledge and company policies that store employees can acquire using Nike's e-learning training solution, called **Sports Knowledge Underground.**

two-and-a-half-hour, instructor-led training sessions as a team approximately once per month.[19] They meet in the stores before or after business hours to get training on the latest products, services, drive times, and issues of concern to their department. During this time, employees engage in role-playing scenarios to practice interacting with customers and apply what they've learned. Associates also complete e-learning courses available on their learning management system, which includes audio modules that allow associates to interact with products while listening to instruction through headphones and an interactive video game that allows associates to practice interacting with virtual customers.

Analyzing Successes and Failures   Every new employee makes mistakes. Store managers should provide an atmosphere in which sales associates try out different approaches for providing customer service and selling merchandise. Store managers need to recognize that some of these new approaches are going to fail, and when they do, managers shouldn't criticize the sales associate. Instead, they should talk about the situation, analyze why the approach didn't work, and discuss how the associate could avoid the problem in the future. Similarly, managers should work with employees to help them understand and learn from their successes. For example, associate shouldn't consider a large, multiple-item sale to be simply due to luck. They should be encouraged to reflect on the sale, identify their key behaviors that facilitated the sale, and then remember these sales behaviors for future use.

It's important to help sales associates assign the right kinds of reasons for their performance. For example, some sales associates take credit for successes and blame the company, the buyers, or the merchandise for their failures. This tendency to avoid taking responsibility for failures doesn't encourage learning. When sales associates adopt this reasoning pattern, they aren't motivated to change their sales behavior because they don't take personal responsibility for losing a sale.

Managers can help sales associates constructively analyze their successes and failures by asking "why" questions that force them to analyze the reasons for effective and ineffective performance. To encourage learning, managers should get salespeople to recognize that they could have satisfied the customer if they had used a different approach or been more persistent. When sales associates accept such responsibility, they'll be motivated to search for ways to improve their sales skills.

MOTIVATING AND MANAGING STORE EMPLOYEES

After employees have received their initial training, managers need to work with them to help them meet their performance goals by being effective leaders and providing appropriate motivation (refer to Exhibit 17–2).

Leadership

Leadership is the process by which one person attempts to influence another to accomplish some goal or goals. Store managers are leaders of their group of employees. Managers use a variety of motivational techniques to increase productivity by helping employees achieve personal goals that are consistent with their firm's objectives.[20]

Leader Behaviors   Leaders engage in task performance and group maintenance behaviors. **Task performance behaviors** are the store manager's efforts to plan, organize, motivate, evaluate, and coordinate store employees' activities. **Group maintenance behaviors** are those activities store managers undertake to make sure that employees are satisfied and work well together. These activities include considering employees' needs, showing concern for their well-being, and creating a pleasant work environment.

The manager of this Sandy Hill, Utah, Shopko store is a democratic leader who holds meetings to keep employees informed about company and store activities. He encourages them to make suggestions about improving store performance.

Leader Decision Making   Store managers vary in how much they involve employees in making decisions. **Autocratic leaders** make all decisions on their own and then announce them to employees. They use the authority of their position to tell employees what to do. For example, an autocratic store manager determines who will work in each area of the store, when they'll take breaks, and what days they'll have off.

In contrast, a **democratic leader** seeks information and opinions from employees and bases his or her decisions on this information. Democratic store managers share their power and information with their employees. The democratic store manager asks employees where and when they want to work and makes schedules to accommodate those employee desires.

Leadership Styles   Store managers tend to develop a specific leadership style. They emphasize either task performance or group maintenance behaviors. They range from autocratic to democratic in their decision-making styles.

After 80 years of research, psychologists have concluded there's no one best style. Effective managers use all styles, selecting the style most appropriate for each situation. For example, a store manager might be autocratic and relations oriented with an insecure new trainee but democratic and task oriented with an effective, experienced employee.

The previous discussion and most of this chapter describe specific behaviors, activities, and programs that store managers use to influence their employees. But the greatest leaders and store managers go beyond influencing employee behaviors to change the beliefs, values, and needs of their employees. **Transformational leaders** get people to transcend their personal needs for the sake of the group or organization. They generate excitement and revitalize organizations.

Transformational store managers create this enthusiasm in their employees through their personal charisma. They are self-confident, have a clear vision that grabs employees' attention, and communicate this vision through words and symbols. Finally, transformational leaders delegate challenging work to subordinates, have free and open communication with them, and provide personal mentoring to develop subordinates.

Retailing View 17.2 examines the inherent difficulties of leading employees with diverse values.

Motivating Employees

Motivating employees to perform up to their potential may be store managers' most important but also most frustrating task. The following hypothetical situation illustrates some issues pertaining to employee motivation and evaluation.

After getting an associate's degree at a local community college, Jim Taylor was hired for a sales position at a department store in San Jose's Eastridge Mall. The position offered firsthand knowledge of the firm's customers, managers, and policies. Taylor was told that if he did well in this assignment, he could become a management trainee.

His performance as a sales associate was average. After observing Taylor on the sales floor, his manager, Jennifer Chen, felt he was effective only when working with customers like himself: young, career-oriented men and women. To encourage Taylor to sell to other types of customers, Chen reduced his fixed salary and increased his commission rate. She also reviewed Taylor's performance goals with him.

Taylor now feels a lot of pressure to increase his sales level. He's beginning to dread coming to work in the morning and is thinking about getting out of retailing and working for a bank.

In this hypothetical situation, Chen focused on increasing Taylor's motivation by providing more incentive compensation. In discussing this illustration, we'll examine the appropriateness of this approach versus other approaches for improving Taylor's performance.

Setting Goals or Quotas

Employee performance improves when employees feel that (1) their efforts will enable them to achieve the goals set for them by their managers and (2) they'll receive rewards they value if they achieve their goals. Thus, managers can motivate employees by setting realistic goals and offering those rewards that employees want.[21]

effort meet goals reward.

For example, Jennifer Chen set specific selling goals for Jim Taylor when he started to work in her department. Taylor, like other store sales associates, has goals in five selling areas: sales per hour, average size of each sale, number of multiple-item (add-on) sales, number of preferred clients, and number of appointments made with preferred clients. (**Preferred clients** are the platinum customer referred to in Chapter 11 with whom salespeople communicate regularly, send notes or e-mails to about new merchandise and sales in the department, and make appointments for special presentations of merchandise.) In addition to selling goals, salespeople are evaluated on the overall department shrinkage due to stolen merchandise, the errors

Should Managers Make Them Do It?   RETAILING VIEW   17.2

In an increasingly diverse work environment, it is likely that conflict will arise among management, individual managers, and employees. Both Wal-Mart and Kroger recently made headlines because a staff pharmacist refused to dispense the Plan B "morning after" contraceptive pill. He said it ran counter to his religious beliefs. In another situation, Muslims who work at grocery checkouts in a Target supercenter said their strict interpretation of the Qur'an prohibited their handling of pork products or even packaged pork products. So they refused to touch, scan, or bag products that contain any pork.

Do managers have the right or the corporate responsibility to force employees to take actions that are contrary to their beliefs, even if they are within the law? Should the pharmacist or the checkout clerks cast aside their personal beliefs to do the job they have been hired to do?

These questions have no clear answer, but it is the retailer's responsibility to recognize the values of their employees while at the same time being able to conduct normal business and satisfy

Should employees who have certain ethical or religious beliefs be required to perform activities that compromise their beliefs if the activities are an integral part of their job?

their customers. The U.S. Food and Drug Administration (FDA) has helped solve the contraceptives conflict by ruling that the Plan B pill can be dispensed without a prescription to women over the age of 18 years but requires that it be kept behind the counter to prevent underage girls from gaining access to it without a parent's permission. Retailers can therefore have more flexibility in handling the situation, because an employee who is not morally opposed to the product can conduct the transaction. Although the practicality of the solution is not as clear, Target could also have other employees step in and help in situations in which Muslim checkout clerks were about to handle pork.

What would you do if you were faced with these or similar ethically sensitive situations?

Source: Curt Woodward, "Court: Druggists May Deny Emergency Pill," *Associated Press*, November 12, 2007; Kevin Coupe, "We Are the World," *Chain Store Age*, May 2007 (accessed January 25, 2008); Chris Serres and Matt McKinney, "Customer Service and Faith Clash at Registers," *Star Tribune*, March 12, 2007.

they make in using the POS terminal, and their contribution to maintaining the department's appearance.

Chen also designed a program for Taylor's development as a sales associate. The activities she outlined over the next six months required Taylor to attend classes to improve his selling skills. Chen needs to be careful in setting goals for Taylor though. If she sets the goals too high, he might become discouraged, feel the goals are unattainable, and thus not be motivated to work harder. However, if she sets the goals too low, Taylor can achieve them easily and won't be motivated to work to his full potential.

Rather than setting specific goals for each salesperson, this retailer uses the average performance for all salespeople as its goal. However, goals are most effective at motivating employees when they're based on the employee's experience and confidence. Experienced salespeople have confidence in their abilities and should have "stretch" goals (high goals that will make them work hard). New salespeople need lower goals that they have a good chance of achieving. The initial good experience of achieving and surpassing goals builds new salespeople's confidence and motivates them to improve their skills.[22] The use of rewards to motivate employees is discussed later in this chapter.

Maintaining Morale

Store morale is important in motivating employees. Typically, morale goes up when things are going well and employees are highly motivated. But when sales aren't going well, morale tends to decrease and employee motivation declines. Some approaches used to build morale are

- Storewide or department meetings prior to the store opening, during which managers pass along information about new merchandise and programs and solicit opinions and suggestions from employees.
- Educating employees about the firm's finances, setting achievable goals, and throwing a party when the goals are met.
- Dividing the charity budget by the number of employees and inviting employees to suggest how their "share" should be used.
- Creating stickers that tell customers that this sandwich was "wrapped by Roger" or this dress was "dry cleaned by Sarah."
- Giving every employee a business card with the company mission printed on its back.

For example, one store manager used real-time sales data collected in her firm's information system to build excitement among her employees. On the first day of the Christmas season, she wrote $3,159 on a blackboard in the store. That was the store's sales during the first day of the Christmas season last year. She told her sales associates that beating that number was not enough. She wanted to see a 36 percent increase, the same sales increase the store achieved over the prior Christmas season.

By setting financial objectives and keeping sales associates informed of up-to-the-minute results, an eight-hour shift of clock watchers gets converted into an excited team of racers. All day, as customers come and go, sales associates take turns consulting the back-room computer that records sales from the store's POS terminals. Retailing View 17.3 describes the distinct efforts that may be required to motivate various generational cohorts.

The Sears manager builds morale and motivates her sales associates by holding "ready meetings" before the store opens. At this meeting, the manager is discussing approaches for improving customer service.

Sexual Harassment

Sexual harassment is an important issue in terms of the productivity of the work environment. Managers must avoid and make sure that store employees avoid any actions that are, or can be interpreted as, sexual harassment. Otherwise, the work environment may be compromised and the retailer and the manager may be held liable for the harassment. The EEOC guidelines define **sexual harassment** as a form of gender discrimination, as follows:

> Unwelcome sexual advances, requests for sexual favors, and other verbal or physical conduct of a sexual nature constitutes sexual harassment when . . . submission to or rejection of such conduct by an individual is used as a basis for employment decisions affecting such individual, or . . . such conduct has the purpose or effect of unreasonably interfering with an individual's work performance or creating an intimidating, hostile, or offensive working environment.

Motivating Different Generational Cohorts   **RETAILING VIEW**   17.3

The major generational cohorts working in retail stores include Baby Boomers (born between 1946 and 1960), Generation X (born 1961–1979), and Generation Y (1980–present). Because employees in each of these age cohorts grew up in different environments, they need to be managed and motivated differently.

Baby Boomers grew up during a period of economic growth, which has given them greater expectations of success. Thus, they are optimistic and self-motivated. They feel that they will earn rewards if they work hard enough.

Generation X employees perceive corporations as less supportive, largely because of the experiences of their parents when economic problems arose. They are skeptical about the firms they work for, and their loyalty to their employer is limited. Instead, they are more concerned about job security and being treated fairly. In turn, they desire a more informal and flexible work environment instead of one that embraces a hierarchical authority.

Generation Y is the first in history to have lived their entire lives with information technology. It is not easy for them to even understand a world without it. Their childhood was comfortable and prosperous, making them more individualistic than earlier generations. Although they demand autonomy in their opinions and behavior, they also remain very interested in personal relationships with their managers and co-workers.

Younger people in general are not motivated by an inherent loyalty to their employer but rather develop high expectations for themselves and want to work for managers who will help them grow and develop their professional skills. These younger workers thus are transforming the workplace from the "get rich quick" attitude of the 1990s to a culture of empowerment and

These Generation Y store employees want to feel they are involved in making decisions that affect their store's performance and are recognized for their achievement.

contribution. At the end of the day, they want to feel as though they are part of something essential and that they have contributed to its achievement. A key to managing this generation therefore is to create excitement about the company's achievements, but even more important, to help them recognize their role in accomplishing that mission.

Generation Y employees further want a role in the decision-making process. Meetings shouldn't be just a method to broadcast decisions that already have been made. Rather than simply being a way to disseminate decisions, meetings should be considered two-way communication forums for asking other employees to contribute their ideas and letting them know that their contribution is not only welcome but valued and carefully considered.

Generational Y employees also want their managers to be mentors, not taskmasters. Unlike their parents, who may have found fulfillment in a steady paycheck, the new generation of employee wants a relationship with someone they feel understands them and their goals. Young people don't want to show up every day to just do the same thing. They look for meaning—in their work, in their lives, and in their interactions with their bosses. An important component of mentoring requires managers to know their employees and understand their goals. One person's goal might be to express herself creatively in her job, whereas another person might aspire to a specific position in the organization or industry.

Sources: "Dueling Age Groups in Today's Workforce; From Baby Boomers to Generations X and Y," *Knowledge@Wharton*, April 22, 2007; "How To Be a Better Boss," *Marketing Magazine*, October 15, 2007, p. 16; Camine Gallo, "Digg This: Talking to Gen Y," *BusinessWeek Online* (accessed January 15, 2008).

Tolerating sexual harassment can significantly decrease morale and productivity.

An appropriate procedure for dealing with a sexual harassment allegation is outlined below:

Step 1: Establish and post an anti–sexual harassment policy, including a complaint procedure outside the normal supervisory channels. Supervisors are often accused of sexual harassment.

Step 2: If a complaint is made, always treat it seriously.

Step 3: Get information from the alleged victim. Ask questions like

- Tell me what happened. Who was involved?
- What did the harasser do and say?
- When did this happen? If this wasn't the first time, when has it happened before?
- Where did it happen?
- Were there any witnesses?
- Have you told anyone else about this or these instances?
- Has anyone else been the object of harassment?
- How did you react to the harasser's behavior?
- Would you care to speak with someone else: another member of management, the personnel department, or the company employment assistance plan person?

Step 4: Document the meeting with the alleged victim.

Step 5: Inform the human resource department or the next higher level of company management of the complaint and of the meeting with the alleged victim.[23]

EVALUATING STORE EMPLOYEES AND PROVIDING FEEDBACK

The fourth step in the management process (Exhibit 17–2) is evaluating and providing feedback to employees. The objective of the evaluation process is to identify those employees who are performing well and those who aren't. On the basis of the evaluation, high-performing employees should be rewarded and considered for positions of greater responsibility. Plans need to be developed to increase the productivity of those employees performing below expectations. Should poor performers be terminated? Do they need additional training? What kind of training do they need?

Who Should Do the Evaluation?

In large retail firms, the evaluation system is usually designed by the human resources department. But the evaluation itself should be done by the employee's immediate supervisor—the manager who works most closely with the employee. For example, in a discount store, the department manager is in the best position to observe a salesperson in action and understand the reasons for the salesperson's performance. The department manager also oversees the recommendations that come out of the evaluation process. Inexperienced supervisors are often assisted by a senior manager in evaluating employees.

How Often Should Evaluations Be Made?

Most retailers evaluate employees annually or semiannually. Feedback from evaluations is the most effective method for improving employee skills. Thus, evaluations should be done more frequently when managers are developing inexperienced

Factors Used to Evaluate Sales Associates at a Specialty Store   **EXHIBIT 17–5**

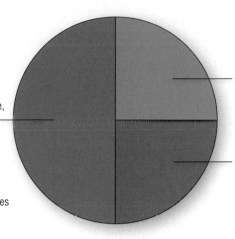

50%
SALES/CUSTOMER RELATIONS

1. Greeting. Approaches customers within 1 to 2 minutes with a smile and friendly manner. Uses open-ended questions.

2. Product knowledge. Demonstrates knowledge of product, fit, shrinkage, and price and can relay this information to the customer.

3. Suggests additional merchandise. Approaches customers at fitting room and cash/wrap areas.

4. Asks customers to buy and reinforces decisions. Lets customers know they've made a wise choice and thanks them.

25%
OPERATIONS

1. Store appearance. Demonstrates an eye for detail (color and finesse) in the areas of display, coordination of merchandise on tables, floor fixtures, and wall faceouts. Takes initiative in maintaining store presentation standards.

2. Loss prevention. Actively follows all loss prevention procedures.

3. Merchandise control and handling. Consistently achieves established requirements in price change activity, shipment processing, and inventory control.

4. Cash/wrap procedures. Accurately and efficiently follows all register policies and cash/wrap procedures.

25%
COMPLIANCE

1. Dress code and appearance. Complies with dress code. Appears neat and well groomed. Projects current fashionable store image.

2. Flexibility. Able to switch from one assignment to another, open to schedule adjustments. Shows initiative, awareness of store priorities and needs.

3. Working relations. Cooperates with other employees, willingly accepts direction and guidance from management. Communicates to management.

employees' skills. However, frequent formal evaluations are time consuming for managers and may not give employees enough time to respond to suggestions before the next evaluation. Managers should supplement these formal evaluations with frequent informal ones. For example, Jennifer Chen should work with Jim Taylor informally and not wait for the formal six-month evaluation. The best time for Chen to provide this informal feedback is immediately after she has obtained, through observations or reports, positive or negative information about Taylor's performance.

Format for Evaluations

Evaluations are only meaningful if employees know what they're required to do, the expected level of performance, and how they'll be evaluated. Exhibit 17–5 shows a specialty retailer's criteria for evaluating sales associates.

In this case, the employee's overall evaluation is based on subjective evaluations made by the store manager and assistant managers. It places equal weight on individual sales/customer relations activities and activities associated with overall store performance. By emphasizing overall store operations and performance, the assessment criteria motivate sales associates to work together as a team.

The criteria used at the department store to evaluate Jim Taylor are objective sales measures based on point-of-sale data, not subjective measures like those used by the specialty store. Exhibit 17–6 summarizes Taylor's formal six-month evaluation. The evaluation form lists results for various factors in terms of both what's considered average performance for company salespeople and Taylor's actual performance. His department has done better than average on shrinkage control, and he has done well on system errors and merchandise presentation. However, his sales performance is below average, even though he made more than the average number of presentations to preferred customers. These results suggest that Taylor's effort is good but his selling skills may need improvement.

	Average Performance for Sales Associates in Department	Actual Performance for Jim Taylor
Sales per hour	$75	$65
Average amount per transaction	$45	$35
Percentage multiple transactions	55%	55%
Number of preferred customers	115	125
Number of preferred customer appointments	95	120
Departmental shrinkage	2.00%	1.80%
Systems errors	10	2
Merchandise presentation (10-point scale)	5	8

Evaluation Errors

Managers can make evaluation errors by first forming an overall opinion of the employee's performance and then allowing this opinion to influence their ratings of each performance factor (haloing). For example, a store manager might feel a salesperson's overall performance is below average and then rate the salesperson below average on selling skills, punctuality, appearance, and stocking. When an overall evaluation casts such a halo on multiple aspects of a salesperson's performance, the evaluation is no longer useful for identifying specific areas that need improvement.

In making evaluations, managers are often unduly influenced by recent events (recency) and their evaluations of other salespeople (contrast). For example, a manager might remember a salesperson's poor performance with a customer the day before and forget the salesperson's outstanding performance over the past three months. Similarly, a manager might be unduly harsh in evaluating an average salesperson just after completing an evaluation of an outstanding salesperson. Finally, managers have a natural tendency to attribute performance (particularly poor performance) to the salesperson and not to the environment in which the salesperson is working. When making evaluations, managers tend to underemphasize effects of external factors, such as merchandise, attractiveness and competitors' actions.

The department store's evaluation of sales associates (Exhibit 17–6) avoids many of these potential biases because most of its ratings are based on objective data. In contrast, the specialty store evaluation (Exhibit 17–5) considers a wider range of activities but uses more subjective measures of performance. Because subjective information about specific skills, attitudes about the store and customers, interactions with coworkers, enthusiasm, and appearance aren't used in the department store's evaluation, performance on these factors might not have been explicitly communicated to Jim Taylor. The subjective characteristics in the specialty store evaluation are more prone to bias, but they also might be more helpful to salespeople as they try to improve their performance. To avoid bias when making subjective ratings, managers need to observe performance regularly, record their observations, avoid evaluating many salespeople at one time, and remain conscious of the various potential biases.

COMPENSATE AND REWARD STORE EMPLOYEES

The fifth and final step in improving employee productivity in Exhibit 17–2 is to compensate and reward employees. Store employees receive two types of rewards from their work: extrinsic and intrinsic. **Extrinsic rewards** are rewards provided by either the employee's manager or the firm, such as compensation, promotion, and recognition. **Intrinsic rewards** are rewards employees get personally from doing their job well. For example, salespeople often like to sell because they think it's challenging and fun. Of course, they want to be paid, but they also find it rewarding to help customers and make sales.[25]

Extrinsic Rewards

Managers can offer a variety of extrinsic rewards to motivate employees. However, store employees don't all seek the same rewards. For example, some salespeople want more compensation; others strive for a promotion in the company or public recognition of their performance. Jim Taylor wants a favorable evaluation from his manager so he can enter the management training program. Part-time salespeople often take a sales job to get out of the house and meet people. Their primary work objective isn't to make money.

Because of these different needs, managers may not be able to use the same rewards to motivate all employees. Large retailers, however, find it hard to develop unique reward programs for each individual. One response is to offer **à la carte plans** that give effective employees a choice of rewards for their good performance. For example, salespeople who achieve their goals could choose a cash bonus, extra days off, or a better discount on merchandise sold in the store. This type of compensation plan enables employees to select the rewards they want. Recognition is another important nonmonetary extrinsic reward for many employees. Although telling employees they've done a job well is appreciated, it's typically more rewarding for them when their good performance is recognized publicly. In addition, public recognition can motivate all store employees, not just the star performers, because it demonstrates management's interest in rewarding employees.

Most managers focus on extrinsic rewards to motivate employees. For example, a store manager might provide additional compensation if a salesperson achieves a sales goal. However, an emphasis on extrinsic rewards can make employees lose sight of their job's intrinsic rewards. Employees can begin to feel that their only reason for working is to earn money and that the job isn't fun.

Intrinsic Rewards

Note that Jennifer Chen tried to motivate Jim Taylor by using extrinsic rewards when she linked his compensation to how much he sold. This increased emphasis on financial rewards may be one reason Taylor now dreads coming to work in the morning. He might not think his job is fun anymore.

When employees find their jobs intrinsically rewarding, they're motivated to learn how to do them better. They act like a person playing a video game: The game itself is so interesting that the player gets rewards from just trying to master it. For example, at a high-fashion, music-inspired apparel store like Hot Topic, employees are intrinsically rewarded by getting involved. Because trends change so quickly, the company encourages store associates to call the buyers after they come back from a club or a concert to tell them what everyone is wearing. The associates thus feel appreciated and involved.

Another approach to making work fun is to hold contests with relatively small prizes. Contests are most effective when everyone has a chance to win. Contests in which the best salespeople always win aren't exciting and may even be demoralizing.

For example, consider a contest in which a playing card is given to salespeople for each men's suit they sell during a two-week period. At the end of two weeks, the best poker hand wins. This contest motivates all salespeople during the entire period of the contest. A salesperson who sells only four suits can win with four aces. Contests should be used to create excitement and make selling challenging for everyone, not to pay the best salespeople more money.

Experienced employees often lose interest in their jobs. Extrinsic rewards, such as pay or promotion, may not be particularly motivating because they might

Public recognition programs make employees feel they are appreciated and motivate them to improve their performance. Marshalls stores that deliver exceptional customer service are recognized for their outstanding efforts.

be satisfied with their present income and job responsibilities. But these employees can be motivated by intrinsic rewards presented as job enrichment. **Job enrichment** is the redesign of a job to include a greater range of tasks and responsibilities. For example, an experienced sales associate who has lost some interest in his or her job could be given responsibility for merchandising a particular area, training new salespeople, or planning and managing a special event.

Compensation Programs

The objectives of a compensation program are to attract and keep good employees, motivate them to undertake activities consistent with the retailer's objectives, and reward them for their effort. In developing a compensation program, the store manager must strike a balance between controlling labor costs and providing enough compensation to keep high-quality employees.

A compensation plan is most effective for motivating and retaining employees when the employees feel the plan is fair and that their compensation is related to their efforts. In general, simple plans are preferred to complex plans. Simple plans are easier to administer, and employees have no trouble understanding them.

Types of Compensation Plans   Retail firms typically use one or more of the following compensation plans: straight salary, straight commission, salary plus commission, and quota–bonus.

With **straight salary compensation,** salespeople or managers receive a fixed amount of compensation for each hour or week they work. For example, a salesperson might be paid $12 per hour or a department manager $1000 per week. This plan is easy for the employee to understand and for the store to administer. Under a straight salary plan, the retailer has flexibility in assigning salespeople to different activities and sales areas. For example, salaried salespeople will undertake nonselling activities, such as stocking shelves, and won't be upset if they're transferred from a high sales-volume department to a low sales-volume department.

The major disadvantage of the straight salary plan is employees' lack of immediate incentives to improve their productivity. They know their compensation won't change in the short run, whether they work hard or slack off. Another disadvantage for the retailer is that a straight salary becomes a fixed cost that the firm incurs even if sales decline.

Incentive compensation plans reward employees on the basis of their productivity. Many retailers now use incentives to motivate greater sales productivity by their employees. With some incentive plans, a salesperson's income is based entirely on commission—called a **straight commission.** For example, a salesperson might be paid a commission based on a percentage of sales made minus the merchandise returned. Normally, the percentage is the same for all merchandise sold (such as 7 percent). But some retailers use different percentages for different categories of merchandise (such as 4 percent for low-margin items and 10 percent for high-margin items). Different percentages provide additional incentives for salespeople to sell specific items. Typically, the compensation of salespeople selling high-priced items such as men's suits, cars, furniture, and appliances is based largely on their commissions.

Incentive plans also may include a fixed salary plus a commission on total sales or a commission on sales over quota. For example, a salesperson might receive a salary of $200 per week plus a commission of 2 percent on all sales over a quota of $50 per hour.

Incentive compensation plans are a powerful motivator for salespeople to sell merchandise, but they have a number of disadvantages. For example, it's hard to get salespeople who are compensated largely by commission to perform nonselling activities. Understandably, they're reluctant to spend time stocking shelves when they could be making money by selling. Also, salespeople will concentrate on the more expensive, fast-moving merchandise and neglect other merchandise. Sales incentives can also discourage salespeople from providing customer service. Finally, salespeople compensated primarily by incentives don't develop loyalty to their employer. The employer doesn't guarantee them an income, so they feel no obligation to the firm.

Under a straight commission plan, salespeople's incomes can fluctuate from week to week, depending on their sales. Because retail sales are seasonal, salespeople might earn most of their income during the Christmas season but much less during the summer months. To provide a more steady income for salespeople who are paid by high-incentive plans, some retailers offer a **drawing account.** With a drawing account, salespeople receive a weekly check based on their estimated annual income, and commissions earned are credited against the weekly payments. Periodically, the weekly draw is compared with the commission earned. If the draw exceeds the earned commissions, the salespeople return the excess money they've been paid, and their weekly draw is reduced. If the commissions earned exceed the draw, salespeople are paid the difference.

Quotas are often used with compensation plans. A **quota** is a target level used to motivate and evaluate performance. Examples might include sales per hour for salespeople or maintained margin and inventory turnover for buyers. For department store salespeople, selling quotas vary across departments due to differences in sales productivity levels.

A **quota–bonus plan** provides sales associates with a bonus when their performance exceeds their quota. A quota–bonus plan's effectiveness depends on setting reasonable, fair quotas, which can be hard. Usually, quotas are set at the same level for everyone in a department, but salespeople in the same department may have different abilities or face different selling environments. For example, in the men's department, salespeople in the suit area have much greater sales potential than salespeople in the accessories area. Newly hired salespeople might have a harder time achieving a quota than more experienced salespeople. Thus, a quota based on average productivity may be too high to motivate the new salesperson and too low to motivate the experienced salesperson effectively. Quotas should be developed for each salesperson on the basis of his or her experience and the nature of the store area in which he or she works.[26]

Group Incentives   To encourage employees in a department or store to work together, some retailers provide additional incentives based on the performance of the department or store as a whole. For example, salespeople might be paid a commission based on their individual sales and then receive additional compensation according to the amount of sales over plan, or quota, generated by all salespeople in the store. The group incentive encourages salespeople to work together in their nonselling activities and while handling customers so the department sales target will be achieved.[27]

Designing the Compensation Program

A compensation program's two elements are the amount of compensation and the percentage of compensation based on incentives. Typically, market conditions determine the amount of compensation. When economic conditions are good and labor is scarce, retailers pay higher wages. Retailers that hire inexperienced salespeople pay lower wages than those that recruit experienced salespeople with good skills and abilities.

Incentive compensation is most effective when a salesperson's performance can be measured easily and precisely. It's difficult to measure individual performance when salespeople work in teams or must perform a lot of nonselling activities. Retailers can easily measure a salesperson's actual sales, but it's hard to measure their customer service or merchandising performance.

When the salesperson's activities have a great impact on sales, incentives can provide additional motivation. For example, salespeople who are simply cashiers have little effect on sales and thus shouldn't be compensated with sales incentives. However, incentives are appropriate for salespeople who provide a lot of information and assistance about complex products, such as designer dresses or home theatre systems. Incentives are less effective with inexperienced salespeople, who are less confident in their skills, because they inhibit learning and thereby can cause excessive stress.

Finally, compensation plans in which too much of the incentive is based on sales may not promote good customer service. Salespeople on commission become interested in selling anything they can to customers, but they aren't willing to spend time helping customers buy the merchandise they need. They tend to stay close to the cash register or the dressing room exits so they can ring up a sale for a customer who's ready to buy.

Setting the Commission Percentage   Assume that a specialty store manager wants to hire experienced salespeople. To get the type of person she wants, she feels she must pay $12 per hour, and her selling costs are budgeted at 8 percent of sales. With compensation of $12 per hour, salespeople need to sell $150 worth of merchandise per hour ($12 divided by 8 percent) for the store to keep within its sales cost budget. The manager believes the best compensation would be one-third salary and two-thirds commission, so she decides to offer a compensation plan of $4 per hour salary (33 percent of $12) and a 5.33 percent commission on sales. If salespeople sell $150 worth of merchandise per hour, they'll earn $12 per hour ($4 per hour in salary plus $150 multiplied by 5.33 percent, which equals $8 per hour in commission).

Legal Issues in Compensation

The **Fair Labor Standards Act** of 1938 set minimum wages, maximum hours, child labor standards, and overtime pay provisions. Enforcement of this law is particularly important to retailers because they hire many low-wage employees and teenagers and ask their employees to work long hours.

The **Equal Pay Act,** now enforced by the EEOC, prohibits unequal pay for men and women who perform equal work or work of comparable worth. Equal work means that the jobs require the same skills, effort, and responsibility and are performed in the same working environment. Comparable worth implies that men and women who perform different jobs of equal worth should be compensated the same. Differences in compensation are legal when compensation is determined by a seniority system, an incentive compensation plan, or market demand.

CONTROLLING COSTS

Labor scheduling, making stores "green" and more energy efficient, and store maintenance offer three opportunities to reduce store operating expenses. Retailing View 17.4 describes how a convenience store chain reengineered its operations to reduce costs and increase customer service.

Labor Scheduling

Using store employees efficiently is an important and challenging problem. Although store employees provide important customer service and merchandising functions that can increase sales, they also are the store's largest operating expense. **Labor scheduling** (determining the number of employees assigned to each area of the store) is difficult because of the multiple shifts and part-time workers needed to staff stores up to 24 hours a day, seven days a week. In addition, customer traffic varies greatly during the day and the week. Bad weather, holidays, and sales can dramatically alter normal shopping patterns and staffing needs.

Managers can spot obvious inefficiencies like long checkout lines and sales associates with nothing to do. But some inefficiencies are more subtle. For example, if 6 percent of a store's sales volume and 9 percent of the total labor hours occur between 2:00 and 3:00 PM, the store might be overstaffed during this time period. Many retailers utilize computer software to deal with the complexities of labor scheduling.[29] This software tracks individual store sales, transactions, units sold, and customer traffic in 15-minute increments over seven weeks, then compares the data to the prior year's, before scheduling workers. It also considers factors like how much time it takes to sell particular merchandise or unload a truck to predict how many workers will be needed at certain times. Although these scheduling systems benefit both retailers and customers, they can burden workers with unpredictable schedules. Workers may be asked to be "on call" to meet customer surges or sent home because of a lull.

Sheetz, a convenience store chain with 310 stores based in Altoona, Pennsylvania, started a series of detailed studies to determine how store-level tasks could be performed more efficiently. It looked at everything from how the store managers closed out the day to how the staff emptied the trash. Two years after the company implemented the recommendations from the study, it had saved $5.1 million in payroll costs alone.

Sheetz, a Pennsylvania-based convenience store chain, reengineered its operations to reduce costs and increase customer service.

too many redundant reports. Thus, the 204 reports that had been available on the store managers' computers were reduced to 23.

Sheetz saved 55 employee hours per week per store by reexamining its labor scheduling. Prior to the study, staffing for stores was based on sales. However, this approach did not consider that some stores generate a lot of sales from labor-intensive activities such as food service, while others derive sales from labor-free, pay-at-the-pump transactions (called *outside sales* by convenience store operators). Some tasks performed in the store were eliminated. For example, the company stopped tracking newspapers at the SKU level. On some newspapers, Sheetz only makes a two-cent margin. When store employees spend time receiving and tracking them by SKU, the firm loses money on each paper it sells.

Sheetz found that store managers were taking three to four hours to close out their sales day. Each day, they had to fill out 40 computer screens of information and would spend an hour looking for a $5 error. Furthermore, the time spent on closing was affecting customer service. Managers would do the paperwork during the morning of the following day, the busiest traffic time, when they should have been out in the stores managing. When Sheetz reexamined these practices, it eliminated over 160,000 hours annually of time the store managers were spending on nonproductive administrative tasks.

Sheetz also found that a lot of the information being sent to store managers was of questionable value. There were

Sources: "Sheetz Hits the Mark," *Retail Merchandiser,* September/October 2007, pp. 28–31; Neil Stern, "Convenience REBORN," *Chain Store Age,* May 2007, pp. 34–39; Rick Romel, "Convenience Stores with a Little Extra," *Knight Ridder Tribune Business,* May 9, 2005, p. 1.

REFACT

In France, the average number of hours worked annually is 1,568, compared with 1,976 in the United States. French workers have 253 paid hours off, compared with 160 hours for U.S. workers.[28]

Retailers also consider the mix of full- versus part-time employees when scheduling labor.[30] Although full-time employees provide stability in the workforce, part-time workers typically receive lower per hour wages and no benefits. Retailers trying to trim labor costs often shift to more part-time employees. Some employees prefer part-time work because it fits in with their lifestyle, whereas others are concerned that a shift toward more part-time work will reduce their incomes and benefits. They also assert that there is a movement to force out longtime, higher-wage, full-time workers to make way for lower-wage, part-time workers.

Labor scheduling is even more difficult in some European countries. For example, in France, a store manager works only 35 hours a week, rarely works at night or on weekends, and has six weeks of annual paid vacation. A store manager in the United States with similar responsibilities works 44 hours a week, including evening and weekend shifts; frequently brings work home at night; and spends some off-time shopping the competitors. Workers in France are guaranteed five weeks paid vacation by law. Most stores other than discount stores are closed during lunch and after 7:00 PM. Few stores are open on Sunday. Store hours are even more restricted in Germany and Italy.

Green and Energy-Efficient Stores

Increasing energy costs, coupled with a greater awareness of business and society's impact on the environment, have caused retailers to make their buildings more energy efficient and **green**—made or maintained in an environmentally and ecologically friendly way, such as by using renewable resources. For example, the Maine-based grocery chain Hannaford Bros. Co. is building a new, state-of-the-art, green supermarket.[31] Plants growing on part of the store's roof add insulation and control storm water. On another part of the roof, photovoltaic panels generate solar energy. The store also relies on geothermal heating and cooling, high-efficiency refrigeration, energy-efficient lighting, and an advanced recycling program.

Wal-Mart also is controlling the energy consumption in all its stores at its corporate headquarters with a team of 100 specialists.[32] If a store manager wants the temperature lowered, the corporate energy team asks a series of questions, such as the exact spot in the store that feels too warm, and then possibly approves the request. Wal-Mart is also reducing its energy costs by buying more produce closer to its stores, which minimizes food-delivery trips; building "high-efficiency" stores that employ wind power and "waterless" urinals; and installing state-of-the-art air conditioning/heating, refrigeration, and lighting systems.

Wal-Mart also is implementing a strategy to ensure it has a positive impact on the environment by reducing packaging across its global supply chain by 5 percent by 2013.[33] In addition to preventing millions of pounds of trash from reaching landfills, it is also saving energy and reducing emissions. Wal-Mart and its suppliers have developed a packaging scorecard to evaluate their performance, using metrics known as the "7Rs of Packaging": remove, reduce, reuse, recycle, renew, revenue, and read.

Store Maintenance

Store maintenance entails the activities involved with managing the exterior and interior physical facilities associated with the store. The exterior facilities include the parking lot, entrances to the store, and signs on the outside of the store. The interior facilities include the walls, flooring, ceiling, and displays and signs. Store maintenance affects both the sales generated in the store and the cost of running the store. A store's cleanliness and neatness affect consumer perceptions of the quality of its merchandise, but maintenance is costly. For instance, floor maintenance for a 40,000 square foot home center runs about $10,000 a year. Poor maintenance shortens the useful life of air conditioning units, floors, and fixtures.

REDUCING INVENTORY SHRINKAGE

An important issue facing store management is reducing inventory losses due to employee theft, shoplifting, mistakes, inaccurate records, and vendor errors. Examples of employee mistakes are failing to ring up an item when it's sold and miscounting merchandise when it's received or during physical inventories. Inventory shrinkage due to vendor mistakes arises when vendor shipments contain less than the amount indicated on the packing slip.

Although shoplifting receives the most publicity, employee theft accounts for more inventory loss. A recent survey attributes 47 percent of inventory shrinkage to employee theft, 32 percent to shoplifting, 14 percent to mistakes and inaccurate records, and 4 percent to vendor fraud, and 3 percent to other reasons.[34]

In developing a loss prevention program, retailers confront a trade-off between providing shopping convenience and a pleasant work environment on the one hand and preventing losses due to shoplifting and employee theft on the other. The key to an effective loss prevention program is determining the most effective way to protect merchandise while preserving an open, attractive store atmosphere and a feeling among employees that they are trusted. Loss prevention requires coordination among store management, visual merchandising, and store design.

REFACT

Total shrinkage in the United States is estimated at $40.5 billion annually.[35]

Calculating Shrinkage

Shrinkage is the difference between the recorded value of inventory (at retail prices) based on merchandise bought and received and the value of the actual inventory (at retail prices) in stores and distribution centers, divided by retail sales during the period. For example, if accounting records indicate inventory should be $1,500,000, the actual count of the inventory reveals $1,236,000, and sales were $4,225,000, the shrinkage is 6.2 percent [($1,500,000 − $1,236,000) ÷ $4,225,000]. Reducing shrinkage is an important store management issue. Retailers' annual loss from shrinkage averages about 1.6 percent of sales.[36] Every dollar of inventory shrinkage translates into a dollar of lost profit.

Organized and High-Tech Retail Theft

Although more than 70 percent of shoplifting is performed by amateurs, professional shoplifters now account for an estimated $15–$30 billion in losses annually, representing almost 25 percent of reported shoplifting cases. These gangs of professional thieves concentrate in over-the-counter medications, infant formula, health and beauty aids, electronics and specialty clothing. This stolen merchandise is often sold by shoplifters on Internet auction sites.

One popular scam is to create counterfeit bar codes at lower prices.[37] For example, a thief created $19 bar codes for $100 Lego sets and got away with sets worth approximately $600,000. Bar-code thieves are hard to catch, because when an alert cashier notices the mispriced item, the thief can either pay the difference or just walk out the door.

Another technology-based scam is tampering with gift cards by professional and amateur shoplifters and employees. The thieves may create duplicate gift cards that can be used by the thief or resold online, or the thief may use active gift card account information to create duplicate cards or make Web purchases. Thieves also have been known to steal merchandise, then return it to the store for credit in the form of gift cards. eBay has become an excellent market for gift cards. It is estimated that 70 percent of gift cards sold on eBay were fraudulently obtained.[39]

Some gangs also are using store credits to steal.[40] In one case, a valid $500 store credit receipt was scanned and digitally altered to $1,200. Then gang members printed copies and presented them in 16 stores across 12 states within an hour of one another.

REFACT

Target Corp. estimates that more than 50 percent of theft at the Target chain involves some high-tech twist—whether in how the goods are stolen or how they are unloaded.[38]

REFACT

As many as one in twelve customers is a shoplifter in the United States. Shoplifters commit an average of 50 thefts before being caught. It is estimated that only 10–15 percent are apprehended.[42]

Detecting and Preventing Shoplifting

Losses due to shoplifting can be reduced by store design, merchandise policies, special security measures, personnel policies, and prosecution of shoplifters.[41]

Store Design   The following store design issues are used to reduce inventory shinkage:

- Do not place expensive or small merchandise near an entrance.
- Keep the height of fixtures low and arranged with no "blind spots," so that the store maintains open sight lines to store entrances and and dressing rooms so employees can see customers in the store and watch for shoplifters while providing better service.
- Use mirrors. Strategically placed one-way observation mirrors and hanging mirrors can help store employees observe customers.
- Because cash wraps are always staffed, they should be near areas that theft is likely to occur. **Cash wraps** are the places in a store where customers can buy their purchases and have them "wrapped"—placed in a bag.
- Alternate clothing hanger directions. Professional shoplifters can steal a tremendous amount of clothing by grabbing it off the rack. If the hangers are alternated, it is difficult for thieves to steal a lot at once.

Merchandise Policies   The following merchandise policies are utilized to reduce inventory shrinkage:

- Require a receipt for all returns, because many shoplifters steal with the intent of returning the merchandise for a cash refund.
- Lock up small, expensive items. Expensive apparel items can be chained. While locking merchandise in a cabinet or chaining expensive apparel decreases shrinkage, it may decrease sales by making it more difficult for customers to look at merchandise of interest.

Security Measures   The following security measures help reduce inventory shrinkage:

Retailers use EAS tags to reduce shoplifting. The price tags contain a device that is deactivated when the merchandise is purchased. If a customer has not purchased the merchandise, an alarm is triggered when the stolen merchandise passes through sensor gates at the store's exit.

- Use closed-circuit TV cameras that can be monitored from a central location. Because purchasing the equipment and hiring people to monitor the system can be expensive, some retailers install nonoperating equipment that looks like a TV camera to provide a psychological deterrent to shoplifters but saves costs compared with purchasing real TV cameras.
- Use **electronic article surveillance (EAS) systems.** These special tags are placed on merchandise. When the merchandise is purchased, the tags are deactivated by the point-of-sale (POS) scanner. If a shoplifter tries to steal the merchandise, the active tags are sensed when the shoplifter passes a detection device at the store exit, and an alarm is triggered. If the store cannot afford an EAS system, it can still use the EAS tags to deter prospective thieves. The EAS tags do not affect shopping behavior, because most customers do not realize they're on the merchandise. Due to the effectiveness of tags in reducing shoplifting, retailers can increase sales by displaying theft-prone, expensive merchandise openly rather than locking or chaining it up.

EXHIBIT 17–7
Spotting Shoplifters

DON'T ASSUME THAT ALL SHOPLIFTERS ARE POORLY DRESSED
To avoid detection, professional shoplifters dress in the same manner as customers patronizing the store. Over 90 percent of all amateur shoplifters arrested have the cash, checks, or credit to purchase the merchandise they stole.

SPOT LOITERERS
Amateur shoplifters frequently loiter in areas as they build up the nerve to steal something. Professionals also spend time waiting for the right opportunity but less conspicuously than amateurs.

LOOK FOR GROUPS
Teenagers planning to shoplift often travel in groups. Some members of the group divert employees' attention while others take the merchandise. Professional shoplifters often work in pairs. One person takes the merchandise and passes it to a partner in the store's restroom, phone booths, or restaurant.

LOOK FOR PEOPLE WITH LOOSE CLOTHING
Shoplifters frequently hide stolen merchandise under loose-fitting clothing or in large shopping bags. People wearing a winter coat in the summer or a raincoat on a sunny day may be potential shoplifters.

WATCH THE EYES, HANDS, AND BODY
Professional shoplifters avoid looking at merchandise and concentrate on searching for store employees who might observe their activities. Shoplifters' movements might be unusual as they try to conceal merchandise.

Personnel Policies   The following personnel policies may help deter shoplifting:

- Use mystery and honesty shoppers—people posing as real shoppers—to watch for employee and customer theft.
- Have store employees monitor fitting rooms. Fitting rooms provide a good environment for stealing.
- Store employees should be trained to be aware, visible, and alert to potential shoplifting situations. Exhibit 17–7 outlines some rules for spotting shoplifters. Perhaps the best deterrent to shoplifting is an alert employee who is very visible.
- Provide excellent customer service. If employees know the customers and offer assistance, shoplifters will be detered.

Prosecution   Many retailers have a policy of prosecuting all shoplifters. They feel a strictly enforced prosecution policy deters shoplifters. Some retailers also sue shoplifters in civil proceedings for restitution of the stolen merchandise and the time spent in the prosecution.

Although many of these measures reduce shoplifting, they can also make the shopping experience more unpleasant for honest customers. The atmosphere of an apparel store is diminished when guards, mirrors, and TV cameras are highly visible. Customers may find it hard to try on clothing secured with a lock and chain or an electronic tag. They can also be uncomfortable trying on clothing if they think they're secretly being watched via a surveillance monitor. Thus, when evaluating security measures, retailers need to balance the benefits of reducing shoplifting with the potential losses in sales.

Reducing Employee Theft

The most effective approach for reducing employee theft and shoplifting is to create a trusting, supportive work environment. When employees feel they're respected members of a team, they identify their goals with the retailer's goals. Stealing from their employer thus becomes equivalent to stealing from themselves or their family, and they go out of their way to prevent others from stealing from the "family." Thus,

REFACT
A dishonest employee typically takes over $1,300 worth of goods and cash, whereas the average customer shoplifter takes $347 in merchandise.[43]

REFACT

Total inventory shrinkage attributed to employee theft is approximately $19 billion annually in the United States.[44]

retailers with a highly committed workforce and low turnover typically have low inventory shrinkage. Additional approaches for reducing employee theft are carefully screening employees, creating an atmosphere that encourages honesty and integrity, and establishing security policies and control systems.

Screening Prospective Employees   As mentioned previously, many retailers use paper-and-pencil honesty tests and undertake extensive reference checks to screen out potential employees with theft problems. A major problem related to employee theft is drug use. Some retailers now require prospective employees to submit to drug tests as a condition of employment. Employees with documented performance problems, an unusual number of accidents, or erratic time and attendance records are also tested. Unless they're involved in selling drugs, employees

17.5   RETAILING VIEW   Technology Stops Thieves

Retailers are turning to technology to help stop shoplifting. Some stores have installed a system called the Video Investigator that examines a shopper's movements to recognize unusual activity. If a customer removes a number of items from a shelf at once, or opens a case that's normally kept closed and locked, the system alerts guards via alarms or handheld devices. If someone opens a back door at 2:00 AM, the system records who sneaked in and links the alert with photos of the previous and next persons to use the door.

A favorite trick of professional shoplifters is to load up carts and simply run out of the store. To thwart this activity, carts are equipped with radio frequency identification chips (RFID) on the cartwheels and antennas around the periphery of the store that broadcast signals to the chips. When a cart approaches the store boundary, its wheels lock up so thieves cannot walk out with it.

Shoplifters also may use the rungs underneath the cart to sneak out items. In response, stores are mounting cameras in the cashiers' stands to scrutinize the bottom racks of carts. If an item matches an image in a database, the system computes the price of the product and adds it to the customer's bill.

Although stores already are using RFID tags to keep track of inventory in the supply chain, as the price of the tags continue to decrease, they likely will replace EAS tags altogether, because they are a more precise and inconspicuous way of tracking items on a sales floor. The tags, which come in different shapes, many smaller than postage stamps, can communicate with a handheld device, telling workers when a large number of items is being moved or leaving the store.

Because almost half of inventory shrinkage is due to employee theft, new transaction-monitoring software also pulls information from registers into a central database and looks for unusual patterns. An excess of manually entered credit-card numbers could be a signal that employees are stealing customers' information. Returns of the same type of sweater 10 times in a row at one register, for instance, could indicate that an employee is processing fake returns for a friend or being conned into making fraudulent returns.

Data-mining programs combined with video technology permit a more comprehensive look at cash register activity. Managers can highlight irregular register transactions on their computers and pull up corresponding videos. This function could enable managers to catch cashiers who cut deals for their friends or pocket cash refunds. It could also curtail fraudulent returns by tracking the route customers take to the customer service desk;

Flashfog is a security product that fills a room with nontoxic smoke when triggered.

do they head straight there, or do they meander through the store, picking up their "return" merchandise along the way?

Sources: "Attention, Shoplifters," *BusinessWeek*, September 11, 2006 (accessed January 25, 2008): Jennifer Davies, "Retailers Use Technology to Thwart Would-be Thieves," *San Diego Union Tribune*, June 13, 2007 (accessed January 25, 2008).

who test positive are often offered an opportunity to complete a company-paid drug program, submit to random testing in the future, and remain with the firm.

Establishing Security Policies and Control Systems   To control employee theft, retailers adopt policies related to certain activities that may facilitate theft. Some of the most prevalent policies are

- Randomly search containers, such as trash bins, where stolen merchandise can be stored.
- Require store employees to enter and leave the store through designated entrances.
- Assign salespeople to specific POS terminals and require all transactions to be handled through those terminals.
- Restrict employee purchases to working hours.
- Provide customer receipts for all transactions.
- Have all refunds, returns, and discounts cosigned by a department or store manager.
- Change locks periodically and issue keys to authorized personnel only.
- Provide a locker room where all employees' handbags, purses, packages, and coats must be checked before the employees leave.
- Maintain rotating employee assignments. Team different employees together.

In the end, it is important that employees do not feel that management is overly suspicious of their actions or that they are treated with disrespect, as this sense will erode morale. Retailing View 17.5 looks at how some new technology is helping retailers curb shoplifting.

REFACT
The average shoplifting loss due to employee theft is approximately $350.[45]

SUMMARY

Effective store management can have a significant impact on a retail firm's financial performance. Store managers increase profits by increasing labor productivity, decrease costs through labor deployment decisions, and reduce inventory loss by developing a dedicated workforce.

Increasing store employees' productivity is challenging because of the difficulties in recruiting, selecting, and motivating store employees.

Employees typically have a range of skills and seek a spectrum of rewards. Effective store managers need to motivate their employees to work hard and develop skills so they improve their productivity. To motivate employees, store managers need to understand what rewards each employee is seeking and then provide an opportunity for that employee to realize those rewards. Store managers must establish realistic goals for employees that are consistent with the store's goals and motivate each employee to achieve them.

Store managers also must control inventory losses due to employee theft, shoplifting, and clerical errors. Managers use a wide variety of methods to develop loss prevention programs, including security devices and employee screening during the selection process. However, the critical element of any loss prevention program is building employee loyalty to reduce employee interest in stealing and increase attention to shoplifting.

KEY TERMS

Age Discrimination and Employment Act, *482*
à la carte plan, *493*
Americans with Disabilities Act (ADA), *482*
autocratic leader, *486*
cash wraps, *500*
democratic leader, *486*
disability, *482*

discrimination, *482*
disparate impact, *482*
disparate treatment, *482*
drawing account, *495*
electronic article surveillance (EAS) system, *500*
Equal Employment Opportunity Commission (EEOC), *482*
Equal Pay Act, *496*

extrinsic reward, *492*
Fair Labor Standards Act, *496*
green, *498*
group maintenance behavior, *485*
incentive compensation plan, *494*
intrinsic reward, *492*
job analysis, *477*
job application form, *479*

GET OUT AND DO IT!

1. **CONTINUING CASE ASSIGN-MENT** Go to the store you have selected for the continuing case assignment and meet with the person responsible for personnel scheduling. Report on the following:

- Who is responsible for employee scheduling?
- How far in advance is the schedule made?
- How are breaks and lunch periods planned?
- How are overtime hours determined?
- On what is the total number of budgeted employee hours for each department based?
- How is flexibility introduced into the schedule?
- How are special requests for days off handled?
- How are peak periods (hourly, days, or seasons) planned for?
- What happens when an employee calls in sick at the last minute?
- What are the strengths and weakness of the personnel scheduling system from the manager's and employees' perspectives?

2. **CONTINUING CASE ASSIGN-MENT** Go to the store you have selected for the continuing case assignment and talk to the person responsible for human resource management to find out how sales associates are compensated and evaluated for job performance.

- How are sales associates trained? What are the criteria for evaluation?
- How often are they evaluated?
- Do salespeople have quotas? If they do, how are they set? What are the rewards of exceeding quotas? What are the consequences of not meeting these objectives?
- Can sales associates make a commission? If yes, how does the commission system work? What are the advantages of a commission system? What are the disadvantages?
- If there is no commission system, are any incentive programs offered? Give an example of a specific program or project used by the store to boost employee morale and productivity.

Evaluate each of the answers to these questions and make recommendations for improvement where appropriate.

3. Go to a store, observe the security measures in the store, and talk with a manager about the store's loss prevention program.

- Are there surveillance cameras? Where are they located? Are the cameras monitored, or are they just there to thwart shoplifting?
- What is the store's policy against shoplifters?
- What are the procedures for approaching a suspected shoplifter?
- What roles do sales associates and executives play in the security programs?
- Is employee theft a problem? Elaborate.
- How is employee theft prevented in the store?
- How is customer service related to loss prevention in the store?
- What is this retailer doing well in terms of security and loss prevention, and in which areas should it improve its policies and procedures?

4. Go online and research the shoplifting laws implemented by the state where you live or attend school. What are the fines, jail time, community service, or punishments for perpetrators in your local jurisdiction? What factors are weighed and evaluated in shoplifting cases? Are the laws in your state a deterrent to shoplifting? Please explain.

5. Go to the homepage for IntelliVid, the leading video surveillance provider, which offers insights into retail best practices, at www.intellivid.com. How do this company's high-tech products and services help retailers reduce shrinkage, track suspicious behavior, and support loss prevention staff?

DISCUSSION QUESTIONS AND PROBLEMS

1. How do on-the-job training, Internet training, and classroom training differ? What are the benefits and limitations of each approach?

2. Give examples of a situation in which a manager of a McDonald's fast-food restaurant should utilize different leadership styles.

3. Use the interview questions in Exhibit 17–4 and role-play with another student in the class as both the interviewer and the applicant for an Assistant Store Manager position with a store of your choice.

4. Name some laws and regulations that affect the employee management process. Which do you believe are the easiest for retailers to adhere to? Which are violated the most often?

5. What's the difference between extrinsic and intrinsic rewards? What are the effects of these rewards on the behavior of retail employees? Under what conditions would you recommend that a retailer emphasize intrinsic rewards over extrinsic rewards?

6. Many large department stores, such as JCPenney, Sears, and Macy's, are changing their salespeople's reward system from a traditional salary to a commission-based system. What problems can incentive compensation systems cause? How can department managers avoid these problems?

7. When evaluating retail employees, some stores use a quantitative approach that relies on checklists and numerical scores similar to the form in Exhibit 17–6. Other stores use a more qualitative approach, whereby less time is spent checking and adding and more time is devoted to discussing strengths and weaknesses in written form. Which is the best evaluation approach? Why?

8. Explain how changing demographics of the workforce are affecting staffing and recruiting efforts for retail sales and management positions.

9. List the skills, knowledge, and abilities that can be successfully taught to new retail employees through an orientation program, a formal training program, and on-the-job training.

10. Discuss how retailers can reduce shrinkage from shoplifting and employee theft.

11. Drugstore retailers, such as CVS, place diabetic test strips and perfume behind locked glass cabinets and nearly all over-the-counter medicines behind plexiglass panels. These efforts are designed to deter theft. Describe how these security measures influence honest customers.

SUGGESTED READINGS

Aberson, Christopher L. "Diversity, Merit, Fairness, and Discrimination Beliefs as Predictors of Support for Affirmative-Action Policy Actions." *Journal of Applied Social Psychology* 37, no. 10 (2007), pp. 2451–74.

Ackfeldt, Anna-Lena, and Leonard Coote. "A Study of Organizational Citizenship Behaviors in a Retail Setting." *Journal of Business Research* 58 (February 2005), pp. 151–63.

Baker, Stacey Menzel; Jonna Holland; and Carol Kaufman-Scarborough. "How Consumers with Disabilities Perceive "Welcome" in Retail Servicescapes: A Critical Incident Study." *Journal of Services Marketing* 21, no. 3 (2007), pp. 160–73.

Bernardin, H. John. *Human Resource Management: An Experiential Approach*, 4th ed. Burr Ridge, IL: McGraw-Hill, 2007.

Cascio, Wayne, and Herman Aguinis. *Applied Psychology in Human Resource Management*, 7th ed. Upper Saddle River, NJ: Pearson/Prentice Hall, 2007.

Hollinger, Richard, and Amanda Adams. *2007 National Retail Security Survey Final Report*. Gainesville, FL: Security Research Project, University of Florida, 2008.

Hornsby, Jeffrey, and Donald Kuratko. *Frontline HR: A Handbook for the Emerging Manager*. Mason, OH: Thomson, 2005.

Lessons Learned: Hiring and Firing. Boston: Harvard Business School Press, 2008.

Noe, Raymond; John Hollenbeck; Barry Gerhart; and Patrick Wright. *Fundamentals of Human Resource Management*, 2nd ed. Burr Ridge, IL: McGraw-Hill, 2006.

Podmoroff, Dianna. *How to Hire, Train & Keep the Best Employees for Your Small Business*. Ocala, FL: Atlantic Publishing Group, 2004.

Rothstein, Mark, and Lance Leibman. *Employment Law*, 6th ed. St. Paul, MN: Thomson/West, 2007.

Store Layout, Design, and Visual Merchandising

EXECUTIVE BRIEFING

Lori Anderson, Owner/Operator, suitcase

impetus for my Master's thesis study. I found that working in this upscale specialty store offered plenty of opportunity for me to demonstrate my creative abilities and decided to open my own store.

My strategy is to target 25 to 55-year-old, affluent, professional women that are style savvy and quality driven. My goal is to not only offer my customers of-the-moment fashion pieces but also to expand their style preferences by exposing them to burgeoning designers—designers that are fresh, inventive, and have yet to be discovered by national chains and large department stores.

After writing a business plan for my store and obtaining the appropriate financing, I had to find a location. I found a great location but the basic shell of the store was less than ideal. It was long and narrow (measuring a mere 18 feet across); thus, it was essential for me to employ various design elements that draw my customers to the back of the store, ensuring they experience the full array of merchandise being offered. My cash wrap is in the center of the store with the fitting rooms toward the back. In order to delineate key zones within the shop, I applied a special wall treatment to these areas. A seating area that typifies a home-like living room was also implemented in the back of the store across from the fitting rooms. Despite some people advising me that this sitting zone

I have always been interested in the aesthetics of design. Initially, upon entering college, I wanted to study architecture and design. However, after realizing that the creation of magnificent buildings involved a bigger commitment than I was prepared to take on at that point in my life, I opted to express my creativity by attaining a degree in marketing.

After graduation, I worked for several large corporations as a marketing representative, all the while still passionate about design and its intricacies. So, back to school it was. While attending the University of Florida's Interior Design graduate program, I worked part-time at a local women's clothing boutique, which ultimately became the

CHAPTER 18

QUESTIONS

What are the critical issues retailers consider in designing a store?

What are the advantages and disadvantages of alternative store layouts?

How is store floor space assigned to merchandise and departments?

What are the best techniques for merchandise presentation?

How exciting should a store be?

impedes upon available selling space (i.e., reducing the amount of merchandise that can be displayed), I have found that this component is the single most effective design element within the store. It enables the customer to feel relaxed and at ease by creating a social environment that encourages shoppers and their friends to engage one another, as well as the sales staff. Because of this, very often shoppers' stays are extended, and as a result, their proclivity to buy more merchandise increases.

My merchandising technique is quite simple. Rather than displaying my product grouped by designer or by size, I assemble my merchandise by color. I have found that many of my customers like outfit ideas presented to them; thus, arranging ensembles together within a color group enables shoppers to more easily facilitate their individual style ideas.

Owning and managing my own store greatly satisfies my needs to be creative, to interact with people, and to make a good living. I have the opportunity to experiment with novel designers, innovative store design elements, and special promotions for attracting new customers and maintaining the loyalty of my existing clientele. The combination of my marketing business background and interior design education, coupled with an innate passion for fashion, has been manifested in a dream come true!

Recognizing the significant impact of the store environment on shopping behavior, retailers have devoted considerable resources to their store design and merchandise presentations. For example, The Apple Store on Fifth Avenue in Manhattan reinforces the company's image of developing products with innovative design features.[1] Its most striking feature is a transparent glass cube, 32 feet on each side, marking the entrance to the store. The cube houses a cylindrical glass elevator and a spiral glass staircase leading to a 10,000-square-foot subterranean retail space.

A well-designed store is like a good story,[2] with a beginning, middle, and end. The story begins at the entrance, which creates expectations and offers promises. As for the first impression, the storefront says, "I have low prices," or "I have the latest fashions," or "I'm easy to shop." Rather than launching right into "Here's what we've got to sell," the store entrance should entice, hint, and tease.

A single message at the entrance is the most effective approach for creating a positive store image. Customers need a few seconds to orient themselves when they enter the store. Thus, cluttering the entrance with a lot of products and signage can create confusion and an uncomfortable feeling for customers.

The middle of the story comes from inside the store. It starts off slow and builds to a crescendo. The store design leads customers on a journey through the store. Using lighting, signage, displays, and aisles, the design creates destinations and guides customers down a path of discovery. During this journey, the store engages shoppers by using design elements to relate the merchandise and services offered to their own needs.

Finally, the cash wrap or checkout counter is the story's climactic finale. It provides an opportunity for

The Apple Store in New York City reinforces the company's image of developing products with innovative design features.

customers to quickly and easily purchase merchandise and conclude their store visit.

This chapter is part of the store management section because store managers are responsible for implementing the design and visual merchandising developed by specialists at the retailer's corporate headquarters. They adapt the prototype plans to the unique characteristics of their store and then make sure the image and experience provided by the design is consistent over time. However, as discussed in this chapter, store design and visual merchandising are also elements of a retailer's communication mix. Store design plays an important role in creating and reinforcing a retailer's brand image.

The chapter begins with a discussion of store design objectives. Next, the three elements of store design—layout, signage, and feature areas—are discussed. Then the decisions about how much space to allocate to different merchandise categories and where the categories should be located in the store are reviewed. The chapter concludes with an examination of store design elements, such as the use of color, lighting, and music, that affect the customer's shopping experience.

STORE DESIGN OBJECTIVES

REFACT

Retailers remodel their stores every eight years on average.[3]

Some objectives for a store design are to (1) implement the retailer's strategy, (2) influence customer buying behavior, (3) provide flexibility, (4) control design and maintenance costs, and (5) meet legal requirements.

Store Design and Retail Strategy

The primary objective of a store design is to implement the retailer's strategy. The design must be consistent with and reinforce the retailer's strategy by meeting the needs of the target market and building a sustainable competitive advantage.[4] For example, to appeal better to European customers, McDonald's remodeled its stores with lime-green designer chairs and dark leather upholstery to create a more relaxed experience in a sophisticated atmosphere.[5] It also implemented nine different designs for different location types and target markets, ranging from "purely simple," with minimalist décor in neutral colors, to "Qualité," featuring large pictures of lettuces and tomatoes and gleaming stainless steel kitchen utensils, like meat grinders. In developing these redesigns, McDonald's had to make sure that the new designs projected a more appealing image but still enabled customers to recognize the store as a McDonald's and continue to have favorable associations with the McDonald's brand.

Retailing View 18.1 illustrates that effective store design differs across cultures and traditions. What works in the U.S may fail in other countries. In India, clutter and noise help sell merchandise.

This McDonald's restaurant in Europe features an innovative design that creates an appealing brand image.

Influence Customer Buying Behavior

A second design objective is to influence customer buying behavior. Specifically, retailers want the store design to attract customers to the store; enable them to locate merchandise of interest easily; motivate them to make unplanned, impulse purchases; and provide them with a satisfying shopping experience.

The influence of store design on buying behavior is increasing with the rise in two-income and single head-of-household families. Due to the limited time these families have, they are spending less time planning shopping trips and making more purchase decisions in stores. So retailers are making adjustments to their stores to get people in and out quicker. For example, at some Whole Foods stores, the checkout area has been redesigned so that customers form a serpentine single line that feeds into the cash registers.[6] Although banks and other service providers have used a similar system for decades, supermarkets and other retailers

Some Whole Foods stores use one line that feeds into all cash registers—a system that can reduce wait times by 50 to 75 percent over a traditional system.

Like a Cluttered Store? Go to India   RETAILING VIEW   18.1

Kishore Biyani's supermarkets in Mumbai, India, were initially designed like most Western-style supermarkets. But customers walked down the wide aisles, past neatly stocked shelves, and out the door without buying. Biyani soon recognized that part of his target market, lower middle–income customers, did not like the sterile environment. His other target market segment, wealthier families, generally employed servants to do the grocery shopping. These servants were accustomed to shopping in small, cramped stores filled with haggling customers. Most Indians buy fresh produce from street vendors or small stores, and the merchandise is kept under burlap sacks.

Biyani therefore redesigned his stores to make them cluttered and noisier, much like a public market. He spent about $50,000 to replace the long wide aisles with narrow crooked ones. The stores have floors of gray granite tiling, common in markets and train stations, so his customers will feel at home. Instead of long aisles and tall shelves, the stores place bins on low shelves, which allows customers to handle the products from all different sides. Indian customers are used to buying

Supermarket customers in India prefer to shop in stores using design elements they are familiar with rather than more "efficiently" designed western supermarkets.

bulk commodities like wheat, rice, and lentils. Although bulk displays can be messy, store employees are instructed not to clean them up because customers are less likely to check out the merchandise if it is in neat stacks.

Because Indian markets are noisy and full of bartering, Biyani's stores employ people to walk around using megaphones to announce promotions, adding to the din of music and commercials playing in the background. Many of the stores aren't air conditioned, not in an effort to save money but rather because the heat adds to the ambiance. There is no quiet, relaxed atmosphere here.

Biyani's approach to store design has worked. His company, Panaloon Retail (India), Ltd., is now the country's largest retailer with annual sales of approximately $900 million.

Source: Eric Bellman, "In India, a Retailer Finds Key to Success Is Clutter," *The Wall Street Journal*, August 8, 2007, p. A1; Curt Hazletter, "Controlled Explosion," *Shopping Centers Today* 28, no. 3 (2007), pp. 63–67; Ritu Upadhyay, "Retailing's Rapid Rise in India," *WWD: Women's Wear Daily*, February 20, 2007.

have generally favored the one-line-per-register system, because they thought a long line would scare off shoppers. Because people stand in the same line though, there are no "slow" lines, delayed by a coupon-counting customer or slow cashier. Using this system, the wait can be reduced 50 to 75 percent compared with using a traditional system.

Flexibility

Retailing is a very dynamic business. Competitors might enter a market and cause existing retailers to change the mix of merchandise offered. As the merchandise mix changes, so must the space allocated to merchandise categories and the layout of the store change. Thus, store designers attempt to design stores with maximum flexibility.[7] Flexibility can take two forms: the ability to physically move and store components, and the ease with which components can be modified.

Most stores are designed with flexibility in mind. For instance, Wallace's Bookstores, one of the nation's largest operators of college bookstores, has an innovative concept with built-in merchandising and design flexibility called *flexsmart*. The format allows the book stores to expand or contract their spaces to accommodate the seasonal fluctuations inherent in the college-bookstore business. College bookstores need to change their space allocations to accommodate the rush for textbooks at the beginning of each semester and the slower in-between periods. During the semester, the allocation of space to books or apparel can be increased or decreased by as much as 30 percent. The key to Wallace's flexibility lies in an innovative fixturing and wall system that portions off the textbook area. **Fixtures** are the equipment used to display merchandise.

Cost

The fourth design objective is to control the cost of implementing the store design and maintain the store's appearance. For instance, the free-form design found in many specialty stores is more costly to construct and can handle less merchandise than a design involving rows of shelves in a discount store. But the free-form design also can encourage customers to explore more of the store and thus increase sales.

Certain types of lighting that highlight expensive jewelry and crystal use more electricity and are less ecologically friendly than rows of bare fluorescent bulbs. However, the more expensive lighting can make the merchandise look better and thus increase sales.

The store design can also affect labor costs and inventory shrinkage. Traditional department stores typically are organized into departments that are isolated from one another. This design provides an intimate and comfortable shopping experience that can result in more sales. However, the design prevents sales associates from observing and covering adjacent departments, which makes it necessary to have at least one sales associate permanently stationed in each department to provide customer service and prevent shoplifting.

Retailing View 18.2 describes how Wal-Mart is building environmentally sensitive stores that reduce energy costs and help build Wal-Mart's image as a socially responsible retailer.

Legal Considerations—Americans with Disabilities Act

A critical objective in any store design or redesign decision is to ensure compliance with the 1990 Americans with Disabilities Act (ADA).[8] This law protects people with disabilities from discrimination in employment, transportation, public accommodations, telecommunications, and the activities of state and local government. It affects store design because the act calls for "reasonable access" to merchandise and services in retail stores that were built before 1993. Stores built after 1993 must be fully accessible.

The Act also states that retailers should not have to incur "undue burdens" to comply with ADA requirements. Although retailers are concerned about the needs of their disabled customers, they are also worried that making merchandise completely accessible to people in a wheelchair or a motorized cart will result in less space available to display merchandise and thus reduce sales. However, providing for wider aisles and more space around fixtures can result in a more pleasant shopping experience for able-bodied as well as disabled customers.

The ADA does not clearly define critical terms such as "reasonable access," "fully accessible," or "undue burden." So the actual ADA requirements are being defined through a series of court cases in which disabled plaintiffs have filed class-action suits against retailers.[9] Based on these court cases, retailers are typically required to (1) provide 32-inch-wide pathways in the main aisle, to bathrooms, fitting rooms, and elevators, and around most fixtures; (2) lower most cash wraps (checkout stations) and fixtures so they can be reached by a person in a wheelchair; and (3) make bathrooms and fitting rooms fully accessible. These accessibility requirements are somewhat relaxed for retailers in very small spaces and during peak sales periods such as the Christmas holidays.[10]

Design Trade-Offs

Typically, a store design cannot achieve all of these objectives, so managers need to make trade-offs among them. Home Depot's traditional warehouse design can efficiently store and display a lot of merchandise with long rows of floor-to-ceiling racks, but this design is not conducive for a pleasant shopping experience, particularly for the female customers who account for more that half of the sales in home

---

Wal-Mart Goes Green   **RETAILING VIEW**   18.2

Wal-Mart is designing new stores and retrofitting older stores to be more energy efficient. These stores are among the "greenest" in the world. The three main design objectives for these stores are to (1) reduce the amount of energy and natural resources required to operate and maintain a store; (2) reduce the amount of raw materials needed to construct a facility; and (3) use, when appropriate, renewable materials to construct and maintain a facility. Although many of the design features reduce its impact on the environment, these stores are expensive to build, and some of their elements make economic sense only if energy costs increase. Initial projections call for the energy used at these stores to be 30–50 percent less, reducing a store's energy costs by $500,000 annually.

Some of its sustainable features are as follows:

• A wind turbine on top of a store produces enough energy to reduce a store's electricity consumption by 5 percent.

• A rainwater harvesting and treatment system provides 95 percent of the water needed for onsite irrigation and reduces demand on the local stormwater system.

• Grass for landscaping should be of varieties that do not need irrigation or mowing.

• Stores are lower in height than a typical Supercenter. The height reduction means fewer building materials are needed, plus it reduces heating and cooling needs.

• Instead of fluorescent lighting, refrigerated cases use LEDs (GE's Lumination Refrigerated Lighting System). Unlike fluorescent lights, LEDs can be switched on and off in cold temperatures without any loss of life expectancy. So the lights stay off until the customer opens the case. In addition to saving energy, the lights add a theatrical appeal for customers.

• The main store area lighting uses high-output linear fluorescent lamps that, in combination with natural daylight and dimming controls, are expected to generate a lighting savings of 300,000 kilowatt hours a year.

• Heat generated by the building's refrigeration system is captured and redirected to heat the water used in the restroom sinks and help heat the water used in the radiant floor-heating system beneath the entries and other areas.

• Cooking oil from the fryers and waste engine oil are burned in a bio-fuel boiler to generate heat that is directed into the heating, ventilation, and radiant floor-heating systems, conserving energy. The boiler generates heat for the building, reducing the demand for natural gas to operate mechanical equipment.

Sources: Marianne Wilson, "Lighting the Way," *Chain Store Age*, October 2007, p. 112; Marianne Wilson, "Supercenter Is Super Efficient," *Chain Store Age*, October 2007, p. 112; Marianne Wilson, "The Machine Goes Green," *Chain Store Age*, August 2005, pp. 110–12.

improvement centers. Women preferred to shop in Lowes' stores. So Home Depot lowered the ceilings, increased the lighting, widened the aisles, and provided better signage—design aspects that tend to appeal to women.[11]

Retailers often make trade-offs between stimulating impulse purchases and making it easy to buy products. For example, supermarkets place milk, a commonly purchased item, at the back of the store to make customers walk through the entire store and thus stimulate more impulse purchases. Realizing that some customers may only want to buy milk, Walgreen's places its milk at the front of the store, enabling it to compete more effectively with convenience stores.

The trade-off between the ease of finding merchandise and providing an interesting shopping experience is determined by the customer's shopping needs. For example, supermarket shoppers typically want to minimize the time they spend shopping, so supermarkets emphasize the ease of locating merchandise. In contrast, customers shopping for specialty goods like a computer, a home entertainment center, or furniture are more likely to spend time in the store browsing, comparing products, and talking with the salesperson. Thus, specialty store retailers that offer this type of merchandise place more emphasis on encouraging exploration rather than the ease of finding merchandise.

Another trade-off is the balance between giving customers adequate space in which to shop and productively using this scarce resource for displaying merchandise. For example, customers are attracted to stores with wide aisles and fixtures whose primary purpose is to display rather than hold the merchandise. However, this type of design reduces the amount of merchandise that can be available to buy, which may also reduce impulse purchases and the customers' chances of finding what they are looking for. But too many racks and displays in a store can cause customers to feel uncomfortable and even confused. The issue of overcrowded display fixtures and merchandise is particularly important when retailers consider the special needs of the disabled.

STORE DESIGN

Retailers first need to determine the basic layout of the store. Then they use signage and other techniques to guide customers through the store and assist them in locating and finding information about merchandise. Finally, a variety of approaches enable them to feature specific products.

Layouts

One method of encouraging customer exploration is to present a layout that facilitates a specific traffic pattern. Customers can be enticed to follow what amounts to a yellow brick road, as in *The Wizard of Oz*. For instance, Toys "R" Us uses a layout that almost forces customers to move through sections of inexpensive impulse-purchase products to get to larger, more expensive goods. It takes a strong-willed parent to navigate through the balloons and party favors without making a purchase. Retailers use three general types of store layout design: grid, racetrack, and free-form. Each of these layouts has advantages and disadvantages that are discussed later in this section.

Another method of helping customers move through the store is to provide interesting design elements. For example, antique stores have little nooks and crannies that entice shoppers to wander around. Off-price retailers intentionally create some degree of messiness so that people will be encouraged to look through the racks for bargains. These feature design elements are also discussed later in this section.

Grid Layout The **grid layout,** illustrated in Exhibit 18–1, has parallel aisles with merchandise on shelves on both sides of the aisles. Cash registers are located at the entrances/exits of the stores.

EXHIBIT 18-1
Grid Store Layout

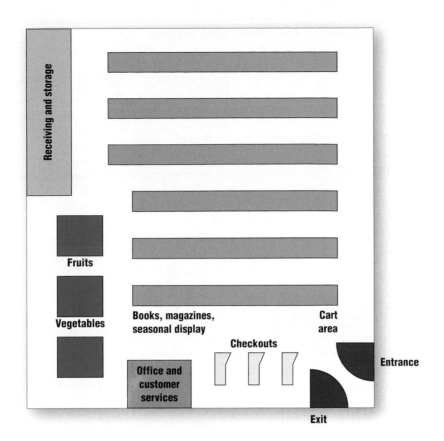

A grid layout does not provide a visually exciting design, but it's well suited for shopping trips in which customers need to move throughout the entire store and easily locate products they want to buy. For instance, when customers do their weekly grocery shopping, they can weave in and out of the specific aisles, easily picking up their desired products every week. Because they know where everything is, they can minimize the time spent on a task that many don't especially enjoy. Thus, most supermarkets use a grid layout.

The grid layout is also cost efficient. There's less wasted space with the grid layout than with other layouts because the aisles are all the same width and designed to be just wide enough to accommodate shoppers and their carts. The use of shelves for merchandise enables more merchandise to be on the sales floor compared with other layouts. Finally, because the fixtures are generally standardized, the cost of the fixtures is low.

One problem with the grid layout is that customers typically aren't exposed to all of the merchandise in the store. This limitation generally isn't an issue in grocery stores, because most customers have a good notion of the types of products they are going to purchase before they enter the store. But other retailers, such as department stores, use a layout that pulls customers through stores and encourages them to explore and seek out new and interesting merchandise available in the store.

Racetrack Layout   The **racetrack layout,** also known as a **loop,** is a store layout that provides a major aisle that loops around the store to guide customer traffic around different departments within the store. Cash register stations are typically located in each department bordering the racetrack.

The racetrack layout facilitates the goal of getting customers to see the merchandise available in multiple departments and thus encourages impulse purchasing. As customers go around the racetrack, their eyes are forced to take different viewing angles rather than looking down one aisle, as in the grid design.

EXHIBIT 18–2   JCPenney Racetrack Layout at NorthPark Center in Dallas

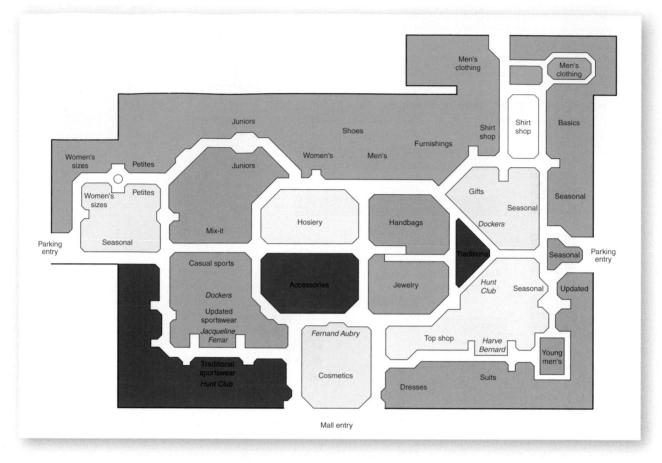

Exhibit 18–2 shows the layout of the JCPenney store in the NorthPark Center in Dallas, Texas. Because the store has multiple entrances, the racetrack layout tends to place all departments on the main aisle by drawing customers through the store in a series of major and minor loops. To entice customers through the various departments, the design places some of the more popular departments, like juniors, toward the rear of the store. The newest items are featured on the aisles to draw customers into departments and around the loop.

To direct customers through the store, the aisles must be defined by a change in surface or color. For instance, the aisle flooring in the store is marble-like tile, whereas the department floors vary in material, texture, and color, depending on the desired ambiance.

Kohl's has modified the racetrack layout to increase shopper convenience. Retailers used to believe that the longer customers were in the store, the more they would buy. But that theory is waning as time-poor customers demand quick and easy access to what they want to buy. Kohl's stores, at 86,000 square feet, are about half the size of most department stores. Although management's objective is to help busy shoppers get in and out quickly, there is ample room to roam from department to department. A wide aisle that forms the racetrack provides room for shoppers with carts or families with children in tow. A middle aisle divides the track, serving as a shortcut for shoppers who don't need to finish the whole circuit. During clearance periods, Kohl's lines the track with markdown merchandise to get shoppers' attention. Cash register stations are located at the start and the halfway point of the racetrack.[12]

Free-Form Layout   A **free-form layout,** also known as **boutique layout,** arranges fixtures and aisles in an asymmetric pattern (Exhibit 18–3). It provides an

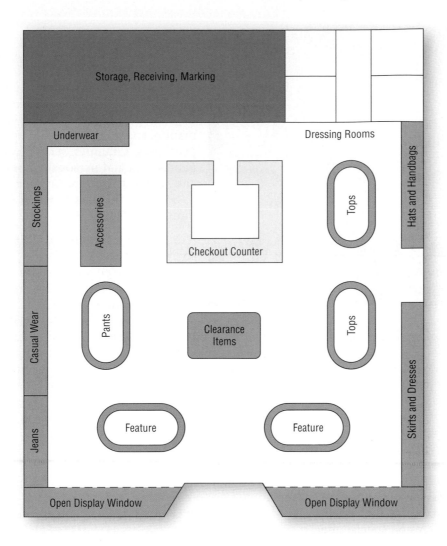

EXHIBIT 18–3
Free-Form Store Layout

intimate, relaxing environment that facilitates shopping and browsing. This layout is typically used in small specialty stores or within the departments of large stores.

However, creating this pleasing shopping environment is costly. Because there is no well-defined traffic pattern, like the racetrack and grid layouts, customers aren't naturally drawn around the store, and personal selling becomes more important for providing guidance. In addition, the layout sacrifices some storage and display space to create the more spacious environment.

To illustrate a free-form boutique within a racetrack layout, consider the Kohl's Chaps by Ralph Lauren boutique in the picture on this page. The designers' objective was to create a simple, clear space that draws customers into the area. Fixtures with the latest garments are placed along the perimeter of the boutique. Yet the flooring and lighting clearly delineate the area from adjacent departments and the walkway. Retailing View 18.3 describes Diesel's own unique approach to store layout.

This Kohl's Chaps by Ralph Lauren boutique uses a free-form layout that provides a comfortable shopping experience, but cannot display as much merchandise to other layout types.

H&M effectively uses graphic photo panels to add personality, beauty, and romance to its store's image.

Signage and Graphics

The grid and racetrack layouts guide customers through the store. Signage and graphics also help customers locate specific products and departments, provide product information, and suggest items or special purchases. Graphics, such as photo panels, can add personality, beauty, and romance to the store's image.

Some of the uses of visual communications are:

• *Location* Retailers use signage to identify the location of merchandise. Large stores often need to display directional signage to guide customers around the store and from one area to another. Hanging signs from the ceiling is often used to enhance their visibility. Larger stores, particularly stores with more than one level, also have a store guide. The location of this guide should be clearly visible from the entrance, with the path to the guide clearly marked so that even a first-time customer can see where to go.

• *Category signage* Used within a particular department or sector of the store, category signs are usually smaller than directional signs. Their purpose is to identify types of products offered. They are usually located near the goods to which they refer.

• *Promotional signage* This signage describing special offers may be displayed in windows to entice the customer into the store. For instance, value apparel stores for young women often display large posters in their windows of models wearing the items on special offer.

• *Point of sale* These signs are placed near the merchandise they refer to so that customers know its price and other detailed information. Some of this information may already be on product labels or packaging. However, point-of-sale signage

---

18.3   RETAILING VIEW   Diesel Breaks Store Design Rules

Diesel jeans stores are so confusing that they beg a question: Are they the worst designed stores ever, or is there method to their madness? Walking into a Diesel jeans store feels a lot like stumbling into a rave. Techno music pounds at a mind-rattling level. A television plays a videotape of a Japanese boxing match, inexplicably. There are no helpful signs pointing to the men's or women's departments and no obvious staff members in sight.

Customers who are industrious, or simply brave enough to reach the "denim bar"—Diesel's name for the counter separating shoppers from the wall of jeans at the back of the store—find themselves confronted by 35 different types of blue jeans costing $115 to $260 a pair. A placard intending to explain the various options looks like an organizational chart for a decent-sized federal agency.

Diesel jeans are a gas for the fashion-forward. Despite its high prices, Diesel prides itself on producing unusual yet modish men's and women's casual wear and a complementary store environment. Diesel's products are sold in over 80 countries through department stores and specialty retailers, as well as more than 50 company-owned stores.

Whereas apparel chains like Banana Republic and The Gap have standardized and simplified the layout of their stores in an effort to put customers at ease, Diesel's approach is based on the unconventional premise that the best customer is a disoriented one. The company intentionally designed an intimidating, user-unfriendly environment so that customers have to interact with the sales staff. Indeed, it is at just the moment when a potential Diesel customer reaches a kind of shopping vertigo that members of the company's with-it staff make their move. Acting as salespeople-in-shining-armor, they rescue—or prey upon, depending on one's point of view—wayward shoppers.

Source: Matthew Hall, "Fueling Sales," *VM&SD,* November 16, 2006; www.couturecandy.com/diesel/designer.html (accessed November 19, 2007); John Holusha, "A Shopping Destination for the Young and Hip," *The New York Times,* August 29, 2004, p. 11.

can quickly identify for the customer those aspects likely to be of greater interest, such as whether the product is on special offer.

• *Lifestyle images* The retailer may use various images, such as pictures of people and places, to create moods that encourage customers to buy the products. These are part of the visual merchandising that the store uses.

Some techniques for effectively using signage are:

• *Coordinate signs and graphics with the store's image* Signs and graphics should act as a bridge between the merchandise and the retailer's target market. The colors and tone of the signs and graphics should complement the merchandise. For example, a formally worded, black-and-white, rectangular sign doesn't relate to a children's display as well as a red-and-yellow circus tent design does. Color combinations should appeal to specific target customers or highlight specific merchandise— primary colors for kids, hot vivid colors for teens, pastel shades for lingerie, bright hues for sportswear, and so forth. New Balance, for instance, is a performance athletic footwear and apparel maker that wants to convey its image of technical innovation.[13] Therefore, it developed an in-store communications/ graphics system that focuses on its wear-test program, in which the company sends new and current products to consumers who subsequently report back their findings. It then puts pictures of these testers using the product, along with their vital statistics, on five foot tall graphic panels, interspersed with fitting benches, in the center of the store.

To convey its image of technical innovation, New Balance uses an in-store communications/graphics system that focuses on its wear-test program, in which the company sends new and current products to consumers who subsequently report back their findings.

• *Inform customers* Informative signs and graphics make merchandise more desirable. For instance, Target's consumer electronics department posts "Why to Buy" signs over the televisions to help consumers sort out the nuances of the different models.[14]

• *Use signs and graphics as props* Using signs or graphics that masquerade as props, or vice versa, is a great way to unify a theme and merchandise for an appealing overall presentation. For instance, Alphabet Soup, a small, Iowa-based chain of educational toy stores, uses lively graphics and props in a unifying theme that is consistent with the store's image.

• *Keep signs and graphics fresh* Signs and graphics should be relevant to the items displayed and should never be left in the store or in windows after the associated displays are removed. New signs imply new merchandise.

• *Limit the text on signs* Because a sign's main purpose is to catch attention and inform customers, the copy is important to its overall success. Yet as a general rule, signs with too much copy won't be read. Customers must be able to grasp the information on the sign quickly as they walk through the store.

• *Use appropriate typefaces on signs* Using the appropriate typeface is critical to a sign's success. Different typefaces impart different messages and moods. For instance, carefully done calligraphy in an Old English script provides a very different message than a hastily written price-reduction sign.

Digital Signage   Traditional print signage is typically developed and produced at corporate headquarters, distributed to stores, and installed by store employees or contractors.[15] Many retailers are beginning to replace traditional signage with digital signage systems. **Digital signage** includes signs whose visual content is delivered digitally through a centrally managed and controlled network and displayed on a television monitor or flat-panel screen. The content delivered can range from entertaining video clips to simple displays of the price of merchandise.

Digital signage provides a number of benefits over traditional static signage. Due to their dynamic nature, digital signs are superior in attracting the attention of customers and helping them recall the messages displayed. Digital signage also offers the opportunity to enhance a store's environment by displaying complex graphics and videos and providing an atmosphere that customers find appealing.

Digital signage also overcomes the time-to-message hurdle associated with traditional print signage. Changing market developments or events can immediately be incorporated into the digital sign. The ease, speed, and flexibility of content development and deployment of digital signage enables the content to be varied within and across stores at different times of the day or days of the week, such as reflecting different weather conditions.

Because the content is delivered digitally, it can easily be tailored to a store's market and changed during the week or even the day and hour. For example, Eddie Bauer analyzed its customer data warehouse and discovered that price-sensitive customers tended to shop in the mornings and that more brand-conscious customers tended to shop in the afternoon and evenings. Subsequently, it experimented with changing the content of its storefront digital signage. In the morning, the signage emphasized merchandise with lower price points and sale items. The merchandise at higher price points and brand image content was displayed later in the day. The result was targeted merchandising messaging to its customers. Messages thus can be targeted on the basis of demographics, merchandise location, store location, and location within a store.

The ability to control digital signage content centrally ensures that the retailer's strategy for communicating with its customers is properly executed systemwide. Digital signage thus eliminates the challenge facing retailers that send out static signage to stores announcing a special promotion or a new marketing initiative, namely, ensuring that the signage is installed in the right place at the right time.

Finally, digital signage eliminates the costs associated with printing, distributing, and installing static signage. In addition, it may decrease store labor costs while improving labor productivity. However, the drawback to using digital signage is the initial cost of the display devices and the system that supports the delivery of the signage. Retailing View 18.4 describes how the U.S. Postal Service is using digital signage as part of its new store design to increase revenue.

Feature Areas

In addition to layout and signage, retailers can guide customers through stores according to the placement of feature areas. **Feature areas** are those areas within a store designed to get the customers' attention. They include entrances, freestanding displays, cash wraps, end caps, promotional aisles or areas, walls, windows, and fitting rooms.

Entrances   The entry area is often referred to as the "decompression zone," because customers are making an adjustment to the new environment: getting a respite from the noisy street or mall, taking off their sunglasses, closing their umbrellas, and developing a visual impression of the entire store.[16] A women's apparel store might feature high-volume, high-profit goods such as handbags or cosmetics. A store catering to teens would feature a trendy "hot" item. Electronics stores display high-tech products that are new on the market.

Freestanding Displays   **Freestanding displays** are fixtures or mannequins located on aisles designed primarily to attract customers' attention and bring them into a department. Similar in purpose to entrances, these fixtures often display and store the newest, most exciting merchandise in the particular department.

Cash Wraps   **Cash wraps**, also known as **point-of-purchase (POP) counters** or **checkout areas**, are places in the store where customers can purchase merchandise. Because many customers go to these areas and may wait in line to make a purchase, they are often used to display impulse items. For example, in supermarkets, batteries, candy, razors, and magazines are often shelved at the checkout counter.

Discount and extreme value retailers and category specialists use centralized checkouts at the front of their stores. But department stores have traditionally placed cash wraps off the main aisle within each department. Several department store chains, such as Kohl's, Sears, and JCPenney, are now switching to centralized cash wraps. By centralizing the checkout areas, these department stores increase customer convenience, reduce staff, and reduce customer complaints arising from slow or poor checkout service.[17]

End Caps   **End caps** are displays located at the end of an aisle. Due to the high visibility of end caps, product sales increase dramatically when that merchandise is featured on an end cap. Thus, retailers use end caps for higher margin, impulse merchandise. In the supermarket industry, vendors often negotiate for their products to be on end cap displays when offering special promotional prices.

Natural and organic foods retailer Whole Foods makes excellent use of its end caps to merchandise seasonal, temporary, or promotional items, as well as

---

The U.S. Postal Service Goes Retail   RETAILING VIEW   18.4

The 32,000 post offices in the United States offer a variety of products and services for consumers. In addition to core products (e.g., stamps, Express Mail, Priority Mail), they accept passport applications and sell shipping supplies, money orders, licensed products, and phone cards. These services generate more than $17 billion in annual retail sales. However, retail revenue has been threatened by the increased usage of e-mail and electronic fund transfers, as well as the decline in first-class stamp sales.

To improve customers' experiences and increase its retail revenues, the postal service is updating the appearance of its retail space using retail merchandising principles and digital signage. Traditionally, postmasters, the store managers, focused more of their attention on mail delivery operations, not on the retail space. Thus, retail space rarely was consistently maintained, and there was no standard for merchandising products in the various post offices.

Through its standardization program, the U.S. Post Office uses Starbucks coffee shops as a role model. Most Starbucks stores have different foot prints, but each contains a well-defined set of design elements: signage with the menu, a POS counter for placing orders, a pickup counter, displays of other merchandise for sale, tables and chairs, and so forth. When customers walk into any Starbucks around the world, they encounter a similar environment. Like Starbucks, post offices do not have a standard foot print, but as a result of standardization efforts, customers now should encounter a familiar environment when they walk into any post office. They will see the same design elements— service counters, point-of-sale displays, and so on—and the offices will offer a consistent, reliable retail environment.

The U.S. Postal Services uses digital signage to inform customers about the services it offers.

The key benefit of digital signage in the Postal Service's environment is message flexibility. With digital signage, it can economically tailor the information provided to customers in different post offices and at different times during the day. For example, the messaging displayed when the retail area is operating informs customers about the services it offers and helps them make purchase decisions before they get to the counter. When the retail space is closed, the messaging changes to inform customers about nearby offices with extended retail hours or recommends www.usps.com as an alternate retail channel.

Sources: Margot Myers, U.S. Postal Service; Steven Keith Platt, Platt Retail Institute; www.usps.com (accessed February 29, 2008).

End caps at Whole Foods are used to merchandise seasonal, temporary, promotional or high margin items.

REFACT

An international survey of supermarket shoppers found that end caps are noticed by more than three-quarters of shoppers and could influence 60 percent into making a purchase.[18]

on high-margin items. For instance, one store featured a huge sign on the sidewalk in front of the store advertising buffalo mozzarella cheese. Upon entering the store, an end cap display features the cheese attractively laid out on ice so customers can grab some while the sign is still fresh in their minds.

Promotional Aisle or Area   A **promotional aisle** or **area** is a space used to display merchandise that is being promoted. Walgreens and CVS, for instance, use promotional aisles to sell seasonal merchandise, such as lawn and garden products in the summer and Christmas decorations in the fall. Shaws supermarkets contain "10 for $10" aisles. From this promotional aisle, customers can purchase 10 selected items for $10. The products change each week and are highlighted in weekly grocery ads. Products can also be mixed, so that customers do not have to buy 10 of the same item. Apparel stores, like The Gap, often place their sale merchandise at the back of the store so customers must pass through the full-price merchandise to get to the sale merchandise.

Walls   Because retail floor space is often limited, many retailers increase their ability to store extra stock, display merchandise, and creatively present a message by utilizing wall space. Merchandise can be stored on shelving and racks and coordinated with displays, photographs, or graphics featuring the merchandise. At the French clothier Lacoste, for instance, merchandise is displayed in bold color swaths relatively high on the wall. Not only does this allow the merchandise to "tell a story," it also helps customers feel more comfortable because they aren't crowded by racks or other people, and they can get a perspective on the merchandise by viewing it from a distance.

Windows   Windows can be an important component of the store layout. Attractive, eye-catching window displays can help draw customers into the store. They provide a visual message about the type of merchandise offered in the store and the type of image the store wishes to portray.

Window displays should be tied to the merchandise and other displays in the store. For instance, if beach towels are displayed in a Bed, Bath & Beyond window, they should also be prominently displayed inside. Otherwise, the drawing power of the window display is lost. Finally, windows can be used to set the shopping mood for a season or holiday like Christmas or Valentine's Day.

Abercrombie & Fitch's Hollister and Ruehl chains take a different approach to window design: They don't use them at all.[19] The outside of a Hollister store looks like a California surf shack whose

Lacoste displays merchandise in bold color swaths relatively high on the wall.

residents have shuttered the windows and hidden the front door to keep out people who are not in their target market. Ruehl is even more extreme. Its storefront is a brick wall, rising up behind cast-iron gates. This retailer is trying to send a specific message: "You either belong in this store, or you don't." The target customers know exactly what the store is and what's behind the façade.

Fitting Rooms   Fitting rooms are a crucial space in which customers decide whether to make a purchase. Depending on their ambiance and the technology they offer, these spaces can add a lot of value to the customer experience.[20]

In particular, fitting rooms must be large, clean, and comfortable. A fitting room that makes a person feel good also makes that shopper more likely to get in the mood to buy something. Bloomingdale's goes beyond other retailers by hanging photographs of local communities on its walls. The women's dressing room, with its fresh flowers and natural light, differs in feel from the men's dressing room, done up in dark wood, leather furniture, and linen wall coverings.

Even as they get more attractive, fitting rooms are introducing new technology that enhances the buying experience. Inside the room, shoppers can find items in stock in the store, similar to shopping online, and see demonstrations of accessory options. Some fitting rooms offer customers the capability of e-mailing friends a photo of the outfit they're considering. Or virtual models can "try on" an outfit to show the shopper how it looks, though this development is still in progress. One system known as The Dressing Room Assistant™ consists of a kiosk in the dressing room, with which customers can request different sizes or colors to try on without leaving the dressing room or having to wait for a store associate.[21] An interactive screen in the dressing room provides pictures and text describing complementary items and promotional messages.

Although technology and décor can enhance the experience of trying on clothing, retailers must ensure they still offer service rather than automating the entire process. Neiman Marcus is cautious about the extent to which it will use technology; salespeople remain at customers' service while they try on clothes in the fitting room. But customers who enjoy a comfortable environment in which to try on clothes likely will provide higher sales for savvy retailers in the future.

SPACE MANAGEMENT

The space within stores and on the stores' shelves and fixtures is a scare resource. Space management thus involves two resource decisions: (1) the allocation of store space to merchandise categories and brands and (2) the location of departments or merchandise categories in the store.

Space Allocated to Merchandise Categories

Some factors that retailers consider when deciding how much floor or shelf space to allocate to merchandise categories and brands are (1) the productivity of the allocated space, (2) the merchandise's inventory turnover, (3) impact on store sales, and (4) the display needs for the merchandise.

Space Productivity   A simple rule of thumb for allocating space is to allocate on the basis of the merchandise's sales. For example, if artificial plants represent 15 percent of the total expected sales for a hobby and craft retailer such as Michaels, then 15 percent of the store's space is allocated to artificial plants.

But, as the discussion of marginal analysis for advertising allocations in Chapter 16 indicates, retailers should allocate space to a merchandise category on the basis of its effect on the profitability of the entire store. In practice, this recommendation means that Michaels should add more space to the artificial plant section as long as the profitability of the additional space is greater that the profitability of the category from which space was taken away. In this condition, the additional space for artificial plants will increase the profitability of the entire store. However, at some point, it will be more profitable to not take away space from other categories.

Two commonly used measures of space productivity are **sales per square foot** and **sales per linear foot.** Apparel retailers that display most of their merchandise on freestanding fixtures typically measure space productivity as sales per square foot. In supermarkets, most merchandise is displayed on shelves. Because the shelves have approximately the same width, only the length, sales per linear foot, is used to assess space productivity.

A more sophisticated productivity measure, such as gross margin per square foot, would consider the profits generated by the merchandise, not just the sales. Thus, if salty snacks generate $400 in gross margin per linear foot and canned soup only generates $300 per linear foot, more space should be allocated to salty snacks. However, factors other than marginal productivity need to be considered when making space allocation decisions.

Inventory Turnover   Inventory turnover affects space allocations in two ways. First, as discussed in Chapter 12, both inventory turnover and gross margin contribute to GMROI—a measure of the retailer's return on its merchandise inventory investment. Thus, merchandise categories with higher inventory turnover merit more space than merchandise categories with lower inventory turnover.

Second, the merchandise displayed on the shelf is depleted quicker for fast selling items with high inventory turnover. Thus, more space needs to be allocated to fast selling merchandise to minimize the need to restock the shelf frequently to reduce stockouts.

Impact on Store Sales   When allocating space to merchandise categories, retailers need to consider the allocation impact on the entire store. The objective of space management is to maximize the profitability of the store, not just a particular merchandise category or department. Thus, supermarkets "overallocate" space to some low productivity categories such as milk because an extensive assortment in these categories attracts customers to the store and positively affects the sales of categories with higher GMROIs. Retailers might also overallocate space to categories purchased by their platinum customers, the customers with the highest lifetime value.

Display Considerations   The physical limitations of the store and its fixtures affect space allocation. For example, the store planner needs to provide enough merchandise to fill an entire fixture dedicated to a particular item.

A retailer might decide that it wants to use a merchandise display as a form of promotion, as if to say, "We have a great assortment of this merchandise." For example, JCPenney has a very appealing offering of its private-label bath towels. To emphasize this offering, it might overallocate space for bath towels and present a wide range of colors.

Location of Merchandise Categories and Design Elements

As discussed previously, the store layout, signage, and feature areas can guide customers through the store. The location of merchandise categories also plays a role in how customers navigate through the store.[22]

By strategically placing impulse and demand/destination merchandise throughout the store, retailers increase the chances that customers will shop the entire store and that their attention will be focused on the merchandise that the retailer is most interested in selling—merchandise with a high GMROI. **Demand/destination merchandise** refers to products that customers have decided to buy before entering the store.

As customers enter the store and pass through the decompression zone, they are welcomed with introductory displays, including graphics. Once through the decompression zone, they often turn right (in Western cultures) and observe the prices and quality of the first items they encounter. This area, referred to as the "strike zone," is critical because it creates the customer's first impression of the store's offering. Thus, retailers should display some of their most compelling merchandise in the strike zone.

After passing through the strike zone, the most heavily trafficked and viewed area is the right-hand side of the store. By this point in their journey through the store, customers have become accustomed to the environment, developed a first impression, and are ready to make purchase decisions. Thus, the right-hand side is a prime area for displaying high GMROI merchandise. For example, supermarkets typically locate the produce section in this area because produce appeals to the shoppers' senses. The smell of fresh fruits and vegetables gets a shopper's mouth watering, and the best grocery store customer is a hungry one.

Some additional implications for store design based on Envirosell's research findings are described in Retailing View 18.5.

Impulse Merchandise   The prime store locations for selling merchandise are heavily trafficked areas such as the entrance, right side of the store, and areas near escalators and cash wraps. In multilevel stores, a space's value decreases the farther it is from the entry-level floor. Thus, **impulse products,** or products that are purchased without prior plans, like fragrances and cosmetics in department stores and magazines in supermarkets, are almost always located near the front of the store, where they're seen by everyone and may actually draw people into the store.

Demand Merchandise   Demand merchandise and promotional merchandise are often placed in the back, left-hand corner of the store. Placing high-demand merchandise in this location pulls customers through the store, increasing the visibility of other products along the way. So supermarkets typically display items almost everyone buys—milk, eggs, butter, and bread—in the back, left-hand corner. In department stores, children's merchandise and furniture, as well as customer-service areas like beauty salons, credit offices, and photography studios, are demand or destination areas and thus located in lightly trafficked areas of the store.

Special Merchandise   Some merchandise categories involve a buying process that is best accomplished in a lightly trafficked area. For example, Steuben glass sculptures are unique, expensive art pieces that require thought and concentration for their purchase decision. Thus, Neiman Marcus locates this merchandise in a lightly trafficked area to minimize distractions to customers contemplating a purchase. Similarly, women's lingerie is typically located in a remote area to offer a more private shopping experience.

Categories that require large amounts of floor space, like furniture, are often located in less desirable locations. Some categories, like curtains, need significant wall space, whereas others, like shoes, require accessible storage.

Adjacencies   Retailers often cluster complementary products together to facilitate multiple purchases. For example, men's dress shirts and ties are located next to each other. On the basis of the market basket analyses described in Chapter 11, supermarkets locate some items in traditional areas and also adjacent to complementary items. For example, salsa is typically located with other condiments, next to corn chips in the salty snacks aisle, and in the Mexican section in the international aisle.

Neiman Marcus locates its Steuben glass sculptures in a lightly trafficked area to minimize distractions to customers contemplating a purchase.

Envirosell, a consulting firm in New York, has made a science out of determining the best ways to lay out a department or a store. Although the firm utilizes lots of hidden video cameras and other high-tech equipment, its most important research tool is a piece of paper called a track sheet in the hands of people called trackers. Trackers follow shoppers and note everything they do. They also make inferences about consumer behavior on the basis of what they've observed. Examples of their quantitative research findings appear in Exhibits 18–4 and 18–5. Here are just a few of the things, that they have learned:

• *Avoid the butt-brush effect* The "butt-brush effect" was discovered at a New York City Bloomingdale's. The researchers taped shoppers attempting to reach the tie rack while negotiating an entrance during busy times. They noticed that after being bumped once or twice, most shoppers abandoned their search for neckwear. The conclusion: Shoppers don't like to shop when their personal space is invaded.

• *Place merchandise where customers can readily access it* Toy store designers are, for the most part, still designing stores as if the customer were taller than 5 feet. Designers should be made to get down on their hands and knees (sitting on a skateboard also works quite well) and tour the store from a child's point of view.

• *Make information accessible* Older shoppers often have a hard time reading the small print on the boxes and the prices. Thus, selective displays should take some of the information off the boxes and enlarge it with a simple 80″ × 80″ sign.

Source: www.envirosell.com (accessed November 19, 2007); "Customer Behavior Insights of Paco Underhill," *Inside Retailing,* November 2, 2007; Paco Underhill, *Call of the Mall: The Geography of Shopping* (New York: Simon & Schuster, 2004); Paco Underhill, *Why We Buy: The Science of Shopping* (New York: Simon & Schuster, 2000).

EXHIBIT 18–4
Percentage of Shoppers Visiting Different Areas of the Store

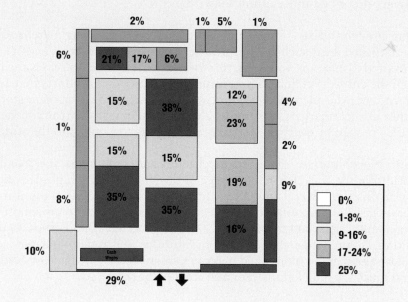

EXHIBIT 18–5
Number of Shoppers Entering the Store at Different Times of the Day

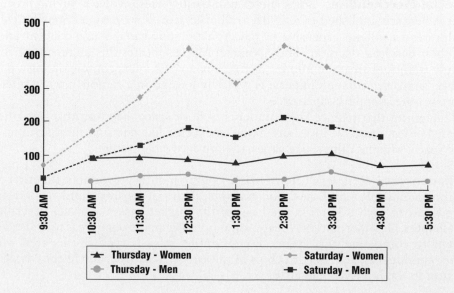

Location of Merchandise within a Category: The Use of Planograms

Retailers devote considerable attention to the location of specific SKUs within a category. For instance, supermarkets and drugstores place private-label brands to the right of national brands. Because Western consumers read from left to right, they will see the higher-priced national brand first and then see and (possibly) purchase the lower-priced, higher margin, private-label item on the right. Produce departments in grocery stores are arranged so apples are the first item most customers see, because apples are the most popular produce item and thus can best initiate a buying pattern. To determine where items should be located within a category or department, retailers generate maps known as planograms, videotape consumers as they move through the store, and utilize virtual store software.

Planograms   A **planogram** is a diagram that shows how and where specific SKUs should be placed on retail shelves or displays to increase customer purchases. The locations can be illustrated using photographs, computer output, or artists' renderings (see the planogram in Retailing View 18.6 on this page).

Marks & Spencer Automates Planograms   RETAILING VIEW   18.6

Marks & Spencer is a large retailer of clothing, home goods, and high-quality food products in the United Kingdom. Its food business, specializing in high-quality convenience and fresh foods, such as sandwiches and take-home dinners, occupies a prominent position in the U.K. food retailing sector.

The retailer is continuously updating its product range with new products developed in conjunction with leading manufacturers of short-life food products. Until recently, this process has been labor intensive. For example, the adjustment of 50 displays in 50 stores requires 2,500 new individual planograms, unless some stores are exactly the same, which is not likely. It would take between 80 and 100 full-time planogrammers to implement weekly changes in its 310 stores.

The $8.6 billion retailer began looking for a planogramming system for its fresh food products. Store-specific space plans were necessary to reflect each store's individual needs.

Working with SAS Retail, the retailer was able to develop an automated planogramming system that could optimize weekly fresh food assortments to individual stores, as well as improve product layout and customer satisfaction.

The Marks & Spencer SAS Retail system calculates an optimal layout by determining how many shelf facings are needed for each SKU in each store. At the same time, the system maintains a consistent look but considers specific fixtures and store layouts.

By implementing automated space planning, Marks & Spencer has greatly increased the productivity of its centralized space planning team and gained control over store layout and product presentation. It can now do weekly plans with 20 planogrammers—and it does a much better job. Product placement is now more efficient and uniform throughout the chain, and customers can more easily find specific products. This ease is of particular importance to Marks & Spencer, as many of its customers shop in more than one of its stores.

Source: Communication with SAS Retail.

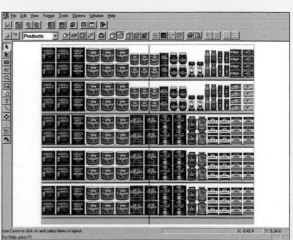

Marks & Spencer in the United Kingdom uses a planogram system developed by SAS Retail to develop a layout that maximizes space productivity.

In developing the planogram, retailers need to make the category visually appealing, consider the manner in which customers shop (or the manner in which the retailer would like customers to shop), and achieve the retailer's strategic and financial objectives. There is an art and a science to planogramming. The art is in ensuring that the proper visual impact and presentation is maintained; the science is in the financial analysis portion. A planogrammer must be able to balance these two elements to create a planogram that is best for the store.

Technology for computer-generated planograms is quite sophisticated. On the basis of analyses of historical sales, gross margins, turnover, the sizes of product packaging for each SKU, and the retailer's design criteria, the software determines the optimal shelf space and location for each SKU.

Planograms are also useful for merchandise that doesn't fit nicely on shelves in a grocery or discount store. Most specialty apparel retailers provide their managers with photographs and diagrams of how merchandise should be displayed. Retailing View 18.6 describes how the SAS planogramming system automated Marks & Spencer's food business.

Videotaping Consumers   Some retailers are using consulting firms, like EnviroSell, or VideoIntelligence software, like that provided by IntelliVid, to analyze in-store video and better understand how customers move through and interact with the store. These videos can be used to improve layouts and planograms by identifying the causes of slow-selling merchandise, such as poor shelf placement. By studying customers' movements, retailers can also learn where they pause or move quickly, or where there is congestion. This information can help the retailers decide, for instance, if the layout and merchandise placement is operating as expected, or if new or promoted merchandise is getting the attention it deserves. Videotapes also could be used to check the effectiveness of Whole food's new "one-line" method of checkout, described previously in this chapter.

To identify "hot" and "cold" spots—areas within the store that receive more, versus less traffic, IntelliVid creates maps like the one on this page. Note, for instance, that the hottest spot (red) in the store is the entrance, a place where too much congestion could dissuade customers from entering the store. Certain end of aisle displays are warm (light blue), getting a moderate amount of traffic; other parts of the store are frigid (dark blue), indicating a lack of traffic.

Virtual Store Software   Another tool used to determine the best place to put merchandise and test how customers will react to new products is an innovation being used by Kimberly-Clark in conjunction with its retail customers.[23] The customer stands in front of three screens showing a store aisle while a retina-tracking device

To identify "hot" and "cold" spots—areas within the store that receive more, versus less traffic, IntelliVid creates maps like this one. Which areas get the most/least traffic?

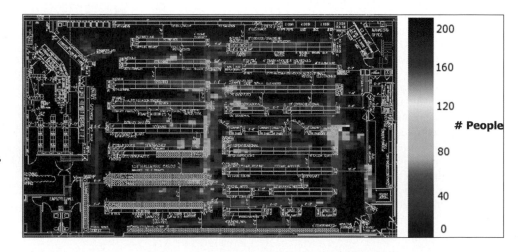

records his or her every glance. When the customer is asked to find a large box of Huggies® diapers in size three, he or she pushes forward on a handle, similar to the handle on a shopping cart, and the video simulates progress down the aisle. Spotting the red packages of Huggies diapers, the customer turns the handle to the right to face the display of diapers. After pushing a button to get a kneeling view of the shelves, the customer virtually reaches forward and taps the screen to put the box in the virtual cart. These virtual shopping trips allows retailers and their suppliers to get a fast read on new product designs and displays without having to stage real-life tests in the early stages of development.

Kimberly-Clark is using virtual store software that uses a retina-tracking device to record a customer's glances. The information obtained from the software enables them to get a fast read on new product designs and displays without having to stage real-life tests in the early stages of product development. Virtual Baby Aisle, © 2005 Kimberly-Clark Worldwide, Inc. Used with permission.

VISUAL MERCHANDISING

Visual merchandising is the presentation of a store and its merchandise in ways that will attract the attention of potential customers. This section examines issues related to the presentation of merchandise, and the following section explores more sensory aspects of the store's environment. This section begins with a review of the fixtures used to display merchandise and then discusses some merchandise presentation techniques.

Fixtures

The primary purposes of fixtures are to efficiently hold and display merchandise. At the same time, they must help define areas of a store and encourage traffic flow. Fixtures must work in concert with other design elements, such as floor coverings and lighting, as well as the overall image of the store. For instance, in stores designed to convey a sense of tradition or history, customers automatically expect to see lots of wood rather than plastic or metal fixtures. Wood mixed with metal, acrylic, or stone modernizes a traditional orientation.

Fixtures come in an infinite variety of styles, colors, sizes, and textures, but only a few basic types are commonly used. For apparel, retailers utilize the straight rack, rounder, and four-way. The mainstay fixture for most other merchandise is the gondola.

The **straight rack** consists of a long pipe suspended from supports in the floor or attached to a wall (Exhibit 18–6A). Although the straight rack can hold a lot of apparel, it cannot effectively feature specific styles or colors. All the customer can see is a sleeve or a pant leg. As a result, straight racks are often found in discount and off-price apparel stores.

A **rounder,** also known as a **bulk fixture** or **capacity fixture,** is a round fixture that sits on a pedestal (Exhibit 18–6B). Although smaller than the straight rack, it's designed to hold a maximum amount of merchandise. Because they're easy to move and efficiently store apparel, rounders are found in most types of apparel stores. But as with the straight rack, customers can't get a frontal view of the merchandise.

A **four-way fixture,** also known as a **feature fixture,** has two crossbars that sit perpendicular on a pedestal (Exhibit 18–6C). This fixture holds a large amount of merchandise and allows the customer to view the entire garment. The four-way is harder to maintain properly than is the rounder or straight rack however. All merchandise on an arm must be of a similar style and color, or the customer may

(A) Straight rack

(B) Rounder

(C) Four-way

(D) Gondola

become confused. Due to their superior display properties, four-way fixtures are commonly utilized by fashion-oriented apparel retailers to display outfits as well as individual garments.

Gondolas are extremely versatile (Exhibit 18–6D). They're used extensively, but not exclusively, in grocery and discount stores to display everything from canned foods to baseball gloves. Gondolas are also found displaying towels, sheets, and housewares in department stores. Folded apparel too can be efficiently displayed on gondolas, but because the items are folded, it's even harder for customers to view apparel on gondolas than on straight racks.

Presentation Techniques

Some presentation techniques are idea-oriented, style/item, color, price lining, vertical merchandising, tonnage merchandising, and frontage presentation.

Idea-Oriented Presentation   Some retailers use an **idea-oriented presentation**—a method of presenting merchandise based on a specific idea or the image of the store. Women's fashions, for instance, are often displayed to present an overall image or idea. Also, furniture is combined in room settings to give customers an idea of how it would look in their homes. Individual items are grouped to show customers how the items could be used and combined. This approach encourages the customer to make multiple complementary purchases. At Sony Style, mini-living rooms showcase what a particular flat-panel TV might look like over a fireplace or a dresser.

Brands that draw strong consumer demand, such as Ralph Lauren Polo, are often merchandised together in the boutique layout described previously in this chapter. This technique is similar to the idea-oriented presentation, in that

REFACT

Fifty percent of women get their ideas for clothes from store displays or window shopping.

merchandise made by the same vendor will tend to be coordinated. Some apparel manufacturers like Liz Claiborne and St. John coordinate both style and color to influence multiple purchases within the line and enhance the line's overall image.

Style/Item Presentation   Probably the most common technique of organizing stock is by style or item. Discount stores, grocery stores, hardware stores, and drugstores employ this method for nearly every category of merchandise, as do many apparel retailers. When customers look for a particular type of merchandise, such as breakfast cereals, they expect to find all items in the same location.

Arranging items by size is a common method of organizing many types of merchandise, from nuts and bolts to apparel. Because the customer usually knows the desired size, it's easy to locate items organized in this manner.

Color Presentation   A bold merchandising technique is by color. For instance, in winter months, women's apparel stores may display all white cruisewear together to let customers know that the store is "the place" to purchase clothing for their winter vacation.

Price Lining   Price lining is when retailers offer a limited number of predetermined price points and/or price categories within another classification. This approach helps customers easily find merchandise at the price they wish to pay. For instance, men's dress shirts may be organized into three groups selling for $49, $69, and $99—good, better, best.

Benetton displays its merchandise by color.

Vertical Merchandising   Another common way of organizing merchandise is **vertical merchandising.** In this approach, merchandise is presented vertically using walls and high gondolas. Customers shop much as they read a newspaper—from left to right, going down each column, top to bottom. Stores can effectively organize merchandise to follow the eye's natural movement. Retailers take advantage of this tendency in several ways. Many grocery stores put national brands at eye level and store brands on lower shelves because customers scan from eye level down. In addition, retailers often display merchandise in bold vertical bands of an item. For instance, you might see vertical columns of towels of the same color displayed in a department store or a vertical band of yellow-and-orange boxes of Tide detergent followed by a band of blue Cheer boxes in a supermarket.

Tonnage Merchandising   As the name implies, **tonnage merchandising** is a display technique in which large quantities of merchandise are displayed together. Customers have come to equate tonnage with low price, following the retail adage, "stock it high and let it fly." Tonnage merchandising is therefore used to enhance and reinforce a store's price image. Using this display concept, the merchandise itself is the display. The retailer hopes customers will notice the merchandise and be drawn to it. For instance, before many holidays, grocery stores use an entire end of a gondola (i.e., an end cap) to display six-packs of Pepsi.

Frontal Presentation   Often, it's not possible to create effective displays and efficiently store items at the same time.

The towel display at this Macy's store uses vertical merchandising.

But it's important to show as much of the merchandise as possible. One solution to this dilemma is the **frontal presentation,** a method of displaying merchandise in which the retailer exposes as much of the product as possible to catch the customer's eye. Book manufacturers, for instance, make great efforts to create eye-catching covers. But bookstores usually display books exposing only the spine. To create an effective display and break the monotony, book retailers often face an occasional cover out like a billboard to catch the customer's attention. A similar frontal presentation can be achieved on a rack of apparel by simply turning one item out to show the merchandise.

ATMOSPHERICS

Atmospherics refer to the design of an environment through visual communications, lighting, colors, music, and scent that stimulate customers' perceptual and emotional responses and ultimately affect their purchase behavior.[24] Many retailers have discovered the subtle benefits of developing atmospherics that complement other aspects of the store design and the merchandise. Research has shown that it is important for these atmospheric elements to work together—for example, the right music with the right scent.[25]

Lighting

Good lighting in a store involves more than simply illuminating space. Lighting can highlight merchandise, sculpt space, and capture a mood or feeling that enhances the store's image. Retailers are exploring ways to save energy with technologically advanced lighting. Having the appropriate lighting has been shown to positively influence customer shopping behavior.[26]

Highlighting Merchandise   A good lighting system helps create a sense of excitement in the store. At the same time, lighting must provide an accurate color rendition of the merchandise. For instance, Wal-Mart has been putting skylights into the roofs of its stores.[27] This addition cuts energy costs and creates more natural light, which is excellent for hardware and home goods. However, it is best to use artificial light for apparel so customers can clearly see details.

Another key use of lighting is called **popping the merchandise**—focusing spotlights on special feature areas and items. Using lighting to focus on strategic pockets of merchandise trains shoppers' eyes on the merchandise and draws customers strategically through the store. Nike, for example, uses a lot of contrast and shadows, highlighting the merchandise but not necessarily the architecture.[28]

Mood Creation   Traditionally, U.S. specialty and department stores have employed incandescent lighting sources to promote a warm and cozy ambience. Overall lighting sources were reduced, and accent lighting was pronounced to call attention to merchandise and displays. It was meant to feel like someone's home—dim lighting overall, with artwork and other areas of interest highlighted. Abercrombie & Fitch's Ruehl No. 925 and Hollister chains use very low levels of light to coordinate with their overall ambiance of resembling a townhouse or a surfshop.[29] Department and mass market retailers, in contrast, tend to be more brightly lit overall.

Energy Efficient Lighting   As the price of energy increases and retailers and their customers become more energy conscious, retailers are looking for ways to cut their energy costs and be more ecological. One obvious source of energy consumption is the lighting in a store. Stores are switching from incandescent lighting to more energy efficient florescent lights.

Color

The creative use of color can enhance a retailer's image and help create a mood. Warm colors (red, gold, and yellow) produce emotional, vibrant, hot, and active responses, whereas cool colors (white, blue, and green) have a peaceful, gentle, calming effect. Colors may have a different impact depending on the culture of the customers. For instance, research suggests that French-Canadians respond more to warm color decors, whereas Anglo-Canadians respond more positively to cool colors.[30]

Music

Like color and lighting, music can either add to or detract from a retailer's total atmospheric package.[31] Unlike other atmospheric elements, however, music can be easily changed. For example, JCPenney has just finished installing a new system for its stores that allows certain music to be played at certain times of the day. It can play jazzy music in the morning and adult contemporary in the afternoon, though only in stores on the East Coast. These selections mirror JCPenney's findings that most of its morning shoppers are older, whereas afternoon shoppers tend to be in the 35–40 year age range. For its West Coast stores, it wants modern rock in the morning and Caribbean beats in the afternoon. And in Texas, it's country music all day, every day. The retailer also can "zone" music by demographics, playing more Latin music in stores that attract a higher Hispanic population. The entire system is controlled by headquarters in Plano, Texas.[32]

Retailers also can use music to affect customers' behavior. Music can control the pace of store traffic, create an image, and attract or direct consumers' attention. For instance, one U.K. toy store switched from children's songs like "Baa Baa Black Sheep" to relaxed classical music and watched sales jump by 10 percent.[33] Managers realized that though children are the consumers of their products, adults are the customers. In general though, slow is good. A mix of classical or otherwise soothing music encourages shoppers to slow down, relax, and take a good look at the merchandise.

REFACT

The U.S. firm Muzak supplies 400,000 shops, restaurants, and hotels around the world—including The Gap, McDonald's, and Burger King—with songs tailored to reflect their identities.[34]

Scent

Many buying decisions are based on emotions, and smell has a large impact on our emotions, such as happiness, hunger, disgust, and nostalgia. Scent, in conjunction with music, has a positive impact on impulse buying behavior and customer satisfaction.[35] Scents that are neutral produce better perceptions of the store than no scent. Customers in scented stores think they spent less time in the store than subjects in unscented stores. Stores using scents thus may improve customers' subjective shopping experience by making them feel that they are spending less time examining merchandise or waiting for sales help or to check out.

Bloomingdale's uses different essences in different departments: baby powder in the baby store; suntan lotion in the bathing suit area; lilacs in lingerie; and cinnamon and pine scents during the holiday season.[36] Upscale shirt retailer Thomas Pink pipes the smell of clean, pressed shirts into its stores. The essence of lavender wafts out of L'Occitane skin-care stores. The scents from frequent cooking demonstrations at Williams-Sonoma kitchen stores help get customers in the cooking and buying mood. Even Sony Style stores have adopted the scent of cinnamon sticks simmering on a wood-burning stove during the holiday season and a mandarin orange and vanilla fragrance year round. KB Toys has experimented with scents of Creamsicle, cotton candy, and Play-Doh. Some customers, however, find the scents annoying, and for some, it even aggravates their allergies and asthma.

REFACT

It is estimated that the industry that supplies scents to retailers and other businesses will be worth $500 million to $1 billion in 2016, up from $40 million to $60 million today.[37]

How Exciting Should a Store Be?

Retailers such as REI, Build-A-Bear Workshop, Bass Pro Shops, and Barnes & Noble attempt to create an entertaining shopping environment by viewing their stores as theatrical scenes: The floor and walls constitute the stage and scenery; the lighting, fixtures, and displays are the props; and the merchandise represents the performance. This creation of a theatrical experience in stores has resulted in the combination of retailing and entertainment. In contrast, retail chains such as Costco and Home Depot successfully use minimalist, warehouse-style shopping environments.

Does providing an exciting, entertaining store environment lead customers to patronize a store more frequently and spend more time and money during each visit? The answer to this question is: It depends.[38]

The impact of the store's environment depends on the customer's shopping goals. The two basic shopping goals are task completion, such as buying a new suit for a job interview, and recreation, such as spending a Saturday afternoon with a friend wandering through a mall. When customers are shopping to complete a task that they view as inherently unrewarding, they prefer to be in a soothing, calming environment—a simple atmosphere with slow music, dimmer lighting, and blue/green colors. However, when customers go shopping for fun, an inherently rewarding activity, they want to be in an exciting atmosphere—a complex environment with fast music, bright lighting, and red/yellow colors.

What does this mean for retailers? They must consider the typical shopping goals for their customers when designing their store environments. For example, grocery shopping is typically viewed as an unpleasant task, and thus, supermarkets should be designed in soothing colors and use slow background music. In contrast, shopping for fashion apparel is typically viewed as fun, so an arousing environment in apparel retail outlets will have a positive impact on the shopping behavior of their customers.

The level of excitement caused by the environment might vary across the store. For example, a consumer electronics retailer might create a low-arousal environment in the accessories area to accommodate customers who typically are task-oriented when shopping for print cartridges and batteries, but then create a high-arousal environment in the home-entertainment centers that are typically visited by more pleasure-seeking shopping customers.

Finally, retailers might vary the nature of their Web sites for customers depending on their shopping goals. For example, research suggests that Amazon should serve up complex, high-arousal Web sites with rich media to customers who indicate they are browsing but simpler, low-arousal sites to customers looking for a specific book.[39] Some similar parallels between store and Web site designs are drawn in the following section.

WEB SITE DESIGN

In many, but not all, cases, good design principles that apply to a physical store can also be applied to a Web site.[40] Consider the following examples.

Simplicity Matters

A good store design allows shoppers to move freely, unencumbered by clutter. There is a fine line between providing customers with a good assortment and confusing them with too much merchandise.[41]

Similarly in a Web site, it is not necessary to mention all the merchandise available at a site on each page. It is better to present a limited selection tailored to the customer's needs and then provide links to related merchandise and alternative assortments. It is also important to include navigation headings and a search engine feature on each page in case a customer gets lost. The search feature in the virtual world is similar to having sales associates readily available in the physical world. Also, less is more. Having a small number of standard links on every page makes it more likely that users can learn the navigation scheme for the site.

Getting Around

When a store is properly designed, customers should be able to find what they are looking for easily. The products that customers frequently purchase together are often displayed together. For example, umbrellas are displayed with raincoats, soft drinks with snack foods, and tomato sauce with pasta. One way to help customers get around a Web site is by using links to other sections of the site. When establishing local links, Web sites should connect:

- Products that are similar in price.
- Complementary products.
- Products that differ from the product shown on some important dimension (e.g., a link to organic produce if the user is looking at natural breakfast cereals).
- Different versions of the shown product (e.g., the same blouse in yellow if the customer is viewing a red blouse).

Let Them See It

Stores are designed so customers can easily view the merchandise and read the signs. But in a store, if the lighting isn't good or a sign is too small to read, the customer can always move around to get a better view. Customers don't have this flexibility on the Internet. Web designers should assume that all potential viewers lack perfect vision. They should strive for realistic colors and sharpness. Some retailers that use the Internet channel have developed interesting ways of viewing merchandise in multiple dimensions (see, for instance, www.landsend.com).

Blend the Web Site with the Store

It is important to visually reassure customers that they're going to have the same satisfactory experience on the Web site that they have in stores. Even if the electronic store is designed for navigation efficiency, there should still be some design elements that are common to both channels. For instance, though very different store types, www.tiffany.com and www.officedepot.com, each have similar looks and feels to those of their stores.

Prioritize

Stores become annoying if everything jumps out at you as if to say, "Buy me! No buy me!" Other stores are so bland that the merchandise appears boring. Setting priorities for merchandise displays and locations is just as important on the Web site as it is in a physical store. A common mistake on many Internet sites is that everything is too prominent, resulting from an overuse of colors, animation, blinking, and graphics. If everything is equally prominent, then *nothing* is prominent. Being too bland is equally troublesome. The site should be designed to advise the customers and guide them to the most important or most promising choices, while also ensuring their freedom to go anywhere they please. Like a newspaper, the most important items or categories should be given the bigger headlines and more prominent placement.

Type of Layout

Some stores are laid out to be functional, like supermarkets and discount stores. They use a grid design to make it easy to locate merchandise. Other stores, like department stores or bookstores, use a more relaxed layout to encourage browsing. The trick is to pick the appropriate layout that matches the typical motives of the shopper.

Here is where store layout and Web site layout differ. Although many higher-end multichannel retailers experimented with fancy and complex designs in their early years on the Internet, most have become much more simple and utilitarian than their bricks-and-mortar counterparts (see, for instance, www.polo.com, www.neimanmarcus.com, and www.bloomingdales.com). When shopping on the Web, customers are interested in speed, convenience, and ease of navigation, not necessarily fancy graphics.[42]

Store designers also strive to make their stores seem different, to stand out in the crowd. A Web site, however, must strike a balance between keeping customers' interest and providing them with a basic comfort level based on convention. Users spend most of their time on *other* sites, so that's where they form their expectations about how most sites work.

When trying to make a decision about Web site design, good designers look at the most visited sites on the Internet to see how they organize their information. If 90 percent or more of the big sites do things in a single way, then it is the de facto standard.

Checkout

Physical stores recognize the perils of long lines at checkout, and some have taken steps to alleviate the problem, as we discussed earlier in this chapter. The problem of abandoned carts at checkout is even more accute with Internet sites. Approximately half of all online customers abandon their purchases during the checkout process—one of the greatest causes of lost revenue for online retailers.[43] Some tips for lessening the abandoned online cart problem are as follows:[44]

- *Make the process seem clear and simple* Make sure the customer knows what to expect from the checkout process, how long it will take, and what details he or she must provide. Because customers hate hidden charges and delivery costs, make this information clear at the beginning of the process. Giving some visible signs of progress through the checkout stages also helps.
- *Close off the checkout process* Remove links to any parts of the site other than the specific stages of the checkout process to focus the customer's mind. Once in the checkout area, there should be only one place customers can go: purchase confirmation.
- *Make the process navigable without threatening the loss of information* Customers may need to make changes at different stages, so making it possible for them to go back and forth through the process without losing any of the details they have already entered is vital to minimize frustration. Back buttons on the form, which save data when clicked, are a good way to achieve this functionality and offer an alternative to hitting the back button on a browser, which causes customers to lose information. Enabling them to use the browser to navigate through checkout and still not lose their data would be even better.
- *Reinforce trust in the checkout process* Display clear signs of server security and third-party verification logos. The company's full address and phone number should also be provided, as well as links to information about the terms and conditions, delivery, and payment rules.

SUMMARY

Some objectives for a store design are to (1) implement the retailer's strategy, (2) influence customer buying behavior, (3) provide flexibility, (4) control design and maintenance costs, and (5) meet legal requirements. Typically, a store design cannot achieve all of these objectives, so managers make trade-offs among objectives, such as providing convenience versus encouraging exploration.

The basic elements in a design that guide customers through the store are the layout, signage, and feature areas. A good store layout helps customers find and purchase merchandise. Several types of layouts commonly used by retailers are the grid, race track, and free-form. The grid design is best for stores in which customers are expected to explore the entire store, such as grocery stores and drugstores. Racetrack designs are more common in large upscale stores like department stores. Free-form designs are usually found in small specialty stores and within large stores' departments.

Signage and graphics help customers locate specific products and departments, provide product information, and suggest items or special purchases. In addition, graphics, such as photo panels, can enhance the store environment and the store's image. Digital signage has several advantages over traditional printed signage, but the initial fixed costs have made the adoption of this technology slow. Feature areas are areas within a store designed to get the customer's attention. They include freestanding displays, end caps, promotional aisles or areas, windows, cash wraps or point-of-sale areas, and walls.

Space management involves two decisions: (1) the allocation of store space to merchandise categories and brands and (2) the location of departments or merchandise categories in the store. Some factors that retailers consider when deciding how much floor or shelf space to allocate to merchandise categories and brands are (1) the productivity of the allocated space, (2) the merchandise's inventory turnover, (3) impact on store sales, and (4) the display needs for the merchandise. When evaluating the productivity of retail space, retailers generally use sales per square foot or sales per linear foot.

The location of merchandise categories also plays a role in how customers navigate through the store. By strategically placing impulse and demand/destination merchandise throughout the store, retailers can increase the chances that customers will shop the entire store and that their attention will be focused on the merchandise that the retailer is most interested in selling. In locating merchandise categories, retailers need to consider typical consumer shopping patterns.

Retailers utilize various forms of atmospherics—lighting, colors, music, and scent—to influence shopping behavior. The use of these atmospherics can create a calming environment for task-oriented shoppers or an exciting environment for recreational shoppers.

Although a retailer's Web site is different than its physical store, in many but not all cases, good design principles that apply to a physical store space can also be applied to a Web site.

KEY TERMS

atmospherics, *530*

boutique layout, *514*

bulk fixture, *527*

capacity fixture, *527*

cash wrap, *515*

checkout area, *518*

demand/destination merchandise, *523*

digital signage, *517*

end cap, *519*

feature area, *518*

feature fixture, *527*

fixture, *510*

four-way fixture, *527*

free-form layout, *514*

freestanding display, *518*

frontal presentation, *530*

gondola, *528*

grid layout, *512*

idea-oriented presentation, *528*

impulse product, *523*

loop, *513*

planogram, *525*

point-of-purchase counter, *518*

popping the merchandise, *530*

price lining, *529*

promotional aisle or area, *520*

racetrack layout, *513*

rounder, *527*

sales per linear foot, *522*

sales per square foot, *522*

straight rack, *527*

tonnage merchandising, *529*

vertical merchandising, *529*

visual merchandising, *527*

GET OUT AND DO IT!

1. **CONTINUING EXERCISE** Go into the physical store location of the retailer you have chosen for the continuing exercise and evaluate the store layout, design, and visual merchandising techniques employed. Explain your answers to the following questions:

(*a*) In general, are the store layout, design, and visual merchandising techniques used consistent with the exterior of the store and location?

(*b*) Is the store's ambience consistent with the merchandise presented and the customer's expectations?

(c) Does the store look like it needs to be redesigned?

(d) To what extent are the store's layout, design, and merchandising techniques flexible?

(e) Notice the lighting. Does it do a good job highlighting merchandise, structuring space, capturing a mood, and downplaying unwanted features?

(f) How does the store utilize atmospheric elements like color, music, or scent? Are these uses appropriate given the store's target markets?

(g) Are the fixtures consistent with the merchandise and the overall ambience of the store? Are they flexible?

(h) Evaluate the store's signage. Does it do an effective job of selling merchandise?

(i) Has the retailer used any theatrical effects to help sell merchandise?

(j) Does the store layout help draw people through the store?

(k) Has the retailer taken advantage of the opportunity to sell merchandise in feature areas?

(l) Does the store make creative use of wall space?

(m) What type of layout does the store use? Is it appropriate for the type of store? Would another type of layout be better?

(n) Ask the store manager how the profitability of space is evaluated (e.g., profit per square foot). Is there a better approach?

(o) Ask the store manager how space is assigned to merchandise. Critically evaluate the answer.

(p) Ask the store manager if planograms are used. If so, try to determine what factors are considered when putting together a planogram.

(q) Are departments in the most appropriate locations? Would you move any departments?

(r) What method(s) has the retailer used to organize merchandise? Is this the best way? Suggest any appropriate changes.

2. Go to your favorite multichannel retailer's Internet site. Evaluate its degree of simplicity, its ease of navigation, its readability, its use of color, its consistency with the brand image, the consistency of its pricing and merchandise with its bricks-and-mortar stores, its checkout process, the number of days required to receive an item, and the time it takes to answer e-mails.

3. Go to the homepage for ACNielsen (www2.acnielsen.com/site/index.shtml) click on "solutions," sort "by product," click on "assortment and in-store space." Read about its retail measurement products, "Shelfbuilder" and "Spaceman." How can retailers use planograms to evaluate the best shelf placement for new products in terms of visual impact, consumers' shopping patterns, and financial earnings potential?

4. Go to www.visualstore.com/ and develop a list that highlights the latest trends in visual merchandising.

5. Go to the homepages for Envirosell (http://envirosell.com/index.php) and IntelliVid (www.intellivid.com/). How do each of these marketing research consulting firms support retailers by collecting consumer information to assist with store layout, design, and visual merchandising?

DISCUSSION QUESTIONS AND PROBLEMS

1. One of the fastest growing sectors of the population is the over-60 years age group. But these customers may have limitations in their vision, hearing, and movement. How can retailers develop store designs with the older population's needs in mind?

2. Assume you have been hired as a consultant to assess a local discount store's floor plan and space productivity. Look back to Chapters 6 and 12 and decide which analytical tools and ratios you would use to assess the situation.

3. What are the different types of design that can be used in a store layout? Why are some stores more suited for a particular type of layout than others?

4. Generally speaking, departments located near entrances, on major aisles, and on the main level of multilevel stores have the best profit-generating potential. What additional factors help determine the location of departments? Give examples of each factor.

5. A department store is building an addition. The merchandise manager for furniture is trying to convince the vice president to allot this new space to the furniture department. The merchandise manager for men's clothing is also trying to gain the space. What points should each manager use when presenting his or her rationale?

6. As a manager for a large department store, you are responsible for ADA compliance. But your performance evaluation is based on bottom-line profitability. How would you make sure your store is accessible to people in wheelchairs and at the same time not lose any sales?

7. Describe the ways in which designing a Web site is similar to and different from designing a store.

8. What are the pros and cons for both centralized cash wraps and departmental cash wraps for stores such as JCPenney and Kohl's?

9. Most department store anchors place cosmetics counters at a ground-floor mall entrance. Explain why this is the preferred location in lieu of other potential locations.

10. If you were the manager of an apparel specialty store targeting men and women, how would you use information about sales per square foot for the various merchandise categories listed in the table below when making merchandise location decisions within the retail space?

ICSC RESEARCH—MONTHLY MERCHANDISE INDEX NON-ANCHOR MALL TENANTS	
Category	Sales per Square Foot
Women's apparel	$25
Women's accessories	$47
Men's apparel	$25
Children's apparel	$23
Women's shoes	$34
Men's shoes	$39
Children's shoes	$27

11. Consider the following types of retail formats that you likely have visited in the past: discount store, department store, office super store, food store, clothing specialty store, and a card and gift store. Describe which retail formats have implemented the best practices for coordinating signs and graphics with each store's image and which formats should improve this aspect of their store layout, design, and visual merchandising. What was appealing to you as a shopper in the stores with a coordinated strategy for store signage and retail brand image?

SUGGESTED READING

Burt, Steve; Ulf Johansson; and Åsa Thelander. "Retail Image as Seen through Consumers' Eyes: Studying International Retail Image through Consumer Photographs of Stores." *International Review of Retail, Distribution & Consumer Research* 17, no. 5 (2007), pp. 447–67.

Chung, Chanjin; Todd M. Schmit; Diansheng Dong; and Harry M. Kaiser. "Economic Evaluation of Shelf-Space Management in Grocery Stores." *Agribusiness* 23, no. 4 (2007), pp. 583–97.

Dean, Corrina. *Inspired Retail Space: Attract Customers, Build Branding, Increase Volume.* Rockport, ME: Rockport Publishers, 2005.

Diamond, Jay, and Ellen Diamond. *Contemporary Visual Merchandising and Environmental Design.* 4th ed. Upper Saddle River, NJ: Prentice Hall, 2006.

Greely, Dave, and Joe Cataudella. *Creating Stores on the Web.* Atlanta: Peachpit Press, 1999.

Kalchteva, Velitchka, and Barton Weitz. "How Exciting Should a Store Be?" *Journal of Marketing*, Winter 2006, pp. 34–62.

Kent, Tony, and Dominic Stone. "The Body Shop and the Role of Design in Retail Branding." *International Journal of Retail & Distribution Management* 35, no. 7 (2007), pp. 531–43.

Lam, Shun Yin, and Avinandan Mukherjee. "The Effects of Merchandise Coordination and Juxtaposition on Consumers' Product Evaluation and Purchase Intention in Store-Based Retailing." *Journal of Retailing* 81, no. 3 (2005), pp. 231–45.

Mostaedi, Arian. *Cool Shops.* Singapore: Page One, 2004.

Underhill, Paco. *Call of the Mall.* New York: Simon and Schuster, 2004.

Underhill, Paco. *Why We Buy: The Science of Shopping.* New York: Simon and Schuster, 2000.

Customer Service

AT&T Inc. is the largest communications holding company in the United States and worldwide by revenue. Operating globally under the AT&T brand, AT&T is recognized as the leading worldwide provider of IP-based communications services to businesses and the leading U.S. provider of wireless, high-speed Internet access, local and long distance, and directory publishing and advertising services.

AT&T is the largest provider of wireless services in the United States, serving more than 67 million wireless subscribers with the nation's largest digital voice and data network. We are dedicated to providing customers with mobile solutions that will enrich their lives.

My role in the enterprise is to gain and care for customers at the retail level. I am responsible for the company's retail operations in North Florida, consisting of our company-owned stores, local dealers, and national retailers like Radio Shack and Best Buy.

The wireless industry is highly competitive. Consumers often are bewildered by the different options available. Thus, customer service plays a critical role in differentiating our offerings and service from those of our competitors. The sales associates in our retail outlets are given extensive training to effectively serve our customers.

In addition to product knowledge, they learn to help customers select the service and equipment best for them—that meets their needs at an attractive price. My team also provides the training for the store employees working for our partners in other retail outlets in my territory.

To make sure customers have a satisfying experience after signing up for our services, we provide each customer with a customer service summary. The summary reviews the information provided by our sales associates, describing the services the customer has selected in easily understandable language, and an estimate of their first bill. It guides them in initiating their service, including setting up voicemail, checking their balance, paying their bill, and

CHAPTER 19

QUESTIONS

What services do retailers offer customers?

How can customer service build a competitive advantage?

How do customers evaluate a retailer's service?

What activities does a retailer have to undertake to provide high-quality customer service?

How can retailers recover from a service failure?

checking their minutes. We also provide a contact person at the local store they can call.

To provide an even more satisfying shopping opportunity, every new store will be an AT&T Experience Store. In these new stores, customers can touch and use the entire array of AT&T's services in one place. For example, an entertainment area features demonstrations of high-definition programming and the company's video-on-demand catalog. In another area, customers learn how to customize Web pages and use remote monitoring.

A music area lets customers test XM Satellite Radio on wireless phones, try out Bluetooth headphones, and test Apple's iPhone, for which AT&T is the exclusive carrier. A gaming station features phones optimized for game-playing and allows customers to use store equipment to download games to their wireless phones. The Productivity Solutions area is where business customers can try out phones and hand-held organizers and discover how to synchronize e-mail, calendar, and contact information between devices and laptops. Each of these areas is staffed with sales associates to assist customers.

These are some of the tools and processes my team uses to ensure we provide customers with the specific wireless technology and service that enriches their lives and keeps them satisfied AT&T customers.

S uppose you are surfing the Internet for a digital camera. At RealCheapCameras.com (www.realcheapcameras.com), a hypothetical site, you are asked to type in the name of the specific brand and model number you want. Then you are quoted a price with shipping charges and asked for your credit card number and a shipping address. In contrast, when you go to www.circuitcity.com, you can buy a specific digital camera, review the specifications for different cameras, and look through reviews by experts and other consumers of different cameras. You can then go to a store to see the cameras, get additional information about the cameras from a sales associate, and look at accessories, such as a carrying case and additional memory units. Circuit City thus is providing some valuable services to its customers—services that they cannot get from RealCheapCameras.com.

Customer service is the set of activities and programs undertaken by retailers to make the shopping experience more rewarding for their customers. These activities increase the value customers receive from the merchandise and services they purchase. Retailing View 19.1 describes some new health services being offered by drug and discount stores.

Some of these services are derived from the retailer's store design or Web site or from policies established by the retailer. However, this chapter focuses on some of the most important personalized services, provided by sales associates interacting directly with customers.

The first section discusses retailers' opportunities to develop strategic advantages through customer service, followed by an examination of how retailers can take advantage of this opportunity by providing high-quality service.

REFACT

Shopping carts were first introduced in 1937 in a Humpty Dumpty store in Oklahoma City.[1]

REFACT

The word service is from the Latin term *servus*, meaning "slave."[2]

STRATEGIC ADVANTAGE THROUGH CUSTOMER SERVICE

REFACT

Nearly one out of four shoppers who have a bad service experience will either tell their friends about their experience and urge them not to shop there or will stop shopping at the store.[3]

Many stores differentiate their retail offerings, build customer loyalty, and develop sustainable competitive advantages by providing excellent customer service. Good service keeps customers returning to a retailer and generates positive word-of-mouth communication, which attracts new customers.[4]

All employees of a retail firm and all elements of the retailing mix provide services that increase the value of merchandise. For example, employees in the distribution center contribute to customer service by making sure the merchandise is in stock. The employees responsible for store location and design contribute by increasing the customer's convenience in getting to the store and finding merchandise in the store.

Exhibit 19–1 lists some of the services provided by retailers. Most of these services furnish information about the retailer's offering and make it easier for customers to locate and buy products and services. Services such as alterations and assembly of merchandise actually change merchandise to fit the needs of specific customers.

Providing high-quality service is difficult for retailers. Automated manufacturing makes the quality of most merchandise consistent from item to item. For example, all Super Twist Skil electric screwdrivers look alike and typically perform alike. But the quality of retail service can vary dramatically from store to store and from salesperson to salesperson within a store. It's hard for retailers to control the performance of employees who provide the service. A sales associate may provide

19.1   RETAILING VIEW   Retailers Provide Health Care Services

To offer customers a one-stop provider for health care solutions, drug and discount store chains are opening in-store health clinics. These clinics offer customers fast access to routine medical services such as strep-throat tests, sports physicals, and flu shots. The clinics, which typically charge between $25 and $99 per visit, don't require an appointment and are open during pharmacy hours, including evenings and weekends. To keep costs down, they are staffed by nurse practitioners, who can legally treat patients and write prescriptions in most states.

The clinics target a broad range of customers, from harried parents dropping by with sick children on the weekends who otherwise could not get an appointment with their doctor to busy professionals ducking in for a prescription during work hours. Clinics increase sales for the retailer when customers fill their prescriptions at the store pharmacy or pick up other items on their way out.

For example, Terri Whitesel, of Minneapolis, had an allergic reaction to a bug bite. She dashed into a MinuteClinic at a Target in between meetings at work. "I didn't want to go to the doctor and sit around waiting with a bunch of people who are really sick," said Whitesel. The nurse practitioner was busy with another patient, but Whitesel wrote down her name, got a beeper at the check-in counter, and shopped for birthday cards until the nurse beeped her five minutes later. The entire visit took less than fifteen minutes, and she wound up with a prescription for an anti-inflammatory drug.

Health insurers support the concept because the clinics promise considerable savings. Whereas a typical doctor visit for a basic illness costs an insurer about $110, a visit to one of the clinics usually costs under $60. Some of the clinics also use technology to increase the efficiency of care. When patients arrive, they check themselves in at a touch screen computer terminal, where they can swipe a credit card and enter basic

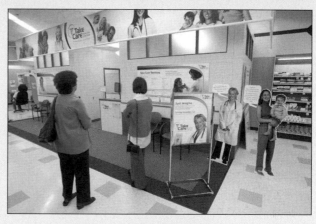

To provide one-stop shopping solutions for its customers' health care needs, Rite Aid is adding these Take Care Clinics to its drugstores.

information about their symptoms and family history. The patient's sign-in information is transmitted electronically to a computer terminal inside the treatment room where the nurses can enter additional information about the patient's symptoms and conditions as they talk with the patient. In one of the more novel uses of technology, the Take Care computer software program eventually will be involved in actually diagnosing illnesses.

Source: Tyler Chin, "Walgreens Plans to Expand In-Store Clinics," *AMNews*, January 29, 2007; Jane Spencer, "Getting Your Health Care at Wal-Mart," *The Wall Street Journal*, October 5, 2005, p. D1. Used by permission of Dow Jones & Co., Inc., via the Copyright Clearance Center; Berkeley Rice, "In-Store Clinics: Should You Worry?" *Medical Economics*, September 16, 2005.

Acceptance of credit cards	Free shipping
Alterations of merchandise	Gift wrapping and notes
Assembly of merchandise	Layaway plans
ATM terminals	Online chat
Blogs	Online customization
Bridal registry	Online inventory search
Check cashing	Parking
Child-care facilities	Personal assistance in selecting merchandise
Coat checks	Personal shoppers
Credit	Repair services
Customer reviews	Restrooms
Deep selection	Return privileges
Delivery to home or work	Shipping to store or home address
Demonstrations of merchandise	Shopping carts
Display of merchandise	Signage to locate and identify merchandise
Dressing rooms	Special orders
Extended store hours	Valet parking
Easy returns to bricks-and-mortar location or online	Warranties
Facilities for shoppers with special needs (physically handicapped)	

EXHIBIT 19–1
Services Offered by Retailers

good service to one customer and poor service to the next. In addition, most services provided by retailers are intangible; customers can't see or feel them. Clothing can be held and examined, but the assistance provided by a sales associate or an electronic agent can't. Intangibility makes it hard to provide and maintain high-quality service because retailers can't count, measure, or check service before it's delivered to customers.

The challenge of providing consistent, high-quality service offers an opportunity for a retailer to develop a sustainable competitive advantage. For example, Nordstrom devotes much time and effort to developing an organizational culture that stimulates and supports excellent customer service. Competing department stores would like to offer the same level of service but find it hard to match Nordstrom's performance.[5]

Customer Service Strategies

Personalized and standardized are two approaches retailers use to develop a sustainable customer service advantage. Successful implementation of the personalized approach relies on the performance of sales associates or the degree to which customer interactions can be personalized using an electronic channel. The standardization approach relies more on policy, procedures, and store and Web site design and layout.

Personalized Approach The **personalized approach** encourages service providers to tailor their service to meet each customer's personal needs.[7] For example, Nine West uses a combintion of workbooks and DVDs to teach its associates how to assess shoppers' needs and present ideas that complement their choices.[8] If a customer chooses a pair of black boots, associates are taught to bring out two other pairs of shoes in a similar style or different color, as well as a handbag or belt to match.

Some retailers are using technology to help personalize their service. The electronics superstore Best Buy uses radio frequency identification (RFID) technology to personalize and enhance the customer experience.[9] Customers receive a card with an embedded RFID transmitter. From home, those customers can browse the Best Buy Web site for information on the products in which he or she is interested. This information can be downloaded to the RFID transmitter, so store employees know exactly who the customer is and what he or she is interested in the moment that person enters the store. The customer can add information about whether he or she wants help from a personal shopping assistant, whether he or she wants to be left to shop alone, or whether he or she wants the customer service representative to allow some time to browse before offering to help. Thus, each customer can tailor the shopping experience exactly to his or her likes and dislikes. The information on the chip also enables Best Buy to offer instant rebates and validate warranty information on the spot, without the customer having to fill out reams of paperwork.

The personalized approach typically results in most customers receiving superior service. But because the service is personalized, its delivery might be more inconsistent than it would with a standardization approach, because the service delivery depends on the judgment and capabilities of each service provider. Some service providers are better than others, and even the best service providers can have a bad day. In addition, providing personalized service is costly because it requires more well-trained service providers or complex computer software.

Standardized Approach   The **standardized approach** is based on establishing a set of rules and procedures and ensuring they get implemented consistently.[10] By strictly enforcing these procedures, retailers minimize inconsistencies in the service they provide. Standardization is one of the keys to franchisors' success. At McDonald's restaurants, for instance, customers receive a reliable quality of food and service across the globe. The food may not be considered gourmet, but it's consistently served in a timely manner at a relatively low cost.

Store or Web site design and layout also play important roles in the standardization approach. In many situations, customers don't utilize the services employees provide. They know what they want to buy, and their objective is to find it in the store and buy it quickly. In these situations, retailers offer good service by providing a layout and signs that enable customers to locate merchandise easily, having relevant information on display, and minimizing the time required to make a purchase.

Retailing View 19.2 describes how IKEA uses a standardized, self-service approach with some unique elements to attract customers who expect the traditional customized approach common to furniture retailing.

Cost of Customer Service   As indicated previously, providing high-quality service, particularly customized service, can be very costly. As such, retailers need to consider the costs versus benefits of service policies.

Starbucks was trying to decide whether to spend $40 million systemwide to add 20 hours of labor per week to each store and thus speed up service.[11] Looking at this change purely from a cost perspective revealed that this expense would reduce net profit by $.07 a share. A different study also found that speed of service is

The office supply category specialist (left) uses signage as part of its standardized approach for improving customer service, while Target's sales associates (right) use a customized approach to tailor their service to match the needs of their individual customers.

crucial to customers' satisfaction and that highly satisfied customers spend 9 percent more than those who are simply satisfied. On the basis of these findings, Starbucks invested in the additional employees.

A "no questions asked" return policy has been offered as a form of customer service by many retailers for years. But because of the high costs when customers abuse the policy, many retailers have modified their return policy. Some large retailers, for instance, now limit their returns to 90 days, considered a reasonable amount of time for customers to return an item. Home Depot's return policy originally would take back all merchandise, but now, if customers don't have a receipt, they can only get store credit based on the lowest selling price of the item. If they have a receipt, they can get cash back. Target requires that customers have a receipt and return the merchandise in 90 days to get a refund. In addition, for some consumer electronics products that have been opened, customers must pay a 15 percent restocking fee. The next section examines how customers evaluate service quality.[12]

Customer Evaluations of Service Quality

When customers evaluate retail service, they compare their perceptions of the service they receive with their expectations. Customers are satisfied when the perceived service meets or exceeds their expectations. They're dissatisfied when they feel the service falls below their expectations.[14]

Role of Expectations   Customer expectations are based on a customer's knowledge and experiences. For example, based on past experiences, customers have different perceived time frames for receiving a response to a letter, a phone call, or an e-mail. An e-mail response is expected to be quicker than a letter response.

Technology is dramatically changing customer expectations. Customers expect to be able to interact with companies through automated voice response systems and place orders and check on delivery status through the Internet. Multichannel

REFACT
Retailers lose nearly $30 billion, or 1.7 percent of sales, because of fraud, and roughly half of that may be related to bad returns.[13]

Customer Service at IKEA   RETAILING VIEW   19.2

IKEA, a global furniture retailer based in Sweden, employs a concept of service unlike that of traditional furniture stores. The typical furniture store uses a showroom to display some of the merchandise sold in the store. Complementing the inventory are books of fabric swatches, veneers, and alternative styles customers can order. Salespeople assist customers in going through the books. When the customer makes a selection, the order is placed with the factory, and the furniture is delivered to the customer's home in six to eight weeks. This system maximizes customization, but the costs are high.

In contrast, IKEA uses a self-service model based on extensive in-store displays. At information desks in the store, shoppers can pick up a map of the store, plus a pencil, order form, clipboard, and tape measure. After studying the catalog and displays, customers proceed to a self-service storage area and locate their selections using codes copied from the sales tags. Every product available is displayed in over 70 room-like settings throughout the 150,000 square foot warehouse stores. Thus, customers don't need a decorator to help them picture how the furniture will go together. Adjacent to the display rooms is a warehouse with ready-to-assemble furniture in boxes that customers can pick up when they leave the store.

Although IKEA uses a "customers do it themselves" approach, it also offers some services that traditional furniture stores do not, such as in-store child-care centers, restaurants serving fast food, and extensive information about the quality of the furniture. Toddlers can be left in a supervised ballroom filled with 50,000

IKEA effectively uses a self-service method to provide customer service through signage and information in displays and on the merchandise.

brightly colored plastic balls. There are changing rooms in each store, complete with bottle warmers and disposable diaper dispensers. Displays cover the quality of products in terms of design features and materials, with demonstrations of testing procedures.

Sources: Deena M. Amato-McCoy, "Checkout Or Bust," *Chain Store Age* 82, 2006 Supplement; www.ikea.com/ms/en_US/about_ikea/store_experience/self-serve_area.html (accessed November 7, 2007); Youngme Moon, "IKEA Invades America," Boston: Harvard Business Press, 2004.

REFACT

Organizations that effectively meet customers' expectations spend only 10 percent of their operating budget fixing issues related to poor customer service, whereas ineffective organizations can spend up to 40 percent of their operating budget.[15]

retailers that do not offer these basic services are not favorably viewed. Customers still expect good services such as dependable outcomes, easy access, responsive systems, flexibility, apologies, and compensation when things go wrong. But now they expect this level of service even when people are not involved.[16]

Expectations vary depending on the type of store. Customers expect a traditional supermarket to provide convenient parking, be open from early morning to late evening, have a wide variety of fresh and packaged food that can be located easily, display products, and offer fast checkout. They don't expect the supermarket to have store employees stationed in the aisle to offer information about groceries or how to prepare meals. When these unexpected services are offered, and the services are important to them, then customers are delighted—the retailer has exceeded their expectations.[17] However, when these same customers shop in a specialty food store like Whole Foods Market, they expect the store to have knowledgeable store employees who can provide expert information and courteous assistance.

Some examples of unexpected positive service experiences are

- A restaurant that sends customers who have had too much to drink home in a taxi and then delivers their cars in the morning.

- A jewelry store that cleans customers' jewelry and replaces batteries in watches for free.

- A men's store that sews numbered tags on each garment so the customer will know what goes together.

Customer service expectations vary around the world. Although Germany's manufacturing capability is world renowned, its poor customer service is also well known. People wait years to have telephone service installed. Many restaurants do not accept credit cards, and customers who walk into stores near closing time often receive rude stares. Customers typically have to bag merchandise they buy themselves. Because Germans are unaccustomed to good service, they don't demand it. But as retailing becomes global and new foreign competitors enter, German retailers are becoming more concerned about how they service their customers.

In contrast, the Japanese expect excellent customer service from their higher-end stores. In the United States, it's said that "the customer is always right." In Japan, the equivalent expression is *okyakusama wa kamisama desu*, "the customer is God." When a customer comes back to a store to return merchandise, he or she is dealt with even more cordially than when the original purchase was made. Customer satisfaction isn't negotiable. The customer is assumed to never be wrong. Even if the customer misused the product, retailers generally feel they were responsible for not telling the customer how to use it properly. The first person in the store who hears about the problem must take full responsibility for dealing with the customer, even if the problem involved another department.

Perceived Service   Customers base their evaluations of store service on their perceptions. Although these perceptions are affected by the actual service provided, service, due to its intangibility, is often hard to evaluate accurately. Five customer service characteristics that customers use to evaluate service quality are discussed next.[18]

- **Reliability** is the ability to perform the service dependably and accurately, such as performing the service as promised/contracted or meeting promised delivery dates.

This salesperson at a Kelo Department Store is providing the excellent personalized service that Japanese customers expect. The computer system scans the customer's feet and suggests shoes that will provide a good fit.

- **Assurance** is the knowledge and courtesy of employees and their ability to convey trust and confidence, such as having salespeople who are thoroughly trained.
- **Tangibles** are the appearances of physical facilities, equipment, personnel, and communication materials.
- **Empathy** refers to the caring, individualized attention provided to customers, such as personalized service, receipts of notes and e-mails, or recognition by name.
- **Responsiveness** is the willingness to help customers and provide prompt service, such as returning calls and e-mails immediately.

Retailing View 19.3 describes how the Broadmoor Hotel maintains its five-star rating by focusing on these five service characteristics.

The Broadmoor Manages Service Quality for Five-Star Rating   **RETAILING VIEW**   **19.3**

Established in 1891 as a gambling casino, and transformed into a "grand resort" in 1918, the Broadmoor, in Colorado Springs, Colorado, is one of the world's premier resorts. It has received a record 47 consecutive years of five-star ratings from the *Mobil Travel Guide*. Perry Goodbar, former vice president of marketing for the Broadmoor, emphasizes, "It's the people who truly make this place special. Exceptional service quality begins with exceptional people." Some aspects of its service quality are as follows:

Reliability   Every new Broadmoor employee, before ever encountering a customer, attends a two-and-a-half day orientation session and receives an employee handbook. Making and keeping promises to customers is a central part of this orientation. Employees are trained always to give an estimated time for service, whether it be room service,

Although the Broadmoor in Colorado Springs has first class amenities, it is its customer service that gives it a five star rating.

laundry service, or simply how long it will take to be seated at one of the resort's restaurants. When employees make promises they keep them. Employees are trained to never guess if they don't know the answer to a question. Inaccurate information only frustrates customers. When employees are unable to answer questions accurately, they immediately contact someone who can.

Assurance   The Broadmoor conveys trust by empowering its employees. An example of an employee empowerment policy is the service recovery program. If a guest problem arises, employees are given discretionary resources to rectify the problem or present the customer with something special to help mollify them. For example, if a meal is delivered and there's a mistake in the order or how it was prepared, a waiter can offer the guest a free item such as a dessert or, if the service was well below expectations, simply take care of the bill. Managers then review expenses to understand the nature of the problem and help prevent it from occurring again.

Tangibles   One of the greatest challenges for the Broadmoor in recent years has been updating rooms built in the early part of the twentieth century to meet the needs of twenty-first

century visitors. To accomplish this, it spent $200 million between 1992 and 2002 in improvements, renovating rooms, and adding a new outdoor pool complex.

Empathy   One approach used to demonstrate empathy is personalizing communications. Employees are instructed to always address a guest by name, if possible. To accomplish this, employees are trained to listen and observe carefully to determine a guest's name. Subtle sources for this information include convention name tags, luggage ID tags, credit cards, or checks. In addition, all phones within the Broadmoor display a guest's room number and name on a screen.

Responsiveness   Every employee is instructed to follow the HEART model of taking care of problems.[19] First, employees must "Hear what a guest has to say." Second, they must "Empathize with them" and then "Apologize for the situation." Third, they must "Respond to the guest's needs" by "Taking action and following up."

Source: Bill Radford, "Broadmoor's Penrose Room Dons a 5th Gem," *The Colorado Springs Gazette*, November 7, 2007; "Grand Plans for a Grande Dame," *Lodging Hospitality*, September 1, 2007, pp. 17–18; www.broadmoor.com (accessed November 7, 2007).

REFACT

More than one-quarter of shoppers cite unsatisfactory service as more likely to drive them away from a store permanently than any other aspect of the shopping experience.[20]

As Retailing View 19.3 indicates, employees can play an important role in customer perceptions of service quality. Customer evaluations of service quality are often based on the manner in which store employees provide the service, not just the outcome. Consider the following situation: A customer goes to return an electric toothbrush that isn't working properly to a store that has a no questions asked, money-back return policy. In one case, the employee asks the customer for a receipt, checks to see if the receipt shows the toothbrush was bought at the store, examines the toothbrush to see if it really doesn't work properly, completes some paperwork while the customer is waiting, and finally gives the customer the amount paid for the toothbrush in cash. In a second case, the store employee simply asks the customer how much he paid and gives him a cash refund. The two cases have the same outcome: The customer gets a cash refund. But the customer might be dissatisfied in the first case because the employee appeared not to trust the customer and took too much time providing the refund. In most situations, employees have a great effect on the process of providing services and thus on the customer's eventual satisfaction with the services.

THE GAPS MODEL FOR IMPROVING RETAIL SERVICE QUALITY

Customers have certain expectations about how a service should be delivered. When the delivery of that service fails to meet those expectations, a **service gap** results. The Gaps Model (Exhibit 19–2) is designed to facilitate the systematic examination of all aspects of the service delivery process and prescribe the steps needed to develop an optimal service strategy.[21]

EXHIBIT 19–2   Gaps Model for Improving Retail Service Quality

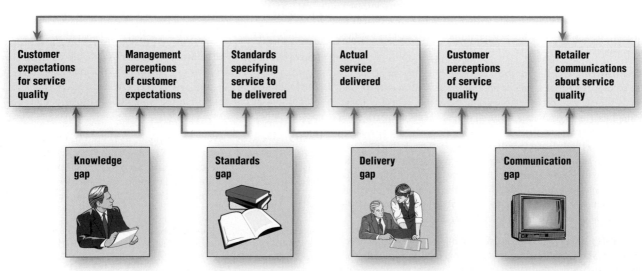

As Exhibit 19–2 shows, there are four service gaps:

1. The **knowledge gap** reflects the difference between customers' expectations and the firm's perception of those customer expectations. Firms can use market research to close this gap by matching customer expectations with actual service provided.

2. The **standards gap** pertains to the difference between the firm's perceptions of customers' expectations and the service standards it sets. By setting appropriate service standards and measuring service performance, firms can attempt to close this gap.

3. The **delivery gap** is the difference between the firm's service standards and the actual service it provides to customers. This gap can be closed by getting employees to meet or exceed service standards through training and/or appropriate incentives.

4. The **communication gap** refers to the difference between the actual service provided to customers and the service that the firm's communication program promises. When firms are more realistic about the services they can provide, they can manage customer expectations effectively and close this gap.

Knowing What Customers Want: The Knowledge Gap

The most critical step in providing good service is to know what the customer wants, needs, or expects, and then use this information to provide the appropriate service level. Yet retailers often lack this information, which can result in poor decisions. For example, a supermarket might hire extra people to make sure the shelves are stocked so customers will always find what they want, but it may fail to realize that customers are most concerned about waiting in the checkout line. From the customer's perspective, the supermarket's service would improve if the extra employees were used to open more checkout lines rather than to stock shelves.

Retailers can reduce the knowledge gap and develop a better understanding of customer expectations by undertaking customer research, increasing interactions between retail managers and customers, and improving communication between managers and the employees who provide customer service.

Market research also can be used to better understand customers' expectations and the quality of service provided by a retailer. Methods for obtaining this information range from comprehensive studies to simply asking customers about the store's service.

Comprehensive Studies   Some retailers have established programs to assess customers' expectations and service perceptions. For example, Best Buy works with a team of engineers, technologists, and product experts from Apple, Xerox, Kodak, and other leading companies.[24] The team receives input from customers about how they live and use consumer electronic products. As a result of this research, Best Buy has increased the number of Geek Squad agents (PC consultants) to 5,000 and moved home theater installation services in-house to provide a better and more consistent customer experience. Membership in the Reward Zone customer loyalty program has reached 7.2 million, and as a result, Best Buy has learned more about customer purchase patterns than ever before.

Gauging Satisfaction with Individual Transactions   Another method for customer research is to survey customers immediately after a retail transaction has occurred. For example, airlines, automobile dealers, hotels, and restaurants give customers surveys, encourage them to take an online survey, or call them on the phone to ask them questions about their service experience, such as how helpful, friendly, and professional the employees were.

REFACT

Just 16 percent of traditional, retail store shoppers are extremely satisfied with their most recent customer service experience, whereas online shoppers are nearly three times as likely to be extremely satisfied with their online customer service experience (44 percent).[22]

REFACT

Eighty percent of Americans are willing to share personal information with companies if it means getting more personal service while shopping.[23]

Customer research on individual transactions provides up-to-date information about customers' expectations and perceptions. The research also indicates the retailer's interest in providing good service. Because the responses can be linked to a specific encounter, this research provides a method for rewarding employees who provide good service and correcting those who exhibit poor performance.

Customer Panels and Interviews   Rather than surveying many customers, retailers can use panels of 10–15 customers to gain insights into expectations and perceptions. For example, some store managers might meet once a month for an hour with a select group of customers who are asked to provide information about their experiences in the stores and offer suggestions for improving service. To reduce the knowledge gap, some supermarket managers go through the personal checks they receive each day and select customers who've made large and small purchases. They call these customers and ask them what they liked and didn't like about the store. With small purchasers, they probe to find out why the customers didn't buy more. Could they find everything they wanted? Did they get the assistance they expected from store employees?

Some retailers have consumer advisory boards composed of a cross-section of their preferred customers. Members of the board complete questionnaires three to four times a year on subjects like holiday shopping problems, in-store signage, and service quality. In exchange for their inputs, members receive gift certificates.

Interacting with Customers   Owner managers of small retail firms typically have daily contact with their customers and thus have accurate, firsthand information about them. In large retail firms, managers often learn about customers through reports, so they may miss the rich information provided by direct contact with customers.

JetBlue pilots go out of their way to make a connection with their customers.

To help ensure that JetBlue consistently monitors customers' wants and needs, the airline surveys at least six customers from every flight it operates.[25] It then brings together top executives to discuss what customers are saying and how it should respond. It learned, for instance, that when its pilots stand in the aisle in the cabin to talk to passengers over the plane's public-address system, the response is extremely favorable—especially when the pilot appears at the beginning of the flight or when there is some kind of delay. As a result, new pilots are now taught how to address passengers, including practicing announcements as part of their training in flight simulators. And every JetBlue pilot is given a printed guide to making announcements.

Customer Complaints   Complaints allow retailers to interact with their customers and acquire detailed information about their service and merchandise. Handling complaints is an inexpensive means to isolate and correct service problems.[27]

Catalog/Internet retailer L.L. Bean keeps track of all complaints and reasons for returned merchandise. These complaints and returns are summarized daily and given to customer service representatives so they can improve their service.

For example, a customer who returns a sweater might indicate the sweater was too large or the color tone differed from the picture in the catalog. With this information, customer service representatives can inform other customers when placing an order for the sweater that it tends to be large and has a slightly different color than shown in the catalog. The information can also be used by buyers to improve vendor merchandise.

Although customer complaints can provide useful information, retailers can't rely solely on this source of market information. In the past, dissatisfied customers didn't typically complain, though this tendency is changing as customers utilize blogs, retailers' own online review systems, and customer service messaging systems more frequently.[28] Although the majority of the complaints are about specific merchandise, service issues are also addressed. These online contributions to blogs and interactions with retailers are very useful because they tend to be very frank compared with information gathered through more traditional research methods.

Using Technology   New, affordable information technology packages are enabling even small retailers to improve their customer service by maintaining and providing customer information to sales associates. The sales staff at Tina's Closet, a Lisle, Illinois-based women's apparel specialty store, uses a clienteling software application with its customer database to track the buying history of its 15,000 customers and provide better customer service. For example, when the store puts Bali bras on sale, it sends postcards to every customer who has bought one. The sales staff is provided with lists of customers who need to be contacted when the merchandise they have on hold is about to be put out for sale, their alterations are ready, or a new line of products is coming in from their favorite designer.[31]

Feedback from Store Employees   Salespeople and other employees in regular contact with customers often have a good understanding of customer service expectations and problems. This information can improve service quality only if the employees are encouraged to communicate their experiences to high-level managers who can act on it.

Some retailers regularly survey their employees, asking questions like,

1. What is the biggest problem you face in delivering high-quality service to your customers?
2. If you could make one change in the company to improve customer service, what would it be?

Using Customer Research   Collecting information about customer expectations and perceptions isn't enough. The service gap is reduced only when retailers use this information to improve service. For example, store managers should review the suggestions and comments made by customers daily, summarize the information, and distribute it to store employees and managers.

Feedback on service performance needs to be provided to employees in a timely manner. Reporting the July service performance in December makes it hard for employees to reflect on the reason for the reported performance. Finally, feedback must be prominently presented so service providers are aware of their performance. For example, at Marriott, front desk personnel's performance feedback is displayed behind the front desk, while restaurant personnel's performance feedback is displayed behind the door to the kitchen. In the next section, approaches for reducing the standards gap are reviewed.

Setting Service Standards: The Standards Gap

After retailers gather information about customer service expectations and perceptions, the next step is to use this information to set standards and develop systems for delivering high-quality service. Service standards should be based on customers' perceptions rather than internal operations. For example, a supermarket chain might set an operations standard of a warehouse delivery every day to each store. But frequent warehouse deliveries may not result in more merchandise on the shelves and therefore may not improve customers' impressions of product availability. To close the standards gap, retailers need to (1) commit their firms to providing high-quality service, (2) define the role of service providers, (3) set service goals, and (4) measure service performance.

Commitment to Service Quality   Service excellence occurs only when top management provides leadership and demonstrates commitment. Top management must be willing to accept the temporary difficulties and even the increased costs associated with improving service quality. This commitment needs to be demonstrated to the employees charged with providing the service.

Pulte Homes Inc., which has earned more top-three finishes than any other homebuilder in the annual J.D. Power and Associates New Home Builder Customer Satisfaction Study has a strong commitment to customer service.[32] It surveys customers immediately after they close on a new home and then at the one-year mark to make sure they are still satisfied. Several years ago, recognizing that customer satisfaction was critically important in the ability to differentiate Pulte in the market, the company developed a seven-step process to interact with the consumer throughout the construction and ownership process—a departure from most homebuilders' typical focus on corrective fixes.

Top management's commitment sets service quality standards, but store managers are the key to achieving those standards. Store managers must see that their efforts to provide service quality are noticed and rewarded. Providing incentives based on service quality makes service an important personal goal. Rather than basing bonuses only on store sales and profit, part of store managers' bonuses should be determined by the level of service provided. For example, some retailers use the results of customer satisfaction studies to help determine bonuses.

Defining the Role of Service Providers   Managers can tell service providers that they need to provide excellent service but not clearly indicate what excellent service means. Without a clear definition of the retailer's expectations, service providers are directionless.

The Ritz-Carlton Hotel Company, winner of the Malcolm Baldrige National Quality Award, has its "Gold Standards" printed on a wallet-size card carried by all employees. The card contains the hotel's motto ("We Are Ladies and Gentlemen Serving Ladies and Gentlemen"), the three steps for high-quality service (warm and sincere greeting, anticipation and compliance with guests' needs, and fond farewell), and 12 basic rules for Ritz-Carlton employees, including "I build strong relationships and create Ritz-Carlton guests for life" (No. 1) and "I am proud of my professional appearance, language, and behavior" (No. 10).[33]

Setting Service Goals   To deliver consistent, high-quality service, retailers need to establish goals or standards to guide employees. Retailers often develop service goals that are based on their beliefs about the proper operation of the business rather than the customers' needs and expectations. For example, a retailer might set a goal that all monthly bills are to be mailed five days before the end of the month. This goal reduces the retailer's accounts receivable but offers no benefit to customers. Research undertaken by American Express showed that customer evaluations of its service were based on perceptions of timeliness, accuracy, and responsiveness. Management then established goals (e.g., responding to all questions about bills within 24 hours) related to these customer-based criteria.

Employees are motivated to achieve service goals when the goals are specific and measurable, and when they participate in setting the goals. Vague goals—such as "Approach customers when they enter the selling area" or "Respond to e-mails as soon as possible"—don't fully specify what employees should do, nor do they offer an opportunity to assess employee performance. Better goals would be "All customers should be approached by a salesperson within 30 seconds after entering a selling area" or "All e-mails should be responded to within three hours." These goals are both specific and measurable.

Employee participation in setting service standards leads to better understanding and greater acceptance of the goals. Store employees resent and resist goals arbitrarily imposed on them by management. Chapter 17 says more about goal setting.

Measuring Service Performance Retailers need to assess service quality continuously to ensure that goals will be achieved.[34] Many retailers conduct periodic customer surveys to assess service quality. Retailers also use mystery shoppers to assess their service quality. **Mystery shoppers** are professional shoppers who "shop" at a store to determine the service provided by store employees and the presentation of merchandise in the store. Some retailers use their own employees as mystery shoppers, but most contract with an outside firm to provide the assessment. Information typically reported by the mystery shoppers includes (1) How long before a sales associate greeted you? (2) Did the sales associate act as if he or she wanted your business? and (3) Was the sales associate knowledgeable about the merchandise?

Retailers typically inform salespeople that they have "been shopped" and provide feedback from the mystery shopper's report. Some retailers offer rewards to sales associates who receive high marks and schedule follow-up visits to sales associates who get low evaluations.[35]

Avero LLC helps restaurants track and break down sales data.[36] Its software measures how often servers sell particular items, like wine and dessert, and averages them across the number of guests an employee has served to offer a more accurate comparison among servers. The software helped one client discover that a particular server had never sold a bottle of wine. It turned out that server simply didn't know the proper way to open the wine at the table and, as a result, avoided selling it.

Giving Information and Training Finally, store employees need to know about the retailer's service standards and the merchandise they offer, as well as their customers' needs. With this information, employees can answer customers' questions and suggest products. This knowledge also instills confidence and a sense of competence, needed to overcome service problems. JCPenney uses interactive distance learning to train its employees.[37] The company uses satellite technology to broadcast its biweekly store manager training sessions, called "News You Can Use," that highlight upcoming marketing initiatives, retail operations, new system rollouts, and any other changes that may affect managers. Along with video, shows include questions for learners to respond to using keypads. Each store has a training room where employees sign onto the satellite program via a keypad while they watch the "news" on a TV screen. Even though it's not live, they're able to respond to a series of questions included in the broadcast.

In addition, store employees need training in interpersonal skills. Dealing with customers is hard—particularly when they're upset or angry. All store employees, even those who work for retailers that provide excellent service, will encounter dissatisfied customers. Through training, employees can learn to provide better service and cope with the stress caused by disgruntled customers. Specific retail employees (salespeople and customer service representatives) are typically designated to interact with and provide service to customers. However, all retail employees should be prepared to deal with customers. For example, Walt Disney World provides

Mystery shoppers are professional shoppers who "shop" at a store to determine the service provided by store employees and the presentation of merchandise in the store.

four days of training for its maintenance workers, even though people can learn how to pick up trash and sweep streets in much less time. Disney has found that its customers are more likely to direct questions to maintenance people than to the clean-cut assistants wearing "ASK ME, I'M IN GUEST RELATIONS" buttons. Thus, Disney trains maintenance people to confidently handle the myriad of questions they'll be asked rather than responding, "Gee, I dunno. Ask her."[38]

Meeting and Exceeding Service Standards: The Delivery Gap

To reduce the delivery gap and provide service that exceeds standards, retailers must give service providers the necessary knowledge and skills, provide instrumental and emotional support, improve internal communications, reduce conflicts, and empower employees to act in the customers' and firm's best interests.[39] Retailing View 19.4 describes how home-cooked meals get distributed to thousands of workers in India.

Providing Instrumental and Emotional Support   Service providers need to have the **instrumental support** (appropriate systems and equipment) to deliver the service desired by customers. For instance, JCPenney has connected its cash registers to the Internet so salespeople can help customers order a size or style not found in the store.[40] Similarly, Barnes & Noble and Kohl's have computer kiosks in stores so customers and employees can order out-of-stock books or clothing items. Target uses its kiosks to enable customers to create gift registries, check prices, and buy gift cards.

19.4   RETAILING VIEW   Home-Cooked Lunch Delivery in India

Throughout large cities in India and in a few large U.S. cities like New York and San Francisco that have large South Asian populations, the 100-year traditional practice of delivering a home-cooked lunch is alive and well. It is almost impossible for workers to get home for lunch in sprawling cities like Mumbai, with its estimated 25 million people. So an intricately organized, labor-intensive operation that would put FedEx or UPS to shame arranges for pickup and delivery.

Dabbawallas rival FedEx or UPS when it comes to on-time deliveries.

Men, called dabbawallas, pick up boxed lunches from customers' homes or from people who cook lunches to order, then deliver the meals to a local railway station. The boxes are hand-sorted for delivery to the different locations within the city, then consolidated and carried to their destinations. After lunch, the service reverses, and the empty boxes are delivered back to their source.

The secret of the system is the color codes painted on the boxes, which tell the dabbawallas where the food comes from and which railway station it must pass through on its way to its customer. The boxes are hauled on a wooden cart through Mumbai and personally delivered to each person.

Anand Sahasrebuddhe, who works for India's largest cement and concrete makers in downtown Mumbai, has been depending on the dabbawallas for his lunch for 26 years. According to his mother Suman, "He simply loves home-cooked food."

Sources: www.mydabbawala.com (accessed November 7, 2007); "Banking Out of the Lunch Box," *Mumbai,* May 7, 2007; Saritha Rai, "In India, Grandma Cooks, They Deliver," *The New York Times,* May 29, 2007 (accessed January 26, 2008.).

In addition to instrumental support, service providers need emotional support from their coworkers and supervisors. **Emotional support** involves demonstrating a concern for the well-being of others. Dealing with customer problems and maintaining a smile in difficult. Stressful situations can be psychologically demanding. Service providers need to maintain a supportive, understanding atmosphere and attitude to deal with these demands effectively.[41]

Although "the customer is always right" may be a common business mantra, employees on the receiving end of a service interaction face incredible pressure to simply "grin and bear it." Retailers need to be aware of how these stressful customer interactions affect the morale and performance of their service providers.

Matt Friedman, the CEO and co-founder of Wing Zone, understands the stress that angry customers can cause his employees, who take the majority of the company's food orders over the phone. Friedman says his entry-level employees, who are mostly college students, simply lack the experience to handle these customers. Therefore, Wing Zone trains them to hand off overly demanding customers to the nearest manager immediately. The manager then turns the complaints back to the customers, asking how they'd like the company to handle the problem. When both parties can't find some middle ground, managers refer the customer to the corporate office's toll-free number or Web site to file a formal complaint.

Robert Girau, the point person at corporate headquarters for complaints that escalate, thinks the company's strategy works because the service providers know how to handle angry customers, managers understand what they can offer and are empowered to solve problems, and complaints with no easy solution can be routed up the organization. The procedures at the store level make life easier for everyone in the company.[42]

Improving Internal Communications   When providing customer service, store employees often must manage the conflict between customers' and the retail firm's needs.[43] For example, while retailers expect their sales associates to encourage customers to make multiple purchases and buy more expensive items, customers are looking for the best value choices to fit their needs. The sales associates therefore may be conflicted between meeting corporate and customers' goals.

Retailers can reduce such conflicts by issuing clear guidelines and policies concerning service and explaining the rationale for these policies. For example, many retailers have a no questions asked return policy. Under such a policy, the retailer will provide a refund at the customer's request even if the merchandise wasn't purchased at the store or was clearly used improperly. When JCPenney inaugurated this policy, some employees refused to provide refunds on merchandise that had been worn or damaged by the customer. They were loyal JCPenney employees and didn't want customers to take advantage of their firm. Once JCPenney employees recognized that the goodwill created by the no-questions-asked policy generated more sales than the losses due to customers' abusing the policy, they implemented the policy enthusiastically.

Conflicts can also arise when retailers set goals inconsistent with the other behaviors expected from store employees. For example, as discussed in Chapter 17, if salespeople are expected to provide customer service, they should be evaluated and compensated on the service they provide, not just the sales they make.

Finally, conflicts can arise between different areas of the firm. A men's specialty store known for its high levels of customer service has salespeople who promise rapid alterations and deliveries to please their customers. Unfortunately, the alterations department includes two elderly tailors who work at their own speed, regardless of the workload. From time to time, management must step in to temper the salepeople's promises and reallocate priorites for the tailors.

REFACT

Trader Joe's, a gourmet supermarket chain, found that a change in its service policy that empowered employees to solve customer problems was accompanied by an increase in annual sales growth from 15 to 26 percent.[44]

Empowering Store Employees   **Empowerment** means allowing employees at the firm's lowest levels to make important decisions regarding how service will be provided to customers. When the employees responsible for providing service are authorized to make important decisions, service quality improves. Retailing View 19.5 describes how the FISH management philosophy helps empower store employees to have fun, be creative and give exceptional customer service.

Nordstrom provides an overall objective—satisfy customer needs—and then encourages employees to do whatever is necessary to achieve the objective. For example, a Nordstrom department manager bought 12 dozen pairs of hosiery from a competitor in the mall when her stock was depleted because the new shipment was delayed. Even though Nordstrom lost money on this hosiery, management applauded her actions to make sure customers found hosiery when they came to the store looking for it. Empowering service providers with only a rule like "Use your best judgment" can also cause chaos. At Nordstrom, department managers avoid abuses by coaching and training salespeople. They help salespeople understand what "Use your best judgment" means.

19.5   RETAILING VIEW   FISH! Empowers Employees

FISH! is a management philosophy developed by ChartHouse and inspired by the Pike Place Fish Market in Seattle. The selling atmosphere at Pike Place is unusual. Employees, known as fishmongers, throw fish over the counter to coworkers for wrapping. The fishmongers also invite customers to get in on the action and try to catch fish. What could be a dull store is transformed into a place where customers and employees are smiling, laughing, and connecting with one another, while keeping an eye out for flying fish.

Amy's Ice Cream (a 13-store chain of premium ice cream shops in Austin, San Antonio, and Houston, Texas) has similarly transformed what could be a boring transaction into a fun experience. Visit an Amy's store, and you'll see employees performing in a manner you won't forget. They juggle with their serving spades, toss scoops of ice cream to one another behind the counter, and break-dance on the freezer top. If there's a line out the door, they might pass out samples or offer free ice cream to any customer who'll sing or dance or recite a poem or mimic a barnyard animal or win a 60-second cone-eating contest.

The four FISH! principles are:

1. Choose your attitude—look for the worst and you'll find it; choose to look for the best and you'll find opportunities heretofore unimagined;

2. Be there—being fully present for one another and diving into every task with your whole heart;

3. Make their day—small kindnesses turn even routine encouters into special memories;

4. Play—serious tasks are made fun through spontaneity and creativity.

By empowering employees to implement the FISH! principles the best way they can, companies facilitate great customer

By giving employees the freedom to have fun at work, Pike Place Fish Markets employees reduce the delivery gap and improve customer service.

service. For example, "choose your attitude" can empower employees to effect change from within themselves. Positive attitudes spread to other employees and onto customers. Empowering employees to "play" on the job makes the working and buying atmosphere fun, and happy customers buy more.

Sources: www.charthouse.com (accessed November 12, 2007); www.amysicecream.com (accessed November 11, 2007); Laura Gee, "Some Companies Work to Put Fun in the Office," www.dailypress.com, October 23, 2007; Tanya Rutledge, "Amy Miller, Sweet Success," *Austin Business Journal*, December 24, 2004, p. 16; Marcia Hicks, "Revitalizing Your Call Center Via FISH! Philosophy," *Direct Marketing Magazine*, December 1, 2003; Stephen C. Lundin, Harry Paul, and John Christensen, *Fish! A Remarkable Way to Boost Morale and Improve Results* (New York: Hyperion, 2000).

However, empowering service providers can be difficult. Some employees prefer to have the appropriate behaviors clearly defined for them. They don't want to spend the time learning how to make decisions or assume the risks of making mistakes. For example, a bank found that when it empowered its tellers, the tellers were reluctant to make decisions about large sums of money. The bank had to develop decision guideposts and rules until tellers felt more comfortable.

In some cases, the benefits of empowering service providers may not justify the costs. For example, if a retailer uses a standardized service delivery approach like McDonald's, the cost of hiring, training, and supporting empowerment may not lead to consistent and superior service delivery. Also, studies have found that empowerment is not embraced by employees in different cultures. For example, employees in Latin America expect their managers to possess all the information needed to make good business decisions. The role of employees is not to make business decisions; their job is to carry out the decisions of managers.[45]

Providing Incentives   As discussed in Chapter 17, many retailers use incentives, like paying commissions on sales, to motivate employees. But retailers have found that commissions on sales can decrease customer service and job satisfaction and motivate high-pressure selling, which leads to customer dissatisfaction. However, incentives can also be used effectively to improve customer service.

Home Depot has a customer service initiative that includes an "Orange Juiced" program, named after employees' signature orange aprons, that earmarks as much as $25,000 per quarter to stores that provide the best customer service.[46] Individual employees can receive bonuses of as much as $2,000 per month or $10,000 per quarter. Home Depot determines which store is rewarded by looking at several factors: reviews by peers and managers, focus groups, and "voice of the customer" surveys. Between 150,000 and 250,000 customers call the company's 800 number each week or visit its Internet site—the address for which is printed at the bottom of receipts—to rate their customer service experience.

Developing Novel Solutions for Improving Service   The previously discussed approaches for closing the service gap rely on informing, empowering, and motivating store personnel to provide better service. Retailers also use systems and technology to close the delivery gap.

Developing New Systems   Finding ways to overcome service problems can improve customer satisfaction and, in some cases, reduce costs. For example, Massachusetts-based Zoots dry cleaners doesn't want to be like its competitors, which are open from 8:00 AM to 6:00 PM—when most customers are at work. So it devised an automated system for 24/7 pickup and delivery. When customers swipe their credit cards, the machine automatically identifies their garments and retrieves the order from the clothes rack into a pickup window or accepts a new dry cleaning order.[47]

Using Technology   Many retailers are installing kiosks with broadband Internet access in their stores. In addition to offering customers the opportunity to order merchandise not available in the store, kiosks can provide routine customer service, freeing employees to deal with more demanding customer requests and problems. For example, customers can use kiosks to locate merchandise in the store and determine whether specific products, brands, and sizes are available. Kiosks can also be used to automate existing store services, such as gift registry management, rain checks, film drop-off, credit applications, and preordering services for bakeries and delicatessens.

Customers can use a kiosk to find more information about products and how they are used. For example, a Best Buy customer might use a kiosk to look at

REFACT

Self-service technology for gas pumps originated in 1947, when two Californians simultaneously hit on the idea. About 90 percent of gasoline purchases now are made at self-serve stations.[48]

The Retail Store Assistant facilitates shopping and reduces the delivery gap by providing customers with information and coupons.

side-by-side comparisons of two DVRs and find more detailed information than is available from the shelf tags or a sales associate. The customer can also access evaluations of the models reported in *Consumer Reports*. The information provided by the kiosk could be tailored to the specific customer, based on the retailer's customer database. For example, a customer who is considering a new set of speakers might not remember the preamplifier he or she purchased previously from Best Buy. This customer might not know whether the speakers are compatible with the preamplifier or what cables are needed to connect the new speakers. These concerns could be addressed by accessing the retailer's customer database through the kiosk. Such applications can complement the efforts of salespeople and improve the service they can offer to customers.

Instead of bringing a shopping list to the store, a customer also can swipe a loyalty card or enter a phone number at a kiosk called a Retail Store Assistant (RSA),[49] or use a similar device attached to his or her shopping cart.[50] Any information the customer has entered online from home will show up on the associated profile. On the basis of this customer's shopping habits, which are stored in the retailer's database, the RSA provides special offers that match the customer's purchase record. On the back of the coupons that the RSA provides is a map of the store and the location of each item, eliminating the need to explore every aisle. If a printed piece of paper is too cumbersome, this list and information also could be transferred via Bluetooth technology to a mobile device, such as a phone.

Some retailers use hand-held scanners to provide customer service. At The Container Store in Manhattan, customers can register a credit card number at the front counter and get a wireless hand-held scanner. As they walk the aisles, they scan in the barcodes of their desired items and then pay for the purchases when they are finished shopping. The items scanned are then delivered to their homes the same day. The use of these hand-held scanners eliminates the need for customers to carry around bulky items in the store and transport them home. The physical and psychological limits on how much is purchased in a single trip are reduced, so the average customer purchase using this service is ten times greater than that of customers not using the service.[51]

Communicating the Service Promise: The Communications Gap

The fourth factor leading to a customer service gap is the difference between the service promised by the retailer and the service actually delivered. Overstating the service offered raises customer expectations. Then, if the retailer doesn't follow through, expectations exceed perceived service, and customers are dissatisfied. For example, if an Internet site store offers free alterations, but then the customer finds that the alterations are only available for purchases greater than $200, then the customer may be disappointed. Raising expectations too high might bring in more customers initially, but it can also create dissatisfaction and reduce repeat business. The communications gap can be reduced by making realistic commitments and managing customer expectations.

Realistic Commitments   Advertising programs are typically developed by the marketing department, whereas the store operations division delivers the service. Poor communication between these areas can result in a mismatch between an ad campaign's promises and the service the store can actually offer. This problem is illustrated by Holiday Inn's "No Surprises" ad campaign. Market research indicated hotel customers wanted greater reliability in lodging, so Holiday Inn's agency developed a campaign promising no unpleasant surprises. Even though hotel managers didn't feel they could meet the claims promised in the ads, top management accepted the campaign. The campaign raised customer expectations to an unrealistic level and gave customers who did confront an unpleasant surprise an additional reason to be dissatisfied. The campaign was discontinued soon after it started.

Managing Customer Expectations   How can a retailer communicate realistic service expectations without losing business to a competitor that makes inflated service claims? American Airlines' "Why Does It Seem Every Airline Flight Is Late?" ad campaign is an example of a communication program that addresses this issue. In print ads, American recognized its customers' frustration and explained some uncontrollable factors causing the problem: overcrowded airports, scheduling problems, and intense price competition. Then the ads described how American was improving the situation.

Information presented at the point of sale can be used to manage expectations. For example, theme parks and restaurants indicate the waiting time for an attraction or a table. Electronic retailers tell their customers if merchandise is in stock and when customers can expect to receive it. Providing accurate information can increase customer satisfaction even when customers must wait longer than desired.

Sometimes service problems are caused by customers. Customers may use an invalid credit card to pay for merchandise, not take time to try on a suit and have it altered properly, or use a product incorrectly because they fail to read the instructions. Communication programs also can inform customers about their role and responsibility in getting good service and give tips on how to get better service, such as the best times of the day to shop and the retailer's policies and procedures for handling problems.

SERVICE RECOVERY

The delivery of customer service is inherently inconsistent, so service failures are bound to arise. Rather than dwelling on negative aspects of customer problems, retailers should focus on the positive opportunities they generate. Service problems and complaints are an excellent source of information about the retailer's offering (its merchandise and service). Armed with this information, retailers can make changes to increase their customers' satisfaction.

Service problems also enable a retailer to demonstrate its commitment to providing high-quality customer service. By encouraging complaints and handling problems, a retailer has an opportunity to strengthen its relationship with its customers. Effective service recovery efforts significantly increase customer satisfaction, purchase intentions, and positive word of mouth. However, postrecovery satisfaction generally is less than the satisfaction level prior to the service failure.

Most retailers have standard policies for handling problems. If a correctable problem is identified, such as defective merchandise, many retailers will make restitution on the spot and apologize for inconveniencing the customer. The retailer will offer replacement merchandise, a credit toward future purchases, or a cash refund.

In many cases, the cause of the problem may be hard to identify (did the salesperson really insult the customer?), uncorrectable (the store had to close due to bad weather), or a result of the customer's unusual expectations (the customer didn't like his haircut). In these cases, service recovery might be more difficult. The steps in effective service recovery are (1) listen to the customer, (2) provide a fair solution, and (3) resolve the problem quickly.[52]

Listening to Customers

Customers can become very emotional about their real or imaginary problems with a retailer. Often this emotional reaction can be reduced by simply giving customers a chance to get their complaints off their chests.

Store employees should allow customers to air their complaints without interruption. Interruptions can further irritate customers who may already be emotionally upset. It's very hard to reason with or satisfy an angry customer.

Customers want a sympathetic response to their complaints. Thus, store employees need to make it clear that they're happy the problem has been brought to their attention. Satisfactory solutions rarely arise when store employees have an antagonistic attitude or assume that the customer is trying to cheat the store.

Employees also need to listen carefully to determine what the customer perceives to be a fair solution. For example, a hotel employee might assume that a customer who's irritated about a long wait to check in will be satisfied with an apology. But the customer might be expecting to receive a free drink as compensation for the wait. A supermarket employee may brusquely offer a refund for spoiled fruit when the customer is also seeking an apology for the inconvenience of having to return to the store. Store employees shouldn't assume they know what the customer is complaining about or what solution the customer is seeking.[53]

Providing a Fair Solution

When resolving customers' problems, service representatives should listen to customers, provide a fair solution, and resolve the problems quickly.

Customers like to feel that they are being treated fairly. They base their perception of fairness on how they think others were treated in similar situations by the retailer and with other retailers. Customers' evaluations of complaint resolutions are based on distributive fairness and procedural fairness.[54]

Distributive Fairness   **Distributive fairness** is a customer's perception of the benefits received compared with their costs in terms of inconvenience or monetary loss. What seems to be a fair compensation for a service failure for one customer may not be adequate for another. For example, one customer might be satisfied with a rain check for a food processor that was advertised at a discounted price but sold out. This customer feels the low price for the food processor offsets the inconvenience of returning to the store. But another customer may need the food processor immediately, so a rain check won't be adequate compensation for him. To really satisfy this customer, the salesperson would have to locate a store that has the food processor and have it delivered to the customer's house.

Customers typically prefer tangible rather than intangible resolutions to their complaints. A low-cost reward, such as a free soft drink or a $1 discount, communicates more concern to the customer than a verbal apology.

Procedural Fairness   **Procedural fairness** is the perceived fairness of the process used to resolve complaints. Customers consider three questions when evaluating procedural fairness:

1. Did the employee collect information about the situation?
2. Was this information used to resolve the complaint?
3. Did the customer have some influence over the outcome?

Customers typically feel they have been dealt with fairly when store employees follow company guidelines. Guidelines reduce variability in handling complaints and lead customers to believe they're being treated like everyone else. But rigid adherence to guidelines can have negative effects. Store employees need some flexibility in resolving complaints, or customers may feel they had no influence on the resolution.

Resolving Problems Quickly

Customer satisfaction is affected by the time it takes to get an issue resolved. As a general rule, store employees who deal with customers should be made as self-sufficient as possible to handle problems. Customers are more satisfied when the first person they contact can resolve a problem. When customers are referred to several different employees, they waste a lot of time repeating their story. Also, the chance of conflicting responses by store employees increases. Retailers can minimize the time to resolve complaints by reducing the number of people the customer must contact and providing clear instructions.

Resolving customer complaints increases satisfaction. But when complaints are resolved too abruptly, customers might feel dissatisfied because they haven't received enough personal attention. Retailers must recognize the trade-off between resolving the problem quickly and taking time to listen to and show concern for the customer.[55]

SUMMARY

Due to the inherent intangibility and inconsistency of services, providing high-quality customer service is challenging. However, customer service also provides an opportunity for retailers to develop a strategic advantage. Retailers use two basic strategies for providing customer service: the personalized and the standardized approach. The personalized approach relies primarily on sales associates. The standardized approach places more emphasis on developing appropriate rules, consistent procedures, and optimum store designs.

Customers evaluate customer service by comparing their perceptions of the service delivered with their expec-

tations. Thus, to improve service, retailers need to close the gaps between the service delivered and the customer's expectations. This gap may be reduced by knowing what customers expect, setting standards to provide the expected service, providing support so store employees can meet the standards, and realistically communicating the service offered to customers.

Due to inherent inconsistency, service failures are bound to arise. These lapses in service provide an opportunity for retailers to build even stronger relationships with their customers.

KEY TERMS

communication gap, *547*

customer service, *539*

delivery gap, *547*

distributive fairness, *558*

emotional support, *553*

empowerment, *554*

instrumental support, *552*

knowledge gap, *547*

mystery shopper, *551*

personalized approach, *541*

procedural fairness, *559*

service gap, *546*

standardized approach, *542*

standards gap, *547*

GET OUT AND DO IT!

1. **CONTINUING ASSIGNMENT** Go to a local store outlet of the retailer you have selected for the continuing assignment and describe and evaluate the service it offers. What services are offered? Is the service personalized or standardized? Ask the store manager if you can talk to some customers and employees. Choose customers who have made a purchase, customers who have not made a purchase, and customers with a problem (refund, exchange, or complaint). Talk with them about their experiences, write a report describing your conversations, and make suggestions for improving the store's customer service. Ask employees what the retailer does to assist and motivate them to provide good service.

2. Bizrate (www.bizrate.com) is a company that collects information about consumer shopping experiences with electronic retailers. Go to Bizrate's Web site and review the evaluations of different retailers that sell products electronically. How useful is this information to you? What could Bizrate do to make the information more useful?

3. Visit the Lands' End Web site (www.landsend.com) and look for a shirt. How does the Web site help you locate the shirt that you might be interested in buying? How does the customer service offered by the Web site compare to the service you would get at a specialty store like The Gap? A department store? Over the phone with a Lands' End representative?

4. Go to a discount store such as Wal-Mart, a department store, and a specialty store to buy a pair of jeans. Compare and contrast the level of customer service you received in each of the stores. Which store made it easiest to find the pair of jeans you would be interested in buying? Why?

DISCUSSION QUESTIONS AND PROBLEMS

1. For each of these services, give an example of a retailer for which providing the service is critical to its success, then give an example of a retailer for which providing the service is not critical: (a) personal shoppers, (b) home delivery, (c) money-back guarantees, and (d) credit.

2. Nordstrom and McDonald's both are noted for their high-quality customer service, but their approaches to providing this quality service are different. Describe this difference. Why have the retailers elected to use these different approaches?

3. Have you ever worked in a job that required you to provide customer service? If yes, describe the skills you needed and tasks performed for this job. If no, what skills and abilities would you highlight to a potential employer that was interviewing you for a position that included customer service in the job description.

4. Retailing View 19.1 describes how drugstores and discounters are providing health care services for customers. In addition to one-stop shopping convenience, how does this customer service mesh with the store's merchandise to create a strategic advantage and increase customer loyalty?

5. Assume you're the department manager for menswear in a local department store that emphasizes empowering its managers. A customer returns a dress shirt that's no longer in the package in which it was sold. The customer has no receipt, says that when he opened the package he found that the shirt was torn, and wants cash for the price at which the shirt is being sold now.

The shirt was on sale last week when the customer claims to have bought it. What would you do?

6. Consider a situation in which you received poor customer service in a retail store or from a service provider. Did you make the store's management aware of your experience? Whom did you relay this experience to? Have you returned to this retailer? For each of these questions, explain why you did what you did.

7. Gaps analysis provides a systematic method for examining a customer service program's effectiveness. Top management has told an information systems manager that customers are complaining about the long wait to pay for merchandise at the checkout station. Take the role of the systems manager and use the gaps analysis table below to evaluate this problem and suggest possible strategies for reducing the wait time

	Problem Encountered	Strategies to Close this Gap
Knowledge Gap		
Standards Gap		
Delivery Gap		
Communication Gap		

8. How could an effective customer service strategy cut a retailer's costs?

9. Give an example of how a retailer would resolve a customer complaint through procedural fairness. Does the resolution depend on the channel or store format? Explain your reasoning.

10. Consider a recent retail service experience you have had, such as a haircut, doctor's appointment, dinner in a restaurant, bank transaction, or product repair (not an exhaustive list), and answer the questions below:
   a. Describe an excellent service delivery experience.
   b. What made this quality experience possible?
   c. Describe a service delivery experience in which you did not receive the performance that you expected.
   d. What were the problems encountered, and how could they have been resolved?

SUGGESTED READINGS

Bolton, Ruth N.; Grewal, Dhruv; and Michael Levy. "Six Strategies for Competing through Service: An Agenda for Future Research." *Journal of Retailing* 83, no. 1 (2007), pp. 1–4.

Bonomo, Timothy P. *Customer Service: Aiming for Excellence.* Victoria, BC: Trafford Publishing, 2006.

Doane, Darryl, and Rose Slout. *The Customer Service Activity Book: 50 Activities for Inspiring Exceptional Service.* New York: American Management Association, 2005.

Hess, Ronald L., Jr.; Shankar Ganesan; and Noreen M. Klein. "Interactional Service Failures in a Pseudorelationship: The Role of Organizational Attributions." *Journal of Retailing* 83, no. 1 (2007), pp. 79–95.

Lusch, Robert F.; Stephen L. Vargo; and Matthew O'Brien. "Competing through Service: Insights from Service-Dominant Logic." *Journal of Retailing* 83, no. 1 (2007), pp. 5–18.

Rayport, Jeffrey, and Bernard Jaworski. *Best Face Forward: Why Companies Must Improve Their Service Interfaces with Customers.* Boston, MA: Harvard Business School Press, 2005.

Spector, Robert, and Patrick McCarthy. *The Nordstrom Way to Customer Service Excellence.* Hoboken, NJ: John Wiley & Sons, 2005.

Wiles, Michael A. "The Effect of Customer Service on Retailers' Shareholder Wealth: The Role of Availability and Reputation Cues." *Journal of Retailing* 83, no. 1 (2007), pp. 19–31.

Zeithaml, Valarie; Mary Jo Bitner; and Dwayne D. Gremler. *Services Marketing,* 5th ed. New York: McGraw-Hill/Irwin, 2008.

Starting Your Own Retail Business

Starting a retail business can be an enticing and daunting prospect. On the one hand, you can be your own boss, enjoy complete creative control, and reap the full rewards of your hard work. On the other hand, retail business owners must assume large amounts of responsibility, bear the consequences of poor decisions, and ultimately shoulder the blame for the success or failure of the business. Owning your own business involves a great deal of effort, sacrifice, and patience. It is inherently risky, and consequently, fewer than 20 percent of new retail businesses survive to the five-year mark. Yet the rewards of successfully navigating the unpredictable landscape of business ownership can be enormous, both personally and financially. You might grow your business and become the next Sam Walton (Wal-Mart), Maxine Clark (Build-A-Bear Workshop), or John Mackey (Whole Food Markets).

The sense of accomplishment garnered from creating and sustaining a thriving enterprise of one's own is immense. Retail owners have the uniquely satisfying opportunity to craft a tangible expression of their own professional visions, talents, and hard work. In addition, they can contribute value to their communities by creating jobs, strengthening the economy, and providing excellent service to customers. Those who join the successful 20 percent of retail entrepreneurs often earn sufficient financial rewards to live securely and comfortably according to their own standards.

The purpose of this appendix is to demonstrate broadly how practically to achieve these goals by starting a retail business. A wealth of information discusses entrepreneurship, retailing, and business startups—and all of it could not possibly be contained within the confines of an appendix. Instead, this appendix provides an overview of the process and offers some further resources that anyone with serious aspirations for starting their own retail business can use to take the first step.

DO YOU HAVE WHAT IT TAKES TO BE A SUCCESSFUL ENTREPRENEUR?

Before starting a business, it is important to take an inventory of skills. Debate continues about the inherent nature of entrepreneurial success. Can someone acquire entrepreneurial skills, or are successful entrepreneurs just people with an innate ability to see and seize an opportunity? It seems that the answer lies somewhere in between.

The skills needed to be a successful entrepreneur can by divided into two broad skill categories: technical training and personal characteristics. To start a retail business, it is very important that the owner possess business skills. Do you understand how to read a financial statement and evaluate your performance and viability? Can you make an effective presentation to potential investors? Do you have an understanding of what customers want? Can you manage the people who work for you? Do you have an understanding of how to launch an electronic channel for your retail business?

For those lacking these business skills, many major universities offer online degrees in a wide variety of disciplines, including business, as well as the option of full-time enrollment. It may be difficult to balance family, work, and school, but owning a business will be just as time consuming. This process can be a litmus test for a person's entrepreneurial work ethic.

A work ethic is a quality that cannot be taught, and for entrepreneurs, it is vital. Passion for a chosen business is another quality that cannot be taught. No one will be looking over a retail business owner's shoulder to ensure he or she is doing everything possible to guarantee

*This appendix was prepared by Christian Tassin MSE 2008, University of Florida, under the supervision of Professor Barton Weitz.

the success of the venture. Can you maintain the level of energy required to sustain a business? Can you handle rejection from investors and still have the confidence to keep going? Seeing opportunity is another skill that is difficult to acquire, but it can be learned through practice. A person can train his or her mind to look for ways to improve the things that need improvement. Visit a retail store to evaluate their practices. What works? What does not? Where is the opportunity to improve on the qualities that do not work? How can value be created from improving on the shortcomings of current business practices?

DEVELOPING A CONCEPT FOR THE RETAIL VENTURE

The genesis of any business venture starts with an idea. A retail store concept should satisfy three objectives. First, the pursuit should be something that the retailer is passionate about. With the intense effort required for successful entrepreneurship, why would a person want to be involved in something that he or she does not enjoy? Sustainability in a retail business becomes virtually impossible if the owner does not have a burning desire to see it succeed. Second, the concept must provide sufficient value to its customers. The purpose of a business is to make a profit, and if people are not willing to pay for the products or services offered, then failure is assured. Third, the concept must provide an offering that is differentiated—not available from competitors and not something that competitors can easily copy.

An important issue to consider is the application of intellectual property to the retail concept. Do you have a patentable concept? Do you have a trademark for your brand name and logo? If an entrepreneur crafts a business venture on company time at his or her day job, it is considered that company's property. Working in an industry related to the retail concept can make this ownership even easier to prove. Will the concept compete with an existing employer? Many companies require that employees sign non-compete clauses. If an idea violates one of those agreements, the business could be over before it even gets started. If you believe your concept or business processes is unique, or are not sure if you can legally execute your retail concept, an attorney who deals in intellectual property can be a great resource.

THE "QUICK SCREEN"

The first step in deciding whether to start a retail business is to examine the retail concept in detail. Essentially, the prospective retailer wants to determine whether he or she merely has an interesting idea or a viable opportunity. Four questions that help determine the viability of an opportunity are as follows:

1. Does it create or add significant value for customers?
2. Does it solve a significant problem or meet a significant demand or need in the marketplace for which someone is willing to pay a premium?
3. Is there a large enough market and sufficient margins to generate profits?
4. Is there a good fit between the skills of the management team and the skills required to operate the business?

If an idea does not fulfill these four requirements, the potential retailer needs to revise it, or else create a new one. For example, if you love the beach and want to start a retail store that sells bathing suits and beach accessories, but you also live in Colorado, the concept lacks the key elements of success. The market for beach goods will not be significant enough, no financially realizable value is being created for the people in the community, and even with a competent team, the idea would be unattractive. Answers to these questions may not be as readily apparent for different concepts, but this simplified example illustrates the effectiveness that the "Quick Screen" can have in testing an idea for true value. Revising an idea is much more efficient in the planning stages than it would be mid-execution.

A potential revision of the beachwear retail concept in Colorado would be to open a sporting goods store named, say, "Mountain Sporting Goods," that caters to people who participate in mountain sports such as skiing, hiking, climbing, and rafting. This concept passes the "Quick Screen," in that it creates value for customers, fulfills a need, has good market potential, and has a suitable risk/reward balance. If a potential venture passes this quick test, it is time to become immersed in the details of its potential by preparing a business plan.

PREPARING A BUSINESS PLAN

The preparation of a business plan is an excellent way to take a hard look at the concept in a structured, practical way. A well-done business plan can help mitigate or address the potential risks involved in starting a business before they actually occur. By thoroughly considering both the merit and the execution strategy of a vision, a prospective retailer can significantly improve its chances of success. A good business plan should concisely and effectively demonstrate the value of the concept to others—especially potential investors. The more prepared the retailer is to demonstrate and execute the value of the proposition, the less risk it poses, and the better investment opportunity the retail concept presents.

Business plans are dynamic and should evolve with the business. There is no set formula for a business plan, but there are some elements that every good business plan should include. First and foremost, a business plan should be well written, concise, and professional. No one will ever invest in a new venture if the business plan is verbose, boring, sloppy, or unprofessional. Nowhere is this more important than in the executive summary. Investors often see hundreds of business plans, and many of them read no further than the executive summary. If a plan does not grab their attention, or inadvertently casts a negative light, the venture proposal will not make it past a cursory reading at best. Structurally, a business plan should include at least the following content:

1. Executive summary.
2. Environmental analysis (trends, customers, competitors, economy).
3. Description of the retail concept and strategy (target market, retail format, competitive advantage).
4. Implementation plan, including the approach for attracting customers.
5. Team, or the other people involved in business.
6. Funding request.
7. Financial plan.

The key points of writing a retail business plan are illustrated here with the creation of a fictitious retail business. The examples include less detail than an actual business plan would require, but they are designed as a starting point from which the entrepreneur can initiate further research. The overarching themes also can be applied to a wide variety of retail businesses.

Environmental Analysis

The scope of the environmental analysis depends on the long-term objective. If the retailer's objective is simply to operate one or two outlets, the environmental analysis should focus on the local environment, such as the trade area of the store, as discussed in Chapter 8. However, if the long-term objective is to open and operate multiple retail outlets, the retailer needs to examine all the elements in the macro environment, such as industry size and trends and the competition and profitability of the industry, as discussed in Chapter 5. The elements in the environmental analysis detailed next apply to supporting a venture that starts in Colorado Springs, with ambitions to expand regionally and potentially nationally.

Industry Size and Trends   Various databases can provide detailed information about industry-wide figures. For example, Hoover's Online and IBISWorld US Industry reports both provide detailed industry data, analyses of publicly traded companies, and customer demographics. Many libraries subscribe to these types of services, and a local librarian can be helpful in providing guidance to access to them. Many publicly traded companies offer information on their Web sites, and they are required to publish financial data with the Securities and Exchange Commission. Trade organizations and publications such as the Sporting Goods Manufacturers Association (www.sgma.com), the National Sporting Goods Association (www.nsga.com), and *Sporting Goods Dealer* often provide detailed information about specific retail sectors. Census data, available at www.census.gov/, give great insight into the population of the focal community in terms of companies and people. For example, there are 625 specialty-line sporting goods establishments in Colorado, according to the Census Bureau.

For smaller local businesses, it can more difficult to find information. Knowledge of the local area therefore can be a great asset. Also, gathering information from the customers and suppliers of competitors in the industry can provide valuable information. Resourcefulness and persistence is a key to discovering certain information, and it can be very beneficial to take the time to do so. Visit similar retailers and look at what they have to offer. Where is the unmet need? How can a new retailer rise to meet it?

Market size also is critical. How much money is being generated in the specific retail area? How is the money distributed within the industry? For example, the sporting goods industry in the United States is expected to generate $53.7 billion in sales in 2007. This number is a significant starting point, in that it illustrates the overall monetary potential of the industry, but more focused data also are necessary.

Research shows that the sporting goods industry is highly fragmented, with many small retailers rather than dominant control by larger players. Therefore, opportunity appears to exist for the growth and expansion of a smaller retailer. Information like this is important to investors, because it can be used to illustrate that the industry is ready for a new retail business concept. For example, the implementation plan for the new store could demonstrate the growth potential that would enable it to consolidate smaller businesses and gain a significant market share in the sporting goods industry. The correlation of industry data to real opportunity makes for a compelling narrative that entices financiers to invest in the company. In other words, a implementation plan should demonstrate how an interesting opportunity can provide a high return on investment.

To find where the specific opportunity lies, industry data must be whittled down to the niche level. In the United States, sporting goods sales derive from retailers such as Sports Authority, Wal-Mart, and a multitude of smaller retailers. These stores sell equipment, apparel, and shoes for every sporting need imaginable and all across the country. For simplicity, Mountain Sporting Goods might focus only on sporting equipment, which comprises 46 percent of the sporting goods industry. It can further narrow its focus by defining what mountain sports mean for "Mountain Sporting Goods." What mountain sports segments will be targeted?

Examination of the sports equipment data makes it apparent that camping, fishing tackle, hunting, and firearms account for 6.9, 9.0, and 12.1 percent (hunting and firearms combined) of the sports equipment market, respectively. Should the concept therefore be expanded to include these segments, in addition to skiing, hiking, rafting, and climbing? A moral disagreement with hunting might be a factor to consider as well. Does the significant financial opportunity outweigh the ethical uncertainty that selling hunting equipment might cause? What are the federal and local licenses required to sell firearms? Will the store sell tags for hunting certain animals? The reconciliation of these types of conflicting issues will help refine the concept.

Target Customers   Another critical element is defining the target market. What age demographic is the typical customer? What is his or her socioeconomic status and gender? Where do they live in relation to the proposed store location? Where do they work? Will the store provide goods for the whole family or focus on individuals? How will the retail concept provide them with value? Will it compete on the basis of low prices or differentiated, higher-quality products? Finding the right balance of these factors is key. An overly narrow focus can be problematic, because it implies insufficient demand for the offering. A focus that is too broad also can hinder the retailer's ability to forge its own identity. Research findings might narrow these options. For example, if Mountain Sporting Goods opened in Aspen, Colorado, it would be reasonable for it to deal in specialty, high-quality, high-price goods because of the affluent customer base that resides there.

Competitors   The final step in analyzing the retail environment is to study potential competitors. How does the retail concept compare with those of others who offer similar merchandise? How do these competitors reach their customers? What kind of advertising strategy do they use? How long have they been in business? Do they have an e-commerce component to their business? How similar are the products they sell? How high are their goods priced? How well do their employees know their product? What is their store layout like?

Many larger sporting goods retailers carry a broad array of sporting products, so naturally, there will be some overlap in what Wal-Mart sells and what Mountain Sporting Goods offers. How important is this overlap? Wal-Mart may take a small portion of customers, but it offers only a general sampling of what Mountain Sporting Goods specializes in providing. Sports Authority would be a bigger threat though, because it offers only sporting goods, spanning the spectrum of equipment, shoes, apparel, camping equipment, and more. Wal-Mart and Sports Authority also can leverage their sizes to compete on price more easily than can a small retail business. Factors such as these must be considered when establishing the new retailer's strategic position. Initially, Mountain Sporting Goods would have to compete on the basis of its ability to offer more differentiated specialty products than some of the bigger chains, and create an environment that draws customers to the store. After a good deal of growth, it might achieve economies of scale by purchasing high volumes of products, which lowers costs and increases its ability to compete on price.

The other segment of sporting goods retailers, which makes up the majority of the industry, is local businesses. Local research as described in the Appendix to Chapter 2, will be very important in determining local competitors' strengths and weaknesses. Do some reconnaissance work to see how competitors operate, and put yourself in the role of the customer to browse their shops. How big is the store? Does it feel cramped? Were you treated well by employees? How knowledgeable were they about the products they sell? Did they have the range of goods that you desire? Were their hours of operation adequate to meet local needs? How can a new store create a more pleasurable shopping experience?

Other issues to consider are the location of competitors, their proximity to the desired demographic, parking lot layout, building condition, and so forth. If Mountain Sporting Goods sells almost the same goods for the same price as a competitor, but customers do not have to drive as far, can park more easily, and can enjoy a nicer facility, Mountain Sporting Goods gains a distinct competitive advantage.

Retail Concept

After completing the industry analysis, it is time to combine the original conceptual idea with the data uncovered through industry research in the form of a company description. Who is Mountain Sporting Goods? To whom will it sell its products? How does it do so better than others? How can it exploit competitive advantages to make the company grow?

Mountain Sporting Goods has decided to include the following information in its company description: It will locate in Colorado Springs, Colorado, to exploit the rapid growth of the community and the prevalence of a young, ecocentric population. Colorado Springs has an unmet need for ecofriendly stores and a large enough population of people who are willing to pay a premium for that attribute. Therefore, the store will sell the best quality, most environmentally friendly skiing, hiking, whitewater rafting, mountain climbing, and camping equipment available. Customers will range in age from 23 to 35 years, and they will place environmental friendliness at the top of their priority list. These young single or coupled professionals without children have a fair amount of disposable income.

In turn, the management for the company must have an extensive background in sustainability and a passion for outdoor activities. As Mountain Sporting Goods gains customers and increases sales revenue, it might begin to acquire other, similarly sized firms to gain market share. These firms must be geographically accessible so that the company can pool resources and increase its purchasing power, as well as reduce costs through the consolidation of tasks such as distribution, purchasing, and accounting. In this way, the firm will be able to achieve the benefits of size and develop economies of scale.

A business plan must present these facets of the business in such a way that they draw the reader into the concept. The company description segment therefore should illustrate the founder's passion for the concept. It should also emphasize the opportunities that it creates and explain the competitive advantages that enable those opportunities to reach fruition.

The research and brainstorming accomplished thus far are detailed in the remainder of the business plan, so the following portions are the most finely detailed. The potential investor should have been able to recognize the value of the potential business already; the remainder of the plan provides proof of that value. The marketing, operations, management, and financial segments of the business plan thus tell the investor how the concept will be executed, what the retailer intends to sell, who will execute the process, how much money will be required to make it happen, and the money that can be earned as a result.

THE IMPLEMENTATION PLAN

The main goal of an implementation plan is to determine how the retail business will attract consumers in the target market and convert them into loyal customers. This essential portion of a retail business plan not only describes how the company will position itself in the market but also outlines the components required to make it a reality. The plan should describe the following elements in detail:

1. *Merchandise offered* Number and breadth of lines to be carried, styles of merchandise and accessories, names of suppliers, supplier credit terms, quality of merchandise, opening stock, inventory levels, and expected turnover rate (see Chapters 12–14).

2. *Customer Services Offered* Customer service levels and contact provided, credit policies, exchange and return policies, alterations, and gift wrapping (Chapter 19).

3. *Facilities* Store appearance, any renovation required, interior décor, storefront, layout, lighting, window displays, wall displays, and overall atmosphere (Chapter 18).

4. *Location* Buy, lease, or rent; terms of contract; local ordinances; zoning regulations; parking; accessibility; local demographics; and conditions for remodeling (Chapters 7 and 8).

5. *Pricing* Price ranges to offer, competitive pricing, profitable pricing, margins, markdowns, and discount prices (Chapter 15)

6. *Promotion* One-year promotional plan, advertising budgets, selection of media, cost of local media options, promotional displays, cooperative advertising efforts, and public relations (Chapter 16).

7. *Employees* Compensational plan and wage scale to be offered, job specifications, employee training program, career and promotion schedule, employee benefits, social security taxes, sources and types of employees to hire (e.g., age, gender, appearance, education level), and policy on family employees (Chapters 9 and 17).

8. *Security* Security guards, fire and theft alarms, computer security system, windows, locks, merchandise protection services, liability insurance, and other insurance (Chapter 17).

9. *Equipment* Cash registers, sales desk, computer systems, display racks, office equipment, office supplies, telephone systems, management information system, software, security, and personal computer requirements (Chapter 10).

10. *Controls* Inventory control and replenishment methods and financial performance analysis. (Chapters 6 and 13).

Team

Who will help to execute the vision? One of the most important factors in starting a business is finding a group of people whose skill sets compliment those of the founder. It is virtually impossible for one person to possess all of the requisite skills for creating and growing a business. For example, if Mountain Sporting Goods intends to follow through with its plans to acquire other businesses, it would be beneficial to bring someone into the group with experience in the area of mergers and acquisitions. Also, the owner/manager of Mountain Sporting Goods has a background in sustainability, which represents a great asset in setting up a business whose cornerstone is environmental awareness.

The team section showcases the talent of the people who will run the retail startup. It is both a "who's who" of the business venture and a way to assure investors that their money will be handled by people of quality. This assurance is especially effective if someone with experience in starting retail stores joins the team. Such a person lends significant credibility to the business endeavor, as well as a great deal of sage advice. Experienced people do not necessarily have to be paid employees or managers but instead could serve on a board of advisors or board of directors. Each person should be listed, with his or her credentials outlined and role within the company clarified.

Funding Request

One of the objectives of a business plan is to seek financing and show how the firm might use investors' money, whether debt or equity financing. For a small retailer, a loan request (debt financing) is more common. If Mountain Sporting Goods' aspiration is to be a local lifestyle business, it still needs to show where the money is going and how the lender will receive a return on its investment through the company's ability to generate enough revenue to repay the loan, as well as the timing of the repayments.

A company with higher aims might seek venture capital support for its major growth. The owner/manager of this company would negotiate with venture capitalists about what portion of their equity should be provided for the desired financial support. Investors would receive shares (equity) in the company in exchange for the financing that they provide.

At a certain point, probably within a few years, venture capitalists typically can monitize those shares after the company is bought by another company, has its initial public offering (IPO), or buys the investors' share of the company back. For example, Mountain Sporting Goods might explain how it will execute its growth plans and generate a return on investment for its financiers. At a specified time, Mountain Sporting Goods will have enough revenue growth and profits to go public, represent a significant enough threat to larger competitors that they buy it out, or pay back the investors at the desired rate of return. Investors base their evaluation of the venture on how much they predict the company will be worth at the designated time of sale, IPO, or buy back. If they believe the company can generate the intended value that they seek, they will invest.

Financial Plan

The financial plan can be one of the more intimidating aspects of business plan writing, but it also is essential to determine the value of the retail business. The financial plan provides investors with information that enables them to decide whether the business concept is worth their risk. Taking the time to learn how to create the financial plan therefore has great value. Moreover, the financial plan offers the prospective retailer a detailed understanding of the major contributing factors that might result in success or failure. With this knowledge, the retailer can safeguard the business and deal with accomplished businesspeople and investors with greater confidence. Financial projections vary depending on the degree of complexity sought for the financing, but the following discussion provides a simple overview of the process. The only way to learn, though, is to roll up your sleeves and do it.

Financial projections for a completely new business are especially difficult, in that they must be based solely on assumptions because there are no historical data. No one has uncovered the secret to predicting the future, but it is possible to make educated estimates. The key is finding where to start. What are the initial elements that an entrepreneur requires to build a financial model of a potential venture?

The income statement, cash flow, balance sheet, financing, and break-even analysis constitute the basics that must be included. The purpose of these projections is to tell investors when the business will actually become profitable and how fast it will grow. The groundwork laid by the implementation plan is a good place to start.

The elements required to reach target customers indicate both startup and fixed costs, which represent the basis of the financial projections. For example, if Mountain Sporting Goods has done enough research, it will have narrowed down how much the location lease or mortgage will cost and, from merchandise sources, learned how much the inventory will cost. These and many other factors will be "known" entities, from which the fixed startup and operating costs can be established. Other miscellaneous startup elements, such as legal fees, also should be included.

After the costs have been established, sales figures must be projected. There are two methods for estimating financial statements: the comparable method and the build-up method. The retailer should employ both methods and compare their results to come up with the final projection. The comparable method uses financial data from a similar company or ratios from the industry, then compares them to the projected data for the concept company. The build-up method examines sales and builds expected revenues and expenses by determining what they might be on an average day, such as the products sold on an average day, the types of products, the buyers and how many people buy, and the amount each would spend. By establishing an average day's sales, the retailer can extrapolate these data to months, years, and so on. The data also can be adjusted for seasonal variances, which is important for any retail business. After reconciling any differences between the estimates produced by the two different methods, all that remains is to construct the financial statements for inclusion in the business plan.

The business plan requires perpetual refining and updating as new information, such as opportunities and threats in the environment that prompt a change in the retail concept, becomes available. The business plan also should be referred to and used at all stages of growth. Just as in a business's infancy, it remains important to evaluate who it is, what it does, and how it will do so on a continuing basis.

GETTING STARTED

Now that the business plan has been completed, there are a few other miscellaneous costs and issues that must be considered. With a strong retail concept, the business must address certain procedural processes. One of the most important is to set up its legal structure. Will the company be a sole proprietorship, a partnership, or an incorporated firm? These structures all incur unique costs, though the least expensive is a sole proprietorship. Sole proprietorship, however, does not remove any personal assets from the responsibility owed to creditors for the failure or success of the business. If an entrepreneur elects to sell shares of the company to investors, he or she will need to have the appropriate structure in place, which often requires the assistance of an attorney, who can help file for the appropriate business structure that shields personal assets from certain risks and that has the most advantageous tax implications. Another necessary regulatory step is to file for an Employer Identification Number (EIN) or Federal Tax Identification Number, which is required by law to operate a business.

Assuming that the company finds the financing required to launch the retail concept, the entrepreneur is now staring at the precipice of opportunity. The groundwork laid by the business plan now can be put to excellent use. It is a time of mixed emotions. The plan that the retailer has toiled so long and hard to craft will soon be battle tested. Theory will be put into practice, and the owner will determine its true value according to the response of the market. Will you achieve the fulfilling personal and financial success to which you aspire? The only way to know is take that first step off the edge.

ADDITIONAL SOURCES OF INFORMATION

Bond, Ronald L. *Retail in Detail: How to Start and Manage a Small Retail Business.* Irvine, CA: Entrepreneur Press, 2005.

Davis, Charlene. *Start Your Own Clothing Store and More.* Irvine, CA: Entrepreneur Press, 2007.

Dion, Jim and Ted Topping. *Start & Run a Retail Business.* 2nd ed. Bellingham, WA: Self-Counsel Press, 2007.

Entrepreneur Press. *Start Your Own Successful Retail Business.* Irvine, CA: Entrepreneur Press, 2003.

Mikaelsen, Debbra and Pamela Skillings. *FabJob Guide to Become a Boutique Owner.* Calgary, Alberta, Canada: FabJob Guides, 2007.

Schroeder, Carol L. *Specialty Shop Retailing: Everything You Need to Know to Run Your Own Store.* 3rd ed. Indianapolis, IN: John Wiley & Sons, 2007.

APPENDIX B
Starting a Franchise Business

Like hot dogs, baseball, and apple pie, franchising in an American institution. A proven means to realize the entrepreneurial dream, franchising also is taking over much of the retail trade in the United States. This appendix explores franchising options in terms of their merits and drawbacks. With more than 2,300 franchises to choose from, finding the best one can be almost as hard as starting a business.

Franchises are popular largely because of their historical success. A 1999 study by the U.S. Chamber of Commerce found that 91 percent of new franchises remained in business after seven years, compared with only 20 percent of new, individual start-up businesses.[1] But not all franchises are secure investments. Arthur Treacher's Fish and Chips, Jerry Lewis Theaters, and Chicken Delight all have one thing in common: They failed. As a result, thousands of dreams were shattered, and millions of dollars were lost. Buying a franchise can be a dream come true, or it can be a nightmare. The key is buying smart, which requires planning and investigating before signing a contract. Franchising can be a very satisfactory method of starting a business. It also can be extremely rewarding, both personally and financially, and it offers ownership and decision-making privileges not afforded by working for someone else.

Some interesting franchise facts to consider:

- The franchise concept began in the 1850s when Singer Sewing Machine Company (franchisor) sold sales rights to independent entrepreneurs (franchisees) in an effort to raise business capital.
- Today, more than 70 percent of all hotel properties are franchises.
- McDonald's was one of the first companies to sell franchises internationally in the 1970s.
- Fast food is the top franchise industry.
- Subway has the most franchised stores in the world, with more than 26,000 units.
- Subway's international growth initiatives include the addition of 1,000 stores to China by 2017.
- Top U.S. franchise trends include children's specialty services, do-it-yourself meal preparation, and senior-care services.

THE BASICS OF FRANCHISING

So how does franchising work? Basically, the franchisor (the company) sells the rights to use the business trademark, service mark, trade name, or other commercial symbol of that company to the franchisee for a one-time franchise fee, which might range anywhere from $0 to $225,000 (the franchise fee for Subway is approximately $15,000). In addition to the franchise fee, the franchisor charges an ongoing royalty fee, typically expressed as a percentage of gross monthly sales. Ongoing royalty fees range from nothing to 10 percent (the royalty fee for Subway is 8 percent). So for example, if a Subway shop generates $20,000 in sales in a given month, the franchisee must pay the franchisor $1,600 (8 percent × $20,000). Some franchisors instead calculate the ongoing royalty fee on a sliding scale, such that the percentage fee decreases as sales increase beyond preestablished thresholds. Suppose the monthly sales threshold for a hypothetical franchise is $50,000. For the first $50,000 of sales, the ongoing royalty fee charged is 6 percent, or $3,000, but for sales of more than

*This appendix was prepared by Professor Tracy Meyer, University of North Carolina Wilmington.

$50,000, the franchisor collects a 3 percent royalty fee. Therefore, if sales for a one-month period total $80,000, the royalty fee equals $3,900, rather than the $4,800 that would have been due if the sliding scale were not in place. The sliding scale thus encourages franchisees to continue to find ways to increase sales volume.

Attractions of Franchise Ownership

When considering the franchise option, potential franchisees must understand the attractions and drawbacks of buying a franchise versus starting a retail business from scratch. There are many reasons to consider franchise ownership, including the success rate, which results partially from the proven business model that the franchisor offers. Success also results from the unique relationship between the franchisor and the franchisee, in which both parties benefit from the success of the franchisee. To get franchisees off to a good start, most franchisors provide off- and onsite training, location analysis assistance, advertising, and sometimes a protected territory (i.e., no other franchise may open a store within a certain radius of the first store). Some franchisors even provide financing or offer third-party financing opportunities.

Drawbacks to Franchise Ownership

However, there are also several drawbacks to franchise ownership. In addition to money that must be paid to the franchisor, the franchisee needs financing available for start-up costs, including renting or purchasing office/retail space, modifying the space according to the guidelines of the franchisor (e.g., paint colors, flooring, lighting, layout), signage, opening inventory, and equipment. For example, a traditional Subway restaurant in the United States creates upfront costs ranging from $79,050 to $212,800, excluding the $15,000 franchise fee. The variation in the cost estimates is primarily due to the cost of leasehold improvements, which can range from $42,000 to $105,000.[2]

In addition to the capital costs, the franchisee must adhere to the franchisor's rules and operating guidelines. In many cases, the franchisee is required to purchase its operating materials from the franchisor, especially in fast-food franchises that rely on standardized products across franchises for the success of the brand. The franchisor also might require the franchisee to purchase the equipment needed to offer a new product, such as fryers at a Burger King or beds at a Holiday Inn. The hours of operation and days of the year that the business is allowed to close also may be dictated by the franchisor.

Finally, sales and profits can be hurt by events outside the control of the franchisee. For example, in 2005, a scam artist reported she had found a severed finger in her Wendy's chili; in response, franchise sales dropped significantly in the subsequent weeks.[3] In another case, a Jackson-Hewitt franchisee actually was caught falsifying tax returns to get larger refunds for its clients, which enabled it to collect higher fees.[4] Whether true or false, such incidents harm the image of the entire franchise system and materially influence consumers' future purchase decisions.

FRANCHISE EVALUATION PROCESS

The key to making a smart purchase of a franchise is taking the necessary time to research franchise opportunities thoroughly. The five steps outlined next offer a methodical approach to the decision process.

Step 1: Initial investigation.
Step 2: Formal request for information from franchisors.
Step 3: Interviews.
Step 4: Evaluation of fit.
Step 5: Choice of franchise.

Step 1: Initial Investigation

As a potential franchisee, the best way to begin a search for franchise opportunities is to consider franchise businesses that seem fundamentally appealing. To determine if a business operates as a franchise, look through *The Franchise Handbook*, a quarterly magazine, or simply visit the company's Web site. Also consider attending franchise trade shows, such as the National Franchise & Business Opportunities Show. Shows travel throughout cities all over North America and offer an excellent way to gain a closer look at what the industry has to offer (www.franchiseshowinfo.com). Potential franchisees should pick five to ten franchises that look interesting and affordable. The due diligence process starts with collecting all information available about each business.

Step 2: Formal Request for Information from Franchisors

After completing the initial information review, if the franchise is still of interest, the potential franchisee should formally request information directly from the franchisor. Most franchisors provide a link on their Web sites (usually at the very bottom of the page) that allows potential franchisees to fill out an online form requesting information. The forms vary dramatically in the amount of information they require. Beyond the basics of name and address, the form may require information relative to education, work experience, personal financial status, and references.

Franchising is governed by the Federal Trade Commission's Franchise and Business Opportunity Rule,[5] which requires franchisors to provide full disclosure of the information that a prospective franchisee needs to make a rational decision about whether to invest in the franchise. The information appears in the form of a Uniform Franchise Offering Circular (UFOC). All 50 states use the same UFOC, though each state retains the right to impose stricter provisions if it so desires. The UFOC lists lawsuits against the company and provides revenue and earnings figures. Franchisors must provide a copy of the UFOC at least 10 days prior to the signing of any contract or the exchange of any money. A side-by-side comparison of the UFOCs of several franchisors can reveal crucial differences in costs and corporate support.

Step 3: Interviews

Potential Franchisee Interviews Franchisor   The interview process goes both ways. The potential franchisee interviews the franchisor, and at the same time, the franchisor is interviewing the potential franchisee. From the perspective of the potential franchisee, understanding the historical success rate of franchisees, the territories that are available, the extent of training and ongoing support provided, and the advertising support offered represent key questions. The financial strength of the franchisor is also of great consequence, because it is important to be confident that the franchisor will be successful for many years ahead.

Franchisor Interviews Potential Franchisee   The franchisor will want to interview the prospective franchisee to determine if he or she possesses the desire and skill set needed to succeed, such as the prospective franchisee's management and people skills and willingness to learn. Does the applicant possess basic business skills? Does the prospective franchisee have access to sufficient capital? These qualities are important to the successful operation of a franchise. The franchisor also wants to be sure that the applicant understands what owning a franchise will require, in terms of both time and money.

Potential Franchisee Interviews Other Franchisees   Assuming the process is proceeding satisfactorily, the prospective franchisee should interview existing franchisees to gain information about any issues or problems that existing franchisees have experienced with the franchisor. The prospective franchisee should ask tough questions, such as the following: Do you have any complaints about the business? How many hours a week do you devote to the business? Is it hard to find staffing? If you had to do it over again, would you purchase the same franchise? The existing franchisee also might have advice to offer. At this point, it may become apparent that some aspects of operating this franchise business had not been previously considered, good and bad!

Step 4: Evaluation of Fit

The gathered information can now be used to determine if the franchise represents a good opportunity. An evaluation of fit requires the prospective franchisee to sift through the information he or she has obtained and outline both the positives and the negatives associated with owing the business. Assuming the financial commitment is plausible and the amount of time required to run the business sounds reasonable, the potential franchisee also should consider if this work is what he or she wants to do. The purchase also may require the move to a new city. These are all things to consider before narrowing the search too much.

Step 5: Choice of a Franchise

This is it! Having completed the information gathering and evaluation process, the time is right to choose a franchise. Recall that the most important element is making sure that the basic idea of the business sounds appealing. At this point, the potential franchisee should solicit the advice of an accountant to review the financials, a lawyer to review the franchise agreement, and potentially a banker to assist with the financing. The potential franchisee also should know exactly what he or she is getting into before committing.

Diligence in following these five steps improves the odds that the potential franchisee transforms into a proud owner of a *successful* franchise.

ADDITIONAL READING

Federal Trade Commission Facts for Consumers: Franchise and Business Opportunities
www.ftc.gov/bcp/edu/pubs/consumer/invest/inv07.pdf

International Franchise Association
www.franchise.org/defaultindustry.aspx

The American Franchisee Association
www.franchisee.org/

Entrepreneur magazine
www.entrepreneur.com/franchiseopportunities/index.html

The U.S. Chamber of Commerce Small Business Center
www.uschamber.com/sb/business/tools/franch_m.asp

1. www.atfranchise.com/franchise_facts.php (accessed July 19, 2007).
2. www.subway.com/subwayroot/development/05dev/financial/index.aspx (accessed July 18, 2007).
3. www.snopes.com/horrors/food/chili.asp (accessed July 19, 2007).
4. money.cnn.com/2007/04/16/smbusiness/jackson_hewitt/index.htm?section= money_topstories (accessed July 19, 2007).
5. www.ftc.gov/bcp/franchise/16cfr436.shtm (accessed July 19, 2007).

Cases

Cases	1	2	3	4	5	6	7	8	9	10	11	12	13	14	15	16	17	18	19	C
																				CHAPTER
1 Tractor Supply Company	P	P			P														S	
2 Rainforest Café	P	S					S											S		
3 Build-A-Bear Workshop	P	P																		C
4 Wal-Mart and Corporate Social Responsibility	P								S							S				
5 Should Retailers Use Blogs?			P	S												S				
6 Mall Away	S	S	P																	
7 Sanchez Family Buys Bicycles				P																
8 Retailing in India	P	S		S	P															
9 Diamonds: From Mine to Market				S	P					P			S							
10 Sav A Lot		P			P													S		C
11 Ahold						P			S											
12 College Age Apparel Market	S	S			P											P				
13 Tiffany's/Blue Nile					S	P														
14 Stephanie's Boutique							P													
15 Hutch								P												
16 Home Depot					S				P											
17 Avon			S		S				P											
18 Nordstrom Revamps its Loyalty Program											P								S	
19 Nolan's												P							S	
20 Hughe's													P							
21 McFadden's													P							
22 Selling A Product to Wal-Mart														P						
23 How Much for a Good Smell?															P					
24 Promoting a Sale															S	P				
25 Macy's Rebranding					S											P				
26 Restaurant Promotion	S	S														P	P			
27 Enterprise					S												P		S	
28 Diamond in the Rough																	P			
29 Grocery Store Layout																		P		
30 Sephora			S		S													P	S	
31 Discmart																	S	P		
32 Nordstrom						S			S									P		
33 Lindy's Bridal Shoppe						S	S						S					S		C
34 Apple			S	S												S	P		S	
35 Starbucks					P											S	S			C
36 Yankee Candle														S						C
37 PetSmart		S		S	S				S							P		S		
38 Interviewing for a Management Trainee Position	P								S							S				

P Primary Use

S Secondary Use

C Comprehensive

CASE 1   Tractor Supply Company—Targeting the Hobby Farmer

Most people have never heard of the Tractor Supply (TSC) Company, a large and fast growing retailer with over $2 billion in annual sales and 700 stores. Its origins date to 1938, when Charles E. Schmidt Sr. established a mail-order tractor parts business. Pursuant to the success of his first retail store in Minot, North Dakota, he opened additional stores to serve the needs of local farmers. But eventually the TSC's sales stagnated because small farms and ranches were being acquired by large farming and ranching corporations. These large agricultural firms buy supplies and equipment directly from manufacturers rather than through local farm supply stores like TSC.

TARGET MARKET

Since the early 1990's, TSC has targeted a growing group of people interested in recreational farming and ranching. Called "sundowners," "U-turners," "hobby farmers," "ruralpolitans," "micropolitans", "gentlemen farmers", and "X-urbanites," these people have turned to farming to escape the hubbub of urban and suburban life. They are drawn to what they believe is a more private, simple, and stressfree lifestyle. They typically live on five to 20 acres in a rural community outside a metropolitan area where they work at a full-time profession, using some of their earnings to keep their farm in operation. Many of them are the sons and daughters of traditional production farmers who inherited the family farm and decided to keep it running. Today less than 10 percent of the company's customers classify themselves as full-time farmers or ranchers, and many of its customers do not farm at all.

RETAIL OFFERING

The typical TSC store has 15,000 to 40,000 square feet of inside selling space with a similar amount of outside space used to display agricultural fencing, livestock equipment, and horse stalls. It tries to locate stores in the prime retail corridor of rural communities two or three counties away from major metropolitan areas. Fifty percent of its stores are in previously occupied buildings. For instance, TSC occupies many of Wal-Mart's vacated discount store locations because the stores are the perfect size and have garden space for outdoor merchandise.

The typical store stocks about 15,000 SKUS, using a combination of national and private label brands. TSC constantly tests new merchandise programs in its stores. For instance, based on a successful test of expanded clothing and footwear categories, TSC doubled the size of these areas of the store and added more lifestyle clothes and workwear for both men and women.

TSC's stores are designed to make shopping an enjoyable experience, while at the same time maximizing sales and operating efficiencies. Their environment allows plenty of space for individual departments and visual displays. Informative signs assist customers with purchasing decisions by delineating "good, better, best" qualities, pointing out their "every day low" pricing policy, and providing useful information regarding product benefits and suggestions for appropriate accessories.

TSC emphasizes customer service. The company tries to hire store employees with previous farming and ranching backgrounds. Its training programs include (i) a full

EXHIBIT 1
TSC's Value and Mission Statement

management training program which covers all aspects of its operations, (ii) product knowledge modules produced in conjunction with key vendors, (iii) frequent management skills training classes, (iv) semi-annual store managers' meetings, with vendor product presentations, (v) vendor sponsored in-store training programs; and (vi) ongoing product information updates at its management headquarters. This extensive training, coupled with a management philosophy that stresses empowerment, enables store employees to assist customers in making their purchase decisions, and solve customer problems as they arise. Store employees wear highly visible red vests, aprons or smocks and nametags. TSC uses a variety of incentive programs that provide the opportunity for store employees to receive additional compensation based on their team, store, and/or company performance.

While TSC creates a "hometown farmer" shopping experience for customers, there is nothing "small-town" or "laid back" about its operations and use of technology. Its management information and control systems include a point-of-sale system, a supply chain management and replenishment system, a radio frequency picking system in the distribution centers, a vendor purchase order control system and a merchandise presentation system. These systems work together to track merchandise from the initial order through to the ultimate sale.

TSC has a centralized supply chain management team to focus on replenishment and forecasting and a buying team that selects merchandise, develops assortments, and evaluates new products and programs. Almost all purchase orders and vendor invoices are transmitted through an electronic data interchange (EDI) system.

VALUES AND MISSION

Despite changes to the TSC's retail strategy in the past 70 years, its values and mission have remained constant. The company's values and mission statement appear on its Web site (Exhibit 1), on cards handed out to all employees, and on the walls of every store. According to TSC management, the first discussion with new employees centers on the firm's values and mission because the firm steadfastly maintains that "being a great place to work enables the company to be a great place to shop and invest.

DISCUSSION QUESTIONS

1. What is Tractor Supply Company's growth strategy? What retail mix does TSC provide?
2. Why and how has TSC's target customer changed over time?
3. How does TSC's retail mix provide the benefits sought by its target market?
4. How vulnerable is TSC to competition? Why is this the case?
5. Why does TSC place so much emphasis on training employees?

Source: This case was written by Barton Weitz, University of Florida.

CASE 2   Rainforest Café: A Wild Place to Shop and Eat

Steve Schussler opened the first Rainforest Café in the Mall of America, the largest enclosed mall in the world, in 1994. Before opening this unique retail store and theme restaurant, Schussler tested the concept for 12 years, eventually building a prototype in his Minneapolis home. It was not easy sharing a house with parrots, butterflies, tortoises, and tropical fish, but Schussler's creativity resulted in a highly profitable and fast-growing chain.

In 1996, the Rainforest Cafés (www.rainforestcafe.com), had locations in Chicago; Washington, DC; Fort Lauderdale, Florida; and Disney World in Orlando, Florida, in addition to the Mall of America in Minneapolis, Minnesota. It generated $48.7 million in sales and $5.9 million in profits. The restaurants offer a unique and exciting atmosphere, with state-of-the-art décor, animatronics, and a tropical rain forest in 20,000 to 30,000 square feet. The cafés are divided into a restaurant that seats 300 to 600 people and a retail store that stocks 3,000 SKUs of unique merchandise, compared with most theme restaurants that stock fewer than 20 SKUs.

Retail merchandise accounts for 30 percent of the revenues generated by the cafés. At Rainforest, the merchandise emphasizes eight proprietary jungle animals, featured as animated characters in the restaurant, including Bamba the gorilla, Cha Cha the tree frog, and Ozzie the orangutan. In addition to stuffed animals and toys, the characters appear on clothing and gifts and star in animated films and children's books.

The menu features dishes such as Leaping Lizard Lettuce Wraps, Rasta Pasta, Seafood Galapagos, Jamaica Me Crazy, and Eye of the Ocelot (meatloaf topped with sautéed mushrooms on a bed of caramelized onions). The restaurants host live tropical birds and fish, plus animated crocodiles and monkeys, trumpeting elephants, gorillas beating their chests, cascading waterfalls surrounded by cool mist, simulated thunder and lightning, continuous tropical rainstorms, and huge mushroom canapés. As Schussler notes, "Our cafés feature the sophistication of a Warner Brothers store with the animation of Disney."

Rainforest Cafés also contribute to their local communities through outreach programs. More than 300,000 schoolchildren visit the cafés each year to hear curators talk about the vanishing rain forests and endangered species. All coins dropped into the Wishing Pond and Parking Meters in the cafés are donated to causes involving endangered species and tropical deforestation.

The setting may seem a bit primitive, but Rainforest Cafés use technology extensively to increase their efficiency and profits. When a party enters the restaurant, the host (called a tour guide) enters the party's name in a computer, which prints a "passport" indicating the party's name, size, and estimated seating time. The party can then go shopping or sightseeing, knowing it will be ushered into the dining room within 5 to 10 minutes of the assigned seating time. When the party returns, the computer tells the "safari guide" at which table to seat the party. Tour and safari guides communicate using headsets. This use of technology enables the Rainforest Cafés to turn tables five to six times a day, compared with two to three turns in a typical restaurant.

The company expanded rapidly. By 2000, even though it earned annual sales of $200 million, it was only achieving $8 million in profits from 28 locations in 15 states, Canada, China, Mexico, and Europe. Many locations appeared in regional malls rather than the initial high-traffic entertainment centers. Rainforest Café was the only restaurant concept not operated by Disney at all three U.S. Disney locations as well as Disneyland Paris and Japan.

Landry's Restaurant Inc. acquired Rainforest Café for about $75 million in 2000. Landry's operates more than 300 full-service restaurants in 35 states and 7 international locations, including Landry's Seafood Houses, The Crab Houses, Chart Houses, Rainforest Cafés, and Saltgrass Steak Houses. Landry's also acquired the Golden Nugget casino in Las Vegas in 2005. The parent company generates over $1.1 billion in revenues.

Tilman Fertitta, the founder and CEO of Landry's, explains his strategy for operating restaurants: "Put good concepts in good locations. Rainforest is a strong concept. The problem wasn't with sales. The worst stores do $5 million a year. The major problem was poor locations in shopping centers with high lease costs." Following the acquisition, Landry's closed many of Rainforest's mall locations but opened new locations in London's Piccadilly Circus; Euro Disney outside Paris; Niagara Falls, Canada; the MGM Grand Hotel and Casino in Las Vegas; the Trump Plaza in Atlantic City, New Jersey; and Fisherman's Wharf in San Francisco.

DISCUSSION QUESTIONS

1. What is Rainforest Café's retail offering and target market?

2. Were malls in good locations for Rainforest Cafés? Why or why not? What would be the best location types for future growth?

3. Many retailers have tried to make their stores more entertaining. In a number of cases, these efforts have failed. What are the pros and cons of providing a lot of entertainment in a retail store or restaurant?

Source: This case was written by Barton Weitz, University of Florida.

CASE 3   Providing a Retail Experience: Build-A-Bear Workshop

Modern consumers want good value, low prices, and convenience, but they also appreciate a great shopping experience. Build-A-Bear Workshop usually locates its more than 275 stores in malls in Canada, the United Kingdom, and the United States. It generates over $450 million in annual sales offering customers the opportunity to make their own stuffed animals, complete with clothing and accessories.

In 1997, Maxine Clark came up with the idea for Build-A-Bear Workshop and opened a storefront in St. Louis. She had plenty of experience in the corporate side of retailing, working for Payless ShoeSource and May Department Stores. In an interview with *BusinessWeek* magazine, she proclaimed, "I left corporate America on a mission to bring the fun back to retailing and to give back to the industry that had been so good to me." When Build-A-Bear Workshop celebrated its tenth anniversary in 2007, the company had sold more than 50 million furry friends.

The stores mirror the chain's name: Customers, or builders, choose an unstuffed animal and, working with the retailer's staff, move through eight "creation stations" to build their own bear (or other animal). At the first station, the Stuffiteria, children can pick fluff from bins marked "Love," "Hugs and Kisses," "Friendship," and "Kindness." The stuffing is sent through a long, clear tube and into a stuffing machine. A sales associate holds the bear to a small tube while the builder pumps a foot peddle. In seconds, the bear takes its form. Before the stitching, builders must insert a heart. The builders follow the sales associates' instructions and rub the heart between their hands to make it warm. They then close their eyes, make a wish, and kiss the heart before putting it inside the bear. After selecting a name and having it stitched on their animal, builders take their bears to the Fluff Me station, where they brush their bears on a "bathtub" that features spigots blowing air. Finally, they move to a computer station to create a birth certificate.

Bears go home in Cub Condo carrying cases, which act as mini-houses complete with windows and doors. In addition to serving as playhouses, the boxes advertise Build-A-Bear Workshop to the child's friends. "[You] could buy a bear anywhere," says Clark, Chief Executive Bear. "It's the experience that customers are looking for." The experience isn't limited to the stores themselves. The retailer's Web site, www.buildabear.com, embraces the same theme.

Customers pay about $25 for the basic bear, but they can also buy music, clothing, and accessories. To keep the experience fresh, Build-A-Bear Workshop regularly introduces new and limited-edition animals. Clothes and accessories are also updated to reflect current fashion trends. Outfits for the bears complement the owner's interests and personalities with themes such as sports, colleges, hobbies, and careers. Some children and their parents hold in-store birthday parties, with music playing from the store's official CD. To ensure customers enjoy a great experience every time they visit, all sales associates attend a three-week training program at "Bear University," and the firm offers incentive programs and bonuses. The inventory in the stores changes frequently,

REFACT

The teddy bear came into being in 1903, when President Teddy Roosevelt refused to shoot a cub while bear hunting. The spared animal was thereafter referred to as the Teddy Bear.

with different bear styles arriving weekly. Build-A-Bear Workshops also feature seasonal merchandise, such as a King of the Grill bear for Father's Day; mummy, wizard, and witch bears for Halloween; and a Sweetheart bear for Valentine's Day.

DISCUSSION QUESTIONS

1. Is the Build-A-Bear Workshop concept a fad, or does it have staying power?
2. Describe the target customer for this retailer.
3. What can Build-A-Bear Workshop do to generate repeat visits to the store?

Source: This case was written by Barton Weitz, University of Florida.

CASE 4 Wal-Mart and Corporate Social Responsibility

Fortune magazine named Wal-Mart the "most admired company in America," and the *Financial Times* included it on its "Most Respected in the World" list. Wal-Mart has received various honors and accolades, such as being selected as among the "Top 50 Companies for Diversity" by *Diversity Inc.*, "Top 35 Companies for Executive Women" by the National Association for Female Executives, and "Top 50 Companies for African American MBAs" by *Black MBAs Magazine*—for two years in a row.

As the world's largest retailer, Wal-Mart has over $360 billion in sales a net profit from continuing operations of over $12.2 billion, and a 3.5 percent profit margin. It operates more than 4,000 facilities in the United States and more than 2,800 more store locations in 11 countries. More than 180 million customers visit Wal-Mart stores worldwide in a week, including 127 million in the United States. In turn, through its relationships with 61,000 U.S. suppliers, it spends more than $250 billion buying merchandise, which the company estimates supports more than 3 million American jobs, including its 1.3 million employees.

Wal-Mart's astounding success is based mainly on its ability to sell merchandise at low prices. It keeps prices down through cost reductions, which it realizes from a highly efficient supply chain management system, aggressive vendor negotiations, and low overhead. These efforts to control costs save U.S. shoppers an estimated $50 billion in food costs and five times that amount in total merchandise—savings that can be especially important to poor and moderate-income families, which spend a greater proportion of their income on food and other basics. The average Wal-Mart customer earns $35,000 a year, compared with $50,000 at Target and $74,000 at Costco.

Low prices and accolades for Wal-Mart also have been countered by a chorus of critics of the company's sourcing policies, employee wages and benefits, adverse effects on small businesses, and contributions to urban sprawl. Many such concerns are dramatically illustrated in Robert Greenwald's 2005 documentary film, *Wal-Mart: The High Cost of Low Prices*. Throughout the documentary, former senior managers tell of being trained to change employee records to avoid paying overtime; supervising factories in Central and South America with deplorable working conditions; and driving through communities to identify small business that would close when a new Wal-Mart store opened. To illustrate the effects that Wal-Mart stores have on local businesses, the film focuses on H & H Hardware, a

family-owned business in a small town in northeastern Ohio. The owner explains that he needs a loan to survive but complains that the local bank has refused his loan application because of the pending opening of the local Wal-Mart store. The film features a headline in the local newspaper, "Wal-Mart Descends On Middlefield!" followed by bulldozers in action.

To offer low prices to its customers, Wal-Mart demands that its 30,000 suppliers continually decrease their costs and prices. Unlike many grocery retailers, Wal-Mart does not charge "slotting fees," but it does establish strict delivery schedules and inventory levels and exerts heavy influence over product specifications. For some of its suppliers, Wal-Mart represents their primary customer, and suppliers that cannot meet Wal-Mart's cost and operational requirements risk losing its business. To achieve Wal-Mart's cost requirements, many suppliers turn to manufacturing facilities overseas, leading Wal-Mart's critics to assert that the retailer's pursuit of lower-cost goods contributes to the accelerating loss of U.S. manufacturing jobs to China and other low-wage paying countries while supporting the low standard of living of employees in these countries.

Many communities have taken legal steps to prevent Wal-Mart and other big box retailers from locating stores there. In California, the Alameda County Board of Supervisors and local governments in the San Francisco Bay passed an ordinance forbidding any store that sells grocery items from exceeding 100,000 square feet (Wal-Mart Supercenters range from 150,000 to 220,000 square feet).

These local governments claim that Wal-Mart stores lower the quality of life and standard of living in a community. When a Wal-Mart opens, they contend, traffic increases; small, local retailers are driven out of business; jobs are lost; the tax base shrinks; the number of workers with health benefits declines; and the number of workers eligible for welfare increases. Thus, in the critics' views, the addition of a Wal-Mart store transforms local retail store owners and family-supporting, middle-class retail jobs into lower-paying jobs that often leave people unable to maintain a reasonable lifestyle. Some economists estimate that Wal-Mart business practices annually cause a $4.7 billion loss of wages for workers in the retail sector.

Greenwald's film portrays Wal-Mart's socially unacceptable personnel policies in the person of a middle-aged African American woman, who relates a conversation she says she had with her boss when she was again passed up for a promotion: "He bluntly told me, 'There's no place for people like you in management.'" To which the employee responded, "What do you mean, people like me? That I'm female or that I'm black?" The manager's reported response: "Two out of two ain't bad."

Wal-Mart also has been criticized for its low wages, poor health care benefits, and aggressive resistance to unions. Approximately 70 percent of Wal-Mart's employees work full time, and full-time workers are eligible for health insurance after they've been on the job for six months; part-time workers get coverage after two years. Under fire because fewer than 45 percent of its workers receive company health insurance, Wal-Mart announced a new benefits plan that seeks to increase participation by allowing some employees to pay just $11 a month in premiums. Some health experts praised the plan for making coverage more affordable, but others criticized it, noting that full-time Wal-Mart employees, who earn on average around $17,500 a year, could face out-of-pocket expenses of $2,500 a year or more.

The Maryland legislature passed a bill forcing any company with more than 10,000 workers to spend at least 8 percent of its payroll on employee health care. The law clearly targeted Wal-Mart, the only company with more than 10,000 employees in Maryland. It thus was ruled unconstitutional, but similar "fair share" bills are pending or planned in 30 other states.

In response to these criticisms, analysts suggest Wal-Mart's compensation and benefits actually may reflect common practices in the retail and services industries. Companies in these industries tend to hire unskilled employees, use part-time workers to staff the long operating hours, and offer low wages and limited benefits. Wal-Mart's hourly wage is higher than the average wages in the retail industry, and more Wal-Mart employees are eligible for health insurance than in the retail industry as a whole,

as well as slightly more than the nationwide total. Other observers, however, compare the personnel policies of Wal-Mart with those of another successful retailer, Costco, and wonder why Wal-Mart cannot be as generous with its employees. For example, Costco's average wages are $16 per hour compared with Wal-Mart's $10; Costco employees pay between 5 and 8 percent of heath care premiums. Wal-Mart employees pay 34 percent with a high deductible; and 82 percent of Costco's employees receive health care benefits, but only 48 percent of Wal-Mart's employees do.

Sources: Jason Furman, "Wal-Mart: A Progressive Success Story," November 28, 2005 (accessed September 25, 2007); Arindrajit Dube, T. William Lester, and Barry Eidlin, "Firm Entry and Wages: Impact of Wal-Mart Growth on Earnings Throughout the Retail Sector," August 6, 2007, Institute for Research on Labor and Employment Working Paper Series, paper iirwps-126-05, http://repositories.cdlib.org/iir/iirwps/iirwps-126-05; Wayne F Cascio, "The High Cost of Low Wages," *Harvard Business Review* 84, No. 12 (December 2006), p. 23 1p, 1c; Joshua Green, "The New War Over Wal-Mart," *Atlantic Monthly*, June 2006 (accessed September 27, 2007).

DISCUSSION QUESTIONS

1. Is Wal-Mart good for society? Would society be better off with or without Wal-Mart?

2. Do you support towns banning the opening of a Wal-Mart store to protect local small businesses? Why or why not?

3. Should Wal-Mart pay higher wages, offer more health care benefits, and pay suppliers higher costs to improve the plight of workers? Why or why not?

Source: This case was written by Barton Weitz, University of Florida.

CASE 5   Should Retailers Use Blogs?

What do eBay, Amazon.com, and Dell share in common, beyond being top Internet retailers? They are all using blogging to their advantage, making them part of a growing trend. According to Jupiter Research, a leading authority on the impact of the Internet and emerging consumer technologies, 35 percent of large companies plan to institute corporate Weblogs (another name for blogs) this year. Marketers have found that blogs can be an excellent tool for developing buzz about new products or services and helping them serve the needs of their customers. Blogging allows customers to give their positive or negative feedback about a brand or store in an open forum. According to *Adweek*, blog feedback tends to be cheaper and quicker to obtain than traditional research, as well as free of the biases inherent to paying people to participate in focus groups.

Consumers use blogs to make comments and express their views in a shared chronological journal, create a personal diary, or disseminate news. Businesses employ them to generate discussion about a specific topic, create an open dialogue with customers to collect key information, or evaluate new opportunities. When Web retailers require customers to create an account before posting to their blog, they gain insight into the perspective of contributors.

This relatively new medium also provides an excellent means to harness the power of word of mouth. When a company's most loyal customers share their satisfaction on a blog, it adds credibility to the company's traditional advertising message. Changes within the company provide another key topic for blogs. People who participate in the blog usually are the same people who have a high level of interest in the company. Finally, bloggers are more likely to share news with others, which creates a great surge in word of mouth.

In one example, Honda is using blogs to evaluate new cars and identify features that customers want. Similar to a research group, Honda uses blogs to determine what gets customers excited or disappointed and then applies that information to build more appealing cars. Customers also benefit. They get to evaluate which products they might want to buy and obtain recommendations from their peers about particular product or service aspects. Whereas traditional advertising only highlights the benefits of a product, blogging points out the good, the bad, and everything in between.

Other retailers allow consumers to use their blogs to communicate with one another in forums. Although

Mall Anchors Away! The Franklins Discover Online Shopping   CASE 6

581

consumers do not direct their comments at the company, the retailers actively monitor the blogs so they can answer questions and clarify problems, which in many cases increases both credibility and customer loyalty.

Amazon.com's editors post blogs about new products and invite bloggers to respond on a forum that both the editors and potential customers can view. Using its famous technology, Amazon.com also sorts blog topics according to a customer's prior product purchases and recently viewed items and sends customers blog feeds that might interest them.

Yet despite these benefits, blogs also create concerns for both retailers and customers. In the past, dissatisfied customers had few ways to voice a complaint, but today, a multitude of open forums allow them to express their honest opinions. If bloggers point out weaknesses or even outright defects in products, product sales will suffer, especially as more and more online consumers use the Web to research products before buying them.

Dissatisfied bloggers also engage in word of mouth and spread negative information. In some cases, the information is completely justified and should encourage retailers to improve their offerings. But in other cases, the customer may not be right, and an inaccurate or punitive posting could cause serious harm to a company that does not necessarily deserve it.

When faced with such a posting, companies have little recourse, because blogs reduce the control companies have over their message and reputation. Many modern consumers value independent information that does not come directly from the company, which makes it even more difficult for retailers to counteract negative information. In essence, blogs have created a new forum for customer complaints that disseminates information about problems to a wide range of potential customers.

The current debate centers on whether blogs will prove to be lasting marketing tools. Statistics from www.technorati.com reveal that 75,000 new blogs appear each day, and 50,000 are updated each hour. With both powerful potential benefits and significant risks, it remains unclear whether retailers can achieve positive results from blogs. Some major players, including Wal-Mart, Home Depot, and Costco, reject the medium, but the trend seems to point to ever greater usage. As consumers learn to avoid traditional advertising media, retailers need new ways to reach out and communicate. Blogging may be a way to close the gap. In the short run, it is at least a rapidly growing trend that any company that wants to exploit the power of the Internet must consider carefully.

Sources: Kathie Paine, "How Do Blogs Measure Up?" *Communication World*, September 2007, pp. 30–33; John Voight, "How Consumers Help Build a Brand's DNA," *Adweek*, January 2, 2007, pp. 16–18; "Jupiter Research Finds that Deployment of Corporate Weblogs Will Double in 2006," *Jupiter Research*, June 26, 2005; Greg Brooks, "The Risks and Rewards of the Branded Blog," *Marketing*, December 6, 2006, pp. 44–46; Holly Dolezalek, "Blog Power," Incentive, July 2007, p. 8; Elizabeth Krietsch, "PR Technique: Staying on Top of Online Influence," *PR Week*, September 4, 2006, p. 18; Brain Morrissey, "Blogs Growing into the Ultimate Focus Group," *Adweek*, June 20, 2005, p. 12.

DISCUSSION QUESTIONS

1. Will blogging become an essential part of the corporate marketing strategy for retailers and product manufacturers?

2. What benefits can a retailer gain from using blogs?

3. If you were assigned the task of improving the marketing efforts of a new Internet retailer, would you use blogging? Why or why not? Does it depend on what your company is selling?

4. Have you ever posted comments in a blog about a company or its products? Was it positive or negative information? Have you every read a blog that affected your buying decision? In what ways?

Source: This case was written by David Rosage, an evening MBA student at Loyola College in Maryland, under the supervision of Professor Hope Corrigan.

CASE 6   Mall Anchors Away! The Franklins Discover Online Shopping

Drew Franklin put the box back on the shelf, to the protests of his son Ian: "But Dad! I really want that one, please!" Drew knelt and looked into the pleading face of his six-year-old child. He took a deep breath and exhaled slowly, wondering whether buying a model ship was a good idea after all. He and Ian had visited four stores in the past two hours. From Toys "R" Us to Wal-Mart, and now this specialty store, Hobby Lobby. The story was the same—limited selections and seemingly unlimited prices. In the discount stores, only a model of the Titanic was available, a model that Ian had already built.

"Ian, this is the fourth store we've been in today. I just think . . ." Drew looked at the box he had just replaced, marked $30 for a small model of a World War II–era destroyer. He corrected himself: "I *know* this is too much to pay."

"You never do anything I want to do!" Ian pouted. Drew thought for a moment and decided to look for models on the Internet. He picked up the destroyer model again and read the manufacturer's information: Tamiya of Japan. No Internet address. He picked up a model of the Titanic and read the box. This model was made by Revell-Monogram and featured the company's Internet address (www.revell-monogram.com) on the package. Drew put the model back on the shelf and looked at Ian. "Let's go home and look at what Revell has on its Web site. If we don't find anything there, we'll buy one of the models we've seen today, probably that aircraft carrier at Toys "R" Us."

At home, Drew and Ian logged on to the Revell-Monogram site and found current models and new releases. But nowhere on the site was there any information about ordering models. Drew was frustrated, and Ian was confused, wondering, "Why won't they sell them to us Dad? Can we go buy that one at the last store we went to today?"

Drew answered slowly: "First, though, let's try searching for other stores that might sell online." He clicked on his Google icon to begin searching, not really knowing what to look for. Ian sat and fidgeted while Drew typed in several different queries. He keyed in "models" and got more than 5,000 sites in return. He changed his keyword to "model ships," and Yahoo found about 80 sites. Looking these over, Drew saw nearly all of them related to museums. Next, he used "hobby shops" and found more than 200 sites. "Let's look at a few of these, and if we don't see anything, we'll go buy one today," Drew promised.

Several of the Web sites were run by model building enthusiasts, offering articles, tips, and pictures of their collections. But two sites stood out: Model Expo (www.modelexpoinc.com) and Internet Hobbies (www.internethobbies.com). Drew and Ian looked through the exhaustive online catalogs. Model Expo featured many types of model planes, trains, ships, trucks, and cars at prices ranging from a few dollars to more that $200 for remote-controlled, large-scale vehicles. One wooden steamboat model featured an optional miniature steam engine and remote control for $250! Drew clicked on the plastic ships on the catalog's opening page, remembering the type of model he had assembled 30 years before. On the page that popped up, he and Ian saw pictures, descriptions, and prices for dozens of ships available from several manufacturers. Prices were one-half to one-third, and sometimes even less, of the prices they had seen in the stores earlier that day.

The story was the same at Internet Hobbies. This online store featured similar prices but more manufacturers than Model Expo. "Still," Drew thought, "the basic types of models I'd like to start with are the same at both places." The *Arizona* and *Missouri* battleships were $7.49 at Model Expo and $6.99 at Internet Hobbies, while the *Nimitz* aircraft carrier was available for $9.99 at Model Expo and $8.99 at Internet Hobbies. "I wonder about shipping costs," Drew thought. He checked and found very similar charges. Internet Hobbies charged a flat rate of $7.50 for orders up to $75, then the percentage stayed at 10 percent of the order. Model Expo had a flat $5 per order charge that rose to 10 percent of the order after $50.

DISCUSSION QUESTIONS

1. What actions could brick-and-mortar retailers take to maintain their model sales? How important is this portion of their business?

2. What could Model Expo and Internet Hobbies do to protect their business if Revell-Monogram and other model kit makers decided to sell directly from their Web sites? Why haven't these manufacturers done so?

3. Construct a multiattribute attitude model for this purchase. Use two brick-and-mortar stores, the two featured online retailers, and at least four appropriate attributes. How might shoppers like Drew and Ian use this model? How could brick-and-mortar retailers use the results? Online retailers?

4. How do sales taxes on electronic commerce transactions change the model-buying scenario in the case?

Source: This case was written by Terence L. Holmes, Murray State University.

CASE 7   The Sanchez Family Buys Bicycles

The Sanchez family lives in Corona, California, west of Los Angeles. Jorge is a physics professor at the University of California, Riverside. His wife Anna is a volunteer, working 10 hours a week at the Crisis Center. They have two children: Nadia, age 10, and Miguel, age 8.

In February, Anna's parents sent her $100 to buy a bicycle for Nadia's birthday. They bought Nadia her first bike when she was five. Now they wanted to buy her a full-size bike for her eleventh birthday. Even though Anna's parents felt every child should have a bike, Anna didn't think Nadia really wanted one. Nadia and most of her friends didn't ride their bikes often, and she was afraid to ride to school because of the traffic. So Anna decided to buy her the cheapest full-size bicycle she could find.

Since most of Nadia's friends didn't have full-size bikes, she didn't know much about them and had no preferences for a brand or type. To learn more about the types available and their prices, Anna and Nadia checked the catalog for Performance Bicycle, a large, mail-order bicycling equipment retailer. The catalog was given to them by a friend of Anna's, who was an avid biker. After looking through the catalog, Nadia said the only thing she cared about was the color. She wanted a blue bike, blue being her favorite color.

Using the Internet, Anna located and called several local retail outlets selling bikes. To her surprise, she found that the local Kmart store actually had the best price for a 26-inch bicycle, even lower than Toys "R" Us and Wal-Mart.

Anna drove to Kmart, went straight to the sporting goods department, and selected a blue bicycle before a salesperson approached her. She took the bike to the cash register and paid for it. After making the purchase, the Sanchezes found out that the bike was cheap in all senses. The chrome plating on the wheels was very thin and rusted away in six months. Both tires split and had to be replaced.

A year later, Anna's grandparents sent another $200 for a bike for Miguel. From their experience with Nadia's bike, the Sanchezes realized that the lowest-priced bike might not be the least expensive option in the long run. Miguel is very active and somewhat careless, so they want to buy a sturdy bike. Miguel said he wanted a red, 21-speed, lightweight mountain bike with a full-suspension aluminum frame and cross-country tires.

The Sanchezes were concerned that Miguel wouldn't maintain an expensive bike with full suspension. When they saw an ad for a bicycle sale at Target, Anna and Jorge went to the store with Miguel. A salesperson approached them at an outdoor display of bikes and directed them to the sporting goods department inside the store. There they found row after row of red, single-speed BMX bikes with no suspension and minimal accessories to maintain—just the type of bike Anna and Jorge felt was ideal for Miguel.

Another salesperson approached them and tried to interest them in a more expensive bike. Jorge dislikes salespeople trying to push something on him and interrupted her in mid-sentence. He said he wanted to look at the bikes on his own. With a little suggestion, Miguel decided he wanted one of these bikes. His desire for accessories was satisfied when they bought a multifunction cyclocomputer for the bike. After buying a bike for Miguel, Jorge decided he'd like a bike for himself to ride on weekends. Jorge had ridden bikes since he was five. In graduate school, before he was married, he'd owned a 10-speed road bike. He frequently took 50-mile rides with friends, but he hadn't owned a bike since moving to Riverside 15 years ago.

Jorge didn't know much about current types of bicycles. He bought a copy of *Bicycling* at a newsstand to see what was available. He also went online to read *Consumer Reports*' evaluation of road, mountain, and hybrid bikes. Based on this information, he decided he wanted a Cannondale. It had all the features he wanted: a lightweight frame, durable construction, and a comfort sports saddle. When Jorge called the discount stores and bicycle shops, he found they didn't carry the Cannondale brand. He thought about buying the bicycle from an Internet site but was concerned about making such a large purchase without a test ride. He then decided he might not really need a bike. After all, he'd been without one for 15 years.

One day, after lunch, he was walking back to his office and saw a small bicycle shop. The shop was run down, with bicycle parts scattered across the floor. The owner, a young man in grease-covered shorts, was fixing a bike. As Jorge was looking around, the owner approached him and asked him if he liked to bicycle. Jorge said he used to but had given it up when he moved to Riverside. The owner said that was a shame because there were a lot of nice places to tour around Riverside.

As their conversation continued, Jorge mentioned his interest in a Cannondale and his disappointment in not finding a store in Riverside that sold them. The owner said that he could order a Cannondale for Jorge but that they weren't in inventory and delivery took between six and eight weeks. He suggested a Trek and showed Jorge one he currently had in stock. Jorge thought the $700 price was too high, but the owner convinced him to try it next weekend. They would ride together in the country. The owner and some of his friends took a 60-mile tour with Jorge. Jorge enjoyed the experience, recalling his college days. After the tour, Jorge bought the Trek.

DISCUSSION QUESTIONS

1. Outline the decision-making process for each of the Sanchezes' bicycle purchases.

2. Compare the different purchase processes for the three bikes. What stimulated each of them? What factors were considered in making the store choice decisions and purchase decisions?

3. Go to the student site of the Online Learning Center (OLC) and click on the multiattribute model. Construct a multiattribute model for each purchase decision. How do the attributes considered and importance weights vary for each decision?

Source: This case was written by Dan Rice and Barton Weitz, University of Florida.

CASE 8 Retailing in India: The Impact of Hypermarkets

The history of India contains a wealth of change and alteration, and the modern era is no different as the country blossoms into a major player in the global economy. Sizable economic growth during the past decade, particularly in the retail sector, has changed the way consumers behave. Though the size of the current Indian retail sector is impressive, its potential really speaks to what retailing will mean in the future. *The Economist* estimates that the retail market in India, approximately $200 billion in 2004, will reach $275 billion by 2010.

In response to such predictions, international retailers such as Wal-Mart, Tesco, and Carrefour are investigating opening hypermarkets in India. These large retail outlets combine the products found in a department store and supermarket with the goal of turning shopping into an experience. The large store layouts and variety of merchandise force customers to spend more time in the stores, which in turn leads to more sales. The potential for hypermarkets in India sheds light on the country's changing retail landscape and the shopping habits of its consumers.

Prior to 2000, Indian consumers generally purchased many of their retail goods from local mom-and-pop stores called *kiranas*, which sold mainly provisions and groceries. Shopping at *kiranas* is easy and convenient, because the small stores service specific neighborhoods and establish personal relationships with their customers. The new infusion of hypermarkets threatens to rob local storeowners of their customer base.

As John Elliott wrote in *Fortune*, "6,000 to 8,000 supermarkets will open across India in the next five to seven years, and each might draw customers from 20 to 25 *kiranas* and fruit and vegetable stands, affecting at most 150,000 vendors." This simple calculation doesn't represent the total effects on all local vendors, but it does demonstrate how hypermarkets influence local retail scenes and the livelihoods of local vendors.

Most *kiranas* cannot compete with hypermarkets, because these larger retail outlets create more efficiency within the supply chain. Much local produce in India currently gets wasted, because the country lacks sufficient infrastructure. Even as it progresses through rapid development,

India still lacks some amenities that Westerners take for granted, like refrigeration in retail operations. If a large retailer wants to open a hypermarket in India, it will have to invest capital to ensure freshness throughout the supply chain and help reduce waste. The Indian government is also expected to spend $150 billion (U.S.) over the next few years to develop a world-class infrastructure, which should spur growth in the retail sector.

The lack of infrastructure underlies a related issue facing hypermarkets. Unlike in Western nations, India's rather poor roads and transportation systems do not allow retailers to locate on large plots of land on the outskirts of town, since fewer consumers can reach them. Therefore, hypermarkets must look for retail space in more urban areas, which provide little available real estate. Buying up space from existing stores means displacing local corner shops already inhabiting that space, which may prompt protests from Indian consumers and store owners who value the Indian tradition that the kiranas represent. Yet larger retail outlets in India could have a dramatic impact on the economy, possibly creating 8 million jobs in the next 10 years. Although many Indians may not appreciate the notion of hypermarkets immediately, their presence is likely inevitable.

Much of the impetus for the emergence of hypermarkets in India also comes from changes among Indian consumers. The country's younger generations are exposed to a host of innovative products that were unknown to their parents. They are far more receptive to new products and ideas. In addition, this segment of the population reflects the shifting age demographics; more than half of India's current population is younger than 25 years of age. With such a large percentage of younger consumers, it seems inevitable that India's cultural tastes will evolve. The strength and abundance of local *kiranas* have been a cultural mainstay, but they cannot efficiently offer Indians access to new and technologically advanced products. Because hypermarkets combine department stores and supermarkets, they carry product lines that local vendors cannot. They sell brand name products at affordable prices, which enables Indians to purchase a wide assortment of goods that they otherwise could not have.

Although hypermarkets may be enabling younger, more worldly Indian consumers to experience the products the rest of the world enjoys, they still are meeting some resistance. As Dharmendra Kumar of India Foreign Direct Investment Watch observed, "This is the country where Gandhi taught people to live on minimum resources. These large retail companies will push us aggressively to consume more and more." For many Indians, the availability of luxury goods, cosmopolitan fashions, and cellular technology means living beyond their means, which directly contradicts Indian traditions.

This shift, from local mom-and-pop stores to more organized retail outlets, is happening very quickly in India. It is embraced by many consumers despite the cultural and legal considerations associated with hypermarkets. Furthermore, because of their potential benefits for both the economy and the national infrastructure, local governments generally support the arrival of a hypermarket. The ultimate target market, however, is not the government but the consumers, and just as in any country at any time, the challenge lies in understanding what those consumers want and how to get it to them.

Sources: "Coming to Market–Retailing in India," *The Economist*, April 15, 2006, p. 69; "Despite Growing Debt, the Indian Consumer Banks on Tomorrow," *India Knowledge@Wharton*, October 31, 2006; Ranjan Biswas, "India's Changing Consumers," *Chain Store Age*, May 2006, p. S2; John Elliott, "Retail Revolution," *Fortune*, August 9, 2007, pp. 14–16; Amelia Gentleman, "Indians Protest Wal-Mart's Wholesale Entry," *The New York Times*, August 10, 2007, p. B1.

DISCUSSION QUESTIONS

1. How might a hypermarket located in India appeal to consumers and orient them to shopping in the larger stores?

2. Is the Indian government's willingness to spend $150 billion to improve the nation's infrastructure good news for international retailers? Why or why not?

3. Identify the main changes that mark Indian consumers. How can international retailers learn more about India's youthful demographic?

Source: This case was written by Todd Nicolini, an evening MBA student at Loyola College in Maryland, under the supervision of Professor Hope Corrigan.

CASE 9   Diamonds: From Mine to Market

According to the American Museum of Natural History, a diamond is carbon in its most concentrated form. Because of their chemical makeup and crystalline structure, diamonds possess unique characteristics, including transparency. They are the hardest known natural substance. These traits determine their status as the "king of gems," a reference to their vast popularity as jewelry and decoration.

To provide diamonds to the millions of consumers who demand them, the supply chain consists of six steps: exploration, mining, sorting, cutting and polishing, jewelry design and production, and retail display. According to the Web site for De Beers, the producer of approximately 40 percent of the world's supply of rough or uncut diamonds, members of this extensive supply chain include geologists, engineers, environmentalists, miners, sorters, distributors, cutters, polishers, traders, manufacturers, exporters, and sales people, who in turn employ vast technology, artistic, and skill-related resources to discover, produce, and distribute jewelry-quality diamonds.

EXHIBIT 1
De Beers' Description of the Four Cs for Diamond Quality

Cut	Cut refers to the angles and proportions a skilled craftsman creates in transforming a rough diamond into a polished diamond.
	A well-cut diamond will reflect light internally from one mirror-like facet to another, dispersing it through the top of the stone.
	To cut a diamond perfectly, a craftsman will often need to cut away more than 50 percent of the rough diamond.
	Cut also refers to the shape of a diamond: round, emerald, heart, marquise, or pear.
Carat Weight	Carat is often confused with size, even though it is actually a measure of weight. The cut of a diamond can make it appear much larger or smaller than its actual weight.
	One carat is the equivalent of 200 milligrams. One carat can also be divided into 100 "points." A .75 carat diamond is the same as a 75-point or a three-quarter carat diamond.
Color	Most diamonds appear icy white, but many have tiny hints of color. Diamonds are graded on a color scale established by the Gemological Institute of America (GIA), ranging from D (colorless) to Z.
	Colorless diamonds are extremely rare and therefore very valuable.
	Diamonds are also sometimes found in "fancy" colors: pink, blue, green, yellow, brown, orange and, very rarely, red. These diamonds, called "fancies" are incredibly rare and valuable. These colors extend beyond the GIA color grading system.
Clarity	Diamonds, like people, have natural blemishes in their make up. Minerals or fractures form these tiny faults, or inclusions, while the diamond is forming in the earth.
	When light enters a diamond, it is reflected and refracted. If anything disrupts the flow of light in the diamond, such as an inclusion, a proportion of the light reflected will be lost.
	Most inclusions are not visible to the naked eye unless magnified.
	To view inclusions, trained gemologists use a magnifying loupe. This tool allows experts to see a diamond at 10 times its actual size. Even with a loupe, the birthmarks in the VVS (Very, Very Slightly Included) to VS (Very Slightly Included) range can be very difficult to find. It is only when a diamond is graded 'I' that it is possible to see the birthmarks with the naked eye.

The jewelry-quality designation refers to a particular rating according to four key elements of a diamond, better known as the 4Cs: cut, carat, color, and clarity. The De Beers Corporation introduced these criteria in 1939 to provide consumers with a reference for evaluating diamonds, as Exhibit 1 summarizes.

Before they reach showrooms to be evaluated on these criteria, diamonds have endured approximately 3 billion years of hot temperatures and intense pressures under the Earth's surface. Production estimates from the World Diamond Council indicate diamond mining operations are in more than 20 countries, including Australia, the Democratic Republic of the Congo, Botswana, Russia, South Africa, Angola, Canada, Namibia, Brazil, and Sierra Leone.

Thus, though "an estimated 65% of the world's diamonds come from African countries," other key sources for diamonds span the globe, for example the remote northern regions of Western Australia, which produce roughly 30 million carats (20 percent of global production) each year from both open pit and underground operations. These diamonds are known for the range of their colored diamonds, especially pink stones.

Diamonds prompt significant competition, as depicted in the movie *Blood Diamond*, which portrays the gruesome conflict and violence in Sierra Leone over diamonds. In many countries, profits from diamonds go to fund civil wars that take millions of lives. To prevent such abuses, the Kimberly Process, an international diamond certification scheme, was established to abolish trade in diamonds that fund conflict. Since its launch in 2003, the Kimberly Process has become law in 69 countries and received backing from the United Nations. It requires that governments of diamond-producing nations certify that shipments of rough diamonds have not prompted greater conflict.

Even with a certification process though, some diamonds continue to be smuggled out of African countries and support rebel armies. Violent groups find ways to exploit the Kimberley Process to traffic in illicit diamonds. "Conflict diamonds continue to be certified in countries that are members of the Kimberley Process, legitimized by the very scheme which was designed to eradicate them." However, a contrasting report from the World Diamond Council claims that "because of the Kimberly Process, more than 99% of the world's diamond supply is from sources free from conflict."

When the international diamond industry agreed to implement a voluntary system of warranties, it promised consumers it could track diamond jewelry up to the point of sale. Invoices for the sale of conflict-free diamond jewelry must include a written guarantee of that status. To ensure the diamonds they purchase for their spouses, fiancées, or themselves are indeed sourced appropriately, consumers are expected to take some responsibility, such as asking a series of questions of the jeweler from which they are purchasing:

What is the country of origin for the diamonds in your jewelry?

Can I see a copy of your company's policy on conflict-free diamonds?

Can you show me a copy of the written warranty from your diamond supplier stating that your diamonds are conflict-free?

Sources: "About Us," Argyle Diamonds, www.argylediamonds.com.au/home.asp; Blood Diamonds are Still a Reality," Amnesty International, http://web.amnesty.org/pages/ec-230107-feature-eng; "Combating Conflict Diamonds," Global Witness, www.globalwitness.org/pages/en/conflict_diamonds.html; "Conflict Free Diamond Jewelry," Brilliant Earth, www.brilliantearth.com/index.aspx; "Diamond Pipe," De Beers, www.debeersgroup.com/debeersweb/Diamond+Journey/The+Diamond+pipeline/; "Forever Diamonds." Gemnation, www.gemnation.com/base?processor=getPage&pageName=forever_diamonds_1; "Four Cs," De Beers, www.debeersgroup.com/debeersweb/Diamond+Industry/The+Four+cs/.

DISCUSSION QUESTIONS

1. How important is it for consumers to buy conflict-free diamonds? Why?

2. What could the jewelry industry do to inform diamond customers about buying conflict-free gems and the Kimberly Process?

3. Select a retail jewelry store in your area to visit. Is its policy on conflict diamonds posted anywhere, such as in the store or on the company's Web site? Ask store personnel the three questions posed at the end of the case. What did you learn from the Web page and site visit?

Source: This case was written by Hope Bober Corrigan, Loyola College, Maryland.

CASE 10 Save-A-Lot

In 1977, Bill Moran was the Vice-President of Sales for a food wholesaler in St. Louis. His customers, independent grocers, were facing a weak economy and stiff competition from the growth of regional supermarket chains. He developed an extreme value, limited assortment concept to give small grocery stores a way to compete. He then tested the concept in several stores. Even though the concept worked in the test stores, the wholesaler believed the concept would not work when the economy improved.

Today, Save-A-Lot has more than 1,300 stores across the United States and enjoys consistent, double-digit sales growth. Seventy-five percent of the stores are operated by licensees, and the remainder are operated by the company.

Save-A-Lot targets a value- and convenience-oriented psychographic segment. The consumers in this segment are looking for a good value, namely, quality merchandise at low prices. Its stores average about 14,000–18,000 square feet, less than half the size of a conventional supermarket. These smaller stores appeal to shoppers who don't want to park half a mile from the storefront and search for merchandise in a 100,000 square foot store.

Stores stock approximately 1,250 SKUs of the most popular items, compared with 30,000 SKUs in a traditional supermarket. Save-A-Lot's large customer base and edited assortment format equate to high sales volume and lower costs. For example, a traditional supermarket may carry 35 SKUs of ketchup—different brands, sizes, and flavors. Save-A-Lot carries just one, made to the same specifications as the leading national brand. The chain has buying power with its vendors by purchasing one size and variety of an item for more than 1,150 stores and 4 million weekly shoppers. In addition, vendors give Save-A-Lot low prices because Save-A-Lot doesn't ask for advertising allowance, fees for stocking items, merchandise return privileges, or charge backs.

To offer quality merchandise at low prices and remain profitable, Save-A-Lot tightly controls its operating costs. Stores are located on inexpensive real estate, and staff in the stores is limited. Merchandise is displayed on shelves in cut-off shipping boxes to reduce the labor costs incurred by taking cans and bottles out of the boxes and placing them on the shelves. Save-A-Lot customers typically bag their own groceries. Some stores charge extra for bags, such as three cents for plastic "t-shirt" bags, five cents for paper grocery bags, and 10 cents for reusable/polyurethane bags. Due to these cost-cutting approaches, Save-A-Lot can offer quality merchandise to its customers at prices 40 percent less than those of traditional supermarkets.

When Save-A-Lot started, it focused simply on providing value to customers by selling the basics: bread, eggs, milk, flour, sugar, and canned goods. It charged low prices in a bare-bones atmosphere. Over time, as its market research revealed that customers' concept of value was changing, Save-A-Lot began adding more unique items to its assortment. The stores' customers, regardless of their income levels, sometimes want to treat themselves to something special, so Save-A-Lot included frozen shrimp, now one of its best selling items. By buying at half the price charged by traditional supermarkets, its customers can still have a special meal at a reasonable price.

Save-A-Lot's success has attracted competitors, such as the extreme value general merchandise chains (e.g., Dollar General, Family Dollar) that are now offering more food items. But Save-A-Lot's efficient food distribution system might be difficult to duplicate. At the same time, Save-A-Lot faces more competition in the United States from ALDI, the German company that originated the extreme value business model in food retailing. ALDI now operates more than 8,000 stores in 24 counties including, approximately 800 in the United States.

DISCUSSION QUESTIONS

1. What is Save-A-Lot's retail strategy—its target market, format, and bases of competitive advantage?

2. How do the elements in the strategic profit model for Save-A-Lot differ from those of a traditional supermarket?

3. What are the pluses and minuses of offering a limited assortment from the perspective of the consumer and the perspective of the retailer?

4. What are the advantages and disadvantages of stores operated by licensees rather than by the company directly?

Source: This case was written by Barton Weitz, University of Florida.

CASE 11   Royal Ahold: The Biggest Supermarket Retailer You Have Never Heard Of

In 1887, 22-year-old Albert Heijn took over his father's small grocery store, near Zaandam in west Holland, which sold everything from groceries to dredging nets. In 1948, Ahold (an abbreviation of Albert Heijn Holding) had become the largest food retailer in the Netherlands. Then Ahold, like its Dutch ancestors, took to the high seas to find new opportunities outside its small home. It went public and made its first acquisition, a Spanish supermarket chain. By 1987, Ahold joined the corporate elite when Queen Beatrix marked its 100th anniversary by awarding it the designation "Koninklijke" (Royal). As the result of a flurry of acquisitions in the 1990s, Royal Ahold was the world's second-largest food retailer in 2003, operating 1,600 stores in 27 countries with sales of more than 72 billion Euros. But the name Royal Ahold does not appear on a single store it owns. In addition to acquiring supermarket chains, in 1999, the company bought U.S. Foodservice, America's second-largest supplier of ready-made meals, prepared foods, and ingredients sold to restaurants, hotels, hospitals, and other institutions.

In 1999, Ahold USA's retail operations consisted of Stop & Shop, Giant-Landover, Giant-Carlisle, Tops, Bi-Lo, and Bruno's. These six supermarket chains stretched from New England to Alabama. In addition, Ahold USA owned Peapod, a leading Internet grocer. Furthermore, Royal Ahold operated under 26 different names in Europe, America, Asia, and Latin America. It uses 10 different formats for its stores, ranging from tiny gas station outlets in the Netherlands to 150,000-square-foot hypermarkets in northern Brazil. The company refers to its strategy as "multilocal, multiformat, multichannel." According to Cees van der Hoeven, Royal Ahold's former CEO, "Our culture is first and foremost the culture of the local operating company. What makes Ahold unique is that we're perceived by our customers as the local guy." Very few customers at a Bruno's supermarket in Alabama or a Disco store in Argentina realize that their store is part of a global retail giant headquartered in the Netherlands.

Wal-Mart and Carrefour, the two largest food retailers, use a different approach. From Paris to Shanghai, all Carrefour stores look the same and have identical layouts (to reach the deli counter, for example, you always turn left at the entrance). Wal-Mart also uses its name on most of its stores across the world. Three years ago, it acquired the Asada chain in the United Kingdom and still operates the stores under the Asada name. But when it bought the Wertkauf chain and some Spar stores in Germany, it converted the stores to Wal-Marts. However, poor profits forced the company to sell its German chain soon thereafter.

Royal Ahold is, first and foremost, a food retailer. Food sales account for 90 percent of its revenues. Recognizing the lifestyle trend toward more out-of-home food consumption, Ahold is attempting to increase its share of the wallet through its acquisition of food-service companies. In contrast, Wal-Mart and Carrefour focus on operating larger supercenters or hypermarkets that offer general merchandise as well as food.

Another difference between Royal Ahold and its major international competitors is its growth strategy. Although Wal-Mart has made some acquisitions, most of its international growth, and all of Carrefour's, has been internally generated. In contrast, Ahold has grown primarily through acquisitions. Over two-thirds of Royal Ahold's sales now come from its U.S. acquisitions. No other European retailer has been as successful in entering the U.S. market. Carrefour tried opening two stores in suburban Philadelphia in the late 1980s but gave up quickly when it faced labor problems and the enduring loyalty customers had to their local supermarket chains.

CEO van der Hoeven had a vision of a future in which Royal Ahold's stores in Guatemala would offer tips on pricing to their colleagues in the United States, and the flooring for every Ahold supermarket from Boston to São Paulo would be ordered from the same supplier. The payoff from this networked global juggernaut would be the ability to leverage its size to get rock-bottom prices from its vendors on everything from corn flakes to oranges. Meanwhile, Royal Ahold's companies in Europe, America, Asia, and Latin America would lower their costs by using the same trucks, sharing accountants, and exchanging ideas over the corporate Intranet. But this global network would be invisible to the 20 million customers who pass through Ahold stores every week.

Royal Ahold has yet to realize this vision. Although Ahold has centralized the procurement of fresh and chilled products across its six U.S. chains, only five percent of all merchandise in Ahold's stores is ordered on a cross-continental basis, about the same as Wal-Mart and Carrefour. Royal Ahold's U.S. managers are just beginning to exchange best practices with their counterparts overseas. For example, Stop & Shop and Peapod are trying to improve their fulfillment accuracy by learning how Royal Ahold's Scandinavian Internet home-delivery service has achieved its successes in performing these activities. However, Royal Ahold's goal remains the same: Bring the same supply chain efficiencies achieved by Wal-Mart and Carrefour in general merchandise distribution to food distribution.

In 2002, Royal Ahold announced, for the first time, that it had lost money during the second quarter. The announcement preceded a scandal that resulted in the resignations of both van der Hoeven and the CFO, Michael Meurs, in February 2003. In the aftermath, the company announced it would restate its financial results by at least 500 million Euros to rectify the errors caused by accounting irregularities and fraud. More than three years after it teetered on the brink of bankruptcy in one of Europe's largest financial scandals, a Dutch court found former CEO van der Hoeven and former CFO Meurs guilty of fraud for improperly booking sales from four subsidiaries in Scandinavia, Argentina, and Brazil. Both men were fined and given suspended sentences.

Then in 2006, Royal Ahold implemented a new strategic plan to focus on its food retail stores in the United States and Europe. Stores in Asia and South America were sold, along with U.S. Foodservice and other food service divisions, as well as some underperforming Tops stores. It already had divested Bruno's. As a result of these divestments, Royal Ahold dropped from second to twelfth in the rankings of the largest global food retailers.

Although Royal Ahold is now organized into relatively independent U.S. and European divisions, each division is organized along geographical areas to coordinate the activities of the stores in that region.

Source: www.ahold.com/ (accessed September 27, 2007); Stewart Hamilton and Alicia Micklethwait, "Too Much Too Fast?" *European Business Forum*, Spring 2007, pp. 47–50; Jim Frederick, "Ahold Trims Down and Focuses on Profit Message," *Drug Store News*, April 23, 2007, pp. 110–11.

DISCUSSION QUESTIONS

1. What are the advantages and disadvantages of the growth strategies pursued by Royal Ahold, Carrefour, and Wal-Mart?

2. Should Royal Ahold use its name on all of its stores like Wal-Mart and Carrefour? Why or why not?

3. What are the advantages and disadvantages of Wal-Mart's and Carrefour's more centralized decision making compared with Royal Ahold's decentralized decision making?

4. Do you think Royal Ahold should have divested its food service divisions? Why or why not?

Source: This case was written by Barton Weitz, University of Florida.

CASE 12 The Competitive Environment in the 18- to 22-Year-Old Apparel Market

Jennifer Shaffer, a 19-year-old college student living in Cupertino, California, used to shop at Abercrombie & Fitch (A&F) once a month. She thought the prices were high, but the brand name and image appealed to her. As she says, "It's like I really had to have Abercrombie." Then an American Eagle (AE) store opened about 15 minutes from her home. Now she shops at the AE store about twice a month and rarely goes to the A&F store. "They look the same, and they're both really cute," she says. "But American Eagle's prices are a little cheaper."

Both A&F and AE are still growing into their present strategy of selling casual apparel to the teen/college market. When A&F was established as an outdoor sporting goods retailer over 100 years ago, it sold the highest quality hunting, fishing, and camping goods. It also outfitted some of the greatest explorations in the early part of the twentieth century, including Robert Perry's expedition to the North Pole and Theodore Roosevelt's trips to the Amazon and Africa.

Over time, its safari image became less attractive to consumers. The chain experienced a significant decline in sales and profits, and in 1977, it was forced to declare bankruptcy. The company, initially acquired by Oshman's Sporting Goods, did not experience a turnaround until The Limited Inc. acquired it in 1988. Initially, The Limited positioned A&F as a tailored clothing store for men. In 1995, The Limited repositioned A&F to target both men and women in the teen and college market, with an emphasis on casual American style and youth.

In 1999, The Limited sold A&F. Now the company operates 361 Abercrombie & Fitch stores, 190 abercrombie stores, 422 Hollister Co. stores, and 17 RUEHL No. 925 stores in the United States, as well as three Abercrombie & Fitch stores and three Hollister Co. stores in Canada and one Abercrombie & Fitch store in London, England. Furthermore, A&F offers its merchandise online at www.abercrombie.com, www.abercrombiekids.com, and www.hollisterco.com.

American Eagle, though lacking the rich tradition of A&F, also was positioned as an outfitter when it started in 1977. Initially offering apparel only for men, AE shifted its focus to teens and college students in 1995. Its merchandise includes jeans, graphic t-shirts, accessories, outerwear, footwear, and swimwear. American Eagle operates about 850 stores in the United States and Puerto Rico, along with 74 AE stores in Canada. The retailer also operates www.ae.com, which offers additional sizes and styles online. Under the aerie brand name, AE offers a collection of dorm wear and intimate apparel, available in 13 aerie stores, AE stores, and www.aerie.com.

Even though A&F and AE have evolved from their roots, their apparel still features an outdoor, rugged aspect. Both retail chains carry a similar assortment of polos, pants, t-shirts, shorts, jeans, outerwear, and sweaters. All the apparel and accessories appear under the store's private-label brand. The Ivy League- and sportswear-inspired merchandise aims to fit the campus lifestyle of its target customer.

With these similarities, the rivalry between A&F and AE is intense; A&F even filed a lawsuit in 1998 in federal court accusing AE of copying its clothing styles and catalog. The courts found that though the designs were similar, there was nothing inherently distinctive in A&F's clothing designs that could be protected by a trademark. But the courts also have ruled that Abercrombie's catalog design and image are worthy of trade dress protection. (Trade dress is the overall image of a product used in its marketing or sales, composed of the nonfunctional elements of its design, packaging, or labeling, such as colors, package shape, or symbols.) However, the court also noted that AE's catalog had a different image that did not infringe upon the image of the A&F catalog.

It was the catalog and home page that first drew Jennifer to an A&F store a couple of years ago. She recalls going through the catalog and browsing the Web page with some girlfriends and looking at the muscular young men featured. "The guys in the magazine—that's what made us all go," she says. This young and sexy image is enhanced by store signage featuring scantily clad lacrosse players and young beachgoers. Abercrombie & Fitch exploited this image by introducing a line of intimate apparel in 2001, now one of the best selling merchandise categories in stores.

Even though A&F devotes its advertising and marketing resources to reaching college-age consumers, many younger teenagers also patronize its stores. The company thus faces concerns that the image of its stores will suffer if they become a hangout for teenagers. The development of the Hollister chain, which targets 14–18-year-old students, represents one of its responses to preserve the A&F image while also catering to the growing teenage market.

Hollister stores are unique. Merchandise is 20–30 percent less expensive than A&F's merchandise, and the styling features brighter colors and larger logos. However, many teenagers fail to recognize the subtle differences. They contend that it is essentially the same merchandise except at lower prices.

Furthermore, Hollister stores are roughly 2,000 square feet smaller than A&F stores, and the store design is completely distinct. Whereas A&F stores still convey outdoor ruggedness in their décor, Hollister stores present a California beach–inspired theme. The retailer wants customers to feel as though they are part of a beach party. This casual atmosphere provides young consumers with an enjoyable shopping experience, as the décor inspires and evokes memories of hot summer days, experienced at any time of the year.

DISCUSSION QUESTIONS

1. What, if any, are the differences in A&F's and AE's retail strategies?

2. What are the brand images of A&F and AE? What words and phrases are associated with each retailer's brand name?

3. List other specialty apparel retailers that target the same customers as A&F and AE. How do these brands differentiate themselves in the competitive retail environment? Construct a product positioning map to illustrate each retailer's positioning.

4. Which retailer(s) has (have) the stronger competitive position?

Source: This case was written by Kristina Pacca, Loyola College of Maryland.

CASE 13   Tiffany's and Blue Nile: Comparing Financial Performance

Charles Lewis Tiffany and John Young founded Tiffany & Young in New York City in 1837. The store sold stationery and costume jewelry and offered a unique, fixed price, no-haggling approach. In 1845, the company began selling fine jewelry, primarily to the growing number of wealthy Americans. The company moved in 1940 to its landmark Fifth Avenue location, showcased in Truman Capote's 1958 novella *Breakfast at Tiffany's* and the 1961 movie of the same name, starring Audrey Hepburn.

Tiffany's offers fine jewelry and watches, silverware, china, stationery, and other luxury items with outstanding customer service. Almost 85 percent of its sales are from jewelry, including exclusive designs by Frank Gehry, Elsa Peretti, and Paloma Picasso. When sold, its merchandise is packaged in the company's trademarked Tiffany Blue Box. Sixty-five percent of the merchandise sold is manufactured by Tiffany's in two plants located in the United States.

Tiffany's operates over 65 stores in the United States and more than 100 stores in international markets. About 50 percent of the sales come from the domestic stores, with the flagship store in Manhattan accounting for 20 percent of U.S. sales. Tiffany's retail stores range from approximately 1,300 to 18,000 square feet, with an average size of approximately 7,100 square feet. New stores are typically 5,000 square feet.

To entice budget-minded, younger customers, Tiffany has broadened its merchandise mix to include key chains and other items that sell for much less than the typical Tiffany price tag. However, expanding its product line and broadening its market has had mixed results. The company's more moderately priced silver products, introduced in the late 1990s, increased sales but also threatened Tiffany's image. The business was by far the fastest growing segment in the company, but the increased store traffic diluted the Tiffany retail experience for its traditional customer base. In early 2002, the company pulled back on its silver offerings and increased its diamond selection. Both entry-level and average prices for the silver items increased, and product line advertising was reduced.

In contrast to Tiffany's 175-year-old tradition, Blue Nile was founded in 1999 but already has grown to become the largest online retailer of certified diamonds and fine jewelry. The company's primary value proposition stems from offering a simple way for men to select diamond engagement rings, which account for some

70 percent of Blue Nile's annual revenue. Customers also can create their own jewelry by choosing a particular diamond, which Blue Nile will set in their preferred earring, pendant, or ring design. Every order is shipped free, guaranteed and returnable within 30 days, so the customer's uncertainty and risk is reduced.

Due to the significant costs of diamonds and lack of customer knowledge about them, a diamond purchasing decision requires extensive problem solving. Customers need substantial information and trusted guidance throughout their purchasing process. Blue Nile's Web sites and trained customer service people provide education and detailed product information that enable customers to compare diamonds and fine jewelry products objectively and make informed decisions. The Web sites feature an interactive search functionality that enables customers to find products that meet their exact needs from a broad selection of diamonds and fine jewelry. The average shopper on Blue Nile spends more than $1,500, though the average spent on an engagement ring is $5,500—close to double the industry average.

Although Blue Nile maintains a modest inventory of diamonds, it also offers diamonds available from its wholesaler's inventory and buys diamonds from the wholesalers after customers order them. As a result, Blue Nile minimizes the costs associated with carrying diamond inventory.

DISCUSSION QUESTIONS

1. Using a the financial information in Exhibit 1, construct a strategic profit models (shown in Exhibit 2) for Tiffany's and Blue Nile using data from the abbreviated income statements and balance sheets in Exhibit 1. You can do these calculations by hand or go to the student side of the Online Learning Center (OLC) and use the Strategic Profit Model Excel spreadsheet that is available. Click on Strategic Profit Model. Then click through to "Try It Yourself—the SPM Calculations." Click on "Spreadsheets: The Strategic Profit Model" at the lower left corner of your screen.

2. Tiffany's manufactures most of the merchandise it sells, whereas Blue Nile outsources the manufacturing of its diamond engagement rings. How are these differences reflected in the financial statements and key ratios?

3. Explain, from a retail strategy perspective, why you would expect the gross margin percentage, operating expenses-to-sales ratio, net profit margin, inventory turnover, and asset turnover to be different for Tiffany's and Blue Nile.

4. Assess which retailer has better overall financial performance now. Why? Which retailer do you think will have overall better performance in the future. Why?

Source: This case was written by Barton Weitz, University of Florida.

EXHIBIT I

Financial Statements for Tiffany's and Blue Nile

ANNUAL INCOME STATEMENT (all dollar amounts in millions)						
	TIFFANY'S			BLUE NILE		
	Jan 07	Jan 06	Jan 05	Dec 06	Dec 05	Dec 04
Net Sales	$2,648.3	$2,395.1	$2,204.8	$251.6	$203.2	$169.2
Costs of Goods Sold	1,172.7	1,052.8	974.3	200.7	158.0	131.6
Gross Margin	1,475.7	1,342.3	1,230.6	50.9	45.1	37.7
SG&A Expense	942.4	850.2	827.9	32.4	25.4	21.3
Depreciation & Amortization	117.8	109.4	108.2	1.9	1.7	1.5
Operating Income	415.4	382.7	294.5	16.6	18.0	14.9
Extraordinary Expenses	−11.0	−14.8	177.6	3.4	2.5	0.8
Net Profit before Taxes	404.4	368.0	472.1	20.0	20.5	15.6
Income Taxes	150.5	113.3	167.9	6.9	7.4	5.6
Net Income after Taxes	253.9	254.7	304.3	13.1	13.1	10.0
Number of employees	8,900	8,120	7,341	161	146	120
Square feet in stores	792,000	745,000	729,000			
Square feet in offices, warehouse	601,000	601,000	601,000	37,000	37,000	37,000

ANNUAL BALANCE SHEET (All dollar amounts in millions except per share amounts.)						
	Jan 07	Jan 06	Jan 05	Dec 06	Dec 05	Dec 04
Cash	$192.0	$393.6	$326.9	$98.4	$114.8	$101.4
Accounts Receivable	242.4	211.9	198.3	2.2	5.1	9.2
Merchandise Inventory	1,214.6	1,060.2	1,057.2	14.6	11.8	9.9
Other Current Assets	57.6	33.2	25.4	0.7	0.8	1.0
Total Current Assets	1,706.6	1,698.8	1,607.9	116.0	132.5	121.5
Total Fixed Assets	1138.9	1978.4	1958.2	6.1	56	6.8
Total Assets	2,845.5	2,777.3	2,666.1	122.1	138.0	128.4

Strategic Profit Model   **EXHIBIT 2**

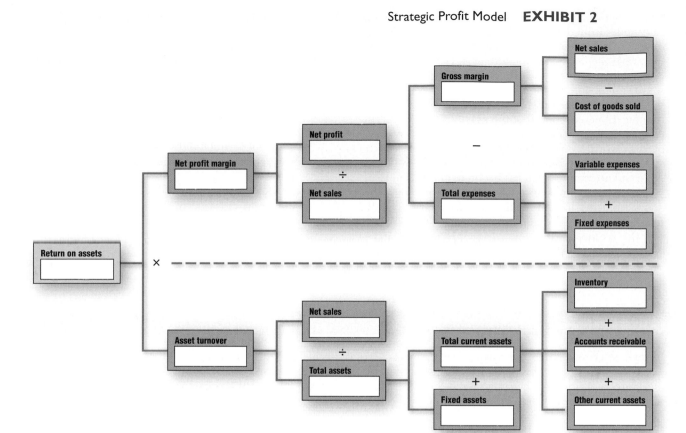

CASE 14   Stephanie's Boutique: Selecting a Store Location

Stephanie Wilson must decide where to open a ready-to-wear boutique she's been contemplating for several years. Now in her late 30s, she's been working in municipal government ever since leaving college, where she majored in fine arts. She's divorced with two children (ages five and eight) and wants her own business, at least partly to be able to spend more time with her children. She loves fashion, feels she has a flair for it, and has taken evening courses in fashion design and retail management. Recently, she heard about a plan to rehabilitate an old arcade building in the downtown section of her Midwestern city. This news crystallized her resolve to move now. She's considering three locations.

THE DOWNTOWN ARCADE

The city's central business district has been ailing for some time. The proposed arcade renovation is part of a master redevelopment plan, with a new department store and several office buildings already operating. Completion of the entire master plan is expected to take another six years.

Dating from 1912, the arcade building was once the center of downtown trade, but it's been vacant for the past 15 years. The proposed renovation includes a three-level shopping facility, low-rate garage with validated parking, and convention center complex. Forty shops are planned for the first (ground) floor, 28 more on the second, and a series of restaurants on the third.

The location Stephanie is considering is 900 square feet and situated near the main ground floor entrance. Rent is $20 per square foot, for an annual total of $18,000. If sales exceed $225,000, rent will be calculated at 8 percent of sales. She'll have to sign a three-year lease.

TENDERLOIN VILLAGE

The gentrified urban area of the city where Stephanie lives is called Tenderloin Village because of its lurid past. Today, however, the neat, well-kept brownstones and comfortable neighborhood make it feel like a trendy enclave. Many residents have done the remodeling work themselves and take great pride in their neighborhood.

About 20 small retailers are now in an area of the Village adjacent to the convention center complex, along with some vegetarian or nouveau cuisine restaurants. There are also three small women's specialty clothing stores.

The site available to Stephanie is on the Village's main street on the ground floor of an old house. Its space is also about 900 square feet. Rent is $15,000 annually with no extra charge based on the level of sales. The landlord knows Stephanie and will require a two-year lease.

APPLETREE MALL

This suburban mall has been open for eight years. A successful regional center, it has three department stores and

100 smaller shops just off a major interstate highway about eight miles from downtown. Of its nine women's clothing retailers, three are in a price category considerably higher than what Stephanie has in mind.

Appletree has captured the retail business in the city's southwest quadrant, though growth in that sector has slowed in the past year. Nevertheless, mall sales are still running 12 percent ahead of the previous year. Stephanie learned of plans to develop a second shopping center east of town, which would be about the same size and character as Appletree Mall. But groundbreaking is still 18 months away, and no renting agent has begun to enlist tenants.

The location available to Stephanie in Appletree is two doors from the local department store chain. At 1,200 square feet, it's slightly larger than the other two possibilities. But it's long and narrow—24 feet in front by 50 feet deep. Rent is $24 per square foot ($28,800 annually). In addition, on sales that exceed $411,500, rent is 8 percent of sales. There's an additional charge of 1 percent of sales to cover common-area maintenance and mall promotions. The mall's five-year lease includes an escape clause if sales don't reach $411,500 after two years.

DISCUSSION QUESTIONS

1. List the pluses and minuses of each location.
2. What type of store would be most appropriate for each location?
3. If you were Stephanie, which location would you choose? Why?

Source: This case was prepared by Professor David Ehrlich, Marymount University.

CASE 15   Hutch: Locating a New Store

In June, after returning from a trip to the Bahamas, Dale Abell, vice president of new business development for the Hutch Corporation, began a search for a good location to open a new store. After a preliminary search, Abell narrowed the choice to two locations, both in Georgia. He now faces the difficult task of thoroughly analyzing each location and determining which will be the site of the next store.

COMPANY BACKGROUND

The Hutch store chain was founded in 1952 by John Henry Hutchison, a musician and extremely successful insurance salesman. Hutchison established the headquarters in Richmond, Virginia, where both the executive offices and one of two warehouse distribution centers are located. Hutch currently operates 350 popularly priced women's clothing stores throughout the Southeast and Midwest. Manufacturers ship all goods to these distribution centers. They are delivered floor-ready, in that the vendor has attached price labels, UPC identifying codes, and source tags for security purposes and placed appropriate merchandise on hangers. Once at the distribution centers, the merchandise is consolidated for reshipment to the stores. Some staple merchandise, such as hosiery, is stored at these distribution centers. All Hutch stores are located within 400 miles of a distribution center. This way, as Abell explains, "A truck driver can deliver to every location in two days."

HUTCH FASHIONS

Hutch Fashions is considered one of the leading popularly priced women's fashion apparel chains in the Southeast. The stores carry trendy apparel selections in juniors', misses', and women's sizes, all at popular prices. The chain offers a complementary array of accessories in addition to its main features of dresses, coats, and sportswear. Located mainly in strip centers and malls, these shops typically require 4,000 to 5,000 square feet.

HUTCH EXTRA

Hutch Extra stores are primarily located in strip centers and malls. They bear a strong resemblance to Hutch Fashions. The difference is that Hutch Extra stores require less space (2,000–3,000 square feet) and cater to women requiring large and half-size apparel. (Women who wear half-sizes require a larger size but are not tall enough to wear a standard large size. In other words, a size 18½ is the same as size 18 except that it is cut for a shorter woman.)

HUTCH FASHIONS* HUTCH EXTRA

Although Hutch Fashions and Hutch Extra stores selectively appear as separate entries, the corporate goal is to position both as a single entity. The combination store emerged in 1986 and is now used for all new stores. The Hutch Fashions* Hutch Extra combination occupies a combined space of 6,000–7,000 square feet, with separate entrances for each entity. A partial wall separates the two frontal areas of the store but allows for a combined checkout/customer service area in the rear. These stores are primarily located in strip centers and can occasionally be found in malls. (Exhibit 1 shows a typical layout.)

MARKETING STRATEGY

Customers

Hutch's target market is women between the ages of 18 and 40 years who are in the lower–middle to middle-income range. Abell explains, "We don't cater to any specific ethnic group, only to women who like to wear the latest fashions."

EXHIBIT I
Layout of Hutch Fashions* Hutch Extra Store

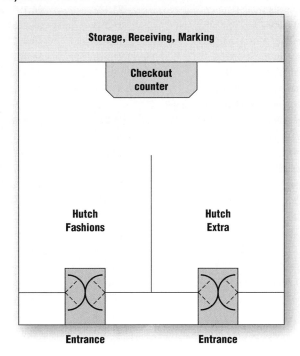

Product/Price

Hutch positions merchandise and price levels between the mass merchandisers and the department stores. You won't find any bluelight specials or designer boutiques in a Hutch store. By avoiding direct competition for customers with the large discounters (Target, Wal-Mart) and the high-fashion department stores and specialty shops, Hutch has secured a comfortable niche for itself. "Our products must be priced at a level where our customers perceive our products to be elegant and fashionable but not too expensive," notes Abell.

Location

Hutch stores are located throughout the Southeast and Midwest and must be within a 400-mile radius of a Hutch distribution center. Within this geographic area, Hutch stores are located in communities with a population range of 10,000 to 50,000 and a trade area of 50,000 to 150,000. These locations are characterized by a large concentration of people in the low- to middle-income brackets who work in agriculture and industry.

Hutch stores are primarily located in strip malls or strip centers—generally ones anchored by either a regional or national discount store (Wal-Mart or Target). In addition, these centers contain a mix of several nationally recognized and popular local tenants. Hutch stores are primarily located adjacent to the center's anchor. Mall locations must be on the main corridor, as close to "center court," as economics (rent) will allow. Abell remarked, "We don't care if it's the only center in the region. If the only space available is at the end of the mall, we won't go in there. Our plan is to be a complement to the anchor and to feed off the traffic coming to it. We may have a rep-

utation for being picky and having one of the toughest lease agreements in the business, but it's one of the main reasons for our continued success."

DATA SOURCES

Abell is using several reports generated by Claritas to help him decide which location to choose for the next Hutch store. He has chosen reports that describe the 10-mile ring around each of the proposed locations. Exhibits 2 and 3 summarize these reports. They contain detailed population, household, race, income, education, and employment data, plus figures on retail sales and number of establishments. The reports also provide information about women's apparel sales and give a market index that estimates the annual per-person spending potential for the trade area divided by the national average (see Exhibit 3). Dalton's 99 index means that the spending potential for women's clothing is slightly lower than the national average of 100. Finally, Abell is using Claritas/UDS's PRIZM lifestyle reports. These reports contain numeric figures and percentages on the population, households, families, sex, age, household size, and ownership of housing. An excerpt from the report is given in Exhibit 4. Some of the cluster group names are described in Exhibit 5.

THE POTENTIAL LOCATIONS

Dalton

Dalton produces most of the carpeting in the United States. Consequently, carpet mills are the major employers in Dalton. Stain Master carpeting has been putting a strain on the city's water supply. Stain Master is said to require seven times the amount of water as regular carpeting and is rapidly becoming the largest proportion of carpeting produced. Expressing concern over market viability, Abell said, "If the Dalton area were ever to experience a severe drought, the carpet mills would be forced to drastically reduce production. The ensuing layoffs could put half the population on unemployment."

The proposed site for the new store is the Whitfield Square shopping center located off the main highway, approximately two miles from the center of town (see Exhibit 6). After meeting with the developer, Abell was pleased with several aspects of the strip center. He learned that the center has good visibility from the highway, will be anchored by both Wal-Mart and Kroger (a large grocery chain), and has ample parking. Abell is also reasonably pleased with the available location within the center, which is one spot away from Wal-Mart. However, he is concerned about the presence of two large outparcels in front of the center that would reduce the number of parking spaces and direct visibility of the center. (An outparcel is a freestanding structure at the front of a mall, commonly a fast-food outlet, a bank, or a gas station.) Other tenants in the center include a nationally recognized shoe store, a beauty salon, two popular restaurants (Chinese and Mexican), and McSpeedy's Pizza at the end of the center, as well as a Century 21 real estate training school in the middle.

EXHIBIT 2

Population and Competitive Profile, 10-Mile Ring from Centers of Dalton and Hinesville, Georgia

		Dalton	Hinesville
Population	2015 projection	93,182	64,195
	2008 estimate	87,293	57,945
	1999 Census	79,420	49,853
	1990 Census	71,373	34,125
	% change, 1999–2008	9.9%	16.2%
	% change, 1990–1999	11.3%	46.1%
	In group quarters (military base) 2008	.9%	11.2%
Household	2015 projection	35,570	20,010
	2008 estimate	33,140	17,541
	1999 Census	29,340	14,061
	1990 Census	24,302	8,557
	% change, 1999–2008	12.9%	24.7%
	% change, 1990–1999	20.7%	64.3%
Families	2008 estimate	24,347	14,277
Race, 2008	White	92.0%	54.1%
	Black	4.9%	38.3%
	American Indian	0.2%	0.5%
	Asian or Pacific Islander	0.6%	3.1%
	Other	2.3%	4.0%
Age, 2008	0–20	31.2%	40.2%
	21–44	37.1%	47.0%
	45–64	21.7%	9.2%
	65+	9.9%	3.4%
	Median age, 2008	33.7	23.9
	Male	32.5	23.6
	Female	35.0	24.6
Household size, 2008	1 person	21.0%	15.2%
	2 persons	32.3%	26.6%
	3–4 persons	38.1%	45.7%
	5+ persons	8.7%	12.6%
Income, 2008	Median household income	$30,516	$23,686
	Average household income	$40,397	$28,677
Sex (% male)		49.1%	55.8%
Education, 2008	Population age 25+	49,298	22,455
	No high school diploma	41.0%	15.5%
	High school only	28.6%	41.2%
	College, 1–3 years	19.1%	29.7%
	College, 4+ years	11.3%	13.5%
Industry	Manufacturing: nondurable goods	42.3%	7.2%
	Retail trade	12.6%	23.3%
	Professional and related services	13.3%	21.4%
	Public administration	2.2%	20.0%
Retail sales ($ thousands)	Total	$706,209	$172,802
	General merchandise stores Apparel stores	$26,634	$9,339
Retail establishments	General merchandise stores	12	3
	Women's apparel stores	21	8

EXHIBIT 3

Sales Potential Index for Women's Apparel

	Area Sales ($ mil.)	Area Sales per Capita	U.S. Sales per Capita	Index (area sales ÷ U.S. sales)
Dalton	$18.01	$206.26	$207.65	99
Hinesville	$8.97	$154.74	$207.65	75

PRIZM Neighborhood Clusters   **EXHIBIT 4**

Prizm Cluster	Population, 2008	Percentage of Population	Prizm Cluster	Population, 2008	Percentage of Population
Dalton			Mines & mills	7,694	8.8
Big fish, small pond	4,727	5.4%	Back country folks	4,293	4.9
New homesteaders	6,030	6.9			
Red, white, & blues	31,123	35.7	**Hinesville**		
Shotguns & pickups	8,881	10.2	Military quarters	45,127	77.9
Rural industrial	12,757	14.6	Scrub pine flats	3,476	6.0

PRIZM Lifestyle Clusters   **EXHIBIT 5**

Big Fish, Small Pond

Small-town executive families; upper-middle incomes; age groups 35–44, 45–54; predominantly white. This group is married, family-oriented, and conservative. Their neighborhoods are older. Best described as captains of local industry, they invest in their homes and clubs and vacation by car in the United States.

Rural Industrial

Low-income, blue-collar families; lower-middle incomes; age groups <24, 25–34; predominantly white, high Hispanic. Nonunion labor found in this cluster, which is comprised of hundreds of blue-collar mill towns on American's rural backroads.

Mines & Mills

Older families; mine and mill towns; poor; age groups 55–64, 65+; predominantly white. Down the Appalachians, across the Ozarks to Arizona, and up the Missouri, this cluster is exactly as its name implies. This older, mostly single population with a few children lives in the midst of scenic splendor.

Shotguns & Pickups

Rural blue-collar workers and families; middle income; age groups 35–44, 45–54; predominantly white. This cluster is found in the Northeast, the Southeast, and the Great Lakes and Piedmont industrial regions. They are in blue-collar jobs; most are married with school-age kids. They are churchgoers who also enjoy bowling, hunting, sewing, and attending car races.

Back Country Folks

Older farm families; lower-middle income; age groups 55–64, 65+; predominantly white. This cluster is centered in the eastern uplands along a wide path from the Pennsylvania Poconos to the Arkansas Ozarks. Anyone who visits their playground in Branson, Missouri, or Gatlinburg, Tennessee, can attest that these are the most blue-collar

neighborhoods in America. Centered in the Bible Belt, many back country folks are hooked on Christianity and country music.

Scrub Pine Flats

Older African-American farm families; poor; age groups 55–64, 65+; predominantly black. This cluster is found mainly in the coastal flatlands of the Atlantic and Gulf states from the James to the Mississippi rivers. These humid, sleepy rural communities, with a mix of blacks and whites, live in a seemingly timeless, agrarian rhythm.

New Homesteaders

Young middle-class families; middle income; age groups 35–44, 45–54; predominantly white. This cluster is above-average for college education. Executives and professionals work in local service fields such as administration, communications, health, and retail. Most are married; the young have children, the elders do not. Life is homespun with a focus on crafts, camping, and sports.

Red, White, & Blues

Small-town blue-collar families; middle income; age groups 35–54, 55–64; predominantly white, with skilled workers primarily employed in mining, milling, manufacturing, and construction. Geocentered in the Appalachians, Great Lakes industrial region, and western highlands, these folks love the outdoors.

Military Quarters

GIs and surrounding off-base families; lower-middle income; age groups under 24, 25–34; ethnically diverse. Since this cluster depicts military life with personnel living in group quarters, its demographics are wholly atypical because they are located on or near military bases. Racially integrated and with the highest index for adults under 35, "Military Quarters" like fast cars, bars, and action sports.

Hinesville

Like Dalton, Hinesville has one major employer, the Fort Stuart army base. Abell recalls that popularly priced stores generally do very well in military towns. In addition, Fort Stuart is a rapid-deployment force base. Because the United States currently is involved in a number of international activities, Abell is concerned with a comment by a Hinesville native: "If these guys have to ship out, this place will be a ghost town." The location under consideration is the Target Plaza at the junction of State Route 119 and U.S. Highway 82 (see Exhibit 7). The center is anchored by Target and a grocery store that is part of a popular Eastern U.S. chain. The two anchors are located side by side in the middle of the center. The spot available in the center is a 6,800-square-foot combination of three smaller

units immediately adjacent to Target. Other tenants in the center include a bookstore, a waterbed store, a shoe store, an electronics retailer, a yogurt store, a video store, and a movie theater.

DISCUSSION QUESTIONS

1. How do the people living in the trade areas compare with Hutch's target customer?
2. How do the proposed locations, including the cities, tenant mix, and the locations within the malls, fit with Hutch's location requirements?
3. Which location would you select? Why?

Source: This case was written by Michael Levy, Babson College

EXHIBIT 6
Whitfield Square Shopping
Center, Dalton, Georgia

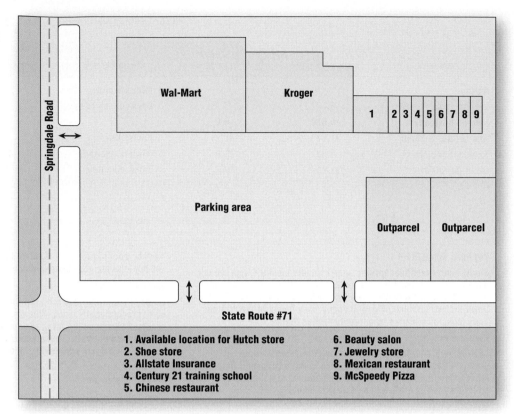

1. Available location for Hutch store
2. Shoe store
3. Allstate Insurance
4. Century 21 training school
5. Chinese restaurant
6. Beauty salon
7. Jewelry store
8. Mexican restaurant
9. McSpeedy Pizza

EXHIBIT 7
Target Plaza, Hinesville,
Georgia

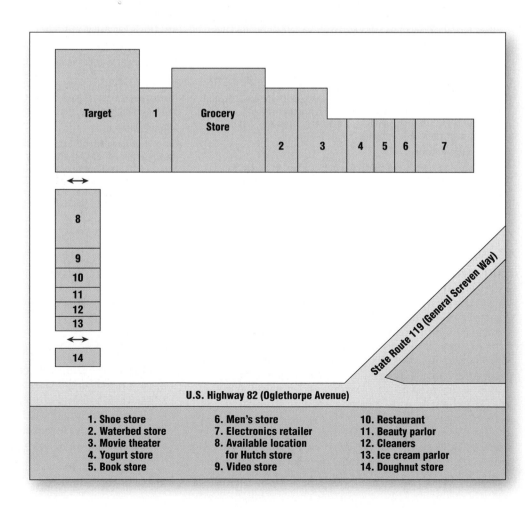

1. Shoe store
2. Waterbed store
3. Movie theater
4. Yogurt store
5. Book store
6. Men's store
7. Electronics retailer
8. Available location for Hutch store
9. Video store
10. Restaurant
11. Beauty parlor
12. Cleaners
13. Ice cream parlor
14. Doughnut store

CASE 16   Home Depot Changes Directions

Home Depot is one of the great success stories in retailing. Founded in Atlanta, Georgia, by Bernard Marcus and Arthur Blank in 1978, the company grew to more than 1,100 big-box stores by the end of 2000, reaching annual sales of $40 billion faster than any retailer in history. The company targets do-it-yourself customers and offers a vast array of home improvement products in a warehouse environment. However, sales associates also are available to answer questions and help customers with projects they are undertaking. The company takes customer service even further by offering how-to clinics and longer four-week courses in its Home Depot University to educate customers about various home improvement projects, such as laying tile and caulking bathrooms. Many store employees possess strong background experience in home improvement and are able to pass their knowledge along to customers. Thus, Home Depot effectively combines the strategies of low price and high service, not commonly seen in retailing.

Marcus (known by most employees as Bernie) created a unique organizational culture, characterized by entrepreneurship, risk taking, a passion for satisfying customer needs, and an aversion to bureaucracy and red tape. Store managers were typically do-it-yourselfers and had a significant amount of control over decisions about merchandising, advertising, and inventory selection for their particular store. Thus, Home Depot stores tended to be less homogeneous in their merchandise offerings than many other national retail chains. Communications and paperwork requirements from headquarters were often ignored, because they distracted managers from their primary function of being on the sales floor helping customers.

Empowering store managers to run their stores with limited restrictions created a strong sense of ownership. Store employees and managers had a great deal of loyalty and pride in the company and their store. By building an enthusiastic staff, Home Depot delivered on its promise of exceptional customer service.

With a market share of 24 percent, Home Depot exuded success. However, historical success and future success are different concepts. Home Depot's board of directors was becoming increasingly unhappy. The company's performance at the time was faltering, with a sharp drop in stock price in October 2000. Costs were increasing because Home Depot could not effectively pool orders from stores to gain scale economies for dealing with vendors. The firm also was having trouble developing mid- and upper-level managers. So Home Depot's directors took action and set out to find a leader capable, in their view, of continuing the firm's growth in sales and profits and transforming it from an entrepreneurial venture to a well managed, large cooperation.

The board found their man in Bob Nardelli. At the time, Nardelli was vying for Jack Welch's position as CEO of GE but lost the battle to Jeff Immelt. Although he was passed up by GE, Nardelli's career had been impressive. From starting as a manufacturing engineer at GE, Nardelli worked his way up to become the head of

GE Transportation and CEO of GE Power Systems. Throughout his career at GE, Nardelli was recognized for his ability to improve operations and execute.

IMPROVING EFFICIENCY

When Nardelli became the CEO of Home Depot, he laid out a three-part strategy: (1) improve the efficiency of the core business, (2) extend the business by offering related services such as tool rental and home installation; and (3) expand Home Depot's market, both geographically and by serving new kinds of customers, such as big construction contractors. To improve the efficiency of the company's operations, he consolidated several business functions. For example, merchandise buying, previously handled by nine regional offices that consolidated requests from store managers, was centralized in the corporate headquarters in Atlanta. By consolidating merchandise buying, Home Depot could get better prices and deliveries from vendors. The company invested $1 billion in new technology, such as self-checkout aisles and inventory management systems. In the past, Home Depot's customer return policy was simply to give cash back, no matter what. Although customers appreciated this policy, the stores suffered widespread abuse because of it. Home Depot saved close to $10 million annually with its new return policy of only store credit without a receipt.

Other cost-cutting efforts were not as successful. For example, to cut costs and gain the flexibility to adjust coverage during busy times of the day, Nardelli tried to shift the staff mix on the sales floor from 30 percent to 50 percent part-time workers. The move was a disaster. Customers complained about bad service, and employees complained that part-timers weren't sufficiently committed, leading Nardelli to abandon this change.

CHANGING THE CULTURE

Shortly after arriving, Nardelli hired a colleague from GE, Dennis Donovan, as his head of human resources. By making a trusted HR executive one of Home Depot's highest paid managers, Nardelli signaled that changing Home Depot's culture would be central to getting the company where it needed to go. Donovan and Nardelli applied the GE mindset, one characterized by strict measurements that emphasized efficiency. Instituting a common set of metrics produced companywide data in areas that hadn't been consistently measured before. These new performance measurements were designed to improve operations, but they also had an important psychological effect.

Initially, the metrics indicated things weren't going as well as employees may have thought. For example, data quantifying customer perceptions of the Home Depot shopping experience replaced anecdotal reports of customer satisfaction and identified several problems in providing a good shopping experience. Other metrics focused on associate training and evaluation. Prior to Nardelli's ascendance, Home Depot had 157 different associate appraisal forms. Now, all 295,000 Home Depot associates are reviewed using just two different forms.

The objective of these performance metrics is to measure virtually everything that happens at the company and hold managers strictly accountable for meeting their numbers. All this information was new to a relatively laid-back organization known for the independence of its store managers and the folksy, entrepreneurial style of the cofounders. These changes did not mean that the company became less interested in developing its people. In fact, Nardelli tried to create an environment that best highlighted each individual's abilities. At Home Depot's headquarters in Atlanta, the company formed a leadership institute offering courses on leadership, merchandising, store planning, financial operations, and Six Sigma to executives with high potential. Nardelli also created a "coaching environment" that promotes succession planning and avoids the need to hire a CEO from outside the company.

Although gross margins and profits increased, the stock price remained the same. Store employees and managers expressed considerable dissatisfaction. Since 2001, 98 percent of Home Depot's top 170 executives were new to their positions; 56 percent of those changes involved bringing new managers in from outside the company. In 2005, Home Depot slipped to last among major U.S. retailers in the University of Michigan's annual American Consumer Satisfaction Index. Even though he produced good financial numbers, Nardelli was asked to resign.

Sources: Dean Foust, Emily Thornton, Roben Farzad, Jena McGregor, Susa Zegel, and Eamon Javers, "Out At Home Depot," *BusinessWeek*, January 15, 2007; Ram Charan, "Home Depot's Blueprint for Culture Change," *Harvard Business Review*, 84 (April 2006); "Home Depot Boots CEO Nardelli," *USA Today*, January 4, 2007.

DISCUSSION QUESTIONS

1. What are the differences in Home Depot's culture before Nardelli and during Narelli's reign as CEO?
2. What effect did Nardelli's policies have on Home Depot's operating efficiency?
3. What were the positive and negative effects of the new programs that Nardelli instituted?
4. How did the shifts in corporate culture affect executives, management, and associates?

Sources: This case was written by Cynthia Wongsuwan and Barton Weitz, University of Florida.

CASE 17 Avon Embraces Diversity

Women have always played an important role at Avon, the largest cosmetics firm in the United States. Mrs. P. F. Albee of Winchester, New Hampshire, pioneered the company's now-famous direct-selling method. Women have been selling Avon since 1886—34 years before women in the United States won the right to vote! Today, Avon is a leading global beauty company, with almost $9 billion in annual revenue. As the world's largest direct seller, Avon markets to women in well over 110 countries through the efforts of more than five million independent Avon Sales Representatives. Avon's merchandise includes beauty products, fashion jewelry, and apparel.

Although most of Avon's employees and customers are women, until recently, the company has been run by men. However, a series of poor strategic decisions in the 1980s led the company to increase aggressively the number of women and minorities in its executive ranks. This decision to increase diversity among its managers was a major factor in Avon's improved financial performance.

Today, Avon is recognized as a leader in management diversity. It has more women in management positions (86 percent) than any other *Fortune* 500 company. Half of the members of its Board of Directors are women. The company also has undertaken various programs to ensure that women and minorities have opportunities for development and advancement. In the United States and elsewhere, Avon has internal networks of associates, including a parents' network, a Hispanic network, a black professional association, an Asian network, and a gay and lesbian network. The networks act as liaisons between associates and management to bring their voices to bear on critical issues that affect both the workplace and the marketplace.

In the 1970s, Avon's top management team was composed solely of men. Avon essentially ignored its own marketing research that indicated more women were entering the workforce and seeking professional careers. It also failed to realize that cosmetic needs were changing, and new approaches for selling products to their customers were needed. Sales growth slowed, and the company reacted by seeking growth through unrelated diversifications. Finally, as the firm was on the brink of bankruptcy, a new top management team entered. Led by CEO Jim Preston, Avon refocused itself on its roots and developed strategies to reach women in a changing marketplace.

Preston realized that Avon's customers needed to be represented in the senior management team. He enacted policies to promote more women into higher-level positions. In addition, Preston shifted the firm's organizational culture to be more accommodating of all its employees.

Avon has also turned to foreign markets for additional growth. In February 2006, the company earned the first direct-selling license in China. According to China's Ministry of Commerce, Avon was the first company to be categorized as a foreign direct-selling enterprise. Avon obtained permission to test its direct-selling approach in two cities, Beijing and Tianjin, and in the province of Guangdong.

Preston's vision also is reflected in Avon's senior management. Andrea Jung is Chair of the Board and Chief Executive Officer; Elizabeth (Liz) Smith is President, Avon Products; and Gina R. Boswell is Senior Vice President and Chief Operating Officer. Half the members of the executive committee, the senior management of the firm, are women. Clearly, Avon has changed its own culture and appreciates the power of diversity and multiculturalism.

The current management team launched several growth initiatives to build on Avon's strong brand name and distribution channel through its customer representative network. Avon product lines include private label brands such as Avon Color, Anew, Skin-So-Soft, Advance Techniques Hair Care, Avon Fragrance, Avon Naturals, mark, and Avon Wellness. Avon also markets an extensive line of fashion jewelry and apparel (see www.avoncompany.com).

Recently, Avon representatives in North America sold more than 40 million lipsticks, making Avon the top seller of lipstick in the mass market. Its Anew brand also is the number one line of anti-aging skin care products in the world. The Advance Techniques hair care line offers high-performance hair products for every hair type, age group, and ethnic background to accommodate a diverse, worldwide consumer base.

Avon Wellness promotes a balanced, healthy lifestyle for women and their families and includes nutritional supplements, a weight management line, and therapeutic products. Avon partnered with the fitness phenomenon Curves, an international fitness franchise, to help women look and feel their best. Through this partnership, Avon Wellness offers an array of Curves-branded exercise videos and DVDs, fitness apparel, accessories, and comfortable footwear that support an active lifestyle.

For the first time in its 121-year history, Avon began focusing on the needs and desires of men by offering grooming products and accessories in one catalog. The Men's Catalog, or M, offers a wide variety of skin care products for men.

Finally, Avon is using technology to support the efforts of its 5 million independent sales representatives. An electronic ordering system allows the representatives to run their businesses more efficiently and improve order processing accuracy. Avon representatives use the Internet to manage their business electronically. In the United States, Avon representatives use an online marketing tool called youravon.com, which helps them build their own Avon business by selling through personalized Web pages, developed in partnership with Avon. Avon e-representatives can promote special products, target specific groups of customers, place and track orders online, and capitalize on e-mail to share product information, selling tips, and marketing incentives.

DISCUSSION QUESTIONS

1. Why is Avon so committed to diversity?
2. Select another retailer that also values diversity. How does this commitment affect its financial results?
3. Make a projection for the results of the test market of Avon's direct-selling strategy in China. How did you develop this projection?

Source: This case was written by Barton Weitz, University of Florida, and Hope Bober Corrigan, Loyola College in Maryland.

CASE 18   Nordstrom Revamps Its Loyalty Program

When members of Nordstrom's Reward program use the store's Visa credit card and spend $1,000 in the store, they receive a $25 gift certificate. If they use it elsewhere and spend $2,000, they earn another $25 certificate. Customers receive notes from sales associates, free gift boxes and access to a complimentary personal shopper. Hence, Nordstrom is using its varied loyalty programs to retain and increase its share of wallet among key customers. The retailer's research indicates customers who have relationships with Nordstrom through either the Rewards program or a salesperson spend more with Nordstrom than those who do not.

Following six months of focus group studies and surveys, Nordstrom launched a new loyalty program in April 2007 to focus on customers who are less interested in discounts and more interested in perks. Nordstrom Fashion Rewards incorporates the company's current points system but provides more benefits in return for shopping at Nordstrom. It calculates customers' spending levels each quarter, rather than every year, and considers usage of any Nordstrom credit or debit card. Benefits available at different levels include complimentary shipping and alterations, invitations to private shopping events, Nordstrom On Call (a 24-hour fashion emergency

hotline), access to exclusive apparel and accessories, tickets to Nordstrom fashion shows, and the opportunity to preselect merchandise prior to Nordstrom's Anniversary Sale, the biggest sale of the year. At its highest levels, the program even offers customers the ability to design private shopping parties or purchase Nordstrom shopping packages, such as trips to store openings, holiday shopping in cities like Chicago and San Francisco, and spa-and-shop getaways. Customers also may buy packages for red carpet events, including travel and accommodation arrangements and a personal wardrobe stylist to help prepare for the occasion.

Nordstrom is not alone in its efforts. Its competitors have also ramped up their loyalty programs. Saks Fifth Avenue introduced a Saks World Elite MasterCard, with which shoppers can earn points on dollars spent outside the store. Diamond Plus customers, who spend at least $25,000 a year at the store, receive free local delivery, complimentary valet parking, storage of one fur item at no cost, advance notice of sales, and invitations to special

REFACT
The average U.S. household belongs to 12 customer loyalty programs and only uses 4 of them actively.

events. Saks also hosts a dinner at a top restaurant once a year for its best customers, who spend between $25,000 and $200,000 a year, and gives them a gift at the end of the evening.

Of the various programs though, Neiman Marcus's In-Circle, launched more that 25 years ago, remains the granddaddy of them all. Its 20 different tiers include a top tier, achieved by earning five million points. Customers usually get one point for each dollar they spend, though at the highest tiers, the point-earning formulas become more generous. Neiman changes its awards each year. For example, the "Rewards Issue" of the program's glossy *Entree* magazine recently featured a model in a Russian red fox stole from fur designer Pologeorgis on its cover, described as a $1,500 value, offered free to those who earn and redeem 50,000 InCircle points. For earning five million points, customers can receive a limited-edition Lexus car, lunch at the Condé Nast headquarters in New York, a visit to the *Vogue* fashion closet, and a private tour of the Metropolitan Museum of Art Costume Institute's fashion exhibit. At Neiman Marcus, the top 100,000 customers each spend an average of $12,333 a year at the store, whereas other shoppers spend an average of $600 a year there.

Sources: Bill Brohaugh, "Neiman Marcus Sweet Rewards Target Loyalty," *Colloquy*, March 23, 2007, p. 2; "Nordstrom Launches 'Fashion Rewards'," PR newswire-First Call (accessed April 26, 2007); Vanessa O'Connell, "Posh Retailers Pile on Perks for Top Customers," *The Wall Street Journal*, April 26, 2007, p. D1.

DISCUSSION QUESTIONS

1. What are the design charateristics of an effective loyalty program?
2. How effective is Nordstrom's new program in terms of developing customer loyalty?
3. Whom should Nordstrom target for its loyalty program?
4. Is the Nordstrom program worth what it spends to reward customers? Why or why not? Explain.
5. Are luxury consumers more drawn to reward/loyalty programs than are those in other economic groups? Are they drawn to different types of programs?
6. What do you see as the strength or weakness of loyalty programs such as Nordstrom's Fashion Rewards or InCircle at Neiman Marcus?

Source: This case was written by Barton Weitz, University of Florida.

CASE 19 Nolan's Finest Foods: Category Management

Nolan's Finest Foods is a full-service retailer that offers shoppers the convenience of one-stop shopping at its high-end, food-and-drug combo stores in the San Francisco Bay area. The chain features a variety of high-quality products at competitive prices but uses promotional pricing as well. Historically, Nolan's has enjoyed great success in its markets and led the region for several years. However, on this winter morning, Roberto Ignacio, the director of strategic planning, had a more immediate concern. The wire services had reported a few weeks ago that the Valumart grocery chain had announced plans for the construction of 10 new food-and-drug combo centers throughout Nolan's markets. After poring over current research and financial results, Ignacio had decided to examine category management as a defense against the encroachment of Valumart.

To date, Nolan's did not have any experience with category management. A decision was made to pilot test category management in some categories before implementing a systemwide rollout. One of the categories chosen for the test was shampoo. Ignacio's immediate assignment was to review the product category and report back to management with an initial recommendation. As Ignacio looked out of his window at the scenic sunset over the San Francisco Bay, he reviewed the events of the past few weeks and the information that he had obtained on the shampoo category. He had several third-party reports (Exhibits 1, 2, and 3) that provided background information about national trends in the shampoo category and trends in supermarkets. Another report (Exhibit 4) provided him with information on how Nolan's shampoo sales compared to the rest of the market.

EXHIBIT 1
Total U.S. Supermarket Dynamics: Shampoo

52 Weeks	# Active SKUs	% New SKUs	# SKUs Handled	SKU Dollar Velocity
Category	1,974	15%	235	$1.64
Brands	1,714	16	229	1.65
Private label	241	12	5	1.33
Generic	19	—	1	1.00

EXHIBIT 2
Shampoo Dollar Share

Trade Channel	12 Months Last Year	12 Months This Year
Food	51.7%	50.5%
Drug	25.6	25.0
Mass merchant	22.7	24.5

EXHIBIT 3
Shampoo Growth

Trade Channel	Dollar Sales % Change versus a Year Ago
Food	0.9%
Drug	4.2
Mass merchant	8.1

EXHIBIT 4
Dollar Sales: Percent Change versus a Year Ago

	MARKET		NOLAN'S FINEST	
	13 Weeks	52 Weeks	13 Weeks	52 Weeks
Total dollar sales	+.1	+1.2	−10.6	−4.5
HBA department	+1.5	+4.2	−8.5	−4.3
Shampoo category	−3.5	+.7	−19.6	−9.7

EXHIBIT 5
Competitive Price Comparison for Shampoo: Counts of Items Showing Differences from the Base Zone (Nolan's Finest Foods)

	Nolan's	Food #1	Mass Merch.	Chain Drug	Food #2
Competition is higher	0	87	0	101	0
Competition is same	103	0	0	0	59
Competition is lower	0	16	103	2	44
Competition does not carry	0	0	0	0	0

However, these reports did not provide Ignacio with information about how Nolan's stacked up against the competition in terms of its assortment and pricing. After some checking around, Ignacio found that he could order reports from third-party vendors that would provide him with an analysis of Nolan's and the competition in terms of product mix and pricing. He had placed an urgent order for these analyses, which arrived this morning through courier (Exhibits 5, 6, and 7).

A few terms in the analyses require explanation:

SKU dollar velocity	Revenue per SKU per store per week
HBA	Health and beauty aids
Market	All food stores
Remaining market	All food stores excluding Nolan's

As Ignacio headed for the water cooler, feeling upbeat by the thought that he had a handle on the shampoo cate-

gory, he ran into Hal Jeffreys, a longtime veteran at Nolan's and vice president of information systems. Knowing that Jeffreys had at one time managed health and beauty aids at Nolan's, Ignacio mentioned his review of the shampoo category and the category management initiative. Jeffreys responded that for years he had a simple approach for category management. He would begin by generating a list of slow sellers in the category and then try to replace these slow sellers with new products or increase the shelf space for existing products. With the new information systems that Nolan's had installed in the past year, generating a slow seller list was very easy. To prove his point, Jeffreys walked back with Ignacio to his office and, using his PC,

Brand Importance Report for Shampoo: Nolan's Foods versus Remaining Market for 13 Weeks   EXHIBIT 6

Description	Chain Sales	Chain Rank	Rem. Mkt. Rank	Rem. Mkt. Sales	Chain Mkt. Share	Chain Category Impt.	Rem. Mkt. Cat. Impt.
Clean & Soft	$108,826	1	1	$512,345	17.5%	14.5	13.0
1st Impressions	77,672	2	3	370,341	17.3	10.3	9.4
Mane Tame	64,446	3	4	244,160	20.9	8.6	6.2
Bargain Bubbles	56,864	4	2	433,300	11.6	7.6	11.0
Silky Style	43,198	5	6	147,773	22.6	5.8	3.7
Elegance	30,869	6	5	181,075	14.6	4.1	4.6

Product Mix Summary Report: Shampoo Dollar Sales—13 Weeks   EXHIBIT 7

	Clean & Soft	1st Impressions	Mane Tame	Bargain Bubbles	Silky Style	Elegance	Private Label
Items carried							
Nolan's	25	25	15	21	13	5	7
Rem. mkt.	25	39	28	42	20	16	28
Sizes carried							
Nolan's	6	6	6	2	4	1	4
Rem. mkt.	7	10	11	3	5	4	6
Types carried							
Nolan's	6	7	6	19	4	5	6
Rem. mkt.	6	10	8	32	5	7	21

EXHIBIT 8   Slow Seller Report: Shampoo for Nolan's Foods, 13 Weeks versus a Year Ago

Item	Chain Sales	Chain Mkt. Share	Chain Subcat. Impt.	Rem. Mkt. Growth	Chain Growth	Chain Avg. % Stores Selling
Golden JJB Lq T 3 oz.	$ 3	9.9%	.0	−51.2-	−50.0	0%
1st Imprs. DF ND Lot. 11 oz.	10	.7	.0	−59.4	−99.4	0
Gentle GLD Lq. 11 oz.	11	100.0	.0	−100.0	9.6	0
Golden AV Lq. T 3 oz.	12	22.4	.0	13.2	−69.2	1
Suds PB Lq. 8 oz.	14	6	.0	107.1	2.9	0
Silky Style X-B Lq. 18 oz.	14	1.6	.0	−65.6	−99.5	0

generated a slow seller report for the shampoo category (Exhibit 8).

"See, technology has made this a real cinch," said Jeffreys and wondered aloud whether the expense and effort of category management would produce net improvements over and above this very simple "knock off the slow seller" approach. "I'll try to come to your presentation tomorrow," said Jeffreys as he left Ignacio's office.

As Jeffreys left his office, Ignacio sank back into his chair with a knot in his stomach. He felt that he had jumped the gun in thinking that he had a handle on the shampoo category. Things seemed to be more complicated than they had appeared earlier in the day. Ignacio wondered whether the shampoo category seemed so difficult because it was the first attempt at category management. In any case, his immediate concern was to prepare for his presentation tomorrow. Since Hal Jeffreys would be in the audience, he knew that he would have to address the "knock out the slow sellers" perspective.

DISCUSSION QUESTIONS

1. What are the national sales trends in the shampoo category?
2. What are the differences in shampoo sales trends at Nolan's compared with national trends?
3. What would be causing these differences?
4. Suggest a plan of action.

Source: This case was written by Kirthi Kalyanam, Retail Management Institute, Santa Clara University. © Dr. Kirthi Kalyanam.

CASE 20   Developing a Buying Plan for Hughe's

A well-established, medium-size department store in the Midwest, Hughe's satisfies consumers' needs by featuring popular names in fashion for the individual consumer, family, and home. It tries to offer a distinctive, wide assortment of quality merchandise with personalized customer service. The customer services include personal shoppers; credit through in-house charge, American Express, and Visa; and an interior design studio. Hughe's pricing policy permits it to draw customers from several income brackets. Moderate-income consumers seeking value and fashion-predictable soft goods are target customers, as are upscale customers with a special interest in fashion.

The department store is implementing new marketing strategies to prepare for continuing growth and expansion.

Hughe's merchandising philosophy is to attract the discerning middle-market customer who comprises 70 percent of the population as well as sophisticated fashion-conscious consumers who expect to buy high-quality, brand-name merchandise at competitive prices.

One portion of Hughe's buying staff is responsible for the Oriental rug department within home furnishings. The open-to-buy figure for this classification within the home furnishings division will be based on last year's sales history (Exhibit 1).

It has been projected that a 15 percent increase over last year's sales volume can be attained due to Oriental rugs' continued popularity. This year's open-to-buy for fall/winter will be $66,200.

EXHIBIT I
Previous Year's Fall/ Winter Sales Results for Oriental Rugs

Sales Volume	$120,000			
Markup	51.5%			
Size	Percentage of Sales		Fabrication	Percentage of Sales
3′ × 5′	20%		Silk	15%
4′ × 6′	40		Cotton	25
6′ × 9′	15		Wool	60
8′ × 10′	10			
9′ × 12′	15			

The buying staff will be making its purchases for fall/ winter in Amritsar, India, a city known for top-quality carpets. Ghuman Export Private, Ltd., of Amritsar, Punjab, India, is the manufacturer the buyers will contact. Exhibit 2 shows information about Ghuman to use in the decision-making process.

DISCUSSION QUESTION

1. Work up a buying plan to use when purchasing merchandise from Ghuman's.
2. How should Hughe's distribute the allotted open-to-buy dollars among the available sizes, colors, and fabrications?
3. Because it is dealing with an overseas manufacturer, how should Hughe's address additional costs, such as duties and shipping, that need to be covered by the allocated open-to-buy dollars?

Source: This case was prepared by Ann Fairhurst, Indiana University.

EXHIBIT 2
Ghuman's Wholesales Price List

	FABRICATION		
Size	Silk	Wool	Cotton
3 × 5′	$400	$250	—
4 × 6′	700	500	$200
6 × 9′	850	700	275
8 × 10′	1,200	1,000	350
9 × 12′	1,400	1,300	500

Colors: Background colors available are navy, burgundy, black, and cream.

Quantities required for purchase: No minimum orders required.

Payment plan: Payment can be made in American dollars or Indian rupees. Letter of credit needs to be established prior to market trip.

Delivery: Air freight—10 to 14 days delivery time; cost is usually 25 percent of total order.

Ocean freight—39 days plus inland time is necessary; cost is usually 8–10 percent of total order.

Customer loyalty: Loyalty to customers is exceptional. Damaged shipments can be returned. Ghuman's philosophy is to help the retailers obtain a profit on their product lines.

CASE 21   McFadden's Department Store: Preparation of a Merchandise Budget Plan

McFadden's Department Store has been a profitable, family-owned business since its beginning in 1910. Last year's sales volume was $180 million. More recently, however, many of its departments have been losing ground to national chains that have moved into the area. To complicate this problem, the National Retail Federation (NRF) predicts a recession, including a 6.5 percent drop in sales, in the coming year for the Pacific Coast, where McFadden's operates.

Department 121 has one of the more profitable departments in the store, maintaining a gross margin of 55 percent. Its basic merchandise is young men's clothing. Last year, sales reached $2,780,750 for the July–December season. The highest sales period is the back-to-school period in August, when autumn fashions are supported by strong promotional advertising. Reductions (including markdowns, discounts to employees, and shrinkages) typically run 20 percent of sales. The percentages of reductions are spread throughout the season as follows:

July	August	September	October	November	December
10	20	15	10	10	35

By month, the percentage of annual sales for Department 121 within this six-month period is distributed as follows:

	July	August	September	October	November	December
2004	3.5	10.1	9.2	6.4	4.8	9.1
2005	3.5	10.3	9.5	6.8	5.3	8.8
2006	3.5	10.5	9.6	6.2	5.5	8.2
2007	3.0	10.3	9.8	6.6	5.5	8.0

The store has planned a pre-Christmas sale in an attempt to counterbalance the slackened sales period following the first of the year. The buyer has decided to bring in some new merchandise for the sale to go along with the remaining fall fashion merchandise. The buyer expects that these efforts will increase December's percentage of annual sales to 30 percent above what it would be without the sale. Top management has emphasized that the department should achieve a gross margin return on investment (GMROI) of 250 percent. The forecasted ending stock level in December is $758,000.

Additional information about the historical stock-to-sales ratio for this type of department is available from a similar department in another store that happens to have a lower average stock-to-sales ratio:

July	August	September	October	November	December
3.0	1.9	2.1	2.4	2.5	2.2

EXHIBIT I   Form for Merchandise Budget Plan

McFadden's Merchandise Budget

Planning Data

SALES FORECAST $ _____

Planned GMROI	=	$\dfrac{\text{Gross Margin}}{\text{Net Sales}}$	×	$\dfrac{\text{Net Sales}}{\text{Inventory Costs}}$	$\dfrac{\text{Sales}}{\text{Inventory Costs}}$ × (100% − GM%) = Inventory Turnover	12 ÷ Inventory Turnover = B.O.M. Stock/Sales

Planned GMROI = $\dfrac{\$\_\_\_}{\$\_\_\_} \times \dfrac{\$\_\_\_}{\$\_\_\_}$

$\boxed{X} \times \boxed{\%} = \boxed{X}$ $\div \boxed{X} = \boxed{X}$

Forecasted Ending Inventory $\boxed{\$\quad}$

			The Plan
Markdowns	%	$	
Discounts +	%	$	
Shortages +	%	$	
Total Reductions	%	$	

		Jan	Feb	Mar	Apr	May	Jun	Jul	Aug	Sept	Oct	Nov	Dec	Total (Average)	Remarks
% Distribution of Sales by Month	1													100.0%	History/Projection
Monthly Sales	2														Step (1) × Net Sales
% Distribution of Reductions/Mo	3													100.0%	History/Projection
Monthly Reductions	4														Step (3) × Total Reductions
B.O.M. Stock/Sales Ratios	5														Adjusted by Mo. Sales Fluctuations
B.O.M. Stock ($000)	6														Step (2) × Step (5)
E.O.M. Stock ($000)	7												(Forecasted End Inventory)		EOM Jan = BOM Feb
Monthly Additions to Stock ($000)	8														Steps 2 + 4 + 7−6 Sales + Reductions + EOM−BOM

DISCUSSION QUESTIONS

1. Prepare a merchandise budget plan. You may do the plan by hand by using the form in Exhibit 1, or you may prepare the plan using the Excel spreadsheet on the student side of the Online Learning Center (OLC). You will need to prepare some intermediate calculations before inputting your answers onto the spreadsheet. Click on the Merchandise Management Module. Click through the exercises until you get to "The Calculation Section." You can access an Excel-based, six-month merchandise budget plan by clicking on the link "merchandise budget." Plug in the numbers from the case.

2. On a separate sheet of paper, explain how you determined the sales forecast, percentage of sales per month, and monthly stock-to-sales ratios.

Source: This case was prepared by Michael Levy, Babson College, and Harold Koenig, Oregon State University.

CASE 22   Selling Pens to Wal-Mart

Wednesday was one of the most important days in Colin Roche's and Bobby Ronsse's careers. The pair had an appointment with a Wal-Mart buyer in Bentonville, Arkansas, to present their ergonomic pen, the PenAgain, to the world's largest retailer. Getting into Wal-Mart is an entrepreneur's equivalent of playing in the Super Bowl. A favor-able response from Wal-Mart would transform their invention from a niche product into a household name. But getting Wal-Mart to stock a new product in the mature writing instrument market was a real challenge.

Roche's path to Bentonville, Arkansas, began during a Saturday detention at his Palo Alto, California, high school. Roche was playing with a toy robot that doubled as a pen and discovered that when he wrote with one index finger between the robot's legs, he didn't need to grip the pen as tightly, and he no longer experienced writer's cramp. He refined the design while in college, and then after graduation, he teamed with his fraternity brother Ronsse to launch Pacific Writing Instruments. They filed for a patent, launched a Web site (www.penagain.com), and set up production in the San Francisco Bay area. The aging population of Baby Boomers dealing with carpal-tunnel syndrome and arthritis created a vast need for ergonomic pens, but their design was truly radical. Traditional pen manufacturers had been attempting to satisfy the market's need by adjusting a pen's length or width or the texture of the grip—never by varying its basic stick design.

Initially, PenAgain focused on small retailers and eventually produced $2 million in annual revenue from 5,000 independent stationery and office supply stores, 200 Staples in Canada, and various other chain outlets, including Fred Meyer and Hobby Lobby. To provide an attractive offering to large retailers like Wal-Mart, PenAgain needed to lower its prices and obtain high-volume manufacturing capability, which meant moving production overseas. It lowered its manufacturing costs so that it could offer a $3.99 pen and expanded its product line to 10 items, including a pencil, highlighter, hobby knife, white-board marker, and children's writing instrument, all in a wide variety of colors and textures.

After talking to local Wal-Mart store managers and attending a trade show hosted by the School, Home, & Office Products Association, the partners landed an appointment with a Wal-Mart buyer. The meeting opened with some bad news: "I've seen this design before and passed," the buyer said, mentioning a competitor's product manufactured in Korea with a similar shape. Roche quickly responded, "The difference is that we are building a brand. Rather than going to you first, we've got a base of independent retailers and distributors worldwide who have already picked us up." (Wal-Mart doesn't like to account for more than 30 percent of a supplier's total business.) He showed her the testimonials, media write-ups, and product extensions. Finally, as their time allotment came to a close, the buyer closed her notebook and said simply, "Okay. We'll give you a trial period."

But that acceptance was just the beginning. Over the next 10 months, PenAgain's founders completed the intensive paperwork required to become an official Wal-Mart vendor. Wal-Mart placed an order for 48,000 pens and

located them on end caps in 500 stores. To earn a more permanent shelf position throughout the entire chain, PenAgain had to sell 85 percent of the pens during the one-month trial period. The PenAgain model sold for $3.76, compared with a nearly identical pen priced at $6.49 on www.amazon.com and more than $12 elsewhere.

Wal-Mart did not provide any marketing support for the pens, and PenAgain was too small to afford traditional print or television advertising. So the partners developed a viral marketing program, reaching out to their national fraternity headquarters and consumer groups that had already shown interest in the PenAgain. The company also marketed through its general e-mail list of some 10,000 customers who regularly bought the pens.

The Wal-Mart buyer did not have time to monitor pen sales, so the partners tracked daily sales over the Internet, using Wal-Mart's Retail Link software system. The PenAgain founders also produced an extra 100 displays for use in Wal-Mart stores and kept them in their own warehouse. PenAgain then hired a merchant service organization, a third-party group that sends representatives into stores to check out display placement and consumer traffic and then report back electronically to the supplier.

In providing its products, PenAgain had to adhere to Wal-Mart's detailed packaging and shipping requirements, which specified the thickness of the cardboard used for display cartons; the placement of a reddish stripe around the shipping container to help Wal-Mart employees know where to place the merchandise in the stores; and shipping labels that included purchase order numbers, distribution center details, and other information.

As the PenAgain partners prepare for what may be the most crucial 30 days of their business careers, they seem realistic about the challenges ahead. "There are things that could go tremendously well, and things that could sink," Roche says. "We have a lot on the line, and honestly, we are nervous as hell."

Sources: http://www.penagain.com (accessed November 15, 2007); Gwendolyn Bounds, "The Long Road to Wal-Mart," *The Wall Street Journal*, September 19, 2005, p. R1; Gwendolyn Bounds, "One Mount to Make It," *The Wall Street Journal*, May 30, 2006, p. B1

DISCUSSION QUESTIONS

1. What are the key steps that PenAgain took to get Wal-Mart to stock its products?
2. If you were one of PenAgain's small retail customers, how would you react to the company selling it products through Wal-Mart?
3. Forecast sales for PenAgain in the 30-days trial.

Source: This case was written by Barton Weitz, University of Florida.

CASE 23 How Much for a Good Smell?

For the past two Christmas seasons, Courtney's, an upscale gift store, has carried a sweet-smelling potpourri in a plastic bag with an attractive ribbon. Heavily scented with cloves, the mixture gives a pleasant holiday aroma to any room, including the store.

Two years ago, the mixture cost $4.50 a bag. Courtney's (the only store in town that carried it) sold 300 pieces for $9.50. Courtney's supply ran out 10 days before Christmas, and it was too late to get any more.

Last year, the manufacturer raised the price to $5.00, so Courtney's raised its retail price to $9.95. Even though the markup was lower than the previous year, the store owner felt there was "magic" in the $10 price. As before, the store had a complete sellout, this time five days before Christmas. Sales last year were 600 units.

This year, the wholesale price has gone up to $5.50, and store personnel are trying to determine the correct retail price. The owner once again wants to hold the price at $10 ($9.95), but the buyer disagrees: "It's my job to push for the highest possible markup wherever I can. This item is a sure seller, as we're still the only store around with it, and we had some unsatisfied demand last year. I think we should mark it $12.50, which will improve the markup to 56 percent. Staying at $10 will penalize us unnecessarily, especially considering the markup would be even lower than last year. Even if we run into price resistance, we'll only have to sell 480 to maintain the same dollar volume."

The owner demurs, saying, "This scent is part of our store's ambiance. It acts as a draw to get people into the store, and its pleasant smell keeps them in a free-spending state of mind. I think we should keep the price at $9.95, despite the poorer markup. And if we can sell many more at this price, we'll realize the same dollar gross margin as last year. I think we should buy 1,000. Furthermore, if people see us raising a familiar item's price 25 percent, they might wonder whether our other prices are fair."

DISCUSSION QUESTIONS

1. What prices caused Courtney's new charges?
2. Which price would result in the highest profit?
3. What other factors should Courtney's consider?
4. What price would you charge, and how many units would you order?

Source: This case was written by Professor David Ehrlich, Marymount University.

CASE 24   Promoting a Sale

A consumer electronics chain in the Washington, DC, area is planning a big sale in its suburban Virginia warehouse over the three-day President's Day weekend (Saturday through Monday). On sale will be nearly $2 million worth of consumer electronic products, 50 percent of the merchandise sold in the store. The company hopes to realize at least $900,000 in sales during the three days. In the retailer's past experience, the first day's sales were 50 percent of the total. The second day's were 35 percent, and the last day's, 15 percent. One of every two customers who came made a purchase.

Furthermore, the retailer knows that large numbers of people always flock to such sales, some driving as far as 50 miles. They come from all economic levels, but all are confirmed bargain hunters. You're the assistant to the general merchandise manager, who has asked you to plan the event's marketing campaign. You have the following information:

1. A full-page *Washington Post* ad costs $10,000, a half-page ad costs $6,000, and a quarter-page ad costs $3,500. To get the maximum value from a newspaper campaign, it is company policy to run two ads (not necessarily the same size) for such events.

2. The local northern Virginia paper is printed weekly and distributed free to some 15,000 households. It costs $700 for a full page and $400 for a half-page ad.

3. To get adequate TV coverage, at least three channels must be used, with a minimum of eight 30-second spots on each at $500 per spot, spread over three or more days. Producing a television advertisement costs $3,000.

4. The store has contracts with three radio stations. One appeals to a broad general audience aged 25 to 34 years. One is popular with the 18-to-25 age group. The third, a classical music station, has a small but wealthy audience. Minimum costs for a saturation radio campaign, including production, on all three stations are $8,000, $5,000, and $3,000, respectively.

5. To produce and mail a full-color flyer to the store's 80,000 charge customers costs $10,000. When the company used such a mailing piece before, about 3 percent of recipients responded.

DISCUSSION QUESTIONS

1. Knowing that the company wants a mixed-media ad campaign to support this event, prepare an ad plan for the general merchandise manager that costs no more than $40,000.
2. Work out the daily scheduling of all advertising.
3. Work out the dollars to be devoted to each medium.
4. Justify your plan.

Source: This case was prepared by David Ehrlich, Marymount University.

CASE 25   Macy's: A National Department Store Brand

In August 2005, Federated Department Stores paid $11.5 billion to acquire the May Company. By adding 400 May stores to its own more than 450 outlets, Federated planned to create a national department store chain that would allow it to compete more effectively against national chains such as Target, JCPenney, and Kohl's. Central to the acquisition was Federated's intention to use the Macy's brand to create a unified image for its regional department store chains, including the newly acquired regional chains owned by May Company.

Federated Department Stores dates back to 1929, when Shillito's (Cincinnati), Bloomingdale's (New York), Jordan Marsh (Boston), and F&R Lazarus (Columbus, Ohio) joined together to form a holding company. All the founding retailers were family-owned chains that traced their origins to the mid-nineteenth century, and all were dominant merchants in their respective regional markets. Abraham & Straus (New York) joined Federated in 1930, and during the decades that followed, other major regional department store chains, including Bon Marche (Seattle), Rich's (Atlanta), Burdine's (Miami), Bullock's (southern California), and Broadway (Los Angeles), also became Federated members. In December 1994, R.H. Macy & Co. merged with Federated. These regional chains remained very involved in their local communities, supporting community events and charities. The multistory, downtown headquarter locations for the chains were well-known landmarks in cities such as Miami, Boston, Atlanta, and Seattle.

The annual Thanksgiving Parade, the classic Christmas film *Miracle on 34th Street*, and a flagship store in New York (one of the city's leading tourist destinations) all contributed to making Macy's one of the best known retail names in the United States. Recognizing the value of this identity, Federated began to expand the brand in 1995, when it renamed the Abraham & Straus stores in New York City. The next year, the Macy's name replaced Jordan Marsh in New England and Bullock's and Broadway in southern California. Then in 2003, Federated added the Macy's name to its regional stores—Rich's became Rich's-Macy's, Burdine's became Burdine's-Macy's, and Bon Marche became Bon-Macy's. On March 6, 2005, however, Federated dismantled the hyphenated names and substituted a single Macy's nameplate. At the time of the May Company acquisition, Federated operated more than 420 Macy's stores and 36 more upscale Bloomingdale's stores.

The 400 stores that Federated acquired from May were organized into 10 regional chains. Similar to other Federated stores, Hecht's (Washington, DC, Virginia), Kaufmann's (Pittsburgh, western New York), Filene's-Foley's (Massachusetts, Texas), Meir and Frank (Oregon), Robinson-May (California), and Marshall Field's (Chicago and the upper Midwest) were long-established, well-loved retailers in their respective trading areas. Nonetheless, shortly after buying the stores, Federated announced that the stores would be rebranded as Macy's, because as CEO Terry Lundgren noted, "We need to think of being a national retailer. . . . We were competing as regional department stores, and not winning." With a single name, the retailer could use a national advertising campaign, strengthen its negotiating power with vendors, expand its private-label programs, and improve its online presence.

To accomplish the brand transition, Federated hired Anne MacDonald, who had overseen marketing for Citibank and been vice president of brand management for Pizza Hut, as Macy's new chief marketing officer. When asked about changing the century-old store names of former May stores, MacDonald stated that "with an acquisition, you have to understand what the brand is currently delivering and the emotional connection consumers have with the brand." She further commented that customers

would accept the Macy's name if the company "was very upfront, very respectful and very involving of the people in each of the communities."

In 2006, Federated surveyed more than 400,000 customers. On the basis of its research, Federated planned to improve customer service in all of its stores, expand its offerings of private-label and exclusive merchandise, improve store layout, and provide amenities such as larger dressing rooms. To avoid offering "cookie-cutter" merchandise assortments across the country, the company grouped its stores into seven regions so that it could tailor product assortments to each area. Federated also promised to continue cherished holiday traditions associated with the former May stores. In Chicago, the company pledged to maintain the Christmas windows at the State Street store, as well as the 45-foot tree in its Walnut Room. In Portland, it assumed sponsorship of the parade on the day after Thanksgiving; and in Pittsburgh, it continued to underwrite local production of *The Nutcracker* ballet.

On September 9, 2006, Federated officially renamed all former May stores. Celebrations at the renamed stores, which were freshly stocked with private-label merchandise, featured block parties, ribbon-cutting ceremonies, and gift card giveaways. The company also launched a major advertising campaign on national and cable television, newspapers, magazines, radio, billboards, and online and sent 54-page catalogs to 3.8 million residents of areas new to Macy's.

Not all customers approved the change. Chicago proved an especially difficult market. More than 60,000 people signed an online petition protesting the loss of Marshall Field's, and "Fields Fans, Chicago" began boycotting Macy's stores. One customer noted, "There was a sense of New York coming here and cramming something down our throat."

Retail analysts and other observers also questioned Federated's strategy. They noted that the May stores had catered to budget-minded customers and wondered whether the Macy's formula of offering higher fashion at higher prices would appeal to those shoppers. One analyst estimated that during the first year of Federated ownership, May stores lost 10 to 20 percent of their customer base. Another attributed the decline to the rapid conversion to the Macy's nameplate, and Macy's emphasis on its private labels, rather than national brands. Tim Calkins, a marketing professor at Northwestern University, argued that a "sharp" transition in retail names and brands "is difficult to pull off, and certainly risks a backlash."

In the months following the name change, sales fell at the former May stores but increased at Macy's other stores. Lundgren used the divergent results to point out that "Time does matter, and it will matter here." In February 2007, Federated announced it would change its corporate name to Macy's Group Inc., because "Most customers don't know what Federated Department Stores stands for, and obviously the name-brand recognition for our new name is an easy decision for us." When the New York Stock Exchange made available the one-letter stock symbol "M," the company chose to rename itself Macy's Inc. The name change took effect in June 2007.

DISCUSSION QUESTIONS

1. What do you think of when you hear the name "Macy's"? Do those brand associations hurt or harm the renamed department stores?

2. What are the advantages of a common brand, Macy's, versus the use of regional department store names?

3. Federated gradually renamed the stores it acquired prior to 2003; by contrast, it rapidly renamed the May stores. Which transition do you think was more effective?

4. Could Federated have delayed the name change? What problems would it have faced? For example, would delaying the change have forced it to continue losing sales to mass merchandisers and operations like JCPenney? Will the disgruntled customers who opposed the name change ever be willing to accept the Macy's name?

Source: This case was written by Marilyn Lavin, University of Wisconsin-Whitewater.

CASE 26   Discount Dining Draws a Crowd: Restaurant Weeks in Major Cities

Growing in popularity, Restaurant Week promotions are springing up all across the country. New York City pioneered the concept in 1992. Since then, copycat events have cropped up in major cities such as Baltimore, Boston, Washington, Philadelphia, San Diego, Pittsburgh, Atlanta, and Denver.

Often organized by local tourism boards and area restaurant associations, the promotions can generate millions of dollars in restaurant revenue each year by bringing in new guests, increasing the volume of business during the week, and inspiring return visits to participating restaurants. Depending on the size of the city and the years in which Restaurant Week promotions take place, anywhere from 60 to more than 200 restaurants participate in the promotions by agreeing to offer specials and deals for a set duration on particular days and times.

A typical promotion includes a multicourse lunch or dinner offer from a selective menu for a price significantly below normal menu prices. During this year's Baltimore Restaurant Week, for example, restaurants such as Oceanaire Seafood Room offered a three-course dinner deal for $30.07, with a lunch version for $20.07. Even diners who normally might prefer a quick salad to a three-course lunch have trouble resisting such a great deal—close to $20 below the set menu price in this case. Instead of grabbing fast food for a rushed meal, diners can take their time, savor food from a renowned restaurant, and enjoy the atmosphere. In some cases, the events have developed a cult-like following, with diners searching for and reserving Restaurant Week spots as soon as they become available.

The offers are not unending though. Restaurant Week promotions generally run for a short period of time, such as a week or 10 days at most. Potential diners thus know that the meal they can get for $30 today will be back up to $70 next week.

This sense of urgency can work several ways. Restaurants lose some money during Restaurant Week because they lower prices. But consumers, prompted by their sense of urgency and the feeling of going somewhere special to eat, spend their food savings on high-margin wine and spirits.

Increasing gasoline, utility, and food costs create tight competition for consumer dining dollars and discretionary income. If Restaurant Week promotions can convince diners that they are treating themselves at the same time as they get a great deal, they may be able to appeal to a wide swath of consumers.

Even tourists can get in on the fun. Restaurant Week promotions are all about location, location, location. As more epicurean tourists plan their vacations around culinary interests, major cities are recognizing the benefits of hosting Restaurant Weeks. Travelers want "experiences" and "excitement" in their social activities, and most want to visit the "downtown" area when they tour a new city.

The challenge, then, lies in finding ways to communicate about the events. Restaurant Week promotions require widespread distribution of time-sensitive information, including last-minute changes in restaurant listings, menus, and pricing. Most promotions employ a dedicated Web site (e.g., www.washington.org.restaurantwk) that features all participating restaurants, information on how to make reservations, and the special meals or menus being offered. With one click, diners gather all the information they need to plan their restaurant visit and take advantage of the deals.

For the restaurants and cities involved, the benefits are multilayered. It is an opportunity for a city to showcase its restaurants. Many restaurants experience significant immediate new and then long-term repeat business as a result of the promotion. But the impact is difficult to quantify. The restaurants cannot, for instance, measure how many regular customers take advantage of the promotion, or whether those taking advantage of the promotion will come back when the prices are back to normal levels.

Sources: "Welcome to the Club," *Restaurants & Institutions* 115, no. 20 (November 1, 2005), pp. 23–23; June Arney, "Discount Dining Draws a Crowd; Owners Say New Patrons Come Back for More after Taste of Restaurant Week," *The Baltimore Sun*, July 27, 2007, p. 1D; Patricia Hochwarth, "The Genius of Restaurant Week," *Restaurant Hospitality* 89, no. 7 (July 2005), pp. 62–68; Scott Hume, "Clip Art," *Restaurants & Institutions* 116, no. 22 (December 1, 2006), pp. 53–54; Ann Shepherd, "Restaurant Week Promotions, When Properly Executed, Fill Seats when Business Is Slow," *Nation's Restaurant News* 41, no. 28 (July 16, 2007), pp. 26–39

DISCUSSION QUESTIONS

1. Does the city where you live have a Restaurant Week promotion?

2. If so, when is it held? Do you believe it is successful? How are you measuring success? What might be some reasons for its success or lack of success?

3. If no, could your city host a Restaurant Week? Why or why not? Which restaurants should participate? When should it be held?

4. Why have Restaurant Week promotions been so successful in general? What is the appeal?

5. To communicate with as many potential diners as possible, Restaurant Week promoters tend to rely on the Internet. Are there any dangers of using only one communication medium? Other than the Internet, what other types of advertising might help promote Restaurant Weeks?

6. Why is a short duration so important to the success of Restaurant Week?

Source: This case was written by Tina Creegan, an evening MBA student at Loyola College in Maryland, under the supervision of Hope Corrigan.

CASE 27 Enterprise Builds on People

When most people think of car rental firms, they may think of Hertz or Avis, but in reality, Enterprise, with annual sales of more than $9 billion, is the largest and most profitable car rental business in North America. The company runs more than 7,000 locations that fall within 15 miles of 90 percent of the U.S. population. Enterprise also operates in Canada, Germany, Ireland, and the United Kingdom. Although it acquired Vanguard (Alamo and National brands) in 2007, Enterprise continues to operate this division as a wholly owned subsidiary.

When Jack Taylor started Enterprise in 1957, he adopted a unique strategy. Most car rental firms targeted business and leisure travel customers who arrived at an airport and needed to rent a car for local transportation. Taylor decided to target a different segment—drivers whose own cars were being repaired or who were driving on vacation, hauling home improvement materials, in need of an extra vehicle for an out-of-town guest, or, for some other reason, simply needed an extra car for a few days.

Traditional car rental companies must charge relatively high daily rates because their locations in or near airports are expensive. In addition, their business customers are price insensitive, because their companies pay for the rental expenses. While the airport locations are convenient for business customers, these locations are inconvenient for people seeking a replacement car while their car is in the shop. Although Enterprise has airport locations, it also maintains rental offices in downtown and suburban areas, near where its target market lives and works. The firm provides local pickup and delivery service in most areas.

Enterprise also rewards entrepreneurship at a local level. The company fosters a sense of ownership among its employees. For example, its management training program starts by defining a clear career path for each management trainee. Then it teaches them how to build their own business. Their compensation is tied directly to the financial results of the local operation. Employees from the rental branch offices often advance to the highest levels of operating management.

The firm hires college graduates—more than 7,000 each year from 220 campuses—for its management trainee positions, because it believes a college degree demonstrates intelligence and motivation. Rather than recruiting students with the highest GPA, it focuses on hiring people who were athletes or officers of social organizations, such as fraternities, sororities, and clubs, because they typically have the good interpersonal skills needed to deal effectively with Enterprise's varied customers.

Jack Taylor's growth strategy is based on providing high-quality, personalized service so that customers would return to Enterprise when they needed to rent a car again. One of his often quoted sayings summarizes his philosophy: "If you take care of your customers and employees, the bottom line will take care of itself." But because operating managers initially were compensated on the basis of sales growth, not customer satisfaction, service quality declined.

The first step Enterprise took to improve customer service was to develop a customer satisfaction measure, called the Enterprise Service Quality Index. The questionnaire that customers complete to assess ESQI was developed on the basis of input from operating managers, which in turn gave those managers a sense of ownership of the measurement tool. As ESQI gained legitimacy, Enterprise made a bigger deal of it. It posted the scores for each location prominently in its monthly operating reports—right next to the net profit numbers that determined managers' pay. The operating managers were able to track how they were doing, and how all their peers were doing, because all of the locations were ranked.

Feedback is also provided to service providers. If a customer mentions in the questionnaire that "I really liked Jill behind the counter; she just was terrific," that comment gets sent the very next morning to the local branch so Jill knows that she did a great job and that a customer said something nice about her. Likewise, if somebody said that a car was dirty, the next day, the local manager knows it and can determine why it happened.

To increase motivation among managers and improve service at their locations, Enterprise also announced that managers could be promoted only if their customer satisfaction scores were above the company average. Then it demonstrated that it would abide by this policy by failing to promote some star performers who had achieved good growth and profit numbers but had below-average satisfaction scores.

To provide a high level of service, new employees generally work long, grueling hours for what many see as relatively low pay. Before they are put in a branch and learn how to rent a car, Enterprise tells new hires about what the company means, what is important to customers, and what it deems important in terms of being a good team member. The company operates like a confederation of small businesses. New employees, like all Enterprise managers, are expected to jump in and help wash or vacuum cars when the location gets backed up. But all this hard work can pay off. The firm does not hire outsiders for other than entry-level jobs. At Enterprise, every position is filled by promoting someone already inside the company. Thus, Enterprise employees know that if they work hard and do their best, they may very well succeed in moving up the corporate ladder to earn a significant income.

Sources: "Enterprise Asks What Customer's Thinking and Acts," *USA Today*, May 22, 2006, p. 6B; John O'Dell, "Rental-Car Giant Rewrites the Rules," *Los Angeles Times*, December 30, 2006, p. C.1; Carol Loomis, "The Big Surprise Is Enterprise," *Fortune*, July 24, 2006, p. 140.

DISCUSSION QUESTIONS

1. What are the pros and cons of Enterprise's human resource management strategy?

2. Would you want to work for Enterprise? Why or why not?

3. How does its human resource strategy complement the quality of customer service delivered by its representatives?

Source: This case was written by Barton Weitz, University of Florida.

CASE 28   Diamond in the Rough

Ruth Diamond, president of Diamond Furriers, was concerned that sales in her store appeared to have flattened out. She was considering establishing a different method for compensating her salespeople.

Diamond was located in an affluent suburb of Nashville, Tennessee. Ruth's father had founded the company 40 years earlier, and she had grown up working in the business. After his retirement in 1980, she moved the store into an upscale shopping mall not far from its previous location, and sales had boomed almost immediately, rising to just over $1 million in five years. However, once it had reached that sales volume, it remained there for the next three years, making Ruth wonder whether her salespeople had sufficient incentive to sell more aggressively.

Diamond's staff was all women, ranging in age from 27 to 58 years. There were four full-timers and four part-timers (20 hours a week), all of whom had at least three years of experience in the store. All of them were paid at the same hourly rate, $10, with liberal health benefits. Employee morale was excellent, and the entire staff displayed strong personal loyalty to Diamond.

The store was open 78 hours a week, which meant that there was nearly always a minimum staff of three on the floor, rising to six at peak periods. Diamond's merchandise consisted exclusively of fur coats and jackets, ranging in price from $750 to more than $5,000. The average unit sale was about $2,000. Full-timers' annual sales averaged about $160,000, and the part-timers' were a little over half of that.

Diamond's concern about sales transcended her appreciation for her loyalty towards her employees. She had asked them, for example, to maintain customer files and call their customers when the new styles came in. Although some of them had been more diligent about this than others, none of them appeared to want to be especially aggressive about promoting sales.

She began to investigate commission systems and discussed them with some of her contacts in the trade. All suggested lowering the salespeople's base pay and installing either a fixed or a variable commission rate system.

One idea was to lower the base hourly rate from $10 to $7 and let them make up the difference through a 4 percent commission on all sales, to be paid monthly. Such an arrangement would allow them all to earn the same as they currently do.

However, she also realized that such a system would provide no incentive to sell the higher-priced furs, which she recognized might be a way to improve overall sales. So she also considered offering to pay 3 percent on items priced below $2,000 and 5 percent on all those above.

Either of these systems would require considerable extra bookkeeping. Returns would have to be deducted from commissions. And she was also concerned that disputes might arise among her people from time to time over who had actually made the sale. So she conceived of a third alternative, which was to leave the hourly rates the same but pay a flat bonus of 4 percent of all sales over $1 million, and then divide it among the salespeople on the basis of the proportion of hours each had actually worked. This "commission" would be paid annually, in the form of a Christmas bonus.

DISCUSSION QUESTIONS

1. What are the advantages and disadvantages of the various alternatives Ruth Diamond is considering?

2. Do you have any other suggestions for improving the store's sales?

3. What would you recommend? Why?

Source: This case was prepared by Professor David Ehrlich, Marymount University.

CASE 29   Fresh Ideas in Grocery Store Layout

Research conducted by faculty at the Wharton School at the University of Pennsylvania tracked and studied consumers' behavior as they were food shopping. The study was conducted at a West Coast supermarket, in which the bottoms of grocery carts were equipped with radio frequency identification (RFID) devices that recorded the travel pattern of individual shoppers. The RFID tags tracked how long customers spent shopping, where they went in the store, and how many items they purchased.

The results of the study showed that shoppers moved through the store in a different way than retailers had expected. People do not weave sequentially up and down every aisle, but instead move in a clockwise direction, stick to the perimeter of the store, and skip entire sections. Often they leave their cart at the end of an aisle and walk down the aisle to get a specific item. Therefore, many customers never see merchandise in the center of the aisle, and end-of-aisle displays are especially important promotional tools.

The study indicated that more time needs to be spent on store layout in the grocery industry to meet shoppers' needs and purchasing patterns. Customers are making more quick trips to the food store, deciding what to serve for dinner on the way home from work, and only purchasing what they need for the next day or two. The once-per-week stock-up trip, which takes 55 minutes or more, accounts for only 10 percent of all grocery store visits.

Based on the Food Marketing Institute's annual "U.S. Grocery Shopper Trends" report, Americans go to food stores on average 2.2 times a week. Nearly two-thirds of shoppers visit a grocery store three or four times per week. On average, each U.S. household spends $92.50 per week at the food store. More than half of those surveyed shop multiple channels, including discounters and warehouse clubs for groceries. The report also found that 54 percent of shoppers make a list. Finally, younger shoppers felt that self-checkout is an important feature when selecting a food store.

Grocery retailers further have noted the following key trends affecting the industry, which call for related improvements in the store:

- Time-strapped customers—grouping items together, offering meal solutions, and improving checkout for speed and convenience.
- Competition for customer loyalty—offering bonus programs and private-label brands.
- Increased pressure from discounters—differentiating the store on benefits other than price.
- Growing interest in nutrition—providing heath information, fresh produce and meat, and organic options.
- Internet shopping—giving technologically savvy shoppers the opportunity to place orders and shop online.

DISCUSSION QUESTIONS

1. How is the supermarket that you shop at most frequently laid out? Describe the store's entry, departments around the perimeter, dry goods, frozen foods, special displays, and checkout.
2. According to the information in the case and your own shopping behavior, what store layout and design features would improve the supermarket and make the experience more enjoyable and convenient for shoppers and more profitable for retailers?

Source: This case was written by Hope Bober Corrigan, Loyola College, Maryland.

CASE 30   Sephora

Sephora, a division of Moet Hennessy Louis Vuitton SA (LVMH), the world's largest luxury goods company, is an innovative retail concept from France that is changing the way cosmetics are sold. Sephora dares to be different in its store design and product offerings. In fact, it defines its fashion retail concept as a means to give customers what they want: "freedom, beauty, and pleasure." Some of Sephora's product offerings include hair care, cosmetics, fragrances, bath and body, and skin care, as well as its own private-label brand of beauty products that account for about 10 percent of sales. The retailer works to ensure that every woman can find the products she desires to pamper herself like a queen.

Sephora takes beauty offerings in a new, exciting direction, allowing the customer to choose her own level of service. The customer may opt for "an individual experience and reflection to detailed expert advice," whether in Sephora's store locations or on its highly interactive Web site (www.sephora.com). This multichannel retailer also issues catalogs several times a year that include beauty tips and trends and showcase a variety of brands and products.

Sephora thus has been taking the U.S. market by storm since it arrived in mid-1998 with two store locations in New York and Miami. Its flagship store, encompassing 21,000 square feet, opened in Rockefeller Center in New York City in October 1999. Now, Sephora operates approximately 515 stores in 14 countries worldwide, with an expanding base of more than 126 stores across North America. Sephora opened its first Canadian store in Toronto in 2004. In addition to its strong presence throughout the United States, it also runs stores in Canada, the Czech Republic, England, France, Greece, Italy, Luxembourg, Monaco, Spain, Poland, Portugal, Romania, Russia, and Turkey. The company plans to open 25 stores in China over the next few years.

Most fashion-oriented cosmetics still are sold in department stores. The scent and cosmetics areas in department stores consist of areas devoted to products made by each manufacturer. Salespeople specializing in a specific line stand behind a counter and assist customers in selecting merchandise.

In contrast, Sephora represents what it calls "the future of beauty," so it should be no surprise that its store designs reflect what beauty consumers might expect in the future. It lures customers into stores with a bright red carpet that immediately induces excitement and intrigue. Once customers enter the store, they are surrounded by what Sephora likes to call "the temple of beauty." An extraordinary assortment of products is arranged alphabetically and by category along the walls. Customers are encouraged to sample the beauty products on their own from self-serve modules. The stores also sell a tremendous variety of brands, including new lines, best sellers, classics, and an exclusive Sephora collection.

For those who cannot get to a store, Sephora offers its cosmetic products online. Speculation in recent years has suggested that beauty products cannot be displayed properly on a two-dimensional Web page. Many other retailers that have been unsuccessful selling cosmetics over the Internet. Yet Sephora again has managed to set itself apart by making its Web site work while still yielding a profit. Sephora offers more than 250 classic and prestige brands, some that consumers have a difficult time finding in de-

partment stores, such as Philosophy, Bare Escentuals, and Lip Fusion.

Women who purchase on the Sephora Web site usually cannot find these products in their hometown malls. To many customers' dismay, Sephora stores are not located in every regional mall across the country. For these customers, Sephora.com represents a one-stop shop for all of their beauty needs. They know that they can find the brands they love at a reasonable price with no hassles. What else could a person ask for?

DISCUSSION QUESTIONS

1. Describe Sephora's target market.
2. Why would women prefer the self-service environment of Sephora rather than the service-oriented environment in department store cosmetic areas?
3. Sephora was unsuccessful in Japan and Germany. Why has this retailer been so successful in other foreign countries?
4. How can a beauty retailer make a seamless transition to online selling? What makes Sephora's online site so successful?

Source: This case was written by Kristina Pacca, University of Florida.

CASE 31   A Stockout at Discmart: Will Substitution Lead to Salvation?

Robert Honda, the manager of a Discmart store (a discount retailer similar to Target and Wal-Mart) in Cupertino, California, was surveying the Sunday morning activity at his store. Shoppers were bustling around with carts; some had children in tow. On the front side of the store, a steady stream of shoppers was heading through the checkout counters. Almost all the cash registers that he could see from his vantage point were open and active. The line in front of register 7 was longer than the other lines, but other than that, things seemed to be going quite smoothly.

The intercom beeped and interrupted his thoughts. A delivery truck had just arrived at the rear of the store. The driver wanted to know which loading dock to use to unload merchandise. Honda decided to inspect the available space before directing the driver to a specific loading dock. As he passed the cash registers on his way to the rear of the store, he noticed that the line at register 7 had gotten a little bit longer. The light over the register was flashing, indicating that the customer service associate (CSA) requested assistance. (At Discmart, all frontline personnel who interact with customers are called CSAs.) As he passed by the register, he could not help overhearing the exchange between what seemed to be a somewhat irate customer and the CSA. The customer was demanding that another item should be substituted for an item that was on sale but currently out of stock, and the CSA was explaining the store policy to the customer. Normally, during a busy time like this, Honda would have tried to help the CSA resolve the situation, but he knew that the truck driver was waiting to unload merchandise that was needed

right away on the floor. Hence, he quickly walked to the rear of the store.

After assigning the truck to a docking bay for unloading, Honda headed back toward the front of the store. On the way back, he ducked into the breakroom to get a Coke and noticed that Sally Johnson, the CSA who had been at register 7, was on a break. Sally had been on the Discmart team for about a year and was considered a very capable employee who always kept the store's interests at heart.

Robert: Hi Sally, I noticed that you had quite a line in front of your register earlier today.

Sally: Hi Robert. Yes, I had a very irate customer, and it took us a while to resolve the issue.

Robert: Oh really! What was he irate about?

Sally: We are out of stock on the 100-ounce Tide Liquid Detergent that was advertised in our flyer and was on sale at 20 percent off. I offered the customer a rain check or the same discount on the same size of another brand, but he kept insisting that he wanted us to substitute a 200-ounce container of Tide Liquid Detergent at the same discount. Apparently, Joe Chang [the assistant manager] had told the customer that we would substitute the 200-ounce size.

Robert: Did you point out to the customer that our sale prices are valid only while supplies last?

Sally: I did mention this to him, but he thought it was strange that we ran out of stock on the morning of the first day of the sale.

Robert: Well, I guess you should have gone ahead and given him what he wanted.

Sally: As you know, our point-of-sale systems allow me to make adjustments only on designated items. Since the 200-ounce sizes were not designated as substitutes, I had to request a supervisor to help me.

Robert: I am glad that you got it resolved.

Sally: Well, the customer got tired of waiting for the supervisor, who was busy helping another customer, so he decided to take a rain check instead. He seemed quite dissatisfied with the whole episode and mentioned that we should stop running these TV ads claiming that we are always in stock and that we guarantee satisfaction.

Robert: I do hate it when they run these ad campaigns and we have to take the heat on the floor, trying to figure out what those cowboys in marketing promised the customer.

Sally: Well, my break is nearly over. I have to get back.

Honda pondered the encounter that Johnson had with the customer. He wondered whether to discuss this issue with Joe Chang. He remembered talking to him about inventory policies a couple of days ago. Chang had indicated that their current inventory levels were fairly high and that any further increases would be hard to justify from a financial perspective. He mentioned some market research that had surveyed a random sample of customers who had redeemed rain checks. The results of the survey indicated that customers by and large were satisfied with Discmart's rain check procedures. Based on this finding, Chang had argued that current inventory levels, supplemented with a rain check policy, would keep customers satisfied.

DISCUSSION QUESTIONS

1. Why did this service breakdown occur?
2. How was this service gap related to the other gaps (standards, knowledge, delivery, and communications) described in the Gaps model in Chapter 19?

Source: This case was prepared by Kirthi Kalyanam, Retail Management Institute, Santa Clara University. © Dr. Kirthi Kalyanam.

CASE 32   Customer Service and Relationship Management at Nordstrom

Nordstrom's unwavering customer-focused philosophy traces its roots to founder Johan Nordstrom's values. Johan Nordstrom believed in people and realized that consistently exceeding their expectations would lead to success and a good conscience. He built his organization around a customer-oriented philosophy. The organization focuses on people, and its policies and selections are designed to satisfy people. As simple as this philosophy sounds, few of Nordstrom's competitors have truly been able to grasp it.

A FOCUS ON PEOPLE

Nordstrom employees treat customers like royalty. Employees are instructed to do whatever is in the customer's best interest. Customer delight drives the values of the company. Customers are taken seriously and are at the heart of the business. Customers are even at the top of the Nordstrom's so-called organization chart, which is an inverted pyramid. Following customers from the top of the inverted pyramid are the salespeople, department managers, and general managers. Finally, at the bottom is the board of directors. All lower levels work toward supporting the salespeople, who in turn work to serve the customer.

Employee incentives are tied to customer service. Salespeople are given personalized business cards to help them build relationships with customers. Uniquely, salespeople are not tied to their respective departments but to the customer. Salespeople can travel from department to department within the store to assist their customer, if that is needed. For example, a Nordstrom salesperson assisting a woman shopping for business apparel helps her shop for suits, blouses, shoes, hosiery, and accessories. The salesperson becomes the "personal shopper" of the customer to show her merchandise and provide fashion expertise. This approach is also conducive to building long-term relationships with customers, as over time, the salesperson comes to understand each customer's fashion sense and personality.

The opportunity to sell across departments enables salespeople to maximize sales and commissions while providing superior customer service. As noted on a *60 Minutes* segment, "[Nordstrom's service is] not service like it used to be, but service that never was."

Despite the obsession with customer service at Nordstrom, ironically, the customer actually comes second. Nordstrom understands that customers will be treated well by its employees only if the employees themselves are treated well by the company. Nordstrom employees are treated almost like the extended Nordstrom family, and employee satisfaction is a closely watched business variable.

Nordstrom is known for promoting employees from within its ranks. The fundamental traits of a successful Nordstrom salesperson (e.g., commitment to excellence, customer service) are the same traits emphasized in successful Nordstrom executives.

Nordstrom hires people with a positive attitude, a sense of ownership, initiative, heroism, and the ability to handle high expectations. This sense of ownership is reflected in Nordstrom's low rate of shrinkage. Shrinkage, or loss due to theft and record-keeping errors, at Nordstrom is under 1.5 percent of sales, roughly half the industry average. The low shrinkage can be attributed in large part to the diligence of salespeople caring for the merchandise as if it were their own.

Employees at all levels are treated like businesspeople and empowered to make independent decisions. They are given the latitude to do whatever they believe is the right thing, with the customers' best interests at heart. All employees are given the tools and authority to do whatever is necessary to satisfy customers, and management almost always backs subordinates' decisions.

In summary, Nordstrom's product is its people. The loyal Nordstrom shopper goes to Nordstrom for the service received—not necessarily the products. Of course, Nordstrom does offer quality merchandise, but that is secondary for many customers.

CUSTOMER-FOCUSED POLICIES

One of the most famous examples of Nordstrom's customer service occurred in 1975 when a Nordstrom salesperson gladly took back a set of used automobile tires and gave the customer a refund, even though Nordstrom had never sold tires! The customer had purchased the tires from a Northern Commercial Company store, whose retail space Nordstrom had since acquired. Not wanting the customer to leave the Nordstrom store unhappy, the salesperson refunded the price of the tires.

Nordstrom's policies focus on the concept of the "Lifetime Value of the Customer." Although little money is made on the first sale, when the lifetime value of a customer is calculated, the positive dollar amount of a loyal customer is staggering. The lifetime value of a customer is the sum of all sales and profits generated from that customer, directly or indirectly. To keep its customers for a "lifetime," Nordstrom employees go to incredible lengths. In a Nordstrom store in Seattle, a customer wanted to buy a pair of brand-name slacks that had gone on sale. The store was out of her size, and the salesperson was unable to locate a pair at other Nordstrom stores. Knowing that the same slacks were available at a competitor nearby, the sales clerk went to the rival, purchased the slacks at full price using petty cash from her department, and sold the slacks to the customer at Nordstrom's sale price. Although this sale resulted in an immediate loss for the store, the investment in promoting the loyalty of the happy customer went a long way.

Nordstrom's employees try to "Never Say No" to the customer. Nordstrom has an unconditional return policy. If a customer is not completely satisfied, he or she can return the new and generally even heavily used merchandise at any time for a full refund. Ironically, this is not a company policy; rather, it is implemented at the discretion of the salesperson to maximize customer satisfaction. Nordstrom's advice to its employees is simply, "Use good judgment in all situations." Employees are given the freedom, support, and resources to make the best decisions to enhance customer satisfaction. The cost of Nordstrom's high service, such as its return policy, coupled with its competitive pricing would, on the surface, seem to cut into profit margins. This cost, however, is recouped through increased sales from repeat customers, limited markdowns, and, if necessary, the "squeezing" of suppliers.

Nordstrom's vendor relationships also focus on maximizing customer satisfaction. According to former CEO Bruce Nordstrom, "[Vendors] know that we are liberal with our customers. And if you're going to do business with us, then there should be a liberal influence on their return policies. If somebody has worn a shoe and it doesn't wear satisfactorily for them, and we think that person is being honest about it, then we will send it back." Nordstrom realizes some customers will abuse the unconditional return policy, but it refuses to impose that abuse back onto their vendors. Here again, the rule of "doing what is right" comes into play.

Nordstrom's merchandising and purchasing policies are also extremely customer focused. A full selection of merchandise in a wide variety of sizes is seen as a measure of customer service. An average Nordstrom store carries roughly 150,000 pairs of shoes with a variety of sizes, widths, colors, and models. Typical shoe sizes for women range from 2½ to 14, in widths of A to EEE. Nordstrom is fanatical about stocking only high-quality merchandise. Once when the upper parts of some women's shoes were separating from the soles, *every* shoe from that delivery was shipped back to the manufacturer.

DISCUSSION QUESTIONS

1. What steps does Nordstrom take to implement its strategy of providing outstanding customer service?
2. How do these activities enable Nordstrom to reduce the gaps between perceived service and customer expectations, as described in Chapter 19?
3. What are the pros and cons of Nordstrom's approach to developing a competitive advantage through customer service?

Source: This case was written by Alicia Lueddemann, the Management Mind Group, and Sunil Erevelles, University of North Carolina, Charlotte.

CASE 33   Lindy's Bridal Shoppe

Located in Lake City (population 80,000), Lindy's Bridal Shoppe, a small bridal store, sells bridal gowns, prom gowns, accessories, and silk flowers. It also rents men's formal wear and performs various alteration services.

Lindy Armstrong, age 33, has owned the store since its founding in March 1997. She is married to a high school teacher and the mother of three young children. A former nurse, she found the demands of hospital schedules left too little time for her young family. An energetic, active woman with many interests, she wanted to continue to work but also have time with her children.

The silk flowers market initially enabled Lindy to combine an in-home career with child rearing. She started Lindy's Silk Flowers with $75 of flower inventory in Vernon, a small town of about 10,000 people 10 miles from Lake City. Working out of her home, she depended on word-of-mouth communication among her customers, mainly brides, to bring in business. As Lindy's Silk Flowers prospered, a room was added onto the house to provide more space for the business. Lindy was still making all the flowers herself. Her flower-making schedule kept her extremely busy. Long hours were the norm.

Lindy was approached by a young photographer named Dan Morgan, who proposed establishing a one-stop bridal shop. In this new business, Dan would provide photography, Lindy would provide silk flowers, and another partner, Karen Ross (who had expertise in the bridal market), would provide gowns and accessories. The new store would be located in Vernon in a rented structure. Shortly before the store was to open, Dan and Karen decided not to become partners, and Lindy became the sole owner. She knew nothing about the bridal business. Having no merchandise or equipment, Lindy was drawn to an ad announcing that a bridal store in a major city was going out of business. She immediately called and arranged to meet the owner. Subsequently, she bought all his stock (mannequins, racks, and carpet) for $4,000. The owner also gave her a crash course in the bridal business.

From March 1997 to December 2008, Lindy owned and operated a bridal gown and silk flowers store named Lindy's Bridal Shoppe in Vernon. The location was chosen primarily because it was close to her home. While Vernon is a very small town, Lindy felt that location was not a critical factor in her store's success. She maintained that people would travel some distance to make a purchase as important as a bridal gown. Rent was $250 per month plus utilities. Parking was a problem.

During this period, Lindy's Bridal Shoppe grew. Bridal gowns and accessories as well as prom dresses sold well. As the time approached for Lindy to renew her lease, she wondered about the importance of location. She decided to move to a much larger town than Vernon. Lake City also is the site of a state university. Lindy decided to move.

GENERAL BUSINESS DESCRIPTION

The majority of Lindy's Bridal Shoppe's current sales are made to individuals who order bridal gowns from the rack or from the catalogs of three major suppliers. At the time of the order, the customer pays a deposit, usually half of the purchase price. The balance is due in 30 days. Lindy would like payment in full at the time of ordering, regardless of the delivery date, but payment is often delayed until delivery. Once ordered, a gown must be taken and the bill paid when delivered.

No tuxedos are carried in the store, so customers must order from catalogs. Fitting jackets and shoes are provided to help patrons size their purchases. Lindy's Bridal Shoppe rents its men's formal wear from suppliers. Payment from the customer is due on delivery.

Certain times of the year see more formal events than others. Many school proms are held during late April and May, and June, July, and August are big months for weddings. Since traditional dates for weddings are followed less and less closely, Lindy believes that the business is becoming less seasonal, though January and February are quite slow.

PROMOTION PRACTICES

Lindy's Bridal Shoppe engages in various promotional activities but is constrained by limited finances. The firm has no operating budget and thus no formal appropriation for advertising expenses.

Newspaper ads constitute the primary promotional medium, though radio is occasionally used. Ads for prom dresses are run only during prom season. These ads usually feature a photograph of a local high school student in a Lindy's Bridal Shoppe gown plus a brief description of the student's activities.

Other promotional activities include bridal shows at a local mall. Lindy feels these have been very successful, though they're a lot of work. A recent prom show in a local high school used students as models, which proved to be an excellent way to stimulate sales. Lindy hopes to go into several other area high schools during the next prom season, though this expansion will demand much planning.

PERSONNEL

Lindy, the sole owner and also the manager of the firm, finds it hard to maintain a capable workforce. A small company, Lindy's Bridal Shoppe can't offer premium salaries for its few positions. There's one full-time salesperson. The part-time staff includes a salesperson, alterations person, bookkeeper, and custodian.

Lindy handles all the paperwork. Her responsibilities include paying bills, ordering merchandise and supplies, hiring and firing personnel, fitting customers, and selling various items. She makes all the major decisions that directly affect the firm's operations. She also makes all the silk flowers herself. It's time consuming, but she isn't satisfied with how anyone else makes them.

MERCHANDISE OFFERINGS

Lindy's Bridal Shoppe's major product lines are new wedding, prom, and party gowns. No used gowns are sold. Discontinued styles or gowns that have been on the rack for a year are sold at reduced prices, primarily because discoloration is a major problem. Gowns tend to yellow after hanging on the racks for a year.

A wide variety of accessories are provided. Lindy believes it's important that her customers do not have to go anywhere else for them. These accessories include shoes, veils, headpieces, jewelry, and foundations. Slips may be rented instead of purchased. One room of Lindy's Bridal Shoppe is used only to prepare silk flowers.

SERVICE OFFERINGS

Lindy's Bridal Shoppe's major service offering is fitting and alteration. Most gowns must be altered, for which there's a nominal charge. Lindy feels that personal attention and personal service set her apart from her competitors. Emphasizing customer satisfaction, she works hard to please each customer. This isn't always easy. Customers can be picky, and it takes time to deal with unhappy people.

LOCATION

Lindy's Bridal Shoppe is located at the end of Lake City's main through street. Initially Lindy didn't think location was important to her bridal store's success, but she's changed her mind. Whereas business was good in Vernon, it's booming in Lake City. Vehicular traffic is high, and there's adequate, if not excess, parking.

Lindy's Bridal Shoppe has a 12-year lease. Rent ($1,800 per month) includes heat and water, but Lindy's Bridal Shoppe must pay for interior decoration. The physical facility is generally attractive, with open and inviting interior display areas. But some areas both inside and outside the store have an unfinished look.

Some storage areas require doors or screens to enhance the interior's appearance. The fitting room ceilings are unfinished, and the carpeting inside the front door may be unsafe. One other interior problem is insufficient space; there seems to be inadequate space for supporting activities such as flower preparation, customer fittings, and merchandise storage, which gives the store a cluttered look.

Several external problems exist. The signs are ineffective, and there's a strong glare on the front windows, which detracts from the effectiveness of the overall appearance and interior window displays. The parking lot needs minor maintenance: Parking lines should be painted, and curbs must be repaired. Much should be done to add color and atmosphere through basic landscaping.

COMPETITION

Lindy's Bridal Shoppe is the only bridal shop in Lake City. Lindy believes she has four main competitors. Whitney's Bridal Shoppe is 30 miles from Lake City; Ender's Brides, a new shop with a good operation, is in Spartan City, 50 miles away; Carole's is a large, established bridal shop in Smithtown, 70 miles distant; and Gowns-n-Such is in Andersonville, 75 miles away. A new store in Yorktown (15 miles away) is selling used gowns and discontinued styles at very reduced prices. Lindy watches this new- and used-gown store closely.

Some of her potential customers are buying wedding gowns from electronic retailers such as The Knot (www.theknot.com) and the Wedding Channel (www.weddingchannel.com). Although these electronic retailers are not yet generating significant sales in her trading area, Lindy is concerned that some of the services offered by these electronic retailers (such as gift registries, e-mail notices, wedding planning, and wedding picture displays) will attract more of her customers.

FINANCIAL CONSIDERATIONS

Basic financial information includes

1. Markup: 50 percent.
2. 2006 sales: $200,000 (estimated).
3. Average inventory: $70,000.
4. Turnover: 3.0 (approximately).
5. Annual expenses: rent $19,200, labor $24,000, utilities $7,000, supplies $12,000, equipment $4,000, and miscellaneous $4,000.
6. Estimated total costs ($200,000 sales): $170,200.
7. Implied profit including owner's salary: $29,800.
8. Capital invested (equipment, $8,000; inventory, $70,000): $78,000.
9. ROI: $5,800/$78,000 & equal; 7.4 percent. (Assume owner salary of $24,000 per year.)

THE FUTURE

Lindy Armstrong is uncertain about the future. She enjoys the business but feels that she's working very hard and not making much money. During all the years of Lindy's Bridal Shoppe's operation, she hasn't taken a salary. She works 60 hours or more a week. Business is excellent and growing, but she's tired. She has even discussed selling the business and returning to nursing.

DISCUSSION QUESTIONS

1. Could Lindy change the emphasis of her merchandise mix to increase her sales?
2. Which products should have more emphasis? Which should have less?
3. What personnel decisions must Lindy face to improve her business?
4. How could someone like Lindy Armstrong balance the demands of her family and her business?
5. If one of Lindy's competitors were to offer her $150,000 for her business, should she sell?

Source: This case was prepared by Linda F. Felicetti and Joseph P. Grunewald, Clarion University of Pennsylvania.

CASE 34   Is Apple America's Best Retailer?

Founded in 1976 by Steve Jobs and Steve Wozniak, Apple has become an innovative leader in the consumer electronics industry. In addition to offering traditional desktop and laptop computers, all of which feature Apple's OS X operating system, Apple essentially founded the digital music player and online music store markets; launches innovative mobile phones; and provides servers, wireless networking equipment, and publishing and multimedia software. Early in 2006, Apple began offering Multi-Pass, a service by which subscribers gain access to select television content. Later that year, it launched an online movie service and introduced iTV to give users access to downloaded shows and movies on their televisions. Its television device, renamed AppleTV, became available early the following year. Although Apple is virtually a household name today, the electronics giant faced numerous challenges on its climb to the top.

CHALLENGES FACING APPLE

During the early 1990s, Apple struggled as computer sales began shifting from specialized computer stores to mainstream retail stores. Big box retailers such as Best Buy and Circuit City could offer a wider selection of computers at lower prices, though they lacked adequate customer service and support. These big box retailers and specialized stores faced even more competition in the form of mail order outlets, including CompuAdd, Gateway, and Dell.

Beginning in 1990, Dell shifted from selling its computers in warehouse and specialized computer stores to operating as an online direct-mail order company. Dell facilitated its online operations with an efficient online store that could handle high-volume sales.

The online Dell store represented a new strategy for manufacturing: Computers built as they were ordered. In turn, Dell could reduce inventory, because it no longer produced computers in mass quantities and then pushed inventory through the channel to resellers.

While establishing its online store, Apple needed to balance its direct orders with the sales initiated by its channel partners, mail order resellers, independent dealers, and CompUSA, with which it initiated a "stores within a store" strategy to focus on Apple's products. Apple's partnership with CompUSA paid off. When the San Francisco CompUSA store was equipped with Macs, Apple's sales jumped from 15 percent to 35 percent of overall store sales.

Apple also put its own employees to work in various retail outlets to help inform and educate customers, as well as ensure its products were being displayed in working order. The company estimated it spent between $25,000 and $75,000 per month on this initiative.

Apple executives soon realized they could not compete with PC brands by selling just laptops and desktops in big box retail stores, because retailers could earn greater profits by selling lower-quality PC models. They had little to no incentive to sell Macs. Without its own retail store, Apple would always be at the mercy of the independent dealers and partners that operated with different strategic goals.

THE SOLUTION: THE APPLE STORE

To compete with the PCs sold by big box retailers, Apple needed to shift from selling its electronics through intermediaries to offering products directly through Apple stores. This shift would not come easily. Steve Jobs, Apple's dynamic founder, first looked to bring in new executives. Mickey Drexler, former CEO of The Gap and J. Crew, was hired in 1999 as part of Apple's Board of Directors. Next, Jobs brought in Ron Johnson, who had been a merchandising executive with Target, to run Apple's retail division as Vice President of Retail Operations.

Instead of launching stores from the start, Drexler suggested that Jobs rent a warehouse and build a prototype store, coined Apple Store Version 0.0. Apple executives then continuously redesigned the store until they achieved a layout that would entice shoppers to not only enter but make purchases. The first store prototype was configured by product category, with hardware laid out according to the internal organization of the company rather than by how customers logically shop. Executives quickly decided to redesign the store to match customer interests better. Although the redesign cost Apple more

than six months, the executives believed this time investment was necessary to achieve a successful store that could compete with well-established electronics retailers and remain consistent with the Apple brand. Its first store opened in Tyson's Corner, Virginia, in May 2001.

THE APPLE STORE LAYOUT

When considering a site for a retail store, Apple uses its customer base to forecast visitor volume and revenues. Most Apple stores locate within existing shopping malls or lifestyle centers, where retail traffic is already present. There are two types of full-size stores, a street-facing building or an in-mall store. The stores range from 3,600 to 20,000 square feet, though most fall in the 3,000–6,000 square feet range. Storefronts are typically all glass with a back-lit Apple logo, and the front display windows change occasionally to focus on the newest marketing campaign. Apple's internal team designs the window displays, often using slot and cable systems to suspend design elements within the window. In some cases, the swinging entrance doors are in the middle, but in other stores, a logo wall appears in the middle with two doors located on either side. Store interiors feature only three materials: glass, stainless steel, and wood.

In addition to the retail floor, Apple stores have backroom areas that sometimes include a public restroom, offices, and the inventory area. At some sites that lack sufficient space, inventory storage is located at a separate facility, though always within walking distance.

The store layout changes multiple times throughout the year. Apple executives organize planograms to coincide with the introduction of new products or heavily marketed merchandise. The layouts depend on the size of the store. A typical in-mall store locates merchandise in the front half of the store and customer service and support areas in the rear. Apple stores carry fewer than 20 products, and every display piece is available for hands-on use. Every computer is hooked up to video camcorders, digital cameras, iPods, and music keyboards so that customers can get an accurate feel for the available hardware and software.

On tables along the right wall, iPhones and iPods take up the front half of the store, whereas the iPod Bar holds court in the rear half. Along the left wall, tables hold various models of general and high-end desktop and laptop computers. These displays give way to The Studio, a newer section hosted by experts who will answer application-oriented, creative questions. Two to three island tables in the front center display software on Apple computers; additional island tables exhibit peripherals such as iPod docking stations and printers. A small children's area houses Apple computers running children's software; the checkout area is nearby. The Genius Bar takes up the back wall with stools before a counter staffed with Apple experts for repairs and consultations. Larger stores also have a theater area in the back, featuring a rear-projection screen with an audience area of either U-shaped wooden benches or full theater seats in rows. This store layout is typical for a store located in a super regional malls.

Apple stores thus follow a free-form layout, which allows customers to browse the store according to their own interests. Signage hanging from the ceiling, for greater visibility, directs customers to specific areas within the store. Bright lighting draws attention to merchandise and creates a sense of excitement. Highlighted merchandise also helps draw customers strategically through the store. As customers browse the products, employees wearing Apple t-shirts and lanyards make themselves available to answer any questions.

In addition, Apple has introduced a series of "mini-stores" that range in size from 500 to 2,000 square feet usually are located within 30 miles of a full-size store. With the goal of expanding Apple's presence in the retail market, mini-stores feature Apple's full line of notebook and desktop computers, iPods, an assortment of third-party products, a small Genius Bar, and onsite repair of all Apple products. Their layout mirrors that of the full-size stores, with merchandise located in the front of the store and customer service in the rear.

Through its intensive development efforts, Apple has created a unique, customer service–oriented shopping experience. Customers can schedule face-to-face appointments at an Apple store to test drive products. One-to-one personal training sessions help customers become familiar with the array of Apple products. The company also offers free, one-hour instructional or informational workshops every day for iPod and Mac owners. Its "Creatives" service offers support for business customers by providing insight and advice about how to create a presentation from start to finish using Apple products.

Sources: "A Preview of Apple's Mini-Stores," *Ifo Apple Store* 2004 http://www.ifoapplestore.com/stores/mini_store_tour/index.html (accessed October 23, 2007); Apple Retail Store, http://www.apple.com/retail (accessed September 25, 2007); Daniel Eran, "Apple's Retail Challenge," 2006 http://www.roughlydrafted.com/RD/Q4.06/1DDD598A-7CE0-479E-A6F9-912777CAB484.html (accessed September 25, 2007); Josh Lower, "Apple, Inc," *Hoover's*, http://premium.hoovers.com/subscribe/co/overview.xhtml?ID=ffffrtjccfjfkfckxf (accessed September 22, 2007); "The Stores," *Ifo Apple Store*, 2007 http://www.ifoapplestore.com/the_stores.html (accessed September 25, 2007); Jerry Useem "Apple: America's Best Retailer," *CNNMoney* http://money.cnn.com/magazines/fortune/fortune_archive/2007/03/19/8402321/index.htm (accessed August 24, 2007).

DISCUSSION QUESTIONS

1. Have you ever visited an Apple store? If yes, did you make a purchase? Why or why not?
2. Why is Apple's store layout and atmosphere important?
3. Do you agree with the way Apple addressed the challenges it faced from competition?
4. Is Apple America's best retailer?
5. Visit your local Apple store. What has changed about the store layout and merchandise from the layout described in this case?

Source: This case was written by Brienne Curley, an evening MBA student at Loyola College in Maryland, under the supervision of Hope Corrigan.

CASE 35   Starbucks Coffee Company

Starbucks is the leading retailer of specialty coffee beverages and beans and related food and merchandise. Its annual sales of more than $6.0 billion earn it profits of more than $400 million. Starbucks owns and operates more than 6,600 retail stores and has licensed an additional 3,700 airport and shopping center stores in 41 countries. The average Starbucks customer visits the store 18 times a month; 10 percent visit twice a day.

In addition to its direct retailing activities, Starbucks has formed strategic alliances with Breyer's Grand Ice Cream, Kraft Foods, Barnes & Noble Booksellers, Jim Beam, United Airlines, and PepsiCo to expand its product and distribution portfolios. Howard Schultz, chairperson and CEO, and his senior management team are focussed on how to sustain the company's phenomenal growth and maintain its market leadership position.

THE COFFEE MARKET

The commercial market for coffee began in AD 1000, when Arab traders brought the coffee tree from its native Ethiopia to the Middle East. Over the next 200 years, coffee drinking spread through the Arab world and was eventually introduced in Europe in the 1500s by Italian traders. By 1650, coffeehouses emerged as popular meeting places in England and France. Well-known public figures would frequent London coffeehouses to discuss political and literary issues.

Coffee consumption flourished in the mid-twentieth century, aided by developments in manufacturing and cultivation. By 1940, large coffee processors such as Nestlé (Hills Bros. brand), Kraft General Foods (Maxwell House), and Procter & Gamble (Folgers) developed instant and decaffeinated coffee varieties in addition to their staple regular ground. Supermarkets emerged as the primary distribution channel for traditional coffee sales.

In the late 1980s, per capita coffee consumption fell slowly and steadily as consumers turned to soft drinks, bottled water, juices, and iced teas. The three major manufacturers—Procter & Gamble, Nestlé, and Kraft—fought for market share in a stagnant market. All the major coffee brands were unprofitable. In an effort to regain profitability, the majors decreased their historically high expenditures on image advertising, increased the use of robusta beans (as opposed to high-quality Arabica beans) to reduce costs, and converted from 16-ounce to 13-ounce cans, claiming that the contents produced the same amount of coffee. Coupons and in-store promotions dominated manufacturer marketing plans as the price wars continued.

THE STARBUCKS COFFEE COMPANY: BACKGROUND

Inspiration for the present Starbucks concept came to Howard Schultz when he went to Italy on a buying trip in 1983. While wandering through the ancient piazzas of Milan, Schultz took particular note of the many cheerful espresso bars and cafés he passed. Italians, he felt, had captured the true romance of the beverage. Coffee drinking was an integral part of the Italian culture. Italians started their day at the espresso bar and returned there later. "There's such a strong sense of community in those coffee bars," he mused. "People come together every single day and in many cases they don't even know each other's names. In Italy, coffee is the conduit to the social experience."

Schultz realized that Americans lacked the opportunity to savor a good cup of coffee while engaging in good conversation in a relaxed atmosphere. He returned to the United States convinced that Americans would find the Italian coffee house culture attractive. In 1987, Schultz bought Starbucks.

RETAIL OFFERING

Starbucks offers more than a cup of coffee. As the vice president of marketing elaborates:

> Our product is not just that which resides in the cup. The product is the store and the service you get in the store. We need to help people appreciate at a higher level why that coffee break feels the way it does, why it's worth the time it takes to prepare a good cup of coffee. I like to think that Starbucks is not so much *food* for thought, but *brewed* for thought. Coffee has for centuries been for thought. I have sometimes thought to myself, "Get out of this chair. You hit the wall." It's that private time for me between 2:00 and 3:00 PM when I walk down to the Commons area here and make myself an Americano and think something through. I think that's maybe what Starbucks has to offer people: that safe harbor, that place to kind of make sense of the world. In the long run, what distinguishes us from our competitors, what is the most enduring competitive advantage we have, is that we are able to give our customers an experience at the store level . . . better than any competitor out there, even the small ones. Starbucks should be a place, an experience, tied up in inspired thought.

Although designs vary in any particular store to match the local market, the typical Starbucks store works around a planned mix of organic and manufactured components: light wood tones at the counters and signage areas, brown bags, polished dark marble countertops, glass shelves, thin modern white track lighting, and pure white cups. Even the logo delivers the double organic/modern message: The Starbucks icon is earthy looking, yet rendered in a modern abstract form, in black and white with a band of color around the center only. The colors of the lamps, walls, and tables mimic coffee tones, from green (raw beans) to light and darker browns. Special package and cup designs are coordinated to create livelier, more colorful tones around holidays. Starbucks also keeps its look lively with rotating in-store variations based on timely themes.

Starbucks stores are spacious so that customers can wander around the store, drinking their coffee and considering the purchase of coffee paraphernalia ranging from coffee beans to brushes for cleaning coffee grinders to $1,000 home cappuccino machines. Starbucks also sells CDs, including 775,000 copies of Ray Charles's *Genius Loves Company* CD and 115,000 units of Coldplay's *X&Y*, two of more than three dozen compact discs offered for $8 to $15.95 each. As it expanded into exclusive distribution of music, it scored a coup by landing Paul McCartney to release his latest album for sale only through Starbucks outlets. Although coffee beverages are standardized across outlets, food offerings vary from store to store.

Starbucks also has strict quality standards. For example, espresso is brewed precisely 18 to 23 seconds and thrown away if it is not served within 10 seconds of brewing. Coffee beans are donated to charities if they are still in the store seven days after coming out of their vacuum-sealed packs. Drip coffee is thrown away if it is not served within an hour of making it. Throughout the store, there exists a keen attention to aroma: Employees are not allowed to wear colognes, stores use no scented cleaning products, and smoking is *verboten*.

HUMAN RESOURCE MANAGEMENT

The company, recognizing that its frontline employees are critical to providing "the perfect cup," has built an organizational culture based on two principles: (1) strict standards for how coffee should be prepared and delivered to customers and (2) a laid-back, supportive, and empowering attitude toward its employees.

All new hires, referred to as partners, go through a 24-hour training program that instills a sense of purpose, commitment, and enthusiasm for the job. New employees are treated with the dignity and respect that goes along with their title as *baristas* (Italian for bartender). To emphasize their responsibility in pleasing customers, baristas are presented with scenarios describing customers complaining about beans that were ground incorrectly. The preferred response, baristas learn, is to replace the beans on the spot without checking with the manager or questioning the complaint. Baristas learn to customize each espresso drink, explain the origins of different coffees, and to distinguish Sumatran from Ethiopian coffees by the way it "flows over the tongue."

Starbucks's Coffee Master program teaches the staff how to discern the subtleties of regional flavor. Graduates (there are now 25,000) earn a special black apron and an insignia on their business cards. The highlight is the "cupping ceremony," a tasting ritual traditionally used by coffee traders. After the grounds have steeped in boiling water, tasters "crest" the mixture, penetrating the crust on top with a spoon and inhaling the aroma. As employees slurp the brew, a Starbucks Coffee Educator encourages them to taste a Kenyan coffee's "citrusy" notes or the "mushroomy" flavor of a Sumatran blend. If the ritual reminds you of a wine tasting, that's intentional. Schultz has long wanted to emulate the wine business.

Holding on to its motivated, well-trained employees is important, so all partners are eligible for health benefits and a stock option plan called "Bean Stock." Each employee receives stock options worth 12 percent of his or her annual base pay. (Starbucks now allows options at 14 percent of base pay in light of "good profits.") Employees are also given a free pound of coffee each week and a 30 percent discount on all retail offerings. Baristas know about and are encouraged to apply for promotions to store management positions. Every quarter, the company has open meetings at which company news, corporate values, and financial performance data are presented and discussed.

Due to the training, empowerment, benefits, and growth opportunities, Starbucks's turnover is only 70 percent, considerably less than the 150 to 200 percent turnover at other firms in the food service business. "We treat our employees like true partners and our customers like stars," comments Schultz.

LOCATION STRATEGY

Starbucks's retail expansion strategy was based on conquering one area of a city or region at a time. Centralized cities served as hubs or regional centers for rollout expansion into nearby markets (e.g., Chicago as a hub for the Midwest). "Clustering" was also key to its location strategy. Major markets were saturated with stores before new markets were entered. For example, there were over 100 Starbucks outlets in the Seattle area before the company expanded to a new region. Having many stores in close proximity to one another generally increased overall revenues. However, comparable store sales growth eventually slowed due to cannibalization.

Traffic was the major determinant in selecting cities and locations. "We want to be in highly visible locations," the senior vice president of real estate explains, "with access to customers that value quality and great coffee. You want a store in the path of people's weekly shopping experience, their route to work, their way home from a movie. You want to be America's porch that no longer exists."

SUPPLY CHAIN

In the 1990s, the specialty coffee market experienced substantial growth, driven largely by the coffee-drinking habits of college graduates and young professionals. While retailers like Starbucks benefited from this growth, coffee growers and supplies did not, due to the worldwide oversupply of lower-grade coffee beans. Although Starbucks purchased the highest quality, Arabica beans and paid premium prices, all growers suffered from the oversupply. Even though Starbucks dominated the specialty coffee industry, it did not use its purchasing power to negotiate lower prices from growers and suppliers and squeeze their profits. Instead, the company decided to use its market power to implement social change within its supply chain. It partnered with Conservation International, an environmental nonprofit organization, to develop CAFE (Coffee and Farmer Equity) practices with the following objectives:

1. Build mutually beneficial relationships with coffee growers and suppliers.
2. Increase economic, social, and environmental sustainability in the industry, including conservation and biodiversity.
3. Provide economic incentives for suppliers who adhere to CAFE standards.
4. Promote transparency and economic fairness within the supply chain.

The CAFE practices thus represent a minimum set of requirements, including coffee quality, social issues, and economic transparency (i.e., disclosing how much growers actually received), that growers and suppliers had to meet to be considered a viable source for Starbucks's coffee beans.

All suppliers were evaluated not just on their performance but also on their supply networks. Farmers were rewarded for coffee growing and processing practices that contributed positively to the conservation of soil, water, energy, and biological diversity and had minimal impact on the environment. The CAFE practices further encouraged farmers to ensure that their workers' wages and safety standards met or exceeded the minimum requirements established under local and national laws. Suppliers that scored well on the independently assessed CAFE practices received a price premium and the largest orders. Starbucks's ultimate goal is to buy the majority of its beans from suppliers that meet is CAFE standards.

GROWTH STRATEGIES

In addition to locations stores in more than 40 countries, Starbucks has taken additional opportunities to capitalize on its strong brand name.

• *Frappuccino.* The Frappuccino bottled beverage combines milk, coffee, and ice. After its great success when introduced to cafés in 1995, Starbucks entered a joint venture with PepsiCo to bottle a ready-to-drink (RTD) version. Frappuccino coffee drinks come in six varieties (Mocha, Decaf Mocha, Vanilla, Coffee, Caramel, and Mocha Lite) and are available at convenience or grocery stores.

• *MAZAGRAN* MAZAGRAN, a carbonated coffee RTD beverage, is manufactured, bottled, and distributed by PepsiCo, but Starbucks shares in the research and development of the product and sets its flavor standards.

• *Breyer's Grand Ice Cream* Breyer's Grand Ice Cream agreed to produce a line of premium ice cream products flavored with Starbucks coffee. The first products in this line, five coffee-flavored gourmet ice creams, sold under the Starbucks name were distributed through supermarket outlets. The leading brand of gourmet coffee ice cream on the market, Starbucks's flavors include Java Chip Big, Mud Pie,

Coffee Almond Fudge, Coffee Fudge Brownie, Low Fat Latte, Classic Coffee, and Caramel Cappuccino Swirl. Frozen Frappuccino ice cream bar novelties also are available in three varieties: Mocha, Java Fudge, and Caffe Vanilla.

• *Kraft and supermarkets* Through an agreement with Kraft, Starbucks sells its branded coffee beans in supermarkets, which command 80 percent of all coffee sales and generate nearly $3 billion in sales annually. The company designed a line of specialty coffees just for supermarkets and opened Starbucks-operated kiosks in selected grocery chains. Kraft manages all distribution, marketing, advertising, and promotions for Starbucks's whole bean and ground coffee in grocery and mass-merchandise stores. During fiscal year 2007, the company's whole bean and ground coffees were available throughout the United States in approximately 30,000 supermarkets, as well as in 4,000 stores outside the United States.

• *Jim Beam* Through a partnership with Jim Beam, Starbucks developed a coffee liqueur.

• Several alternative channels include the sale of whole beans through Nordstrom department stores and coffee by the cup in cafés in Barnes & Noble bookstores. Additional channels include distribution through service providers like Holland America Cruise Lines, United Airlines, and Sheraton and Westin Hotels.

CHANGING CUSTOMER BASE

As Starbucks grew, its customer base evolved. Starbucks's historical customer profile—affluent, well-educated, white-collar women between the ages of 24 and 44 years—had expanded. For example, about half of the stores in southern California welcome large numbers of Hispanic customers. Newer customers tend to be younger, less well educated, and in a lower income bracket than Starbucks's more established customers. These newer customers are more interested in convenience than the experience. In response to improve service perceptions, especially the time it takes to place an order and receive the coffee, Starbucks has started installing automatic espresso machines in its stores.

DISCUSSION QUESTIONS

1. What is Starbucks's retail strategy? What is its target market, and how does it try to develop an advantage over its competition?

2. Describe Starbucks's retail mix: location, merchandise assortment, pricing, advertising and promotion, store design and visual merchandising, customer service, and personal selling. How does its retail mix support its strategy?

3. What factors in the environment provided the opportunity for Starbucks to develop a new, successful retail chain? What demand and supply conditions prevailed in the U.S. coffee market when Howard Schultz purchased Starbucks in 1987? What insight did Schultz have that other players in the coffee market did not possess?

4. What have been the principal drivers behind Starbucks's success in the marketplace? What does the Starbucks brand mean to consumers? How have the growth opportunities that Starbucks has pursued affected the value of its brand name?

5. What are the major challenges facing Starbucks as it goes forward? Is the brand advantage sustainable going forward? Can Starbucks defend its position against other specialty coffee retailers?

Source: This case was written by Barton Weitz, University of Florida.

CASE 36 New Product Development at Yankee Candle Company

COMPANY OVERVIEW

Yankee Candle Company, Inc. (YCC), is a leading manufacturer, wholesaler, and retailer of premium scented candles in the $55 billion giftware industry. Gross sales (wholesale and retail combined) are greater than $600 million. YCC has maintained steady growth since its inception in 1969 and has displayed consistently impressive sales performance.

Yankee Candle products and accessory items are distributed through a network of 15,600 wholesale customers operating gift stores (e.g., Hallmark) nationwide, an expanding retail base of 385 company-owned stores in 42 states, a mail-order catalog, a Web site (www.yankeecandle.com), and a growing network of European retailers. Headquartered in Whately, Massachusetts, YCC employs 5,500 people nationwide. Its flagship store in South Deerfield is the second-largest tourist destination in Massachusetts, attracting more than 2.5 million visitors annually.

CORE PRODUCT LINES

The two core product lines for YCC are scented candles and candle accessories. The premium-quality scented candles feature approximately 125 fragrances. All candles are produced onsite at the Whately facility. Candles are manufactured with strict quality control standards to ensure a true scent, long burn time, and consistency of fragrance over the life of the candle. Candles are available in clear or frosted glass Housewarmer jars, Sampler votive candles, wax potpourri Tarts, pillars, tapers, Cocktail Candles, and tea lights.

Coordinating candle accessory products include jar toppers (decorative lids for the Housewarmer jar candles); taper holders; pillar and jar bases; matching jar shades, plates, and sleeves; votive holders; and tea light holders. One additional accessory product line, "Car Jars," is an assortment of air fresheners in the shape of the Housewarmer jar designed to hang from a car or truck rearview mirror. The full line of product offerings is available on YCC's Web site.

NEW PRODUCT DEVELOPMENT ACTIVITY

New product development is a key activity for members of the YCC management team. A core committee meets weekly to discuss new product ideas, strategies, and other marketing-related issues. This six-person team consists of senior vice presidents, vice presidents, directors, and buyers from three key functional areas: marketing, retailing, and wholesaling.

New product ideas are discussed in a "roundtable" format. Ideas come from the core committee team members and sources outside the team (e.g., other YCC employees, wholesale customers, retail customers, suppliers). Ideas typically surface in response to industry trends, observations from trade shows, and information in syndicated marketing research reports purchased by YCC. One notable idea that became a successful product is the Car Jar. On the basis of prior discussions with Robert Nelson, manager of the testing lab at YCC, a supplier representative presented the idea for the Car Jar to the core committee. The product development team gave the representative some latitude to explore the idea, and he came back with a finished prototype. After YCC endorsed the idea, it grew into a successful line for the company.

The core committee regularly discusses upcoming seasonal additions to the line as new products. For example, in the holiday season (Christmas, Hanukah), YCC offers candles in three limited edition fragrances, such as Starry Night, Icicles, and Poinsettia, to complement its four established holiday fragrances—Nutcracker, Peace on Earth, Holiday Spirit, and Christmas Wish.

NEW PRODUCT DEVELOPMENT PROCESS

The launch of a new product line, Country Classics (CC), provided YCC with another strong performer in the form of a line of candles and accessories decorated with artwork by folk artist Warren Kimble. The CC line introduced candles in an additional type of container, a ceramic crock, as well as a host of non-candle kitchen and home decorating products (e.g., clocks, coaster/trivet set, picture frames). The process involved in launching the CC line relied heavily on a new product development framework.

Stage 1: Idea Generation

The core committee began considering the CC line in December, when Gail Flood, Senior VP Retailing, brought in samples of Kimble's artwork and proposed a joint product/marketing effort. She began thinking of licensing possibilities after seeing two Kimble patterns on dinnerware in a Kitchen Etc. store in Boston. After an initial positive reaction, Erin O'Connor, Director New Product Package Design, and her staff developed concept boards pairing Kimble artwork with YCC fragrances. The core committee continued to discuss particular fragrance options and artwork pairings during December.

Stage 2: Screening

In early January, the idea for CC had been refined; Chuck Murphy, Senior Retail Buyer, worked with his counterparts in purchasing/operations to gather pricing information from candle, glass, and fragrance suppliers. Information on licensing arrangements between YCC and the Warren Kimble organization was obtained by John Cummo, VP Marketing, and his staff. Additional team members joined the core committee at some of the weekly meetings to discuss CC and screen this new idea further. These additional team members included Tom Sweeney, Senior Candle Buyer, Retail; Robert Nelson, Director of Product Testing; and Jane Tate, Production/Manufacturing Manager.

By mid-January, the core committee felt that CC was a feasible idea for a new product line. In one final screening activity, the committee brought in five managers of YCC retail stores in the eastern Massachusetts area to get their opinions about the concept. The retail managers were in agreement that the "look" of the Kimble folk art was a strong complement to the general YCC image. Harlen Kent, VP Wholesaling, and Sean Gillespie, Director of Wholesaling, coordinated a similar meeting of several prominent wholesale customers in the Massachusetts area to get their evaluations and reactions to the CC concept.

Stage 3: Product Development

After a presentation to senior management in late January, the core committee moved forward to begin converting the CC concept into a reality. Robert Nelson and his staff in the testing lab worked closely with members of the core committee to develop 10 fragrances to pair with 10 chosen pieces of Kimble artwork. Representatives from manufacturing, along with Jane Tate, began to plan production runs for the chosen fragrance/candle products. Gail Flood and her staff finalized the licensing arrangement details with Warren Kimble. A prototype candle had been developed by mid-February.

Stage 4: Product/Market Testing

Product testing included a limited production run so that candle prototypes could be tested in a lab setting for quality control variables, such as burn time, fragrance dispersion, and fragrance quality. Quality control testing was completed by mid-March.

Next, a limited production run was manufactured for shipment to the Deerfield store and 10 New England–area retail stores in a limited market test. The product became available in test market stores on April 1. Product sales were monitored, and the retail managers were contacted often to report on consumer reaction to the CC products. Consumer response was extremely favorable; the limited inventory was sold within four weeks of delivery to the stores, exceeding the expectations of the core committee.

Stage 5: Business Analysis

The development process for CC was not as sequential. The business analysis activity occurred at approximately the same time as product prototype development (Stage 3). New team members from the operations side of YCC entered the process to conduct a feasibility analysis for CC. Jennifer Flynn, Business Analyst Leader, worked with the core committee to complete the financial projections for CC. Financial projections were based on demand for Warren Kimble merchandise, current market information from syndicated research reports, and past YCC sales history data.

Stage 6: Commercialization

The limited test market was judged successful on the basis of the level of sales achieved compared with expectations. According to YCC's VP of marketing, John Cummo, "The CC situation is like all our new product decisions. We go to test market with a target sales goal in mind. If a new product meets the goal and we feel good about it, we go with it; if it doesn't meet the target, we probably won't go forward." In June, YCC introduced the CC line to wholesalers and made the initial line of 10 fragrances available in its retail stores.

As the CC line moved into commercial rollout, an unusual thing happened: One member of the core committee saw a decorative, three-dimensional, resin-based lid for a glass jar at a giftware trade show. After quickly securing a vendor and extending the licensing with Warren Kimble, YCC began offering coordinating Jar Toppers in retail stores shortly after the June 23 rollout. Although this part of the product line was an afterthought, the flexibility demonstrated by the YCC core committee and other members of the firm made it possible to get this complementary item into the market quickly.

Sales of the CC line represented another success for YCC. As with other YCC lines, CC is constantly scrutinized and updated. Two new fragrances, Sage and Citrus and Fruit Basket, were introduced with matching jar toppers in March of the following year.

NEW PRODUCT STRATEGY AND TRENDS: WHAT'S ON THE HORIZON?

CEO Craig Rydin summarized YCC's market situation: "The combination of our brand strength, breadth of product offering, and new product development and merchandising initiatives have enabled us to continue to generate very strong growth and market share gains." But YCC did not simply rest on its laurels. First quarter sales were up 12 percent and earnings per share were up 10 percent.

So where does YCC go from here? New product development continues at a fast pace, including newly added fragrances such as Balsam and Cedar, Peppermint Cocoa, Hot Buttered Rum, Jack Frost, and Snow Angels. The company introduced room perfume in spring scents, such as Ginger and Green Tea, Rain Washed, and Sweet Pea, which match existing candle scents. During the fall season, it offered Macintosh and Peach and Pineapple Citrus scents in the Housewarmer candle collection, as well as in the form of potpourri, room spray, and Car Jars. For summer, Yankee Candle pushes Cocktail Candles in Apple Martini, Mandarin Mimosa, and Strawberry Daiquiri scents. These six-ounce candles sell for $12.99.

DISCUSSION QUESTIONS

1. Was the new product development process for Country Classics cross-functional? Explain.
2. What are the strengths of YCC's approach to new product development?
3. What are some weaknesses of YCC's approach to new product development?
4. What other new products should the company introduce that might appeal to its target audience of women, aged 20 to 60 years, and that would complement its existing product lines and brand?

Source: This case was written by Elizabeth J. Wilson, Suffolk University. The author gratefully acknowledges the Sawyer School of Management, Suffolk University, and the Carroll School of Management, Boston College, for support in preparation of this case.

CASE 37   PetSmart: Where Pets Are Family

In the animal-loving society of the United States, 63 percent of households, or 71.1 million homes, own pets. The resulting pet retail industry has benefited from pet owners' tendency to humanize and treat their pets like family members, which has increased industry revenues rapidly. As depicted in Exhibit 1, pet industry expenditures have more than doubled since 1994, making pet care the second fastest growing retail category with an average annual growth rate of 6 percent. By 2008, U.S. pet industry expenditures exceeded $40 billion and are projected to continue to grow.

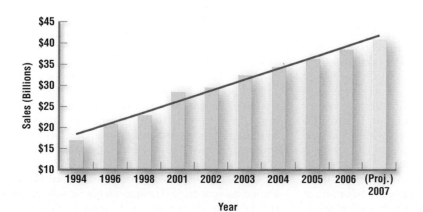

EXHIBIT 1

U.S. Pet Industry Expenditures

EXHIBIT 2
U.S. Pet Expenditures by Category

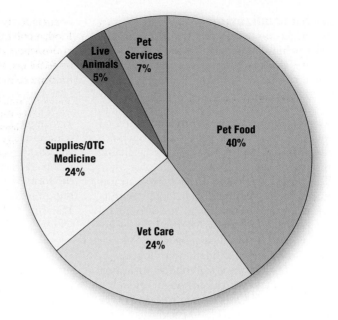

An industry once dominated by bland pet food and basic supplies thus has transformed into a highly differentiated market with diverse and creative offerings including pet fashions and accessories, gourmet pet cuisine, and even pet massages. Exhibit 2 depicts the ever-expanding composition of the pet industry, including the sale of pet food, supplies, veterinary care, medicine, animal purchases, and pet services such as grooming and boarding.

PETSMART CAPITALIZES ON INDUSTRY TRENDS

A recent survey conducted by the Washington-based Pew Research Center found that 85 percent of pet owners called their dogs members of the family, as do 78 percent of those with cats. The study also noted that 80 percent of the owners buy holiday and birthday gifts for their pets, and nearly half of the female respondents said that they relied more on their pet's affection than on their spouse's or children's. As these statistics reveal, pet owners have become emotionally tied to their pets and, in turn, treat their pets like humans by dressing them in the latest fashions, prolonging their lives through expensive medical treatments, and buckling them into specially designed car seats.

PetSmart has taken advantage of this pet humanization trend and thereby increased its revenues and profitability. Three key features mark the expanded pet retail industry: (1) increased product offerings, (2) more licensing agreements for pet products, and (3) innovative pet services.

Pet ownership drives demand, profitability for retailers depends on the ability to generate store traffic and merchandise effectively. To meet growing demand, PetSmart has expanded its store offerings to include a wider range of merchandise and services. A typical PetSmart store stocks 12,900 in-store products and offers an even larger variety of products online. In addition, it has increased its product assortment within each product category. PetSmart presently stocks a deep selection of pet foods from a large array of suppliers, including low-cost, all natural, breed-specific, preservative-free, diet, organic, and premium foods with real meats and vegetables. To provide total solutions to its customers, the company introduced a wide range of private-label brands, positioned as low-cost alternatives to national brands. According to the Private Label Manufacturers Association, store brands account for 11 percent of cat food, 12 percent of dog food, 13 percent of pet supplies, and 21 percent of cat litter sales.

Consumers interested in spoiling their pet often walk into a pet store to buy and coordinate outfits for their cat or dog, with choices ranging from personalized t-shirts to dresses to water-activated cooling bandanas. Through partnerships with PetSmart, renowned companies are leveraging their own brands within the pet sector. Store aisles are lined with toys, clothing, accessories, bedding, and aquariums displaying popular cartoon characters such as SpongeBob SquarePants, Clifford the Big Red Dog, Barbie, Blues Clues, Disney, and Peanuts characters. In addition, companies from a diverse collection of industries, such as Paul Mitchell, Polo Ralph Lauren, Harley Davidson, and Old Navy, have developed their own pet product lines. Even Jeep has released its own line of branded strollers and pet ramps for cars and trucks to attempt to profit from the endless licensing opportunities within the pet retailing industry.

In the past, pet retailers provided just the most basic products. Today, they aim to create lasting relationships with customers. The service sector of the pet retail industry has higher profit margins, so PetSmart is incorporating various service offerings into its business model, including in-store grooming, six- to eight-week training sessions, Doggie Day care with supervised group play, and "Pet Hotel" boarding with cozy beds and televisions airing Animal Planet programming. As a result, PetSmart earned more than $500 million from its service businesses, representing 10 percent of its annual sales revenue. Pet service industry competitors similarly attempt to position themselves to reach a portion of the market. Doggie spas, for example, offer high-end services such as massage therapy and pedicures, while pet walking and waste pick-up services enjoy greater success within the industry.

HUMAN RESOURCES AS A BRAND STRATEGY

Through various employee development programs, PetSmart trains its employees to reinforce the firm's brand image. It hires people who love pets and thus helps provide customers with value, quality, and service. For example, PetSmart administers a 120-hour educational program for its trainers, a six-month instructional program for its groomers, and 16 hours of role-play training before any store opens to the public. As a result, the cheerful demeanor of PetSmart employees remains consistent across the country. PetSmart's staff passionately converses with customers, asks pet-related questions, and gives recommendations. This sense of helpfulness and friendliness aligns the service staff with the company's overall brand strategy and creates an emotional customer connection to the brand. Moreover, well-behaved pets are allowed to shop with their owners, which prompts a pleasant, comfortable, animal-loving store atmosphere that furthers the business's brand equity.

PetSmart regularly displays highly visible corporate charity and donation-related signs for animal-related causes at its checkout counters to reinforce the company's animal-loving culture. The business made a conscious decision to encourage adoption from shelters instead of selling cats and dogs, even though sales of cats and dogs would generate higher annual revenues. The decision to encourage and facilitate adoptions is decreasing euthanization of abandoned animals. PetSmart CEO Philip

Francis notes that "But by the time you factor in the bed, food, a collar, a leash, a training program, a bath, and a vet appointment, this adopted dog or cat could be a $300 to $400 event for us, and could be the opportunity for a lifetime relationship with that pet and that pet parent."

Sources: Diane Brady, Paula Lehman, Christopher Megerian, Christopher Palmeri, and Arlene Weintraub, "The Pet Economy; Americans Spend an Astonishing $41 Billion a Year on their Furry Friends," *BusinessWeek*, August 6, 2007 (accessed September 30, 2007); Catherine M. Dalton, "A Passion for Pets: An Interview with Philip L. Francis, Chairperson and CEO of PETsMART, Inc.," *Business Horizons*, 2005, pp. 469–75; Doug Desjardins, "Off and Running: Pet Products Lure Licensed Brands," *Retailing Today*, June 18, 2007 (accessed September 30, 2007); "Industry Statistics and Trends," *American Pet Products Manufacturers Association, Inc.*, 2007 (accessed September 30, 2007); Joseph Tarnowski, "Pet Care: Furry Forecast," *Progressive Grocer*, January 1, 2006 (accessed September 30, 2007); Mike Troy, "Global Pet Expo: Booming Pet Industry Fetches Strong Returns," *Retailing Today*, March 5, 2007; Constantine Von Hoffman, "Upscale Amenities Go to the Dogs," *Brandweek*, January 8, 2007.

DISCUSSION QUESTIONS

1. What else could PetSmart do to increase its store traffic, revenues, and profitability?

2. Consider other retailers that might begin to sell a larger assortment of pet products and services. How will this competition affect PetSmart?

3. Should PetSmart expand its operations internationally? Why or why not?

Source: This case was written by James Pope, an evening MBA student at Loyola College in Maryland, under the supervision of Professor Hope Corrigan.

CASE 38 Interviewing for a Management Trainee Position

1. Assume the role of the college recruiter for a national retail chain that is reviewing résumés to select candidates to interview for a management trainee position. Which of the three résumés on the following pages do you find effective? Ineffective? Why? Which would you select to interview? Why?

2. Update your résumé and prepare for an interview for a manager training program with a large lumber and building supply retailer. This full-time position promises rapid advancement upon completion of the training period. A college degree and experience in retail, sales, and marketing are preferred. The base pay is between $35,000 to $45,000 per year, plus a bonus of up to $7,000. This retailer promotes from within, and a new manager trainee can become a store manager within two to three years, with earnings potential of $100,000 or more. The benefits package is generous, including medical, hospitalization, dental, disability, and life insurance, a 401k plan, profit sharing, awards and incentives, paid vacations, and holidays. Your résumé should include your contact information, education and training, skills, experience and accomplishments, and honors and awards.

3. Role play a practice interview for this position. In pairs, read each other's résumés and then spend 20 to 30 minutes representing each side of the interview. One student should be the human resource manager screening applicants, and the other person should be the candidate for the manager training program. As the human resource manager, ask appropriate questions of the applicant, such as the following:

- Why are you applying for this position?
- What are your strengths and weaknesses for this position?
- Why should this organization consider you for this position?
- Why are you interested in working for this company?
- What are your career goals for the next five to ten years?
- Describe your skills when working in a team setting.
- What questions do you have about the company?

Source: This case was written by Cecelia Schulz, University of Florida.

Martin L. Cox

xxxx@ufl.edu, (xxx) 3xx-xxxx
123 Your Street, Apt. 301
Gainesville, Florida 32605

OBJECTIVE
Seeking a marketing internship utilizing leadership experience, strong work ethic, and interpersonal skills with a focus in product planning.

EDUCATION
Bachelor of Science in Business Administration   May 2009
University of Florida, Gainesville, Florida   GPA 3.69
Major in Marketing

LEADERSHIP
Student Government

Theatre Nights Chair	Jan. 2008-Present
Emerging Leaders Conference Executive Assistant	Sept. 2007-Present
Student Integrity Court Justice	May 2007-Present
Banquet Cabinet Assistant Director	May 2007-Present
Innovate Party House Representative	Jan. 2007-April 2007
Homecoming Supper Staff	Oct. 2006, 2007 Pan-Hellenic Council
Assistant Director of Jr. Pan-Hellenic	Dec. 2006-Present
Jr. Pan-Hellenic Executive VP Int. Relations	Sept. 2006-Jan. 2007 Tri-Delta

Philanthropy   Triple Play

Intramural Soccer-Captain	Oct. 2006, 2007
Intramural Basketball-Captain	Sept. 2007-Present
Member since Aug. 2003	Jan. 2007-Present

HONORS

Savant UF Leadership Honorary	Oct. 2007-Present
Sandra Day O'Connor Pre-Law Society	Sept. 2007-Present
Alpha Lambda Delta Honor Society	Inducted March 2007
Phi Eta Sigma Honor Society	Inducted March 2007

COMMUNITY SERVICE

Mentor to Freshmen Students for SG Mentor/Mentee	Sept. 2007-Present
Basketball On Wheels Volunteer	Sept. 2007-Present
Dance Marathon Dancer	Jan. 2007-March 2007
After School Gators Volunteer	Jan. 2007-April 2007
Pillows for Patriots Service Project Volunteer	Sept. 2006-Dec. 2006

WORK EXPERIENCE

Senior Customer Service Associate, Video-R-Us, Tampa, FL	Jan. 2005-Aug. 2006
Secretarial Assistant, Law Firm, Mount Dora, FL	June-Aug. 2005

References available upon request.

Tina Acosta
123 Your Street #335
Gainesville, FL 32608
(727) xxx-xxxx
lxxx@ufl.edu

OBJECTIVE

To integrate my financial and business background with my creative and artistic skills in a fast-paced industry

EDUCATION

University of Florida	International Baccalaureate Program
Warrington College of Business	St. Petersburg High School
Bachelor of Science in Finance	Focus in Theatre, English, and History
Minor in Spanish	Graduation 2005
Graduation: May 2009	GPA: 4.0
GPA: 3.73	

RELEVANT CLASSES

Retail Management, Study Abroad in Spain, Business Finance, Managerial Accounting, Problem Solving Using Computer Software, Debt and Money Markets

EXPERIENCE

Abercrombie & Fitch—Gainesville, FL   Brand Representative (October 2007-Present)
- Oversaw customer service on the sales floor
- Maintained and updated the sales floor design
- Handled purchases and returns at the register
- Prepared shipments and the floor for an internal audit
- Promoted the brand name for the women's fashion line

Olive Garden—St. Petersburg, FL   Server (April 2006-August 2006)
- Used a computerized food and beverage ordering system
- Maintained the management's expectations through customer service
- Interacted with customers
- Memorized an extensive menu and recommended foods satisfying customer's needs while maximizing the restaurant's profits

Sacino's Formalwear—St. Petersburg, FL   Sales Representative (August 2004-August 2005)
- Managed incoming and outgoing shipment responsibilities
- Organized financial paperwork
- Oversaw customer service on the sales floor
- Headed the formal wear department for young women

SKILLS

Proficient in Spanish
Office XP: Word-Document Formatting, Letters, Tables, Flyers, and Macros
            Excel-Spreadsheets, Formulas, and Graph Database Analysis, Functions, and Simples Macros
            PowerPoint-Professional Presentations

HONORS

Third place in the preliminary competition for the University of Florida's Center for
    Entrepreneurship and Innovation
Florida's Bright Futures Scholar
University of Florida Dean's List Student 2006

Richard Kates
xxxxxx@ufl.edu

123 Your Street. #164	123 8th Ave N
Gainesville, Florida 32608	Tampa, Florida 33713
(352) xxx-xxxx	(813) xxx-xxxx

Objective	Seeking a position utilizing marketing, management, and organizational abilities, as well as interpersonal skills.

Education	**Marketing Major**	May 2009
	University of Florida	Gainesville, Florida
	Minor in Mass Communications and Minor in	
	Entrepreneurship GPA 3.7	

Experience	**Entrepreneur/CEO,** Long River PC, LLC	August 2005 to
	Tampa, FL	Present
	-Helped create and manage a new software company based in South Florida.	
	-Helped develop revolutionary program that will aid the visually impaired. Researched and developed multiple original non-disclosure as well as non-compete agreements.	
	-Responsible for hiring, funding, managing, and controlling progress of almost a dozen private software engineers. Reported to and allocated funds of angel investors.	
	Server, Carraba's	April 2007 to
	Gainesville, Florida	Present
	-Help train new employees through shadowing and demonstration.	
	-Serve over 70 guests per day, and ensure customer satisfaction and attentiveness.	
	-Multiple top sales, as well as winner of "Perfect Check" contest.	
	Usher/Security/Technician, Ben Hill Griffin Stadium	August 2005 to
	Gainesville, Florida	August 2007
	Pool/Health Club Attendant, Don Cesar Resort	May 2004 to
	St. Petersburg, Florida	August 2006

Leadership	**Executive Board Member, Varsity Tennis Team. Social Chair**
	University of Florida August 2006 to Present
	Organized, planned, and financed all Tennis Team social events. In charge of planning large events, gatherings at home and away meets, coordinating the activities of over 60 members.
	Executive Board Member, Fisher School of Accounting
	University of Florida January 2007 to May 2007
	Aided in revision and draft of new official Fisher School of Accounting Council's by-laws.
	Drafted a new 5 year program for the expansion and direction of the new Fisher School including member growth, activities, graduate prerequisites, and facility uses.
	CHAMPS Mentoring Volunteer Program
	Gainesville Florida January 2007 to Present
	Met with an "at risk" elementary school student 2 hours per week each semester to spend quality time encouraging the child's healthy growth and development.

Affiliations	**Phi Eta Sigma Honor Society,** Member active 2005 to present
	Florida Tennis Team, Fall 2005 to Spring 2007. Varsity Fall 2006 to Spring 2007
	Team Florida Cycling, Spring 2007 to present
	Student Alumni Association Member, Fall 2006 to present
	American Marketing Association, Member Fall 2007
	International Business Society, Fall 2007
	Business Administration College Council, Fall 2007 Member-at-Large
	The Entrepreneurs Club, Fall 2007

Skills	Computer-Fluent in Microsoft Word, Excel, PowerPoint, Explorer, and Media Player, Fluent-Spanish

References	Available upon request.

ABC analysis An analysis that rank orders SKUs by a profitability measure to determine which items should never be out of stock, which should be allowed to be out of stock occasionally, and which should be deleted from the stock selection.

accessibility (1) The degree to which customers can easily get into and out of a shopping center; (2) ability of the retailer to deliver the appropriate retail mix to customers in the segment.

accessories Merchandise in apparel, department, and specialty stores used to complement apparel outfits. Examples include gloves, hosiery, handbags, jewelry, handkerchiefs, and scarves.

accordion theory A cyclical theory of retailer evolution suggesting that changes in retail institutions are explained in terms of depth versus breadth of assortment. Retail institutions cycle from high-depth/low-breadth to low-depth/high-breadth stores and back again.

account opener A premium or special promotion item offered to induce the opening of a new account, especially in financial institutions and stores operating on an installment credit basis.

accounts payable The amount of money owed to vendors, primarily for merchandise inventory.

accounts receivable The amount of money due to the retailer from selling merchandise on credit.

actionability Criteria for evaluating a market segment scheme indicating what the retailer should do to satisfy its needs.

activity-based costing (ABC) A financial management tool in which all major activities within a cost center are identified, calculated, and then charged to cost objects, such as stores, product categories, product lines, specific products, customers, and suppliers.

additional markup An increase in retail price after and in addition to an original markup.

additional markup cancellation The percentage by which the retail price is lowered after a markup is taken.

additional markup percentage The addition of a further markup to the original markup as a percentage of net sales.

add-on selling Selling additional new products and services to existing customers, such as a bank encouraging a customer with a checking account to apply for a home improvement loan from the bank.

administered vertical marketing system A form of vertical marketing system designed to control a line or classification of merchandise as opposed to an entire store's operation. Such systems involve the development of comprehensive programs for specified lines of merchandise. Vertically aligned companies—manufacturers or wholesalers—even though in non-ownership positions, may work together to reduce the total systems cost of such activities as advertising, transportation, and data processing. See also *contractual vertical marketing system* and *corporate vertical marketing system*.

advanced shipping notice (ASN) An electronic document received by the retailer's computer from a supplier in advance of a shipment.

advertising Paid communications delivered to customers through nonpersonal mass media such as newspapers, television, radio, direct mail, and the Internet.

advertising manager A retail manager who manages advertising activities such as determining the advertising budget, allocating the budget, developing ads, selecting media, and monitoring advertising effectiveness.

advertising reach The percentage of customers in the target market exposed to an ad at least once.

affinity marketing Marketing activities that enable consumers to express their identification with an organization. An example is offering credit cards tied to reference groups like the consumer's university or an NFL team.

affordable budgeting method A budgeting method in which a retailer first sets a budget for every element of the retail mix except promotion and then allocates the leftover funds to a promotional budget.

Age Discrimination and Employment Act A federal act that makes it illegal to discriminate in hiring and termination decisions concerning people between the ages of 40 and 70 years.

agent (1) A business unit that negotiates purchases, sales, or both but does not take title to the goods in which it deals; (2) a person who represents the principal (who, in the case of retailing, is the store or merchant) and acts under authority, whether in buying or in bringing the principal into business relations with third parties.

aging The length of time merchandise has been in stock.

aided recall When consumers indicate they know the brand when the name is presented to them.

à la carte plans An employee reward program giving employees a choice of rewards and thus tailoring the rewards to the desires of individual employees.

allocator Position in merchandise management responsible for allocating merchandise and tailoring the assortment in several categories for specific stores in a geographic area.

alteration costs Expenses incurred to change the appearance or fit, to assemble, or to repair merchandise.

Americans with Disabilities Act (ADA) A federal civil rights law that protects people with disabilities from discrimination in employment, transportation, public accommodations, telecommunications, and the activities of state and local government.

analog approach A method of trade area analysis also known as the *similar store* or *mapping* approach. The analysis is divided into four steps: (1) describing the current trade areas through the technique of customer spotting; (2) plotting the customers on a map; (3) defining the primary, secondary, and tertiary area zones; and (4) matching the characteristics of stores in the trade areas with the potential new store to estimate its sales potential.

anchor store A large, well-known retail operation located in a shopping center or Internet mall and serving as an attracting force for consumers to the center.

ancillary services Services such as layaway, gift wrap, and credit that are not directly related to the actual sale of a specific product within the store.

anticipation discount A discount offered by a vendor to a retailer in addition to the cash discount or dating, if the retailer pays the invoice before the end of the cash discount period.

anticompetitive leasing arrangement A lease that limits the type and amount of competition a particular retailer faces within a trading area.

antitrust legislation A set of laws directed at preventing unreasonable restraint of trade or unfair trade practices. Aim is to foster a competitive environment. See also *restraint of trade*.

application form A form used to collect information on a job applicant's education, employment experience, hobbies, and references.

artificial barriers In site evaluations for accessibility, barriers such as railroad tracks, major highways, or parks.

asset management path One of the two paths in the strategic profit model affecting a retailer's return on assets.

assets Economic resources, such as inventory or store fixtures, owned or controlled by an enterprise as a result of past transactions or events.

asset turnover Net sales divided by total assets.

assortment The number of SKUs within a merchandise category. Also called *depth of merchandise*.

assortment plan A list of merchandise that indicates in very general terms what should be carried in a particular merchandise category.

atmospherics The design of an environment through visual communications, lighting, colors, music, and scent to stimulate customers' perceptual and emotional responses and ultimately to affect their purchase behavior.

auction A market in which goods are sold to the highest bidder; usually well publicized in advance or held at specific times that are well known in the trade. Auctions are becoming very popular over the Internet.

autocratic leader A manager who makes all decisions on his or her own and then announces them to employees.

automatic reordering system A system for ordering staple merchandise in which an automatic reorder is generated by a computer on the basis of a perpetual inventory system and reorder point calculations.

average BOM stock-to-sales ratio The number of months in the period divided by planned inventory turnover for the period.

average inventory The sum of inventory on hand at several periods in time divided by the number of periods.

Baby Boomer The generational cohort of people born between 1946 and 1964.

back order A part of an order that the vendor has not filled completely and that the vendor intends to ship as soon as the goods in question are available.

backup stock The inventory used to guard against going out of stock when demand exceeds forecasts or merchandise is delayed. Also called *safety stock* or *buffer stock*.

backward integration A form of vertical integration in which a retailer owns some or all of its suppliers.

bait-and-switch An unlawful deceptive practice that lures customers into a store by advertising a product at lower than usual prices (the bait), then inducing the customers to switch to a higher-price model (the switch).

balance sheet The summary of a retailer's financial resources and claims against the resources at a particular date; indicates the relationship between assets, liabilities, and owners' equity.

bank card Credit card issued by a bank, such as Visa and MasterCard.

bar code See *Universal Product Code (UPC)*.

bargain branding A branding strategy that targets a price-sensitive segment by offering a no-frills product at a discount price.

bargaining power of vendors A characteristic of a market in which retailers are so dependent on large, important vendors that their profits are adversely affected.

barriers to entry Conditions in a retail market that make it difficult for firms to enter the market.

base stock See *cycle stock*.

basic merchandise See *staple merchandise*.

basic stock list The descriptive and record-keeping function of an inventory control system; includes the stock number, item description, number of units on hand and on order, and sales for the previous periods.

basic stock method An inventory management method used to determine the beginning-of-month (BOM) inventory by considering both the forecast sales for the month and the safety stock.

benchmarking The practice of evaluating performance by comparing one retailer's performance with that of other retailers using a similar retail strategy.

benefits The customer's specific needs that are satisfied when the customer buys a product.

benefit segmentation A method of segmenting a retail market on the basis of similar benefits sought in merchandise or services.

big box stores Large, limited service retailers.

black market The availability of merchandise at a high price when it is difficult or impossible to purchase under normal market circumstances; commonly involves illegal transactions.

block group A collection of adjacent census blocks that contain between 300 and 3,000 people that is the smallest unit for the sample data.

blog A public Web site where users post informal journals of their thoughts, comments, and philosophies.

blue laws Laws prohibiting retailers from being open two consecutive days of the weekend—ostensibly to allow employees a day of rest or religious observance. Most states no longer have blue laws.

bonus Additional compensation awarded periodically, based on a subjective evaluation of the employee's performance.

book inventory system See *retail inventory method.*

bottom-up planning When goals are set at the bottom of the organization and filter up through the operating levels.

boutique (1) Departments in a store designed to resemble small, self-contained stores; (2) a relatively small specialty store.

boutique layout See *free-form layout.*

brand A distinguishing name or symbol (such as a logo, design, symbol, or trademark) that identifies the products or services offered by a seller and differentiates those products and services from the offerings of competitors.

brand association Anything linked to or connected with the brand name in a consumer's memory.

brand awareness The ability of a potential customer to recognize or recall that a particular brand name belongs to a retailer or product/service.

brand building The design and implementation of a retail communication program to create an image in the customer's mind of the retailer relative to its competitors. Also called *positioning.*

brand equity The value that brand image offers retailers.

brand image Set of associations consumers have about a brand that are usually organized around some meaningful themes.

brand loyalty Indicates customers like and consistently buy a specific brand in a product category. They are reluctant to switch to other brands if their favorite brand isn't available.

breadth of merchandise See *variety.*

break-even analysis A technique that evaluates the relationship between total revenue and total cost to determine profitability at various sales levels.

break-even point quantity The quantity at which total revenue equals total cost and beyond which profit occurs.

breaking bulk A function performed by retailers or wholesalers in which they receive large quantities of merchandise and sell them in smaller quantities.

breaking sizes Running out of stock on particular sizes.

broker A middleman that serves as a go-between for the buyer or seller; assumes no title risks, does not usually have physical custody of products, and is not looked upon as a permanent representative of either the buyer or seller.

buffer stock Merchandise inventory used as a safety cushion for cycle stock so the retailer won't run out of stock if demand exceeds the sales forecast. Also called *safety stock.*

building codes Legal restrictions describing the size and type of building, signs, type of parking lot, and so on that can be used at a particular location.

bulk fixture See *rounder.*

bullwhip effect The buildup of inventory in an uncoordinated channel.

buyback A strategy vendors and retailers use to get products into retail stores, either when a retailer allows a vendor to create space for goods by "buying back" a competitor's inventory and removing it from a retailer's system or when the retailer forces a vendor to buy back slow-moving merchandise.

buyer Person in a retailing organization responsible for the purchase and profitability of a merchandise category. Similar to *category manager.*

buyer's market Market occurring in economic conditions that favor the position of the retail buyer (or merchandiser) rather than the vendor; in other words, economic conditions are such that the retailer can demand and usually get concessions from suppliers in terms of price, delivery, and other market advantages. Opposite of a *seller's market.*

buyer's report Information on the velocity of sales, availability of inventory, amount of order, inventory turnover, forecast sales, and, most important, the quantity that should be ordered for each SKU.

buying behavior The activities customers undertake when purchasing a good or service.

buying calendar A plan of a store buyer's market activities, generally covering a six-month merchandising season based on a selling calendar that indicates planned promotional events.

buying committee A committee that has the authority for final judgment and decision making on such matters as adding or eliminating new products.

buying power The customer's financial resources available for making purchases.

buying process The stages customers go through to purchase merchandise or services.

buying situation A method of segmenting a retail market based on customer needs in a specific buying situation, such as a fill-in shopping trip versus a weekly shopping trip.

buzz Genuine, street-level excitement about a hot new product.

capacity fixture See *rounder.*

career path The set of positions to which management employees are promoted within a particular organization as their careers progress.

cash Money on hand.

cash discounts Reductions in the invoice cost that the vendor allows the retailer for paying the invoice prior to the end of the discount period.

cash wraps The places in a store where customers can purchase merchandise and have it "wrapped"—placed in a bag.

catalog retailer A nonstore retailer that communicates directly with customers using catalogs sent through the mail.

catalog retailing Nonstore retail format in which the retail offering is communicated to a customer through a catalog.

category An assortment of items (SKUs) the customer sees as reasonable substitutes for one another.

category captain A supplier that forms an alliance with a retailer to help gain consumer insight, satisfy consumer needs, and improve the performance and profit potential across the entire category.

category killer A discount retailer that offers a narrow but deep assortment of merchandise in a category and thus dominates the category from the customers' perspective. Also called a *category specialist.*

category life cycle A merchandise category's sales pattern over time.

category management The process of managing a retail business with the objective of maximizing the sales and profits of a category.

category manager See *buyer*.

category specialist See *category killer*.

caveat emptor Latin term for "let the buyer beware."

census A count of the population of a country as of a specified date.

census block An area bounded on all sides by visible (roads, rivers, etc.) and/or invisible (county, state boundaries) features that is the smallest geographic entity for which census data are available.

census tracts Subdivisions of a Metropolitan Statistical Area (MSA), with an average population of 4,000.

central business district (CBD) The traditional downtown business area of a city or town.

centralization The degree to which authority for making retail decisions is delegated to corporate managers rather than to geographically dispersed regional, district, and store management.

centralized buying A situation in which a retailer makes all purchase decisions at one location, typically the firm's headquarters.

central market See *market*.

central place A center of retailing activity such as a town or city.

central place theory Christaller's theory of retail location suggesting that retailers tend to locate in a central place. As more retailers locate together, more customers are attracted to the central place. See also *central place*.

chain discount A number of different discounts taken sequentially from the suggested retail price.

chargeback A practice used by retailers in which they deduct money from the amount they owe a vendor.

chat room Location in an Internet site at which customers can engage in interactive, real-time, text-based discussions.

checking The process of going through goods upon receipt to make sure that they arrived undamaged and that the merchandise received matches the merchandise ordered.

checkout areas See *cash wraps*.

cherry picking Customers visiting a store and buying only merchandise sold at big discounts or buying only the best styles or colors.

classification A group of items or SKUs for the same type of merchandise, such as pants (as opposed to jackets or suits), supplied by different vendors.

classification dominance An assortment so broad that customers should be able to satisfy all of their consumption needs for a particular category by visiting one retailer.

classification merchandising Divisions of departments into related types of merchandise for reporting and control purposes.

Clayton Act (1914) An act passed as a response to the deficiencies of the Sherman Act; it specifically prohibits price discrimination, tying arrangements, and exclusive dealing contracts that have the effect of limiting free trade, and it provides for damages to parties injured as a result of violations of the act.

clearance sale An end-of-season sale to make room for new goods; also pushing the sale of slow-moving, shopworn, and demonstration model goods.

closeout (1) An offer at a reduced price to sell a group of slow-moving or incomplete stock; (2) an incomplete assortment, the remainder of a line of merchandise that is to be discontinued and so is offered at a low price to ensure immediate sale.

closeout retailer Off-price retailer that sells a broad but inconsistent assortment of general merchandise as well as apparel and soft home goods, obtained through retail liquidations and bankruptcy proceedings.

COD (cash on delivery) Purchase terms in which payment for a product is collected at the time of delivery.

collaboration, planning, forecasting, and replenishment (CPFR) A collaborative inventory management system in which a retailer shares information with vendors. CPFR software uses data to construct a computer-generated replenishment forecast that is shared by the retailer and vendor before it's executed.

commercial bribery A vendor's offer of money or gifts to a retailer's employee for the purpose of influencing purchasing decisions.

commission Compensation based on a fixed formula, such as percentage of sales.

committee buying The situation whenever the buying decision is made by a group of people rather than by a single buyer. A multiunit operation is usually the type of firm that uses this procedure.

common stock The type of stock most frequently issued by corporations. Owners of common stock usually have voting rights in the retail corporation.

communication gap The difference between the actual service provided to customers and the service promised in the retailer's promotion program. This factor is one of the four factors identified by the Gaps model for improving service quality.

communication objectives Specific goals for a communication program related to the effects of the communication program on the customer's decision-making process.

community shopping centers See *neighborhood centers*.

comparable store sales growth See *same store sales growth*.

comparative price advertising A common retailing practice that compares the price of merchandise offered for sale with a higher "regular" price or a manufacturer's list price.

comparison shopping A market research method in which retailers shop at competitive stores, comparing the merchandise, pricing, visual display, and service to their own offering.

compatibility The degree to which the fashion is consistent with existing norms, values, and behaviors.

compensation Monetary payments including salary, commission, and bonuses; also, paid vacations, health and insurance benefits, and a retirement plan.

competition-oriented pricing A pricing method in which a retailer uses competitors' prices, rather than demand or cost considerations, as guides.

competitive parity method An approach for setting a promotion budget so that the retailer's share of promotion expenses is equal to its market share.

competitive rivalry The frequency and intensity of reactions to actions undertaken by competitors.

competitor analysis An examination of the strategic direction that competitors are likely to pursue and their ability to successfully implement their strategy.

complexity The ease with which consumers can understand and use a new fashion.

composite segmentation A method of segmenting a retail market using multiple variables, including benefits sought, lifestyles, and demographics.

computerized checkout See *point-of-sale (POS) terminal*.

conditions of sale See *terms of sale*.

conflict of interest A situation in which a decision maker's personal interest influences or has the potential to influence his or her professional decision.

congestion The amount of crowding of either cars or people.

consideration set The set of alternatives the customer evaluates when making a merchandise selection.

consignment goods Items not paid for by the retailer until they are sold. The retailer can return unsold merchandise; however, the retailer does not take title until final sale is made.

consortium exchange A retail exchange that is owned by several firms within one industry.

consumer cooperative Customers own and operate this type of retail establishment. Customers have ownership shares and share in the store's profits through price reductions or dividends.

Consumer Goods Pricing Act (1975) The statute that repealed all resale price maintenance laws and made it possible for retailers to sell products below suggested retail prices.

consumerism The activities of government, business, and independent organizations designed to protect individuals from practices that infringe on their rights as consumers.

contest Promotional activity in which customers compete for rewards through games of chance. Contests can also be used to motivate retail employees.

contract distribution service company Firm that performs all of the distribution functions for retailers or vendors, including transportation to the contract company's distribution center, merchandise processing, storage, and transportation to retailers.

contractual vertical marketing system A form of vertical marketing system in which independent firms at different levels in the channel operate contractually to obtain the economies and market impacts that could not be obtained by unilateral action. Under this system, the identity of the individual firm and its autonomy of operations remain intact. See also *administered vertical marketing system* and *corporate vertical marketing system*.

contribution margin Gross margin less any expense that can be directly assigned to the merchandise.

convenience center A shopping center that typically includes such stores as a convenience market, a dry cleaner, or a liquor store.

convenience goods Products that the consumer is not willing to spend the effort to evaluate prior to purchase, such as milk or bread.

convenience shopping situation When consumers are primarily concerned with minimizing their effort to get the product or service they want.

convenience store A store that provides a limited variety and assortment of merchandise at a convenient location in a 2,000- to 3,000-square-foot store with speedy checkout.

conventional supermarket A self-service food store that offers groceries, meat, and produce with limited sales of nonfood items, such as health and beauty aids and general merchandise.

conversion rates Percentage of consumers who buy the product after viewing it.

cookies Computer text files that identify visitors when they return to a Web site.

coop advertising Enables a retailer to associate its name with well-known national brands and use attractive art work created by the national brand. Also a method a retailer uses to share the cost of advertising with a vendor.

cooperative (co-op) advertising A program undertaken by a vendor in which the vendor agrees to pay all or part of a promotion for its products.

cooperative buying When a group of independent retailers work together to make large purchases from a single supplier.

copy The text in an advertisement.

copycat branding A branding strategy that imitates the manufacturer brand in appearance and trade dress but generally is perceived as lower quality and is offered at a lower price.

copyright A regulation that protects original works of authors, painters, sculptors, musicians, and others who produce works of artistic or intellectual merit.

core assortment A relatively large proportion of the total assortment that is carried by each store in the chain, regardless of size.

corporate social responsibility Voluntary actions taken by a company to address the ethical, social, and environmental impacts of its business operations and the concerns of its stakeholders.

corporate vertical marketing system A form of vertical marketing system in which all of the functions from production to distribution are at least partially owned and controlled by a single enterprise. Corporate systems typically operate manufacturing plants, warehouse facilities, and retail outlets. See also *administered vertical marketing system* and *contractual vertical marketing system*.

cost The financial expenditure required to obtain something in return.

cost code The item cost information indicated on price tickets in code. A common method of coding is the use of letters from an easily remembered word or expression with nonrepeating letters corresponding to numerals. For example, y o u n g b l a d e 1 2 3 4 5 6 7 8 9 0.

cost complement Used in the cost method of accounting, the percentage of net sales represented by the cost of goods sold.

cost method of accounting A method in which retailers record the cost of every item on an accounting sheet or include a cost code on the price tag or merchandise container. When a physical inventory is conducted, the cost of each item must be determined, the quantity in stock is counted, and the total inventory value at cost is calculated. See *retail inventory method*.

cost multiplier Used in the cost method of accounting, the cumulative markup multiplied by 100 percent minus cumulative markup percentage.

cost-oriented method A method for determining the retail price by adding a fixed percentage to the cost of the merchandise; also known as *cost-plus pricing*.

cost per thousand (CPM) A measure that is often used to compare media. CPM is calculated by dividing an ad's cost by its reach.

counterfeit merchandise Goods that are made and sold without permission of the owner of a trademark, a copyright, or a patented invention that is legally protected in the country where it is marketed.

coupons Documents that entitle the holder to a reduced price or X cents off the actual price of a product or service.

courtesy days The days on which stores extend to loyalty club customers the privilege of making purchases at sale prices in advance of public sale.

coverage The theoretical number of potential customers in the retailer's target market that could be exposed to an ad in a given medium.

credit Money placed at a consumer's disposal by a retailer, financial or other institution. For purchases made on credit, payment is due in the future.

credit limit The quantitative limit that indicates the maximum amount of credit that may be allowed to be outstanding on each individual customer account.

crossdocked Items that are unloaded from the shippers' truck and within a few hours reloaded onto trucks going to stores. These items are prepackaged by the vendor for a specific store, such that the UPC labels on a carton indicate the store to which it is to be sent.

cross-docking distribution area An area in a distribution center in which merchandise is delivered to one side of the facility by vendors, is unloaded, and is immediately reloaded onto trucks that deliver merchandise to the stores. With cross-docking, merchandise spends very little time in the warehouse.

cross-selling When sales associates in one department attempt to sell complementary merchandise from other departments to their customers.

cross-shopping A pattern of buying both premium and low-priced merchandise or patronizing expensive, status-oriented retailers and price-oriented retailers.

culture The meaning and values shared by most members of a society.

cumulative attraction The principle that a cluster of similar and complementary retailing activities will generally have greater drawing power than isolated stores that engage in the same retailing activities.

cumulative markup Used in the cost method of accounting, the average percentage markup for the period; the total retail price minus cost divided by retail price.

cumulative quantity discounts Discounts earned by retailers when purchasing certain quantities over a specified period of time.

cumulative reach The cumulative number of potential customers that would see an ad that runs several times.

current assets Cash or any assets that can normally be converted into cash within one year.

current liabilities Debts that are expected to be paid in less than one year.

customer allowance An additional price reduction given to the customer.

customer buying process The stages a customer goes through in purchasing a good or service. Stages include need recognition, information search, evaluation and choice of alternatives, purchase, and postpurchase evaluation.

customer database See *data warehouse*.

customer delight A high level of customer satisfaction created by retailers providing greatly unexpected services.

customer loyalty Customers' commitment to shopping at a store.

customer relationship management (CRM) A business philosophy and set of strategies, programs, and systems that focuses on identifying and building loyalty with a retailer's most valued customers.

customer returns The value of merchandise that customers return because it is damaged, doesn't fit, and so forth.

customer service The set of retail activities that increase the value customers receive when they shop and purchase merchandise.

customer service department The department in a retail organization that handles customer inquiries and complaints.

customer spotting A technique used in trade area analysis that "spots" (locates) residences of customers for a store or shopping center.

customization approach An approach used by retailers to provide customer service that is tailored to meet each customer's personal needs.

cycle stock The inventory that goes up and down due to the replenishment process. Also known as *base stock*.

cycle time The time between the decision to place an order and the receipt of merchandise and placement in the store.

cyclical theories Theories of institutional change based on the premise that retail institutions change on the basis of cycles. See also *wheel of retailing* and *accordion theory*.

data mining Technique used to identify patterns in data found in data warehouses, typically patterns that the analyst is unaware of prior to searching through the data.

data warehouse The coordinated and periodic copying of data from various sources, both inside and outside the enterprise, into an environment ready for analytical and informational processing. It contains all of the data the firm has collected about its customers and is the foundation for subsequent CRM activities.

dating A series of options that tells retailers when discounts can be taken from vendors and when the full invoice amount is due.

deal period A limited time period allowed by manufacturers for retailers to purchase merchandise at a special price.

decentralization When authority for retail decisions is made at lower levels in the organization.

deceptive advertising Any advertisement that contains a false statement or misrepresents a product or service.

decile analysis A method of identifying customers in a CRM program that breaks customers into ten deciles based on their LTV (lifetime value). When using decile analysis, the top 10 percent of the customers would be the most valued group.

deferred billing An arrangement that enables customers to buy merchandise and not pay for it for several months, with no interest charge.

delivery gap The difference between the retailer's service standards and the actual service provided to customers. This factor is one of the four factors identified by the Gaps model for improving service quality.

demalling The activity of revitalizing a mall by demolishing a mall's small shops, scrapping its common space and food courts, enlarging the sites once occupied by department stores, and adding more entrances into the parking lot.

demand/destination area Department or area in a store in which demand for the products or services offered is created before customers get to their destination.

demand/destination merchandise Products that customers have decided to buy before entering the store.

demand-oriented method A method of setting prices based on what the customers would expect or be willing to pay.

democratic leader A store manager who seeks information and opinions from employees and bases decisions on this information.

demographics Vital statistics about populations such as age, sex, and income.

demographic segmentation A method of segmenting a retail market that groups consumers on the basis of easily measured, objective characteristics such as age, gender, income, and education.

department A segment of a store with merchandise that represents a group of classifications the consumer views as being complementary.

department store A retailer that carries a wide variety and deep assortment, offers considerable customer services, and is organized into separate departments for displaying merchandise.

depth interview An unstructured personal interview in which the interviewer uses extensive probing to get individual respondents to talk in detail about a subject.

depth of merchandise See *assortment*.

deseasonalized demand The forecast demand without the influence of seasonality.

destination store A retail store in which the merchandise, selection, presentation, pricing, or other unique feature acts as a magnet for customers.

dialectic theory An evolutionary theory based on the premise that retail institutions evolve. The theory suggests that new retail formats emerge by adopting characteristics from other forms of retailers in much the same way that a child is the product of the pooled genes of two very different parents.

digital signage Signs whose visual content is delivered digitally through a centrally managed and controlled network and displayed on a television monitor or flat panel screen.

direct investment The investment and ownership by a retail firm of a division or subsidiary that builds and operates stores in a foreign country.

direct mail Any brochure, catalog, advertisement, or other printed marketing material delivered directly to the consumer through the mail or a private delivery company.

direct-mail catalog retailer A retailer offering merchandise or services through catalogs mailed directly to customers.

direct-mail retailer A nonstore retailer that communicates directly with customers using mail brochures and pamphlets to sell a specific product or service to customers at one point in time.

direct marketing A form of nonstore retailing in which customers are exposed to merchandise through print or electronic media and then purchase the merchandise by telephone, mail, or over the Internet.

direct product profitability (DPP) The profit associated with each category or unit of merchandise. DPP is equal to the per-unit gross margin less all variable costs associated with the merchandise such as procurement, distribution, sales, and the cost of carrying the assets.

direct-response advertising Advertisements on TV and radio that describe products and provide an opportunity for customers to order them.

direct retailing See *nonstore retailing*.

direct selling A retail format in which a salesperson, frequently an independent distributor, contacts a customer directly in a convenient location (either at a customer's home or at work), demonstrates merchandise benefits, takes an order, and delivers the merchandise to the customer.

disability Any physical or mental impairment that substantially limits one or more of an individual's major life activities or any condition that is regarded as being such an impairment.

disclosure of confidential information An unethical situation in which a retail employee discloses proprietary or confidential information about the firm's business to anyone outside the firm.

discount A reduction in the original retail price granted to store employees as a special benefit or to customers under certain circumstances.

discount-oriented center See *promotional center*.

discount store A general merchandise retailer that offers a wide variety of merchandise, limited service, and low prices.

discrimination An illegal action of a company or its managers when a member of a protected class (women, minorities, etc.) is treated differently from nonmembers of that class (see *disparate treatment*) or when an apparently neutral rule has an unjustified discriminatory effect (see *disparate impact*).

disintermediation When a manufacturer sells directly to consumers, thus competing directly with its retailers.

disparate impact The case of discrimination when an apparently neutral rule has an unjustified discriminatory effect, such as if a retailer requires high school graduation for all its employees, thereby excluding a larger proportion of disadvantaged minorities, when at least some of the jobs (e.g., custodian) could be performed just as well by people who did not graduate from high school.

disparate treatment The case of discrimination when members of a protected class are treated differently from nonmembers of that class—if a qualified woman (protected class), for example, does not receive a promotion given to a lesser qualified man.

dispatcher A person who coordinates deliveries from the vendor to the distribution center or stores or from the distribution center to stores.

distribution See *logistics*.

distribution center A warehouse that receives merchandise from multiple vendors and distributes it to multiple stores.

distribution channel A set of firms that facilitate the movement of products from the point of production to the point of sale to the ultimate consumer. Similar to a supply chain.

distribution intensity The number of retailers carrying a particular category.

distributive fairness A customer's perception of the benefits received compared to their costs (inconvenience or loss) when resolving a complaint.

distributive justice Arises when outcomes received are viewed as fair with respect to outcomes received by others.

diversification growth opportunity A strategic investment opportunity that involves an entirely new retail format directed toward a market segment not presently being served.

diversionary pricing A practice sometimes used by retailers in which low price is stated for one or a few goods or services (emphasized in promotion) to give the illusion that the retailer's prices are all low.

diverted merchandise Merchandise that is diverted from its legitimate channel of distribution; similar to *gray-market merchandise* except there need not be distribution across international boundaries.

diverter A firm that buys diverted merchandise from retailers and manufacturers and then resells the merchandise to other retailers. See *diverted merchandise*.

double coupon A retail promotion that allows the customer to double the face value of a coupon.

drawing account A method of sales compensation in which salespeople receive a weekly check based on their estimated annual income.

drugstore Specialty retail store that concentrates on pharmaceuticals and health and personal grooming merchandise.

duty See *tariff*.

economic order quantity (EOQ) The order quantity that minimizes the total cost of processing orders and holding inventory.

editing the assortment Selecting the right assortment of merchandise.

efficient customer response (ECR) The set of programs supermarket chains have undertaken to manage inventory and increase inventory turnover.

80–20 rule A general management principle where 80 percent of the sales or profits come from 20 percent of the customers.

electronic agent Computer program that locates and selects alternatives based on some predetermined characteristics.

electronic article surveillance system (EAS) A loss prevention system in which special tags placed on merchandise in retail stores are deactivated when the merchandise is purchased. The tags are used to discourage shoplifting.

electronic data interchange (EDI) The computer-to-computer exchange of business documents from retailer to vendor and back.

electronic retailing A retail format in which the retailers communicate with customers and offer products and services for sale over the Internet.

e-mail A paid personal communication vehicle that involves sending messages over the Internet.

emotional support Supporting retail service providers with the understanding and positive regard to enable them to deal with the emotional stress created by disgruntled customers.

employee discount A discount from retail price offered by most retailers to employees.

employee productivity Output generated by employee activities. One measure of employee productivity is the retailer's sales or profit divided by its employee costs.

employee turnover The number of employees occupying a set of positions during a period (usually a year) divided by the number of positions.

employment branding Programs undertaken by employers to understand what potential employees are seeking, as well as what they think about the retailer; developing a value proposition and an employment brand image; communicating that brand image to potential employees; and then fulfilling the brand promise by ensuring the employee experience matches that which was advertised.

employment marketing See *employment branding*.

empowerment The process of managers sharing power and decision-making authority with employees.

empty nest A stage in a family life cycle where children have grown up and left home.

empty nester Household where all children are grown and have left home.

end cap Display fixture located at the end of an aisle.

end-of-month (EOM) dating A method of dating in which the discount period starts at the end of the month in which the invoice is dated (except when the invoice is dated the 25th or later).

energy management The coordination of heating, air conditioning, and lighting to improve efficiencies and reduce energy costs.

environmental apparel Merchandise produced with few or no harmful effects on the environment. Part of a green marketing program.

Equal Employment Opportunity Commission (EEOC) A federal commission that was established for the purpose of taking legal action against employers that violate Title VII of the Civil Rights Act. Title VII prohibits discrimination in company personnel practices.

Equal Pay Act A federal act enforced by the Equal Employment Opportunity Commission that prohibits unequal pay for men and women who perform equal work or work of comparable worth.

escape clause A clause in a lease that allows the retailer to terminate its lease if sales don't reach a certain level after a specified number of years or if a specific cotenant in the center terminates its lease.

e-tailing See *electronic retailing.*

ethics A system or code of conduct based on universal moral duties and obligations that indicate how one should behave.

evaluation of alternatives The stage in the buying process in which the customer compares the benefits offered by various retailers.

everyday low pricing (EDLP) A pricing strategy that stresses continuity of retail prices at a level somewhere between the regular nonsale price and the deep-discount sale price of the retailer's competitors.

evolutionary theories Theories of institutional change based on the premise that retail institutions evolve. See *dialectic theory* and *natural selection.*

exclusive co-brand A brand developed by a national brand vendor, often in conjunction with a retailer, and sold exclusively by the retailer.

exclusive dealing agreement Restriction a manufacturer or wholesaler places on a retailer to carry only its products and no competing vendors' products.

exclusive geographical territory A policy in which only one retailer in a certain territory is allowed to sell a particular brand.

exclusive use clause A clause in a lease that prohibits the landlord from leasing to retailers selling competing products.

executive training program (ETP) A training program for retail supervisors, managers, and executives.

expenses Costs incurred in the normal course of doing business to generate revenues.

express warranty A guarantee supplied by either the retailer or the manufacturer that details the terms of the warranty in simple, easily understood language so customers know what is and what is not covered by the warranty.

extended problem solving A buying process in which customers spend considerable time at each stage of the decision-making process because the decision is important and they have limited knowledge of alternatives.

external sources of information Information provided by the media and other people.

extra dating A discount offered by a vendor in which the retailer receives extra time to pay the invoice and still take the cash discount.

extranet A collaborative network that uses Internet technology to link businesses with their suppliers, customers, or other businesses.

extreme value food retailers See *limited assortment supermarkets.*

extreme value retailers Small, full-line discount stores that offer a limited merchandise assortment at very low prices.

extrinsic reward Reward (such as money, promotion, or recognition) given to employees by their manager or the firm.

factoring A specialized financial function whereby manufacturers, wholesalers, or retailers sell accounts receivable to financial institutions, including factors or banks.

factory outlet Outlet store owned by a manufacturer.

fad A merchandise category that generates a lot of sales for a relatively short time—often less than a season.

Fair Labor Standards Act A federal law, enacted in 1938, that sets minimum wages, maximum hours, child labor standards, and overtime pay provisions.

fair trade Purchasing practices that require producers to pay workers a living wage, well more than the prevailing minimum wage, and offer other benefits, like onsite medical treatment.

fair trade laws See *resale price maintenance laws.*

fashion A type of product or a way of behaving that is temporarily adopted by a large number of consumers because the product, service, or behavior is considered to be socially appropriate for the time and place.

fashion merchandise Category of merchandise that typically lasts several seasons, and sales can vary dramatically from one season to the next.

fashion/specialty center A shopping center that is composed mainly of upscale apparel shops, boutiques, and gift shops carrying selected fashions or unique merchandise of high quality and price.

feature area Area designed to get the customer's attention that includes end caps, promotional aisles or areas, freestanding fixtures and mannequins that introduce a soft goods department, windows, and point-of-sale areas.

feature fixture See *four-way fixture.*

features The qualities or characteristics of a product that provide benefits to customers.

Federal Trade Commission Act (1914) The congressional act that created the Federal Trade Commission (FTC) and gave it the power to enforce federal trade laws.

fill rate The percentage of an order that is shipped by the vendor.

financial leverage A financial measure based on the relationship between the retailer's liabilities and owners' equity that indicates financial stability of the firm.

first-degree price discrimination Charging customers different prices on the basis of their willingness to pay.

fixed assets Assets that require more than a year to convert to cash.

fixed costs Costs that are stable and don't change with the quantity of product produced and sold.

fixed expenses Expenses that remain constant for a given period of time regardless of the sales volume.

fixed-rate lease A lease that requires the retailer to pay a fixed amount per month over the life of the lease.

fixtures The equipment used to display merchandise.

flexible pricing A pricing strategy that allows consumers to bargain over selling prices.

flextime A job scheduling system that enables employees to choose the times they work.

floor-ready merchandise Merchandise received at the store ready to be sold, without the need for any additional preparation by retail employees.

FOB (free-on-board) destination A term of sale designating that the shipper owns the merchandise until it is delivered to the retailer and is therefore responsible for transportation and any damage claims.

FOB (free-on-board) origin A term of sale designating that the retailer takes ownership of the merchandise at the point of origin and is therefore responsible for transportation and any damage claims.

focus group A marketing research technique in which a small group of respondents is interviewed by a moderator using a loosely structured format.

forward buy An opportunity to purchase at an extra discount more merchandise than the retailer normally needs to fill demand.

forward integration A form of vertical integration in which a manufacturer owns wholesalers or retailers.

four-way fixture A fixture with two cross-bars that sit perpendicular to each other on a pedestal.

franchisee The owner of an individual store in a franchise agreement.

franchising A contractual agreement between a franchisor and a franchisee that allows the franchisee to operate a retail outlet using a name and format developed and supported by the franchisor.

franchisor The owner of a franchise in a franchise agreement.

free-form layout A store design, used primarily in small specialty stores or within the boutiques of large stores, that arranges fixtures and aisles asymmetrically. Also called *boutique layout*.

free riding A situation in which a retailer, such as a discount store, takes more than its fair share of the benefits derived by another retailer's promotional or service efforts but does not incur its fair share of the costs and is thus able to sell the merchandise at a lower price.

freestanding fixture Fixtures and mannequins located on aisles that are designed primarily to get customers' attention and bring them into a department.

freestanding insert (FSI) An ad printed at a retailer's expense and distributed as a freestanding insert in the newspaper. Also called a *preprint*.

freestanding site A retail location that is not connected to other retailers.

free trade zone A special area within a country that can be used for warehousing, packaging, inspection, labeling, exhibition, assembly, fabrication, or transshipment of imports without being subject to that country's tariffs.

freight collect When the retailer pays the freight from the vendor.

freight forwarders Companies that purchase transport services. They then consolidate small shipments from a number of shippers into large shipments that move at a lower freight rate.

freight prepaid When the freight is paid by the vendor to the retailer.

frequency The number of times a potential customer is exposed to an ad.

frequent shopper program A reward and communication program used by a retailer to encourage continued purchases from the retailer's best customers. See *loyalty program*.

fringe trade area See *tertiary trade area*.

frontal presentation A method of displaying merchandise in which the retailer exposes as much of the product as possible to catch the customer's eye.

full-line discount store Retailers that offer a broad variety of merchandise, limited service, and low prices.

full-line forcing When a supplier requires a retailer to carry the supplier's full line of products if the retailer wants to carry any part of that line.

full warranty A guarantee provided by either the retailer or manufacturer to repair or replace merchandise without charge and within a reasonable amount of time in the event of a defect.

functional discount See *trade discount*.

functional needs The needs satisfied by a product or service that are directly related to its performance.

functional product grouping Categorizing and displaying merchandise by common end uses.

functional relationships A series of one-time market exchanges linked together over time.

future dating A method of dating that allows the buyer additional time to take advantage of the cash discount or to pay the net amount of the invoice.

Gaps model A conceptual model that indicates what retailers need to do to provide high-quality customer service. When customers' expectations are greater than their perceptions of the delivered service, customers are dissatisfied and feel the quality of the retailer's service is poor. Thus, retailers need to reduce the service gap—the difference between customers' expectations and perceptions of customer service to improve customers' satisfaction with their service.

general merchandise catalog retailers Nonstore retailers that offer a broad variety of merchandise in catalogs that are periodically mailed to their customers.

generational cohort People within the same generation who have similar purchase behaviors because they have shared experiences and are in the same stage of life.

Generation X The generational cohort of people born between 1965 and 1976.

Generation Y The generational cohort of people born between 1977 and 1995.

generic brand Unbranded, unadvertised merchandise found mainly in drug, grocery, and discount stores.

gentrification A process in which old buildings are torn down or restored to create new offices, housing developments, and retailers.

geodemographic segmentation A market segmentation system that uses both geographic and demographic characteristics to classify consumers.

geographic information system (GIS) A computerized system that enables analysts to visualize information about their customers' demographics, buying behavior, and other data in a map format.

geographic segmentation Segmentation of potential customers by where they live. A retail market can be segmented by countries, states, cities, and neighborhoods.

glass ceiling An invisible barrier that makes it difficult for minorities and women to be promoted beyond a certain level.

gondola An island type of self-service counter with tiers of shelves, bins, or pegs.

graduated lease A lease that requires rent to increase by a fixed amount over a specified period of time.

gray-market goods Merchandise that possesses a valid U.S. registered trademark and is made by a foreign manufacturer but is imported into the United States without permission of the U.S. trademark owner.

green marketing A strategic focus by retailers and their vendors to supply customers with environmentally friendly merchandise.

greeter A retail employee who greets customers as they enter a store and who provides information or assistance.

grid layout A store design, typically used by grocery stores, in which merchandise is displayed on long gondolas in aisles with a repetitive pattern.

gross margin The difference between the price the customer pays for merchandise and the cost of the merchandise (the price the retailer paid the supplier of the merchandise). More specifically, gross margin is net sales minus cost of goods sold.

gross margin return on investment (GMROI) Gross margin dollars divided by average (cost) inventory.

gross profit See *gross margin*.

gross sales The total dollar revenues received from the sales of merchandise and services.

group maintenance behaviors Activities store managers undertake to make sure that employees are satisfied and work well together.

habitual decision making A purchase decision involving little or no conscious effort.

hedonic needs Needs motivating consumers to go shopping for pleasure.

high-assay principle A resource allocation principle emphasizing allocating marketing expenditures on the basis of marginal return.

high/low pricing A strategy in which retailers offer prices that are sometimes above their competition's everyday low price, but they use advertising to promote frequent sales.

home improvement center A category specialist offering equipment and material used by do-it-yourselfers and construction contractors to make home improvements.

horizontal price fixing An agreement between retailers in direct competition with each other to charge the same prices.

house brand See *generic brand*.

Huff's gravity model A trade area analysis model used to determine the probability that a customer residing in a particular area will shop at a particular store or shopping center.

human resource management Management of a retailer's employees.

hype Artificially generated word of mouth, manufactured by public relations people.

hypermarket Large (100,000–300,000 square feet) combination food (60–70 percent) and general merchandise (30–40 percent) retailer.

idea-oriented presentation A method of presenting merchandise based on a specific idea or the image of the store.

identifiability A criteria for evaluating market segments in which retailers must be able to identify the customers in a target segment for the segmentation scheme to be effective. By identifying the segment, it allows retailers to determine (1) the segment's size and (2) with whom the retailer should communicate when promoting its retail offering.

illegal discrimination The actions of a company or its managers that result in a number of a protected class being treated unfairly and differently than others.

impact An ad's effect on the audience.

implied warranty of merchantability A guarantee that accompanies all merchandise sold by a retailer, assuring customers that the merchandise is up to standards for the ordinary purposes for which such goods are used.

impulse buying A buying decision made by customers on the spot after seeing the merchandise.

impulse merchandise See *impulse products*.

impulse products Products that are purchased by customers without prior plans. These products are almost always located near the front of the store, where they're seen by everyone and may actually draw people into the store.

impulse purchase An unplanned purchase by a customer.

incentive compensation plan A compensation plan that rewards employees on the basis of their productivity.

income statement A summary of the financial performance of a firm for a certain period of time.

independent exchange A retail exchange owned by a third party that provides the electronic platform to perform the exchange functions.

infomercials TV programs, typically 30 minutes long, that mix entertainment with product demonstrations and solicit orders placed by telephone from consumers.

information search The stage in the buying process in which a customer seeks additional information to satisfy a need.

infringement Unauthorized use of a registered trademark.

ingress/egress The means of entering/exiting the parking lot of a retail site.

in-house credit system See *proprietary store credit card system*.

initial markup The retail selling price initially placed on the merchandise less the cost of goods sold.

inner city Typically a high-density urban area consisting of apartment buildings populated primarily by ethnic groups.

input measure A performance measure used to assess the amount of resources or money used by the retailer to achieve outputs.

installment credit plan A plan that enables consumers to pay their total purchase price (less down payment) in equal installment payments over a specified time period.

institutional advertisement An advertisement that emphasizes the retailer's name and positioning rather than specific merchandise or prices.

in-store kiosk Spaces located within stores containing a computer connected to the store's central offices or the Internet.

instrumental support Support for retail service providers such as appropriate systems and equipment to deliver the service desired by customers.

integrated marketing communication (IMC) program The strategic integration of multiple communication methods to form a comprehensive, consistent message.

intellectual property Property that is intangible and created by intellectual (mental) effort as opposed to physical effort.

intelligent agent A computer program that locates and selects alternatives based on some predetermined characteristics.

interactive electronic retailing A system in which a retailer transmits data and graphics over cable or telephone lines to a consumer's TV or computer terminal.

interest The amount charged by a financial institution to borrow money.

interest income The income a retailer can generate through proprietary credit cards, bank deposits, bonds, treasury bills, fixed income investments, and other investments.

internal sources of information Information in a customer's memory such as names, images, and past experiences with different stores.

Internet retailing See *electronic retailing.*

intertype competition Competition between retailers that sell similar merchandise using different formats, such as discount and department stores.

intranet A secure communication system that takes place within one company.

intratype competition Competition between the same type of retailers (e.g., Kroger versus Safeway).

intrinsic rewards Nonmonetary rewards employees get from doing their jobs.

inventory Goods or merchandise available for resale.

inventory management The process of acquiring and maintaining a proper assortment of merchandise while keeping ordering, shipping, handling, and other related costs in check.

inventory shrinkage See *shrinkage.*

inventory turnover Net sales divided by average retail inventory; used to evaluate how effectively managers utilize their investment in inventory.

invoice cost The actual amount due for the merchandise after both trade and quantity discounts are taken.

irregulars Merchandise that has minor mistakes in construction.

job analysis Identifying essential activities and determining the qualifications employees need to perform them effectively.

job application form A form a job applicant completes that contains information about the applicant's employment history, previous compensation, reasons for leaving previous employment, education and training, personal health, and references.

job description A description of the activities the employee needs to perform and the firm's performance expectations.

job enrichment The redesign of a job to include a greater range of tasks and responsibilities.

job sharing When two or more employees voluntarily are responsible for a job that was previously held by one person.

joint venture In the case of global expansion, an entity formed when the entering retailer pools its resources with a local retailer to form a new company in which ownership, control, and profits are shared. More generally, any business venture in which two or more firms pool resources to form a new business entity.

key items The items that are in greatest demand. Also referred to as best sellers or "A" items (in the case of an ABC analysis).

keystone method A method of setting retail prices in which retailers simply double the cost of the merchandise to obtain the original retail selling price.

kickback See *commercial bribery.*

kiosk See *merchandise kiosk.*

knockoff A copy of the latest styles displayed at designer fashion shows and sold in exclusive specialty stores. These copies are sold at lower prices through retailers targeting a broader market.

knowledge gap The difference between customer expectations and the retailer's perception of customer expectations. This factor is one of four identified by the Gaps model for improving service quality.

labor scheduling The process of determining the number of employees assigned to each area of the store at each hour the store is open.

layaway A method of deferred payment in which merchandise is held by the store for the customer until it is completely paid for.

leader pricing A pricing strategy in which certain items are priced lower than normal to increase the traffic flow of customers or to increase the sale of complementary products.

leadership The process by which a person attempts to influence another to accomplish some goal or goals.

lead time The amount of time between recognition that an order needs to be placed and the point at which the merchandise arrives in the store and is ready for sale.

leased department An area in a retail store leased or rented to an independent company. The leaseholder is typically responsible for all retail mix decisions involved in operating the department and pays the store a percentage of its sales as rent.

lessee The party signing the lease.

lessor The party owning a property that is for rent.

less-than-carload (LCL) The transportation rate that applies to less-than-full carload shipments.

level of support See *service level.*

liabilities Obligations of a retail enterprise to pay cash or other economic resources in return for past, present, or future benefits.

licensed brand Brand for which the licensor (owner of a well-known name) enters a contractual arrangement with a licensee (a retailer or third party). The licensee either manufactures or contracts with a manufacturer to produce the licensed product and pays a royalty to the licensor.

lifestyle Refers to how people live, how they spend their time and money, what activities they pursue, and their attitudes and opinions about the world they live in.

lifestyle center A shopping center with an outdoor traditional streetscape layout with sit-down restaurants and a conglomeration of specialty retailers.

lifestyle segmentation A method of segmenting a retail market based on how consumers live, how they spend their time and money, what activities they pursue, and their attitudes and opinions about the world they live in.

lifetime customer value (LTV) The expected contribution from the customer to the retailer's profits over his or her entire relationship with the retailer.

lift-out See *buyback.*

limited assortment supermarkets A supermarket offering a limited number of SKUs.

limited problem solving A purchase decision process involving a moderate amount of effort and time. Customers engage in this type of buying process when they have some prior experience with the product or service and their risk is moderate.

limited warranty A type of guarantee in which any limitations must be stated conspicuously so that customers are not misled.

local links A way to help customers get around a Web site on the Internet by using links that are internal to the Web site.

logistics Part of the supply chain process that plans, implements, and controls the efficient, effective flow and storage of goods, services, and related information from the point of origin to the point of consumption to meet customers' requirements.

long-term liabilities Debts that will be paid after one year.

loop layout See *racetrack layout.*

loss leader An item priced near or below cost to attract customer traffic into the store.

low-price guarantee policy A policy that guarantees that the retailer will have the lowest possible price for a product or group of products and usually promises to match or better any lower price found in the local market.

loyalty program A program set up to reward customers with incentives such as discounts on purchases, free food, gifts, or even cruises or trips in return for their repeated business.

magalog Combination of magazine and catalog.

mail-order retailer See *direct-mail catalog retailer.*

Main Street The central business district located in the traditional shopping area of smaller towns, or a secondary business district in a suburb or within a larger city.

maintained markup The amount of markup the retailer wishes to maintain on a particular category of merchandise; net sales minus cost of goods sold.

maintenance-increase-recoupment lease A provision of a lease that can be used with either a percentage or straight lease. This type of lease allows the landlord to increase the rent if insurance, property taxes, or utility bills increase beyond a certain point.

mall A shopping center with a pedestrian focus where customers park in outlying areas and walk to the stores.

management by objectives A popular method for linking the goals of a firm to goals for each employee and providing information to employees about their role.

managing diversity A set of human resource management programs designed to realize the benefits of a diverse workforce.

manufacturer brand A line of products designed, produced, and marketed by a vendor. Also called a *national brand.*

manufacturer's agent An agent who generally operates on an extended contractual basis, often sells within an exclusive territory, handles noncompeting but related lines of goods, and possesses limited authority with regard to prices and terms of sale.

manufacturer's outlet store A discount retail store owned and operated by a manufacturer.

manufacturer's suggested retail price (MSRP) The lowest price specified by a manufacturer at which a retailer can sell the manufacturer's product.

maquiladoras An assembly plant in Mexico, especially one along the border between the United States and Mexico, to which foreign materials and parts are shipped and from which the finished product is returned to the original market.

marginal analysis A method of analysis used in setting a promotional budget or allocating retail space, based on the economic principle that firms should increase expenditures as long as each additional dollar spent generates more than a dollar of additional contribution.

markdown The percentage reduction in the initial retail price.

markdown cancellation The percentage increase in the retail price after a markdown is taken.

markdown money Funds provided by a vendor to a retailer to cover decreased gross margin from markdowns and other merchandising issues.

market A group of vendors in a concentrated geographic location or even under one roof or over the Internet; also known as a *central market.*

market attractiveness/competitive position matrix A method for analyzing opportunities that explicitly considers the capabilities of the retailer and the attractiveness of retail markets.

market basket analysis Specific type of data analysis that focuses on the composition of the basket (or bundle) of products purchased by a household during a single shopping occasion.

market development See *market penetration growth opportunity.*

market expansion growth opportunity A strategic investment opportunity that employs the existing retailing format in new market segments.

marketing segmentation The process of dividing a retail market into homogeneous groups. See *retail market segment.*

market penetration growth opportunity An investment opportunity strategy that focuses on increasing sales to present customers using the present retailing format.

market research The systematic collection and analysis of information about a retail market.

market share A retailer's sales divided by the sales of all competitors within the same market.

market week See *trade show.*

markup The increase in the retail price of an item after the initial markup percentage has been applied but before the item is placed on the selling floor.

markup percentage The markup as a percent of retail price.

marquee A sign used to display a store's name or logo.

mass customization The production of individually customized products at costs similar to mass-produced products.

mass-market theory A theory of how fashion spreads that suggests that each social class has its own fashion leaders who play a key role in their own social networks. Fashion information trickles across social classes rather than down from the upper classes to the lower classes.

Mazur plan A method of retail organization in which all retail activities fall into four functional areas: merchandising, marketing communications, store management, and accounting and control.

m-commerce (mobile commerce) Communicating with and even selling to customers through wireless handheld devices, such as cellular telephones and personal digital assistants.

media coverage The theoretical number of potential customers in a retailer's market who could be exposed to an ad.

memorandum purchases Items not paid for by a retailer until they are sold. The retailer can return unsold merchandise; however, the retailer takes title on delivery and is responsible for damages. See *consignment goods.*

mentoring program The assigning of higher-level managers to help lower-level managers learn the firm's values and meet other senior executives.

merchandise budget plan A plan used by buyers to determine how much money to spend in each month on a particular fashion merchandise category, given the firm's sales forecast, inventory turnover, and profit goals.

merchandise category See *category.*

merchandise classification See *classification.*

merchandise group A group within an organization managed by the senior vice presidents of merchandise and responsible for several departments.

merchandise kiosks Small, temporary selling spaces typically located in the walkways of enclosed malls, airports, train stations, or office building lobbies.

merchandise management The process by which a retailer attempts to offer the right quantity of the right merchandise in the right place at the right time while meeting the company's financial goal.

merchandise show See *trade show.*

merchandising See *merchandise management.*

merchandising optimization software Set of algorithms (computer programs) that monitors merchandise sales, promotions, competitors' actions, and other factors to determine the optimal (most profitable) price and timing for merchandising activities, especially markdowns.

merchandising planner A retail employee responsible for allocating merchandise and tailoring the assortment in several categories for specific stores in a geographic area.

message board Location in an Internet site at which customers can post comments.

Metropolitan Statistical Area (MSA) A city with 50,000 or more inhabitants or an urbanized area of at least 50,000 inhabitants and a total MSA population of at least 100,000 (75,000 in New England).

metro renters One of ESRI's Community Tapestry segmentation scheme clusters. Young, well-educated singles beginning their professional careers in the largest cities, such as New York, Chicago, and Los Angeles.

micropolitan statistical area A city with only 10,000 inhabitants in its core urban area.

mission statement A broad description of the scope of activities a business plans to undertake.

mixed-use development (MXD) Development that combines several uses in one complex—for example, shopping center, office tower, hotel, residential complex, civic center, and convention center.

model stock list A list of fashion merchandise that indicates in very general terms (product lines, colors, and size distributions) what should be carried in a particular merchandise category; also known as a model stock plan.

model stock plan A summary of the desired inventory levels of each SKU stocked in a store for a merchandise category.

monthly additions to stock The amount to be ordered for delivery in each month, given the firm's turnover and sales objectives.

months of supply The amount of inventory on hand at the beginning of the month expressed in terms of the time it will take to sell. A six-month supply means it will take six months for the merchandise to sell. A six-month supply is equivalent to an inventory turnover of two.

multiattribute analysis A method for evaluating vendors that uses a weighted average score for each vendor, which is based on the importance of various issues and the vendor's performance on those issues.

multiattribute attitude model A model of customer decision making based on the notion that customers see a retailer or a product as a collection of attributes or characteristics. The model can also be used for evaluating a retailer, product, or vendor. The model uses a weighted average score based on the importance of various issues and performance on those issues.

multichannel retailer Retailer that sells merchandise or services through more than one channel.

multilevel network A retail format in which people serve as master distributors, recruiting other people to become distributors in their network.

multiple-unit pricing Practice of offering two or more similar products or services for sale at one price. Also known as *quantity discounts.*

mystery shopper Professional shopper who "shops" a store to assess the service provided by store employees.

national brand See *manufacturer brand.*

natural barrier A barrier, such as a river or mountain, that impacts accessibility to a site.

natural selection A theory of retail evolution that argues that those institutions best able to adapt to changes in customers, technology, competition, and legal environments have the greatest chance for success.

needs The basic psychological forces that motivate customers to act.

negligence A product liability suit that occurs if a retailer or a retail employee fails to exercise the care that a prudent person usually would.

negotiation An interaction between two or more parties to reach an agreement.

neighborhood shopping center A shopping center that includes a supermarket, drugstore, home improvement center, or variety store. Neighborhood centers often include small stores, such as apparel, shoe, camera, and other shopping goods stores.

net invoice price The net value of the invoice or the total invoice minus all other discounts.

net lease A lease that requires all maintenance expenses such as heat, insurance, and interior repairs to be paid by the retailer.

net profit A measure of the overall performance of a firm; revenues (sales) minus expenses and losses for the period.

net profit margin Profit a firm makes divided by its net sales.

net sales The total number of dollars received by a retailer after all refunds have been paid to customers for returned merchandise.

network direct selling See *multilevel direct selling.*

net worth See *owners' equity.*

never-out list A list of key items or best sellers that are separately planned and controlled. These items account for large sales volume and are stocked in a manner so they are always available. These are "A" items in an ABC analysis.

noncumulative quantity discount Discount offered to retailers as an incentive to purchase more merchandise on a single order.

nondurable Perishable product consumed in one or a few uses.

nonstore retailing A form of retailing to ultimate consumers that is not store-based. Nonstore retailing is conducted through the Internet, vending machines, mail, direct selling, and direct marketing.

North American Industry Classification System (NAICS) Classification of retail firms into a hierarchical set of six-digit codes based on the types of products and services they produce and sell.

notes payable Current liabilities representing principal and interest the retailer owes to financial institutions (banks) that are due and payable in less than a year.

objective-and-task method A method for setting a promotion budget in which the retailer first establishes a set of communication objectives and then determines the necessary tasks and their costs.

observability The degree to which a new fashion is visible and easily communicated to others in a social group.

observation A type of market research in which customer behavior is observed and recorded.

odd pricing The practice of ending prices with an odd number (such as 69 cents) or just under a round number (such as $98 instead of $100).

off-price retailer A retailer that offers an inconsistent assortment of brand-name, fashion-oriented soft goods at low prices.

off-the-job training Training conducted in centralized classrooms away from the employee's work environment.

omnicenter A combination of mall, lifestyle, and power center components in a unified, open-air layout.

one hundred percent location The retail site in a major business district or mall that has the greatest exposure to a retail store's target market customers.

one-price policy A policy that, at a given time, all customers pay the same price for any given item of merchandise.

one-price retailer A store that offers all merchandise at a single fixed price.

1-to-1 retailing Developing retail programs for small groups or individual customers.

online chat A customer service offering that provides customers with an opportunity to click a button at anytime and have an instant messaging, e-mail, or voice conversation with a customer service representative.

online retailing See *electronic retailing.*

on-the-job training A decentralized approach in which job training occurs in the work environment where employees perform their jobs.

open-to-buy The plan that keeps track of how much is spent in each month and how much is left to spend.

operating expenses Costs, other than the cost of merchandise, incurred in the normal course of doing business, such as salaries for sales associates and managers, advertising, utilities, office supplies, and rent.

opinion leader Person whose attitudes, opinions, preferences, and actions influence those of others.

opportunity cost of capital The rate available on the next best use of the capital invested in the project at hand. The opportunity cost should be no lower than the rate at which a firm borrows funds, since one alternative is to pay back borrowed money. It can be higher, however, depending on the range of other opportunities available. Typically, the opportunity cost rises with investment risk.

optical character recognition (OCR) An industrywide classification system for coding information onto merchandise; enables retailers to record information on each SKU when it is sold and transmit the information to a computer.

opt in A customer privacy issue prevalent in the European Union. Takes the perspective that consumers "own" their personal information. Retailers must get consumers to explicitly agree to share this personal information.

option credit account A revolving account that allows partial payments without interest charges if a bill is paid in full when due.

option-term revolving credit A credit arrangement that offers customers two payment options: (1) pay the full amount within a specified number of days and avoid any finance charges or (2) make a minimum payment and be assessed finance charges on the unpaid balance.

opt out A customer privacy issue prevalent in the United States. Takes the perspective that personal information is generally viewed as being in the public domain and retailers can use it in any way they desire. Consumers must explicitly tell retailers not to use their personal information.

order form When signed by both parties, a legally binding contract specifying the terms and conditions under which a purchase transaction is to be conducted.

order point The amount of inventory below which the quantity available shouldn't go or the item will be out of stock before the next order arrives.

organization chart A graphic that displays the reporting relationships within a firm.

organization culture A firm's set of values, traditions, and customs that guide employee behavior.

organization structure A plan that identifies the activities to be performed by specific employees and determines the lines of authority and responsibility in the firm.

outlet center Typically stores owned by retail chains or manufacturers that sell excess and out-of-season merchandise at reduced prices.

outlet store Off-price retailer owned by a manufacturer or a department or specialty store chain.

outparcel A building or kiosk that is in the parking lot of a shopping center but isn't physically attached to a shopping center.

output measure Measure that assesses the results of retailers' investment decisions.

outshopping Customers shopping in other areas because their needs are not being met locally.

outsourcing Obtaining a service from outside the company that had previously been done by the firm itself.

overstored trade area An area having so many stores selling a specific good or service that some stores will fail.

own brand See *private-label brand.*

owners' equity The amount of assets belonging to the owners of the retail firm after all obligations (liabilities) have been met; also known as *net worth* and *stockholders' equity.*

pallet A platform, usually made of wood, that provides stable support for several cartons. Pallets are used to help move and store merchandise.

parallel branding A branding strategy that represents a private label that closely imitates the trade dress (packaging) and product attributes of leading manufacturer brands but with a clearly articulated "invitation to compare" in its merchandising approach and on its product label.

parallel import See *gray-market goods.*

parasite store A store that does not create its own traffic and whose trade area is determined by the dominant retailer in the shopping center or retail area.

partnering relationship See *strategic relationship.*

party plan system Salespeople encourage people to act as hosts and invite friends or coworkers to a "party" at which the merchandise is demonstrated. The host or hostess receives a gift or commission for arranging the meeting.

patent A law that gives the owner of a patent control over the right to make, sell, and use a product for a period of 17 years (14 years for a design).

penetration A low-pricing strategy for newly introduced products or categories.

percentage lease A lease in which rent is based on a percentage of sales.

percentage lease with specified maximum A lease that pays the lessor, or landlord, a percentage of sales up to a maximum amount.

percentage lease with specified minimum The retailer must pay a minimum rent no matter how low sales are.

percentage-of-sales method A method for setting a promotion budget based on a fixed percentage of forecast sales.

periodic reordering system An inventory management system in which the review time is a fixed period (e.g., two weeks), but the order quantity can vary.

perpetual book inventory See *retail inventory method.*

perpetual ordering system The stock level is monitored perpetually and a fixed quantity is purchased when the inventory available reaches a prescribed level.

personalized approach A customer service strategy that encourages service providers to tailor their service to meet each customer's personal needs.

personal selling A communication process in which salespeople assist customers in satisfying their needs through face-to-face exchange of information.

physical inventory A method of gathering stock information by using an actual physical count and inspection of the merchandise items.

pick ticket A document that tells the order filler how much of each item to get from the storage area.

pilferage The stealing of a store's merchandise. See also *shoplifting.*

planners Employees in merchandise management responsible for the financial planning and analysis of the merchandise category and, in some cases, the allocation of merchandise to stores.

planogram A diagram created from photographs, computer output, or artists' renderings that illustrates exactly where every SKU should be placed.

point-of-purchase (POP) area See *point-of-sale area*.

point-of-sale area An area where the customer waits at checkout. This area can be the most valuable piece of real estate in the store, because the customer is almost held captive in that spot.

point-of-sale (POS) terminal A cash register that can electronically scan a UPC code with a laser and electronically record a sale; also known as *computerized checkout*.

polygon Trade area whose boundaries conform to streets and other map features rather than being concentric circles.

popping the merchandise Focusing spotlights on special feature areas and items.

population density The number of people per unit area (usually square mile) who live within a geographic area.

positioning The design and implementation of a retail mix to create in the customer's mind an image of the retailer relative to its competitors. Also called *brand building*.

postpurchase evaluation The evaluation of merchandise or services after the customer has purchased and consumed them.

poverty of time A condition in which greater affluence results in less, rather than more, free time because the alternatives competing for customers' time increase.

power center Shopping center that is dominated by several large anchors, including discount stores (Target), off-price stores (Marshalls), warehouse clubs (Costco), or category specialists such as Home Depot, Office Depot, Circuit City, Sports Authority, Best Buy, and Toys "R" Us.

power perimeter The areas around the outside walls of supermarket that have fresh merchandise categories.

power retailer See *category killer* or *category specialist*.

power shopping center An open-air shopping center with the majority of space leased to several well-known anchor retail tenants—category specialists.

predatory pricing A method for establishing merchandise prices for the purpose of driving competition from the marketplace.

preferred client High-purchasing customers salespeople communicate with regularly, send notes to about new merchandise and sales in the department, and make appointments with for special presentations of merchandise.

premarking Marking of the price by the manufacturer or other supplier before goods are shipped to a retail store. Also called *prepricing*.

premium branding A branding strategy that offers the consumer a private label at a comparable manufacturer-brand quality, usually with a modest price savings.

premium merchandise Offered at a reduced price, or free, as an incentive for a customer to make a purchase.

prepricing See *premarking*.

preprint An advertisement printed at the retailer's expense and distributed as a freestanding insert in a newspaper. Also called a *freestanding insert (FSI)*.

press conference A meeting with representatives of the news media that is called by a retailer.

press release A statement of facts or opinions that the retailer would like to see published by the news media.

prestige pricing A system of pricing based on the assumption that consumers will not buy goods and services at prices they feel are too low.

price bundling The practice of offering two or more different products or services for sale at one price.

price comparison A comparison of the price of merchandise offered for sale with a higher "regular" price or a manufacturer's list price.

price discrimination An illegal practice in which a vendor sells the same product to two or more customers at different prices. See *first-degree price discrimination* and *second-degree price discrimination*.

price elasticity of demand A measure of the effect a price change has on consumer demand; percentage change in demand divided by percentage change in price.

price fixing An illegal pricing activity in which several marketing channel members establish a fixed retail selling price for a product line within a market area. See *vertical price fixing* and *horizontal price fixing*.

price lining A pricing policy in which a retailer offers a limited number of predetermined price points within a classification.

pricing experiment An experiment in which a retailer actually changes the price of an item in a systematic manner to observe changes in customers' purchases or purchase intentions.

primary data Marketing research information collected through surveys, observations, and experiments to address a problem confronting a retailer.

primary trade area The geographic area from which a store or shopping center derives 50 to 70 percent of its customers.

private exchanges Exchanges that are operated for the exclusive use of a single firm.

private-label brands Products developed and marketed by a retailer and only available for sale by that retailer. Also called *store brands*.

private-label store credit card system A system in which credit cards have the store's name on them, but the accounts receivable are sold to a financial institution.

PRIZM (potential rating index for zip markets) A database combining census data, nationwide consumer surveys, and interviews with hundreds of people across the country into a geodemographic segmentation system.

procedural fairness The perceived fairness of the process used to resolve customer complaints.

procedural justice An employee's perception of fairness (how he or she is treated) that is based on the process used to determine the outcome.

product attributes Characteristics of a product that affect customer evaluations.

product availability A measurement of the percentage of demand for a particular SKU that is satisfied.

productivity measure The ratio of an output to an input determining how effectively a firm uses a resource.

product liability A tort (or wrong) that occurs when an injury results from the use of a product.

product line A group of related products.

profitability A company's ability to generate revenues in excess of the costs incurred in producing those revenues.

profit margin Net profit divided by net sales.

profit margin management path One of two paths in the strategic profit model to increasing return on assets.

prohibited use clause A clause in a lease that keeps a landlord from leasing to certain kinds of tenants.

promotion Activities undertaken by a retailer to provide consumers with information about a retailer's store, its image, and its retail mix.

promotional aisle Area aisle or area of a store designed to get the customer's attention. An example might be a special "trim-the-tree" department that seems to magically appear right after Thanksgiving every year for the Christmas holidays.

promotional allowance An allowance given by vendors to retailers to compensate the latter for money spent in advertising a particular item.

promotional area A feature area in a store in which merchandise on sale is displayed.

promotional center A type of specialty shopping center that contains one or more discount stores plus smaller retail tenants. Also called *discount-oriented center.*

promotional department store A department store that concentrates on apparel and sells a substantial portion of its merchandise on weekly promotion.

promotional stock A retailer's stock of goods offered at an unusually attractive price in order to obtain sales volume; it often represents special purchases from vendors.

promotion from within A staffing policy that involves hiring new employees only for positions at the lowest level in the job hierarchy and then promoting employees for openings at higher levels in the hierarchy.

promotion mix A communication program made up of advertising, sales promotions, Web sites, store atmosphere, publicity, personal selling, and word of mouth.

proprietary EDI systems Data exchange systems that are developed and used primarily by large retailers for the purpose of exchanging data with their vendors.

proprietary store credit card system A system in which credit cards have the store's name on them and the accounts receivable are administered by the retailer; also known as *in-house credit system.*

providing assortments A function performed by retailers that enables customers to choose from a selection of brands, designs, sizes, and prices at one location.

psychographics Refers to how people live, how they spend their time and money, what activities they pursue, and their attitudes and opinions about the world they live in.

publicity Communications through significant unpaid presentations about the retailer (usually a news story) in impersonal media.

public warehouse Warehouse that is owned and operated by a third party.

puffing An advertising or personal selling practice in which the seller exaggerates the benefits or quality of a product in very broad terms.

pull supply chain Strategy in which orders for merchandise are generated at the store level on the basis of demand data captured by point-of-sale terminals.

push money (PM) An incentive for retail salespeople provided by a vendor to promote, or push, a particular product; also known as *spiff.*

push supply chain Strategy in which merchandise is allocated to stores on the basis of historical demand, the inventory position at the distribution center, and the stores' needs.

pyramid scheme When the firm and its program are designed to sell merchandise and services to other distributors rather than to end users.

quantity discount The policy of granting lower prices for higher quantities. Also known as *multiple-unit pricing.*

quick response (QR) delivery system System designed to reduce the lead time for receiving merchandise, thereby lowering inventory investment, improving customer service levels, and reducing distribution expenses; also known as a just-in-time inventory management system.

quota Target level used to motivate and evaluate performance.

quota–bonus plan Compensation plan that has a performance goal or objective established to evaluate employee performance, such as sales per hour for salespeople and maintained margin and turnover for buyers.

racetrack layout A type of store layout that provides a major aisle to facilitate customer traffic that has access to the store's multiple entrances. Also known as a *loop layout.*

radio frequency identification device (RFID) A technology that allows an object or person to be identified at a distance using radio waves.

rain check When sale merchandise is out of stock, a written promise to customers to sell them that merchandise at the sale price when it arrives.

reach The actual number of customers in the target market exposed to an advertising medium. See *advertising reach.*

reachable A requirement of a viable market segment that the retailer can target promotions and other elements of the retail mix to the consumers in that segment.

rebate Money returned to the buyer in the form of cash based on a portion of the purchase price.

receipt of goods (ROG) dating A dating policy in which the cash discount period starts on the day the merchandise is received.

receiving The process of filling out paperwork to record the receipt of merchandise that arrives at a store or distribution center.

recruitment Activity performed by a retailer to generate job applicants.

reductions Includes three things: markdowns, discounts to employees and customers, and inventory shrinkage due to shoplifting, breakage, or loss.

reference group One or more people whom a person uses as a basis of comparison for his or her beliefs, feelings, and behaviors.

reference price A price point in the consumer's memory for a good or service that can consist of the price last paid, the price most frequently paid, or the average of all prices customers have paid for similar offerings. A benchmark for what consumers believe the "real" price of the merchandise should be.

refusal to deal A legal issue in which either a vendor or a retailer reserves the right to deal or refuse to deal with anyone it chooses.

region In retail location analysis, refers to part of the country, a particular city, or Metropolitan Statistical Area (MSA).

regional mall Shopping malls less than 1 million square feet.

regression analysis A statistical approach for evaluating retail locations based on the assumption that factors that affect the sales of existing stores in a chain will have the same impact on stores located at new sites being considered.

Reilly's law A model used in trade area analysis to define the relative ability of two cities to attract customers from the area between them.

related diversification growth opportunity A diversification opportunity strategy in which the retailer's present offering and market share something in common with the market and format being considered.

relational partnership Long-term business relationship in which the buyer and vendor have a close, trusting interpersonal relationship.

reorder point The stock level at which a new order is placed.

resale price maintenance laws Laws enacted in the early 1900s to curb vertical price fixing. These laws were designed to help protect small retailers by prohibiting retailers from selling below manufacturer's suggested retail price. Also called *fair trade laws*. In 1975, these laws were repealed by the Consumer Goods Pricing Act.

resale price management (RPM) A requirement imposed by a vendor that a retailer cannot sell an item for less than the specific price (the manufacturer's suggested retail price).

resident buying office An organization located in a major buying center that provides services to help retailers buy merchandise.

restraint of trade Any contract that tends to eliminate or stifle competition, create a monopoly, artificially maintain prices, or otherwise hamper or obstruct the course of trade and commerce as it would be carried on if left to the control of natural forces; also known as unfair trade practices.

retail audit See *situation audit*.

retail chain A firm that consists of multiple retail units under common ownership and usually has some centralization of decision making in defining and implementing its strategy.

retailer A business that sells products and services to consumers for their personal or family use.

retail exchanges Electronic marketplaces operated by organizations that facilitate the buying and selling of merchandise using the Internet.

retail format The retailers' type of retail mix (nature of merchandise and services offered, pricing policy, advertising and promotion program, approach to store design and visual merchandising, and typical location).

retail format development growth opportunity An investment opportunity strategy in which a retailer offers a new retail format—a format involving a different retail mix—to the same target market.

retail information system System that provides the information needed by retail managers by collecting, organizing, and storing relevant data continuously and directing the information to the appropriate managers.

retailing A set of business activities that adds value to the products and services sold to consumers for their personal or family use.

retailing concept A management orientation that holds that the key task of a retailer is to determine the needs and wants of its target markets and direct the firm toward satisfying those needs and wants more effectively and efficiently than competitors do.

retail inventory method (RIM) An accounting procedure whose objectives are to maintain a perpetual or book inventory in retail dollar amounts and to maintain records that make it possible to determine the cost value of the inventory at any time without taking a physical inventory; also known as *book inventory system* or *perpetual book inventory*.

retail market A group of consumers with similar needs (a market segment) and a group of retailers using a similar retail format to satisfy those consumer needs.

retail market segment A group of customers whose needs will be satisfied by the same retail offering because they have similar needs and go through similar buying processes.

retail mix The combination of factors used by a retailer to satisfy customer needs and influence their purchase decisions; includes merchandise and services offered, pricing, advertising and promotions, store design and location, and visual merchandising.

retail-sponsored cooperative An organization owned and operated by small, independent retailers to improve operating efficiency and buying power. Typically, the retail-sponsored cooperative operates a wholesale buying and distribution system and requires its members to concentrate their purchases from the cooperative wholesale operation.

retail strategy A statement that indicates (1) the target market toward which a retailer plans to commit its resources, (2) the nature of the retail offering that the retailer plans to use to satisfy the needs of the target market, and (3) the bases upon which the retailer will attempt to build a sustainable competitive advantage over competitors.

retained earnings The portion of owners' equity that has accumulated over time through profits but has not been paid out in dividends to owners.

return on assets Net profit after taxes divided by total assets.

return on owners' equity Net profit after taxes divided by owners' equity; also known as return on net worth.

reverse auction Auction conducted by retailer buyers. Known as a *reverse auction* because there is one buyer and many potential sellers. In reverse auctions, retail buyers provide a specification for what they want to a group of potential vendors. The competing vendors then bid down the price at which they are willing to sell until the buyer accepts a bid.

reverse logistics The process of moving returned goods back through the supply chain from the customer, to the stores, distribution centers, and vendors.

review time The period of time between reviews of a line for purchase decisions.

revolving credit A consumer credit plan that combines the convenience of a continuous charge account and the privileges of installment payment.

RFM (recency, frequency, monetary) analysis Often used by catalog retailers and direct marketers, a scheme for segmenting customers on the basis of how recently they have made a purchase, how frequently they make purchases, and how much they have bought.

ribbon center See *strip shopping center.*

road condition Includes the age, number of lanes, number of stoplights, congestion, and general state of repair of roads in a trade area.

road pattern A consideration used in measuring the accessibility of a retail location from major arteries, freeways, or roads.

Robinson-Patman Act (1946) The Congressional act that revised Section 2 of the Clayton Act and specifically prohibits certain types of price discrimination.

rounder A round fixture that sits on a pedestal. Smaller than the straight rack, it is designed to hold a maximum amount of merchandise. Also known as a *bulk* or *capacity fixture.*

routine decision making See *habitual decision making.*

rule-of-thumb method A type of approach for setting a promotion budget that uses past sales and communication activity to determine the present communications budget.

safety stock See *buffer stock.*

sale-leaseback The practice in which retailers build new stores and sell them to real estate investors who then lease the buildings back to the retailers on a long-term basis.

sales associate The same as a salesperson. The term is used to recognize the importance and professional nature of the sales function and avoids the negative image sometimes linked with the term "salesperson."

sales consultant See *sales associate.*

sales per cubic foot A measure of space productivity appropriate for stores such as wholesale clubs that use multiple layers of merchandise.

sales per linear foot A measure of space productivity used when most merchandise is displayed on multiple shelves of long gondolas, such as in grocery stores.

sales per square foot A measure of space productivity used by most retailers since rent and land purchases are assessed on a per-square-foot basis.

sales promotions Paid impersonal communication activities that offer extra value and incentives to customers to visit a store or purchase merchandise during a specific period of time.

sales-to-stock ratio The net sales divided by average inventory at cost. It is one component of GMROI and is similar in concept to inventory turnover except the numerator is expressed at retail (net sales) rather than at cost (cost of good sold)

same store sales growth The sales growth in stores that have been open for over one year.

satisfaction A postconsumption evaluation of the degree to which a store or product meets or exceeds customer expectations.

saturated trade area A trade area that offers customers a good selection of goods and services, while allowing competing retailers to make good profits.

scale economies Cost advantages due to the size of a retailer.

scanning The process in point-of-sale systems wherein the input into the terminal is accomplished by passing a coded ticket over a reader or having a hand-held wand pass over the ticket.

scrambled merchandising An offering of merchandise not typically associated with the store type, such as clothing in a drugstore.

search engines Computer programs that search for and provide a listing of all Internet sites selling a product category or brand with the price of the merchandise offered. Also called *shopping bots.*

seasonal discount Discount offered as an incentive to retailers to place orders for merchandise in advance of the normal buying season.

seasonal merchandise Inventory whose sales fluctuate dramatically according to the time of the year.

secondary data Market research information previously gathered for purposes other than solving the current problem under investigation.

secondary trade area The geographic area of secondary importance in terms of customer sales, generating about 20 percent of a store's sales.

second-degree price discrimination Charging different prices to different people on the basis of the nature of the offering.

security An operating unit within a retail organization that is responsible for protecting merchandise and other assets from pilferage (internal or external). Those working in security may be employees or outside agency people.

security policy Set of rules that apply to activities in the computer and communications resources that belong to an organization.

self-analysis An internally focused examination of a business's strengths and weaknesses.

self-service retailer A retailer that offers minimal customer service.

selling agent An agent (sales organization) that operates on an extended contractual basis; the agent sells all of a specified line of merchandise or the entire output of the principal (manufacturer) and usually has full authority with regard to prices, terms, and other conditions of sale. The agent occasionally renders financial aid to the principal.

selling, general, and administrative expenses (SG&A) Operating expenses, plus the depreciation and amortization of assets.

selling process A set of activities that salespeople undertake to facilitate the customer's buying decision.

selling space The area set aside for displays of merchandise, interactions between sales personnel and customers, demonstrations, and so on.

sell-through analysis A comparison of actual and planned sales to determine whether early markdowns are required or more merchandise is needed to satisfy demand.

seniors The generational cohort of people born before 1946.

service gap The difference between customers' expectations and perceptions of customer service to improve customers' satisfaction with their service.

service level A measure used in inventory management to define the level of support or level of product availability; the number of items sold divided by the number of items demanded. Service level should not be confused with customer service. Compare *customer service*.

services retailer Organization that offers consumers services rather than merchandise. Examples include banks, hospital, health spas, doctors, legal clinics, entertainment firms, and universities.

sexual harassment Unwelcome sexual advances, requests for sexual favors, or other verbal or physical conduct with sexual elements.

share of wallet The percentage of total purchases made by a customer in a store.

shelf talkers Signs on the shelf providing information about the merchandise and its price.

Sherman Antitrust Act (1890) An act protecting small businesses and consumers from large corporations by outlawing any person, corporation, or association from engaging in activities that restrain trade or commerce.

shoplifting The act of stealing merchandise from a store by employees, customers, or people posing as customers.

shopping bots See *search engines*.

shopping center A group of retail and other commercial establishments that is planned, developed, owned, and managed as a single property.

shopping goods Products for which consumers will spend time comparing alternatives.

shopping guide Free paper delivered to all residents in a specific area.

shopping mall Enclosed, climate-controlled, lighted shopping centers with retail stores on one or both sides of an enclosed walkway.

shortage See *shrinkage*.

shrinkage An inventory reduction that is caused by shoplifting by employees or customers, by merchandise being misplaced or damaged, or by poor bookkeeping.

situation audit An analysis of the opportunities and threats in the retail environment and the strengths and weaknesses of the retail business relative to its competitors.

skimming A high-pricing strategy for newly introduced categories or products.

SKU See *stockkeeping unit*.

sliding scale lease A part of some leases that stipulates how much the percentage of sales paid as rent will decrease as sales go up.

slotting allowance Fee paid by a vendor for space in a retail store. Also called *slotting fee*.

slotting fee See *slotting allowance*.

socialization The steps taken to transform new employees into effective, committed members of the firm.

social shoppers People who participate in virtual communities to obtain not just information for future use but also an enhanced emotional connection to other participants in the shopping experience.

sole proprietorship An arrangement in which an unincorporated retail firm is owned by one person.

span of control The number of subordinates reporting to a manager.

special event Sales promotion program comprising a number of sales promotion techniques built around a seasonal, cultural, sporting, musical, or other event.

specialization The organizational structure in which employees are typically responsible for only one or two tasks rather than performing all tasks. This approach enables employees to develop expertise and increase productivity.

specialty catalog retailer A nonstore retailer that focuses on specific categories of merchandise, such as fruit (Harry and David), gardening tools (Smith & Hawken), or seeds and plants (Burpee).

specialty department store A store with a department store format that focuses primarily on apparel and soft home goods (such as Neiman Marcus or Saks Fifth Avenue).

specialty product A product which the customer will expend considerable effort to buy.

specialty shopping Shopping experiences when consumers know what they want and will not accept a substitute.

specialty store A type of store concentrating on a limited number of complementary merchandise categories and providing a high level of service.

spending potential index (SPI) Compares the average expenditure in a particular area for a product to the amount spent on that product nationally.

spiff See *push money*.

split shipment A vendor ships part of a shipment to a retailer and back orders the remainder because the entire shipment could not be shipped at the same time.

spot A local television commercial.

spot check Used particularly in receiving operations when goods come in for reshipping to branch stores in packing cartons. Certain cartons are opened in the receiving area of the central distribution point and spot-checked for quality and quantity.

spotting technique See *analog approach*.

staging area Area in which merchandise is accumulated from different parts of the distribution center and prepared for shipment to stores.

standardization approach An approach used by retailers to provide customer service by using a set of rules and procedures so that all customers consistently receive the same service.

standards gap The difference between the retailer's perceptions of customers' expectations and the customer service standards it sets. This factor is one of four factors identified by the Gaps model for improving service quality.

staple merchandise Inventory that has continuous demand by customers over an extended period of time. Also known as *basic merchandise.*

stockholders' equity See *owners' equity.*

stockkeeping unit (SKU) The smallest unit available for keeping inventory control. In soft goods merchandise, an SKU usually means a size, color, and style.

stocklift See *buyback.*

stockout A situation occurring when an SKU that a customer wants is not available.

stock overage The amount by which a retail book inventory figure exceeds a physical count of the ending inventory.

stock-to-sales ratio Specifies the amount of inventory that should be on hand at the beginning of the month to support the sales forecast and maintain the inventory turnover objective. The beginning-of-month (BOM) inventory divided by sales for the month. The average stock-to-sales ratio is 12 divided by planned inventory turnover. This ratio is an integral component of the merchandise budget plan.

store advocates Customers who like a store so much that they actively share their positive experiences with friends and family.

store atmosphere The combination of the store's physical characteristics (such as architecture, layout, signs and displays, colors, lighting, temperature, sounds, and smells), which together create an image in the customers' mind. See *atmospherics.*

store brand See *private-label brand.*

store image The way a store is defined in a shopper's mind. The store image is based on the store's physical characteristics, its retail mix, and a set of psychological attributes.

store loyalty A condition in which customers like and habitually visit the same store to purchase a type of merchandise.

store maintenance The activities involved with managing the exterior and interior physical facilities associated with the store.

straight commission A form of salesperson's compensation in which the amount paid is based on a percentage of sales made minus merchandise returned.

straight lease A type of lease in which the retailer pays a fixed amount per month over the life of the lease.

straight rack A type of fixture that consists of a long pipe suspended with supports going to the floor or attached to a wall.

straight salary compensation A compensation plan in which salespeople or managers receive a fixed amount of compensation for each hour or week they work.

strategic alliance Collaborative relationship between independent firms. For example, a foreign retailer might enter an international market through direct investment but develop an alliance with a local firm to perform logistical and warehousing activities.

strategic profit model (SPM) A tool used for planning a retailer's financial strategy based on both margin management (net profit margin) and asset management (asset turnover). Using the SPM, a retailer's objective is to achieve a target return on assets.

strategic relationship Long-term relationship in which partners make significant investments to improve both parties' profitability.

strategic retail planning process The steps a retailer goes through to develop a strategic retail plan. It describes how retailers select target market segments, determine the appropriate retail format, and build sustainable competitive advantages.

strengths and weaknesses analysis A critical aspect of the situation audit in which a retailer determines its unique capabilities—its strengths and weaknesses relative to its competition.

strip shopping center A shopping center that usually has parking directly in front of the stores and does not have enclosed walkways linking the stores.

structured training program Training that teaches new employees the basic skills and knowledge they will need to do their job.

style The characteristic or distinctive form, outline, or shape of a product.

subculture A distinctive group of people within a culture. Members of a subculture share some customs and norms with the overall society but also have some unique perspectives.

subculture theory A theory of how fashion spreads that suggests that subcultures of mostly young and less affluent consumers, such as motorcycle riders and urban rappers, have started fashions for such things as colorful fabrics, t-shirts, sneakers, jeans, black leather jackets, and surplus military clothing.

supercenter Large store (150,000 to 220,000 square feet) combining a discount store with a supermarket.

superregional mall Shopping center that is similar to a regional center, but because of its larger size, it has more anchors and a deeper selection of merchandise, and it draws from a larger population base.

superstore A large supermarket between 20,000 and 50,000 square feet in size.

supply chain A set of firms that make and deliver a given set of goods and services to the ultimate consumer.

supply chain management The set of approaches and techniques firms employ to efficiently and effectively integrate their suppliers, manufacturers, warehouses, stores, and transportation intermediaries to efficiently have the right quantities at the right locations, and at the right time.

survey A method of data collection, using telephone, personal interview, mail, or any combination thereof.

sustainable competitive advantage A distinct competency of a retailer relative to its competitors that can be maintained over a considerable time period.

sweepstakes A promotion in which customers win prizes based on chance.

target market The market segment(s) toward which the retailer plans to focus its resources and retail mix.

tariff A tax placed by a government upon imports. Also known as *duty*.

task performance behaviors Planning, organizing, motivating, evaluating, and coordinating store employees' activities.

teleshopping See *television home shopping*.

television home shopping A retail format in which customers watch a TV program demonstrating merchandise and then place orders for the merchandise by phone.

terms of purchase Conditions in a purchase agreement between a retailer and a vendor that include the type(s) of discounts available and responsibility for transportation costs.

terms of sale Conditions in a sales contract with customers including such issues as charges for alterations, delivery, or gift wrapping or the store's exchange policies.

tertiary trade area The outermost ring of a trade area; includes customers who occasionally shop at the store or shopping center.

theme/festival center A shopping center that typically employs a unifying theme that is carried out by the individual shops in their architectural design and, to an extent, their merchandise.

third-degree price discrimination Charging different prices to different demographic market segments.

third-party logistics company Firm that facilitates the movement of merchandise from manufacturer to retailer but is independently owned.

thrift store A retail format offering used merchandise.

ticketing and marking Procedures for making price labels and placing them on the merchandise.

tie-in An approach used to attract attention to a store's offering by associating the offering with an event.

timing The determination of when and how often an ad should run.

tonnage merchandising A display technique in which large quantities of merchandise are displayed together.

top-down planning One side of the process of developing an overall retail strategy where goals are set at the top of the organization and filter down through the operating levels.

top-of-mind awareness The highest level of brand awareness; arises when consumers mention a brand name first when they are asked about a type of retailer, a merchandise category, or a type of service.

trade area A geographic sector that contains potential customers for a particular retailer or shopping center.

trade discount Reduction in a retailer's suggested retail price granted to wholesalers and retailers; also known as a *functional discount*.

trade dress A product's physical appearance, including its size, shape, color, design, and texture. For instance, the shape and color of a Coca-Cola bottle is its trade dress.

trademark Any mark, work, picture, or design associated with a particular line of merchandise or product.

trade show A temporary concentration of vendors that provides retailers opportunities to place orders and view what is available in the marketplace; also known as a *merchandise show* or *market week*.

traditional distribution center Warehouse in which merchandise is unloaded from trucks and placed on racks or shelves for storage.

traffic appliance Small portable appliance.

traffic flow The balance between a substantial number of cars and not so many that congestion impedes access to the store.

transformational leader A leader who gets people to transcend their personal needs for the sake of realizing the group goal.

travel time contours Used in trade area analysis to define the rings around a particular site based on travel time instead of distances.

trialability The costs and commitment required to initially adopt a fashion.

trickle-down theory A theory of how fashion spreads that suggests that the fashion leaders are consumers with the highest social status—wealthy, well-educated consumers. After they adopt a fashion, the fashion trickles down to consumers in lower social classes. When the fashion is accepted in the lowest social class, it is no longer acceptable to the fashion leaders in the highest social class.

triple-coupon promotion A retail promotion that allows the customer triple the face value of the coupon.

trust A belief that a partner is honest (reliable, stands by its word, sincere, fulfills obligations) and benevolent (concerned about the other party's welfare).

tying contract An agreement between a vendor and a retailer requiring the retailer to take a product it does not necessarily desire (the tied product) to ensure that it can buy a product it does desire (the tying product).

understored trade area An area that has too few stores selling a specific good or service to satisfy the needs of the population.

unit pricing The practice of expressing price in terms of both the total price of an item and the price per unit of measure.

Universal Product Code (UPC) The black-and-white bar code found on most merchandise; used to collect sales information at the point of sale using computer terminals that read the code. This information is transmitted computer to computer to buyers, distribution centers, and then to vendors, who in turn quickly ship replenishment merchandise.

unrelated diversification Diversification in which there is no commonality between the present business and the new business.

UPC See *Universal Product Code*.

URL (uniform resource locator) The standard for a page on the World Wide Web (e.g., www.nrf.org).

utilitarian needs Needs motivating consumers to go shopping to accomplish a specific task.

value Relationship of what a customer gets (goods/services) to what he or she has to pay for it.

values of lifestyle survey (VALS2) A tool used to categorize customers into eight lifestyle segments. Based on responses to surveys conducted by SRI Consulting Business Intelligence.

variable costs Costs that vary with the level of sales and can be applied directly to the decision in question.

variable pricing Charging different prices in different stores, markets, or zones.

variety The number of different merchandise categories within a store or department.

vending machine retailing A nonstore format in which merchandise or services are stored in a machine and dispensed to customers when they deposit cash or use a credit card.

vendor Any firm from which a retailer obtains merchandise.

vendor-managed inventory (VMI) An approach for improving supply chain efficiency in which the vendor is responsible for maintaining the retailer's inventory levels in each of its stores.

vertical integration An example of diversification by retailers involving investments by retailers in wholesaling or manufacturing merchandise.

vertical merchandising A method whereby merchandise is organized to follow the eye's natural up-and-down movement.

vertical price fixing Agreements to fix prices between parties at different levels of the same marketing channel (for example, retailers and their vendors).

virtual community A network of people who seek information, products, and services and communicate with one another about specific issues.

virtual mall A group of retailers and service providers that can be accessed over the Internet at one location.

visibility Customers' ability to see the store and enter the parking lot safely.

visual communications The act of providing information to customers through graphics, signs, and theatrical effects—both in the store and in windows—to help boost sales by providing information on products and suggesting items or special purchases.

visual merchandising The presentation of a store and its merchandise in ways that will attract the attention of potential customers.

want book Information collected by retail salespeople to record out-of-stock or requested merchandise.

warehouse club A retailer that offers a limited assortment of food and general merchandise with little service and low prices to ultimate consumers and small businesses.

weeks of supply An inventory management method most similar to the stock-to-sales method. The difference is that everything is expressed in weeks rather than months.

wheel of retailing A cyclical theory of retail evolution whose premise is that retailing institutions evolve from low-price/service to higher-price/service operations.

wholesale market A concentration of vendors within a specific geographic location, perhaps even under one roof or over the Internet.

wholesaler A merchant establishment operated by a concern that is primarily engaged in buying, taking title to, usually storing, and physically handling goods in large quantities, and reselling the goods (usually in smaller quantities) to retailers or industrial or business users.

wholesale-sponsored voluntary cooperative group An organization operated by a wholesaler offering a merchandising program to small, independent retailers on a voluntary basis.

word of mouth Communications among people about a retailer.

yield management The practice of adjusting prices up or down in response to demand to control sales generated.

zone pricing Charging different prices for the same merchandise in different geographic locations to be competitive in local markets.

zoning The regulation of the construction and use of buildings in certain areas of a municipality.

ENDNOTES

Chapter 1

1. Susan Reda, "Service That Stacks Up," *Stores*, March 2007 (accessed December 22, 2007); www.brooksbrothers.com (accessed February 14, 2008).
2. "2007 Global Powers of Retailing," *Stores*, January 2007, pp. 16–32. http://www.nxtbook.com/nxtbooks/nrfe/stores-globalretail07 (accessed May 22, 2007).
3. http://www.bsr.org (accessed May 21, 2007).
4. http://www.census.gov/svsd/retlann/pdf/sales.pdf (accessed June 18, 2007).
5. factfinder.consus.gov/servlet/IBQTable?_bm=Y&-NAICS2002=22, May 23, 2007 (accessed June 8, 2007).
6. Ibid.
7. Retail Industry Indicators, Washington, DC: National Retail Foundation, August 2006, p. 19. Courtesy of the NRF Foundation.
8. John Dawson, "Retailer Internationalisation: What Is Being Internationalised?" Workshop on Globalizing Retail: Transnational Retail, Supply Chains and the Global Economy. July 17, 2006, University of Surrey School of Management.
9. Retail Industry Indicators; "2007 Global Powers of Retailing."
10. Michael Barbaro, "Candles, Jeans, Lipsticks: Products with Ulterior Motives," *New York Times*, November 13, 2006 (accessed December 22, 2007).
11. Sarah Butler, "Would You Like a Bag with That, Madam?" *The London Times*, October 7, 2006 (accessed December 22, 2007).
12. "2007 Global Powers of Retailing."
13. www.gradcareers.com (accessed May 25, 2007).
14. www.achievement.org/autodoc/printmember/bez0bio-1 (accessed May 25, 2007); "Jeff Bezos: The Wizard of Web Retailing," *BusinessWeek*, December 2004, p. 13.
15. "Jeff Bezos," en.wikipedia.org/wiki/Jeff_Bezos (accessed May 25, 2007).
16. http://www.anitaroddick.com/aboutanita.php (accessed June 4, 2007); http://www.thebodyshopinternational.com/About+Us/Our+History/Home.htm (accessed June 4, 2007).
17. "Ingvar Kamprad," en.wikipedia.org/wiki/Ingvar_Kamprad (accessed May 25, 2007).
18. "Ingvar Kamprad."
19. "Rating the Stores," *Consumer Reports*, November 1994, p. 714.
20. Rusty Williamson and Mathew W. Evans, "Walgreens Raising its Fashion Quotient," *WWD*, December 13, 2006 (accessed December 22, 2007)
21. Bill Hare, *Celebration of Fools: An Inside Look at the Rise and Fall of JCPenney* (New York: AMACOM 2004); Kelly Nolan, "America's Mid-Tier Darling Gets on Track with Off-Mall," *Retailing Today*, April 2007 (accessed December 22, 2007); Maria Halkias, "Penney's New Image Turns Heads," *The Dallas Morning News*, April 19, 2007 (accessed December 22, 2007); "JCPenney Creates 'American Living,'" *Apparel Magazine*, 48, no. 8 (April 2007), p. 9; Maria Halkias, "Penney Hoping Love Is in Store," *The Dallas Morning News*, February 13, 2007 (accessed December 22, 2007).

22. Dan Scheraga, "Penney's Net Advantage," *Chain Store Age*, September 2000, pp. 114–18.
23. "Whole Foods Delays Wild Oats Deal," *Austin Business Journal*, May 22, 2007 (accessed December 22, 2007.)
24. Christopher Thompson, "Whole Foods Hits the Land of Mushy Peas," *Time*, June 14, 2007 (accessed December 22, 2007.)
25. "Whole Foods Market, Inc.," Hoovers.com (accessed May 29, 2007).
26. Ibid.
27. Ibid.
28. Whole Foods Market, "Declaration of Interdependence," company philosophy, www.wholefoodsmarket.com/company/declaration.html (accessed May 29, 2007).
29. Mathew Enis, "John Mackey," *Supermarket News*, July 24, 2006 (accessed December 22, 2007).
30. Bruce Horowitz, "A Whole New Ballgame in Grocery Shopping," *USA TODAY*, March 9, 2005, p. A1.
31. Mark Hamstra, "Slow Start for Newest Whole Foods," *Supermarket News*, April 9, 2007 (accessed December 22, 2007).
32. "Whole Foods Market® Launches Weekly Online Cooking Show," *PRNewswire*, May 7, 2007 (accessed December 22, 2007).
33. Retail Industry Indicators.

Chapter 2

1. factfinder.census.gov/servlet/IBQTable?_bm=Y&-NAICS2002=22. Created May 23, 2007.
2. *Annual Revision of Monthly Retail and Food Services: Sales and Inventories—January 1992 Through February 2007*. Washington, DC: U.S. Department of Commerce, 2007; Economics and Statistics Administration, U.S. Census Bureau, March 2007, p. 1; *Retail Industry Indicators 2004*. Washington, DC: NRF Foundation, 2004, p. 7.
3. *Industry Outlook: Food Channel* (Columbus, OH: Retail Forward, April 2007).
4. Ibid, p. 12
5. Ibid., p.13.
6. http://www.fmi.org/facts_figs/superfact.htm (accessed May 22, 2007).
7. http://www.fmi.org/facts_figs/keyfacts/grocerydept.htm (accessed June 8, 2007).
8. http://www.fmi.org/facts_figs/superfact.htm (accessed June 1, 2007).
9. "Roaring 20's Ends in Depression," *Chain Store Age Executive*, June 1994, p. 49.
10. Wikipedia.com (accessed May 31, 2007).
11. Dan Sewell, "Grocery Competition, Choices Grow," *Fort Worth Star-Telegram*, January 25, 2007 (accessed December 24, 2007).
12. www.wegmans.com/about/pressRoom/overview.asp (accessed June 1, 2007); Roseanne Harper, "All in the Family," *Supermarket News*, September 18, 2006, pp. 49–53.
13. "Voting with Your Trolly," *The Economist*, December 7, 2006 (accessed December 24, 2007).

14. Julie Gallagher, "Private Eye," *Supermarket News* 55, no. 20 (May 14, 2007), pp. 57–58.

15. *Natural/Organics Trend Here to Stay* (Columbus, OH: Retail Forward Retail Perspectives, August 2006).

16. www.infoplese,cm/spot/hhmcensus1.html (accessed June 1, 2007).

17. "The Top 10 Ethnic Retailers," *Supermarket News*, November 6, 2006 (accessed December 24, 2007).

18. Jennifer Halterman, *Taking the Online Grocery Plunge* (Columbus, OH: Retail Forward Retail Perspectives, July 2006); Bob Tedeschi, "After Delving Into 33 Other Lines, Amazon Finally Gets Around to Food," *The New York Times*, July 24, 2006 (accessed December 24, 2007); Robert Manor, "Online Grocers Seek Method that Clicks," *Chicago Tribune*, July 22, 2006 (accessed December 24, 2007); Christopher Conkey, "Internet Grocers Can Help You Avoid Supermarket, But Is It Worth the Price?" *The Wall Street Journal*, July 22, 2006 (accessed December 24, 2007).

19. "Private Label," http://en.widipedia.org/wiki/Private_label (accessed December 24, 2007); http://plma.com/storeBrands/sbt07.html (accessed June 1, 2007).

20. Marcelle S. Fischler, "Super-Duper Markets," *The New York Times*, July 29, 2006 (accessed December 24, 2007).

21. "The Value-Focused Consumer, Consumer Behavior" (Loganville, GA: Richard K. Miller & Associates, 2007).

22. Mike Troy, "Sam's Club Seeks New Growth," *Retailing Today*, March 2007, pp. 1–5.

23. Jennifer Halterman, *Industry Outlook: Convenience Stores* (Columbus, OH: Retail Forward, February 2007).

24. Peter O'Dowd, "The British Are Coming to Change our Grocery Stores," *ABC News Business Unit*, April 19, 2007; Jennifer Halterman, *Tesco's U.S. Invasion Update* (Columbus, OH: Retail Forward, September 2006).

25. http://www.Sheetz.com (accessed June 1, 2007).

26. http://www.Kamcity.com (accessed July 12, 2007).

27. Kelly Trackett, *Industry Outlook: Department Stores* (Columbus, OH: Retail Forward, July 2006), p. 7.

28. David Moin, "Department Stores: The Issues," *WWD Infotracs*, June 1997, pp. 4–6.

29. Vanessa O'Connell, "Reinventing the Luxury Department Store," *The Wall Street Journal*, July 15, 2006, pp. 1, 6.

30. *Industry Outlook: Department Stores*, p. 16.

31. Ibid,

32. Ibid, p. 15

33. "J.C. Penney Gets the Net," *BusinessWeek*, May 7, 2007 (accessed December 24, 2007)

34. "Wal-Mart" http://www.Wikipedia.com (accessed June 4, 2007).

35. *Industry Outlook: Mass Channel* (Columbus, OH: Retail Forward, June 2006), p. 29.

36. http://www.hbc.com/hbc/history/ (accessed June 18, 2007).

37. http://www.limitedbrands.com/brands/vs/index.jsp (accessed June 3, 2007).

38. Steven Vames, "Hot Topics Aims to Stay Ahead of Teen Trends," *The Wall Street Journal*, January 28, 2004, p. A1.

39. Adam Smith, "How Topshop Changed Fashion," *Time*, May 24, 2007; Kristin Miller, "Fashion's New Fast Lane," *Forbes*, September 12, 2006; Jim Lovejoy, "Fast-Fashion vs. Speed to Market," http://www.techexchange.com/thelibrary/fastfashvs.html, April 2007; Kasra Ferdows, Michael A. Lewis, and Jose A.D. Machuca, "Zara's Secret for Fast Fashion," http://hbswk.hbs.edu/archive/4652.html,

40. Sandra J. Skrovan, *Drug Stores on Acquisition Trail* (Columbus, OH: Retail Forward, August 2006).

41. Rusty Williamson, "Walgreens Raising Its Fashion Quotient," *WWD*, December 13, 2006.

42. Jennifer Halterman, "Industry Outlook: Drug Channel," Columbus OH: Retail Forward, Inc. November 2006, p. 3.

43. Ibid., p. 22.

44. "Variety Store," http://en.wikipedia.org/wiki/Variety_store (accessed June 13, 2007).

45. Ibid.

46. John Dobosz, "Putting Family Dollar On The Shopping List," *Forbes*, August 23, 2006 (accessed December 24, 2007); http://www.dollargeneral.com (accessed June 18, 2007).

47. "T.J. Maxx," http://en.wikipedia.org/wiki/T.J._Maxx (accessed June 18, 2007).

48. "Back to the Future," *New York Times Magazine*, April 6, 1997, pp. 48–49.

49. Kelly Trackett, "The State of Multi-Channel Shopping," *Retail Perspectives*, November 2006, p. 1.

50. Richard S. Hodgson, "It's Still the 'Catalog Age,'" *Catalog Age*, June 1, 2001.

51. *Statistical Factbook 2007* (Washington, DC: Direct Marketing Association, 2006).

52. http://www.luxist.com/2006/10/03/neiman-marcus-christmas-book-2006/ (accessed June 15, 2007).

53. "Fact Sheet," http://www.dsa.org (accessed June 7, 2007).

54. http://www.dsa.org/pubs/numbers/calendar05factsheet.pdf (accessed June 7, 2007).

55. "Fact Sheet."

56. Ibid.

57. Charles Duhigg, "Why Short Sellers Want to Crash the Tupperware Party," *The New York Times*, November 13, 2006 (accessed December 24, 2007).

58. "T-Commerce!: On Sale Now for a Limited Time!" *Cableworld*, December 4–17, 2006 (accessed December 24, 2007); "Will Viewers Buy into Shopping Via iTV ads?" *NMA*, October 13, 2005 (accessed December 24, 2007).

59. "T-Commerce!"

60. "High-End TV Retailing," *Chain Store Age* 82, no. 12 (December 2006), pp. 30, 34.

61. http://inventors.about.com/library/inventors/blvendingmachine.htm (accessed June 14, 2007).

62. Ylan Q. Mui, "Redbox Finds Its Niche," *Washington Post*, April 28, 2007, p. D01.

63. Eric Benderoff, "Retail CDs Get Personal," *Chicago Tribune*, May 3, 2007 (accessed December 24, 2007).

64. Mehgan Belanger, "Convenience to the Max," *Convenience Store News* 42, no. 14 (November 13, 2006), pp. 57–58.

65. http://www.zoots.com (accessed June 7, 2007).

66. Valarie A. Zeithaml, A. Parasuraman, and Leonard L. Berry, *Delivering Quality Service: Balancing Customer Perceptions and Expectations* (New York: The Free Press, 1990).

67. Dhruv Grewal, Gopalkrishnan R. Iyer, Jerry Gotlieb, and Michael Levy, "Developing a Deeper Understanding of Post-Purchase Perceived Risk and Behavioral Intentions in a Service Setting," *Journal of the Academy of Marketing Science* 35 (2007), pp. 250–58: Margy P. Conchar, George M. Zinkhan, Cara Peters, and Sergio Olavarrrieta. "An Integrated Framework for the Conceptualization of

February 21, 2005; Rana Foroohar, "Fabulous Fashion," *Newsweek*, October 17, 2005.

Consumers' Perceived-Risk Processing," *Journal of the Academy of Marketing Science* Winter 2004, pp. 418–36; Dhruv Grewal, Jerry Gotlieb, and Howard Marmorstein, "The Moderating Effects of Message Framing and Source Credibility on the Price-perceived Risk Relationship," *Journal of Consumer Research* 21 (June 1994), pp. 145–53.

68. http://www.franchisefunding.net/fran_industry_info.html (accessed June 14, 2007).

Chapter 3

1. Kelly Tackett, "The State of Multi-Channel Shopping," *Retail Perspectives*, Columbus OH: Retail Forward, November 2006, p. 1.

2. Kenneth Hein, "Web Research Nets In-Store Sales," *Brandweek*, May 7, 2007 (accessed December 24, 2007).

3. Stacy Gilliam, "Sweet Delivery," *Black Enterprise*, November 2006 (accessed December 24, 2007).

4. "Shopping Center Developer Sheldon Gordon Announces Location Secured for the World's First Epicenter Collection," *E-Commerce Technology Guide*, May 21, 2007 (accessed December 24, 2007).

5. Bob Tedeschi, "Small Internet Retailers Are Using Web Tools to Level the Selling Field," December 19, 2005 (accessed December 24, 2007).

6. Ruud T. Frambach, Henk C. A. Roest, and Trichy V. Krishnan, "The Impact of Consumer Internet Experience on Channel Preference and Usage Intentions Across the Different Stages of the Buying Process," *Journal of Interactive Marketing* 21, no. 2 (2007), pp. 26–41.

7. Susan Kuchinskas, "A Decade of E-Commerce," October 18, 2004, http://www.internetnews.com (accessed February 14, 2008).

8. "Can't Find that Dress on the Rack? Retailers Are Pushing More Shoppers to the Net," *Knowledge@Wharton*, November 1, 2006.

9. Mary Brett Whitfield, "E-Retailing Point of View," *Shopper Update*, Columbus OH: Retail Forward, March 2006.

10. Michelle Slatalla, "A Narrow Window into the Future," *The New York Times*, April 26, 2007 (accessed December 24, 2007).

11. John P. Mello Jr., "Solo Hunters, Social Gatherers and the Online Marketplace," *E-Commerce Times*, May 25, 2007 (accessed December 24, 2007).

12. James Covert, "Online Clothes Reviews Give 'Love That Dress' New Clout," *The Wall Street Journal*, December 7, 2006, p. B1.

13. Bob Tedeschi, "Like Shopping? Social Networking? Try Social Shopping," *The New York Times*, September 11, 2006 (accessed December 24, 2007).

14. Satish Nambisan, and Robert A. Baron, "Interactions in Virtual Customer Environments: Implications for Product Support and Customer Relationship Management," *Journal of Interactive Marketing* 21, no. 2 (2007), pp. 42–62.

15. Kenneth Hein, "Research: Study: Web Research Nets In-Store Sales," *Brandweek*, May 7, 2007 (accessed December 24, 2007).

16. Ibid.

17. Bob Tedeschi, "Salesmanship Comes to the Online Stores, but Please Call It a Chat," *The New York Times*, August 7, 2006 (accessed December 24, 2007); Sumbramanian Sivaramakrishnan, Fang Wan, and Zaiyong Tang, "Giving an 'E-human Touch' to E-tailing: The Moderating Roles of Static Information Quantity and Consumption Motive in

the Effectiveness of an Anthropomorphic Information Agent," *Journal of Interactive Marketing* 21, no. 1 (2007), pp. 60–75.

18. Jessica E. Vascellaro, "Online Retailers Are Watching You," *The Wall Street Journal*, November 28, 2006, p. D1.

19. Michele Chandler, "More Companies Using Instant-Connect Tools to Answer Questions from Shoppers Online," *San Jose Mercury News*, October 2, 2006 (accessed December 24, 2007).

20. "Internet Retailer Best of the Web 2007," *Internet Retailer*, June 18, 2007 (accessed December 24, 2007).

21. Alexandria Sage, "Consumers Find a Personal Shopper in the Web," *Boston Globe*, August 19, 2006 (accessed December 24, 2007).

22. Michael Barbaro, "Less Risk Seen in Purchasing Clothes Online," *The New York Times*, May 14, 2007 (accessed December 24, 2007).

23. Gianluigi Guido, Mauro Capestro and Alessandro M. Peluso, "Experimental Analysis of Consumer Stimulation and Motivational States in Shopping Experiences," *International Journal of Market Research* 49, no. 3 (2007), pp. 365–86.

24. Sandra Forsythe, Liu Chuanlan Liu, David Shannon, and Liu Chun Gardner, "Development of a Scale to Measure the Perceived Benefits and Risks of Online Shopping," *Journal of Interactive Marketing* 20, no. 2 (2006), pp. 55–75.

25. Jon Brodkin, "TJX Breach: Rethinking Corp. Security," *Network World* 24, no. 13 (2007), (accessed December 24, 2007).

26. Ibid.

27. Forrester Research, "State of Consumers and Technology," 2006.

28. For more information on approaches for increasing share of wallet, see Tom Osten, *Customer Share Marketing*, Upper Saddle River, NJ: Prentice Hall, 2002.

29. Maria Halkias, "Catalogs Make Paper Trails to Retailers," *The Dallas Morning News*, October 9, 2006 (accessed December 24, 2007).

30. Ibid.

31. Venkatesh Shankar, and Russell S. Winer, "Interactive Marketing Goes Multichannel," *Journal of Interactive Marketing* 19, no. 2 (2005), pp. 2–3.

32. Evan Schuman, "E-Commerce Satisfaction Survey: The Good, The Bad, The Crashey," http://www.storefront Backtalk.com, May 31, 2007 (accessed December 24, 2007).

33. http://www.thetalbotsinc.com/corporate.asp (accessed June 13, 2007).

34. Mark Brohan, "The Top 500 Guide," *Internet Retailer*, July 2007 (accessed August 13, 2007).

35. http://www.naturalizer.com (accessed June 14, 2007).

36. http://www.lacoste.com (accessed June 13, 2007).

37. http://premium.hoovers.com/subscribe/co/factsheet.xhtml?ID=ffffhrcsyxxckchhyf (accessed June 15, 2007).

38. http://www.patagonia.com (accessed June 13, 2007).

39. "Internet Retailer Best of the Web 2007."

40. Cate Corcoran, "Latest Search Engines Boost Local Stores," *Women's Wear Daily*, December 1, 2006 (accessed December 24, 2007).

41. Iconix Brand Group Inc.'s Rampage brand currently provides this feature. See Vauhini Vara, "'That Looks Great on You': Online Salespeople Get Pushy," *The Wall Street Journal*, January 3, 2007 (accessed December 24, 2007).

Chapter 4

1. For a detailed discussion of customer behavior, see J. Paul Peter and Jerry C. Olson, *Consumer Behavior and Marketing Strategy*, 8th ed. (New York: McGraw-Hill, 2008); Michael R. Solomon, *Consumer Behavior: Buying, Having, and Being*, 7th ed. (Upper Saddle River, NJ: Prentice Hall, 2006).

2. Liz C. Wang, Julie Baker, Judy A. Wagner, and Kirk Wakefield, "Can a Retail Website be Social?" *Journal of Marketing* 71, no. 3 (2007), pp. 143–57; Gianluigi Guido, Mauro Capestro, and Alessandro M. Peluso, "Experimental Analysis of Consumer Stimulation and Motivational States in Shopping Experiences," *International Journal of Market Research* 49, no. 3 (2007), pp. 365–86.

3. Gianluigi, Capestro, and Peluso, "Experimental Analysis"; Woonbong Na, Youngseok Son, and Roger Marshall, "Why Buy Second-Best? The Behavioral Dynamics of Market Leadership," *Journal of Product & Brand Management* 15, no. 1 (2007), pp. 16–22; Min-Young Lee, Kelly Green Atkins, Youn-Kyung Kim, and Soo-Hee Park, "Competitive Analyses Between Regional Malls and Big-Box Retailers: A Correspondence Analysis for Segmentation and Positioning," *Journal of Shopping Center Research*, April 2006, pp. 81–98.

4. Sylvie Morin, Laurette Dube, and Jean-Charles Chebat, "The Role of Pleasant Music in Servicescapes: A Test of the Dual Model of Environmental Perception," *Journal of Retailing* 83, no. 1 (2007), pp. 115–30; Nicole Bailey and Charles S. Areni, "When a Few Minutes Sound Like a Lifetime: Does Atmospheric Music Expand or Contract Perceived Time?" *Journal of Retailing* 82, no. 3 (2006), pp. 189–202; Michael A. Jones and Kristy E. Reynolds, "The Role of Retailer Interest on Shopping Behavior," *Journal of Retailing* 82, no. 2 (2006), pp. 115–26; Shu pei Tai, "Impact of Personal Orientation on Luxury-Brand Purchase Value," *International Journal of Marketing Research* 47, no. 4 (2005), pp. 429–54.

5. Jess W.J. Weltrereden, "Substitution or Complementarity? How the Internet Changed City Centre Shopping," *Journal of Retailing and Consumer Services* 14, no. 3 (2007), pp. 192–207; Shun Yin Lam, Albert Wai-Lap Chau, and Tsunhin John Wong, "Thumbnails as Online Product Displays: How Consumers Process Them," *Journal of Interactive Marketing* 21, no. 1 (2007), pp. 36–59.

6. Melody Vargas, "Frequent Leisure Time Shoppers Spend More per Trip," *About Retailing*, July 11, 2006 (accessed December 24, 2007).

7. Brian T. Ratchford, Debabrata Talukdar, and Myung-Soo Lee, "The Impact of the Internet on Consumers' Use of Information Sources for Automobiles: A Re-Inquiry," *Journal of Consumer Research* 34, no. 1 (2007), pp. 111–19; Glenn J. Browne, Mitzi G. Pitts, and James C. Wetherbe, "Cognitive Shopping Rules for Terminating Information Search in Online Tasks," *MIS Quarterly* 31, no. 1 (2007), pp. 89–104; John Graham, "How to Profit from Customer Buying-Cycle Basics," *Printer and Publisher* 69, no. 2 (2006).

8. http://www.nearbynow.com (accessed June 27, 2007).

9. John P. Mello Jr., "Solo Hunters, Social Gatherers and the Online Marketplace," *E-Commerce Times*, May 25, 2007 (accessed December 24, 2007); Helene F. Jaillet, "Web Metrics: Measuring Patterns in Online Shopping," *Journal of Consumer Behavior* 2, no. 4 (2003), pp. 369–81.

10. Bob Tedeschi, "Shopping Site Offers a Way to Raid a Celebrity's Closet," *The New York Times*, November 13, 2006 (accessed December 24, 2007); Steven Bellman, Eric J. Johnson, Gerald L. Lohse, and Naomi Mandel, "Designing Marketplaces of the Artificial with Consumers in Mind: Four Approaches to Understanding Consumer Behavior in Electronic Environments," *Journal of Interactive Marketing* 20, no. 1 (2006), pp. 21–33.

11. Bob Tedeschi, "A Richer Trip to the Mall, Guided by Text Messages," *The New York Times*, March 5, 2007 (accessed December 24, 2007); Alice Z. Cuneo, "'Yard' Sale? Sprite Talks to Teens with Mobile Promotions," *Advertising Age* (Midwest region edition), June 11, 2007, p. 23.

12. Paul Dwyer, "Measuring the Value of Electronic Word of Mouth and its Impact in Consumer Communities," *Journal of Interactive Marketing* 21, no. 2 (2007), pp. 63–79; Pallavi Gogoi, "Retailers Take a Tip from MySpace," *BusinessWeek*, February 13, 2007.

13. Gogoi, "Retailers Take a Tip."

14. Hollie Shaw, "Converting Retail Browsers into Buyers," *Financial Post*, June 30, 2007 (accessed December 24, 2007); Catarina Sismeiro and Randolph E Bucklin, "Modeling Purchase Behavior at an E-Commerce Web Site: A Task-Completion Approach," *Journal of Marketing Research* 41, no. 3 (2004), pp. 306–23.

15. Cecilie Rohwedder, "For a Delicate Sale, a Retailer Deploys 'Stocking Fellas,'" *The Wall Street Journal*, December 21, 2006, p. A1.

16. Teresa F. Lindeman, "Macy's Sees Food as the Way to the Wallet," *Boston Globe*, May 14, 2007.

17. Teresa Lindeman, "Retailers Try to Convince Customers to Stick Around," *Miami Herald*, April 26, 2007. Statistics taken from the work force management firm H.B. Maynard and Co.

18. Chris T. Allen, Karen A. Machleit, Susan Schultz Kleine, and Arti Sahni Notani, "A Place for Emotion in *Attitude* Models," *Journal of Business Research* 58, no. 4 (2005), pp. 494–99; Armin Scholl, Laura Manthey, Roland Helm, and Michael Steiner, "Solving Multiattribute Design Problems with Analytic Hierarchy Process and Conjoint Analysis: An Empirical Comparison," *European Journal of Operational Research* 164, no. 3 (2005), pp. 760–77; Richard Lutz, "Changing Brands Attitudes through Modification of Cognitive Structure," *Journal of Consumer Research* 1, no. 1 (1975), pp. 125–36.

19. Dong-il Yoo and Hiroshi Ohta, "Optimal Pricing and Product-Planning for New Multiattribute Products Based on Conjoint Analysis," *International Journal of Production Economics* 38, no. 2,3 (1995), pp. 245–53; Richard J. Lutz and James R. Bettman, "Multi-Attribute Models in Marketing: A Bicentennial Review," in *Consumer and Industrial Buying Behavior*, eds. A.G. Woodside, J.N. Sheth, and P.D. Bennett (New York: Elsevier-North Holland, 1977), pp. 13–50; William L. Wilkie and Edgar D. Pessimier, "Issues in Marketing's Use of Multi-Attribute Attitude Models," *Journal of Marketing Research*, November 1973, pp. 428–41.

20. Pat West, P. Brockett, and Linda Golden, "A Comparative Analysis of Neural Networks and Statistical Methods for Predicting Consumer Choice," *Marketing Science* 16, no. 4 (1997), pp. 370–91.

21. Peter R. Darke, Amitava Chattopadhyay, and Laurence Ashworth, "The Importance and Functional Significance of Affective Cues in Consumer Choice," *Journal of Consumer Research* 33, no. 3 (2006), pp. 322–28; David Bell, Tech-Hua Ho, and Christopher Tang, "Determining Where to Shop: Fixed and Variable Costs of Shopping," *Journal of Marketing Research* 35 (August 1998), pp. 352–70.

22. John G. Lynch and Gal Zauberman, "Construing Consumer Decision Making," *Journal of Consumer Psychology* 17, no. 2

(2007), pp. 107–12; Wayne D. Hoyer and Steven Brown, "Effects of Brand Awareness of Choice for a Common, Repeat-Purchase Product," *Journal of Consumer Research*, September 1990, pp. 141–49.

23. Pallavi Gogoi, "I Am Woman, Hear Me Shop," *BusinessWeek*, February 14, 2005, p. 23.

24. Dylan T. Lovan, "Fast Repair a Priority at Geek Center," *USA Today*, May 11, 2007.

25. Peter N. Child, Suzanne Heywood, and Michael Kliger, "Do Retail Brands Travel?" *McKinsey Quarterly*, no. 1 (2002), pp. 25–34.

26. Andras Vag, "Simulating Changing Consumer Preferences: A Dynamic Conjoint Model," *Journal of Business Research* 60, no. 8 (2007), pp. 904–11; Richard J. Lutz, "Changing Brand Attitudes through Modification of Cognitive Structure," *Journal of Consumer Research* 1 (March 1975), pp. 49–59.

27. Jeanette Borzo, "From Lands' End to Fair Trade," *Business 2.0*, December 2006, p. 31.

28. Joan Voight, "Getting a Handle on Customer Reviews," *Adweek* 48, no. 26 (June 25–July 2, 2007), pp. 16–17; Nanda Kumar and Izak Benbasat, "The Influence of Recommendations and Consumer Reviews on Evaluations of Websites," *Information Systems Research* 17, no. 4 (2006), pp. 425–41; Bob Tedeschi, "Help for the Merchant in Navigating a Sea of Shopper Opinions," *The New York Times*, September 4, 2006.

29. Ibid.

30. "Beware of Dissatisfied Consumers: They Like to Blab," *Knowledge @ Wharton*, March 8, 2006, based on "Retail Customer Dissatisfaction Study 2006," conducted by the Jay H. Baker Retailing Initiative at Wharton and The Verde Group (accessed December 24, 2007); "The Lowdown on Customer Loyalty Programs: Which Are the Most Effective and Why," *Knowledge @ Wharton*, September 6, 2006; Sandra Kennedy, "Keeping Customers Happy," *Chain Store Age*, February 2005, p. 24; Heiner Evanschitzky, Gopalkrishnan Iyer, Josef Hesse, and Dieter Ahlert, "E-Satisfaction: A Re-Examination," *Journal of Retailing* 80, no. 3 (2004), pp. 239–52; Emin Babakus, Carol Bienstock, and James Van Scotter, "Linking Perceived Quality and Customer Satisfaction to Store Traffic and Revenue Growth," *Decision Sciences*, 35 (Fall 2004), pp. 713–38; Jarrad Dunning, Anthony Pecotich, and Aron O'Cass, "What Happens When Things Go Wrong? Retail Sales Explanations and Their Effects," *Psychology & Marketing* July 2004, pp. 553–68; Richard Oliver, Roland Rust, and Sajeev Varki, "Customer Delight: Foundations, Findings, and Managerial Insights," *Journal of Retailing* 73 (Fall 1997), pp. 311–36; Chezy Ofir and Itamar Simonson, "The Effect of Stating Expectations on Customer Satisfaction and Shopping Experience," *Journal of Marketing Research* 44, no. 1 (2007), pp. 164–74.

31. "Beware of Dissatisfied Consumers."

32. Roy Baumeister and David Mick, "Yielding to Temptation: Self-Control Failure, Impulsive Purchasing, and Consumer Behavior," *Journal of Consumer Research* 28 (March 2002), pp. 670–77; Seounmi Youn and Ronald Faber, "The Dimensional Structure of Consumer Buying Impulsivity: Measurement and Validation," *Advances in Consumer Research* 29, no. 1 (2002) p. 280; Angela Hausman, "A Multi-Method Investigation of Consumer Motivations in Impulse Buying Behavior," *Journal of Consumer Marketing* 17, no. 4/5 (2000), pp. 403–20; Ramanathan Suresh and Patti Williams, "Immediate and Delayed Emotional Consequences of Indulgence: The Moderating Influence of Personality Type on Mixed Emotions," *Journal of Consumer Research* 34, no. 2 (2007), pp. 212–23.

33. Marc Levy, "Big Retail Indulges Customers in Candy," *Sacramento Bee*, December 10, 2006 (accessed December 24, 2007).

34. Debbie Howell, "National Brands Feel the Pressure," *DSN Retailing Today*, October 25, 2004, pp. 22–28.

35. Margaret Magnarelli, "Big Spenders," *Parents*, March 2004 (accessed December 24, 2007).

36. Susan Reda, "What Are Shoppers Saying About You?" *Stores*, February 2007 (accessed December 24, 2007).

37. Ibid.

38. Bruce Horovits, "Alpha Moms Leap to Top of Trendsetters," *USA Today*, March 27, 2007 (accessed December 24, 2007); Alexander Frenzel Baudisch, "Consumer Heterogeneity Evolving from Social Group Dynamics: Latent Class Analyses of German Footwear Consumption 1980–1991," *Journal of Business Research* 60, no. 8 (2007), pp. 836–47; Julie Juan Li and Chenting Su, "How Face Influences Consumption: A Comparative Study of American and Chinese Consumers," *International Journal of Market Research* 49, no. 2 (2007), pp. 237–56.

39. David Ackerman and Gerald Tellis, "Can Culture Affect Prices? A Cross-Cultural Study of Shopping and Retail Prices," *Journal of Retailing* 77 (Spring 2001), pp. 57–63; Aaron Ahuvia and Nancy Wong, "The Effect of Cultural Orientation in Luxury Consumption," in *Advances in Consumer Research*, vol. 25, eds. Eric J. Arnould and Linda M. Scott (Ann Arbor MI: Association for Consumer Research, 1998), pp. 29–32.

40. James Areddy, "Chinese Consumers Overwhelm Retailers With Team Tactics," *The Wall Street Journal*, February 28, 2006, p. A.1.

41. Cyndee Miller, "Top Marketers Take a Bolder Approach in Targeting Gays," *Marketing News*, July 4, 1994, pp. 1–2.

42. Liz Grubow, "Values Shape Purchasing Styles," *Global Cosmetic Industry* 175, no. 3 (2007), pp. 26–27; Thomas W. Leigh, Cara Peters, and Jeremy Shelton, "The Consumer Quest for Authenticity: The Multiplicity of Meanings within the MG Subculture of Consumption," *Journal of the Academy of Marketing Science* 34, no. 4 (2006), pp. 481–93; Deborah C. Fowler, Scarlett C. Wesley, and Maria Elena Vazquez, "How May Retailers Respond to the Hispanic Immigration and Ethnicity Trends in Non-traditional Growth Areas," *Journal of Shopping Center Research* 12, no. 2 (2005), pp. 131–50.

43. Ann Zimmerman, "To Boost Sales, Wal-Mart Drops One-Size-Fits-All Approach," *The Wall Street Journal*, September 7, 2006, p. A1.

44. Robert Rugimbana, "Generation Y: How Cultural Values Can Be Used to Predict their Choice of Electronic Financial Services," *Journal of Financial Services Marketing* 11, no. 4 (2007), pp. 301–13; Stephanie Kang, "Retailers Scramble to Serve a Glut of Twentysomethings: Cashmere, DJs, Celebrity Vibe," *The Wall Street Journal*, September 1, 2006, p. A1; Jung-Wan Less and Simon Tai, "Young Consumers' Perceptions of Multinational Firms and their Acculturation Channels Towards Western Products in Transition Economies," *International Journal of Emerging Markets* 1, no. 3 (2006), pp. 212–24.

45. Óscar González-Benito, César A. Bustos-Reyes, and Pablo A. Muñoz-Gallego, "Isolating the Geodemographic Characterisation of Retail Format Choice from the Effects of Spatial Convenience," *Marketing Letters* 18, no. 1-2 (2007),

pp. 45–59; Michael J. Weiss, *The Clustered World* (Boston: Little, Brown, 2000).

46. Irina B. Grafova, "Your Money or Your Life: Managing Health, Managing Money," *Journal of Family and Economic Issues* 28, no. 2 (2007), pp. 285–303; Jagdish Sheth, Banwari Mittal, and Bruce I. Newman, *Customer Behavior: Consumer Behavior and Beyond* (Fort Worth, TX; The Dryden Press, 1999).

47. VALS 1, the original lifestyle survey, assessed general values and lifestyles. The VALS 2 survey focuses more on values and lifestyles related to consumer behavior and thus has more commercial applications. Another lifestyle segmentation systems is Yankelovich's Monitor Mindbase.

48. Sabrina M. Neeley and Tim Coffey, "Understanding the 'Four-Eyed, Four Legged' Consumer: A Segmentation Analysis of U.S. Moms," *Journal of Marketing Theory and Practice* 15, no. 3 (2007), pp. 251–61; Stuart J. Barnes, Hans H. Bauer, Marcus M. Neumann, and Frank Huber, "Segmenting Cyberspace: A Customer Typology for the Internet," *European Journal of Marketing* 41, no. 1/2 (2007), pp. 71–93; Michael D. Lam, "Psychographic Demonstration: Segmentation Studies Prepare to Prove their Worth," *Pharmaceutical Executive*, January 2004.

49. Deena M Amato-McCoy, "A Point of Differentiation," *Chain Store Age*, January 2007, pp. 26–27; Jeff Zabin, "The Importance of Being Analytical," *Brandweek*, July 24, 2006, pp. 21; Mindy Fetterman, "Best Buy Gets in Touch with its Feminine Side," *USA Today*, December 20, 2006 (accessed December 21, 2006).

50. Jeannette Jarnow and Kitty G. Dickerson, *Inside the Fashion Business*, 7th ed. (Englewood Cliffs, NJ: Prentice Hall, 2002); Mike Easy, ed., *Fashion Marketing* (Oxford, England: Blackwell, 2001).

51. Vanessa O'Connell, "How Fashion Makes Its Way From the Runway to the Rack," *The Wall Street Journal*, February 8, 2007, p. D1. For additional information about fashion and the fashion industry, see Giannino Malossi, ed., *The Style Engine: Spectacle, Identity, Design, and Business: How the Fashion Industry Uses Style to Create Wealth* (New York: Monacelli Press, 1998).

52. Teri Agins, "Rethinking Expensive Clothes," *The New York Times*, April 12, 2007, p. D8.

53. "The Fashion Innovators," *WWD*, March 20, 1997, p. 2.

54. Teri Agins, "Goodbye, Mainstream," *The Wall Street Journal*, January 22, 2007, p. R 7.

Chapter 5

1. See David Aaker, *Strategic Market Management*, 8th ed. (New York: Wiley, 2007); Russ Winer, *Marketing Management*, 3rd ed. (Upper Saddle River, NJ: Prentice Hall, 2006).

2. Roger Evered, "So What Is Strategy?" *Long Range Planning* 16 (Fall 1983), p. 120.

3. Michael E. Porter and Mark R. Kramer, "Strategy and Society: The Link Between Competitive Advantage and Corporate Social Responsibility," *Harvard Business Review*, December 2006; Michael Porter, *On Competition* (Boston: Harvard Business School Press, 1998); Michael Porter, "What Is Strategy?" *Harvard Business Review*, November–December 1996, pp. 61–78.

4. Masha Zager, "The Steve & Barry's Strategy," *Apparel Magazine*, July 2007 (accessed January 4, 2008); Robert Berner, "Steve & Barry's Rules the Mall," *BusinessWeek*, April 10, 2006 (accessed January 4, 2008).

5. Debbie Howell, "Putting Loyalty to Work," *Chain Store Age* 82, no. 12 (2006) (accessed January 4, 2008); Georgia Lee, "Chico's Touts Expansion," *WWD*, April 12, 2007; Georgia Lee, "Chico's Outlines Plan to Improve on Results," *WWD*, March 8, 2007; Michael Cole, "The Apparel Top 50: A Rising Tide," *Apparel Magazine* 46, no. 11 (2005), pp. 24–35 (accessed January 4, 2008).

6. http://www.curves.com; Alison Stein Wellner, "Gary Heavin Is on a Mission from God," *Inc.*, October 2006, pp. 116–24; Shelley Widhalm, "Women Weigh Need for Exercise; More Are Drawn to Benefits of Regular Workouts at the Gym," *The Washington Times*, June 19, 2007, p. B01.

7. Rob Katz, "How Magazine Luiza Courts the Poor," *HBS Working Knowledge*, April 18, 2007 (accessed January 4, 2008); Todd Benson, "Courting the Poor, a Retailer Rises to No. 3 in Brazil," *The New York Times*, July 14, 2004.

8. Anthony Boardman and Aidan Vining, "Defining Your Business Using Product-Customer Matrices," *Long Range Planning* 29 (February 1996), pp. 38–48.

9. Rajagopal, "Leisure Shopping Behavior and Recreational Retailing: A Symbiotic Analysis of Marketplace Strategy and Consumer Response," *Journal of Hospitality & Leisure* 15, no. 2 (2006), pp. 531–58; Morten Hansen and Nitin Nohria, "How to Build Collaborative Advantage," *MIT Sloan Management Review* 46 (Fall 2004), pp. 22–28; Jeffrey Dyer and Harbir Singh, "The Relational View: Cooperative Strategy and Sources of Interorganizational Competitive Advantage," *Academy of Management Review* 23 (October 1998), pp. 660–80; Cynthia Montgomery, "Creating Corporate Advantage," *Harvard Business Review*, May–June 1998, pp. 71–80; Shelby Hunt and Robert Morgan, "The Comparative Advantage Theory of Competition," *Journal of Marketing* 59 (April 1995), pp. 1–15; Kathleen Conner and C. K. Prahalad, "A Resource-Based Theory of the Firm: Knowledge versus Opportunism," *Organizational Science* 7 (September-October 1996), pp. 477–501.

10. Lars Meyer-Waarden, "The Effects of Loyalty Programs on Customer Lifetime Duration and Share of Wallet," *Journal of Retailing* 83, no. 2 (2007), pp. 223–36; Lynette Ryals, "Measuring and Managing Customer Relationship Risk in Business Markets," *Industrial Marketing Management* 36, no. 6 (2007), pp. 823–33.

11. Jochen Wirtz, Anna S. Mattila, and May O. Lwin, "How Effective Are Loyalty Reward Programs in Driving Share of Wallet?" *Journal of Service Research* 9, no. 4 (2007), pp. 327–34; Jorna Leenheer, Harald J. van Heerde, Tammo H. A. Bijmolt, and Ale Smidts, "Do Loyalty Programs Really Enhance Behavioral Loyalty? An Empirical Analysis Accounting for Self-Selecting Members," *International Journal of Research in Marketing* 24, no. 1 (2007), pp. 31–47.

12. http://www.llbean.com (accessed July 30, 2007).

13. Darin W. White and Keith Absher, "Positioning of Retail Stores in Central and Eastern European Accession States," *European Journal of Marketing* 41, no. 3–4 (2007), pp. 292–306; Robert Morgan, Carolyn Strong, and Tony Mcguinness, "Product-Market Positioning and Prospector Strategy: An Analysis of Strategic Patterns from the Resource-Based Perspective," *European Journal of Marketing* 10 (2003), pp. 1409–40; Richard Czerniawski and Michael Maloney, *Creating Brand Loyalty: The Management of Power Positioning and Really Great Advertising* (New York: AMACOM, 1999); S. Chandrasekhar, Vinod Sawhney, Rafique Malik, S. Ramesh Kumar, and Pranab Dutta, "The Case of Brand Positioning," *Business Today*, June 7, 1999, pp. 131–40; Bernard Schmitt, Alex Simonson, and Joshua Marcus, "Managing Corporate Image and Identity," *Long Range Planning* 28 (October 1995), pp. 82–92; Tim Ambler, "Category

Management Is Best Deployed for Brand Positioning," *Marketing*, November 29, 2001, p. 18; Harriet Marsh, "What New Look Must Take Stock," *Marketing*, March 29, 2001, p. 17.

14. David Lei and John Slocum Jr., "Strategic and Organizational Requirements for Competitive Advantage," *Academy of Management Executive*, February 2005, pp. 31–46.

15. Maria Halkias, "Penney Remakes Culture to Remake Image," *The Dallas Morning News*, February 12, 2007 (accessed January 4, 2008).

16. Richard Cuthbertson, Gerd Islei, Peter Franke, and Balkan Cetinkaya, "What Will the Best Retail Supply Chains Look Like in the Future?" *European Retail Digest*, Summer 2006, pp. 7–15; "Competitive Advantage Through Supply-Chain Innovation," *Logistics & Transport Focus*, December 2004, pp. 56–59.

17. Nawel Amrouche, and Georges Zaccour, "Shelf-Space Allocation of National and Private Brands," *European Journal of Operational Research* 180, no. 2 (2007), pp. 648–63; Miguel Gomez, Vithala Rao, and Edward W. McLaughlin, "Empirical Analysis of Budget and Allocation of Trade Promotions in the U.S. Supermarket Industry," *Journal of Marketing Research* 44, no. 3 (2007), pp. 410–24.

18. Robert Berner, "The New Alchemy At Sears," *Business Week*, April 16, 2007, pp. 58–60.

19. Murali Mantrala, Suman Basuroy, and Shailendra Gajanan, "Do Style-Goods Retailer's Demands for Guaranteed Profit Margins Unfairly Exploit Vendors?" *Marketing Letters* 16, no. 1 (2005), pp. 53–66.

20. Youngme Moon, "IKEA Invades America," *Harvard Business Review*, September 14, 2004; Christopher A. Bartlett, Vincent Dessain, and Anders Sioman, "Ikea's Global Sourcing Challenge: Indian Rugs and Child Labor," *Harvard Business Review*, May 3, 2006.

21. Frances X. Frei and Amy C. Edmondson, "Influencing Customer Behavior in Service Operations," Harvard Business School Publications, Case 9-606-061, March 10, 2006; Rajnish Jain and Sangeeta Jain, "Towards Relational Exchange in Services Marketing: Insights from Hospitality Industry," *Journal of Services Research* 5, no. 2 (2006), pp. 139–50; Tim Matanovich, "Know Your Service Strategy," *Marketing Management*, July/August 2004, pp. 14–16.

22. Vaidyanathan Jayaraman and Luo Yadong, "Creating Competitive Advantages Through New Value Creation: A Reverse Logistics Perspective," *Academy of Management Perspectives* 21, no. 2 (2007), pp. 56–73; David Bryce and Jeffrey H. Dyer, "Strategies to Crack: Well-Guarded Markets," *Harvard Business Review* 85, no. 5 (2007), pp. 84–92; Rajagopal, "Leisure Shopping Behavior."

23. Richard O. Jones, "An Examination of Tenant Evolution Within the UK Factory Outlet Channel," *International Journal of Retail and Distribution Management* 25, no. 1 (2007), pp. 35–53; "Growth Mining, The New Retail Imperative for Retailers," Columbus, OH: Retail Forward, May 2004; Susan Mudambi, "A Topology of Strategic Choice in Retailing," *International Journal of Retail & Distribution Management* 22 (1994), pp. 22–25.

24. http://link.brightcove.com/services/link/bcpid86195573/bclid86272812/bctid1114968515 (accessed July 18, 2007).

25. Ibid.

26. Janet Adamy, "Dunkin' Donuts Whips Up A Recipe for Expansion," *The Wall Street Journal*, May 3, 2007, p. B1.

27. Ross Tucker, "Hollister Helps A&F Rebound," *WWD*, May 12, 2004, p. 22; Kristin Young, "Ramping Up at Hollister," *WWD*, April 23, 2003, p. 8.

28. http://www.tescocorporate.com/page.aspx?pointerid=3DB554FCAE344BD88EEEEFA63D71B831 (accessed July 30, 2007).

29. Andrew Sorkin and Michael De La Merced, "Home Depot Sells a Unit That Never Fit," *The New York Times*, June 20, 2007, p. C.1; Andrew Sorkin and Michael De La Merced, "Home Depot Supply Unit May Be Sold," *The New York Times*, February 13, 2007, p. C.1.

30. Nobuo Matsubayashi, "Price and Quality Competition: The Effect of Differentiation and Vertical Integration," *European Journal of Operational Research* 180, no. 2 (2007), pp. 907–21; Yanni Yan, John Child, and Chan Yan Chong, "Vertical Integration of Corporate Management in International Firms: Implementation of HRM and the Asset Specificities of Firms in China," *International Journal of Human Resource Management* 18, no. 5 (2007), pp. 788–807; Anita McGahan, "Sustaining Superior Profits: Customer and Supplier Relationships," *Harvard Business Online*, March 1, 1999, pp. 1–7, http://harvardbusinessonline.hbsp.harvard.edu; Randolph Beard, "Regulation, Vertical Integration and Sabotage," *Journal of Industrial Economics* 49, no. 3 (2001), pp. 319–33.

31. Rebecca Mead, "Brooks Brothers a Go-Go," *The New Yorker*, March 22, 1999, p. 88.

32. "2007 Global Powers of Retailing," *Stores*, January 2007, pp. G17–21.

33. http://www.businessweek.com/magazine/content/05_46/b3959003.htm (accessed July 30, 2007).

34. Kristin Acker, "Internationalisation of German Retailers: The case of *Aldi* in the United States," *European Retail Digest* 50 (2006), pp. 43–46; Nirmalya Kumar, "Strategies to Fight Low-Cost Rivals," *Harvard Business Review* 84, no. 12 (2006), pp. 104–12; Lisa M. Wood and Barry J. Pierson, "The Brand Description of Sainsbury's and Aldi: Price and Quality Positioning," *International Journal of Retail and Distribution Management* 34, no. 12 (2006), pp. 904–17; "Going Global," *DSN Retailing Today*, December 14, 2005, pp. G17–21; Jay McIntosh and Julie Kunkel, "Top 100 Global Retailers," *Chain Store Age*, December 2004, pp. 76–78.

35. This section is adapted from "Winning Moves on a Global Chessboard: Wal-Mart and Costco in a Global Context," Goldman Sachs Investment Research, May 12, 2000.

36. Daniel Nilsson, "A Cross-Cultural Comparison of Self-service Technology Use," *European Journal of Marketing* 41, no. 3/4 (2007), pp. 367–81; Lisa Penaloza and Mary Gilly, "Marketer Acculturation: The Changer and the Changed," *Journal of Marketing* 63 (Summer 1999), pp. 84–95.

37. Don Lee, "A Chinese Lesson for Big Retailers," *Los Angeles Times*, July 2, 2006; Peter N. Child, "Lessons from a Global Retailer: An Interview with the President of Carrefour China," *The McKinsey Quarterly*, 2006; "Company Spotlight: Carrefour," *MarketWatch: Global Round-up* 6, no. 4 (2007), pp. 67–72; "Carrefour," http://en.wikipedia.org/wiki/Carrefour (accessed July 12, 2007).

38. Janet Adamy, "Starbucks Chairman Says Trouble May Be Brewing," *The Wall Street Journal*, February 24, 2007.

39. "Carrefour."

40. This sections draws heavily from Ayuna Kidder, "Global Retail Outlook," Columbus, OH: Retail Forward, Inc., March 2007.

41. "Taking the Field," *Soap, Perfumery & Cosmetics*, September 2006, pp. 32–34.

42. "A Focus on Emerging Markets," *European Retail Digest*, no. 49 (Spring 2006), pp. 49–51.

43. Ibid.

44. Ibid.

45. "Taking the Field."

46. "India Retail: Foreign Chains Eye the Potential, but Will they Succeed?" *Knowledge at INSTEAD*, May 28, 2007 (accessed January 4, 2008), quotation from Paddy Padmanabhan.

47. Michael R. Czinkota and Ilkka A. Ronkainen, *International Marketing*, 8th ed. (Mason, OH: Thomson South-Western, 2007).

48. http://www.marksandspencer.com (accessed July 17, 2007).

49. Donald Lehman and Russell Winer, *Analysis for Marketing Planning*, 6th ed. (Burr Ridge, IL: McGraw-Hill/Irwin, 2004); Aaker, *Strategic Market Management*.

50. Neal M. Ashkanasy, "Revisiting JOB's Mission," *Journal of Organizational Behavior* 28, no. 4 (2007), pp. 353–55; Lehman and Winer, *Analysis for Marketing Planning*.

51. Alfred Rappaport, *Creating Shareholder Value: The New Standard for Business Performance* (New York: Wiley, 1988).

52. See Linda Gatley and David Clutterbuck, "Superdrug Crafts a Mission Statement," *International Journal of Retail and Distribution Management* 26 (October–November 1998), pp. 10–11, for an interesting example of the process used by a U.K. drugstore chain to develop a mission statement.

53. Aaker, *Strategic Market Management*.

54. http://www.catofashions.com (accessed July 19, 2007).

55. Tony Grundy, "Rethinking and Reinventing Michael Porter's Five Forces Model," *Strategic Change* 15, no. 5 (2006), pp. 213–29; Michael Porter, "Strategy and the Internet," *Harvard Business Review*, March 2001, pp. 63–78; Michael Porter, *Competitive Strategy* (New York: The Free Press, 1980).

56. Susan Reda, "Sights Set on the Subcontinent," *Stores*, September 2006 (accessed January 4, 2008).

57. Linda Matchan, "The Sleek, Smooth Design of Apple's iPod Is not Mirrored in the Architecture of Some of the Company's High-Profile Stores," *Boston Globe*, June 29, 2006; Stephanie Kang, "Questions For . . . Wendy Clark," *The Wall Street Journal*, June 20, 2007.

58. See Aaker, *Strategic Market Management*, Ch. 7. Another matrix often used in strategic planning is the Boston Consulting Group (BCG) market growth/market share matrix. Rather than considering all of the factors that determine market attractiveness and competitive position, the BCG matrix focuses on just two factors: market growth and market share. Research indicates that concentrating on these two factors may result in poor strategic decisions. See Robin Wensley, "Strategic Marketing: Betas, Boxes, and Basics," *Journal of Marketing* 45 (Summer 1981), pp. 173–82, for a critical analysis of these approaches.

Chapter 6

1. Robert Kaplan and David Norton, "How Strategy Maps Frame an Organization's Objectives," *Financial Executive*, March/April 2004, pp. 40–46.

2. Patrick Dunne and Robert Lusch, *Retailing*, 6th ed. (Mason, OH: South-Western, 2007).

3. Stephanie Thompson, "Ben & Jerry's: A Green Pioneer," *Advertising Age*, June 11, 2007; http://www.benjerry.com (accessed July 11, 2007).

4. Ibid.

5. http://www.macysjobs.com/common/about/diversity.asp (accessed July 10, 2007).

6. Some entries are combined to improve the pedagogy.

7. http://southernstudies.org/facingsouth/2006/04/costco-spreading-responsible-retail.asp (accessed July 10, 2007).

8. Jane O'Donnel, "Retailers Want a Place in Your Wallet," *USA Today*, July 10, 2006 (accessed January 4, 2008).

9. Terry Pristin, "Owning Your Retail Space Is Not Just for The Big Guys Anymore," *The New York Times*, March 29, 2006 (accessed January 4, 2008).

10. Although the use of asset turnover presented here is helpful for gaining an appreciation of the performance ratio, capital budgeting or present value analyses are more appropriate for determining the long-term return of a fixed asset.

11. http://www.bizstats.com/inventory.htm (accessed July 10, 2007).

12. Ibid.

13. http://bizstats.com/emprodretail.htm (accessed July 10, 2007).

Chapter 7

1. Underhill, Paco, *The Call of the Mall*, New York: Simon & Schuster, 2004. http://www.icsc.org/srch/sct/sct0405/by_the_numbers_042005.pdf (accessed July 24, 2007).

2. Mike Boyer, "J.C.Penney's Leaves Malls," *The Enquirer*, June 29, 2007.

3. Ylan Q. Mui, "Redbox Finds Its Niche," *Washington Post*, April 28, 2007, p. D01.

4. Fiona Soltes, "New Take on Retail Verticals," *Stores*, January 2007 (accessed January 4, 2008).

5. Ford Motors, "Ford Announces New Green Retail Development in Allen Park," August 8, 2005, http://media.ford.com/newsroom/feature_display.cfm?release=21279 (accessed February 20, 2008).

6. *Cushman & Wakefield's Main Streets Across the World*, http://www.cushmanwakefield.com/cwglobal/jsp/newsDetail.jsp?Language=EN&repId=c8000027p&Country=Canada (accessed January 4, 2008).

7. Elaine Cavanagh, "Room for Plenty Abroad," *Estates Gazette*, April 29, 2006.

8. http://www.colliers.com/Content/Repositories/Base/Corporate/English/Market_Report_Corporate/PDFs/RetailNAHighlights2006.pdf (accessed July 25, 2007).

9. http://www.icsc.org, April 26, 2007 (accessed July 24, 2007); Elaine Walker, "Study: Inner-City Economies Are Undervalued," *Miami Herald*, April 26, 2007.

10. Deirdre Pfeiffer, "Displacement through Discourse: Implementing and Contesting Public Housing Redevelopment in Cabrini Green," March 22, 2006, http://www.accessmylibrary.com/comsite5/bin/comsite5.pl (accessed January 4, 2008).

11. Claire Wilson, "The Harlem Revival Brings in the Shops," *The New York Times*, April 18, 2007 (accessed January 4, 2008).

12. http://www.simon.com/about_simon/index.aspx (accessed July 25, 2007).

13. http://history.sandiego.edu/gen/soc/shoppingcenter.html (accessed July 25, 2007); http://www.icsc.org/srch/sct/sct0707/center_stage_art_deco.php (accessed July 25, 2007).

14. "Back to the Future," *The New York Times Magazine*, April 6, 1997, pp. 48–49.

15. http://www.mallofamerica.com (accessed July 25, 2007).

16. http://www.kingofprussiamall.com (accessed July 25, 2007).

17. Ibid.

18. Sana Siwolop, "Going Beyond the Simple Food Court," *The New York Times*, August 2, 2006, (accessed January 4, 2008).

19. Amy Cortese, "At the Mall, Mariachi Instead of Muzak," *The New York Times*, May 20, 2007 (accessed January 4, 2008).

20. Ibid.

21. Ibid.

22. "Mall-Based Stores Losing Market Share," *Chain Store Age*, August 2004, p. 33; research conducted by New Canaan, Connecticut-based Customer Growth Partners.

23. Jayne O'Donnell, "Shoppers Turn to Town Centers," *USA Today*, January 31, 2007 (accessedJanuary 4, 2008).

24. Greg Lindsay, "Say Goodbye to the Mall," *Advertising Age*, November 2, 2006 (accessed August 23, 2007).

25. Jenifer Goodwin, "Chula Vista 'Lifestyle Center' Trumps Mall," *Union Tribune*, October 27, 2006.

26. Erika D. Smith, "Where Men Go To Shop," indystar.com, December 14, 2006.

27. "R.I. Reform School to Be Lifestyle Center," *Shopping Centers Today*, July 2004.

28. Presentation by Michael P. Kercheval, President and CEO, International Council of Shopping Centers, Executive Advisory Board Meeting for the Miller Center for Retailing Education and Research, University of Florida, October 2004.

29. http://www.tangeroutlet.com (accessed August 24, 2007).

30. Ray A. Smith, "Outlet Centers in the U.S. Turn Upmarket in Amenities," *The Wall Street Journal*, June 8, 2002, p. B11.

31. Matt Hudgins, "Factory Outlets Gain International Appeal," *National Real Estate Investor*, August 2007, p. 58; Amy Cortese, "Outlet Shopping, The European Way," *The New York Times*, July 15, 2007, p. BU28.

32. Amy Choi, "The Ins and Outs of Outlet Centers," *DNR*, March 26, 2007, p. 25.

33. J.K. Wall, "Cashing in on Asia," *Knight Ridder Tribune Business News*, July 16, 2006 (accessed January 4, 2008); Izumi Yuasa, "Gotemba, Japan, Outlet's Cheap Brand Goods Are Explosively Popular," *Knight Ridder Tribune Business News*, October 15, 2004, p. 1.

34. Presentation by Jay Starr, 2007 Retailing Smarter Symposium, June.

35. Debra Hazel, "Omnicenters Blend Aspects of Malls and Power and Lifestyle Centers," *ICSC.org*, March 21, 2005; http://www.stjohnsphase2.com/ (accessed August 1, 2007).

36. http://www.miznerpark.com/html/index19.asp (accessed September 3, 2007); Gretel Sarmiento, "Boca 'Spine' Faces Closer Inspection," *Palm Beach Post*, August 27, 2007; Matt Valley, "The Remalling of America," *National Real Estate Investor*, May 2002, pp. 18–23.

37. Jerath, Kinshukn and Z. John Zhang, "Store-within-a-Store," *Wharton School*, June 2007.

38. Betsy Spethmann, "For a Limited Time Only," *Promo: Ideas, Connections and Brand*, 2004, http://promomagazine.cm/mag/marketing_limited_time/ (accessed February 20, 2008).

39. Sandra Jones, "Pop-Up Stores Aim to Create a Buzz in Fleeting Existence," *Tribune*, February 27, 2007.

40. Elizabeth Holmes, "View From the Market Booth," *The Wall Street Journal*, December 8, 2006, p. B1.

41. Hazel, "Omnicenters Blend."

Chapter 8

1. U.S. Bureau of Census, http://www.census.gov/population/www/estimates/metroarea.html.

2. Ibid.

3. "Company Profile," *Hoovers Online*, July 2007, www.hoovers.com.

4. Mike Duff, "Wal-Mart Stores Inc.," *DSN Retailing Today*, February 2005, p. 44; Don Longo, "Wal-Mart Says Cannibalization Is Good," *Retail Merchandiser*, January 2005, p. 14.

5. Molly Knight, "Untangling the Wires," *Shopping Centers Today*, May 2007; www.wirelesstoyz.com (accessed July 31, 2007); Connie Robbins, "Small Chains with Big Growth Plans," *Chain Store Age*, March 2005, pp. 121–24.

6. Cherie Jacobs, "'Cumulative Attraction' Draws Lowe's, Home Depot Locations Together," *Knight Ridder Tribune Business News*, April 2003, p. 1.

7. http://www.partycity.com (accessed August 1, 2007); John Beaney, "A Growing Party," *Chain Store Age*, December 2005.

8. *Census 2000 Basics*. (Washington DC: U.S. Census Bureau, September 2002).

9. http://en.wikipedia.org/wiki/List_of_U.S._states_by_population (accessed July 31, 2007).

10. Ibid.

11. Connie Gentry, "Science Validates Art," *Chain Store Age*, April 2005, pp. 83–84.

12. http://www.esri.com/library/brochures/pdfs/community-tapestry-handbook.pdf.

13. David L. Huff, "Defining and Estimating a Trade Area," *Journal of Marketing* 28 (1964), pp. 34–38; David L. Huff and William Black, "The Huff Model in Retrospect," *Applied Geographic Studies* 1, no. 2 (1997), pp. 22–34.

14. Giuseppe Bruno and Gennaro Improta, "Using Gravity Models for the Evaluation of New University Site Locations: A Case Study," *Computers & Operations Research* 35, no. 2 (2008), pp. 436–44; Tammy Drezner and Zvi Drezner, "Validating the Gravity-Based Competitive Location Model Using Inferred Attractiveness," *Annuals of Operations Research* 111 (March 2002), pp. 227–41.

Chapter 9

1. Susan Jackson and Randall Schuler, *Managing Human Resources Through Strategic Relationships*, 9th ed. (Mason, OH: Southwestern, 2005), p. 5.

2. Personal communication.

3. Anthony Rucci, Steven Kirn, and Richard T. Quinn, "The Employee-Customer-Profit Chain at Sears," *Harvard Business Review*, January-February 1998, pp. 82–97.

4. Jeffrey Pfeffer, *What Were They Thinking?: Unconventional Wisdom About Management* (Boston: Harvard Business School Press, 2007).

5. *Retail Industry Indicators* (Washington, DC: National Retail Federation, August 2006), p. 27.

6. "Out of Stock? It Might Be Your Employee Payroll—Not Your Supply Chain—That's to Blame," *Knowledge@Wharton*, April 4, 2007, based on research by Marshall L. Fisher, Serguei Netessine, and Jayanth Krishnan.

7. *Retail Industry Indicators*, p. 25.

8. Ibid.

9. "Dueling Age Groups in Today's Workforce; From Baby Boomers to Generations X and Y," *Knowledge@Wharton*, April 22, 2007.

10. David M. Walker, "Older Workers: Some Best Practices and Strategies for Engaging and Retaining Older Workers: GAO-07-433T," *GAO Reports*, February 28, 2007; Amy Joyce, "Retired, and Rehired to Sell," *Washington Post*, July 27, 2006.

11. Shali Wu and Boaz Keysar, "The Effect of Culture on Perspective Taking," *Psychological Science* 18, no. 7 (2007), pp. 600–606; Fred O. Walumbwa, John J. Lawler, and Bruce J. Avolio, "Leadership, Individual Differences, and Work-related Attitudes: A Cross-Culture Investigation," *Applied Psychology: An International Review* 56, no. 2 (2007), pp. 212–30; Yuka Fujimoto and Charmine E.J. Hortel, "A Self-Representation Analysis of the Effects of Individualist Collectivist Interactions within Organizations in Individualistic Cultures: Lessons for Diversity Management," *Cross-Cultural Management* 13, no. 3 (2006), pp. 204–18.

12. William K.W. Choy, "Globalisation and Workforce Diversity: HRM Implications for Multinational Corporations in Singapore," *Singapore Management Review* 29, no. 2 (2007), pp. 1–19; Betty Jane Punnett, *International Perspectives on Organizational Behavior and Human Resource Management* (Armonk, NY: M.E. Sharpe, 2004); Pawan S. Budhwar and Yaw A. Debrah, eds., *Human Resource Management in Developing Countries* (London & New York: Routledge, 2004).

13. Catherine Fredman, "HR Takes Center Stage," *Chief Executive*, November 2003, pp. 36–42.

14. *Retail Industry Indicators*, p. 35.

15. "Business Antiquities," *The Wall Street Journal*, November 17, 1999.

16. Paul M. Mazur, *Principles of Organization Applied to Modern Retailing* (New York: Harper & Brothers, 1927).

17. 2007 Corporate Fact Book (Cincinnati, OH: Federated Department Stores, 2007).

18. Stefan Stern, "Simply Recruit from the Ranks to Win the War for Talent," *Financial Times*, March 6, 2007, p. 11; Vinod Mahanta and Vikas Kumar, "It's a Battle Out There for Talent," *Knight Ridder Tribune Business News*. April 21, 2006 (accessed October 4, 2007).

19. Stewart Black, "The Employee Value Proposition: How To Be the Employer of Choice," Knowledge @ INSEAD (accessed October 9, 2007), Dina Berta, "Chains Build Employment Brands to Compete for Workers," *Nation's Restaurant News*, December 18, 2006, pp. 10–18; "'Brand' Your Company to Get—and Keep—Top Employees," *HR Focus*, October 2006, pp. 7–10.

20. Niala Boodhoo, "Wanted: 180 New Starbucks Employees," *Miami Herald*, September 24, 2007 (accessed September 27, 2007).

21. "State of the Industry Operational Management," *Chain Store Age*, August 1, 1998, p. 17A.

22. Jackson and Schuler, *Managing Human Resources*.

23. Deborah Alexander, "A Grocer's Recipe for Success," Gannett News Service, May 7, 2007 (accessed January 9, 2008).

24. Katherine Field, "The Training Game," *Chain Store Age* 82, no. 9, (September 2006), p. 38.

25. Philip Cheng-Fei Tsai, Yu-Fang Yen, Liang-Chih Huang, and Ing-Chung Huang, "A Study on Motivating Employees' Learning Commitment in the Post-Downsizing Era: Job Satisfaction Perspective," *Journal of World Business* 42, no. 2 (2007), pp. 157–69; Jay B. Barney, "An Interview with William Ouchi," *Academy of Management Executive* 18, no. 4 (2004), pp. 108–16.

26. Jackson and Schuler, *Managing Human Resources*, p. 405.

27. Alison Coleman, "Reading the Signs of Reward's Progress," *Employee Benefits*, July 2007; "A Total View of Employee Rewards," *HR Magazine*, August 2007; Ruth N. Bolton, Dhruv Grewal, and Michael Levy, "Six Strategies for Competing Through Service: An Agenda for Future Research," *Journal of Retailing* 83, no. 1 (2007), pp. 1–4; Jeffrey Pfeffer, "Sins of Commission: Performance-Based Pay Isn't Just for CEOs and Salespeople Anymore. But Short-Term Rewards Could Be Costly in the Long Run," *Business 2.0*, May 2004, pp. 56–61.

28. Robert Spector and Patrick D. McCarthy, *The Nordstrom Way to Customer Service Excellence: A Handbook for Implementing Great Service in Your Organization* (New York: Wiley, 2005).

29. Jackson and Schuler, *Managing Human Resources*.

30. Bronwen Bartley, Gomibuchi Seishi, and Robin Mann, "Best Practices in Achieving a Customer-Focused Culture," *Benchmarking: An International Journal* 14, no. 4 (2007), pp. 482–96; Donna McAleese and Owen Hargie, "Five Guiding Principles of Culture Management: A Synthesis of Best Practice," *Journal of Communication Management* 9 (2004), pp. 155–65.

31. Carmine Gallo, "How Ritz-Carlton Maintains Its Mystique," *BusinessWeek Online*, February 14, 2007.

32. Tamara J. Erickson and Lynda Gratton, "What It Means to Work Here," *Harvard Business Review* 85, No. 3 (March 2007), pp. 104–12; John R. Wells and Travis Haglock, "Whole Foods Market, Inc." 9-705-476, Harvard Business School Publications, June 1, 2005.

33. Gary Desller, "How to Earn Your Employee's Commitment," *Academy of Management Executive* 13 (May 1999), pp. 58–59; Deb McCusker, "Loyalty in the Eyes of Employer and Employees," *Workforce*, November 1998, pp. 23–28; David L. Stum, "Five Ingredients for an Employee Retention Formula," *HR Focus*, September 1998, pp. S9–11.

34. Yahya Melhem, "The Antecedents of Customer-Contact Employees' Empowerment," *Employee Relations* 26 (2004), pp. 72–78.

35. Heloneida C. Kataoka, Nina D. Cole, and Douglas A. Flint, "Due Process Model of Procedural Justice in Performance Appraisal: Promotion Versus Termination Scenarios," *Psychological Reports* 99, no. 3 (2006), pp. 819–32; Shankar Ganesan and Barton Weitz, "The Impact of Staffing Policies on Retail Buyer Job Attitudes and Behaviors," *Journal of Retailing*, Spring 1996, pp. 231–45.

36. Suzanne C. De Janasz and Scott J. Behson, "Cognitive Capacity for Processing Work-Family Conflict: An Initial Examination," *Career Development International* 12, no. 4 (2007), pp. 397–411; Cath Sullivan and Janet Smithson, "Perspectives of Homeworkers and their Partners on Working Flexibility and Gender Equity," *International Journal of Human Resource Management* 18, no. 3 (2007), pp. 448–61.

37. Charlotte Huff, "With Flextime, Less Can Be More," *Workforce Management*, May 2005, pp. 65–69; Joe Mullich, "Giving Employees Something They Can't Buy With A Bonus Check," *Workforce Management*, July 2004, pp. 66–68; John Brandon, "Best Buy Rethinks the Time Clock," *Business 2.0*, March 15, 2007 (accessed March 19, 2007).

38. Nancy Shallow, "Changes to Workforce Diversity Reports," *Stores* 89, no. 6 (2007); Glenda Strachan, John Burgess, and Anne Sullivan, "Affirmative Action or Managing Diversity: What Is the Future of Equal Opportunity Policies in Organizations?" *Women in Management Review* 18 (2004), pp. 196–205.

39. Aldred H. Neufeldt, James Watzke, Gary Birch, and Denise Buchner, "Engaging the Business/Industrial Sector in Accessibility Research: Lessons in Bridge Building," *Information Society* 23, no. 3 (2007), pp. 169–81.

40. "80 Most Influential People in Sales and Marketing," *Sales & Marketing Management*, October 1998, p. 78.

41. Ann Zimmerman, "Big Retailers Face Overtime Suits as Bosses Do More 'Hourly' Work," *The Wall Street Journal*, May 26, 2004, p. B1.

42. Jon Ortiz, "Local Grocery Industry Keeps Eye on Tense Talks Down South," *The Sacramento Bee*, April 16, 2007; Doug Desjardins, "Between Grocers and UFCW, Something's Gotta Give," *Retailing Today*, April 21, 2007.

43. William Atkinson, "Safety, Service Equals Satisfaction," *Beverage World* 126, no. 7 (2007); Tahira M. Probst, and Ty L. Brubaker, "Organizational Safety Climate and Supervisory Layoff Decisions: Preferences Versus Predictions," *Journal of Applied Social Psychology* 37, no. 7 (2007), pp. 1630–48; Daniel Corcoran and Joshua D. Shackman, "A Theoretical and Empirical Analysis of the Strategic Value of Beyond Compliance Occupational Health and Safety Programs," *Journal of Business Strategies* 24, no. 1 (2007), pp. 49–68; http://www.osca.com/ (accessed August 20, 2007).

44. "Employers Beware: You're Liable for Harassment by Customers, Too," http://www.ppspublishers.com/articles/beware.htm (accessed August 11, 2007).

45. Paul Dolan, Richard Edlin, Aki Tsuchiya, and Allan Wailoo, "It Ain't What You Do, It's the Way that You Do It: Characteristics of Procedural Justice and their Importance in Social Decision-Making," *Journal of Economic Behavior and Organization* 64, no. 1 (2007), pp. 157–70.

46. Dina Berta, "NAFE Survey: Women Must Start at Bottom Line to Reach Top Posts," *National's Restaurant News*, February 9, 2004, pp. 16–17; Tony Wilbert, "Women Climbing Corporate Ladder at Home Depot," *The Atlanta Journal*, February 3, 2004, p. B1; Ann Zimmerman, "Federal Judge Will Consider Wal-Mart Suit for Class Action," *The Wall Street Journal*, September 23, 2003, p. B2; Linda Wirth, *Breaking through the Glass Ceiling: Women in Management* (Washington, DC: International Labor Office, 2001).

Chapter 10

1. David Simchi-Levi, Philip Karminsky, and Edith Simchi-Levi, *Designing and Managing the Supply Chain: Concepts, Strategies, and Case Studies*, 3rd ed. (New York: McGraw-Hill/Irwin, 2007).

2. Mike Griswold, "Out Of Stock," *Forbes*, December 14, 2006 (accessed January 8, 2008), data from Information Resources.

3. Standard Analytics, "Retail Heartbeat: Real Time Shelf Out of Stock Alert & Response System," April 2, 2006.

4. "Understanding the Problems of Assortment and Allocation," Profitlogic, a division of Oracle, undated.

5. Serguei Roumiantsev and Serguei Netessine, "Should Inventory Policy be Lean or Responsive?: Evidence for US Public Companies," Unpublished Working Paper, The Wharton School, December 2005.

6. "Bharti Enterprises and Wal-Mart Join Hands in Wholesale Cash-and-Carry to Serve Small Retailers, Manufacturers and Farmers," PR Newswire, August 6, 2007 (accessed January 8, 2008).

7. Kristine Miller, "Fashion's New Fast Lane," Forbes, September 12, 2006.

8. http://www.uc.countil/org/glossary/index.cfm; Steve Lohr, "Bar Code Détente: U.S. Finally Adds One More Digit," *The New York Times*, July 12, 2004, p. C3 (accessed February 23, 2008).

9. "Bar Codes Change the Way Retailers Stocked, Priced Products," *Boston Globe*, June 29, 2004, p. C1.

10. Constance Hays, "What Wal-Mart Knows about Customers' Habits," *The New York Times*, November 14, 2004, p. C1.

11. http://www.uc-council.org/ean_ucc_system/stnds_and_tech/ucs.html (accessed February 23, 2008).

12. http://www.vics.org/about/value_proposition/ (accessed February 23, 2008).

13. Tom Zeller Jr., "The Scramble to Protect Personal Information," *The New York Times*, June 9, 2005, p. B1.

14. Eve Tahmincioglu, "Data Security Is No Longer an Option," *The New York Times*, June 29, 2006 (accessed January 8, 2008).

15. Lingxziu Dong and Kaijie Zhu, "Two-Wholesale-Price Contracts: Push, Pull, and Advance-Purchase Discount Contracts," *Manufacturing & Service Operations Management* 9, no. 3 (2007), pp. 291–311; Hyun-Soo Ahn, and Philip Kaminsky, "Production and Distribution Policy in a Two-Stage Stochastic Push-Pull Supply Chain," *IIE Transactions* 37, no. 7 (2005), pp. 609–21; W. Masuchun, S. Davis, and J. Patterson, "Comparison of Push and Pull Control Strategies for Supply Network Management in a Make-to-Stock Environment," *International Journal of Production Research* 42, no. 20 (2004), pp. 4401–20.

16. Council of Supply Chain Management Professionals, Anaheim, CA, http://cscmp.org/ (accessed August 18, 2007).

17. "ProFlowers Streamlines Floral Business," *DSN Retailing Today*, May 9, 2005, p. 29.

18. See Arnold Maltz and Nichole Denoratius, *Warehousing: The Education and Research Council*, 2004, http://www.werc.com (accessed February 23, 2008).

19. Susan Reda, "Crossdocking: Can Supermarkets Catch Up?" *Stores Online*, November 9, 2001, http://www.stores.org (accessed February 23, 2008).

20. Susan Elzey, "Location Part of Store Closing," *Knight Ridder Tribune Business News*, July 19, 2007; Dollar General Corporation, 10-K Form, filed with the SEC on February 2, 2007; Amy Sung, "Dollar General Cites Progress with Store Receiving System," *Supermarket News*, October 10, 2005, p. 49.

21. David Blanchard, "Supply Chains also Work in Reverse," *Industry Weekly*, May 1, 2007 (accessed January 8, 2008).

22. Ibid.

23. Ibid.

24. Noel P. Bodenburg, "Better Conveyor Returns, *Modern Materials Handling* 62, no. 6 (June 2007), p. 53.

25. Sherry Chiger, "Reverse Logistics: Every Department's Challenge," *Multichannel Merchant* 3, no. 6 (2007).

26. "LUSH Showers U.S. Market with Enhanced Service," http://www.ups.com/media/en/cs_lush.pdf (accessed August 24, 2007).

27. Huynh Trung Luong and Nguyen Huu Phien, "Measure of Bullwhip Effect in Supply Chains: The Case of High Order Autoregressive Demand Process," *European Journal of Operational Research* 183, no. 1 (2007), pp. 197–209; Hau Lee, V. Padmanabhan, and Seungjin Whang, "The Bullwhip Effect in Supply Chains," *Sloan Management Review*, Spring 1997, pp. 93–102.

28. Mattias Holweg, Stephen Disney, Jan Holmstrom, and Johanna Smaros, "Supply Chain Collaboration: Making Sense of the Strategy Continuum," *European Management Journal* 23 (April 2005), pp. 170–81.

29. V.G. Narayanan and Ananth Raman, "Aligning Incentives in Supply Chains," *Harvard Business Review*, November 2004, pp. 94–102.

30. http://www.vendormanagedinventory.net (accessed August 15, 2007).

31. http://www.ecrnet.org (accessed August 15, 2007).

32. Kurt Salmon Associates, *Efficient Consumer Response: Enhancing Customer Value in the Grocery Industry* (Washington, DC: The Food Marketing Institute, 1993).

33. Ibid.

34. S.P. Nachiappan, A. Gunasekaran, and N. Jawahar, "Knowledge Management System for Operating Parameters in Two-Echelon VMI Supply Chains," *International Journal of Production Research* 45, no. 11 (2007), pp. 2479–2505; Andres Angulo, Heather Nachtmann, and Matthew A. Waller, "Supply Chain Information Sharing in a Vendor Managed Inventory Partnership", *Journal of Business Logistics* 25 (2004), pp. 101–20.

35. Lisa Harrington, "The Consumer Products Supply Chain: Shopping for Solutions," http://inboundlogistics.com (accessed January 8, 2008) August 2006; January 8, 2008; Jamie Swedberg, "Collaboration Can Speed Fashion Cycle," *Apparel Magazine*, June 2004, p. 33.

36. http://www.i2.com/industries/consumer_industries/vmi/vendor_managed_inventory.cfm (accessed August 15, 2007).

37. Mohsen Attaran and Sharmin Attaran, "Collaborative Supply Chain Management: The Most Promising Practice for Building Efficient and Sustainable Supply Chains," *Business Process Management Journal* 13, no. 3 (2007), pp. 390–404; http://www.ediuniversity.com/glossary (accessed January 8, 2008); Mark Barratt, "Positioning the Role of Collaborative Planning in Grocery Supply Chains," *International Journal of Logistics Management* 14 (2003), pp. 53–67.

38. Attaran and Attaran, "Collaborative Supply Chain Management."

39. Gary McWilliams, "Wal-Mart's Radio-Tracked Inventory Hits Static," *The Wall Street Journal*, February 15, 2007, p. B1.

40. Ibid; see also Zeynep Ton, Vincent Dessain, and Monika Stachowiak-Joulain, "RFID at the Metro Group," Harvard Business School Publications, 9-606-053, November 9, 2005.

41. Rhonda Ascierto, "IBM Updates WebSphere RFID with Drug ePedigree," *CBR*, August 9, 2007.

42. Claire Swedberg, "Magicmirror Could Assist Retail Customers," *RFID Journal*, November 29, 2006.

43. Jennifer Davies, "Retailers Use Technology to Thwart Would-be Thieves," *San Diego Union Tribute*, June 13, 2007 (accessed January 8, 2008).

44. B. Hardgrave, Matthew Waller, and R. Miller, "Does RFID Reduce Out of Stocks? A Preliminary Analysis," Sam M. Walton College of Business, University of Arkansas, Information Technology Research Institute, November 2005, http://itri.uark.edu/research/display.asp?articles=ITRI-WP058-1105 (accessed February 23, 2008).

45. Ibid.

46. Simon Holloway, "The Benefits of RFID Will Soon Be Realized," http://www.it-director.com/business/content.php?cid=9653 (accessed August 20, 2007).

47. Lynn A. Fish and Wayne C. Forrest, "A Worldwise Look at RFID," *Supply Chain Management Review*, April 2007, pp. 48–55.

Chapter 11

1. Werner Reinartz and V. Kumar, "The Mismanagement of Customer Loyalty," *Harvard Business Review*, July 2002, pp. 86–94.

2. Matthew Budman, "Customer Loyalty: Are You Satisfying the Right Ones?" *Across the Board* 42, no. 2 (March/April 2005), pp. 51–52.

3. Rajagopal, "Stimulating Retail Sales and Upholding Customer Value," *Journal of Retail & Leisure Property* 6, no. 2 (2007), pp. 117–35; Timothy L. Keiningham, Bruce Cooil, Lerzan Aksoy, Tor W. Andreassen, and Jay Weiner, "The Value of Different Customer Satisfaction and Loyalty Metrics in Predicting Customer Retention, Recommendation, and Share-of-Wallet," *Managing Service Quality* 17, no. 4 (2007), pp. 361–84; Deborah Brown McCabe, Mark S. Rosenbaum, and Jennifer Yurchisin, "Perceived Service Quality and Shopping Motivations: A Dynamic Relationship," *Services Marketing Quarterly* 29, no. 1 (2007), pp. 1–21.

4. Vanessa O'Connell, "Posh Retailers Pile on Perks for Top Customers," *The Wall Street Journal*, April 26, 2007, p. D1.

5. Mark Albright, "Peddling Prestige," *St. Petersburg Times*, August 22, 2001, p. 8E.

6. Personal experience of the author.

7. Phil Cordell, "Why Improve Your Service?" *Sales & Service Excellence* 7, no. 6 (2007), p. 6-6; Lawrence A. Crosby and Sheree L. Johnson, "Experience REQUIRED," *Marketing Management* 16, no. 4 (2007), pp. 20–28; Lawrence A. Crosby and Sheree L. Johnson, "Make It Memorable," *Marketing Management* 15, no. 4 (2006), pp. 12–13; Samantha Murphy, "Relationship Woes," *Chain Store Age* 83, no. 5 (2007).

8. Kelly Hlavinka and Rick Ferguson, *Quo Vadis: Sizing Up the U.S. Loyalty Marketing Industry* (Milford, OH: Colloquy, April 2007).

9. Susan Reda, "Service that Stacks Up," *Stores*, March 2007 (accessed January 8, 2008).

10. Amy C. Edmondson, "Mitchells/Richards," *Harvard Business School Publications*, Case Number 9-604-010, December 2003.

11. Bryan Dorfler, "Use CRM to Extend F&I," *Ward's Dealer Business* 40, no. 8 (2006); Laurie Sullivan, "Car Dealers Rev CRM to Manage Net Leads," *Information Week*, September 13, 2004, p. 40.

12. Personal communication with stores, August 23, 2007.

13. *Marketing News*, August 15, 2004, p. 3.

14. Joseph A. Bellizzi and Terry Bristol, "An Assessment of Supermarket Loyalty Cards in One Major US Market," *Journal of Consumer Marketing* 21, no. 2 (2004), pp. 144–54.

15. http://www.cmbinfo.com/pdf/WSJ_Nordstrom.pdf (accessed September 8, 2007).

16. Sudhir H. Kale and Peter Klugsberger, "Reaping Rewards," *Marketing Management*, July/August 2007.

17. Bill Brohaugh, "Three Women," *Colloquy* 15, no. 2 (2007).

18. "Grocer Launches Biometric Service for Shoppers," *Business Courier of Cincinnati*, July 10, 2007 (accessed January 8, 2008).

19. Ylan Q. Mui, "Retailers Reward Loyalty—and Reap the Rewards," *Washington Post*, December 7, 2006, p. D01.

20. Natalie Petouhoff, "How Much Is Your Customers' Trust Worth?" *Customer Relationship Management*, September 2006.

21. Martha Neil, "Thinking Globally," *ABA Journal* 91 (2005), p. 62.

22. Sara Dolnicar and Yolanda Jordaan, "A Market-Oriented Approach to Responsibly Managing Information Privacy Concerns in Direct Marketing," *Journal of Advertising* 36, no. 2 (2007), pp. 123–149; William E. Spangler, Kathleen S. Hartzel, and Mordechai Gal-Or, "Exploring the Privacy Implications of Addressable Advertising and Viewer Profiling," *Communications of the ACM* 49, no. 5 (2006), pp. 119–23.

23. *Marketing News*, August 15, 2004, p. 3.

24. Junko Yoshida, "Sounding the Alarm as Big Brother Goes Digital," *Electronic Engineering Times*, April 4, 2005, pp. 1–2; Orin S. Kerr, "The Fourth Amendment and New Technologies: Constitutional Myths and the Case for Caution," *Michigan Law Review* 102, no. 5 (March 2004), pp. 801–89;

Mary Culnan, "Protecting Privacy Online: Is Self-Regulation Working?" *Journal of Public Policy & Marketing* 19 (Spring 2000), pp. 20–26.

25. http://www.ftc.gov/bcp/conline/pubs/alerts/privprotalrt.shtm (accessed September 6, 2007).

26. http://www.ftc.gov/reports/privacy3/fairinfo.shtm (accessed September 6, 2007).

27. Deena M. Amato-McCoy, "The Power of Knowledge," *Chain Store Age* 82, no. 6 (2006), p. 48.

28. George Stalk Jr., "In Praise of the Heavy Spender," *Toronto Global and Mail*, May 21, 2007 (accessed January 9, 2008).

29. V. Kumar, Denish Shah, and Rajkumar Venkatesan, "Managing Retailer Profitability—One Customer at a Time!" *Journal of Retailing* 84, no. 2 (2006), pp. 277–94.

30. Dennis Pitta, Frank Franzak, and Danielle Fowler, "A Strategic Approach to Building Online Customer Loyalty: Integrating Customer Profitability Tiers," *Journal of Consumer Marketing* 23, no. 7 (2006), pp. 421–29; Werner Reinartz and V. Kumar, "The Mismanagement of Customer Loyalty," *Harvard Business Review*, July 2002; Valarie Zeithaml, Roland Rust, and Katherine Lemon, "The Customer Pyramid: Creating and Serving Profitable Customers," *California Management Review* 43 (Summer 2001), p. 124.

31. V. Kumar and Denish Shah, "Building and Sustaining Profitable Customer Loyalty for the 21st Century," *Journal of Retailing* 80, no. 4 (2004), pp. 317–29.

32. Ibid.; see also Werner Reinartz and V. Kumar, "On the Profitability of Long-Life Customers in a Noncontractual Setting: An Empirical Investigation and Implications for Marketing," *Journal of Marketing* 64 (October 2000), pp. 17–33, for an examination of programs designed to develop long-term relationships.

33. "The Lowdown on Customer Loyalty Programs: Which Are the Most Effective and Why," *Knowledge@Wharton*, September 6, 2006 (accessed January 9, 2008).

34. Stephanie M. Noble and Joanna Phillips, "Relationship Hindrance: Why Would Consumers Not Want a Relationship with a Retailer?" *Journal of Retailing* 80, no. 4 (Winter 2004), pp. 289–303.

35. "At Sentry Foods, a Changing of the Card," *Chain Store Age* 81, no. 5 (May 2005).

36. Kate Fitzgerald, "Grocery Cards Get an Extra Scan," *Credit Card Management* 16, no. 13 (March 2004), p. 34.

37. Ed McKinley, "Custom-Fit Solutions," *Stores*, June 2005, p. 23.

38. Joe Lichtman, "Is 'Personalized Merchandising' Becoming an E-Commerce Reality?" *E-Commerce Times*, August 20, 2007 (accessed January 9, 2008).

39. Jonathan Birchall, "Just Do It, Marketers Say," *Financial Times*, April 30, 2007.

40. Roland Rust, Valerie Zeithaml, and Katherine Lemon, *Driving Customer Equity* (New York: The Free Press, 2002), Ch. 13; Zeithaml, Rust, and Lemon, "The Customer Pyramid."

41. http://www.oprah.com (accessed September 19, 2007); Linda Zebian, "The Mass-Consumer Magazine Web Dilemma," *Folio: The Magazine for Magazine Management* 36, no. 8 (2007), pp. 8–9; Robert C. Blattberg, Gary Getz, and Jacquelyn S. Thomas, *Customer Equity: Building and Managing Relationships as Valuable Assets* (Boston: Harvard Business School Press, 2001), pp. 112–15; "Oprah on Oprah: Perfectionist," *Newsweek International*, January 8, 2001, pp. 33–35

42. http://www.stopandshop.com/stores/shopping_buddy.htm (accessed September 19, 2007); David Pinto, "The Shopping Buddy," *Mass Market Retailers*, October 8, 2003.

43. Rust, Zeithaml, and Lemon, *Driving Customer Equity*, Ch. 13.

Chapter 12

1. Personal communication with the authors.

2. Renee M. Covino, "Breakfast of Champions," *Frozen Food Age* 54, no. 3 (October 2005), (accessed January 15, 2008).

3. Shailendra Gajanan, Suman Basuroy, and Srinath Beldona, "Category Management, Product Assortment and Consumer Welfare," *Marketing Letters* 18, no. 3 (July 2007), pp. 135–48.

4. "Captains of Excellence," *Convenience Store News* 43, no. 3 (March 5, 2007), (accessed January 15, 2008).

5. Gérard P. Cachon and A. Gürhan Kök, "Category Management and Coordination in Retail Assortment Planning in the Presence of Basket Shopping Consumers," *Management Science* 53, no. 6 (2007), pp. 934–51; Neil A. Morgan, Anna Kaleka, and Richard A. Gooner, "Focal Supplier Opportunism in Supermarket Retailer Category Management," *Journal of Operations Management* 25, no. 2 (2007), pp. 512–27.

6. Daniel J. Sweeney, "Improving the Profitability of Retail Merchandising Decisions," *Journal of Marketing*, January 1973, pp. 60–68.

7. http://www.hidefster.com/history (accessed September 23, 2007).

8. http://www.ncta.com/IssueBrief.aspx?contentId=2688&view=4 (accessed September 24, 2007).

9. http://unspun.amazon.com/Top-Current-Fads-of-2006/list/show/1787 (accessed January 15, 2008).

10. Pia Sarkar, "Retailers Use Weather to Forecast Their Sales," *San Francisco Chronicle*, December 4, 2006, (accessed January 15, 2008). Attributed to Mike Niemira, Chief Economist at the International Council of Shopping Centers.

11. http://www.papermag.com (accessed September 18, 2007); Samantha Graham, "Paper Round," *RunwayReporter.com*, September 13, 2007; Robin Givha, "Paper Rocks Hipsters: 20 Years of Cool Hunting," *Washington Post*, September 24, 2004, p. C2.

12. Ian Rowley and Hiroko Tashiro, "Testing What's Hot in the Cradle of Cool," *Business Week* online, May 7, 2007.

13. Vanessa O'Connell, "How Fashion Makes Its Way From the Runway to the Rack," *The Wall Street Journal*, February 8, 2007, p. D1.

14. Steven Shugan and Jinhong Xie, "Advance Selling for Services," *California Management Review* 46 (Spring 2004), pp. 37–45.

15. Ellen Byron, "To Refurbish Its Image, Tiffany Risks Profits," *The Wall Street Journal*, January 10, 2007, p. A1.

16. Laurens M. Sloot, Dennis Fok, and Peter C. Verhoef, "The Short- and Long-Term Impact of an Assortment Reduction on Category Sales," *Journal of Marketing Research* 43, no. 4 (2006), pp. 536–48; John T. Gourville and Dilip Soman, "Overchoice and Assortment Type: When and Why Variety Backfires," *Marketing Science* 24, no. 3 (2005), pp. 382–395; Barbara Kahn and Brian Wansink, "The Influence of Assortment Structure on Perceived Variety and Consumption Quantities," *Journal of Consumer Research*, March 2004, pp. 519–34.

17. Alan Wolf, "Circuit City Will Cut Assortment of Flat Panels," www.twice.com, June 18, 2007, p. 41, 42.

18. Brett Nelson and Maureen Farrell, "Note to Online Retailers: Less is More," *Forbes*, October 12, 2006 (accessed January 15, 2008), taken from Barry Schwartz, *The Paradox of Choice: Why More is Less* (New York: Ecco, 2005).

Chapter 13

1. "Inventory Management 2003: An Overview," *Chain Store Age*, December 2003, p. 3A.

2. "Robbery, Employee Theft, Leading Causes of Supermarket Losses," *Chain Store Age*, August 1998, p. 84; based on the Food Marketing Institute's annual security survey.

3. Susan M. Broniarczyk and Wayne D. Hoyer, "Retail Assortment: More Does Not Equal Better," in *Retailing in the 21st Century*, ed. Manfred Krafft and Murali K. Mantrala (Berlin: Springer, 2006); Murali Mantrala, "Allocating Marketing Resources," in *Handbook of Marketing*, eds. Barton Weitz and Robin Wensley (London: Sage Publications, 2002).

Chapter 14

1. "Best Global Brands 2007," *BusinessWeek*, August 6, 2007.

2. http://www.factsfiguresfuture.com/archive/november_2005.htm (accessed October 22, 2007); Noreen O'Leary, "New & Improved Private Label Brands," *Adweek*, October 22, 2007.

3. http://www.privatelabelmag.com/pdf/pli_fall2004/13.cfm (accessed October 22, 2007); Nirmalya Kumar and Jan-Benedict E.M. Steenkamp, *Private Label Strategy: How to Meet the Store Brand Challenge* (Boston: Harvard Business Press, 2007).

4. http://www2.acnielsen.com/news/20030916.shtml (accessed October 18, 2007).

5. Ann Zimmerman, David Kesmodel, and Julie Jargon, "From Cheap Stand-In to Shelf Star," *The Wall Street Journal*, August 29, 2007, p. B1, according to market-research firm Nielsen Co. (Wal-Mart does not supply sales data to Nielsen or any other data-tracking firm).

6. http://www.federated-fds.com/home.asp (accessed August 2, 2005).

7. Kumar and Steenkamp, *Private Label Strategy*.

8. Ibid.

9. Mark Bergen, Shantanu Dutta, and Steven Shugan, "Branded Variants: A Retail Perspective," *Journal of Marketing Research*, February 1996, pp. 9–20.

10. Christopher Lawton, "Tweaking the Standard-Issue PC," *The Wall Street Journal*, June 14, 2007, p. D1.

11. Ibid.

12. Teresa F. Lindeman, "Brands Expand: Retailers Work to Create Exclusive Products to Set Themselves Apart," *Pittsburgh Post-Gazette*, August 24, 2007 (accessed January 25, 2008).

13. Ibid.

14. Sandra Jones, "Retailers Sold on Exclusives," *Chicago Tribune*, December 15, 2006 (accessed January 25, 2008). http://www.fashioncenter.com (accessed October 22, 2007).

15. http://www.dallasmarketcenter.com (accessed October 15, 2007).

16. Ibid.

17. http://www.cesweb.org/about_ces/fact_sheet.asp (accessed October 11, 2007).

18. http://www.mccormickplace.com (accessed October 11, 2007).

19. http://www.hollander.com (accessed October 11, 2007).

20. Ted Fishman, "The Chinese Century," *The New York Times Magazine*, July 4, 2004, p. 26.

21. David Barboze, "In Roaring China, Sweaters Are West of Socks City," *The New York Times*, December 24, 2004, p. C2.

22. J.C. Penney 2007 10-K Report, filed with the Securities and Exchange Commission, February 3, 2007, p. 2.

23. Tobias Schoenherr and Vincent Mabert, "Online Reverse Auctions: Common Myths Versus Evolving Reality," *Business Horizons* 50 (September 2007), pp. 373–84; Elisa Martinelli and Gianluca Marchi, "Enabling and Inhibiting Factors in Adoption of Electronic-Reverse Auctions: A Longitudinal Case Study in Grocery Retailing," *International Review of Retail, Distribution & Consumer Research* 17(July 2007), pp. 203–18; Mya Frazier, "Look Who's Putting the Squeeze on Brands," *Advertising Age*, March 27, 2006, pp. 1, 46.

24. Bruce Fox, "Arizona Chain Pioneers Reverse Auctions for Grocery Buying," *Stores*, January 2002, pp. 62–64.

25. Frazier, "Look Who's Putting the Squeeze on Brands."

26. Max Chafkin, "Reverse Auctions: A Supplier's Survival Guide," *Inc.* 29, no. 5 (May 2007); Michael B. Baker, "Price-Focused RFPs Not Driving Deals," *Business Travel News*, July 17, 2006; Joe Nowlan, "Think TWICE, Bid ONCE," *Industrial Distribution* 95, no. 7 (July 2006).

27. Dexter Roberts, Pete Engardio, Aaron Bernstein, Stanley Holmes, and Xiang Ji, "Secrets, Lies and Sweatshops," *Business-Week*, November 27, 2006;

28. http://www.coopamerica.org/programs/rs/profile.cfm?id=278 (accessed October 11, 2007); http://www.coopamerica.org/programs/rs/profile.cfm?id=259 (accessed October 11, 2007); http://www.sweatshopwatch.org (accessed October 23, 2007).

29. http://www.limitedbrands.com/social_responsibility/labor/labor.jsp (accessed October 23, 2007).

30. Cheryl Dahle, "Gap; New Look: The See-Through," *Fast Company*, September 2004, pp. 69–70.

31. Dmitr Kuksov and Amit Pazgal, "The Effects of Costs and Competition on Slotting Allowances," *Marketing Science* 26 (March/April 2007), pp. 259–67; Paula Bone, France Fitzgerald, Karen Russo, and Richard Riley, "A Multifirm Analysis of Slotting Fees," *Journal of Public Policy & Marketing* 25 (Fall 2006), pp. 224–37; K. Sudhir and Vithala Rao, "Do Slotting Allowances Enhance Efficiency or Hinder Competition?" *Journal of Marketing Research* 43 (May 2006), pp. 137–55.

32. Richard G. Shell, *Bargaining for Advantage: Negotiation Strategies for Reasonable People*, 2d ed. (New York: Penguin, 2006). These guidelines are based on Roger Fisher and William Ury, *Getting to Yes* (New York: Penguin, 1981).

33. Thomas Powers and William Reagan, "Factors Influencing Successful Buyer–Seller Relationships," *Journal of Business Research* 60 (December 2007), pp. 1234–42; Kevin Celuch, John Bantham, and Chickery Kasouf, "An Extension of the Marriage Metaphor in Buyer–Seller Relationships: An Exploration of Individual-Level Process Dynamics," *Journal of Business Research* 59 (May 2006), pp. 573–81; Olaf Ploetner and Michael Ehret, "From Relationships to Partnerships—New Forms of Cooperation Between Buyer and Seller," *Industrial Marketing Management* 35 (January 2006), pp. 4–9; Erin Anderson and Anne Coughlan, "Structure, Governance, and Relationship Management," in *Handbook of Marketing*, eds. B. Weitz and R. Wensley (London: Sage, 2002), pp. 223–47; Barton Weitz and Sandy Jap, "Relationship Marketing and Distribution Channels," *Journal of the Academy of Marketing Sciences* 23 (Fall 1995), pp. 305–20; F. Robert Dwyer, Paul Shurr, and Sejo Oh, "Developing Buyer–Seller Relationships," *Journal of Marketing* 51 (April 1987), pp. 11–27.

34. Anne Coughlan, "Michaels Craft Stores: Integrated Channel Management and Vendor-Retail Relations," Kellogg School of Management, Northwestern University, KEL036, 2004.

35. http://www.bentonville-ar-relocation.com/ (accessed October 22, 2007); Jim Yardley, "Vendorville," *The New York Times Magazine*, March 8, 1998, p. 62.

36. Anne Coughlan, Erin Anderson, Louis W. Stern, and Adel El-Ansary, *Marketing Channels*, 7th ed. (New York: Prentice Hall, 2005).

37. Fabio Caldieraro and Anne T. Coughlan, "Spiffed-Up Channels: The Role of Spiffs in Hierarchical Selling Organizations," *Marketing Science* 26, no. 1 (2007), pp. 31–51.

38. William H. Kitchens, "Is It Legal?" *Refrigerated & Frozen Foods Retailer* 5, no. 5 (June 2007); Paul Stancil, "Still Crazy after All These Years: Understanding the Robinson-Patman Act Today," *Business Law Today*, September/October 2004, pp. 34–44.

39. "Retail Price Maintenance Policies: A Bane for Retailers, but a Boon for Consumers?," *Knowledge@Wharton*, August 8, 2007; Stephen Labaton, "Century-Old Ban Lifted on Minimum Retail Pricing," *The New York Times*, June 29, 2007 (accessed January 25, 2008).

40. Patti Bond and Duane D. Stanford, "Home Depot Issues Ban on Accepting Gifts," *The Atlanta Journal-Constitution*, August 2, 2007 (accessed January 25, 2008); Michelle Nichols, "When Customers Want Kickbacks," *BusinessWeek*, May 6, 2005, p. 30; Tracie Rozhom, "Stores and Vendors Take Their Haggling Over Payments to Court," *The New York Times*, May 17, 2005, p. B1.

41. Robin Givhan, "The Grim Reality of the Bottom Line," *The Washington Post*, May 27, 2005, p. C02.

42. TJX Annual 10K Report, 2006.

43. *In re Toys R Us AntiTrust Litigation*, 191 F.R.D. 347 (E.D.N.Y. 2000).

Chapter 15

1. Roger Kerin, Steven Hartley, Eric Berkowitz, and William Rudelius, *Marketing*, 9th ed. (New York: McGraw-Hill, 2008).

2. Pallavi Gogoi, "How Wal-Mart's TV Prices Crushed Rivals," *BusinessWeek*, April 23, 2007 (accessed January 25, 2008); Gary McWilliams, "Hefty Discounting of Flat-Panel TVs Pinches Retailers," *The Wall Street Journal*, December 20, 2006, p. A1.

3. "Focus French Retailers Pin Hopes on Liberalisation of Price Negotiations," *AFX News*, October 16, 2007; Robert Matthews, "With Profit Falling, Carrefour Rethinks Strategy," *The Wall Street Journal*, March 11, 2005, p. B3.

4. Tom Grant, "Pricing and Price Discrimination," *American Drycleaner*, March 2006, pp. 30–31; Frances Cerra Whittelsey and Marcis Carroll, *Why Women Pay More* (New York: New Press, 1995).

5. Jessica E. Vascellaro, "Online Retailers are Watching You," *The Wall Street Journal*, November 28, 2006, p. D1.

6. Donald Lehmann, "Perceptions of Price Fairness Influence Consumer Behavior," *Marketing News*, October 15, 2004, p. 52.

7. Ted Bridis, "Customers in Dark about Retail Pricing," *Houston Chronicle*, June 1, 2005, p. B3.

8. Stephen Labaton, "Century-Old Ban Lifted on Minimum Retail Pricing," *The New York Times*, June 29, 2007 (accessed January 25, 2008).

9. Richard Clodfelter, "Price Strategy and Practice: An Examination of Pricing Accuracy at Retail Stores that Use Scanners," *Journal of Product and Brand Management* 13 (2004), pp. 269–83.

10. Ibid.

11. Brian Bergstein, "Pricing Software Could Reshape Retail," *The Associated Press*, April 27, 2007 (accessed January 25, 2008).

12. Ibid.

13. Victoria Murphy Barret, "What the Traffic Will Bear," *Forbes*, July 3, 2006 (accessed January 25, 2008).

14. Amy Merrick, "Prices to Move: Retailers Try to Get Leg Up on Markdowns with New Software," *The Wall Street Journal*, August 7, 2001, p. A1.

15. Michael Levy, Dhruv Grewal, Praveen K. Kopalle, and James D. Hess, "Emerging Trends in Retail Pricing Practice: Implications for Research," *Journal of Retailing* 80, no. 3 (2004), pp. xiii–xxi; Marc Millstein, "Banking on Optimization," *wwd*, January 12, 2005, p. 12B; Dan Scheraga, "Pricing to Sell," *Chain Store Age*, March 2004, p. 52; Scott Friend and Patricia Walker, "Welcome to the New World of Merchandising," *Harvard Business Review*, November 2001, pp. 133–41; Murali Mantrala and Surya Rao, "A Decision-Support System that Helps Retailers Decide Order Quantities and Markdowns for Fashion Goods," *Interfaces*, May/June 2001, Part 2, pp. S146–63.

16. Liz Parks, "Bloomie's Revamps Buyer's Culture," *Stores*, December 2004, pp. 35–38.

17. "80 Most Influential People in Sales and Marketing," *Sales & Marketing Management*, October 1998, p. 78.

18. "Levi Strauss Reacquires a Pair of Jeans, at Markup," *The Wall Street Journal*, May 29, 2001, p. B13A.

19. Vascellaro, "Online Retailers."

20. Cotten Timberlake, "Macy's Loses Sales as It Weans Shoppers From Coupons," www.bloomberg.com, May 16, 2007.

21. Michael Johnsen, "Ukrop's Launches Personalized Loyalty Shopper Program," *C Drug Store News*, May 15, 2007 (accessed January 25, 2008).

22. Valarie A. Zeithaml and Mary Jo Bitner, *Service Marketing: Integrating Customer Focus across the Firm*, 4th ed. (New York: McGraw-Hill, 2005).

23. Arvind Sahay, "How to Reap Higher Profits With Dynamic Pricing," *MIT Sloan Management Review* 48, no. 4 (2007), pp. 53–60; Barry Berman, "Applying Yield Management Pricing to Your Service Business," *Business Horizons* 48 (March/April 2005), pp. 169–82; Ramao Desiraju and Steven Shugan, "Strategic Service Pricing and Yield Management," *Journal of Marketing* 63 (January 1999), pp. 44–56.

24. Howard Marmorstein, Jeanne Rossome, and Dan Sarel, "Unleashing the Power of Yield Management in the Internet Era: Opportunities and Challenges," *California Management Review* 45 (Spring 2003), pp. 147–67.

25. Priceline.com 10-K report, filed with the Securities and Exchange Commission, December 26, 2006.

26. Thomas T. Nagle and Reed K. Holden, *The Strategy and Tactics of Pricing*, 3rd ed. (Upper Saddle River, NJ: Pearson, 2002); Glenn Voss, A. Parasuraman, and Dhruv Grewal, "The Roles of Price, Performance and Expectations in Determining Satisfaction in Services Exchanges," *Journal of Marketing* 62, no. 4 (October 1998), pp. 46–61.

27. Ed Christman, "Market Making and Loss Leading," *Billboard*, October 13, 2007 (accessed January 25, 2008).

28. Susanne Ault, "Fry's Heats Up High-Def Prices," *Video Business*, July 30, 2007, p. 5, 22.

29. Edward J. Fox and Stephen J. Hoch, "Cherry-Picking," *Journal of Marketing* 69, no. 1 (2005), pp. 46–62.

30. Itamar Simonson, "Shoppers Easily Influenced Choices," *The New York Times*, November 6, 1994, p. 311. Based on research by Itamar Simonson and Amos Tversky.

31. Marc Vanhuele, Gilles Laurent, and Xavier Dreze, "Consumers' Immediate Memory for Prices," *Journal of Consumer Research* 33, no. 2 (2006), pp. 163–72.

32. This discussion has been going on for at least 70 years; see Louis Bader and James De Weinland, "Do Odd Prices Earn Money?" *Journal of Retailing* 8 (1932), pp. 102–104. For recent research in this area, see Robert M. Schindler, "The 99-Price Ending as a Signal of a Low-Price Appeal," *Journal of Retailing* 82, no. 1 (2006), pp. 71–77; Eric Anderson and Duncan Simester, "Effects of $9 Price Endings on Retail Sales: Evidence form Field Experiments," *Quantitative Marketing and Economics*, March 2003, pp. 93–110; Mark Striving, "Price-Endings When Prices Signal Quality," *Management Science* 12, no. 46 (2000), pp. 1617–29.

33. Robert Schindler, "Fine Tuning a Retail Price," *Retail Navigator* (Gainesville, FL: Miller Center for Retailing Education and Research, April 2004).

34. Ibid.

Chapter 16

1. David A. Aaker, *Brand Portfolio Strategy: Creating Relevance, Differentiation, Energy, Leverage, and Clarity* (New York: The Free Press, 2004).

2. Linda Hyde and Elaine Pollack, *What's in a Name?* (Columbus, OH: Retail Forward, Inc., June 1999), p. 9.

3. "History in the Making: A Look at 16 Campaigns that Helped Redefine Promotion Marketing," *Promo*, March 2002, p. 23.

4. Stephanie Kang, "Finish Line Hopes to Become Destination," *The Wall Street Journal*, July 19, 2007, p. B4.

5. "Integrating Online and Store Images Pays Off for American Eagle," www.internetretailer.com, August 3, 2005.

6. "100 Leading National Advertisers," *Advertising Age*, Supplement, June 20, 2007.

7. *100 Leading Advertisers: 2007 Marketers Profile Yearbook* (Advertising Age: New York, 2007).

8. Eric Pfanner, "Reins Off, French Retailers Rush to Buy TV Time," *The New York Times*, January 9, 2007.

9. www.marketingpower.com/mg-dictionary.php?SearchFor=special+event&Searched=1 (accessed November 24, 2007).

10. Peter Sanders, "D'Oh! Simpsons Campaign Uses a Backward Approach," *The Wall Street Journal*, July 26, 2007, p. B1.

11. Chris Serres and Jon Bream, "Macy's Hopes Prince Strikes Youthful Chord," *Minneapolis St. Paul Star Tribune*, May 30, 2007 (accessed January 25, 2008).

12. "The Man Who Created Rudolph from an Idea That Almost Didn't Fly," *Chicago Tribune*, December 13, 1990, p. 1C.

13. Christopher Megerian, "On the Digital Catwalk at H&M," *BusinessWeek*, June 29, 2007 (accessed January 25, 2008).

14. "The Man Who Created Rudolph."

15. Mya Frazier, "Research Team Develops Shopping-Cart Ad System," *Ad Age*, August 30, 2006 (accessed January 25, 2008).

16. Jessica Tsai, "Coupons Without the Clipping," *CRM Magazine* 11, no. 10 (October 2007).

17. Dhruv Grewal and Michael Levy, "Journal of Retailing: What Have We Learned in the Last Six Years? Where Should We Focus Our Attention?" *Journal of Retailing* 84 (forthcoming 2008); Sylvie Morin, Laurette Dube, and Jean-Charles Chebat, "The Role of Pleasant Music in Servicescapes: A Test of the Dual Model of Environmental Perception," *Journal of Retailing* 2007, 83, no. 1, pp. 115–130; Nicole Bailey and Charles S. Areni, "When a Few Minutes Sound like a Lifetime: Does Atmospheric Music Expand or Contract Perceived Time?" *Journal of Retailing* 2006, 82, no. 3, pp. 189–202; Julie Baker, A. Parasuraman, Dhruv Grewal, and Glenn Voss, "The Influence of Multiple Store Environment Cues on Perceived Merchandise Value and Patronage Intentions," *Journal of Marketing* 66 (April 2002), pp. 120–41; Dhruv Grewal, Julie Baker, Michael Levy, and Glenn B. Voss, "Wait Expectations, Store Atmosphere and Store Patronage Intentions," *Journal of Retailing* 79, no. 4 (2003), pp. 259–68; Sevgin Eroglu, Karen Machleit, and Jean-Charles Chebat, "The Interaction of Retail Density and Music Tempo: Effects on Shopper Responses," *Psychology & Marketing*, July 2005, pp. 577–59.

18. Enid Burns, "The State of Retail E-Mail," www.clickz.com/stats/sectors/email/ (accessed November 5, 2007).

19. http://www.frederiksamuel.com/blog/ad-dictionary (accessed October 29, 2007).

20. http://about.telus.com/investors/en/glossaryBot.html (accessed October 26, 2007).

21. Joseph Tarnowski, "Technology: The 'Extended Peripheral'," *Progressive Grocer*, September 14, 2006 (accessed January 25, 2008).

22. Jayne O'Donnell, "Teens Targeted With Cellphone Marketing," *USA Today*, March 20, 2007.

23. Ibid.

24. Louise Story, "New Form of Impulse: Shopping via Text Message," *The New York Times*, April 16, 2007 (accessed January 25, 2008).

25. Bob Tedeschi, "Reaching More Customers with a Simple Text Message," *The New York Times*, July 16, 2007, according to Greg Sterling, an analyst with the Internet consultancy Sterling Market Intelligence (accessed January 25, 2008).

26. Leo Jakobson, "A Gift Card that Gives Back," *Incentive*, July 19, 2007 (accessed January 25, 2008).

27. Kris Hudson, "Behind the Scenes, PR Firm Remakes Wal-Mart's Image," *The Wall Street Journal*, December 7, 2006, p. A1.

28. Frederick Reichheld, "Loyalty-Based Management," *Harvard Business Review*, March–April 1993, p. 65.

29. Greet Van Hoye and Filip Lievens, "Social Influences on Organizational Attractiveness: Investigating If and When Word of Mouth Matters," *Journal of Applied Social Psychology* 37, no. 9 (2007), pp. 2024–47; Robert East, Kathy Hammond, and Malcolm Wright, "The Relative Incidence of Positive and Negative Word of Mouth: A Multi-Category Study," *International Journal of Research in Marketing* 24, no. 2 (2007), pp. 175–84; Tom Brown, Thomas Barry, Peter Dacin, and Richard Gunst, "Spreading the Word: Investigating Antecedents of Consumers' Positive Word-of-Mouth Intentions and Behaviors in a Retailing Context," *Journal of the Academy of Marketing Science* 33 (Spring 2005), pp. 123–39.

30. Bob Tedeschi, "Like Shopping? Social Networking? Try Social Shopping," *The New York Times*, September 16, 2006 (accessed January 25, 2008).

31. Joan Voight, "Getting a Handle on Customer Reviews," *Adweek*, July 5, 2007, based on research by Top 40 Online Retail from Foresee Results and the University of Michigan (accessed January 25, 2008).

32. Cheryl Lu-Lien Tan, "That's So You! Just Click Here to Buy It," *The Wall Street Journal*, June 7, 2007, p. D8.

33. Ibid.

34. Voight, "Getting a Handle on Customer Reviews."

35. Ibid., using the 2007 Edeman Trust Barometer which surveys nearly 2,000 opinion leaders in 11 countries.

36. Valerie Seckler, "Buzz Brightens as TV Spots Fade," *WWD*, June 29, 2005, p. 13.

37. "Perry Ellis Links with Dolphins, Dolphins Stadium," *Sporting Goods Business*, September 27, 2005 (accessed January 25, 2008).

38. George Belch and Michael Belch, *Advertising and Promotion*, 7th ed. (New York: McGraw-Hill, 2006).

39. Leonard Lodish, *Advertisers and Promotion Challenge: Vaguely Right or Precisely Wrong* (New York: Oxford University Press, 1986).

40. Belch and Belch, *Advertising and Promotion*.

41. Murali Mantrala, "Allocating Marketing Resources," in *Handbook of Marketing*, ed. Barton Weitz and Robin Wensley (London: Sage, 2002), pp. 409–35.

42. Teresa A. Summers and Paulette R. Hebert, "Shedding Some Light on Store Atmospherics; Influence of Illumination on Consumer Behavior," *Journal of Business Research* 54, no. 2 (November 2001), pp. 145–50.

43. Ronald Curhan and Robert Kopp, "Obtaining Retailer Support for Trade Deals: Key Success Factors," *Journal of Advertising Research* 27 (December 1987–January 1988), pp. 51–60.

44. Stefano Puntoni and Nader T. Tavassoli, "Social Context and Advertising Memory," *Journal of Marketing* Research 44, no. 2 (2007), pp. 284–296; Donald Ziccardi and David Moin, *Master Minding the Store: Advertising, Sales Promotion, and the New Marketing Reality* (New York: Wiley, 1997).

45. *100 Leading Advertisers*, p. 3

46. Ibid.

47. Kim T. Gordon, "4 Keys to Radio Advertising," *Entrepreneur*, April 13, 2007.

Chapter 17

1. H. John Bernardin, *Human Resource Management: An Experiential Approach*, 4th ed. (Burr Ridge, IL: McGraw-Hill, 2007); Raymond Noe, John Hollenbeck, Barry Gerhart, and Patrick Wright, *Fundamentals of Human Resource Management*, 2nd ed. (Burr Ridge, IL: McGraw-Hill, 2005).

2. Amy Joyce, "Retired, and Rehired to Sell," *Washington Post*, July 27, 2006, p. D01; Lauri Giesen, "Seniors' Moment," *Stores* June 2005, p. 80.

3. Mark Schoeff Jr., "CVS Optimas Award Winner for Partnership," *Workforce Management*, March 26, 2007, p. 30.

4. Vicki Powers, "Finding Workers Who Fit the Container Store Built a Booming Business for Neatnicks Who Turned Out to Be Their Best Employees," *Business 2.0*, November 2004, p. 74.

5. Katherine Field, "High-Speed Hiring," *Chain Store Age*, June 2006.

6. Susan Jackson and Randall Schuler, *Managing Human Resources: Through Strategic Relationships*, 8th ed. (Mason, OH: South-Western, 2003), p. 328.

7. Diane Coutu, "We Googled You," *Harvard Business Review*, June 2007, pp. 37–47.

8. Richard C. Hollinger and Amanda Adams, *2006 National Retail Security Survey* (Gainesville: University of Florida, 2007), p. 16.

9. Mina Kimes, "Faster Drug Tests," *Fortune Small Business*, November 2007 (accessed January 25, 2008), according to the U.S. Department of Health and Human Services

10. Shari L. Peterson, "Managerial Turnover in US Retail Organizations," *Journal of Management Development* 26, no. 7/8

(2007), pp. 770–89; Aaron Arndt, Todd J. Arnold, and Timothy D. Landry, "The Effects of Polychronic-Orientation upon Retail Employee Satisfaction and Turnover," *Journal of Retailing* 82, no. 4 (2006), pp. 319–30; Hiram Barksdale Jr., Danny Bellender, James Boles, and Thomas Brashear, "The Impact of Realistic Job Previews and Perceptions of Training on Sales Force Performance and Continuance Commitment: A Longitudinal Test," *Journal of Personal Selling and Sales Management* 23 (Spring 2003), pp. 125–40.

11. John Kador, *The Manager's Book of Questions: 1001 Great Interview Questions for Hiring the Best Person*, 2nd ed. (Burr Ridge, IL: McGraw-Hill, 2006); Robin Kessler, *Competency-Based Interviews: Master the Tough New Interview Style And Give Them the Answers That Will Win You the Job*, (Franklin Lakes, NJ: Career Press, 2006); Deborah Walker, "Behavioral Interviews: 3 Steps to Great Answers," *PA Times* 30, no. 9 (2007), p. 22; John Sullican, "Be Correctly Prepared," *PM Network* 20, no. 4 (2006), p. 24.

12. Mya Frazier, "Help Wanted," *Chain Store Age*, April 2005, pp. 37–40.

13. Keith Rollag, "Defining the Term 'New' in New Employee Research," *Journal of Occupational & Organizational Psychology* 80, no. 1 (2007), pp. 63–75; Keith Rollag, "The Impact of Relative Tenure on Newcomer Socialization Dynamics," *Journal of Organizational Behavior* 25 (November 2004), pp. 853–73.

14. Vicki Powers, "Finding Workers Who Fit," *Business 2.0*, November 2004, p. 74.

15. Jessica Marquez, "Faced with High Turnover, Retailers Boot Up E-Learning Programs for Quick Training," *Workforce Management*, August 2005, pp. 74–75.

16. Ibid.

17. W. Arthur Jr., B.D. Edwards, S.T. Bell, A.J. Villado, and W. Bennett Jr., "Team Task Analysis: Identifying Tasks and Jobs that Are Team-Based," *Human Factors* 47, pp. 654–69.

18. George Anders, "Companies Find Online Training Has Its Limits," *The Wall Street Journal*, March 26, 2007, p. B3.

19. Lorri Freifeld, "Focus on Retail: Best Buy Connects with Customers," *Sales and Marketing Management*, August 1, 2007 (accessed January 25, 2008).

20. Annie McKee, Richard Boyatzis, and Fran Johnston, *Becoming a Resonant Leader: Develop Your Emotional Intelligence, Renew Your Relationships, Sustain Your Effectiveness* (Boston: Harvard Business School Press, 2008).

21. C. Fred Miao and Kenneth R. Evans, "The Impact of Salesperson Motivation on Role Perceptions and Job Performance—A Cognitive and Affective Perspective," *Journal of Personal Selling & Sales Management* 27, no. 1 (2007), pp. 89–101.

22. Tará Burnthorne Lopez, Christopher D. Hopkins, and Mary Anne Raymond, "Reward Preferences of Salespeople: How do Commissions Rate?" *Journal of Personal Selling & Sales Management* 26, no. 4 (2006), pp. 381–90; Richard G. McFarland and Blair Kidwell, "An Examination of Instrumental and Expressive Traits on Performance: The Mediating Role of Learning, Prove, and Avoid Goal Orientations," *Journal of Personal Selling & Sales Management* 26, no. 2 (2006), pp. 143–59.

23. Ross Petty and John Farr, "Sexual Harassment: Handling the 'He-Said-She-Said' Hot Potato," *Chain Store Age*, April 1998, pp. 56–59.

24. **Mark Albright, "Hiring the Right Person," St. Petersburg Times, March 25, 2002, p. 8E.**

25. Arthur C. Brooks, "I Love My Work," *American: A Magazine of Ideas* 1, no. 6 (2007), pp. 20–28; John H. Fleming and Jim Asplund, *Human Sigma: Managing the Employee–Customer Encounter* (New York: Gallup Press, 2007).

26. Karolin Fellner, Royce Kallesen, Antonio Ruggiero, and Benson Yuen, "Improving Revenue Through Fare Rationalization and a New Business Process Between Revenue Management and Sales," *Journal of Revenue & Pricing Management* 5, no. 2 (2006), pp. 118–27.

27. James P. Guthrie and Elaine C. Hollensbe, "Group Incentives and Performance: A Study of Spontaneous Goal Setting, Goal Choice and Commitment," *Journal of Management* 30, no. 2 (2004), pp. 263–85.

28. Lisa Girion, "Working Longer?" *Los Angeles Times,* September 10, 2000, p. G1.

29. Kris Maher, "Wal-Mart Seeks New Flexibility in Worker Shifts," *The Wall Street Journal,* January 3, 2007, p. A1.

30. Steven Greenhouse and Michael Barbaro, "Wal-Mart to Add Wage Caps and Part-Timers," *The New York Times,* October 2, 2006 (accessed January 25, 2008).

31. Glenn Adams, "Grocer Pushes Earth-Friendly Store Design," *Los Angeles Times,* October 22, 2007 (accessed January 25, 2008).

32. Leila Abboud and John Biers, "Business Goes on an Energy Diet," *The Wall Street Journal,* August 24, 2007 (accessed January 25, 2008).

33. www.walmartfacts.com/articles/4564.aspx (accessed November 30, 2007).

34. Hollinger and Adams.

35. Ibid.

36. Ibid.

37. Ann Zimmerman, "As Shoplifters Use High-Tech Scams, Retail Losses Rise," *The Wall Street Journal,* October 25, 2006, p. A1.

38. Ibid., estimate by Brad Brekke, vice president of assets protection at Target Corp.

39. Ibid., based on a study by the National Retail Federation.

40. Ylan Q. Mui, "Not-So-Happy Returns," *Washington Post,* December 25, 2006, p. D01.

41. Mike Delaney, "How to Beat Shoplifting," about.com, April 26, 2006 (accessed January 25, 2008); Ronald Bond, "Preventing Retail Theft," www.entrepreneur.com, July 18, 2007 (accessed January 25, 2008).

42. Delaney.

43. Hollinger and Adams, p. 28.

44. Hollinger and Adams.

45. Ibid.

Chapter 18

1. Linda Matchan, "The Sleek, Smooth Design of Apple's iPod Is Now Mirrored in the Architecture of Some of the Company's High-Profile Stores," *Boston Globe,* June 29, 2006 (accessed December 28, 2007).

2. Raymond Burke, "Exploring Shopability," *Chain Store Age,* September 2005, p. 57; Mitchell Mauk, "The Store as Story," *VM & SD,* October 2000, pp. 23, 25.

3. "Growing Pains," *Chain Store Age,* August 2005, p. 31A.

4. Eun Joo Park, Eun Young Kim, and Judith Cardona Forney, "A Structural Model of Fashion-Oriented Impulse Buying Behavior," *Journal of Fashion Marketing & Management* 10, no. 4 (2006), pp. 433–46.

5. Julia Werdigier, "To Woo Europeans, McDonald's Goes Upscale," *The New York Times,* August 25, 2007 (accessed December 28, 2007).

6. Michael Barbaro, "A Long Line for a Shorter Wait at the Supermarket," *The New York Times,* June 23, 2007 (accessed December 28, 2007).

7. Jonathan Reynolds, Elizabeth Howard, Christine Cuthbertson, and Latchezar Hristov, "Perspectives on Retail Format Innovation: Relating Theory and Practice," *International Journal of Retail & Distribution Management* 35, no. 8 (2007), pp. 647–60.

8. Rosemary D. F. Bromley and David L. Matthew, "Reducing Consumer Disadvantage: Reassessing Access in the Retail Environment," *International Review of Retail, Distribution & Consumer Research* 17, no. 5 (2007), pp. 483–501; Stacey Menzel Baker, Jonna Holland, and Carol Kaufman-Scarborough, "How Consumers with Disabilities Perceive 'Welcome' in Retail Servicescapes: A Critical Incident Study," *Journal of Services Marketing* 21, no. 3 (2007), pp. 160–73; Marianne Wilson, "Accessible Fixtures," *Chain Store Age* 83, no. 2 (February 2007).

9. See, for example, *Disabled in Action of Metropolitan New York, Inc. et al. v. Duane Reade, Inc.,* U.S. District Court Southern District of New York, Civil Action No.: 01 Civ. 4692 (WHP), 2004; *Californians for Disability Rights v. Mervyn's, Superior Court of California,* No. 2002-051738 (RMS), 2003; *Shimozono, et al. v. May Department Stores Co. d/b/a Robinsons-May,* Federal Court, Central District of California, Case No. 00-04261 (WJR), 2001; *Access Now, et al., v. Burdines, Inc.,* Federal Court, Southern District of Florida, Case No. 99-3214 (CIV), 2000.

10. Michael Barbaro, "Department Stores Settle Disability Lawsuit," *The Washington Post,* February 9, 2005, p. E.02.

11. Lisa Eckelbecker, "Female Persuasion; Lowe's, Others Learn How to Design Stores with Women Shoppers in Mind," *Worcester Telegram & Gazette,* February 13, 2005, p. E.1.

12. Willard N. Ander Jr. and Neil Z. Stern, *Winning At Retail: Developing a Sustained Model for Retail Success* (New York: Wiley, 2004).

13. Marianne Wilson, "Spotlight on Performance," *Chain Store Age,* October 2007, pp. 116–17.

14. Alan Wolf, "Target Revamps CE Departments," *Twice,* October 22, 2007, p. 26.

15. Fiona Soltes, "It's the Message, Not the Medium," *Stores,* October 2007, p. 26; Michael Curran, "Now Playing: Interactive Retail Marketing 2.0," *Stores,* August 2007, p. 92; Katherine Field, "Digital Signage: A Powerful New Medium," *Chain Store Age,* May 2006, p. 204; Steven Keith Platt, Kingshuck Sinha, and Barton Weitz, *Implications for Retail Adoption of Digital Signage Systems* (Chicago, IL: Platt Retail Institute, 2004).

16. Mindy Fetterman and Jayne O'Donnell, "Just Browsing at the Mall? That's What You Think," *USA Today,* September 1, 2006 (accessed December 28, 2007).

17. Doris Hajewski, "JCPenney Now Hot on Kohl's Heels, Retail Industry Watchers Say," *Knight Ridder Tribune Business News,* November 7, 2004, p. 1.

18. Michael Applebaum, "More Eyeballs at Checkout," *Brandweek,* June 27–July 4, 2005, p. 54.

19. Michael Barbaro, "Are We Shopping? Is This a Store?" *The New York Times,* November 1, 2006 (accessed December 28, 2007).

20. Lorrie Grant, "Give Customers Some Space," *Stores,* April 2007 (accessed December 28, 2007).

21. www.ribastoresolutions.com/index.html (accessed December 28, 2007).

22. Ron Bond, "The Art and Science of Retail Displays," *Entrepreneur.com,* August 15, 2005.

23. Ellen Byron, "A Virtual View of the Store Aisle," *The Wall Street Journal,* October 3, 2007, p. B1.

24. The concept of atmospherics was introduced by Philip Kotler, "Atmosphere as a Marketing Tool," *Journal of Retailing* 49 (Winter 1973), pp. 48–64. The definition is adapted from Richard Yalch and Eric Spangenberg, "Effects of Store Music on Shopping Behavior," *Journal of Service Marketing* 4, no. 1 (Winter 1990), pp. 31–39.

25. Eric R. Spangenberg, David E. Sprott, Bianca Grohmann, and Daniel L. Tracy, "Gender-Congruent Ambient Scent Influences on Approach and Avoidance Behaviors in a Retail Store," *Journal of Business Research* 59, no. 12 (2006), pp. 1281–87; Anna S. Mattila and Jochen Wirtz, "Congruency of Scent and Music as a Driver of In-Store Evaluations and Behavior," *Journal of Retailing* 77, no. 2 (Summer 2001), pp. 273–89.

26. Julie Baker, Dhruv Grewal, Michael Levy, and Glenn Voss, "Wait Expectations, Store Atmosphere and Store Patronage Intentions." *Journal of Retailing* 79, no. 4 (2003), pp. 259–68.

27. Cate T. Corcoran, "Stores Lighten Up," *WWD: Women's Wear Daily*, September 6, 2007, p. 24.

28. Ibid.

29. Ibid.

30. Jean-Charles Chebat and Maureen Morrin, "Colors and Cultures: Exploring the Effects of Mall Décor on Consumer Perceptions," *Journal of Business Research* 60, no. 3 (2007), pp. 189–96; Malaika Brengman and Maggie Geuens, "The Four Dimensional Impact of Color on Shopper's Emotions," *Advances in Consumer Research* 31 (2003), pp. 122–25; Barry Babin, David Hardesty, and Tracy Suter, "Color and Shopping Intentions: The Intervening Effect of Price Fairness and Perceived Affect," *Journal of Business Research* 56 (July 2003), pp. 541–55.

31. Michael John Healy, Michael Beverland, Harmen Oppewal, and Sean Sands, "Understanding Retail Experiences—The Case for Ethnography," *International Journal of Market Research* 49, no. 6 (2007), pp. 751–78; Nicole Bailey and Charles S. Areni, "When a Few Minutes Sound Like a Lifetime: Does Atmospheric Music Expand or Contract Perceived Time?" *Journal of Retailing* 82, no. 1 (2006), pp. 189–202; Sevgin Erolglu, Karen Machleit, and Jean-Charles Chebat, "The Interaction of Retail Density and Music Temp: Effects on Shopper Responses," *Psychology & Marketing* 22 (July 2005), pp. 577–90; Michael Morrison and Michael Beverland, "In Search of the Right In-Store Music," *Business Horizons* 46 (November/December 2003), pp. 77–87.

32. Fetterman and O'Donnell.

33. Theunis Bates, "Volume Control," *Time*, August 2, 2007 (accessed December 28, 2007)

34. Ibid.

35. Spangenberg, Sprott, Grohmann, and Tracy; Jean-Charles Chebat and Richard Michon, "Impact of Ambient Odors on Mall Shoppers' Emotions, Cognition, and Spending: A Test of Competitive Causal Theories," *Journal of Business Research* 56 (July 2003), pp. 529–45.

36. Ylan Q. Mui, "Dollars and Scents," *Washington Post*, December 19, 2006, p. D01; Keith McArthur, "Marketers Next Hit? Right at Your Nose," *Toronto Globe and Mail*, January 26, 2006 (accessed December 28, 2007).

37. Earl Print, "Euro Lighting," *VM&SD*, May 1999, pp. 38, 40.

38. Velitchka Kalchteva and Barton Weitz, "How Exciting Should a Store Be?" *Journal of Marketing*, Winter 2006, pp. 34–62.

39. Ibid.

40. Jung-Hwan Kim, Minjeong Kim, and Jay Kandampully, "The Impact of Buying Environment Characteristics of Retail Websites," *Service Industries Journal* 27, no. 7 (2007), pp. 865–80;David Cunningham, Liz Thach, and Karen Thompson, "Innovative E-Commerce Site Design: A Conceptual Model to Match Consumer MBTI Dimensions to Website Design," *Journal of Internet Commerce* 6, no. 3 (2007), pp. 1–27.

41. James J. Cappel and Zhenyu Huang, "A Usability Analysis of Company Websites," *Journal of Computer Information Systems* 48, no. 1 (2007), pp. 117–23.

42. Yen, Benjamin P. C. Yen, "The Design and Evaluation of Accessibility on Web Navigation," *Decision Support Systems* 42, no. 4 (2007), pp. 2219–35.

43. "Tips on Improving the Checkout Process," www.e-consulatancy.com, August 17, 2007.

44. Ibid.

Chapter 19

1. "Retailers Join the War Effort," *Chain Store Age*, June 1994, p. 15.

2. Murray Raphael, "Tell Me What You Want and the Answer Is Yes," *Direct Marketing*, October 1996, p. 22.

3. "Driving Customers Away," *Chain Store Age*, June 2001, p. 39; Clay M. Voorhees, Michael K. Brady, and David M. Horowitz, "A Voice From the Silent Masses: An Exploratory and Comparative Analysis of Noncomplainers," *Journal of the Academy of Marketing Science* 34 (October 2006), pp. 514–27; Sijun Wang and Lenard C. Huff, "Explaining Buyers' Responses to Sellers' Violation of Trust," *European Journal of Marketing* 41 (September 2007), pp. 1033–52.

4. Valarie Zeithaml, Leonard Berry, and A. Parasuraman, "The Behavioral Consequences of Service Quality," *Journal of Marketing* 60 (April 1996), pp. 31–46; Tom DeWitt and Michael K. Brady, "Rethinking Service Recovery Strategies," *Journal of Service Research* 6 (November 2003), pp. 193–207.

5. Robert Spector and Patrick McCarthy, *The Nordstrom Way: The Inside Story of America's #1 Customer Service Company*, 3d ed. (New York: John Wiley & Sons, 2005).

6. Joyce Smith, "Positive Customer Service Pays Off," *Myrtle Beach Sun News*, November 5, 2006, based on a National Retail Foundation survey.

7. Dwayne Ball, Pedro S. Coelho, and Manuel J. Vilares, "Service Personalization and Loyalty," *Journal of Services Marketing* 20 (September 2006), pp. 391–403; Carol F. Suprenant and Michael R. Solomon, "Predictability and Personalization in the Service Encounter," *Journal of Marketing* 51 (April 1987), p. 86.

8. Deena M. Amato-McCoy, "Putting the Best Foot Forward," *Retail Technology Quarterly*, October 2007, pp. 4A–6A.

9. Jason Friedman, "Tracking Success In-Store," www.marketingatretail.com, December 21, 2006; Dennis Viehland and Aaron Wong, "The Future of Radio Frequency Identification," *Journal of Theoretical and Applied Electronic Commerce Research* 2 (August 2007), pp. 74–81; Claudia Loebbecke, "Use of Innovative Content Integration Information Technology at the Point of Sale," *European Journal of Information Systems* 16 (July 2007), pp. 228–36.

10. James Kohnen, "Beyond Six Sigma: Profitable Growth through Customer Value Creation," *The Quality Management Journal* 14 (April 2007), p. 41; Jiju Antony, Frenie Jiju Antony, Maneesh Kumar, and Byung Rae Cho, "Six Sigma in Service Organisations: Benefits, Challenges and Difficulties, Common Myths, Empirical Observations and Success Factors," *The International Journal of Quality & Reliability Management* 24 (March 2007), pp. 294–311.

11. Ryan Chittum, "Good Customer Service Costs Money. Some Expenses are Worth It—and Some Aren't," *The Wall Street Journal*, October 30, 2006, p. R7, based on a study conducted by the Harvard Business School.

12. www.consumerreports.org/cro/home-garden/resource-center/home-improvement/return-policies-of-the-leading-home-improvement-retailers-9-07/retailers-return-policies/home-improvement-return-policies-retailers-return-policies.htm (accessed November 7, 2007); Zhen Zhu, K. Sivakumar, and A. Parasuraman, "A Mathematical Model of Service Failure and Recovery Strategies," *Decision Science* 35 (Summer 2004), pp. 493–525; Roland T. Rust and Tuck Siong Chung, "Marketing Models of Service and Relationships," *Marketing Science* 25 (November 2006), pp. 560–80; A. Parasuraman, "Modeling Opportunities in Service Recovery and Customer-Managed Interactions," *Marketing Science* 25 (November 2006), pp. 590–93.

13. Ariana Eunjung Cha, "Finding Fewer Happy Returns," *Washington Post*, November 7, 2004, p. A.01.

14. Stephen L. Vargo, Kaori Nagao, Yi He, and Fred W. Morgan, "Satisfiers, Dissatisfiers, Criticals, and Neutrals: A Review of Their Relative Effects on Customer (Dis)Satisfaction," *Academy of Marketing Science Review* (January 2007), p. 1; Chezy Ofir and Itamar Simonson, "The Effect of Stating Expectations on Customer Satisfaction and Shopping Experience," *Journal of Marketing Research* 44 (February 2007), p. 37; Torsten Ringberg, Gaby Odekerken-Schröder, and Glenn L Christensen, "A Cultural Models Approach to Service Recovery," *Journal of Marketing* 71 (July 2007), p. 194; A. Parasuraman and Valarie Zeithaml, "Understanding and Improving Service Quality: A Literature Review and Research Agenda," in *Handbook of Marketing*, eds. B. Weitz and R. Wensley (London: Sage, 2002); Praveen Kopalle and Donald Lehmann, "Strategic Management of Expectations: The Role of Disconfirmation Sensitivity and Perfectionism," *Journal of Marketing Research* 38 (August 2001), pp. 386–401.

15. Todd Beck, "Want Loyal Customers? Don't Stop at Satisfaction," *Customer Inter@ction Solutions*, February 2005, pp. 36–49.

16. Mary Jo Bitner, "Self-Service Technologies: What Do Customers Expect? In This High-Tech World, Customers Haven't Changed—They Still Want Good Service," *Marketing Management*, Spring 2001, pp. 10–15; Ofir and Simonson; Jackie L. M. Tam, "Managing Customer Expectations in Financial Services: Opportunities and Challenges," *Journal of Financial Services Marketing* 11 (May 2007), pp. 281–89; Deirdre O'Loughlin and Isabelle Szmigin, "External and Internal Accountability of Financial Services Suppliers: Current Paradoxes in Managing Expectations and Experience," *Journal of Strategic Marketing* 13 (June 2005), pp. 133–47.

17. Timothy Keiningham and Terry Vavra, *The Customer Delight Principle* (Chicago: American Marketing Association, 2002); Kenneth B. Yap and Jillian C. Sweeney, "Zone-of-Tolerance Moderates the Service Quality-Outcome Relationship," *Journal of Services Marketing* 21 (February 2007), p. 137; Roland T. Rust and Richard L. Oliver, "Should We Delight the Customer?" *Journal of the Academy of Marketing Science* 28 (January 2000), pp. 86–94.

18. Parasuraman and Zeithaml, "Understanding and Improving Service Quality."

19. Andrew J. Czaplewski, Eric M. Olson, and Stanley F. Slater, "Applying the RATER Model for Service Success: Five Service Attributes Can Help Maintain Five-Star Ratings," *Marketing Management*, January–February 2002, pp. 14–20.

20. Valerie Seckler, "The Shopping Experience: Service Is Key," *WWD*, August 10, 2005, p. 10.

21. The discussion of the Gaps model and its implications is based on Doen Nel and Leyland Pitt, "Service Quality in a Retail Environment: Closing the Gaps," *Journal of General Management* 18 (Spring 1993), pp. 37–57; Valarie Zeithaml, A. Parasuraman, and Leonard Berry, *Delivering Quality Customer Service* (New York: The Free Press, 1990); Valarie Zeithaml, Leonard Berry, and A. Parasuraman, "Communication and Control Processes in the Delivery of Service Quality," *Journal of Marketing* 52 (April 1988), pp. 35–48; Nitin Seth, S.G. Deshmukh, and Prem Vrat, "A Conceptual Model for Quality of Service in the Supply Chain," *International Journal of Physical Distribution & Logistics Management* 36 (August 2006), pp. 547–75; R. Rohini and B. Mahadevappa, "Service Quality in Bangalore Hospitals: An Empirical Study," *Journal of Services Research* 6 (April 2006), pp. 59–84.

22. Linda Abu-Shalback Zid, "Another Satisfied Customer," *Marketing Management*, March/April 2005, p. 5.

23. www.retailindustry.about.com, April 4, 2001 (accessed January 26, 2008).

24. Devendra Mishra, "How Best Buy Uses Customer Input to Develop Private Label Line," *Dealerscope*, June 2007 (accessed January 26, 2008).

25. Kemba J. Dunham, "Beyond Satisfaction," *The Wall Street Journal*, October 30, 2006, p. R4.

26. "Driving Customers Away," *Chain Store Age*, June 2001, p. 39.

27. Xueming Luo, "Consumer Negative Voice and Firm-Idiosyncratic Stock Returns," *Journal of Marketing* 71 (July 2007), p. 75; James C. Ward and Amy L. Ostrom, "Complaining to the Masses: The Role of Protest Framing in Customer-Created Complaint Web Sites," *Journal of Consumer Research* 33 (September 2006), pp. 220–30; Simon J. Bell and James A. Luddington, "Coping With Customer Complaints," *Journal of Service Research* 8 (February 2006), pp. 221–33; Thorsten Gruber, Isabelle Szmigin, and Roediger Voss, "The Desired Qualities of Customer Contact Employees in Complaint Handling Encounters," *Journal of Marketing Management* 22 (June 2006), p. 619; Christian Homburg and Andrea Furst, "How Organizational Complaint Handling Drives Customer Loyalty: An Analysis of the Mechanistic and the Organic Approach," *Journal of Marketing* 69 (July 2005), pp. 95–107; Moshe Davidow, "Organizational Responses to Customer Complaints: What Works and What Doesn't," *Journal of Service Research* 5 (February 2003), pp. 225–51; U. Chapman and George Argyros, "An Investigation into Whether Complaining Can Cause Increased Consumer Satisfaction," *Journal of Consumer Marketing* 17 (2000), pp. 9–19.

28. James Covert, "Online Clothes Reviews Give 'Love That Dress' New Clout," *The Wall Street Journal*, December 7, 2006, p. B1.

29. "Customers Seek Self-Service Alternatives," www.nacsonline.com, January 25, 2007.

30. Ryan Schuster, "Frustrated with Poor Service?" *Bakersfield Californian*, April 14, 2007.

31. Staci Kusterbeck, "Clienteling: Retailers Get Up Close and Personal with Customers," *Apparel*, May 2005, pp. 38–42.

32. Dunham.

33. Carmine Gallo, "How Ritz-Carlton Maintains its Mystique," *Business Week*, February 13, 2007 (accessed January 26, 2008); Peter Sanders, "Takin' Off the Ritz—a Tad," *The Wall Street Journal*, June 23, 2006, p. B1; Jagdip Singh, "Performance Productivity and Quality of Frontline Employees in Service

Organizations," *Journal of Marketing*, 64 (April 2000), pp. 15–34; Benjamin Schneider, William H. Macey, and Scott A Young, "The Climate for Service: A Review of the Construct with Implications for Achieving CLV Goals," *Journal of Relationship Marketing*, January 2006, p. 111; Mark Wickham and Melissa Parker, "Reconceptualising Organisational Role Theory for Contemporary Organisational Contexts." *Journal of Managerial Psychology* 22 (July 2007), pp. 440–64.

34. See Chuck Chakrapani, *How to Measure Service Quality and Customer Satisfaction: The Informal Field Guide for Tools and Techniques* (Chicago: American Marketing Association, 1998); Linda C. Ueltschy, Michel Laroche, Axel Eggert, and Uta Bindl, "Service Quality and Satisfaction: An International Comparison of Professional Services Perceptions," *Journal of Services Marketing* 21 (September 2007), pp. 410–23; María Elisa Alén González, Lorenzo Rodríguez Comesaña, and José Antonio Fraiz Brea, "Assessing Tourist Behavioral Intentions Through Perceived Service Quality and Customer Satisfaction," *Journal of Business Research* 60 (February 2007), p. 153.

35. Emily Le Coz, "Mystery Shoppers Help Businesses Improve Customer Service," *Knight Ridder Tribune Business News*, April 25, 2005, p. 1; Adam Finn, "Mystery Shopper Benchmarking of Durable-Goods Chains and Stores," *Journal of Service Research* 3 (May 2001), pp. 310–20; Margaret Erstad, "Mystery Shopping Programmes and Human Resource Management," *International Journal of Contemporary Hospitality Management* 10 (January 1998), pp. 34–38.

36. Janet Adamy, "A Menu of Options," *The Wall Street Journal*, October 30, 2006, p. R6.

37. Margery Weinstein, "Satellite Success," *Training*, January/February 2007 (accessed January 26, 2008); Barbara Allan and Dina Lewis, "Virtual Learning Communities as a Vehicle for Workforce Development: A Case Study," *Journal of Workplace Learning* 18 (August 2006), pp. 367–83.

38. Disney Institute and Michael Eisner, *Be Our Guest: Perfecting the Art of Customer Service* (New York: Disney Editions, 2001); Lance A. Bettencourt and Stephen W. Brown, "Role Stressors and Customer-Oriented Boundary-Spanning Behaviors in Service Organizations," *Journal of the Academy of Marketing Science* 31 (Fall 2003), pp. 394–408; Linda L. Price, Eric J. Arnould, and Patrick Tierney, "Going to Extremes: Managing Service Encounters and Assessing Provider Performance," *Journal of Marketing* 59 (April 1995), pp. 83–97; Charles H. Schwepker Jr. and Michael D. Hartline, "Managing the Ethical Climate of Customer-Contact Service Employees," *Journal of Service Research* 7 (May 2005), pp. 377–97.

39. James R. Detert and Ethan R. Burris, "Leadership Behavior and Employee Voice: Is the Door Really Open?" *Academy of Management Journal* 50 (August 2007), pp. 869–84; Gilad Chen, Bradley L. Kirkman, Ruth Kanfer, Don Allen, and Benson Rosen, "A Multilevel Study of Leadership, Empowerment, and Performance in Teams," *Journal of Applied Psychology* 92 (March 2007), p. 331; Adam Rapp, Michael Ahearne, John Mathieu, and Niels Schillewaert, "The Impact of Knowledge and Empowerment on Working Smart and Working Hard: The Moderating Role of Experience," *International Journal of Research in Marketing* 23 (September 2006), pp. 279–93; Jim Poisand, *Creating and Sustaining a Superior Customer Service Organization: A Book about Taking Care of the People Who Take Care of the Customers* (Westport, CT: Quorum Books, 2002); O.C. Hartline, James Maxham III, and Daryl McKee, "Corridors of Influence in the Dissemination of Customer-Oriented Strategy to Customer Contact Service Employees," *Journal of Marketing* 64 (April 2000), pp. 25–41.

40. Sheryl Jean, "Seeking the 'Seamless' Shopping Experience," *Star-Telegram*, October 16, 2007.

41. Julie Holliday Wayne, Amy E. Randel, and Jaclyn Stevens, "The Role of Identity and Work-Family Support in Work-Family Enrichment and Its Work-Related Consequences," *Journal of Vocational Behavior* 69 (December 2006), p. 445; Alicia Grandey and Analea Brauburger, "The Emotion Regulation Behind the Customer Service Smile," in *Emotions in the Workplace: Understanding the Structure and Role of Emotions in Organizational Behavior*, eds. R. Lord, R. Klimoski, and R. Kanfer (San Francisco: Jossey-Bass, 2002); Jill Kickul and Margaret Posig, "Supervisory Emotional Support and Burnout: An Explanation of Reverse Buffering Effects," *Journal of Managerial Issues* 13 (October 2001), pp. 328–44.

42. Hazel-Anne Johnson and Paul Spector, "Service With a Smile: Do Emotional Intelligence, Gender, and Autonomy Moderate the Emotional Labor Process?" *Journal of Occupational Health Psychology*, October 2007, pp. 319–33; Merran Toerien and Celia Kitzinger, "Emotional Labour in Action: Navigating Multiple Involvements in the Beauty Salon," *Sociology*, August 2007, pp. 645–62; Jarrad Dunning, Aron O'Cass, and Anthony Pecotich, "Retail Sales Explanations: Resolving Unsatisfactory Sales Encounters," *European Journal of Marketing* 38 (2004), pp. 1541–61; Margaret Pressler, "The Customer Isn't Always Right; Retail Staff Say Shoppers' Behavior Is Going From Bad to Worse," *Washington Post*, March 24, 2002, p. H.05; Chris Penttila, "Touch Customer: Managing Abusive Customers," *Entrepreneur*, May 2001, pp. 5, 95.

43. Fons Naus, Ad van Iterson, and Robert Roe, "Organizational Cynicism: Extending the Exit, Voice, Loyalty, and Neglect Model of Employees' Responses to Adverse Conditions in the Workplace," *Human Relations* 60 (May 2007), pp. 683-718; Richard Netemeyer and James G. Maxham III, "Employee Versus Supervisor Ratings of Performance in the Retail Customer Service Sector: Differences in Predictive Validity for Customer Outcomes," *Journal of Retailing* 83 (January 2007), pp. 131–46.

44. Alan Randolph and Marshall Sashkin, "Can Organizational Empowerment Work in Multinational Settings?" *Academy of Management Executive* 16 (February 2002), pp. 102–16.

45. Graham Bradley and Beverly Sparks, "Customer Reactions to Staff Empowerment: Mediators and Moderators," *Group and Organization Management* 26 (March 2001), pp. 53–68.

46. Joyce Smith, "Positive Customer Service Pays Off Consumer, Loyalty May Take Financial Investment," *Myrtle Beach Sun News*, November 5, 2006 (accessed January 26, 2008).

47. Jenn Abelson, "Bar-Code Tags, ATM-style Machines Drive High-Tech Laundry Business," *Boston Globe*, July 3, 2006; www.zoots.com (accessed November 5, 2007); Francoise Simon and Jean-Claude Usunier, "Cognitive, Demographic, and Situational Determinants of Service Customer Preference for Personnel-in-Contact over Self-Service Technology," *International Journal of Research in Marketing* 24 (June 2007), pp. 163–73; Matthew L. Meuter, Mary Jo Bitner, Amy L. Ostrom, and Stephen W. Brown, "Choosing Among Alternative Service Delivery Modes: An Investigation of Customer Trial of Self-Service Technologies," *Journal of Marketing* 69 (April 2005), pp. 61–83.

48. Tammy Joyner, "More Businesses Telling Customers: Do It Yourself," *The Atlanta Journal-Constitution*, August 10, 2003, p. B2.

49. Erica Ogg, "HP Developing Shopping Kiosks of the Future," www.silicon.com, May 30, 2007 (accessed January 26, 2008).

50. www.stopandshop.com/stores/shopping_buddy.htm (accessed November 7, 2007); Shia Kapos, "High-Tech Shopping Lists Guide Grocery Shoppers," *Chicago Tribune*, June 20, 2005, p. C1.

51. Bert Weijters, Devarajan Rangarajan, Tomas Falk, and Niels Schillewaert, "Determinants and Outcomes of Customers' Use of Self-Service Technology in a Retail Setting," *Journal of Service Research* 10 (August 2007), pp. 3–21; Daniel Nilsson, "A Cross-Cultural Comparison of Self-Service Technology Use," *European Journal of Marketing* 41 (March 2007), pp. 367–81; Alex Kuczynski, "A Weapon of Self-Destruction for Buyers," *The New York Times*, March 23, 2006.

52. Chihyung Ok, Ki-Joon Back, and Carol W Shanklin, "Mixed Findings on the Service Recovery Paradox," *The Service Industries Journal* 27 (September 2007), p. 671; Celso Augusto de Matos, Jorge Luiz Henrique, and Carlos Alberto Vargas Rossi, "Service Recovery Paradox: A Meta-Analysis," *Journal of Service Research* 10 (August 2007), pp. 60–77; Ringberg, Odekerken-Schröder, and Christensen; Mahesh S. Bhandari, Yelena Tsarenko, and Michael Jay Polonsky, "A Proposed Multi-Dimensional Approach to Evaluating Service Recovery," *The Journal of Services Marketing*, 21 (April 2007), pp. 174-185; James G. Maxham III and Richard G. Netemeyer, "A Longitudinal Study of Complaining Customers' Evaluations of Multiple Service Failures and Recovery Efforts," *Journal of Marketing* 66 (October 2002), pp. 57–71.

53. Hui Liao, "Do It Right This Time: The Role of Employee Service Recovery Performance in Customer-Perceived Justice and Customer Loyalty After Service Failures," *Journal of Applied Psychology* 92 (March 2007), p. 475; Kate L. Reynolds and Lloyd C. Harris, "When Service Failure Is Not Service Failure: An Exploration of the Forms and Motives of 'Illegitimate' Customer Complaining," *Journal of Services Marketing* 19 (July 2005), pp. 321–35; Gillian Naylor, "The Complaining Customer: A Service Provider's Best Friend?" *Journal of Consumer Satisfaction, Dissatisfaction and Complaining Behavior* 16 (January 2003), pp. 241–48.

54. Betsy Bugg Holloway, Sijun Wang, and Janet Turner Parish, "The Role of Cumulative Online Purchasing Experience in Service Recovery Management," *Journal of Interactive Marketing* 19 (July 2005), pp. 54–66; Anna S. Mattila and Paul G. Patterson, "Service Recovery and Fairness Perceptions in Collectivist and Individualist Contexts," *Journal of Service Research* 6 (May 2004), pp. 336–46; Stephen S. Tax, Stephen W. Brown, and Murali Chandrashekaran, "Customer Evaluations of Service Complaint Experiences: Implications for Relationship Marketing," *Journal of Marketing* 62 (April 1998), pp. 60–76.

55. Seokhwa Yun, Riki Takeuchi, and Wei Liu, "Employee Self-Enhancement Motives and Job Performance Behaviors: Investigating the Moderating Effects of Employee Role Ambiguity and Managerial Perceptions of Employee Commitment," *Journal of Applied Psychology* 92 (May 2007), p. 745; Ringberg, Odekerken-Schröder, and Christensen; Amy K. Smith, Ruth N. Bolton, and Janet Wagner, "A Model of Customer Satisfaction with Service Encounters Involving Failure and Recover," *Journal of Marketing Research* 36 (August 1999), pp. 356–72.

CREDITS

Chapter 1

2 © PhotoLink/Getty Images; **4** Courtesy of Maxine Clark; **8** © AP Photo/Keith Ferris; **10** Courtesy of Edun; **12** © Medio-Images/Getty Images; **14** © Stephen Pumphrey; **15** Used with permission of Inter IKEA Systems B.V.; **17** left © Mark Richards/PhotoEdit; **17** right © Myrleen Ferguson Cate/PhotoEdit; **20** left Courtesy of J.C. Penney Company, Inc.; **20** right Courtesy of J.C. Penney Company, Inc.; **22** © Bob Daemmrich/The Image Works; **27** © Tom Stack; **29** Courtesy of John Tighe

Chapter 2

34 Courtesy of Keith Koenig; **38** Courtesy of Bag Borrow or Steal™; **39** Courtesy of Eastern Mountain Sports; **42** Courtesy of ALDI; **43** Courtesy of Wegmans Food Markets, Inc.; **45** Courtesy of Costco; **48** Courtesy of Kohl's; **50** Courtesy of SEPHORA; **52** Courtesy of Bass Pro Shops; **54** © Jeff Greenberg/PhotoEdit; **56** © Bonnie Kamin/PhotoEdit; **58** Courtesy of Get & Go Corp.; **59** Courtesy of Penzoil-Quaker State Co.; **62** © PG/Magnum Photos; **64** © Getty Images

Chapter 3

70 Courtesy of Kristin Micalizo; **74** © Mark Scott/Getty Images; **75** Courtesy of Circuit City; **77** Courtesy of WeddingChannel.com; **78** Courtesy of Bluefly, Inc.; **80** Courtesy of Blue Nile, Inc.; **81** Courtesy of H&M; **82** Courtesy of REI; **84** Courtesy of Zingerman's Creamery; **85** © Susan Van Etten/PhotoEdit; **87** Courtesy of Talbots; **88** © Eveready Battery Company, Inc. Printed with permission; **89** Courtesy of Patagonia, Inc.; **90** © David Young-Wolff/PhotoEdit

Chapter 4

96 Courtesy of Cynthia Cohen; **100** © BananaStock/Supter-Stock; **101** © AP Photo/Mary Altaffer; **102** www.seenon.com; **104** Photo provided by the Southern Daily Echo; **107** left © Digital Vision/Getty Images; **107** right © Tony Freeman/PhotoEdit; **109** Courtesy of Lowe's; **112** © Bill Aron/PhotoEdit; **113** Used with permission of Inter IKEA Systems B.V.; **115** Courtesy of Club Libby Lu; **116** Courtesy of Costco; **121** © Justin Pumfrey/Getty Images; **127** left © Getty Images; **127** right © Getty Images

Chapter 5

130 © Alistair Berg/Photodisc/Getty Images; **132** Courtesy of Jim Cossin; **135** Courtesy of Steve & Barry's; **140** © Nick Daly/Getty Images; **141** © Rob Crandall/The Image Works; **142** © Getty Images; **143** Courtesy of The Container Store; **147** © Najilah Feanny/Corbis; **149** © AP Photo/str; **151** © AP Photo/Greg Baker; **156** Courtesy of Quill & Press; **160** left Courtesy of Blockbuster Inc.; **160** right Reproduced by permission of Netflix, Inc., Copyright © 2007 Netflix, Inc. All rights reserved.

Chapter 6

166 Courtesy of Steve Stagner; **169** © Getty Images; **171** Courtesy of Macy's; **172** Courtesy of Costco Wholesale Corporation; **177** © Martin Riedl/Getty Images; **178** top © Jeff Greenberg/PhotoEdit; **178** bottom Courtesy of Costco Wholesale Corporation; **188** © AP Photo/Gregory Smith

Chapter 7

192 Courtesy of Michael Kercheval; **194** Courtesy of Doctor's Associates Inc.; **196** © Getty Images; **198** © Nik Wheeler/Corbis; **199** © AP Photo/Berry Sweet; **200** © The McGraw-Hill Companies, Inc./Andrew Resek, photographer; **202** © Tim Mouncer; **204** © Manuel Llaneras Photography; **205** Courtesy of San Jose Town and Country Village, LLC; **206** Courtesy of Ghirardelli Square; **207** Courtesy of General Growth Properties, Inc.; **208** Second Life is a trademark of Linden Research, Inc.

Certain materials have been reproduced with the permission of Linden Research, Inc. COPYRIGHT © 2001-2007 LINDEN RESEARCH, INC. ALL RIGHTS RESERVED; **209** © AP Photo/Tina Fineberg; **211** right Courtesy of Beall's Inc.; **211** left © Bill Serne/St. Petersburg Times; **213** © Atlantide Phototravel/Corbis

Chapter 8

216 Courtesy of Juan del Valle; **220** © Tom Iannuzzi/Mercury Pictures; **222** © Christopher Barth/epa/Corbis; **224** © Keri Johnson; **225** left © The McGraw-Hill Companies, Inc./John Flournoy, photographer; **225** right © Author's Image/Punch-stock; **227** © Mike Hillyer; **229** © James Paul Photographers; **230** Courtesy of Talbots; **234** © Hoby Finn/Getty Images; **238** left Courtesy of The Edward Beiner Group; **238** right Courtesy of The Edward Beiner Group

Chapter 9

246 Courtesy of Derek Jenkins; **249** Courtesy of The Men's Wearhouse; **254** Courtesy of PetSmart; **261** © Stephen Pumphrey; **262** Courtesy of J.C. Penney Company, Inc.; **264** Courtesy Peet's Coffee & Tea ®; **265** © AP Photo/Elaine Thompson; **267** © Dennis MacDonald/PhotoEdit; **271** © Getty Images

Chapter 10

276 Courtesy of Jim LaBounty; **281** © AP Photo/Denis Doyle; **283** Courtesy of Zoots; **288** © Spencer Grant/PhotoEdit; **290** top © Walter Hodges/Photodisc/Getty Images; **290** bottom © Charles Gupton; **293** top Courtesy of Wal-Mart; **293** bottom Courtesy of Wal-Mart; **292** Courtesy of L.L. Bean; **294** Courtesy of Kiva Systems, Inc.; **295** Courtesy of LUSH Fresh Handmade Cosmetics; **299** Courtesy of J.C. Penney Company, Inc.; **300** Courtesy of West Marine; **301** Courtesy of thebigspace Ltd.

Chapter 11

304 Courtesy of Bari Harlam; **306** © Jim Cummins/Getty Images; **307** Courtesy of Neiman Marcus Group, Inc.; **309** © Don Mason/Corbis; **310** © AP Photo/Tribune Newspapers, Darryl Webb; **311** © Getty Images; **314** © Elusive Photography; **315** Courtesy of Tesco Stores Limited; **316** © AP Photo/Janet Hostetter; **321** top © 2005 Amazon.com, Inc. All Rights Reserved; **321** bottom © AP Photo/Doug Mills; **322** Courtesy of Cuesol, Inc.

Chapter 12

326 © Getty Images; **328** © James Paul Photographers; **330** © Ryan McVay/Getty Images; **333** © Mark E. Gibson/Corbis; **335** left © Michael Newman/PhotoEdit; **335** right © AP Photo/Columbia Daily Tribune, G.J. McCarthy; **337** © Getty Images; **339** © Getty Images; **340** © Annie Reynolds/PhotoLink/Getty Images; **341** © AP Photo/Ed Andrieski; **343** © Thomas Concordia/WireImage/Getty Images; **345** © Getty Images; **347** © Alan Becker/Still Media; **348** © The McGraw-Hill Companies, Inc./Lars A. Niki, photographer; **351** © AP Photo/Kenneth Lambert

Chapter 13

356 Courtesy of Latoya Parker; **358** Courtesy of Loehmann's; **360** top Courtesy of Lowe's; **360** bottom Courtesy of Rubbermaid; **363** © Vic Bider/PhotoEdit; **364** © Tony Freeman/PhotoEdit; **368** © Antony Nagelmann/Getty Images; **371** left © The McGraw-Hill Companies, Inc./Lars A. Niki, photographer; **371** right © Digital Vision/Getty Images; **372** left Courtesy of Saks Incorporated; **372** right Courtesy of Saks Incorporated; **374** © James Paul Photographers; **375** Courtesy of Cognos Incorporated

Chapter 14

382 Courtesy of Michael Jeppesen;   **384** © Barbara J. Norman Photography;   **385** © Ashley Cooper/Corbis;   **386** Courtesy of Macy's;   **387** top PRESIDENT'S CHOICE, DECADENT, THE DECADENT and THE DECADENT CHOCOLATE CHIP COOKIE & Design are registered trademarks of Loblaws Inc. Used with permission;   **387** bottom © AP Photo/Kohl's, Phelan M. Ebenhack;   **389** © WWD/Conde Nast/Corbis;   **391** Courtesy of the Consumer Electronics Association;   **393** © Paula Bronstein/Liaison Agency;   **395** © Stephen Alvarez/National Geographic/Getty Images;   **396** Courtesy of William Alcorn;   **397** © Comstock/PictureQuest;   **405** © AP Photo/Bebeto Matthews;   **406** © Getty Images;   **408** © Suzanne DeChillo/The New York Times/Redux

Chapter 15

412 Courtesy of Mike Pepe;   **417** © Getty Images;   **418** © Jack Hollingsworth/Corbis;   **424** © Getty Images;   **426** Courtesy of Oracle Retail;   **429** © Glenn Paulina/TRANSTOCK;   **428** Courtesy of Reesycakes.com;   **430** © Matthew Abourezk/Entry Point Communications;   **431** © Getty Images;   **432** left © AP Photo/Mark Lennihan;   **432** right © Annette Coolidge/PhotoEdit;   **433** © Jeff Greenberg/PhotoEdit;   **434** © AP Photo/Jennifer Graylock;   **436** © Mary Kate Denny/PhotoEdit

Chapter 16

440 Courtesy of Spencer Knisely;   **442** right © PRNewsFoto/Old Navy;   **442** left Courtesy of Ace Hardware;   **443** Courtesy of J.C. Penney Company, Inc.;   **444** © AP Photo/Jeff Christensen;   **445** Courtesy of Patagonia, Inc.;   **446** Courtesy of L.L. Bean;   **448** © Katie Orlinsky/Sipa Press/Newscom;   **449** Courtesy of MediaCart;   **450** Courtesy of Del Monte Foods;   **451** Courtesy of The Knot;   **452** © AP Photo/Noah Berger;   **454** © Geof Kern;   **455** Used with permission of Sugar Inc.;   **456** Courtesy of Perry Ellis®;   **465** © Bonnie Kamin/PhotoEdit;   **468** Courtesy of Back To Bed;   **469** © Michael J. Hruby;   **470** © Michael J. Hruby

Chapter 17

472 © Getty Images;   **474** Courtesy of Lee Donnelly;   **483** © Getty Images;   **484** Courtesy of Nike, Inc.;   **486** Courtesy of ShopKo Stores, Inc.;   **487** bottom © Kaveh Kazemi/Corbis;   **489** © Jon Riley/Getty Images;   **490** © Jack Star/PhotoLink;   **494** Courtesy of The TJX Companies, Inc.;   **497** Courtesy of Sheetz, Inc.;   **500** Courtesy of Checkpoint Systems, Inc.;   **502** © Dan Trevan/Copley News Service

Chapter 18

506 Courtesy of Lori Anderson;   **508** top © AP Photo/Mark Lennihan;   **508** bottom © Steve Forrest/The New York Times/Redux;   **509** top © Panoramic Images/Getty Images;   **509** bottom © Robert Caplin/The New York Times/Redux;   **515** © Jim Stem/The New York Times/Redux;   **516** © Andy Kropa/Redux;   **517** © Mark A. Steele Photography, Inc.;   **519** © United States Postal Service;   **520** top Courtesy of Whole Foods Market, Inc.;   **520** bottom © Taku Kumabe;   **523** Courtesy of Steuben Glass;   **525** Courtesy of SAS Institute Inc.;   **525** Courtesy of SAS Institute Inc.;   **526** Courtesy of IntelliVid Corporation;   **527** Virtual Baby Aisle, © 2005 Kimberly-Clark Worldwide, Inc. Used with permission;   **528** © Sharon Hoogstraten;   **528** © Sharon Hoogstraten;   **528** © Sharon Hoogstraten;   **528** © Sharon Hoogstraten;   **529** top © Amy Etra/PhotoEdit;   **529** bottom Courtesy of Macy's

Chapter 19

538 Courtesy of Rudy Hermond;   **540** © Craig Mitchelldyer/Mitchellyder Photography;   **542** left © Bill Aron/PhotoEdit;   **542** right Discount Store News;   **543** © Getty Images;   **544** © Fujifotos/The Image Works, Inc.;   **545** Courtesy of The BROADMOOR;   **548** Courtesy of JetBlue;   **551** © James Darell/Getty Images;   **552** © Dr. Tarique Sani;   **554** © David Kadlubowski/DIT/Corbis;   **556** Courtesy of IBM Corporation;   **558** © Bruce Forster/Getty Images

COMPANY INDEX

art.com/ www.carrefour.com www.homedepot.com www.metr

o.com/ www.searsholdings.com/ www.aldifoods.com/ www.inte

eens.com www.lowes.com www.itoyokado.iyg.co.jp/ www.teng

ww.americanexpress.com www.edeka.de www.e-leclerc.fr www.

.autonation.com www.mcdonalds.com www.publix.com/ www.

ated-fds.com www.loews.com/ www.morrisons.co.uk/ www.dai

izegroup.com www.tjx.com www.marksandspencer.com www.r

ww.winndixie.com/ www.otto.nl www.toysrusinc.com/ www.dix

ed.com www.marriott.com www.yum.com/ www.boots.com w

ww.johnlewis.com/ www.bjs.com/ www.lesechos.fr/ www.nordstr

ww.metcash.com/ www.coxenterprises.com www.barnesandnoble

notive.com/ www.hm.com/ www.footlocker-inc.com/ www.fami

ww.radioshack.com/ www.longs.com/ www.harrahs.com/ www.b

www.rossstores.com/ www.hrblock.com/ www.bordersgroupinc.

ww.nytco.com/ www.walmart.com/ www.carrefour.com www.ho

w.ahold.com/ www.costco.com/ www.searsholdings.com/ www.

nney.com www.walgreens.com www.lowes.com www.itoyokado

ww.tiaa-cref.org www.americanexpress.com www.edeka.de www

www.autonation.com www.mcdonalds.com www.publix.com/ w

ated-fds.com www.loews.com/ www.morrisons.co.uk/ www.dai

izegroup.com www.tjx.com www.marksandspencer.com www.r

ww.winndixie.com/ www.otto.nl www.toysrusinc.com/ www.dix